S0-BZK-774

APPLIED DATA COMMUNICATIONS

A Business-Oriented Approach

THIRD EDITION

James E. Goldman
Phillip T. Rawles
Purdue University

JOHN WILEY & SONS, INC.

New York • Chichester • Weinheim
Brisbane • Singapore • Toronto

James E. Goldman/*To Susan, Eric, and Grant*
Phillip T. Rawles/*To Cheri*

ACQUISITIONS EDITOR	Beth Lang Golub
MARKETING MANAGER	Jessica Garcia
SENIOR PRODUCTION EDITOR	Patricia McFadden
SENIOR DESIGNER	Kevin Murphy
ILLUSTRATION EDITOR	Anna Melhorn
PRODUCTION MANAGEMENT SERVICES	Hermitage Publishing Services

Cover illustration © Bob Commander/Stock Illustration Source, Inc.

This book was set in 10/12 Palatino by Hermitage Publishing Services and printed and bound by R. R. Donnelley & Sons. The cover was printed by Lehigh Press, Inc.

This book is printed on acid-free paper. ∞

Copyright 2001 © John Wiley & Sons, Inc. All rights reserved.

No part of this publication may be reproduced, stored in a retrieval system or transmitted in any form or by any means, electronic, mechanical, photocopying, recording, scanning or otherwise, except as permitted under Sections 107 or 108 of the 1976 United States Copyright Act, without either the prior written permission of the Publisher, or authorization through payment of the appropriate per-copy fee to the Copyright Clearance Center, 222 Rosewood Drive, Danvers, MA 01923, (978) 750-8400, fax (978) 750-4470. Requests to the Publisher for permission should be addressed to the Permissions Department, John Wiley & Sons, Inc., 605 Third Avenue, New York, NY 10158-0012, (212) 850-6011, fax (212) 850-6008, E-Mail: PERMREQ@WILEY.COM. To order books please call 1(800)-225-5945.

ISBN 0-471-37161-0

Printed in the United States of America

10 9 8 7 6 5 4 3 2 1

PREFACE

NEW TO THE THIRD EDITION

The field of data communications continues to evolve at a rapid pace. To provide the reader with the most timely and important information possible, several changes have been made to the third edition while preserving those unique aspects of the first and second editions that contributed to its wide acceptance and popularity. Among the significant changes to the third edition are the following:

- All new case studies in every chapter.
- Increased technical depth as well as breadth of coverage throughout the text.
- Updated business implications of the Telecommunications Act of 1996.
- IT Economics orientation added to Chapter 11 (network development life cycle) including such topics as total cost of ownership, return on investment, and IT project portfolio management.
- Increased coverage of Unix including Linux.
- Increased coverage of wavelength division multiplexing and optical switching in Chapter 8 (WAN).
- Increased and updated coverage of wireless protocols (Bluetooth, WAP, 802.11, HiperLAN).
- More emphasis on organizing the entire text according to the OSI 7 layer model.

THE NEED FOR THIS BOOK

The field of information systems has undergone major paradigm shifts over the past several years from mainframe oriented, hierarchical information systems architectures through distributed, LAN-based, client-server information systems architectures, to browser/Internet-based information systems. However, this transition is far from complete as information systems architectures continue to evolve to include seamless integration with World Wide Web and Internet technologies such as application service providers as well as more transparent interoperability with legacy or mainframe systems. Today's resultant information systems architecture is comprised of a complicated array of interacting technologies combining elements of client-server, web-based, Internet, intranet, legacy applications, and database management systems. Data communications is the key building block to all of these interacting technologies.

Designing, implementing, and managing a successful data communications system requires sophisticated business-oriented analysis, design, and problem-solving skills. Furthermore, the collaborative computing and multimedia applications that are likely to be executed on these information systems are highly dependent on properly designed networks for successful delivery of interactive content. The interdependency of application and network development required for successful deployment of distributed information systems is all too often overlooked by information systems professionals.

To effectively design today's highly integrated, distributed data communications networks, a comprehensive systems engineering approach that incorporated business analysis, application development, database systems integration, distributed network design, and structured technology analysis is required. Such a business-first, technology-last, top-down model was introduced in the first edition of *Applied Data Communications: A Business-Oriented Approach* by James E. Goldman of Purdue University. The highly successful second edition of *Applied Data Communications* and the subsequent texts *Local Area Networks* and *Client Server Information Systems* have solidified the top-down approach as the preferred design methodology for complex network-based information systems.

Unlike many of the currently available books and texts on data communications that seem to be either too broadly focused and conceptual or too narrowly focused and technical, this text strikes a balance between the two extremes while offering the reader a structured approach to data communications analysis and design from initial business considerations through final technology choices.

DESCRIPTION

Applied Data Communications: A Business-Oriented Approach, Third Edition, provides a thorough explanation of the analysis, design, integration, and technology choices involved with deploying, managing, and securing effective data communications systems, local area networks, internetworks, and wide area networks.

The text is flexibly organized so as to cater to a variety of course orientations. The general organization and key features of the text are as follows:

- Text is divided into four major sections to maximize flexible use by a wide variety of course orientations:
    - Part 1: Data and Voice Communications Fundamentals
    - Part 2: Local Area Networks
    - Part 3: Wide Area Networks and Internetworking
    - Part 4: Network Development and Administration
- Thirteen chapters of manageable length allow instructors to pick and choose chapters as appropriate for course content, focus, length, and intended audience.
- Written in a logical, problem-solving style applauded by both students and faculty from academia and industry.
- Text material is organized into overall architectures or models. By providing students with the "big picture" first, the text assists students in understanding how particular individual topics relate to other topics and to the overall scheme of things.
- Stresses analytical questioning and problem-solving skills as being key to successful design of information systems.

- Provides working models into which students can organize their problem solving approach. These models are reinforced and used throughout the text. Examples include
  - Top down model
  - TCP/IP model
  - OSI model
- Business cases reprinted from professional periodicals are included in each chapter. Questions guide students toward development of analytical skills and business-oriented client-server information systems design capabilities.

The text equips students with real-world skills. In a fashion similar to Professor Goldman's previous texts, *Applied Data Communications: A Business Oriented Appraoch, Third Edition,* teaches students how to *do* data communications design rather than merely reading about it.

APPROACH

The reviews and current level of adoptions of the first two editions of *Applied Data Communications: A Business Oriented Appraoch,* the first two editions of *Local Area Networks: A Business Oriented Approach,* and *Client/Server Information Systems: A Business Oriented Approach* indicate that the same proven, practical approach should be applied to the third edition of this book. The text follows the top-down model, examining the many options, standards, interfaces, implications, advantages, and disadvantages in each of the top-down model's five layers:

- Business
- Application
- Data
- Network
- Technology

Concept roadmaps are located throughout the text that stress the relationship between chapters and their relationship to a data communications systems architecture as well as between topics within chapters.

Each chapter begins with an outline of new concepts introduced, previous concepts reinforced, and the learning objectives for that chapter.

Section and paragraph headings help students to organize and identify key concepts introduced in each chapter.

End of chapter material includes chapter summaries, key terms listings, abundant review questions, and activities and problems for active student learning.

As previously mentioned, business cases from professional periodicals are reprinted at the close of each chapter with associated analysis questions to be answered by students or used as the basis for classroom discussion.

A liberal use (two to three times as many as competing texts) of clear, concise diagrams add to the usability of the text and to the understanding of the students.

TARGET AUDIENCES/COURSES

Due to the modular nature of this text, a variety of audience/courses could be well served. Among the courses as potential adopters of this text are the following:

- An introductory level course on data communications: the practical nature of the text would be appealing as well as its broad coverage and architectural orientation. Advanced sections of the text could be easily avoided. This course could also serve as the foundation course for a concentration or degree program in data communications/telecommunications, and networking technology.
- A business-oriented course in data communications as part of an MBA program, especially those with concentration in MIS
- Continuing education or industrial seminars offered in data communications fundamentals for professional development.

SPECIAL FEATURES

Although some of these features have been mentioned previously, they are repeated here to stress the unique nature of this text as a purveyor of practical, business-oriented data communications analysis skills and problem-solving abilities rather than a mere collection of concepts and facts.

- Modular approach allows flexible use of text to fit instructor and course needs.
- Real business case studies stressing the business impact of data communications, thereby assisting students in sharpening their analysis and problem solving skills. Directed questions accompanying each case stimulate classroom discussion as well.
- "In Sharper Focus" sections highlight more detailed, more advanced, or background information for concepts introduced within a chapter. These sections can be included or excluded at the instructor's discretion.
- "Managerial Perspective" sections take a "bottom-line" approach to client server information systems analysis and design. The potential impact of management decisions in a variety of situations is highlighted in these sections that may be of particular interest to MBA audiences.
- "Applied Problem Solving" sections of chapters focusing on the use of analytical models for applied problem-solving activities are highlighted for the benefit of both instructors and students. By stressing problem-solving activities, students can be assured of learning how to *do* data communications analysis and design.
- Emphasizing the practical nature of the text, instances of practical advice or warnings are highlighted to call the reader's attention to important but often overlooked information.

OSI NETWORK REFERENCE MODEL ORGANIZATION

Previous editions of *Applied Data Communications* have attempted to strike a balance between stressing a systems integration approach to teaching data communications against a strict organization of material according to the seven layers of the OSI network reference mode. The authors feel that the key to comprehending data communications lies in the understanding of the interfaces between OSI layer components rather than in the categorization of components according to OSI layer. As a result, although the material in the text is loosely organized according to the layers of the OSI model, the key theme to the overall organization of the text is the appreciation of how data communications components must be integrated to produce a functional end-to-end system. As an aid for those instructors wishing to organize their course according to the OSI model, the table below provides a cross-reference.

OSI Model Layer	Topics	Chapter(s)
Layer 1-Physical	Media, signaling, modulation	3, 4, 6
Layer 2-Data Link	LAN architectures	5
Layer 3-Network	LAN protocols and NOS	7
Layer 4-Transport	LAN protocols, internetworking	7,9
Layer 5-Session	LAN protocols and NOS	7
Layer 6-Presentation	LAN protocols and NOS	7
Layer 7-Application	LAN protocols and NOS	7

SUPPLEMENT PACKAGE

A CD-ROM containing the Instructor's Resource Guide and PowerPoints is provided to adopters. The IRG contains thorough answers to all review questions featured at the end of each chapter, solutions to case study questions, and an abundant selection of additional questions in a variety of formats for each chapter. In addition, all illustrations are in PowerPoint format to expedite the production of transparencies and class notes to accompany the text.

ACKNOWLEDGMENTS

We are indebted to a number of people whose efforts were crucial in the development of this book.

For the outstanding quality illustrations that appear in the book, as well as for his unwavering support, we'd like to thank Curt Snyder our wonderful and talented illustrator.

For their collaborative efforts in turning a manuscript into a professional published book, we'd like to thank the following professionals at John Wiley & Sons: Beth Golub, Acquisitions Editor, and Jessica Garcia, Marketing Manager.

Reviewers

A special debt of gratitude is owed to the professionals who were kind enough to review the manuscript of this book before publication. It is through your effort that an accurate text of high quality can be produced.

George Scheets, *Oklahoma State University*

Michael E. Whitman, *Kennesaw State University*

Gusteau Duclos, *DeVry Institute of Technology, NY*

Mary Brabston, *University of Manitoba*

Alan Runge, *DeVry Institute of Technology, MO*

Jerry Feinstein, *George Washington University*

Kent Webb, *San Jose State*

ABOUT THE AUTHORS

James E. Goldman, Principal Author James E. Goldman is currently Professor of Computer Information Systems and Assistant Department Head for Telecommunications and Networking in the nationally prominent Department of Computer Technology at Purdue University. An award winning teacher, Professor Goldman is the only faculty member in the history of the School of Technology to win all three school-level teaching awards: The James G. Dwyer Outstanding Teacher Award, the School of Technology Outstanding Non-Tenured Faculty Award, and the School of Technology Tenured Faculty Award, as well as the Purdue University Charles B. Murphy Award for Outstanding Undergraduate Teaching. In 1999, Professor Goldman was named as a University Faculty Scholar at Purdue.

Professor Goldman is also the author of *Local Area Networks: A Business Oriented Approach, Second Edition* (2000), and *Client/Server Information Systems: A Business Oriented Approach,* which was published in 1998 with fellow Purdue professors Phillip Rawles and Julie Mariga. Professor Goldman has an active consulting practice and is a MCSE (Microsoft-certified systems engineer).

Phillip T. Rawles, Co-Author Phillip T. Rawles is an Associate Professor of Computer Information Systems and Technology for Telecommunications and Networking in the nationally prominent Department of Computer Technology at Purdue University. Professor Rawles has won various student and faculty selected teaching awards for his performance in the classroom for his work in developing ad delivering courses in local area networking, systems administration, enterprise network management, and enterprise network design.

Professor Rawles is also the author of *Local Area Networks: A Business Oriented Approach, Second Edition* (2000), and *Client/Server Information Systems: A Business Oriented Approach*, which was published in 1998 with fellow Purdue professors James Goldman and Julie Mariga. Professor Rawles has an active consulting practice and is a MCSE (Microsoft-certified systems engineer), certified Solaris system administrator, and Cisco-certified network associate.

CONTENTS

CHAPTER 7 Local Area Network Communications Protocols and Operating Systems /245

CHAPTER 8 Wide Area Networking Concepts, Architectures, and Services /301

CHAPTER 9 Internetworking /357

CHAPTER 10 Remote Access and Wireless Networking /419

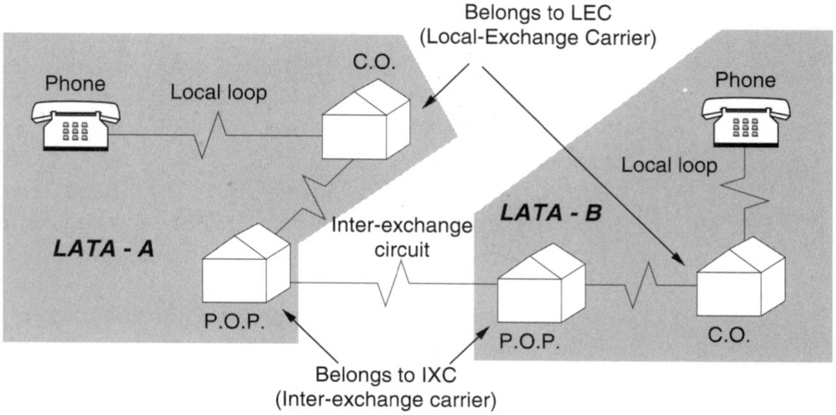

Figure 1-3 Basic Telecommunications Infrastructure

(IXC) of the customer's choice. Competing long-distance carriers wishing to do business in a given LATA maintain a switching office in that LATA known as a **point of presence** or **POP.** This POP handles billing information and routes the call over the long-distance carrier's switched network to its POP in the destination's LATA. The circuit between the POPs may be via satellite, microwave, fiber optic cable, traditional wiring, or some combination of these media. Depending on traffic levels on the long-distance carrier's network, calls may be routed through any combination of switches before reaching their final destination.

Deregulation and Divestiture: 1980s After one understands the overall interaction of carriers and regulatory agencies as well as the basic infrastructure of today's

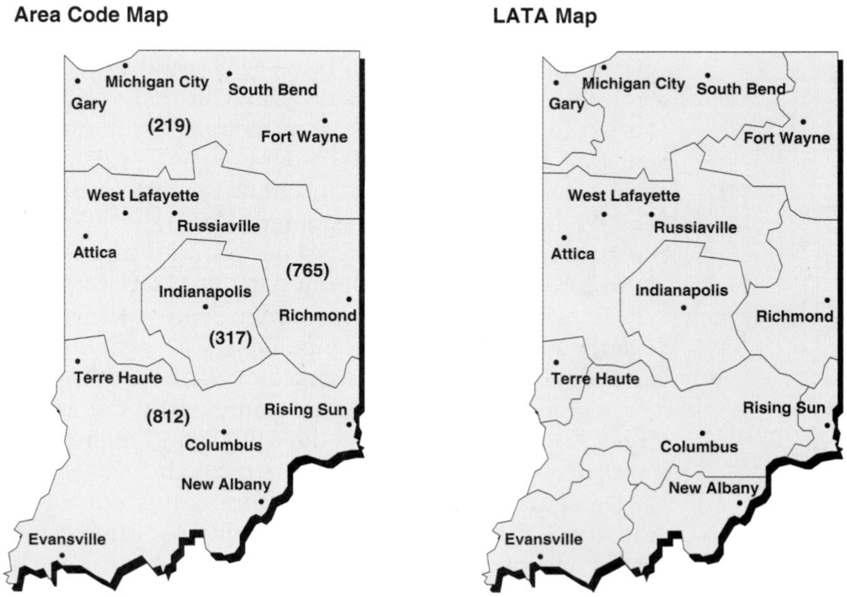

Figure 1-4 Area Codes vs. LATAs

telecommunications industry, the historical aspects of this regulatory relationship must be explored to better understand how today's regulatory environment evolved. Today's competitive telecommunications industry in the United States is largely the result of rulings by the Justice Department in the early 1980s. These rulings are generally referred to as **deregulation** and **divestiture.** These two terms are related but not synonymous.

Before deregulation and divestiture, America's telecommunications needs (data and voice), (hardware and services) were supplied, with few exceptions, by a single vendor: AT&T (American Telephone and Telegraph). At that time, homeowners were not allowed to purchase and install their own phones. AT&T owned all equipment connected to the PSTN. Customers rented their phones from AT&T.

Local Bell operating companies provided local service but were still part of AT&T. All telephone service, both local and long distance, was coordinated through one telecommunications organization. Most indoor wiring was also the responsibility of AT&T, not the owner of the building in which the wiring existed. This top-to-bottom integration allowed for excellent coordination and interoperability. It was easy to know who to call for new service or a repair problem because installation and maintenance of hardware, as well as long-distance and local service for voice or data were all coordinated through one company. On the other hand, the total control of the telecommunications industry by one company severely limited customer choice. If you wanted a telephone, you became an AT&T customer. If you were not happy with AT&T's service or pricing, the only option was to terminate your service. This top-to-bottom control of the telecommunications industry was seen as a monopoly, especially by other vendors wishing to compete in the telecommunications industry.

The single company telecommunications industry model came to an end through deregulation and divestiture in the late 1970s and early 1980s. It is important to note that the initial divestiture and deregulation of the telecommunications industry was not the result of a purely regulatory process. This enormously important event was primarily a judicial process, fought out in the courtrooms and largely fostered by one man, Bill McGowan, former president of MCI.

Although the Federal Communications Committee (FCC), a federal regulatory agency, initially ruled in 1971 that MCI could compete with AT&T for long-distance service, it was McGowan's 1974 lawsuit that got the Justice Department involved and led to the actual breakup of the telecommunications monopoly in the United States. AT&T was declared a monopoly and broken into several smaller companies in a process known as divestiture as set forth by Federal Judge Harold Greene in the 1982 **Modified Final Judgment (MFJ).** By interpreting the MFJ, Judge Greene effectively controlled the U.S. telecommunications industry from the original ruling in 1982 until the Telecommunications Act of 1996 expressly ended his control.

Divestiture broke up the telephone network services of AT&T into separate long-distance and local service companies. AT&T would retain the right to offer long-distance services, while the former local Bell operating companies were grouped into new regional Bell operating companies **(RBOCs)** to offer local telecommunications service. Figure 1-5 illustrates the RBOCs and their constituent former Bell operating companies (BOCs) after divestiture through 1996.

Deregulation introduced an entirely different aspect of the telecommunications industry in the United States: the ability of "phone companies" in America to compete in an unrestricted manner in other industries such as the computer and information systems fields. Before deregulation, phone companies were either banned from doing business in other industries or were subject to having their profits

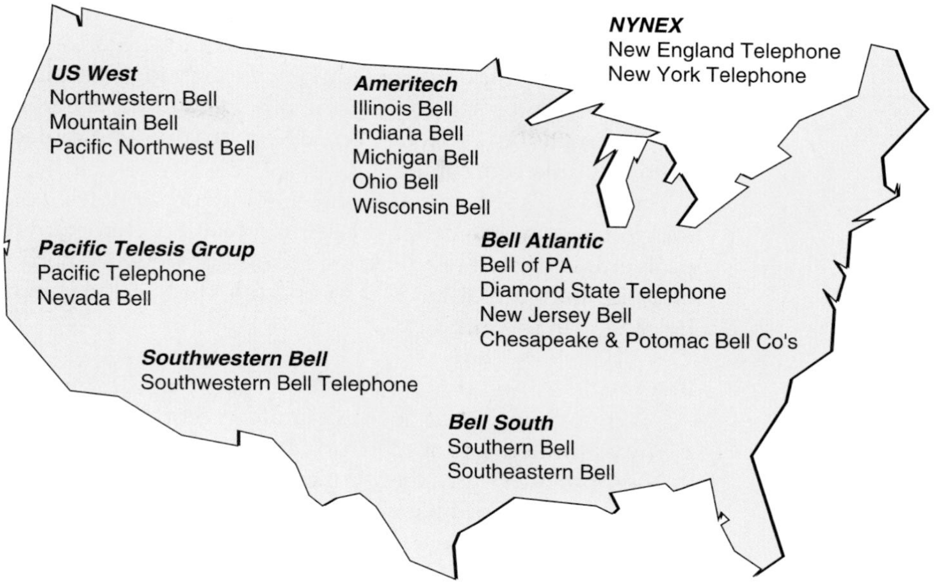

Figure 1-5 Post Divestiture/Pre-Telecommunications Act of 1996 RBOC and BOC Alignment

and/or rates monitored or "regulated" in a fashion similar to the way in which their rates for phone service were regulated.

As a result of deregulation, both AT&T and the RBOCs were allowed to enter into other industries by forming additional subsidiaries. For the first time, phone companies were competing in a market-driven, customer-dictated economy. A common misconception about deregulation is that phone companies became totally deregulated and could charge whatever the market would bear for phone services. This is not the case. Phone companies today have both regulated and deregulated portions of their business, which are often segregated into separate companies.

Network services offered by phone companies are still regulated. New rate proposals from phone companies are filed as tariffs with state or federal regulatory authorities. Local service rate changes are filed on the state level with a particular state's Public Utilities Commission and on a federal level with the FCC for interstate service proposals and rate change requests. These commissions must balance objectives that are sometimes contradictory:

- Basic phone service must remain affordable enough that all residents of a state can afford it. This guarantee is sometimes known as **universal service** or **universal access.**
- Phone companies must remain profitable to be able to afford to constantly reinvest in upgrading their physical resources (hardware, cables, buildings) as well as in educating and training their human resources.

The divestiture and deregulation activities of the 1980s allowed competing long-distance carriers such as MCI and US Sprint to sell long-distance services on a level playing field with AT&T thanks to a ruling known as **equal access.** This means that all long-distance carriers must be treated equally by the local BOCs in terms of access to the local carrier switching equipment, and ultimately to their customers.

From the end-user's perspective, the divestiture and deregulation activities of the 1980s enabled freedom of choice for long-distance carriers. The competition for business and residential customers' long-distance business has forced down prices for long-distance service. On the other hand, the simplicity of ordering, installing, and maintaining services from one company was replaced by a series of services from multiple companies.

This loss of coordinated installation and troubleshooting is perhaps the biggest loss to telecommunications users as a result of deregulation and divestiture. Service problems can often result in finger-pointing between hardware vendors, local service carriers, and long distance carriers while the telecommunications users are left rather helplessly in the middle.

Deregulation, Divestiture, and Realignment: 1990s In September 1992, the FCC enacted additional rulings that enabled limited competition in the local loop. The competition was limited to leased or private lines that bypass the phone company's switching equipment. Before these rulings, only the RBOCs were allowed to transport calls from a residence or business to the local central office and ultimately to the point of presence of any of the long-distance carriers.

After this ruling, a company could use a leased line to transport voice and/or data between corporate locations on a 24 hr/day, 7 day/week basis. Leased lines have no dial tone. They are private, point-to-point, "pipes" into which customers can transport voice and data to only the predetermined ends of those pipes. The differences among all of the various switched and leased voice and data services are explored further in Chapters 2, 3, and 4.

Through a mandated process known as **co-location,** RBOCs had to allow alternate local loop carriers to install their equipment in the RBOC's CO. In return, RBOCs were allowed to charge **access charges** for co-location of the alternate carrier's equipment in their COs. End-users could also co-locate networking equipment in the RBOC's CO. Businesses could now build their own virtual private networks by co-locating their own networking equipment in local phone company COs.

Remembering that this ruling only affected leased line traffic, only those businesses that had a need for point-to-point or multipoint leased lines, usually for data transmission, were likely to benefit from this ruling. However, this local loop leased line deregulation was but a shadow of things to come.

In 1995, AT&T reacted to a changing marketplace in an unusual manner. To free its various divisions to seek business opportunities without regard for the interests of other AT&T divisions, AT&T split into three separate companies. Whereas the divestiture of AT&T in the 1980s was vigorously fought by AT&T and eventually government-imposed, the trivestiture of AT&T in 1995 was self-imposed. The three companies are as follows:

1. AT&T—The carrier services, wireless services, and half of Bell Labs retain the AT&T name.
2. Lucent Technologies—Data, voice, and networking equipment and the other half of Bell Labs.
3. NCR—Known as AT&T Global Information Solutions after the 1991 takeover, NCR is once again an independent computer manufacturer.

The Telecommunications Act of 1996 sought to encourage competition in all aspects and markets of telecommunications services including switched and dedicated local and inter-LATA traffic, cable TV, and wireless services such as paging, cellular, and satellite services. The legislation directs the FCC to produce the rules that will allow LECs and IXCs to compete in each other's markets. Companies that wish to offer local access service in competition with RBOCs are known as **competitive local exchange carriers (CLEC).**

Perhaps most importantly the law completely changed the regulatory environment of the telecommunications marketplace by expressly preempting the authority of Judge Greene to dictate the operation of the telecommunications industry in the United States. As a result of the act, the FCC has been given the task of establishing a fair and equitable market environment in which a variety of companies can compete in a deregulated manner. The goal of the Telecommunications Act of 1996 can be summarized in three words: *free market economy.* Figure 1-6 summarizes the major implications of the Telecommunications Act of 1996 from a variety of perspectives.

Managerial Perspective

TELECOMMUNICATIONS ACT OF 1996 IMPACT

In addition to its primary goal of creating competition in all aspects of the U.S. telecommunication market, the Telecommunications Act of 1996 has had several other effects on the various players in the marketplace. One of the most visible impacts is the merger and acquisition of telecommunications vendors in an attempt to gain competitive advantage. Because traditional long-distance carriers (IXCs) can potentially enter their marketplace, RBOCs have merged to increase territory size, capitalize major new ventures, and create a more formidable competitor for IXCs. The major RBOC realignments are as follows:

1. NYNEX and Bell Atlantic combined as Bell Atlantic to control the northeast corridor region from Washington D.C. to Boston.
2. Bell Atlantic and GTE are combining operations to expand their service offerings under the Verizon brand name.
3. PacTel (Pacific Telesis) and Southwestern Bell combined as SBC Communications to control telecommunications in the Texas to California high-tech region.
4. SBC then merged with Ameritech to add a large section of the Midwest to their portfolio.

Similarly traditional long-distance companies are merging to consolidate market position and capitalize on research and development dollars. In addition to mergers within the long-distance company ranks, IXCs have merged with companies that cover other sectors of the telecommunications industry.

1. European based WorldCom communications purchased UUNET, a leading Internet carrier.
2. MCI merged with WorldCom to form MCI-WorldCom.
3. America Online is currently trying to acquire Sprint.
4. MCI-WorldCom is also acquiring SkyTel, a leading two-way pager service provider.

Perspective	Implication/Importance
Strategic Intent	• Provides for a procompetitive deregulatory national policy framework by opening all telecommunications markets to competition • Directs the FCC to create rulemakings to produce this deregulated environment
FCC	• Imposes a significant burden on the FCC to produce new rules so that the deregulated market operates fairly for all competitors • Examines all regulations imposed on carriers and eliminates any that no longer serve a productive purpose
IXCs	• Eliminates the need for long distance carriers to file tariffs. Rates are determined by competitive pricing and the free market • Can enter into local access markets, thereby gaining access to local loops on a national basis • Will likely resell access to RBOC's local networks rather than building their own
CLECs	• Gain access to RBOCs local loop markets • Will likely resell access to RBOC's local networks rather than building their own • Looking at wireless solutions as an alternative to using the RBOC's local loops
LECs	• Can compete for IXC business within their own region as long as they can prove there is at least potential for competition in the local loop • Can enter into equipment manufacturing businesses
Cable TV Companies	• Can enter telephone business but must wait until cable rates are deregulated
Users	• Will be offered more opportunities for bundled services from a single vendor • May regain single source for voice and data services lost in original divestiture/deregulation • Increased competition in a variety of markets may produce lower costs

Figure 1-6 Telecommunications Act of 1996

5. AT&T has acquired TCI cable systems to expand its presence in the cable television and high-speed Internet via cable marketplaces.
6. Various IXCs are merging with or acquiring wireless carriers.

Although the resulting companies do not have the market position of the prebreakup AT&T, the market seems to be moving toward a scenario in which a few companies can offer all types of communications services from traditional telephony to wireless telephony, cable television, and Internet service. These companies, also known as

universal carriers, hope that by bundling various services together, they can become a one-stop solution for all of their customers' communications needs.

One of the key aspects of the Telecommunications Act of 1996 was that it opened the door for competition in the local phone service market. However, there has been little headway in this area. As of late 1999, CLECs accounted for less than 1% of the US local telephone marketplace. The main reason that CLECs are having trouble breaking into the marketplace is local loop access. A CLEC can deliver local telephone access in one of two ways: lease the existing local loop from the incumbent local service provider or provide an alternate means of customer connection.

If the CLEC chooses to lease local loop access from the incumbent LEC, it is limited to a retailer's profit, as the Act ensures the incumbent LEC of a reasonable profit for maintaining the local loops by setting the cost of local loop access to wholesale levels. The economics of this model simply have not spawned much interest in local access competition. However, new wireless technologies are making the second option, providing an alternate connection to the customer, far more viable. By implementing fixed-point wireless solutions, a CLEC can offer customers not only multiple lines of local telephone service, but also high-speed Internet access. By combining these new technologies with traditional local loop service, CLECs such as US Xchange are aggressively beginning to enter the local service marketplace.

Interestingly, this competition in the local service marketplace is welcomed by the incumbent LECs. According to the Act, LECs cannot enter the highly lucrative long-distance marketplace until they can show meaningful competition in the local service marketplace. In this case, the potential profit lost on local service (which is usually fixed) will be more than made up for in increased revenue from long-distance services.

Another key player in the industry that has been affected by the Act is the cable television (CATV) industry. The CATV industry has an inherent advantage over traditional local service providers: Its connection to the user natively provides significantly greater bandwidth than the traditional telephone local loop. This increased bandwidth allows multiple phone lines and high-speed Internet access to be bundled with traditional cable service.

Although they are well positioned from a cable plant basis to deliver service in the local market, most cable companies are poorly positioned economically to do so. Bearing large debt loads as a result of rapid expansion, CATV providers are too undercapitalized to make the required investment to upgrade their traditional one-way analog networks to support the two-way digital transmission required to deliver local telephone service. Besides the economic issue, CATV providers also lack expertise in switching environments to implement telephony over the cable infrastructure. These issues are currently driving multiple mergers and partnerships between CATV companies and traditional long-distance carriers. The combined companies can offer bundled local and long-distance service along with television and Internet access.

The importance of the Internet and the ability to offer high-speed Internet access to telephone service providers cannot be overstated. New technologies such as Voice Over IP (VOIP) have the potential to replace traditional circuit-switched telephone technologies with packet-switched voice. The impact of such a shift will likely be more dramatic on the telecommunications industry than all legislative and regulatory rulings combined.

Due to the distance insensitivity of packet-switched Internet telephone technologies, the concept of pay per minute long distance could become obsolete. Instead it might soon be possible to pay a monthly fee for access to long-distance network and make an unlimited number of calls to anywhere in the world for no additional charge. Several IXCs including MCI and AT&T are experimenting with using Internet technologies in the core of their network between POPs to leverage the distance insensitivity of packet-switched voice.

The ability of Internet telephony to compete with traditional telephone networks may ultimately depend as much on the regulatory environment as it does on the quality and reliability of the technology. It remains to be seen what influence, if any, the FCC will have on packet-switched Internet telephony. Recent rulings are inconclusive because the FCC has expressed concern about the impact of such technologies on universal access, but has yet to place any new barriers to their implementation.

The Standards Process

While the regulatory process is most important to carriers and their customers, the standards process is important to all constituencies of the data communications industry. Without standards, data communications would be nearly impossible, as single-vendor, customized transmission solutions would probably be the only way to achieve end-to-end transmissions. **Standards** allow multiple vendors to manufacture competing products that work together effectively. End-users can be confident that devices will operate as specified and will interoperate successfully. Standards can have a tremendous potential economic impact on vendors of data communications equipment, and the standards-making process is affected by both political and financial influences.

Although the charter of each standards-making organization dictates the exact procedure for standards development, the process can be generalized as follows:

1. Recognition of the need for a standard
2. Formation of some type of committee or task force
3. Information/recommendation gathering phase
4. Tentative/alternative standards issued
5. Feedback on tentative/alternative standards
6. Final standards issued
7. Compliance with final standards

Standards-Making Organizations Standards-making organizations for the data communications industry fall into two major categories:

- Officially sanctioned
- Ad hoc

Some of the most significant officially sanctioned standards-making organizations, whose standards are referred to throughout the book, are listed in Figure 1-7.

Because of the lag time often required to produce standards in an officially sanctioned standards-making organization, or perhaps in response to the ever-broadening scope of data communications-related technology, many ad hoc

Organization Name	Abbreviation	Authority/Charter	Mission/Contribution
International Organization for Standardization	ISO	International; voluntary	OSI 7 layer model
Comite Consultif International Telegraphique et Telephonique	CCITT	International; U.N. chartered	Telecommunications standards
International Telecommunications Union	ITU-T	International; U.N. chartered	Parent organization and successor to CCITT
American National Standards Institute	ANSI	U.S. government representative to ISO	Information systems standards
Institute of Electrical and Electronics Engineers	IEEE	Industrial professional society	Local area network standards
Internet Engineering Task Force	IETF	International, open	Design protocol and other standards for the Internet
Internet Architecture Board	IAB	International, open	Oversees the standards process for Internet standards as developed by the IETF
Internet Society	ISOC	International, open	Parent organization of the IETF and IAB
Electronics Industries Association	EIA	Trade organization	Electrical signaling standards, wiring standards

Figure 1-7 Officially Sanctioned Standards-Making Organizations

standards-making organizations continue to be formed. Known by a variety of terms including *task forces, user groups, interest groups, consortium, forum, alliances,* or *institutes,* these groups have developed standards for specific areas of the data communications industry.

Although these ad hoc organizations are able to produce standards faster, in most cases, than official standards-making organizations, their existence and operation pose a few potential problems. Vendor-initiated ad hoc standards-making organizations are occasionally organized into opposing camps, with users left as victims caught between multiple standards for a single item. These vendor-driven consortia do not necessarily have the best interests of end-users as their highest priority. Some ad hoc standards groups do not produce final standards, but rather seek to expedite the standards-making process by hammering out technical debates and issuing unified recommendations to official standards-making organizations for official sanction and ratification.

Business Impacts of Standards The standards-making process is important to manufacturers and they monitor it closely and participate in it actively. The development of new technology most often precedes its standardization. The development process is usually performed by either individual manufacturers or groups of manufacturers as part of their research and development work. Competing manufacturers may propose differing technological solutions for a given opportunity. It is often only after these competing technologies are about to come to market that the need for standardization prompts the formation of a standards committee.

It should be obvious that competing manufacturers have a strong desire to get their own technology declared as "the standard." To capture early market share and thereby influence the standards-making process, manufacturers often produce and sell equipment before standards are issued. Make no mistake about it: standards making can be a very political process. Furthermore, by the time standards are actually adopted for a given technology, the next generation of that technology is sometimes ready to be introduced to the market. Figure 1-8 attempts to illustrate this time lag between technological development and standards creation.

Practical Advice and Information

PROPRIETARY STANDARDS

Purchasers of data communications equipment should be wary of buying equipment that complies with proprietary prestandards. Have accommodations been made to upgrade the equipment to comply with official standards once they are issued? Will there be a charge for this upgrade? Will the upgrade require a return to the factory, or is it a software upgrade that can be downloaded and installed in the field?

In general, standards work to the advantage of the data communications consumer, as they allow interoperability of equipment manufactured by a variety of vendors. However, users should be aware of at least two standards-related issues that can cause confusion and potentially lead to bad purchase decisions and operational nightmares.

Standards Extensions Recalling the potentially competitive nature of the standards-making process, it should come as no surprise that final standards are sometimes "least common denominator" implementations of competing proposals. To differentiate their own product offerings, vendors are likely to offer "extensions" to a given "standard." Naturally, one vendor's "extensions" do not necessarily match all the other vendors' "extensions." Users must be careful not only to make sure that a particular vendor's equipment meets industry standards, but also to know *how* the equipment meets the standards and whether or not the vendor has implemented extensions to the standard.

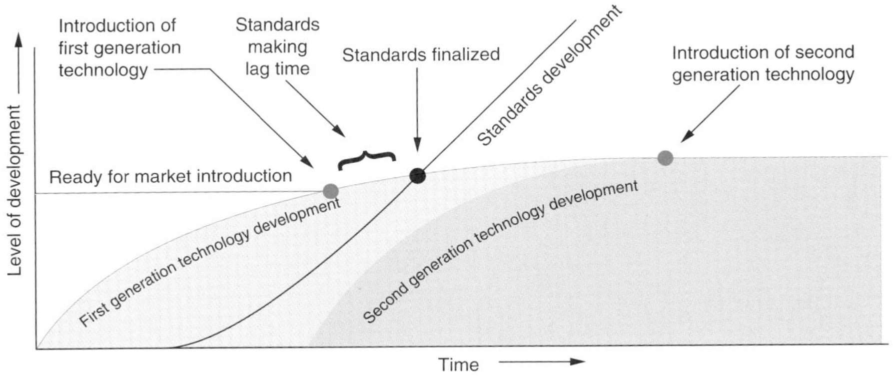

Figure 1-8 Technology Development and Standards Creation

The Jargon Jungle Unfortunately, standards do not apply to the vocabulary used by salespeople and marketing agencies to describe data communications hardware and software technology. There is no standards-making body to regulate data communications vocabulary and its use. As a result, the data communications user is trapped in a situation sometimes referred to as the "jargon jungle." Competing manufacturers often call similar features or operational characteristics by different names, leaving it to the data communications consumer to sort out the differences.

Put another way:

- **Law 3.** There are no data communications police.

The best way to prevent being lost in the "jargon jungle" is to ask lots of questions. Be prepared to determine functionality of equipment based on operational characteristics rather than on package labels.

Manufacturing, Research, and Technology

Just as the regulatory and carriers components of the data communications environment were grouped together based on their respective interactions, many of the remaining component entities portrayed in Figure 1-1 can be legitimately grouped together based on their most important interactive force: business.

Supply and Demand Unlike the formal interactions of proposals and rulings that join regulatory and carrier components, the interacting forces that join the remaining components as well as carriers are supply and demand, basic economic concepts. That's right, *data communications is business.* Figure 1-9 attempts to graphically illustrate the complex relationship among these many data communications environment components. The present status and near-term trends of any particular component are directly related to the net effect of the supply and demand forces of all other components combined.

This same phenomenon is sometimes referred to as **technology push/demand pull.** In a technology push scenario, new technologies may be introduced to the market to spawn innovative uses for this technology and thereby generate demand. Conversely, business needs may create a demand for services or technological innovation that are not currently available. However, the demand pull causes research and development efforts to accelerate, thereby introducing the new technology sooner than it would have otherwise been brought to market.

As an example, business and users may demand faster transfer of data. However, if research has not supplied the technology to accomplish these faster transfers, then manufacturers cannot produce and supply (sell) these products to business and users. Nor can vendors and consultants distribute and recommend their use.

Available technology also plays a key role in the relationship between business and carriers. Understanding that the phone companies are in business to make a profit and therefore need to sell the network services that business is willing to buy at a price business is willing to pay, it should follow that these enabling technologies tie the business demand for network services to the carrier's supply of network services. Stated another way, a carrier cannot provide the network services that businesses demand unless the proper technology is in place. Carriers can afford to invest in new technology only through profitable operations. This dynamic relationship can be expressed in the following equation:

Business Demand + Available Technology = Emerging Network Services

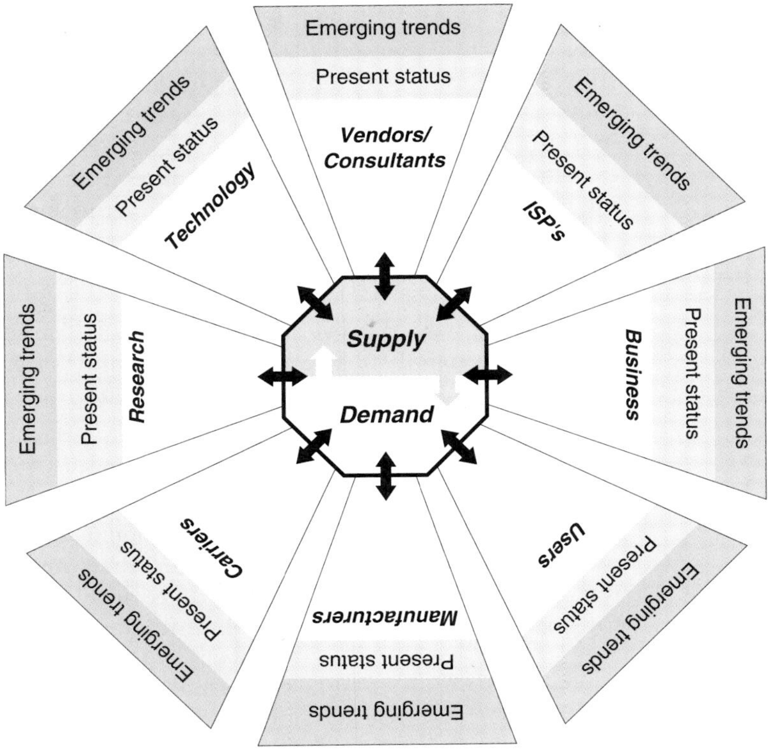

Figure 1-9 Supply and Demand as Driving Forces of the Data Communications Industry

CHALLENGES AND SOLUTIONS TO BUSINESS-ORIENTED DATA COMMUNICATIONS ANALYSIS

Having explored the interacting components of the data communications industry to gain an appreciation of its dynamic nature, the network analyst must next identify the key challenges to success in the data communications field and the potential solutions to those challenges. One of the most important things to realize is that corporations are not interested in investing in technology merely for technology's sake. Rather, implemented technology must produce measurable impact on business goals and requirements. Ensuring and accounting for this technological impact on business goals is a significant challenge.

Challenge: Information Technology Investment vs. Productivity Gains, Ensuring Implemented Technology Meets Business Needs

In the past decade, over $1 trillion dollars has been invested by business in information technology. Despite this massive investment, carefully conducted research indicates that there has been little if any increase in productivity as a direct result of this investment. This dilemma is known as the **productivity paradox.** How did so much money get invested in technology that failed to deliver increases in productivity? What was the nature of the analysis and design process that recommended the purchase of this technology? Clearly, something is wrong with an analysis and design process that recommends technology implementations that fail to meet the strategic business objective of increased productivity.

What are the characteristics required of an analysis and design process that has the potential to overcome the productivity paradox? How can a network analyst remain properly focused on business requirements while performing technology analysis? Bringing this general investment in technology issue down to a particular investment in data communications and networking it may be safe to say that:

- **Law 4.** If the network doesn't make good business sense, it probably makes no sense.

To overcome the productivity paradox, a structured methodology must be followed to ensure that the implemented network technology meets the communications and business needs of the intended business, organization, or individual. The top-down approach and benchmarking are two potential solutions to the productivity paradox.

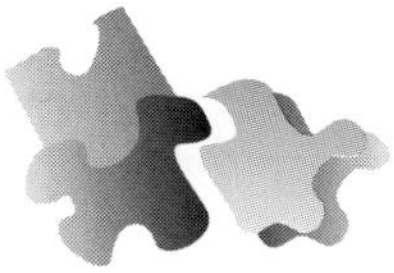

Applied Problem Solving

SOLUTION: THE TOP-DOWN APPROACH

One such structured methodology is known as the top-down approach. Such an approach can be graphically illustrated in a **top-down model** shown in Figure 1-10. Use of the top-down approach as illustrated in the top-down model is relatively straightforward. Insisting that a top-down approach to network analysis and design is undertaken should ensure that the network design implemented meets the business needs and objectives that motivated the design in the first place.

This top-down approach requires network analysts to understand business constraints and objectives, as well as information systems applications and the data on which those applications run, before considering data communications and networking options.

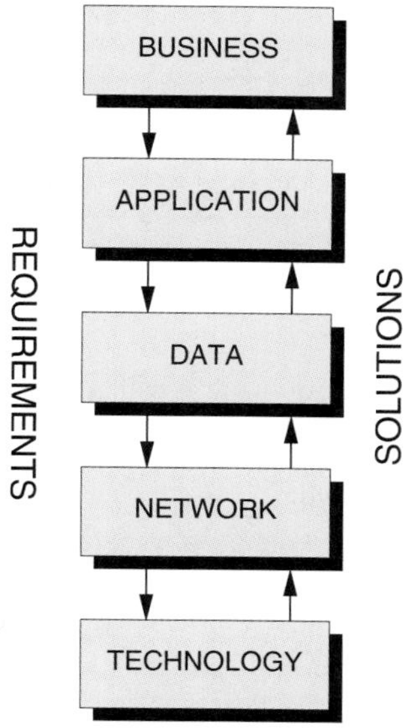

Figure 1-10 The Top-Down Model

Notice where the network layer occurs in the top-down model. It is no accident that data communications and networking form the foundation of today's sophisticated information systems. A properly designed network supports flexible delivery of data to distributed application programs, allowing businesses to respond quickly to customer needs and rapidly changing market conditions.

The Top-Down Model How does the proper use of the top-down model ensure effective, business-oriented network analysis and design? Figure 1-11 lists the analysis processes associated with each layer of the top-down model. One must start with the *business* level objectives. What is the company (organization, individual) trying to accomplish by installing this network? Without a clear understanding of business level objectives it is nearly impossible to configure and implement a successful network. In many cases, businesses take this opportunity to critically reexamine their business processes in an analysis methodology known as **business process reengineering (BPR).**

Top-Down Model Layer	Associated Analysis Processes
Business Layer	• Strategic business planning • Business process reengineering • Identify major business functions • Identify business processes • Identify business opportunities
Applications Layer	• Applications development • Systems analysis and design • Identify information needs • Relate information needs to business processes and opportunities
Data Layer	• Database analysis and design • Data modeling • Data distribution analysis • Client/server architecture design • Distributed database design • Relate data collection and distribution to information and business needs
Network Layer	• Network analysis and design • Logical network design (what) • Network implementation planning • Network management and performance monitoring • Relate logical network design to data collection and distribution design
Technology Layer	• Technology analysis grids • Hardware software-media technology analysis • Physical network design (how) • Physical network implementation • Relate physical network design to logical network design

Figure 1-11 Analysis Processes of the Top-Down Model

Once business level objectives are understood, one must understand the *applications* that will be running on the computer systems attached to these networks. After all, it is the applications that will be generating the traffic that will travel over the implemented network.

Once applications are understood and have been documented, the *data* that the applications generate must be examined. In this case, the term *data* is used in a general sense, as today's networks are likely to transport a variety of payloads including voice, video, image, and fax in addition to true data. Data traffic analysis must determine not only the amount of data to be transported, but also important characteristics about the nature of that data.

Once data traffic analysis has been completed, the following should be known:

1. Physical locations of data (Where?)
2. Data characteristics and compatibility issues (What?)
3. Amount of data generated and transported (How much?)

Given these requirements as determined by the upper layers of the top-down model, the next job is to determine the requirements of the *network* that will possess the capability to deliver this data in a timely, cost-effective manner. These network performance criteria could be referred to as *what* the implemented network must do to meet the business objectives outlined at the outset of this top-down analysis. These requirements are also referred to as the **logical network design.**

The *technology* layer analysis, in contrast, determines *how* various hardware and software components are combined to build a functional network that meets the predetermined business objectives. The delineation of required technology is referred to as the **physical network design.**

Overall, the relationship between the layers of the top-down model can be described as follows: analysis at upper layers produces requirements that are passed down to lower layers, while solutions meeting these requirements are passed back to upper layers. If this relationship among layers holds true throughout the business oriented network analysis, then the implemented technology (bottom layer) should meet the initially outlined business objectives (top layer). Hence, the name, top-down approach.

Applied Problem Solving

SOLUTION: BENCHMARKING

If using the top-down approach ensures that implemented technology meets business objectives, how can the impact of implemented technology on business objectives be measured? Without measurement, the top-down approach can't be proven to be any more effective at overcoming the productivity paradox than any other analysis and design methodology. In the age of limited professional staffs and operating budgets, network managers must be able to prove the strategic importance of networking resources to achieve overall business objectives. Without such proof, network managers may soon find themselves and their staffs replaced by outside contractors.

One way to demonstrate the impact of implemented technology is to tie networking costs to business value through a process known as **benchmarking.** Benchmarking can be summarized into the following three major steps:

1. Examine and document quantifiable improvements to business processes.
2. Perform surveys to measure customer satisfaction with deployed network services.
3. Compare actual implementation costs with the cost to purchase similar services from outside vendors **(outsourcing)** or examine other companies in the same vertical market to compare costs.

Benchmarking the impact of networking technology is not an exact science. Although costs are relatively easy to quantify, the same cannot be said for benefits. Controlling all variables affecting business improvement is difficult at best. For example, how can improved business performance be directly attributed to network improvements while eliminating such variables as an improved economy or a reduction in competition?

Challenge: Analysis of Complex Data Communications Connectivity and Compatibility Issues

Assuming that the proper use of the top-down model will ensure that implemented technical solutions will meet stated business requirements, the more technical challenges of network analysis and design must be addressed.

Introduction to Protocols and Compatibility Solving incompatibility problems is at the heart of successful network implementation. Compatibility can be thought of as successfully bridging the gap or communicating between two or more technology components, whether hardware or software. This logical gap between components is commonly referred to as an **interface.**

Interfaces may be physical (hardware to hardware) in nature:

- Cables physically connecting to serial ports on a computer.
- A network interface card physically plugging into the expansion bus inside a computer.

Interfaces may also be logical or software-oriented (software to software),

- A network operating system client software (Windows for Workgroups) communicating with the client PC's operating system (DOS).
- A client-based data query tool (Microsoft Excel) gathering data from a large database management system (Oracle).

Finally, interfaces may cross the hardware to software boundary:

- A network operating system specific piece of software known as a driver that interfaces to an installed network interface card (NIC).
- A piece of operating system software known as a kernel that interfaces to a computer's CPU chip.

These various interfaces can be successfully bridged to support compatibility between components because of **protocols.** Protocols are nothing more than rules for how communicating hardware and software components bridge interfaces or talk to one another. Protocols may be proprietary (used exclusively by one or more vendors) or open (used freely by all interested parties). Protocols may be officially sanctioned

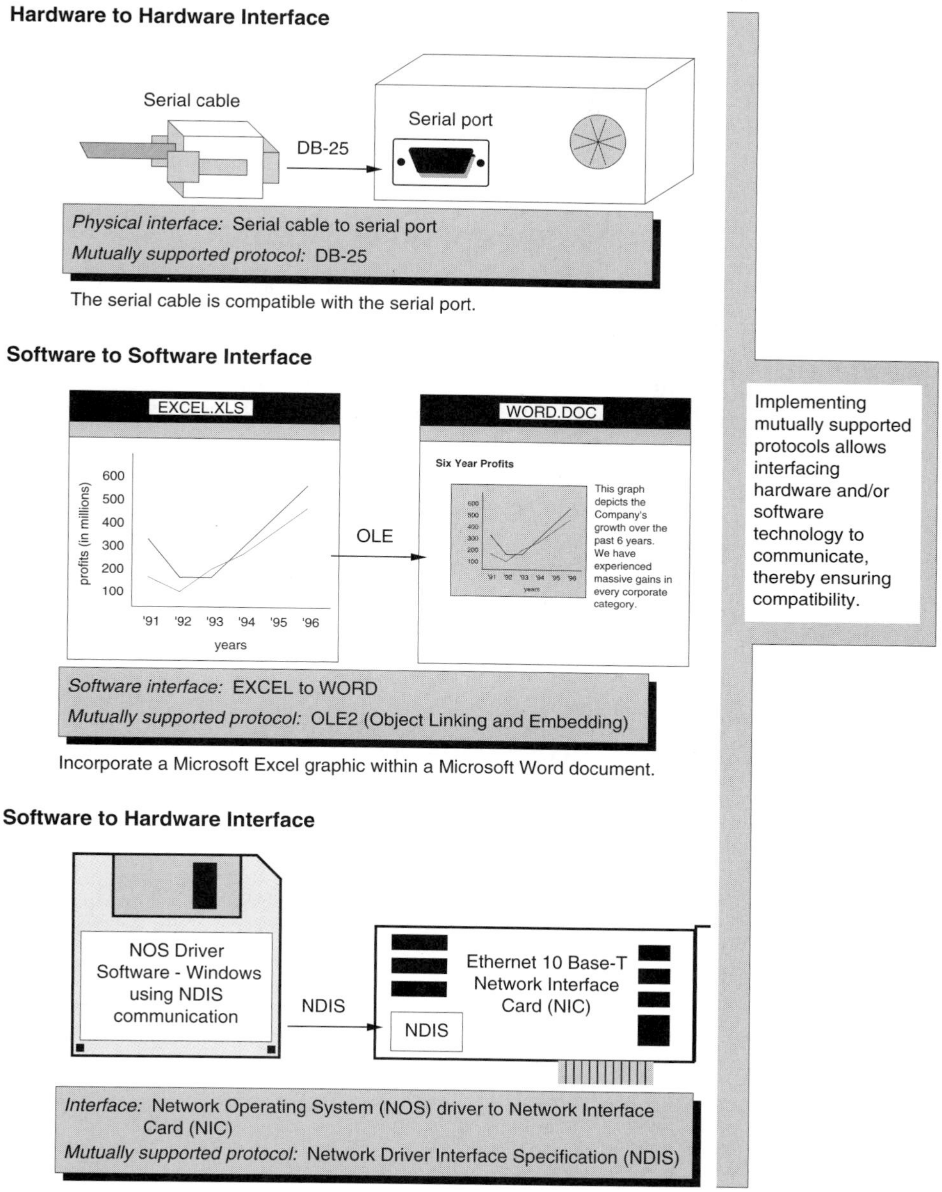

Figure 1-12 Interfaces, Protocols, and Compatibility

by international standards-making bodies such as the International Organization for Standardization (ISO), or they may be purely market driven (de facto protocols). Figure 1-12 illustrates the relationship between interfaces, protocols, and compatibility.

For every potential hardware-to-hardware, software-to-software, and hardware-to-software interface, there is likely to be one or more protocols supported. The sum of all of the protocols employed in a particular computer is sometimes referred to as that computer's **protocol stack.** Successfully determining which protocols must be supported in which instances for the multitude of possible interfaces in a complicated network design is likely to mean the difference between the success or failure of a network implementation.

How can a network analyst possibly keep track of all potential interfaces and their associated protocols? What is needed is a framework in which to organize the various interfaces and protocols in complicated network designs. More than one such framework, otherwise known as communications architectures, exists. Two of the most popular communications architectures are the seven-layer OSI model and the four-layer internet suite of protocols model.

Applied Problem Solving

SOLUTION: THE OSI NETWORK REFERENCE MODEL

Choosing the technology and protocols that can meet the requirements as determined in the logical network design from the network layer of the top down model requires a structured methodology of its own. Fortunately, the ISO has developed a framework for organizing networking technology and protocol solutions known as the open systems interconnection (OSI) network reference model or OSI model for short. The following section offers the reader only a brief introduction to the overall functionality of the OSI model as a network analysis tool; more detailed information on the model is provided throughout the remainder of the text. The OSI model should be looked on as a powerful, but somewhat complex, tool.

This section is intended as an overview of the OSI model. In Chapter 5, the model is explored in much greater detail in terms of both architecture and functionality in the discussion of LAN architectures and internetwork connectivity. The **OSI seven-layer model** is illustrated in Figure 1-13.

OSI Model Layer	Functionality	Automobile Assembly Line
7: Application	Layer where application programs interact and receive services	Dealer Installed Options: Options desired by users are added at the dealership
6: Presentation	Ensures reliable session transmission between applications; takes care of differences in data representation	Painting and Finish Work: Vehicle is painted and trim is applied
5: Session	Enables two applications to communicate across the network	Interior: Seats and dashboard are added to passenger compartment
4: Transport	Ensures reliable transmission from end-to-end, usually across multiple nodes	Electrical: Electrical system and components are added
3: Network	Sets up the pathways or end-to-end connections, usually across a long distance, or multiple nodes	Body: Passenger compartment and fenders are attached to the chassis
2: Data Link	Puts messages together, attaches proper headers to be sent out or received, ensures messages are delivered between two points	Engine/Drive Train: Engine and transmission components pro provide the vehicle with propulsion
1: Physical	Concerned with transmitting bits of data over a physical medium	Chassis/Frame: Steel is fabricated to form the chassis on which all other components will travel

Figure 1-13 The OSI Model

The OSI model divides the communication between any two networked computing devices into seven layers or categories. Network analysts literally talk in terms of the OSI model. When troubleshooting network problems, inevitably the savvy network analyst starts with the physical layer (layer 1) and ensures that protocols and interfaces are operational at each layer before moving up the OSI model. Another benefit of the OSI model is that it allows data communications technology developers and standards developers to talk about the interconnection of two networks or computers in common terms without dealing in proprietary vendor jargon. These "common terms" are the result of the layered architecture of the seven layer OSI model. The architecture breaks the task of two computers communicating with each other into separate but interrelated tasks, each represented by its own layer. As can be seen in Figure 1-13, the top layer (layer 7) represents services offered to the application programs running on each computer and is therefore aptly named the application layer. The bottom layer (layer 1) is concerned with the actual physical connection of the two computers or networks and is therefore named the physical layer. The remaining layers (2–6) may not be as obvious but, nonetheless, represent a sufficiently distinct logical group of functions required to connect two computers, as to justify a separate layer. As will be seen later in the text, some of the layers are divided into sublayers.

To use the OSI model, a network analyst lists the known protocols for each computing device or network node in the proper layer of its own seven-layer OSI model. The collection of these categorized protocols is known as the protocol stack of the network node. For example, the physical media employed, such as unshielded twisted pair, coaxial cable, or fiber optic cable, would be entered as a layer 1 protocol, while Ethernet or token ring network architectures might be entered as a layer 2 protocol. As will be seen later in Chapter 5, a given computer may employ more than one protocol on one or more layers of the OSI model. In these cases, such computers are described as supporting multiple protocol stacks or simply as multiprotocol.

The OSI model allows network analysts to produce an accurate inventory of protocols present on any given network node. This protocol profile represents a unique personality of each network node and gives the network analyst some insight into what **protocol conversion,** if any, may be necessary to allow any two network nodes to communicate successfully. Ultimately, the OSI model provides a structured methodology for determining the hardware and software technology required in the physical network design to meet the requirements of the logical network design.

Perhaps the best analogy for the OSI model is an assembly line producing an automobile. Although each process or step is independently managed and performed, each step also depends on previous steps to be performed according to standardized specifications or protocols for the overall process to be successful. Similarly, each layer of the OSI model operates independently while depending on neighboring layers to perform tasks according to specification while cooperating in the attainment of the overall task of communication between two computers or networks.

The OSI model is not a protocol or group of protocols. It is a standardized, empty framework into which protocols can be listed to perform an effective network analysis and design. As will be seen later in the text, however, the ISO has also produced a set of OSI protocols that correspond to some of the layers of the OSI model. It is important to differentiate between the OSI model and OSI protocols.

The OSI model is used throughout the remainder of the text as the protocol stacks of various network operating systems are analyzed and in the analysis and design of advanced network connectivity alternatives.

Applied Problem Solving

SOLUTION: THE INTERNET SUITE OF PROTOCOLS MODEL

Although the OSI model is perhaps more famous than any OSI protocol, just the opposite is true for the **internet suite of protocols model** and its associated protocols. Also known as the **TCP/IP** protocol suite, or **TCP/IP** architecture, this communications architecture takes its name from **transmission control protocol/internet protocol,** the de facto standard protocols for open systems internetworking. As can be seen in Figure 1-14, TCP and IP are just two of the protocols associated with this model.

Like the OSI model, the TCP/IP model is a layered communications architecture in which upper layers use the functionality offered by lower layer protocols. Each layer's protocols are able to operate independently from the protocols of other layers. For example, protocols on a given layer can be updated or modified without having to change the protocols in any other layers. A recent example of this independence is the new version of IP known as IPng (IP next generation) developed in response to a pending shortage of IP addresses. This proposed change is possible without the need to change all other protocols in the TCP/IP communication architecture. The exact mechanics of how TCP/IP and related protocols work are explored in greater depth in Chapter 7.

Figure 1-14 compares the four layer Internet suite of protocols model with the seven-layer OSI model. Either communications architecture can be used to analyze and design communication networks. In the case of the internet suite of protocols model, the full functionality of internetwork communications is divided into four layers rather than seven. Because of the fewer layers and the dominant market position of TCP/IP, some network analysts consider the internet suite of protocols model to be more simple and practical than the OSI model.

Layer	OSI	INTERNET	Data Format	Protocols
7	Application	Application	Messages or Streams	TELNET FTP TFTP SMTP SNMP CMOT MIB
6	Presentation			
5	Session			
4	Transport	Transport or Host-Host	Transport Protocol Packets	TCP UDP
3	Network	Internet	IP Diagrams	IP
2	Data Link	Network Access	Frames	
1	Physical			

Figure 1-14 Internet Suite of Protocols vs. OSI

Applied Problem Solving

SOLUTION: THE I-P-O MODEL

Once the protocols are determined for two or more computers that wish to communicate, the next step is to determine the technology required to deliver the identified internetworking functionality and protocols.

To understand the basic function of any piece of networking equipment, one really need only understand the differences between the characteristics of the data that came in and the data that went out. Those differences identified were processed by the data communications equipment.

This input-processing-output or **I-P-O model** is another key model used throughout the textbook to analyze a wide variety of networking equipment and opportunities. The I-P-O model provides a framework in which to focus on the difference between the data that came into a particular networked device (I) and the data that came out of that same device (O). By defining this difference, the processing (P) performed by the device is documented.

As a simple example of the use of the I-P-O model, let's assume that we wish to hook a particular PC to a particular printer. After some investigation, we discover that the PC can provide input (I) to the printer (O) only through the PC's serial port. However, the printer (O) only has a parallel interface. As a result, we have a serial interface (perhaps DB-25, RS-232) as an input and have a parallel interface (centronics connector) as an output. What is required is a device to provide the necessary (P) recessing to convert our serial input to the required parallel output. Such devices are readily available. However, before purchasing such a device, it is essential to have organized and documented the required electrical and mechanical protocols that must be interfaced and converted between. By organizing such interfaces in a simple I-P-O model, the exact conversions that must take place are immediately evident.

Although at first glance the I-P-O model may seem overly simplistic, it is another valuable model that can assist network analysts in organizing thoughts, documenting requirements, and articulating needs.

THE DATA COMMUNICATIONS PROFESSION

Where Does Data Communications Fit in an Overall Information Systems Architecture?

How is a top-down approach to data communications analysis and design actually implemented in today's corporations? What is the overall information systems structure into which this top-down approach fits? Figure 1-15 illustrates one way in which a top-down approach could be implemented within the overall framework of an information systems architecture.

Several key points illustrated in the diagram are worth noting. Predictably, the entire information systems development process begins with the business analysis process. What is important to note, however, is that all major sections of the top-down approach model—business, applications, data, and network—take part in the business analysis process.

In some cases, a separate technology assessment group exists within a corporation and partakes in the business analysis phase of the information systems development process. In so doing, each layer of the top-down model is represented by trained individuals and complementary processes in the top-down approach to information systems development. This initial participation of all segments of the

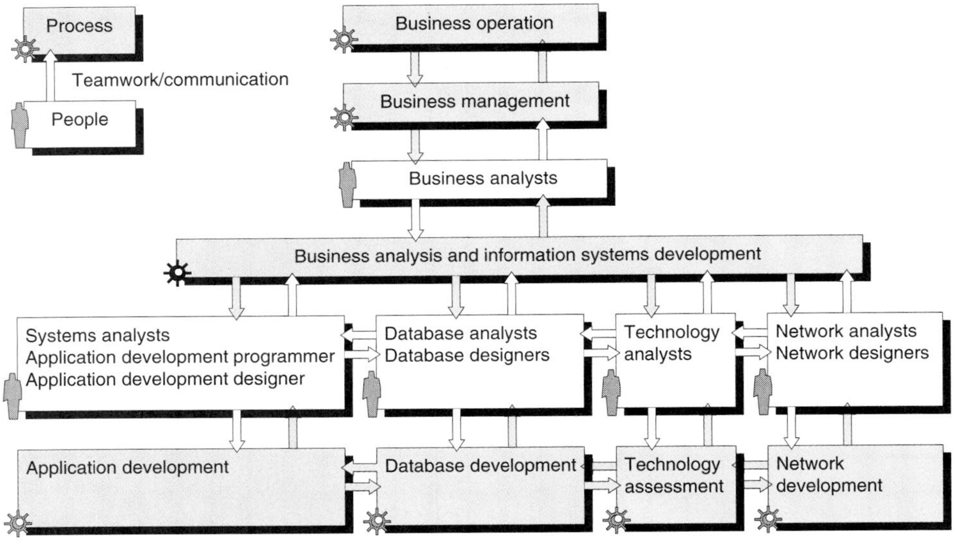

Figure 1-15 The Top-Down Approach to Information Systems Development

information systems development team in the business analysis portion of the process ensures that the implemented system will adequately support the business functions for which it was intended.

After this initial participation of all segments of the team in the business analysis phase, each segment develops its portion of the information system. However, merely knowing the business needs that an information system is trying to meet is an insufficient guarantee of successful implementation. It is essential that during the development process, the applications, database, network, and technology development teams continually communicate to ensure that their finished subsystems will interoperate effectively enough to support the identified business needs. This critical communication between subsystems as well as between the individuals who developed these subsystems is illustrated in Figure 1-15.

Professional Development

The accomplishment of this communication between business, application, database, network, and technology analysts should not be taken for granted. These analysts must be able to speak each other's languages and jargon to communicate effectively. The need to understand all aspects of the information systems architecture has major implications for the proper training of data communications and networking professionals.

Unless one understands "the big picture" of the top-down model, one cannot effectively design and implement the data communications and networking foundation to support this same big picture. Put another way, data communications cannot be studied in a vacuum. The study of data communications and networking must be approached from "the big picture" perspective, ever-mindful of the tremendous potential effect that data communications and networking decisions have on this same big picture.

Critical Skills for Data Communications Professionals To understand the critical skills required of data communications professionals, one must first thoroughly understand the business environment in which these professionals operate. Today's economic environment has been alternatively described as the information age or a knowledge-based economy. Characteristics of such an economy are the recognition of information as a corporate asset to be leveraged for competitive advantage and the need for highly reliable networks to support the mission-critical applications that deliver valuable information to key decision makers.

Such an economic environment requires data communications professionals who can move beyond their technical expertise and specialization by demonstrating the ability to solve business problems. In this role, data communications professionals will be seen increasingly as change agents and partners and less as technology experts and consultants.

So what do the current trends in data communications indicate in terms of employment opportunities? Given the recognition by business of the importance of networks and given the complicated nature of both the data communications technology and the integration of that technology to carrier-provided network services, job opportunities should be excellent for data communications professionals who

- Understand and can speak "business."
- Demonstrate an ability to own and solve business problems in a partnership rather than consultative role.
- Demonstrate an ability to look outside their own expertise for solutions.
- Exhibit an understanding of the need for lifelong learning.
- Demonstrate an ability to evaluate technology with a critical eye as to cost/benefit and potential for significant business impact of that technology.
- Understand comparative value and proper application of available network services and can work effectively with carriers to see that implementations are completed properly and cost effectively.
- Communicate effectively, both verbally and orally, with both technically oriented people and business management personnel.

The multitalented nature of these data communications professionals is illustrated in Figure 1-16.

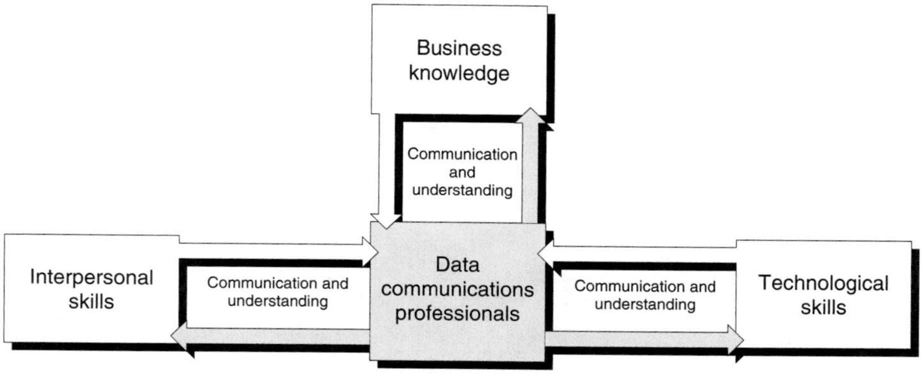

Figure 1-16 Critical Skills for Data Communications Professionals

The Certification Question Certification as an indication of mastery of a particular vendor's technology may be important in some employment situations. Figure 1-17 lists some of the vendor-specific certifications available to data communications professionals.

Some concerns with certification programs are

- The amount of practical, hands-on experience required to earn a given certification.
- The amount of continuing education and experience required to retain a certification.
- Vendor-specific certifications do not provide the broad background required for today's multivendor internetworks.

In an effort to address these concerns, the Network Professional Association has developed a certification known as the Certified Network Professional (CNP). To earn the CNP certification, applicants must

- Already have earned at least two of the vendor-specific certifications listed in Figure 1-17.
- Have at least 2 years of employment as a network professional.
- Pass the CNP examination, which includes sections on client operating systems, network operating systems, hardware, protocols, and topologies.

To remain certified as a CNP, an individual must participate in between 60 and 120 hours of continuing education per year and must remain employed in the networking profession. As the networking profession matures, the importance of certification to the profession remains to be seen.

The Opportunity To say that these are exciting times in the field of data communications is an understatement of untold proportions. The opportunities are indeed significant for those individuals properly prepared. We invite you to enter the exciting world of data communications with us. We are confident that it is a journey you will not soon forget. For a more humorous view of pursuing a career in data communications, see the Ten Top Reasons to be in Data Communications in Appendix B.

Vendor	Certification
Compaq	Accredited system engineer
Lotus	Certified Lotus professional
Microsoft	Certified systems engineer (MCSE)
Novell	Certified Novell engineer (CNE)
Cisco Systems	Cisco Certified Network Associate (CCNA) Cisco certified internetwork expert (CCIE)

Figure 1-17 Vendor-Specific Certifications

SUMMARY

Today's data communications industry is characterized by an environment consisting of a group of interacting components such a business, technology and research, standards-making organizations, regulatory agencies, and common carriers. The state of the overall industry at any time is the product of the interaction of these components. To be an effective participant in the data communications field, one must be aware of the forces at work that are shaping the industry.

The data communications industry was traditionally tightly regulated. Although recent changes such as the breakup of AT&T in the early 1980s and the Telecommunications Act of 1996 have moved the marketplace toward a competitive model, local telephone and cable rates are still tightly regulated.

Data communications and networking are integral parts of an overall information systems architecture. The ultimate success of an implemented information system depends largely on the design of the network that forms the foundation of that system. This high degree of integration between networking and other information system architecture components is graphically illustrated in the top-down model.

The top-down model implies that any information system design must begin with a thorough understanding of business requirements before subsequent issues such as applications, data, networking, and technology are addressed.

The integrated nature of the network layer of an information systems architecture is mirrored in the skills required of today's data communications professionals. The demand is high for individuals well versed in business analysis, information systems, and networking design combined with outstanding written and verbal communications skills.

Remember—if the network does not make good business sense, it probably makes no sense at all.

KEY TERMS

access charges
benchmarking
business process reengineering
carriers
central office
CLEC
CO
co-location
competitive local exchange carriers
data communications
demand pull
deregulation
divestiture
equal access
I-P-O model
interexchange carriers
interface
Internet suite of protocols model
IXC
LATA
LEC
local access transport area
local exchange carrier
local loops
logical network design
MFJ
modified final judgment
OSI seven layer model
outsourcing
physical network design
point of presence
POP
productivity paradox
protocol conversion
protocol stack
protocols
PSTN
public switched telephone network
RBOC
regional Bell operating companies
regulatory [agencies]
standards
TCP/IP
technology push
telecommunications
Telecommunications Act of 1996
top-down model
transmission control protocol/internet protocol
universal access
universal carriers
universal service

REVIEW QUESTIONS

1. What are the major interacting components that make up today's data communications industry?
2. What are the specific interaction scenarios between the following components: Manufacturers and standards-making organizations, Business and manufacturers, Carriers and regulatory agencies, Carriers and political/judicial/legislative?
3. Where does data communications and networking fit in an overall information systems architecture?
4. What is the role of business requirements analysis in network analysis and design?
5. What is the top-down model and how is it employed in network analysis and design?
6. Define the relationship between the following terms: inter-LATA and intra-LATA, CO and POP, local loop and RBOC.
7. What is the overall intent of the Telecommunications Act of 1996?
8. What has been the impact of the Telecommunications Act of 1996 on the traditional telecommunications players?
9. What skills are required of today's data communications professional?
10. What is divestiture and how does it differ from deregulation?
11. What is an RBOC?
12. Why is the data communications industry in such a state of change?
13. What is the Modified Final Judgment and why is it important?
14. What are the key events that led up to divestiture and deregulation?
15. Who were the big winners and losers as a result of divestiture?
16. From a data communications user's perspective, what have been the most important impacts of divestiture and deregulation?
17. Explain how carriers can engage in both regulated and unregulated business ventures.
18. Which agencies are responsible for regulation of carriers on both a state and federal level?
19. What is the OSI model and why is it important?
20. Why is the standards-making process so politically charged at times?
21. Why do standards often lag behind technological development?
22. What are the possible business impacts of standards on a manufacturer of data communications equipment?
23. How do the laws of supply and demand apply to the data communications industry? Give examples.
24. What is benchmarking and how is it related to the top-down model?
25. What is the I-P-O model and of what value is it?
26. What are the major processes performed by most data communications equipment?
27. Distinguish between and give an example of each of the three types of interfaces discussed in the chapter.
28. What is the relationship between interfaces, protocols, and standards?
29. What is meant by the statement, "Data communications solutions are business solutions"?
30. What is the internet suite of protocols model?
31. Describe the similarities and differences between the OSI model and the internet suite of protocols model.
32. What are the benefits and shortcomings of vendor-specific certifications?
33. What are the major differences between logical network design and physical network design?
34. Explain how the processes associated with each layer of the top-down model contribute to effective information systems development.
35. How can one avoid wasting money on technology that does not improve productivity?
36. What kinds of opportunities are available in the data communications industry for properly trained graduates?
37. How can equations such as "Business Demands + Available Technology = Emerging Network Services" remain useful to you in the future?
38. What is the productivity paradox and why should a network analyst be concerned with it?

ACTIVITIES

1. Contact the local provider of telecommunications services to your home or business. Inquire as to how long-distance calls are passed along to user-specified long distance carriers.
2. If your local telecommunications provider is not one of the seven RBOCs, inquire as to the history of this company's providing telecommunications service in this area. Why doesn't one of the RBOCs supply local telecommunications service in this area?
3. Ask your public utilities commission about the regulations in your state for shutting off phone service due to nonpayment. Is phone service seen more as a right or privilege in your state?
4. Ask your local telecommunications carrier or RBOC which aspects of its business are regulated vs. unregulated. Draw a diagram.
5. Are any of your local carrier's unregulated activities being considered for regulation?
6. Invite a telecommunications professional who was in the business at the time of divestiture to speak to your class regarding life before and after divestiture. Try to get speakers representing both the user's and carrier's perspective.
7. Find out if there are any CLECs currently marketing telecommunications services in your area. If so, compare their service offerings and pricing plans against the incumbent LEC.
8. Gather job postings for networking-related careers. Put together a scrap book or bulletin board display. What types of technical and non-technical skills are required? What are the salary ranges? Do all jobs require experience?
9. What types of professional certifications, if any, are currently available to people in the field of data communications and networking? How are such certifications viewed by companies hiring networking professionals?
10. Who is the current chairman of the FCC and what are his/her qualifications?
11. Who are the Public Utility Commissioners in your home state? What are their qualifications for the position?
12. Which committees in the House of Representatives and Senate consider legislation related to telecommunications?
13. Which representatives/senators currently serve on those committees? How much financial support do these elected officials receive from telecommunications companies or lobbyists?
14. What, if any, telecommunications-related legislation is currently being considered by Congress?
15. Do standards always lag behind technological development? If not, give an example.

CASE STUDY

QuikOrder Brings Domino's Pizza to You in 30 Minutes or Less

You know you get cranky when your pizza isn't delivered on time – Domino's does too. That's why when the company decided to take pizza orders online, it brought in a fault-tolerant ordering system that keeps servers up and pizza orders flowing.

The pizza company is so convinced online services are the way to go, it expects that 50% of its business will be conducted over the Internet or interactive TV – such as Web TV – in the next five years, says Glen Mueller, president of Domino's franchisee RPM Pizza in Gulfport, Miss.

To prepare for that growth, individual Domino's franchises are contracting with QuikOrder, an e-commerce service provider in Chicago. In the eight months QuikOrder has been taking orders for Domino's, it has logged more than 10,000 orders. When the project is complete, over 300 stores in 15 states will use the online system. In Mueller's case, he is installing QuikOrder software in 160 stores.

QuikOrder, which supplies the e-commerce software, installed a fault-tolerant cluster called the Endurance 4000 from

Marathon Technologies in its Chicago headquarters to keep its servers functioning 24–7. "The competition to online ordering is people ordering over the phone," says Ray Anderson, president of QuikOrder. "We wanted dial-tone reliability, just like the telephone company offers. We can't have any downtime. In fact, if a user was on the system and something failed, we wouldn't want the user to know it."

When a customer visits the quikorder.com site, he enters his zip code, name, address, e-mail or ICQ address, and other pertinent information. If the store is open, he orders the pizza he wants. If the store is closed, he will be directed to check back later. Comments, such as "Watch out for hungry pit bull," or "Deliver to pool in backyard" can be added to the order, and the system will tell the customer how long delivery will take or when his carry-out will be ready.

The QuikOrder system automatically dispatches the order to the closest Domino's store. Domino's sends a confirmation to the user's e-mail. Pizza reorders take less than 30 seconds because information is saved about each customer in QuikOrder's system.

QuikOrder's online delivery system runs on four Pentium II 400-MHz Windows NT servers connected to each other via Gigabit Ethernet links. Two servers act as compute servers that handle application processing; the other two handle I/O for the system and share a storage subsystem.

The two compute servers run Marathon software, which sends data to and receives data from both compute servers simultaneously, and synchronizes operations so the pizza-ordering application runs in lockstep fashion across the servers. Data is written to the disks on each server or mirrored, thereby providing redundant backup for the entire system. The I/O processors (IOP) handle processing with peripherals such as disk drives and printers.

Each compute server is paired with an IOP. If a component in a compute element or IOP fails or if the pair fails, the other pair continues processing.

"We've been operational for eight months with not a minute of downtime," Anderson says. "Every minute of downtime is a potential lost pizza order."

Source: Deni Connor, "Quikorder brings Domino's pizza to you in 30 munutes or less," *Network World,* vol. 17, no. 10 (March 6, 2000), p. 20. Copyright Network World. Reprinted with permission.

BUSINESS CASE STUDY QUESTIONS

Activities

1. Complete a top-down model for this case by gleaning facts from the case and placing them in the proper layer of the top-down model. After having completed the top-down model, analyze and detail those instances where requirements were clearly passed down from upper layers to lower layers of the model and where solutions to those requirements were passed up from lower layers to upper layers of the model.
2. Detail any questions about the case that may occur to you for which answers are not clearly stated in the article.

Business

1. What was the business motivation or problem that initiated the search for the implemented solution?
2. Were business performance metrics and associated infrastructure performance metrics identified? If so, were they achieved? If not, what might be some suitable business and infrastructure performance metrics for this case?
3. Is this business opportunity primarily marketing or profit driven?

Application

1. What does the application do?
2. What are the basic steps in the process?

Data

1. What types of data does the application provide to the customers?
2. What types of data does the customer provide to Domino's?

Network

1. There are two networks associated with this application: the Internet and an Intranet. What are the characteristics of the Intranet?
2. How many Internet servers are used? Where are they located?

Technology

1. What specific technologies were employed to deliver the described solution?

CHAPTER 2

VOICE COMMUNICATIONS CONCEPTS AND TECHNOLOGY

Concepts Reinforced

Top-Down Model
OSI Model
Protocols and Interoperability

Concepts Introduced

Voice Digitization
Voice Compression
PBX Functionality and Architecture
Voice Transmission Alternatives
Data/Voice Integration
Voice Network Concepts
Computer Telephony Integration
Voice Over the Internet

OBJECTIVES

Upon successful completion of this chapter, you should:

1. Understand the underlying technical concepts for voice transmission, voice digitization, voice compression, and data/voice integration.
2. Understand currently available voice-related technology including PBX's, voice digitizers, and voice/data multiplexers and modems.
3. Understand the functionality, standards, business impact, and technology involved with computer telephony integration.
4. Understand the functionality, concepts, standards, business impact, and technology involved with voice network services, voice transmission alternatives, and voice/data integration.

INTRODUCTION

Network analysts must be qualified to design networks that are capable of carrying voice as well as data. Before designing such networks, it is essential for the network analyst to understand the nature of voice signals, as well as how voice signals can be processed and integrated into a cohesive network with data transmissions.

Once the exclusive province of analog transmission, voice communication is increasingly becoming more digital in nature. Once the voice signal has been digitized, a wide variety of transmission services can potentially be employed to complete the transmission of the voice signal to its designated destination. In some cases, these voice transmissions can be easily integrated with simultaneous data transmission. As is the case with any type of communications system involving the interoperability of multiple pieces of hardware and software technology, standards play an essential role in ensuring end-to-end interoperability.

This chapter first explains voice transmission basic concepts such as voice digitization and compression. Next a key piece of voice processing technology known as the PBX or private branch exchange is introduced. Increasingly, the PBX is seen as a voice server to be integrated into a client/server information system like any other server. The final sections of this chapter cover key technologies that can be used to converge voice and data onto a single network.

VOICE TRANSMISSION BASIC CONCEPTS

A voice conversation consists of sound waves that are of varying frequency and amplitude and represented as a continuously varying analog waveform. The **POTS (plain old telephone service)** network employed analog transmission methodologies to transmit the voice signals from source to destination.

How does this analog waveform get from a person's mouth, the human transmitter, onto the PSTN and subsequently into the ear, the human receiver, of the person who was called? Figure 2-1 illustrates the mechanics of a typical phone handset, which consists of both transmitter and receiver components.

The telephone handset, consisting of both a transmitter and receiver, is a fairly simple device that works largely based on the properties of electromagnetism. The **transmitter,** or mouthpiece, is composed of a movable diaphragm that is sensitive to changes in voice frequency and amplitude. The diaphragm contains carbon granules that have the ability to conduct electricity. As the human voice spoken into the transmitter varies, the amount of carbon granules striking the electrical contacts in the mouthpiece varies, sending a varying analog electrical signal out onto the voice network.

This constantly varying analog electrical wave is transmitted over the voice network to the phone of the receiving person. The **receiver** or earpiece portion of the handset works in the opposite fashion of the mouthpiece. The varying electrical waves produced by the transmitter are received at an electromagnet in the receiver. Varying levels of electricity produce varying levels of magnetism that in turn cause the diaphragm to move in direct proportion to the magnetic variance. The moving diaphragm produces varying sound waves that correspond to the sound waves that were input at the transmitter. The electromagnetically reproduced sound produced at the receiver resembles the actual sound waves input at the transmitter closely enough to allow for voice recognition by the receiving party.

Voice Bandwidth

Although the approximate range of hearing of the human ear is between 15,000 and 20,000 Hz, significantly less bandwidth is used to transmit the electromagnetic representations of analog voice signals over the analog PSTN (public switched telephone

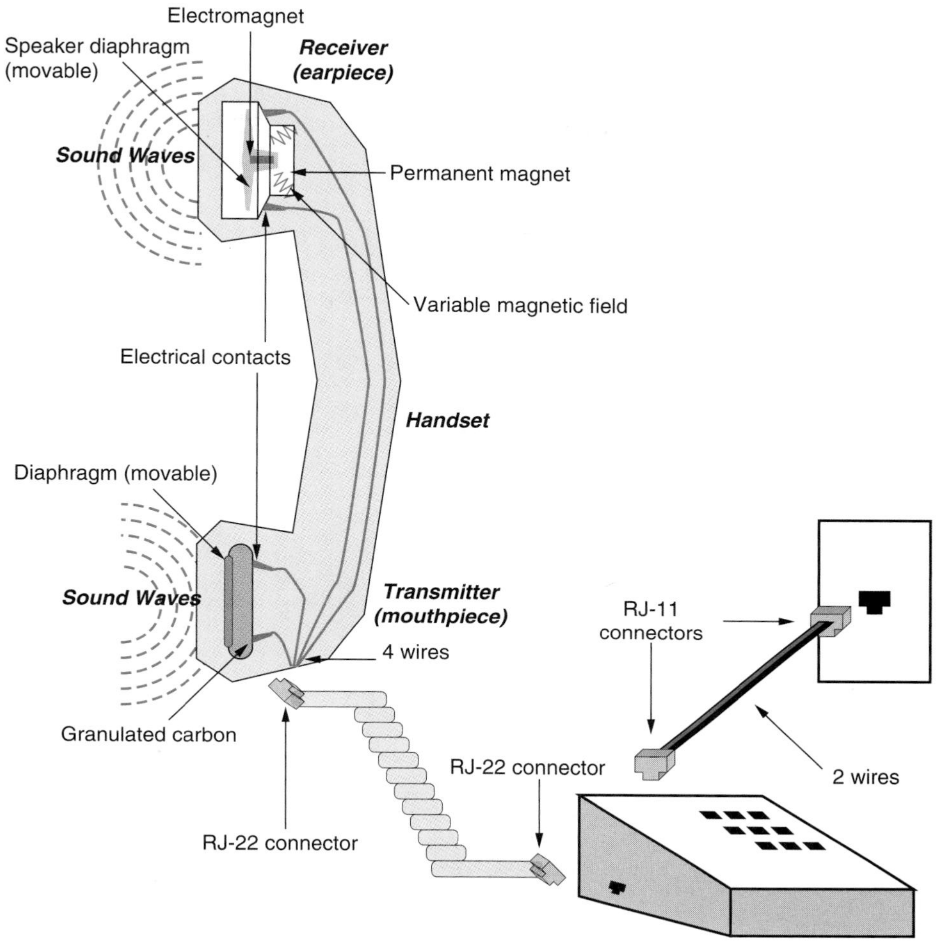

Figure 2-1 Getting Voice Onto and Off the Network

network). POTS uses a bandwidth of 4000 Hz including two **guardbands** to prevent interference from adjacent frequencies from interfering with the voice signal. As a result, the usable bandwidth on the local loop circuit connecting an individual's home or business to the phone company's central office for dial-up analog voice transmission is 3000 Hz, ranging from 300 to 3300 Hz. Figure 2-2 illustrates the comparative bandwidths of human speech and the analog phone network. This limited bandwidth is why people sound less lifelike on the telephone than in person.

VOICE NETWORK CONCEPTS

Telephone calls are connected from source via circuit switching. Circuit switching is an analog telecommunications term that originally meant that a physical electrical circuit was created from the source telephone handset to the destination telephone handset. In the early days of the telephone system, a telephone system operator man-

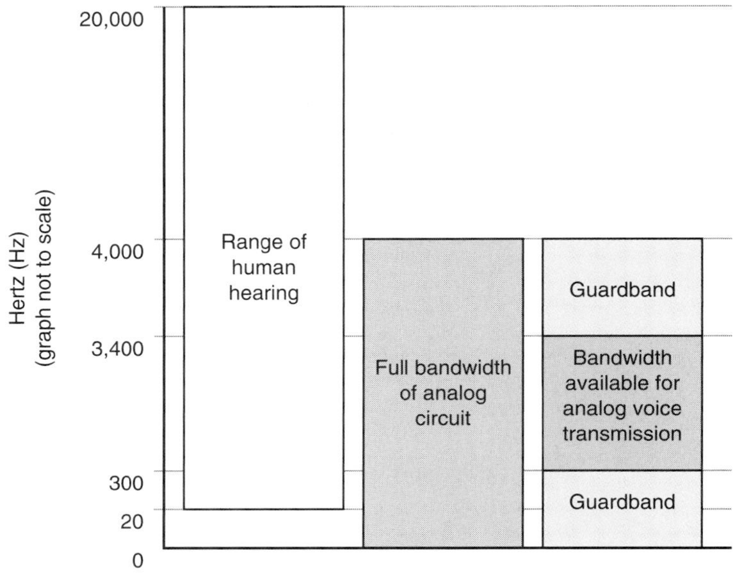

Figure 2-2 Voice Bandwidth

ually made these connections at a switchboard. Later the rotary telephone and automatic switching was introduced.

A better definition of a switch in the modern phone system is a reserved bandwidth connection between two telephone handsets. While there is no longer a physical circuit in place between the handsets, the capacity on the telephone network required to deliver the call is reserved for the exclusive use of the call: The same amount of telephone system capacity is used by two people who are being perfectly quiet as is used by two people who are talking at the same time. The capacity is dedicated to the call as soon as it is placed.

Basic Telecommunications Infrastructure

The modern telephone system is commonly known as the **public switched telephone network (PSTN).** Figure 2-3 illustrates the major components of the PSTN. The circuits between a residence or business and the local **central office** or **CO** are known as **local loops.** A central office is a facility belonging to the local phone company in which calls are switched to their proper destination. As covered in Chapter 1, the LATA is an area within which the local carrier completed all of the calls during the period between the breakup of AT&T and the Telecommunications Act of 1996.

Telephone calls are established by a device located at the local telephone company's central office (CO) known as a **telephone switch.** The telephone switch is directly connected to the customer's telephone handset via the local loop. The telephone switch routes calls to the destination telephone handset. Requested destinations for phone calls are indicated to the telephone switch by dialing a series of numbers. These numbers tell the telephone switch whether the call will be local, intra-LATA, or inter-LATA and subsequently which circuits must be accessed and combined to complete the call as requested.

All voice traffic destined for locations outside of the local LATA, and some traffic within the LATA, must be handed off to the long-distance or **inter-exchange carrier (IXC)** of the customer's choice. Competing long distance carriers wishing to do business in a given LATA maintain a switching office in that LATA known as a **POP** or **point of presence.** This POP handles billing information and routes the call over the long distance carrier's switched network to its POP in the destination's LATA. The circuit between the POPs may be via satellite, microwave, fiber optic cable, traditional wiring, or some combination of these media. Depending on traffic levels on the long-distance carrier's network, calls may be routed through any combination of switches before reaching their final destination.

In the basic infrastructure illustrated in Figure 2-3, the only analog links in the PSTN are the local loops running from the end points to the COs. Once the voice signal hits the central office, it is converted into a digital signal for transmission across the PSTN to the destination central office where it is converted back into an analog signal for transmission across the local loop to the destination telephone. The processes used to convert the phone call from analog to digital signals are covered later in this chapter.

Because these local loops are the sole remaining analog links in the modern PSTN and cover relatively short distances, they are commonly referred to as the **last mile** in the telephone system. In the next few chapters you will see how the analog local loops pose a serious limitation in terms of the rate of data transmission across the PSTN.

PSTN Network Hierarchy

As can be seen in Figure 2-4, a residential or business call is first processed in the local central office, also known as an end office or local office. In terms of the network hierarchy, an end office is known as a **Class 5 office.** This local central office contains a switch that processes incoming calls, determines the best path to the call destination, and establishes the circuit connection.

Local calls come into the local central office via a local loop and travel to their local destination via a local loop. If a call is destined to another telephone on the same telephone switch, the call is switched at the CO to the destination local loop.

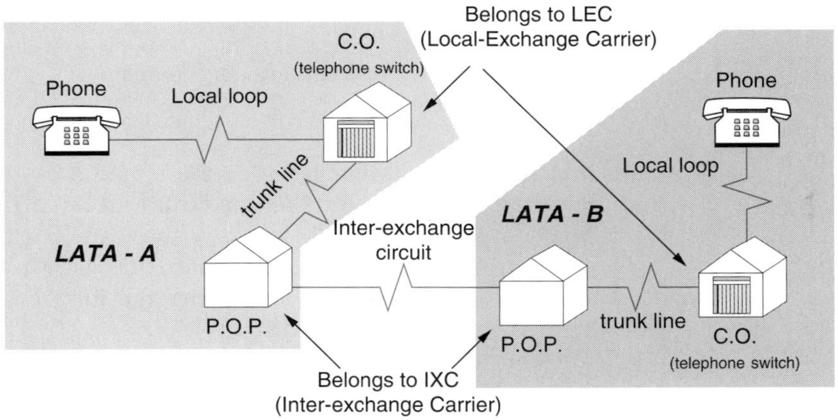

Figure 2-3 Basic Telecommunications Infrastructure

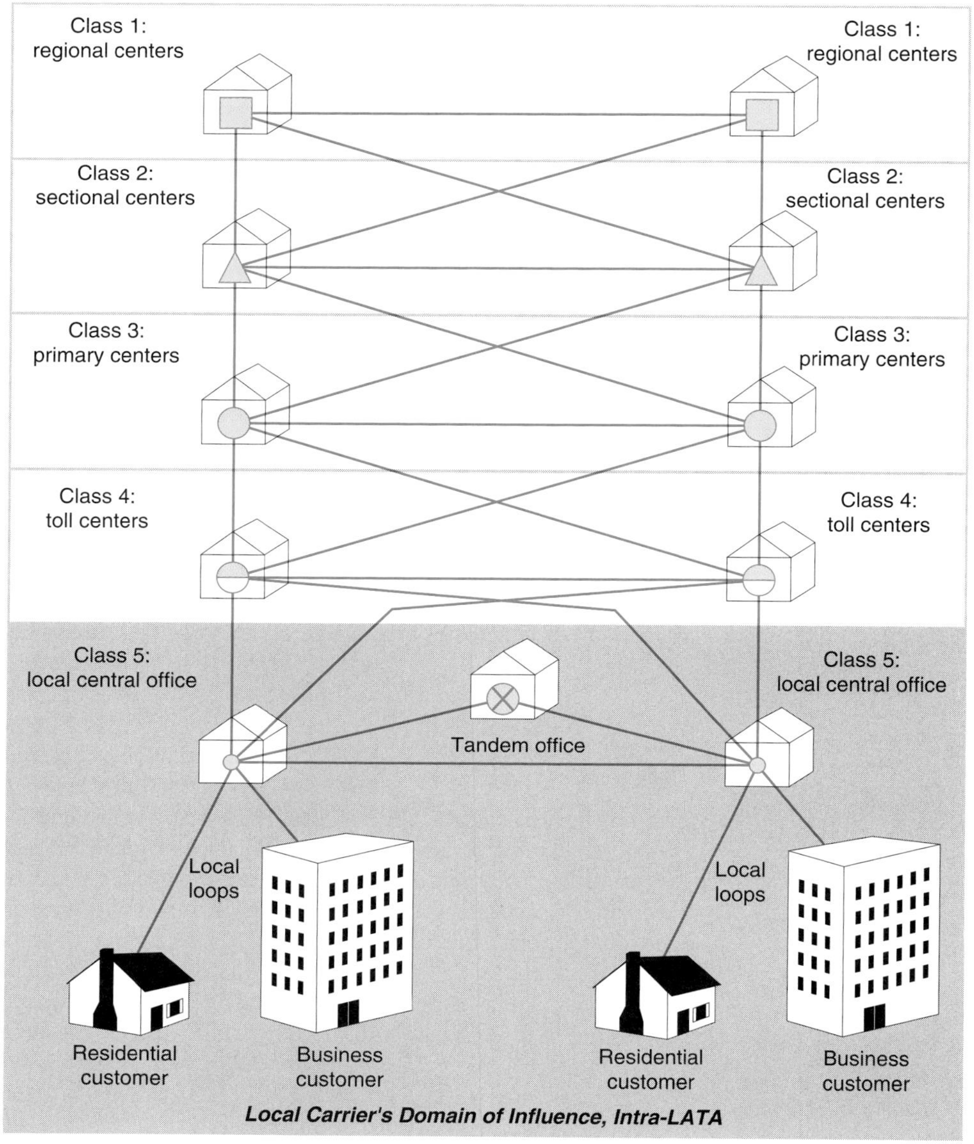

Figure 2-4 Representative Voice Network Hierarchy

Calls that are not local but still within the same LATA are known as intra-LATA calls and are handled by the caller's selected intra-LATA carrier, most often a regional Bell operating company (RBOC). Technically, these are long distance calls, and a local CO may not have a direct line to the destination CO. In this case, the call is routed through a **tandem office** that establishes the intra-LATA circuit and also handles billing procedures for the long distance call.

If the call is bound for a destination in another LATA, it must be turned over from the local carrier to a long-distance carrier such as AT&T, MCI, or Sprint. In most cases, the IXC will have been chosen by individual residential and business subscribers. The local CO still receives such inter-LATA calls from subscribers. However, rather than routing the call itself, the CO merely forwards the call to the local POP of the long-distance carrier of choice.

Such a long-distance switching office is also known as a POP, or a **Class 4 toll center.** The term *toll center* implies that long-distance billing calculation and switching activities are performed at these locations. A given local CO may have trunks to more than one toll center. As will be seen, circuit redundancy offering multiple alternative paths for call routing is a central premise of the voice network hierarchy. If the local toll center can find adequate space on a trunk headed to the destination CO, then the connection between source and destination COs is completed. If no paths to the destination are directly available to the local toll center, then the call is escalated up the network hierarchy to the next level of switching office. The overall desire is to keep the call as low on the hierarchy as possible. This provides both quicker call completion for the subscriber and maximization of the cost-effective use of the lowest and least expensive switching offices possible.

Higher levels on the network hierarchy imply greater switching and transmission capacity as well as greater expense. When calls cannot be completed directly, Class 4 toll centers turn to **Class 3 primary centers** that subsequently turn to **Class 2 sectional centers** that turn finally to **Class 1 regional centers.** These categories of switching and transmission centers were originally AT&T's, and not all inter-LATA or long-distance carriers have such a five-level network hierarchy. However, the five-level hierarchy has become industry standard terminology.

Telephone Number Plans

Telephone numbers are built using a hierarchical address method. Telephone numbers in the United States can be divided into three basic parts: a three-digit area code, a three-digit exchange, and a four-digit subscriber number. To make a telephone call, at a minimum the exchange plus the subscriber number must be dialed. If the call is to a destination phone outside the source phone's area code, the destination area code must be dialed as well.

Originally assigned to geographic areas, area codes are the top level of the hierarchy. When the US telephone system was originally designed, all area codes had either a 1 or a 0 as the center digit. Conversely exchanges were not allowed to have a 0 or a 1 as the center digit. This technique allowed the telephone switches at the CO to easily distinguish between area codes and exchanges. Because of this differentiation, long-distance calls placed within an area code could simply be dialed by adding a 1 to the beginning of the local telephone number.

This system worked well until the number of area codes increased to the point that all of the area codes with 1s and 0s in the center were in use. At that point there was no choice but to add an area code with a different number as the center digit. The first area code placed in service that did not have a 1 or 0 as the center digit was the 770 area code that serves the area outside of Atlanta, Georgia.

The implementation of these nonstandard area codes originally caused some problems. Telephone switches and PBXs had to be reprogrammed to support the new number scheme. When the 770 area code first went into use, several areas could not place a call to it. This new area code number scheme created another problem. Because the telephone switch cannot tell the difference between an exchange and an area code based on number structure, it is now usually necessary to dial all 10 digits when placing a long distance call even if the call is within the same area code.

While the area code + exchange + subscriber number system is used in the United States, a broader ranging system is used internationally. To place an international call, you must dial 011 + country code + city code + number. The numbering systems for country codes, city codes, and local numbers can vary between countries. It is important to carefully research the dialing pattern before placing an international call.

In Sharper Focus

TELEPHONE NUMBER SHORTAGES AND NEW AREA CODES

The need for new area codes results from the increasing need for new telephone numbers. The proliferation of fax machines, cellular phones, pagers, and second lines for use to connect to the Internet has caused an exponential increase in the number of telephone numbers currently in use. Each exchange supports 10,000 telephone numbers. Each area code supports 1000 exchanges or 10 million separate telephone numbers. When the required amount of telephone numbers exceeds the available capacity, there is no choice but to add another area code to the geographic area served by the original area code.

There are two basic approaches to adding area codes. The geographic area served by the original area code can be broken into two smaller sections. One section retains the original area code and the new section is given a new area code. Although this approach is true to the original concept of an area code, it changes the area code for half the telephones in the old area code. This change affects the calling patterns of every subscriber in the area code and of everyone who needs to place a long distance call to them. Each business that experiences an area code change must replace all of their business cards, letterhead, and any other items that contain their telephone number, often at a significant expense.

To resolve these issues, an alternate concept known as overlaying is becoming common. In an overlay solution, a new area code is added to the original area code's geographic area. New telephone numbers are simply assigned to this new area code. In this scenario, no existing customers are forced to change their area code. It is possible, however, that your neighbor might be in a different area code than you are. In this case, you would dial the full 10-digit telephone number to place a local call to your neighbor.

System Signaling

In addition to carrying the actual voice signals, the telephone system must also carry information about the call itself. This information is commonly referred to as **system signaling** or **interoffice signaling.** At a bare minimum, system signaling needs to provide a means of accomplishing call set-up and call termination. In addition to these basic functions, many other advanced functions are available including call waiting, caller ID, and three-way calling. Each of these functions requires the source telephone set to send data to the local phone switch or for the local phone switch to send data to the destination phone switch and telephone set in addition to the basic voice data transmission.

There are two basic approaches to sending system signaling data across the PSTN: in band and out of band. In an **in-band** system, the signals are sent on the same channel as the voice data itself. This method is used to send signals across the analog local loop for most home telephones. When you pick up the phone, you listen for a **dial tone** to make sure the telephone switch at the CO is ready to serve you. At that point, you dial (sending the phone number across in the voice bandwidth) and listen for the phone to ring. If the called party answers the phone, the remote telephone switch comes off the hook and the connection is established.

The destination telephone number can be communicated to the telephone switch in two ways. Older style rotary phones, like the one taken apart to draw Figure 2-1, have a round dial that causes a certain number of pulses of electricity to be generated depending on the number dialed. Dialing a "1" produces one electrical pulse, dialing a "2" produces two electrical pulses, and so on. These pulses were used to physically operate relays in the first automatic phone switches. Modern phone switches no longer use mechanical relays and therefore do not require electrical pulses to indicate the destination telephone number.

Many of today's phones no longer have rotary dials on them. Instead, they contain 12 buttons that correspond to the 10 numbers on the rotary dial plus two additional characters, the star (*) and the pound (#). A switch is often included, which can be set to have the telephone set issue a series of **pulses** to emulate the dialing process of the older style of phone for areas where CO switches have not yet been upgraded to understand **touch-tone** dialing.

In Sharper Focus

TOUCH TONE DIALING

Touch-tone dialing is technically called **DTMF,** or **dual tone multifrequency,** because the tone associated with each number dialed is really a combination of two tones selected from a matrix of multiple possible frequencies. Figure 2-5 illustrates the numbers and symbols found on a typical telephone touch panel and their associated dual tone frequencies.

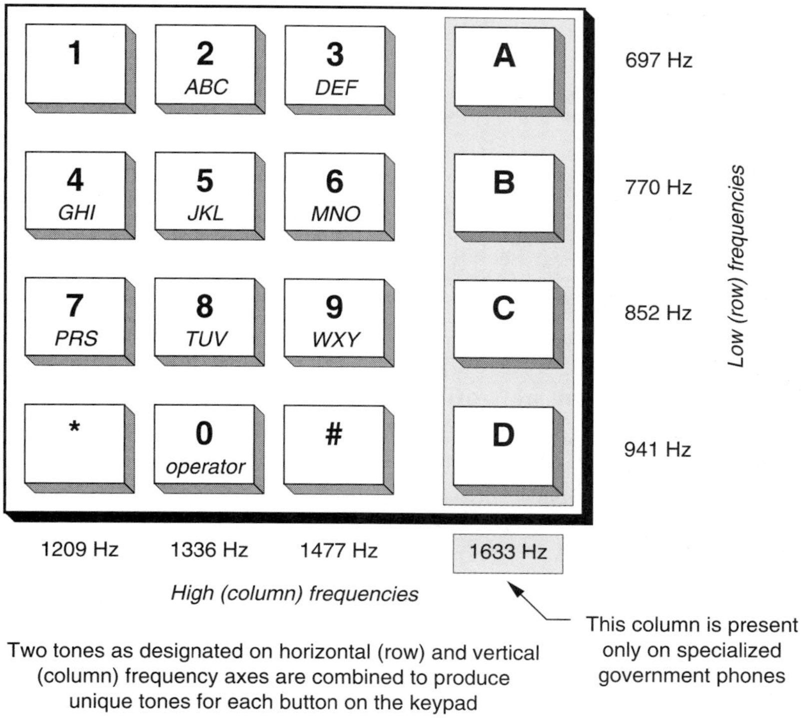

Figure 2-5 Tone Dialing with DTMF

The tones generated by DTMF phones can be used for much more than merely dialing destination telephone numbers. As will be seen later in the chapter, these same tones can be used to enable specialized services from PBXs, carriers, banks, information services, and retail establishments.

When you decide to terminate the call, you hang up or change the status of your local loop to on-hook. At that time, the local telephone switch changes from off-hook to on-hook, and the telephone switch knows you are off the phone and are ready to receive a telephone call. Call waiting, three-way calling, and caller ID all use similar in-band means to communicate information between the telephone handset and the local telephone switch.

Although in-band signaling works well for communication between telephone handsets and the local telephone switch across the analog local loop, the inter-switch connections on the digital PSTN make use of a separate channel to carry system signaling data. This **out-of-band signaling** approach provides a means to manage the network itself by handling the routing of calls and circuit establishment as well as the monitoring of circuit status and notification and rerouting in the case of alarms or circuit problems. By moving the call setup and management data to a separate network, it becomes easier to support transparent operation between different digital encoding mechanisms. The management data is readily available to each piece of telephone network equipment regardless of the encoding mechanism used.

Signaling System 7 The worldwide CCITT-approved standard for out-of-band signaling is known as **signaling system 7 (SS7).** SS7 controls the structure and transmission of both circuit-related and non-circuit-related information via out-of-band signaling between CO switches. SS7 delivers the out-of-band signaling via a packet-switched network physically separate from the circuit switched network that carries the actual voice traffic. Each node on the PSTN must connect to both the voice network and the SS7 network.

The SS7 network is nothing more than a packet-switched network, not unlike other suites of protocols examined in Chapter 7. Like most protocol suites, SS7 can be modeled in comparison to the OSI 7 Layer Reference Model. Figure 2-6 summarizes the major characteristics of the SS7 protocols and compares the SS7 protocol suite to the OSI model.

SS7 and the intelligent services that it enables are often described as part of an all-encompassing interface between users and the PSTN known as the **AIN** or **advanced intelligent network.** The AIN is sometimes simply referred to as the **intelligent network (IN).**

The AIN provides a great deal of flexibility to customers. The use of AIN services provides a means of achieving many different applications. Services enabled by AIN include:

- **Alternate billing service (ABS)**—This service allows a long-distance call to be billed to a calling card, third party, or receiver (collect call).
- **Custom local area signaling service (CLASS)**—A group of services that allow many services local to the customer's telephone. Examples include call waiting, call forwarding, call blocking, caller ID blocking, busy number redial, and automatic redial of missed calls.

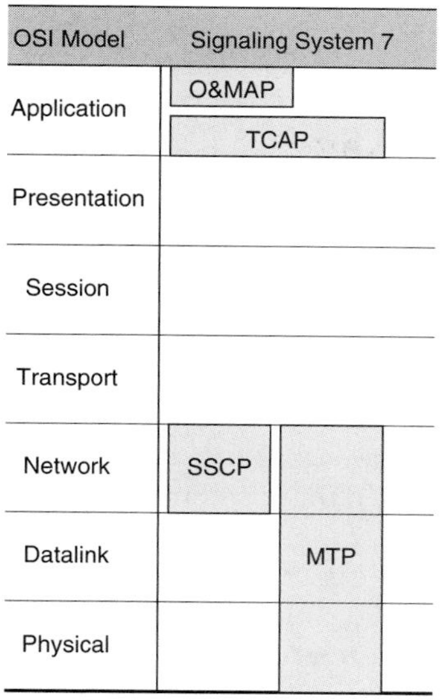

Protocol Name	Description/Function
Operations Maintenance Application Part *(O&MAP)*	*O&MAP* provides standards for routing and management of messages related to network operations and maintenance
Transaction Capabilities Application Part *(TCAP)*	*TCAP* provides standards for routing and management of noncircuit related information for transaction processing applications requiring out-of-band signaling
Signaling Connection Control Part *(SCCP)*	*SCCP* provides standards for routing and management of signaling messages. Not related to call set-up between switches. A connection-oriented service providing reliable message delivery
Message Transfer Part *(MTP)*	*MTP* provides standards for routing of signaling messages between switches. A connectionless, datagram service
Network Service Part *(NSP)*	*Another term for the combination of the SCCP and the MTP3*

Figure 2-6 Signaling System 7 Protocols and the OSI Model

- **Enhanced 800 service**—This service allows 800 number portability. Originally 800 numbers were tied to a specific area code and long distance provider. This service resolves those limitations.
- **Intelligent call processing (ICP)**—Using this service customers are able to reroute incoming 800 calls among multiple customer service centers in a matter of seconds. This rerouting is done completely transparent to the calling customer. ICP allows multiple call centers geographically dispersed throughout the country to function as one logical call center, with the overall number of incoming calls distributed in a balanced manner across all centers.

User oriented network, services such as the AIN are being offered in response to user demands for in-house control over a key element of their business: their telecommunications systems and the links from those systems to the wide area PSTN. Catalog sales organizations are literally out of business without their phones and must have contingency plans and disaster recovery plans in place to deal with and avoid possible catastrophes.

Voice Digitization

The analog POTS system has largely been supplanted in the modern telephone system by a combination of analog and digital transmission technologies. Although analog signaling is effective, it is limited in terms of quality, distance, and capacity. The longer the signal has to travel, the poorer the quality. Also significant capacity issues are associated with analog transmission. In general only one voice conversation can be carried on a single set of wires using analog transmission. Although it is possible to partially overcome this limitation through the use of multiplexing, as illustrated in detail in Chapter 8, digital transmission offers better quality and higher capacity than analog transmission over a given media. The modern voice network is almost entirely digital in nature.

Although the local loop between the local CO and a residence or place of business may be an analog circuit, it is highly unlikely that the continuously varying analog signal representing a person's voice will stay in analog form all the way to the destination location's phone receiver. Rather, high-capacity digital circuits will likely be employed to transport that call, especially between COs or carriers. That carriers may be converting a voice conversation to digital format and reconverting it back to analog form before it reaches its destination is completely transparent to phone network users.

The basic technique for **voice digitization** is relatively simple. The constantly varying analog voice conversation must be sampled frequently enough so that when the digitized version of the voice is converted back to an analog signal, the resultant conversation resembles the voice of the call initiator. Most voice digitization techniques employ a sampling rate of 8000 samples per second.

Recalling that a digital signal is just a discrete electrical voltage, there are only a limited number of ways in which the electrical pulses can be varied to represent characteristics of an analog voice signal:

Pulse amplitude modulation, or **PAM,** varies the amplitude or voltage of the electrical pulses in relation to the varying characteristics of the voice signal. PAM was the voice digitization technique used in some earlier PBXs.

Pulse duration modulation (PDM), otherwise known as **pulse width modulation (PWM),** varies the duration of each electrical pulse in relation to the variances in the analog signal.

Pulse position modulation (PPM) varies the duration between pulses in relation to variances in the analog signal. By varying the spaces in between the discrete electrical pulses on the digital circuit, PPM focuses on the relative position of the pulses to one another as a means of representing the continuously varying analog signal. Figure 2-7 illustrates these three voice digitization techniques.

Pulse Code Modulation (PCM) Although any of the above methods may be used for voice digitization, the most common voice digitization technique in use today is **pulse code modulation** or **PCM.** Figure 2-8 illustrates the basics of PCM.

As can be seen from Figure 2-8, eight bits or one byte are required to transmit the sampled amplitude of an analog signal. Since an 8 bit code allows 2^8 or 256 different possible values, each time the actual analog wave is sampled, it is assigned a value from 0 to 255 depending on its location or amplitude at the instant it is sampled. Some simple mathematics will reveal the bandwidth required to transmit digitized voice using PCM. This required bandwidth, by no coincidence, corresponds exactly to a common digital circuit bandwidth.

The device that samples the analog POTS transmission coming in from the local loop and transforms it into a stream of binary digits using PCM is known as a

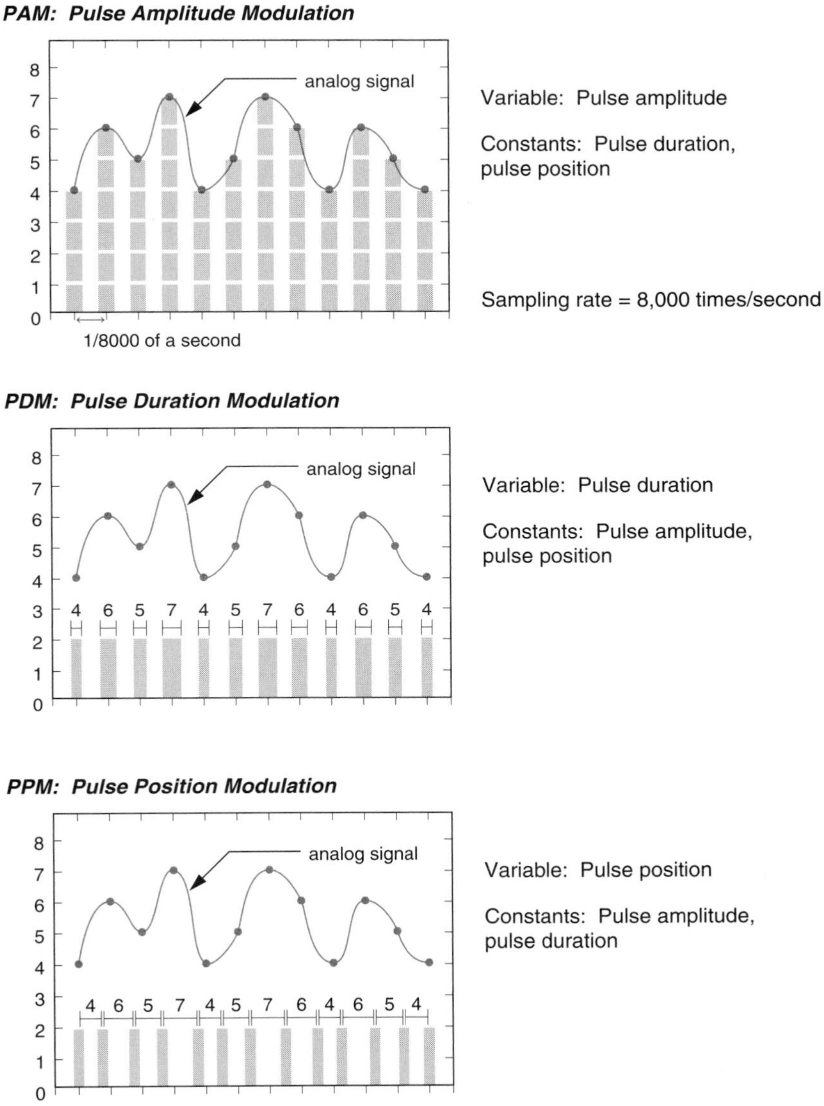

Figure 2-7 Voice Digitization: PAM, PDM, PPM

coder/decoder or **codec.** As mentioned in the following section, each codec outputs a digital signal at a data rate of 64 Kbps. This data rate, known as a DS-0, is the basic unit of voice data transmission in a PCM-based telephone system. All higher speed voice connections will operate at some multiple of this DS-0 speed. Codecs are usually deployed as part of a channel bank. A channel bank is a hybrid device consisting of 24 codecs, and the circuitry required to place the digitized PCM voice signals onto a T-1 circuit. Codecs and channel banks may be integrated into telephone switches or purchased separately.

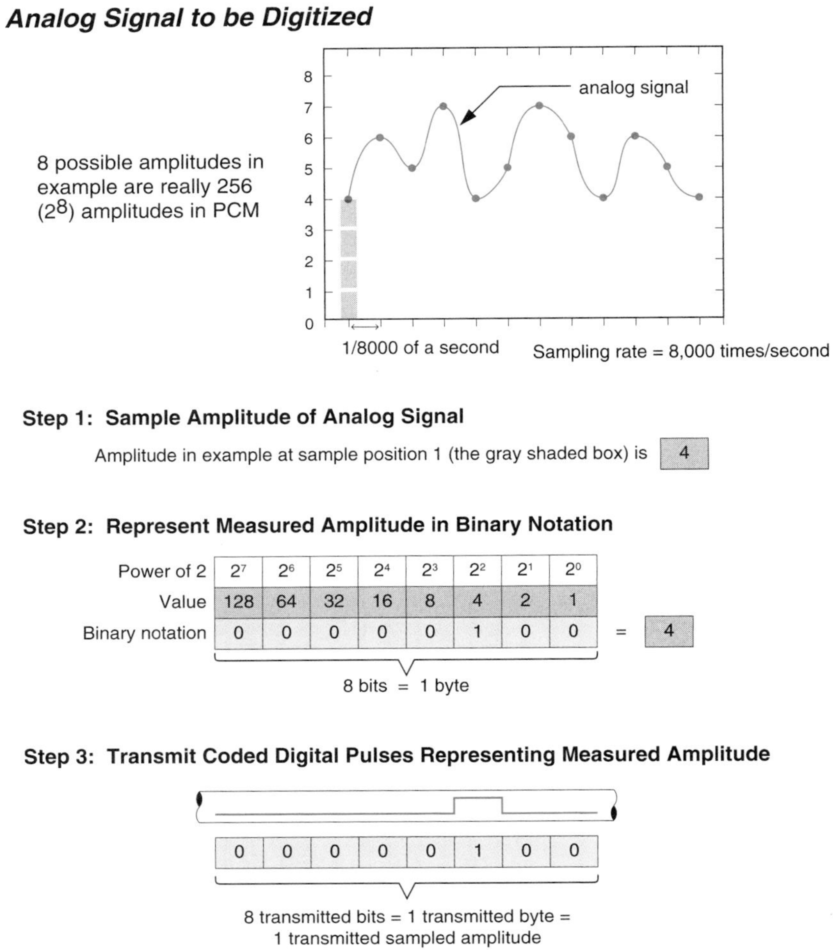

Figure 2-8 Voice Digitization: Pulse Code Modulation (PCM)

In Sharper Focus

VOICE DIGITIZATION BANDWIDTH REQUIREMENTS

Since 8000 samples per second are required to ensure quality transmission of digitized voice, and each sample requires eight bits to represent that sampled bandwidth in binary (1s and 0s) notation, the following equation reveals that 64,000 bits/psec is the required bandwidth for transmission of voice digitized via PCM. A DS-0 circuit has a transmission capacity of exactly 64 Kbps. Twenty-four DS-0s are combined to form a T-1, so that a T-1 can carry 24 simultaneous voice conversations digitized via PCM. Following is the mathematical proof:

$$8{,}000 \text{ samples/sec} \times 8 \text{ bits/sample} = 64{,}000 \text{ bits/sec (bps)}$$

$$64{,}000 \text{ bits/sec} = 64 \text{ Kbps} = \text{DS-0 Circuit}$$

$$24 \text{ DS-0s} = 24 \times 64 \text{ Kbps} = 1{,}536 \text{ Kbps} = 1.536 \text{ Mbps}$$

Plus: 1 framing bit/sample × 8,000 samples/sec = 8,000 framing bits/sec

8 Kbps + 1,536 Kbp = 1,544 Kbps = 1.544 Mbps = Transmission capacity of T-1 circuit

The maximum data-carrying capacity of a T-1 circuit is only 1.536 Mbps, as the framing bits cannot be used to carry data.

ADPCM A variation of this digitization technique known as **Adaptive Differential Pulse Code Modulation,** or **ADPCM,** is most commonly used in Europe. ADPCM is a CCITT (ITU) standard that takes a slightly different approach to coding sampled amplitudes in order to use transmission bandwidth more efficiently; ADPCM requires roughly half the bandwidth for each digitized conversation compared with PCM. By transmitting only the approximate difference or change in amplitude of consecutive amplitude samples, rather than the absolute amplitude, only 32 Kbps of bandwidth is required for each conversation digitized via ADPCM.

Using a specialized circuit known as an adaptive predictor, ADPCM calculates the difference between the predicted and actual incoming signals and specifies that difference as one of 16 different levels using 4 bits ($2^4 = 16$). Since each voice channel can be represented by just 4 bits, ADPCM can support 48 simultaneous voice conversations over a T-1 circuit.

The ITU standard for 32 Kbps ADPCM is known as G.721 and is generally used as a reference point for the quality of voice transmission known as **toll quality.** G.721 has been superseded by other ADPCM standards that use less than 32 Kbps per voice channel. For example, G.723 defines ADPCM for 24 Kbps and 40 Kbps, whereas G.726 defines ADPCM for 40, 32, 24, and 16 Kbps.

Fortunately, voice signals can be readily converted between any of these digital formats, enabling transparent telephone conversations regardless of the voice digitization technique used at either end of the call.

Voice Compression

ADPCM is also known as a voice compression technique because of its ability to transmit 24 digitized voice conversations in half the bandwidth required by PCM. Other more advanced techniques employ specially programmed microprocessors known as **digital signal processors** that take the digitized PCM code and further manipulate and compress it. In doing so, DSPs are able to transmit and reconstruct digitized voice conversations in as little as 4800 bps per conversation, an increase in transmission efficiency of more than 13 times over PCM!

Numerous voice compression technological approaches exist. Voice compression can be performed by stand-alone units or by integral modules within other pieces of equipment. The particular method by which the voice is compressed may be according to an open standard or by a proprietary methodology. Proprietary methods require that a given vendor's equipment must be present on both ends of the voice circuit in question. Each voice compression technique seeks to reduce the amount of transmitted voice information in one way or another.

Some voice compression techniques attempt to synthesize the human voice, other techniques attempt to predict the actual voice transmission patterns, and still others attempt to transmit only changes in voice patterns. Regardless of the voice compression technique employed, one thing is certain. The quality of compressed voice transmissions does not match the quality of an analog voice transmission over an analog dial-up line or a PCM-digitized voice transmission using a full 64 Kbps of digital bandwidth. The transmission quality degradation varies from one instance to another. However, only the end-users of the compressed voice system can determine whether the reduced voice quality is worth the bandwidth and related cost savings.

PBX CONCEPTS

PBX Market

To provide flexible voice communications capability among people within a business organization as well as with the outside world, a switching device known as a **PBX,** or **private branch exchange,** is often employed. Sales of PBXs in the United States represent approximately a $4 billion annual market with service on these PBXs accounting for an additional $2 billion in additional revenue. The PBX market is currently dominated by Nortel (Northern Telecom), with its line of Meridian PBXs, and by Lucent Technologies (formerly AT&T Global Business Communications Systems), with its line of Definity PBXs. Each of these two major players control about 25% market share. The major players in the PBX market and their approximate market shares are displayed in Figure 2-9.

PBX Functionality and Architecture

As illustrated in the I-P-O (Input-Processing-Output) diagram of Figure 2-10, a PBX provides an interface between users and the shared private or public network connections available for carrying users' voice and data traffic. The additional intelligent services offered by a PBX allow users to use their phones more efficiently and effectively.

A PBX is really just a privately owned, smaller version of the switch in telephone company COs that control circuit switching for the general public. Depending on the requested destination, switched circuits are established, maintained, and terminated on a per call basis by the PBX **switching matrix.**

Beyond the switching capabilities of a PBX, programmable features offer advanced functionality to users. These features and the overall performance of the PBX are controlled by software programs running on specialized computers within

Approximate PBX Market Share	PBX Vendors
25–30%	Nortel, Lucent Technologies
10–20%	NEC and Mitel
5–10%	Siemens Rolm
2–5%	Fujitsu, Intecom, Ericsson, Hitachi
Less than 2%	Toshiba, Executone, Tadrian, SRX, Harris Digital

Figure 2-9 PBX Vendors and Market Share

I(Input)	P (Processing)	O (Output)
Users access PBX connections and services via desktop phones or access devices	Provides necessary switching to allow connections among PBX users or to outside network services	Other local PBX users or outside local loops and PSTN connections. Outside connections may also be to shared high-speed digital lines
Input traffic may be voice, data, or video	Provides additional intelligent services to track PBX usage, offer conference calling, call-forwarding, least cost routing, automatic call distribution, automated attendant, links to computer databases	

Figure 2-10 IPO Diagram of PBX Functionality

the PBX in an area sometimes referred to as the **PBX CPU, stored program control,** or **common control area.**

Telephone sets in user offices are connected to the PBX via slide-in modules or cards known as **line cards, port cards,** or **station cards.** Connection to an outside network (usually the PSTN) is accomplished via **trunk cards.** Trunk cards vary in design from easily scalable cards to specialized cards for a particular type of network line.

Some PBXs allow any chassis slot to be used for any type of card or module, whereas other PBXs specify certain slots for line cards and others for trunk cards. Starting with an open chassis or cabinet with power supply and backbone or backplane, modules or cards are added to increase PBX capacity for either user extensions or connections to the outside network. Additional cabinets can often be cascaded to offer PBX expandability. Figure 2-11 illustrates the physical attributes of a representative PBX.

PBX Technology Analysis

Before reviewing PBX technology, it is essential to have performed a thorough top-down analysis beginning with the business needs and functionality that must be met by the chosen PBX technology. Having identified those PBX features that are most important to a given business, the following information could be used as a representative sample of typical PBX features and services.

PBX features and services tend to fall into three broad categories:

- Features and services that provide users with flexible usage of PBX resources
- Features and services that provide for data/voice integration
- Features and services that control and monitor the use of those PBX resources

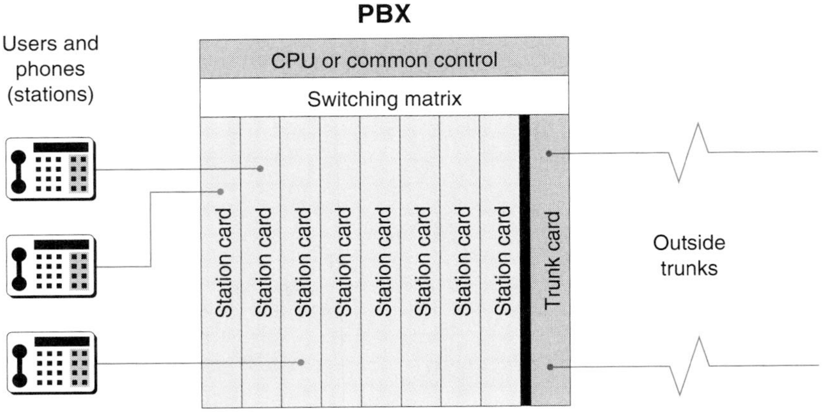

Figure 2-11 PBX Physical Architecture

Voice-Based Features and Services In the flexible usage category, features such as conference calling, call forwarding, call transfer, speed dialing, redialing, and call hold are commonplace and should not require further explanation. Other voice-based PBX features and services that support flexible usage of PBX resources are summarized in Figure 2-12.

Data/Voice Integration Features & Services Data/Voice integration by PBXs is increasingly common, although PBXs can vary significantly in their extent of support for data transmission. Differences in data interfaces and whether or not those interfaces and associated software represent an upgrade at additional cost should be investigated thoroughly before any PBX purchase. In some cases, data are transmitted through the PBX via a dedicated connection, and in other cases a specialized hybrid voice/data phone is used to transmit both voice and data simultaneously over a single connection to the PBX. Data and data/voice integration-related features and issues are summarized in Figure 2–13.

Control and Monitoring Features and Services Control and monitoring features range from the simple, such as limiting access to outside lines from certain extensions, to the complex, such as entire stand-alone **call accounting systems.** Call accounting systems are often run on separate PCs that interface directly to the PBX and execute specially written software. Accounting reports or bills sorted by department or extension can be run on a scheduled basis or on demand. Exception reports can be generated to spot possible abuses for calls over a certain length or cost, or calls made to a particular area code. Both incoming and outgoing calls can be tracked. Call accounting systems can pay for themselves in a short time by spotting and curtailing abuse, as well as by allocating phone usage charges on a departmental basis.

The information on which such a call accounting system depends is generated by the PBX. In a process known as **SMDR,** or **station message detail recording,** an individual detail record is generated for each call. This data record can then be transferred from the PBX to the call accounting system computer, usually from an RS-232 DB-25 port on the PBX to the serial port on the PC. Data records can be stored and summarized on the call accounting system computer depending on available disk space. Figure 2-14 illustrates the setup of a call accounting system.

Feature/Service	Description
Least Cost Routing (LCR)	Using routing and pricing information supplied by the user, the PBX chooses the most economical path for any given call. This feature was especially important when WATS (Wide Area Telecommunications Service) lines were more prevalent. These days, thanks to competition and discount programs among long distance carriers, PBXs can access any outgoing trunk rather than trying to get certain calls onto certain trunks.
Automatic Call Distribution (ACD)	Incoming calls are routed directly to certain extensions without going through a central switchboard. Calls can be routed according to the incoming trunk or phone number. Often used in customer service organizations in which calls may be distributed to the first available agent.
Call Pickup	Allows a user to pickup or answer another user's phone without the need to actually forward calls.
Paging	Ability to use paging speakers in a building. May be limited to specific paging zones.
Direct Inward Dialing (DID)	Allows calls to bypass the central switchboard and go directly to a particular user's phone.
Hunting	Hunt groups are established to allow incoming calls to get through on alternate trunks when a primary trunk is busy. For example, most businesses publish only one phone number even though they may have multiple incoming trunks. If the primary trunk is busy, the PBX hunts for an open trunk transparently to the user.
Prioritization	Individual extensions can be given priority access to certain trunks or groups of trunks. In most cases, PBXs are equipped with fewer outgoing trunks than internal extensions or station lines. If certain users *must* have access to outside lines, prioritization features are important.
Night mode	Many companies close their switchboard at night but still have employees working who must be able to receive and make phone calls.

Figure 2-12 Voice-Based PBX Features and Services

Auxiliary Voice-Related Services Just as the previously mentioned call accounting systems are most often an add-on device for PBXs, other auxiliary systems exist to enhance PBX capability. The auxiliary nature of these systems implies that they are often not included as standard features on PBXs but may be purchased separately from either the PBX vendor or third-party manufacturers. Sometimes these services are available as a combination of specialized PC boards and associated TAPI

Feature/Service	Description
ISDN Support	Are WAN interfaces for ISDN (Integrated Services Digital Network) supplied or available as upgrades? ISDN BRI (Basic rate interface) service is two 64Kbps channels. ISDN PRI service is twenty-three 64 Kbps channels.
T-1 Support	Are T-1 (1.544 Mbps) interfaces supported? Outside of North America, are E-1 (2.048 Mbps) supported? Are codecs included? Are channel banks included?
Data Interfaces	Are computer data interfaces included on the PBX? Are hybrid voice/data phones available? Are LAN interfaces such as Ethernet and Token Ring as well as serial interfaces such as RS-232 supported? How many of the following services are supported: fax transmission, modem pooling, printer sharing, file sharing, video conferencing?
PBX-to-Host Interfaces	Before the advent of open systems computer telephony integration APIs such as TAPI and TSAPI, each PBX vendor had its own PBX-Host interface specification. How many of the following vendor-specific PBX-Host interfaces are supported: Nortel: Meridian Link; Rolm: CallBridge; IBM: CallPath; AT&T: Passageway; Siemens: Applications Connectivity Link (ACL); Mitel: NeVaDa (Networked Voice and Data)?

Figure 2-13 Data and Data/Voice Integration PBX Features and Services

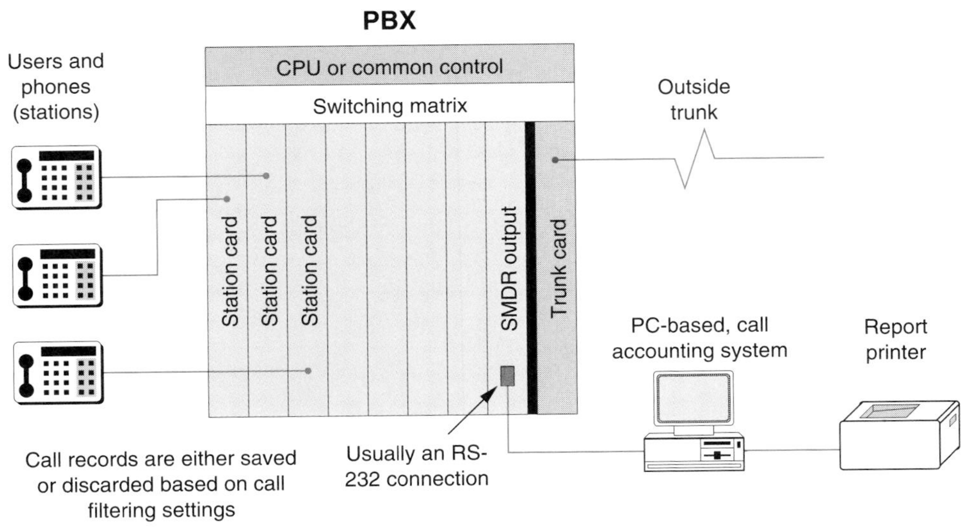

Figure 2-14 Call Accounting Systems Installation

Service/Device	Description
Automated Attendant	A recorded message that works with a touch-tone phone that requests callers to press the number of the extension they wish to reach. Those wishing to speak to an operator are transferred.
Voice Mail	Voice mail systems can vary widely in cost and sophistication. After recording an initial message for someone, voice mail systems may allow the voice mail to be handled like a written phone message. It can be forwarded, copied, appended to, saved, recalled, or deleted.
Voice Response Units (VRUs) Interactive Voice Response	Menu selections are offered to callers who use the touch pad to navigate through menu selections. Some answering machines include VRUs that allow the owner to check remotely for messages. Banks allows customers to make account inquiries and transactions via VRUs, and airlines provide arrival and departure information via VRUs.
Voice Processor	Performs same basic functions as VRU but may also provide additional services based on voice response, speech recognition, or tone detection.
Voice Server	A LAN-based server that stores, processes, and delivers digitized voice messages Often used as the processing and storage component of a voice mail system.
Music/ads on Hold	When customers are put on hold, music plays, or alternatively a tape-recorded sales message interrupts periodically with messages such as "Your call is important to us. Please stay on the line."

Figure 2-15 Auxiliary Voice-Related Services/Devices

(telephony API) or TSAPI-compliant software. Figure 2-15 lists and describes a few of the more popular auxiliary PBX systems.

PBX Trends

Architecture Trends PBX vendors must respond to the demands of their market. PBX users are demanding:

- Better connectivity between phones and desktop PCs
- Better connectivity between PBXs and LANs
- More open PBX architectures for easier access to PBX features and services from a variety of computing platforms
- Better integration of PBX management programs with enterprise network management packages

In many ways, the PBX is becoming nothing more than a specialized communications or voice server that must integrate with all other servers as part of an overall enterprise network. To achieve this transparent integration as part of the enterprise network, PBXs have had to undergo a radical change in their overall design from proprietary, monolithic devices to more open architectures based on industry standard hardware and software components. Figure 2-16 summarizes some of the transitions involved in the migration to the new open PBX architecture, and Figure 2-17 portrays a logical architecture for an open architecture PBX.

One of the key architectural features of the open PBX architecture illustrated in Figure 2-17 is the logical separation of the call processing functionality from the underlying switching fabric. This independence between call processing and switching functionality allows PBX vendors to introduce newer and faster switching technologies such as ATM (Asynchronous Transfer Mode) without having to re-design their entire PBX from top to bottom.

Another important benefit of the open PBX architecture is that by supporting industry standard APIs (application program interfaces) such as TAPI and TSAPI for telephony applications, third-party software developers are able to produce a variety of telephony applications that are able to interface to a variety of PBXs and computers. This frees the PBX vendors from the cost and obligation of developing proprietary telephony applications software for their PBXs. Likewise, by writing to these industry standard APIs, third-party software developers do not need to write numerous PBX-specific versions of a particular telephony application program. TAPI and TSAPI are discussed in more detail in this chapter's section on computer telephony integration.

Multivendor Interoperability Standards Just as open systems has become a major emphasis in the computer industry, interoperability between PBXs from various manufacturers has been receiving increased attention. An international standard sponsored by the ISO known as **Q.Sig** seeks to allow PBXs of any manufactures to

PBX Attribute	Traditional PBX	New Open Architecture PBX
Name	Private Branch Exchange (PBX)	Enterprise Communications Server (ECS)
Processor	Proprietary	Industry standard processors
Operating Systems	Proprietary	Unix
Applications Software	Proprietary	Object-oriented applications written in C or C++
Design Strategy	Monolithic	Modular
Transmission Media	Wireline only	Integrated wireline and wireless
Computer Hardware Interface	Proprietary	Ethernet
Computer Interface Transport Protocol	Proprietary	TCP/IP
Management Information Database Format	Proprietary	Industry standard
Management Interface	Proprietary	Industry standard via SNMP protocol
Application Program Interface	Proprietary	Industry standard APIs: TAPI and TSAPI

Figure 2-16 Trends in PBX Architectures

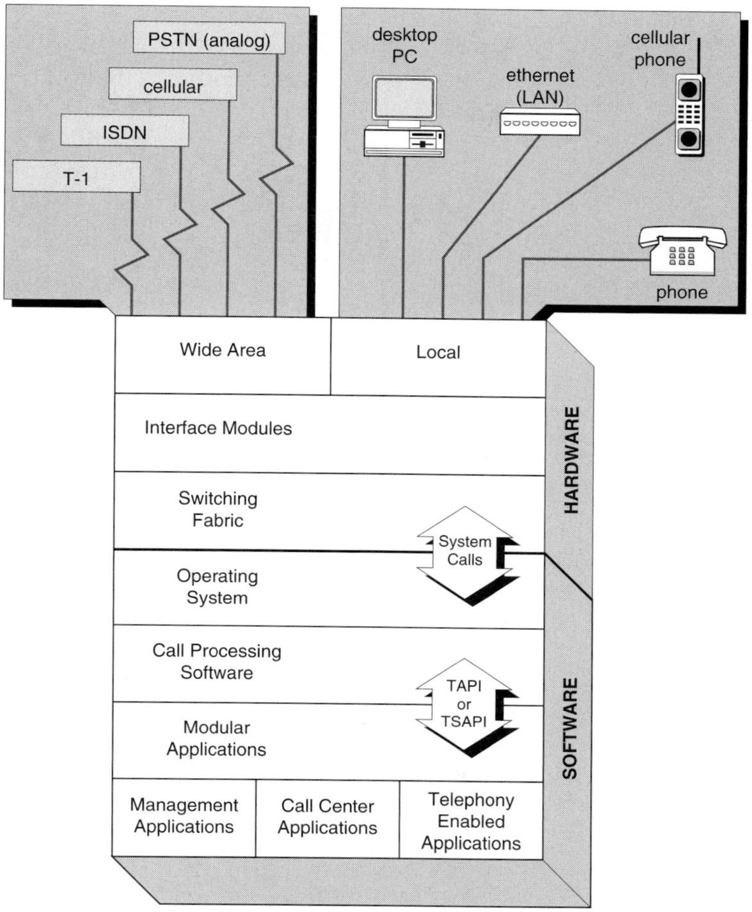

Figure 2-17 Open PBX Architecture

interoperate with each other and with ISDN networks. As a matter of fact, Q.Sig is an extension of an ISDN standard known as **Q.931,** which allows PBX features to interoperate with public switched telephone network features.

Q.Sig standardizes features among different PBX manufacturers and delivers them within the limitations of the feature set offered by ISDN. Among the standardized PBX features are call establishment and termination, call waiting, caller ID and caller ID blocking, as well as other ISDN-supported features. As with any multivendor interoperability standard, only those features common to all supported technology are implemented in the interoperability standard. This represents a least common denominator of common functionality, thereby bypassing any vendor-specific more advanced features.

PBX Integration with Wireless Phones It seemed inevitable that with the explosion in the use of portable wireless telephones, a demand would arise for transparent integration of those wireless phones with the traditional PBX architecture. Northern Telecom, one of the world's largest and most successful PBX manufacturers, has created such a link between the wireless phones and PBXs. Their system, the Companion, allows wireless phones to take advantage of PBX features such as call forwarding, conference calling, and speed dialing. In addition, a person's portable phone can be "twinned" with the office phone so that both ring when the extension is called. The portable phone becomes just another PBX extension, rather than a unintegrated remote phone, reachable only by dialing a full 7-digit number.

Standards support is important in wireless phones as in any other type of data communications. These PBX-integrated wireless phones support the **CT2 (cordless telephony generation 2) common air interface (CAI)** global standard for low-power wireless transmission. Such systems are especially useful in large hospitals, hotels, convention centers, and office buildings where key support people spend a great deal of time at various locations throughout the building.

Mini-PBXs for the Small Office Home Office Market As the number of professionals working out of a small or home office has skyrocketed, an entire market known as **SOHO (small office home office)** has developed that demands **mini-PBXs** with all of the sophistication of large and expensive PBXs at a fraction of the cost. Also known as **multifunction telephony boards,** these PC expansion boards offer multiple workers the ability to share a small number of phone lines with integrated advanced features such as:

- Auto-attendant software
- Integrated with cell phones, pagers, and voice mail systems
- ISDN support
- Integrated with auto-dialer applications, universal mailboxes, and caller ID applications
- Integrated with bundled call control software
- Compatible with computer telephony integration software and APIs

The SOHO marketplace is a major growth area in the telephony marketplace. Every telecommunications vendor is rapidly working to develop and release products for this lucrative market.

COMPUTER TELEPHONY INTEGRATION

CTI Functionality

CTI or **computer telephony integration** seeks to integrate the two most common productivity devices, the computer and the telephone, to enable increased productivity not otherwise possible by using the two devices in a nonintegrated fashion. CTI is not a single application, but an ever widening array of possibilities spawned by the integration of telephony and computing. Figure 2-18 briefly describes some of the subcategories of CTI applications.

CTI Architectures

Computer telephony integration is commonly implemented in one of the following three architectures:

CTI Application Category	Application Description
Call Control	Using computer-based applications users are more easily able to use all of the features of their phone system or PBX, especially the more complicated but seldom used features Includes use of features like on-line phone books, auto-dialing, click-and-point conference calls, on-line display and processing of voice mail messages
Automated Attendant	Allows callers to direct calls to a desired individual at a given business without necessarily knowing their extension number
Automated Call Distribution	Used primarily in call centers staffed by large numbers of customer service agents; incoming calls are automatically distributed to the first available rep, or in some cases, the rep that serves a given geographic region as automatically determined by the computer based on the incoming phone number.
Audiotex	These systems deliver audio information to callers based on responses on the touch-tone keypad to prerecorded questions. Primarily used for information hot lines.
Fax-on-Demand	By combining computer-based faxing with interactive voice response, users can dial in and request that specific information be faxed to their fax machine.
Interactive Voice Response	Interactive Voice Response systems differ from audiotex systems in that IVR systems support on-line transaction processing rather than just information hot-line applications. As an example, banks use IVR systems to allow users to transfer funds between accounts by using only a touch-tone phone.
Outbound Dialing	Also known as **predictive dialing,** this merger of computing and telephony uses a database of phone numbers, automatically dials those numbers, recognizes when calls are answered by people, and quickly passes those calls to available agents.
Unified Messaging	Perhaps the most interesting for the LAN-based user, unified messaging, also known as the **universal in-box** will allow voice mail, e-mail, faxes, and pager messages to be displayed on a single graphical screen. Messages can then be forwarded, deleted, or replied to easily in point-and-click fashion. Waiting calls can also be displayed in the same universal in-box.

Figure 2-18 Computer Telephony Integration Functionality

- PBX-to-host interfaces
- Desktop CTI
- Client/server CTI

Traditionally, computer telephony integration was achieved by linking mainframes to PBX via proprietary PBX-to-host interfaces. Applications were required to be compatible with both the model of mainframe computer and PBX installed. In many cases, these systems actually linked to an ancillary device known as an **ACD** or **automatic call distribution** unit. These systems were very expensive and were usually only employed in large customer service call centers. In this CTI architecture, all phones are controlled by the CTI application running on the mainframe computer.

Desktop CTI, also known as **first-party call control,** is a much less expensive and simpler alternative to the PBX-to-host interface architecture. In this CTI architecture, individual PCs are equipped with telephony boards and associated call control software. Each desktop CTI-equipped PC controls only the phone to which it is directly attached. There is no overall automatic call distribution across multiple agents and their phones, and there is no sharing of call-related data among the desktop CTI PCs.

Finally, client/server CTI offers the overall shared control of the PBX-to-host CTI architecture at a cost much closer to the desktop CTI architecture. In this CTI architecture, a CTI server computer interfaces to the PBX or ACD to provide overall system management while individual client-based CTI applications execute on multiple client PCs. The advantage to such an architecture is that multiple CTI applications on multiple client PCs can share the information supplied by the single CTI server. Figure 2-19 illustrates the various CTI architectures.

CTI Application Development and Implementation

CTI applications, like any client/server application, must be able to integrate easily with a variety of computing platforms and operating systems. Such application portability is possible only if those applications support common commands and systems calls referred to as **application program interfaces (API).** In the case of CTI applications, **TAPI (telephony API),** jointly developed and sponsored by Intel and Microsoft, is the primary API used for CTI.

Applications written to use TAPI should be able to operate transparently in a Windows environment. Figure 2-20 illustrates the key technology required to develop and implement a working CTI application. More specifically, an **interactive voice response (IVR)** application is illustrated. Examples of such applications are automated systems to check account balances at banks or to check arrival and departure information at airlines.

Before the CTI application can be developed, it is essential to first understand the business process that is to be automated using CTI. In addition, it is also essential to know the details of the database system to/from which data will be stored and retrieved with the CTI application.

CTI applications must first be developed using a **CTI application development tool.** Most of these tools automatically generate programming code in either Visual Basic or Visual C++ programming languages. The ease with which this code is designed and generated and the amount of programming knowledge required to use these tools can vary significantly among currently available offerings. If the CTI application is to include faxback or fax-on-demand capabilities, then an optional networked faxing program may need to be integrated during the application development effort. Following are some key characteristics of CTI application development tools:

- Graphical code generators allow easy application development with a minimum of programming background.

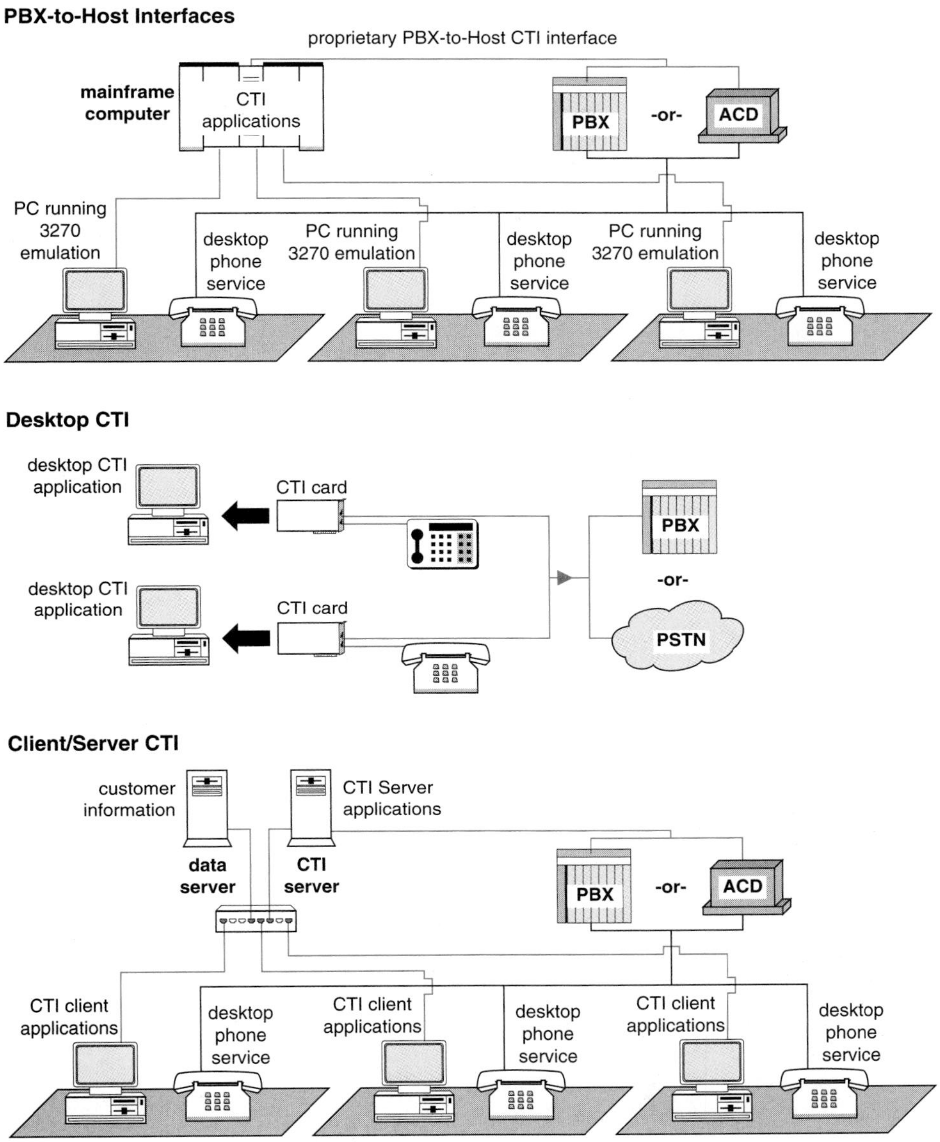

Figure 2-19 CTI Architectures

- Debugging tools, also known as test utilities or virtual phone utilities, allow applications to be tested without the need for voice cards or phones. Log files that record all user responses and program interactions can also aid in debugging new programs.
- Interfaces to fax software for incoming or outbound fax control can add faxback or fax-on-demand capabilities.
- Sound editors can edit and translate between .WAV and .VOX sound files.
- Prerecorded sound bites with standard greetings and responses can lend a professional image to developed CTI applications.

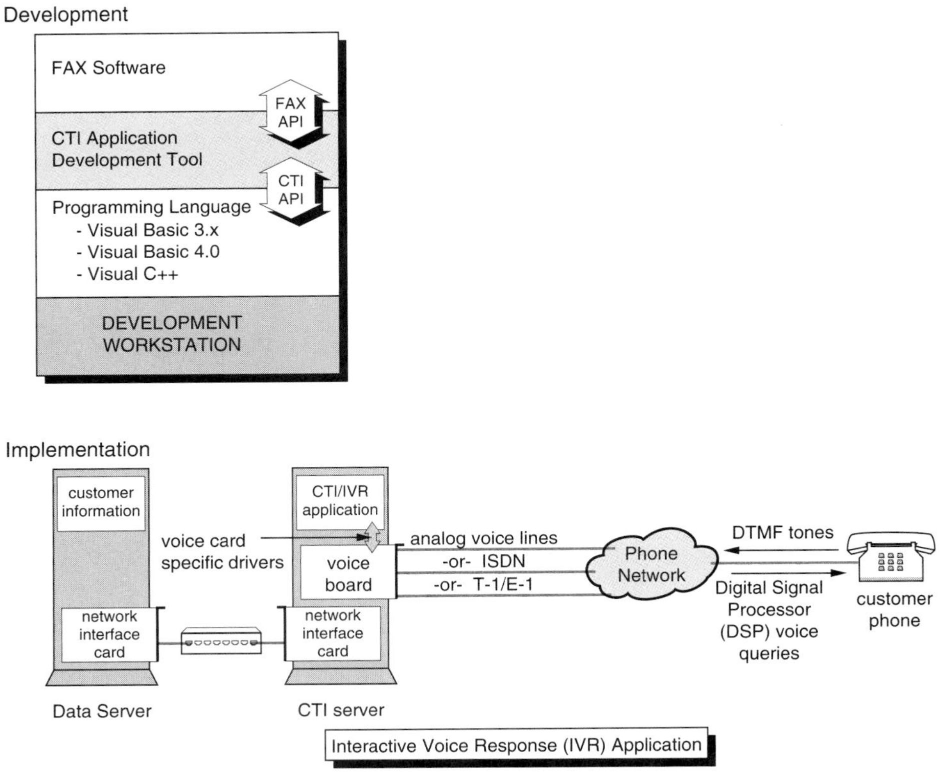

Figure 2-20 Technology Required to Develop and Implement CTI Applications

- CTI applications developed with a given CTI application development tool may or may not need to pay royalties on copies of the finished application.
- Among the types of CTI applications that can be developed with such application development tools are voice mail, interactive voice response, inbound/outbound fax-on-demand, and call center CTI.

Examples of popular CTI application development tools and their respective vendors are shown in Figure 2-21.

The final version of the CTI program must be deployed in a CTI server with a compatible **CTI voice card.** Compatibility between voice cards and CTI applications is ensured by mutual support of the TAPI API. The key functions of a CTI voice card are as follows:

Vendor	**CTI Application Development Tool**
Artisoft, Inc.	Visual Voice Pro
Parity Software Development Corp.	CallSuite
Pronexus	VBVoice

Figure 2-21 Popular CTI Vendors

- Record and playback digitized video.
- Create and recognize DTMF tones (dual tone multifrequency).
- Answer and place phone calls.
- Recognize and process incoming Caller ID (automatic number identification) information.

Once the CTI application is installed, users are able to interact with the application by using a touch-tone phone to respond to voice queries generated by the CTI voice card. Authorized requests for data are passed from the voice card to the networked database server. Responses to database requests are returned to the caller via the CTI voice card.

VOICE TRANSMISSION ALTERNATIVES

Although the PSTN has traditionally been seen as the cheapest and most effective way to transmit voice, alternative methods for voice transmission do exist. Several such methods are briefly explored in terms of configuration requirements, advantages, and disadvantages.

Voice over IP (VOIP)

Although this alternative voice transmission methodology is also commonly referred to as voice over the Internet, it is actually the underlying transport protocols of the Internet that deliver the voice conversations. **Voice over IP** refers to any technology used to transmit voice over any network running the IP protocol. The important point about VOIP technologies is that they are not exclusively confined to use on the Internet. They can be used just as effectively in any of the following topologies:

- Modem-based point-to-point connections
- Local area networks
- Private networks, also known as **intranets**

VOIP can be successfully deployed in any of the previously mentioned topologies provided that required technology is properly implemented. Figure 2-22 illustrates the technology required to implement both IP-based voice transmission and sample topologies.

Required client hardware and software technology for VOIP transmission includes the following:

- VOIP client software
- PC workstation with sufficiently fast CPU to digitize and compress the analog voice signal (200 MHz pentium CPU minimum)
- Sound card for local playback of received voice transmission
- Microphone for local input of transmitted voice signals
- Speakers for local output of received voice signals

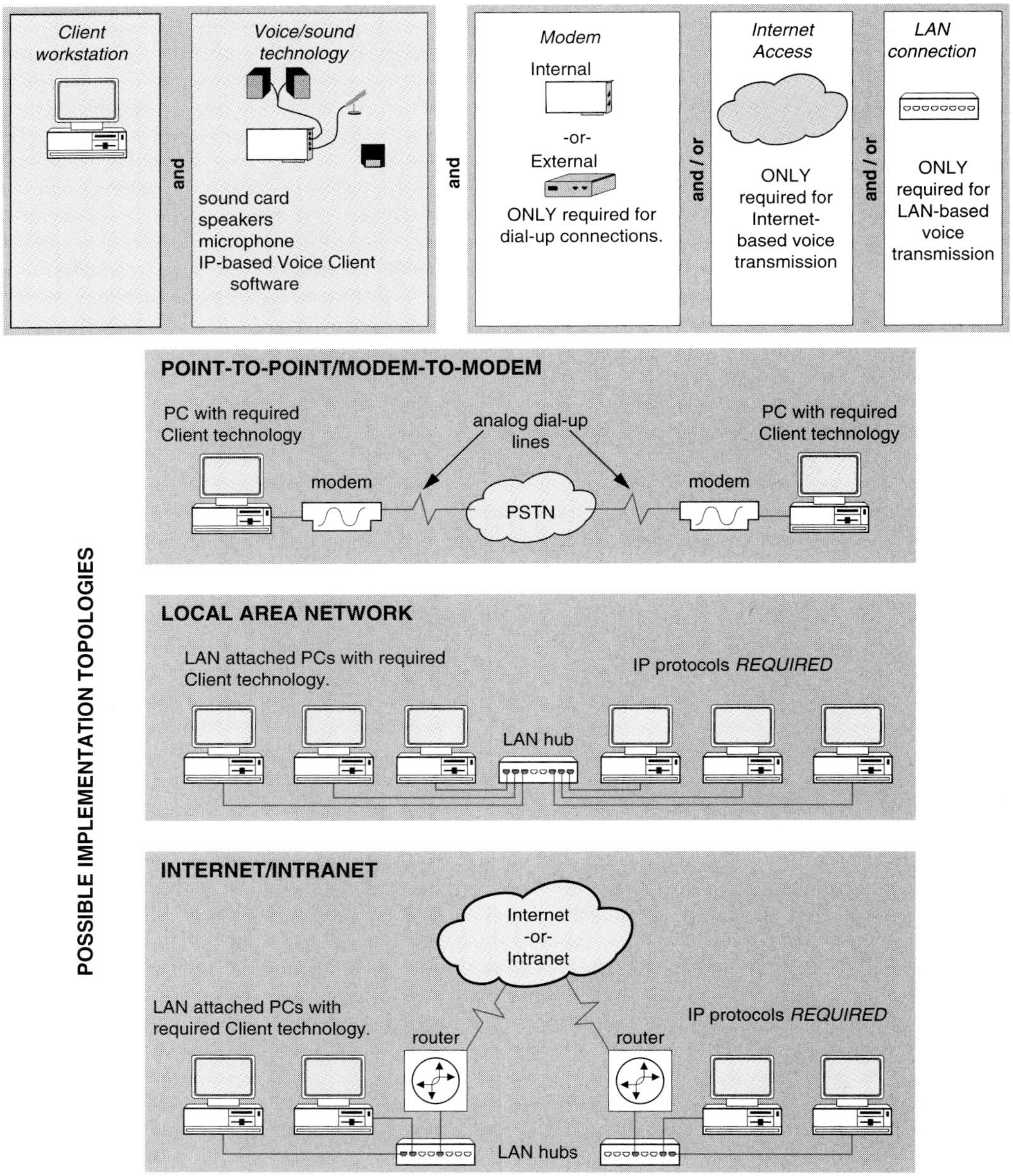

Figure 2-22 VOIP Transmission Technology and Topologies

Figure 2-23 summarizes many of the key features and functionality of VOIP client software.

One of the hottest areas in networking today, VOIP is evolving rapidly. In such a fast-moving marketplace, there is uncertainty that any product or company will survive. However, some of the currently available VOIP software and associated vendors are listed in Figure 2-24.

Feature	Importance/Implication
Client Platform Support	Most IP-based voice transmission software supports Windows 9x, with fewer packages supporting Windows NT and Windows 2000.
Interoperability	The **ITU H.323** standard for interoperability among client software for low bandwidth audio (voice) and video conferencing is supported by some, but not all, client IP-based voice transmission software.
Transmission Quality	Although transmission quality has improved thanks to improved voice compression algorithms, shared IP networks were designed to carry data that could tolerate delays. Voice networks are designed with dedicated circuits offering guaranteed bandwidth and delivery times to voice transmissions.
Multipoint Audioconferences	Some packages may employ proprietary methods and others may support the **T.120** conferencing standard.
Addressing for Call Creation	IP-based software packages employ a variety of different addressing techniques to create calls. In some cases, a directory server must be established listing all potential voice call destinations. In other cases, e-mail addresses or IP addresses may be used to initiate an IP-based voice call. Third-party directory services may also be supported.
Bandwidth Reservation on Shared Networks	To more closely emulate the dedicated bandwidth circuits of the PSTN, an IP-based protocol known as **RSVP** (resource reservation protocol) enables routing software to reserve a portion of network bandwidth known as **a virtual circuit.** This dedicated, guaranteed bandwidth is assigned to a particular IP-based voice transmission session, thereby minimizing transmission delay and increasing overall transmitted voice quality.
Voice Compression	Depending on the particular codec algorithm used, voice compression can cause a major difference in required bandwidth. Among the more popular codec standards are high bandwidth **GSM** (global systems mobile communication), which uses 9600 to 11,000 bps, and low-bandwidth **RT24,** which uses 2400 bps.
Auxiliary Features	Many IP-based voice packages support a variety of other functions that may be important to some organizations. Examples of such functions include answering machine/recorded message capabilities, on-line rolodex with photographs of called parties, text-chat when sufficient voice quality cannot be maintained, electronic whiteboard for long distance brainstorming, file transfer and application sharing, incorporation of voice transmission into HTML documents for web pages, and API to integrate voice transmission in customized applications.

Figure 2-23 Features and Functionality of VOIP Software

Vendor	IP-Based Voice Transmission Software
VocalTec Inc.	Internet Phone
Microsoft Corporation	Microsoft NetMeeting
Netspeak Corporation	Netspeak
Net2Phone Corporation	Net2Phone
Phonefree Corporation	Phonefree
Voxware, Inc.	TeleVox

Figure 2-24 VOIP Client Software

Managerial Perspective

COST/BENEFIT ANALYSIS FOR IP-BASED VOICE TRANSMISSION

The spreadsheet in Figure 2-25 identifies many of the potential costs associated with implementing an IP-based voice transmission network. All cost categories listed will

Costs	
Client Platforms	
Workstation (with sufficiently fast CPU) if not already available	$
Modem (28.8 Kbps minimum, 56 Kbps recommended	$
Speakers	$
Microphone	$
Sound card	$
Client voice software	$
Total cost per voice client	$
Total cost for all voice clients	$
Server Platforms	
Directory servers	$
Directory server software	$
Total server costs	$
Access Charges	
Internet access (monthly charge to ISP)	$
Access line (paid to phone carrier)	$
Total access charges	$
Other Costs	
Training & support	$
Other costs	
Total other costs	$
Total Costs	$
Benefits	
Savings from reduced phone bills to phone service provider	$
Total Benefits	$
Net Cost/Benefit	$

Figure 2-25 Cost/Benefit Analysis for IP-Based Voice Transmission

not apply in all situations. Benefits will be most significant for those organizations with large domestic or international long-distance calling expenses. However, it should be noted that such organizations often already have large volume discounted rate contracts with their phone service providers, which minimize or negate any potential savings that might be achieved by shifting to an IP-based voice transmission network.

A more subjective criterion that must be considered is the minimum acceptable transmitted voice quality. Higher transmission quality demands higher amounts of dedicated bandwidth. Lower amounts of shared bandwidth can cause transmission delays that will be manifested as voice dropouts or clipped words. Typical delays on voice transmission networks such as PSTN are in the 50 to 70 msec range, and IP-based voice transmission networks can exhibit delays of 500 msec to 1.5 secs. Many corporations may conclude that the current generation of IP-based voice transmission technology is sufficient for internal corporate communication but is unacceptable for external communication with clients and customers.

Finally, if large amounts of revenue begin to bypass phone carriers as a result of a massive use of IP-based voice transmission over the Internet, it is likely that the Federal Communications Commission may take steps to ensure that internet service providers (ISP) do not have an unfair competitive advantage.

Voice Over Frame Relay

IP-based voice transmission via the Internet is not the only alternative to traditional voice transmission over wide areas. **Frame relay** is another wide area transmission service that was primarily or initially deployed for data transmission but is now capable of delivering voice transmissions as well. Although frame relay is discussed further in Chapter 8, the implications of transmitting voice over this service are detailed here.

To be able to adapt dynamically to transmit data as efficiently as possible, frame relay encapsulates segments of a data transfer session into variable length frames. For longer data transfers, longer frames with larger data payloads are used and for short messages, shorter frames are used. These variable length frames introduce varying amounts of delay resulting from processing by intermediate switches on the frame relay network. This variable length delay introduced by the variable length frames works well for data but is unacceptable to voice payloads that are sensitive to delay.

The **FRAD** or **frame relay access device** can accommodate both voice and data traffic by using any or all of the following techniques:

- Voice prioritization—FRADs can distinguish between voice and data traffic and prioritize voice traffic over data traffic.
- Data frame size limitation—Long data frames must be segmented into multiple smaller frames so that pending voice traffic can have priority access. However, data must not be delayed to unacceptable levels.
- Separate voice and data queues—To more effectively manage pending data and voice messages, separate queues for data and voice messages can be maintained within the FRAD.

Voice conversations transmitted over frame relay networks require 4 to 16 Kbps of bandwidth each. This dedicated bandwidth is reserved as an end-to-end connection through the frame relay network known as a PVC or permanent virtual circuit. For prioritization schemes established by FRADs to be maintained throughout a voice conversation's end-to-end journey, intermediate frame relay switches within the frame relay network must support the same prioritization schemes. At this point, voice conversations can take place only between locations connected directly to a frame relay network. There are currently no interoperability standards or network–network interface standards defined between frame relay networks and the voice-based PSTN. Figure 2-26 illustrates voice transmission over a frame relay network.

Voice Over ATM

Whereas frame relay is a switch-based WAN service using variable length frames, **ATM (asynchronous transfer mode)** is a switch-based WAN service using fixed length frames, more properly referred to as **cells.** Fixed length cells ensure fixed length processing time by ATM switches, thereby enabling predictable, rather than variable, delay and delivery time. Voice is currently transmitted across ATM networks using a bandwidth reservation scheme known as **CBR** or **constant bit rate,** which is analogous to a frame relay virtual circuit. However, constant bit rate does not make optimal use of available bandwidth because during the course of a given voice conversation, moments of silence intermingle with periods of conversation. The most common method for currently transmitting voice over an ATM network is to reserve a CBR of 64 Kbps for one voice conversation digitized via PCM (pulse code modulation).

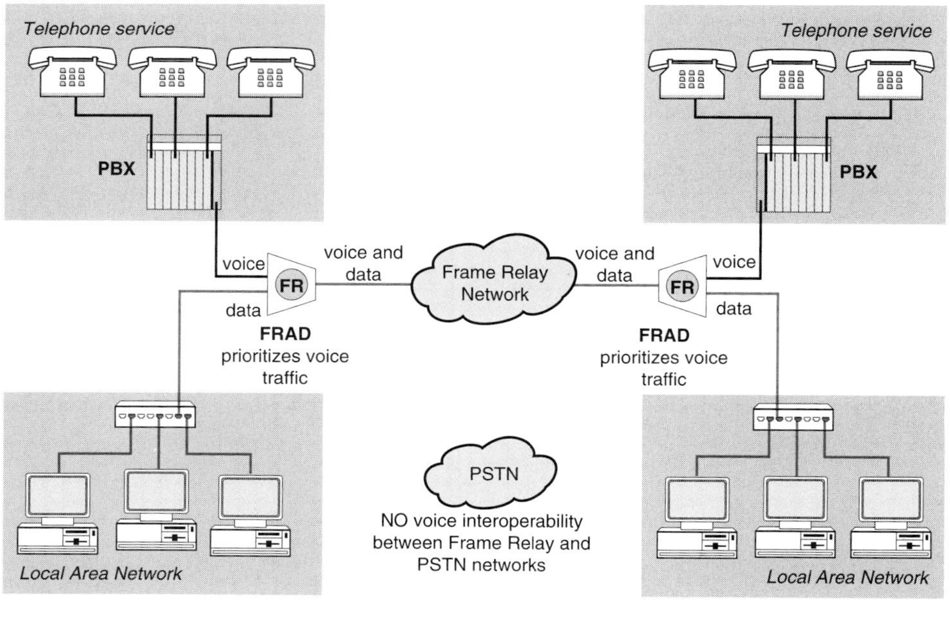

Figure 2-26 Voice Transmission over a Frame Relay Network

In Sharper Focus

OPTIMIZING VOICE OVER ATM

More efficient use of ATM network capacity for voice transmission can be achieved in one of the following ways:

- Voice compression—The ITU standardized voice compression algorithms via the G series of standards. Algorithms vary in the amount of bandwidth required to transmit toll quality voice. (G.726: 48, 32, 24, or 16 Kbps; G.728: 16 Kbps; G.729: 8 Kbps). An important point to remember with voice compression is that the greater the compression ratio achieved, the more complicated and processing intensive the compression process. In such cases, the greatest delay is introduced by the voice compression algorithm, with the highest compression ratio requiring the least bandwidth.
- Silence suppression—All cells are examined as to contents. Any voice cell that contains silence is not allowed to enter the ATM network. At the destination end, the nontransmitted silence is replaced with synthesized background noise. Silence suppression can reduce the amount of cells transmitted for a given voice conversation by 50%.
- Use of **VBR (variable bit rate)** rather than CBR—By combining the positive attributes of voice compression and silence suppression, ATM-based voice conversation are able to be transmitted using variable bit rate bandwidth management. By using only bandwidth when someone is talking, remaining bandwidth is available for data transmission or other voice conversations. Use of VBR is controlled via two parameters:
  - Peak voice bit rate controls the maximum amount of bandwidth a voice conversation can be given when there is little or no contention for bandwidth.
  - Guaranteed voice bit rate controls the minimum amount of bandwidth that must be available to a voice conversation regardless of how much contention exists for bandwidth.

Standards for voice transmission over ATM (VTOA) networks are being developed by the ATM Forum. Among the standards available or under development are the following:

- CES, Circuit emulation standard—Defines voice transport over ATM networks using CBR (constant bit rate). Equivalent to PVCs over frame relay nets.
- VTOA–ATM—For use on private or public ATM networks, defines voice transmission using:
  - **ISDN (integrated services digital network)** as a voice source network.
  - Transport of compressed voice over ATM.
  - Virtual tunnel groups that are able to handle multiple calls simultaneously between two locations.
- VTOA to the desktop—Defines interoperability between ATM and non-ATM networks.

Figure 2-27 illustrates the transmission of voice conversations over an ATM network.

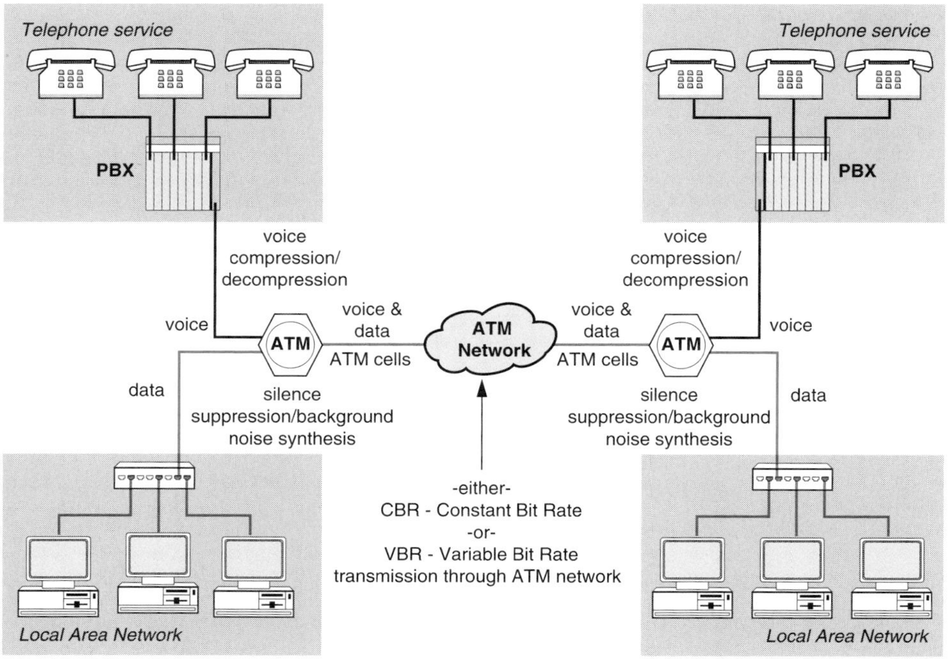

Figure 2-27 Voice Transmission Over an ATM Network

Voice/Data Multiplexers

As opposed to using a switch-based frame relay or ATM network for wide area transmission of voice and data, organizations have traditionally chosen to link combined voice and data transmission over long distances via leased digital transmission services such as T-1. From a business perspective, a key difference between switched services such as frame relay or ATM and leased services such as T-1 is that switched services are usually tariffed according to usage, and leased services are usually tariffed according to a flat monthly rate. As a result, leased services are being paid for 24 hr/day, 7 days/week, whether or not they are being used.

Many corporations that once maintained a private network of **voice/data multiplexers** linked via T-1 or other high speed digital services have found that usage-based pricing of frame relay networks can produce significant savings. A voice/data multiplexer can simultaneously transmit digitized voice and data over a single digital transmission service by assigning the voice and data transmissions to separate channels. Multiplexing is explored in more depth in Chapter 8.

Voice/Data Modems

With the increase in home businesses and telecommuting, the idea of transmitting voice and data simultaneously over a single analog phone line has gathered increased interest. In this manner, a technical support specialist could be speaking with a customer while simultaneously taking over remote control of the PC to run diagnostics or downloading files for inspection, editing, and reinstallation. Such a simultaneous conversation/data session would not require a second phone line on either end but would require modems that support simultaneous transmission of voice and data on both ends of the transmission.

Two different standards currently exist for simultaneous transmission of voice and data over a single analog phone line:

- **ASVD—Analog simultaneous voice and data** does not transmit voice and data in a truly simultaneous manner. Instead, it switches quickly between voice and data transmission. Voice transmission always takes priority, so data transfers are paused during data transmissions. ASVD has been formalized as ITU standard V.61 and is incorporated into voice view software from Radish Communications Systems.
- **DSVD—Digital simultaneous voice and data** digitizes all voice transmissions and combines the digitized voice and data over the single analog transmission line. The digitized voice is compressed into between 9.6 and 12 Kbps, leaving between 16.8 and 19.2 Kbps for data of the total 28.8 Kbps transmission rate of a V.34 DSVD-compliant modem. The DSVD standard has been formalized as ITU V.70.

ISDN

ISDN (integrated services digital network) is a switched digital, rather than analog, service that is also capable of transmitting voice and data simultaneously. Rather than using modems, ISDN requires devices that are officially known as terminal adapters but that are frequently marketed as **ISDN data/voice modems.** ISDN BRI (basic rate interface) service offers two 64 Kbps channels. One of these channels is used for data and the other is used to simultaneously transmit voice. Analog phones or fax machines can be interfaced to the ISDN data/voice modem to allow these analog devices to access ISDN's digital transmission service. Point-to-point ISDN connections require both ends of the transmission to be able to access ISDN services via ISDN data/voice modems.

ISDN is not nearly as available as switched analog voice phone service. In addition, pricing policies for ISDN can include both a monthly flat fee and an additional usage based tariff. ISDN is explored further in Chapter 8. Figure 2 - 28 illustrates the differences between simultaneous voice and data transmission using DSVD modems on analog services and ISDN data/voice modems over ISDN services.

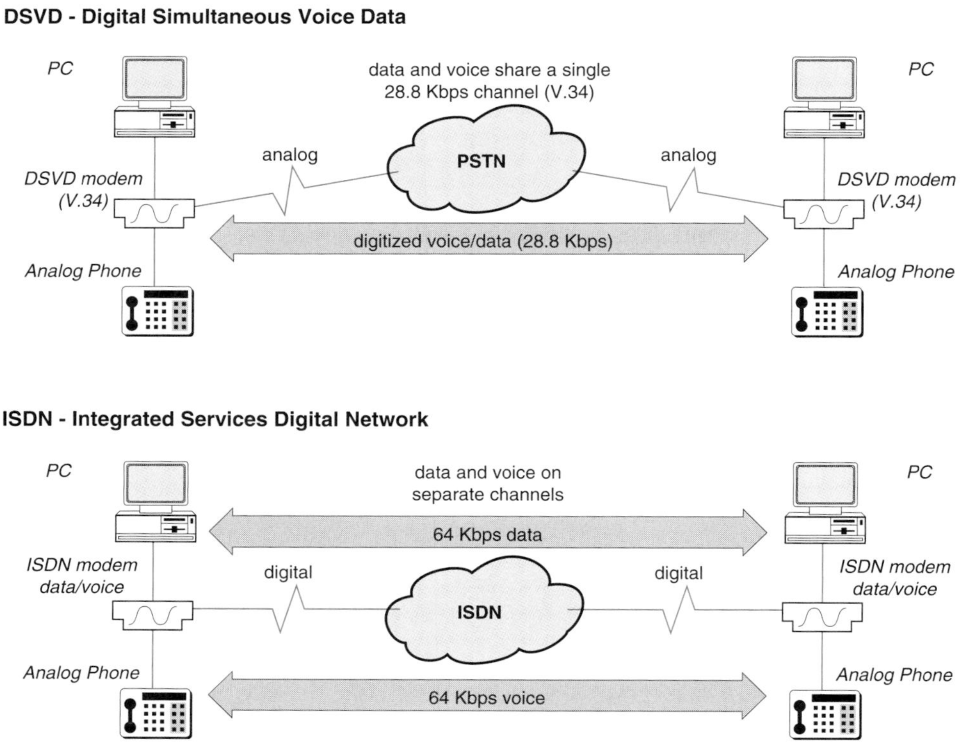

Figure 2-28 Simultaneous Voice/Data Transmission with DSVD and ISDN

SUMMARY

Network analysts must be qualified to design networks that are capable of carrying voice as well as data. Before designing such networks, the network analyst must understand the nature of voice signals and how voice signals can be processed and integrated into a cohesive network with data transmissions.

Voice bandwidth on the analog public switched telephone network (PSTN) is limited to 3100 Hz. To combine voice with data over a single transmission link, voice signals must first be digitized. Pulse code modulation or one of its derivatives is the most popular voice digitization technique. Depending on voice compression algorithms employed, digitized voice requires between 64 and 8 Kbps of bandwidth.

The PBX is the voice server or switch that links users' phones with their intended destinations. Today's PBXs have evolved from proprietary monolithic architectures to open, standards-based architectures.

PBXs are being increasingly seen as a specialized server for distributed client/server information systems. Computer telephony integration seeks to optimize the use of the telephone and the desktop computer by being able to share the information and functionality offered by each. Standardized APIs and PBX-to-host interfaces are required if CTI is to ever reach its full potential.

The voice network is comprised of a hierarchy of switching offices designed to offer fast, reliable service. Switches are able to communicate with each other via a common language known as signaling system 7. End-users are able to now use SS7 to monitor and control their carrier-based transmission circuits through the advanced intelligent network.

Alternative voice transmission architectures include voice over IP, voice over frame relay, voice over ATM, voice/data multiplexers, voice/data modems, and ISDN modems.

KEY TERMS

ACD
Adaptive Differential Pulse Code Modulation
ADPCM
advanced intelligent network
AIN
analog simultaneous voice and data
API
application program interfaces
ASVD
asynchronous transfer mode
ATM
Audiotex
automated attendant
automatic call distribution
CAI
call accounting system
call control
call pickup
CBR
cells
central office
Class 1 regional center
Class 2 sectional center
Class 3 primary center
Class 4 toll center
Class 5 office
CO
codec
common air interface
common channel interoffice signaling
common control area
computer telephony integration
constant bit rate
Cordless Telephony Generation 2
CT2
CTI
CTI application development tool
CTI voice card
DID
digital signal processors
digital simultaneous voice and data
direct inward dialing
DSVD
DTMF
dual tone multifrequency
fax-on-demand
first-party call control
FRAD
frame relay access device
frame relay
GSM
guardbands
hunting
ICP
integrated service digital network
IN
intelligent call processing
intelligent network
interactive voice response
inter-exchange carrier
inter office signaling
intranets
ISDN
ISDN data/voice modem
ITU H.323
IVR
last mile
LCR
least cost routing
line cards
local loops
mini-PBX
multifunction telephony boards
night mode
out-of-band signaling
paging
PAM
PBX
PBX CPU
PBX-to-host interfaces
PCM
PDM
plain old telephone service
point of presence
POP
port cards
POTS
PPM
predictive dialing
prioritization
private branch exchange
PSTN
public switched telephone network
pulse
pulse amplitude modulation
pulse code modulation
pulse duration modulation
pulse position modulation
pulse width modulation
PWM
Q.931
Q.Sig
receiver
RSVP
RT24
signaling System 7
Small Office Home Office
SMDR
SOHO
SS7
station cards
station message detail recording
stored program control
switching matrix
system signaling
T.120
tandem office
TAPI
telephone switch
telephony API
toll quality
transmitter
trunk cards
unified messaging
universal in-box
variable bit rate
VBR
virtual circuit
voice digitization
voice over IP
voice/data multiplexers

REVIEW QUESTIONS

1. How do the sound waves of the human voice actually get transferred onto and off the voice network?
2. What is DTMF, and what are its potential uses beyond assisting in completing a call?
3. What are the differences between the various voice digitization techniques?
4. How does PCM differ from ADPCM in terms of bandwidth requirements?
5. How is voice compression accomplished? What technology is involved?
6. What is the business motivation for voice compression? What is the potential tradeoff?
7. What are the major architectural elements of a PBX?
8. Explain how voice transmission can be integrated with computers to produce a service known as computer telephony integration.
9. What are some practical business applications of CTI?
10. What are some potential uses of voice processing or interactive voice response?
11. What is the voice network hierarchy, and what are the fundamental implications of such a hierarchical design?
12. What is out-of band signaling, and of what importance is such a technical ability in terms of emerging network services?
13. Why might a voice conversation not be totally transmitted via analog transmission even if the source and destination loops are analog?
14. How does sampling rate in voice digitization relate to the quality of the transmitted voice signal?
15. How does ADPCM accomplish digitized voice transmission in less than 64 Kbps?
16. Why is DS-0 considered a standard circuit for transmission of digitized voice?
17. How does PCM differ from other voice digitization techniques such as PAM?
18. What are the benefits of PCM over other voice digitization methods?
19. What is the role of a codec in voice digitization?
20. What are some of the interoperability issues surrounding CTI?
21. How can the cost of call accounting systems be justified?
22. What are some the PBX features required to support a call accounting system?
23. What are some of the issues surrounding interoperability of PBXs from various vendors?
24. What is signaling system?
25. What is the AIN and what role does SS7 play in such a network?
26. Why is it important for network analysts to be qualified to design voice networks?
27. Compare the bandwidth of the PSTN with that of human hearing.
28. What is a channel bank?
29. What is toll quality and how is it related to ADPCM?
30. Show the mathematical proof of why a T-1 circuit is 1.544 Mbps.
31. Describe the basic architecture of a PBX. How is it like and unlike the switch in a CO?
32. What are some important architectural trends in PBX design, and what is the driving force behind these trends?
33. What is automatic call distribution, and what is an effective application of ACD?
34. Differentiate among the three major CTI architectures in terms of physical topology and delivered functionality.
35. What is predictive dialing?
36. What is a universal in-box and why might this be of benefit to its users?
37. What are some of the important functions of CTI application development tools?
38. What is the function of the CTI voice card in the CTI implementation?
39. What is a tandem office?
40. What is required to transmit voice over the Internet?
41. What are some important features of VOIPclient software?
42. How is voice compression related to bandwidth requirements and delay?
43. What characteristic of frame relay must be overcome for effective voice transmission?
44. What are some of the issues surrounding voice over ATM?
45. Differentiate between ASVD and DSVD.
46. How does an ISDN data/voice modem differ from a DSVD modem?
47. What is the difference between CBR and VBR for voice over ATM?
48. Differentiate between peak voice bit rate and guaranteed voice bit rate.
49. How does a FRAD assist in optimizing voice transmission over frame relay?

ACTIVITIES

1. Suppose a normal voice grade circuit had a bandwidth of 3000 Hz. What would be the maximum sampling rate of an analog signal on such a circuit? How much bandwidth would be required to transmit a digitized conversation from such a circuit using PCM? Using ADPCM? How many conversations could be transmitted over a T-1 using PCM? Using ADPCM?
2. Request product literature from a variety of PBX vendors. Note differences in functionality and pricing. Prepare presentations concerning PBX options and price ranges for small, medium, and large companies.
3. Investigate the level of support for CTI from the major PBX vendors. Which computing platforms are compatible with which PBXs? What impact has TAPI had on the CTI market?
4. What are the approximate costs of various CTI systems? Assuming a maximum payback period of 2 years, how much additional revenue would the various CTI options have to generate? Which CTI functionality is most often implemented? (IVR, predictive dialing, ACD, etc.)
5. Take apart a modern telephone handset and compare it with the handset illustrated in Figure 2-1. Draw a detailed diagram of your handset. Try to explain any differences between the two diagrams.
6. Investigate and report on which government agencies use the specialized keys illustrated in Figure 2-5 and for what purpose such keys are used.
7. Arrange a tour of a large school or business PBX facility. Prepare a detailed report outlining PBX functionality, installation, and architecture, as well as the PBX's ability to meet business level requirements and objectives.
8. Find out if your school or business uses a call acounting system. Speak to the person in charge of the system to investigate how it is used, as well as its effectiveness at spotting and curtailing abuse of phone privileges. Report on your results.
9. Conduct a survey on how people feel about doing business with companies that employ voice processing or automated attendant systems.
10. Contact your local phone company to investigate the nearest location of each of the various classes of switching offices illustrated in Figure 2-4.
11. Investigate the current market penetration of TAPI-based applications. Explain your results.

CASE STUDY

Bloomberg Goes IP

Giant financial information firm scraps proprietary network, embraces the 'Net.

NEW YORK – It sounds like a headline Bloomberg might carry: Network upgrade gets information services firm ready for the dot-com era. But in this story, the company that redesigned its network is financial information powerhouse Bloomberg itself.

Bloomberg recently migrated its private network from dedicated terminals and home-grown black boxes running proprietary network protocols to standard PCs, Unix workstations and off-the-shelf routers running IP.

In overhauling its network, Bloomberg spent "far in excess of $50 million" on network equipment and personnel, says Tom Secunda, a Bloomberg founder and the company's head of development. But Bloomberg is already reaping the rewards of the project in terms of cost savings from not having to build its own network gear and from the ability to offer new Internet-based services, he says.

"The greatest advantage to us with the new network is that we can take advantage of new products and technologies," Secunda says. "We're able to buy someone else's hardware, although we tend to build a lot of the software ourselves."

By using IP, Bloomberg can make its information service interoperate with existing Internet content and can take advantage of Internet applications such as Real Network's RealAudio and Microsoft's NetShow to create multimedia news feeds.

"Bloomberg is now, in a loose sense, a portal," Secunda explains. "We provide our customers with Internet content, and we direct them to the appropriate content on the Web. For example, if you were looking at IBM information on Bloomberg, we can add a URL that you can click on to get to IBM's Web site."

Founded in 1982 and headquartered in New York, Bloomberg provides breaking news and stock ticker information to banks and other financial institutions. Bloomberg has two data centers – in New York and Princeton, N.J. – that are connected via a private frame relay network to tens of thousands of customer sites around the world. Bloomberg supports more than 120,000 terminals, which are usually owned and maintained by the customer.

Bloomberg relies on a handful of carriers to lease the portion of the network from its data centers to points of presence (POP) in major cities and then to customer sites. The POPs house routers for passing data. From the POPs, the information goes to routers at the customer sites and then to individual terminals.

In the past, Bloomberg used custom-made Intel multibus terminals that communicated with Unix servers – and before that, minicomputers in the data centers.

"We created a protocol that talked over our frame relay network. It ran on a proprietary box, built on Intel technology by us, to do screen display and protocol conversion at the customer site." Similar special-purpose boxes that supported the proprietary protocols were located in Bloomberg's data centers and POP sites.

The new network, which most Bloomberg customers had converted to by October, still relies on frame relay for the transport layer, but it supports traffic using both the IP and User Datagram Protocol (UDP) standards. Bloomberg uses off-the-shelf routers from Nortel Networks and commercial network management software such as Hewlett-Packard's Open View.

During the network migration, Bloomberg customers ran into some problems sending UDP-based multimedia traffic through commercial firewalls. To resolve these problems, Bloomberg chose the SOCKS 5 protocol. In fact, NEC Systems announced in November a special version of its SOCKS 5 server – the EBorder Special Edition – that is customized for Bloomberg's services. Users of the special NEC SOCKS 5 server include Dresdner Bank and Merrill Lynch.

Dresdner Bank has migrated all 600 of its Bloomberg terminals – located in Frankfurt, Germany, New York, London, Tokyo, Hong Kong and Singapore – to the new IP router system. At each site, Dresdner has set up a firewall complex based on NEC's SOCKS 5 server to protect Dresdner's corporate network from third-party networks such as Bloomberg's, says Norbert Schaar, network and security consultant for Dresdner Bank's Global IT Services. Schaar says NEC's special server "ensures the enforcement of our security policy, provides proxy services for a lot of services and applications, and enhances the security and availability."

With its IP network in place, Bloomberg plans to roll out new offerings in such areas as streaming audio and video as well as conference calling. "We have hundreds of different concepts," Secunda says.

Bloomberg is already offering improved services for mobile users. In the past, customers could access information services on a portable computer via a dial-up connection. To support such services, Bloomberg had massive phone banks in New York and other major financial centers around the world. Maintaining those phone banks was expensive. Now the same services are provided over the Internet at a reduced cost to Bloomberg, Secunda says.

By linking to existing Web content, Bloomberg can put its internal resources into developing new services. "We had a way of looking up ZIP codes and looking up plane schedules. Now we're deciding whether our systems are better, or if we should just link to the Web," Secunda says. "We have more options because we have the ability to transport Web content to our customers."

Source: Carolyn Duffy Marsan, "Bloomberg goes IP," *Network World*, vol. 17, no. 3 (January 17, 2000), p. 1. Copyright Network World. Reprinted with permission.

BUSINESS CASE STUDY QUESTIONS

Activities

1. Complete a top-down model for this case by gleaning facts from the case and placing them in the proper layer of the top-down model. After having completed the top-down model, analyze and detail those instances where requirements were clearly passed down from upper layers to lower layers of the model and where solutions to those requirements were passed up from lower layers to upper layers of the model.
2. Detail any questions about the case that may occur to you for which answers are not clearly stated in the article.

Business

1. What was the business motivation or problem that initiated the search for the implemented solution?
2. What was the primary reason for Bloomberg converting their network to IP?
3. Were business performance metrics and associated infrastructure performance metrics identified? If so, were they achieved? If not, what might be some suitable business and infrastructure performance metrics for this case?
4. What other company (ies) have taken advantage of Bloomberg's network conversion?

Application

1. What is the application that Bloomberg has implemented IP to deliver?
2. Is Bloomberg truly becoming a "portal" as the case mentions?
3. What new applications is Bloomberg looking to roll out onto their new network?
4. What are the network management applications used in the new Bloomberg network?

Data

1. What types of data does the upgraded network currently carry?
2. What types of data does the upgraded network have the capability to carry upon which Bloomberg can build new applications?

Network

1. What layer two technology does Bloomberg utilize in their core network?
2. What protocols does the new network utilize?
3. How has the network upgrade helped Bloomberg reduce costs?

Technology

1. What specific technologies were employed to deliver the described solution?

CHAPTER 3

DATA COMMUNICATIONS CONCEPTS

Concepts Reinforced

I-P-O Model	Basic Telecommunications Infrastructure
Protocols and Compatibility	

Concepts Introduced

Character Encoding	Analog vs. Digital
Serial vs. Parallel	Physical Interfaces vs. Transmission Protocols
Serial Transmission Standards	Carrier Waves
Modulation Techniques	Half-Duplex vs. Full-Duplex
Two-Wire vs. Four-Wire Circuits	Synchronous vs. Asynchronous Transmission
Dial-up vs. Leased Line	Echo Cancellation
Baud Rate vs. Transmission Rate	
Transmission Services	
Modulation/Demodulation	

OBJECTIVES

Upon successful completion of this chapter, you should:

1. Distinguish between the following related concepts and understand the proper application of each:

analog	digital
synchronous	asynchronous
full duplex	half duplex
two wire	four wire
serial	parallel
bps	baud rate
leased line	dial-up/switched line

2. Understand the concepts, processes, and protocols involved with completing a modem-based, point-to-point data communications session, including the following:

   character encoding
   serial/parallel conversion

serial transmission
modulation/demodulation

3. Understand the impact and limitations of various modulation techniques.
4. Understand the differences and proper application of a variety of carrier transmission services

INTRODUCTION

As new vocabulary and concepts are introduced in this chapter, it's important to understand that these words and concepts will be used throughout your study of data communications. Future concepts will be built on the foundation of a thorough understanding of the vocabulary in this chapter. This is the time to begin to speak this foreign language that we call data communications. Don't be timid. Try to get together with other data communications students or professionals outside of class and practice your new vocabulary.

Discussions of specific technology will be kept to a minimum in this chapter. We concentrate instead on the conceptual aspects of the "how" of data transmission. Although modems are mentioned in this chapter, the in-depth study of technology, including its business impact, begins in Chapter 4.

End-to-End Data Communications

Figure 3-1 serves as a roadmap for all of the concepts to be studied in Chapter 3. An end-to-end communication session between two PCs (personal computers) and their associated modems via a dial-up phone line offers an overall scenario into which most data communication concepts can be introduced. In this manner, each concept can be understood individually as well as in terms of its contribution to the overall end-to-end data communications session.

Another reason for choosing a modem-based communication session as a means of introducing basic data communications concepts is the likelihood of encountering modems and dial-up connections in real life. This contributes to familiarity with the process as we begin this study and a greater understanding of this common data communications opportunity at the conclusion of the chapter.

However, it is important to understand that the concepts outlined in Figure 3-1 and explained throughout the chapter are not specific to only PCs or modems. These are basic data communications concepts that form the basis of the vast majority of data communications technology. Likewise, although PC modems are discussed in this chapter, modems also have many other applications such as communicating with mainframe computers as described in Chapter 8.

The end-to-end data communications session between two PCs is illustrated in Figure 3-1. The constituent concepts and processes can be logically subdivided into three major sections:

- From the computer to the modem
- Within the modem
- From the modem to the phone service

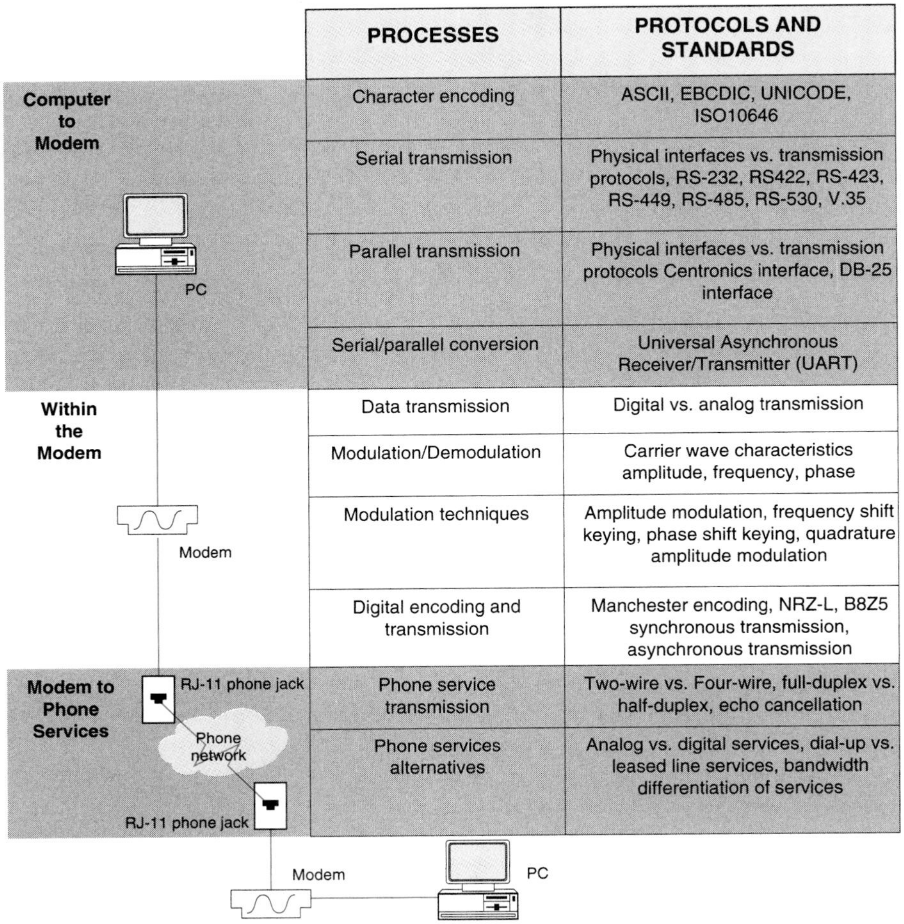

PROCESSES	PROTOCOLS AND STANDARDS
Character encoding	ASCII, EBCDIC, UNICODE, ISO10646
Serial transmission	Physical interfaces vs. transmission protocols, RS-232, RS422, RS-423, RS-449, RS-485, RS-530, V.35
Parallel transmission	Physical interfaces vs. transmission protocols Centronics interface, DB-25 interface
Serial/parallel conversion	Universal Asynchronous Receiver/Transmitter (UART)
Data transmission	Digital vs. analog transmission
Modulation/Demodulation	Carrier wave characteristics amplitude, frequency, phase
Modulation techniques	Amplitude modulation, frequency shift keying, phase shift keying, quadrature amplitude modulation
Digital encoding and transmission	Manchester encoding, NRZ-L, B8Z5 synchronous transmission, asynchronous transmission
Phone service transmission	Two-wire vs. Four-wire, full-duplex vs. half-duplex, echo cancellation
Phone services alternatives	Analog vs. digital services, dial-up vs. leased line services, bandwidth differentiation of services

Figure 3-1 Basic Data Communications Concepts: End-to-End Modem-Based Data Communications Session

In turn, each of these major subsections is divided into several constituent processes. Each of these processes is described conceptually. In addition, any significant protocols or standards currently governing these processes, as listed in Figure 3-1, are explored.

More detailed information on the operation of the carrier network and services are provided in Chapters 2 and 8.

COMPUTER TO MODEM

Character Encoding

To get data from the source PC to the destination PC, it must first be transformed from a humanly understandable form (letters, numbers, voices, images) to an electronic machine understandable form. The process of transforming humanly readable characters into machine readable code is known as **character encoding.**

Using a particular encoding scheme, characters are turned into a series of 1s and 0s. Why 1s and 0s? The 1 and 0 are used as symbols to represent two discrete states, much like a light switch being on or off. These two discrete states can be represented by discrete voltages of electricity or level of light. In turn, these discrete voltages of electricity or levels of light representing coded characters can then be easily transmitted, received, and examined by data communications equipment.

The individual 1s and 0s that constitute a given character are known as **bits.** The series of bits representing the entire encoded letter (usually 8 bits) is known as a **byte.** These 1s and 0s, or digits, represented by discrete signals are said to be in a **digital** format and are known as digital data. Now that the character is in a machine-readable form, it can be transmitted through the process generally known as data communications.

Multiple protocols or standards can be used to code characters. The most commonly used standards are ASCII, EBCDIC, and UNICODE.

ASCII **American Standard Code for Information Interchange (ASCII)** is one standardized method for encoding humanly readable characters. Standardized by ANSI, ASCII uses a series of seven bits to represent 128 ($2^7 = 128$) different characters including upper and lower case letters, numerals, punctuation and symbols, and specialized control characters. One use of control characters is explained further in Chapter 4. An eight bit, known as a parity bit, is added to seven-bit ASCII for error detection. Error detection and parity checking are also described in Chapter 4. Figure 3-2 is an ASCII table that illustrates the relationship between characters and their associated ASCII codes.

MSB Bit 6				0	0	0	0	1	1	1	1
MSB Bit 5				0	0	1	1	0	0	1	1
MSB Bit 4				0	1	0	1	0	1	0	1
LSB Bit 0	Bit 1	Bit 2	Bit 3								
0	0	0	0	NUL	DLE	SP	0	@	P		p
1	0	0	0	SOH	DC1	!	1	A	Q	a	q
0	1	0	0	STX	DC2		2	B	R	b	r
1	1	0	0	ETX	DC3	#	3	C	S	c	s
0	0	1	0	EOT	DC4	$	4	D	T	d	t
1	0	1	0	ENQ	NAK	%	5	E	U	e	u
0	1	1	0	ACK	SYN	&	6	F	V	f	v
1	1	1	0	BEL	ETB		7	G	W	g	w
0	0	0	1	BS	CAN	(	8	H	X	h	x
1	0	0	1	HT	EM	)	9	I	Y	i	y
0	1	0	1	LF	SUB	*	:	J	Z	j	z
1	1	0	1	VT	ESC	+	;	K	[	k	{
0	0	1	1	FF	FS	,	<	L	\	l	|
1	0	1	1	CR	GS		=	M	]	m	}
0	1	1	1	SO	RS	.	>	N	^	n	~
1	1	1	1	SI	US		?	O	-	o	DEL

Figure 3-2 ASCII Table

			MSB Bit 0	0	0	0	0	0	0	0	0	1	1	1	1	1	1	1	1
			MSB Bit 1	0	0	0	0	1	1	1	1	0	0	0	0	1	1	1	1
			MSB Bit 2	0	0	1	1	0	0	1	1	0	0	1	1	0	0	1	1
			MSB Bit 3	0	1	0	1	0	1	0	1	0	1	0	1	0	1	0	1
LSB Bit 7	Bit 6	Bit 5	Bit 4																
0	0	0	0	NUL	DLE	DS		SP	&	-									0
1	0	0	0	SOH	DC1	SOS						a	j			A	J		1
0	1	0	0	STX	DC2	FS	SYN					b	k	s		B	K	S	2
1	1	0	0	ETX	DC3							c	l	t		C	L	T	3
0	0	1	0	PF	RES	BYP	PN					d	m	u		D	M	U	4
1	0	1	0	HT	NL	LF	RS					e	n	v		E	N	V	5
0	1	1	0	LC	BS	EOB	UC					f	o	w		F	O	W	6
1	1	1	0	DEL	IL	PRE	EOT					g	p	x		G	P	X	7
0	0	0	1		CAN							h	q	y		H	Q	Y	8
1	0	0	1		EM						\	i	r	z		I	R	Z	9
0	1	0	1	SMM	CC	SM		>>	!		:								
1	1	0	1	VT				.	$	,	#								
0	0	1	1	FF	IFS		DC4	<	*	%	@								
1	0	1	1	CR	IGS	ENQ	NAK	(	)										
0	1	1	1	SO	IRS	ACK		+	;	>	=								
1	1	1	1	SI	IUS	BEL	SUB	|	-	?									

Figure 3-3 EBCDIC Table

EBCDIC **Extended Binary Coded Decimal Interchange Code (EBCDIC)** is an IBM proprietary eight-bit code capable of representing 256 different characters, numerals, and control characters ($2^8 = 256$). EBCDIC is the primary coding method used in IBM mainframe applications. Figure 3-3 is an EBCDIC table that illustrates the relationship between characters and their associated EBCDIC codes.

Practical Advice and Information

USING ASCII AND EBCDIC TABLES

Using ASCII or EBCDIC tables to interpret character encoding is relatively straightforward. The tables are arranged according to groups of bits otherwise known as bit patterns. The bit patterns are divided into groups. In the case of ASCII, bits 6 through 4 are known as the most significant bits (MSB), and bits 3 through 0 are known as the least significant bits (LSB). In the case of EBCDIC, bits 0 through 3 are known as the MSB and bits 4 through 7 are known as the LSB.

To find the bit pattern of a particular character, one needs to combine the bit patterns that intersect in the table at the character in question, remembering that most significant bits always come before least significant bits. In the case of ASCII,

Humanly Readable	ASCII	EBCDIC
A	1000001	11000001
x	1111000	10100111
5	0110101	11110101
LF (Line Feed)	0001010	00100101

Figure 3-4 Human Readable Characters and Their Corresponding ASCII and EBCDIC Codes

this means that bits are arranged from bit 6 to bit 0, whereas EBCDIC is arranged from bit 0 to bit 7. As an example, representative characters, numerals, and control characters and their bit patterns are highlighted with shading in the ASCII and EBCDIC tables and are displayed in Figure 3-4 in humanly readable, ASCII, and EBCDIC formats.

UNICODE and ISO 10646 ASCII and EBCDIC coding schemes have sufficient capacity to represent letters and characters familiar to people whose alphabets use the letters A,B,C etc. However, what happens if the computer needs to support communication in Chinese or Arabic? It should be obvious that 128 or 256 possible characters will not suffice when other languages and alphabets are considered.

To resolve this issue, two different efforts were undertaken to establish a new coding standard that could support many more alphabets and symbols than could ASCII or EBCDIC. The efforts were ultimately combined and a single standard, **ISO** (International Organization for Standardization) **10646,** also known as **UNICODE.** Unicode version 1.1 was released in 1993.

UNICODE is a 16-bit code supporting up to 65,536 possible characters (2^{16}= 65,536). It is backward compatible with ASCII, as the first 128 characters are identical to the ASCII table. In addition, UNICODE includes more than 2000 Han characters for languages such as Chinese, Japanese, and Korean. It also includes Hebrew, Greek, Russian, and Sanskrit alphabets, as well as mathematical and technical symbols, publishing symbols, geometric shapes, and punctuation marks.

Application programs that display text on a monitor must encode characters according to an encoding scheme understood by the computer's operating system. It is up to the operating systems vendors to include support for particular encoding schemes such as UNICODE/ISO 10646. Microsoft's Windows NT and Windows 2000 are examples of operating systems that support UNICODE.

Serial vs. Parallel Transmission

The bits that represent human-readable characters can be transmitted in either of two basic transmission methodologies: either simultaneously **(parallel transmission)** or in a linear fashion, one after the other **(serial transmission).** The advantages, limitations, and typical applications of each of these transmission methodologies are summarized in Figure 3-5 and illustrated in Figure 3-6.

Transmission Characteristic	Serial	Parallel
Transmission Description	One bit after another, one at a time	All bits in a single character transmitted simultaneously
Comparative Speed	Slower	Faster
Distance Limitation	Farther	Shorter
Application	Between two computers, from a computer to an external modem, from a computer to a relatively slow printer	Within a computer along the computer's bus, from a computer to parallel high speed printers
Cable Description	All bits travel down a single wire, one bit at a time	Each bit travels down its own wire simultaneously with other bits.

Figure 3-5 Serial Transmission vs. Parallel Transmission

Practical Advice and Information

PHYSICAL INTERFACES VS. TRANSMISSION PROTOCOLS

With either parallel or serial transmission, it is important to distinguish between those standards that describe the connectors or physical interfaces that are used to connect appropriate cables to a computer's parallel or serial ports, and the standards that describe the electrical characteristics, or transmission protocol of either serial or parallel transmission. These differences in standards are highlighted in the sections on serial and parallel transmission that follow.

Serial Interface Standards Figure 3-7 illustrates five of the most common physical interfaces for serial transmission:

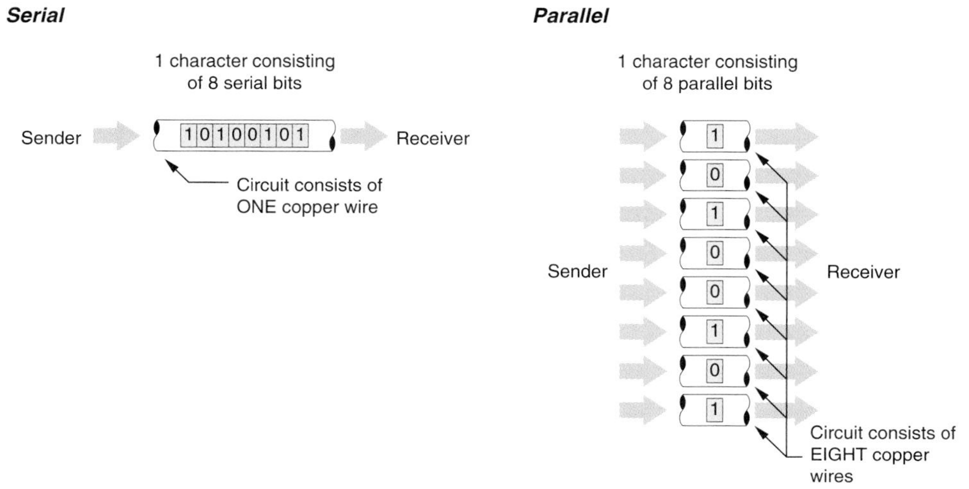

Figure 3-6 Serial and Parallel Transmission Illustrated

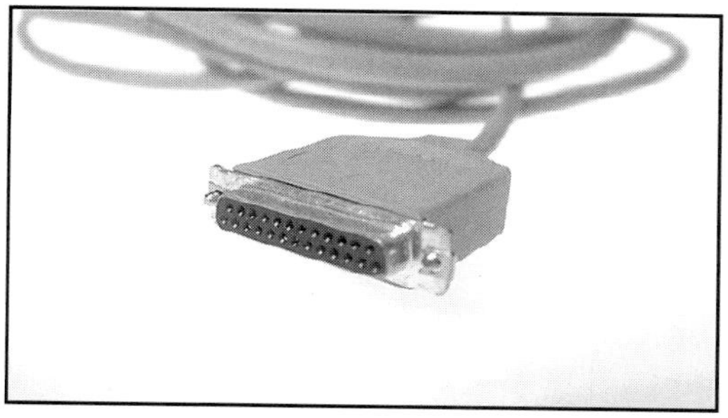

DB-25 connector (female)

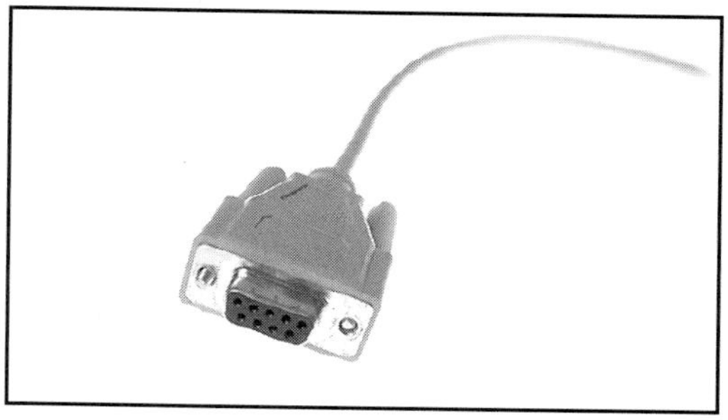

DB-9 connector (female)

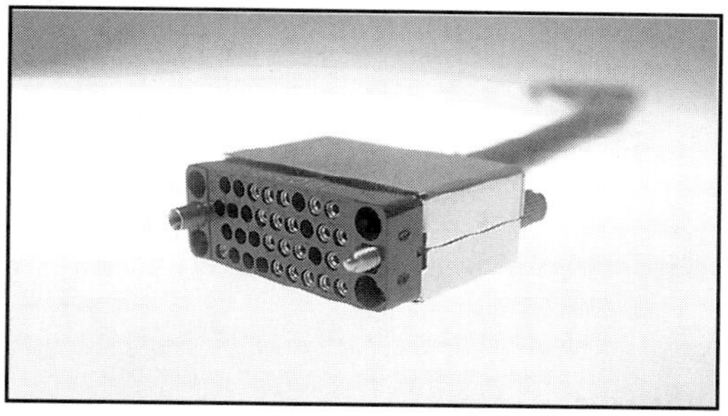

M-Block connector

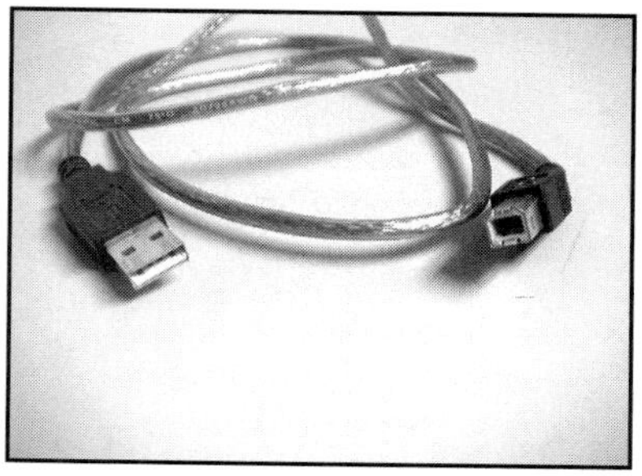

USB-A (on left) and USB-B (on right) connectors

Figure 3-7 Serial Transmission Physical Interfaces

- A typical 25-pin serial port, known as a **DB-25** connector
- A 9-pin serial port most often found on personal computers, known as a **DB-9** connector
- An **M block connector** used in high speed serial transmission
- A **USB** "A" or "B" connector used with **universal serial bus** transmission

It is important to note that the designators DB-25, DB-9, and M block describe only the physical connectors and do not imply anything regarding the transmission protocol that defines the electrical specifications for transmission using one of these physical interfaces. As will be seen, these physical interfaces can be used with a variety of different transmission protocols. The USB "A" and "B" interfaces are unique to the USB standard and also contain power connectors for USB devices.

Serial Transmission Standards Serial transmission is the basis of most data communications between computers and, therefore, deserves further investigation. The transmission of data between two PCs via modems, as illustrated in Figure 3-1, is an example of serial transmission.

RS-232

RS-232 is currently the most commonly used serial standard for modem communication. The prevalence of RS-232 in the PC marketplace is so great that the term "serial port" has come to mean an RS-232 serial connection. Although newer serial standards threaten to replace RS-232 as the predominant serial standard in the not too distant future, it still merits close inspection.

RS-232 can be implemented on a multitude of data connectors. In the case of the DB-25 connector illustrated in Figure 3-7, the presence or absence of an electrical charge on each of these 25 pins has been designated as having a specific meaning in data communications. These standard definitions, officially known as **RS-232-C,** were issued by the Electronics Industries Association (EIA), and are listed in Figure 3-8.

Although all 25 pins are defined, in most cases 10 or fewer of the pins are actually used in the majority of serial transmission applications. On some PCs, such as personal computers and many notebook and laptop computers, the serial port has only nine pins (DB-9 connector), and the RS-232 serial transmission protocol is supported as listed in Figure 3-8. Other RS-232 implementations rely on mini-DIN connectors or phono plug style connectors.

Recalling that character encoding ensures that all characters can be represented as a series of 1s and 0s, it is the job of the transmission protocol to represent these 1s and 0s as discrete electrical signals. RS-232 defines voltages of between +5 and +15 volts DC on a given pin to represent a logical zero, otherwise known as a space, and

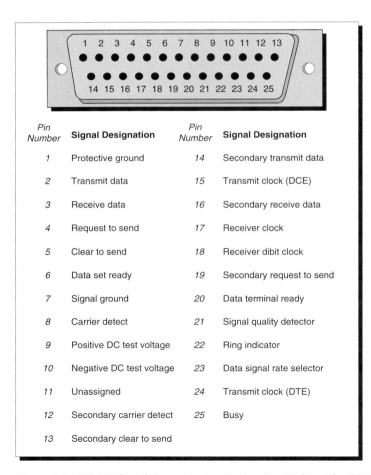

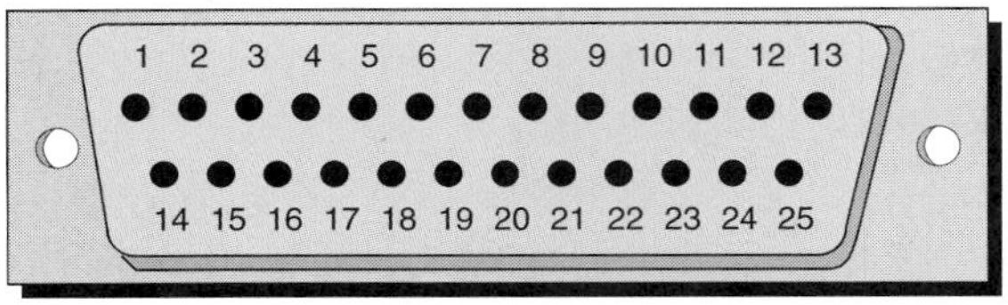

Pin Number	Signal Designation	Pin Number	Signal Designation
1	Protective ground	14	Secondary transmit data
2	Transmit data	15	Transmit clock (DCE)
3	Receive data	16	Secondary receive data
4	Request to send	17	Receiver clock
5	Clear to send	18	Receiver dibit clock
6	Data set ready	19	Secondary request to send
7	Signal ground	20	Data terminal ready
8	Carrier detect	21	Signal quality detector
9	Positive DC test voltage	22	Ring indicator
10	Negative DC test voltage	23	Data signal rate selector
11	Unassigned	24	Transmit clock (DTE)
12	Secondary carrier detect	25	Busy
13	Secondary clear to send		

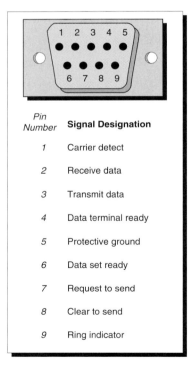

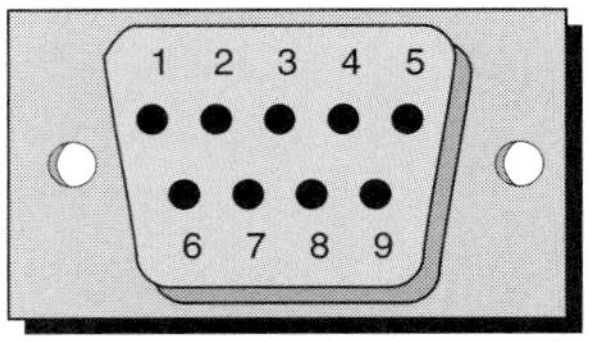

Pin Number	Signal Designation
1	Carrier detect
2	Receive data
3	Transmit data
4	Data terminal ready
5	Protective ground
6	Data set ready
7	Request to send
8	Clear to send
9	Ring indicator

Figure 3-8 RS-232 Serial Transmission Protocol as Defined for DB-25 and DB-9 Connectors

voltages of between –5 and –15 volts DC to represent logical ones, otherwise known as a mark.

Modem Cables

To transport these meaningful electrical signals from the serial port on the local PC to a similar looking port, or interface, on the local modem you must buy or make a data cable in a configuration known as a **modem cable.**

The cable has several small, insulated wires within an outer jacket. These cables come with different numbers of "inner" wires depending on how many signals need to be transferred from one serial port to another. Each signal to be carried, or RS-232 pin to be supported, requires its own individual inner wire.

The next question is: Which of the possible 25 signals are most meaningful and therefore worth transferring over the modem cable in this example? Figure 3-9 summarizes the 12 signals that are most commonly included in modem cables and designates which signals are assigned to which pins on both DB-9 and DB-25 connectors. The RS-232 signals described in Figure 3-9 are arranged in logical pairs to increase understanding rather than in order of DB-25 pin number.

The modem cables will have 12 data leads or inner wires, one for each of the commonly used RS-232 pins outlined in Figure 3-9. The wires will be pinned "straight-through", in other words, the wire from pin #2 on the DTE(PC) end will go "straight through" to pin #2 on the DCE (modem) end, and so on with the remaining pins.

Constructing modem cables or connecting any two devices for data communications involves choosing among a variety of media types. Coaxial cable, unshielded twisted pair, shielded twisted pair, and fiber optic cable are but a few of the possible options. Although media alternatives are explored in detail in Chapter 5, it is important to understand that media choices are present in every data communications opportunity.

DCE vs. DTE

The original application of RS-232 was to connect computing devices to modems. To make cabling this "standard" solution easier, two classifications of RS-232 devices were created. The pin-outs for these classifications were established so that the cable could be "straight through" in nature, where each pin is connected to the same pin on the other end of the cable. Pin 1 connects to pin 1, pin 2 to pin 2, etc. The PC and modem in our scenario are examples of these two classifications: **DTE (data terminal equipment)** and **DCE (data communications equipment),** respectively. DCE can also be expanded as **data circuit terminating equipment.**

Although this approach made sense for modem applications, the use of RS-232 has expanded to include all sorts of electronic equipment ranging from modems to scanners and personal digital assistants (PDAs). It is critical, therefore, to establish exactly which signals are associated with each pin on the connector. You cannot rely on any standard mapping, as each device may have deviated from the loosely enforced standard.

Many of the RS-232 pins and signals are implemented in directional pairs. In other words, either the terminal is informing the modem of something by raising or lowering electrical voltages to a certain pin, or the modem is informing the terminal of something by the same means. Figure 3-9 outlines the directionality of the signals of commonly used RS-232 pins in the columns labeled "FROM" and "TO".

RS-232 Signal	DB –25 Pin	DB –9 Pin	Abbr.	From	To	Explanation
Protective Ground	1	5	PG			A reference voltage used to protect circuit boards inside PC
Signal Ground	7	5	SG			A reference voltage used to determine proper signal voltage for 1s and 0s.
Transmit Data	2	3	TXD	DTE	DCE	Discrete voltages representing characters encoded as 1s and 0s are transmitted on this pin to deliver the actual data message
Receive Data	3	2	RXD	DCE	DTE	Discrete voltages representing characters encoded as 1s and 0s are received on this pin to receive the actual data message
Request to Send	4	7	RTS	DTE	DCE	Used in conjunction with CTS to perform modem-to-modem flow control, allowing modems to take turns transmitting to each other
Clear to Send	5	8	CTS	DCE	DTE	Used in conjunction with RTS to perform modem-to-modem flow control, allowing modems to take turns transmitting to each other
Data Set Ready	6	6	DSR	DCE	DTE	Used for initial handshaking between local modem and local PC to indicate local modem is functional
Data Terminal Ready	20	4	DTR	DTE	DCE	Used for initial handshaking between local modem and local PC to indicate local PC is functional
Transmit Clock	15		TC	DTE	DCE	Clocking signal transmitted on this pin. Required for synchronous modems only.
Receive Clock	17		RC	DCE	DTE	Clocking signal received on this pin. Required for synchronous modems only.
Carrier Detect	8	1	CD	DCE	DTE	Indicates that the local modem has successfully contacted the remote modem and is ready to transmit data
Ring Indicator	22	9	RI	DCE	DTE	Indicates to the local modem that a call is incoming and that the modem should auto-answer the call

Figure 3-9 Most Commonly Used RS-232 Signals

In Sharper Focus

OTHER TRADITIONAL SERIAL TRANSMISSION STANDARDS

RS-232 is officially limited to 20 Kbps for a maximum distance of 50 ft. Depending on the type of media used and the amount of external interference present, RS-232 can be transmitted at higher speeds and/or over greater distances. Using 16,550 family UARTS (see the following section), it is common for RS-232 to support speeds up to 115 Kbps.

To resolve the speed and distance limitations of RS-232, several other serial transmission standards have been developed. Several of these standards also include the ability to connect more than two devices at the same time. A serial standard that can connect three or more devices together concurrently is known as a multipoint serial communications standard. A list of common serial standards is provided in Figure 3-10.

Standard Name	Standards Body	Physical Interface Connector	Description
RS-422	EIA	DB9 DB25 DB37	An electrical specification usually associated with RS-449 (DB37 connector). Each signal pin has its own ground line (balanced) rather than sharing a common ground. Up to 10 Mbps over 1200. Use of DB25 or DB9 also possible.
RS-423	EIA	DB9 DB25 DB37	An electrical specification usually associated with RS-449 (DB37 connector). Signal pins share a common ground wire (unbalanced signaling). Up to 10 Mbps over 1200. Use of DB25 or DB9 also possible.
RS-449	EIA	DB37 plus DB9	A physical/mechanical specification for a DB-37 (37-pin connector) plus an additional DB-9 if required. Usually associated with either RS-422 or RS-423 electrical specifications.
RS-485	EIA	DB9 DB25 DB37	Can be used in multipoint applications in which one computer controls multiple (up to 64) devices. Often used in computer integrated manufacturing operations or in telecommunications management networks.
RS-530	EIA	DB25	A physical/mechanical specification that works with RS-422 or RS-423 over a DB-25 connector rather than a DB-37 connector. Allows speeds of up to 2 Mbps.
V.35	ITU	M-Block	An international standard for serial transmission up to 48 Kbps defined for an M-block connector. Often used on data communications equipment that must interface to high speed carrier services.

Figure 3-10 Other Traditional Serial Transmission Standards

Universal Serial Bus (USB)

Although RS-232 is historically the most commonly implemented serial standard, a new standard recently developed and rapidly becoming ubiquitous threatens to replace RS-232 in all but the most basic applications. RS-232 is a standard solution and is widely implemented, but there are three basic architectural limitations in the technology that limit its application to new devices such as scanners, digital still cameras, digital motion cameras, and personal digital assistants. RS-232 is relatively slow (only up to 115 Kbps), it only supports one device per port, and it requires significant configuration to attach a device.

The universal serial bus (USB) is a high-speed, multipoint serial communications technology developed by the USB Implementer's Forum, a consortium of computer companies to resolve these shortcomings of RS-232. Two versions of USB are currently available, the original USB 1.1 specification and a new higher speed USB 2.0 specification. USB 2.0 is backwards compatible with USB 1.1, although to gain the higher speeds offered by USB 2.0 compatible devices must be attached either directly to the computer or to a USB 2.0 compatible hub.

USB version 1.1 operates at either 1.5 Mbps or 12 Mbps or over 1000 times the maximum speed of RS-232. USB 2.0 can operate at even higher speeds, up to 480 Mbps. This increased speed is especially important when supporting such high data devices such as scanners and digital cameras. As described in Chapter 5, it is even possible to connect to a local area network (LAN) via a USB network interface card (NIC). USB can support up to 126 devices on each port. Some devices come with two USB ports so that the user can simply "daisy-chain" the devices together. Although this solution is functional for a couple of devices, a better solution for larger USB implementations is to use a USB hub. As illustrated in Figure 3-11, a USB hub is a device that connects directly to the computer's USB port and offers multiple ports to connect other USB devices.

To reduce the configuration hassles traditionally associated with serial connectivity using RS-232, USB is designed to be "plug and play." Devices are automatically assigned an address, select a speed, and identify themselves to the computer's operating system. As long as the operating system supports USB, all that is required to connect a device is to plug it into either the computer itself or to a USB hub connected

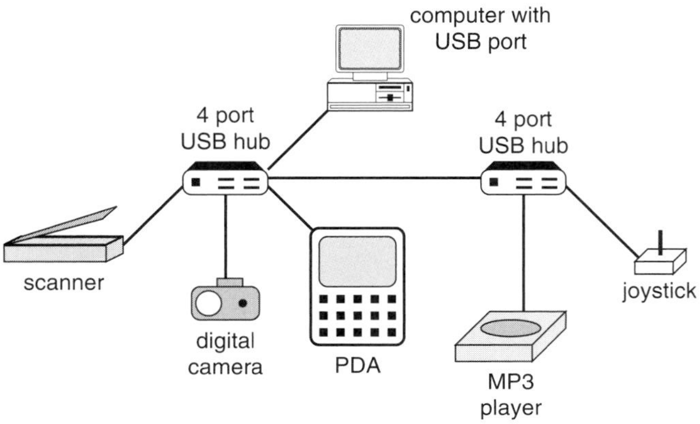

Figure 3-11 USB Hub Implementation

to the computer. To make the process of attaching devices even easier, the USB ports and cables also include the power to the device, eliminating the need to have a separate power supply for each peripheral.

Two connector types are associated with USB. The USB "A" connector is used to connect to computers, and the USB "B" connector is used to connect to the devices. The ability to disconnect the USB cable at the device end of the connection makes it significantly easier to change devices than having to reach behind the computer to disconnect the cables.

IEEE-1394

Another emerging serial standard is IEEE 1394. Originally developed by Apple Computer Inc. as the proprietary "Firewire", the interface was standardized by the IEEE in 1995. Sony has trademarked the name i.Link for its implementation of IEEE-1394, and that moniker seems to be gaining popularity at least among Japanese consumer electronics manufacturers.

IEEE-1394 is a multipoint serial bus-based solution. Devices can be added or removed from the live bus. Devices can be daisy chained or connected to an IEEE-1394 hub for connectivity between more than two devices. Although similar to USB in many ways, IEEE-1394 is not intended to directly compete with USB but rather to complement USB. USB offers a low-to medium-speed serial solution, whereas IEEE-1394 offers a high-speed solution. By having two separate serial standards, each can be optimized for specific applications.

IEEE-1394 is a high-speed serial solution operating at speeds up to 1 Gbps. One of the key differentiators between IEEE-1394 and other serial bus standards is that in addition to standard asynchronous communication, IEEE-1394 includes support for isochronous communication. Isochronous communication guarantees data delivery at a constant, predetermined rate. This allows IEEE-1394 to be used in time-critical, multimedia applications. The constant data delivery rate reduces the need to buffer data, thereby greatly reducing the cost of implementing the technology compared with a traditional asynchronous solution.

Taking advantage of its isochronous capabilities, the main applications of IEEE-1394 at the present time are in the transmission of digital data between consumer electronics devices. IEEE-1394 has been adopted by the digital VCR Manufacturers Association as their standard interconnection technology. The ongoing conversion of television from an analog format to digital HDTV technologies will increase the marketplace for IEEE-1394 technologies in the consumer electronics marketplace.

IEEE-1394 ports are also being introduced in multimedia capable computers. In addition to allowing the computer to connect to digital camcorders and VCRs, the availability of these ports will allow data network solutions to be deployed using the technology. To support the use of IEEE-1394 on computer platforms, the IEEE-1394 Trade Association is currently working on an updated version of the standard known as IEEE-1394b. The IEEE-1394b standard is designed to increase speeds to 3.2 Gbps at 100 meters on UTP and fiber optic media and reduce latency by streamlining the protocol. IEEE-1394b is designed to be backward compatible with the original IEEE-1394 standard IEEE-1394-1995.

Parallel Transmission As can be seen from Figure 3-6, parallel transmission is primarily limited to transmission of data within a computer and between a computer's parallel port and a parallel printer. Common physical interfaces associated with par-

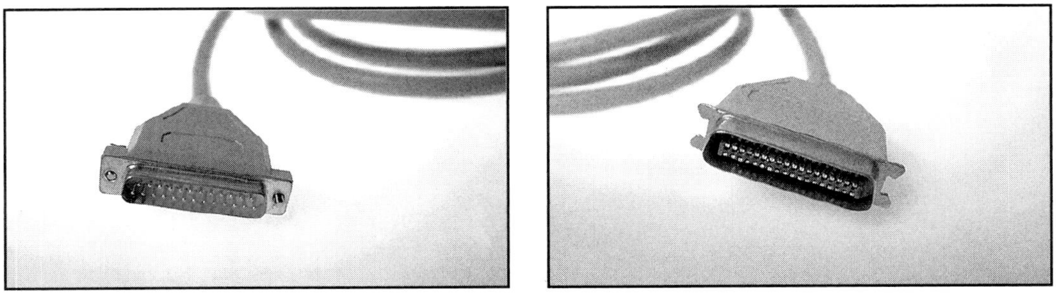

DB-25 (male) parallel interface   Centronics parallel interface

Figure 3-12 Parallel Transmission Physical Interfaces

allel transmission are the DB-25 connector and the Centronics connector. The Centronics connector is a 36-pin parallel interface. In addition to the physical plug and socket, the Centronics parallel standard also defines electrical signaling for parallel transmission and is a de facto standard. DB-25 and Centronics parallel physical interfaces are illustrated in Figure 3-12.

Serial/Parallel Conversion: UARTs Remember that data travel via parallel transmission within a PC over the PC's main data highway, known as a bus; however, the data emerging from the serial port and out into a modem must be in serial format. Therefore, somewhere inside the PC a parallel to serial conversion must be taking place. A specialized computer chip known as a **UART (universal asynchronous receiver transmitter)** acts as the interface between the parallel transmission of the computer bus and the serial transmission of the serial port. UARTs differ in performance capabilities based on the amount of on-chip buffer memory. The 16550 UART chip contains a 16-byte on-chip buffer memory for improved serial/parallel conversion performance. In the case of internal modems, the UART is included on the internal modem card, thereby bypassing the system UART.

Practical Advice and Information

MODERN UARTS

Given the transmission speed of today's modems, it is especially important that PCs are equipped with the 16550 family UART with its 16-byte FIFO (buffer) rather than with previous generation UARTs that contained only a 1-byte FIFO. A 16550 family UART can deliver speeds up to 115 Kbps, but the older 8250 UART family can deliver speeds up to only 20 Kbps.

Transmission Monitoring and Manipulation: Breakout Boxes To effectively troubleshoot serial or parallel transmissions, it is necessary to be able to monitor and manipulate the electrical signaling on individual signaling pins. Devices known as **breakout boxes** are used to monitor and manipulate electrical signaling. Breakout boxes are built to monitor a particular electrical transmission specification. As a result, separate breakout boxes are required to monitor RS-232, V.35, RS-449, or parallel transmission. Figure 3-13 illustrates a typical breakout box.

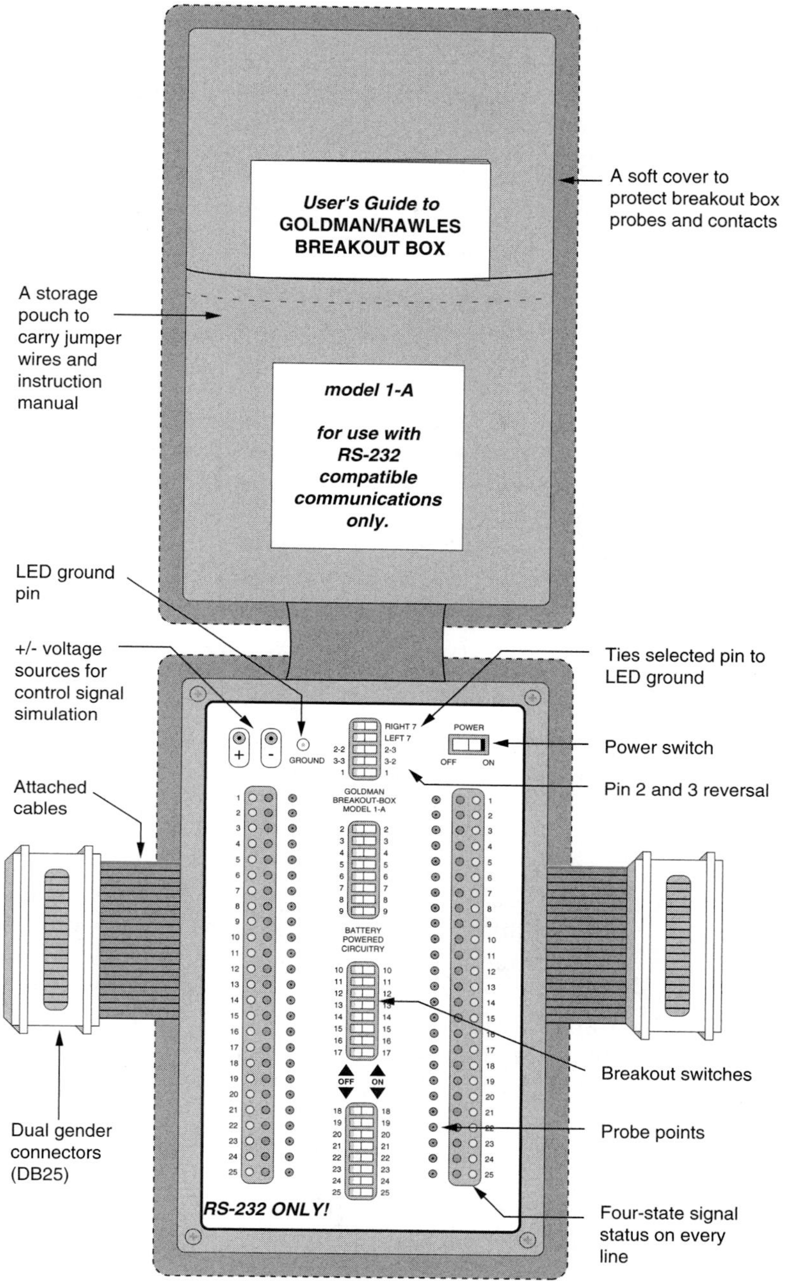

Figure 3-13 Breakout Box

WITHIN THE MODEM

What does a modem do? To analyze what any piece of data communications equipment does, the Input-Processing-Output or I-P-O analysis model, introduced in Chapter 1, is employed.

Applied Problem Solving

THE I-P-O MODEL

The I-P-O model provides a framework in which to focus on the difference between the data that came into the modem (I) and the data that came out of the modem (O). By defining this difference, we have defined how the modem processed the data (P). In general terms, based on what we have learned thus far, we could say:

- Input data (I)—From the PC: A series of 1s and 0s representing characters and transmitted as discrete voltages of electricity in digital format.
- Output data (O)—To the public switched telephone network on a normal phone line.

It should be obvious that to better understand processing *(P)* that goes on in a modem, it is first necessary to have a better understanding of *(O)* data transmission over a "normal" or dial-up phone line.

Digital vs. Analog Transmission

A **switched** or **dial-up line** is the type of phone line that you would typically have installed in your home or place of business. To place a call, you pick up the receiver or handset, wait for a dial tone, and dial the number of the location you wish to call. This ordinary type of phone service is sometimes called **POTS** or **plain old telephone service.** More formally, the phone network is referred to as the **public switched telephone network (PSTN).**

As introduced in Chapter 2, a large switch in a telephone company building called a central office, or CO, connects your phone equipment to the phone equipment of the party you wished to call by finding an available circuit or path to your desired destination. It is important to understand at this point that the CO switch tries to find a path as quickly as possible to your destination. The actual circuits it chooses represent the best path available at that time. The particular circuits or path chosen may vary from one occasion to another, even for calls to the same location. Calls placed over dial-up lines through CO switches that have connections built from available circuits are called circuit-switched connections. To interface transparently to the PSTN, modems must be able to dial and answer phone calls to and from other modems.

The next important characteristic related to transmitting data over a dial-up phone line involves how the data are represented on that phone line. First, it is important to realize that today's dial-up phone network was originally designed to carry voice conversations efficiently and with reasonable sound quality. This "efficiency of design with reasonable sound quality" meant reproducing a range of the frequencies of human speech and hearing just wide enough to produce reasonable sound quality. That range of frequencies, or **bandwidth,** is 3100 Hz (from 300 Hz to 3400 Hz) and is the standard bandwidth of today's voice-grade dial-up circuits (phone lines). Hz is the abbreviation for hertz: 1 hertz is 1 cycle per second. The higher the number of hertz or cycles per second, the higher the frequency. Frequency, wavelength, hertz, and cycles per second are explained further later in this chapter.

This 3100 Hz is all the bandwidth with which the modem operating over a dial-up circuit has to work. Remember also that because today's dial-up phone network was designed to be able to mimic the constantly varying tones or frequencies that

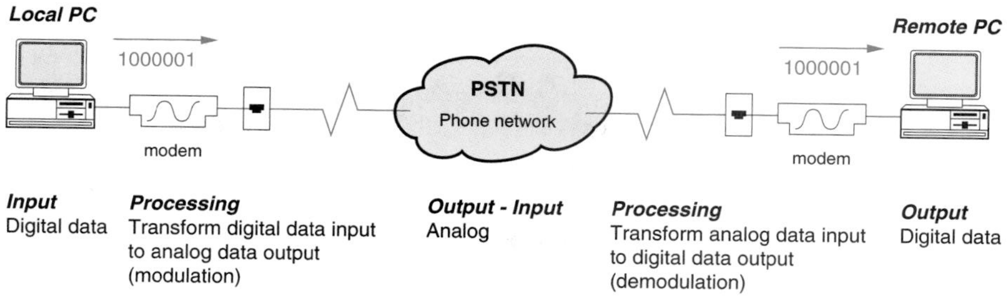

Figure 3-14 I-P-O Analysis: Modems and the PSTN

characterize human speech, only these continuous, wavelike tones or frequencies can travel over the dial-up phone network in this limited bandwidth.

The challenge for the modem, then, is to represent the discrete, digitized 1s and 0s from the input (PC) side of the modem in a continuous or **analog** form within a limited bandwidth so that the data may be transmitted over the dial-up network. Figure 3-14 summarizes the results of I-P-O analysis involving modems and the PSTN.

Modulation/Demodulation

It should be clear that a modem's job must be to convert digital data into analog data for transmission over the dial-up phone network and to convert analog data received from the dial-up network into digital data for the terminal or PC. The proper names for these processes are **modulation** and **demodulation** as illustrated in Figure 3-15. In fact, the word **modem** is actually a contraction for **Mo**dulator/**dem**odulator.

Carrier Waves To represent the discrete-state 1s and 0s or bits of digitized data on a dial-up phone line, an analog or voice-like wave must be able to be changed between at least two different states. This implies that a "normal" or "neutral" wave must exist to start with that can be changed to represent these 1s and 0s.

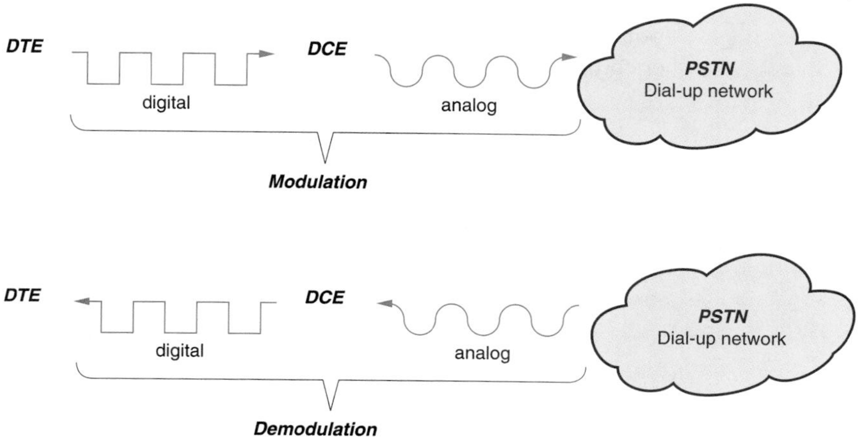

Figure 3-15 Modulation vs. Demodulation

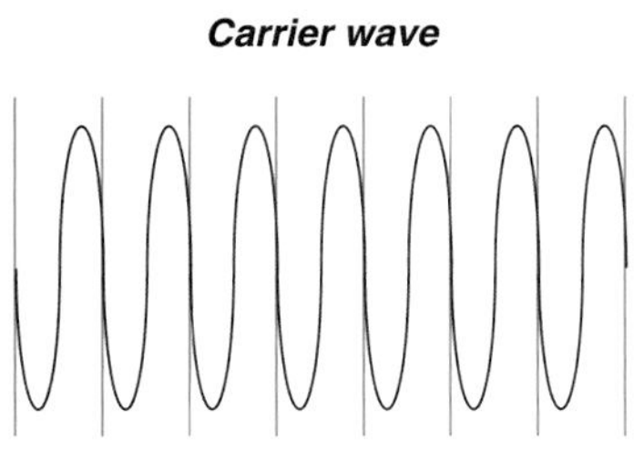

Figure 3-16 Carrier Wave

This "normal" or "neutral" wave is called a **carrier wave.** A sample carrier wave is illustrated in Figure 3-16. Modems generate carrier waves that are then altered (modulated) to represent bits of data as 1s and 0s. When local and remote modems are trying to establish communications, you may have heard a series of high-pitched screeches before the carrier detect indicator lights on your modem. These screeches are the two modems trying to detect a common carrier wave to establish communication. Once the carrier wave has been detected by both modems, the actual data transmission can begin as the modems manipulate this common carrier wave to represent 1s and 0s.

How can the carrier wave be manipulated to represent 1s and 0s? Only three physical characteristics of this wave can be altered or modulated:

1. **Amplitude.**
2. **Frequency.**
3. **Phase.**

As will be seen later in this section, in some modulation schemes, more than one of these characteristics can be modulated simultaneously.

Amplitude Modulation Figure 3-17 illustrates the **amplitude modulation** of a carrier wave. Notice how only the amplitude changes while frequency and phase remain constant. In this example, the portions of the wave with increased height (altered amplitude) represent 1s and the lower wave amplitude represent 0s. Together, this portion of the wave would represent the letter "A" using the ASCII-7 character encoding scheme.

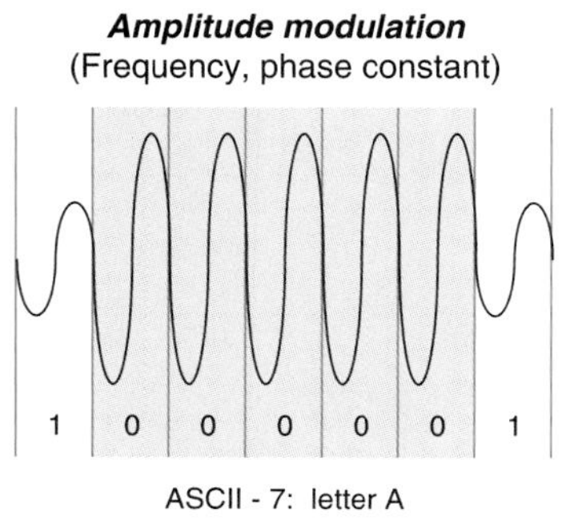

Figure 3-17 Amplitude Modulation

The vertical lines in Figure 3-17 separate opportunities to identify a 1 or 0 from another. These timed opportunities to identify 1s and 0s by sampling the carrier wave are known as signaling events. The proper name for one signaling event is a **baud.**

Frequency Modulation Figure 3-18 represents **frequency modulation** of a carrier wave. Frequency modulation is often referred to as **frequency shift keying** or **FSK.** The frequency can be thought of as how frequently the same spot on two subsequent waves pass a given point. Waves with a higher frequency take less time to pass than waves with a lower frequency.

The distance between the same spots on two subsequent waves is called the **wavelength.** The longer the wavelength, the lower the frequency; the shorter the wavelength, the greater the frequency. Notice in Figure 3-18 how the higher frequency (shorter wavelength) part of the wave represents a 1 and the lower frequency (longer wavelength) part of the wave represents a 0, whereas amplitude and phase remain constant. Again, the entire bit stream represents the letter "A" in ASCII-7.

Phase Modulation Figure 3-19 illustrates an example of **phase modulation** also known as **phase shift keying** or **PSK.** Notice how the frequency and amplitude remain constant in the diagram. Phase modulation can be thought of as a shift or departure from the "normal" continuous pattern of the wave. Notice in Figure 3-19 how we would expect the pattern of the wave to follow the broken line, but suddenly the phase shifts and heads off in another direction. This phase shift of 180 degrees is a detectable event with each change in phase representing a change in state from 0 to 1 or 1 to 0 in this example.

Measuring Phase Shift In Figure 3-19, the detected analog wave was either the carrier wave with no phase shift, or it was phase shifted 180 degrees. Given that phase shifts are measured in degrees, it should stand to reason that we could shift the phase of carrier waves by varying degrees other than just 180 degrees. By increasing the number of possible phase shifts, we increase the number of potential detectable

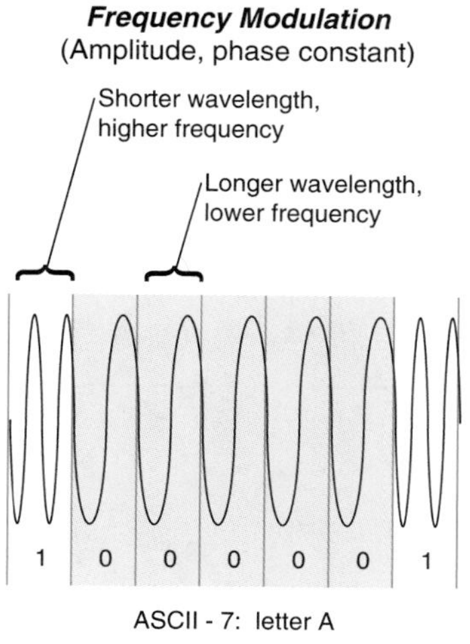

Figure 3-18 Frequency Modulation

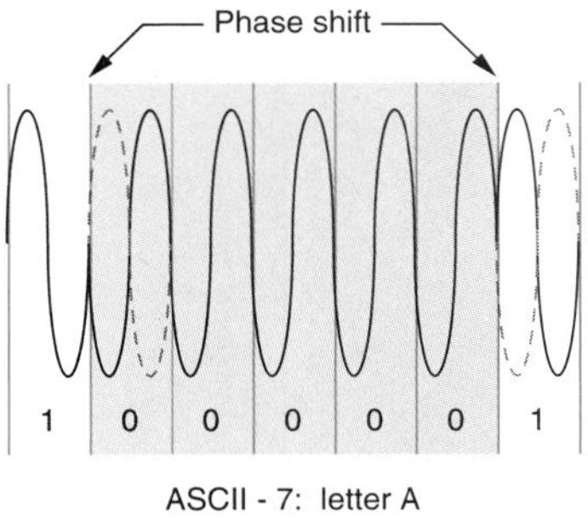

Figure 3-19 Phase Modulation

events. As illustrated in Figure 3-20, when we had just two potential detectable events (no phase shift, or 180 degree phase shift), those two events represented a 0 or a 1, respectively. However, by introducing four potential phase shifts (0, 90, 180, 270), we are able to associate two bits with each potential detectable event.

A simpler and perhaps clearer way to represent phase shifts, as illustrated in Figure 3-20, is through the use of **constellation points.** Using a four-quadrant representation of the 360 degrees of possible phase shift, individual points represent each different shifted wave. Note that when represented in a constellation diagram, a phase shift of 270 degrees is represented as –90 degrees. Phase shift modulation with

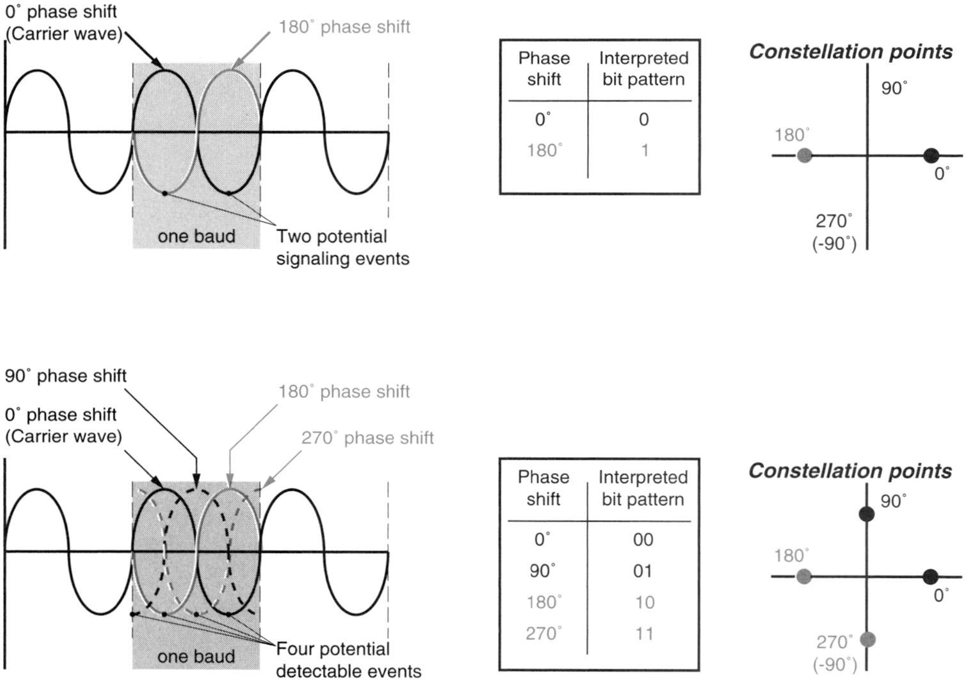

Figure 3-20 Relationship Between Number of Phase Shifts and Number of Potential Detectable Events

four different phases is more properly referred to as **quadrature phase shift keying** or **QPSK.**

Baud Rate vs. Transmission Rate The number of signaling events per second is more properly known as the **baud rate.** Although baud rate and **bps** (bits/second) or **transmission rate** are often used interchangeably, the two terms are in fact related, but not identical. In the first illustration in Figure 3-20, only two detectable events were possible, meaning that only one bit was interpreted at each signaling event (1 bit/baud). Therefore, in this case the baud rate was equal to the transmission rate as expressed in bps.

However, in the second illustration in Figure 3-20, four detectable events are possible for each signaling event, making it possible to interpret two bits per baud. In this case, the bit rate or transmission rate as measured in bps would be twice the baud rate.

More sophisticated modulation techniques are able to interpret more than 1 bit/baud. In these cases, the bps is greater than the baud rate. For example, if the baud rate of a modem was 2400 signaling events per second and the modem was able to interpret 2 bits per signaling event, then the transmission speed would be 4800 bps. Mathematically, the relationship between baud rate and transmission rate can be expressed as:

$$\text{Transmission rate (bps)} = \text{Baud rate} \times \text{bits/baud}$$

In Sharper Focus

MORE THAN 1 BIT/BAUD

There are really only two ways by which a given modem can transmit data faster:

1. Increase the signaling events per second, or baud rate.
2. Find a way for the modem to interpret more than 1 bit/baud.

By modifying a phase modulation technique such as that illustrated in Figure 3-20, a modem can detect, interpret, and transmit more than 1 bit/baud. The mathematical equation that describes the relationship between the number of potential detectable events and the numbers of bits per baud that can be interpreted is as follows:

$$\text{Number of potential detectable events} = \text{Number of states}^{\text{bits/baud}}$$

- Number of states = always 2 (data are either a 1 or 0).
- Number of potential detectable events = 4 different phase angles (0, 90, 180, 270) as shown in the second illustration in Figure 3-20.

To solve:

- 2 (the number of states) raised to what power equals 4 (the number of different detectable events)?

The answer is 2, meaning that 2 bits/baud can be interpreted at a time. Two bits at a time are known as a **dibit.** By extending the preceding mathematical equation, it should be obvious that:

Number of Potential Detectable Events	Number of Bits/Baud	Also Known As
8	3	tribit
16	4	quadbit
32	5	
64	6	
128	7	
256	8	
512	9	

Figure 3-21 shows the encoding of an ASCII "A" using dibits in differential quadrature phase shift keying. In this differential approach the phase change is measured in relationship to the previous baud rather than from the original carrier phase. Before the ASCII "A" can be encoded, an eighth bit is appended to make the total number of bits divisible by 2. This eighth bit is known as a parity bit and is further explained in Chapter 4.

Compare Figure 3-21 with two state phase modulation as illustrated in Figure 3-19. Notice that only four baud periods are required to transmit the ASCII "A" using dibits compared to the seven baud periods required for two state phase modulation.

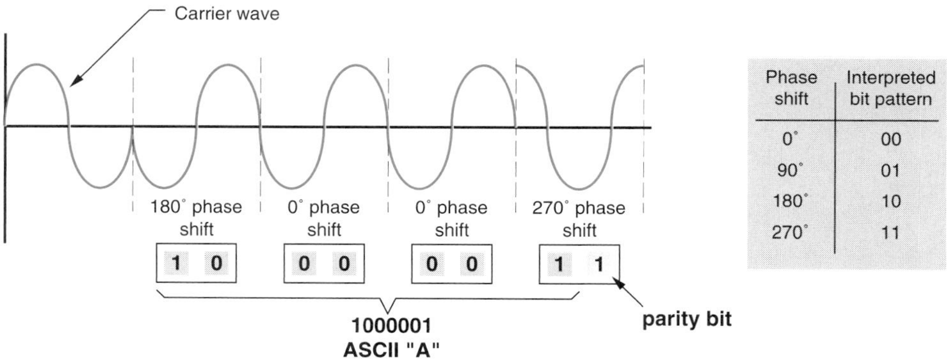

Figure 3-21 Differential Quadrature Phase Shift Keying

Quadrature Amplitude Modulation How far can we go with increasing the number of phase shift angles or potential detectable events? One limiting factor to increasing the bits/baud in phase shift modulation is the quality of the telephone line.

Given that that the modem is being used on a dial-up line of unpredictable quality, how small (least number of degrees) a phase shift can be reliably detected? Sixteen different phase shifts would require reliable detection of phase shifts of as little as 22.5°. Remembering that phase is not the only wave characteristic that can be varied, 16 different detectable events can also be produced by varying both phase and amplitude. Many of today's high-speed modems use a modulation technique that

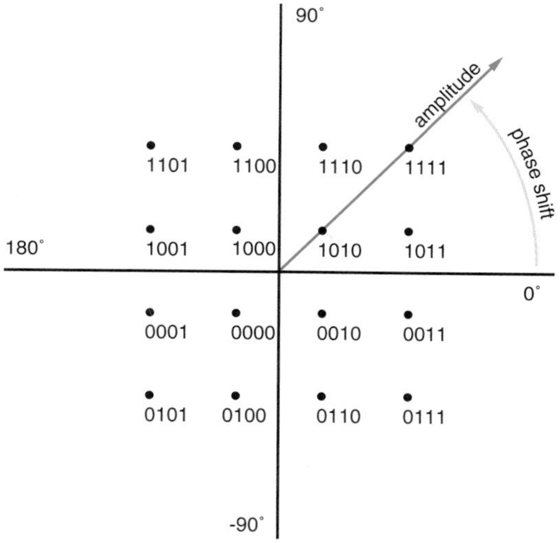

Figure 3-22 QAM Constellation Points and Quadbits

varies both phase and amplitude known as **quadrature amplitude modulation** or **QAM.**

16QAM, with its 16 different potential detectable events, would allow 4 bits/baud or quadbits to be produced or detected per signaling event. In this case the transmission rate in bps would be 4 times the baud rate. Figure 3-22 illustrates a representative set of constellation points and associated quadbits for a QAM modulation scheme. Differences in phase are represented in degrees around the center of the diagram, whereas differences in amplitude are represented by linear distance from the center of the diagram. Each point is uniquely identified by combining one of three potential amplitudes (.311V, .850V, and 1.161V) with one of twelve potential phase shifts (15, 45, 75, 105, 135, 175, –165, –135, –105, –75, –45, and –15°). Obviously, all potential combinations of these two sets of variables are not used in 16QAM.

In Sharper Focus

NYQUIST'S THEOREM AND SHANNON'S LAW

What are the underlying factors that limit the carrying capacity of a given circuit? The work of Harry Nyquist and Claude Shannon help to answer that question.

Nyquist's Theorem

The constellation points illustrated in Figure 3-22 are sometimes referred to as symbols. It should stand to reason that as the number of constellation points (symbols) increases and symbols are in closer proximity to each other on the constellation diagram, the chance for a modem to misinterpret constellation points increases. Interference between symbols that can cause misinterpretation is known as **intersymbol interference.** Nyquist investigated the maximum data rate (measured in bps) that can be supported by a given bandwidth (measured in Hz) due to the effect of intersymbol interference. He found the relationship between bandwidth *(W)* and maximum data rate *(C)* to be

$$C = 2W$$

Consider a voice grade circuit: $W = 3{,}100\ Hz$; therefore maximum theoretical data rate $C = 6{,}200\ bps$. However, this fails to account for the ability of modern modems to interpret more than 1 bit/baud by being able to distinguish between more than just two symbols or potential detectable events. Taking this ability into account, if we call the number of potential detectable events M, Nyquist's Theorem becomes

$$C = 2W \log_2 M$$

Again, considering a voice grade circuit: if $M = 16$ potential detectable events, then $\log_2 M = 4$ and $C = 24{,}800\ bps$.

Shannon's Law

The data rates theorized by Nyquist's Theorem are not achieved in reality due to the presence of noise on phone lines. Noise is measured as a ratio of the strength of the data signal to the strength of the background noise. This ratio is known as the **signal to noise ratio (S/N)** and is computed as follows:

$$(S/N)_{dB} = 10 \log \text{(signal power/noise power)}$$

S/N is expressed in decibels (dB). Decibels are a logarithmic measurement using a reference of 0_{dB} for comparison. As a result, a noise level of 10_{dB} is 10 times more intense than a noise level of 0_{dB}, a noise level of 20_{dB} is 100 times more intense than a noise level of 0_{dB}, and a noise level of 30_{dB} is 1000 times more intense than a noise level of 0_{dB}.

Shannon found that the higher the data rate, the more interference is caused by a given amount of noise, thus causing a higher error rate. This should make sense since at higher data rates, more bits are traveling over a circuit in a fixed length of time, and a burst of noise for the same length of time will affect more bits at higher data rates. By taking into account the signal to noise ratio, Shannon expresses the maximum data rate of a circuit (C) as

$$C = W \log_2 (1 + S/N)$$

To make calculating Shannon's Law easier for calculators that aren't capable of calculating a $\log_2$, this equation is mathematically equivalent to

$$C = 3.32\ W \log 10\ (1 + S/N)$$

Consider a voice grade circuit: if $W = 3100\ Hz$ and the $S/N = 30_{dB}$, and remembering that a S/N of 30_{dB} yields a ratio of 1000, then $C = 30{,}894\ bps$. Depending on the value inserted into Shannon's Law for S/N or for W, C will vary accordingly. The value 24,000 bps is also commonly used for C in Shannon's Law. By substituting different values for W and for S/N, it should become obvious that data channel capacity (C) can be more drastically effected by changes in bandwidth (W), than by changes in the signal to noise ratio (S/N).

Finally, it should be noted that there are numerous other line impairments such as attenuation, delay distortion, and impulse noise that Shannon's Law does not take into account. As a result, the data channel capacity (C) derived from Shannon's Law is theoretical and is sometimes referred to as error-free capacity.

Synchronous vs. Asynchronous Transmission Potential detectable events must be produced on one modem, transmitted over the public phone network, and detected reliably on a remote modem. In a modem with a baud rate of 2400 baud (signaling events) per second, the remote modem has exactly 0.416 msec (1 divided by 2400) to accurately detect and interpret the incoming data.

Obviously, modems must have a reliable way to know exactly when to sample the line for data. Somehow, local and remote modems must establish and maintain some type of timing between them so that these detectable events are produced, transmitted, and detected accurately. There are two main alternatives to establishing and maintaining the timing for the sampling of detectable events: **asynchronous** and **synchronous transmission.**

Figure 3-23 summarizes some important characteristics about asynchronous and synchronous transmission methods. First the most noticeable difference is that the synchronization, or detectable event timing, itself is reestablished with the transmission of each character in asynchronous transmission via the use of start and stop bits and with each block of characters in synchronous transmission. In asynchronous transmission, there may be 1, 1.5, or 2 stop bits. The timing for synchronous transmission is provided by a clocking signal that may be supplied by either modem, or by the carrier.

Second, when comparing idle time activity, synchronization is maintained, thanks to the ever-present clocking signal, in synchronous transmission and dropped in asynchronous transmission while no characters are being transmitted. The effect of these characteristics on transmission efficiency is illustrated in Figure 3-23.

Asynchronous transmission

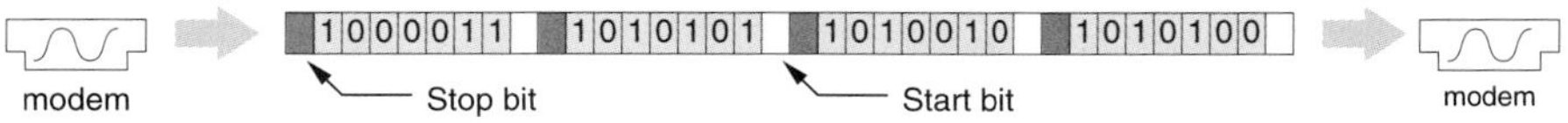

Characteristics:

Data is sent one character at a time
Each character has a start and 1, 1.5, or 2 stop bits
Synchronization is reestablished for each character
Time between character is unsynchronized and of random length

Efficiency (1000 character transmission)

Control / overhead bits: 1 start and stop bits per character
2 control bits per character x 1000 characters = 2000 control bits
7000 data bits / 9000 total bits = 77.7% efficient

Synchronous transmission

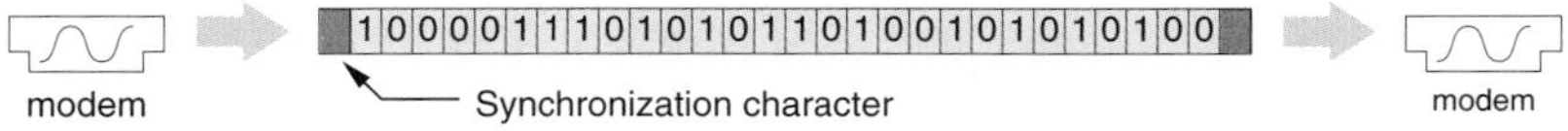

Characteristics:

Data are sent as a block of uninterrupted characters
Synchronization characters precede and follow the data block
The data block may be 1000 uninterrupted characters
Synchronization is maintained whether data are actually being sent and detected or not
Modems remain synchronized during idle time

Efficiency (1000 character transmission)

Control / overhead bits: 48 total control bits per block using HDLC
48 control bits per block x 1 block = 48 control bits
7000 data bits / 7048 total bits = 99.3% efficient

Figure 3-23 Asynchronous vs. Synchronous Transmission

In terms of application, PC modems use asynchronous transmission as do asynchronous terminals such as a VT-100 to an asynchronous minicomputer such as a VAX. Synchronous transmission is used between mainframe terminals such as IBM 3270 and IBM mainframe computers. Synchronous transmission is also used for most high-speed WAN services such as 64 Kbps or T-1.

MODEM TO PHONE SERVICE

Transmission Concepts

To understand the capabilities and limitations of a variety of phone services available to the consumer, it is first necessary to gain a better understanding of some of the concepts of the phone network infrastructure responsible for delivering those services.

Two-Wire vs. Four-Wire Circuits Most local loops that are used for connection to the PSTN to supply switched, dial-up phone service are physically described as **two-wire circuits.** Since one of these two wires serves as a ground wire for the circuit, that leaves only one wire between the two ends of the circuit for data signaling. Dial-up or switched circuits generate a dial tone and are connected at a central office-based switch that completes connections to the circuit corresponding to the dialed phone number.

A **four-wire circuit** consists of two wires capable of simultaneously carrying a data signal each with its own dedicated ground wire. Typically, four-wire circuits are reserved for **leased lines,** otherwise known as dedicated lines or private lines. These circuits bypass telephone company switching equipment. They have no dial tone and are always operational between the locations specified by the customers ordering the leased lines.

Half-Duplex vs. Full-Duplex Given that two-wire dial-up circuits have only one wire for data signaling, only one modem could be transmitting at a time while the other modem could only be receiving data. This one direction at a time transmission is known as **half-duplex.**

Modems that interfaced to a dial-up circuit had to support this half-duplex transmission method. This meant that once the two modems completed initial **handshaking,** one modem would agree to transmit while the other received. For the modems to reverse roles, the initially transmitting DTE (terminal or computer) drops its RTS (request to send) (RS-232 pin 4) and the transmitting DCE (modem) drops its CTS (clear to send) (RS-232 pin 5) and perhaps its carrier wave. Next, the initially receiving DTE must raise RTS, the initially receiving DCE (modem) must generate a carrier wave and raise CTS, and the role reversal is complete.

This role reversal is known as **turnaround time** and can take 0.2 sec or longer. This may not seem like a very long time, but if this role reversal needs to be done several thousand times over a long-distance circuit, charged by usage time, it may have a large dollar impact.

Full-duplex transmission supports simultaneous data signaling in both directions. Full-duplex transmission might seem to be impossible on two-wire circuits. Until the advent of the V.32 9600 bps full-duplex modem, the only way to get full-duplex transmission was to lease a four-wire circuit. Two wires (signal and ground) were for transmitting data and two wires (signal and ground) were for receiving data. There was no "role reversal" necessary and therefore no modem turnaround time delays.

Modems manufactured to the CCITT's V.32 standard (and the later V.34 standard) can transmit in full-duplex mode, thereby receiving and transmitting simultaneously over dial-up two-wire circuits. These modems use sophisticated **echo cancellation** techniques and, at least when they were first introduced, were significantly more expensive than slower, half-duplex modems. Figure 3-24 highlights the differences between half-duplex and full-duplex transmission.

Echo Cancellation Echo cancellation takes advantage of sophisticated technology known as **digital signal processors (DSP),** which are included in modems that offer echo cancellation. By first testing the echo characteristics of a given phone line at modem initialization time, these DSPs are able to actually distinguish the echoed transmission of the local modem from the intended transmission of the remote modem. By subtracting or canceling the echoed local transmission from the total data signal received, only the intended transmission from the remote modem remains to be processed by the modem and passed on to the local PC.

Transmission Services

After reviewing the processes involved to move a data signal from a computer through a modem, the final step in the overall process is to interface that modem to a transmission service purchased from the local carrier or phone company. Figure 3-25 summarizes some of the potential transmission services that can be purchased from local carriers. Most of these services are explored further in later chapters.

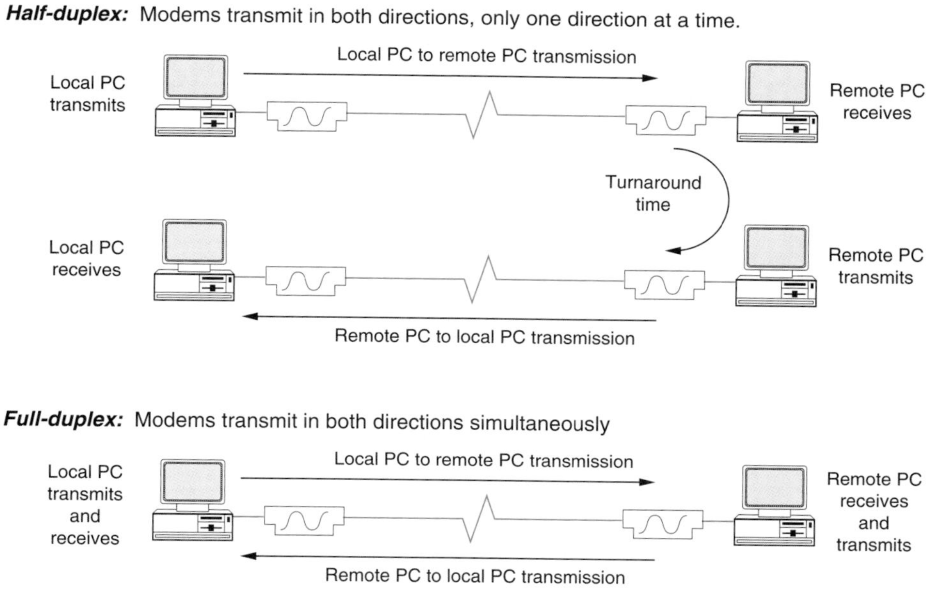

Figure 3-24 Half-Duplex vs. Full-Duplex Transmission

Service Name	Dial-up/ Leased	Analog/ Digital	2-Wire/ 4-Wire	Rates: Flat or Usage	Transmission Rate
Analog					
• **POTS**	D	A	2	U	28.8 Kbps w/V.34 modem
• **Voice-Grade Leased**	L	A	4	F	28.8 Kbps w/V.34 modem
Narrow-Band Digital					
• **DDS**	L	D	4	F	9.6 Kbps, 19.2 Kbps, 56 Kbps
• **DS-0**	L	D	4	F	64 Kbps
Broad-Band Digital					
• **T-1**	L	D	4	F	1.544 Mbps
• **T-3**	L	D	Fiber	F	44.736 Mbps
Digital Dial-Up					
• **ISDN**	D	D	2 or 4	U	144 Kbps
• **Switched 56K**	D	D	4	U	56 Kbps
Alternative Services					
• **Cable Modems**		A	Coaxial cable	F	10 to 60 Mbps one-way with highly variable return
• **Digital Subscriber Line (DSL)**		A	2	F	Up to 8 Mbps one-way with 640 Kbps return

Figure 3-25 Transmission Services

Analog Services Modems modulate digital input from computers into analog output compatible with the phone company's analog voice network. As will be seen in our study of data communications technology in Chapter 4, modems may be able to interface to analog dial-up services, analog leased lines, or both.

An analog or **voice-grade leased line** is a normal voice grade line that bypasses the carrier's switching equipment. When the service is ordered, you must name the two or more locations that are to be connected. A new circuit is installed into these locations, with a new RJ-11 jack interface added at each circuit location. There is no dial tone on this new line because it does not go through any switching equipment. With only two locations connected, the circuit is called point-to-point; with more than two locations, the circuit is called multipoint.

For leased lines, charges include both an installation charge and a flat monthly charge. The installation charge may be significant, especially if the circuit crosses LATAs. The flat monthly fee does not vary by usage, unlike the dial-up voice-grade circuits. The circuit is exclusively the user's, 24 hr/day 7 days/week.

Digital Services As can be seen in Figure 3-25, digital transmission services available from carriers can be either dial-up or leased. One very important point to remember about interfacing to digital services is that a modem is not used since there is no need to modulate the computer's digital signaling into an analog signal. Rather than terminating the circuit with a modem, a **CSU/DSU (channel service unit/data service unit)** is employed. CSU/DSUs are explored further in Chapter 8.

Narrowband Digital Services In addition to being differentiated as either dial-up or leased, digital services can also be differentiated as to amount of bandwidth delivered. Digital services that deliver less than 1.544 Mbps of bandwidth are generally considered as **narrowband digital services.**

When ordering a narrowband digital circuit, the speed of that circuit must be specified to the phone company at the time the order is placed. Typical choices are

- **Digital data services (DDS)** at speeds of 2400, 4800, 9600, 19,200, or 56 Kbps.
- **DS-0** (digital service level 0) at 64 Kbps.

This "declaring your speed" brings up a key difference in operation of analog and digital circuits. When an analog circuit, dial-up or leased, degrades or has some kind of transmission impairment, many modems use **fallback** or lower speeds automatically and continue with data transmissions. With a digital circuit, the speed of the circuit is set at the CO, the CSU/DSUs are set to the speed of the circuit, and if there is a problem with the line, the data transmission ceases. It should be pointed out that digital circuits tend to be more error free than analog circuits. Simply stated, the key determining factor in the transmission speed of an analog circuit is the modem, and the key determining factor in the case of a digital circuit is the configured speed of the circuit itself.

Broadband Digital Services Higher capacity digital services are also available. **T-1** (1.544 Mbps) and **T-3** (45 Mbps) leased lines are among the most popular services available. Although these services offer flat monthly rates, these rates usually vary with distance. T-1 lines can easily cost thousands of dollars per month, and T-3 lines can easily cost tens of thousands of dollars per month.

Dial-up Digital Services Digital dial-up services have become increasingly popular and more available with the tremendous increase in interest in Internet access. **Integrated services digital network (ISDN)** is a dial-up digital service that can offer up to 144 Kbps (most often 128 Kbps). Accessing an ISDN service from your home computer requires a device that performs the same basic functions as a CSU/DSU but is called a **terminal adapter, network termination unit (NTU),** or a **digital modem.** The term *digital modem* is really a contradiction in terms. Another digital dial-up service is known as **switched 56K.** Interfacing to a switched 56K service requires a switched 56K CSU/DSU.

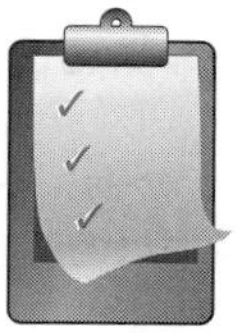

Practical Advice and Information

SERVICE AVAILABILITY

ISDN service, switched 56K service, or any of the digital services listed in Figure 3-25, are not necessarily available at any given home or business location. One should never assume that any particular transmission service is available at any network location when performing network planning and design.

Alternative Services In addition to traditional dial-up and leased line point-to-point services, a new breed of network connections are being introduced. **Digital subscriber line (DSL)** services use frequency division multiplexing to analog encode a high-speed data channel over a traditional POTS local loop connection to the central office. This high-speed channel can be used to carry data to and from a data network, usually the Internet. DSL technology is available in a myriad of choices with many different speeds and characteristics. For a more in-depth analysis of DSL technology refer to Chapter 8.

Cable modems are another alternative service. Like DSL, cable modems are designed to place a single data channel over the top of an existing connection into the home or business, in this case the cable television connection. Due to the high bandwidth available on the installed coaxial cable plant, cable modem technologies have the potential of offering extremely high-speed network access. However, many limiting factors are associated with cable modem technologies, which may or may not hinder their widespread usage. For more information on cable modem technology please refer to Chapter 8.

SUMMARY

Using the transmission of data from one PC to another via a dial-up phone line as an example of a simple data communications opportunity, many key concepts were introduced in this chapter.

Because the dial-up phone network was initially designed for voice or analog traffic only, the modem's major task is to transform digital data to analog and vice versa (modulation/demodulation). Modems can accomplish this modulation by any combination of amplitude, frequency, or phase modulation. The greater the number of bits that can be interpreted per baud, or signaling event, the greater the overall transmission rate of bits as measured in bits per second (bps).

The timing of signaling events between distant modems is crucial to successful data transmission. Asynchronous transmission uses start and stop bits surrounding each character to achieve this intermodem timing, while synchronous transmission uses a constant clocking signal to keep modems constantly synchronized.

Once the parallel data of the PC have been modulated into serial format onto the phone network, it may reach its remote destination by using a variety of available network services. Circuits may be switched, more commonly known as dial-up, or may be leased, in which case a customer would have access to these lines 24 hr/day, 7 days/week. Charges would be based on the length of this permanent circuit rather than on circuit usage time, as is the case with dial-up lines.

Digital network services are also available, in which case a CSU/DSU rather than a modem is employed, since there is no need for analog to digital conversion on an all-digital link.

Data communications devices such as modems and CSU/DSUs combine with available network services to provide end-to-end transmission between computers. The complicated interaction between hardware, software, and network services is transparent to the end-user. In analyzing and designing such a network, data communications professionals concentrate on how changes in one aspect of a design affect other aspects of a design. For example, changing from analog to digital leased lines would have a major impact on the type of data communications devices employed.

Using network analysis models such as the I-P-O (input-processing-output) model provides a framework in which to plan network connections from a simple modem-to-modem transmission to a complex transcontinental wide-area network.

KEY TERMS

16QAM
American standard code for information interchange
amplitude
amplitude modulation
analog
ASCII
asynchronous transmission
bandwidth
baud
baud rate
bit
bps
breakout boxes
byte

cable modems
carrier wave
channel service unit/data service unit
character encoding
constellation points
CSU/DSU
data circuit terminating equipment
data communications equipment
data terminal equipment
DB-25
DB-9
DCE
DDS
demodulation
dial-up line
dibit
digital
digital data services
digital modum
digital signal processors
digital subscriber line
DS-0
DSL
DSP
DTE
EBCDIC
echo cancellation
Extended Binary Coded Decimal Interchange Code
fallback
four-wire circuit
frequency
frequency modulation
frequency shift keying
FSK
full-duplex
half-duplex
handshaking
integrated services digital network
intersymbol interference
ISDN
ISO 10646
leased lines
M block connector
modem
modem cable
modulation
narrowband digital services
network termination unit
NTU
parallel transmission
phase
phase modulation
phase shift keying
plain old telephone service
POTS
PSK
PSTN
public switched telephone network
QAM
QPSK
quadrature amplitude modulation
quadrature phase shift keying
RS-232-C
S/N
serial transmission
signal to noise ratio
switched 56K
switched line
synchronous transmission
T-1
T-3
terminal adapter
transmission rate
turnaround time
two-wire circuits
UART
UNICODE
universal asynchronous receiver/transmitter
universal serial bus
USB
voice-grade leased line
wavelength

REVIEW QUESTIONS

1. What is the difference between analog transmission and digital transmission?
2. What is the difference between asynchronous transmission and synchronous transmission? Which is more efficient?
3. What is a carrier wave?
4. What three characteristics of a carrier wave can be varied?
5. How are the number of detectable events related to the baud rate and bits/p second (bps)?
6. Why do high-speed modems vary more than one characteristic of a carrier wave?
7. What is the difference between full-duplex and half-duplex data transmission?
8. What is the difference between bps and baud rate?
9. What is the difference between a leased line and a dial-up line?
10. What is character encoding and why is it necessary?
11. What are the two major encoding standards?
12. Why isn't there a single encoding standard?
13. What is a bit and how is it represented within a computer?
14. How must bits be represented on a voice-grade dial-up line?
15. What are the primary differences between serial and parallel transmission?
16. Which type of transmission (serial or parallel) is most often used in data communications and why?
17. What is a UART and what role does it play in the overall process of getting data from a local PC to a remote PC?
18. List the 10 most commonly used RS-232 pins including name, abbreviation, and DCE/DTE orientation.
19. What is the name of the device employed to monitor and manipulate RS-232 signals?

20. At what speeds does USB operate?
21. List three advantages of USB over RS-232.
22. What is currently the primary application for IEEE-1394?
23. What is the purpose of the I-P-O model and how can it be used to model both ends of given circuit?
24. Explain in simple terms how a circuit-switched or dial-up call is established.
25. What is the bandwidth of a dial-up circuit?
26. What is the significance of the range of frequencies of a dial-up circuit?
27. What are some of the shortcomings of a dial-up circuit in terms of data communications?
28. Modem is actually a contraction for what two words?
29. Complete an I-P-O chart illustrating the required functionality of a modem.
30. What role does a carrier wave play in data transmission over a dial-up line?
31. How is the fact that different modems can use carrier waves with different frequencies resolved?
32. What is the relationship between wavelength and frequency?
33. What is a signaling event?
34. How long (in seconds) is a signaling event on a 1200 baud modem?
35. How long (in seconds) is a signaling event on a 2400 baud modem?
36. Which transmission methodology requires an external clocking source? Why?
37. What are the two ways in which modems can be modified to transmit data faster?
38. How are two-wire and four-wire circuits related to full-duplex and half-duplex transmission?
39. How are handshaking and turnaround time related to full-duplex and half-duplex transmission?
40. What is a CSU/DSU and how does it differ from a modem?
41. What are the differences in functionality between a modem and a CSU/DSU when encountering line problems?
42. What is the importance of encoding standards such as Unicode/ISO 10646?
43. What is a disadvantage of encoding standards such as Unicode/ISO 10646?
44. Give an example of how physical interfaces or connectors don't necessarily imply a transmission protocol.
45. What is a constellation point?
46. What is intersymbol interference and what impact does it have on modulation scheme design?
47. What is the importance of signal to noise ratio in terms of modem design and operation?
48. What is echo cancellation and why is it important?
49. How is echo cancellation enabled?
50. Which types of transmission services are becoming popular for Internet access?
51. What are some of the shortcomings of RS-232 C and how are they overcome?
52. What type of device must you purchase to interface your PC to ISDN services?

ACTIVITIES

1. Gather advertisements or product specifications for modems of various types. What are the price ranges of these modems? What are the various modulation techniques employed by these modems?
2. Contact your local phone service provider. Inquire as to how many of the services listed in Figure 3-20 are available in your area? Are other services available that are not listed? Are there any current plans to provide additional services?
3. Inquire of your local phone company how the decision is made whether or not to provide a particular data service in a given area.
4. Inquire of your local phone company the approximate time it takes to "roll out" a new service from conception, through regulatory approval, to actual deployment.
5. Contact the Electrical Engineering or Electrical Engineering Technology department at your school. Inquire as to the availability of a guest speaker who might be able to bring an oscilliscope to class to demonstrate the wave characteristics described in Chapter 4.
6. Inquire from your local phone company whether most local loops supplied to homes in your area are two or four wire.
7. Inquire as to the difference between ground start and loop start subscriber trunks (local loops).
8. Gather advertisements or product specifications for digital modems, CSU/DSUs, NTUs, and ISDN modems. What are the price ranges of these modems?
9. Research the deployment levels of Unicode and ISO 10646. How many operating systems support

these character encoding schemes? How must application programs be modified to support them?

10. Find examples of cables or connectors used for serial transmission methods other than RS-232C. What differences are noticable about these cables and connectors?

11. Research advertisements for breakout boxes. Prepare a technology analysis grid detailing the technical differences and price differences among the models researched.

12. Research the current revisions of USB and IEEE-1394. Prepare a report on any new developments since the publication of this book.

CASE STUDY

Ford Paves Employees' Road to 'Net

DETROIT — Ford wants its workers to get wired. That's why company and union leaders last week announced a groundbreaking program to provide all 300,000 Ford employees with the opportunity to buy a new PC and printer, and receive Internet access for home use at a nominal monthly fee.

Ford's Internet access program — the largest deal of its kind — is being hailed as a sign of how the Net is reshaping the way American companies do business. Experts expect other automotive and manufacturing companies to follow suit.

"It's going to be very difficult for the other car companies not to grant their employees the same kind of deal." says Rob Enderle, vice president of desktop and mobile technology at Giga Information Group in Santa Clara, Calif. "It's hard to believe that other largely unionized industries aren't going to get pressure to offer this kind of benefit."

In fact, Delta Airlines announced Friday it is offering a similar program to its 72,000 employees. Delta's goal is to improve communications with mobile workers, many of whom do not have corporate desktop systems. The home PCs under the Delta plan come equipped with a link into DeltaNet, the company's intranet.

Deals of this magnitude are made possible by the plummeting costs of computer hardware, software and Internet access, says Steven Clemons, senior vice president of the New America Foundation, a Washington, D.C., think tank that tracks Internet access issues.

"Ford and the [United Auto Workers] are punching a hole in the connectivity problem for the people they work with." Clemons says. "I see all of the trends moving very quickly to the point where everyone will have Internet access at work, at home and at the community center."

Ford's three-year Internet access program is the latest in a series of e-business announcements from America's No. 2 car maker. Ford recently announced deals with Oracle. Microsoft CarPoint. TeleTech. Yahoo, Bolt.com, Village.com and UPS Logistics Group.

"Ford is recasting itself as not an old smokestack, steel and rubber-tire type of company, but as a more modern. IT-friendly company." Clemons says, "It's very clear that it's a top-down strategy."

Ford officials say they are subsidizing Internet access for their employees to ensure that the workforce is technically savvy and to provide a new channel of interactive communication for employees.

"The automotive industry is at the bleeding edge of technology." Ford CEO Jac Nasser says. "In product development. customer satisfaction, customer service and in the manufacturing plant — everything is touched by technology. We want our employees to experience what's going on in technology."

The Ford program is being coordinated by PeoplePC.a San Francisco start-up that offers

PCs. printers and unlimited Internet access for $25 per month to members who agree to receive e-mail pitches from companies that help underwrite the costs of the service.

In the U.S., Ford employees will have a $5 monthly copayment for the subscription service. Ford employees have the option of upgrading the PC., printer and Internet access at an additional cost.

"Ford employees should be dancing in the streets." Enderle says. "These are extremely reliable systems that won't break. It's more technology than the average user could ever have wished for."

PeoplePC officials expect to begin shipping systems in April, with service availability around the world within 12 months. The program is set to last three years, after which the employees own the systems.

Ford officials declined to comment on the cost of the program, but estimates ranged as high as $200 million. Enderle argues that Ford will actually save money by improving the computer literacy of its employees and by cutting down on other telecommuting expenditures, such as laptops.

"When Ford considers the productivity benefit they're going to get out of this program, they may end up being ahead moneywise even after the subsidy," Enderle says.

Delta also is coordinating its program through PeoplePC at a copayment of $12 per month. Delta has yet to pick a hardware supplier, but Internet access will be provided by AT&T.

Source: Carolyn Duffy Marsan, "Ford paves employees' road to "Net," *Network World*, vol. 17, no. 19 (February 7, 2000), p. 1. Copyright Network World. Reprinted with permission.

BUSINESS CASE STUDY QUESTIONS

Activities

1. Complete a top-down model for this case by gleaning facts from the case and placing them in the proper layer of the top-down model. After having completed the top-down model, analyze and detail those instances where requirements were clearly passed down from upper layers to lower layers of the model and where solutions to those requirements were passed up from lower layers to upper layers of the model.
2. Detail any questions about the case that may occur to you for which answers are not clearly stated in the article.

Business

1. What was the business motivation or problem that initiated the search for the implemented solution?
2. What was the productivity impact of the implemented solution?
3. What is the primary reason for Ford and Delta to offer the PC/Internet access benefit to their employees?
4. Is this just an employee benefit or does it offer a legitimate payback to Ford and Delta? Explain your answer.

Application

1. What applications do Ford and Delta plan for their employees to use in addition to merely gaining PC literacy?
2. What company is providing the turnkey solution for Ford?

Data

1. What types of data will be carried on the employee computers?
2. Are there any special data types for this solution that differ from general Internet access?

Network

1. What underlying network technologies were key to the achievement of stated business objectives?

Technology

1. What specific technologies were employed to deliver the described solution?
2. What has enabled Ford and Delta to be able to deliver such a solution to their employees?

CHAPTER 4

BASIC DATA COMMUNICATIONS TECHNOLOGY

Concepts Reinforced

Top-Down Model
Modulation Techniques
Transmission Services
I-P-O Model
Protocols and Compatibility
Analog vs. Digital

Concepts Introduced

Modem Standards
Error Prevention
Error Detection
Flow Control
Modem Trends
Communications Software Analysis
Data Compression
Error Correction
Dial Backup and Restoral

OBJECTIVES

Upon successful completion of this chapter, you should:

1. Understand modem operation, comparative modem features, the importance of modem standards, and the cost/benefit analysis of various modem purchases.
2. Understand the comparative features and proper business application of communications software.
3. Understand the implications in terms of technology and cost/benefit of the use of various carrier services.

INTRODUCTION

In Chapter 3, PC-to-PC communications via modems was described as a means of explaining many introductory concepts. This chapter describes in detail the operation and comparative features of modems. The role of communications software in the establishment, maintenance, and termination of reliable data communications is also explored. An introduction to the world of digital carrier services includes studies of the required technology as well as the cost/benefit analysis of employing such services.

MODERN TECHNOLOGY ANALYSIS

Applied Problem Solving

GAUGING BUSINESS IMPACT OF TECHNOLOGY

How does one gauge the business impact of investment in modem technology? How does one justify upgrading to newer modem technology?

By first understanding business needs, one is better able to make informed technology purchase decisions. As Figure 4-1 illustrates, potential business impacts of modem technology purchases include the ability to transfer data in a manner that is

- Faster.
- More efficient.
- More reliable.
- More secure.

These four business layer characteristics become the frame of reference through which potential modem purchases are evaluated. In other words, if purchasing the technology in question will not make data transmissions faster, more efficient, more reliable, or more secure, why should we invest in such technology?

The concepts, standards, and technology listed in Figure 4-1 serve as a roadmap for topics covered in this section of the chapter.

Business Layer	Concepts	Standards and Technology
Faster	• New modem standards	• V.90, V.34. and older standards
	• Digital transmission services	• DDS services, ISDN, CSU/DSUs
More Efficient	• Data compression	• V.42bis, MNP 5, throughput, transmission rate
	• Backward compatibility	• Handshaking, Hayes AT command set
More Reliable	• Error prevention	• Line conditioning, adaptive protocols, TCM
	• Error detection	• Parity, LRC, checksums, CRC
	• Error correction	• ARQ, ACK/NAK
	• Line-failure backup	• Auto-dial backup and date restoral
	• Flow control	• RTS/CTS, XON/XOFF
	• Error control standards	• V.42, MNP4
More Secure	• Unauthorized access prevention	• Password protection, callback security
	• Encryption	• Standards, stand-alone vs. integrated

Figure 4-1 Gauging Business Impact of Modem Technology

Future Value of Business Analysis As new modem-related technologies are introduced, their business value can be judged using such a model and by asking the following questions:

1. Does the new technology or feature fit into one of the listed supporting concept categories?
2. If not, does it represent a new category or does it not meet any currently perceived business need?
3. Does the new technology identify a new as yet unlisted business data communications need?
4. If so, add it to your business model layer.
5. If not, then perhaps the newly evaluated technology is either ahead of its time or not currently cost justifiable.

The entries listed on each model layer are based on the authors' experience and observations in business data communications. If your experience yields differing results, then by all means change the entries in the model. If you use *your* top-down model as a frame of reference for data communications technology evaluation, it will assist you in making sense of the current explosion of technology while maintaining an objective so-what attitude toward that technology.

Faster

Modem Standards For modems manufactured by different vendors to interoperate successfully, they must adhere to common operational standards. These standards must define methods of modulation, data compression, error correction, auto-dialing, and backward compatibility with older standards. Figure 4-2 summarizes significant dial-up modem standards of the last 20 years.

Modem Standard	Transmission Rate	Baud Rate	Data Compression	Error Correction	Modulation Method
V.90	56 Kbps down, 28.8 Kbps up	3200, 3000, 2400, 2743, 2800, 3429	V.42bis/MNP5	V.42/MNP4	Digital downlink and 9 QAM and TCM uplink
V.34	28.8 Kbps 33.6 Kbps (optional)	3200, 3000, 2400, 2743, 2800, 3429	V.42bis/MNP5	V.42/MNP4	9QAM and TCM
V.32ter	19.2 Kbps	2400	V.42bis/MNP5	V.42/MNP4	8QAM and TCM
V.32bis	14.4 Kbps	2400	V.42bis/MNP5	V.42/MNP4	6QAM and TCM
V.32	9.6 Kbps	2400	V.42bis/MNP5	V.42/MNP4	4QAM and TCM
V.22bis	2400 bps	600	V.42bis/MNP5	V.42/MNP4	4QAM and TCM
Bell 212A	1200 bps	600			4PSK
Bell 103	300 bps	300			FSK

Figure 4-2 Modem Standards

The V series standards featured in Figure 4-2 are officially sanctioned by ITU-T (International Telecommunications Union—Telephony Sector). The Bell standards listed in Figure 4-2 are predivestiture standards from the time when AT&T dictated modem specifications in the United States and compliance with international standards was not an option. The suffix *bis* refers to the second standard issued by a given standard committee while the suffix *ter* refers to the third standard issued by that same committee.

Practical Advice and Information

NONSTANDARD STANDARDS

In an effort to gain market share during the time when standards-making organizations are deliberating new standards, vendors often introduce proprietary versions of pending standards. Before the standardization of V.90, there were two proprietary 56 Kbps modem technologies: X2 from 3COM/US Robotics and K56flex from Lucent Technologies.

One very important point to keep in mind when purchasing prestandard data communications equipment is the ability of the vendor to upgrade that equipment to meet the specifications of the official standard once it is issued. In some cases, software upgrades are possible, whereas in other cases, hardware upgrades or chip replacement is required. In some cases, these upgrades may be free and easily accomplished via the Internet, whereas in other cases, the upgrade may involve returning the equipment to the factory involving upgrade fees of several hundred dollars. Be sure to understand all of the details regarding standards compliance upgrades before ever purchasing prestandards data communications equipment.

V.34 V.34 is the most current analog modem standard. V.34 offers a transmission rate of up to 33.6 Kbps (33,600 bps) over the standard analog local loop. The highest required speed for a V.34 compliant modem is 28.8 Kbps. The 33.6 Kbps speed is available for modems that make use of an optional baud rate. As shown in Figure 4-2, the higher speed is achieved by using a lower baud rate with more bits per baud than the required 28.8 Kbps speed.

It is important to note in Figure 4-2 that although modulation standards have changed to produce higher transmission rates, the associated data compression and error correction standards have remained constant. The V.34 modem standard instituted a variety of technical innovations to achieve this transmission rate over dial-up lines of variable quality. The overall effect of technical innovations is that the V.34 modem is better able than any previous modem standard to easily and dynamically adjust to variable line conditions to optimize transmission rate.

In Sharper Focus

V.34 TECHNICAL INNOVATIONS

Figure 4-3 summarizes the technical innovations introduced with the V.34 modem standard and their associated importance or implication.

V.34 Technical Innovation	Importance/Implication
Multiple Baud Rates/Carrier Frequencies	The V.34 standard specifies three required baud rates (3200, 3000, 2400) and three optional baud rates (3429, 2800, 2743). Multiple potential baud rates increase the V.34 modem's ability to adapt to variable line conditions. Each baud rate supports two different carrier frequencies to optimize transmission speed on dial-up lines of variable quality.
Baud Rates Greater Than 2400	The V.34 standard is the first to attempt baud rates of greater than 2400. The 28.8 Kbps transmission rate is achieved by interpreting 9 data bits/baud at a baud rate of 3200. The 33.6 Kbps transmission rate is achieved by interpreting 12 bits/baud at a baud rate of 2800.
Auxiliary Management Channel	An auxiliary or side channel, separate from the data channel, is available for transmission of management or configuration data. This channel would be particularly important if the V.34 modem were attached to a router or similar internetworking device that might require monitoring or management without disrupting the main data traffic.
Asymmetrical Transmit/Receive Speeds	Some applications such as database queries/responses, or Web requests/downloads, may require wide bandwidth in one direction only. V.34 specifies a method for allocating the data with a larger bandwidth in one direction than the other.
Adaptive Line Probing	Adaptive line probing tests the characteristics of the transmission line not just at call initiation time, but throughout the transmission. Baud rate, carrier frequency, constellation size and shape, and other parameters can be changed to optimize transmission rate.
Precoding and Nonlinear Encoding	Reduces high frequency line noise and increases immunity to interference on analog to digital conversion by plotting constellation points in areas with less interference.
Fallback/Fallforward	Although many modem standards support fallback, V.34 supports fallforward features that allow increases in transmission rates as line conditions improve.
Trellis-Coded Modulation	A forward error correction methodology that helps support higher baud rates on dirty phone lines by predicting the location of a given constellation point. Can add significant processing overhead.
V.8 Training Specification	Also known as fast training, this specification allows two V.34 modems that support V.8 training to setup and initialize a call faster than modems that do not support V.8

Figure 4-3 V.34 Technical Innovations

Although all of the technical innovations listed in Figure 4-3 are considered part of the V.34 standard, it is not safe to assume that they are all included in any V.34 modem. In addition, several other optional features that may or may not be supported on any given V.34 modem are as follows:

- Support of leased lines as well as dial-up lines
- Inclusion of four-wire as well as two-wire physical interfaces
- Password protection and callback security
- Ability to connect to fax machines via the V.17 FAX standard
- Ability to auto-dial via the V.25bis auto-dial standard
- Auto-dial backup for failed leased lines or lost carrier
- Auto-restoral to repaired leased lines

This lack of assurance as to the exact features supported on any given V.34 can lead to interoperability problems among V.34 modems. The best solution to this dilemma is to purchase identical modems from a single manufacturer. If this is not practical, then the time invested to carefully investigate which features of the V.34 standard are implemented in a given modem would be a wise investment indeed.

V.90 According to Shannon's Law, the highest V.34 transmission rate of 33.6 Kbps should be the maximum transmission rate that a voice grade telephone line can support. However, Figure 4-2 claims that modems that adhere to the V.90 standard are capable of transferring data in at least one direction at speeds up to 56 Kbps/sec. How can this be? Were telecommunications engineers able to change the laws of physics?

The answer is obviously no. Shannon's law is still intact for data transmission across the PSTN. The telecommunications engineers instead changed the paradigm to alleviate one of the largest components of noise in a traditional modem implementation. The resulting standard, known as **V.90,** is a hybrid analog/digital standard that offers transmission rates of almost double V.34 levels.

A review of Chapter 2 shows that the majority of the telephone system is currently digital in nature, with the local loops from the central offices (COs) to the end users being the only remaining analog connections. As you recall from Chapter 2, an analog telephone signal is converted into a digital signal at the CO for transmission across this digital telephone system and then converted back into an analog signal at the destination CO for transmission to the destination telephone.

The limiting factor in exceeding V.34 speeds is the quantization noise associated with the conversion of the analog signal to a digital signal for transmission across the digital telephone system. To exceed V.34 speeds, this analog to digital conversion and its associated quantization noise must be eliminated. Fortunately the digital nature of the modern PSTN makes this possible.

In Sharper Focus

QUANTIZATION NOISE

Conversion of a signal from an analog format to a digital format imparts "noise" into the signal. This can be readily explained by considering the nature of both analog and digital signals. Analog signals can consist of any possible level. Digital signals on the other hand can consist of only fixed levels.

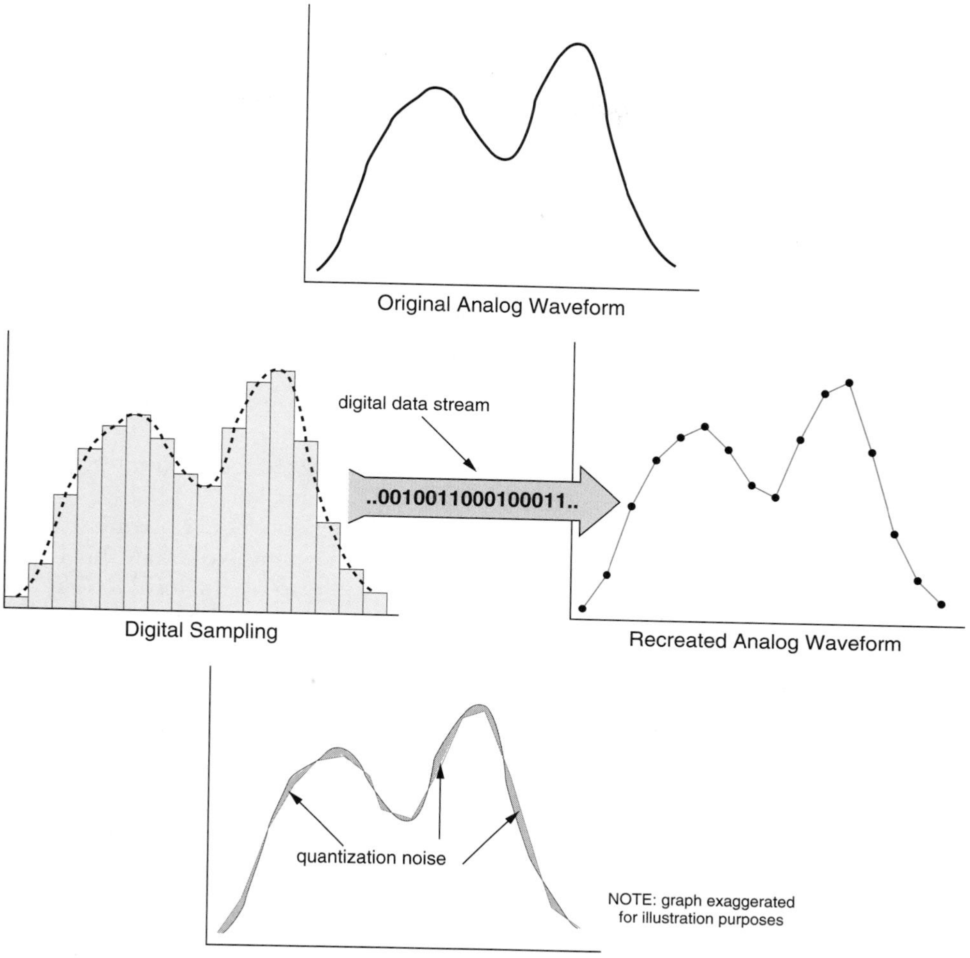

Figure 4-4 Quantization Noise

As shown in Figure 4-4, when an analog signal is sampled and converted into a digital signal, a certain level of detail is lost. When the digital signal is converted back into an analog signal at the destination end of the call, the resulting analog waveform is not exactly equal to the source waveform. This error is known as **quantization noise.**

While quantization noise is not perceivable by humans on normal telephone calls, it affects the ability of modems to use the entire bandwidth of the call, thus limiting the potential transmission rate. It is important to note that quantization noise is created by the analog to digital conversion process, although it does not manifest itself until subsequent digital to analog conversion.

The V.90 modem standard makes use of the digital PSTN to overcome quantization noise by replacing the analog modem on one end of the connection with a digital server. This server connects directly to its CO via a digital connection such as an ISDN PRI or T-1 line. By using a direct digital connection, the server avoids any ana-

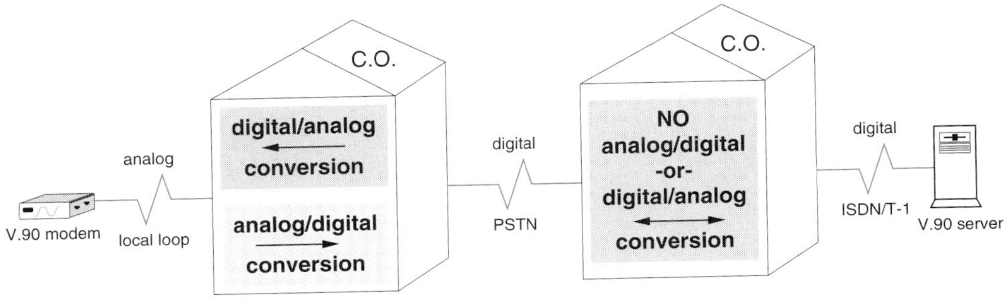

Figure 4-5 V.90 Implementation

log to digital conversions for outgoing transmission, thereby eliminating quantization noise. At the other end of the connection, the CO converts the digital signal into a clean analog signal and transmits it to the destination modem. This process is illustrated in Figure 4-5.

By using this technique, a theoretical transmission rate of 56 Kbps can be achieved from the server to the modem. Note that this is a theoretical rate. An FCC limit on the amount of power allowed on the local loop reduces this theoretical limit to around 53 Kbps. Physical limitations in the local loop, including the distance from the modem to the CO, the number of connections or splices in the local loop, and the overall quality of the local loop, can limit the actual transmission rates further. In the authors' experience it is far more common to achieve transmission rates of around 44 Kbps, although connections at rates in excess of 50 Kbps have been noted.

A close examination of Figure 4-5 shows the increased speed offered by V.90 is limited to the half of the connection originating at the server and terminating at the modem. The other half of the connection, originating at the modem and terminating at the server, must undergo an analog to digital conversion and therefore incurs quantization error, limiting speeds to V.34 levels. Because the speeds are different in each direction, V.90 is said to be an **asymmetrical transmission** technology.

Fortunately the asymmetrical characteristic of V.90 matches the asymmetrical nature of the most common modem application: accessing the Internet. In a normal session, a user sends a fairly short request (such as the address of a web page) to a server. The server responds with a much larger collection of data (such as the text and graphics that make up the web page) to the user, making V.90 a natural fit for Internet access.

As with all modem standards, V.90-compliant modems are backwards compatible with earlier standards. When a connection is initially made, the modem attempts to connect at the highest possible V.90 speed. It then drops back to slower V.90 levels, then resorts to V.34 levels, V.32 levels, etc. until a carrier wave can be established. Because of this automatic rate fallback strategy, it is common for first-time users to comment on the long time required for a V.90 modem to establish a carrier and begin communicating.

MNP Standards **Microcom Networking Protocols (MNP)** are error correction and data compression protocols originally developed by the modem manufacturer Microcom. MNP classes or groups of protocols are excellent examples of de facto standards. They are supported by most modems even though they are not mandated by any officially sanctioned standards making organization. However, MNP classes often form the basis for officially sanctioned international standards. For example,

MNP Class	Explanation/Importance
1	• Early error control protocol superseded by later classes.
2	• Defined a method for asynchronous byte-oriented full-duplex data transmission.
3	• Defined a method for synchronous bit-oriented communication between modems, even if the communication session between PCs was asynchronous. Removed start bits and stop bits to increase efficiency by up to 8%.
4	• Adaptive size packet assembly: Size of data packets is adjusted according to the quality of the line to avoid errors and retransmissions. • Data phase packet format optimization: Eliminates the portions of the overhead or framing bytes in the data packets that do not change during data transfer. • Implementation of MNP Class 4 protocols can increase transmission efficiency by up to 20%.
5	• Data compression protocol that can increase throughput by up to 200%. See section on data compression for further explanation. See the section on data compression for further explanation.
6	• Universal link negotiation: Allows modems supporting a variety of standards to interoperate at speeds from 50 to 19.2 Kbps. Eliminates incompatibilities between Bell standards and V series standards. • Statistical duplexing: Also known as simulated full-duplex transmission. Allows half-duplex modems to support fast turnaround time based on which direction has more data waiting to be transmitted.
7 8	• Enhanced data compression protocol that can increase throughput by up to 300%. • Enhancement to MNP Class 6 simulated full-duplex by combining MNP Class 7 data compression with V.29 fast-train protocol (9600 bps, half-duplex).
9	• MNP Class 7 data compression plus V. 32 (9600 bps, full-duplex). • Enhanced universal link negotiation: Allows MNP and non-MNP modems to establish optimum performance communications sessions.
10	• Consists of four protocols known collectively as **adverse channel enhancements (ACE)** that were designed for inherently unreliable circuits such as cellular transmission. 1. Robust auto-reliable: Multiple attempts of link setup at highest common protocol level. 2. Aggressive adaptive packet assembly: Packet size is quickly and dynamically changed in response to changing line conditions. 3. Dynamic speed shifts: Transmission speed and modulation scheme can vary dynamically in response to changing line conditions. 4. Negotiated speed upshifts: Transmission session is initially established at a negotiated speed that will provide the highest reliability. If line conditions improve, higher speeds will be supported.

Figure 4-6 MNP Classes

the ITU's V.42 error correction standard incorporates MNP classes 2, 3, and 4. Figure 4-6 summarizes the current MNP classes. Further explanation of selected MNP classes is provided in later sections of this chapter.

Cheaper (More Efficient)

By operating more efficiently, modems are able to offer more transmitted data in a given amount of time. Although several factors can lead to increased modem efficiency, data compression can have the most significant impact in the amount of data actually delivered by a given modem in a given amount of time.

Data Compression **Data compression** replaces large strings of repeating character patterns with a special code that represents the pattern. The code is then sent to the other modem. From that point forward the sending modem sends the code instead of the original pattern. As the code is significantly smaller than the pattern it represents, the amount of data sent between the two modems is reduced by up to 400% under optimal conditions. The process of data reduction is similar to the concept of having more than 1 bit/baud as covered in the previous chapter.

By using data compression, a 28.8 Kbps (V.34) modem could optimally transfer 115.2 Kbps (28.8 Kbps compression factor of 4:1) of data across a dial-up phone line. In this scenario, the 115,200 bps is known as **throughput** while the transmission rate remains at or below the V.34 maximum of 28.8 Kbps. Figure 4-7 illustrates the difference between throughput and transmission rate.

It is important to understand how data compression works and the fact that all of the 115,200 bits/sec do not actually travel across the phone circuit. It is equally important to understand that data compression only works if both modems on the circuit support the same data compression standard. Data compressed by the sending modem must be uncompressed by the receiving modem using an identical algorithm or methodology.

In the case of the common V.42bis compression standard, the data compression software examines the raw data received from the transmitting PC, looking for repetitive patterns of characters, before it sends the data onto the circuit. Having spotted a repetitive pattern of up to 32 characters, the two modems store this pattern, along with an 11-bit code or key, in a constantly updated library. The next time this pattern of data comes along to be sent, the sending modem just sends the 11-bit code that

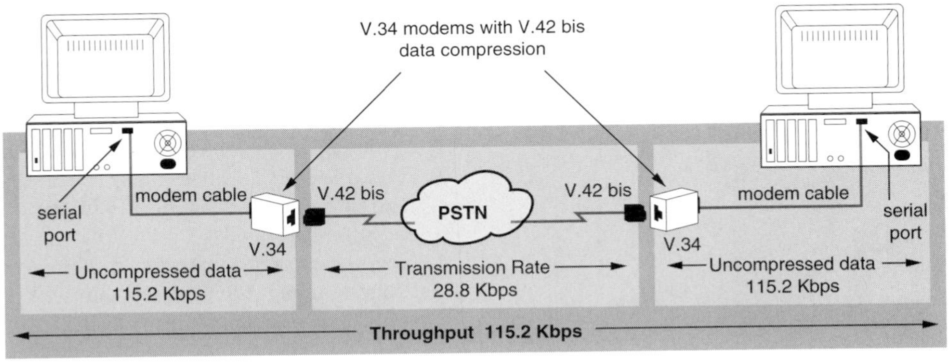

Figure 4-7 Data Compression: Transmission Rate vs. Throughput

represents the 32-byte pattern, rather than the entire data stream itself. The receiving modem then consults its library to see which "uncompressed" pattern is represented by the code character(s) received.

Obviously, the more "repetitive patterns" the data compression software can find in the data, the higher the compression ratio that can be expected. Thus, some data streams are more compressible than other data streams and would yield a higher data compression ratio.

Given the transmission of compressed data in which a single character may "uncompress" into many characters, the importance of error prevention, detection, and correction should be obvious. An erroneously transmitted character could be referenced in the receiving modem's library of repetitive patterns and incorrectly "uncompressed" into the wrong data stream.

V.42bis and MNP 5 The two predominant data compression standards are V.42bis and MNP5. Most modems try to negotiate with each other to implement V.42bis data compression at initialization. The less efficient MNP5 protocol is commonly used as a second option.

V.42bis uses a data compression algorithm known as the Lempel Ziv algorithm as described in the previous section. Ideally, it can compress files and thereby increase throughput by a 4:1 ratio. Proprietary improvements to this algorithm by modem manufacturers can be achieved in two ways:

1. Increase the amount of memory dedicated to the library, also known as the dictionary. (1.5KB standard, some modems use up to 6 KB).
2. Increase the size of the pattern of characters, also known as string size, which can be stored in the dictionary (32 bytes standard, some modems support strings up to 256 bytes).

Proprietary improvements to standards such as V.42bis are effective only when both modems involved in a transmission are identical. It should also be noted that most independent modem testing suggests that compression ratios in the range of 2.5:1 are most likely despite higher optimal claims.

MNP Class 5 yields data compression ratios between 1.3:1 and 2:1. MNP5 uses two data compression algorithms:

1. **Huffman encoding** is a special character encoding scheme that reencodes ASCII characters. Frequently used characters such as *a,e,* and *s* are encoded with only 4 bits, whereas rarely occurring characters such as *x* or *z* are encoded using as many as 11 bits. Overall, the effect of Huffman encoding is that more characters are transmitted using fewer bits.
2. **Run-length encoding** exams a data stream in search of repeating characters. When any character repeats more than three times, the run-length encoding algorithm replaces the entire string of repeated characters with only three repetitions of the character followed by a count field indicating how many times the character is actually repeated. For example, a data string containing 10 consecutive repetitions of the same character would be replaced by three repetitions of that character followed by a 1-byte count character. This would reduce the string in question from 10 bytes to 4 bytes for a savings of 60%. Repeated characters can include nonprinting characters such as spaces, carriage returns, and line feeds.

Practical Advice and Information

SOFTWARE VS. HARDWARE DATA COMPRESSION

The data compression techniques discussed so far are hardware based, implemented in the modems themselves. Many data communication software solutions (such as Microsoft Windows Dial-up Networking) also include data compression. If both software compression and hardware compression are available, software compression is usually more effective because the software packages are typically optimized for their data stream. Hardware compression, as implemented in the modem, by definition must be generic, as the modem designers have no idea of the type of data that might be transmitted.

Regardless of whether hardware or software compression is chosen, you should never turn on both hardware and software compression at the same time. Hardware compression is designed to work with raw (uncompressed) data streams. Attempting to compress a data stream that is already compressed will often cause the hardware "compressed" data stream to be *larger* than the original data stream.

Principle of Shifting Bottlenecks The potential for throughput rates of 115.2 Kbps via V.34 modems with V.42bis data compression introduces a potentially interesting dilemma. By examining Figure 4-7 carefully, it should be obvious that the serial ports of the PCs involved in the end-to-end communications session should be set to 115.2 Kbps. However, some older PC serial ports are able to support transmission speeds of only 19.2 Kbps or 38.4 Kbps. These speed limits are somewhat dependent on the particular UART chip installed. This dilemma is an example of a principle of data communications common to numerous transmission systems known as the **principle of shifting bottlenecks.**

In the case of a modem-based transmission system, the modems themselves traditionally represented the bottleneck, or slowest link of the overall end-to-end transmission. However, as modem technology advanced with the introduction of the V.90 standard and beyond, the transmission bottleneck has shifted from the modem to the PC's serial port. To resolve these serial port speed limitations, the use of USB ports for modem connections is becoming common. As mentioned in Chapter 3, USB supports speeds up to 12 Mbps, more than adequate for any modem applications.

More Reliable

Improving the reliability of the data transmission link between two modems will ultimately make that data transmission faster and more efficient. Fewer retransmissions due to data errors will reduce the overhead associated with correcting errors, thus reducing the time necessary to transmit a given message. This will minimize the cost of the data transmission.

The goal of reliable transmission is to minimize the error rate of a data transmission session. The first category of error correction techniques try to prevent errors from happening by optimizing the condition of the transmission link **(error prevention).** If errors occur, the second category of error correction techniques detect **(error detection)** and correct the errors **(error correction)**

Error Prevention Data transmission errors occur when received data are misinterpreted due to noise or interference on the phone lines over which the data message traveled. Errors can be prevented by

- Reducing the amount of noise or interference on a given transmission line.
- Employing modulation techniques that are able to adapt to and overcome noisy lines.

Line Conditioning, Repeaters, and Amplifiers **Line conditioning** is a value-added service available for analog leased lines from the phone company. Various levels of conditioning are available at prices that increase proportionally to the level of conditioning, or noise reduction, requested. Conditioning represents a promise from the phone company in terms of the noise levels or interference present on a given analog leased line. To deliver on this promise, the phone company may have to install additional equipment.

A **repeater** is often used by a phone company to ensure signal quality over the entire length of a circuit. As a signal travels through a medium such as copper wire, it loses some of its strength due to the resistance of the wire. This loss of signal strength or volume is known as **attenuation.**

A repeater on an analog circuit, sometimes called an **amplifier,** strengthens and repeats the signal. Unfortunately, on an analog circuit, the amplifier cannot distinguish between the voice or data signal and the background noise. As a result, the amplifier strengthens and repeats both signal and background noise.

Repeaters on digital circuits are able to distinguish the digital signals from the background noise. Therefore digital repeaters can retransmit a digital signal free of noise, ensuring that the signal will reliably arrive at its destination without the need for specialized line conditioning. The repeaters in this application are primarily used only by the phone company and should not be confused with local area network repeaters. LAN repeaters are covered in Chapter 9.

As analog leased lines give way to digital leased and dial-up services, the purchase of line conditioning will become a nonissue in the error prevention arena. In fact, the use of DDS or digital leased lines could itself be seen as an error prevention technique.

Adaptive Protocols Another way in which errors can be prevented during data transmission is through the use of **adaptive protocols.** Adaptive protocols adjust transmission session parameters in response to varying line conditions. The MNP classes of networking protocols offer several examples of such adaptive protocols. **Adaptive size packet assembly** is an MNP Class 4 protocol that can increase or decrease the amount of data sent in each packet according to the current condition of the transmission circuit. A packet that includes data and overhead information is analogous to a handwritten message (the data) plus a sealed, addressed envelope (the overhead). This protocol tries to optimize the amount of data per packet by building packets containing the greatest amount of data that can be transmitted reliably and therefore not require retransmission.

Optimal packet size is a moving target, changing with line conditions. Each packet of data contains overhead. Therefore if line conditions are good, it makes sense to use large packets to maximize the data to overhead ration. Returning to the previous analogy, it would be advantageous to write as long a letter as possible for each envelope. Too little data per packet and time is wasted processing overhead (opening envelopes in the analogy).

However, if line conditions are poor, errors will occur. Because the error detection process can only determine that an error occurred in the packet rather than the exact bit in error, the entire packet containing the error must be retransmitted. The larger the packets, the more data that must be retransmitted for each error. In our analogy this correlates to receiving, rewriting and remailing letters for insufficient postage. Adaptive size packet assembly solves the data per packet dilemma by adapting the amount of data included in each packet according to varying line conditions. When errors are detected, packet size is reduced. When no errors are detected over time, packet sizes are increased.

Dynamic speed shifts is an MNP Class 10 adaptive protocol that allows two modems to change speeds up or down (faster or slower) in the midst of their data transmission in response to varying line conditions. The adaptive nature of this protocol ensures that the highest practical transmission speed will be used at all times, depending on current line conditions. This adaptive protocol is especially useful in cellular phone environments in which line quality can vary significantly over short periods of time.

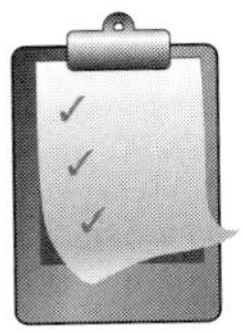

Practical Advice and Information

ADAPTIVE PROTOCOLS CAN MASK PROBLEMS

Dynamic speed shifts or any adaptive protocol can be a double-edged sword. In the event of degraded line quality, MNP 10 modems may automatically downgrade their transmission speeds. Unless a personnel procedure is in place to take note of the lower transmission speed, the problem may go undetected and unreported to the carrier for an extended time.

Error Detection Once everything possible to prevent errors has been done, the next task is to reliably detect the errors that occur. Remembering that transmitted data, on the most elementary level, is merely a stream of 1s and 0s, the role of error detection can be defined as providing the assurance that the receiving modem receives the same 1s and 0s in the exact sequence transmitted by the transmitting modem.

Overall Process This assurance is achieved through the cooperative efforts of the transmitting and receiving modem. In addition to transmitting the actual data, the transmitting modem must also transmit some type of verifiable bit or character that the receiving modem can use to decide whether or not the transmitted data were received correctly. Figure 4-8 illustrates this overall process shared by all error detection techniques.

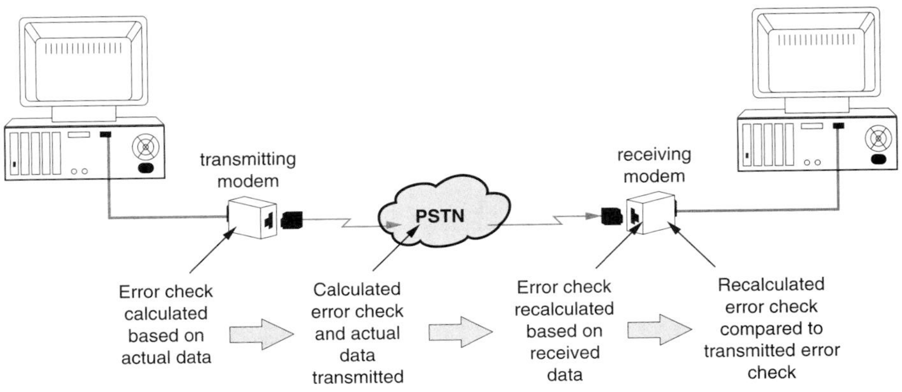

Figure 4-8 The Overall Error Detection Process

A generalized error detection process as illustrated in Figure 4-8 could be summarized as follows:

1. The transmitting and receiving modems agree on how the error check is to be calculated.
2. The transmitting computer calculates and transmits the error check along with the transmitted data.
3. The receiving modem recalculates the error check based on the received data and compares its newly calculated error check to the error check received from the transmitting modem.
4. If the two error checks match, everything is fine. If the receiving modem's calculated error check does not match the transmitted error check, an error has occurred.

Several error detection techniques of varying degrees of complexity have been developed. The following error detection techniques will be discussed further:

- Parity (VRC)
- Longitudinal redundancy checks (LRC)
- Checksums
- Cyclic redundancy checks (CRC)

Parity **Parity,** also known as a **(vertical redundancy check** or **VRC),** is the simplest error detection technique. Parity works by adding an error check bit to each character. For example, since the ASCII 7-bit code for the letter *A* is 1000001, a parity bit is added as the eighth bit. Whether this bit should be a 0 or a 1 depends on whether odd or even parity has been defined or agreed on in advance by communicating devices. These devices can also agree to data transmission with no parity. Examples of the letter *A* with odd and even parity are illustrated in Figure 4-9.

As can be seen in Figure 4-9, when the letter *A* is transmitted with odd parity, the parity bit is set to 1 so that there is an odd number of 1s in the 8-bit character. Conversely, when even parity is used, the parity bit is set to 0 so that there is an even number of 1s in the 8-bit character. If even parity is chosen and the receiving computer detects an odd number of 1s in the character, then it knows that a transmission error has occurred.

Parity checking has a limitation. It can only detect odd numbers of bit substitution errors. If an even number of bit substitution errors occur, the received character

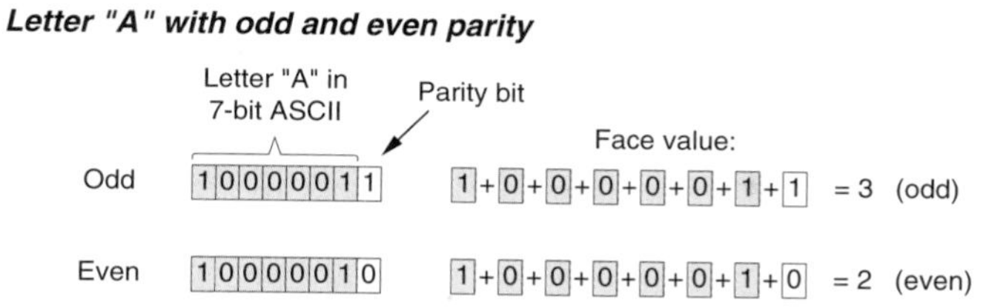

Figure 4-9 Odd and Even Parity

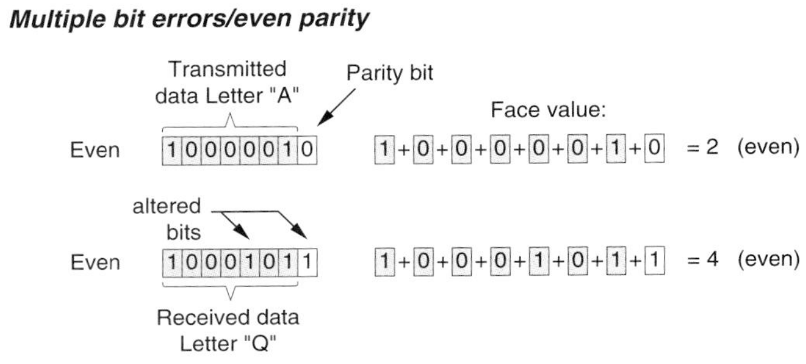

Figure 4-10 Parity Checking's Inability to Detect Multiple Bit Errors

will pass the parity check even though the character received was not the character sent. Figure 4-10 illustrates parity checking's inability to detect even numbers of bit substitution errors within the same character.

As can be seen in Figure 4-10, the received character has an even number of 1s so that the receiving computer thinks everything is fine. However, a letter *Q* was received instead of the letter *A* that was sent.

Longitudinal Redundancy Checks **Longitudinal redundancy checks (LRC)** seek to overcome the weakness of simple bit-oriented one-directional parity checking. One can think of LRC as adding a second dimension to parity. Figure 4-11 illustrates longitudinal redundancy checking with even parity in two dimensions.

As can be seen in Figure 4-11, LRC is a block-oriented parity checking mechanism that adds an entire parity character following a block of data characters. The bits of the parity character are set to establish property parity for each bit position within the block of data characters. In the example illustrated in Figure 4-11, both the parity bits of individual characters (VRC) as well the parity bits of the longitudinal redundancy check character would be checked to be sure that even parity existed in both directions.

Checksums **Checksums** are also block-oriented error detection characters added to a block of data characters. However, rather than checking the number of 1s in the block as was the case with the LRC, a checksum is calculated by adding the decimal face values of all of the characters sent in a given data block and sending only the

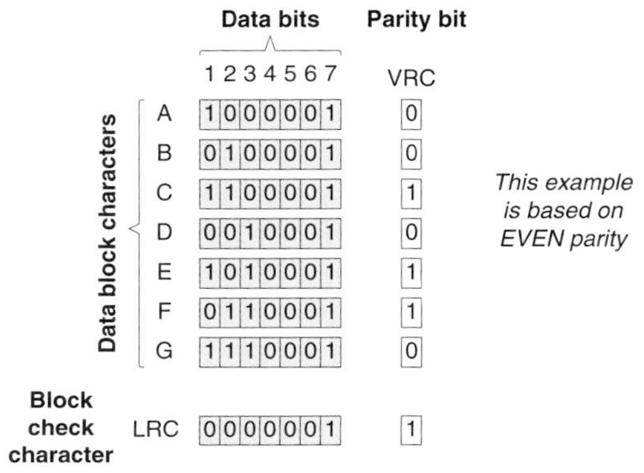

Figure 4-11 Longitudinal Redundancy Checks

least significant byte of that sum. The receiving modem generates its own checksum based on the data it has received and compares the locally calculated checksum with the transmitted checksum.

In Sharper Focus

CHECKSUM CALCULATION

The formula for calculating a checksum is as follows:

1. Add the ASCII decimal face value of each of the 128 characters in the block.
2. Divide this number by 255.
3. The remainder of this answer is the checksum character to be transmitted to and verified by the receiving modem.

To understand the inner workings of this formula, it is necessary to further understand the ASCII table, first introduced in Figure 3-2. Every value in the ASCII table has a decimal equivalent computed by transforming the 1s and 0s of any character, into their base 2 column values and adding the decimal values of those base 2 columns in which 1s appear.

Example:
Capital letter *A* 7-bit ASCII code is 1000001
Now assign base 2 place values to each column

Power of 2	**7**	**6**	**5**	**4**	**3**	**2**	**1**	**0**
Decimal value	128	64	32	16	8	4	2	1
Letter '*A*' code		1	0	0	0	0	0	1

There is a "1" in the "64" column and a "1" in the "1" column. Adding these place values, yields 64 + 1 or 65 (base 10) or decimal 65. Therefore the ASCII decimal face value of the capital letter *A* is 65. Some ASCII and EBCDIC tables supply only decimal values rather than binary values as illustrated in Figures 3-2 and 3-3.

If 128 capital '*A*'s were transferred as a single block of data, the total ASCII face value of the block would be $128 \times 65 = 8320$. Dividing the total ASCII face value by 255 yields 8320/255 = 32 r 160. So the remainder is 160. This remainder is also known as the least significant byte.

To represent the remainder (160) as a single checksum character in binary format, use the decimal values chart of the powers of 2.

Power of 2	**7**	**6**	**5**	**4**	**3**	**2**	**1**	**0**
Decimal value	128	64	32	16	8	4	2	1
Binary value of 160	1	0	1	0	0	0	0	0

Thus, the transmitted checksum character would be 10100000.

When dividing our total ASCII face value by 255, the highest remainder possible would be 254. Decimal 254 would be represented in binary and transmitted in a single checksum character (8 bits) as 11111110.

Cyclic Redundancy Checks **Cyclic redundancy checks (CRC)** seek to improve on the error detection capability of checksums and LRCs. A CRC is really a more sophisticated form of a checksum. Two types of cyclical redundancy checks **(CRC-16** and **CRC-32)** may be used.

To understand CRC-16 and CRC-32, binary division is required. In cyclic redundancy checking, the entire message block of 1s and 0s, even if it's 1000 bits long, is treated as a single, gigantic binary number. This gigantic string of 1s and 0s is divided by a predetermined prime binary number (a 17-bit divisor for CRC-16 and a 33-bit divisor for CRC-32). Remembering that these divisors are prime (only divisible by 1 and themselves), they will produce a 16-bit and 32-bit remainder, respectively.

This remainder is then attached to the actual data message (the original string of 1s and 0s to be transmitted) and transmitted to the receiving modem where the received data string is again divided by the same 16-bit or 32-bit divisor. The remainder calculated at the receiving modem is compared to the remainder received from the transmitting modem.

Using this technique, a CRC-16 modem can detect error bursts of up to 15 bits 100% of the time, and a CRC-32 modem can detect error bursts of up to 31 bits 100% of the time. The CRC-16 modem can detect error bursts equal to 16 bits $(100 - 1/2^{15})\%$ of the time and a CRC-32 modem can detect error bursts equal to 32 bits $(100 - 1/2^{31})\%$ of the time. The CRC-16 modem can detect error bursts larger than 16 bits $(100 - 1/2^{16})\%$ of the time and a CRC-32 modem can detect error bursts of larger than 32 bits than 32 bits $(100 - 1/2^{32})\%$ of the time. Computing the overall percentage for CRC-16 yields an error detection rate of 99.999984742%!

Error Correction Once it is understood how data transmission errors can be detected, they must be reliably and efficiently corrected. In simple terms, error correction amounts to:

- The receiving modem detects an error and requests a retransmission.
- The transmitting modem retransmits the data received in error.

The differences in sophistication between the various error correcting protocols are centered around a few variables:

- How is the retransmission requested?
- How much data must be retransmitted?
- How is retransmission time minimized?

Error correction could easily have been included in the "More efficient" (cheaper) section of the business layer model (Figure 4-1). Retransmissions take time and in business time is money.

Automatic Retransmission Request (ARQ) **ARQ** or **automatic retransmission request** is a general term that really describes the overall process of error detection using one of the previously described methods as well as the subsequent automatic request for retransmission of that data. As noted, the actual request for retransmission can occur in different ways.

Discrete ARQ—ACK/NAK **Discrete ARQ** is sometimes also known as "stop and wait" ARQ. In a protocol using discrete ARQ, the transmitting device sends a block of data and waits until the remote receiving device does the following:

1. Receives the data.
2. Tests for errors using either parity, LRC, checksum, or CRC.
3. Sends an **acknowledgment (ACK)** character back to the transmitting device if the transmitted data was error free or...
4. Sends a **negative acknowledgment (NAK)** character if the data were not successfully received

After waiting for this **ACK/NAK,** the transmitting device does the following:

1. Sends the next block of data if an ACK was received or...
2. Retransmits the original block of data if a NAK was received.

This entire process repeats itself until the conclusion of the data transmission session. Obviously, the transmitting device spends a significant amount of time idly waiting for either an ACK or NAK to be sent by the receiving device. As may have been suspected, there are ARQ methodologies that take a different, more efficient approach to error detection and correction.

Continuous ARQ A variation of ARQ known as **continuous ARQ,** eliminates the requirement for the transmitting device to wait for an ACK or NAK after transmitting each block before transmitting the next block of data. This obviously eliminates a great deal of idle time and increases overall data throughput.

With continuous ARQ, sometimes known as a **sliding window protocol** when implemented in a communications software package, a **block sequence number** is appended to each block of data transmitted. The transmitting device continuously transmits blocks of data without waiting for ACK or NAK from the receiving device after each block of data sent. However, there is often a sliding window block limit to prevent a modem from transmitting indefinitely without having received either an ACK or NAK. The receiving device still checks each block of data for errors just as it did with discrete ARQ.

However, when the receiving device detects an error in a block of data, it sends the block sequence number along with the NAK back to the transmitting device. The transmitting device now knows which particular block of data was received in error, slides the transmission window back to the NAK'd block, and resumes transmission from that point.

Selective ARQ Continuous ARQ's requirement to retransmit *all* blocks of data from the NAK'd block forward is more efficient than discrete ARQ but can still be made more efficient. **Selective ARQ** increases efficiency by requiring only the retransmission of the blocks received in error rather than the block in error and all subsequent blocks.

Flow Control How does the transmitting device remember what data were in which block? Obviously, the data must be stored and saved somewhere in the block sequence order in which it was transmitted. That somewhere is in **buffer memory.** The addition of this buffer memory as well as the sophisticated programming necessary to manage the flow of data into and out of this memory adds additional costs to these devices. The benefits of increased data throughput and resultant reduced phone circuit usage must be weighed against the increased cost of this more sophisticated technology when making informed business decisions on technology acquisition.

The constant storage and retrieval of blocks of data from this finite amount of buffer memory necessitates some type of management of the use of this memory. That management is commonly known as **flow control.** Simply stated, flow control controls the flow of data into and out of the buffer memory to avoid any loss of data. The flow control management software must constantly monitor the amount of free space available in buffer memory and tell the sending device to stop sending data when there is insufficient storage space. That signal to stop sending data, and the subsequent signal to resume sending data, may be either hardware or software based.

Hardware flow control—RTS/CTS **Hardware flow control** was actually introduced in Chapter 3 in the section "RS-232". Pin 4, Request to Send (RTS), and pin 5, Clear to Send (CTS), are the essential elements of hardware flow control. A transmitting device will only send data into buffer memory as long as pin 5, Clear to Send, continues to be "held high" or carry an appropriate voltage. As soon as Clear to Send is "dropped," or the appropriate voltage ceases on pin 5, the transmitting device would immediately cease transmitting data.

Software flow control—XON/XOFF Rather than controlling flow through pins 4 and 5, actual characters could be transmitted on pin 2 and received on pin 3, which would mean either "Stop Sending Data" or "Resume Sending Data." When a device cannot receive data any longer, it sends an XOFF control character to the transmitting device. The more familiar keyboard representation of XOFF is the keystroke combination of CTRL-S. The transmitting device would not resume data transmission until it received an XON control character, CTRL-Q on the keyboard.

Practical Advice and Information

SOFTWARE VS. HARDWARE FLOW CONTROL

It has been the authors' experience that hardware flow control is more reliable and usually faster than software flow control. Remember that software flow control is nothing more than transmitted characters susceptible to the same transmission problems as normal data. Occasionally, an XOFF may be transmitted in error and stop a data transmission session for no apparent reason. Also, because XON and XOFF are characters, they are received in on pin 3 along with all the "normal" data and must be differentiated from that data. This process takes time (adds latency) and is subject to error.

Forward Error Correction Sophisticated error correction techniques exist that send sufficient redundant data to the receiving modem to enable it to not only detect, but also correct data transmission errors without the need for retransmission. Forward error correction works in a manner similar to the data correction techniques previously explained. On the transmitting side, the incoming data signal is processed, and redundant code bits are generated based on that incoming signal. These additional redundant bits are added to the original signal and transmitted to the receiving device. The receiving device processes the incoming data signal in the same manner as the transmitting device and regenerates the redundant code bits. The transmitted redundant code bits are compared with the redundant code bits regenerated by the receiving modem. If they match, then no errors have occurred on the incoming signal. If they don't match, the forward error correction circuitry at the receiving device uses the transmitted redundant bits to correct the incoming data signal, thereby correcting transmission errors without the need for retransmission.

However, there is a downside to forward error correction. In data communications, just as in life, you can't get something for nothing. To give the receiving modem sufficient redundant data to be able to correct its own detected errors, the overall throughput of informational data on the circuit is reduced. This process, known as **forward error correction,** tries to favorably balance how much redundant data can be sent "up front," thereby avoiding retransmissions, to maximize overall throughput on the circuit. It's a bit of a gamble really:

- If not enough redundant data are sent, the overall throughput is reduced due to retransmissions.
- If too much redundant data are sent, the overall throughput is reduced because the redundant data are taking up space and processing power that could be occupied by "new" nonredundant data.

Trellis-Coded Modulation **Trellis-coded modulation (TCM)** is another way in which transmission errors can be overcome without the need for retransmission. Modems that employ TCM are able to overcome twice as much noise on a given circuit as QAM modems, which don't employ TCM. Intersymbol interference can cause a modem to detect the wrong constellation point and subsequently interpret that constellation point into an incorrect sequence of bits. Using a sophisticated technique known as **convolutional encoding,** TCM adds a redundant bit that limits the possible valid constellation points for the current transmission. By limiting the number of possible constellation points that are potentially valid for any given symbol received, the modem is able to avoid misinterpreting symbols that would ordinarily lead to retransmissions to correct the error.

For example, if we wanted to send 6 data bits per baud, that would ordinarily require a 64-point constellation (2^6). However, by adding a seventh TCM code bit to each 6-data bits, a 128-point constellation would be generated (2^7). But remember, only 64 constellation points are required to transmit the original 6 data bits per baud, so only 64 of the 128 possible detectable constellation points are defined as valid. If one of the invalid constellation points is detected, the TCM circuitry selects the most likely valid constellation point and its associated pattern of bits. In this manner, TCM reduces errors and the need for retransmission due to line impairments. However, error detection and correction techniques must still be employed.

The sophistication of a given TCM scheme is measured by the number of potential trellis codes or states. The greater the number of TCM states, the higher the required processing power in the modems, and the higher immunity to intersymbol interference due to line noise. TCM was first introduced as part of the V.32 modem standard and is supported by V.34 and V.90 modems.

Error Control Standards *MNP4* The MNP error control standards were originally developed by Microcom, a modem manufacturer. The MNP standards include Classes 2, 3, and 4. These error control standards optimize the full-duplex transmission of data over dial-up lines through adaptive size packet assembly and the elimination of redundant or overhead information from transmissions.

V.42 Not to be confused with the CCITT V.42bis standard for data compression, **V.42** incorporates MNP Class 4 error control as the first of two possible error control protocols. In addition, a second error control protocol known as **link access protocol for modems,** or **LAP-M,** adds Selective ARQ to the capabilities of MNP Class 4 error control protocol. Selective ARQ, described earlier, only requires retransmission of specific blocks received in error rather than all blocks subsequent to the block in which the error was detected. V.42 also provides for negotiation during modem handshaking to allow two modems to decide whether they will implement MNP 4 or LAP-M as an error control protocol for their data transmission.

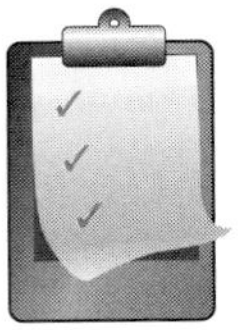

Practical Advice and Information

HARDWARE VS. SOFTWARE ERROR CONTROL

MNP 4 and V.42 are error control protocols implemented within modems. Using these protocols, the modems themselves ensure error-free transmission. There is no need for additional error control protocols supplied by communications software packages running as an application program on a PC.

Dial Backup/Auto Restoral Leasing either an analog or digital dedicated circuit (leased line) from a phone company can provide high bandwidth data transmission of guaranteed quality. That's the good news. The bad news is that, despite what the phone company sales rep may say, *leased lines do periodically fail.* It should stand to reason that the more complicated the circuit, the more likely it is to fail. It has been our experience that multipoint lines are more likely to fail than point-to-point leased lines.

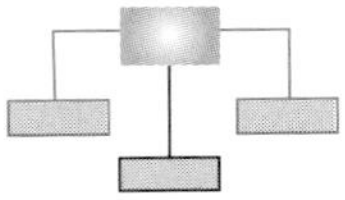

Managerial Perspective

LEASED LINE BACKUP

Coping with leased line failure requires a business decision. The technology is available to backup failed leased lines by automatically establishing connections via dial-up lines between points on the failed circuit. However, at least two incremental costs are involved in this automatic backup. First, there is the cost of the additional technology necessary to detect the leased line failure and establish the dial-up connection. Second, dial-up circuits must be available for the auto dial backup unit to utilize in the event of a leased line failure. These dial-up circuits would incur both installation and monthly charges whether or not they are used. In addition, if the established dial backup connection is long distance, then per minute usage charges for the dial-up lines could amount to a significant incremental cost. The other side of the cost benefit equation would require the following question to be asked, "What is the cost of the business lost during the time that the leased line is down?" If that lost business can be translated into lost sales dollars in excess of the incremental cost of establishing and maintaining the dial-up backup for the failed leased line, then the acquisition of the equipment and phone lines to enable automatic backup would constitute a prudent business decision.

Some leased line modems possess sufficient technology to be able to monitor the failed leased line after establishing the **dial backup,** sense when service on the leased line has been repaired, and automatically restore the data transmission back onto the leased line in a process known as **auto-restoral.** Sometimes this automatic backup and/or restoral capability is built into the modem (analog) or CSU/DSU (digital). These built-in features are known as integral, whereas the dedicated devices that are designed to do only automatic backup and/or restoral are known as stand-alone devices. In this way, the automatic backup and restoral capability can be added after the initial modem or CSU/DSU purchase, if required.

CSU/DSUs used on digital leased lines can offer an additional backup option compared with analog modems. Automatic backup and restoral features on a CSU/DSU have a choice as to which available switched or dial-up services to access when establishing the backup connection. Some digital CSU/DSUs access analog dial-up lines from the public switched telephone network (PSTN) for backup, whereas other CSU/DSUs access switched 56 K or ISDN dial-up digital services in the event of a digital leased line failure.

Practical Advice and Information

CSU/DSU SOURCING

One of the major functions of the CSU/DSU is to perform diagnostic tests to determine the cause of service interruption. A word of warning: If you buy your own CSU/DSUs rather than rent or buy them from the provider of the DDS service, you run the risk of being stuck between the proverbial rock and a hard place during service interruptions when:

- The DDS leased line provider says the problem is in your CSU/DSU.
- The CSU/DSU provider says the problem is in your DDS service.

Many DDS providers also rent or sell the CSU/DSUs. In the authors' experience, there is usually no significant difference in price between buying CSU/DSUs from the carriers or from a data communications equipment distributor. By buying CSU/DSUs from the DDS provider, you will be able to make them totally responsible for the delivery of the service through their DCEs to your DTEs, thereby avoiding any possible fingerpointing.

More Secure

In addition to the need for reliable data communications, there exists an increasing business need for security of both transmitted data and controlled access to the corporate network over which that data are transmitted. Modem technology has been developed that provides solutions to both of these security-related issues. Although network security will be dealt with in detail in Chapter 12, security issues related to modem-based transmission are detailed here.

Granting dial-up network access only to those individuals properly authorized is most often accomplished through either one or both of the following techniques:

- **Password protection**
- **Dial back or callback security**

Password Protection and Callback Units Password protection may already be familiar as a means of controlling access to a local area network, minicomputer, or mainframe. However, it is important to understand that, in this case, it is an additional layer of password protection offered by certain modems or auxiliary add-on devices. Typically, a modem would answer an incoming call and require a password before allowing the calling party access to the network. Failure to enter a valid password in a limited amount of time will cause the answering modem to terminate the call. As telecommuting and remote access have increased in popularity, however, the need for increased levels of dial-in security have increased proportionately.

Some modems add an additional layer of security beyond password protection. Once a valid password and/or user ID has been entered, the answering modem:

1. Terminates the call
2. Looks up and validates the user ID and/or password in a directory
3. Finds the phone number of the valid user in the directory
4. Dials the valid user back and establishes the communication session

Do not confuse this dial back unit with the dial backup unit employed for leased line failure recovery. The advantages of a dial back system include the following:

- Only valid users can gain access to the network.
- Valid users are easily maintained in one central directory. By merely eliminating terminated employees from the directory, one can prevent unauthorized network access. Of course, this assumes that users do not tell each other their passwords, either purposefully or accidentally.
- Users can also have network access restricted according to time of day or day of the week. This information would also be stored in the central directory.
- Some dial back units save and report usage information such as user ID, date and time, length of session, resources accessed, etc.

The disadvantages of a dial back system include the following:

- By always dialing back valid users, the central location of the dial back unit always incurs any long-distance phone charges.
- The fixed dial back phone number for each valid user does not work well for traveling users such as field representatives.

Only calling back users at a previously designated phone number is known as **fixed callback.** To overcome this problem, some dial back units feature **variable callback,** wherein valid users enter both a password and a phone number to which the dial back unit should return the call.

Modem Technology Analysis

Having thoroughly studied the functionality of modems, a technology analysis grid such as the one illustrated in Figure 4-12 can be constructed. As a network analyst, you decide which of the myriad of available modem functions listed along the horizontal axis of the technology analysis grid are most important to your business. This analysis is accomplished using the top-down model as described at the beginning of this chapter (Figure 4-1). Next, the functional characteristics present in various modems from a variety of vendors (vertical axis; modems A through Z) are plotted on the technology analysis grid. In this manner, you are able to graphically see which modems meet the functional requirements of your business.

	Transmission Protocols						Error Control		Data Compression				Physical Characteristics									FAX Features			Transmission Services				Support Services							
	V.90	V.34	V.32bis	V.32	V.32terbo	V.22bis	V.42	MNP4	V.42bis	V.42bis Dictionary Size	V.42bis String Length	MNP5	PCMCIA/External/Internal	Maximum DCE Speed	Maximum DTE Speed	Serial Port	Parallel Port	2-wire Interface	4-wire Interface	Dial-up	Leased Line	Group 3	Class 1	Class 2	POTS	Analog Leased	ISDN	Cellular	Caller ID Support	DSVD	Distinctive Ring	Software Included	Cables Included	Flash ROM Upgradable	Warranty	Tech Support Options/Cost
Modem A																																				
Modem B																																				
Modem C																																				
Modem D																																				
.																																				
.																																				
.																																				
Modem Z																																				

Figure 4-12 Modem Technology Analysis Grid

COMMUNICATIONS SOFTWARE TECHNOLOGY ANALYSIS

The Hardware/Software Interface

Communications software interprets business data communication needs into a language that the data communications hardware can understand. Communications software is an application program that should offer easy to understand screens from which users can initiate, maintain, and terminate data communications sessions. Commands entered or menu items selected in the communications software are passed along to the operating system of the PC in question, which, in turn, interfaces directly to the PC's hardware such as an integral modem card or serial port. Communications software is the interface between data communications needs and the data communication hardware. Figure 4-13 graphically illustrates where communi-

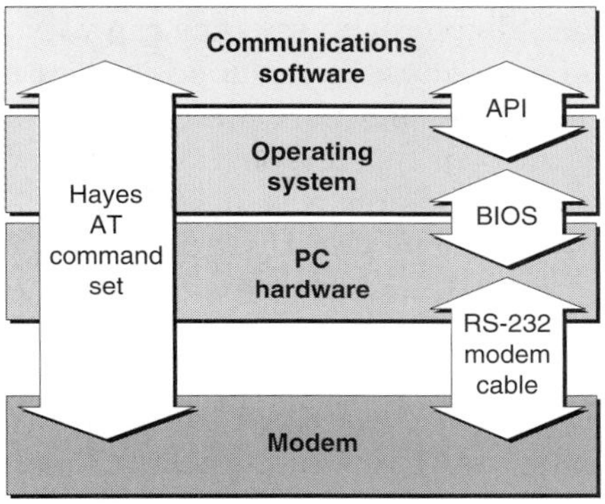

Figure 4-13 The Role of Communications Software

cations software fits into a PC-based data communications session and the numerous interfaces involved.

As can be seen in Figure 4-13, several interfaces are involved in the process of communications software's interaction with a modem.

- The communication software must be compatible with the operating system of the PC. Applications programs such as communication software interact with an operating system via **application program interfaces (API).** APIs are a series of commands embedded within the communication software that are understood by the installed operating system. APIs are discussed further in later chapters.
- The operating system interacts with the PC hardware (CPU, memory, serial port, etc.) via a series of commands known as the **basic input output system (BIOS).**
- The PC is physically connected to the modem either via the PC's bus, an RS-232 port, or a USB port.

Hayes AT Command Set and the Modem Setup Strings The interfaces described in the previous section establish a physical link between the communications software and the modem. But how can the communications software talk to the modem? What language or commands does the modem understand? How does the communications software wake up or initialize the modem?

The answer to all of these questions is that a de facto standard known as the **Hayes AT command set** exists for commands understood by both communication software and modems. The "AT" in Hayes AT command set is itself a command that stands for "attention," a command sent from the communications software to the modem to let it know a command is forthcoming. Other examples of Hayes commands include ATDT followed by a number, which means tone dial the given number, or ATDP, which means pulse dial the given number. Pauses can also be inserted into a dial string to wait for a second dial tone for an outside line. Modems that understand commands from the Hayes AT command set are termed **Hayes compatible.**

One of the most important uses of the Hayes AT command set is to construct and send **modem setup strings** from the communications software to the modem to initiate a communications session. Sending the modem setup string amounts to a handshaking between the PC and the modem. Although nearly all modems support the Hayes AT command set, they can vary widely in the particular commands and parameters that must be included in their modem setup strings. These setup strings are not always straightforward or easily written by novices to the field of data communications. For this reason, it is important that the communications software package purchased includes a setup string for the modem or modems that are to be used. If many different modems from many different manufacturers are to be used, it is essential to purchase a communications software package with numerous setup strings. Numbers of included setup strings may vary from none to several hundred.

Redirection for Local Area Network Based Modems The previous example of a hardware/software interface assumed that a dedicated external modem was attached to the local PC's serial port. What would happen if the local PC were attached to a local area network (LAN) and the modem were attached to the LAN server rather than to the local serial port as illustrated in Figure 4-14?

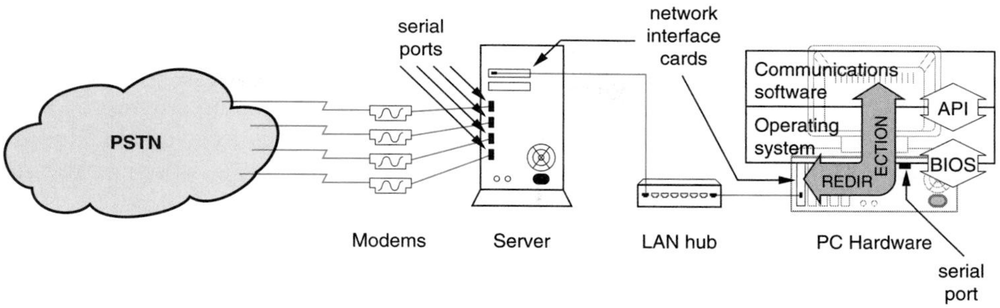

Figure 4-14 Redirection for Local Area Network-Based Modems

Sharing modems in this way can be a very cost-effective alternative to all users having their own dedicated modems. The shared modems are hooked to a high-powered PC known as a server. In some cases, the sole job of this server is to manage modem access and other data communications-related tasks, in which case it is known as a **communications server** or **remote access server.**

Even though a user's PC is hooked to a network, the communications software is still running on the individual user's PC. The difficulty arises in that the modem is not directly attached to the PC as the communications software would normally expect. To access the modem attached to the network's communications server, the communications software must send instructions and data out through the PC's **network interface card** rather than the PC's serial port. A network interface card is a board that plugs into a PC and allows the network cabling to attach this particular PC to other PCs on the same network.

To redirect modem output to a network interface card rather than the local serial port, a communications package must support two specialized interfaces or interrupts.

- If the local area network is using Novell's NetWare network operating system, then the communication software must be able to redirect modem output to a software interface known as NASI (NetWare asynchronous service interface) so that communications can be redirected by the local operating system to the local network interface card rather than the local serial port.
- If the local area network is using a Microsoft network operating system, then the communications software must be able to redirect modem output to a software interface known as **Int14 (Interrupt 14)**

Communication Software Functionality

Applied Problem Solving

TOP-DOWN APPROACH TO COMMUNICATIONS SOFTWARE ANALYSIS

How can a network analyst ensure that the *right* communication software package is purchased? In a manner similar to that employed for modem analysis at the beginning of the chapter, by following a top-down approach, network analysts can ensure that purchased communications software meets stated business objectives.

Business Issues The first concerns in the top-down approach to needs analysis are the business-related needs. In Figure 4-15, the business layer model, has been divided into two distinct segments: business perspectives and business activities. Business perspectives are those overriding business needs that underlie specific business activities. These business perspectives are key assumptions that must be documented before business activity analysis begins. Examples of business perspectives related to communications software might be:

- Communications software must be easy to use.

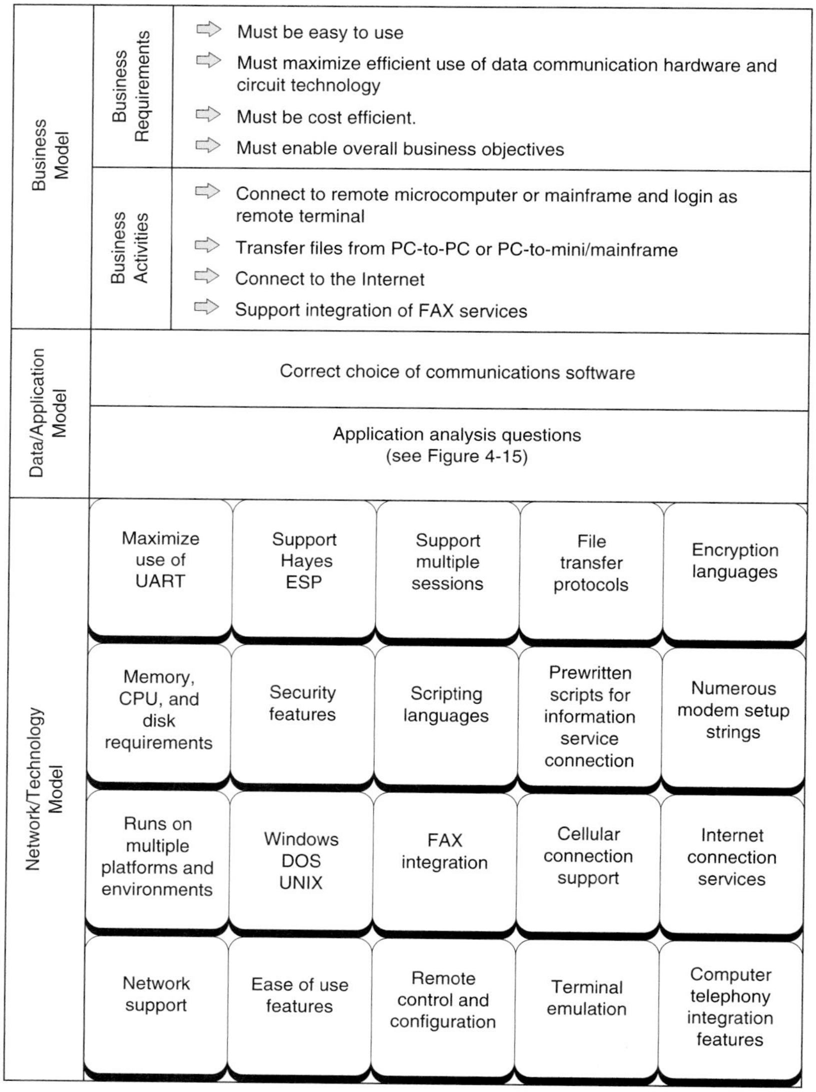

Figure 4-15 Top-Down Approach to Communications Software Analysis

- Communications software must maximize the efficient use of available hardware and transmission services.
- Purchase of communications software must be cost-effective. (Prices can range from free to $400 or more.)
- Communications software must enable overall business objectives such as improved customer service, more efficient operations, and better and faster information to decision makers.

The themes of ease of use, maximum efficiency, cost-effectiveness, and support of overall business objectives serve as the starting point for requirements of the business layer that will be passed down to lower layers of the top-down model. It is important to note that other nonlisted business perspectives as dictated by you or your business should be added to the model.

Broadly speaking, the following items summarize typical business uses of communications software. Again, you should add your own business uses of communications software.

- Connect to a remote minicomputer or mainframe and login as a remote terminal
- Transfer files from PC to PC, or from PC to mini/mainframe
- Connect to the Internet
- Support integration with fax services

Although these general statements summarize the most popular uses of communications software, additional analysis is necessary to determine the best communications software package for an individual or company based on their particular required business activities and perspectives.

Analysis Questions Map Technical Features to Business Needs Notice the placement of the "Correct Choice of Communication Software" in the top-down analysis model (Figure 4-15). It bridges the gap between the business perspectives and activities of the upper business layer and the myriad of technical features found in different communications software packages as listed in the network model or technology layer.

Figure 4-16, summarizes some key analysis questions used to assist in determining the best communications software package for a particular individual or business, as well as the options and implications of those questions. Analysis questions are designed to help the network analyst decide which communications software features are most important to have the purchased communication software meet stated business objectives. Again, add to the list of analysis questions as you see fit.

As the implications of each of the questions listed in Figure 4-16 are explored, each of the technical features listed in the network/technical model layer of Figure 4-15 will be explained. Few, if any communications software packages contain all of these features. Furthermore, few, if any businesses need all of these features. The real challenge is to determine which of these technical features are truly necessary to support business activities and then to find the best-priced communication software package that offers those features.

Analysis Question/Technical Feature	Importance/Implication
What are the hardware requirements of the communications software package?	Minimum processor, memory, and disk requirements
Which minicomputer or mainframe do you wish to log into?	Logging into minicomputers or mainframes requires terminal emulation. Variety of terminals emulated varies from 10 to 36.
Do you wish to transfer files to/from a PC, minicomputer, or mainframe?	Same file transfer protocol must run on each machine. Number of file transfer protocols ranges from 8 to 16. Some packages offer high-performance proprietary transfer protocols.
Is the modem hooked directly to your PC or to a modem server?	Not all communications packages are able to redirect output to network interface cards. Different network operating systems use different redirection interrupts.
Do you want to log onto Internet or other information services?	Software packages vary in the number of browsers included and in the number of prewritten scripts included for automatic access to information services.
What are your security requirements? Will other users be dialing into this computer?	Security features might include password protection/encryption, data encryption, callback security support, or remote file transfer lock out.
Do your modems support V.42 and/or MNP 4 error control?	If not, the file transfer protocols included in the communication software will have to supply their own error control.
Will remote control or configuration be required?	Some packages offer remote control capabilities.
Will you be using a cellular phone network with this software?	Some packages include special enhancements to improve performance over cellular networks.
Will you be sending/receiving faxes through this software?	Some communications software packages include integrated fax functionality.
Will you need to control your phone from your PC?	Some packages offer computer telephony integration functionality such as on-screen telephone pad and dialer or support of CTI APIs.
How many different computers and operating systems does this software run on?	In a multiplatform environment, it would be nice to be able to run all of the same communications software.
Will modems of numerous manufacturers be used?	If so, you will want a communications software package with as many modem setup strings as possible.
Will you need to conduct more than one communication session simultaneously?	Some communications software packages support management of multiple simultaneous communication sessions.

Figure 4-16 Analysis Questions Map Technical Features to Business Needs

In Sharper Focus

FILE TRANSFER PROTOCOLS

As identified on the business activities layer of our top-down model, the establishment, management, and termination of file transfers is one of the most common uses of communications software. Obviously, these file transfers must be free of errors. In some cases, the necessary error control is supplied as a function of the modems employed in the data transmission. MNP Class 4 and V.42, discussed earlier in this chapter, are two of the most common modem-based error control protocols.

File transfer protocols, part of a communications software package, can also offer error control capabilities. As many as 15 or more file transfer protocols may be included in a given communications software package. If the modems to be used for data transmission do not supply their own error control, then be sure to purchase communications software that includes sufficient file transfer protocols with error control. Remember, for modems to furnish error control capabilities over a data transmission circuit, *both* modems must support the same error control protocol. Figure 4-17 summarizes the characteristics of popular file transfer protocols, including their error control capabilities.

As seen in Figure 4-17, file transfer protocols can differ by a relatively few criteria:

- Error checking technique: Checksum, CRC, CRC-16, CRC-32.
- Request for retransmit: Stop and wait ACK/NAK, sliding window, none (Streaming).
- Block size in bytes: 128, 1K, variable depending on line quality.
- Others: Batch capability, multiple platforms, auto-recovery.

File transfer protocols with the suffix of "G" (XMODEM-G, YMODEM-G) are known as **streaming protocols** because they do not stop transmitting a file until they reach an end of file indicator. These file transfer protocols are an appropriate choice if error control is being handled by the modems using MNP Class 4 or V.42 error control protocols. In these cases, since the error control is being handled by the hardware, there is no need for the communications software to add additional error control and its associated overhead.

Block size may be of a fixed length of either 128 or 1024 bytes, or it may vary according the quality of the data transmission circuit. The adaptive packet length protocols will usually produce the greatest throughput on circuits of varying quality. Other features that may be important, depending on the detailed business activities as analyzed in the top-down analysis, might include

- Batch capability that would allow multiple file transfers to take place sequentially without user intervention.
- Multiple platform capability that is essential for those users or businesses who wish to conduct PC to minicomputer or mainframe file transfers. Kermit is an excellent example of a multiplatform file transfer protocol.
- Finally, **ZMODEM** offers a rather unique feature that has become especially popular with BBS (bulletin board service) users who pay by the minute for connection to on-line bulletin boards. An auto-recovery feature

File Transfer Protocol	Differentiating Features	Block Size	Error Control	Application Notes
XMODEM -checksum		128 bytes/block	ACK/NAK stop and wait ARQ, checksum error control	Public domain, widely used; stop and wait ARQ is not efficient
XMODEM-CRC	CRC improves error detection			
XMODEM-1K	1024 bytes (1KB) per block	1024 bytes/block 128 bytes/block fallback		Sometimes called YMODEM; Uses CRC, may have batch capability
XMODEM-G	G implies a streaming protocol			File transfer protocol offers no error control; relies on modems with MNP 4 or V.42
YMODEM -CRC-16	Adds CRC-16 error control to YMODEM		CRC-16	
YMODEM-Batch	Batch capability			Allows transfers to be controlled by separate executable files; supports multiple file transfers at a given time.
ZMODEM	Dynamically adjusts packet size as in MNP 4; automatic recovery from aborted file transfers.		CRC-32 silding window	Widely used by BBS users
Kermit	Multiple platform availability		ACK/NAK; stop and wait ARQ	Great for transfers to minicomputers or mainframes; not very fast.
Sliding Window Kermit	Adds sliding window ARQ to Kermit		Continuous ARQ	Faster; may not be available on all of the platforms that Kermit is available on

Figure 4-17 Comparative Features of File Transfer Protocols

allows an aborted file transfer to resume at the point where the transfer aborted rather than starting the transfer over at the beginning of the file. Amazingly, it also doesn't matter when you resume the transfer, assuming both files still exist.

Technology Analysis

Communications software, like most data communications technology, has undergone significant evolution in the past few years. Modem manufacturers now often include high-quality communications software at no extra cost to differentiate their products from competitors. Operating systems now often include communication software functionality. As a result, many of today's communications software packages are more correctly categorized as remote control or remote access products designed primarily to assist telecommuting professionals in accessing corporate data resources from their offices. Remote control and remote access software are reviewed in Chapter 10.

Figure 4-18 is a communications software technology analysis grid. Technical features of communications software packages are outlined along the horizontal axis. The implications or importance of these features were highlighted in Figure 4-16. Currently available communications software packages would be listed along the vertical axis. The technical features available in any given package would be plotted within the technology analysis grid. Having determined which technical features were most important in meeting stated business objectives, the network analyst could easily and objectively determine which communications software package would offer the greatest required functionality for the best price.

	System Requirements						File Transfer Features			Network Redirection Features			Internet Connections				Security Features						FAX and Phone Features						Program Features								
	RAM Size	Disk Space	CPU Chip Type and Speed	Windows 9x	Windows NT/2000	Other Platforms	Number of File Transfer Protocols	File Transfer in Background	Supports External Protocols	TCP/IP Support	Int 14	NASI	Mail Service	News Reader	Web Browser	FTP File Transfer	Password Protection	Data Encryption	Callback Capability	Remote File Transfer Lock Out	Private Messages/Mail	Log Calls	FAX Support	Switch from Data to Voice	Telephone Pad/Dialer	Answering Machine/Voice Mail	Import/Export from Other Communications Software	Number of Entries per Phone Directory	Context-Sensitive Help	Functions Supplied on Icon Bar	Direct Cable Connection Supported	Maximum Number of Communication Ports Supported	Number of Modem Setup Strings	Number of Terminal Emulations	32 bit Multi-threading Design	Modem Indicator Lights	Unattended Host Mode
Software A																																					
Software B																																					
Software C																																					
Software D																																					
.																																					
.																																					
.																																					
Software Z																																					

Figure 4-18 Communications Software Technology Analysis Grid

SUMMARY

By employing the top-down model in the analysis of currently available modem technology, any modem functionality should deliver on at least one of the following business communications requirements: faster, more efficient (cheaper), more reliable, or more secure.

By focusing on how data communications devices of any type deliver on predetermined business requirements and objectives, one can avoid purchasing technology that may be appealing or cleverly marketed, but which lacks the ability to deliver a positive impact on business objectives.

Current modem standards include V.34 and V.90. V.34 is the newest analog modem standard, offering transmission speeds up to 33.6 Kbps in both directions. V.90 is a hybrid analog/digital standard that offers an asymmetrical transmission rate of up to 56 Kbps from a remote server to the modem and up to 33.6 Kbps from the modem to the server.

Current modulation standards such as V.34 and V.90 can deliver even more throughput over dial-up lines when compression standards such as MNP5 or V.42bis are applied. As this increasing sophistication in dial-up modems has yielded ever faster transmission speeds over dial-up lines, the types of network services offered by carriers have also evolved.

ISDN is a dial-up digital service offering 128 Kbps that has become a popular option for Internet access. Since ISDN is a digital service, it does not require a modem, but rather a device known alternatively as a terminal adapter, digital modem, or NT-1.

Reliability of data transmissions is ensured by the net effect of three related processes: error prevention, error detection, and error correction.

Error prevention can be accomplished via forward error correction techniques such as TCM or through adaptive protocols that adjust transmission characteristics in response to changing line conditions. Error detection is accomplished through a variety of techniques in which the transmitting and receiving modems transmit and verify some sort of error check bit or character in addition to the transmitted data itself. Techniques such as parity, LRC, checksums, CRC-16, and CRC-32 vary in both the level of complexity of their error checking routines and their ability to detect bursts of multiple bit errors.

Error correction is accomplished in general through retransmission of those characters received in error. Techniques such as discrete ARQ, continuous ARQ, and selective ARQ vary in how efficiently their retransmission is accomplished.

Security is provided by a variety of techniques that can be integrated into modems or added via standalone devices. Callback access combined with password protection are typical modem-based security features.

Communications software is a key component in linking a user's communications requirements to the modems and network services that deliver on those desires. Communications software varies widely in features and price. As a result, a careful business-oriented analysis is required using a technology analysis grid such as those supplied in this chapter to objectively compare the many technological alternatives in a structured manner.

KEY TERMS

ACE
ACK/NAK
acknowledgment
adaptive protocols
adaptive size packet assembly
advanced parallel technology
adverse channel enhancements
amplifier
API
application program interfaces
APT
ARQ
asymmetrical transmission
attenuation
auto-restoral

automatic retransmission Request
basic input output system
Bell 103
Bell 212A
BIOS
block sequence number
buffer memory
callback security
checksums
communications server
continuous ARQ
convolutional encoding
CRC
CRC-16
CRC-32
cyclic redundancy checks
data compression
dial backup
Discrete ARQ
dynamic speed shifts
error correction
error detection
error prevention
fixed callback
flow control
forward error correction
hardware flow control
Hayes AT command set
Hayes compatible accelerator
Huffman encoding
Int14
Interrupt 14
Kermit
LAP-M
line conditioning
link access protocol for modems
longitudinal redundancy checks
LRC
Microcom Networking Protocols
MNP
MNP Class 5
modem setup strings
negative acknowledgment
network interface card
parity
password protection
principle of shifting bottlenecks
quantization noise
remote access server
repeater
run-length encoding
selective ARQ
sliding window protocol
software flow control
streaming protocols
TCM
throughput
trellis-coded modulation
V.22bis
V.32
V.32bis
V.32 ter
V.34
V.42
V.42bis
V.90
variable callback
vertical redundancy check
VRC
XMODEM
XON/XOFF
YMODEM
ZMODEM

REVIEW QUESTIONS

1. How is a technology analysis grid employed in a business networking requirements analysis and design?
2. What is the difference between discrete ARQ and continuous ARQ?
3. What inefficiency is inherent in a data transmission session utilizing discrete ARQ over a full-duplex circuit?
4. Which modulation technique is employed in a V.34 modem?
5. How does a V.90 modem system overcome the 33.6 Kbps limit as dictated by Shannon's Law?
6. What is quantization error?
7. Explain why V.90 is asymmetrical in nature?
8. What is the potential throughput of a V.34 modem with V.42bis data compression?
9. Why are standards important when it comes to data compression?
10. How can the top-down model remain useful given the rate of rapidly changing technology?
11. What effect does trellis-coded modulation have on the number of constellation points and the number of data bits interpreted per detectable event?
12. What is meant by an adaptive protocol? Give at least two examples.
13. What are the key differences between V.32 and V.32bis?
14. What does *bis* stand for?
15. Explain the significance of the phrase "fully standard compliant" in terms of modem standards.
16. How does data compression work?
17. Why can't a 4:1 compression ratio always be achieved with V.42bis?
18. What is the difference between V.42 and V.42bis?
19. Why is error-free transmission so important to successful data compression?
20. In general, what are the advantages of DDS over analog leased lines?
21. How can one avoid being caught in the middle of fingerpointing when purchasing a CSU/DSU?
22. Why is a CSU/DSU different in function than a modem?
23. What are some of the most common uses of switched digital services?
24. What is handshaking and what does it have to do with modem interoperability?

25. What is the Hayes AT command set and why is it significant?
26. Elaborate on the relationship between error prevention, error detection, and error correction.
27. What are the major differences between repeaters and amplifiers?
28. Explain how multiple bit errors can remain undetected using simple parity checking.
29. Explain how LRC overcomes parity checking's inability to detect multiple bit errors.
30. Explain in simple terms how checksums and CRCs detect transmission errors.
31. What is meant by a sliding window protocol?
32. What is selective ARQ?
33. How are block sequence numbers related to sliding window protocols?
34. What role does buffer memory play in the implementation of sliding window protocols?
35. Explain the differences between hardware and software flow control.
36. Explain why hardware or software flow control may be more reliable.
37. What is forward error correction and what is the trade-off involved in such a protocol?
38. What is the difference between a dial back unit and a dial backup unit?
39. What is variable callback and when might it be required?
40. What are the potential security risks in variable callback?
41. What are the important issues to consider when purchasing communications software?
42. What are the issues when modems are to be accessed via a LAN rather than directly attached to a PC?
43. What is a UART and how does it relate to communications software choices?
44. What are the key differentiating factors between file transfer protocols?
45. What is the principle of shifting bottlenecks? Give an example.
46. Explain both a short-term and long-term solution to the current PC serial port bottleneck.
47. Explain at least three significant technical innovations introduced as part of the V.34 standard.
48. Differentiate between MNP5 and V.42bis.
49. Differentiate between MNP4 and V.42.
50. What are some of the dangers in buying prestandard data communications equipment?

ACTIVITIES

1. Install a modem and associated communications software. Document your installation procedure as well as any problems encountered and problem-solving techniques employed.
2. Using a modem advertisement of your choice or one chosen by your instructor, write a technical memo to a nontechnically oriented manager explaining the features of the modem in terms of business layer impact. Prepare a cost/benefit analysis and make a recommendation as to whether the modem in question should be purchased.
3. Investigate and report on the difference between modem standards and fax modem standards. Which organizations set fax standards? Does communications software interact with the fax part of the modem, or is other software required?
4. Prepare a comparative budget for a long-distance data transmission between two cities of your choice. Compare the cost vs. available bandwidth of such a transmission for each of the following three scenarios:
   - V.90/V.34 modems, dial-up lines
   - CSU/DSUs, switched 56K lines
   - ISDN lines
   - DSL lines
   - Cable modems
5. Using file transfer or communications software, prepare a graph showing the results of the transfer of various sized files using different file transfer. Record any error messages received as well as transfer time and file size. Abort and restart the transfer mid-way using different file transfer protocols and record results.
6. Research product tests or buyers guides of V.34 modems. Report on the results of performance tests regarding actual throughput. What percentage of the time is the 28.8 Kbps rate maintained?
7. Research and prepare a presentation on the Hayes AT command set. How many commands are sup-

ported? What is the purpose of the registers? What are the limitations?

8. Research and report on the results of the comparative impact of the USB in solving the serial port bottleneck problem.

9. Some communications software packages include scripting languages. What is the business application for such languages and what characteristics or features are important?

CASE STUDY

Ford Steps on Global Web Marketing Gas

GM, Nissan and others making e-comm moves.

DEARBORN, MICH.–Ford Motor Co. last week aired plans to get its 5,000 car dealers on the same e-commerce page.

The broad cooperative Web marketing effort will include designing Web sites for individual dealers that have a common look and feel, and enabling the dealers to offer a similar set of online services, from insurance policies to car sales. To do this, Ford is taking the unusual step of setting up an as-yet-unnamed joint venture with Trilogy Software, which helped design the current Ford.com site.

With Trilogy's founder and CEO Chris Porch in charge, this new Austin, Texas-based venture is expected next month to begin providing Web design services to Ford, its dealers and perhaps other clientele. Ford isn't disclosing its investment in the joint venture, but not surprisingly, the company hinted the undertaking could go public in the future.

"We want to make sure our dealers have the tools to get leads and make sales on the Internet," said Brian Kelley, president of Ford's Consumer-Connect e-commerce division. While Ford's Web site Buyer-Connection.com directs potential buyers to local dealers, the site doesn't support the same type of e-mail negotiation available at rival General Motors' GMBuyPower.com site. That site is where 80% of GM's 7,700 dealers now list their inventories, get customer e-mail and check visitor Web statistics on what cars get the most page views.

The larger issue is how far the big car manufacturers will go to get dealers to support a corporate Web brand. Today, GM dealers have free reign in building Web sites. However, not unlike Ford, GM and its e-Dealers Advisory Council are considering whether to adopt a common look and feel for local dealers, a GM spokeswoman says.

Another competitor, Daimler-Chrysler, has a Web site to generate leads to about 40% of Chrysler's 4,000 dealers on Chrysler car models, but so far the company lacks a unified global Web strategy to reflect its merger with Daimler-Benz.

Ford's upcoming Web makeover might also lead to new pricing mechanisms. "We are looking at invoice pricing for the Internet," Kelley hinted last week. That could mean new cars might be sold more inexpensively on the Web than off.

Analysts say Ford's effort may improve its brand consistency on the Web. Some local Ford dealers' Web sites are so amateurish "they look like their high school sons and daughters must have done them," says Gartner Group Research Director Rob DeSisto.

But the danger is, local individuality could give way to a monolithic look.

DeSisto also warns that Trilogy's strength is in a tool that lets online shoppers put together a desired car model. But he says the company is hardly in a position to provide the wide range of Web services to dealers envisioned by Ford.

"Trilogy's technology footprint will fall far short of what's needed here," DeSisto asserts, pointing out that dealers will need e-mail, customer response management software, mail-campaign software and much more.

LESSONS FROM NISSAN

Global car manufacturer Nissan last year struggled with the daunting task of a Web makeover for purposes of giving potential car buyers a more unified view of car dealerships. Nissan dealers traditionally did their own thing on the Web, but Nissan management decided this was too fragmented an approach in terms of quality and branding.

Nissan is divided into three regional centers – Europe, Japan and North America. For Nissan, the biggest headache in the search for a global Nissan Web brand has been that the nissan.com and nissan.net domain names are held by Nissan Computer, which is now entwined in a trademark dispute with the car maker in a California court.

"This has been a huge drag," says Gary Larsen, manager of brand communications in Europe for the car maker, which had to use nissaneurope.com for his region.

With so many country, language, tax and price differences in Europe, another problem has been maintaining a distinct local flavor on Nissan Web sites while making it easier to find car information. Systems integrator Razorfish has created a Web-based map of Europe for Nissan that lets viewers click on France, for instance, to be linked to nissanfrance.com.

Nissan's new European Web look has meant that local dealers had to agree to turn over control of their Web site content and management to Nissan Europe.

"They felt this was pragmatic, and they agreed to do it," Larsen says. "We now have these microsites in numerous languages so every national Nissan site can link into these."

Dealers now exchange Web files with Nissan's central command for Europe in Amsterdam. While buyers can now configure the Nissan car they want online and get a quote for it, they cannot buy cars via the Web. But Nissan hints that online car sales are on a road it may take in the future.

Source: Ellen Messmer, "Ford steps on global Web marketing gas," *Network World,* vol. 17, no. 9 (February 28, 2000), p. 10. Copyright Network World. Reprinted with permission.

BUSINESS CASE STUDY QUESTIONS

Activities

1. Complete a top-down model for this case by gleaning facts from the case and placing them in the proper layer of the top-down model. After having completed the top-down model, analyze and detail those instances where requirements were clearly passed down from upper layers to lower layers of the model and where solutions to those requirements were passed up from lower layers to upper layers of the model.
2. Detail any questions about the case that may occur to you for which answers are not clearly stated in the article.

Business

1. What was the business motivation or problem that initiated the search for the implemented solution?
2. What was the customer service impact of the proposed solution?
3. What have Ford's competitors done in the area of a integrated web presence?
4. Is this business opportunity primarily marketing or profit driven?

Application

1. What applications in addition to web services will dealers need?
2. Were any of the auto manufacturers mentioned in the article selling cars on the web at the time the article was written?
3. How are the web sites of the Ford, GM, DaimlerChrysler, and Nissan dealers integrated into the manufacturers web page? Are there any key differences in strategy and approach between manufacturers?

Data

1. What types of data will the network be required to carry?
2. What protocols will be required to deliver the required applications?

Network

1. What underlying network technologies were key to the achievement of stated business objectives?

Technology

1. What specific technologies were employed to deliver the described solution?

CHAPTER 5

LOCAL AREA NETWORK ARCHITECTURES

Concepts Reinforced

OSI Model
Hardware/Software Compatibility
Local Area Networks
Top-Down Model
Protocols and Standards

Concepts Introduced

Access Methodologies
Physical Topologies
IEEE 802 Standards
Logical Topologies
Network Architectures
High-Speed Network Architectures

OBJECTIVES

Upon successful completion of this chapter, you should:

1. Understand how access methodologies, logical topologies, and physical topologies combine to form alternative network architectures.
2. Understand the similarities, differences, advantages, and disadvantages of current network architectures such as Ethernet, token ring, and FDDI.
3. Understand the similarities, differences, advantages, and disadvantages of high-speed network architectures such as 100BaseT, ATM, and gigabit Ethernet.
4. Understand the value of the OSI model in the analysis of network architecture alternatives.
5. Understand how proper LAN analysis can help determine which network architecture is most appropriate in any given situation.

INTRODUCTION

Chapter 5 explores the underlying local area network (LAN) architectures that allow hardware and software technologies to interact transparently. Clients and servers are able to communicate and share information thanks to the combined components of the LAN that links them together. These LAN components are able to offer transparent network transmission services to clients and services due to their adherence to standards and protocols. One of the key distinguishing characteristics of a particular LAN is its network architecture. In this chapter, the components of a network architecture are explored, followed by comparative evaluations of the numerous network architectures either currently available or emerging into the networking marketplace.

THE OSI MODEL

Overall Structure and Characteristics

The **OSI model** consists of a hierarchy of seven layers that loosely group the functional requirements for communication between two computing devices regardless of the software, hardware, or geographical differences between the devices. The power of the OSI model, officially known as ISO Standard 7489, lies in its openness and flexibility. It can be used to organize and define protocols involved in communicating between two computing devices located in the same room as effectively as two devices located on opposite sides of the world.

Each layer in the OSI model relies on lower layers to perform more elementary functions and to offer total transparency as to the intricacies of those functions. At the same time, each layer provides incrementally more sophisticated transparent services to upper layers. In theory, if the transparency of this model is supported, changes in the protocols of one layer should not require changes in protocols of other layers. A **protocol** is a set of rules that govern communication between hardware and/or software components.

Physical Layer

The **physical layer,** also known as layer 1, is responsible for the establishment, maintenance, and termination of physical connections between communicating devices. These connections are sometimes referred to as **point-to-point data links.** The physical layer transmits and receives a stream of bits. There is no data recognition at the physical layer.

Specifically, the physical layer operation is controlled by protocols that define the electrical, mechanical, and procedural specifications for data transmission. The RS232-C specification for serial transmission is an example of a physical layer protocol. Strictly speaking, the physical layer does not define the specifications for connectors and cables that are sometimes referred to as belonging to layer 0.

Data-Link Layer

The **data-link layer** is responsible for providing protocols that deliver reliability to upper layers for the point-to-point connections established by the physical layer protocols. The data-link layer is of particular interest to the study of LANs, as this is the layer in which network architecture standards are defined. These standards are debated and established by the **IEEE (Institute of Electrical and Electronic Engineers) 802** committee and are introduced and explained later in this chapter. The number 802 is derived from the date of the committee's formation in 1980 (80) in the month of February (2).

The data-link layer provides reliability to the physical layer transmission by organizing the bit stream into structured **frames** that add addressing and error checking information. Additional information added to the front of data is called a **header,** whereas information added to the back of data is called a **trailer.** Data-link layer protocols provide error detection, notification, and recovery.

The data-link layer frames are built within the **network interface card** installed in a computer according to the predetermined frame layout particular to the network architecture of the installed network interface card. Network interface cards are given a unique address in a format determined by their network architecture. These addresses are usually assigned and preprogrammed by the NIC manufacturer. The network interface card provides the connection to the LAN, transferring any data frames that are addressed to it from the connected network media to the computer's memory for processing.

The first two layers of the OSI model, physical and data-link, are manifested as hardware (media and NICs, respectively), whereas the remaining layers of the OSI model are all installed as software protocols.

Sublayers

To allow the OSI model to more closely adhere to the protocol structure and operation of a local area network, the IEEE 802 committee split the data-link layer into two sublayers.

Media Access Control The **media access control** or **MAC sublayer** interfaces with the physical layer and is represented by protocols that define how the shared LAN media is to be accessed by the many connected computers. As is explained more fully later is this chapter, token ring (IEEE 802.5) and Ethernet (IEEE 802.3) networks use different media access methodologies and are therefore assigned different IEEE 802 protocol numbers. Unique addresses assigned to NICs at the time of manufacture are commonly referred to as MAC addresses or MAC layer addresses.

Logical Link Control The upper sublayer of the data-link layer that interfaces to the network layer is known as the **logical link control** or **LLC sublayer** and is represented by a single IEEE 802 protocol (IEEE 802.2). The LLC sublayer also interfaces transparently to the MAC sublayer protocol beneath it. The advantage to splitting the data-link layer into two sublayers and to having a single, common LLC protocol is that it offers transparency to the upper layers (network and above) while allowing the MAC sublayer protocol to vary independently. In terms of technology, the splitting of the sublayers and the single LLC protocol allow a given network operating system to run equally well over a variety of different network architectures as embodied in network interface cards.

Network Layer

The **network layer** protocols are responsible for the establishment, maintenance, and termination of **end-to-end network links.** Network layer protocols are required when computers that are not physically connected to the same LAN must communicate. Network layer protocols are responsible for providing network layer (end-to-end) addressing schemes and for enabling internetwork routing of network layer data **packets.** The term packets is usually associated with network layer protocols, whereas the term frames is usually associated with data-link layer protocols. Unfortunately, not all networking professionals or texts adhere to this generally accepted convention. Addressing schemes and routing are thoroughly reviewed in the remainder of the text.

Network layer protocols are part of a particular network operating system's protocol stack. Different networking operating systems may use different network layer protocols. Many network operating systems have the ability to use more than one network layer protocol. This capability is especially important to heterogeneous, multiplatform, multivendor client/server computing environments.

Transport Layer

Just as the data-link layer was responsible for providing reliability for the physical layer, the **transport layer** protocols are responsible for providing reliability for the end-to-end network layer connections. Transport layer protocols provide end-to-end error recovery and flow control. Transport layer protocols also provide mechanisms for sequentially organizing multiple network layer packets into a coherent **message.**

Transport layer protocols are supplied by a given network operating system and are most often closely linked with a particular network layer protocol. For example, NetWare uses IPX/SPX in which IPX (Internet Packet Exchange) is the network layer protocol and SPX (Sequenced Packet Exchange) is the transport layer protocol. Another popular transport/network protocol duo is TCP/IP in which TCP (Transmission Control Protocol) is the transport layer protocol that provides reliability services for IP (Internet Protocol), the network layer protocol.

Session Layer

Session layer protocols are responsible for establishing, maintaining, and terminating sessions between user application programs. Sessions are interactive dialogues between networked computers and are of particular importance to distributed computing applications in a client/server environment. As the area of distributed computing is in an evolutionary state, the session layer protocols may be supplied by the distributed application, the network operating system, or a specialized piece of additional software designed to render differences between computing platforms transparent, known as middleware. RPC, or remote procedure call protocol, is one example of a session layer protocol.

Presentation Layer

The **presentation layer** protocols provide an interface between user applications and various presentation-related services required by those applications. For example, data encryption/decryption protocols are considered presentation layer protocols as are protocols that translate between encoding schemes such as ASCII to EBCDIC. A common misconception is that graphical user interfaces such as Microsoft Windows and X-Windows are presentation layer protocols. This is not true. Presentation layer protocols deal with network communications, whereas Microsoft Windows and/or X-Windows are installed on end-user computers.

Application Layer

The **application layer,** layer 7 of the OSI model, is also open to misinterpretation. Application layer protocols do not include end-user application programs. Rather, they include utilities and network-based services that support end-user application programs. Some people include network operating systems in this category. Strictly speaking, the best examples of application layer protocols are the OSI protocols X.400 and X.500. X.400 is an open systems protocol that offers interoperability between different e-mail programs, and X.500 offers e-mail directory synchronization among different e-mail systems. DNS, Domain Name Service, which is an Internet protocol that resolves a computer's common or domain name to a specific IP address, is also considered an application layer protocol.

Figure 5-1 offers a conceptual view of the OSI model and summarizes many of the previous comments.

Encapsulation/Deencapsulation

The previous discussion highlighted the roles of the various OSI model layer protocols in a communication session between two networked computers. How the various protocol layers actually interact with each other to enable an end-to-end communication session is highlighted in Figure 5-2.

As illustrated in Figure 5-2, a data message emerges from a client front-end program and proceeds down the protocol stack of the network operating system installed in the client PC in a process known as **encapsulation.** Each successive layer of the OSI model adds a header according to the syntax of the protocol that occupies that layer. In the case of the data-link layer, both a header and trailer are added. The bit stream is finally passed along the shared media that connects the two computing devices. This is an important point. Although the OSI model may seem to imply that given layers in a protocol stack talk directly to each other on different computers, the computers are only connected physically by the media and that is the only layer that talks directly between computers.

When the full bit stream arrives at the destination server, the reverse process of encapsulation, known as **deencapsulation,** takes place. In this manner, each successive layer of the OSI model removes headers and/or trailers and processes the data that were passed to it from the corresponding layer protocol on the source client. Once the server has processed the client's request for data in the server back-end engine application, the whole process is reversed and the requested data will be encapsulated by the server's protocol stack, transmitted over the communications media, and deencapsulated by the client PC's protocol stack before being ultimately delivered to the client front-end application that requested the data in the first place. Additional examples of the OSI model are provided in Chapter 7.

LAN MEDIA

Although LAN media are technically not part of the OSI network reference model, their importance cannot be understated. When two devices that have been working

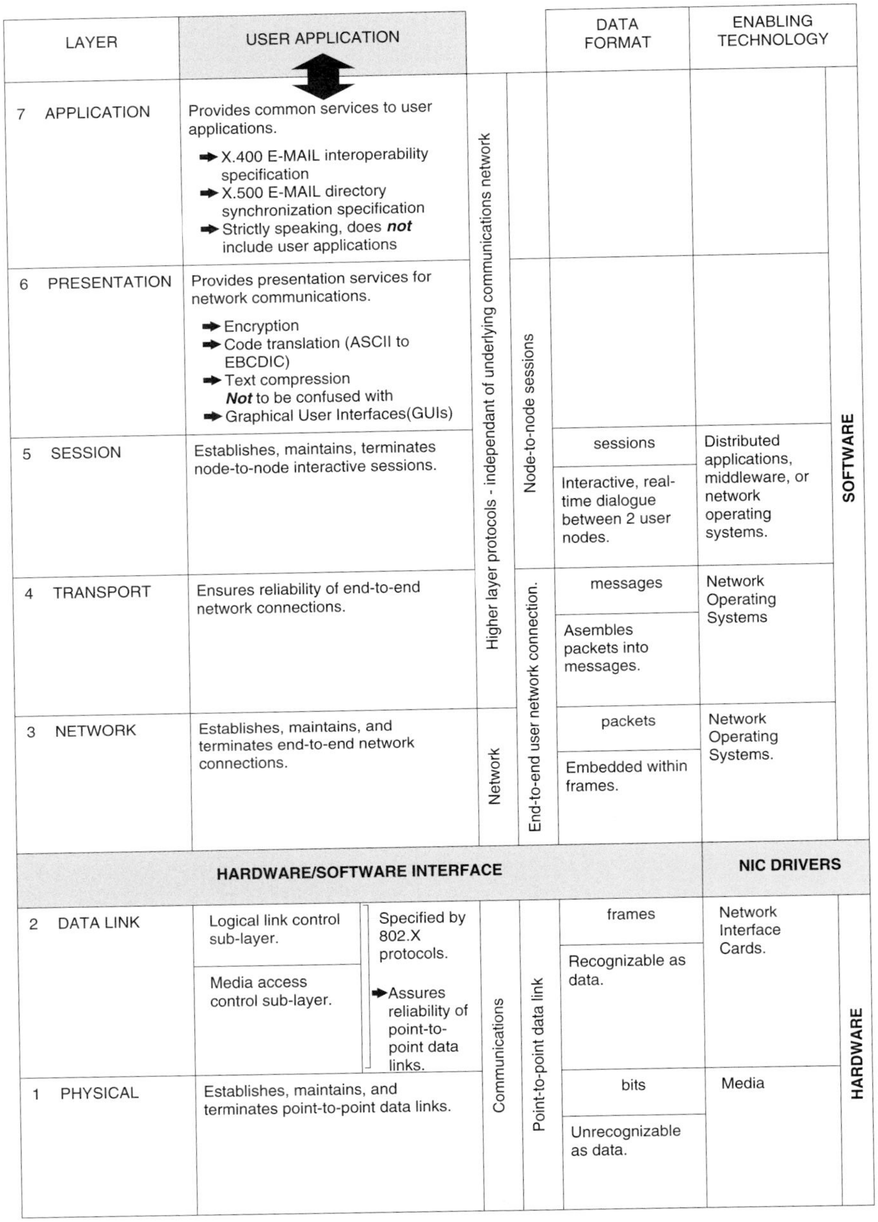

Figure 5-1 OSI Model—A Conceptual View

flawlessly cease to operate, there is a very good chance that the problem can be directly attributed to problems with the media connecting the devices. Perhaps the first mantra of network troubleshooting should be "check the physical layer."

While a variety of wire and fiber media alternatives are reviewed in this section, wireless alternatives for LAN media are explored in the Chapter 10.

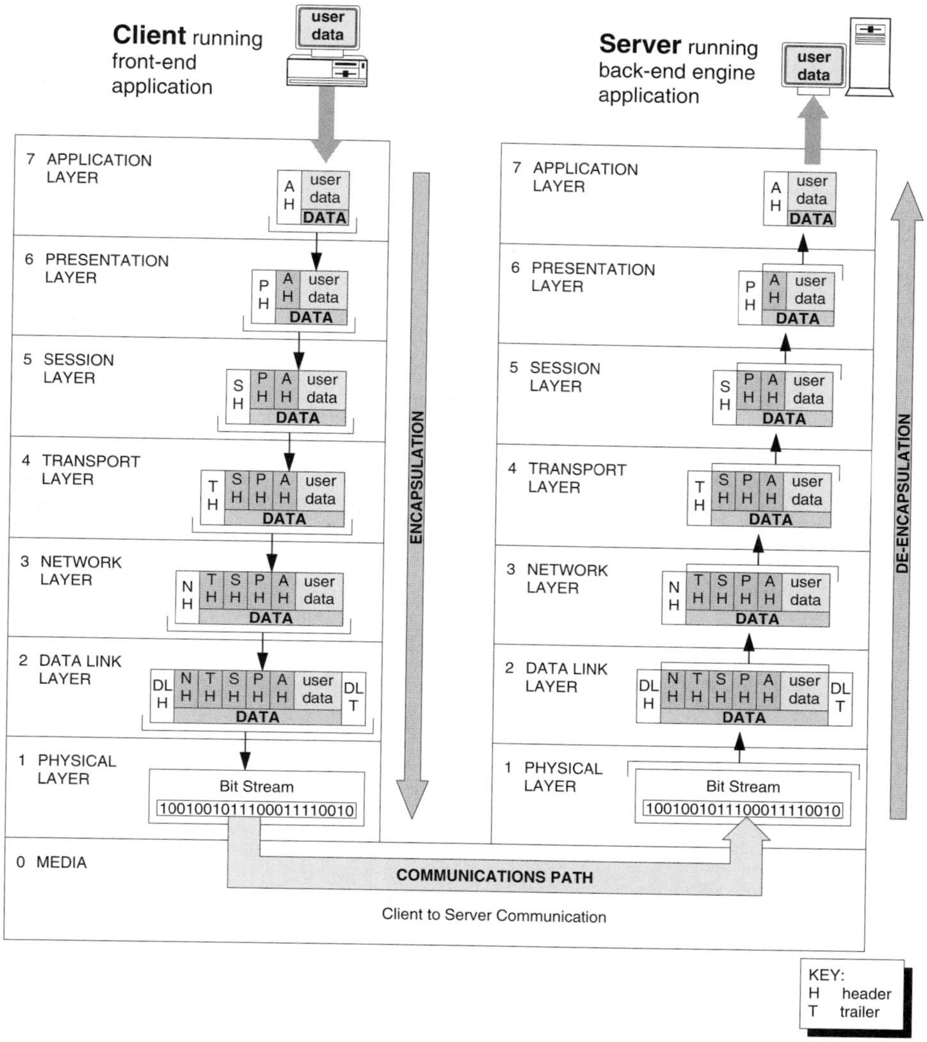

Figure 5-2 OSI Model—An Architectural View

Not Twisted Pair

The type of phone wire installed in most homes consists of a tan plastic jacket containing four untwisted wires: red, yellow, green, and black and is also known as **4 conductor station wire** or **RYGB.** This type of wire is not suitable for data transmission and is not the unshielded twisted pair (UTP) that is so often referred to.

Another popular type of phone wiring is referred to as **flat gray modular** wiring, also known as gray satin or silver satin. Inside this flat gray jacket are either four, six, or eight wires that get crimped into either RJ-11 (4 wire), RJ-12 (6 wire), or RJ-45 plugs (8 wire) using a specialized crimping tool. Premises phone wiring as well as phones, crimp tools, RJ-11 plugs, and flat gray modular wire are attainable at nearly any hardware or department store.

Flat gray modular wire is not the same as twisted pair and is suitable only for carrying data over short distances. For instance, this type of cable is often used between a PC or workstation and a nearby RJ-11 jack for access to premises wiring systems or LAN backbones. Modular NICs with RJ-11 input jacks mounted within RS-232 hoods are available to quickly construct data cables of various pin-out configurations without having to crimp RS-232 pins on individual conductors.

Unshielded Twisted Pair

Twisted pair wiring consists of one or more pairs of insulated copper wire that are twisted at varying lengths, from 2 to 12 twists per foot, to reduce interference both between pairs and from outside sources such as electric motors and fluorescent lights. Interference can cause data errors and necessitate retransmission. These individually twisted pairs are then grouped together and covered with a plastic or vinyl covering or jacket. No additional shielding is added before the pairs are wrapped in the plastic covering. Thus, the completed product is known as **unshielded twisted pair** or **UTP:** 2, 3, 4, and 25 pairs of twisted copper wire are the most common numbers of pairs combined to form the unshielded twisted pair cables.

All UTP are not created equal. One of the common appeals of UTP is that they are often already installed in modern buildings to carry voice conversations through the voice PBX. Most often, when the twisted pair wiring for the voice PBX is installed, extra pairs are wired to each office location. Some people then conclude that they don't need to invest in any new wiring to carry data transmission throughout their buildings. They'll just use the existing extra pairs of unshielded twisted pair wiring. However, five different categories of UTP are specified by **EIA/TIA 568** (Electronics Industry Association/Telecommunications Industry Association). In addition to specifying UTP specifications, EIA/TIA 568 also specifies:

- The topology, cable types, and connector types to be used in EIA/TIA 568 compliant wiring schemes.
- The minimum performance specifications for cabling, connectors, and components such as wall plates, punch down blocks, and patch panels to be used in an EIA/TIA 568 compliant installation.

Although Category 1 UTP, otherwise known as voice-grade, need only carry voice conversations with reasonable clarity, Categories 3–5 (data-grade) cable must meet certain predefined electrical characteristics that ensure transmission quality and speed. Before assuming that the UTP in a building is just fine for data transmission, have its transmission characteristics tested, and ensure that these characteristics meet listed data-grade UTP specifications. Figure 5-3 summarizes the specifications for Categories 1–5 UTP.

Wire thickness is measured by gauge and represented with the unit **AWG** (American Wire Gauge). The higher the gauge number, the thinner the wire. UTP wiring of different categories must meet specifications for resistance to different forces that interfere with signal strength. Two of the more common sources of interference or loss of signal strength are as follows:

1. **Attenuation** is the decrease in the power of signal over a distance in a particular type of wire or media.

UTP Category	Specifications/Applications
Category 1 UTP	22 or 24 AWG. Not recommended for data.
Category 2 UTP	22 or 24 AWG. Only suitable for data transmission of less than 1 Mbps.
Category 3 UTP	24 AWG. Very common in existing installations. Most often used for voice-only installations. Suitable for data up to, but not including 16 Mbps. As a result, it can be used reliably for 4 Mbps token ring and 10 Mbps Ethernet. Tested for attenuation and near-end crosstalk up to 16 MHz.
Category 4 UTP	22 or 24 AWG. Tested for attenuation and near-end crosstalk up to 20 MHz. Not widely used in favor of Category 5 UTP.
Category 5 UTP	22 or 24 AWG. Tested for attenuation and near-end crosstalk to 100 MHz. Capable of transmitting up to 1,000 Mbps when strictly installed to EIA/TIA 568 specifications. Currently the most commonly installed category of UTP.

Figure 5-3 Unshielded Twisted Pair Specifications

2. **Near-end crosstalk (NExT)** is signal interference caused by a strong signal on one-pair (transmitting) overpowering a weaker signal on an adjacent pair (receiving). Near-end crosstalk and attenuation to crosstalk ratio (ACR) are both measured in dB or decibels. A decibel is a logarithmic rather than linear measurement of the ratio between two powers, often a data signal and some type of noise or interference.

Practical Advice and Information

BEYOND CAT 5

Enhanced Category 5 UTP (EC5), otherwise known as **Category 5+** or **CAT5e,** offers enhanced performance over CAT5 UTP due to the following improvements in electrical specifications:

- Attenuation to crosstalk ratio of 10 dB at 155 MHz
- A minimum 400% improvement in capacitance, or ability of a wire to store an electrical charge
- A 250% improvement in frequency
- A 35% improvement in resistance
- An average of 5% improvement in attenuation
- An average of a 6 dB improvement in NET

Although no official Category 6 cable has become standardized, media vendors are attempting to develop cable that is capable of carrying data at frequencies of up to 600 MHz. Some attempts are not truly unshielded twisted pair but rather are FTP or foil-twisted pair cable that is more closely related to shielded twisted pair. Buyers must be wary of so-called Category 6 cable by focusing on whether the cable is truly UTP and whether it is a specified EIA/TIA standard.

Level	Highest Test Frequency	Required Frequency in MHz for Attenuation to Crosstalk Ratio (ACR) at 10 dB (Powersum Bandwidth)
5	200 MHz	80 MHz
6	350 MHz	100 MHz
7	400 MHz	160 MHz

Figure 5-4 UTP Level 5, 6, and 7 Performance Specifications

Anixter, a major cabling manufacturer, has proposed a Levels 97 program to define performance characteristics for cabling tested beyond the 100 MHz required for CAT 5. Since higher speed network architectures such as Fast Ethernet and Gigabit Ethernet require four pair of UTP to be transmitting power simultaneously, it was determined that crosstalk should be measured by taking into account the crosstalk influence from all pairs in the cable, whether four-pair or 25-pair rather than just crosstalk between adjacent pairs, or pair-to-pair, as had been required for CAT5 certification. This type of crosstalk test is called **powersum crosstalk.** Key performance specifications for levels 5, 6, and 7 are detailed in Figure 5-4.

Practical Advice and Information

COMMON UTP INSTALLATION MISTAKES

As mentioned in the Category 5 UTP definition in Figure 5-3, strict adherence to EIA/TIA 568 installation standards is essential to successful transmission at 100 Mbps over UTP CAT 5. Because a less-than-perfect installation will probably transport 10 Mbps traffic without any problem, noncompliant installations may not surface until upgrades to 100 Mbps network architectures are attempted. Among the most common installation mistakes are the following:

- Untwisting the UTP wire more than the maximum 13 mm to secure the UTP to wall plates or punch-down blocks.
- Exceeding the maximum bend radius specified for UTP. Overbending the wire can increase cross-talk between stretched pairs of wires.
- Bundling the groups of UTP together too tightly with cable ties. Excessively pinching the UTP together can increase cross-talk between pairs.

STP-Shielded Twisted Pair

Data transmission characteristics and therefore the data transmission speed can be improved by adding **shielding** around both each individual pair and the entire group of twisted pairs. This shielding may be a metallic foil or copper braid. The function of the shield is rather simple. It "shields" the individual twisted pairs as well as the entire cable from either EMI (electromagnetic interference) or RFI (radiofrequency interference). Installation of shielded twisted pair can be tricky.

Remember that the shielding is metal and is therefore a conductor. Often, the shielding is terminated in a drain wire that must be properly grounded. Improperly installed shielded twisted pair (STP) wiring can actually increase rather than decrease interference and data transmission problems. STP was commonly specified for token ring installations. However, recent specifications for CDDI, fast Ethernet, ATM, and other high-speed network architectures are using Category 5 UTP rather than STP.

Coaxial Cable

Coaxial cable, more commonly known as coax or cable TV cable, has specialized insulators and shielding separating two conductors, allowing reliable, high-speed data transmission over relatively long distances. Figure 5-5 illustrates a cross-section of a typical coaxial cable. Coax comes in various thicknesses and has been historically used in Ethernet network architectures. In some cases, these network architecture specifications include required characteristics of the (physical layer) coaxial cable over which the (data-link layer) MAC layer protocol is transmitted.

Ethernet 10Base5 specifies coaxial cable known as thick coax or more affectionately known as "frozen yellow garden hose," giving a hint as to how easy this media is to work with.

Fiber Optic Cable

Coax was at one time the media of choice for reliable, high-speed data transmission. But times and technology change, and people now often turn to fiber optic cable when seeking reliable, high-bandwidth media for data transmission beyond the capabilities of Category 5 UTP. Price is still a factor, however; as one can see from Figure 5-7, fiber optic cable is still the most expensive media option available. This expensive media delivers high bandwidth in the range of several gigabytes (billions of characters) per second over distances of several kilometers.

Fiberoptic cable is also one of the most secure of all media, as it is relatively untappable, transmitting only pulses of light, unlike all of the aforementioned media that transmit varying levels of electrical pulses. Whereas fiber optic is really a thin fiber of glass rather than copper, this media is immune to electromagnetic interference, contributing to its high bandwidth and data transmission capabilities. Fiber optic cable comes in a number of varieties. Figure 5-6 illustrates a cross-section of a fiber optic cable.

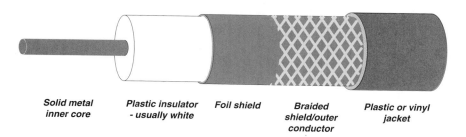

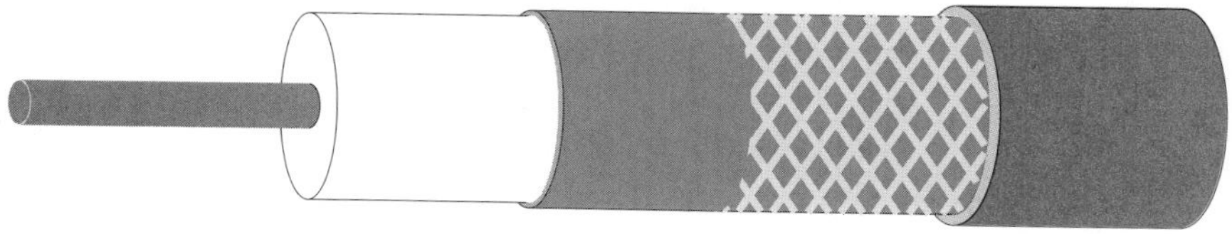

Figure 5-5 Coax Cable: Cross-Section

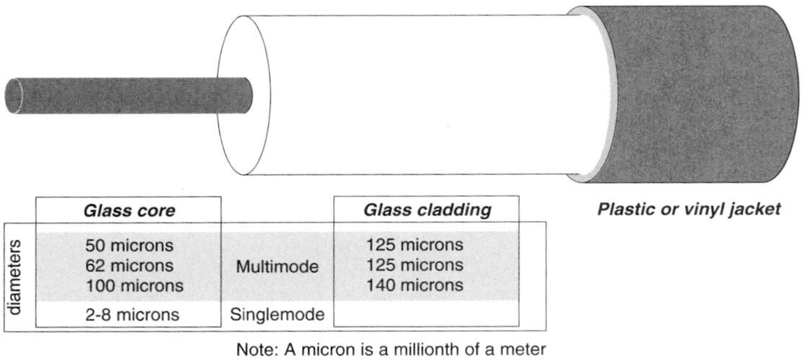

Figure 5-6 Fiber Optic Cable: Cross-Section

Light Transmission Modes Once a pulse of light enters the core of the fiber optic cable, it behaves differently depending on the physical characteristics of the core and cladding of the fiber optic cable. In a **multimode** or **multimode step index** fiber optic cable, some rays of light bounce off the cladding at different angles and continue down the core while others are absorbed in the cladding. These multiple rays at varying angles cause distortion and limit the overall transmission capabilities of the fiber. This type of fiber optic cable is capable of high bandwidth (200 Mbps) transmission, but usually over distances of less than 1 km. By gradually decreasing a characteristic of the core known as the refractive index from the center to the outer edge, reflected rays are focused along the core more efficiently yielding higher bandwidth (3 GBps) over several kilometers. This type of fiber optic cable is known as **multimode graded index fiber.**

The third type of fiber optic cable seeks to focus the rays of light even further so that only a single wavelength can pass through at a time, in a fiber type known as **single mode.** Without numerous reflections of rays at multiple angles, distortion is eliminated and bandwidth is maximized. Single mode is the most expensive fiber optic cable, but it can be used over the longest distances.

Core Thickness The thickness of fiber optic cable's core and cladding is measured in microns (millionths of an inch). The three major core thicknesses are 50, 62, and 100 microns, and their associated claddings are 125, 125, and 140 microns, respectively. The increasing core thicknesses generally allow transmission over longer distances but at a greater expense.

Light Source Wavelength The wavelength of the light that is pulsed onto the fiber optic cable is measured in nanometers (nm), with the optimal light transmitting wavelengths coming in three distinct windows of 820 nm, 1310 nm, and 1500 nm. Wavelengths of 820 nm and 1310 nm are most often used for local and campus-wide networking such as FDDI, whereas 1310 nm and 1500 nm are used by carriers to deliver high bandwidth fiber-based service over long distances. The higher frequency light emitting sources are more expensive.

Applied Problem Solving

LAN MEDIA TECHNOLOGY ANALYSIS

Media Type	Also Called	Bandwidth	Distance Limits	Connectors	Comments/Applications	Token Ring	Ethernet	FDDI	CDDI	Fast Ethernet	Gigabit Ethernet	ATM	Price ($)
4-wire phone station wire	Quad RYGB	3 Kbps	200 feet	RJ-11 jacks	4 insulated wired-red, green, yellow, black. Home phone wiring. Voice applications								0.09/foot
Flat gray modular	Flat satin, telephone cable, silver satin	14.4 Kbps	10-20 feet	RJ-11 or RJ-45 plugs	Comes with 4,6,8 conductors. Used for short data cables using modular (mod-tap) adapters	■	■						0.09-0.18/foot
Unshielded twisted pair	UTP	100 Mbps	100 feet	RJ-45	5 Designated categories. Twists prevent interference, increase bandwidth. Voice grade usually not suitable for data	■	■		■	■	■	■	0.10/foot
Shielded twisted pair	STP	16 Mbps	100 feet	RJ-45 or IBM data connectors	Shielding reduces interference but complicates installation	■	■		■	■		■	0.42/foot
Coax- thick	Frozen yellow garden hose	10 Mbps	500 feet	AUI (attachment unit interface)	Original Ethernet cabling		■						1.10 foot
Coax-thin	RG-58, thinnet, cheaperNet	10 Mbps	200 feet	BNC connector	Looks like cable TV cable. Easier to work with than thick coax.		■						0.32/foot
Coax-thin	RG-62	2.5 Mbps	200 feet	BNC or IBM data connector	Similar to RG-58 (thinnet) but different electrical characteristics make these cables NOT interchangeable	■							0.32/foot
Fiberoptic cable	Fiber glass	several Gbps	several kilometers	SI or SMA 905 or SMA 906	Difficult to install but technology is improving. High bandwidth, long distance, virtually error free, high security	■	■	■			■	■	1.00/foot

Figure 5-7 LAN Media Technology Analysis

THE LOCAL AREA NETWORK ARCHITECTURE MODEL

Although not all network architectures are standardized by the IEEE or some other standards-making organization, all network architectures are made up of the same logical components. To accurately describe a given network architecture, one needs to know the following:

- Access methodology
- Logical topology
- Physical topology

Numerous network architectures are evaluated later in the chapter. Each architecture is examined from each of these three perspectives. The only other variable added to the network architecture of choice is the particular media over which a given network architecture can operate. As will be seen, most network architectures are able to operate over a variety of media types. Although networking vocabulary is by no means standardized, the previously mentioned combinations of variables can be summarized in the following manner:

- Network architecture = access methodology + logical topology + physical topology
- Network configuration = network architecture + media choice

Access Methodology

If the media is to be shared by numerous PC users, then there must be some way to control access by multiple users to that media. Realizing that more than one user is likely to be sending requests onto the shared LAN media at any one time, the need for some way to control which users get to put their messages onto the network and when should be obvious. These media-sharing methods are properly known as **access methodologies.** Sharing the media is an important concept to LAN, also referred to as **media sharing LANs.**

Logically speaking, there are really only two philosophies for controlling access to a shared media. An analogy of access to a crowded freeway can provide a vivid illustration of these access methodology choices.

CSMA/CD One philosophy says, "Let's just let everyone onto the media whenever they want and if two users access the media at the exact same split second, we'll work it out somehow." Or … in the analogy… "Who needs stop as lights! If we have a few collisions, we'll work it out later!"

The access methodology based on this model is known as **carrier sense multiple access with collision detection** or **CSMA/CD** for short. A clearer understanding of how this access methodology works can be achieved by examining the name of this access methodology one phrase at a time.

`Carrier sense': The PC wishing to put data onto the shared media listens to the network to see if any other users are "on the line" by trying to sense a neutral electrical signal known as a carrier. If no transmission is sensed, then *multiple access* allows anyone onto the media with no further permission required. Finally, if two user PCs should both sense a free line and access the media at the same instant, a collision occurs and *collision detection* lets the PCs know that their data were not delivered and controls retransmission in such a way as to avoid further data collisions. Another possible factor leading to data collisions is the **propagation delay** or the time it takes a signal from a source PC to reach a destination PC. Because of propagation delay, it is possible for a workstation to sense that there is no signal on the shared media, when in fact another distant workstation has transmitted a signal that has not yet reached the carrier sensing PC.

In the event of a collision, the station that first detects the collision sends out a special jamming signal to all attached workstations. Each workstation, or more precisely the network interface card in the workstation, stops all transmission instantly and waits a random amount of time before retransmitting, thus reducing the likelihood of recurring collisions. If successive collisions continue to occur, the random time-out interval is doubled.

CSMA/CD is obviously most efficient with relatively little contention for network resources. The ability to allow user PCs to access the network easily without a lot of permission requesting and granting reduces overhead and increases performance at lower network usage rates. As usage increases, however, the increased number of data collisions and retransmissions can negatively affect overall network performance.

Token Passing The second philosophy of access methodology is much more controlling. It says, "Don't you dare access the media until it's your turn. You must first ask permission, and only if I give you the magic token may you put your data onto the shared media." The highway analogy would be the controlled access ramps to freeways in which a driver must wait at a stoplight and somehow immediately get to 65 mph to merge with the traffic.

Token passing ensures that each PC user has 100% of the network channel available for their data requests and transfers by insisting that no PC accesses the network without first possessing a specific packet (24 bits) of data known as a **token.** The token is initially generated by a designated PC known as the **active monitor** and passed among PCs until one PC would like to access the network.

At that point, the requesting PC seizes the token, changes the token status from free to busy, puts its data frame onto the network, and doesn't release the token until it is assured that its data were delivered successfully. Successful delivery of the data frame is confirmed by the destination workstation setting **frame status flags** to indicate successful receipt of the frame and continuing to forward the original frame around the ring to the sending PC. On receipt of the original frame with frame status flags set to "destination address recognized, frame copied successfully," the sending PC resets the token status from busy to free and releases it. After the sending PC releases the token, it is passed along to the next PC, which may either grab the free token or pass it along.

16 Mbps token ring network architectures use a modified form of token passing access methodology in which the token is set to free and released as soon as the transmission of the data frame is completed rather than waiting for the transmitted data frame to return first. This is known as the **early token release mechanism.** The software and protocols that actually handle the token passing and token regeneration, in the case of a lost token, are usually located in the chips on the network adapter card. Figure 5-8 illustrates a simple token passing access methodology LAN.

Token passing's overhead of waiting for the token before transmitting inhibits overall performance at lower network usage rates. However, because all PC users on a token passing access control network are well behaved and always have the magic token before accessing the network, there are, by definition, no collisions, making token passing a more efficient access methodology at higher network utilization rates.

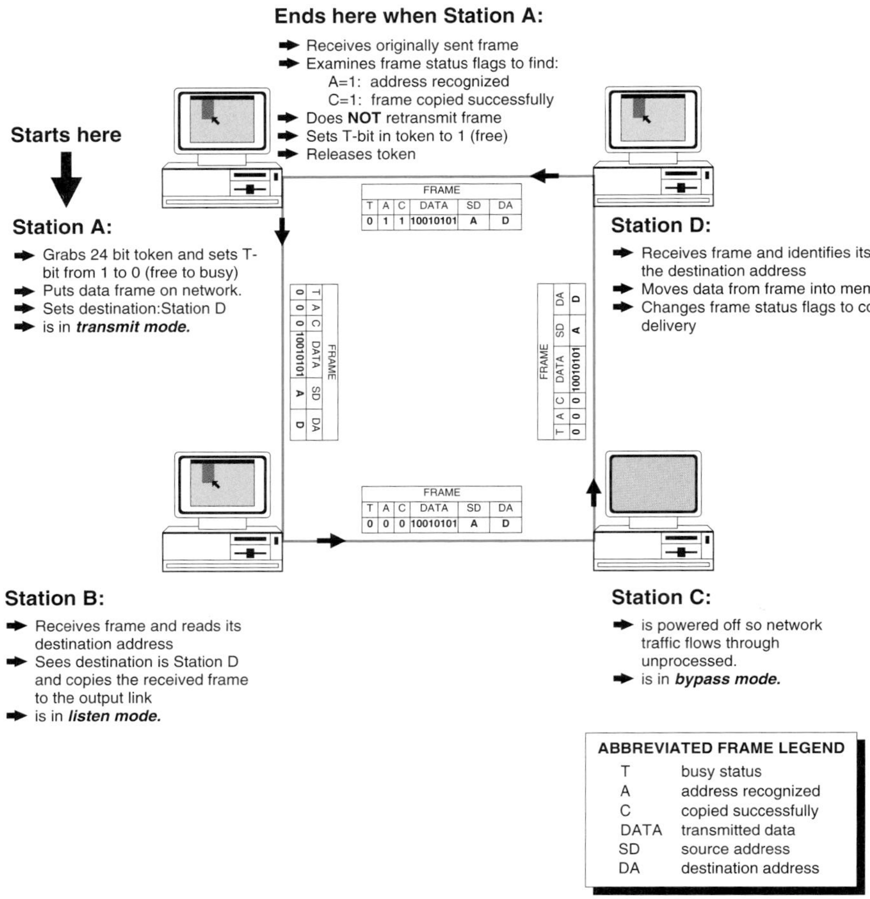

Figure 5-8 Token-Passing Access Methodology

In Sharper Focus

CSMA/CD VS. TOKEN PASSING

Much has been made of the differences between CSMA/CD and token passing over the years. What once burned as a holy war between Ethernet and token ring advocates (see In Sharper Focus section on Ethernet vs. token ring for more detail) has been reduced to academic discussion due to marketplace dynamics.

However, there are real differences in the performance of networks using these two media access techniques. CSMA/CD requires less overhead and is more efficient than token passing at low traffic levels. At higher traffic levels, the inherent collisions and retransmissions make token passing more efficient. While the exact traffic level at which token passing becomes more efficient than CSMA/CD depends on factors such as frame size and segment length, the overall relationship will always look very similar to that shown in Figure 5-9.

In Figure 5-9 the horizontal axis represents the demand for network capacity (or bandwidth) as a percentage. The vertical axis represents the actual capacity delivered by the media access control technique. Ideally, a 1- to-1 mapping, or a line running at a 45-degree angle up the chart would be possible. However, the overhead associated with each technique makes that impossible.

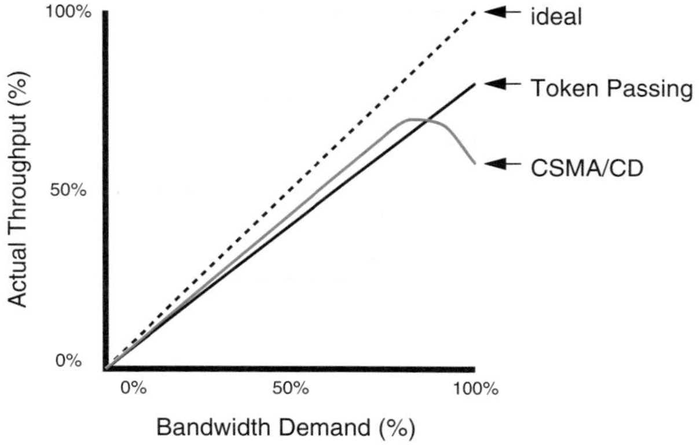

Figure 5-9 CSMA/CD vs. Token Passing

As shown in the figure, CSMA/CD provides nearly perfect efficiency until the number of collisions and retransmits start to erode the performance. This phenomenon starts to seriously affect performance around 60% bandwidth demand and increases until performance actually deteriorates with additional bandwidth demand. Simply put, the number of collisions start to outnumber the number of successful transmissions.

The structured media access approach used in token passing does not suffer this same fate. Because transmission is tightly controlled, performance is predictable until 100% of the bandwidth is demanded. However, the overhead associated with token passing makes it less efficient than CSMA/CD as lower levels of demand.

Logical Topology

Once a data message is onto a shared LAN media that is connected to numerous workstations, the next thing that must be determined is how that message will be passed from workstation to workstation until the message ultimately reaches its intended destination workstation. The particular message passing methodology employed is more properly referred to as the network architecture's **logical topology.** An analogy used to describe logical topologies has to do with how best to put out a fire in a PC user's wastebasket.

Sequential The first topical topology or method of delivering data is known as **sequential.** In a sequential logical topology, also known as a **ring** logical topology, data are passed from one PC (or node) to another. Each node examines the destination address of the data packet to determine if this particular packet is meant for it. If the data were not meant to be delivered at this node, the data is passed along to the next node in the logical ring.

This is analogous to the bucket brigade method of putting out a fire in a PC user's wastebasket. A bucket of water is filled by one PC user and passed to the neighboring PC user. That user determines if his/her wastebasket is on fire. If it is, the user douses the flames with the bucket of water. Otherwise, the user passes the bucket along to the next user in the logical ring.

Broadcast The second logical topology or method of delivering data is known as **broadcast.** In a broadcast logical topology, a data message is sent simultaneously to all nodes on the network. Each node decides individually if the data message was directed toward it. If not, the message is simply ignored. There is no need to pass the message along to a neighboring node. All nodes received the same message at the same time.

This is analogous to the sprinkler system method of putting out a fire in a PC user's wastebasket. Rather than worry about passing a bucket of water around a logical ring until it finally reaches the engulfed wastebasket, the water is just broadcast over the entire network, the result being that the wastebasket that was on fire will know that the water was meant for it.

In summary, to appreciate the key difference between sequential and broadcast logical topologies, focus on the role or responsibility of the intermediate workstations to which a destination message is not actually addressed. In the case of sequential logical topology, the nonrecipient workstation has a job to do. It must continue to pass the message along to its next sequential neighbor. However, in the case of a broadcast logical topology, the nonrecipient workstation has no further responsibilities and simply ignores the message.

Physical Topology

Finally, clients and servers must be physically connected to each other according to some configuration and be linked by the shared media of choice. The physical layout of this configuration can have a significant impact on LAN performance and reliability and is known as a network architecture's **physical topology.**

Bus The **bus** topology is a linear arrangement with terminators on either end and devices connected to the "bus" via connectors and/or transceivers. The purpose of the terminator is to close off the ends of the bus topology, thereby completing the electrical circuit and allowing the data signals to flow. A bus topology without properly matched terminators will not work. The weak link in the bus physical topology is that a break or loose connection anywhere along the entire bus will bring down the whole network.

Ring The **ring** topology suffers from a similar Achilles' heel. Each PC connected via a ring topology is actually an active part of the ring, passing data packets in a sequential pattern around the ring. If one of the PCs dies, or a network adapter card malfunctions, the "sequence" is broken, the token is lost, and the network is down. In addition, any cable breaks bring down the entire network.

Star The **star** physical topology avoids these two aforementioned potential pitfalls by employing some type of central management device. Depending on the network architecture and sophistication of the device, it may be called a hub, a wiring center, a concentrator, a MAU (multiple access unit), a repeater, or a switching hub. All of these devices will be studied later in the text. By isolating each PC or node on its own leg or segment of the network, any node or cable failure only effects that leg, while the remainder of the network continues to function normally.

Since all network data in a star topology is going through this one central location, it makes a marvelous spot to add system monitoring, security, or management capabilities. The other side of the coin is that since all network data are going

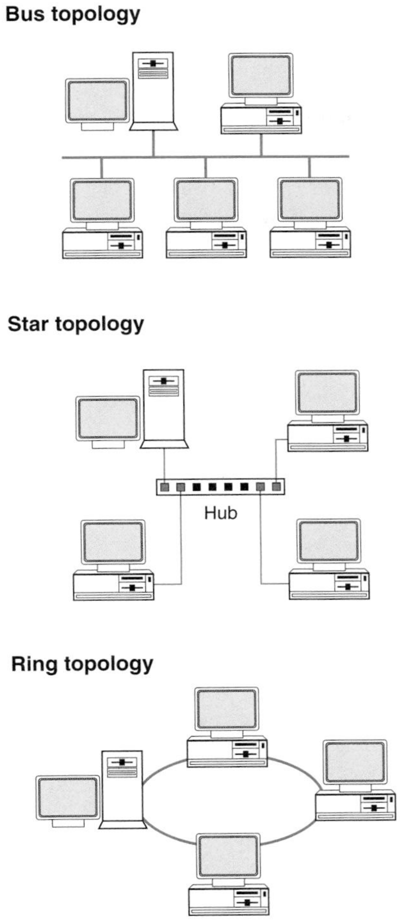

Figure 5-10 LAN Physical Topology Choices

through this one central location, it makes a marvelous networking no-no known as a **single point of failure.** The good news is, any node can be lost and the network will be fine. The bad news is, lose the hub and the whole network goes down.

As we will see shortly in the study of hubs, vendors have risen to the occasion, offering such reliability extras as redundant power supplies, dual buses, and "hot swappable" interface cards. Figure 5-10 highlights the differences between these physical topologies.

NETWORK ARCHITECTURES

Ethernet

Origins The invention of **Ethernet** is generally credited to Robert Metcalfe, who later went on to become the founder of 3COM Corporation. Although strictly speaking Ethernet and **IEEE 802.3** are conflicting standards, the term *Ethernet* is commonly used to refer to any IEEE 802.3 compliant network. Differences between the two standards are outlined shortly.

Functionality

- Access methodology: CSMA/CD
- Logical topology: broadcast
- Physical topology: traditionally, bus; currently, most often star

Standards The first Ethernet standard was developed by Digital, Intel, and Xerox Corporation in 1981 and was known as DIX 1.0, sometimes referred to as Ethernet I. This standard was superseded in 1982 by DIX 2.0, the current Ethernet standard, also known as Ethernet II. The frame layouts for **Ethernet II** and IEEE 802.3 are illustrated in Figure 5-11.

As illustrated in Figure 5-11, both Ethernet II and IEEE 802.3 frames can vary in length from 64 to 1518 octets.

Ethernet II The Ethernet II frame layout consists of the following fields:

- The Ethernet II frame starts with a preamble of eight octets. The purpose of the preamble is to alert and synchronize the Ethernet network interface card to the incoming data.
- The destination and source addresses are each six octets long and are also known as MAC layer addresses. These addresses are permanently burned into the ROM (read-only memory) of the Ethernet II network interface card at the time of manufacture. The first three octets of the address identify the manufacturer of the network interface card and are assigned by the IEEE. The last three octets are assigned by the manufacturer producing unique MAC layer addresses for all Ethernet network interface cards.
- The type field identifies which network protocols are embedded within the data field. For example, if the data field contained Network IPX/SPX proto-

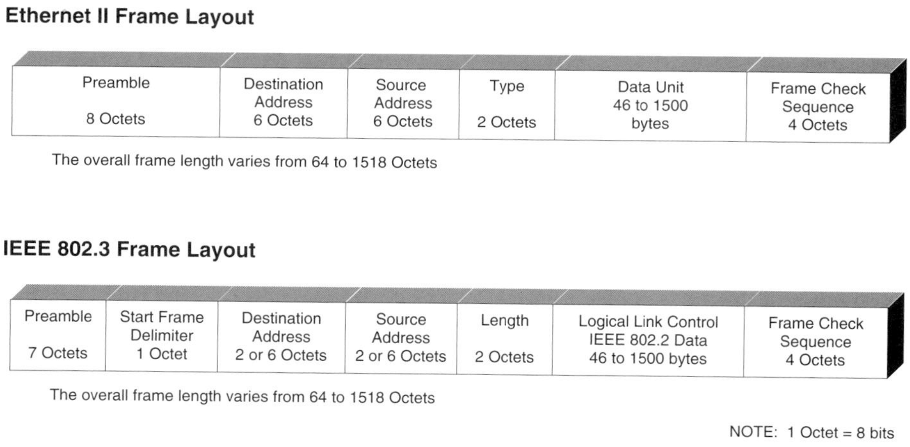

Figure 5-11 Ethernet and IEEE 802.3 Standards

cols, then the type field would have a value of 8137 (hexadecimal); and if the data field contained TCP/IP protocols, then the type field would contain a value of 0800 (hexadecimal). These type values are assigned by the IEEE. The type field is important to enable multiple protocols to be handled by a single network interface card that enables multiple protocol stacks to be loaded in a given client or server. Once the network interface card identifies which protocol is embedded within the data field, it can forward that data field to the proper protocol stack for further processing. Multiple protocol stacks allow communication between clients and servers of different network operating systems, which is essential to transparent distributed computing.

- The data unit field contains all of the encapsulated upper layer (network through application) protocols and can vary in length from 46 to 1500 bytes. The 46-byte minimum data field length combines with the 18 octets of fixed overhead of all of the other fields to produce the minimum frame size of 64 octets.
- The **frame check sequence (FCS)** is an error detection mechanism generated by the transmitting Ethernet network interface card. A 32 bit **cyclical redundancy check (CRC)** is generated over the address, type, and data fields. The receiving Ethernet network interface card regenerates this same CRC on the address, type, and data fields in the received frame and compares the regenerated CRC to the transmitted CRC. If they match, the frame was received error free. CRCs with 32 bits can detect error bursts of up to 31 bits with 100% accuracy.

IEEE 802.3 The IEEE 802.3 frame layout is very similar to the Ethernet II frame layout. Highlights of the IEEE 802.3 frame layout are as follows:

- The seven-octet preamble plus the one-octet starting frame delimiter perform the same basic function as the eight-octet Ethernet II preamble.
- Address fields are defined and assigned in a similar fashion to Ethernet II frames.
- The two-octet length field in the IEEE 802.3 frame takes the place of the type field in the Ethernet frame. The length field indicates the length of the variable-length **LLC (logical link control**—IEEE 802.2) data field that contains all upper layer embedded protocols.
- The type of embedded upper layer protocols is designated by a field within the LLC data unit and is explained more fully in the "In Sharper Focus" section next.
- The frame check sequence is identical to that used in the Ethernet II frame.

In Sharper Focus

IEEE 802.2 AND ETHERNET SNAP

For an IEEE 802.3 compliant network interface card to be able to determine the type of protocols embedded within the data field of an IEEE 802.3 frame, it refers to the header of the **IEEE 802.2** logical link control (LLC) data unit. Figure 5-6 illustrates the fields contained in the IEEE 802.2 data unit.

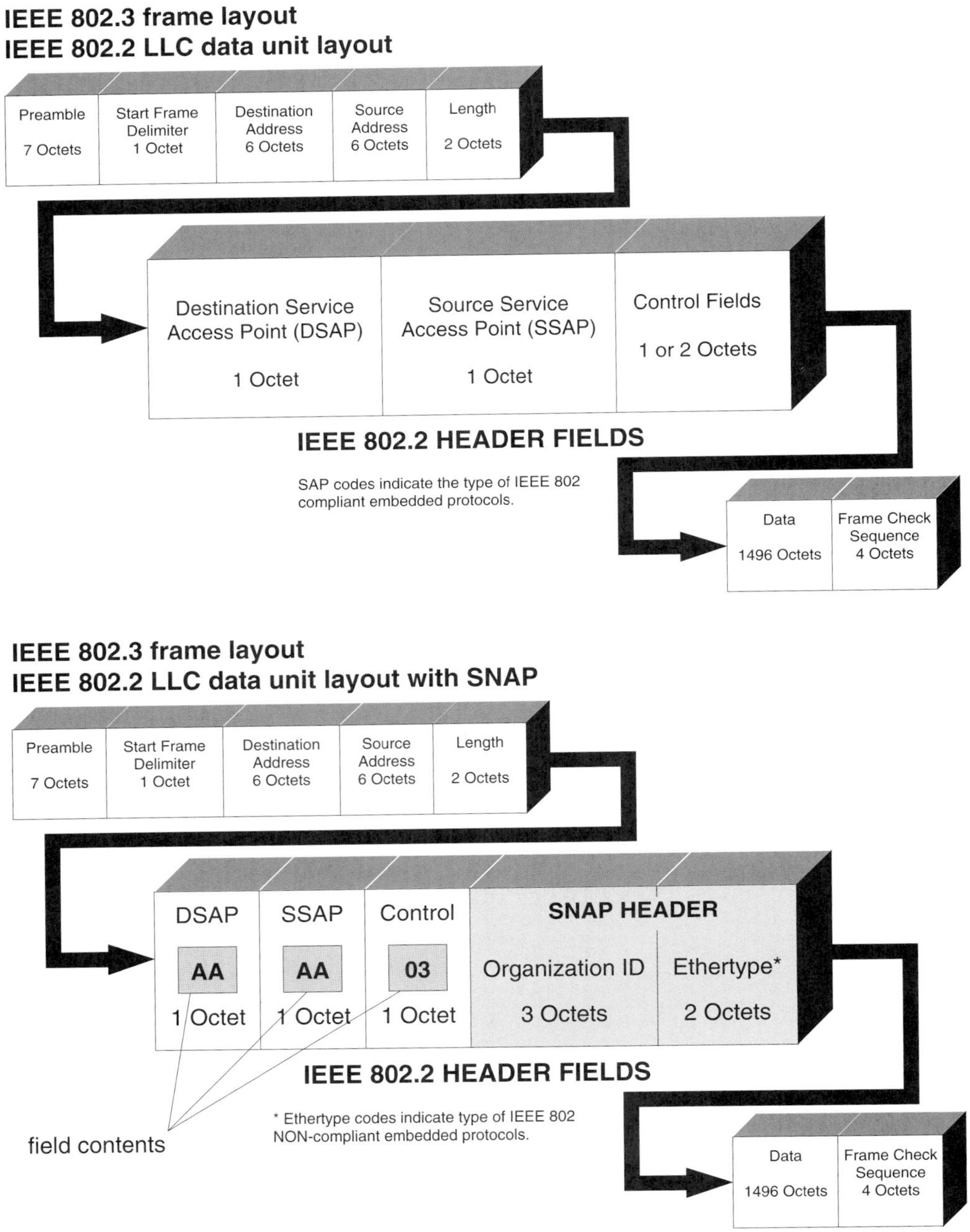

Figure 5-12 IEEE 802.2 and Ethernet SNAP

More specifically, the types of protocols embedded within the data unit are identified within the destination and source service access point fields (**DSAP** and **SSAP**). These fields are analogous to the type field in the Ethernet frame. SAP codes that identify a particular protocol are issued by the IEEE to those companies that register their IEEE-compliant protocols. For example, a SAP code of E0 identifies a Novell protocol, and a SAP code of 06 identifies a TCP/IP protocol. NetWare frames adhering to this standard are referred to as NetWare 802.2 (802.3 plus 802.2).

However, in some cases, rendering network protocols to be IEEE 802 compliant was not an easy task. To ease the transition to IEEE 802 compliance, an alternative method of identifying the embedded upper layer protocols was developed, known as **SNAP** or **subnetwork access protocol.** Any protocol can use SNAP with IEEE 802.2 and appear to be an IEEE 802 compliant protocol. In some cases, network operating systems vendors, such as NetWare used SNAP until modifications were made to bring protocols into compliance with IEEE standards. Now that NetWare is IEEE 802 compliant and has a designated SAP code, NetWare users should choose the NetWare 802.2 frame layout.

In the case of Ethernet SNAP, a single SAP code of AA in both the DSAP and SSAP and a control code of 03 are used to identify all noncompliant protocols. To differentiate which particular noncompliant protocol is embedded, any packet with AA in the DSAP and SSAP fields also has a five-octet SNAP header known as a **protocol discriminator** following the control field as illustrated in Figure 5-12. The first three octets of the protocol discriminator are called the organization ID and indicate to which company the embedded noncompliant protocol belongs, whereas the last two octets are called the EtherType field, which indicates which particular protocol is embedded. If the organization ID field consists entirely of zeroes, a generic Ethernet frame, not unique to any particular company, is indicated. Examples of EtherType values include

- 08-00 for TCP/IP
- 81-37 for NetWare

NetWare frames adhering to this specification are known as NetWare 802.2 SNAP (802.3 plus 802.2 plus SNAP).

Media-Related Ethernet Standards Ethernet can run over numerous media types. Various media alternatives and their electrical and transmission characteristics will be explored in the next chapter. The unshielded twisted pair media employed in an Ethernet standard known as **10BaseT** sells for as little as 6 cents per foot. The "10" in 10BaseT refers to 10 Mbps capacity, the "Base" refers to **baseband transmission,** meaning that the entire bandwidth of the media is devoted to one data channel, and the "T" stands for Twisted Pair, the media of choice. Another important distinction of 10BaseT is that is specifies the use of a star topology with all Ethernet LAN segments connected to a centralized wiring hub. Other 10 Mbps Ethernet standards and associated media are listed in Figure 5-13.

Application The potential for collisions and retransmission on an Ethernet network has already been mentioned. In some cases, Ethernet networks with between 100 and 200 users barely use the 10-Mbps capacity of the network. However, the nature of the data transmitted is the key to determining potential network capacity problems. Character-based transmission, such as typical data entry, in which a few characters at a time are typed and sent over the network, are much less likely to cause network capacity problems than the transfer of graphical user interface, screen-oriented transmission such as Windows-based applications. CAD/CAM images are even more bandwidth intensive.

Simultaneous requests for full-screen Windows-based transfers by 30 or more workstations on a single LAN segment can cause collision and network capacity

Standard	Popular Name	Speed	Media	Maximum Segment Length
10Base5	Frozen yellow garden hose	10 Mbps	Thick coaxial cable (RG-11) (.405-in. diameter)	500 meters
10Base2	ThinNet, CheaperNet	10 Mbps	Thin coaxial cable (RG-58)	185 meters
10BaseT	100BaseT, twisted pair Ethernet	10 Mbps	Unshielded twisted pair	100 meters
10BaseF	Fiber Ethernet FOIRL (Fiber Optic Inter Repeater Link)	10 Mbps	Multimode fiber optic cable	Described by IEEE 802.1j-1993 standard (1000 meters)
10Base5	StarLAN	1 Mbps	Unshielded twisted pair	500 meters
10BaseT	StarLAN10	10 Mbps	Unshielded twisted pair	100 meters

Figure 5-13 Ethernet Media-Specific Standards

problems on an Ethernet network. As with any data communications problem, there are always solutions or workarounds to these problems. The point in relaying these examples is to provide some assurance that although Ethernet is not unlimited in its network capacity, in most cases it provides more than enough bandwidth.

A key advantage to Ethernet is scalability. As will be covered later in this chapter, higher-speed Ethernet network architectures have been developed that allow for a hierarchy of network capacity. The fact that these higher speed Ethernet implementations maintain the standard 10 Mbps Ethernet frame structure allows traffic to be quickly bridged or switched onto these higher capacity networks. Details on bridging and switching are provided in Chapter 9.

Token Ring

Origins The credit for the first token ring network architecture has been attributed to Olaf Soderblum, who proposed such a network in 1969. IBM has been the driving force behind the standardization and adoption of token ring with a prototype in IBM's laboratory in Zurich, Switzerland, serving as a model for the eventual **IEEE 802.5** standard.

Functionality

- Access methodology: token passing
- Logical topology: sequential
- Physical topology: traditionally, ring; currently, most often star

Standards Unlike IEEE 802.3 Ethernet networks, whose speeds are specified as part of the IEEE standard, the IEEE 802.5 token ring standard does not include a speed specification. IBM, the leading advocate of the token ring network architecture, has specified token ring network architectures that operate at 4 Mbps and 16 Mbps.

As mentioned earlier in the discussion of the token-passing access methodology, the token is actually a 24-bit formatted data packet and is illustrated in Figure 5-14 along with the IEEE 802.5 Token ring MAC sublayer frame layout.

The IEEE 802.5 token frame layout consists of the following fields:

- The starting delimiter field alerts the token ring network interface card installed in a workstation that a token ring frame is approaching. Notice that

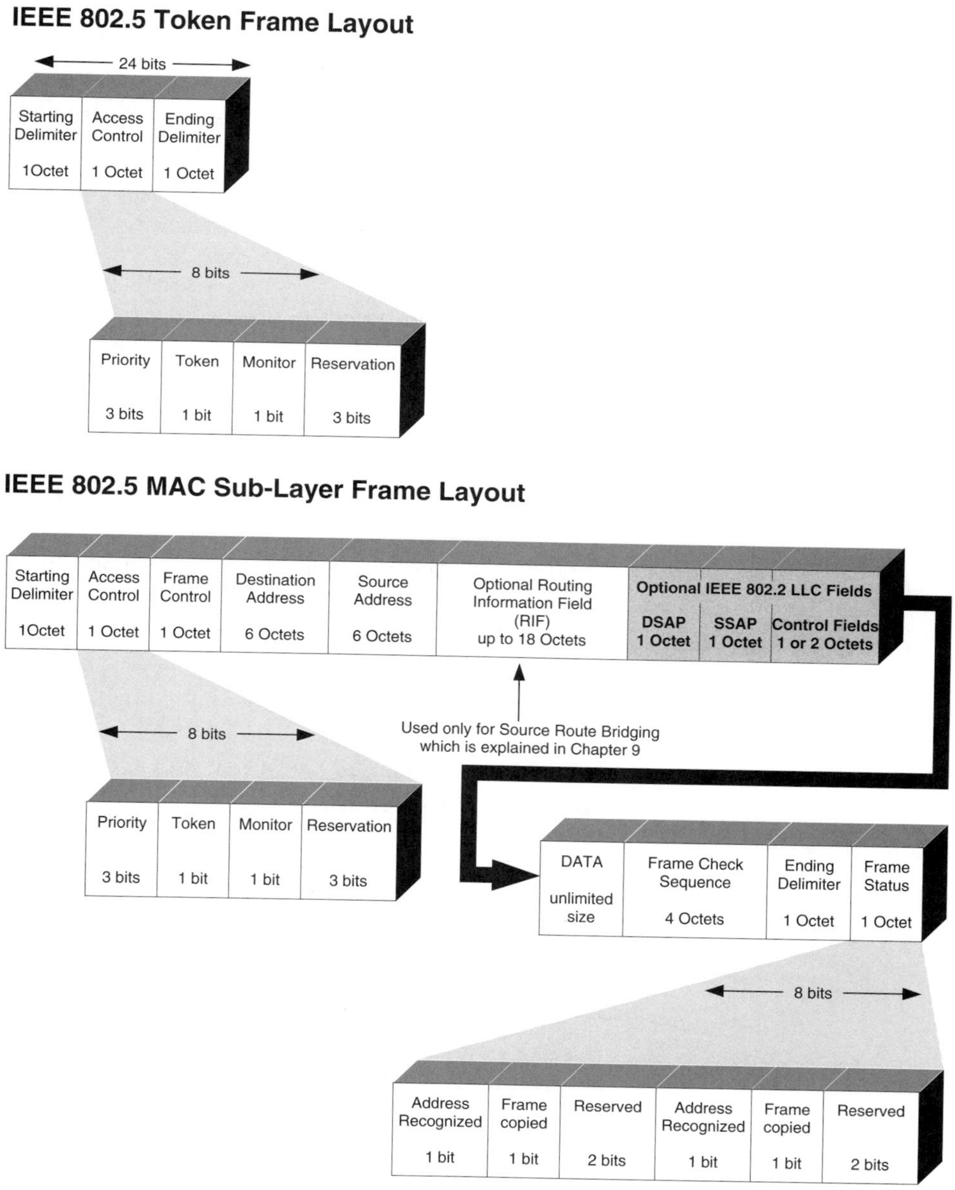

Figure 5-14 IEEE 802.5 Token Ring Token and MAC Sublayer Frame Layout

both the token frame and the MAC sublayer frame both start with the starting delimiter.

- Once the access control field is received, the workstation can distinguish between tokens and MAC sublayer frames. If the token bit within the access control field (see Figure 5-8) is set to 0, then the received frame represents a free token, in which case the access control field would be immediately followed by an ending delimiter. The workstation is welcome to receive the full token frame and change the token bit from 0 to 1 to indicate a busy token. The received starting delimiter field plus the access control field with the T (token) bit now set to 1 form the first two fields of an IEEE 802.5 MAC sublayer data frame, allowing the sending workstation to just append address information, data, and the remaining fields in the data frame layout and transmit this frame onto the ring.
- If the token bit on the received frame was set to 1, then the next field is the frame control field that indicates whether this frame contains data or is a special network management frame.
- Following the frame control field are the destination and source address fields. The receiving network interface card would read the destination address to determine if it was the frame's intended recipient. If it was, then the workstation will read the rest of the frame into memory. If not, then the NIC will simply pass the rest of the bits of the frame along the ring without transferring them to the workstation's memory. No snooping allowed.
- The routing information field is used with devices known as source routing bridges that are able to link together multiple token ring LANs. Source route bridging and other LAN-to-LAN connectivity options are discussed in Chapter 9.
- The IEEE 802.2 header fields are used in an identical manner as they are used with IEEE 802.3 Ethernet MAC sublayer frames. Likewise, IEEE 802.2 SNAP is also supported within the IEEE 802.5 MAC sublayer frame.
- The data field contains data in the form of embedded upper level protocols if this is a data frame and network management information if this is a network management frame as indicated by the frame control field. The data field does not have a fixed maximum length as in the case of Ethernet but is effectively controlled by a timing limit as to how long any workstation can hold onto a token. The timing limit of 10 msec imposes a practical limit on the size of the data field in a 4 Mbps token ring network to about 4500 bytes and on a 16 Mbps token ring network to about 16,000–18,000 bytes. Token ring timing issues are explained further in an In Sharper Focus section later in this chapter.
- The frame check sequence uses a 32-bit cyclical redundancy check in an identical manner to IEEE 802.3.
- The ending delimiter not only can let the workstation know that the end of the frame has arrived, but can also let the workstation know if this was an intermediate frame with more related data to follow immediately behind. The ending delimiter can also indicate if another station has found an error in a frame and has indicated that it should be ignored and returned around the ring to the source address workstation for removal from the ring.

- The frame status field serves an important role in letting the sending workstation know whether the frame was successfully delivered. If the destination workstation recognized its address, then the A (address recognized) bits are set to 1 and if the frame was successfully copied into the destination workstation's memory, then the C (frame copied) bits are set to 1. There are two sets of A and C bits for redundancy in order to help eliminate errors. To be more specific, since the A and C bits are set by destination station after the frame has been received, they are not covered by the frame check sequence error detection mechanism.

One workstation on every token ring LAN is designated as the active monitor and acts as a kind of caretaker of the token ring network architecture. Being the active monitor requires no special hardware or software and all other workstations are designated standby monitors. Among the tasks that can be performed by the active monitor are the following:

- Removes frames from the ring that have not been removed by the sending workstation
- Regenerates lost or damaged tokens
- Provides a special 24-bit buffer if the physical ring is so small that it does not have enough delay or latency to hold the 24-bit token. For more information, see the In Sharper Focus section entitled "Token Ring and Timing."
- Controls the master clock
- Makes sure that there is only one designated active monitor on this ring

Application IBM's token ring network architecture, adhering to the IEEE 802.5 standard, utilizes a star configuration, sequential message delivery, and a token passing access methodology scheme.

Remembering that the sequential logical topology is equivalent to passing messages from neighbor to neighbor around a ring, the token ring network architecture is sometimes referred to as: **logical ring, physical star.**

The token ring's use of the token passing access methodology furnishes one of the key positive attributes of this network architecture. The guarantee of no data collisions with assured data delivery afforded by the token passing access methodology is a key selling point in some environments where immediate, guaranteed delivery is essential.

The second attribute in token ring's favor was the backing of a computer company of the magnitude of IBM. For those businesses facing integration of PCs with existing IBM mainframes and minicomputers, IBM's token ring network architecture offers assurance of the possibility of such integration.

Although token ring is IBM's PC networking architecture, it is neither a closed system nor a monopoly. Third-party suppliers offer choices in the network adapter card and wiring hub (multiple access unit) markets, and numerous network operating systems run over the token ring architecture. Competition encourages research and development of new technology and can eventually drive down prices. Price is an important point about token ring. Network adapter cards for a token ring network tend to cost from one and one-half to two times as much as Ethernet network adapter cards.

In Sharper Focus

ADDRESS BIT ORDER REVERSAL

One small but significant difference between Ethernet and token ring networks is known as **address bit order reversal.** As illustrated in Figure 5-15, both Ethernet and token ring refer to the first (leftmost) octet of the address as byte 0. Also, both Ethernet and token ring believe that bit 0 on byte 0, referred to as the **least significant bit,** should be transmitted first. However, in the case of IEEE 802.3, the least significant bit is the rightmost bit of the byte and in the case of IEEE 802.5, the least significant bit is the leftmost bit of the byte. This bit order reversal is especially troublesome for translating bridges, which must translate between token ring and Ethernet frames.

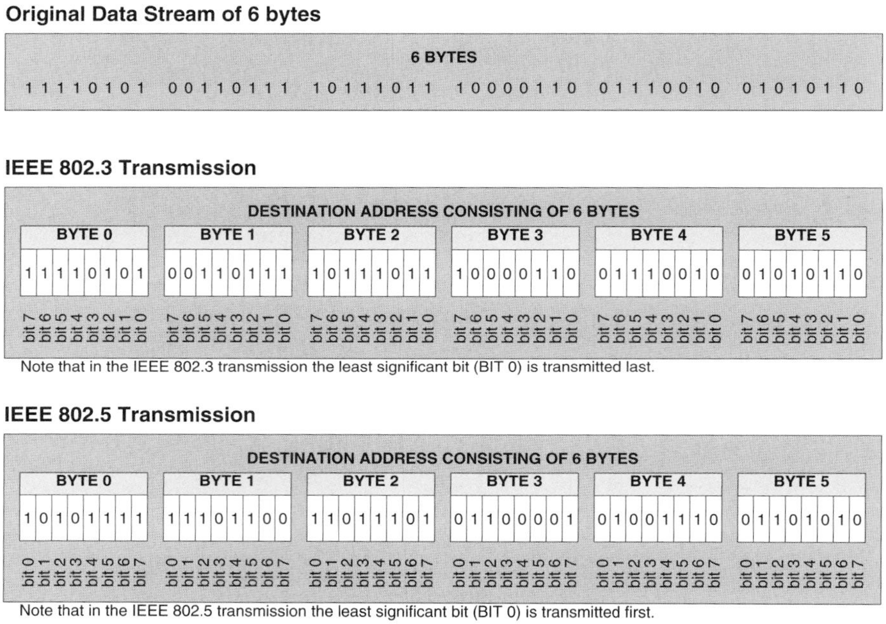

Figure 5-15 Address Bit-Order Reversal in Ethernet and Token Ring

In Sharper Focus

TOKEN RING AND TIMING

For the token ring network architecture to operate correctly, the 24-bit token must circulate continuously even if no workstations are in need of transmitting data. Therefore, the entire token ring network must possess enough delay or latency to hold the entire 24-bit token. This latency or required delay can be computed by dividing the length of the token (24 bits) by the ring's transmission speed (4 Mbps), yielding a required latency of 6 μsec. The next question is, how far can an electrical signal travel in 6 μsec? The answer to that question will depend on the media through which the signal is traveling, with different media possessing different propagation velocities. For example, unshielded twisted pair has a propagation velocity of 0.59 times the speed of light, denoted as *c*. The speed of light is equal to 300,000,000 m/sec. Finally, the minimum ring size to introduce the required 6 μsec of delay can be calculated as follows:

$$
\begin{aligned}
\text{Minimum Ring Size} &= \text{Required Latency} \times \text{propagation velocity of media} \\
&= 0.000006 \text{ seconds} \times .59 \times 300{,}000{,}000 \text{ m/sec} \\
&= 1062 \text{ m} \\
&= 1.062 \text{ km}
\end{aligned}
$$

According to this calculation, the minimum size of a token ring network, even for three or four workstations, would have to be over a kilometer in length. This is obviously not practical. As mentioned earlier, the active monitor station adds a 24-bit delay buffer to the ring to ensure that regardless of the physical size of the ring, the token will be able to circulate continually.

Managerial Perspective

TOKEN RING OR ETHERNET?

Discussions as to the relative merits of token ring or Ethernet network architectures were conducted at one time with all the fervor of a religious war. There seems to be less argument now as Ethernet has clearly surpassed token ring in terms of install base. This is not to say that Ethernet is a better network architecture. The significant advantage in terms of Ethernet market share probably has more to do with the affordability and availability of Ethernet vs. token ring hardware. Ethernet cards sell from $10.00 to $150.00, whereas token ring cards sell from around $200.00 to $475.00. A 16-port 10 Mbps Ethernet hub sells for as little as $60.00, whereas the equivalent token ring MAU (multistation access unit) sells for several hundred dollars.

At one time, token ring network architectures were more easily integrated with minicomputer and mainframe environments. This is no longer true as the mainframe/minicomputer world has evolved to embrace open systems, namely TCP/IP and Ethernet.

In conclusion, the biggest technical difference between token ring and Ethernet is the scalability of Ethernet from the nominal 10 Mbps speed, through 100 Mbps, to gigabit (1000 Mbps). This inherent upgrade path, combined with lower initial costs, has allowed Ethernet to win the war. At this point, 99+% of new network installations are Ethernet based. For existing implementations, interoperability between the two network architectures is possible, although challenges do exist. Ethernet/token ring bridges provide transparent interoperability between the two network architectures and are detailed in Chapter 9.

In Sharper Focus

ARCNET

ARCNet (attached resources computer network) was a popular LAN architecture that was originally developed by Datapoint, Inc. It offered 2.5-Mbps transmission speed and used a token-passing access methodology, a broadcast logical topology, and a star physical topology over RG-62 coaxial cable. Since RG-62 is the same cable used to connect IBM 3270 terminals to cluster controllers, ARCNet was often installed in downsized IBM installations where the cable could be reused. ARCNet was never standardized by the IEEE and has been largely replaced by Ethernet and token ring network architectures.

FDDI

Origins **Fiber distributed data interface (FDDI)** is a 100-Mbps network architecture that was first specified in 1984 by the ANSI (American National Standards Institute) subcommittee entitled X3T9.5. It is important to note that FDDI is not an IEEE standard. However, FDDI does support IEEE 802.2 logical link control protocols offering it transparent interoperability to IEEE-compliant upper layer protocols (layers 3–7).

Functionality

- Access methodology: modified token passing
- Logical topology: sequential
- Physical topology: dual counter–rotating rings

Built-in Reliability and Longer Distance FDDI supplies not only high bandwidth (100 Mbps), but also a high degree of reliability and security while adhering to standards-based protocols not associated with or promoted by any particular vendor.

FDDI's reliability includes the fiber itself. Fiber is immune to both **EMI** (Electromagnetic Interference) and **RFI** (radiofrequency interference). Additional reliability is achieved through the design of the physical topology of FDDI. FDDI's physical topology is comprised of not one, but two, separate rings around which data move simultaneously in opposite directions. One ring is the primary data ring and the other is a secondary or backup data ring to be used only in the case of the failure of the primary ring or an attached workstation. Whereas both rings are attached to a single hub or concentrator, a single point of failure remains in the hub while achieving redundancy in the network media. Figure 5-16 illustrates some of the key features of the FDDI network architecture and technology, whereas Figure 5-17 more specifically illustrates the self-healing capabilities of the dual counter-rotating rings network architecture of FDDI.

In addition to speed and reliability, distance is another key feature of an FDDI LAN. Up to 500 nodes at 2 km apart can be linked to an FDDI network. The total media can stretch for a total circumference of up to 200 km (125 miles) if repeaters are used at least every 2 km. This increased distance capability makes FDDI an excellent choice as a high speed backbone network for campus environments.

Another positive attribute of FDDI, illustrated in Figure 5-16, is its ability to interoperate easily with IEEE 802.3 10-Mbps Ethernet networks. In this way, a business does not have to scrap its entire existing network to upgrade a piece of it to 100 Mbps FDDI. An FDDI-to-Ethernet bridge can be employed in such a setup. Bridges may be able to connect either a single Ethernet or several Ethernet segments to the FDDI LAN.

The technology involved with FDDI network architectures is similar in function to that of other network architectures and is illustrated in Figure 5-16. PCs, workstations, minicomputers, or mainframes that wish to access the FDDI LAN must be equipped with either internal FDDI network adapter cards or external FDDI controllers.

One way in which some network managers cut down on FDDI's cost while still benefiting from the 100-Mbps bandwidth is to only connect to one of FDDI's two fiber rings. This type of connection is sometimes called **SAS,** or **single-attachment stations** as opposed to **DAS,** or **dual-attachment stations,** in which both FDDI rings are accessed. Obviously, if a device is only attached to one FDDI ring, it forgoes the reliability afforded by the redundant secondary data ring.

At the heart of the FDDI LAN is the FDDI concentrator or hub. The design of these hubs is often modular, with backbone connections to both FDDI rings, management modules, and device attachment modules in various media varieties avail-

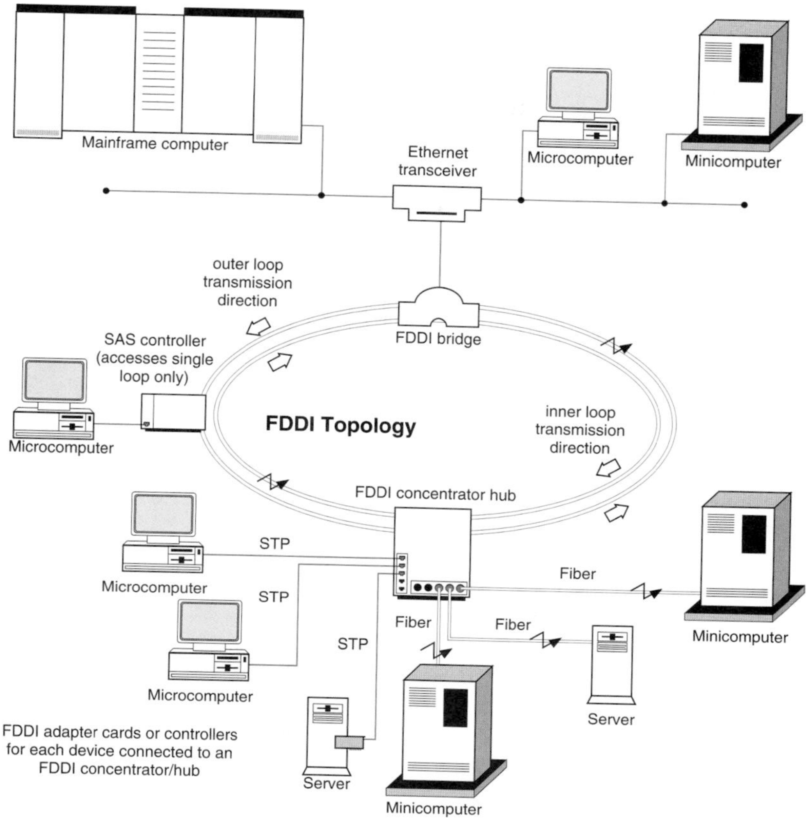

Figure 5-16 FDDI Network Architecture and Technology

able for customized design and ease of installation. In reality, most FDDI traffic is directed through routers with FDDI modules rather than dedicated FDDI hubs or concentrators. Routers are discussed further in Chapter 9.

Standards FDDI uses a modified token-passing access methodology. The word *modified* is used here because it is different from the IEEE 802.5 token ring type token passing in at least two key respects:

- First, due to the great potential distances on an FDDI LAN, it was impractical to turn "free" tokens into "busy" tokens and let a single station monopolize that token until it had received confirmation of successful delivery of its data. Instead, unlike token ring, which just flipped the T bit in the access control byte from 0 to 1 and appended a data frame, FDDI physically removès the token from the ring and transmits a full data frame. On completion of transmission, it immediately releases a new token. Recall that token ring waited until the transmitted frame returned before releasing the token. Collisions are still avoided as only one station can have the free token at a time, and stations cannot put data messages onto the network without a token.

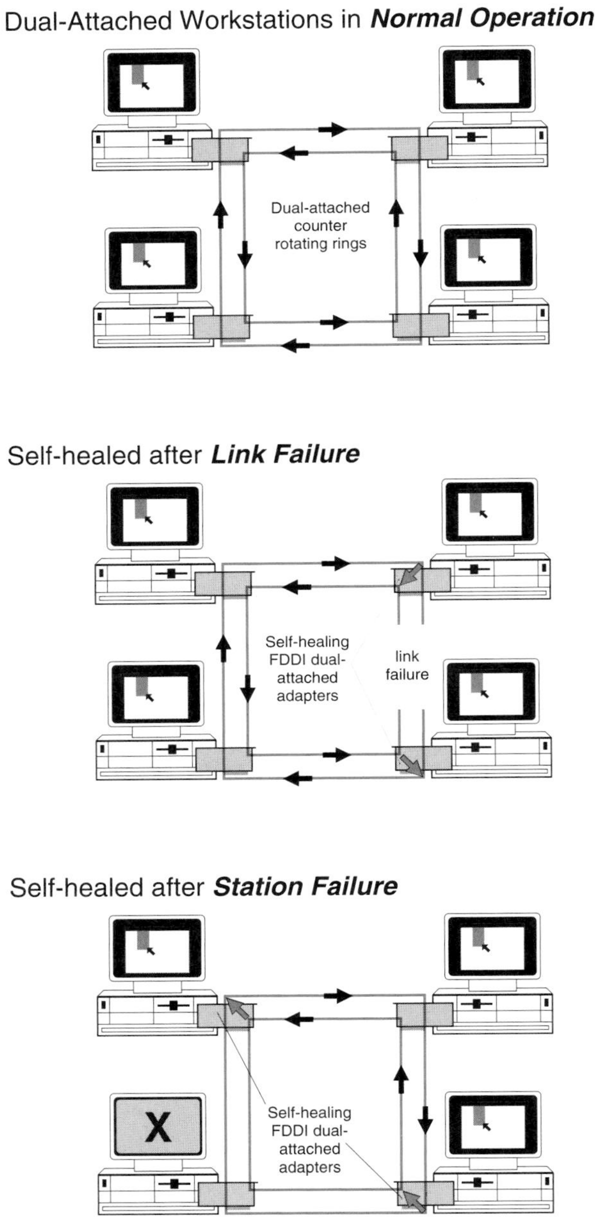

Figure 5-17 FDDI's Self-Healing Ability

- A second token-passing modification in FDDI is that numerous messages may be sent by a single PC before relinquishing the token as opposed to the "one message per token per customer" philosophy of the IEEE 802.5 token-passing access methodology. Frames transmitted in a continuous stream are known as synchronous frames and are prioritized according to a methodology known as synchronous bandwidth allocation or SBA which assigns fixed amounts of bandwidth to given stations. While synchronous frames are being transmitted, any unused network capacity can still be used by other workstations transmitting **asynchronous frames.**

Figure 5-18 illustrates both a FDDI token layout and a FDDI data frame layout.

An alternative to fiber-based FDDI is to run FDDI over copper wiring, either shielded or unshielded twisted pair (UTP), as used in Ethernet and token ring installations. Cost savings of UTP over fiber amount to about 33%. Because running a fiber-based architecture over copper sounds a little strange, this variation of FDDI has been dubbed **CDDI** or **copper distributed data interface.** While it will still support 100 Mbps, distance is limited to 100 m/segment compared with the 2 km/segment of fiber-based FDDI. The official ANSI standard for CDDI is known as **TP-PMD** (twisted pair-physical media dependent). The pinouts or wiring pattern for TP-PMD are different from those of 10 BaseT Ethernet over twisted pair pinouts. CDDI has been largely forgotten with the introduction of 100 Mbps Ethernet alternatives explained later in this chapter.

Application To understand all the fuss about FDDI and CDDI, it is necessary to first understand why 10 Mbps Ethernet and 16 Mbps token ring may not contain sufficient bandwidth for the bandwidth-hungry applications. The major bandwidth drivers fall into two major categories:

1. Network architecture trends
2. Network application trends

As far as trends in network architecture go, as more and more users are attached to LANs, the demand for overall network bandwidth increases. LANs are increasing both in size and overall complexity. Internetworking of LANs of various protocols via bridges and routers means more overall LAN traffic. FDDI is frequently used as a high-speed backbone network architecture servicing multiple lower speed network segments, each of which support multiple workstations, although even higher speed network architectures are being introduced into the network bandwidth hierarchy.

Network applications are driving the demand for increased bandwidth as well. Distributed computing, data distribution, and client/server computing all rely on a network architecture foundation of high bandwidth and high reliability. Imaging, multimedia, and data/voice integration all require high amounts of bandwidth to transport and display these various data formats in "real" time.

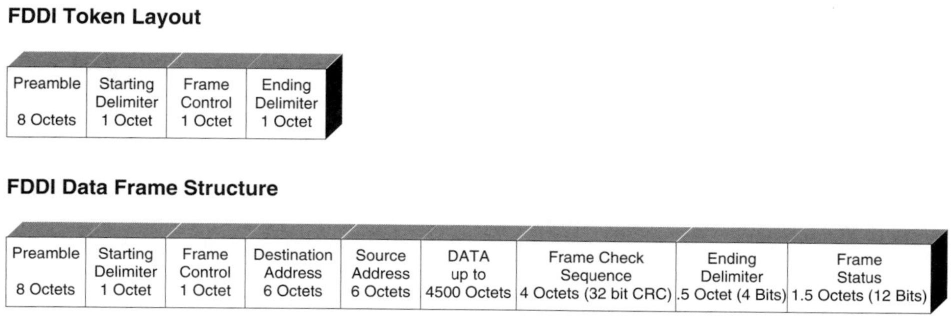

Figure 5-18 FDDI Token and Data Frame Layouts

In other words, if full-motion video is to be transported across the LAN as part of a multimedia program, there should be sufficient bandwidth available on that LAN for the video to run at full speed and not in slow motion. Likewise, digitized voice transmission should sound "normal" when transported across a LAN of sufficient bandwidth.

The uses of the FDDI or other high-speed network architectures seem to fall into three categories. Although FDDI may fulfill any of the listed roles, with the proliferation of relatively inexpensive 100 Mbps Ethernet network interface cards, hubs, and switches, FDDI has been largely relegated to a campus backbone role:

1. Campus backbone—Not necessarily implying a college campus, this implementation is used for connecting LANs located throughout a series of closely situated buildings. Remember that the total ring circumference can equal 200 km. Multiple FDDI LANs are also a possibility. Building backbones would fall into this category as well, with perhaps a 100-Mbps FDDI building backbone going between floors connecting numerous 10-Mbps Ethernet LANs located on the various floors via routers. High-bandwidth devices such as servers can be connected to the FDDI backbone via concentrators. Multiple concentrators attaching multiple devices to the FDDI rings as illustrated in Figure 5-18 are known as a **dual ring of trees.** In some cases, a given server may be connected to more than one FDDI concentrator to provide redundant connections and increased fault tolerance. Connecting servers to more than one network segment in this manner is known as **dual homing.**
2. High-Bandwidth Workgroups—The second application category is when the FDDI LAN is used as a truly local area network, connecting a few (less than 20) PCs or workstations that require high-bandwidth communication with each other. Multimedia workstations, engineering workstations, or CAD/CAM workstations are all good examples of high-bandwidth workstations. As "power users" turn increasingly toward high-bandwidth graphical user interfaces (GUI), this constituency's bandwidth requirements will rise as well.
3. High Bandwidth Subworkgroup Connections—In some cases, only two or three devices, perhaps servers, need high bandwidth requirements. As distributing computing and data distribution increase as part of the downsizing and applications rightsizing trends sweeping the information systems industry, an increasing demand for high-speed server-to-server data transfer will be seen. Figure 5-19 illustrates alternative applications of the FDDI network architecture.

After all of these positive things to say about FDDI, surely there must be something negative about this LAN network architecture. Chief among the negatives is price. As with any other shared-media network architecture, for a PC to access an FDDI LAN, it must be equipped with an FDDI network adapter card. These cards range from $800 to $1000, with the "lower" priced FDDI network adapter cards able to attach to and use only one of the two FDDI data rings. Compare these prices with the average fast Ethernet card at $25 to $200.

The key advantages of FDDI have traditionally been its reliability, speed, and distance capabilities. The ability to support long distances made FDDI the network architecture of choice for campus backbones and metropolitan area networks

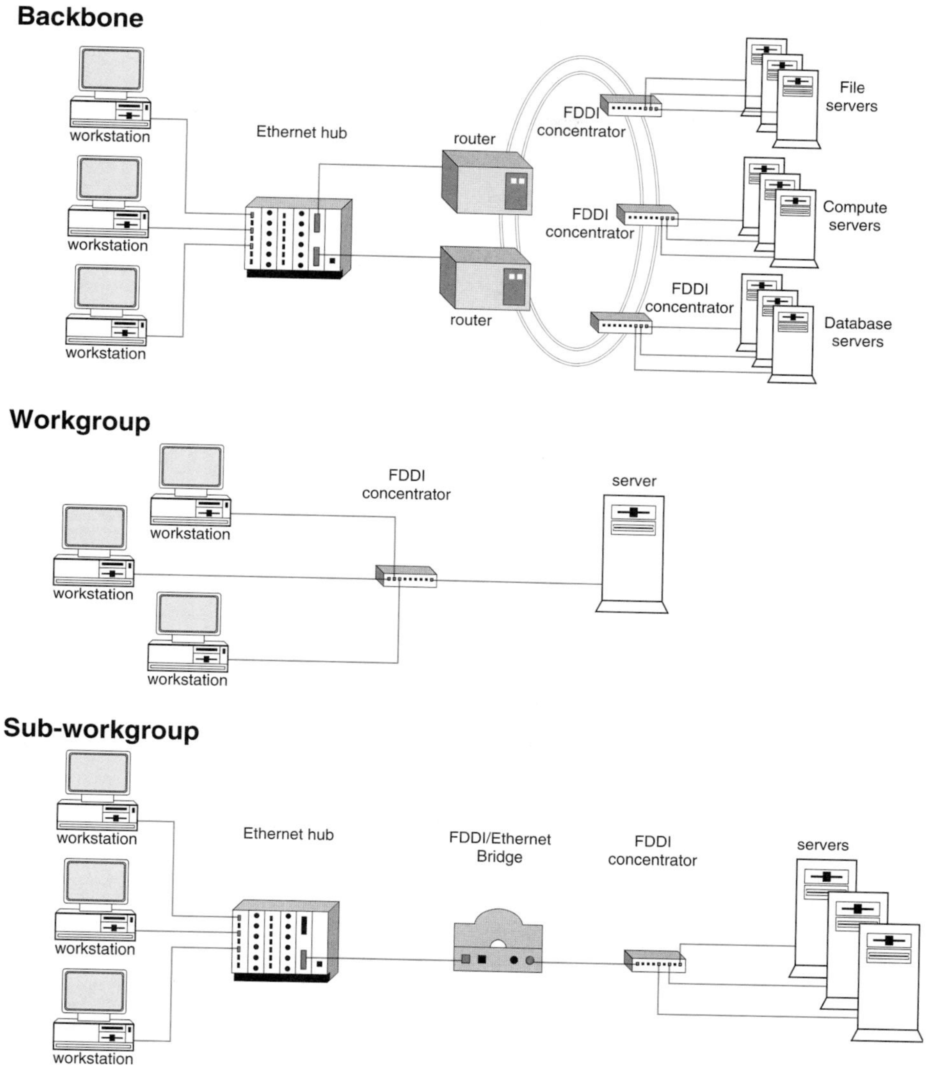

Figure 5-19 Alternative Applications of the FDDI Network Architecture

(MAN). For shorter distances, the fiber media itself has been seen as a negative factor by some detractors. Although fiber is lightweight and can be packed more densely than copper wire, it is made of glass and/or plastic and can easily break. Connecting, terminating, and splicing fiber optic cables require special tools and training. These obstacles can be overcome and, at least in some cases, the "fear of fiber" may be nothing more than the fear of the unknown.

Managerial Perspective

FDDI'S FUTURE

Occasionally in the field of data communications and networking, one technology is eclipsed or replaced by a newer technology that might be cheaper, easier to work with, or both. This has proven to be the case with FDDI. At one time, FDDI was the only network architecture alternative to turn to when Ethernet and token ring could no longer meet demands for robustness, bandwidth, or distance. As will be seen in the next section, there now exist numerous high-speed network architecture alternatives that have eclipsed FDDI in terms of price, performance, and ease of use. Collectively, these newer technologies have made FDDI obsolete. Manufacturing of FDDI controller chips, the heart of a FDDI NIC, ended in 1999. Although major vendors have stockpiled these chips to provide a migration path from FDDI, from a practical perspective FDDI is no longer a viable alternative for a new network. Existing FDDI networks will be migrated to alternative technologies within the next few years.

HIGH-SPEED NETWORK ARCHITECTURES

Fast Ethernet (100BaseT)

100BaseT represents a family of Fast Ethernet standards offering 100-Mbps performance and adhering to the CSMA/CD access methodology. The details of the operation of 100BaseT are in the **IEEE 802.3u** standard. The three media-specific physical layer standards of 100BaseT are as follows:

- **100BaseTX**—This is by far the most common of the three standards and the one for which the most technology is available. It specifies 100-Mbps performance over two pair of Category 5 UTP (unshielded twisted pair) or two pair of Type 1 STP (shielded twisted pair).
- **100BaseT4**—Physical layer standard for 100-Mbps transmission over four pair of Category 3, 4, or 5 UTP.
- **100baseFX**—Physical layer standard for 100-Mbps transmission over duplex multimode fiber optic cable. They key reason to implement 1000BaseFX is the additional distance supported by the fiber media.

Network Architecture 100BaseT standards use the same IEEE802.3 MAC sublayer frame layout and yet transmit it at 10 times faster than 100BaseT. Obviously, there must be a trade-off somewhere. The trade-off comes in the maximum network diameter:

- 100BaseT's maximum network diameter is 2500 m, with up to four repeaters/hubs between any two end nodes.
- 100BaseT's maximum network diameter is 210 m with up to only two repeaters/hubs between end nodes. 100BaseT is implemented as a shared-media LAN network architecture that links 100BaseT workstations via 100BaseT hubs and repeaters.

In Sharper Focus

TIMING ISSUES AND 100BASET NETWORK DIAMETER

Collisions are a fact of life with any CSMA/CD-based network architecture. The time required for a given workstation to detect a collision is known as **slot time** and is measured in bits. When collisions occur, the transmitting station must be notified of the collision so that the affected frame can be retransmitted. However, this collision notification and retransmission must occur before the slot time has expired. The slot time for both 10BaseT and 100BaseT is 512 bits.

The speed of 100BaseT is obviously 10 times as fast as 10BaseT. To be certain that collision notifications are received by 100BaseT network attached workstations before their constant slot time expires, the maximum network diameter had to be reduced proportionately to the increase in network speed. As a result, the maximum network diameter shrinks from 2500 m to 210 m.

Technology Most fast Ethernet NICs are also referred to as **10/100 NICs** because they can support either 10BaseT or 100BaseT. However, a NIC can only operate at one speed at any given time. These cards cost not much more than quality 100-Mbps only cards, allowing network managers to buy fast Ethernet capability now and implement the increased speed later when the requisite fast Ethernet hubs are installed.

Fast Ethernet networks can only interoperate with 10-Mbps Ethernet with the help of internetworking devices such as bridges and routers. These types of technology are discussed in more depth in Chapter 10. Some Ethernet switches, which are discussed in Chapter 6, also have the capability to support fast Ethernet connections and to auto-sense, or distinguish between, 10BaseT and fast Ethernet traffic. Figure 5-20 illustrates a representative fast Ethernet installation.

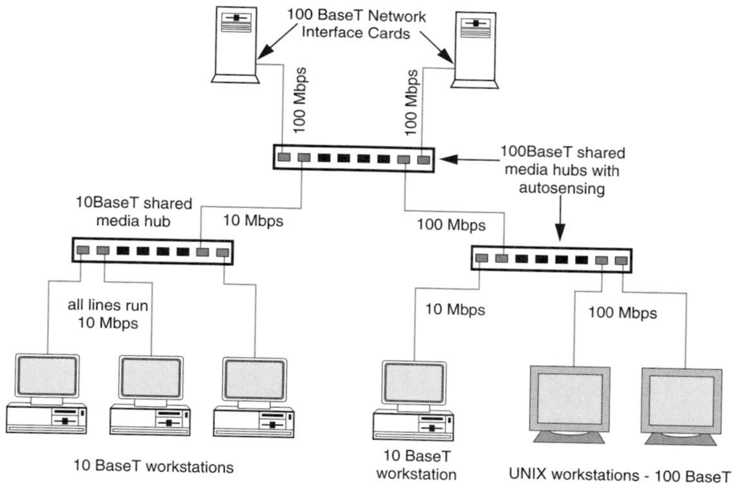

Figure 5-20 100BaseT Network Architecture Implementation

In Sharper Focus

100VG-ANYLAN

100VG-AnyLAN was a 100-Mbps alternative to 100BaseT that replaced the CSMA/CD access methodology with **demand priority access method** or **DPAM.** Details of the 100VG-AnyLAN network architecture are contained in the **IEEE 802.12** standard. The *AnyLAN* part of this network architecture name referred to its ability to deliver standard IEEE 802.3 or IEEE 802.5 MAC layer frames.

Perhaps the most unique aspect of the 100VG-AnyLAN network architecture was the demand priority access methodology, also known as DPMA, demand priority media access. This unique access methodology improved on CSMA/CD by eliminating collisions and transmissions and improved on token ring by eliminating token rotation delays.

Although 100VG-AnyLAN offered the unique ability to easily integrate with both Ethernet and token ring networks, it lost the market penetration (and subsequent price point) war to 100BaseT. Although DPMA can be considered a superior alternative to CSMA/CD, many industry pundits took the viewpoint that "if it isn't CSMA/CD, it isn't Ethernet." Production of 100VG-AnyLAN NICs has ended, effectively killing the technology.

In Sharper Focus

ISOCHRONOUS ETHERNET

One of the key limitations with shared media networks is the inherent variation in the time it takes for a message to transverse the network. Although most data applications can tolerate this variation, it severely limits the network's ability to transport time-sensitive traffic such as voice, video, or multimedia. To combat this limitation, a hybrid Ethernet technology that combined key features of Ethernet and ISDN was developed.

Known as **Isochronous Ethernet** or **Iso-Ethernet,** this hybrid network architecture consisted of a 10-Mbps Ethernet channel combined with 6.144 Mbps ISDN C **channel** that could carry up to 96 telephone conversations at 64 Kbps each. The concept behind Iso-Ethernet was that a single network could offer both data and voice services. However, streaming media technologies such as VOIP have reduced the need for separate media channels effectively sending Iso-Ethernet the way of ARCNET and VG-AnyLAN.

High Speed Token Ring – HSTR

A 100 Mbps token ring network architecture, otherwise known as **high-speed token ring (HSTR)** has been approved by an organization known as the high-speed token ring alliance that is also supposedly working on a gigabit token ring standard. One of the interesting characteristics of the 100-Mbps standard is that it supports a standard for virtual LANs known as IEEE 802.1q, which will allow Ethernet frames to be encapsulated within token ring frames, an important characteristic in organizations that must support both network architectures. Although 100-Mbps token ring NICs, switches, and router modules may be available, remember that compatible driver software must be available for any network operating system to be able to communicate with these devices.

In Sharper Focus

FULL DUPLEX NETWORK ARCHITECTURES

Switched LAN architectures, which are described more thoroughly in the next chapter, depend on specialized LAN wiring centers known as LAN switches and are able to provide dedicated point-to-point links between communicating clients and servers. In the case of Ethernet switches, for example, since the point-to-point link between two communicating PCs is dedicated, there can be no data collisions and there is no longer any need for an access methodology such as CSMA/CD; no other workstations are contending for this dedicated bandwidth connection. As a result, communication between the two computers that serve as the end-points of this switched dedicated connection could both send and receive data to and from each other simultaneously. This switch-dependent capability is known as **full-duplex Ethernet** and requires compliant NICs, NIC drivers, and Ethernet switches. Many

Ethernet switches allow certain ports, such as those attached to servers, to be set to full duplex mode. In such an implementation, only the servers attached to full duplex switch ports would require full duplex NICs. In theory, full duplex Ethernet should allow twice the normal Ethernet performance speed by offering a dedicated 10-Mpbs communication channel in each direction for a total available bandwidth of 20 Mbps.

In practice, the throughput, or actual data transferred, on full duplex Ethernet connections is usually not 20 Mbps. Chief among the reasons for this is that the amount of network transmission is a product of application program design. Most distributed application programs tend to exhibit short requests for services from clients to servers followed by large transfers of data from the server back to the client. However, this is not to say that the technology lacks the ability to deliver higher performance. Controlled tests involving high-bandwidth applications have produced throughput of 20 Mbps. As a result, the most likely implementation scenario for full-duplex Ethernet is in switch-to-switch connections and switch-to-server connections.

Since the full-duplex NIC installed in the computer is both sending and receiving data simultaneously, a multithreaded operating system and network operating system is required to take full advantage of this technology. Examples of such multithreaded operating systems and network operating systems are Windows 2000, Windows NT, NetWare 4 and 5, and most varieties of UNIX. Full-duplex Ethernet has gathered sufficient interest from the networking technology vendor and user communities to warrant the formation of the **IEEE 802.3x** committee to develop standards for full-duplex Ethernet. Full-duplex technology is also either under development or available in full-duplex fast Ethernet (200 Mbps), full-duplex token ring (32 Mbps), and full-duplex FDDI (200 Mbps) varieties.

Gigabit Ethernet

Network Architecture **Gigabit Ethernet,** also known as 1000BaseX, is an upgrade to Fast Ethernet that was standardized as **IEEE 802.3z** by the IEEE on June 25, 1998. The standard defined the following configurations:

- **1000BaseSX:** Uses short wavelength (850 nm) laser multimode fiber optic media, primarily used for horizontal building cabling on a given floor.
- **1000BaseLX:** Uses long wavelength (1300 nm) laser single-mode fiber optic media, primarily used for high speed campus backbone applications.
- **1000BaseCX:** Uses copper twinaxial cable and transceivers for distances of only 25 m, used primarily to link servers within a data center or high-speed network devices within a wiring closet. The subsequent release of 1000BaseTX has effectively killed 1000BaseCX.
- **1000BaseTX:** Ratified in March 1999, this standard uses four pair of Category 5 unshielded twisted pair with a maximum distance of 100 m.

Specifics of the Gigabit Ethernet standard are listed in Figure 5-21. It should be pointed out that the maximum recommended distance over FDDI style multimode fiber optic cable is only 220 m.

Standard	Media	Fiber Core Diameter	Bandwidth	Range
1000BaseTX	4 pair category 5 UTP (unshielded twisted pair)	N/A	N/A	100 m
1000BaseSX	Multimode fiber	62.5 microns	160	2 to 220 m
1000BaseSX	Multimode fiber	62.5 microns	200	2 to 275 m
1000BaseSX	Multimode fiber	50.0 microns	400	2 to 500 m
1000BaseSX	Multimode fiber	50.0 microns	500	2 to 550 m
1000BaseLX	Multimode fiber	62.5 microns	500	2 to 550 m
1000BaseLX	Multimode fiber	50.0 microns	400	2 to 550 m
1000BaseLX	Multimode fiber	50.0 microns	500	2 to 550 m
1000BaseLX	Single mode fiber	9 microns	N/A	2 m to 5 km or more

Figure 5-21 Gigabit Ethernet Fiber-Dependent Configurations

Technology Initially, most Gigabit Ethernet switches and network interface cards only supported either the 1000BaseSX or 1000BaseLX fiber optic-based standards. With the introduction of the 1000BaseTX standard in mid-1999 vendors have rapidly added support for the copper-based standard. Among vendors of Gigabit Ethernet switches and NICs are familiar names such as 3Com, Cabletron, Intel, Lucent, Cisco, Hewlett-Packard, and Nortel, as well as new names such as Foundry, Extreme Networks, and Packet Engines. As with any relatively new technology, multivendor interoperability is a major concern as subtleties of implementation of the Gigabit Ethernet standard are ironed out. Also, beware of switches that merely introduce Gigabit Ethernet interfaces without upgrading the bandwidth of the aggregate switch backplane. Appropriately sized switches should have backplane capacity in the tens of gigabits per second, and tens of millions of packets per second.

The importance of the IEEE 802.3ab 1000BaseT Gigabit Ethernet over copper standard cannot be overstated. Although the fiber-based standards offer a high bandwidth alternative for campus networks, metropolitan area networks, and data centers, the vast majority of installed network media is UTP copper. The introduction of the 1000BaseTX standard was delayed to resolve technical issues associated with maximum transmission distance. The majority of buildings are currently wired with maximum cabling distances up to 100 m, the distance supported by the existing 10BaseT and fast Ethernet over UTP standards. The final 1000BaseTX standard meets this de facto distance requirement.

Although the 1000BaseTX standard supports category 5 UTP, it is important to note that to squeeze gigabit data transfer rates into the limited bandwidth available, the cable installation must be exactly to standard. Unlike the slower 10BaseT and fast Ethernet standards that use only two pair, 1000BaseTX requires all four pair. Organizations that choose to "split pairs" on their existing wiring to carry either two Ethernets or an Ethernet and a telephone line on one cable will be forced to rewire their cable plants. A category 5 wiring plant that exhibits excellent performance under the fast Ethernet standard might not work at all with Gigabit Ethernet.

Although most organizations will implement Gigabit Ethernet in a switch-based configuration, the CSMA/CD MAC protocol was retained for backward compatibility with 10BaseT and fast Ethernet-based full-duplex, shared-media Ethernet implementations. In addition, the minimum and maximum Ethernet frame size has not changed. However, to maintain the required slot time (see In Sharper Focus section earlier in this chapter, "Timing Issues and 100BaseT Network Diameter") given the 10-fold increase in speed over fast Ethernet would have reduced maximum cable lengths to only 10 m. As a solution, Gigabit Ethernet increases the slot size, but not the minimum frame size, from 64 bytes to 512 bytes in a process called carrier extension.

Application Gigabit Ethernet offers two key advantages over previous Ethernet standards: speed and maximum transmission distance when using single mode fiber optic cable. These two advantages directly map to the applications for Gigabit Ethernet.

Support for single mode fiber that can run up to 5 km makes gigabit Ethernet an excellent candidate for campus networks and metropolitan area networks. For networks that do not require bandwidth splitting between telephony and data payloads, gigabit offers a unique combination of speed, distance, cost, and compatibility with existing Ethernet networks. With the imminent demise of FDDI, most FDDI rings will be converted to gigabit Ethernet over the next few years. If streaming media technologies such as VOIP continue to evolve, the domain of gigabit Ethernet in campus and MAN networks may increase to include converged data and voice networks. For more on VOIP and network convergence see Chapter 2.

The raw speed of gigabit Ethernet makes it a natural fit for bandwidth constrained servers and building backbones. By simply adding a gigabit capable switch and gigabit NICs, most server bandwidth constraints can be resolved. However, as the principle of shifting bottlenecks states, fixing one limitation in a network will undoubtedly uncover another. For most applications, both the backbone and server connections must be upgraded to gigabit Ethernet to practically solve bandwidth limitations.

It should be noted that most server hardware and operating systems have a difficult time delivering the speed promise of gigabit Ethernet. Although hardware has improved significantly, most NIC driver designs date back to the days when 10-Mbps Ethernet was considered a "fast" network. From a practical perspective, most current server implementations will have a difficult time delivering over 400 to 600 Mbps on a gigabit Ethernet connection. Although newer hardware and driver architectures will inevitably solve this limitation, 400 to 600 Mbps is in and of itself a vast improvement over the 70 to 80 Mbps commonly delivered via 100 Mbps Ethernet.

Managerial Perspective

ETHERNET BEYOND GIGABIT SPEEDS

Although gigabit Ethernet is in its infancy, researchers are already working on higher-speed Ethernet derivatives. As of October 1999, Lucent had 10 gigabit Ethernet working at short distances in the laboratory. With the continued growth of the Ethernet speed hierarchy, Ethernet (or at least the Ethernet frame) will be a major LAN standard for a long time.

Fibre Channel

Before the introduction of gigabit Ethernet, an alternative network architecture known as **fibre channel,** (ANSI standard X3T9.3) was defined to run at speeds of 133 Mbps to 1.062 Gbps over optical fiber and copper cables. Support for speeds up to 4.268 Gbps are expected in the future. Fibre channel is often used to connect high performance storage devices and RAID subsystems to computers. Fibre channel switches and NICs are also available, although fibre channel is rarely used as an intercomputer architecture.

LAN-Based ATM

ATM (asynchronous transfer mode) is a switched network technology that has been defined at speeds ranging from 25 Mbps to several gigabits per second. Network interface cards are available for both workstations and servers. However, for ATM-based computers to communicate with non-ATM-based computers, a process known as LAN emulation must be implemented. LAN emulation and other ATM-based network architectures fall into the realm of enterprise networking and is described in more detail in Chapter 8. Moreover, for applications to take full advantage of ATM's speed and features, they must be "ATM aware." Although desktop ATM has been implemented in such industries as animation and stock trading, many of the previously mentioned high-speed network architectures are more likely to be implemented for LANs. With that said, however, ATM is a fairly popular choice for high-speed backbone networks. ATM on the LAN is covered in more detail in Chapter 6.

HOME MARKET NETWORK ARCHITECTURES

With the ongoing penetration of computers into the home marketplace, many families are purchasing second or third computers. With the evolution of the multicomputer home, a means to connect these computers becomes desirable. Although most home users do not need a high-speed network, they would like to have a means to gain access to printers, share Internet access (either via modem or broadband connection), and play multiplayer games.

Although any of the traditional networking architectures previously described in this chapter could meet the needs of the average home user, most people are not willing to rewire their homes to install the required media. Nor do they need the bandwidth that traditional network architectures provide. The printer and Internet sharing applications along with multiplayer gaming simply do not require large amounts of bandwidth to implement. In response to this need, vendors have developed new network architectures targeted directly at the home marketplace.

Vendors have developed two basic approaches to providing network connectivity without extensive rewiring of the home: HPNA and wireless solutions.

The HPNA (home phone line networking alliance) is an industry group dedicated to developing a standard approach to providing computer network connectivity over the telephone lines already existing in the home. The term HPNA is commonly used to refer to any network devices that support the standards developed by the HPNA organization. As described in Chapter 2, only a small amount of bandwidth is actually used to make a telephone call. Using a technique known as frequency division multiplexing (see Chapter 2) HPNA works by using the bandwidth in a house's telephone system that is not used by the telephone system. To eliminate potential conflicts with xDSL technologies (see Chapter 8), HPNA also avoids their assigned frequency range. Computers can be installed anywhere in the house as long as they can be connected via cable to a telephone jack. The HPNA system is transparent to use of the telephone. A typical HPNA installation is shown in Figure 5-22. HPNA is essentially Ethernet running over RGYB telephone wiring. The initial specification offered 1 Mbps of bandwidth to up to 25 nodes located within 500 feet of one another. Version 2.0 of the standard has increased base speed to 10 Mbps. HPNA NICs are available in PCMCIA, ISA, and PCI formats, as well as external devices connecting via parallel ports or USB connections.

The second approach to home networking is wireless technologies. Rather than using any existing wires in the home, computers are connected to wireless transmitters. This solution frees users from locating computers near existing phone jacks or adding new phone jacks. However, to keep the cost of wireless home network solutions affordable, most operate at fairly low data speeds of no more than 1.6 Mbps using a media access control technique known as CSMA/CS (carrier sense multiple access with collision avoidance). CSMA/CA induces more overhead into the media access process than traditional CSMA/CD, resulting in less throughput for a given speed than a wired network. Wireless home networks operate in the 2.4 GHz range devoted to public access. Also known as spread spectrum technologies, these devices

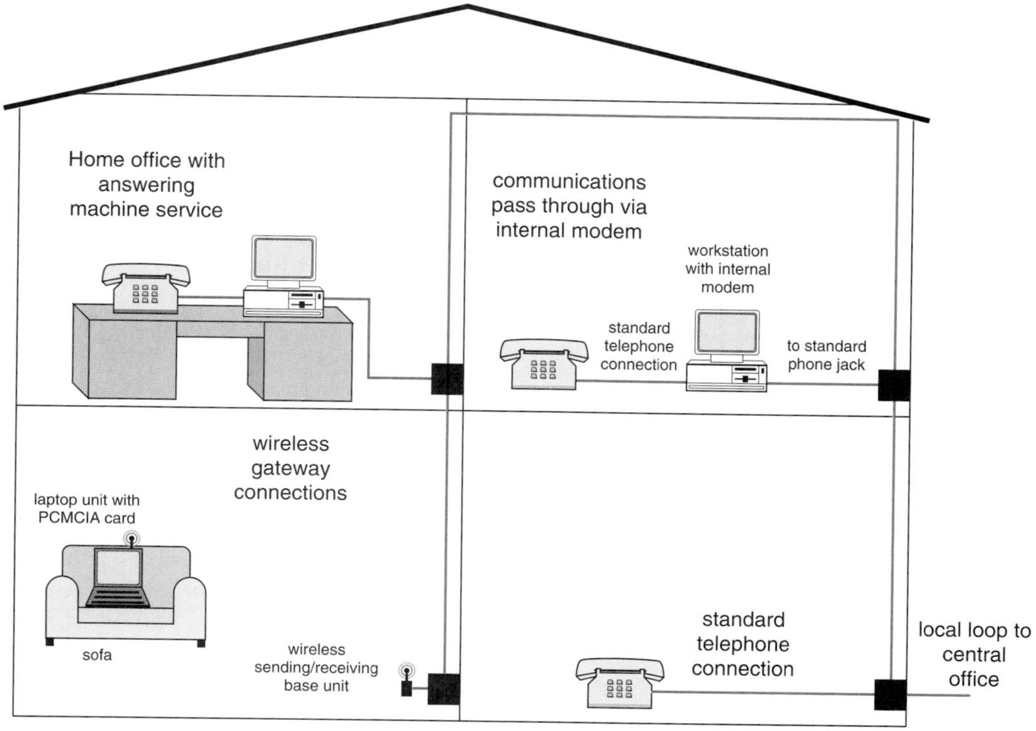

Figure 5-22 HPNA Implementation

change frequencies rapidly to reduce the chance that a conflict with another device will occur. Although there are currently no standards for wireless home networking, most solutions allow for up to 16 nodes to participate on the LAN at ranges up to 150 feet. For more information on spread spectrum technologies, please refer to Chapter 10.

The lack of standardization is likely to be solved through industry cooperation on a new specification for wireless home LANs. One potential solution is the expansion of the HPNA specification to include a wireless version. This would allow for the development of standard wireless/wireline gateways between portable devices and stationary devices attached to the home's telephone system. At costs as low as under $100 per NIC, solutions such as HPNA and wireless home networking are poised to grow rapidly as the Internet and computers become more engrained in popular culture.

Applied Problem Solving

NETWORK ARCHITECTURES IN A NUTSHELL

Many of the shared media network architectures reviewed in this chapter are ideal in certain situations. There is no one "best" network architecture. In addition to all of the shared media network architectures reviewed in this chapter, another entire category of network architectures known as switched network architectures is reviewed in the next chapter. To decide which network architecture is best in any given situation, a top-down approach should be taken:

- What types of applications are required to meet business objectives?
  - Multimedia?
  - Collaborative or distributed computing?
  - Large or frequently distributed database lookups?
  - Specialized applications such as CAD/CAM, medical imaging, or video editing?
  - Internet or IP-Based Telephony?
- What are the bandwidth and network delivery requirements of the data produced by these applications?
  - High bandwidth needs?
  - Guaranteed delivery times for time-sensitive or streaming traffic?
  - Large database downloads or replications?
  - Additional bandwidth is not always the answer. Application or processing latency can vary independently of the amount of bandwidth. Understand bottlenecks well before designing your network.
- What is the cost threshold for upgrading to a high speed network architecture?
  - FDDI NICs traditionally cost about $1000 each and offer 100 Mbps
  - 100BaseT NICs now cost about $50 each and offer 100 Mbps. At these prices, perhaps a company doesn't even need a high bandwidth or time-sensitive application to justify upgrading to a high-speed network architecture. Even traditional applications will be transported much more quickly.
  - Gigabit Ethernet NICs currently cost around $600, with prices consistently falling as the technology becomes more mainstream.

- Which upgrade philosophy is preferred?
  - Replace all NICs, hubs, and possibly cabling?
  - Replace hubs and NICs in a gradual manner?
  - Replace just the hubs and leave the NICs and cabling alone? This option is really only available with switched network architectures, which are studied in the next chapter.
- When considering an upgrade to a particular high-speed network architecture, these are some of issues that may require attention:
  - New NICs
  - New NIC drivers; Can be a real problem. Where is the source of these drivers? As will be explained later in the text, drivers must be compatible with a particular NIC and the network operating system and operating system of the computer in which the NIC is installed.
  - Proper cabling to meet new cable specifications
  - New hubs
  - Management software
  - New distance limitations
  - New rules for cascading hubs or maximum number of repeaters between two end nodes
  - Availability of internetworking hardware such as bridges and routers that are compatible with this particular high-speed network architecture. Without such hardware, the network will not be able to be extended beyond the immediate local network.

SUMMARY

To properly analyze and design local area networks, it is essential to have a thorough understanding of the OSI model and its constituent layers. Of particular interest is the data link layer that serves as the home of the IEEE LAN standards and is subdivided into the MAC and LLC sublayers for that purpose. The processes of encapsulation and deencapsulation as OSI model processes are the basis of understanding communication between two computing devices. The importance of protocol compatibility to network communications can be modeled using the OSI Model as an open framework for protocol compatibility design.

LAN media can differ significantly in cost, supported speeds, ease of use, and network architectures supported. Although fiber optic cable was at one time considered to be the only media suitable for speeds of 100 Mbps and greater, Category 5 unshielded twisted pair seems to be a common media option for high-speed network standards. New advanced testing techniques have been developed to ensure that UTP will be capable of transmitting high-speed network architectures such as gigabit Ethernet.

The local area network architecture model distills all network architectures into three basic components: access methodology, logical topology, and physical topology. Network architectures applied to a variety of media alternatives are known as network configurations. Key access methodologies are CSMA/CD and token passing, logical topologies are either broadcast or sequential, and physical topologies are most often star, although bus and ring are also possible.

Two of the most popular network architectures are Ethernet (IEEE 802.3) and token ring (IEEE 802.5). Comparisons between the two are no longer as intense as they might have once been given Ethernet's market dominance and significant price advantage. The most popular current implementation of Ethernet is 10BaseT, which uses unshielded twisted pair as media.

FDDI is the most robust traditional high-speed network architecture, offering 100-Mbps performance over dual counterrotating rings of fiber optic cable. The dual counterrotating network architecture affords FDDI exceptional fault tolerance, redundancy, and reliability.

Fast Ethernet is a CSMA/CD-based 100-Mps network architecture that operates over the two pair of twisted pair but is limited to a network diameter of only 210 m. With almost all current NICs, hubs, and switches now supporting both 100 Mbps and 10baseT, fast Ethernet has effectively become the introductory Ethernet LAN technology.

Gigabit Ethernet, 1000baseX, offers extremely high bandwidth over fiber optic cable and copper cabling. Gigabit Ethernet is rapidly becoming the network architecture of choice for backbone and server connectivity applications. Other high-speed architectures continue to be proposed and developed as the thirst for more bandwidth continues unabated.

No single network architecture can be considered the best in all situations. Top-down analysis examining business, application, and data issues is required before determining which network architecture is most appropriate in each situation.

KEY TERMS

4 conductor station wire
10/100 NICs
1000BaseSX
1000BaseLX
1000BaseCX
1000BaseTX
100BaseFX
100BaseT4
100BaseTX
10Base2
10Base5
10BaseF
10BaseT
1Base5
access methodologies
active monitor
address bit order reversal
applications layer
asynchronous frames
attachment units
attenuation
AU
AWG
baseband transmission
broadcast
bus
carrier sense multiple access with collision detection
CAT 5+
CAT 5e
CDDI
copper distributed data interface
CRC
CSMA/CD
cyclical redundancy check
DAS
data-link layer
deencapsulation
demand priority access method
DPA
dual attachment stations
dual homing
dual ring of trees
early token release mechanism
EC5
EIA/TIA 568
Enhanced Category 5 UTP
EMI
encapsulation
end-to-end network links
Ethernet
Ethernet II
FCS
FDDI
Fast Ethernet
fibre channel
fiber distributed data interface
flat gray modular
frame check sequence
frame status flags
frames
full-duplex Ethernet
gigabit Ethernet
header
high-speed token ring
HSTR
IEEE
IEEE 802.12
IEEE 802.2
IEEE 802.3
IEEE 802.3u
IEEE 802.3x
IEEE 802.3z
IEEE 802.5
Institute of Electrical and Electronic Engineers
Integrated services digital
Integrated services terminal
ISDN
Iso-Ethernet
Isochronous Ethernet
least significant bit
LLC
LLC sublayer
logical link control
logical ring, physical star
logical topology
MAC sublayer
media access control
media sharing LANs
message
multimode
multimode graded index fiber

multimode step index
near-end crosstalk
network interface card
network layer
NExT
OSI model
packets
physical layer
physical topology
point-to-point data links
powersum crosstalk
presentation layer
propagation delay
protocol
protocol discriminator
RFI
ring
RYGB
SAS
SBA
sequential
session layer
shielding
single attachment stations
single mode
single point of failure
slot time
SNAP
star
subnetwork access protocol
token
token passing
TP-PMD
trailer
transport layer
unshielded twisted pair
UTP

REVIEW QUESTIONS

1. What is the importance of the OSI model to LAN analysis and design?
2. What is a protocol?
3. What is the relationship between protocols and the OSI model?
4. What is the overall purpose of the physical layer?
5. What are the major differences between a point-to-point link and an end-to-end link?
6. Why is the data-link layer of particular interest to LAN network architectures?
7. Define the relationship between the two data-link layer sublayers.
8. What does the introduction of data-link layer sublayers offer in terms of increased interoperability options?
9. In general, what are the purposes of the header and trailer added to data-link layer frames.
10. Where are data-link layer frames built, and why is this an appropriate place?
11. What is the relationship between the network layer and the data-link layer?
12. What is the relationship between the transport layer and the network layer?
13. Why is the session layer of more interest to client/server information systems?
14. Name at least two misconceptions as to the interpretation of layer functionality.
15. Briefly explain the purpose of encapsulation/de-encapsulation.
16. Why is twisted pair twisted?
17. What is the importance of EIA/TIA 568?
18. What is the most common type category of UTP installed today and why?
19. Why is UTP Category 5 favored over shielded twisted pair, coax, and fiber optic cable for many high speed network architectures?
20. Why is shielded twisted pair considered trickier to install than UTP?
21. What is the difference between powersum crosstalk and pair-to-pair crosstalk?
22. How are Levels 5, 6, and 7 different from Category 5?
23. Why are testing and certification specifications required beyond CAT 5?
24. What are the three elements that make up any network architecture?
25. Compare and contrast CSMA/CD and token passing as access methodologies.
26. What are two different potential causes of collisions in Ethernet networks?
27. What does the early token release mechanism accomplish?
28. What actually is a token?
29. What is the difference between a logical and a physical topology?
30. Differentiate between the broadcast and sequential logical topologies.
31. Differentiate between the bus, star, and ring physical topologies.
32. Differentiate between Ethernet II and IEEE 802.3 Ethernet.
33. What is the relationship between IEEE 802.2 and IEEE 802.3?
34. Differentiate between IEEE 802.2 and Ethernet SNAP.
35. What is a protocol discriminator?
36. Differentiate among the various media-specific alternative configurations of 10 Mbps Ethernet.
37. What are the unique characteristics of a token ring network architecture?
38. What is the role of the active monitor in a token ring network?

39. How are timing issues significant to token ring networks?
40. Differentiate between Ethernet and token ring in terms of performance at various traffic levels.
41. What advantages does FDDI offer over Ethernet and token ring?
42. Explain the self-healing powers of FDDI.
43. What are FDDI's primary negative attributes?
44. What are the three primary uses of the FDDI network architecture?
45. What is the advantage of dual homing?
46. Compare the advantages and disadvantages of 100BaseT and FDDI.
47. What is the advantage of buying 10/100 NICs?
48. What are the advantages and disadvantages of gigabit Ethernet?
49. What are the available media alternatives and their maximum distances for gigabit Ethernet?
50. What are the advantages and disadvantages of high-speed token ring?

ACTIVITIES

1. Prepare a presentation or bulletin board consisting of an empty OSI 7 layer model. As local area networks or network operating systems are encountered, place the protocols in the proper layers of the OSI model.
2. From the previous activity, determine which categories of protocols do not conform well to a particular layer of the OSI model.
3. Design an alternative network communications protocol model to the OSI model. Justify why the new model is more effective than the OSI model.
4. Prepare a display including electrical specifications of the various types of LAN media cited in Chapter 5. Detail network architectures and maximum transmission speeds to which each media type is assigned.
5. Choose a particular protocol stack and outline the frame layouts for each protocol in each layer of the OSI model. Be sure to indicate which protocols are encapsulated by which other protocols.
6. Investigate the IEEE 802.4 token bus standard. Report on its history, implementation, available technology, current status, and an explanation of this current status.
7. Survey the local area network implementations in your school or business. Report on the physical topologies found. Explain your results.
8. Investigate the daisy chain physical topology. Is it truly a unique physical topology or a variation of one of three primary physical topologies?
9. Conduct a survey of Ethernet networks in your school or business. What is the media of choice in each installation? Why was each media chosen in each situation?
10. Survey schools or companies that have installed token ring networks. Report on the reasons for their choice and add your own analysis of the results.
11. Survey schools or business that employ FDDI network architectures. Gather information regarding motivation, installation date, satisfaction, problems, and the outcome of a similar decision on network architecture made today.
12. Investigate the gigabit Ethernet market. What vendors are currently manufacturing NICs and switches? What are the statistics on market size for the technology? Analyze and present your results.

CASE STUDY

Fla. School District Gives Data Mining High Marks

A lot of companies use data-mining to comb through databases to figure out which of their products sells best and where. Now a public school district is using equally sophisticated technology to analyze student performance.

Florida's Broward County School District is outfitting each of its 207 schools with an IBM AS/400 running IBM's DB2 so school administrators can record student test scores and absenteeism, and analyze trends using IBM's desktop data-mining tools.

The goal is to give administrators an easy way to get a historical view of each child's academic performance, says Nancy Terrell, director of strategic planning and accounting for the district.

In addition, officials who want to see how their school performance compares with other county schools can get remote access over a private-line network connecting the schools to the central data repository maintained by the county's Education Technology Service (ETS).

This data repository is also based on the IBM AS/400 running DB2. It is now getting daily student updates based on data input by school administrators during the regular course of their jobs at schools that use the new system.

With a population of 250,000 students, Broward County School District is the fifth-largest in the U.S. By next year, all the Broward student data is expected to be searchable online by authorized school administrators using passwords and IBM's Brio data-mining software for the PC or Macintosh. The county is also considering how to make select parts of the repository's information available on the Web to parents.

"We need to see how a child has done historically on standardized tests over a period of time," Terrell says. "We used to have a great many disparate databases, and it was hard to get that information. We had to go through a large, forbidding printout to do a comparison on how well one class did in comparison with another."

Mindful of privacy concerns, Broward County has taken steps to ensure that the central data repository in the ETS office will only display average scores of schools – not individual student scores – when accessed remotely. "I can't pull up an individual student's scores at school unless it's my own school," Terrell says.

Phyllis Chasser, senior data warehouse analyst for the district, says teachers who use the Brio software are discovering more about student learning patterns.

"One math teacher was very upset because his students were only doing average on math tests," Chasser says. "He went online at our data warehouse and found that a good portion of the students were scoring poorly on building graphics. He was surprised, and changed his teaching to focus more on graphics."

Broward County has been able to implement its data-mining project under a $2 million grant from IBM for "reinventing education" that covers the cost of services but not equipment. Data mining is already showing its value in letting school officials complete in an afternoon the kind of analysis that used to take several days, Terrell says.

Source: Ellen Messmer, "Fla. School district give data-mining high marks," *Network World*, vol. 17, no. 9 (February 28, 2000), p. 39.
Copyright Network World. Reprinted with permission.

BUSINESS CASE STUDY QUESTIONS

Activities

1. Complete a top-down model for this case by gleaning facts from the case and placing them in the proper layer of the top-down model. After having completed the top-down model, analyze and detail those instances where requirements were clearly passed down from upper layers to lower layers of the model and where solutions to those requirements were passed up from lower layers to upper layers of the model.
2. Detail any questions about the case that may occur to you for which answers are not clearly stated in the article.

Business

1. What was the motivation or problem that initiated the search for the implemented solution?
2. What was the productivity impact of the implemented solution?
3. What are the key goals for the data-mining solution?
4. What business benefit has the school district already received from the system?

Application

1. For what types of applications is data-mining normally used?
2. What is different about the data-mining solution used in the case from the "normal" data-mining scenario of question 1?
3. What types of comparisons can the system make?
4. What privacy concerns does the system take into account? How are these concerns addressed?

Data

1. What types of data does the system store and analyze?
2. For how many students are data kept?
3. What is the geographical scope of the system?

Network

1. What underlying network technologies were key to the achievement of stated business objectives?

Technology

1. What specific technologies were employed to deliver the described solution?

CHAPTER 6

LOCAL AREA NETWORK HARDWARE

Concepts Reinforced

OSI Model
Network Architectures
IEEE 802 Standards
Protocols and Standards
Top-Down Model
Physical Topologies
High-Speed Network Architectures
Hardware/Software Compatibility

Concepts Introduced

LAN Technology Architecture
Network Interface Card Technology
Network Interface Card Drivers
LAN Media Alternatives
Switched LAN Architectures
Shared-Media LAN Wiring Centers
LAN Switches
Desktop ATM

OBJECTIVES

Upon successful completion of this chapter, you should:

1. Understand the interaction between the various hardware and software components of the local area network (LAN) technology architecture.
2. Understand the differences between switched LAN architectures and shared-media LAN architectures.
3. Understand the importance of compatible network interface card drivers to overall network implementation.
4. Understand the comparative differences between and proper application of available network interface cards.
5. Understand the comparative differences between and the proper application of available hubs, multistation access unit (MAUs), switching hubs, concentrators, and similar devices.
6. Understand the comparative differences between and the proper application of the various available types of LAN media.

INTRODUCTION

Chapter 5 reviewed the relative merits of the various network architectures that can be implemented to link clients and servers. Chapter 6 focuses on the hardware technology that must be employed to implement a given network architecture. The transition from shared-media network architectures to hardware-based switched network architectures represents a major paradigm shift in terms of LAN design. As applications demand more and more bandwidth, numerous alternatives exist for upgrading network capacity. Choosing the right upgrade path requires a thorough understanding of the LAN hardware described in this chapter.

To provide an appreciation for the interaction of all of the various LAN hardware components, Chapter 6 begins by introducing the reader to the LAN technology architecture. To understand the role of LAN switches in network architectures, the differences between switched-based and shared-media LAN architectures are outlined, followed by a detailed review of LAN hardware alternatives.

THE LOCAL AREA NETWORK TECHNOLOGY ARCHITECTURE

In general terms, any LAN, regardless of network architecture, requires the following components:

- A central wiring concentrator of some type that serves as a connection point for all attached local area network devices. Depending on the particular network architecture involved and the capabilities of the wiring center, this device can be known alternatively as a hub, MAU, CAU, concentrator, LAN switch, or a variety of other names.
- Media such as shielded or unshielded twisted pair, coaxial cable, or fiber optic cable must carry network traffic between attached devices and the wiring center of choice.
- **Network interface cards (NICs)** are installed either internally or externally to client and server computers to provide a connection to the LAN of choice.
- Finally, **network interface card drivers** are software programs that bridge the hardware/software interface between the network interface card and the computer's network operating system. Figure 6-1 summarizes the key components of the LAN technology architecture.

Implications of LAN Technology Choices

Within each of the major categories of LAN technology illustrated in Figure 6-1, numerous alternatives exist as to the specific make, model, and manufacturer of the technology that may be chosen. It is important to note that choosing a particular technology in one LAN technology category may have significant implications or limitations on available technology choices in other LAN technology categories. It is also important to fully understand the implications of a given technology decision before purchase. Figure 6-2 attempts to graphically portray some of the relationships

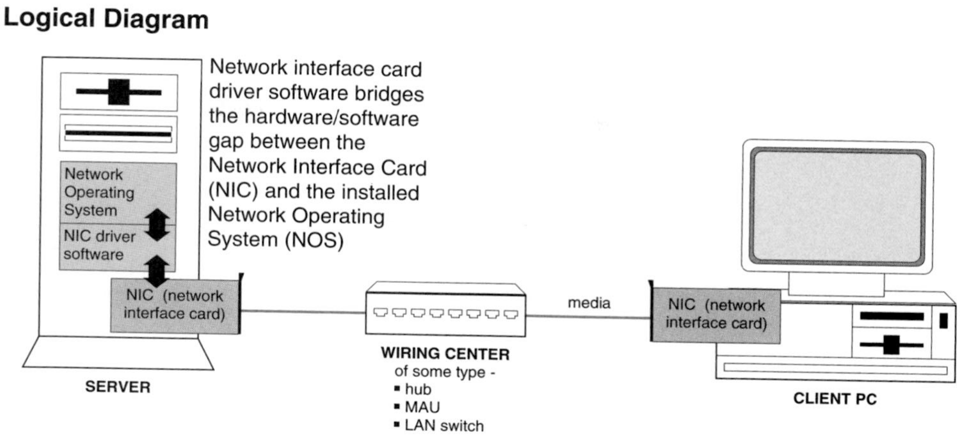

Figure 6-1 The Local Area Network Technology Architecture

and dependencies among technology choices in a variety of LAN technology categories.

MEDIA-SHARING LAN ARCHITECTURES VS. SWITCHED LAN ARCHITECTURES

As client/server information systems and distributed computing applications have put increasing demands on the local area network infrastructure in terms of the amount of data traffic to be transferred, network architects and technology providers have responded with alternative solutions.

As seen in Chapter 5, one solution to the network bandwidth crunch is to offer higher speed **shared-media network architectures** such as high-speed token ring, fast Ethernet, or gigabit Ethernet. Each of these alternatives possess the same basic shared-media structure as Ethernet and token ring, the only difference being that the higher speed alternatives offer more bandwidth for all attached workstations to share. Media-sharing network wiring centers such as hubs offer all attached workstations shared access to a single LAN segment. If the hub happens to be a 10BaseT Ethernet hub, then all attached workstations must share access to the single 10-Mbps LAN segment, whereas 100-BaseT hubs offer shared access for all attached workstations to a single 100-Mbps LAN segment. The shared-media approach is the same in both cases, the only difference being the amount of available bandwidth to be shared. As discussed in Chapter 5, on a shared-media LAN, only one node can transmit at any given time.

Switched LAN architectures depend on wiring centers called LAN switches or switching hubs that resolve the one at a time limitation of shared-media LAN architectures by offering all attached workstations access to a switching matrix that provides point-to-point connections between any two ports. Each port on the LAN switch is effectively a dedicated LAN segment with dedicated bandwidth offered to the attached devices. Each port on the LAN switch may be assigned to a single workstation or to an entire LAN segment linked by a media-sharing network architecture

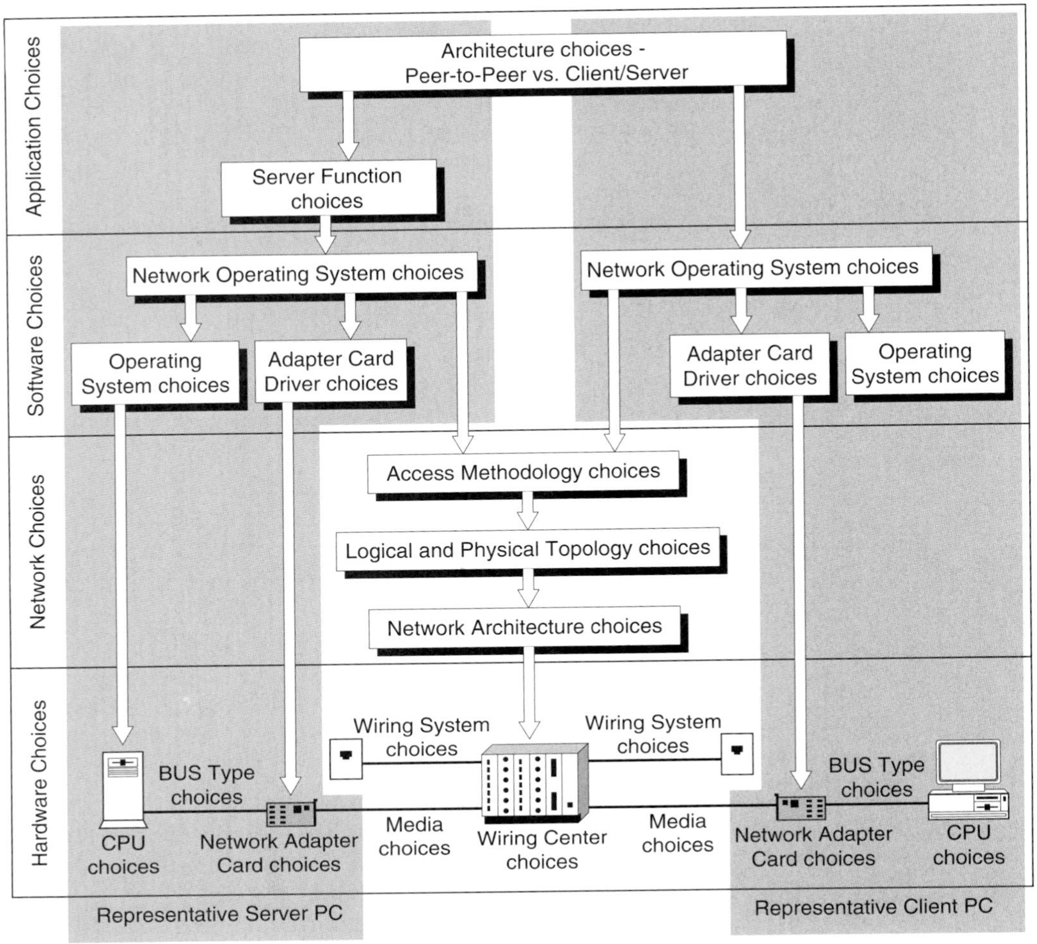

Figure 6-2 Implications of LAN Technology Choices

(nonswitching) hub. Although shared-media LAN segments can link to a LAN switch to take advantage of its dedicated connections and guaranteed bandwidth, there is no shared media or shared bandwidth within the switched LAN architecture itself. The limiting factor in a switch-based LAN architecture is the number of simultaneous point-to-point connections that a given switch can support, commonly referred to as switch **backplane capacity.** Figure 6-3 contrasts the differences in wiring center functionality between media-sharing and switch-based LAN architectures.

Switched LAN architectures are essentially a multiport LAN bridge. As detailed in Chapter 9, a bridge has the ability to connect LANs running at different speeds. In this manner an Ethernet LAN switch can transparently connect nodes or LAN segments running at 10 Mbps with nodes or LAN segments running at 100 Mbps or even gigabit speeds. As shown in Figure 6-4, by exercising this multispeed capability, a network speed hierarchy can be developed that allows network traffic to be aggregated onto a high-speed backbone or a high-speed server link. This ability is essential to build a large network where many client nodes need to communicate with a limited number of centralized servers.

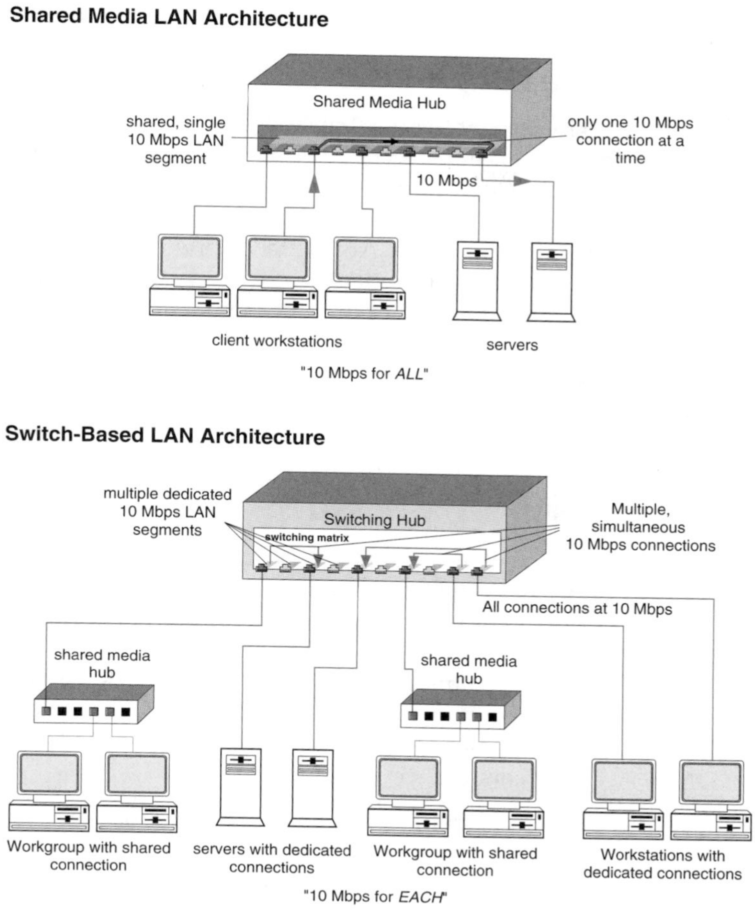

Figure 6-3 Switched LAN Architectures vs. Media-Sharing LAN Architectures Wiring Center Functionality

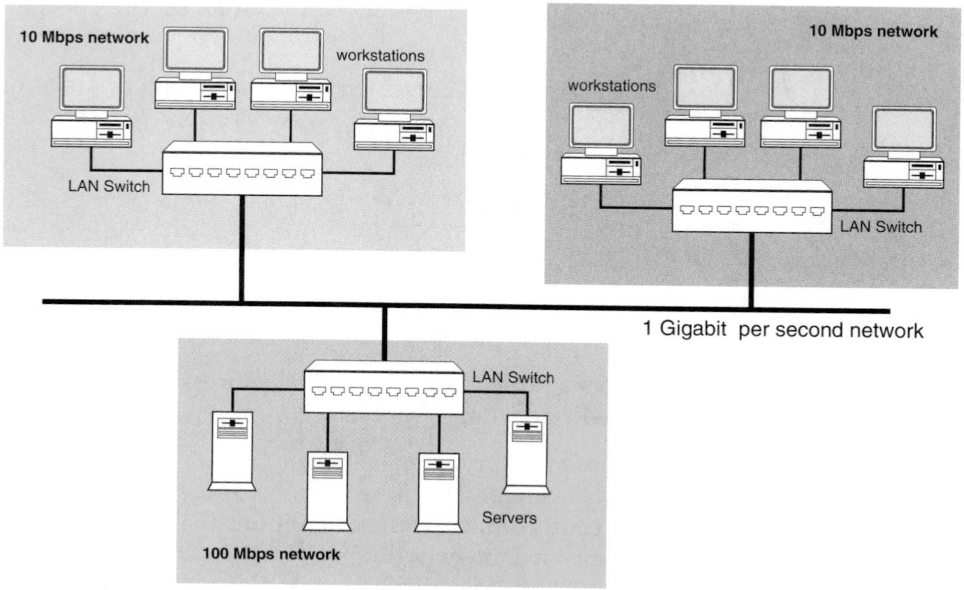

Figure 6-4 Building a Bandwidth Hierarchy with a Switched LAN Architecture

Managerial Perspective

ADVANTAGES OF SWITCHED LAN ARCHITECTURES

It is important to note that switched LAN architectures implementations only change the wiring center technology and, as a result, the manner in which workstations are able to set up point-to-point communications to each other. In other words, network interface cards, network interface card drivers, and media do not change. For this reason, installing a LAN switch is often the first and easiest alternative chosen when network bandwidth demands exceed current supply. To go from an Ethernet shared-media architecture to an Ethernet switch-based architecture, it is only necessary to replace the shared-media hub with an Ethernet LAN switch. To migrate from a token ring shared-media environment to a token ring switch-based architecture, it is only necessary to replace the shared media MAUs (multistation access units) with a token ring LAN switch.

Practical Advice and Information

LAN SWITCH TRAFFIC ANALYSIS

It is important to analyze the traffic patterns between attached clients and servers before swapping out hubs and installing switches. To minimize the interswitch traffic, which represents a potential bottleneck, the following are suggested:

- It is important to have those workstations and servers that communicate most often with each other attached to the same switch since switches differ in their cascadability and in the speed of the interswitch communications connection.
- Another benefit of analyzing traffic patterns before installing the switch is to identify those users and workstations that must have a dedicated switch port and those that can reside on a shared LAN segment attached to a switched port.

The following are a few general guidelines for switch port allocation:

- Servers and high-end workstations should ideally have their own switch port.
- Distributed computing power users with frequent queries to servers should be able to be connected to switch ports via shared LAN segments of up to eight nodes.
- Casual or light traffic users accessing only e-mail and terminal, character-based programs can be connected to switch ports via shared LAN segments of 50 or more nodes.
- The ability of LAN switches to support multiworkstation LAN segments on a single switch port may vary among switches.
- The number of workstation addresses that can be supported by a given switch port may vary as well.

Furthermore, swapping a shared-media hub for a LAN switch will not necessarily improve all network traffic situations. If a server has only one 10-Mbps network interface card installed with which it must service all client requests, a LAN switch will not improve the network performance. In fact, due to the latency introduced by the switch to set up switched connections, the performance may actually degrade.

The power of a LAN switch is its ability to support simultaneous connections between any combination of clients and servers. It is but one piece of a solution to network performance bottlenecks that can be effectively implemented only after a thorough network traffic analysis has been conducted.

Implementation Scenarios for Switched LAN Architectures

Depending on switch capacity and installed components, LAN switches can be implemented to fulfill a variety of different roles.

- **Stand-alone workgroup/departmental LAN switches**—Offer dedicated connections to all attached client and server computers via individual switch ports. Such an implementation is appropriate for multimedia or videoconferencing workstations and servers. In some cases, such as a distributed computing environment, dedicated ports are only necessary for servers, whereas client workstations share a switch port via a cascaded media-sharing hub. This variation is sometimes referred to as a **server front-end LAN switch.**
- **Backbone-attached workgroup/departmental LAN switches**—Offer all of the local switching capabilities of the stand-alone workgroup/departmental LAN switch plus switched access to higher speed backbone networks. This higher speed backbone connection may be to a higher capacity backbone switch or may be to a higher speed shared-media device such as a backbone router.
- **Backbone/data center switches**—Offer high-capacity, fault-tolerant, switching capacity with traffic management capabilities. These high-end switches are really a self-contained backbone network, which is sometimes referred to as a **collapsed backbone network.** These backbone switches most often offer switched connectivity to other workgroup switches, media-sharing hubs, and corporate servers that must be accessed by multiple departments/workgroups. They are often modular in design, allowing different types of switching modules such as Ethernet, token ring, fast Ethernet, and ATM (asynchronous transfer mode) to share access to a high-capacity switching matrix or backplane.

Figure 6-5 highlights the differences between these switched LAN architecture implementation scenarios.

In Sharper Focus

FULL DUPLEX NETWORK ARCHITECTURES

Switched LAN architectures provide dedicated point-to-point links between communicating clients and servers. In the case of Ethernet switches, for example, since the point-to-point link between two communicating PCs is dedicated, there can be no data collisions, and there is no longer any need for an access methodology such as CSMA/CD, because no other workstations are contending for this dedicated bandwidth connection. As a result, two computers that serve as the end-points of this switched dedicated connection could both send and receive data simultaneously. This switch-dependent capability is known as **full-duplex Ethernet** and requires specialized full-duplex Ethernet NICs, NIC drivers, and full-duplex Ethernet switches. Many Ethernet switches allow certain ports, such as those attached to

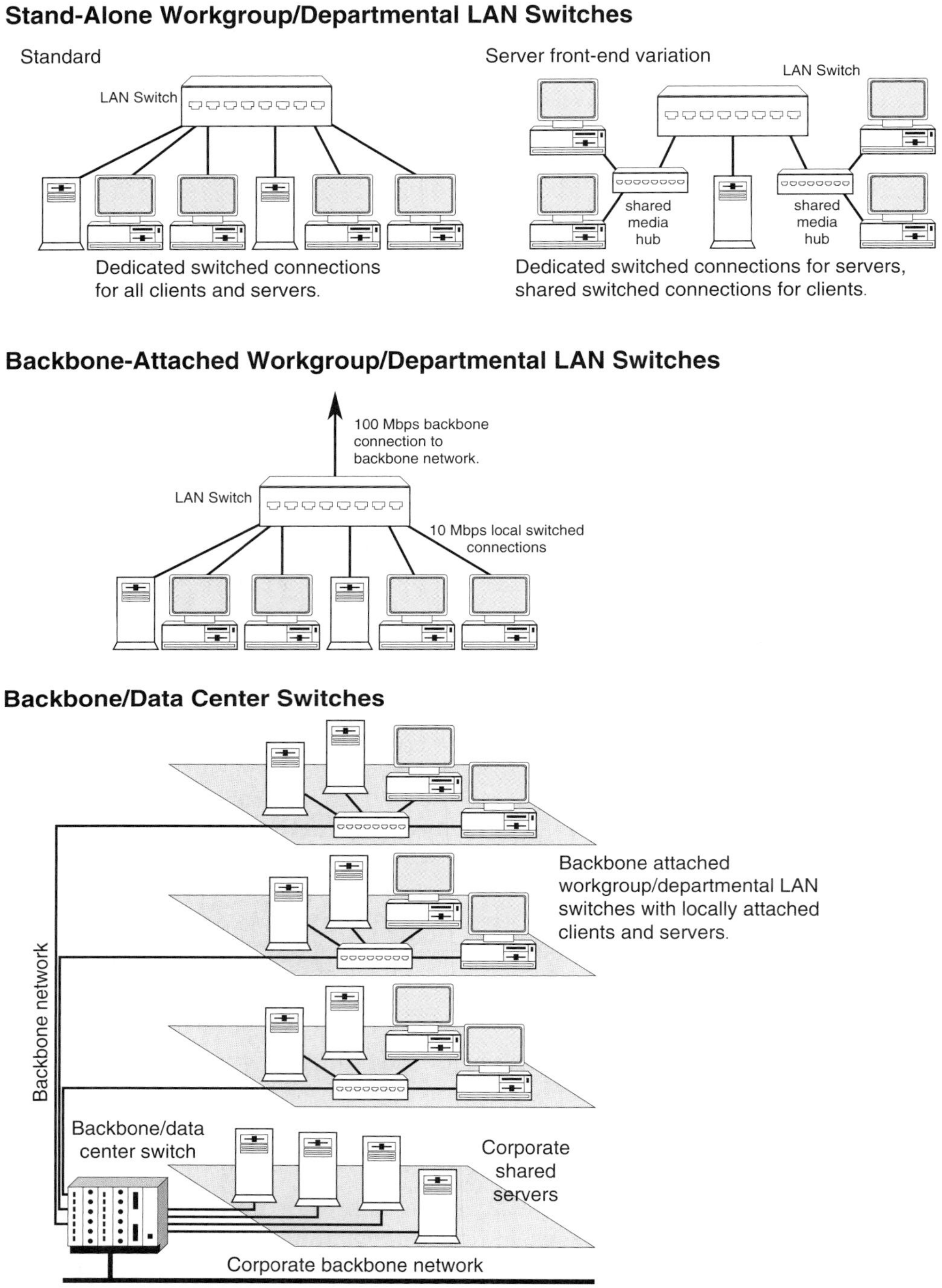

Figure 6-5 Implementation Scenarios for Switched LAN Architectures

servers, to be set for full-duplex Ethernet. In such an implementation, only the servers attached to full-duplex switch ports would require full-duplex NICs. In theory, full-duplex Ethernet should allow twice the normal Ethernet performance speed by offering a dedicated 10-Mbps communication channel in each direction for a total available bandwidth of 20 Mbps for traditional Ethernet, 200 Mbps for fast Ethernet, or 2000 Mbps for gigabit Ethernet.

In practice, the throughput, or actual data transferred, on full-duplex Ethernet connections is not nearly 20 Mbps. Chief among the reasons for this outcome is that the amount of network transmission is a product of application program design. Most distributed application programs tend to exhibit short requests for services from clients to servers followed by large transfers of data from the server back to the client. However, this is not to say that the technology lacks the ability to deliver higher performance. Controlled tests involving high bandwidth applications have produced throughout of 20 Mbps. As a result, the most likely implementation scenarios for full-duplex Ethernet is in switch-to-switch connections and switch-to-server connections.

Since the full-duplex NIC installed in the computer is sending and receiving data simultaneously, a multithreaded operating system and network operating system is required to take full advantage of this technology. Examples of such multithreaded operating systems and network operating systems include Windows NT and 2000, NetWare 3.11 or newer, as well as most varieties of UNIX. Full-duplex Ethernet has garnered sufficient interest from the networking technology vendor and user communities to prompt the **IEEE 802.3x** committee to develop standards for full-duplex Ethernet. Full-duplex technology is also either under development or available in full-duplex token ring (32 Mbps) and full-duplex FDDI (200 Mbps), as well as full-duplex fast Ethernet and gigabit Ethernet varieties.

NETWORK INTERFACE CARDS

Functionality

Network cards, or NICs, are the physical link between a client or server PC and the shared media of the network. Providing this interface between the network and the PC or workstation requires that the network interface card have the ability to adhere to the access methodology (CSMA/CD or token passing) of the network architecture (Ethernet, token ring, FDDI/CDDI, ATM etc.) to which it is attached. These software rules, implemented by the network interface card, that control the access to the shared network media are known as media access control (MAC) protocols and are represented on the MAC sublayer of the data link layer (layer 2) of the OSI seven-layer reference model.

Since these are MAC layer interface cards and are therefore the keepers of the MAC layer interface protocol, it's fair to say that it is the NICs themselves that determine network architecture and its constituent protocols. Take an Ethernet NIC out of the expansion slot of a PC and replace it with a token ring NIC and you have a token ring workstation. In this same scenario, the media may not even need to be changed since Ethernet, token ring, and FDDI/CDDI often work over the same media.

A network interface card is a bit like a mediator or translator. On one side it has the demands of the client or server PC in which it is installed for network-based services, whereas on the other side it has the network architecture with its rules for accessing the shared network media or LAN switch. The network interface card's job is to get the PC all of the network services it desires while adhering to the rules (MAC layer protocols) of the network architecture.

Technology Analysis

The following are some of the key differences in NIC design and available features:

- Bus type
  - ISA (8 or 16 bit)
  - EISA (16 or 32 bit)
  - MCA (Micro-Channel – IBM PS/2)
  - NuBus (Apple)
  - PCI (current generation PCs)
  - PCMCIA (laptops)
  - SBus (Sun)
  - USB (external interfaces)
- On board processor capabilities
- Amount of on-board memory
- Data transfer techniques
  - Bus-mastering DMA
  - DMA
  - Shared memory
  - Programmed I/O
- Media interfaces
- System memory requirements
- Internal NICs vs. external NICs
- Network drivers included
- Network architecture(s) supported

Applied Problem Solving

NETWORK INTERFACE CARD TECHNOLOGY ANALYSIS GRID

Many of these features are listed in Figure 6-6, the network interface card technology analysis grid. A technology analysis grid is a structured analysis tool for mapping functional networking requirements as identified by the logical network design of the networking layer in the top-down model to the technical capabilities and characteristics of available technology. In this manner, technology can be comparatively evaluated in an objective fashion. Recalling the basic premise of the top-down model—that each lower layer offers solutions that meet the requirements of the immediate upper layer—the chosen technology incorporated in the physical network design should meet the original business goals and objectives as identified in the business layer.

As a practical example, whereas servers will need to transfer large quantities of data more quickly than client PCs, technology analysis should be performed to purchase more powerful, faster NICs for servers than for clients to minimize potential bottlenecks.

		Ethernet	Token Ring (4Mbps)	Token Ring (16Mbps)	FDDI	CDDI	Fast Ethernet	Gigabit Ethernet	Full duplex Ethernet	ATM
Bus Type	Internal/external									
	ISA - 8 bit/16 bit									
	MCA - 32 bit									
	EISA - 32 bit									
	PCI - 32 bit/64 bit									
	Macintosh - NUBUS									
	External interface to parallel port/USB									
	PCMCIA (laptops)									
	SBUS (SUN)									
Drivers	NDIS									
	ODI									
	NETBIOS									
	IPX									
	SOLARIS									
	Windows NT									
	Windows 2000									
Cabling Type (media interface)	UTP									
	STP									
	Thin COAX									
	Thick COAX									
	Fiber									
	Wireless									
Data transfer	BUS mastering									
	DMA									
	Programmed I/O									
	Shared memory									
Management	SNMP support									
	RMON support									
	SMON support									
	PROM support									
	Prices									

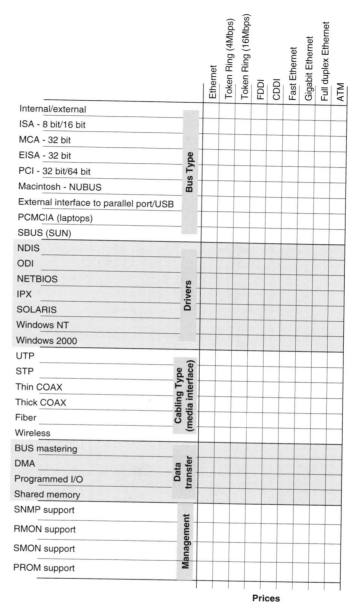

Figure 6-6 Network Interface Card Technology Analysis Grid

Bus Type The bus into which a network interface card is attached allows many different types of add-in cards to be attached to this data transfer pipeline leading to the CPU and RAM memory. The expansion bus in a PC is a lot like a straight line of empty parking spaces waiting to be filled by PC expansion cards of one type or another. These expansion cards draw electricity from and transfer data to/from other system components such as the CPU or memory through the expansion bus. NICs are manufactured to physically interface to a particular type of bus.

The PCI bus offers its own clocking signal and low CPU utilization and seems to be the bus of choice for high-performance NICs. PCI bus-compatible NICs are now available for a variety of network architectures, with some taking advantage of the PCI bus's ability to cascade buses by delivering four network interface ports on a single network interface card. Some PCI-based cards also have full-duplex capabilities. Such high-capacity cards are most appropriate for servers with high data transfer demands.

SBus is the type of bus included in UNIX workstations (SPARCstations) from Sun Microsystems.

The important choice related to bus architecture is that a network interface card is chosen that not only "fits," or is compatible with, the installed bus, but more important, takes full advantage of whatever data transfer capability that given bus may afford.

Data Transfer Method The key job of the NIC is to transfer data between the local PC and the shared network media. Ideally, this should be done as quickly as possible with a minimum of interruption of the PC's main CPU. Two hardware-related NIC characteristics that can have a bearing on data transfer efficiency are the amount of on-board memory and the processing power of the on-board CPU contained on the network interface card. Figure 6-7 summarizes four network interface card-to-PC memory data transfer techniques:

- Programmed I/O (input/output)
- DMA (direct memory access)
- Shared memory
- Bus-mastering DMA

Network interface cards may support more than one of these techniques. Some of these data transfer techniques are possible only with the more sophisticated buses such as EISA, MCA, or PCI, with certain network architectures, or with a certain level of CPU power.

Remembering that one of the objectives of network-to-PC data transfer was to minimize the number of interruptions of the system CPU, it can be seen in Figure 6-7 that only the **bus-mastering DMA** (direct memory access) data transfer technique leaves the system CPU alone to process other applications. In bus-mastering DMA, the CPU on the network interface card manages the movement of data directly into the PC's RAM memory without interruption of the system CPU by taking control of the PC's expansion bus. PCI bus-based NICs also exhibit low utilization of the main CPU thanks to the intelligence of the PCI bus itself.

Bus-mastering DMA as a feature on NICs requires the expansion bus in the PC to support being "mastered" by the CPU on the network interface card. Some buses are more sophisticated (MCA, EISA, and PCI) when it comes to bus mastering by maintaining more control and management over how the mastering of the expansion bus by the network interface card CPU is handled. Also, the CPU and operating system must have the capability to relinquish control of the expansion bus for bus mastering network interface cards to function correctly.

Basic NIC Configuration Once NICs have been physically installed inside a computer, they must be properly configured to interact successfully with that computer. The

Programmed I/O

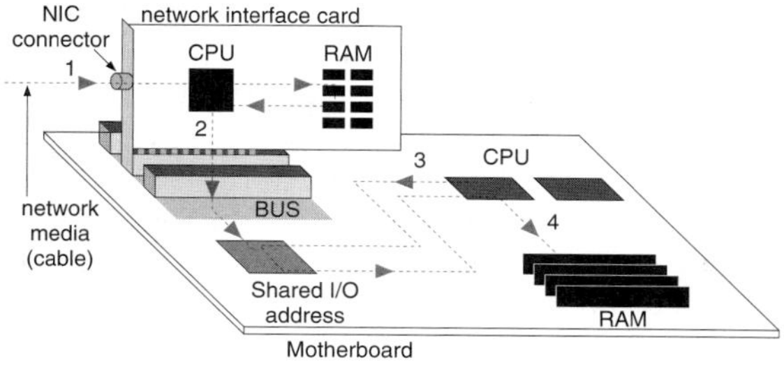

Steps
1. Data enter network interface card through the network media and connector.
2. Adapter card CPU loads network data into a specific I/O address on the motherboard.
3. Main CPU checks I/O area for data
4. If data exist, it is transferred to main memory, RAM, by main CPU.

Keynote
The motherboard's CPU has the ultimate responsibility of data transfer into RAM.

DMA (Direct Memory Access)

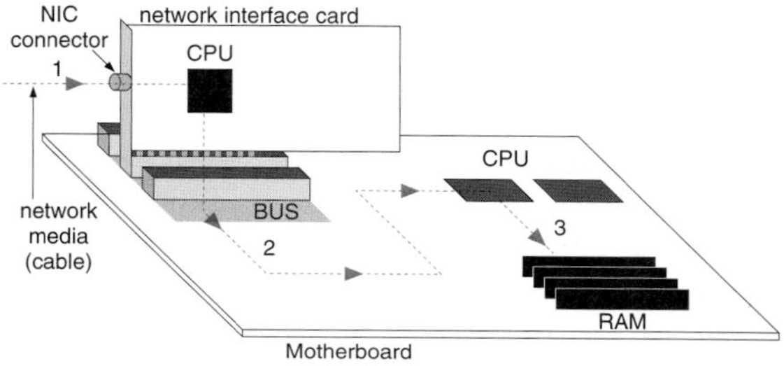

Steps
1. Data enters network interface card through the network media and connector.
2. Adapter card CPU interrupts the motherboard CPU.
3. Main CPU stops other processing and transfers the data to RAM.

Keynote
The motherboard's CPU has the ultimate responsibility of data transfer into RAM.

Shared Memory

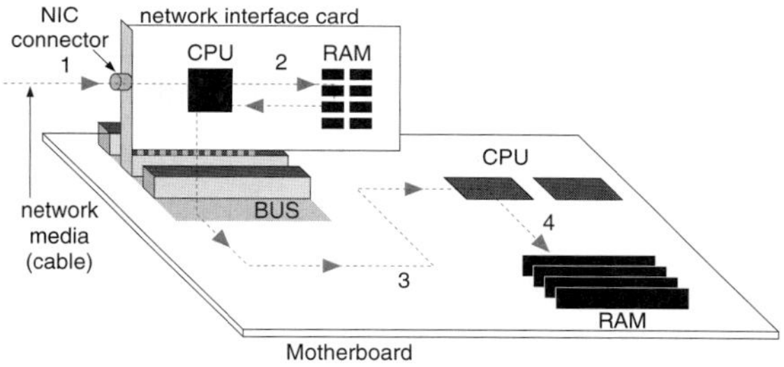

Steps
1. Data enters network interface card through the network media and connector.
2. Adapter card CPU stores data on its RAM.
3. Adapter card CPU interrupts the motherboard CPU.
4. Main CPU stops other processing and transfers data into RAM.

Keynote
The motherboard's CPU has the ultimate responsibility of data transfer into RAM.

Bus Mastering DMA

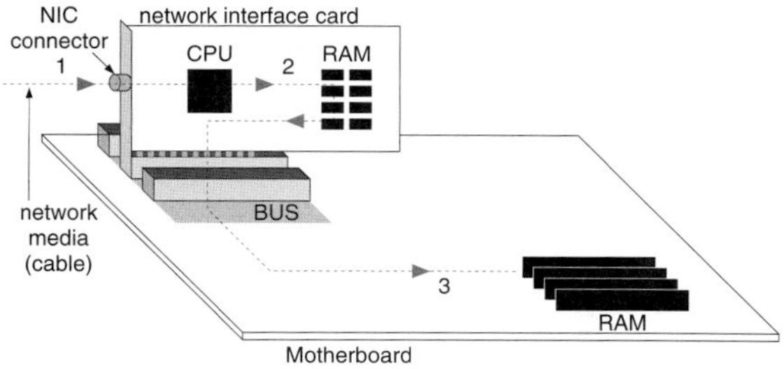

Steps
1. Data enters network interface card through the network media and connector.
2. Adapter card CPU temporarily stores data on its RAM.
3. Adapter card CPU sends data directly to motherboard RAM when network transmission completes (it does NOT interrupt the main CPU).

Keynote
The adapter card's CPU has the ultimate responsibility of data transfer into RAM.

Figure 6-7 Network Interface Cards Data Transfer Methods

role of the NIC driver software is explained in a later section in this chapter. However, there are some other key configuration issues related more to the physical or hardware interaction of the NIC and the computer into which it has been installed. Among these parameters are the following:

- **IRQ-Interrupt request**—The network interface card, like every other hardware device in the computer, must interrupt and request resources such as CPU cycles and memory from the CPU itself. It must be assigned an IRQ or interrupt request number so that the CPU knows that it is the NIC requesting these services. The key issue regarding IRQ assignments is that the IRQ must not be used by any other device and must be supported by the NIC. IRQ 3 and 5 are typically used for NICs. Some NICs are able to use different IRQs, but others are not. Typical IRQ assignments for Intel ×86 architecture computers are listed in Figure 6-8.
- **Base I/O port address**—This address defines a memory location through which the data will flow between the network interface card and the CPU. It is somewhat analogous to a mailbox through which messages are transferred into and out of. All NICs need an available base I/O address as part of their configuration.
- **Base memory address**—Some NICs require a base memory address, not to be confused with base I/O address, to indicate the starting location in the computer's memory that can be used by the NIC as a buffer memory. Not all NICs need to use the computer's memory and therefore would not need a base memory address.

IRQ Number	Typical Use Note: PCI Bus IRQ Settings May Vary
0	Reserved—CPU tick counter
1	Reserved—keyboard controller
2	Reserved—cascade controller
3	Usually COM2 and COM4
4	Usually COM1 and COM3
5	Usually LPT2 or sound card
6	Floppy disk controller
7	LPT1
8	Reserved—real time clock
9	Reserved—slave controller
10	Usually available
11	Usually available
12	Usually available
13	Coprocessor error
14	Non-SCSI fixed disk
15	Usually available

Figure 6-8 Typical IRQ Assignments

Media Interfaces A network interface card must worry about hardware compatibility in two directions. First, the card must be compatible with the expansion bus into which it will be inserted. Secondly, it must be compatible with the chosen media of a particular network architecture implementation. Supported media types are dependent on standards defined for a particular network architecture. All NICs do not support all media types. In addition to the type of media, the physical connector that must interface between the NIC and the media can differ.

Several network interface cards come with interfaces for more than one media type with "jumpers" or switches enabling one media type or another. Ethernet NICs with interfaces for both 10BaseT RJ45 or 8 pin Telco plug) and thin coax connections known as a BNC connector, or with both thick and thin coax connections are quite common. Thick coax connectors are 15-pin interfaces (DB-15) also called AUI connectors. AUI connectors allow Ethernet NICs to be attached to thin or thick coax Ethernet backbone networks via transceivers (transmitter/receivers) and AUI or transceiver cables. Figure 6-9 illustrates the three common Ethernet media interfaces and connection of an Ethernet NIC to an Ethernet backbone network via transceivers.

All of the discussion thus far regarding installation of network interface cards has assumed that NICs are internal or connected directly to the system expansion bus. Alternatively, NICs can be connected externally to a PC via the PC's parallel or USB ports. In these cases, **external NICs,** as small as a pack of cigarettes, are interfaced between the PC's parallel port and the network media. External NICs cannot draw electricity from the expansion bus like internal NICs and therefore require a power source of their own such as an AC NIC in most cases. Some external NICs are able to draw power from the keyboard jack on the notebook computer, eliminating the need for bulky and inconvenient AC NICs.

Although external NICs were originally developed to support laptop computers that lack internal expansion capability, the market for them has shifted to the home

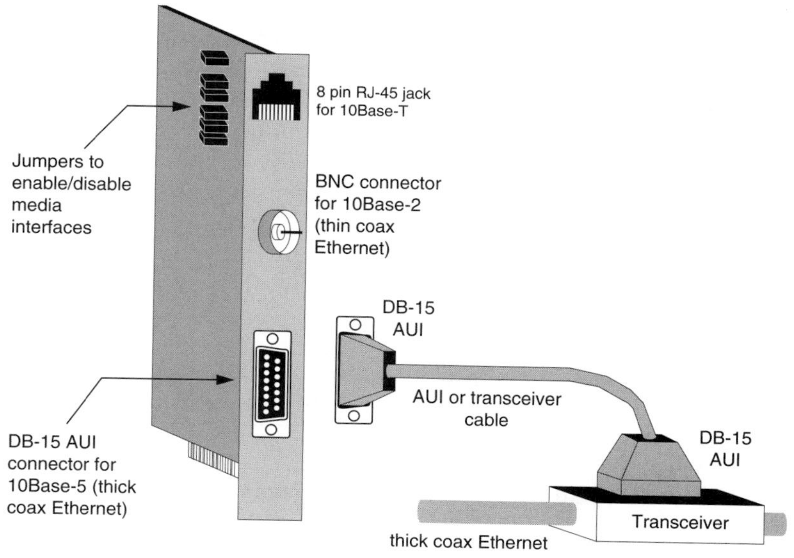

Figure 6-9 Ethernet Media Interfaces

computer market. Home users that lack the sophistication or desire to install internal NICs are utilizing outboard parallel or USB NICs to create networks within their homes to share files, printers, and Internet access. Refer to Chapter 5 for more information on common household LAN architectures.

In a good example of the principle of shifting bottlenecks, although NICs can transfer data at rates of several megabits/second, throughput on existing parallel ports hovers around 130 Kbps, whereas a newer **high-performance parallel port,** also known as **EPP** or **enhanced parallel port,** delivers a throughput of up to 2 Mbps. Remember that the parallel port is a component of the PC, not of the NIC itself. **USB** or **universal serial bus** NICs have the ability to communicate to the PC at speeds of up to 12 Mbps, effectively not creating a bottleneck, although actual USB performance depends on the number of devices sharing the bus and the operating system running on the PC.

PC Card (PCMCIA) Standards To enable network access on portable notebook computers, a means of attaching NICs was required. Although the use of parallel port-based NICs enabled a degree of connectivity, the relatively slow speeds made such solutions undesirable. To resolve this need and the need to expand the notebook computer in general, the PCMCIA was created. The **PCMCIA (personal computer memory card international association)** is a nonprofit trade association and standards body that promotes PC card technology along with miniature card and SmartMedia cards by defining technical standards and educating the market. In the past, cards that supported PCMCIA standards were known as PCMCIA cards, but the industry now refers to products based on the technology as **PC cards** and refers to the association itself as PCMCIA.

The PCMCIA standards are actually a series of specifications that represent the physical and functional/electrical standards for technology adhering to these specs. Figure 6-10 summarizes the physical specifications, and Figure 6-11 summarizes the functional/electrical specifications for the PCMCIA standards.

Types I–III all must support the standard PCMCIA 68-pin interface and the 85.6 × 54 mm credit card size dimensions. Certain vendors are producing disk drives that are 16 mm thick and calling them PC Card Type IV. These standards are strictly proprietary, as the PCMCIA has not approved a Type IV specification.

The introduction of PC card technology has not been without its trials and tribulations. Before the introduction of the PC card version 2.1 specification, incompatibility problems were very common. Version 2.1 has minimized, although not eliminated, many of the previous incompatibility problems through the introduction of card services and socket services, also known as card and socket services or CSS. card and socket services provide a layer of transparency and compatibility between the notebook computer's hardware, the PC card, and the notebook computer's operating system software. Technical aspects of card and socket services are covered later

PC Card/Slot Type	Maximum Thickness	Typical Use
Type I	3.3 mm	Memory cards
Type II	5.5 mm	Modems, network interface cards
Type III	10.5 mm	Disk drives

Figure 6-10 PCMCIA Physical Specifications

PCMCIA Spec. Version	Bus Width	Clock Speed	Comments
1.0	8 bits	up to 6 MHz	Used for memory cards. No I/O functions or software drivers defined
2.0	8–16 bits	up to 6 MHz	Introduced I/O but left software drivers up to card manufacturers
2.1	8–16 bits	up to 6 MHz	Introduced card services and socket services
CardBus (3.0)	32 bits	20–33 MHz	Up to 80 Mbps throughput

Figure 6-11 PCMCIA Functional/Electrical Specifications

in this chapter in the discussion of driver software. Version 2.1 also introduced hot-swappable capabilities, which allow PC cards to be inserted and removed with the computer powered up.

Version 3.0 of the PCMCIA standards vastly improves the throughput of the specification by increasing the bus width to 32 bits and the clock speed to as high as 33 MHz. This new standard, commonly known as **CardBus,** also adds bus-mastering capability to increase the efficiency of moving data from the card to the computer's system memory. CardBus adds multifunction capabilities for cards so that a single card might include a fax/modem, an Ethernet network interface card, and 4 MB of cache memory. In the interest of improving battery life on notebook computers, the CardBus standard also outlines operations at 3.3 volts rather than 5 volts.

The future looks bright for CardBus. In addition to being implemented in all new notebook computers and many other handheld devices, CardBus slots are now being included on desktop computers to allow users to maximize their peripheral investment. The types of PC Cards available have expanded rapidly. New functionality such as SCSI adapters, audio and video adapters, and TV tuner cards have been introduced. With the proliferation of DVD ROM drives in notebook computers DVD decoder cards have been introduced that can decode the DVD stream and display it either directly on the notebooks screen or provide standard video and audio output jacks to display it on an external monitor or television.

Network Interface Card Trends

Among the trends in network interface cards that are either emerging or under development are the following:

- Dual-speed cards—Some 10/100 Ethernet cards feature auto-sensing, which can automatically determine whether traffic is being transmitted and received at 10 or 100 Mbps through a single media interface connector. Others have two separate media interface connectors, one for 10 Mbps Ethernet and one for fast Ethernet. 10/100 Cards are important as a means to ease migration from 10-Mbps network architectures to 100-Mbps network architectures.

- Integrated or on-board NICs—Computer manufacturers now commonly include an Ethernet NIC right on the business and workstation class PC's motherboards, thereby saving a slot on the expansion bus. The explosion in the number of multi-PC households combined with the introduction of the HPNA technologies for home networking has led several manufacturers to include HPNA ports on their computers aimed at the home market. Chapter 5 contains additional information on HPNA.
- Multiport NICs—The cascading ability, otherwise known as the mezzanine architecture of the PCI bus, has allowed multiport NICs to be manufactured on a single card. In this manner, servers with high traffic demands can have up to four links to the network while using only a single expansion slot.
- On-NIC security—As network data security has become an important issue, focus had shifted to the NIC as the entry point for network communications. Some NICs now offer encryption as means of protection against network infiltration.
- Integrated repeater modules—Some NICs have incorporated integrated repeater modules that allow up to seven additional devices to be cascaded from the NIC and attached to the network via a single 10BaseT hub port.
- Full-duplex mode—Some Ethernet NICs have full-duplex capability that can be enabled. Recall that implementation of full-duplex Ethernet is dependent on the full-duplex Ethernet NIC being directly connected to a port on a full-duplex Ethernet switch.
- Performance improvements—Several manufacturers of Ethernet NICs have implemented **packet overlapping** or **fast-packet forwarding** technology to improve overall NIC performance by as much as 50%. Traditionally, Ethernet NICs only forwarded one packet at a time from the CPU bus, through the buffer memory on the NIC, to the network media. With packet overlapping technology, the next packet of information is immediately forwarded as soon as its start of frame is detected rather than waiting for the previous frame to be totally onto the network media before beginning transmission of the next packet.

NETWORK INTERFACE CARD DRIVERS

Role of NIC Drivers

Ensuring that a purchased NIC interfaces successfully to both the bus of the CPU and the chosen media of the network architecture will ensure hardware connectivity. Full interoperability, however, depends on compatibility between the NIC and the network operating system installed in a given computer and is delivered by network interface card drivers. Any driver software must be compatible with the hardware card itself, which is why many NIC manufacturers ship numerous drivers from which to choose with their NICs. A given network interface card may also be required to be compatible with a number of different network operating systems. The network operating systems use the NIC drivers to communicate with the NICs and the network beyond. Without the proper NIC drivers, there can be no communication out through the NIC and, as a result, there is no network.

Driver Availability

Initially, drivers were written for specific combinations of a particular NIC and a particular version of an operating system or network operating system. In was to an NIC vendor's advantage to ship drivers for as many operating systems and network operating systems as possible. Examples of drivers typically included are:

- LANtastic
- LANManager
- LANServer
- NetWare
- Vines
- Windows
- OS/2
- Windows NT
- Windows 2000
- UNIX (many varieties)

This is obviously a fairly long list and drivers may have to be rewritten for each new version of an operating system or network operating system. Drivers written for specific NIC/network operating system combinations are known as **monolithic drivers.** Network interface card drivers were also supplied by network operating system vendors. In these cases, the competition centered around which network operating system vendor could include drivers for the largest number of network interface cards. As the number of possible combinations of network interface cards and network operating systems continued to increase, network interface card vendors and network operating system vendors found themselves spending ever increasing amounts of time and money on driver development.

A more generic approach to the problem was for NIC manufacturers to supply drivers that could interact successfully with either NetBIOS or TCP/IP. The reasoning in this case is that most network operating systems, in turn, communicate with either NetBIOS (PC environment) or TCP/IP (UNIX environment). These drivers were generally successful except for the occasional incompatibilities among NetBIOS versions, so long as a given operating system supported NetBIOS or TCP/IP. Also, specifically written, monolithic drivers were more efficient and better performing in most cases.

Another approach is for network interface card manufacturers to emulate the NIC interface specifications of market-leading network interface cards for which drivers are most commonly available. The NE2000 NIC, originally manufactured by Eagle Technologies and since purchased by Novell, is often emulated by other manufacturers who subsequently claim that their NICs are NE2000 compliant.

Multiprotocol Network Interface Card Drivers

Novell was the first network operating system to attempt to break the need for specially written drivers for every possible NIC/network operating system combination. By allowing NIC vendors to develop one file called IPX.COM, which is linked with a Novell file called IPX.OBJ through a process known as WSGEN, unique drivers could be more easily created and updated. However, even these "bound" drivers were still monolithic in the sense that only a single protocol stack, Novell's IPX/SPX, could communicate with the installed network interface card.

To resolve this issue, an industry initiative was undertaken that would develop driver software that would accomplish two major objectives:

1. NIC-specific drivers should be developed independently from network operating system-specific protocol stack drivers, and the two drivers should be bound together to form a unique driver combination.
2. Driver management software should allow for installation of both multiple network interface cards and multiple protocol stacks per NIC.

This initiative was undertaken by two independent industry coalitions:

1. Microsoft and 3Com, a major NIC manufacturer, developed **NDIS (network driver interface specification).**
2. Novell, producers of NetWare, and Apple joined forces to develop **ODI (open data-link interface).** Most NICs are now shipped with both NDIS and ODI drivers.

The significant operational difference between these two driver specifications and monolithic drivers is that they are able to support multiple protocol stacks over a single NIC. For example, a network interface card with an ODI driver installed could support communications to both a NetWare server via IPX protocols and a UNIX host via TCP/IP protocols. These upper layer communication protocols are introduced in Chapter 7.

In Sharper Focus

NDIS

NDIS is a driver specification that offers standard commands for communications between NDIS-compliant network operating system protocol stacks (NDIS protocol driver) and NDIS-compliant network interface card drivers (NDIS MAC drivers). In addition, NDIS specifies **a binding** operation that is managed by a separate program known as the **protocol manager** (PROTMAN.DOS in DOS-based systems). As will be seen, the protocol manager program does much more than just supervise the binding of protocol drivers to MAC drivers. NDIS also specifies standard commands for communication between the protocol manager program and either protocol or MAC drivers.

Protocol drivers and MAC drivers that adhere to the NDIS specification work as follows:

1. When a DOS-based computer is first booted or powered up, a configuration file known as CONFIG.SYS is executed. One line in this file specifies that the protocol manager program (PROTMAN.DOS) should be initiated.
2. The first job of the program manager is to access a text file known as PROTOCOL.INI, which contains

- Setup information about protocol drivers and MAC drivers.
- Binding statements that link particular protocol drivers to particular MAC drivers.

3. Having read PROTOCOL.INI and parsed its contents into usable form, the protocol manager program loads the PROTOCOL.INI information into a memory resident image.
4. As new protocol drivers or MAC drivers are loaded, they
   - Ask the protocol manager program for the location of the memory resident image of PROTOCOL.INI.
   - Look in PROTOCOL.INI for setup information about the MAC driver or protocol driver with which they wish to bind.
   - Identify themselves to the protocol manager program, which adds their information to the PROTOCOL.INI file.
5. Binding takes place when the protocol manager program oversees the exchange of characteristic tables between protocol drivers and MAC drivers.
6. Once bound and operating, packets of a particular protocol are forwarded from the NIC to the proper protocol stack by a layer of software known as the **vector.**

Figure 6-12 illustrates many of the concepts and components of the NDIS specification.

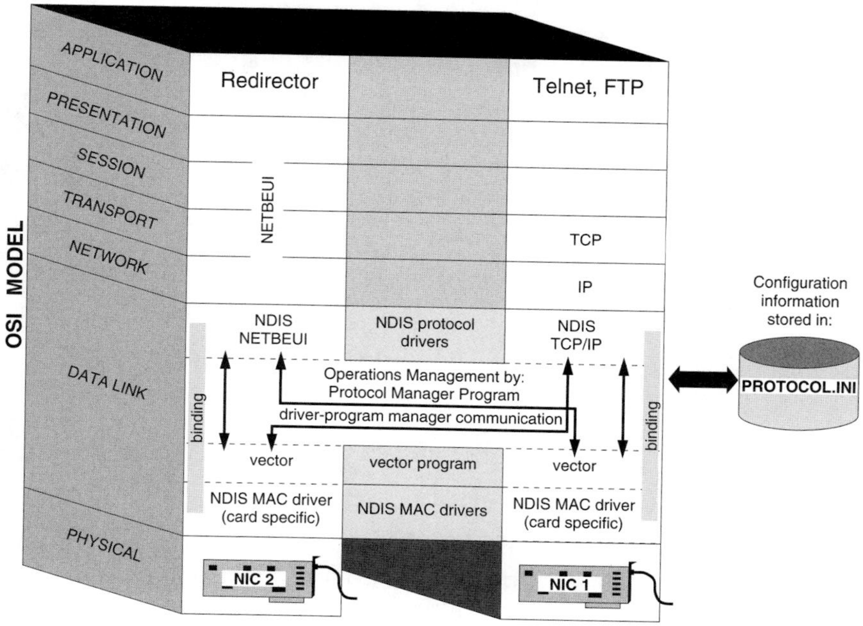

Figure 6-12 Network Device Interface Specification (NDIS) Architecture

In Sharper Focus

ODI

Like NDIS, ODI allows users to load several protocol stacks simultaneously for operation with a single network interface card and supports independent development with subsequent linking of protocol drivers and NIC drivers. In ODI, users enter configuration information regarding NIC settings and protocol driver information into a file named NET.CFG. Operations of ODI are similar to the basic functionality of NDIS and are orchestrated by a program known as LSL.COM, where **LSL** stands for **link support layer.** Network interface card drivers are referred to as **multi-link interface drivers** or **MLID** in an ODI-compliant environment. Figure 6-13 illustrates the basic architecture of an ODI-compliant environment.

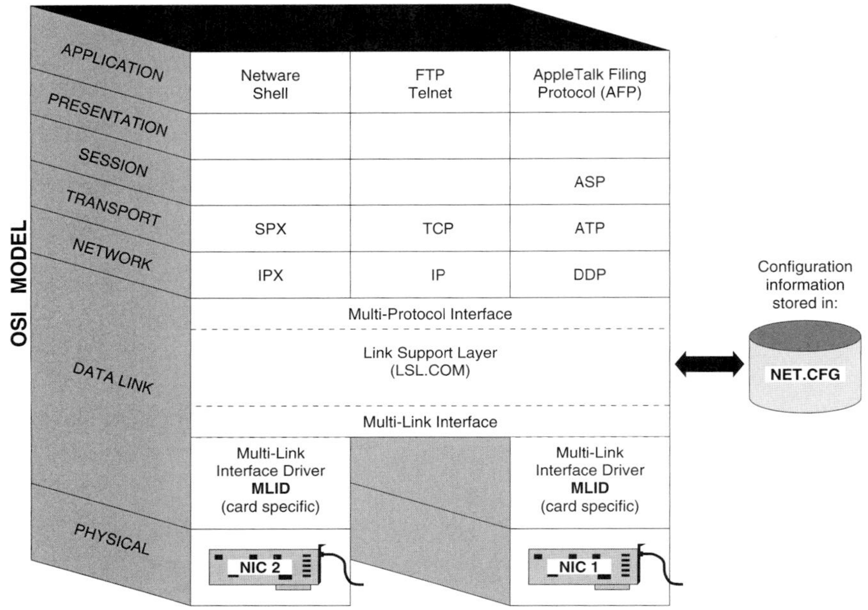

Figure 6-13 Open Data-Link Interface (ODI) Architecture

PC Card (PCMCIA) Drivers

When network interface cards are PCMCIA-based, two levels of driver software are required:

1. Drivers to interface to operating systems and network operating systems such as NDIS 2.0 for DOS and OS/2 and ODI for DOS and OS/2. Occasionally, NetWare-specific drivers may also be available with certain PC cards.
2. Drivers to interface the PCMCIA controller to the PCMCIA card and to the aforementioned client software drivers.

As previously noted in this chapter, the introduction of version 3 of the PCMCIA specification has replaced the term *PCMCIA* with the terms *PC card* to refer to the actual cards themselves and the term *CardBus* to refer to the PC card bus (slots) on the computer.

Compatibility problems and lack of standardized driver software were common occurrences with PCMCIA-based network interface cards before the release of PCMCIA version 2.1. By introducing **card and socket services (CSS)** driver specification, version 2.1 resolved many of these compatibility issues. CSS is relatively self-configuring and enables the following capabilities:

- Hot-swappable devices allowing PC cards to be inserted and removed while the notebook computer is running
- Automatic PC card configuration
- Management of multiple PC cards
- Support for "standby" mode
- I/O conflict management

CSS is split into two logical sublayers:

1. The **card services** sublayer is hardware independent and interfaces to the client operating system or network operating system driver software. Card services deliver error messages and enable resource management and configuration.
2. The **socket services** sublayer is written specifically for the type of PCMCIA controller included in a notebook computer. Socket services are more hardware oriented and provide information concerning insertion and removal of cards from available slots.

If compatible CSS drivers are not available for a particular PC card/controller combination, then lower-level drivers known as **direct enablers** must be configured and installed. Direct enablers, like the socket services of CSS, are controller specific and must be configured for each PC card/controller combination, unlike the card and socket services drivers, which allow multiple cards to be swapped in and out of a given CardBus slot without the need for reconfiguration. Direct enabler drivers are often supplied on diskette along with CSS drivers by the PC card vendors.

Practical Advice and Information

It is in an NIC manufacturer's best interests to include as many drivers as possible with their NICs to ensure that they will work with as many network operating systems as possible. However, before purchasing any NIC, be sure that proven software drivers compatible with the installed or chosen network operating system(s) are included with the purchase of the NICs.

Remember that drivers for various cards are often supplied with the installed networking operating system as well. One of these drivers may be more efficient in terms of operation or required memory than another.

SHARED-MEDIA LAN WIRING CENTERS

The most common network physical topology employed today is the star topology, and the heart of the star topology is the wiring center. A wiring center may be alternatively known as a hub, a concentrator, a repeater, a MAU (multistation access unit) or a variety of other terms. In this section, wiring center functionality, technology, management, and analysis are examined for shared-media network architectures; LAN switches and switching hubs appropriate for switch-based network architectures are covered in the next section.

Wiring Center Categories

In terms of network architectures supported, token ring wiring centers are known as **MAUs (multistation access units),** whereas wiring centers for all other network architectures are known as **hubs.** All hubs, or MAUs, are basically just multiport digital signal repeaters. They do not make logical decisions based on the addresses or content of messages. They merely repeat all digital data received among connected ports. In terms of the OSI model, repeaters or hubs are layer 1 or physical layer devices dealing only with bit streams.

In terms of functionality and features, wiring centers can be separated into three broad categories:

1. **Stand-alone hubs** are fully configured hubs offering a limited number (usually 12 or fewer) of ports of a particular type of network architecture (Ethernet, token ring) and media. They are fully configured and include their own power supply but are not generally expandable, do not include management software, and are the least expensive of the three wiring center categories. Stand-alone hubs typically have the ability to be linked together, or cascaded, via the same media used in the normal data connections. The actual method used to connect the hubs depends on the network architecture. Ethernet hubs are cascaded via uplink ports, whereas token ring hubs are cascaded via ring-in and ring-out ports.
2. **Stackable hubs** add expandability and manageability to the basic capabilities of the stand-alone hub. Stackable hubs can be linked together via proprietary cables to form one larger virtual hub of a single type of network architecture and media. When stacked, all the hubs appear as a single large hub. Given the larger number of ports, management software becomes essential. Most stackable hubs offer some type of local management software as well as links to enterprise management software platforms such as Computer Associates Unicenter, HP Open View, Sun's SunNet Manager, and Tivoli NetView.
3. **Enterprise hubs,** also known as **modular concentrators,** differ from stackable hubs in both physical design and offered functionality. Rather than being fully functional self-contained units, enterprise hubs are modular by design, offering a chassis-based architecture to which a variety of different modules can be inserted. In some cases, these modules can be inserted and/or removed while the hub remains powered up, a capability known as **hot swappable.** Among the possible modules supported by enterprise hubs are
   - Ethernet, token ring, FDDI, and ATM port modules in a variety of speeds, port densities, and media types
   - Management modules

- Router modules
- Bridge modules
- WAN link modules
- Multiple power supplies for redundant power

These broad category definitions and labels are not standards and are not universally adhered to by manufacturers. Signaling standards defined as part of the IEEE or ANSI LAN standards allow hubs and NICs of different vendors to interoperate successfully in most cases. Figure 6-14 illustrates some of the physical differences between the three major categories of hubs, whereas Figure 6-15 differentiates among the functionality of the major categories of wiring centers.

Repeaters

A repeater, as its name would imply, merely "repeats" each bit of digital data it receives. This repeating action actually "cleans up" the digital signals by retiming

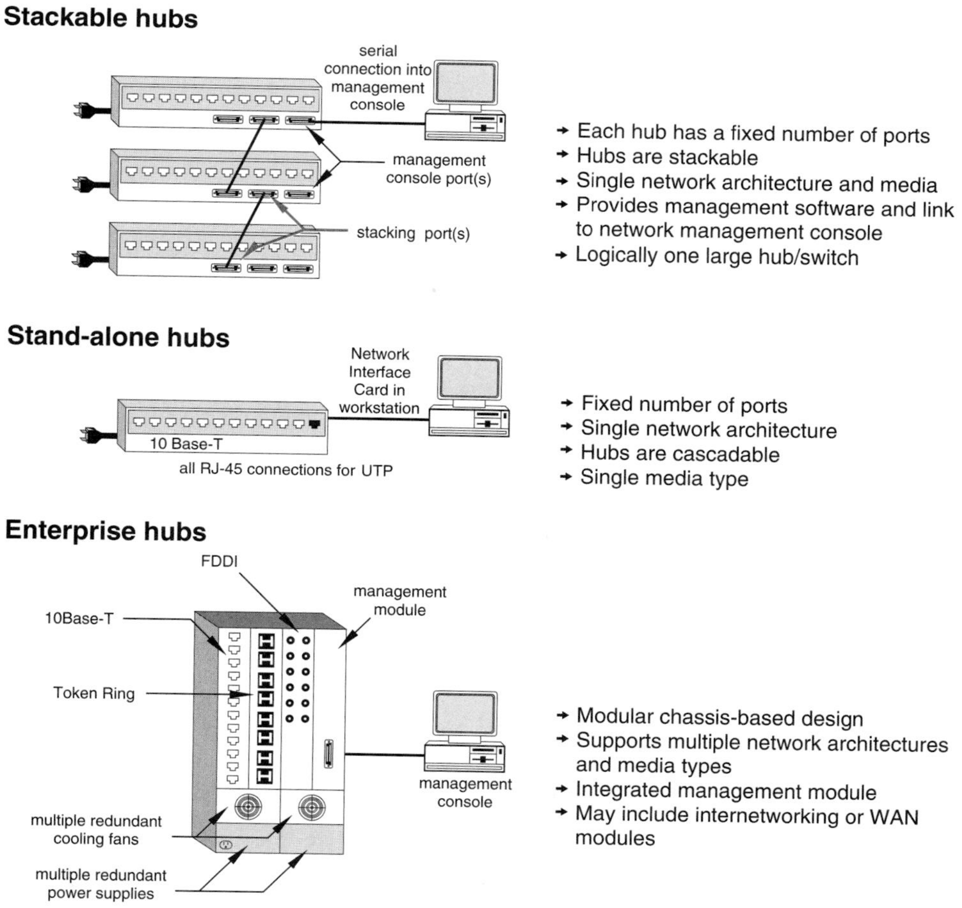

Figure 6-14 Major Categories of Hubs

		Multiport digital signal repeater	Network Architectures: Ethernet	Network Architectures: Token Ring	Network Architectures: FDDI	Network Architectures: Fast Ethernet	Network Architectures: Gigabit Ethernet	Stand-alone	Cascadable	Modular chassis-based	Includes internetworking modules (bridges and routers)	Includes WAN links	Includes network management
Repeaters		●	●	●	●			●					
Stand-alone hubs		●	●		●	●	●	●					
Stackable hubs		●	●		●	●	●		●			●	●
MAUs	stand-alone	●		●				●					
	stackable	●		●					●			●	●
Enterprise hubs		●	●	●	●	●	●		●	●	●	●	

Figure 6-15 Wiring Center Functional Comparison

and regenerating them before passing this repeated data from one attached device or LAN segment to the next. Repeaters can only link devices or LAN segments of similar network architectures.

Hubs

Hubs are a subset of repeaters that allow attachment of single devices rather than LAN segments to each hub port. The terms *hub* and *concentrator* or *intelligent concentrator* are often used interchangeably. Distinctions can be made however between these broad classes of wiring centers, although there is nothing to stop manufacturers from using the terms as they wish.

A hub is often the term reserved for describing a stand-alone device with a fixed number of ports that offers features beyond that of a simple repeater. The type of media connections and network architecture offered by the hub are determined at the time of manufacture as well. For example, a 10BaseT Ethernet hub will offer a fixed number of RJ-45 twisted pair connections for an Ethernet network. Additional types of media or network architectures are not usually supported.

Stackable Hubs

Hubs may also be cascadable or stackable via **cascading ports,** which may be specialized ports on the hub or may be switch configurable "normal" ports, allowing repeated data to flow out of a cascading port to the next hub rather than the normal inbound-only port traffic flow. In general, cascading ports are proprietary in nature, thereby making it impossible to cascade hubs of different vendors together. Specialized hub-to-hub cascading cables may also be required, and the maximum allowable distance between stacked hubs may vary as well. Stackable hubs also vary as to stackability, with the number of stackable hubs ranging from 4 to 20 and the total number of stacked ports ranging from 48 to 768. Cost per port can range from $35 to $147, with most per port costs in the $60–$70 range.

MAUs

A MAU or multistation access unit is IBM's name for a token ring hub. A MAU is manufactured with a fixed number of ports and connections for unshielded or shielded twisted pair. IBM uses special connectors for token ring over shielded twisted pair (STP) connections to a MAU known as Type 1 connectors. Some MAUs support RJ-45 connectors rather than the more bulky and difficult to work with Type 1 connectors. MAUs typically have eight ports with two additional ports labeled RI (ring in) and RO (ring out). These specialized cascading ports allow multiple MAUs to be linked in a single logical ring by connecting the ring in port on one MAU to the ring out port on a second MAU and vice-versa. MAUs may also be cascaded to each other via fiber optic cable as opposed to shielded twisted pair.

MAUs offer varying degrees of management capability. **Active management MAUs** are able to send alerts to management consoles regarding malfunctioning token ring NICs and can also forcibly remove these misbehaving NICs from the ring. Removing malfunctioning nodes is especially critical in token ring LANs because one of the malfunctioning nodes can become disabled while holding onto the token. Although such an event would be at the very least inconvenient, it would not be a catastrophe, as the active monitor workstation is capable of regenerating a new token.

Enterprise Hubs

The terms *concentrator, intelligent concentrator, smart hub,* and *enterprise hub* are often reserved for a device characterized by both its flexibility and expandability. A concentrator starts with a fairly empty, boxlike device often called a chassis. This chassis contains one or more redundant power supplies and a "built-in" network backbone. This backbone might be Ethernet, token ring, FDDI, AppleTalk, fast Ethernet, gigabit Ethernet, or some combination of these. Individual cards or modules are inserted into this "backplane."

For instance, an 8- or 16-port twisted pair Ethernet module could be purchased and slid into place in the concentrator chassis. A network management module supporting the SNMP (simple network management protocol) network management protocol could then be purchased and slid into the chassis next to the previously installed 10BaseT Port module. In this "mix and match" scenario, additional cards could be added for connection of PCs with token ring NICs, PCs or workstations with FDDI NICs, or "dumb" asynchronous terminals. These modules are most often hot swappable, allowing modules to be added or removed without shutting down the entire enterprise hub. Obviously, the capacity of these enterprise hubs is equally as important as the flexibility afforded by the modular design. In fact, enterprise hubs often support several hundred network ports of varying architecture.

This "network in a box" is now ready for workstation to be hooked up to it through twisted pair connections to the media interfaces on the network interface cards of the PCs or workstations. Allowing different media types to be intermixed in the concentrator was one of its first major selling points. Remember that Ethernet can run over UTP, STP, thick and thin coax, and fiber.

Additional modules available for some, but not all, concentrators may allow data traffic from this "network in a box" to travel to other local LANs via bridge or router add-on modules. Bridges and routers are discussed later in the text. These combination concentrators are sometimes called internetworking hubs. Communication to remote LANs or workstations may be available through the addition of other specialized cards, or modules, designed to provide access to wide area network services purchased from common carriers such as the phone company. Whereas all local network traffic travels through this single enterprise hub, it is also an ideal location for security modules to be added for either encryption or authorization functionality.

Backplane design within enterprise hubs is proprietary and, as a result, the modules for enterprise hubs are not interoperable. Therefore, it is important to ensure that the enterprise hub to be purchased has available all required types of modules in terms of network architecture, media type, management, internetworking, WAN interfaces, or security. Vendors' promised delivery dates for required modules should not be depended on.

Hub Management

Since all local area network traffic must pass through the hub, it becomes an ideal place for installation of management software to both monitor and manage network traffic. As previously stated, stand-alone hubs rarely are manufactured with management software. In the case of stackable and enterprise hubs, two layers of management software are most often involved:

1. First, **local hub management software** is usually supplied by the hub vendor and runs over either DOS or Windows. This software allows monitoring and management of the hub from a locally attached management console.
2. Second, since these hubs are just a small part of a vast array of networking devices that might have to be managed on an enterprise basis, most hubs are also capable of sharing management information with **enterprise network management systems** such as Computer Associates Unicenter, HP OpenView, Tivoli NetView, and SunNet Manager.

Although Chapter 13 covers network management in more detail, a small explanation here as to how this hub management information is fed to the enterprise network management system is appropriate.

Network management information transfer between multivendor network devices and enterprise network management systems must be characterized by standards-based communication. The standards that govern this network management communication are part of the TCP/IP family of protocols, more correctly known as the Internet suite of protocols. Specifically, network management information is formatted according to the **SNMP** or **simple network management protocol.** The types of information to be gathered and stored have also been defined as **MIBs** or **management information bases.** There are actually numerous MIBs defined, with the most often used one for network monitoring and management known as the **RMON (remote monitoring) MIB.** RMON collects data from a single network segment. The newest addition to the SNMP family of monitoring standards is **SMON (switch monitoring).** SMON expands RMON's monitoring ability by offering a mechanism to collect data from all network segments connected to a LAN switch.

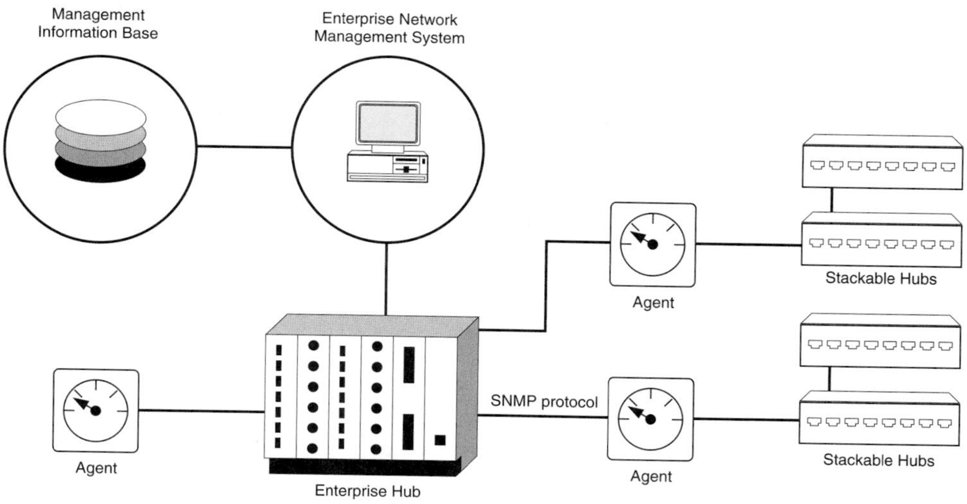

Figure 6-16 Standards-Based Network Management Communications Protocols

Network statistics and information are gathered in the first place and packetized in SNMP format by specialized software known as **agents,** which reside within the monitored network device and are supplied by the network device's manufacturer. Enterprise network management systems, such as HP Openview, are able to interpret, consolidate, and display information and alarms from a variety of different networking equipment manufactured by a variety of different vendors thanks to standards-based communication protocols. Figure 6-16 illustrates the relationship of the various aspects of the standards-based network management communications protocols.

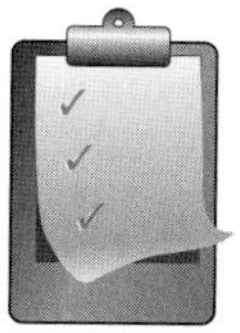

Practical Advice and Information

Some hub management issues are particular to stackable and/or enterprise hubs. For example:

- Many stackable hubs offer network management capabilities as an optional hardware or software upgrade. It is important to fully understand the ease with which this upgrade can be accomplished and whether or not the hubs must be powered off while doing so.
- The network management traffic may exit the hub via a separate serial port or travel along a separate bus within the hub so as not to diminish the amount of bandwidth available for data. These options are sometimes referred to as out-of-band management connections.
- The entire stack of hubs should be viewed, monitored, and managed by the network management software as a single, virtual hub.
- The local hub management software should be simple, easy to use, and preferably Windows-based with the capability to talk to enterprise network management system platforms should that need arise.
- If at all possible, management modules or upgrades should be included with the original purchase to avoid potential upgrade hassles. Buying manage-

ment modules at purchase time is often more economical than buying upgrades later thanks to vendor discount packages.

- An issue particular to token ring modules included in enterprise hubs is that the management software should possess the ability to dynamically assign ports located on the same physical module onto different logical rings to optimize network performance.

Applied Problem Solving

WIRING CENTERS TECHNOLOGY ANALYSIS

Some of the major technical features to be used for comparative analysis are listed in Figure 6-17. Before purchasing a wiring center of any type, consider the implications of the various possible features listed in the wiring center technology analysis.

Wiring Center Characteristic	Implications/Options
Expandability	Most stand-alone hubs are cascadable via the same network technology as is used to connect nodes to the hub. Stackable hubs are cascadable via proprietary cabling that allows the entire stack to appear as one large hub, and enterprise hubs are expandable by adding more LAN modules. Enterprise hubs vary in the number of open slots from approximately 5 to 20. Total backplane capacity (speed) is important, as this is the shared network media that must be shared by all attached modules.
Network Architectures	Options: Ethernet, token ring, FDDI, AppleTalk, fast Ethernet, gigabit Ethernet, ATM. Not all enterprise hubs have all types of network architecture modules available.
Media	Options: UTP, STP, thin coax, thick coax, fiber optic cable. Modules also differ according to supported media. Remember that a NIC is on the other end of the connection to the hub module. Is this hub module media type and connector compatible with installed NICs?
Terminal Communications	Can "dumb" asynchronous terminals be connected directly to the hub? What is the physical connector and serial transmission specification? (DB-25?, RS-232?)
Internetworking	Are bridging and/or routing modules available that can redirect traffic from module to module? Across different types of network architecture modules? Across which different network architecture modules will traffic need to be bridged?
Wide Area Networking	Is this hub connected to other hubs remotely through the use of carrier-based data services? If so, which WAN services are supported? Options: frame relay, ISDN, switched 56K, digital leased lines from 9.6 Kbps to 1.544 Mbps (T-1).

Figure 6-17 Wiring Centers Technology Analysis *(figure continues)*

Management	Is a local hub management program available? Are SNMP management protocols supported? Can individual ports be managed? Is monitoring software included? What security services are available? Can ports be remotely enabled/disabled? Can the hub be controlled by a port attached workstation or only by a special management console? Can the hub be controlled remotely? Via a modem? Are management statistics and alarms graphically displayed? How are alarm thresholds set? How are faults managed? Can port access be limited by day and/or time? What operating systems can the management software run on? Can a map of the network be displayed?
Reliability	Is an integrated UPS included? Are power supplies redundant? Are modules hot swappable? Are cooling fans redundant? Which components are capable of being replaced by the user?

Figure 6-17 (continued)

LAN SWITCHES

The "network in a box" or "backbone in a box" offered by concentrators and hubs shrinks the length of the network backbone but doesn't change the architectural characteristics of a particular network backbone. For instance, in an Ethernet concentrator, multiple workstations may access the built-in Ethernet backbone via a variety of media, but the basic rules of Ethernet such as CSMA/CD access methodology at 10 Mbps still control performance on this "Ethernet in a box." Only one workstation at a time can broadcast its message onto the shared 10 Mbps backbone.

Switch Classification

Supported Network Architectures A **switching hub,** or **LAN switch,** seeks to overcome this "one at a time" broadcast scheme, which leads to data collisions, retransmissions, and reduced throughput between high bandwidth-demanding devices such as engineering workstations or server-to-server communications. By adding the basic design of a data PBX to the modular-designed concentrator, numerous manufacturers have delivered "switched" Ethernet connections at 10 Mbps to multiple users simultaneously through a process known as parallel networking.

The Ethernet switch is actually able to create connections, or switch, between any two attached Ethernet devices on a packet-by-packet basis in as little as 40 msec. Figure 6-3 illustrated the basic functionality of an Ethernet switch. Ethernet is not the only network architecture for which LAN switches are available. Either stand-alone versions or slide-in modules for enterprise switches are also available for token ring, FDDI, fast Ethernet, and gigabit Ethernet.

In addition, many high-end LAN switches also support **ATM (asynchronous transfer mode),** which is a type of switching that not only allows the previously mentioned LAN network architectures to be switched extremely quickly but also can switch voice, video, and image traffic equally well. In fact ATM can switch any type of digital information over LANs or WANs with equal ease at speeds up to 2.4 Gbps.

Super switches or mega-switches support multiple different LAN architectures, ATM, and interface to WAN services.

Functional Differences Switches can vary in ways other than just the types of network architectures supported. Significant functional differences between switches can have a dramatic effect on switch performance. The first major functional difference has to do with how the network architecture frames are processed before they are switched to their destination:

- **Cut-through switches** read only the address information in the MAC layer header before beginning processing. After reading the destination address, the switch consults an address look-up table to determine which port on the switch this frame should be forwarded to. Once the address look-up is completed, the point-to-point connection is created and the frame is immediately forwarded. Cut-through switching is very fast. However, because the frame check sequence on the forwarded frame was not checked, bad frames are forwarded. As a result, the receiving station must send a request for retransmission followed by the sending station retransmitting the original frame leading to overall traffic increases.
- **Store-and-forward switches** read the entire frame into a shared memory area in the switch. The contents of the transmitted frame check sequence field is read and compared to the locally recalculated frame check sequence. If the results match, then the switch consults the address look-up table, builds the appropriate point-to-point connection, and forwards the frame. As a result, store-and-forward switching is slower than cut-through switching but does not forward bad frames.
- **Error-free cut-through switches,** also known as **adaptive switching,** read both the addresses and frame check sequences for every frame. Frames are forwarded immediately to destination nodes in an identical fashion to cut-through switches. However, if bad frames are forwarded, the error-free cut-through switch is able to reconfigure those individual ports producing the bad frames to use store-and-forward switching. As errors diminish to preset thresholds, the port is set back to cut-through switching for higher performance throughput.

Practical Advice and Information

SWITCH TECHNOLOGY ISSUES

Switch Flow Control Switches are very often employed to make switched connections between multiple network architectures. A common role of LAN switches is to provide switched connections between 10- and 100-Mbps network architectures. However, when servers on high-speed (100 Mbps) switched connections blast high-bandwidth data traffic back to clients on shared 10-Mbps port connections, data traffic can get backed up and data frames can be lost once buffers designed to hold overflow data become filled.

Switch vendors have attempted to respond to this situation in a variety of ways. Some switches include so-called deep buffers, which allow more overflow traffic to be buffered before it is discarded. However, the dilemma with this approach is that memory is expensive, and it is difficult to determine how much buffer memory is enough while still keeping switch costs reasonable.

A second approach for Ethernet switches involves implementing a feedback mechanism known as **backpressure.** Backpressure prevents lost frames during overload conditions by sending out false collision detection signals to get transmitting clients and servers to time-out long enough to give the switch a chance to forward buffered data. It is somewhat ironic that the CSMA/CD access methodology that the switch sought to overcome is being used to improve switch performance. The difficulty with backpressure mechanisms in the case of multiple-device LAN segments being linked to a single switch port is that the false collision detection signal stops all traffic on the LAN segment, even peer-to-peer traffic, which could have been delivered directly without the use of the switch. One possible solution to this shortcoming is to enable backpressure only on those switch ports that are connected to single devices such as servers.

Switch Management Another major issue to be faced by network managers before jumping blindly onto the LAN switch bandwagon is the matter of how to monitor and manage switched LAN connections. Unlike shared-media LAN management tools, which are able to access all network traffic from a single interface to the shared-media hub, switched architecture management tools must be able to monitor numerous point-to-point dedicated connections simultaneously. In a switched LAN architecture, each port is the equivalent of a dedicated LAN that must be individually monitored and managed. Switch vendors currently offer three basic approaches to the switch management dilemma:

1. **Port mirroring** copies information from a particular switch port to an attached LAN analyzer. The difficulty with this approach is that it only allows one port to be monitored at a time.
2. **Roving port mirroring** creates a roving RMON (remote monitoring) probe that gathers statistics at regular intervals on multiple switch ports. The shortcoming with this approach is that at any single point in time, only one port is being monitored.
3. **Simultaneous RMON view** allows all network traffic to be monitored simultaneously. Such a monitoring scheme is possible only on those switches that incorporate a shared memory multigigabit bus as opposed to a switching matrix internal architecture. Furthermore, unless this monitoring software is executed on a separate CPU, switch performance is likely to degrade.
4. **SMON** allows traffic to be monitored on a per switch basis rather than a per segment basis. SMON greatly reduces the bandwidth required to collect network statistics.

There is little doubt that properly deployed LAN switches can greatly improve network performance. However, management tools for LAN switches continue to evolve, and network managers should be wary of introducing technology into an enterprise network whose impact cannot be accurately monitored and managed.

LAN SWITCH TECHNOLOGY ANALYSIS

Applied Problem Solving

Some of the important analysis issues surrounding LAN switch selection are highlighted in Figure 6-18.

LAN Switch Characteristic	Implications/Options
Switching Architecture	Options include cut-through, store-and-forward, and error-free store-and-forward.
Token Ring Switches	Some token ring switches also employ store-and-forward switching with buffering on the outbound port so that the outbound port has time to wait until the token reaches that switch port when multiple token ring devices are attached to a single switch port. Token ring switches are also able to reduce NetBIOS and source route bridging broadcast traffic by filtering. Some token ring switches also support full-duplex token ring networking, also known as DTR (dedicated token ring), IEEE 802.5r.
Network Architectures	Switches may support one or more of the following: Ethernet, token ring, FDDI, fast Ethernet, gigabit Ethernet, and ATM. Network architectures may be available in a variety of different media types.
Port Configuration	Switches can vary in both the number of MAC addresses allowed per port and the total number of MAC addresses supported for the entire switch. Some switches only allow single devices to be attached to each LAN switch port. How easily can devices be assigned/reassigned to switch ports? Can devices that are physically attached to different switch ports be assigned to the same virtual LAN?
Full Duplex	Some switches allow some ports to be enabled for full-duplex operation. Full-duplex switch ports will only communicate with full-duplex NICs, whereas "normal" switch ports will communicate with existing NICs.
Switch-to-Switch Connection	Some switches use Ethernet or token ring switched ports, whereas others use higher speed architectures such as FDDI or ATM. These interswitch connections are sometimes referred to as the fat pipe.
Internetworking	In addition to merely establishing switched connections and forwarding traffic, some switches also have the ability to examine the addressing information contained within the data frames and perform bridging and routing functions. Token ring switches may or may not perform source route bridging that is specific to the token ring architecture. Some routing models can also examine embedded protocols and make routing and filtering decisions based on that criteria.
Management	Does the switch support both SNMP and the RMON MIB? Does the switch contain a management port and management software? Which type of RMON probe is supported? Is a separate CPU provided for processing system monitoring software? Does the local management software support enterprise network management software such as HP Openview, IBM NetView, Sun SunNet Manager? Is a port provided to which a protocol analyzer can be attached?

Figure 6-18 LAN Switch Technology Analysis

ATM for the LAN

ATM (asynchronous transfer mode) is a connection-oriented switched transmission methodology that holds great promise for becoming a single solution for the transmission of data, voice, and video over both local and wide area networks. The word "promise" in the previous sentence is significant. Any technology that sounds as if it is the ultimate solution to the world's transmission needs would obviously require an enormous amount of standards-making and interoperability planning efforts. Such is the case with ATM.

One characteristic of ATM that affords it the capability of delivering a variety of traffic over both local and wide area networks is the fixed length 53-byte cells into which all traffic is segmented. This uniform length allows timed, dependable delivery for streaming traffic such as voice and video, while simplifying troubleshooting, administration, setup, and design. Standards-making activities are divided into two major efforts:

1. **UNI or user–network interface** defines standards for interoperability between end-user equipment and ATM equipment and networks. These standards are well defined and equipment is fairly widely available.
2. **NNI or Network–Network Interface** defines interoperability standards between various vendors' ATM equipment and network services. These standards are not as well defined as UNI.

As a result, single vendor solutions are currently the safest bet for network managers requiring ATM's speed and flexibility. Technology support for ATM is shown in Figure 6-19.

Costs for ATM technology vary widely and should decrease significantly with increased demand. Following are some typical cost ranges:

- 25 Mbps NICs: $250–$400 each
- 100 Mbps and 155 Mbps NICs: $400–$1000 each
- 622 Mbps and 2.4 Gbps NICs: $4000–$6000 each
- Per port cost on ATM hubs/switches: $200–$4000 each

As is the case with any high-speed network architecture, migration strategies from existing network architectures to ATM are of critical importance. Three basic migration approaches have been defined:

ATM Speed	Cabling Type
25 Mbps	STP, UTP3 or better
100 Mbps	UTP5
155 Mbps	Single and multimode fiber optic cable and UTP5
622 Mbps	Single and multimode fiber optic cable
2.4 Gbps	Single mode fiber optic cable

Figure 6-19 Available ATM Speed/Cabling Specifications

1. **IP over ATM,** otherwise known as **classical IP,** adapts the TCP/IP protocol stack to employ ATM services as a native transport protocol directly. This is an IP-specific proposal and is not an option for LANs using other protocol stacks such as NetWare's IPX/SPX.
2. **LAN emulation** provides a translation layer that allows ATM to emulate existing Ethernet and token ring LANs and allows all current upper-layer LAN protocols to be transported by the ATM services in an unmodified fashion. With LAN emulation, ATM networks become nothing more than a transparent, high-speed delivery service. LAN emulation is most often implemented by the ATM vendor by the installation of an **address resolution server,** which provides translation between the ATM addressing scheme and the addressing scheme that is native to a particular emulated LAN.
3. **MPOA,** also known as **multi-protocol over ATM,** provides support for multiple local area network protocols running on top of the ATM cell-switched network.

Figure 6-20 illustrates a typical ATM implementation featuring an ATM local workgroup, connection of legacy LANs to a local ATM network, the local ATM switched network itself acting as a local high-speed backbone, and access to wide-area ATM services that may be either a private network or purchased from an ATM WAN service provider.

LAN ENCODING SCHEMES

Regardless of network architecture, all computers attached to a LAN communicate with each other by representing humanly readable characters and symbols in machine-readable format. The process of transforming humanly readable characters into machine readable code is known as character encoding.

Using a particular encoding scheme, characters are turned into a series of 1s and 0s. The 1 and 0 are used as symbols to represent two discrete states, much like a light switch being on or off. These discrete states can be easily represented electrically by discrete voltages of electricity. In turn, these discrete voltages of electricity representing coded characters can then be easily transmitted, received, and examined by data communications equipment.

The individual 1s and 0s that constitute a given character are known as **bits.** The series (usually 8) of bits representing the entire encoded letter is known as a **byte.** These 1s and 0s, or digits, represented by discrete voltages of electricity are in **digital** format and known as digital data. Now that the humanly readable character is in machine readable form, it (these bits) can now be transmitted over the shared LAN media. If the shared LAN media is copper based, the 1s and 0s will be represented by discrete levels of electrical voltages. If the shared LAN media is fiber optic cable, then the 1s and 0s will be represented by discrete levels of light or optical energy.

Characters can be encoded according to a variety of protocols or standards. A few of the currently popular encoding standards are described next.

ASCII

American Standard Code for Information Interchange (ASCII) is one standardized method for encoding humanly readable characters. ASCII uses a series of seven bits

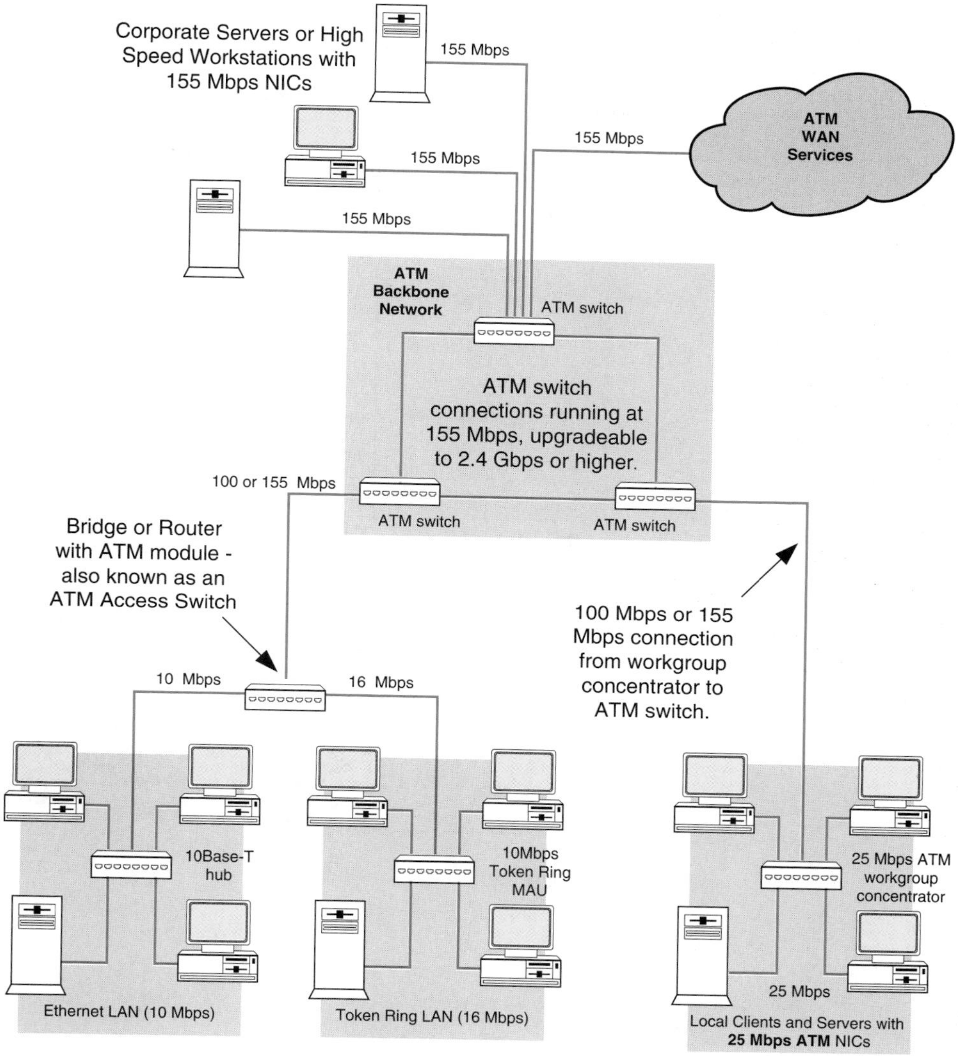

Figure 6-20 ATM Implementation

to represent 128 ($2^7 = 128$) different characters including upper and lowercase letters, numerals, punctuation and symbols, and specialized control characters. Figure 6-21 is an ASCII table.

EBCDIC

Extended Binary Coded Decimal Interchange Code (EBCDIC) is an eight-bit code capable of representing 256 different characters, numerals, and control characters ($2^8 = 256$). EBCDIC is the primary coding method used in IBM mainframe applications. Figure 6-22 is an EBCDIC table.

			MSB								
			Bit 6	0	0	0	0	1	1	1	1
			Bit 5	0	0	1	1	0	0	1	1
			Bit 4	0	1	0	1	0	1	0	1
LSB											
Bit 0	Bit 1	Bit 2	Bit 3								
0	0	0	0	NUL	DLE	SP	0	@	P		p
1	0	0	0	SOH	DC1	!	1	A	Q	a	q
0	1	0	0	STX	DC2		2	B	R	b	r
1	1	0	0	ETX	DC3	#	3	C	S	c	s
0	0	1	0	EOT	DC4	$	4	D	T	d	t
1	0	1	0	ENQ	NAK	%	5	E	U	e	u
0	1	1	0	ACK	SYN	&	6	F	V	f	v
1	1	1	0	BEL	ETB		7	G	W	g	w
0	0	0	1	BS	CAN	(	8	H	X	h	x
1	0	0	1	HT	EM	)	9	I	Y	i	y
0	1	0	1	LF	SUB	*	:	J	Z	j	z
1	1	0	1	VT	ESC	+	;	K	[	k	{
0	0	1	1	FF	FS	,	<	L	\	l	|
1	0	1	1	CR	GS		=	M	]	m	}
0	1	1	1	SO	RS	.	>	N	^	n	~
1	1	1	1	SI	US		?	O	-	o	DEL

Figure 6-21 ASCII Table

Practical Advice and Information

USING ASCII AND EBCDIC TABLES

Using ASCII or EBCDIC tables to interpret character encoding is relatively straightforward. The tables are arranged according to groups of bits otherwise known as bit patterns. The bit patterns are divided into groups. In the case of ASCII, bits 6 through 4 are known as the most significant bits (MSB), whereas bits 3 through 0 are known as the least significant bits (LSB). In the case of EBCDIC, bits 0 through 3 are known as the MSB and bits 4 through 7 are known as the LSB.

To find the bit pattern of a particular character, one needs to just combine the bit patterns that intersect in the table at the character in question, remembering that most significant bits always come before least significant bits. In the case of ASCII, this means that bits are arranged from bit 6 to bit 0, whereas EBCDIC is arranged from bit 0 to bit 7. As an example, representative characters, numerals, and control characters and their bit patterns are highlighted with shading in the ASCII and EBCDIC tables and are displayed in Figure 6-23 in humanly readable, ASCII, and EBCDIC formats.

			MSB Bit 0	0	0	0	0	0	0	0	0	1	1	1	1	1	1	1	1
			Bit 1	0	0	0	0	1	1	1	1	0	0	0	0	1	1	1	1
			Bit 2	0	0	1	1	0	0	1	1	0	0	1	1	0	0	1	1
			Bit 3	0	1	0	1	0	1	0	1	0	1	0	1	0	1	0	1
LSB Bit 7	Bit 6	Bit 5	Bit 4																
0	0	0	0	NUL	DLE	DS		SP	&	-									0
1	0	0	0	SOH	DC1	SOS						a	j			A	J		1
0	1	0	0	STX	DC2	FS	SYN					b	k	s		B	K	S	2
1	1	0	0	ETX	DC3							c	l	t		C	L	T	3
0	0	1	0	PF	RES	BYP	PN					d	m	u		D	M	U	4
1	0	1	0	HT	NL	LF	RS					e	n	v		E	N	V	5
0	1	1	0	LC	BS	EOB	UC					f	o	w		F	O	W	6
1	1	1	0	DEL	IL	PRE	EOT					g	p	x		G	P	X	7
0	0	0	1		CAN							h	q	y		H	Q	Y	8
1	0	0	1		EM						\	i	r	z		I	R	Z	9
0	1	0	1	SMM	CC	SM		>>	!		:								
1	1	0	1	VT				.	$	,	#								
0	0	1	1	FF	IFS		DC4	<	*	%	@								
1	0	1	1	CR	IGS	ENQ	NAK	(	)										
0	1	1	1	SO	IRS	ACK		+	;	>	=								
1	1	1	1	SI	IUS	BEL	SUB	|	-	?									

Figure 6-22 EBCDIC Table

Humanly Readable	ASCII	EBCDIC
A	1000001	11000001
x	1111000	10100111
5	0110101	11110101
LF (line feed)	0001010	00100101

Figure 6-23 Humanly Readable, ASCII, and EBCDIC Coding

Line Encoding

Two of the more popular methodologies in which 1s and 0s are actually represented by discrete levels of voltages are manchester encoding and differential manchester encoding. Both of these encoding schemes ensure sufficient transitions between pos-

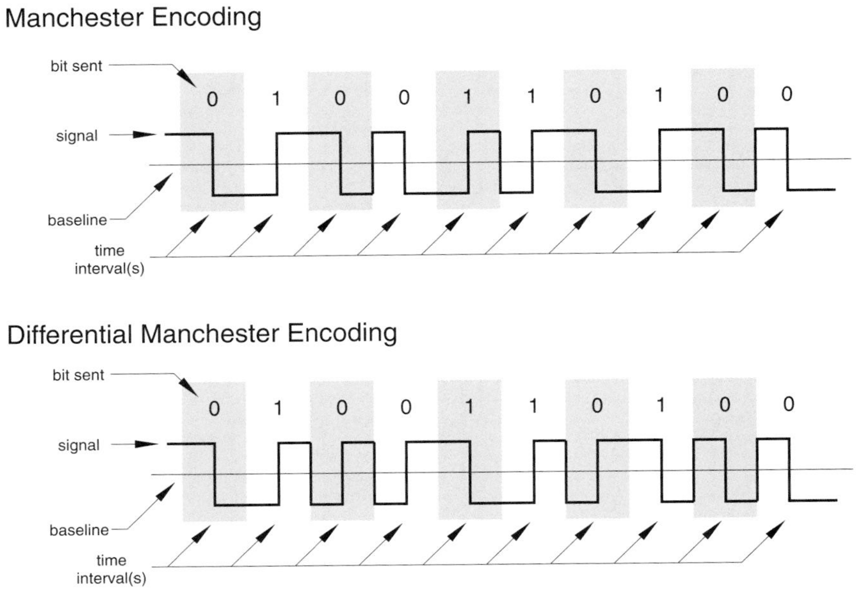

Figure 6-24 Manchester Encoding vs. Differential Manchester Encoding

itive and negative voltages to ensure the required signal timing and reliability. Time slots in which a given signal voltage is sampled are known as bit times. As illustrated in Figure 6-24, transitions between positive and negative voltages occur during these bit times. In the case of manchester encoding, a transition from negative to positive within a bit time represents a binary 1, and a transition from positive to negative voltages within a given bit time slot represents a binary 0. Differential manchester encoding takes into account the additional factor of the *difference* between the voltage level at the beginning of the current bit time and the voltage level at the end of the previous bit time. If these two voltage levels are the same, a 1 is represented. If the voltage level at the beginning of a given bit time is the opposite of the voltage at the end of the previous bit time, a 0 is being represented in that bit time. Figure 6-24 illustrates the difference between manchester encoding and differential manchester encoding.

SUMMARY

The hardware required to implement any local area network architecture falls into a relatively few broad categories: network interface cards, media, and wiring centers. Linking this hardware to the network operating system and operating system software is the network interface card driver. Advances in wiring center technology have enabled an entirely new, switch-based LAN architecture. LAN switches are extremely popular as an upgrade strategy for bandwidth-hungry networks, as they do not require any changes to network interface cards, drivers, or media. However, preupgrade traffic analysis is prudent as interswitch bottlenecks can actually degrade, rather than improve, performance.

PCI-based network interface cards are emerging as the high performance NIC of choice thanks largely to PCI's own clock, CPU, and mezzanine architecture. The key operational characteristics of network interface card drivers are the ability to support multiple protocol stacks on a single network adapter card and the need to avoid having to write monolithic drivers for every possible network interface card/network operating system combination. NDIS and ODI are the two most popular multiprotocol NIC drivers.

Shared-media wiring centers include stand-alone hubs, stackable hubs, enterprise hubs, and MAUs. These shared-media hubs merely collapse the shared-media LAN backbone into a single enclosure, while maintaining the one-at-a-time access methodologies. Hub management is especially important as numbers of users grow into the hundreds. Hub management software should be able to tie into enterprise network management software.

LAN switches offer multiple simultaneous connections to attached workstations as opposed to the one-at-a-time access schemes of the shared media hubs. However, LAN switches are a relatively new technology and have their definite drawbacks. For one, when high-speed ports transfer large amounts of data to shared lower speed ports, data overflow and lost data can occur. Second, management of switched connections that may last only for fractions of a second is not nearly as straightforward as management of a shared media hub. Each of these challenges is being addressed by LAN switch vendors.

KEY TERMS

active management MAUs
adaptive switching
address resolution server
agents
asynchronous transfer mode
ATM
backbone-attached workgroup/departmental LAN switches
backbone/data center switches
backplane capacity
backpressure
base I/O address
base memory address
binding
bus-mastering DMA
byte
card and socket services
card services
CardBus
cascading ports
classical IP
collapsed backbone network
CSS
cut-through switches
digital
direct enablers
EBCDIC
enhanced parallel port
enterprise hubs
enterprise network management systems
EPP
error-free cut-through switches
Extended Binary Coded Decimal Interchange Code
external NICs
fast-packet forwarding
full-duplex Ethernet
high performance parallel port
Home Phoneline Association*
hot swappable
hubs
interrupt request
IRQ
IP over ATM
LAN emulation
LAN switch
link support layer
local hub management software
LSL
management information bases
MAUs
MIBs
MLID
modular concentrators
monolithic drivers
MPOA
multi-link interface drivers
multi-protocol over ATM
multistation access units
NDIS
network device interface specification
network interface card drivers
network interface cards
network-network interface
NICs
NNI
ODI
open data-link interface
packet overlapping
PC card
PCMCIA
personal computer memory card international association
port mirroring
protocol manager
remote monitoring MIB
RMON
roving port mirroring
server front-end LAN switch
shared-media network architecture
simple network management protocol
simultaneous RMON view
SMON
SNMP
socket services
stackable hubs
stand-alone hubs
stand-alone workgroup/departmental LAN switches
store-and-forward switches
switch monitoring

switched LAN architectures
switching hub
UNI
USB
universal serial bus
user-network interface
vector

REVIEW QUESTIONS

1. List the broad functions and interrelationships of each of the major categories of technology cited in the LAN technology architecture.
2. Differentiate between a shared-media network architecture and a switch-based network architecture in terms of advantages and disadvantages of each.
3. What are some of the potential drawbacks or cautions to upgrading to a LAN switch?
4. Differentiate between the three major implementation scenarios for LAN switches in terms of delivered functionality and corresponding required switch technology.
5. Describe the advantages and disadvantages of a collapsed backbone network.
6. What are the advantages and disadvantages of full-duplex network architectures?
7. What do full-duplex architectures require, in terms of both hardware and software, beyond normal switch-based LAN architectures?
8. What applications are full-duplex network architectures especially well suited for?
9. What is the meaning of the phrase "The NIC is the keeper of the MAC layer protocol"?
10. What unique advantages can PCI bus NICs offer?
11. Which NIC data transfer method is most efficient and why?
12. Why is it not safe to assume that a bus-mastering DMA NIC will work on any computer?
13. What is the disadvantage of using external adapters on notebook or laptop computers?
14. What is the functional role of a network interface card driver?
15. What are the disadvantages of monolithic drivers?
16. What are the two major advantages of multiprotocol network adapter card drivers?
17. Compare and contrast NDIS and ODI in terms of architecture and functionality.
18. What is the significance of binding in a NDIS environment?
19. Which files and programs are involved in a binding operation?
20. How are protocols actually directed to the proper protocol stack in an NDIS environment?
21. What are the differences between PCMCIA card services and socket services?
22. What are the differences between PCMCIA CSS and direct enablers?
23. Differentiate the terms PC card, CardBus, and PCMCIA.
24. Differentiate between the three major categories of hubs in terms of delivered functionality and required technology features.
25. What important advantages does an active management MAU offer?
26. Why can't modules from one vendor's enterprise hub be used in another vendor's enterprise hub even though the modules both support the same network architecture?
27. What are the differences between the two levels of management software that hubs should support?
28. How is it possible for an enterprise network management system to compile statistics from networking equipment manufactured by a variety of different vendors?
29. What are the major functional differences between how LAN switches process and forward packets? What are the advantages and disadvantages of each method?
30. In what types of LAN switch implementations is backpressure likely to be an issue?
31. Why is traffic monitoring and management more of a challenge in LAN switches than in shared-media hubs?
32. What new standards have been developed to help alleviate the challenges presented in question 30?
33. Differentiate between the three major LAN switch traffic monitoring and management techniques.
34. What are the advantages and disadvantages of assigning multiple workstations per switch port?
35. What switching issues are unique to token ring switches?
36. What roles can ATM play in a local area network?
37. How can "legacy LANs" be integrated into an ATM network?
38. What are the unique capabilities of ATM that account for all of the interest in this technology?
39. What is LAN emulation and why is it important?
40. What is HPNA and why is it potentially an important technology for your home?

ACTIVITIES

1. Research the relative market sizes of hubs vs. LAN switches over the past 3 years. Interpret your results.
2. Find actual LAN switch implementations and analyze and compare the various implementation scenarios. What function is the LAN switch serving in each case? Are there implementation categories beyond those listed in Chapter 6? Were examples found of each scenario listed?
3. Find actual implementations of full-duplex network architectures and report on the applications served by this technology. Is traffic level measured in this application? If so, report on the findings.
4. Research the network interface card market and report on those features or functions offered by the most advanced NICs.
5. Locate a computer that uses NDIS drivers. Print out the CONFIG.SYS and PROTOCOL.INI files. Trace the binding operation between MAC drivers and protocol drivers.
6. Locate a computer that uses ODI drivers. Print out the CONFIG.SYS and the NET.CFG files. Determine how multiple protocol stacks can be assigned to a single NIC.
7. Research data communications catalogs, buyers' guides, and product literature for the latest information on PCMCIA adapters. Report on the latest trends and capabilities. Are multiple functions, such as modems and NICs, being included on a single card?
8. Research data communications catalogs, buyers' guides, and product literature for the latest information on hubs. Pay special attention to the availability of management features, especially ties to enterprise management systems.
9. Research the topic of the RMON Which standards-making organization is responsible for the definition? What types of information are collected in the RMON MIB? What are RMON probes and how do they function?
10. Research the topic of the SMON MIB. Which standards-making organization is responsible for the definition? What types of information are collected in the SMON MIB? What types of devices perform this data collection?
11. Research data communications catalogs, buyers' guides, and product literature for the latest information on LAN switches. Pay special attention to how the switches handle flow control issues and report on the alternative methods.
12. Research data communications catalogs, buyers' guides, and product literature for the latest information on LAN switches. Pay special attention to how the switches handle monitoring and management of LAN switch traffic and report on the alternative methods.
13. Research data communications catalogs, buyers' guides, and product literature for the latest information on ATM technology for the LAN. What is the availability and cost range for ATM NICs of various speeds? Which vendors seem to have the most complete "single-vendor solutions"?
14. Research the pros and cons and advantages and disadvantages of gigabit Ethernet vs. ATM. What does each architecture do well and not so well? What are the best uses of each? Is either one better in all cases? Present your results in a research paper or panel discussion.
15. Research current vendors of home networking equipment. Compile a chart showing the type of products they offer, technology used (wired or wireless), specifications supported, and cost for a typical configuration that includes two computers and a means to access the Internet.

CASE STUDY

Extreme Networking

No roads lead here. There is no sun for half the year. The nearest place to get supplies is 800 miles away, the nearest city is some 3,000 miles away, and the only way to get here is by plane, weather permitting.

Welcome to the U.S. Amundsen-Scott South Pole station, home to just 250 people during the Antarctic summer and one-fifth that number the rest of the year. Until recently, their communications with the rest of the world were extremely limited. That changed with the arrival of voice over IP.

Jeff Thompson, a network engineer for the United States Antarctic Program (USAP), was responsible for upgrading communications links with the isolated Amundsen-Scott South Pole base.

Clearly, the rudimentary voice links that relied on ham radio and ATS-3, an ancient NASA satellite originally used to support the Apollo lunar missions, were simply not enough to meet the growing requirements of the scientists and support personnel at the South Pole.

But upgrading the system to handle the needs of a world-class research facility wouldn't be easy. Because of the station's isolated location and the frigid environment, building a new communications infrastructure would be very impractical — since there are no roads leading to the station, equipment and workers have to be flown in by special military aircraft during the Antarctic summer. In addition, temperatures reaching minus 110 degrees Fahrenheit the rest of the year not only make prolonged work outside impossible, but also require equipment that can withstand the extreme conditions.

Then there were costs to consider — laying an undersea cable beneath the churning South Atlantic and building a land link from the coast would total more than $200 million, while building a microwave link to McMurdo station, a larger U.S. base on the Antarctic coast with 24-hour T-1 access, would cost an estimated $45 million. Other options were also deemed too expensive.

In the end, Thompson's communications woes were solved by new satellite links and a new technology: voice over IP.

"The implementation of VoIP was the only solution that would allow voice traffic at a very small cost," says Thompson, a former Navy engineer who first came to Antarctica 10 years ago and is now vice president of technology at Holmes & Narver/McClier, one of the primary contractors for the USAP.

The key to setting up the voice-over-IP network was the arrival at the pole of three satellites — GOES-3, LES-9 and TDRS F1 — for data communications. In 1998, the University of Miami, which operates two of the satellites ground stations, installed a Selsius call manager and sent several Selsius IP phones to the South Pole for trials.

Thompson liked what he saw. "We tested them out during the summer of 1998/1999 at South Pole station," he says. "This allowed South Pole to make commercial toll-grade calls for the first time."

Realizing the potential of voice over IP to drastically improve voice communications from the South Pole, Thompson and his colleagues began to explore ways to move from a testing phase to a full-scale implementation.

There were several factors that had to be taken into consideration. Because the South Pole's location falls well outside of the footprints of most geosyncronous satellites, direct links are only possible with satellites in highly inclined orbits that are only visible at certain times of the day.

Because of LES-9s limited bandwidth, it was relegated to handling low-speed Internet traffic only. TDRS F1, however, could easily manage voice-over-IP traffic on its two-way, 1024K bit/sec data link, while the satellite's one-way, 6M bit/sec transmitter could be used for the transmission of large graphic and data files by the astronomers, physicists and climatologists working at the South Pole. GOES-3 was also assigned voice over IP and data traffic.

At the South Pole, and at the satellite ground stations at the University of Miami and White Sands, N.M., Thompson and his colleagues gradually took on the task of expanding the voice-over-IP system. Since last June, a number of new components have been installed at the South Pole station's communications building and several outlying structures, starting with a half-dozen Cisco 12 SP+IP phones, which are plugged into a Catalyst 2924M-XL distribution switch with two 100BaseFX unlinks to a Catalyst 6509 core switch.

From there, the voice-over-IP traffic travels over fiber-optic cable to a Linux-based Netmax Firewall, then to a Packeteer PacketShaper 2000, where quality-of-service standards are applied. The traffic is then passed on to a Cisco 4000 router, and either sent to the satellite dish for GOES-3, or to a Cisco 2500 router that oversees traffic to the TDRS F1 satellite uplink.

The GOES-3 voice-over-IP traffic arrives at a ground station in Florida, where it is channeled via two T-1s to the University of Miami. The TDRS F1 traffic, on the other hand, is downlinked to White Sands and then sent over the NASA backbone, which is connected to the University of Miami by two T-1s.

At the University of Miami, the voice-over-IP traffic arrives at the university's Windows NT-based call manager before being passed off to either a Cisco DT-24+ digital voice-over-IP gateway or to one of two analog Selsius gateways, which are connected to the university's PBX. According to Thompson, there were some integration issues at the university, but these have since been overcome. Still, after his experience building and tweaking the South Pole voice-over-IP system, he hopes future product releases will include "Unix-based call managers and the ability to move phones from subnet to subnet with zero reconfiguration."

Overall, however, Thompson is extremely satisfied with the voice-over-IP phones. He adds that more improvements are on the way, in line with the South Pole Station Modernization (SPSM) project, a $ 128 million endeavor to modernize the living quarters, scientific equipment, support buildings and IT infrastructure at the Amundsen-Scott base and outlying scientific structures by 2005.

"We currently have six phones scattered around the station, and as part of the SPSM we'll [probably] be installing a total Ethernet-based phone system. We will, however, have analog copper lines for 911 services," he says. Other upgrades under consideration involve adding up to 15 more IP phones, incorporating a planned link to the Marisat F2 satellite and building a new ground station at the South Pole.

There is also talk of discarding the Ethernet-based phone system in favor of a different architecture that would include a traditional PBX with a voice-over-IP interface at the pole.

Cost-wise, Thompson is pleased with the way voice over IP has worked out. The Cisco IP phones cost $350 apiece, and much of the other recently purchased gear was included in the budget for the ongoing SPSM network upgrades. "My network upgrade budget for this year, which included a core switch, eight distribution switches and the Packeteer, was around $175,000," he says. "We got really good pricing."

Users who have tried new voice-over-IP system are ecstatic with the improvement in communications. Steve Barwick, a scientist working on the Antarctic Muon and Neutrino Detector Array (AMANDA) astronomy project at the pole, remembers all too well the days before voice over IP.

"When I first started to come to [the] pole in 1992, communication was very restrictive," Barwick says. "Bandwidth was limited, so e-mail was censored to ensure that only business-related communication took place. For personal communication, a ham radio was used to patch to the phone system in the U.S. Sometimes four people were listening to your call, so privacy was not a strong concern."

Barwick says there is a direct correlation between the integrated voice-over-IP/data traffic system and the amount of science that can be conducted by the AMANDA team.

"The voice-over-IP phone is now a useful scientific tool, since we can call from any phone at the station. This is a wonderful advance," Barwick says. "Imagine what it was like two years ago. If there was an unexpected problem and we needed to talk to a colleague in the U.S. or Europe and the satellite was up, we would walk about 1 kilometer to the phone, then usually wait for a clear period, and then get a busy signal or no answer. Compare that to now. We can call from the building that we normally work in. If the person on the other line is out, we can leave a message and that person can call us back. Voice communication becomes a viable tool when there is this level of convenience."

Thompson agrees: "VoIP has really changed the way we do business."

Source: Ian Lamont, "Extreme Networking—VOIP smokes at minus 100 degrees in Antartica," *Network World,* vol. 17, no. 10 (March 6, 2000), p. 57. Copyright Network World. Reprinted with permission.

BUSINESS CASE STUDY QUESTIONS

Activities

1. Complete a top-down model for this case by gleaning facts from the case and placing them in the proper layer of the top-down model. After having completed the top-down model, analyze and detail those instances where requirements were clearly passed down from upper layers to lower layers of the model and where solutions to those requirements were passed up from lower layers to upper layers of the model.
2. Detail any questions about the case that may occur to you for which answers are not clearly stated in the article.

Business

1. What was the business motivation or problem that initiated the search for the implemented solution?
2. What was the productivity impact of the implemented solution?
3. Why is the installation of the VOIP phones critical to the success of the Antarctic base?

Application

1. What is the main application described in the article?
2. What additional applications also make use of the new bandwidth provided by the new sattelites?

Data

1. What types of data are carried by the network?
2. What are the amounts of data that typically must be transferred in this application?

Network

1. What was the solution used before the VOIP phones were implemented?
2. What satellites were used to deliver phone service before and after the VOIP installation?
3. What is the purpose of the Packeteer device? Why is this critical to the delivery of VOIP service?
4. What underlying network technologies were key to the achievement of stated business objectives?

Technology

1. What specific technologies were employed to deliver the described solution?

CHAPTER 7

LOCAL AREA NETWORK COMMUNICATIONS PROTOCOLS AND OPERATING SYSTEMS

Concepts Reinforced

OSI Network Reference Model
Data Link Functionality
Hardware/Software Compatibility
Network Architectures
Protocol Encapsulation
Network Functionality
Client/Server Technology Model
LAN Software Architecture

Concepts Introduced

Network Addressing
Routing
Ports
Network Operating System Functionality
Architectures
Client Network Operating Systems
Address Resolution
Sessions
Sockets
Network Operating Systems
Server Network Operating Systems

OBJECTIVES

Upon successful completion of this chapter, you should:

1. Understand the concept of protocol encapsulation.
2. Understand address resolution and its role in the delivery of data.
3. Understand the network, transport, and session layers of the OSI network reference model.
4. Understand the IPX/SPX, TCP/IP, AppleTalk, NetBEUI, and DLC protocols and their implementation.
5. Understand the basics of network operating system functionality.
6. Understand the important differences between peer-to-peer and client/server network operating systems architectures.
7. Understand the emerging role of the client network operating system and the universal client.

8. Understand how to analyze functional networking requirements and match those requirements to available technology.

INTRODUCTION

Local area network (LAN) communications protocols can be thought of as the language of computer networks: They provide the language and grammatical rules that define communication. Just as humans have to agree on common languages to communicate, local area networks must agree on common protocols to communicate. In this chapter, the general concepts of LAN communications protocols are developed and specific protocol implementations are discussed.

Network operating systems, like most other aspects of data communications, are undergoing tremendous change. As a result, before examining the operational characteristics of a particular network operating system, it is important to gain an overall perspective of network operating systems in general. In particular, network operating systems architectures are in a state of transition from closed environments, in which only clients and servers running the same network operating system could interact, to open environments, in which universal clients are able to interoperate with servers running any network operating system. In this chapter network operating system functionality is examined for both client and server network operating systems.

OSI NETWORK REFERENCE MODEL REVISITED

One of the best ways to categorize network functionality is the OSI network reference model. As illustrated in Figure 7-1, the OSI model provides a means of breaking complex network architectures into a series of layers that provide similar functionality. The bottom two layers of the model are implemented in hardware and were covered in depth in Chapters 5 and 6. The top five layers are implemented in software. This section focuses on providing additional detail into the software layers of the OSI model.

Layer Three—The Network Layer

The third layer of the OSI network reference model is the network layer. The network layer is primarily concerned with providing a means for nodes to communicate with other nodes on different network segments. As explained in Chapter 5, the data link layer provides a means for two nodes on a *common* network segment to communicate. Technologies such as Ethernet and token ring provide this intrasegment connectivity.

Network layer protocols expand the capabilities of the network by providing a means of delivering data (called packets) between network segments. A network layer protocol provides a means of addressing a node on the interconnected network and a means of delivering data across the network to destination nodes. The process of determining the best path to the destination node and delivering the data is known as routing. Network layer addresses can be categorized in terms of these two basic functions: addressing and routing.

LAYER	USER APPLICATION			DATA FORMAT	ENABLING TECHNOLOGY	
7 APPLICATION	Provides common services to user applications. ➡ X.400 E-MAIL interoperability specification ➡ X.500 E-MAIL directory synchronization specification ➡ Strictly speaking, does ***not*** include user applications	Higher layer protocols - independant of underlying communications network				SOFTWARE
6 PRESENTATION	Provides presentation services for network communications. ➡ Encryption ➡ Code translation (ASCII to EBCDIC) ➡ Text compression ***Not*** to be confused with ➡ Graphical User Interfaces(GUIs)	Higher layer protocols - independant of underlying communications network	Node-to-node sessions			SOFTWARE
5 SESSION	Establishes, maintains, terminates node-to-node interactive sessions.	Higher layer protocols - independant of underlying communications network	Node-to-node sessions	sessions Interactive, real-time dialogue between 2 user nodes	Distributed applications, middleware, or network operating systems.	SOFTWARE
4 TRANSPORT	Assures reliability of end-to-end network connections.	Higher layer protocols - independant of underlying communications network	End-to-end user network connection.	messages Asembles packets into messages.	Network Operating Systems	SOFTWARE
3 NETWORK	Establishes, maintains, and terminates end-to-end network connections.	Network	End-to-end user network connection.	packets Embedded within frames.	Network Operating Systems.	SOFTWARE
HARDWARE/SOFTWARE INTERFACE					NIC DRIVERS	
2 DATA LINK	Logical Link control sub-layer. Media access control sub-layer. Specified by 802.X protocols. ➡ Assures reliability of point-to-point data links.	Communications	Point-to-point data link	frames Recognizable as data.	Network Interface Cards.	HARDWARE
1 PHYSICAL	Establishes, maintains, and terminates point-to-point data links.	Communications	Point-to-point data link	bits Unrecognizable as data	Media	HARDWARE

Figure 7-1 OSI Network Reference Model

In Sharper Focus

FRAMES AND PACKETS

It is important to note the difference in the terminology used to describe the data being transmitted at each of these layers of the OSI network reference model. The data link layer (layer two) transmits *frames* of data. The network layer (layer three) transmits *packets* of data.

In Sharper Focus

NETWORKS AND SEGMENTS

A constant source of confusion is the use of multiple terms to describe network architectures. Different sources commonly use different terms to mean the same thing. Regardless of terminology, there are two key levels of networking: single segments, in which every node receives every packet, and multisegment networks, in which some internetworking device forwards packets between network segments.

Single network segments are commonly referred to as segments, subnetworks, or subnets. Interconnected segments are commonly referred to as networks or internetworks. Don't let these varying terms confuse you: If every node sees every frame of data on the LAN, it's a segment. If more than one segment is used, it's an internetwork.

Although this chapter focuses on the network layer of the OSI network reference model, each protocol discussed is part of an overall protocol family that integrates protocols from layers three through seven of the OSI model. These associated protocols are discussed in more detail in subsequent chapters.

Network Layer Addressing The role of network layer addresses is to provide a means to uniquely identify a node on the internetwork. The network layer address is used in the routing process to deliver a packet of data to the correct network segment for delivery. In this manner, network addresses are used for "end-to-end" or "inter-segment" communication.

There are two basic components to a network layer address: a network segment address and a node address. The **network segment address** identifies on which network segment the destination node is located. This address is used by the routing process to determine the destination network segment and deliver the packet to that segment. Once the packet has arrived at the correct network segment, the **node address** is resolved to a physical address and passed to the data link layer for delivery. The relationship between address components and their purpose is illustrated in Figure 7-2.

Collectively these two parts identify a node on the internetwork. The segment address must be unique to the inter-network to ensure that the packet is delivered to the correct network segment. Similarly, node address must be unique *within a network segment*. As shown in Figure 7-3, it is possible to use the same node address on multiple segments. There is no chance for confusion between the nodes, as the packet will be routed to the network segment of the correct node based on the segment address.

Address Component	Layer	Purpose
Network Segment Address	Network	Used by routers to forward data to the correct network segment
Node Address	Network	Used to identify a node within a network segment. Resolved to physical address for actual data delivery
Physical Address	Data Link	Used to deliver data to the destination node

Figure 7-2 Network Address Components

Network layer addresses are assigned on a per-network interface card (NIC) basis. It is possible for a single device to contain more than one NIC. In this case, each NIC will have its own network layer address (segment address + node address). Devices that contain more than one NIC are said to be **multihomed.**

There are several reasons to multihome a device, including performance, reliability, and stability. However, the primary reason a device is multihomed is to allow it to forward packets from one network segment to another. By definition a device that performs packet forwarding is known as a **router.** In Figure 7-3, the device in the center of the diagram that connects to all three network segments is functioning as a router, forwarding packets as needed from one segment to another.

Network Layer vs. Data Link Layer Addressing As previously mentioned, the network layer is primarily responsible for addressing nodes uniquely on an internetwork and providing a means of delivering data across network segments. The responsibility of moving data within a network segment is that of the data link layer. The data link layer uses the physical address (also known as the MAC addresses for Ethernet and token ring technologies) of the NIC to deliver data rather than the network layer node address.

For the network and data link layers to successfully interact to deliver data, a direct, one-to-one mapping must be made between the network layer address and the data link layer physical address. Although the exact method used to make this mapping varies between the various network layer protocols, every network layer protocol has a standardized method for mapping its node address to the physical address associated with the NIC. The process of determining the physical layer address of a NIC from the network layer address is known as **address resolution.**

Each NIC has both a data link layer physical address and a network address associated with it. The network layer address is used by upper layer protocols to denote which node they wish to communicate with. The network layer is also used to transport (route) data through the network to the destination network segment. Once the data arrive at the destination network segment, the network layer address is resolved to a physical address and delivered to the destination node (NIC) by the data link layer.

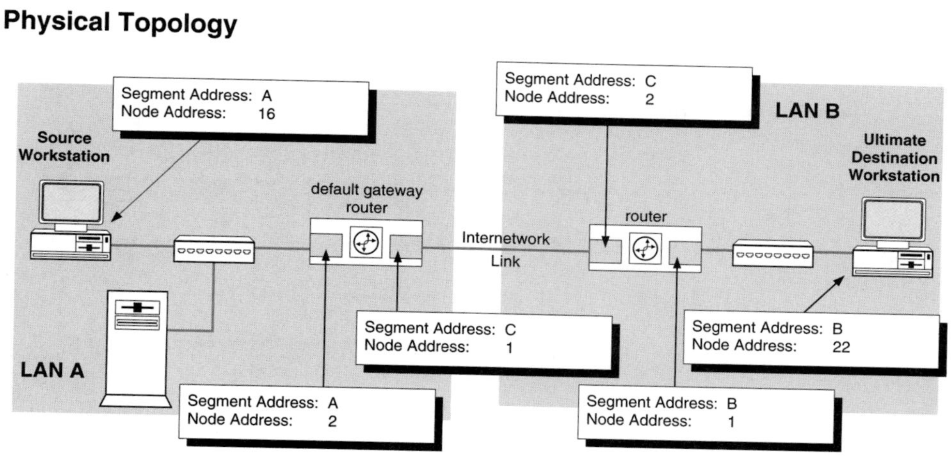

Figure 7-3 Node Addressing

Network Data Delivery	Mail Delivery
Network Segment Address	Zip code
Node Address	Street address
Physical Address	Physical mailbox location

Figure 7-4 Network Data Delivery vs. Mail Delivery

The process of delivering data to a destination node is analogous to the method used to deliver a letter to a person's house. The zip code (network segment address) is used to route the mail to the correct postal route. The mail carrier for that route then looks at the street address (node address) to determine the final destination of the letter. The mail carrier then resolves the street address to a physical mailbox location (physical address) for delivery. This relationship is shown in Figure 7-4.

Protocol Encapsulation/Deencapsulation Whereas different layer three protocols use different techniques for addressing and packet construction, a layer three packet will always contain at least three sections: source network address, destination network address, and data. The source and destination addresses are used in the routing process, and the data are the reason the packet was sent. Packet construction is detailed in subsequent sections for the most common network layer protocols currently in use.

Packets are sent through the network by encapsulating them in data link layer frames. As illustrated in Figure 7-5, a packet of data from the network layer is placed in the data section of a data link layer frame. Known as **encapsulation,** this process adds both a header and trailer to the packet. The bit stream is finally passed along the shared media that connects the two computing devices. When the full bit stream arrives at the destination server, the reverse process of encapsulation, **deencapsulation,** takes place. In this manner, the destination data link layer strips the layer two header and trailer and passes the packet to the network layer for processing.

Fragmentation Every protocol has a maximum overall packet (or frame) length. This length is the maximum size of a packet (or frame) including the header and data. The maximum size of a packet or frame of data is known as the **maximum transmission unit** (MTU).

If a higher level packet will not fit into a lower layer's available payload area, the higher level packet is broken into two or more packet fragments. These packet frag-

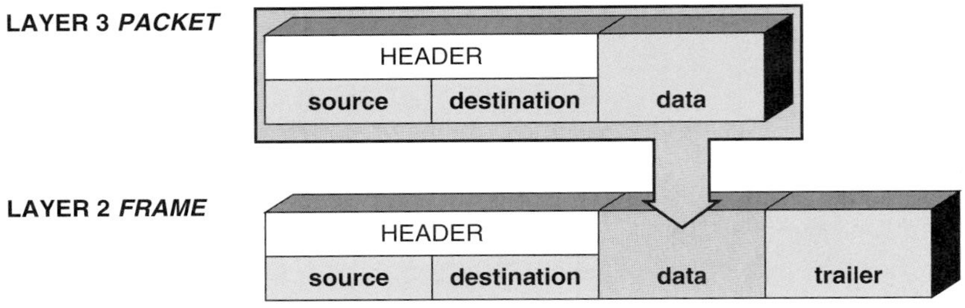

Figure 7-5 Protocol Encapsulation

ments are sent across the network and reassembled into a single packet before being sent back up the protocol stack on the destination node. **Fragmentation** allows large quantities of data to be sent across the network in smaller, more manageable "chunks" of data.

Data fragmentation is required between the application layer and the network layer for large quantities of application layer data (such as a 10 MB file) to be sent across a network. However, data fragmentation between the network layer and the data link layer represents additional overhead and should be avoided if at all possible. Fragmenting network layer packets is required when the underlying layer two frame's data payload is not capable of transporting the entire layer three packet. Such fragmentation requires the layer three packet be broken into multiple layer two frames of data that are sent across the physical network and reassembled at the layer two destination node.

The impact of network layer packet fragmentation is illustrated in Figure 7-6. When the source creates a packet that is larger than the underlying layer two transport protocols, each router on a path between the source and destination must break the packet into multiple fragments and send each fragment across the layer two link to the next router. Each frame that contains a fragment of the packet must also contain a copy of the packet's header to ensure that the packet is properly reassembled.

The next router must collect the fragments, reassemble them into the original network layer packet, and repeat the process for the next hop. Such repeated packet fragmentation and reassembly place a large processing burden on routers, effectively reducing their overall routing capacity.

Compare Figure 7-6 to Figure 7-7. Figure 7-7 represents the same network, but the layer three packet size has been set equal to or lower than the underlying layer two frame data payload. In Figure 7-7, each router merely has to package each network layer packet into a single layer two frame and send it along the route to its destination. Packet fragmentation is currently one of the key capacity limitations on most routed networks, especially when the network includes WAN links, which typically use much smaller frame sizes than LAN links.

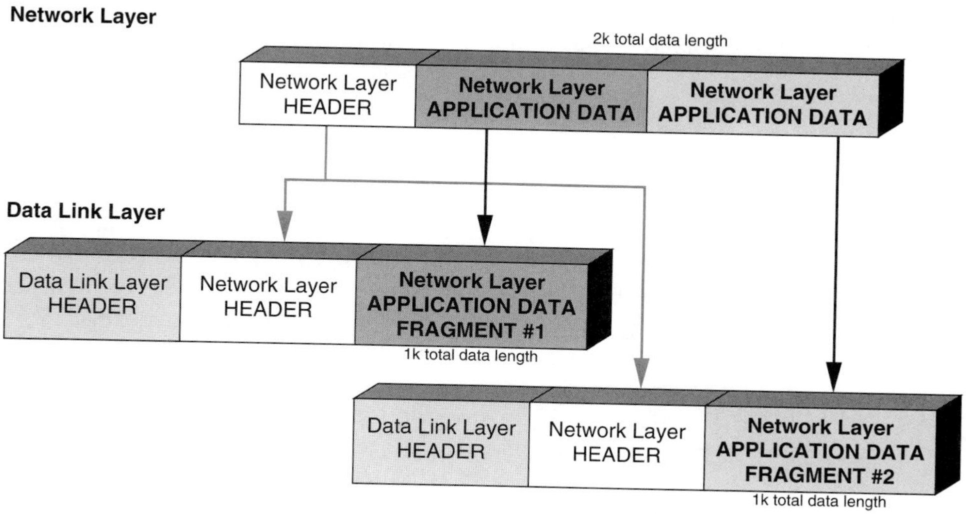

Figure 7-6 Layer Three Packet Fragmentation

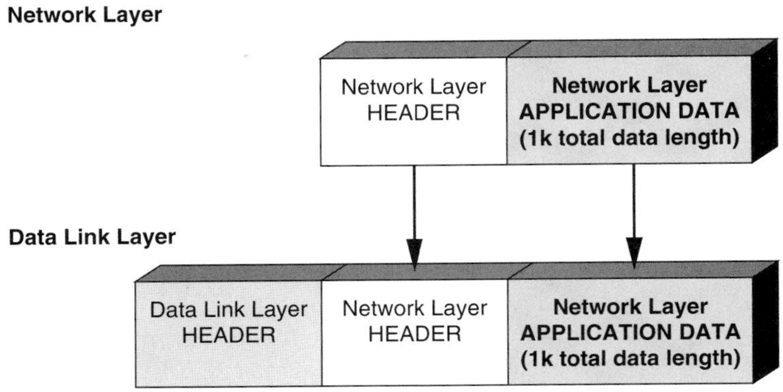

Figure 7-7 Layer Three Packet Fragmentation Eliminated

Routing Routing is the process of moving data across network segments toward its final destination. Routers receive frames of data, deencapsulate the layer three packet, examine the network layer packet header, determine the next hop of the packet, package the packet into a new data frame, and transmit the new frame.

To return to the mail example in the previous section, the routing process is analogous to the method used by the post office to deliver a letter. Someone places a sheet of paper (data) in an envelope (packet), addresses it, places it in the mailbox, and raises the flag (transmits the packet). The mail carrier picks up the letter and places it in a mail bag (data frame) and takes it to the post office (default gateway). At the post office, the letter is taken out of the mail bag (data frame), and the zip code (network segment address) is used by the post office to determine where to send the letter (routing). After the next hop is determined, the letter is placed into a new mail bag (data frame) for transmission to the destination post office (router on the destination network segment). This process continues until the letter reaches the post office that services the destination zip code (router to the destination segment).

At the destination post office, the letter is removed from the mail bag and placed into the mail bag of a mail carrier that services the destination street address. The mail carrier then places the mail in the mailbox of the destination street address for final delivery to the recipient.

Routing Is Address Processing Although routing is explained in detail in Chapter 9, it is important to understand some basic routing concepts to appreciate routing protocol functionality. Perhaps the most important thing to understand about routing is that it is nothing more than address processing performed when messages need to travel beyond the local LAN. By keeping track of the following address-related issues, the entire routing process can be largely demystified. As illustrated in Figure 7-8, the only thing that changes throughout the routing process is that the source and destination physical addresses are changed during each hop on the way to the destination node. For this example, network layer addresses are given in the format letter:number, where letter is the segment address and number is the node address.

The first logical step in the routing process is for the source workstation to fill in the source address field in the network layer header with its own network layer address and the destination address field in the network layer header with the network layer address of the ultimate destination workstation. Since the destination workstation is not on the local LAN, the packet must be forwarded to the local gate-

Physical Topology

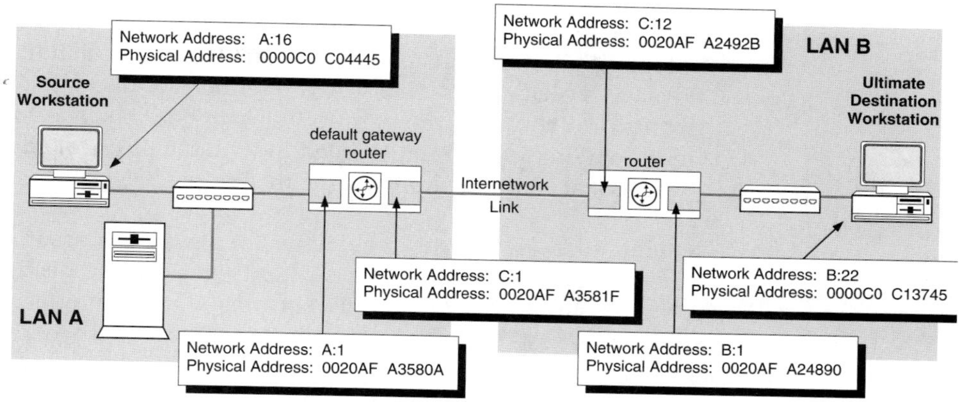

Address Processing

From source workstation to default gateway router found on LAN A:

Data-Link		Network	
source 0000C0 C04445	destination 0020AF A3580A	source A:16	destination B:22

From LAN A router to next hop router towards ultimate destination as noted in routing table:

Data-Link		Network	
source 0020AF A3581F	destination 0020AF A2492B	source A:16	destination B:22

From LAN B router to locally attached ultimate destination workstation:

Data-Link		Network	
source 0020AF A24890	destination 0000C0 C13745	source A:16	destination B:22

Figure 7-8 Routing is Address Processing

way, or router, which will have sufficient information to forward this packet properly.

The source workstation looks in its network layer configuration information to determine the network layer address of its default gateway. The default gateway is the only way out for packets off of the local LAN. To deliver this packet to the router for further processing, the packet must be wrapped in a data link layer frame such as Ethernet, token ring, or FDDI. Addresses that are included in the data link layer header are known as physical addresses. Although the source workstation has the network address of the default router in its network configuration file, it does not know the physical address router. The source workstation determines the physical address of the of the router through address resolution

Once the source workstation determines the physical address, it encapsulates the network layer packet in a data link layer frame. The physical address associated with its own NIC is placed in the source address field of data link layer frame, and the physical address of the default gateway is placed in the destination address of the data link layer frame.

The default gateway or local router receives the data link layer frame explicitly addressed to it and examines the ultimate destination address held in the packet. The router then consults its routing tables to see if it has an entry for a known path to the ultimate destination workstation. That known path may be via another router, or the ultimate destination workstation may be part of a different LAN connected to this same router through a different NIC. In either case, the packet and its addresses are not modified but are instead reencapsulated in a fresh data link layer frame with the physical layer destination address of either the ultimate destination workstation or the next router along the path to that workstation. The source address field on the fresh data link layer frame is filled in with the physical address of the default router that has just completed processing the packet.

Routing Protocols In the previous example, it was assumed that each router intuitively knew where to send a packet to get it to its destination. However, when a router is initially started, it only knows about the interfaces connected to it or **static routes** that have been configured by an administrator. For a network to dynamically build comprehensive routing tables that automatically add new routes and remove old ones, a routing protocol must be used. Routing protocols provide routers a means of automatically exchanging routing tables to ensure that each router knows where to route packets for a given destination.

Routing protocols are discussed in detail in Chapter 9, but a brief introduction is required here to understand the routing capabilities of the various network layer protocols discussed in this chapter. There are two major categories of routing protocol algorithms: distance vector and link state. Distance vector protocols broadcast their entire routing table periodically. In this manner, changes to the network routing tables slowly make their way through the network. A router using a distance vector algorithm knows nothing about the makeup of the network beyond the next hop to the destination; it merely knows that, by sending a packet of data to the next hop, the data should eventually reach the destination.

Link state protocols transmit a more complete picture of the network between routers. Through the use of link state packets (LSP), each router learns the structure of the entire network. In this manner, the link state algorithm can make better routing decisions. Link state routing reacts more quickly to changes in the routing structure than distance vector routing and uses less bandwidth to maintain routing tables. Implementation and maintenance consideration for routing protocols are discussed in Chapter 9.

Layer Four—The Transport Layer

The fourth layer of the OSI network reference model is the transport layer. Also known as the **host-to-host** layer, the transport layer is primarily concerned with creating, maintaining, and tearing down end-to-end network connections. When an application needs to send data to a remote network node, the transport layer is responsible for determining the correct network layer address and initiating the connection to the remote node. The transport layer also performs error control and correction and flow control for host-to-host connections. This includes ensuring that all packets arrive at the destination node without errors caused by dropped packets, duplicate packets, packets arriving out of order, or packets corrupted in transmission.

The transport layer can be thought of as being responsible for creating a communication channel between two nodes on an internetwork. Whereas the network layer actually transports the packets between the two nodes, the transport layer ensures that the packets flow as a data stream rather than a series of independent packets.

From the perspective of higher level protocols, the connection is a pipeline directly to the other node, independent of the routers and network links that must be traversed. For this reason the transport and all higher levels are collectively known as end-to-end layers.

Unlike network layer protocols that are **connectionless** in nature, transport layer protocols are usually **connection-oriented** and therefore provide reliable data transmission. Each packet is assigned a sequence number that uniquely identifies it in the data flowing through the connection. By referencing the sequence numbers, the destination node can ensure packets are arriving in the proper order and that no packets have been dropped. The destination node must then respond to each packet with either an acknowledgment (ACK) of correct receipt or a negative acknowledgement (NAK) to indicate an error condition.

As illustrated in Figure 7-9, the destination node acknowledges the correct receipt of each packet by sending an ACK back to the sender that includes the sequence number of the packet. If a packet fails the error check upon receipt, the destination node responds with a NAK for the sequence number. If a packet arrives out of order, the destination node examines the sequence number, realizes it is not the correct next packet, and responds with a NAK for the missing sequence number. The sending node also keeps track of the time since a packet was sent. If the destination node doesn't respond with an ACK within a preset time period, the sending node assumes that packet was dropped and resends that packet with the original sequence number. This is referred to as a packet timing-out or a time-out error.

Data sent via a connection-oriented transport layer protocol will either arrive at its destination safely, or the sending application will be alerted that the transmission failed. Because of their reliability, most data streams make use of connection-oriented transport protocols. However a connection-oriented protocol adds overhead to the

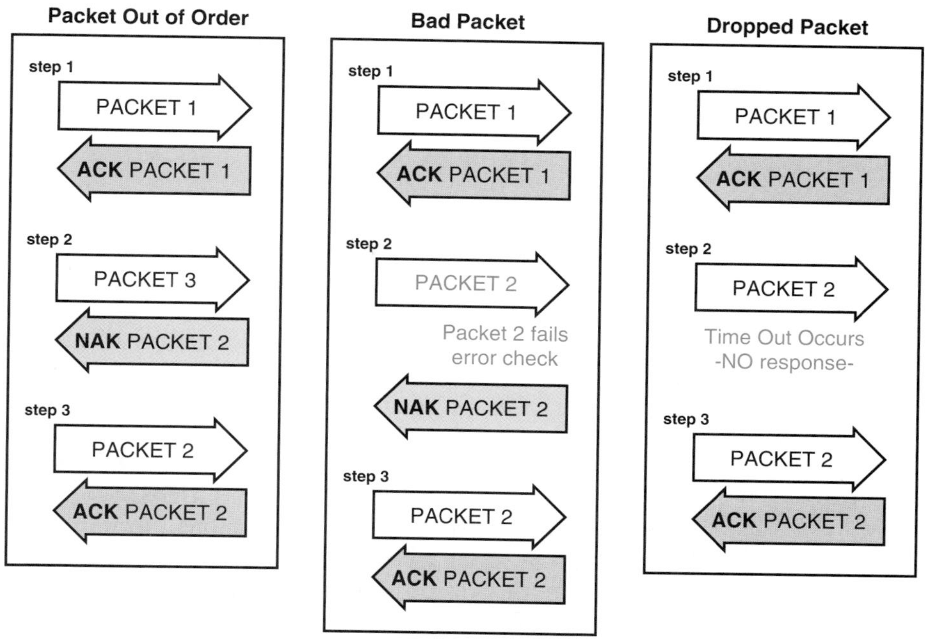

Figure 7-9 Connection-Oriented Error Correction

communication process. A connection must be built between the two nodes before any data is transmitted. The process of building a connection can require that multiple packets of data be exchanged between the two nodes. Each packet that is sent via the connection requires an ACK packet in response. At the end of the communication, the transport layer must also exchange packets to tear down the connection.

In Sharper Focus

CONNECTIONLESS OR CONNECTION-ORIENTED?

Although connection-oriented protocols require more overhead than do connectionless protocols, they ensure that the data will accurately reach its destination. This reliability is important for most data streams, as the data they carry are important or it would not have been sent in the first place. It would certainly make sense for a bank to use a connection-oriented protocol to carry financial transaction data — you wouldn't want any packets to be dropped without notice and error correction!

However, in some cases the use of a connection-oriented protocol may not be required. For messages that can be contained in a single packet, the overhead of establishing and tearing down a connection and processing ACKS can add more overhead than the message is worth. An example of a nonurgent, single-packet message is a routing protocol packet. Because routing protocol packets are routinely sent between routers, dropping a single packet is not a catastrophic event. It makes more sense to risk an occasional dropped packet than to add the overhead associated with a connection-oriented protocol for this application.

Another common application for connectionless protocols is streaming media. Streaming multimedia application layer protocols that can carry audio and video data across data networks are now commonplace. For these protocols to provide clear sound and pictures, it is important that every packet be accurately delivered to the destination. However, it is inevitable that packets will be dropped from the media stream at some point regardless of the protocol used. The issue is what to do when a packet is dropped. Is it worth the additional overhead of a connection-oriented protocol to resend dropped packets, or is it better to simply miss an occasional second of the stream?

Layer Five — The Session Layer

The fifth layer of the OSI network reference model is the session layer. The session layer is responsible for establishing, maintaining, and terminating logical sessions between applications. In the event of session failure, the session layer is responsible for reestablishing the session.

The session layer builds on the functionality of the transport layer by adding a mechanism to differentiate between applications at each end of a connection. It ensures that a packet gets to the correct application on the remote node after it crosses the connection. If there are two different communications sessions running between two nodes (such as a Telnet session and a WWW session), the session layer identifies the packets for each session and keeps them separated.

Session layer protocols identify sessions through the use of **ports** and **sockets.** Although these terms have slightly different meanings depending on the protocol, they represent the "address" of an application on a node. Each application on a node is assigned a unique port number. Most session layer protocols make use of fixed port numbers for commonly used services. This greatly simplifies the establishment of sessions between these services. Other application protocols may use a range of ports that are dynamically assigned. Regardless of the manner in which port numbers are assigned, no two applications can concurrently use the same port. To ensure that a packet is delivered to the correct address on the correct destination node, both the network layer address and port number must be specified.

To return to the letter addressing example used earlier in this chapter, the port or socket number is analogous to the person's name on the letter. The network layer is only concerned with getting the letter to the correct mailbox. It's the responsibility of the session layer to get the letter to the correct person in the house (application).

Although the functionality of the session layer is distinct from that of the transport layer, most protocol suites merge transport and session layer functionality into a single protocol.

Layers Six and Seven — The Presentation and Application Layers

The sixth layer of the OSI network reference model is the presentation layer. The presentation layer is responsible for formatting data for transmission across the network. The presentation layer performs encryption and compaction of data and converts between data communication codes as required.

The seventh layer of the OSI network reference model is the application layer. The application layer is responsible for providing data transmission services to user applications. The application layer provides these services via an **application programming interface (API).** Any application that makes calls to the API can use the services of the application layer and its underlying layers for data communication. Presentation layer functionality is closely related to application layer functionality, and both are commonly integrated into a single protocol. For the remainder of this chapter, the presentation and application layers are grouped as upper layer protocols.

Each protocol suite takes significant liberties in the assignment of functionality to protocols above the network layer. In practical terms, it is impossible to match single end-to-end protocols with a specific layer of the OSI network reference model. However the protocols of a particular protocol suite collectively provide the complete functionality as described in the OSI model.

LOCAL AREA NETWORK PROTOCOLS

Many different network layer protocols are currently in use. IPX, IP, and AppleTalk are the three most commonly used protocols for local and wide area network traffic. This section introduces these protocols.

NetWare (IPX/SPX) Protocol Suite

The IPX/SPX protocol suite was originally developed by Novell for its NetWare network operating system. IPX/SPX has also found its way to Microsoft operating systems and is commonly used to support network computer games owing to its ease of configuration.

Network Layer Protocol — IPX **Internet Packet Exchange (IPX)** was developed for and is still most commonly used in NetWare environments. While the *I* in IPX stands for internet, don't confuse it with the Internet (capital I). The Internet uses IP rather than IPX as its network layer protocol.

IPX, like most other network layer protocols, serves as a basic delivery mechanism for upper layer protocols such as SPX, RIP, SAP, and NCP. This delivery mechanism is accomplished through encapsulation whereby upper layer protocols are encapsulated within properly addressed IPX "envelopes." Network layer protocols are generally characterized as:

- **Connectionless**—implying individual, fully addressed packets, or datagrams, are free to negotiate their way through the network in search of their final destination.
- **Unreliable**—implying that the network layer does not require error checking and acknowledgment of error-free receipt by the destination host.

The entire IPX packet is, in turn, encapsulated within a data link layer frame, which corresponds to the installed network interface card. For example, if the workstation in question has a token ring card, then the entire IPX packet will be inserted into the data field of the token ring frame. If an Ethernet card is present, then the encapsulation of the IPX packet will be into the data field of the designated type of Ethernet frame.

IPX is a fairly small, easily configured protocol primarily designed to support LAN configurations. IPX is supported by many operating systems including Novell NetWare and Microsoft Windows. While IPX was once the default network layer protocol for both NetWare and Windows networking, it has seen its usage decline with the explosion of the IP-based Internet.

Addressing Addressing in IPX is very straightforward and relatively easy. The segment address and node address are kept separate and are automatically determined by most nodes on the network. IPX uses a 32-bit segment address that is usually displayed in hexadecimal (base 16). This gives an available IPX address space ranging from 0000 0000 to FFFF FFFF, which correspond to 4.29 billion different network segments. Segment addresses are hierarchical in nature, allowing easier routing within IPX networks.

As mentioned earlier in this chapter, a network layer node address is associated with a NIC card and must correlate with the underlying NICs physical address (the MAC address for Ethernet and token ring NICs). To keep configuration of IPX networks as simple as possible, the designers of the IPX protocol simply use the NIC's MAC address as the IPX node address.

As mentioned in Chapter 5, MAC addresses are 6 bytes long and are usually reported as six sets of two hexadecimal numbers (such as 00-A0-24-51-3C-D0). Because MAC addresses are by design unique (no two NICs can have the same MAC address), each node address on an IPX segment is therefore unique. In addition to eliminating the need to configure each node on an IPX network, this design also eliminates the need to resolve IPX layer three node addresses to physical addresses: The node address *is* the physical address.

In addition to the required segment and node address, IPX also provides a socket address. Technically a transport layer function, the socket address indicates which process on the destination node is to use the packet. IPX supports up to 50 sockets per computer. Upper layer protocols to which IPX transfers data frequently via encapsulation such as NCP, SAP, RIP, and NetBIOS have reserved socket numbers.

Together the segment address, node address, and socket address make up a complete IPX address.

IPX Routing Protocols IPX supports two basic routing protocols: RIP and NLSP. NLSP is known as a **link-state routing protocol,** whereas RIP is known as a **distance vector routing protocol.** Although the full differentiation between these two categories of routing protocols is explored in Chapter 9, suffice to say here that link-state protocols are more efficient in their updates of routing tables and more intelligent in their routing directions recommendations for data packets than are distance vector protocols.

Transport/Session Layer Protocols Although IPX is technically a network layer protocol, it also provides session layer addressing via sockets. An application layer protocol can directly address a remote application using only IPX as long as it specifies the socket number of the application on the destination node. For simple communication between two nodes such as exchanging routing information, IPX may be the only protocol required. Applications that require a reliable network transport mechanism require the use of SPX.

SPX **Sequenced packet exchange (SPX)** is a transport/session layer protocol that can be used with IPX to provide reliable communication. The key characteristics of SPX are as follows:

- **Connection-oriented**—implying that specific paths known as virtual circuits are explored and determined before the first packet being sent. Once the virtual circuit is established directly from the source host or node to destination node, then all packets bound for that address follow each other in sequence down the same physical path. Virtual circuits are especially important when the source host and destination host reside on different networks.
- **Reliable** — implying that SPX requires error checking and acknowledgment to ensure reliable receipt of transmitted packets. Because transfer of a single file may be broken up across multiple IPX packets, SPX adds sequence numbers to ensure that all pieces are received and that they are reconstructed in the proper order. To ensure that packets are not lost accidentally due to hosts or routers suffering from buffer overflow, SPX also has mechanisms to institute flow control.

SPX provides reliability by adding sequence numbers and acknowledgments to IPX. SPX is encapsulated within IPX and therefore depends on IPX for delivery to the destination workstation via the local network interface card.

The Internet Suite of Protocols: Overall Architecture and Functionality

TCP/IP (transmission control protocol/Internet protocol) is the term generally used to refer to an entire suite of protocols used to provide communication on a variety of layers between widely distributed different types of computers. Strictly speaking, TCP and IP are just two of the protocols contained within the family of protocols more properly known as the Internet suite of protocols. TCP/IP was developed during the 1970s and widely deployed during the 1980s under the auspices of DARPA or the Defense Advanced Research Projects Agency to meet the Department of Defense's need to have a wide variety of different computers interoperate and communicate. TCP/IP became widely available to universities and research agencies and has become the de facto standard for communication between heterogeneous networked computers.

Overall Architecture TCP/IP and the entire family of related protocols are organized into a protocol model. Although not identical to the OSI seven-layer model, the TCP/IP model is no less effective at organizing protocols required to establish and maintain communications between different computers. Figure 7-10 illustrates the TCP/IP model, its constituent protocols, and its relationship to the OSI model network reference model.

As illustrated in Figure 7-10, the OSI model and TCP/IP model are functionally equivalent, although not identical, up through the transport layer. Although the OSI model continues on with the session, presentation, and applications layers, the TCP/IP model has only the application layer remaining with utilities such as Telnet (terminal emulation) and FTP (file transfer protocol) as examples of application layer protocols. As illustrated in Figure 7-10, the functionality equivalent to the OSI model's session, presentation, and application layers is added to the TCP/IP model by combining it with the network file system (NFS) distributed by Sun Microsystems. As a result, to offer equivalent functionality to that represented by the full OSI seven-layer model, the TCP/IP family of protocols must be combined with NFS, sometimes known as the open network computing (ONC) environment.

Individual Protocols: Architecture and Functionality Figure 7-11 illustrates the placement of many of the TCP/IP family of protocols into their respective layers of the TCP/IP model. Each of these protocols, as well as several others, are explained here in detail. Many protocols involved with network management, routing, and remote access do not logically fit into any of the layers of the TCP/IP model and therefore

Layer	OSI	INTERNET	Data Format	Protocols
7	Application	Application	Messages or Streams	TELNET FTP TFTP SMTP SNMP CMOT MIB
6	Presentation			
5	Session			
4	Transport	Transport or Host-Host	Transport Protocol Packets	TCP UDP
3	Network	Internet	IP Diagrams	IP
2	Data Link	Network Access	Frames	
1	Physical			

Figure 7-10 The TCP/IP Model

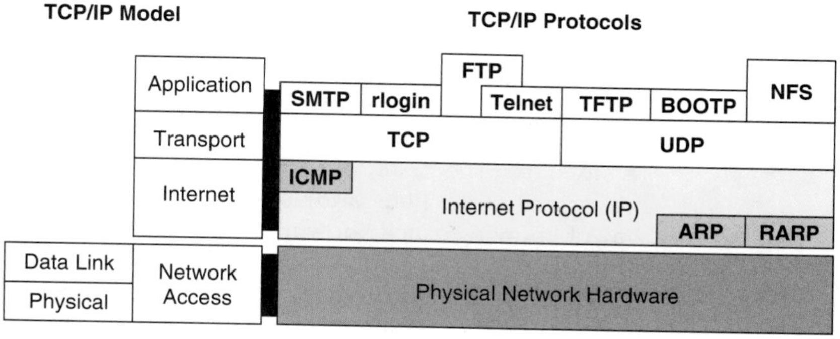

Figure 7-11 TCP/IP Family of Protocols

are not listed. The same lack of a proper layer into which to place such protocols is also true in the OSI model.

Network Layer Protocol — IP The most commonly used network layer protocol is **IP** or the **Internet protocol.** As its name would indicate, IP is the protocol used on the world wide Internet. All World Wide Web browsing, e-mail exchanging, and media streaming on the Internet is carried by IP.

The Internet protocol was the first packet-switched protocol. Originally developed to allow communication on the ARPAnet, IP has continually evolved and remains the most important layer three protocol currently in use. The version of IP most currently used is version four or IPv4. As IP continues to gain acceptance and as the size and traffic levels on the Internet continue to grow, IPv4 is reaching its limits. To resolve these issues, the Internet Engineering Task Force (the standard bearers for IP) has created an updated version of IP: IPv6, also known as **IPng** (for **next generation**). Both IPv4 and IPv6 are discussed in this section.

IP Addressing Rather than breaking the segment and node portions of the network layer address into separate units as was done in IPX, IP combines the two into a single hierarchical IP address. Although the hierarchical nature of IP addresses makes routing of IP packets easier, it makes understanding IP addressing somewhat confusing.

IPv4 addresses are 32 bits long and are represented as a sequence of four **octets.** Each octet is a decimal representation of an 8-bit section of the overall IP address. As shown in Figure 7-12, each 8-bit section of the overall IP address is converted to its

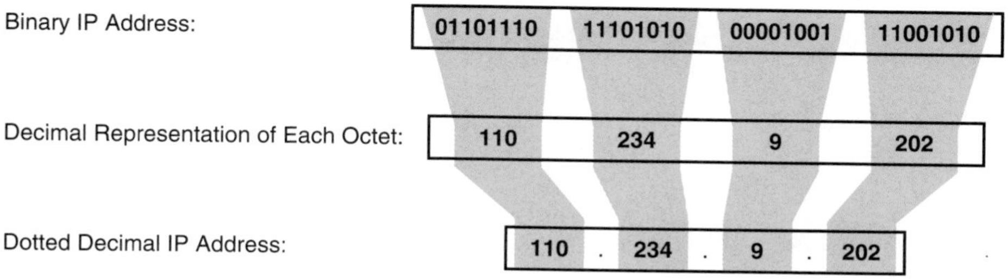

Figure 7-12 IP Address Construction

decimal value and separated by a "." This is commonly referred to as a dotted decimal approach to representing IP addresses. Although people commonly refer to sections of an IP-based network by the IP address, it's important to remember that it's the binary value that determines how the address is parsed and utilized.

An IP address contains both a segment address and a node address for a node ran together. The first X bits represent the segment address, and the remaining 32-X bits represent the node address. However, as illustrated in Figure 7-13, there is no way of knowing exactly how many bits are used for each merely by looking at the IP address.

The separation of an IP address into its segment and node address components is accomplished via a **subnet mask.** A subnet mask is a 32-bit binary sequence that divides the IP address by using a 1 to indicate that the corresponding position in the IP address is part of the segment address and by using a 0 to indicate that the corresponding portion in the IP address is part of the node address. Because the segment address is the first x bits and the node address is the remaining bits, a subnet mask will always consist of x 1s followed by 32-x zeros. The effect of using varying subnet masks on an IP address is shown in Figure 7-14. Just like IP addresses, subnet masks are usually referred to in dotted decimal format.

Once an IP address had been divided into a segment address and a range of node addresses through the application of a subnet mask, the resulting IP addresses may be assigned to the nodes on the network segment. However there are two reserved addresses that may not be assigned to a node: the address that corresponds to all ones in the node section and the address that corresponds to all zeros in the node section. All 1s in the node section of the IP address is the broadcast address for the network segment. This address is used to send a single message to every node on the network segment. All 0s in the node section of the IP address is the address of the network segment itself. This address is used by routers to refer to the network in their routing tables. For a class "C" network these addresses correspond to x.x.x.255 and x.x.x.0, respectively.

IP Address Classes An IP address can be broken into a segment address and a node address anywhere as long as both the segment address and node address consist of at least 2 bits. However, to make IP addresses easier to work with, it's customary to divide them at the octet boundaries. IP addresses divided this way are known as **classfull** addresses. In Figure 7-14, subnet mask B represents a **classfull** address. IP

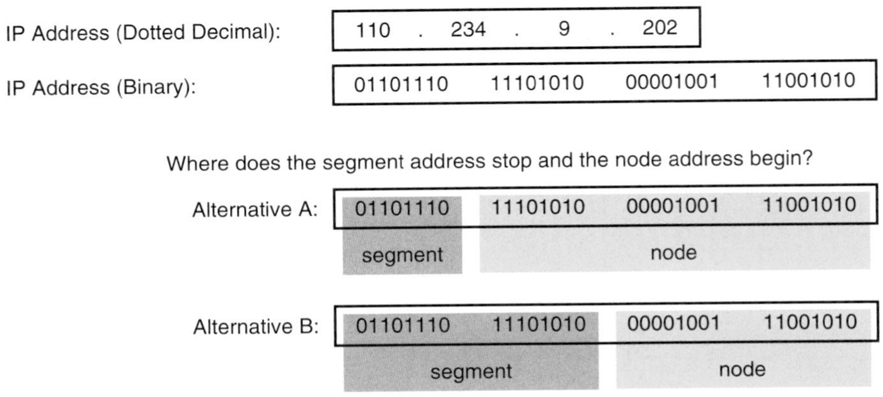

Figure 7-13 IP Segment Address vs. Node Address

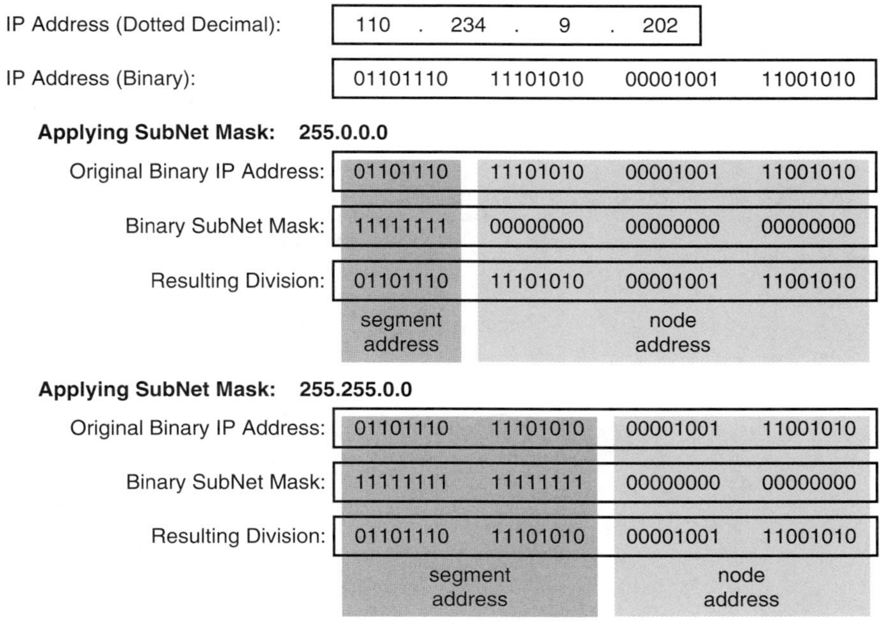

Figure 7-14 Use of Subnet Masks

addresses that are not broken on octet boundaries are known as **classless** addresses. The remainder of this chapter uses classfull addressing.

Classfull addresses are broken apart on octet boundaries; therefore, there are three basic classes of addresses. As illustrated in Figure 7-15, these classes are known as class A, B, or C networks. To distinguish among classes, the first few bits of each segment address are used to denote the address class of the segment.

In addition to these basic address classes, two additional classes, D and E, can be used for IPv4 addressing. Class D addresses are reserved for multicast systems such as routers, and class E addresses are reserved for future use.

The assignment of address classes and network ID ranges to a particular organization wishing to connect to the Internet is the responsibility of the Internet Activities Board (IAB). The IAB ensures that all organizations using the Internet for network communications have unique IP addresses for all of their workstations. If an organization has no intention of ever accessing the Internet, then there may not be a need to register with the IAB for an IP address class and range of valid network IDs. However, even in this case, all workstations on all communicating networks must have IP addresses unique within the internal corporate network.

Within a network segment there are two special addresses: the **broadcast address** and the network address. The broadcast address consists of a node address of all 1s. All nodes on the network segment receive any packet addressed to the broadcast address. The network address consists of a node address of all 0s. The network address is used by routers to refer to the network segment itself, rather than to any particular node on the segment.

For IP networks that consist of a single network segment, the specification of an IP address and a segment mask is adequate to ensure proper packet delivery. However, most IP networks have multiple segments, in fact, support for multiple segments is one of the key reasons to use IP in the first place.

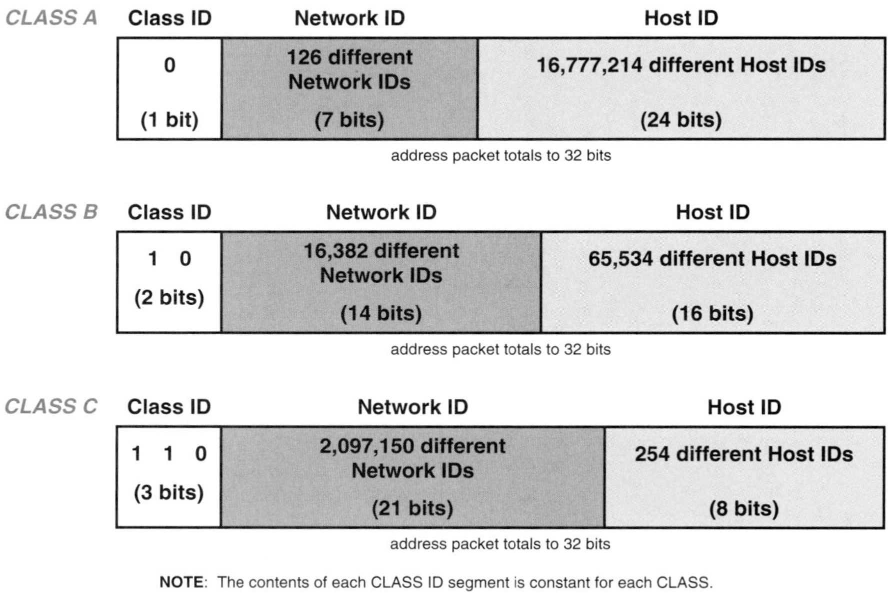

Figure 7-15 IPv4 Address Classes

For IP networks that consist of multiple network segments, each node must also be configured with a **default gateway** address. The default gateway address represents a router that should be used to route packets on remote network segments. The default router must reside on the same network segment as the node: if the node cannot talk to remote segments without a default gateway, how could it talk to a default gateway on a remove segment?

IP to Datalink Address Resolution Unlike IPX, an IP node address has no direct relationship with its associated NIC's datalink (MAC) address. Therefore a mechanism to resolve IP addresses to datalink addresses is required to deliver packets within a LAN. This process is analogous to the use of directory assistance services to find a desired phone number. There are two protocols that resolve between IP addresses and datalink addresses: ARP and RARP.

ARP or **address resolution protocol** is used if an IP address of workstation is known, but a datalink layer address for the same workstation is required. Each node on the network uses ARP to determine the datalink address for each destination.

RARP or **reverse address resolution protocol** is used if the datalink layer address of the workstation is known, but the IP address of the same workstation is required. RARP is most commonly used to provide configuration information to nodes at boot time.

ARP and RARP are broadcast protocols. The requests for addresses are broadcast to an entire IP network segment. It should be obvious that this could represent a significant traffic burden. Routers do not rebroadcast ARP or RARP packets and thereby act as a filter to prevent infinite propagation of ARP/RARP broadcasts. Responses to ARP and RARP requests are sent directly to the requesting workstation rather than being broadcast to all attached workstations. The ARP-response is sent by the workstation whose IP address is found in the destination address field of the broadcast

ARP packets. To reduce the overhead required by ARP requests, ARP responses are stored in an ARP cache so that it will not be necessary to rebroadcast for the same address.

IP Routing Protocols There are two basic nonproprietary routing protocols used to maintain IP routing tables: RIP and OSPF. RIP broadcasts its routing tables to all directly connected routers every 30 seconds. Those directly connected routers then propagate the new routing table information to the routers directly connected to them. This pattern continues, and after about 7 minutes (30 second intervals × 15 hop max.), all routing tables have been updated and, for the moment, are synchronized. **OSPF** or **open shortest path first** is a link state protocol developed to overcome RIP's shortcomings such as the 15-hop limit and full routing table broadcasts every 30 seconds. OSPF sends routing table updates only as required.

IP Version 6 Although IPv4 is the most commonly used network layer protocol, some key limitations affect its usage. Recall that connection to the Internet requires use of an IP address that is absolutely unique. Although the current version of IP could theoretically support 4.3 billion host addresses, far fewer addresses are actually available.

The recent boom in the use of the Internet by commercial entities has put a serious strain on the availability of IP addresses. As the number of nodes on the Internet grows, the 32-bit address space provided by IPv4 is rapidly running out. Although it provides almost 4.3 billion addresses, the hierarchical nature of IP addressing greatly limits the efficiency with which IP addresses can be used. This is largely due to the IP address classes introduced earlier. Class C addresses, with only 256 hosts IDs, are too limiting for many corporations, whereas class B addresses, with 65, 534 host IDs, provide far more host IDs than necessary, leading to wasted and subsequently unavailable addresses in most cases. Although this appears to be a waste of address spaces, the routing benefits of such a hierarchical addressing approach greatly outweigh the inefficiency of address utilization. Nevertheless some method of increasing the IP address space is required.

Another problem associated with IPv4 is that it uses variable length headers, resulting in increased router processing. Other concerns with IPv4 include the need for new functionality that simply isn't included in the current version of the protocol. With the advent of streaming media on the Internet, there is a strong need for multicasting to be supported under IP. **Multicasting** allows a single packet to be sent to multiple nodes (but not all nodes) on multiple network segments. In the current unicast model, if five nodes on one network need to receive the same packet of data, it must be sent five times—one packet addressed to each node. In a multicasting model, only a single packet would have to be sent, thus reducing the load on the routers and reducing the bandwidth required to support the transmission.

The third class of problems with IPv4 has to do with the evolution of data networks. Data networks are now being used to carry data types that the creators of IPv4 couldn't have anticipated. Streaming media, Internet telephone calls, and other time-sensitive data were not considered when the protocol was originally developed. These new applications create another issue that cannot easily be resolved using IPv4: different packets have different levels of importance. Under IPv4 there is no way to indicate that a packet carrying payroll data is more important than a packet carrying a media stream of the radio broadcast of a basketball game. If a router becomes overloaded, it will drop whichever packet comes after the buffer is full. Ideally the router should make a decision to drop lower priority packets from the buffer to allow higher priority packers to reach their destinations. This ability is commonly known as class of service.

The final concern with IPv4 is that there are no security features. Although data in the higher level protocols can be encrypted, the resulting ciphertext is readily available to anyone who wants to "listen" for it anywhere along the route to the destination. There is also no mechanism in IPv4 to prevent a node from pretending to be someone it's not. This process of deception, known as spoofing, presents a serious security threat to IP-based networks.

To address these shortcomings of IPv4, the Internet Engineering Task Force has developed a new version of the Internet protocol: IPv6, also known as IPng (next generation).

Addressing IPv6 resolves the IPv4 address space problem by expanding IP addresses to 128 bits, a 8×10 to the 28th power improvement. Instead of the familiar dotted decimal notation, IPv6 addresses are represented in a manner similar to MAC addresses: as a series of six 4-byte hexadecimal codes separated by colons. An example IPv6 address is FF0E:0:0:A0B9:0:23. As can be seen in this example, a section of all 0s is simply expressed as a single 0. Subnet masks are expressed in a similar manner. An example IPv6 subnet mask is FFFF:FFFF:FFFF:0:0:0.

Other Improvements To reduce the processing load on routers, IPv6 utilizes fixed-length field headers. Although the overall packet header for IPv6 is larger than IPv4 due to the increased length of the source and destination addresses, each header is constructed in exactly the same format, thus removing the requirement that routers parse each packet. Packet header error checking has been removed, as it is somewhat redundant. If a packet header has an error, it is somewhat unlikely it would reach its destination in the first place, so why bother to check for errors?

To address the need for classes of service, IPv6 numbers each data stream and labels it as either congestion controlled or noncongestion controlled. Congestion-controlled data streams can tolerate delays but non-congestion-controlled data streams cannot. An example of a congestion-controlled data stream is a file transfer, an example of a non-congestion-controlled data stream is an Internet telephone call. IPv6 also includes support for multicast addresses and a new unicast address method called anycast that streamlines routing through IPv6 networks along with traditional support for broadcast addresses.

Security has been addressed on two fronts: authentication and encryption. IPv6 packets can be set to authenticate their origin. This prevents another node from spoofing an IP address and fraudulently gaining access to sensitive data. IPv6 packets can also be encrypted at the network layer, thus eliminating the need to each higher level protocol to implement its own encryption methodology.

Transition from IPv4 to IPv6 Although there are compelling technical reasons to transition all IP-based networks to IPv6 as soon as possible, the actual transition itself is problematic. Consider a large corporate private network consisting of 5000 nodes in 17 cities spread across six time zones. It is simply not realistic to say that at midnight GMT on a certain date, every node will change over to IPv6. The Internet exacerbates the problem, with its constituent networks under the control of various organizations spread literally around the globe. What is needed is a mechanism to allow IPv4 and IPv6 to coexist for a period until the transition can be completed.

IPv6 provides three such mechanisms. A NIC can be bound to two IP addresses: one IPv4 and one IPv6. Such a dual-addressed node would respond to either IP address as if it were the node's only address. A second approach is to tunnel IPv6 data across IPv4 network backbones. This approach works well for organizations that interconnect their data networks via the Internet. The third approach provides the most seamless solution to the problem by adding the ability to translate headers between IPv4 and IPv6 at the routers between IPv4 and IPv6 networks. In this manner, an IPv6 node can directly communicate with an IPv4 node.

Transport Layer Protocols As previously mentioned, Internet protocols implement OSI network model functionality in a slightly modified manner. As illustrated in Figure 7-10, Internet transport or host-to-host protocols implement both transport layer functionality and session layer addressing functionality. The remaining OSI session, presentation, and application layer functionality are implemented by Internet application layer protocols. This chapter focuses on Internet protocols through the transport layer. Application layer protocols are covered later in this chapter.

UDP—User Datagram Protocol The **user datagram protocol (UDP)** is used to provide unreliable, connectionless messaging services for applications. The main purpose of the header is to allow UDP to keep track of which applications it is sending a datagram to and from through the use of port addresses and to pass those messages along to IP for subsequent delivery. Because UDP does not provide reliable connection-oriented services, the UDP packet header is small.

Because of the small size of UDP packet headers and the fact that they require no acknowledgments from the receiving node, UDP is the perfect transport/session layer protocol for delivering streaming media packets. The overhead associated with a connection-oriented protocol would greatly reduce the number of clients that a streaming media server could support compared with the relatively efficient UDP protocol.

TCP—Transmission Control Protocol The majority of network traffic requires a more reliable connection than UDP offers. To provide connection-oriented, reliable data transmission, the **transmission control protocol (TCP)** is the transport/session layer protocol of choice. Reliability is ensured through the additional fields contained within the TCP header that offer flow control, acknowledgments of successful receipt of packets after error checking, retransmission of packets as required, and proper sequencing of packets

UDP and TCP Port Numbers UDP and TCP provide session layer addressing through the use of **ports.** Ports are specific 16-bit addresses that are uniquely related to particular applications. Source port and destination port addresses are included in the UDP/TCP header. The unique port address of an application combined with the unique 32-bit IP address of the computer on which the application is executing is known as a **socket.** Some typical port numbers for popular TCP/IP applications are listed in Figure 7-16.

Domain Name System IP addresses are used to uniquely identify nodes on an IP-based network. However, 32-bit IPv4 addresses are difficult for humans to memorize and work with, even in dotted decimal form. IPv6 promises to make this problem even worse with its 128 bit addresses. To make identifying node addresses easier for people, the **domain name system (DNS)** has been created. DNS provides the following key services:

- Uniquely identifies all hosts connected to the Internet by name.
- Resolves, or translates, host names into IP addresses (and vice versa).

TCP/IP Application	Port Number
HTTP	80
Telnet	23
FTP	21
SMTP	25
BootP client	68
BootP server	67
TFTP	69
Finger	79
NetBIOS session service	139
X.400	103
SNMP	161

Figure 7-16 Selected Port Numbers

- Identifies which services are offered by each host such as gateway or mail transfer, and to which networks these services are offered.

DNS is a hierarchical naming structure with the hierarchical layers being separated by dots such as "www.company.com." DNS addresses are listed in inverse order, with the hostname being the first word and the domain name being the following words. In the www.company.com example, www is the hostname and company.com is the domain name. The last section of a domain name is called the top level domain. Top level domains are carefully managed to ensure that there is no confusion between DNS domains. To make DNS as intuitive as possible, consistent naming conventions need to be established. For nodes connected directly to the Internet, standard top level domains such as .edu for educational institutions, .com for commercial entities, and .gov for government agencies are used. Private institutions not directly connecting to the Internet are welcome to establish their own naming schemes for use within their corporate networks.

AppleTalk

The Apple Talk protocol family was originally developed by Apple Computer to provide connectivity among their Macintosh products introduced in 1984. The original implementation, known as LocalTalk, was designed as an inexpensive solution that connected Macintoshes via their serial ports. As the need for more bandwidth grew, AppleTalk Phase 2 was developed to run over Ethernet (EtherTalk) and token ring (TokenTalk) datalink technologies. AppleTalk Phase 2 utilizes IEEE 802.2 compliant datalink interfaces and has an improved address space compared to the original AppleTalk specification. Figure 7-17 shows the

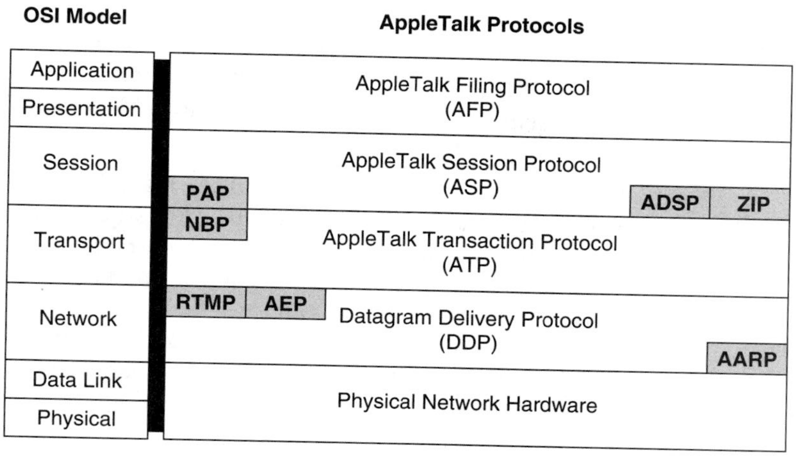

Figure 7-17 The AppleTalk Family of Protocols

AppleTalk family of protocols and their mapping against the OSI network reference model.

DDP The **datagram delivery protocol (DDP)** is the network layer protocol for the AppleTalk protocol suite. DDP is a routable, connectionless, nonreliable protocol that is used to encapsulate all higher level AppleTalk protocols.

Addressing DDP addresses are composed of three parts: network address, node address, and socket address. The network (segment) address is 16 bits long. A network address of all ones (65535) is reserved by Apple Computer and is therefore illegal for normal use. The node address is 8 bits long. A node address of all 1s (255) is used as the broadcast address for the network segment. A node address of 0 specifies the local node. The socket address is 8 bits long and identifies the process on the node that is responsible for the packet.

DDP addresses are resolved to datalink addresses via the AppleTalk Address Resolution Protocol (AARP). Similar to ARP on IP-based networks, AARP is a broadcast-based protocol. When a node needs the datalink address for a DDP address, it broadcasts an AARP packet querying the destination DDP address. The node with the destination DDP address responds with its datalink address, which is then used to address the datalink layer frame to the destination.

AppleTalk Routing Protocols The protocol used to distribute routing information through DDP based networks is the **routing table maintenance protocol (RTMP).** RTMP is a distance vector routing protocol similar to RIP in IP-based networks. Routing information is regularly broadcast through the network, with old routes being removed by a routine aging process where table entries are deleted when they no longer are received via RTMP broadcasts. AppleTalk Phase 2 also includes support for split horizon routing. In split horizon routing, RTMP transfers routing only data about directly attached networks. This helps reduce the overhead traffic associated with distance vector protocols.

Transport Layer Protocols The **AppleTalk transaction protocol (ATP)** is a transport layer protocol that provides connection-oriented, reliable delivery of data across DDP-based networks. ATP uses a bitmap token to provide sequence numbers and handle acknowledgment and flow control. A series of reserved bytes are used by higher level protocols for flow management.

Session Layer Protocols The **AppleTalk session protocol (ASP)** manages sessions for higher layer AppleTalk protocols. ASP issues a unique session identifier for each logical connection and continuously monitors the status of each connection. It maintains idle sessions by periodically exchanging keep-alive frames to verify session status.

The **AppleTalk data stream protocol (ADSP)** provides a data channel for the hosts. It is a connection-oriented protocol that guarantees in-sequence data delivery with flow control.

Stand-Alone Transport Layer Protocols

NetBEUI (NBF) **NetBEUI frame (NBF)** is a simple transport/session layer protocol that does not provide any network layer functionality. The lack of network layer addressing results in a nonroutable protocol limited to use on networks consisting of a single network segment.

As the expansion of NetBEUI (NetBIOS extended user interface) implies, NetBEUI is an extended version of the original NetBIOS API used in Microsoft LAN Manager and OS/2 LAN Server. NetBEUI is a connection-oriented, reliable protocol that makes use of sequence numbers and acknowledgments to ensure correct data transmission. NBF improves on NetBEUI's data transfer performance in connection-oriented sessions by adopting an adaptive sliding window protocol that allows for more efficient data transfer. As will be seen, the word *window* in the name of this protocol is not related to the term *window* as in Windows NT.

NBF is able to adjust the number of packets that can be sent by the sending computer before an acknowledgment must be received. Ideally, the sending computer wants to send the maximum number of packets possible while avoiding the need to retransmit packets because of transmission errors. The number of packets that can be sent before the receipt of an acknowledgment determines the size of the **send window.** If a negative acknowledgment is received, thereby necessitating a packet retransmission, the sending window will slide back to the packet that was received in error and retransmit it.

The second major improvement of NBF over NetBEUI has to do with session limits. Since NetBEUI is NetBIOS-based, it was forced to support the 254-session limit of NetBIOS. The source of this limit is a variable within NetBIOS known as the local session number. The local session number is a 1 byte (8 bit) field with a limit of 256 possible entries (2 to the eighth = 256, less reserved numbers = 254). Since Windows NT servers using the NBF communications protocol could easily need to support more than 254 sessions, some way needed to be found to overcome the 254-session limit. Although a detailed explanation of the mathematical algorithms behind the solution is beyond the scope of this chapter, the key to the solution is a two-dimensional matrix maintained by NBF that maps 254 logical session numbers against the network address of each computer with which it may establish a session. The end result of the maintenance and translation of the various matrices is that each client-to-server connection can support 254 sessions, rather than a grand total for all connections of 254 sessions.

Practical Advice and Information

USE OF NETBEUI

NetBEUI has two selling points: efficiency and ease of configuration. Because NetBEUI is not routable, there is no need to assign network addresses or to reserve space in the packet header to carry them. However, these points are overshadowed by the fact that NetBEUI is nonroutable.

The only reason to use NetBEUI is connection with legacy equipment that requires its use. At this point, there is no reason to install a new NetBEUI-based network.

DLC **DLC** or **data link control** is a communication protocol traditionally reserved for communication with IBM mainframe computers. DLC is used by Microsoft SNA Gateway for Windows NT to allow transparent interoperability between Windows NT clients and IBM mainframe computers. By using a gateway server, the Windows NT clients do not require any hardware or software modifications to communicate with the IBM mainframe. DLC has also been adopted as a means to communicate between print servers and printers directly attached to the network through network interface cards such as Hewlett-Packard JetDirect cards.

Similar to NetBEUI, DLC is a transport layer-only protocol that is nonroutable and applicable only to single-segment networks. DLC adheres to the OSI model principle of independence of the functional layers by running equally well over Ethernet or token ring network interface cards and attached network architectures. In addition, DLC is also compatible with the IEEE 802.2 LLC (logical link control) specification and frame layout.

NETWORK OPERATING SYSTEMS ARCHITECTURES

Traditional Differentiation: Peer-to-Peer Vs. Client/Server

Traditionally, there were two major product categories of network operating systems:

- **Peer-to-peer network operating systems,** also known as DOS-based LANs or Low-cost LANs, offered easy to install and use file and print services for workgroup and departmental networking needs.
- **Client/Server network operating systems** offered more powerful capabilities including the ability to support hundreds of users and the ability to interact with other network operating systems via gateways. These client/server network operating systems were both considerably more expensive and considerably more complicated to install and administer than peer-to-peer network operating systems.

Peer-to-Peer One of the early appeals of peer-to-peer network operating systems was their relatively minimal hardware requirements in terms of memory and disk space. In addition, the fact that they ran as a background application over the DOS operating system made them considerably less complicated to install and administer than client/server network operating systems. When printer sharing and file sharing for less than 50 users represented the major functional requirements of a network operating system, peer-to-peer network operating systems such as Artisoft's LANtastic and Performance Technology's PowerLAN were popular choices in this technology category.

In most peer-to-peer LANs, individual workstations can be configured as a service requester (client) a service provider (server) or a combination of the two. The terms *client* and *server* in this case describe the workstation's functional role in the network. The installed network operating system is still considered a peer-to-peer network operating system, because all workstations in the network use the same networking software. Designed as a low cost, workgroup solution, most peer-to-peer network operating systems lacked the ability to access servers of client/server network operating systems and suffered from exponential performance decreases as the number of users increased. As a result, traditional peer-to-peer network operating systems were characterized as lacking interoperability and scalability.

Client/Server In contrast to the homogeneous peer-to-peer software environment, traditional client/server network operating systems require two distinct software products for client and server computers. The specialized client software required less memory, disk space, and was less expensive than the more complicated and expensive server software. NetWare 3.12 and Microsoft LANManager are examples of traditional client/server network operating systems. The client software was made to interact with the corresponding server software. As a result, although traditional client/server network operating systems overcame the scalability limitation of peer-to-peer network operating systems, they did not necessarily overcome the interoperability limitation. Functionally, client/server network operating systems offered faster, more reliable performance than peer-to-peer LANs, as well as improved administration, scalability, and security. Figure 7-18 illustrates the key differences between traditional peer-to-peer and client/server network operating systems.

Current Differentiation: Client NOS Vs. Server NOS

Functional Requirements of Today's Network Operating Systems Although traditional peer-to-peer and client/server network operating systems successfully met the functional requirements for workgroup and departmental computing, as these departmental LANs needed to be integrated into a single, cohesive, interoperable, enterprise-wide information system, the limitations of these traditional NOS (network operating system) architectures became evident.

To understand the architectural specifications of today's network operating systems, it is first necessary to understand the functional requirements that these network operating systems must deliver. In taking a top-down approach to network operating system requirements analysis, one might ask, "What are users of an enterprise-wide information system demanding of a network operating system in terms of services?" The answer to this question lies in the application layer of the top-down model. Given that distributed applications enables enterprise-wide productivity and decision making, the underlying network operating systems must support these distributed applications by supplying the message services and global directory services required to execute these applications in an enterprise-wide, multiple server environment.

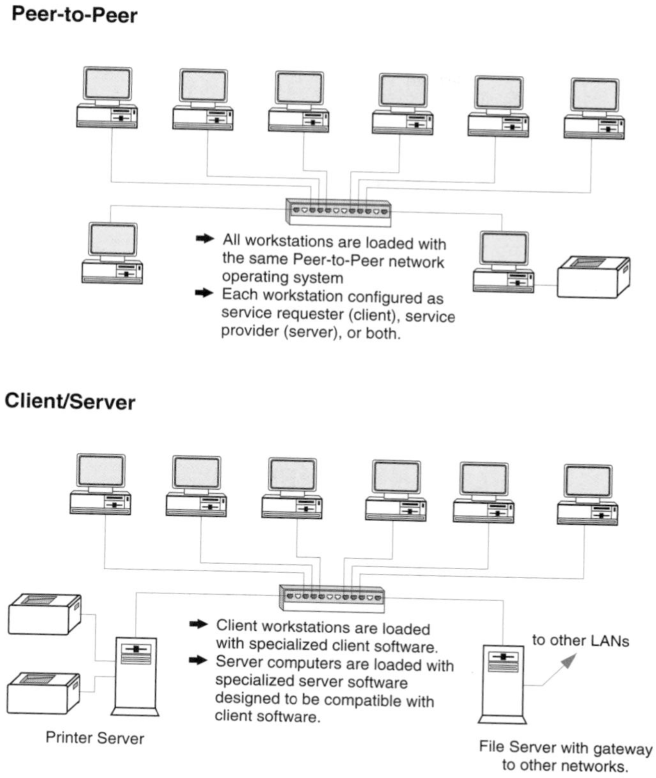

Figure 7-18 Peer-to-Peer vs. Client/Server Network Operating Systems

Figure 7-19 illustrates these functional requirements and contrasts them with the requirements traditionally demanded of client/server and peer-to-peer network operating systems.

As illustrated in Figure 7-19, the new or emerging demands being put on network operating systems are:

- **Application services**
- **Directory services**
- **Integration/migration services**

To successfully meet these functional requirements, network operating system architectures have shifted from integrated, single-vendor client and server network operating systems to independent, distinct, multivendor client and server network operating systems. The functional characteristics of these distinct client and server network operating systems are described in detail later in this chapter. Figure 7-20 illustrates this architectural shift in network operating system development.

Client Network Operating Systems: The Universal Client **Client network operating systems,** as illustrated in Figure 7-20, integrate traditional operating system functionality with highly configurable networking features to enable communication with a variety of network operating system servers. The client workstation's ability to inter-

		All services delivered seamlessly across multiple server platforms regardless of installed network operating system		
Traditional Requirements		Emerging Requirements		
FILE SERVICES	PRINTER SERVICES	APPLICATION SERVICES	DIRECTORY SERVICES	INTEGRATION/MIGRATION SERVICES
		➡ Database back-end engines ➡ Messaging and communication back-end engines ***SUPPORT FOR:*** ➡ 32 bit symmetrical multi-processing ➡ Pre-emptive multi-tasking ➡ Applications run in protected memory mode ➡ Multithreading	➡ Global directory or naming services ➡ All network objects defined in single location and shared by all applications ➡ Directory information is stored in replicated, distributed databases for reliability, redundancy, fault tolerance	➡ Allow multiple different client network operating systems to transparently interoperate with multiple, different server network operating systems ➡ Provide easy-to-implement paths for upgrades to more recent versions or migration to different network operating systems

Figure 7-19 Required Network Operating System Services: Traditional vs. Current

operate transparently with a number of different network operating system servers without the need for additional products or configurations breaks the traditional hard linkage between client and server NOS. This ability is commonly referred to as **universal client** capability.

Server Network Operating Systems Because the client and server platforms have been decoupled, **server network operating systems** can be selected based on their performance characteristics for a given function. For example, NetWare servers are often employed as file and print servers, whereas Windows NT, OS/2, or UNIX servers are more likely to be employed as application servers. Because the universal client has the ability to communicate with any server, and the server has the ability to communicate with any client, the choice of server network operating system can be based on optimizing functional performance rather than whether the system simply provides interoperability.

CLIENT NETWORK OPERATING SYSTEM FUNCTIONALITY

With an understanding of the new architectural arrangement of network operating systems consisting of distinct, interoperable, multivendor client and server network operating systems, we can now examine the functional aspects of client network operating systems categories.

Client network operating systems such as Windows 9x, Windows NT Workstation, and the Macinstosh OS offer three major categories of functionality:

- Operating system capabilities
- Peer-to-peer networking capabilities
- Client software for communicating with various network operating systems

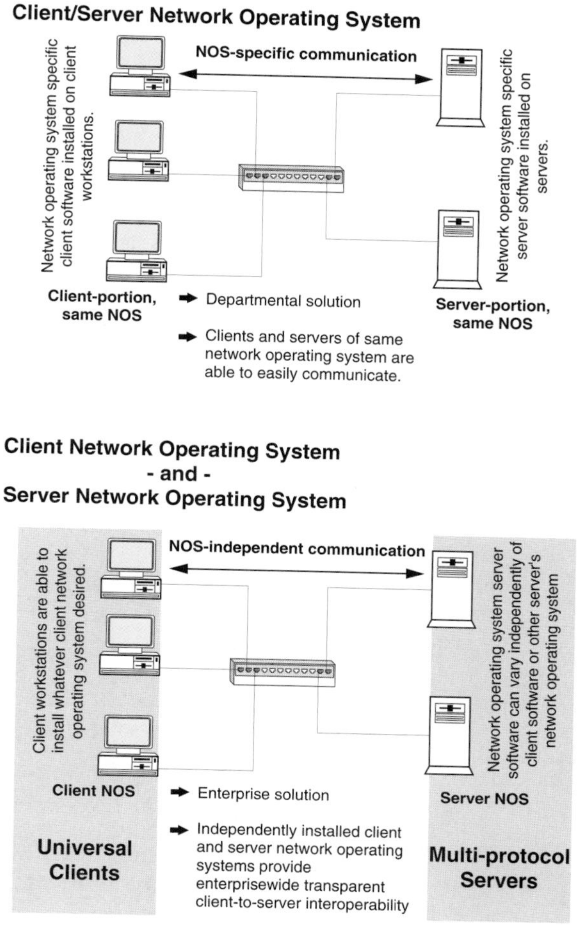
Client/Server Network Operating System
NOS-specific communication
Network operating system specific client software installed on client workstations.
Network operating system specific server software installed on servers.
Client-portion, same NOS
Departmental solution
Clients and servers of same network operating system are able to easily communicate.
Server-portion, same NOS
Client Network Operating System
- and -
Server Network Operating System
NOS-independent communication
Client workstations are able to install whatever client network operating system desired.
Network operating system server software can vary independently of client software or other server's network operating system
Client NOS
Enterprise solution
Independently installed client and server network operating systems provide enterprisewide transparent client-to-server interoperability
Server NOS
Universal Clients
Multi-protocol Servers

Figure 7-20 Client/Server NOS vs. Client and Server NOS

The logical relationship of these three distinct yet complementary categories of functionality is illustrated in Figure 7-21. Figure 7-21 also point out potential areas for compatibility and protocol consideration where the various software and hardware layers interface.

The importance of each of these three functional categories to the overall network operating system is covered in the following sections along with key implementation differences between technologies. From such a review of network operating system functionality, the network analyst should be able to construct a logical network design listing the functionality required to meet the business objectives.

This logical network design is then used as an evaluation mechanism for selecting available technologies. Logical network design functionality can be compared to available technology's delivered functionality in a technology analysis grid. As stated in previous chapters, employing a technology analysis grid in such an endeavor ensures that purchase decisions or recommendations are made based on facts rather than creative packaging or effective marketing.

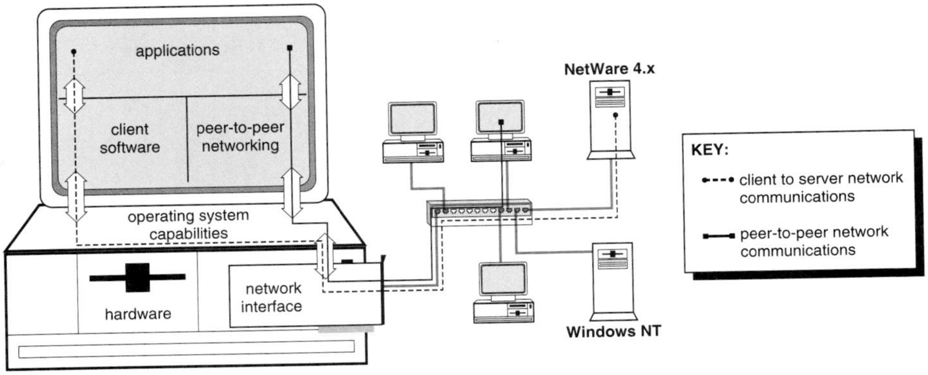

Figure 7-21 Logical Relationship of Client NOS Functional Categories

Operating System Capabilities

The following operating systems characteristics are listed and briefly explained here from the perspective of each characteristic's importance to overall network operating system performance.

- 32-bit operating systems allow more sophisticated and higher performance 32-bit applications to execute more quickly.
- Preemptive multitasking prevents misbehaving programs from monopolizing systems resources at the expense of the performance of other applications.
- Protected memory space prevents application programs from accidentally writing into each other's or the operating system's memory space, thereby causing general protection faults and/or system crashes.
- Support for symmetrical multiprocessing (SMP) is especially important for server network operating systems owing to the processing load imposed by multiple simultaneous requests for services from clients. Some high-powered client applications such as three-dimensional modeling or simulation software may warrant SMP support on client platforms as well.
- Multithreading applications are only able to achieve performance increases if they are executed by an operating system that supports multithreaded applications, allowing more than one subprocess to execute simultaneously.

User Interface **Object-oriented user interfaces** present the user with a graphical desktop on which objects such as files, directories, folders, disk drives, programs, or devices can be arranged according to the user's whim. More important, as objects are moved around the desktop, they retain their characteristic properties. As a result, when a desktop object is clicked upon, only legitimate actions presented in context-sensitive menus appropriate for the object class are available.

Unlike object-oriented user interfaces, Windows-based user interfaces, although graphical, do not allow icons representing directories, files, disk drives, and so on to be broken out of a particular Window and placed directly on the desktop.

Application Program Support A very important aspect of any migration plan to a new client network operating system is the extent of support for **backward compatibility** in terms of application support, also known as **legacy application** support. It should stand to reason that most companies cannot afford to replace or rewrite all of their application software to upgrade to a new client network operating system.

Although 32-bit client network operating systems are desirable and most current network-based applications are 32-bit, many custom software solutions are still 16-bit. In addition, many of these 16-bit application programs bypass supported API calls and commands in favor of directly addressing hardware devices. Initially created to increase performance, these applications significantly limit multitasking and interoperability. Programs or subroutines that write directly to computer hardware are sometimes referred to as employing real-mode device drivers.

Many 32-bit network operating systems do not allow application programs to address or control hardware directly in the interest of security and protecting applications from using each other's assigned memory spaces and causing system crashes. Instead, these more secure 32-bit operating systems control access to hardware and certain system services via **virtual device drivers.** otherwise known as **VxDs.** Windows NT is perhaps the best example of a 32-bit network operating system that prevents direct hardware addressing. As a result, many 16-bit applications, particularly highly graphical computer games, will not execute over the Windows NT network operating system. On the other hand, Windows NT is extremely stable.

Whether or not an application is executable over a particular network operating system depends on whether or not that application issues commands and requests for network-based services in a predetermined format defined by the network operating system's **application program interface (API).** Each network operating system has its own unique API or variation. For example, both Microsoft NT and Windows 9x support variations of the Win32 API.

Some client network operating systems, such as Windows NT, have the ability to support multiple APIs and multiple different operating system subsystems, sometimes known as **virtual machines.** This feature allows applications written for a variety of operating systems, such as OS/2, DOS, or POSIX, to execute over a single client network operating system.

Plug-n-play Features One of the largest problems with installing new devices into a computer was configuring the hardware's resource usage. **Plug-n-play (PnP),** included in varying degrees in most client network operating systems, is designed to free users from having to understand and worry about such things as IRQs (interrupt requests), DMA (direct memory access) channels, memory addresses, COM ports, and editing CONFIG.SYS whenever they want to add a device to their computer.

Although the goal of automatic hardware configuration has not been fully realized, definite progress has been made. Ideally PnP functionality will:

- Automatically detect the addition or removal of PnP devices
- Set all of the previously mentioned settings so that they do not conflict with other devices
- Automatically load necessary drivers to enable the particular device

PnP standards also include support for dynamic reconfiguration that enables:

- PCMCIA cards being inserted into and removed from computers without a need to reboot
- Hot docking (powered up) of laptop computers into docking bays or stations
- Dynamic reconfiguration-aware applications software that could automatically respond to changes in system configuration

Compatibility issues are important to the achievement of full PnP functionality. To be specific, three distinct elements must all support PnP standards:

1. A **PnP BIOS** (basic input output system) is required to interface directly to both PnP and non-PnP-compliant hardware.
2. PnP capabilities must be supported by the client network operating system through interaction with the PnP BIOS. Windows 9x possesses the most PnP capability among currently available client network operating systems.
3. The devices installed must be PnP compliant. This basically means that the manufacturers of these devices must add some additional software and processing power so that these devices can converse transparently with the PnP operating system and BIOS. In some cases, PnP-compliant device drivers may also be required.

To cater to vast majority of legacy (non-PnP-compliant) devices, many PnP-compliant client network operating systems ease configuration hassles by using a variety of detection techniques. Non-PnP devices are detected by the client operating system through an assistant agent program, sometimes referred to as a hardware wizard, which walks the user through the configuration routine. Such programs are often capable of detecting and displaying IRQs and DMA addresses used by other devices, allowing users to accept supplied default answers in this semiautomatic configuration scenario.

Peer-to-Peer Networking Capabilities

Most current network client operating systems also include peer-to-peer networking capability. These features allow each client to interact at a basic level with other clients. By utilizing these features, many small businesses can avoid the expense of implementing a large scale server environment.

File and Printer Sharing Perhaps the most basic peer-to-peer network function is file and printer sharing. In many cases, other resources such as CD-ROM drives and fax modems can also be shared. Network operating systems supporting peer-to-peer networking can vary widely in terms of file access security features. The level at which access can be controlled (disk, directory, or file level) is sometimes referred to as the **granularity** of the access control scheme. Access is controlled on a per user or per group basis. Sophistication of the printer management facility can also vary from one client network operating system to another.

As client network operating systems have grown in sophistication, file and printer sharing services are now available to client platforms other than those configured with identical client network operating systems. Figure 7-22 illustrates some of the cross-platform peer-to-peer file and printer-sharing capabilities of Windows 9x.

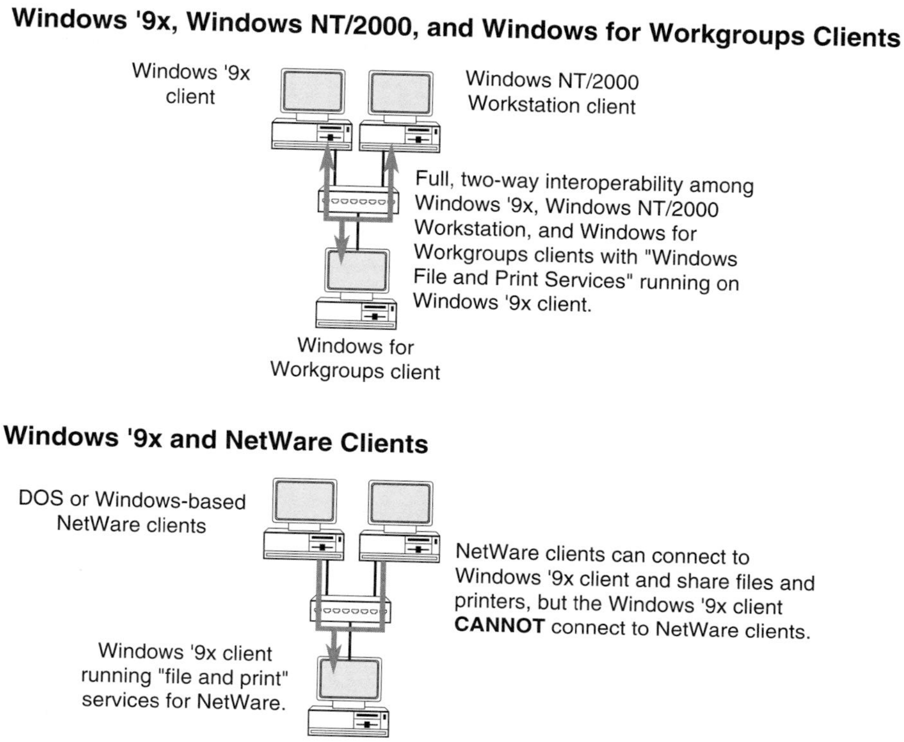

Figure 7-22 Cross-Platform File and Printer Sharing

Client Networking Capabilities

As illustrated architecturally in Figure 7-23, there are three distinct elements of client network functionality in addition to the previously mentioned required application support capabilities. In some cases, more than one alternative is offered for each of the following elements:

1. Client software and network drivers that allow a particular client to communicate with a compatible server. These are MAC (media access control) protocol specifications such as NDIS and ODI.
2. Network transport protocols that package and transport messages between clients and servers. These protocols correspond to the network and transport layers of the OSI model.
3. Network redirectors that trap API (application program interface) calls and process them appropriately. Redirectors are concerned with providing file system related services in support of application programs.

More than one alternative protocol may be provided in a given client network operating system for each of the three network protocol categories. Figure 7-24 displays the protocol stacks for the following three different client network operating systems:

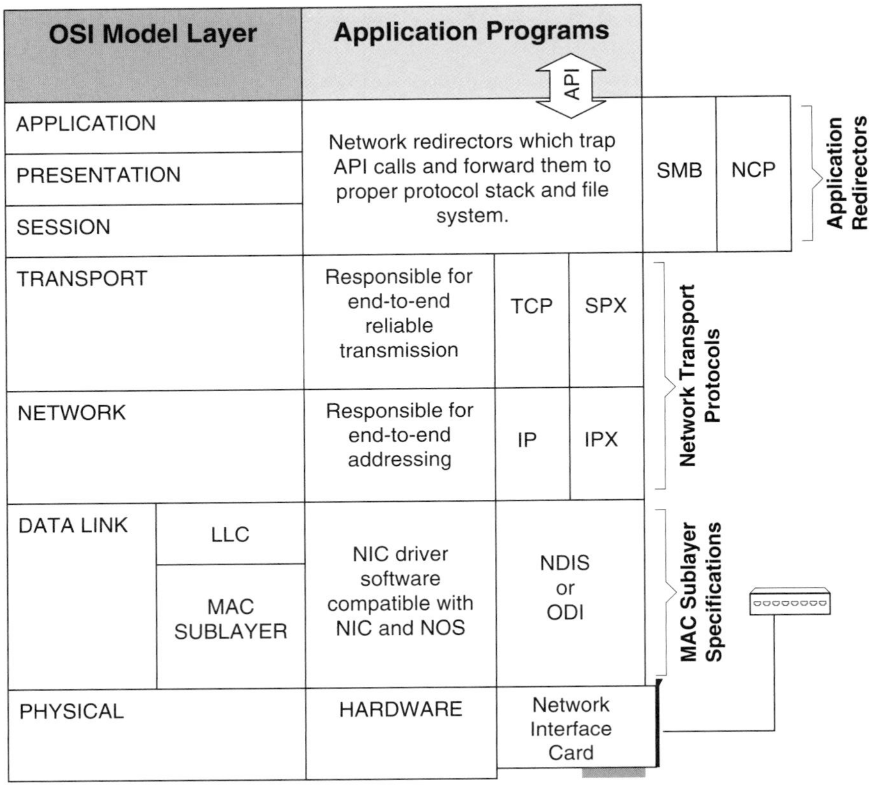

Figure 7-23 Client Network Functionality

1. Windows for Workgroups
2. Windows NT Workstation/2000 Professional
3. Windows 9x

Rather than organize protocols according to the OSI network reference model, Figure 7-24 divides the protocols into layers according to networking functionality.

Connecting Clients to Multiple Servers In most client network operating systems, these three elements of network functionality combine to allow client platforms to automatically find and connect to servers. For example, a properly configured Windows NT client will be able to automatically display network connections and connect to Windows NT and NetWare servers that are physically reachable and to which the client has been assigned access privileges. The client software does not have to be preconfigured with any information about these servers. The server discovery and access is all handled transparently by the client network operating system.

In addition to network operating system client software for specific server network operating systems such as NetWare and Windows NT Server, specialized application-oriented client software is often also included in client network operating systems. Examples of such network applications include:

	Windows for Workgroups	Windows NT/2000 Workstation	Windows '9x
Application Support	WIN16 API 16-bit Windows applications supported	WIN32 API 32-bit and some 16-bit Windows applications supported	WIN32 API 32-bit and most 16-bit Windows applications supported
Application Redirectors and File Systems	SMB Server Message Block Redirector (Microsoft) FAT File Allocation Table File System (DOS/Windows)	NCP Netware Core Protocol Redirector (Novell) SMB Server Message Block Redirector (Microsoft) FAT File Allocation Table File System (DOS/Windows) NTFS NT File System	NCP Netware Core Protocol Redirector (Novell) SMB Server Message Block Redirector (Microsoft) FAT File Allocation Table File System (DOS/Windows)
Network Transport Protocols	IPX/SPX NETBEUI NetBIOS Extended User Interface (Microsoft) TCP/IP	IPX/SPX NETBEUI NetBIOS Extended User Interface (Microsoft) TCP/IP Apple-Talk	IPX/SPX NETBEUI NetBIOS Extended User Interface (Microsoft) TCP/IP
MAC Sublayer Specifications	NDIS Network Data-Link Interface Specification (Microsoft/3Com) ODI Open Data-Link Interface (Novell)	NDIS Network Data-Link Interface Specification (Microsoft/3Com)	NDIS Network Data-Link Interface Specification (Microsoft/3Com) ODI Open Data-Link Interface (Novell)

Figure 7-24 Supported Protocol Stacks for Major Client Network Operating Systems

- Web browsers
- FTP (file transfer protocol) client software
- E-mail client software
- Scheduling systems client software

In the case of the e-mail and scheduling clients, to achieve maximum benefit-compatible e-mail and scheduling, application servers must be available. The client portion is merely the front-end to a back-end application engine executing in some other network-accessible location. Most e-mail clients do support the POP3 and SMTP protocols required to connect to Internet mail servers.

Remote Access With the advent of telecommuting, access to network data from outside the network has become a key concern. Specialized client software written to allow remote access to data contained on network servers is included with or available for most client network operating systems. These remote access clients connect to remote access servers. Remote access servers can be implemented as either specialized software running on a network server operating system or as a specialized hardware solution. The remote access server is specifically designed to handle incoming remote access clients and usually contains specialized security features to ensure the integrity of network data.

Some client network operating systems include not only remote access client software, but also remote access server software. With this capability, other remote access clients can dial-in to each other for file sharing, e-mail exchange, schedule synchronization, etc. Windows NT Workstation and Windows 2000 Professional extend this scenario by offering limited local server capability, as well as remote access server capability.

Applied Problem Solving

CLIENT NETWORK OPERATING SYSTEM TECHNOLOGY ANALYSIS

Figure 7-25 is a technology analysis grid comparing key architectural and functional characteristics of the client network operating systems listed on page 283.

Client Network Operating System Category	Windows for Workgroups	Windows 9x	Windows NT Workstation/ 2000 Professional
Hardware and Platform			
Required recommended memory	4MB-8MB	16MB-32	32MB-64MB
16 or 32 bit	16 bit	32 bit	32 bit
User interface	Windows	Object-oriented desktop	Windows
Operating System Capabilities			
Preemptive multitasking	no	yes	yes
Supports SMP	no	no	yes
Protected memory program execution	no	yes	yes
Multithreading	no	yes	yes
Runs 32-bit apps	no	yes	yes
Runs 16-bit apps	yes	yes	Some. Won't support real mode drivers
Peer-to-Peer Networking			
File and printer sharing	yes	yes	yes
Workgroup applications	yes	yes	yes
Client Networking			
Network clients	Windows NT, Microsoft Mail and Schedule	Windows NT, NetWare, Microsoft Exchange	NetWare, FTP, Internet
Network transport protocols	NetBEUI	NetBEUI, TCP/IP, IPX/SPX	NetBEUI, TCP/IP, IPX/SPX, Appletalk
Remote access	yes	yes	yes
Laptop synchronization	no	yes	no

Figure 7-25 Client Network Operating System Technology Analysis Grid

- Windows for Workgroups
- Windows NT Workstation/Windows 2000 Professional
- Windows 9x

This grid illustrates how technology analysis grids can be used to effectively map required networking functional requirements to available technology solutions in an objective manner. This technology analysis grid is not meant to be absolutely authoritative or all inclusive. Its primary purpose is to provide a concrete example of the type of analysis tool used in a professional, top-down, network analysis and design methodology. It is expected that network analysts will create new technology analysis grids for each networking analysis opportunity based on their own networking functional requirements and the latest technology specifications available from buyer's guides or product reviews.

The client network operating system technology analysis grid is divided into the following major sections:

- Hardware/platform-related characteristics
- Operating system capabilities
- Peer-to-peer networking capabilities
- Client networking capabilities

SERVER NETWORK OPERATING SYSTEM FUNCTIONALITY

Changing Role of the Server Network Operating System

Traditionally, file and printer sharing services were the primary required functionality of server-based network operating systems. However, as client/server information systems have boomed in popularity, **application services** have become one of the most important criteria in server network operating system selection. The distributed applications of the client server model require that distinct client and server portion applications interact to perform the required task as efficiently as possible. The server network operating system is responsible not only for executing the back-end portion of the application, but also for supplying the messaging and communications services that enable interoperability between distributed clients and servers. Figure 7-26 illustrates the evolving role of the server network operating system from an architectural perspective.

Examination of server network operating system functionality in the remainder of the chapter focuses on those aspects of functionality that are most important to the support of distributed applications and their associated distributed clients and users.

In terms of currently available technology, NetWare and Microsoft Windows NT Server are the predominant server network operating systems. When comparing these two network operating systems, it is important to note the historical strong points of each. Novell NetWare has traditionally been stronger in file and print services than in the area of application services. Microsoft NT Server has traditionally been stronger in terms of application services than file and print services. With the release of the latest versions of each product, both are rapidly making progress at improving on their weaknesses.

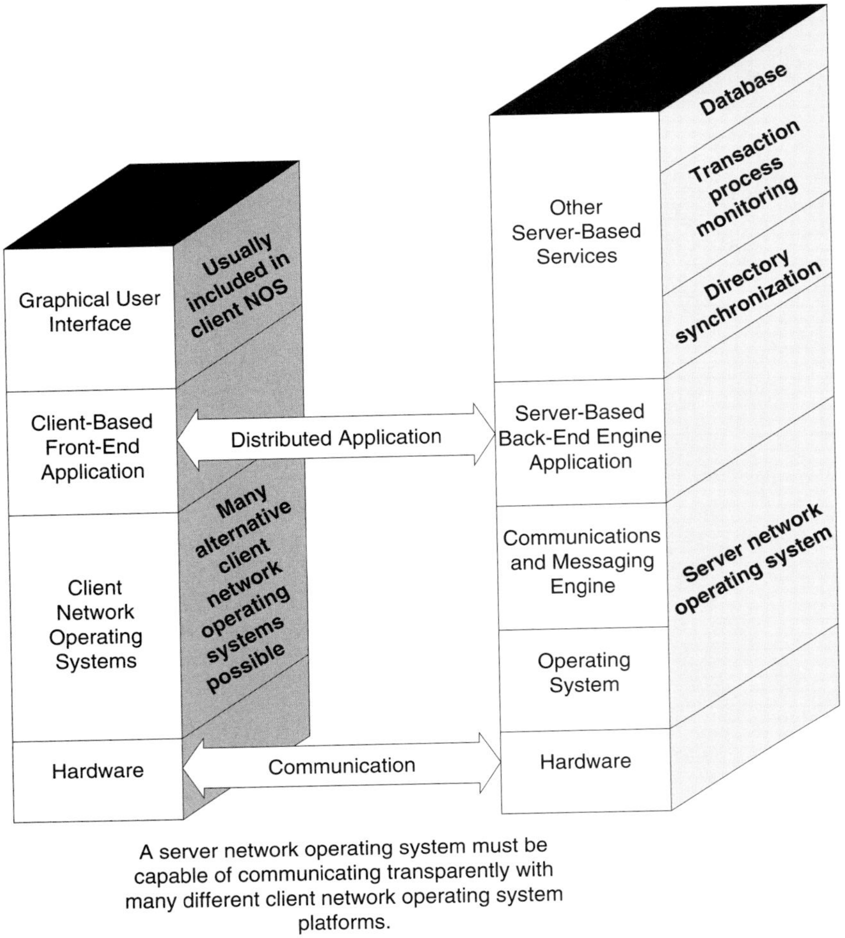

Figure 7-26 Role of Server Network Operating Systems in Distributed Applications

Various flavors of UNIX combined with TCP/IP as a network protocol and NFS as a file system have also been a popular choice of an applications server platform. However, this combination of operating system, network protocols, and file system is not as integrated or feature-rich as either NetWare or Windows NT Server and probably does not deserve the label of "next-generation" NOS.

Directory Services

Network operating systems depend on some sort of naming service or directory in which to store information about users and system resources such as disks, servers, and printers. NetWare 3.x servers stored this type of information in a **bindery.** NetWare 4 and 5 employ a **global directory service** known as **NDS** or **NetWare Directory Services,** and Windows NT uses a **domain directory service.**

Global Directory Services vs. Domain Directory Services Global and domain directory services differ primarily in the organization of information concerning network users and resources. Global directory services organize all network user and resource data into a single hierarchical database, providing a single point of user and resource management. The hierarchical database is based on a hierarchical tree structure. All servers that participate in the directory are part of the global hierarchy and can see all other parts of the network. In this sense, the hierarchical directory database is merely a reflection of the hierarchical network itself.

The global directory database is often distributed; different portions of the data are physically stored on multiple servers connected via the network. In addition, the global directory database is often replicated among multiple servers for redundancy and fault tolerance. In terms of a logical view of the network, global directory services provide a view of a single, enterprise network.

In contrast, domain directory services see the network as a series of linked subdivisions known as **domains.** Domain directory services associate network users and resources with a primary server known as a **PDC** or **primary domain controller.** Each domain's directory must be individually established and maintained. Domains can be individually maintained and controlled in terms of how much of other domains can be seen.

Directory services can also vary in what types of information are stored in the directory services database. In some cases, all users and network resources are considered **network objects,** with information concerning them stored in a single database, arranged by object type. Object attributes can be modified and new network objects can be defined. In other cases, network users and network resources are kept in separate databases. Frequently, separate databases are maintained for network user account information and e-mail user account information.

Application Services

Recalling that the primary objective of the next-generation server NOS is to provide high-performance application services, the most important enabling NOS characteristic required to deliver that objective is the ability to support symmetrical multiprocessing. As numbers of users and sophistication of application programs continue to increase, the only real solution is for the application to be able to utilize more processing power simultaneously. Not all server network operating systems support symmetrical multiprocessing, and those that do may vary in the maximum number of processors supported. Other server network operating system characteristics that are essential to optimization of application program performance are:

- Preemptive multitasking
- 32-bit execution
- Multithreaded application support
- Program execution in protected memory space

File Services Applications programs are stored in a particular file system format. In addition, when these application programs execute, they may request additional services from the resident file system via API calls. Server network operating systems vary in the types and number of supported file systems. Some network operating systems can have multiple partitions on a disk drive supporting multiple file sys-

File System Name	Associated Network Operating System
FAT – File Allocation Table	Windows NT Server
NetWare File System	NetWare 3.x and 4.x
NetWare Storage System	NetWare 5.x
NFS	UNIX (native), most other NOS (optional)
NTFS – NT File System	Windows NT Server
Vines File System	Banyan Vines

Figure 7-27 File Systems and Associated Server Network Operating Systems

tems. Figure 7-27 lists file systems supported by the various server network operating systems in the marketplace.

Other file services offered by some server network operating systems include file compression utilities and **data migration** utilities, which manage the migration of data among different types of storage devices as part of a comprehensive hierarchical storage management (HSM) program.

Just as client network operating systems were either bundling or offering optional workgroup software as part of their package, server network operating systems are offering a variety of bundled back-end engines as part of their offerings. For example, as an option or add-on to Windows NT Server, a bundled product known as Microsoft Back-Office offers the following suite of server applications:

- Exchange server
- System management server
- SQL server
- SNA gateway to IBM mainframe networks

Application Integration Applications integration refers to the extent to which applications program are able to integrate or take advantage of the capabilities of the operating system to optimize application program performance. Successful applications integration with operating system can yield both increased convenience and performance.

From a convenience standpoint, consider these questions:

- Does the application integrate with the operating system's security system, allowing single UserIDs and user accounts, or must two separate security databases be maintained?
- Does the application integrate with the operating system's monitoring capabilities, allowing it to be monitored from within the operating system?
- Can the application be configured and maintained from within the operating system's control panel or setup subsystem?

From a performance standpoint, consider these questions:

- Can the application take advantage of the multithreaded capabilities of the operating system?
- Can the application automatically detect the presence of multiple processors and respond accordingly?
- Can the application use the multitasking capabilities of the operating system, or does it supply its own multitasking environment?
- How easily, and to what extent, can adjustments be made to the operating system to optimize the performance of the application?
- Does the application run as a 32-bit or 16-bit application?

Managerial Perspective

TO UPGRADE OR NOT TO UPGRADE

New versions of server operating systems are released on an annual basis, if not more frequently. When in the market for a server operating system, it is important to take a fresh look at all currently available products. When making this analysis, consider current technology investments, business objectives, the applications that will be executed in the proposed server environment, and the stability and strategic product development direction of the operating system vendor. After completing this analysis, the best solution should be apparent.

Networking and Connectivity Services

Network Clients Supported In addition to the client network operating systems that were previously reviewed, server network operating systems may also need to communicate with client platforms with only the following operating systems installed:

- DOS
- Windows 9x
- Windows NT
- Windows 2000
- Macintosh
- UNIX

Because these operating systems possess no native networking functionality, the server network operating system must provide client software that supplies the necessary operating system-specific network communications capabilities. This software is loaded on the intended networking client, and the required network communication capabilities are merged with the native operating system.

Network Protocol Support The key question concerning network protocols and server network operating systems is not how many different network protocols are supported, but how many network protocols can be supported simultaneously. As the trend toward heterogeneous multivendor enterprise networks continues, it is essential that server network operating systems possess the ability to support multiple network protocols simultaneously. This ability maximizes not only the different types of clients that can be supported, but also the number and type of other servers with which a given server can communicate. The ease with which multiple network protocols can be supported or whether multiple network protocols can be supported at all can vary among different server network operating systems.

Related to the ability of a server network operating system to simultaneously support multiple protocols is the ability of a server network operating system to support multiple network interface cards. If a single NIC is the bottleneck to network communications, additional NICs can be added provided the NOS and computer bus supports them. As PCI buses and PCI-based NICs have increased in popularity, PCI cards containing up to four NICs have been produced. Unless the server network operating system has the ability to communicate with four NICs simultaneously, this four NIC PCI card would be of little use.

Multiprotocol Routing Underlying a server network operating system's ability to process multiple protocols simultaneously is the presence of **multiprotocol routing** software. This software may be either included, optional, or not available, depending on the server network operating system in question. Multiprotocol routing provides the functionality necessary to actually process and understand multiple network protocols as well as translate between them. Without multiprotocol routing software, clients speaking multiple different network protocols cannot be supported. Routing in general and multiprotocol routing in particular are covered in great detail in Chapter 13, LAN Internetworking. Figure 7-28 illustrates the relationship among multiple network protocols, multiple network interface cards per server, and multiprotocol routing software.

Remote Access and Gateway Services Just as client network operating systems supplied the client portion of a remote access communication, server network operating systems can supply the server side of remote access communication. These remote access servers may be included with the server NOS or may be available for an additional fee. It is important that these remote access servers be tightly integrated into the server network operating system to ensure reliable performance, full functionality as offered to locally connected users, and tight security. Windows NT RAS (remote access server) is integrated with Windows NT Server, and NetWare Connect is the remote access server that integrates with NetWare.

In some cases, it may be necessary for either clients or servers to access IBM mainframe computers or AS/400s that are linked on IBM's proprietary network architecture known as **SNA (systems network architecture).** In such cases, it makes more sense for the translation software necessary to access the SNA network to reside on a single server than on multiple clients. In this scenario, the server with the SNA translation software installed becomes a gateway to the SNA network. Windows NT's product for IBM mainframe access is called SNA Gateway, and NetWare's product is called NetWare for SAA (systems application architecture).

Management and Administration Services

Installation, Configuration, and Administration Reviews of server network operating systems consistently list **auto-detection and configuration** of installed controllers, interface cards, and peripherals as the most important installation-related feature. The ability of a server network operating system to automatically configure a controller, adapter, or peripheral is dependent on the network operating system possess-

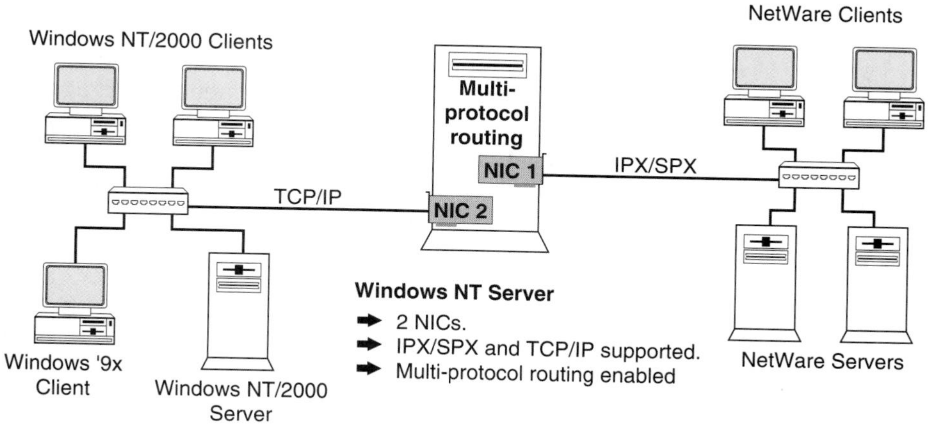

Figure 7-28 Multiple Network Protocols and Server Network Operating Systems

ing a compatible driver for that device. It should stand to reason that the greater the number of drivers supported by a given network operating system, the greater the probability that auto-configuration will be successful.

Another hardware compatibility issue related to installation is on which CPUs a given server network operating system can operate. For example, although NetWare can only operate on Intel chips, Windows NT Server can operate on Intel chips and DEC Alpha chips.

To appreciate the differences in ease of administration offered by server network operating systems, it is important to consider multiserver enterprise network serving hundreds, if not thousands, of users. Simple items that are merely a nuisance on a smaller network can easily become major issues in such a large implementation. With this scenario in mind, some pertinent questions might be:

- How many steps are involved in creating a new user account?
- What is involved in giving a user access to remote servers?
- How easily can a user profile be copied and used as a template to automatically generate other user profiles? This feature is particularly important in academic settings where user profiles must be constantly generated in large numbers.
- What tools are available to assist in managing multiple servers simultaneously?

Server network operating systems can vary widely in the sophistication of the **performance monitoring** software included or available as an add-on. Ideally, the monitoring software should offer the ability to set thresholds for multiple system performance parameters. If these thresholds are exceeded, alerts or alarms should notify network management personnel of the problem, and offer advice as to possible diagnoses or solutions. Event logging and audit trails are often included as part of the performance monitoring package.

In multiple-server environments, it is particularly important that all servers can be monitored and managed from a single management console. Desktop and server management software offers capabilities beyond the monitoring software included in server network operating systems. For example, performance statistics are often gathered and stored in databases known as **MIBs (management information base).** In addition, this performance management information can be communicated to enterprise management systems such as HP OpenView, Computer Associates Uni-Center, or Tivoli's Management Framework using **SNMP (simple network management protocol).** In addition to these enterprise network management platforms, both Microsoft and Novell offer tools designed to ease system administration across large network installations such as Microsoft System Management Server (SMS) and Novell Manage Wise.

Integration and Migration **Migration** features are aimed at easing the transition from one server NOS to another. Key among the migration concerns is the conversion of the directory services information. Utilities are available from third-party software vendors as well as from the NOS vendor's themselves to help automate directory data conversion.

Integration refers to the transitionary period of time in the migration process when both network operating systems are running simultaneously and interacting to some degree. Integration utilities or strategies include:

- NetWare file and print services for NT, which allow a Windows NT server to appear to be a NetWare server by offering native file and print services to NetWare clients.
- NW-Link, which allows Windows NT Workstation clients and Windows '95 clients to communicate with NetWare 3.12 servers.
- File access protocols for NCP (NetWare core protocol) and SMB (server message block) can be loaded simultaneously as redirectors, allowing either NetWare-or Windows-compatible programs to be executed.

Monitoring As more mission-critical applications are deployed on LAN-attached servers, server operating systems must offer more sophisticated management tools to manage those applications effectively. Monitoring ability is essential in determining where potential performance bottlenecks might occur and to react accordingly. Among the server attributes that should capable of being monitored and logged include:

- Processor utilization
- Network I/O
- Disk I/O
- Memory usage including L2 cache
- Individual application performance and system impact
- Process and thread performance

The monitor tool should be able to display data in a variety of ways:

- As a graph
- As a report
- As alarms or alerts if preset thresholds are crossed

A strong and flexible alert system is essential to keep applications running and users happy. Some alert systems have the ability to dial particular pagers for particular alerts and can forward system status information to that pager as well.

A monitoring tool should support multiple open monitoring windows simultaneously so that multiple attributes or applications can be observed. The monitoring or management tool should be open and support industry standard management protocols and APIs so that application-specific management tools can be easily integrated into the overall operating system monitor.

Performance

To take advantage of the increased processing powers of multiple processors, server operating systems must be specially written to operate in a symmetrical multiprocessing (SMP) environment. Server operating systems can differ as to the maximum number of processors they can support. Figure 7-29 summarizes the number of processors supported by some currently available server operating systems.

UNIX-based server operating systems such as Solaris and others have been offering SMP capabilities for many more years than operating systems that have been developed in the Intel chip environment. As a result, UNIX-based server operating systems tend to be more stable with servers having more than 16 or 32 processors.

Security

As local area network operating system based client/server systems have replaced traditional mainframe-type applications, the need for effective security has increased. Overall security features fall into three broad categories:

- Authentication
- Authorization
- Encryption

Authentication **Authentication** is concerned with determining which user is attempting to access the system. There are two key components to authentication: identification and proof of identification. In most network operating system environments, identification is provided by a UserID and proof of identification is provided by a password. Collectively, the UserID and password are known as a set of **authentication credentials.** In the login process, the server NOS checks the supplied

Server Operating System	Vendor	Number of Processors Supported
Windows NT server	Microsoft	2 to 16
Solaris	Sun Microsystems	2 to 64
OpenServer MPX	SCO (Santa Cruz Operation)	2 to 30
NetWare 5.x	Novell	2 to 32

Figure 7-29 Number of Processors Supported by Server Operating Systems

authentication credentials against the directory service to determine if the credentials are valid. If so, the user is allowed to log onto the system.

Most server network operating systems have the facility to support a guest user that is not authenticated. Although such a user usually is assigned minimal access rights to network resources, some situations, such as Internet publishing, require a nonauthenticated user be given access to files and resources on a network server. When browsing the web, a user typically doesn't need to log onto each server they wish to access.

Authorization **Authorization** is the process of controls access rights to network resources. **Access control lists (ACLs)** are the most commonly used authorization technique for local area network operating systems. In an ACL-based authorization scheme, a list of users and groups is attached to each network resource along with their permitted access level. When a user attempts to access a network resource, the server checks the supplied authentication credentials against the access control list. If the credentials support the desired access level, the action is completed. If the credentials do not support the desired access level, the action is prohibited and an error is displayed to the user. A second authorization method is Kerberos, a multiserver authorization method that provides increased security for large client/server applications. Although traditionally used only in mainframe-type applications, Kerberos is rapidly being integrated into PC local area network operating systems to increase the level of available security as more high-end applications are ported to these platforms.

In addition to individual user accounts, it is also possible to create user groups accounts. A group account is a place holder that allows for a single change in user permissions or rights to affect multiple users at the same time. By assigning all authorization rights to groups rather than users, it is possible to greatly reduce the amount of effort required to administrate a system while increasing consistency and alleviating potential security holes. When creating user accounts, considerable time can be saved if UserIDs can be created or modified using a template or group name instead of having to answer numerous questions for every individual UserID.

Encryption **Encryption** is the process of "scrambling" data before the information is sent across a network and "unscrambling" it at the destination. By encrypting data, it is protected from anyone who may make a copy of it along the way. There are multiple methods of data encryption in the marketplace. The two most common are DES and RSA public key encryption. DES is a single key system whereby a single key is used to encrypt and decrypt the message. In RSA public key encryption a combination of private and public keys are used to encrypt and decrypt the message, effectively eliminating potential problems with the transmission of a single key from the source to the destination.

Encryption is especially important when authentication credentials are entered. Encrypted passwords are unreadable while being transmitted between a client workstation and the authorizing server. Two main methods are used to encrypt authentication credentials: PAP and CHAP. The **password authentication protocol (PAP)** provides for the transmission of encrypted passwords between network nodes. The **challenge/handshake authentication protocol (CHAP)** provides a more secure environment for the transmission of authentication credentials by encrypting the UserID as well as the password. Before PAP or CHAP can be implemented, both the client and server must be configured to support the protocol. Some clients cannot support one or the other, so a careful examination of the available options is required before implementing either solution.

Applied Problem Solving

SERVER NETWORK OPERATING SYSTEM TECHNOLOGY ANALYSIS

A network analyst's job is to always seek out the latest information the industry has to offer before making recommendations for purchases that could have a significant bearing on both the company's prosperity and personal job security. The following server networking operating system technology analysis grid (Figure 7-30) is given

Server Network Operating System Characteristic	Windows NT (2000) Server	NetWare	UNIX
Hardware/Platform			
Required memory	32-64 MB	32-64 MB	64 MB +
CPUs	Intel, DEC/Compaq Alpha	Intel	Intel, Sparc, Power PC, DEC/Compaq Alpha, MIPS, etc.
Symmetrical multiprocessing	yes	no	yes
Preemptive multitasking	yes	no	yes
Multithreading	yes	yes	yes
Protected memory application execution	yes	yes, but not with NLMs	yes
Installation and Configuration			
Automatic detection and configuration of adapters and peripherals	yes	no	no
Requires a separate administrator console	no	yes	yes
Networking and Connectivity			
Clients supported	DOS, Windows, Windows for Workgroups, OS/2, Windows NT, Mac, UNIX	DOS, Windows, Windows for Workgroups, UNIX, OS/2, Windows NT, Mac	UNIX, DOS, Windows, Windows for Workgroups, OS/2, Windows NT, Mac
Network protocols supported	TCP/IP, IPX/SPX, NetBEUI, Appletalk, TCP/IP encapsulated NetBIOS	TCP/IP, IPX/SPX, Appletalk, TCP/IP encapsulated IPX, IPX encapsulated NetBIOS	TCP, IPX/SPX

Figure 7-30 Server Network Operating System Technology Analysis Grid (figure continues)

Server Network Operating System Characteristic	Windows NT (2000) Server	NetWare	UNIX
Routing supported	TCP/IP, IPX/SPX	TCP/IP, IPX/SPX, AppleTalk	TCP/IP, IPX/SPX
Remote access services	Windows NT RAS	NetWare Connect	Optional
E-mail gateways	Mail server optional	MHS included	Sendmail
Clients able to access remote resources	yes	yes	yes
Management and Administration			
Can act as SNMP agent for enterprise management system	yes	Optional	yes
Can set performance thresholds and alerts	yes	yes with ManageWise (Optional)	yes
Central management of multiple servers	yes	yes	yes
Audit trails and event logs	yes	yes	yes

Figure 7-30 (continued)

as an example, but is not meant to be either authoritative or all inclusive. The technology analysis grid is divided into the following major categories:

- Hardware/platform characteristics
- Installation and configuration
- Networking and connectivity
- Management and administration

NETWORK OPERATING SYSTEM INTEROPERABILITY

Because of increased demands to share information more quickly and easily within a company, as well as the increased number of corporate mergers and acquisitions, interoperability between different types of network operating systems has become an increasingly important functional characteristic.

Transparent interoperability between different network operating systems does not happen by magic. Compatibility on a variety of levels must be reconciled. A model should be devised that details how identified incompatibilities are to be dealt with. A separate model should be completed for each representative client and server system. Figure 7-31 illustrates representative models for NetWare, Windows NT (2000), and UNIX.

Once the layer one media (UTP, Fiber, Coax) and layer two network architecture (Ethernet, token ring, FDDI, Fast Ethernet) incompatibilities have been settled, the

	NetWare	Windows NT (2000)	UNIX
Directory Services	Bindery, NetWare directory services (NDS)	Domains, active directory	Stand-alone, network information system (NIS)
File Systems	NWFS, NSS	FAT, NTFS	UNIX file system
Application Protocols	NCP	SMB	NFS
Network Protocols	IPX/SPX, TCP/IP	IPX/SPX, TCP/IP, NetBEUI, AppleTalk	TCP/IP

Figure 7-31 Sample Compatibility Model

options for eliminating remaining incompatibilities are straightforward. Incompatibilities on layers four through seven can be dealt with in any combination of the following ways:

- **Communication protocol.** In the case of NetWare/NT interoperability, both IPX/SPX or TCP/IP can be supported by both network operating systems, depending on NOS version numbers.
- **Server-side software or gateways.** Can NT or NetWare clients access each other's servers without adding special client software? Are server-based gateway products available that will give clients access to foreign servers?

Although not specifically noted on a particular layer of the OSI model, at least two other interoperability issues must be resolved before true transparent interoperability can be achieved:

- **File system interoperability** allows servers of different network operating systems and their respective clients to be able to share each other's files. Server-to-server interoperability is not automatically two-way. For example, one interoperability product may be required to allow server A to share server B's file system, and a different product may be required to allow server B to share server A's file system.
- **Directory system interoperability** allows two different network operating systems to share and synchronize their respective directory systems. As was the case with the file system interoperability, two separate products may be required to ensure two-way directory systems interoperability.

SUMMARY

The network layer of the OSI network reference model is concerned with addressing and routing data packets between nodes on connected internetworks. All data from higher level protocols are encapsulated in network layer protocols for transmission across network segments.

Each node must be given a fully qualified network layer address consisting of both a network segment address and a node address. This fully qualified network layer address is resolved to an underlying NIC physical address when the layer three packet is encapsulated in a layer two frame for transmission at the datalink layer of the OSI model.

The transport layer of the OSI network reference model is concerned with the creation, maintenance, and destruction of logical network connections between nodes. Typically connection-oriented in nature, packets sent across a transport layer connection are subject to error correction and flow control.

The session layer of the OSI network reference model is concerned with addressing data streams to particular applications running on each node. These connections, know as sessions, are typically identified via ports and sockets.

Three major network layer protocol suites are currently in use: IPX/SPX, TCP/IP, and AppleTalk. IPX/SPX is the traditional network layer protocol for Novell NetWare systems and provides an easy to configure internetwork protocol.

TCP/IP is the protocol suite used to transmit data across the Internet. The TCP/IP suite consists of three major protocols: IP, TCP, and UDP. The current version of the IP protocol is IPv4. A newer version of the IP protocol (IPv6 or IPng) is currently being prepared for implementation.

AppleTalk is most commonly used in Apple Macintosh installations to support client/server computing applications. Other commonly used protocols for LAN applications include NetBEUI for internode communications on a single segment LAN and DLC for connection to LAN-attached printers.

Network operating systems have traditionally provided shared file and print services among networked clients. With the increase in client/server architectures and the associated increase in distributed applications, network operating systems are now also providing application services, directory services, and messaging and communications services in support of these distributed applications.

Network operating systems were once classified as either peer-to-peer or client/server. As network operating systems have evolved, this categorization no longer holds true. Network operating systems are now classified by their function: client network operating systems or server network operating systems.

Client network operating systems functionality can be categorized into operating systems capabilities, peer-to-peer networking capabilities, and client networking capabilities. Client networking capabilities are largely measured by the number of different server network operating systems with which the client can transparently interoperate. Remote access capability is also important.

Server network operating systems are now primarily concerned with high-performance application services for back-end application programs. Enterprise-wide directory services must also be provided. The two major approaches to enterprise directory services are global directory services and domain directory services.

To communicate with numerous client platforms, server network operating systems must support a variety of different network clients as well as a variety of different network transport protocols. Multiprotocol routing and remote access services are also essential to deliver transparent interoperability to the greatest number of client platforms. In the multiple server environments of the enterprise network, monitoring, management, and administration tools play a critical role.

KEY TERMS

access control lists
ACLs
address resolution
address resolution
address resolution protocol (ARP)
AppleTalk data stream protocol (ADSP)
AppleTalk session protocol (ASP)
AppleTalk transaction protocol (ATP)
application program interface (API)
application services
authentication
authentication credentials

authorization
auto-detection and configuration
backward compatibility
bindery
broadcast address
challenge/handshake authentication protocol
CHAP
classfull
class of service
classless
client network operating systems
client/server network operating systems
connectionless protocols
connection-oriented protocols
data link control protocol (DLC)
data migration
datagram delivery protocol (DDP)
deencapsulation
default gateway
directory services
distance vector routing protocol
domain directory service
domain name system (DNS)
domains
encapsulation
encryption
fragmentation
global directory service
granularity
host-to-host
integration
integration/migration services
Internet Packet Exchange (IPX)
Internet Protocol (IP)
IP next generation (IPng)
IT
LDAP
legacy application
link-state protocols
local session number
management information base
maximum transmission unit
MIBs
migration
multicasting
multihomed
multiprotocol routing
NDS
NetBEUI frame (NBF)
NetWare directory services
network objects
network segment address
node address
object-oriented user interfaces
octets
open shortest path first (OSPF)
PAP
password authentication protocol
PDC
peer-to-peer network operating systems
performance monitoring
plug-n-play (PnP)
PnP BIOS
ports
primary domain controller
protected memory mode
reverse address resolution protocol (RARP)
router
routing table maintenance protocol (RTMP)
sequenced packet exchange protocol (SPX)
server network operating systems
simple network management protocol
SNA
SNMP
socket
static routes
subnet mask
Systems Network Architecture
transmission control protocol/Internet protocol (TCP/IP)
UDP
universal client
user datagram protocol
virtual device drivers
virtual machines
VxDs
Windows NT remote access server

REVIEW QUESTIONS

1. What are the two components of a network layer address?
2. Explain the concept of protocol encapsulation.
3. Explain the concept of address resolution.
4. What layer's address is used to deliver data across an internetwork (end-to-end delivery)?
5. What layer's address is used to deliver data to a NIC within a network segment (point-to-point delivery)?
6. What is meant by protocol fragmentation?
7. What address does a router use to make routing decisions?
8. Why are routing protocols used?
9. What is the difference between a distance vector routing protocol and a link state routing protocol?
10. Explain the difference between connectionless and connection-oriented protocols.
11. Why are all connectionless protocols considered unreliable?
12. Explain the purpose of ports and sockets.
13. List the protocols in the IPX/SPX protocol suite. What is the primary purpose of each protocol?
14. What is the address resolution process used to resolve physical addresses from IPX addresses?
15. List the protocols in the TCP/IP protocol suite. What is the primary purpose of each protocol?
16. How is address resolution accomplished within the IP network layer protocol?
17. Break the IP address 192.168.101.4 (subnet mask 255.255.255.0) into its network segment and node address components.
18. What are the major problems associated with version four of the IP protocol?
19. Explain the purpose of the domain name system.

20. What is the distance vector routing protocol used with IP-based networks?
21. What is the link state protocol used with IP-based networks?
22. What is the difference between broadcasting and multicasting?
23. How does IPv6 solve the address space concerns of IPv4?
24. List three strategies to make the transition from IPv4 to IPv6.
25. List the protocols in the AppleTalk protocol suite. What is the primary purpose of each protocol?
26. What is the network layer protocol used in AppleTalk networks?
27. When is NetBEUI a viable primary LAN protocol?
28. For what applications is DLC commonly used?
29. What network layer protocol is used on the Internet?
30. What effect has the adoption of client/server architectures and distributed applications had on network operating systems architectures?
31. Differentiate between peer-to-peer network operating systems and client/server network operating systems.
32. Differentiate between today's client network operating system and the client portion of traditional client/server network operating systems.
33. How does the combination of today's client and server network operating systems differ from a traditional client/server network operating system implementation?
34. Why is a universal client important to enterprise computing?
35. Describe the importance of the following service categories in more detail: directory services, applications services, integration/migration services.
36. Describe the major categories of functionality of client network operating systems.
37. Describe how 16-bit or 32-bit applications running in their own protected memory space can still cause system crashes.
38. What is the objective of PnP standards?
39. Describe the components required to deliver a PnP solution and the relationship of the described components.
40. Describe the three elements of networking functionality belonging to client network operating systems paying particular attention to the relationship between the elements.
41. Why is it important for a client network operating system to be able to support more than one network transport protocol?
42. Describe the major differences between global directory services and domain directory services in terms of architecture and functionality.
43. What is accomplished by having directory services databases be both distributed and replicated? Differentiate between the two techniques.
44. What is LDAP?
45. What are the two basic parts of an authentication credential set?
46. What is the difference between authentication and authorization?
47. What is the purpose of an ACL?
48. What is the difference in terms of functionality and communication between a client running only an operating system such as Windows and a client running a network operating system such as Windows '95?
49. What are some important functional characteristics of server network operating systems related to integration and migration?
50. Name and describe the issues surrounding at least four areas of NOS functionality that must be addressed when designing interoperability solutions.

ACTIVITIES

1. Prepare a chart that maps the protocols in the IPX/SPX protocol suite against the OSI network reference model. Which protocols are connectionless and which are connection-oriented?
2. Prepare a chart that maps the protocols in the TCP/IP protocol suite against the OSI network reference model. Which protocols are connectionless and which are connection-oriented?
3. The TCP/IP protocol suite was the first packet-switched protocol suite. Research the history of TCP/IP and prepare a report explaining its evolution.
4. Visit the network department of your school or company. Ask about the design of their data network. Prepare a chart that explains the network address scheme used.
5. Visit the network department of your school or company. Ask about their plans for implementing IPv6.
6. Visit the network department of your school or company. Prepare a report that describes the routing protocols used.

7. Using back issues of a publication such as *PC Magazine*, prepare a presentation tracing the functionality of peer-to-peer LANs from 1994 to the present. Prepare a graph detailing price, number of supported users, and required memory over the research period.
8. Using back issues of a publication such as *PC Magazine*, prepare a presentation tracing the functionality of client/server LANs from 1994 to the present. Prepare a graph detailing price, number of supported users, and required memory over the research period.
9. Gather current market share statistics for the following market segments and prepare a presentation: peer-to-peer NOS, client NOS, server NOS.
10. Analyze the results of the previous activity. Which products are gaining market share and which are losing market share? Relate the market shifts to product functionality. Present your results in a top-down model format.
11. Prepare a presentation on the comparative functionality of Windows 9x/Millenium vs. Windows 2000 Professional. Compare marketing campaigns and current market share.
12. Review advertisements and catalogs for devices that support the PnP standard. Prepare a listing detailing which types of devices have the most PnP offerings. Which network operating system (if any) do devices claim to be compatible with?
13. Prepare a product review of dial-up or remote node servers, paying special attention to the source and compatibility of client software. Are most dial-up servers NOS specific? Why or why not?
14. Research and prepare a presentation on LDAP. What software categories supported LDAP specifications originally, currently? What key vendor groups or standards bodies (if any) support LDAP? What is your prediction as to the widespread adoption of LDAP?
15. Compare the performance monitoring capabilities of various server network operating systems. Which are best at monitoring a single server? Multiple servers? Which are best at setting thresholds and alerts? Which are best at linking to enterprise management systems such as HP Open View, CA Unicenter, or Tivoli NetView?

CASE STUDY

Web Switches Open e-Comm Doors at Nettaxi

One of the most difficult tasks facing e-commerce sites today is ensuring that end users can access the content they request in a timely fashion. At Nettaxi.com, a Web site offering e-mail, home pages and domain hosting, switches that can direct requests by URL are doing the job.

"All of our content is mission-critical, but some of our services, like those for premium subscribers, are extremely important to our business," says Brian Stroh, vice president of information services at Nettaxi. "With our new switches, we can set aside a separate bank of servers to make sure they are available for requests coming in for that [premium] content."

Nettaxi gets about 55 million hits and pushes out 7.8 terabytes of data to users on a daily basis, according to Stroh. "Now we can essentially say [to our switches], `If you get a request for this type of content go to this server,' which is something we could not do before. We couldn't drill down and direct traffic at such a fine level."

Nettaxi now uses six ArrowPoint CS-100 switches to route requests to 72 Sun servers running Solaris. Previously, the company used Cisco routers and software to accommodate content requests through a traditional server load-balancing scheme in which requests essentially were directed to whichever server was the least busy at the time of the request.

On the whole, the performance of the Cisco products was good, but Nettaxi could not prioritize requests from premium subscribers, who might have unlimited Web space or e-mail boxes. Stroh also needed a better way to organize traffic on the site to reduce jams.

Unlike basic Layer 2 and 3 switches, which look at media access control and subnet addresses to determine where traffic goes, ArrowPoint devices make traffic direction decisions by identifying URLs within a packet's HTTP payload and by looking at accompanying cookies that include end-user profiles. Nettaxi has defined policies that instruct its switches to give preferred treatment to requests for certain types of content. The switches consult these policies before sending requests to a server.

Nettaxi has clustered the servers supporting its Web site into four groups, each of which serves up a different set of content, such as premium services or e-mail. The technical advantage of this type of arrangement is that Nettaxi can designate more network bandwidth and server horsepower to the cluster hosting the most crucial data.

Stroh says Nettaxi's transition to ArrowPoint switches was relatively painless.

"When you are dealing with the network that we have, in making sure we have 100% uptime, it was a little tricky," he says. "But we had three or four engineers from ArrowPoint and seven or eight of our own people to make it happen. We met at one o'clock in the morning and it took us two hours to make the change."

Source: April Jacobs, "Web switches open e-comm doors at Nettaxi," *Network World,* vol. 16, no. 49 (December 6, 1999), p. 19. Copyright Network World. Reprinted with permission.

BUSINESS CASE STUDY QUESTIONS

Activities

1. Complete a top-down model for this case by gleaning facts from the case and placing them in the proper layer of the top-down model. After having completed the top-down model, analyze and detail those instances where requirements were clearly passed down from upper layers to lower layers of the model and where solutions to those requirements were passed up from lower layers to upper layers of the model.
2. Detail any questions about the case that may occur to you for which answers are not clearly stated in the article.

Business

1. What was the business motivation or problem that initiated the search for the implemented solution?
2. What was the customer service impact of the implemented solution?
3. Were business performance metrics and associated infrastructure performance metrics identified? If so, were they achieved? If not, what might be some suitable business and infrastructure performance metrics for this case?
4. Is this business opportunity primarily marketing or profit driven?

Application

1. How do the web switches do?
2. Upon what parameters do they make decisions?
3. How do the web servers provide a better way to organize traffic on the site to reduce jams?

Data

1. How many hits does the nettaxi site get each day?
2. How much data is transferred on a daily basis?
3. What types of data are transferred?

Network

1. What underlying network technologies were key to the achievement of stated business objectives?

Technology

1. What specific technologies were employed to deliver the described solution?

CHAPTER 8

WIDE AREA NETWORKING CONCEPTS, ARCHITECTURES, AND SERVICES

Concepts Reinforced

OSI Model	Internet Suite of Protocols Model
Top-Down Model	

Concepts Introduced

Wide Area Network Architecture	Switching Architectures
Transmission Architectures	Multiplexing
Packetization	Local Loop Transmission Alternatives
Broadband Transmission	Wide Area Network Services
Wide Area Network Design	Network Convergence

OBJECTIVES

Upon successful completion of this chapter, you should:

1. Understand the concept of multiplexing in general as well as several multiplexing techniques and related technology and applications in particular.
2. Understand the relationship between business motivation, available technology, and carrier services in creating wide area networking solutions.
3. Understand the advantages, limitations, and technology of current and forthcoming packet switching networks.
4. Understand the importance of standards as applied to wide area networking.
5. Understand the interrelationships and dependencies between the components of any wide area network architecture.
6. Understand the impact of the evolution in switching methodologies as it applies specifically to frame relay and cell relay.
7. Understand the business and technical issues surrounding WAN design and network convergence.

INTRODUCTION

When applications must be distributed over widely dispersed geographic areas, it is essential to have an understanding of the wide area networks on which such distribution depends. One of the most significant differences between wide area networks and the local area networks that were studied in previous chapters is the dependency, in most cases, on third-party carriers to provide wide area transmission services. The ability to understand the transmission and switching architecture that underlies and enables the variety of wide area transmission services that are offered by these carriers is of critical importance to successful wide area network managers.

To understand wide area switching and transmission architectures, one must first understand some basic principles or concepts of wide area networking such as multiplexing, packet switching, and circuit switching. Once switching and transmission architectures are understood, the wide area network services, both wireless and wireline, that are enabled by these architectures can be more effectively understood.

BASIC PRINCIPLES OF WIDE AREA NETWORKING

Network Design Principles

Among the strategic wide area network design principles to be considered in a given wide area network design are the following:

- Cost
- Availability/reliability
- Security/auditing
- Manageability and monitoring
- Quality of service/class of service
- Performance
- Support of business recovery planning initiatives

Optimizing for one of the aforementioned network design principles may lead to a diminished focus on other network design principles. For example, if a WAN is to be optimized for availability and performance, it could not simultaneously be optimized for cost. Deciding which principles take priority over other network design principles is the job of senior business and technical managers.

Network Convergence

One of the currently most popular WAN design philosophies is **network convergence.** Simply stated, network convergence is the merging (or converging) of data, voice, and video traffic onto a single physical network. The achievement of network convergence is dependent on a combination of business drivers, technology drivers, and technology industry drivers.

Because of its broad marketing appeal, the term network convergence is used in a variety of ways. In fact, the term network convergence can be used to describe at least three different technical possibilities or development stages as illustrated in Figure 8-1:

- **Stage 1 network convergence** involves the core network and/or cable plant of an organization. This is primarily a carrier network issue and is usually transparent to the end-user. Carriers have been transporting data and voice simultaneously over their networks for years, currently most often with ATM/SONET.
- **Stage 2 network convergence** is sometimes referred to as converged electronics or switch-to-switch network convergence. The technology required to support this level of network convergence is evolving at a rapid rate. The ATM/SONET combination will give way to Packet over SONET or IP over Optics within 5 years. The converged electronics switches may be co-located at the carrier locations or may be on the customer premises.
- **Stage 3 network convergence** involves converged end-user devices, also known as integrated access devices (IADs) or unified services platforms. These devices would be located on the customer premises but may be monitored and managed by the carrier. Research indicates that full, end-to-end network convergence could take 6 to 20 years.

Network Convergence Business Drivers Among the key business drivers behind the recent surge in interest in network convergence are the following:

- Internet traffic is doubling every 3 to 6 months.
- Current network is dominated by voice, but data are quickly catching up.
- 98 Carrier revenue: $200 billion, <$30 billion is voice.
- Internet telephony: $3 to 4 billion by 2004, which still represents only 10% of total US voice.
- Telecommunications Act of 1996 basically allows anyone to sell anything.

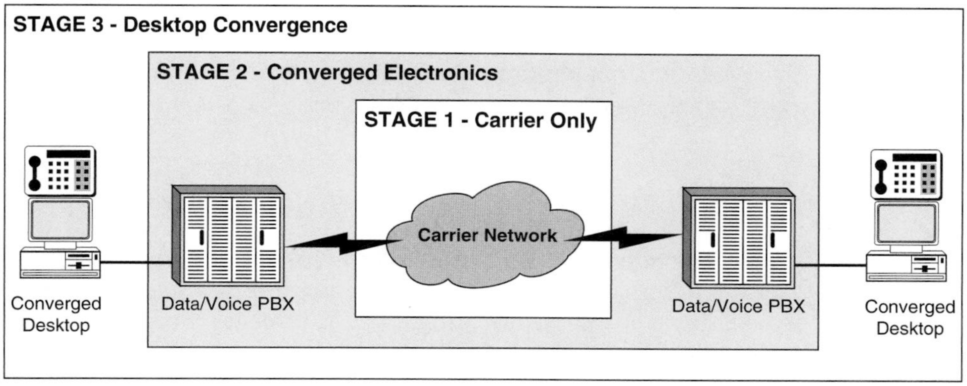

Figure 8-1 Three Stages of Network Convergence

- Consumer view: too many providers or too many different services provides openings for "one stop shopping" converged network vendors.

Network Convergence Technical Drivers Any network architecture is composed of two basic capabilities or subarchitectures; switching and transmission. Converged networks require extremely fast technology in both of these areas. More specifically, following are the most frequently cited technology requirements underlying widespread network convergence:

- In the switching area: optical switching and terabit routers will be required.
- In the transmission area: terabit optical transmission will be required.

Network Convergence Bottom Line If network convergence is the answer, what was the question? As previously stated, any network convergence strategy should start with a solid business case. Much of the hype and excitement surrounding network convergence is being generated by vendors trying to create a market for their newest technology and services. It is essential that organizations have a clear understanding of both what they hope to gain from network convergence and what their current network architecture and traffic patterns are before pursuing a move to a converged network. Without properly documented baseline data on current network performance characteristics, it will be impossible to objectively document the impact of the new converged network architecture.

Underlying Business Issues

To understand the basic technical principles of wide area networking, one must really start by looking at its basic business principles. In wide area networking as in most areas of business, the desire to maximize the impact of any investment in technology is a central focus. Figure 8-2 illustrates the underlying business motivation of wide area networking principles. Given five systems (LANs, computers, terminals to mainframes) that need to be linked over long distances, there are basically two choices of physical configurations. A dedicated wide area link can be provided for each system-to-system connection, or somehow both the principles and technology necessary to share a single wide area link among all five system-to-system connections can be found.

The cost of WAN services has a direct impact on WAN design. Current research shows that while WAN traffic is nearly doubling every year, budgets for WAN services are increasing at an average rate of less than 10% annually.

Underlying Technical Concepts

The two most basic principles involved in sharing a single data link among multiple sessions, as illustrated in Figure 8-2, are **packetizing** and **multiplexing.** Packetizing is the segmenting of data transmissions between devices into structured blocks or packets of data that contain enough "overhead" or management information in addition to the transmitted data itself, to ensure delivery of the packet of data to its intended destination. Multiplexing then takes this packetized data and

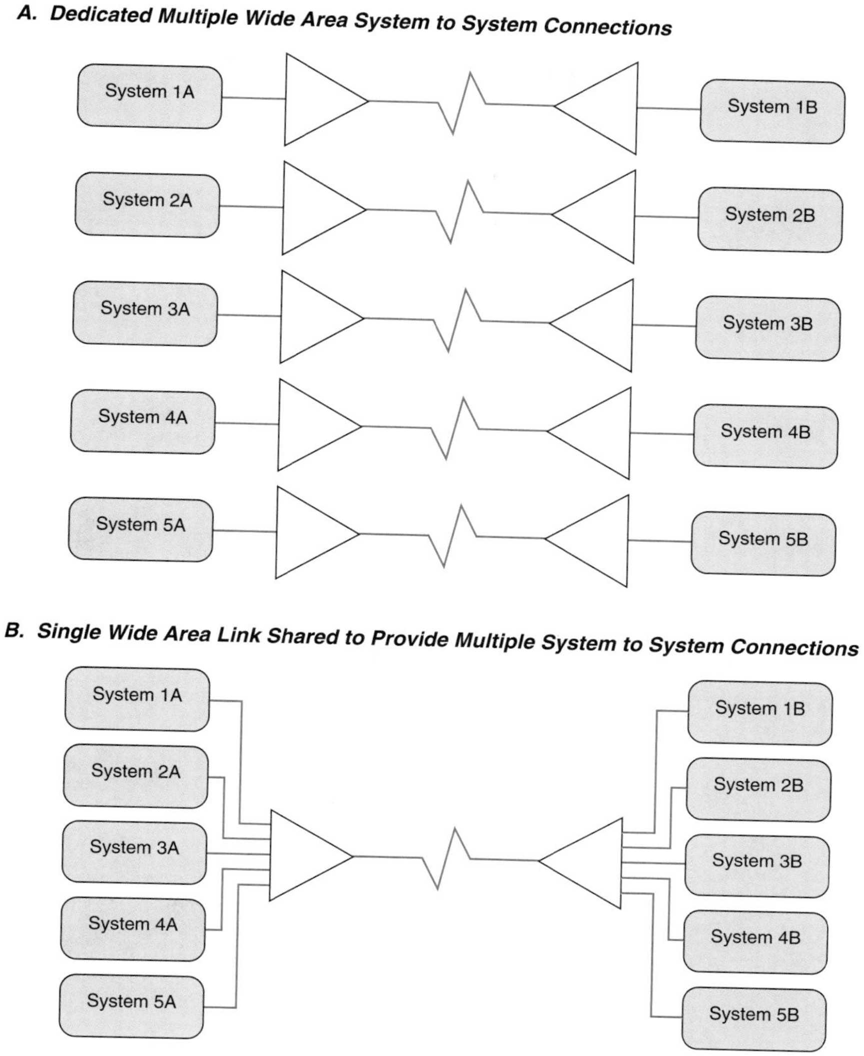

Figure 8-2 WAN Technical Principles Are Motivated by Business Principles

sends it over a shared wide area connection along with other packetized data from other sources. At the far end of the single wide area network link, this stream of multiple source, multiplexed data packets is demultiplexed and the packets sent to their respective destination addresses. A long distance parcel shipping analogy may clarify the underlying technical concepts of packetizing and multiplexing (Figure 8-3).

Multiple packages of several presents each are transported over a long distance via a single transport mechanism and subsequently delivered to their individual destinations. The equivalent wide area data transmission events are listed along the top of Figure 8-3., illustrating several packets of data from multiple sources being transmitted over a single, shared wide area communications link and subsequently demultiplexed and delivered to their individual destination addresses.

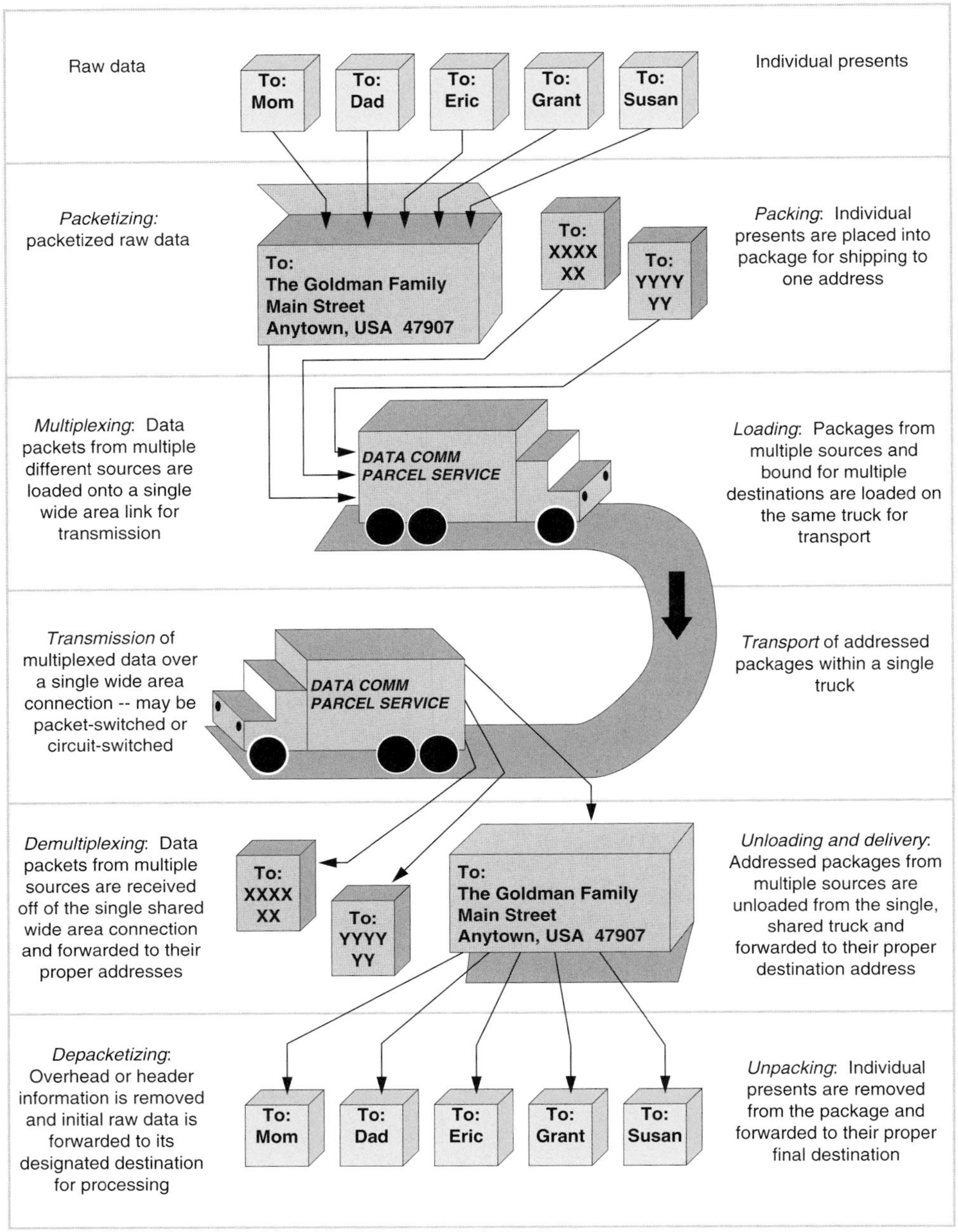

Figure 8-3 Packetizing and Multiplexing: A Parcel Shipping Analogy

Packetizing

A packet is a group of data bits organized in a predetermined, structured manner, to which overhead or management information is added to ensure error-free transmission of the actual data to their intended destination. These generalized packets may be alternatively known as frames, cells, blocks, data units, among other names. The predetermined, structured nature of a packet should not be overlooked. Recall that all of the raw data and any address information or error control information are nothing more than bits of data, 1s and 0s, that will be processed by some type of programmed, computerized communications device.

This programmed data communications device must be able to depend on exactly where certain pieces of key information, such as destination address and error check numbers, are located within a packet containing both raw data and overhead information.

By knowing exactly which bits within a packet represent a destination address and which bits represent data to be forwarded, the data communications device can process incoming data packets more quickly and efficiently. See Figure 8-29 for an example of a WAN-based packet format.

The parcel shipping analogy also illustrates the need for predetermined, structured packets. When shipping a parcel with nearly any parcel shipping company, one must fill out one of their standardized "structured" shipping forms, putting all data in the properly marked spaces. By doing so, the wide area transport mechanism, the parcel shipping company, can process packages more quickly and efficiently by reading only one type of form and knowing where specific data are located on that form. Regulations pertaining to maximum and minimum package size as well as packaging techniques also allow the parcel shipping company to perform more efficiently. As will be seen, maximum and minimum packet lengths in wide area data transmission are also important to overall transmission efficiency.

Multiplexing

Two basic techniques are employed in multiplexing digitized traffic:

- **Frequency division multiplexing (FDM)**
- **Time division multiplexing (TDM)**

A variation of TDM known as **statistical time division multiplexing (STDM)** is also commonly employed for digital data.

The previous three multiplexing techniques are limited to digitized traffic in which bits of data are transmitted as discrete voltages of electricity. In the optical transmission world, in which bits of data are represented by bursts of light energy of varying wavelengths, a relatively new multiplexing technique known as **wavelength division multiplexing (WDM)** has been developed. WDM technology is deployed primarily by telecommunications carriers with extensive long distance fiber optic networks to increase transmission capacity without the need to install additional fiber. WDM is discussed in more detail in the SONET (synchronous optical network) section of this chapter.

Frequency Division Multiplexing In frequency division multiplexing, multiple input signals are modulated to different frequencies within the available output bandwidth of a single composite circuit, often a 3000 Hz dial-up line, and subsequently demodulated back into individual signals on the output end of the composite circuit. Sufficient space in between these separate frequency channels is reserved in **guardbands** to prevent interference between the two or more input signals that are sharing the single circuit. Figure 8-4 illustrates a simple frequency division multiplexing configuration.

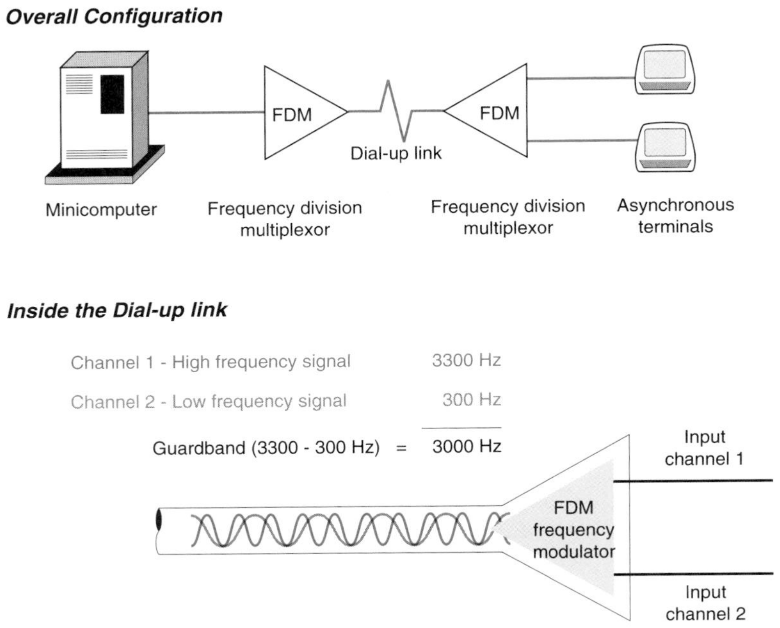

Figure 8-4 Frequency Division Multiplexing

The communications device that employs frequency division multiplexing is known as a frequency division multiplexer (FDM). At one time, FDMs were employed to transmit data from multiple low-speed (less than 1200 bps) terminals over dial-up or leased lines. As the speed of frequency division multiplexed terminals increases, the guardband width between channels in the shared composite circuit must also increase. As terminal speeds and demand for more bandwidth per terminal have risen, frequency division multiplexing is no longer the most practical multiplexing method employed.

Although FDM is seldom if ever still used to multiplex data from multiple terminals, it is still employed in devices known as **data over voice** units or DOV units. DOV units are most often employed where data transmission is desired to a location that is currently wired for phones but which cannot be easily or affordably also be rewired for data. In these cases, both the data and the voice transmission are simultaneously transmitted over the existing phone wiring. What's more, the data and voice transmissions are independent of one another. A person can be talking to someone else across the country while being on-line with a data transmission to the local computing center. It is important to point out that DOV units cannot be used over the PSTN (public switched telephone network). They must be used in environments that are served by a local PBX. College campuses are probably the most popular environment for DOV unit usage.

In FDM, the total bandwidth of the composite channel is divided into multiple subchannels by frequency. With FDM, from a connected terminal's point of view, a portion of the total bandwidth is available 100% of the time, yielding the appearance of a dedicated circuit. As a result the timing of signals between a connected terminal or device and the centralized processor is not affected.

DSL (digital subscriber line) services, a high speed local loop alternative available from some carriers, uses a variation of FDM to send digital data over the same physical pair of copper wires as the analog voice signal.

Time Division Multiplexing In time division multiplexing (TDM), the opposite is true. With TDM, from a connected terminal's point of view, 100% of the bandwidth is available for a portion of the time. The portion of time that is available to each connected input device is constant and controlled by the time division multiplexer. A key point to understand about time slots in a TDM environment is that a fixed portion of time, measured in milliseconds, is reserved for each attached input device whether or not the device is active. As a result, efficiency is sacrificed for the sake of simplicity.

Sometimes in a TDM environment, a terminal with nothing to say is given its full time allotment while other busy terminals are waiting to transmit. A TDM is really a fairly simple device that uses many familiar elements such as buffer memory and flow control. Figure 8-5 illustrates simple time division multiplexing.

As can be seen in Figure 8-5, each input channel has a fixed amount of buffer memory into which it can load data. Flow control, either XON/XOFF or CTS/RTS, tells the terminal to stop transmitting to the buffer memory when the buffer memory fills. **A central clock** or timing device in the TDM gives each input device its allotted time to empty its buffer into an area of the TDM where the combined data from all of the polled input devices are conglomerated into a single message frame for transmission over the composite circuit. This process of checking on each connected terminal to see if any data is ready to be sent is known as **polling.**

If a terminal was inactive and had nothing in its input buffer to contribute to the consolidated message frame, that input terminal's allotted space in the **composite message frame** is filled with blanks. The insertion of blanks, or null characters, into composite message links is the basis of the TDM's inefficient use of the shared composite circuit connecting the two TDMs. Although the data from the various input terminals is combined into a single message frame, each individual terminal's data

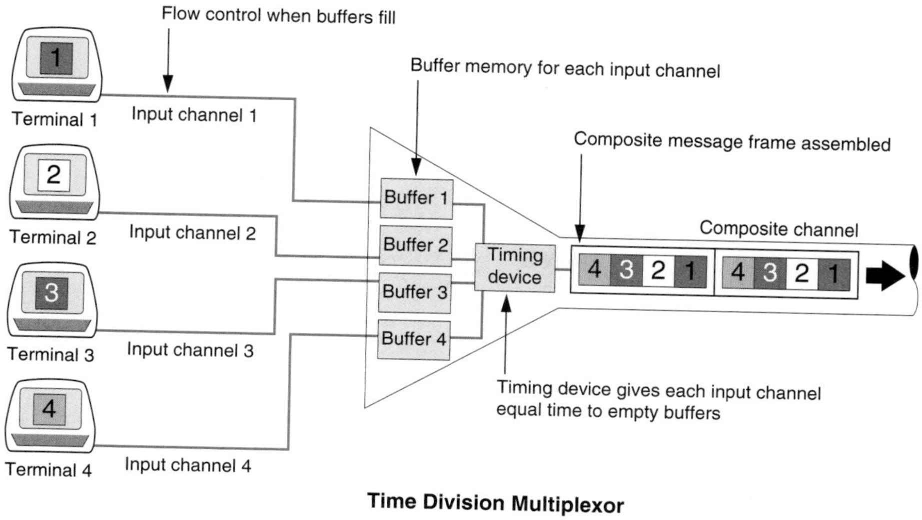

Figure 8-5 Time Division Multiplexing

are still identifiable by position within that composite message frame. This fact is important because once the composite message frame has finished its journey down the transmission link, it must be resegmented back into the individual terminal's original data format.

Statistical Time Division Multiplexing Statistical time division multiplexing (STDM) seeks to offer more efficient use of the composite bandwidth than simple TDM by employing increased monitoring and manipulation of input devices to accomplish two major goals:

1. Eliminate "idle time" allocations to inactive terminals
2. Eliminate padded blanks or null characters in the composite message blocks

In a statistical multiplexer or Stat Mux, allocation time is dynamically allocated to input devices. As terminals become more active, they get more time to send data directly to the Stat Mux. As terminals become less active or inactive, the Stat Mux polls them for input less frequently. This dynamic time slot allocation takes both processing power and additional memory. Statistics are kept relating to terminal activity over time—hence the name *statistical time division multiplexers.* Specially programmed microprocessors and additional buffer memory are key upgrades to STDMs and contribute to their increased costs over the simpler TDMs.

To increase the efficiency of use of the composite link, padded blanks and null characters are not inserted into message frames for inactive terminals. Remember that the purpose of the blanks is to occupy the space in the composite message frame assigned to that particular device. In an STDM, rather than assign space to input devices in the composite message frame by position regardless of activity, the STDM adds control information to each terminal's data within the composite message frame that indicates the source terminal and how many bytes of data came from that terminal. Figure 8-6 illustrates composite message block construction in STDMs.

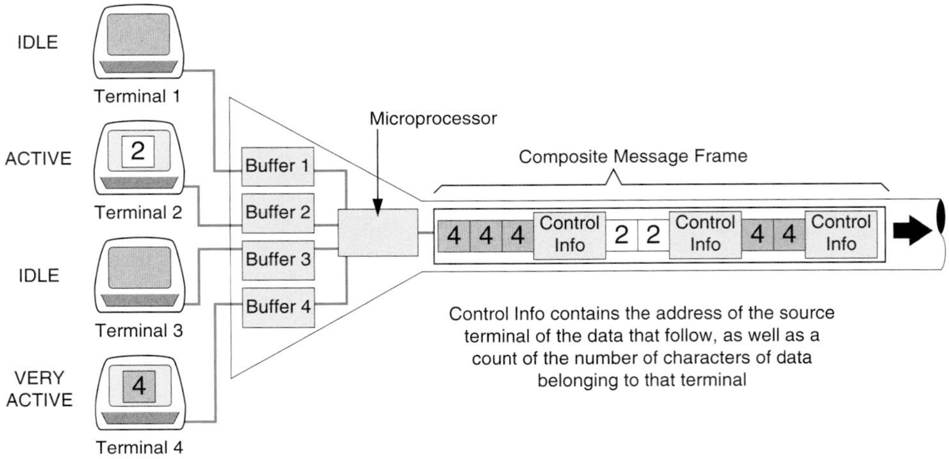

Figure 8-6 STDMs Make Efficient Use of Composite Bandwidth

Practical Advice and Information

A FEW IMPORTANT POINT ABOUT STAT MUXES:

- The time allocation protocols and composite message frame building protocols are proprietary and vary from one manufacturer to the next. As a result, multiplexers from different manufacturers are not interoperable.
- The dynamic allocation of time afforded to individual terminals or devices by the STDM can interfere with any timing, which might have been previously set up between the remote device and the central processor. This is particularly important in manufacturing or process control operations.

Managerial Perspective

STDM COST/BENEFIT ANALYSIS

From a business standpoint, what does a cost/benefit analysis of an STDM reveal? The STDM's increased costs are due to increased buffer memory, more sophisticated programming, and an integral microprocessor. On the benefits side of the equation, STDMs produce increased efficiency in time slot allocation and composite bandwidth usage. Some STDMs also include proprietary data compression techniques. These increased efficiencies in STDMs seem to produce "something for nothing."

For example, it is not unheard of for STDMs to seemingly transmit data at four or even eight times the speed of the composite link. For instance, I have installed 16-

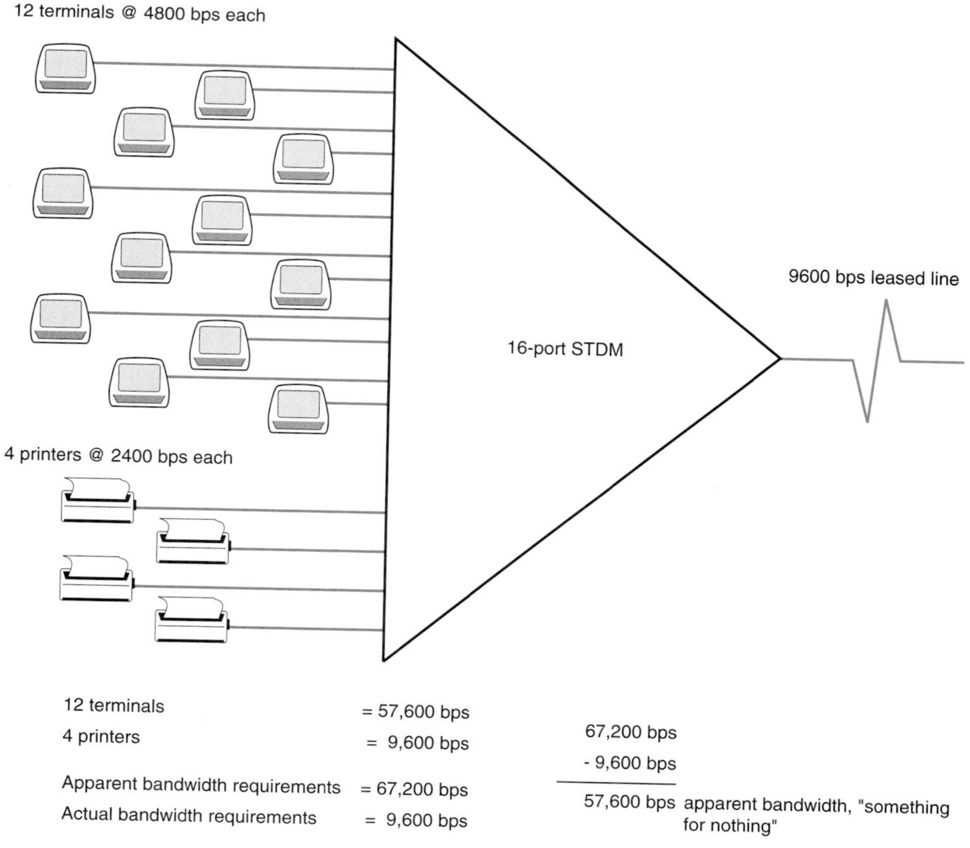

Figure 8-7 STDMs Seem to Offer Something for Nothing

port STDMs with four printers running at 2400 bps and 12 async terminals running at 4800 bps for an apparent bandwidth requirement of 67.2 Kbps (2400 × 4 plus 4800 × 12). The fact is, these 16 devices ran just fine over a 9600 bps leased line! This apparent discrepancy is largely due to the "statistical" nature of data transmission from terminals, which demonstrates the likelihood that only a relatively small percentage of terminals will be transmitting data at any split second in time. The STDM's sophisticated dynamic time slot allocation capabilities take advantage of this relatively large "idle time." Figure 8-7 illustrates the STDM's apparent ability to offer something for nothing.

Wide Area Network Architecture

To better understand how packetizing, multiplexing, and other wide area networking principles combine to create all of the current and emerging wide area networking technologies and services, a simple model defining the major segments and interrelationships of an overall wide area network architecture are included in Figure 8-8.

As can be seen in Figure 8-8, **user demands** are the driving force behind the current and emerging wide area **network services** that are offered to business and residential customers. Companies offering these services are in business to generate profits by implementing the underlying architectures that will enable them to offer the wide area networking services that users are demanding at the lowest possible cost.

For users to take advantage of network services, standardized **interface specifications** must be developed to ensure interoperability among different manufac-

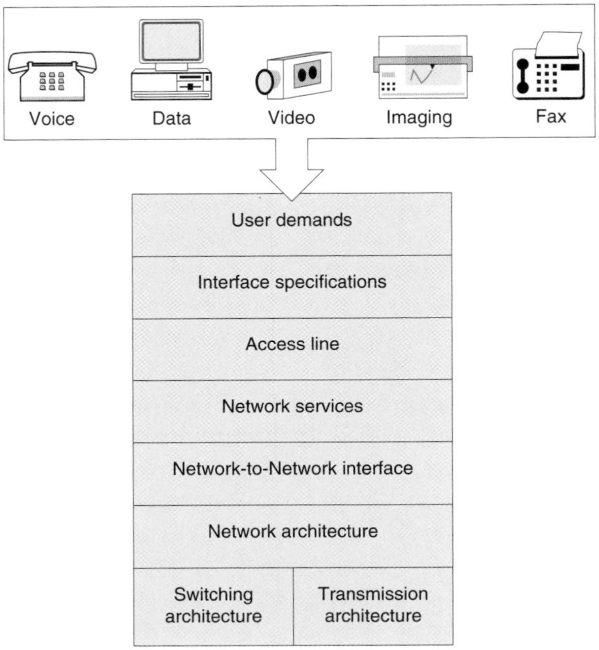

Figure 8-8 Major Components of a Wide Area Network Architecture

turer's end-user equipment. As an example, the X.25 interface specification ensures that users can purchase packet assembler disassemblers from any manufacturer and be able to successfully interface to a packet switched network service. Having packetized user payloads according to standard interface specifications, carrier network services must be accessed via an appropriately sized **access line** running from the user's residence or business to the entry or gateway to the carrier's network service.

To ensure transparent delivery of network services to users regardless of location, several carriers may need to cooperatively hand-off user payloads to each other. The transparent interoperability of network services from different carriers requires predefined **network-to-network interfaces.**

Network services cannot be offered unless the underlying infrastructure of the carriers and companies wishing to offer these services is technically capable of doing so. The combination of sophisticated switches **(switching architecture)** and transmission facilities **(transmission architecture)** that make up this infrastructure is known as the **network architecture.** Switching architectures or methods, such as circuit switching or packet switching, ensure the proper routing of information (data, voice, video, etc.) from the data's source to its destination. Transmission architectures or methods are the circuits or data highways over which the information is actually delivered.

To return to the parcel shipping analogy, switching is the activity that takes place inside depots and warehouses, whereas transmission takes place in the trucks on the highways and in the planes in the air. By adjusting depot organization, manpower, floorspace, or equipment, a parcel shipping company could adjust its switching capacity or sophistication. By utilizing varying numbers of planes or trucks, or by changing truck or plane routes, the same parcel shipping company could adjust its transmission capacity or sophistication.

In the case of wide area or packet-switched networks, the copper, fiber, microwave, and satellite links and the protocols that control access to and monitoring of these circuits constitute the transmission architecture of wide area networks. The central office switches and packet switches that build connections from source to destination utilizing these transmission circuits constitute the switching architecture of the wide area or packet-switched network. The importance of the relationship between the two architectures is well illustrated by the parcel shipping company analogy. If the parcel shipping company were to increase switching capacity and sophistication by building several new depots, but did not upgrade its transmission capacity by increasing numbers of trucks and planes, the result would be less than optimal. Similarly, providers of wide area network services are in the process of upgrading both their switching and transmission facilities to be able to meet future user demands for sophisticated and reasonably priced wide area network services.

WIDE AREA NETWORKING SWITCHING

Switching of some type or another is necessary in wide area network architectures because the alternative is unthinkable. Without some type of switching mechanism or architecture, every possible source of data in the world would have to be directly connected to every possible destination of data in the world, not a very likely prospect. Switching allows temporary connections to be established, maintained, and terminated between message sources and message destinations, sometime called **sinks** in data communications. Two primary switching techniques are employed in switching architectures:

- **Packet switching**
- **Circuit switching**

In packet-switched networks, users' packetized data are transported across circuits between packet switches along with the data of other users of the same packet-switched network. In contrast, in circuit-switched networks, users get dedicated bandwidth on circuits created solely for their use.

Packet Switching

In a **packet-switched network,** packets of data travel one at a time from the message source to the message destination. A packet-switched network, otherwise known as a **public data network (PDN),** is represented in network diagrams by a symbol that resembles a cloud. Figure 8-9 illustrates such a symbol as well as the difference between circuit switching and packet switching. The cloud is an appropriate symbol for a packet-switched network because all that is known is that the packet of data goes in one side of the PDN and comes out the other. The physical path that any packet takes may differ from those of other packets and, in any case, is unknown to the end-users. Beneath the cloud in a packet-switched network is a large number of **packet switches** that pass packets among themselves as the packets are routed from source to destination.

Remember that packets are specially structured groups of data that include control and address information in addition to the data itself. These packets must be assembled (control and address information added to data) somewhere before entry

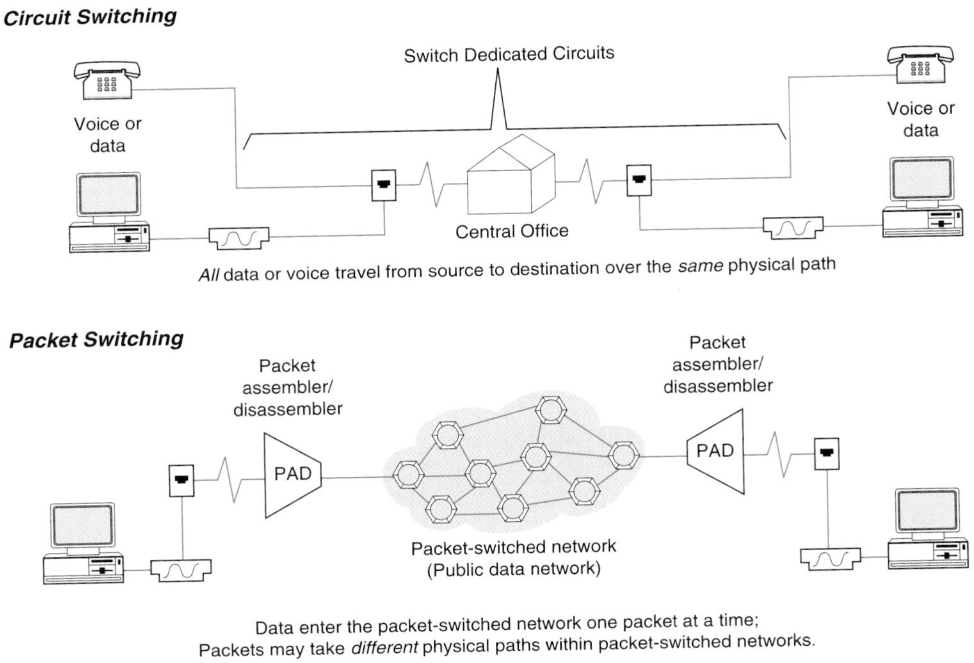
Circuit Switching
Switch Dedicated Circuits
Voice or data
Voice or data
Central Office
All data or voice travel from source to destination over the same physical path
Packet Switching
Packet assembler/ disassembler
Packet assembler/ disassembler
PAD
PAD
Packet-switched network (Public data network)
Data enter the packet-switched network one packet at a time;
Packets may take different physical paths within packet-switched networks.

Figure 8-9 Circuit Switching vs. Packet Switching

into the packet-switched network and must be subsequently disassembled before delivery of the data to the message destination. This packet assembly and disassembly is done by a device known as a **PAD** or **packet assembler disassembler.** PADs may be stand-alone devices or may be integrated into specially built modems or multiplexers. These PADs may be located at and end-user location, or may be located at the entry point to the packet-switched data network. Figure 8-9 illustrates the latter scenario in which the end-users employ regular modems to dial-up to the packet-switched network that provides the PADs to properly assemble the packets before transmission. This set-up is often more convenient for end-users, as they can still employ their modem for other dial-up applications.

The packet switches illustrated inside the PDN cloud in Figure 8-9 are generically known as **DSEs,** data switching exchanges, or **PSEs,** packet switching exchanges. DSE is the packet switching equivalent of the DCE and DTE categorization that were first encountered in the study of modems and dial-up transmission.

Another way in which packet switching differs from circuit switching is that as demand for transmission of data increases on a packet-switched network, additional users are not denied access to the packet-switched network. Overall performance of the network may suffer, errors and retransmission may occur, or packets of data may be lost; but all users experience the same degradation of service. This occurs because, in the case of a packet-switched network, data travels through the network one packet at a time, traveling over any available path within the network rather than waiting for a switched dedicated path, as in the case of the circuit-switched network.

Connectionless vs. Connection-Oriented Packet-Switched Services For any packet switch to process any packet of data bound for anywhere, it is essential that packet address information be included on each packet. Each packet switch then reads and processes each packet by making routing and forwarding decisions based on the packet's destination address and current network conditions. The full destination address uniquely identifying the ultimate destination of each packet is known as the **global address.**

Because an overall data message is broken up into numerous pieces by the packet assembler, these message pieces may actually arrive out of order at the message destination because of the speed and condition of the alternate paths within the packet-switched network over which these message pieces (packets) traveled. The data message must be pieced back together in proper order by the destination PAD before final transmission to the destination address. These self-sufficient packets containing full source and destination address information plus a message segment are known as **datagrams.** Figure 8-10 illustrates this packet-switched network phenomenon.

A switching methodology in which each datagram is handled and routed to its ultimate destination on an individual basis resulting in the possibility of packets traveling over a variety of physical paths on the way to their destination is known as a **connectionless** packet network. It is called connectionless because packets do not follow one another, in order, down a particular path through the network.

There are no error-detection or flow-control techniques applied by a datagram-based or connectionless packet-switched network. Such a network would depend on end-user devices (PCs, modems, communications software) to provide adequate error-control and flow control. Because datagrams are sent along multiple possible paths to the destination address, there is no guarantee of their safe arrival. This lack of inherent error-detection or flow-control abilities is the basis for refering to connectionless packet networks as **unreliable** packet networks.

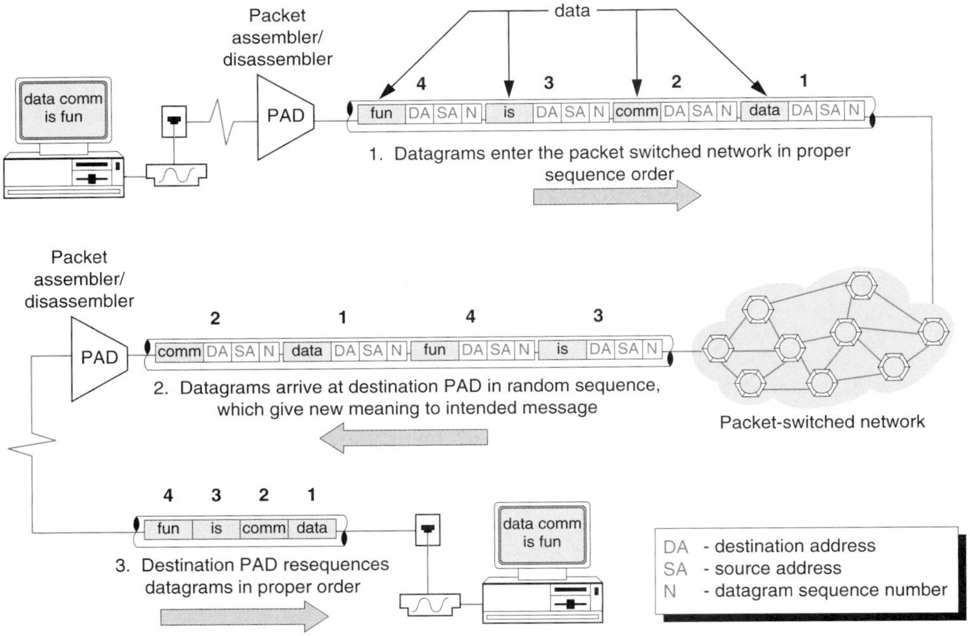

Figure 8-10 Datagram Delivery on a Packet-Switched Network

Virtual Circuits In contrast to the connectionless packet networks, **connection-oriented** or **reliable** packet networks establish **virtual circuits** enabling message packets to follow one another, in sequence, down the same connection or physical circuit. This connection from source to destination is set up by special packets known as **call set-up packets.** Once the call set-up packets have determined the best path from the source to the destination and established the virtual circuit, the message bearing packets follow one another in sequence along the virtual circuit from source to destination. Unlike a connectionless service, a connection-oriented service, because of the establishment of the virtual circuit, can offer check sum error detection with ACK/NAK retransmission control and flow control. These services can be offered by the packet network itself rather than depending on the end-user devices. Because connection-oriented packets all follow the same path, or **logical channel,** from source to destination, they do not require the full global addressing on each packet, as in the case of the connectionless datagram networks. Instead, connection-oriented network packets have an abbreviated **logical channel number, or LCN,** included with each packet. The details that relate the LCN to a physical circuit consisting of an actual series of specific packet switches within the packet-switched network are stored in a **virtual circuit table.**

Connection-oriented packet switching networks actually define two types of virtual circuits: **switched virtual circuits (SVC)** and **permanent virtual circuits (PVC).** The switched virtual circuit connection is terminated when the complete message has been sent, and a special **clear request packet** causes all switched virtual circuit table entries related to this connection to be erased. The virtual circuit table of the permanent virtual circuit is not erased, making the PVC the equivalent of a "virtual" circuit-switched leased line.

Although the use of LCNs as opposed to full global addressing reduces overhead in connection-oriented packet networks, the following elements add to that overhead:

1. Connection set-up
2. Network-based, point-to-point error detection and flow control

Figure 8-11 contrasts the overhead of connectionless vs. connection-oriented packet-switched networks as well as several other key differentiating criteria.

Managerial Perspective

The truth is that unless a company plans to set up its own packet-switched network, decisions regarding the relative merits of connectionless vs. connection-oriented packet-switched networks will not have to be considered. It is more likely that a company will access a major commercial packet-switched network service. In that case, what goes on "inside the cloud" is invisible to the users of that packet-switched network. In such a case, an end-user's only concern is how to interface to "the cloud."

Circuit Switching

In a **circuit-switched network,** a switched-dedicated circuit is created to connect the two or more parties, eliminating the need for source and destination address information such as that provided by packetizing techniques explored earlier. The switched-dedicated circuit established on circuit-switched networks makes it appear to the user of the circuit as if a wire has been run directly between the phones of the calling parties. The physical resources required to create this temporary connection are dedicated to that particular circuit for the duration of the connection. If system usage should increase to the point where insufficient resources are available to create additional connections, users would not get a dial tone.

	Overhead	Greatest Strength	Call Set-up	Addressing	Also Known As...	Virtual Circuit	Error Correction	Flow Control
Connectionless	Less	Ability to dynamically reroute data	None	Global	Datagram unreliable	None	Left to end-user devices	Left to end-user devices
Connection-oriented	More	Reliability	Yes	Local logical channel number	Reliable virtual circuit	Created for each call, virtual circuit table established	By virtual circuit	By virtual circuit

Figure 8-11 Connection-Oriented vs. Connectionless Packet-Switched Networks

Managerial Perspective

A BUSINESS PERSPECTIVE ON CIRCUIT-SWITCHING VS. PACKET SWITCHING

If the top-down model were applied to an analysis of possible switching methodologies, circuit switching and packet switching could be properly placed on either the network or technology layers. In either case, to make the proper switching methodology decision, the top-down model layer directly above the network layer—the data layer—must be thoroughly examined. The key data layer question becomes:

- What is the nature of the data to be transmitted, and which switching methodology best supports those data characteristics?

The first data-related criterion to examine is the data source.

- What is the nature of the application program (application layer) that will produce these data?
- Is it a transaction-oriented program or more of a batch update or file-oriented program?

A transaction-oriented program, producing what is sometimes called interactive data, is characterized by short bursts of data followed by variable length pauses due to users reading screen prompts or pauses between transactions. This bursty transaction-oriented traffic, best categorized by banking transactions at an Anytime Money machine, must be delivered as quickly and reliably as the network can possibly perform. In addition to data burstiness, time pressures and reliability constraints are other important data characteristics that will assist in switching methodology decision making.

Applications programs more oriented to large-file transfers or batch updates have different data characteristics than transaction-oriented programs. Overnight updates from regional offices to corporate headquarters or from local stores to regional offices are typical examples. Rather than being bursty, the data in these types of applications are usually large and steadily flowing. These transfers are important, but not often urgent. If file transfers fail, error detection and correction protocols such as those examined in the study of communications software can retransmit bad data or even restart file transfers at the point of failure.

From a business perspective, the two switching techniques vary as well. Whereas both circuit-switched and packet-switched services usually charge a flat monthly fee for access, the basis for usage charges differs. In general, circuit-switched connections are billed according to time connected to the circuit. Leased lines are billed with a flat monthly fee that varies according to circuit mileage. Packet-switched networks usually charge according to packet transfer volume.

To analyze further, if a company gets charged for connection time to the circuit-switched circuit whether they use it or not, they had better be sure that while they are connected, their data is steady and taking full advantage of available bandwidth.

One other switching difference is worth noting. In terms of the need to deliver bursty, transaction-oriented data quickly and reliably, call set-up time can be critical. With circuit-switched applications, dial tone must be waited for, and the number must be dialed and switched through the network. With connection-oriented packet-switched networks, call set-up packets must explore the network and build virtual circuit tables before the first bits of data are transferred. Datagrams don't require call set-up but offer no guarantee of safe delivery.

By first carefully examining the characteristics of the data traffic to be transported, a network analyst can more reliably narrow the choices of possible network services to consider.

Optical or Photonic Switching

The current generation of telecomm switches is electronic or digital in nature, although transmission between these switching devices has been optical for some time. As a result, optical signals must be converted to electronic signals before they can be switched, introducing an extra layer of complexity to the transmission process. Clearly, if this optical to electronic conversion can be avoided, substantial transmission gains can be achieved. Optical switching is a switching process that can be accomplished directly on optical signals without the need to first convert to electronic or digital signals. Optical switching is an underlying requirement for the converged network of the future.

In the optical switching arena, new optical cross-connect switches have been produced that eliminate the need to demultiplex optical signals into electronic cross-connects. All pass-through traffic is handled optically by preconfiguring matching groups of input fibers and output fibers. Between input and output fibers, the light beams are focused via lenses or mirrors and redirected. Signals can be switched in anywhere from 5 to 150 msec depending on the particular technology. The total number of input and output circuits is organized into a matrix that can be 1152 × 1152 circuits or larger. Such optical switching would be considered optical circuit switching, as the entire optical circuits are redirected from the input fiber to the output fiber.

WIDE AREA NETWORKING TRANSMISSION

WAN transmission technologies and services fall into two overall categories. This categorization is based largely on WAN services as they are organized by and purchased from carriers.

- **Local loop transmission** provides bandwidth to users' residences and businesses, generally offering connectivity between these end-points and the carrier network service of choice. Strictly speaking, the term local loop is a geographic designation.
- **Broadband transmission** usually refers to transmission services offering greater than 1.544 Mbps transmission rates and connectivity between network switches or between different carriers' network services. Large consumers of bandwidth may require broadband transmission services to their various corporate locations as access lines.

Local Loop Transmission Alternatives

Local loop transmission, sometimes referred to as "the last mile," provides a means for users' residences or businesses to connect to the voice or data services of their choice. Local loop services must be properly sized to provide sufficient bandwidth to deliver user payloads efficiently and cost effectively. Although a wide variety of local loop transmission services are possible, among the most popular current or emerging local loop technologies are the following:

- POTS (plain old telephone service)
- ISDN (integrated services digital network)
- ADSL (asymmetric digital subscriber line)
- Cable TV

POTS POTS (plain old telephone service) is what most readers are familiar with as the default local loop technology. Users employ V.34 (28.8 Kbps) or V.34+ (33.6 Kbps) modems for transmitting data over the analog POTS network. Because of line impairments and interference on analog transmission lines, optimal transmission rates are seldom achieved and rarely maintained.

ISDN ISDN is somewhat of a phenomenon in the telecommunications industry. Opinions on it range from a revolutionary breakthrough to conviction that it won't ever materialize. ISDN has brought more humor to telecommunications than nearly any other topic, with the various interpretations of the ISDN acronym such as "**I**t **S**till **D**oes **N**othing" and **I** **S**till **D**on't **N**eed" it. ISDN has been described as a solution in search of an application. The need for dial-up access to Internet services at transmission rates greater than those available via POTS has significantly increased the interest in ISDN as a local loop transmission alternative.

Architecture **Narrowband ISDN** is a switched digital network service offering both voice and nonvoice connectivity to other ISDN end-users. Voice, video, and data are all transportable over a single ISDN connection. Depending on bandwidth requirements, voice, video, and data may even be transported simultaneously over a single network connection. The fact that ISDN is a switched service allows temporary connections to be constructed and terminated dynamically among a variety of ISDN sites unlike other digital services of similar bandwidth that are only available as static point-to-point circuits. Figure 8-12 illustrates a high-level view of possible ISDN use.

Narrowband ISDN is deliverable in two different service levels or interfaces. **Basic rate interface,** or **BRI,** is also referred to as **2B+D.** This 2B+D label refers to the channel configuration of the BRI service in which 2 **B**earer channels (64 Kbps each) and one **D**elta or Data channel (16 Kbps) are combined into a 144 Kbps interface. The **bearer channels** are intended to "bear" or carry services such as voice, video, or data transport, and the **d channel** is intended for network management data for call set-up and teardown, calling number identification and other ISDN specific network signals. In some cases, 9.6 Kbps of the D channel may be used for additional X.25 packet-based transmissions, in a service known as ISDN D channel packet service.

The use of this side D channel for carrying signal data is known as **out-of-band signaling** and is one of the key features of ISDN. The "out of band" refers to the fact that the signal control information does not have to be intermingled with the user data, thereby maximizing the available bandwidth for user data. Before ISDN, control information was passed over the network within the user channels in a technique known as **in-band signaling.** This is why many so-called ISDN services such as **automatic number identification** can be offered without ISDN.

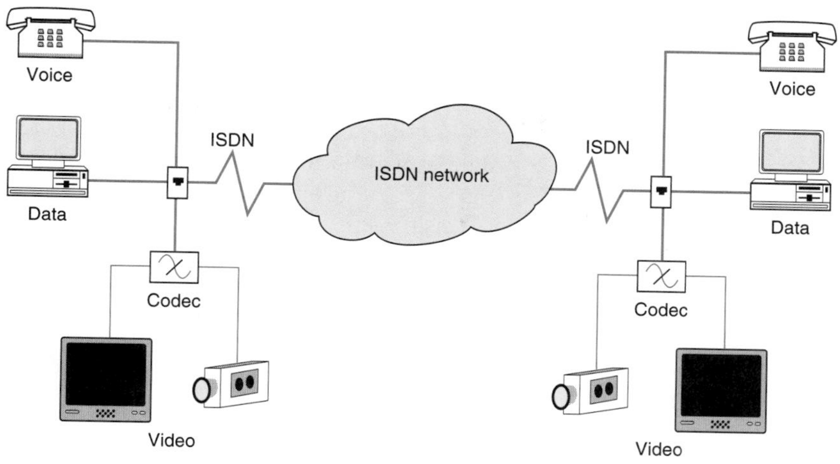

Figure 8-12 ISDN Architecture

A second ISDN service level known as **PRI** or **primary rate interface,** also known as **23B+D,** is composed of 23 64 Kbps Bearer channels and one 64 Kbps data channel for a combined bandwidth of 1.536 Mbps. With a small amount of additional overhead, PRI maps nicely onto the 1.544 Mbps **T-1** circuit. In Europe, ISDN is offered in a **30B+D** configuration yielding 1.984 Mbps. Additional overhead in this case maps nicely to the **E-1** (European digital signal level 1) of 2.048 Mbps. Figure 8-13 summarizes the narrowband ISDN architectural information.

In some cases, users may want variable amounts of bandwidth depending on specific applications and circumstances. In such cases, **multirate ISDN** may be employed. Multirate ISDN uses a technique known as **inverse multiplexing** in which a collection of 64 Kbps B channels are dialed up and combined together into a single logical channel of sufficient bandwidth to meet application needs such as

Services	Video freeze-frame Voice Data	LAN Interconnect Full motion video Voice Data
Transport category	BRI (Basic Rate Interface)	PRI (Primary Rate Interface)
Transport capacity	2 B + D 2 · 64 Kbps 128 Kbps + 16 Kbps 16 Kbps 144 Kbps	23 B + D 23 · 64 Kbps B channels + 64 Kbps D channels 1.536 Mbps
Transport architecture	2-wire Dial-up	T-1
Inter-switch protocol and switching architecture	Signalling System 7 (SS7)	

Figure 8-13 Narrowband ISDN Architectural Information

videoconferencing. To ensure interoperability among inverse multiplexing devices, a standard known as **BONDING (bandwidth on demand interoperability group)** is supported by most ISDN inverse multiplexers.

Services Earlier in its history, ISDN was widely criticized for spotty deployment, leading to "islands of isolation" for those ISDN pioneers who decided to adopt the service. The ISDN coverage situation has improved significantly, but is still not available in all locations throughout the United States. Signaling requirements limit ISDN installations to residences and businesses within 18,000 feet, about 3.4 miles, from the ISDN switch. Another often overlooked service-related issue of ISDN is that, unlike today's analog phones, ISDN customer premises equipment requires external AC power.

Whereas today's POTS customers have grown accustomed to having phone service even during power failures, this would not be the case with ISDN-based phone service. Charges for ISDN vary from carrier to carrier, although most charge a flat monthly rate plus a per minute usage charge.

The heart of an ISDN network is the **ISDN switch.** Before 1992, two competing ISDN switches, **AT&T 5ESS switch** and **Northern Telecom's DMS100 switch,** had slightly different specifications as to interfaces with **customer premises equipment (CPE).** Customer premises equipment that supported the AT&T specification would not operate on Northern Telecom switches and vice-versa. In 1992, the Corporation for Open Systems International and the North American ISDN Users Forum launched an effort entitled Transcontinental ISDN Project 1992 (TRIP `92) to define necessary specifications to eliminate incompatibilities between ISDN networks. The interoperability specification developed is known as **NISDN-1 (National ISDN-1)** and defines a national standard for ISDN switches as well as interswitch communication.

Managerial Perspective

Although deployment and technology incompatibility difficulties may have been overcome, that is not to say that ISDN ordering and implementation are either easy or foolproof. To properly interface an end-user's ISDN equipment to a carrier's ISDN services, desired ISDN features must be specified. In some cases, end-user equipment such as remote access servers must be programmed with **service profile identifier numbers (SPID)** to properly identify the carrier's equipment with which the user equipment must interface. Depending on what combinations of voice, video, or data traffic a user wishes to transmit over ISDN, up to 20 or more **ISDN ordering codes (IOC)** are possible. To try to further simplify this process, an alternative ordering code scheme known as **EZ-ISDN** has been proposed by the National ISDN Users Forum. However, some of the EZ codes duplicate IOC codes, whereas others do not correspond to existing IOC codes, leaving network administrators to do their best to work with carrier personnel to see that required ISDN features are implemented.

Technology Uses of ISDN fall into two broad categories of connectivity:

- Single user-to-office or Internet connectivity
- Office-to-office connectivity

Applications for single user-to-office or Internet connectivity include telecommuting, Internet services access, simultaneous voice and data technical support, and collaborative computing. Applications for office-to-office connectivity include remote office routing, LAN-to-LAN connectivity, and disaster recovery through the use of ISDN lines as a backup to failed leased lines.

To get voice or data onto the ISDN network, the equivalent of an ISDN modem known as an **ISDN terminal adapter** must be employed. A terminal adapter is a type of ISDN CPE (customer premises equipment) that allows analog devices such as phones and fax machines to interface to the all-digital ISDN network. Without the terminal adapter, special digital ISDN phones would have to be purchased to interface directly to the ISDN service. These ISDN terminal adapters are available both as PC cards for installation into a PC's expansion bus, as stand-alone units, or integrated into ISDN data/voice modems.

Practical Advice and Information

Software compatibility issues should not be overlooked. Just as asynchronous modems required compatible communications software with appropriate modem set-up strings, to have ISDN terminal adapters automatically dialing up switched ISDN connections, compatible software and drivers must also be available. This software and drivers must be compatible with installed network operating systems as well as with the purchased terminal adapter. Most often this software complies with NDIS and ODI driver specifications and is supplied by the terminal adapter vendor.

A **network termination unit-1 (NTU-1)** or **(NT-1)** is required to physically connect the ISDN line to a user's ISDN CPE. Most integrated ISDN equipment includes built-in NT-1s, although stand-alone models are available.

To support office-to-office connectivity needs, ISDN terminal adapters and NT-1s are often integrated with internetworking technology such as routers and access servers. It is important at this point to understand why ISDN is well suited to such applications. For occasional communications between offices for LAN to LAN connectivity or database updates, ISDN routers can be much more cost-effective than leased line routers. Although rates may vary according to location, a general rule of thumb is that ISDN access for office-to-office connectivity is cheaper than leased lines of equivalent bandwidth when connectivity needs are 4 hours per day or less. Figure 8-14 illustrates the installation and interaction of a variety of ISDN technology.

ADSL An alternative digital local loop transmission technology is known as **asymmetric digital subscriber line** or **ADSL.** Unlike ISDN, ADSL works along with POTS for traditional voice services. In fact, ADSL works over POTS, at higher frequencies, on the same copper pair that currently carries voice transmission. Unlike using a modem on a voice line, ADSL does not interfere with voice services. That is to say, one could be connected to the Internet via ADSL and still make and receive voice phone calls on the same line.

Architecture The term *asymmetric* in ADSL refers to the service's differing upstream (away from the user) and downstream (toward the user) bandwidths. The bandwidths and associated distance limitations from the carrier's central office of two of the most common ADSL implementations are listed in Figure 8-15. Other transmission speeds and distance limitations are possible.

To transmit high-bandwidth data simultaneously with circuit-switched voice conversation, ADSL employs frequency division multiplexing as described earlier in

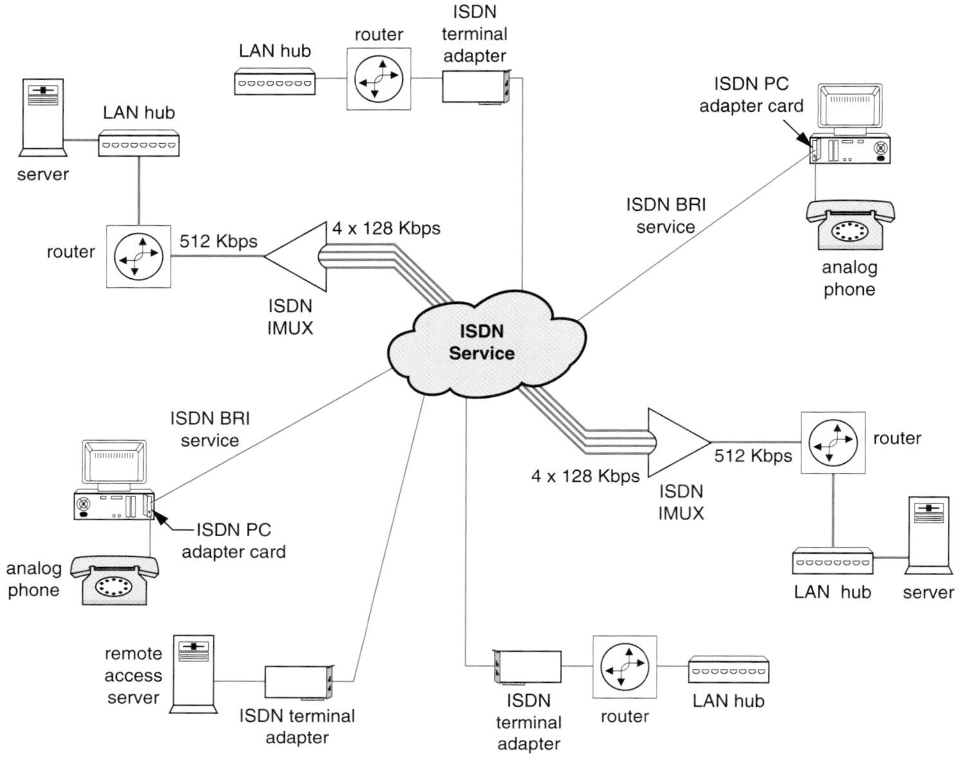

Figure 8-14 ISDN Technology

this chapter. Whereas POTS occupies the lowest frequencies from 0-4 KHz, upstream data use from about 25 KHz to 200 KHz, and downstream data uses from about 250 KHz to 1.1 MHz.

There are currently two competing standards for how ADSL units manage bandwidth for data transmission:

- **Carrierless amplitude and phase (CAP)** treats the frequency range as a single channel and uses a technique similar to quadrature amplitude modulation to build constellations and avoid interference. CAP is a de facto standard, deployed in many trial ADSL units, and was developed by AT&T Paradyne.

ADSL Upstream	ADSL Downstream	Distance Limitation
150 Kbps – 640 Kbps	1.5 Mbps	18,000 ft.
640 Kbps	6.0 Mbps	12,000 ft.
640 Kbps	9.0 Mbps	9,000 ft.

Figure 8-15 ADSL Bandwidth Comparison

- **Discrete multitone (DMT)** divides the 1 MHz of usable bandwidth in 4 KHz channels and adjusts the usage of any of the 4 KHz channels to minimize interference and noise. DMT has been approved as an ADSL standard (ANSI Standard T1.413) by the ANSI T1E1.4 working group.

Several other DSL solutions are currently in various stages of development. All DSL solutions support simultaneous POTS service:

- **VDSL (very high speed digital subscriber line DL)** provides 52 Mbps downstream and between 1.6 and 2.3 Mbps upstream over distances of up to only 1000 ft. It is being explored primarily as a means to bring video on demand services to the home.
- **RADSL (rate adaptive digital subscriber line)** is able to adapt its data rate to the level of noise and interference on a given line. Currently, however, it is not able to support this adaptive rate on a dynamic basis.
- **SDSL (symmetric digital subscriber line)** differs from ADSL in that it offers upstream and downstream channels of equal bandwidth.
- **HDSL (high bit rate digital subscriber line)** offers 1.5 Mbps in each direction at distances of up to 12,000 feet over four wire circuits
- **HDSL2 (high bit rate digital subscriber line—two wire)** has the same performance characteristics as HDSL only over two wire circuits rather than four.

Technology ADSL is an attractive alternative from a carrier's perspective because it does not require carriers to upgrade switching technology. Separate ADSL units, about the size of a modem, are deployed at customer sites and at the central office where voice frequencies are stripped off and passed to existing voice switching equipment, and data frequencies are separated off and forwarded to an Internet service provider. The ADSL units provide an Ethernet 10BaseT interface for data that may be connected to the 10BaseT interface in the user's PC, to a shared 10BaseT hub, or to a 10BaseT router.

Carriers may need to recondition or replace some lines within the 18,000 ft. distance limitation to provide ADSL services. ADSL equipment cannot work through bridge taps and loading coils that carriers have installed over the years to boost voice signals to residences beyond 18,000 ft. from the closest central office. Figure 8-16 illustrates a typical installation of ADSL technology.

Practical Advice and Information

The author participated in an ADSL trial with GTE in West Lafayette, IN, from November 1996 through April 1998. ADSL really works very well. Downstream rates from the Internet were consistently at the expected 1.5 Mbps level, and the data transmission had no effect on existing voice services.

Cable TV as a WAN Service At first glance, it might seem that Cable TV providers have ample bandwidth available for wide area data and voice transmission. When all of the facts are known, however, cable TV as a WAN service may not have such a distinct advantage over carrier-based services such as ADSL.

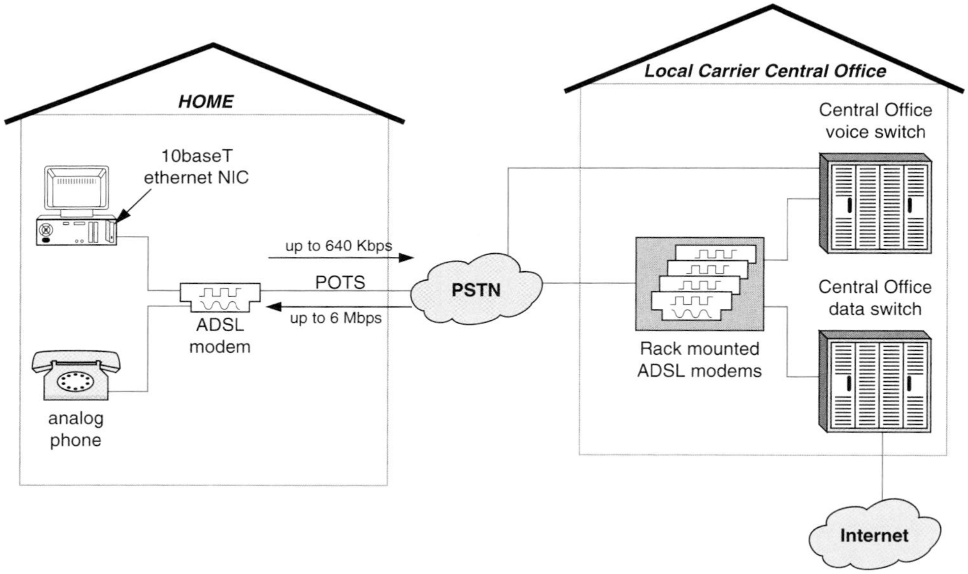

Figure 8-16 ADSL Technology Implementation

Architecture Most cable TV systems were built for one-way broadcast transmission, downstream from the cable head end to the users' residences. To provide the necessary upstream bandwidth, cable providers have two basic options:

- Provide upstream bandwidth over POTS while providing downstream bandwidth in a coordinated fashion over the installed cable plant. This architecture does not deliver simultaneous voice capability as in ADSL architectures.
- Modify cable architecture to support simultaneous upstream and downstream transmission. Current implementations of such an architecture provides up to 30 Mbps downstream and 768 Kbps upstream.

However, providing upstream bandwidth is only one of the architectural obstacles that cable providers must overcome. Whereas phone carriers provide voice service via a switched media architecture (circuit-switching), cable companies provide cable service via a shared media architecture in which an entire neighborhood may be served by the same shared coaxial cable. Therefore, although 30 Mbps downstream bandwidth may sound impressive, one really needs to know among how many users that 30 Mbps will be shared. The access methodologies for sharing cable bandwidth are being standardized as **IEEE 802.14** cable network specifications.

Cable companies, like voice-service carriers, must either develop their own Internet access services or buy these services from an existing Internet service provider to provide transparent Internet access to their customers.

Technology Cable modems will be provided by cable companies and will connect to standard RG-59 coax for the network connection while offering a 10BaseT Ethernet connection for users' local data access. Figure 8-17 illustrates a typical cable modem network implementation.

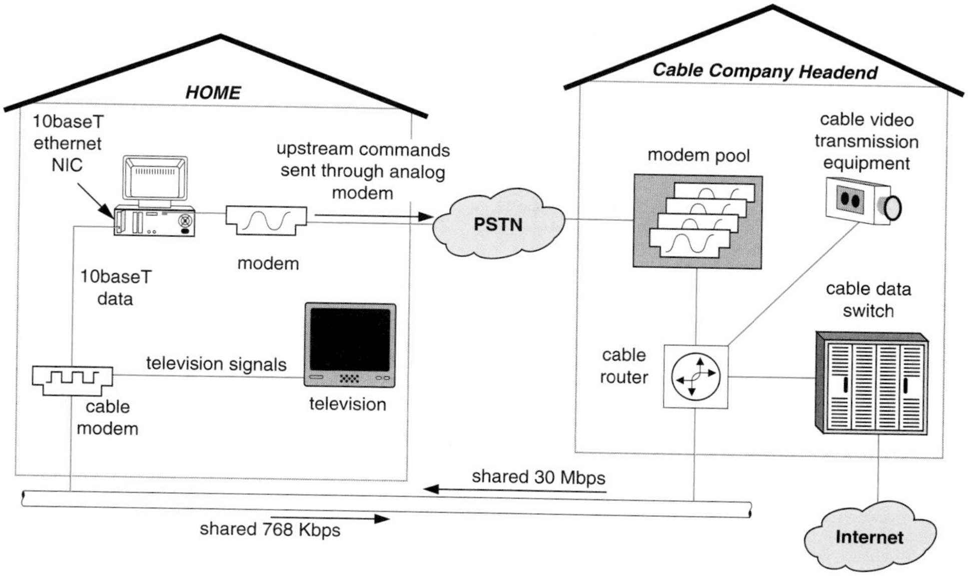

Figure 8-17 Cable Modem Installation

Broadband Transmission

T-1 To effectively establish and manage long-distance telecommunications links between end-user locations as well as between multiple vendors, standards were required to outline both the size and organization of high-capacity digital communications links between carriers. The standard high-capacity digital transmission circuit in North America is known as a **T-1** with a bandwidth of 1.544 Mbps. In other parts of the world, the standard high-capacity digital circuit is known as **an E-1** with a bandwidth of 2.048 Mbps.

T-1 Framing The T-1 circuit is divided into twenty-four 64 Kbps channels to allow more flexible use of the 1.544 Mbps of bandwidth. In this manner, some of the 24 channels can be used for voice while others are used for data. Differentiating between channels is accomplished through a technique known as **framing,** which is really an adaptation of the TDM (time division multiplexing) techniques that were explored earlier in the chapter.

Using a voice digitization technique known as **pulse code modulation (PCM),** eight bits are required to transmit the PCM sampled amplitude of an analog signal. Since 8000 samples/sec are required to ensure quality transmission of digitized voice, and each sample requires eight bits to represent that sampled bandwidth in binary (1s and 0s) notation, 64,000 bits/sec is the required bandwidth for transmission of voice digitized via PCM. A DS-0 circuit has a transmission capacity of exactly 64 Kbps. Twenty-four DS-0s are combined to form a T-1, yielding the fact that a T-1 can carry 24 simultaneous voice conversations digitized via PCM. However, it is important to note that any or all of these 64 Kbps channels could just as easily carry data traffic or any other type of digitized traffic.

In a technique known as **periodic framing** or **synchronous TDM,** 24 channels of eight bits each (192 bits total) are arranged in a **frame.** Each group of eight bits represents one sampling of voice or data traffic to be transmitted on its associated channel.

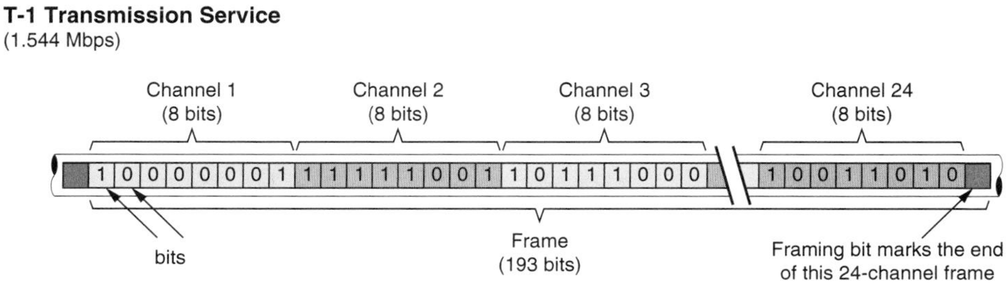

24 channels/frame · 8 bits/channel	= 192 data bits/frame
192 data bits + 1 framing bit	= 193 total bits/frame
193 bits/frame · 8,000 frames/second sampling rate	= 1,544,000 bits/second
	= 1.544 Mbps
	= DS-1
	= T-1

Figure 8-18 T-1 Frame Layout

Each group of eight bits is known as a **time slot.** Twenty-four time slots are grouped into a frame, sometimes also known as a **D-4** frame. Each frame is terminated with a **framing bit** in the 193rd position. Such a frame, sometimes known as a D-4 frame, is illustrated in Figure 8-18.

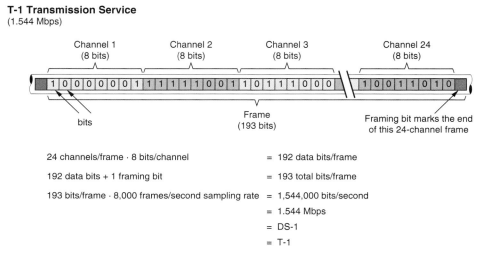

Rather than just using the 193rd bit as a simple frame marker, techniques have been developed to combine the values of sequential framing bits into meaningful arrangements that provide management and error control capabilities for the T-1 transmission service. A group of 12 frames is known as a **superframe,** and a group of 24 frames is known as an **ESF** or **extended superframe.** Superframes and extended superframes are illustrated in Figure 8-19.

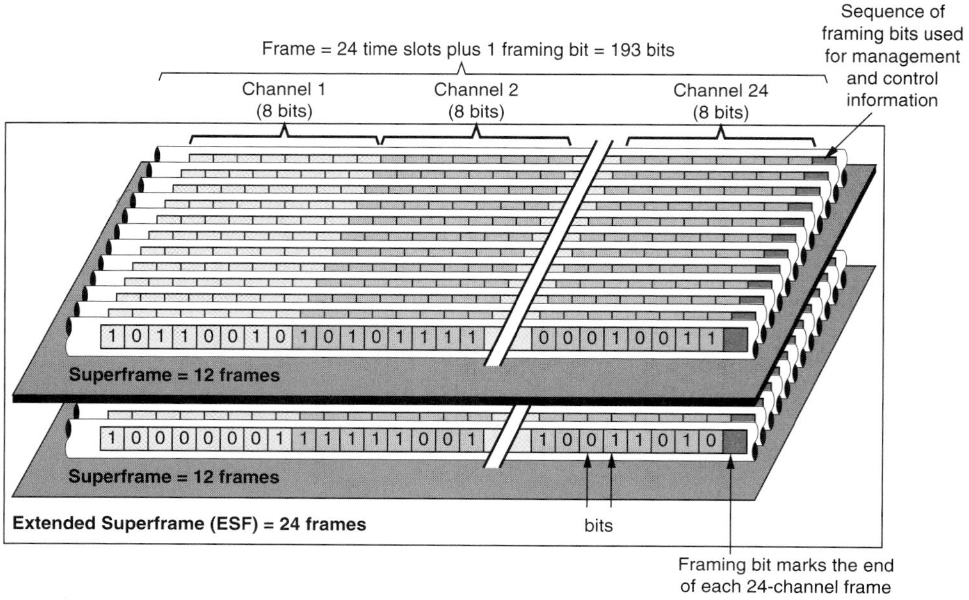

Figure 8-19 Superframes and Extended Superframes

Digital service (DS) hierarchy.

Digital Service Level	Number of Voice Channels	Transmission Rate	Corresponding Transmission Service
DS-0	1	64 Kbps	DS-0 or switched 64K
DS-1	24	1.544 Mbps	T-1 or switched T-1
DS-1C	48	3.152 Mbps	T-1C
DS-2	96	6.312 Mbps	T-2
DS-3	672	44.736 Mbps	T-3
DS-4	4032	274.176 Mbps	T-4

CCITT digital hierarchy.

Digital Service Level	Number of Voice Channels	Transmission Rate	Corresponding Transmission Service
1	30	2.048 Mbps	E-1
2	120	8.448 Mbps	E-2
3	480	34.368 Mbps	E-3
4	1920	139.264 Mbps	E-4
5	7680	565.148 Mbps	E-5

Figure 8-20 Digital Service Hierarchy and CCITT Standards

T-1 Architecture T-1 lines are examples of leased or private lines, also known as dedicated lines, and differ from circuit-switched line usage in several ways.

With leased lines there is no dial tone. The circuit is always open and available. The end-user is billed for the circuit, 24 hours/day, 7 days/week. With leased lines, it is even more imperative than with circuit-switched lines to ensure sufficient data traffic to utilize as close to 100% capacity as possible 100% of the time in order to ensure cost justification of circuit costs. Higher bandwidth leased lines cost more per month than lower bandwidth leased lines.

Before the advent of high-speed packet services and high-speed modems that worked over dial-up (circuit-switched) lines, leased lines were the only available means of high-speed data transfer over a wide area network. Network managers did their best to get the most out of these relatively expensive leased lines through the use of STDMs, explained earlier in the chapter.

Leased lines do not get set up in a matter of seconds in a manner such as circuit-switched lines. In most cases, a 4- to 6-week lead time is required for the installation of a leased line. Leased lines are constructed to circumvent central office switch facilities so as not to monopolize limited circuit-switching capacity.

In some cases, the multiple 64-Kbps channels within a T-1 transport circuit can be manipulated or utilized on an individual basis. A service that offers such capability is known as **fractional T-1** or **FT-1.** The full T-1 circuit must be physically delivered to the customer's premises, but only a given number of 64-Kbps channels within the T-1 are enabled. Fractional T-1 is really just a creative marketing practice on the part of carriers as a means of increasing sales of digital transmission services.

T-1 Technology To access T-1 service offered by carriers users may use a variety of T-1 technology. The most basic piece of T-1 technology is the **T-1 CSU/DSU** (channel service unit/data service unit) that interfaces directly to the carrier's termination of the T-1 service on the customer premises. Physically, a T-1 is delivered as a four-wire service two for transmit, two for receive) most often terminated in a **RJ-48c** jack. Most T-1 CSU/DSUs have a corresponding RJ-48c jack to connect to the carrier's RJ-48c jack. The CSU/DSU will transfer the 1.544 Mbps of T-1 bandwidth to local devices such as routers, PBXs, or channel banks via V.35, RS-530, or RS-449 high-speed serial connectors or RJ-45 connectors for direct connection to 10BaseT or 100BaseT Ethernet networks. Because these T-1 CSU/DSUs play such an important role in a corporation's wide area network, they are often able to communicate status and alarm information to enterprise network management systems via SNMP (simple network management protocol).

T-1 Multiplexers are able to aggregate several lower speed data or voice channels into a single composite T-1 link. T-1 MUXs often have CSU/DSUs built in and require all data input channels to be in digital format adhering to such transmission standards as RS-232, RS-449, or V.35. Voice input to T-1 MUXs must already be digitized in a digital voice PBX and output in a transmission format known as DSX-1. **Fractional T-1 multiplexers** are able to use less than the full 1.544 Mbps of composite T-1 output bandwidth. Obviously, FT-1 multiplexers make good business sense if less than 1.544 Mbps of composite T-1 output bandwidth is sufficient, thereby saving on monthly carrier charges. A **T-1 IMUX** or **inverse multiplexer** is able to combine multiple T-1 output lines to provide high-bandwidth requirements for such applications as LAN-to-LAN communication via routers or high-quality videoconferencing.

A **T-1 channel bank** is similar to but more flexible than a T-1 MUX. A T-1 channel bank is an open chassis-based piece of equipment with a built-in CSU/DSU to which a variety of data and voice input channel cards can be flexibly added. Input data channels may be synchronous or asynchronous at a variety of different speeds and serial transmission protocols. Voice channels may accept analog voice traffic to be digitized by a variety of voice digitization techniques. Output of a T-1 channel bank is typically just a single T-1. Finally, **T-1 switches** can be employed by companies wishing to build their own private wide area networks. T-1 switches are able to switch entire T-1s or particular DSOs among and between other T-1 switches to flexibly deliver voice and data to a variety of corporate locations. Figure 8-21 illustrates the implementation of a variety of T-1 technology.

Sonet **SONET (synchronous optical network)** is an optical transmission service delivering multiple channels of data from various sources thanks to periodic framing or TDM, much like T-1 transmission service. The differences between T-1 and SONET transmission services lie chiefly in the higher transmission capacity of SONET due to its fiber optic media and the slightly different framing techniques used to channelize this higher transmission capacity. SONET is defined by ANSI (American National Standards Institute) T1.105 and T1.106 standards.

Just as the digital service hierarchy defined levels of service for traditional digital service, optical transmission has its own hierarchy of service levels. Rather than being designated as DS levels, optical transmission is categorized by **OC** or **optical carrier** levels and illustrated in Figure 8-22. Because SONET will eventually carry voice, video, and image as well as data, the basic unit of measure is referred to as an **octet** of 8 bits rather than a byte of 8 bits. Byte is usually reserved for referring to data only and is often synonymous with a character.

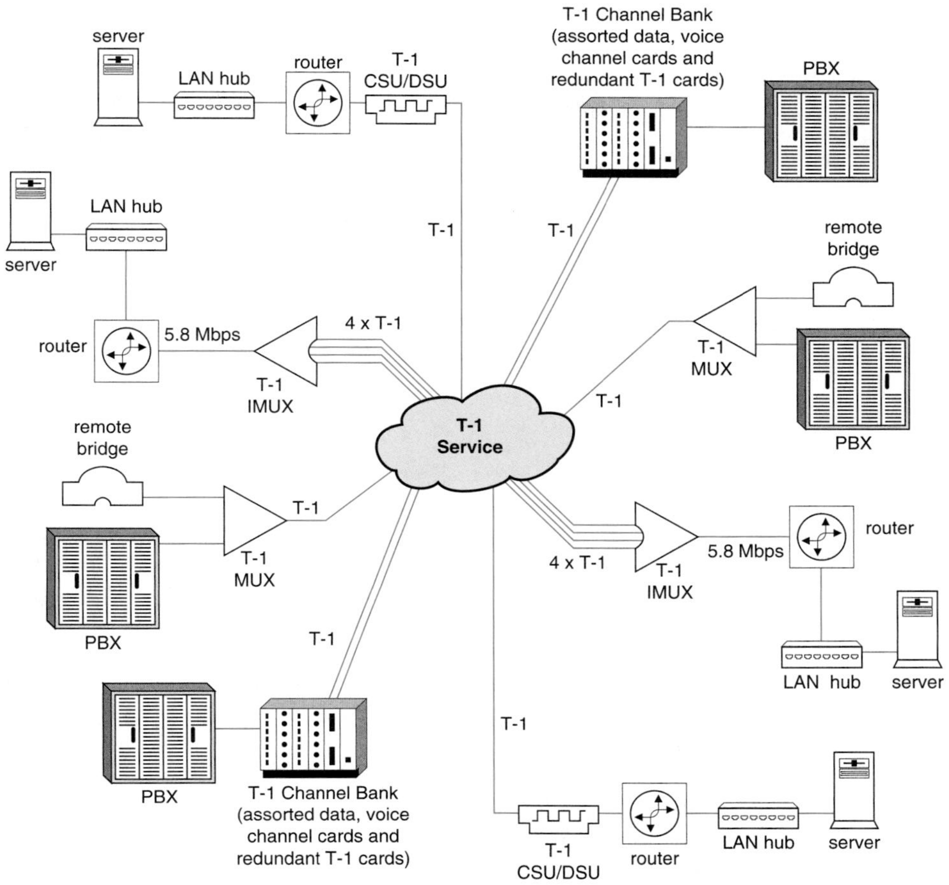

Figure 8-21 T-1 Technology Implementation

SONET's OC (Optical Carrier) standards

Digital Service Level	Transmission Rate
OC-1	51.84 Mbps
OC-3	155.52 Mbps
OC-9	466.56 Mbps
OC-12	622.08 Mbps
OC-18	933.12 Mbps
OC-24	1.244 Gbps
OC-36	1.866 Gbps
OC-48	2.488 Gbps

Figure 8-22 Optical Carrier Levels

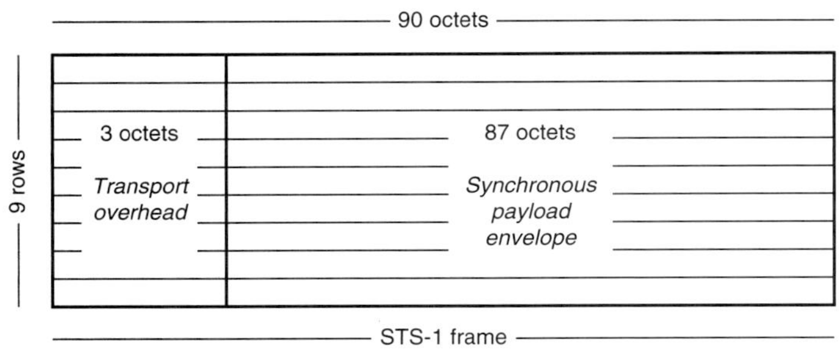

90 octets/row · 8 bits/octet = 720 bits/row

720 bits/row · 9 rows/frame = 6,480 bits/frame

6,480 bits/frame · 8,000 frames/second (sampling rate) = 51,840,000 bits/second

Transfer Rate of 51.84 Mbits/second

Figure 8-23 SONET Framing

SONET Framing In many ways, SONET framing is the same as T-1 framing. The basic purpose of each is to establish markers with which to identify individual channels. Because of the higher bandwidth of SONET (51.84 OC-1 vs. 1.544 Mbps T-1) and potential for sophisticated mixed-media services, more overhead is reserved surrounding each frame than the single bit reserved every 193rd character in a T-1 frame.

Rather than fitting 24 channels per frame delineated by a single framing bit, a single SONET frame or **row** is delineated by 3 octets of overhead for control information followed by 87 octets of **payload.** Nine of these 90 octet rows are grouped together to form a **SONET superframe.** The 87 octets of payload per row in each of the time rows or the Superframe is known as the **synchronous payload envelope** or **SPE.** The electrical equivalent of the **OC-1,** the optical SONET superframe standard, is known as the **STS-1** or synchronous transport signal. The SONET frame structure is illustrated in Figure 8-23.

Virtual Tributaries in SONET Unlike the T-1 frame with its 24 predefined 8-bit channels, SONET is flexible in its definition of the use of its payload area. It can map DS-0 (64 Kbps) channels into the payload area just as easily as it can map an entire T-1 (1.544 Mbps). These flexibly defined channels within the payload area are known as **virtual tributaries or VTs.**

For instance, a T-1 would be mapped into a virtual tributary standard known as **VT-1.5,** with a bandwidth of 1.728 Mbps, the difference between that figure and the 1.544 Mbps T-1 being accounted for by the additional SONET overhead.

The virtual tributaries of SONET are equivalent to circuit-switched transmission services. In addition to the 3 octets per row of transport overhead in OC-1, there is also a variable amount of path overhead imbedded within the SPE to keep track of which virtual tributaries start where within the SPE payload boxcar. This path overhead brings the total overhead to about 4% before any additional overhead embedded within the SPE payload boxcar is considered.

SONET Architecture The architecture of a SONET network is based on a layered hierarchy of transport elements and associated technology. Understanding the differences between these various SONET transport elements, or building blocks, is vital

SONET Building Block	Function/Description
Section	Basic building block of a SONET network. A section is physically built using a single fiber optic cable between two fiber optic transmitter/receivers. A transmitter/receiver is the most basic SONET technology. It is sometimes referred to as an optical repeater or designated as STE (section terminating equipment). All more sophisticated SONET technology includes this capability.
Line	Multiple sections combine to form a SONET line. A SONET line is terminated with LTE (line terminating equipment) such as an add/drop multiplexer.
Path	Multiple lines combine to form a SONET path. A path is an end-to-end circuit most often terminating in SONET access multiplexers that have channel interfaces to lower speed or digital electronic transmission equipment.

Figure 8-24 Hierarchy of SONET Transport Elements

to understanding how to build a SONET and how to decipher the contents of a SONET frame. Figure 8-24 summarizes the characteristics of the various SONET transport elements and Figure 8-25 shows SONET framing with detail as to the overhead associated with each SONET transport element.

Figure 8-25 adds detail to the SONET frame illustrated in Figure 8-23, highlighting where the overhead information for section, line, and path are stored.

SONET Deployment SONET services are currently available within many major metropolitan areas. Accessing such services requires the local carrier to bring the fiber-based ring directly to a corporate location and to assign dedicated bandwidth to each SONET customer. Because of the limited geographic scope of most SONET services, it is most appropriate for those organizations with very high bandwidth needs (OC-1 to OC-192) between multiple locations within the limited SONET service area. Such companies would typically be employing multiple T-3s and looking at SONET as an attractive upgrade path.

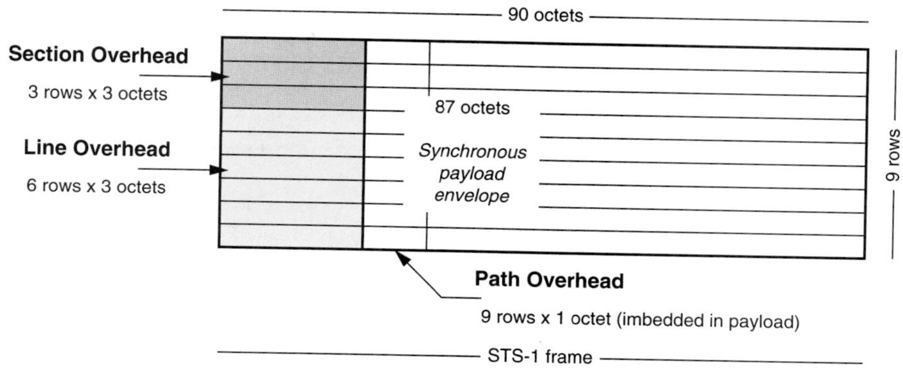

Figure 8-25 Section, Line, and Path Overhead in a SONET Frame

Add-drop multiplexers, sometimes referred to as broadband bandwidth managers or cross-connect switches, are the customary type of hardware used to access SONET services. Such devices are often capable of adding several T-1 or T-3 digital signals together and converting those combined signals into a single, channelized, optical SONET signal, usually OC-3 or higher. In some cases, ATM switches are equipped with SONET interfaces for direct access to either a local SONET ring or commercial SONET services.

Another key advantage of SONET is the fault tolerance and reliability afforded by its fiber-based architecture. In the event of a network failure, traffic can be rerouted. Although numerous SONET architectures are possible, the two principal architectures for SONET deployment are:

- Unidirectional path-switched rings (UPSR) in which all users share transmission capacity around the ring rather than using dedicated segments. UPSRs are most commonly used in access networks and adhere to Bellcore standard GR-1400. UPSRs provide duplicate, geographically diverse paths for each service, thereby protecting against cable cuts and node failures. As the data signal travels in one direction, a duplicate signal travels in the opposite direction for protection. The system automatically switches to the protection signal if there is a problem with the primary data signal. A SONET UPSR topology is illustrated in Figure 8-26.
- Bidirectional line-switched rings (BLSR) in which each user's traffic is specifically rerouted in the case of a fiber failure. BLSR architectures employ two fiber rings with bidirectional traffic flow with each ring's capacity divided equally (by STS) between working and protection bandwidth. BLSR provides survivability in the event of electronic, node, or cable failure by automatically routing traffic away from faults in as little as 50 msec. BLSRs are most commonly used for internode, or carrier backbone networks, and adhere to Bellcore standard GR-1230. A SONET BLSR topology is illustrated in Figure 8-27.

Wavelength Division Multiplexing SONET network capacity can be increased substantially with the introduction of **wavelength division multiplexing.** By transmitting more than one wavelength (color) of light simultaneously on a given single-mode fiber, multiple optical signals and the embedded data contained therein can be transmitted simultaneously. Wavelengths are between 50 and 100 GHz apart. When eight or more distinct wavelengths are simultaneously transmitted, the term

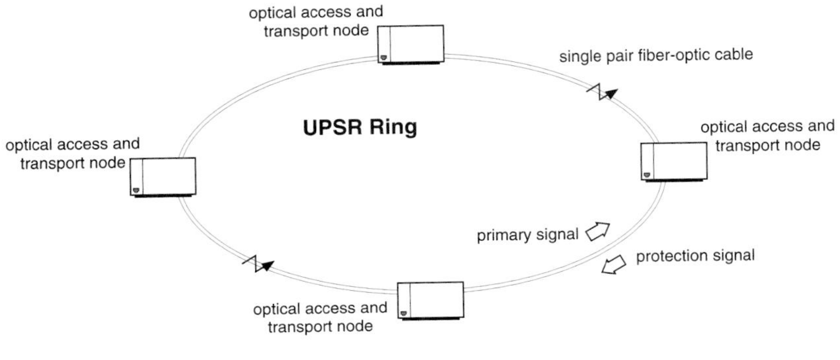

Figure 8-26 SONET UPSR Topology

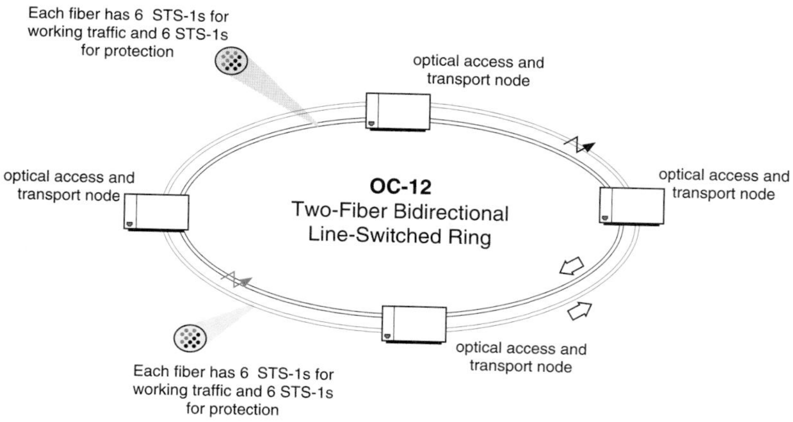

Figure 8-27 SONET BLSR Topology

DWDM (dense wavelength division multiplexing) is often used. WDM should theoretically be able to produce transmission capacity on a single fiber in the Terabit per second (1000 Gbps) range. Individual DWDM wavelengths are referred to as lambdas and have a transmission capacity of 2.4 Gbps each. Sixty-four lambdas per fiber can be transmitted with current technology while hundreds of lambdas per fiber are possible in the future.

Conclusion: So what is SONET? SONET is a service-independent transport function that can carry the services of the future such as B-ISDN (broadband ISDN) or HDTV (high-definition television) as easily as it can carry the circuit-switched traffic of today such as DS-1, and DS-3. It has extensive performance monitoring and fault location capabilities. For instance, if SONET senses a transmission problem, it can switch traffic to an alternate path in as little as 50 msec (1000ths of a second). This network survivability is due to SONET's redundant or dual-ring physical architecture. Based on the OC hierarchy of standard optical interfaces, SONET has the potential to deliver multigigabyte bandwidth transmission capabilities to end-users.

Managerial Perspective

SONET availability is currently limited to large metropolitan areas in most cases. SONET availability implies that a high-capacity, dual-ring, fiber optic cable-based transmission service is available between the customer premises and the carrier central office. SONET services cost about 20% more than conventional digital services of identical bandwidth. The benefit of the 20% premium is the network survivability offered by SONET's dual ring architecture. Unless a corporation has identified mission-critical network transmissions requiring fault-tolerant circuits, SONET's benefits may not be worth the added expense.

WIDE AREA NETWORK SERVICES

As illustrated in Figure 8-8, the foundation of any wide area network architecture depends on the particular switching and transmission architectures employed therein. Wide area network services that are offered to consumers depend on these underlying transmission and switching architectures. Switching architectures and transmission architectures have been reviewed previously in this chapter. In this section, different wide area network services are reviewed and the business aspects of these services, the underlying switching and transmission architectures required, and the technology employed to interface to such services are explained.

X.25

X.25 is an international CCITT standard that defines the interface between terminal equipment (DTE) and any packet-switched network (the cloud). It is important to note that X.25 does *not* define standards for what goes on *inside* the cloud. One of the most common misconceptions is that the X.25 standard defines the specifications for a packet-switching network. On the contrary, X.25 only ensures that an end-user can depend on how to get information into and out of the packet-switched network.

X.25 is a three-layer protocol stack corresponding to the first three layers of the OSI model. The total effect of the three-layer X.25 protocol stack is to produce packets in a standard format acceptable by any X.25-compliant public packet-switched network. X.25 offers network transparency to the upper layers of the OSI protocol stack. Figure 8-28 illustrates the relationship of the X.25 protocol stack to the OSI model.

Architecture The X.25 standard consists of a three-layer protocol that ensures transparent network access to OSI layers 4–7. In other words, applications running on one computer that wish to talk to another computer do not need to be concerned with anything having to do with the packet-switched network connecting the two computers. In this way, the X.25-compliant packet-switched network is nothing more than a transparent delivery service between computers.

The physical layer (layer 1) protocol of the X.25 standard is most often RS-232 or some other serial transmission standard. The data-link layer (layer 2) protocol is

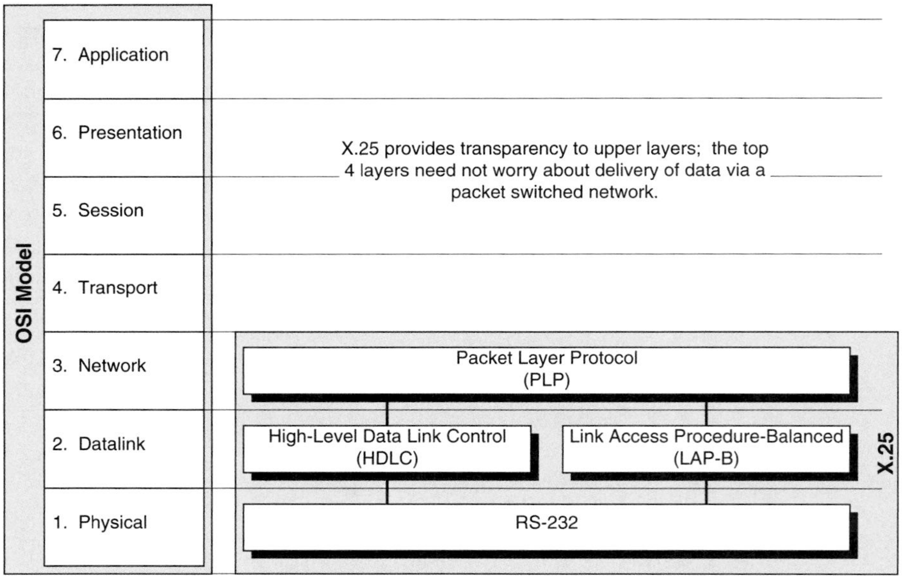

Figure 8-28 X.25 and the OSI Model

Flag	Address field	Control field	Information field	Frame check sequence	Flag
8 bits	8 bits	8 bits	Variable	16 bits	8 bits

Figure 8-29 X.25 Data-Link Layer Protocol: HDLC

known as **HDLC** or **high-level data link control.** HDLC is very similar to IBM's SDLC in structure. Functionally, HDLC accomplishes the same things as any other data-link layer protocol, such as Ethernet or token ring:

- Organizes data into structured frames that may contain more than one packet
- Ensures reliable delivery of data via error checking
- Provides point-to-point data delivery between adjacent nodes

Figure 8-29 illustrates a HDLC frame. In the case of HDLC and X.25, error checking is achieved via a 16-bit frame check sequence, while the Control Field transports important management information such as frame sequence numbers and requests for retransmission. Newer implementations of X.25 use **LAP-B,** or **link access procedure-balanced,** a subset and functional equivalent of the full HDLC frame, as a data-link layer protocol. The network layer (layer 3) X.25 protocol is known as **PLP** or **packet-layer protocol.** Remembering that the job of any OSI layer 3 network layer protocol is the establishment, maintenance, and termination of end-to-end connections, PLP's main job is to establish, maintain, and terminate virtual circuits within a connection-oriented packet-switched network.

Figure 8-30 lists important standards related to X.25 and a brief explanation of their importance:

Standard	Explanation/Importance
X.121—Global Addressing Scheme	As packet switching networks have become global in nature, a global addressing scheme was necessary to allow transparent global access to these networks. X.121 defines zone codes, country codes, and PSN codes within countries. This four-digit global addressing prefix is followed by up to 10 digits to uniquely identify the destination address node.
X.28 and X.32—Dial-Up Access Directly into PADs	X.28 (asynchronous) and X.32 (synchronous) define standards that allow users to dial-up a PAD and subsequently place a call over the packet-switched network.
X.75—Internetworking Packet-Switched Networks	X.25 defined the interface from the end-user device into the packet-switched network cloud. A standard was required to define a standardized interface between different packet-switched networks. X.75 is that standard and has been referred to as the packet-switched network gateway protocol.

Figure 8-30 X.25-Related Standards

Technology X.25 requires data to be properly packetized by the time the information reaches the cloud. Terminals and computers that do not possess the X.25 protocol stack internally to produce properly formatted packets employ a **PAD** or **packet assembler/disassembler** to packetize their output data into X.25 format for entry into the cloud. Such devices usually have several (4–16) RS-232 serial ports for input from PCs, terminals, or host computer ports that wish to transmit traffic via a carrier's X.25 service. These input ports are typically asynchronous. The single composite output port is synchronous and is most often limited to 2 Mbps, although most X.25 carrier services are limited to about 9.6 Kbps. This seemingly excess composite output capacity is due to the fact that many X.25 PADs are also capable of accessing higher speed packet-switched network services such as frame relay, which is explained in the next section. Inside the carrier's X.25 cloud, X.25 switches are connected together in a mesh topology and are most often connected to each other via high-speed digital transmission services such as T-1. Figure 8-31 illustrates X.25 technology implementation.

Frame Relay

Figure 8-32 illustrates the relationship between a packet-switched network service such as X.25 and other packet-switched and circuit-switched network services. The differences between circuit switching and packet switching have already been explained; the differences among the various packet-switched network services are based largely around transmission speed and overhead.

To understand how these packet services could be made faster, the source of the overhead or slowness of the existing X.25 packet-switching networks must first be examined. Recall from the previous discussion of connection-oriented packet-switched networks that error-checking and retransmission requests were done on a

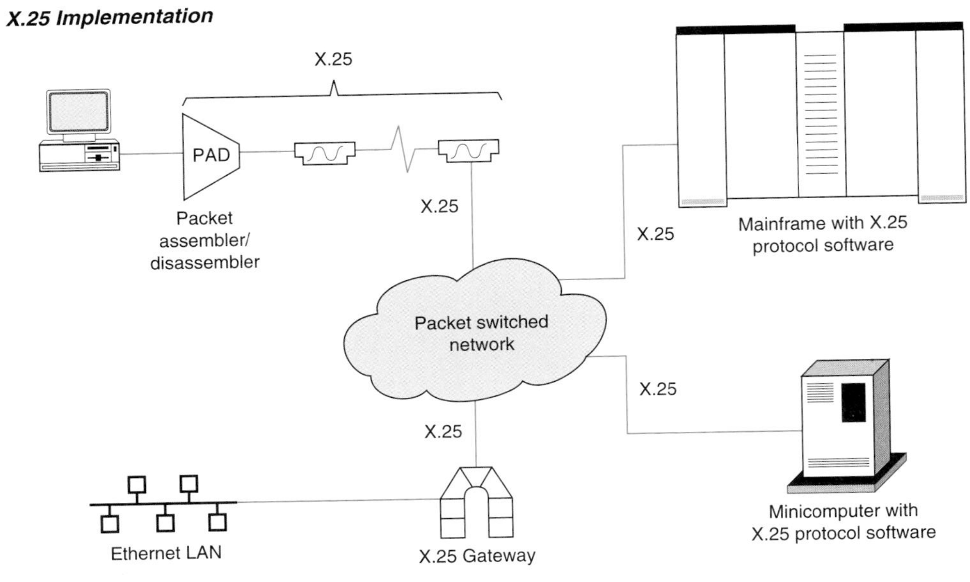

Figure 8-31 X.25 Technology Implementation

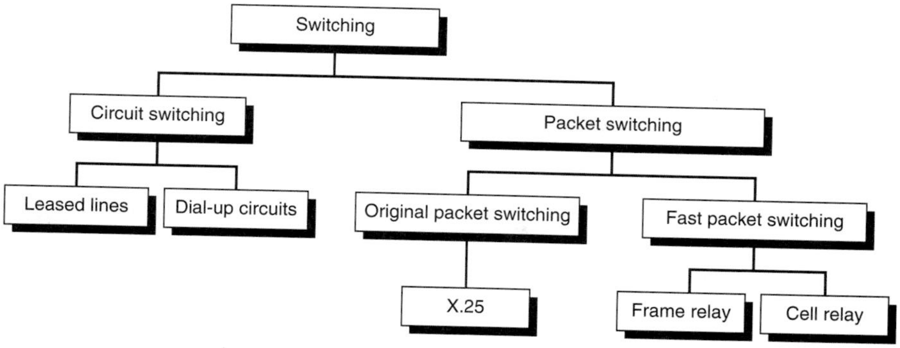

Figure 8-32 Switched Network Services Hierarchy

point-to-point basis, between adjacent packet switches. This point-to-point oriented error checking is sometimes called hop-by-hop error checking.

At the time X.25 was first introduced about 20 years ago, the long-distance circuits connecting the X.25 packet switches were not nearly as error free as they are today. Transmission errors are measured by **bit error rate (BER).** As a result, to guarantee end-to-end error free delivery, it was necessary to check for errors and request retransmissions on a point-to-point or hop-by-hop basis at every X.25 packet switch in the network. Although necessary, this constant error checking and correction added significant overhead and therefore delay to the X.25 packet transmission process.

Today's long-distance digital transmission systems are largely fiber based and far less error prone than those of 20 years ago. As a result, new packet-switching methodologies such as **frame relay** were introduced that sought to take advantage of the decreased bit error rate on today's transmission systems. The basic design philosophy is simple:

- Given the quality of the transmission system, stop all point-to-point error correction and flow control within the network itself and let the end-nodes worry about it!

The end nodes, such as PCs, servers, and mainframes, would use higher level (layers 4–7) protocols to perform their own error checking. In the case of a PC, this would likely be a sliding window file transfer protocol. This philosophy works fine as long as the basic assumption, the low bit error rate of today's transmission system, holds true. If it does not, then retransmissions are end-to-end spanning the entire network, rather than point-to-point between adjacent packet switches.

Architecture

Error Detection and Correction It is important to distinguish between **error detection** and **error correction.** Both frame relay and X.25 perform point-to-point error detection by comparing generated **CRCs (cyclic redundancy checks)** with transmitted CRCs, also known as **FCSs (frame check sequences).** The difference and resultant processing time savings for frame relay occur in the action taken on the detection of an error.

An X.25 switch will always send either a positive ACK or negative NAK acknowledgment on receipt of each packet and will not forward additional packets until it receives an ACK or NAK. If a NAK is received, the packet received in error will be retransmitted. Packets are stored in X.25 switches in case a NAK is received, necessitating retransmission. For this reason X.25 packet switching is sometimes called a **store-and-forward** switching methodology.

On the other hand, if a frame relay switch detects an error when it compares the computed vs. transmitted FCSs, the bad frame is simply discarded. The correction and request for retransmission of bad frames are left to the end-node devices: PCs, modems, computers, and their error-correction protocols. Technically speaking, in frame relay, there is point-to-point error detection, but only end-to-end error correction. Whereas X.25 networks were typically limited to 9.6 Kbps, frame relay networks typically offer transmission speeds of T-1 (1.544 Mbps) and occasionally T-3 (44.736 Mbps). Figure 8-33 illustrates point-to-point vs. end-to-end error correction.

In terms of the OSI model, the difference between X.25 packet switching and frame relay is simple. Frame relay is a two-layer protocol stack (physical and data link) and X.25 is a three-layer protocol stack (physical, data-link, and network). There is no network layer processing in frame relay, accounting for the decreased processing time and increased throughput rate.

Flow Control Although end-node devices such as PCs and modems can handle the error detection and correction duties shed by the frame relay network with relative ease, **flow control** is another matter. End nodes can only manage flow control between themselves and whatever frame relay network access device they are linked

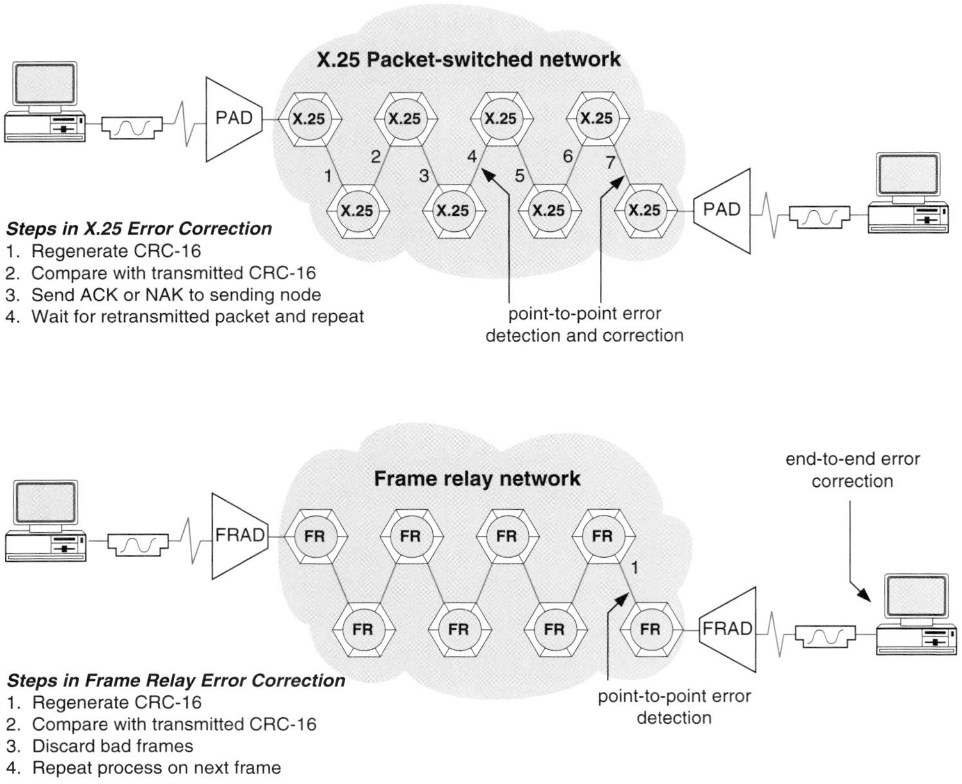

Figure 8-33 Point-to-Point vs. End-to-End Error Correction

to. There is no way for end nodes to either monitor or manage flow control within the frame relay network itself. Some frame relay switch vendors have implemented their own flow control methodologies, which is sufficient if only that vendor's switches are being used.

Referring to the frame relay frame structure diagram in Figure 8-34 there are three bits in the frame definition known as **BECN, FECN,** and **DE,** which stand for **backward explicit congestion notification, forward explicit congestion notification,** and **discard eligibility.** BECN is sent back to the original source user to tell the FRAD to throttle back its transmission onto the frame relay network while FECN warns the destination recipient of this frame of the congested network conditions. If the discard eligible field is set, then the carrier managing the frame relay network is granted permission to discard such frames to relieve network congestion. These bits are the elements of a scheme to allow frame relay devices to dynamically adjust flow control. Some frame relay devices even have the ability to read or write to these fields.

Practical Advice and Information

The only problem is, what action should be taken by a given device in the event that any of these bits indicate a flow control problem has not necessarily been agreed upon or uniformly implemented by frame relay technology manufacturers? Unless you were responsible for setting up your own frame relay network, you might not think much of this problem. On the other hand, it represents the need to have a healthy dose of skepticism when shopping for data communications devices, even when those devices "support all applicable standards." If standards are not uniformly implemented by technology manufacturers, they are of little use.

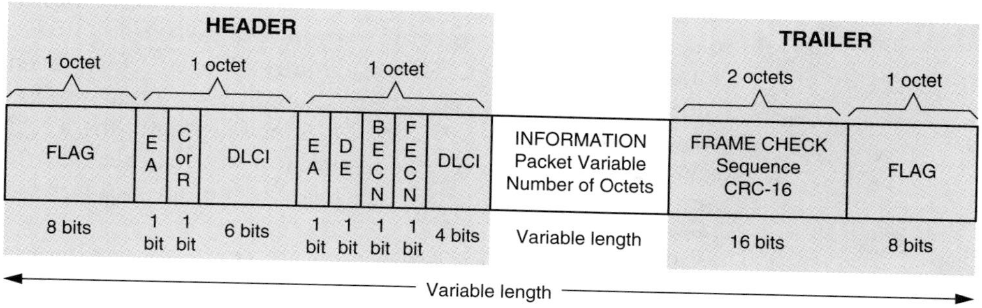

FLAG	unique bit sequence that indicates beginning of frame
EA	extended address — standard address is two octets; this bit setting can extend address to 3 or 4 octets
C or R	command or response — application specific — not used by standard frame relay protocol
DLCI	data-link connection identifier (address) — identifies particular logical connection over a single physical path
EA	extended address — standard address is two octets; this bit setting can extend address to 3 or 4 octets
DE	discard eligibility — used by frame relay switches for flow control
BECN	backward explicit congestion notification — used by frame relay switches for flow control
FECN	forward explicit congestion notification — used by frame relay switches for flow control
DLCI	data-link connection identifier (address) — identifies particular logical connection over a single physical path
INFORMATION	minimum number of octets — enough to make total frame at least 7 octets long. Maximum number of octets is 8000. Carries upper layer data
FRAME CHECK	frame check sequence for error detection — also called cyclic redundancy check
FLAG	unique bit sequence that indicates end of frame

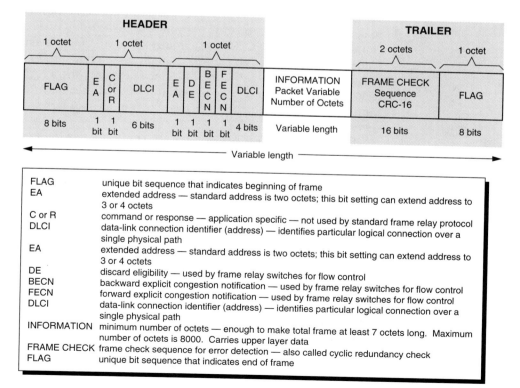

Figure 8-34 Frame Relay Frame Layout

In a similar manner to X.25 packet formation, frame relay frames are formatted within the FRAD, or in computers or PCs that have frame relay protocol software loaded to build frame relay frames directly. The **frames** that a frame relay network forwards are variable in length, with the maximum frame transporting nearly 8000 characters at once. Combining these potentially large, variable length frames with the low overhead and faster processing of the frame relay switching delivers a key characteristic of the frame relay network: High throughput with low delay.

Figure 8-34 illustrates the frame definition for frame relay networks. This frame definition is said to be a subset of the LAP-D protocol. **LAP-D** stands for **link access procedure—D Channel,** where the D channel refers to the 16-Kbps delta channel in BRI (basic rate interface) ISDN (integrated services digital network).

The variable length frames illustrated in Figure 8-34 can be a shortcoming, however. Because there is no guarantee as to the length of a frame, there can be no guarantee as to how quickly a given frame can be forwarded through the network and delivered to its destination. In the case of data, this lack of guaranteed timed delivery or maximum delay is of little consequence.

However, in the case of more time-sensitive information such as voice or video, it could be a real issue. Digitized voice or video can be packetized or put into frames like any other data. The problem arises when framed voice and video do not arrive in a predictable timed fashion for conversion back to understandable voice and video. As a result, frame relay is often described as a data-only service. That's not exactly true. Options do exist to transport digitized, compressed voice transmissions via a frame relay network. However, most voice over frame relay technology is proprietary, requiring all FRADs and/or switches that support voice over frame relay to be purchased from the same vendor.

Virtual Circuits Frame relay networks most often employ **PVCs (permanent virtual circuits)** to forward frames from source to destination through the frame relay cloud. **SVCs (switched virtual circuit)** standards have been defined but are not as readily available from all carriers. Remembering that an SVC is like a dial-up call, to transport data over an SVC-based frame relay network, a LAN NOS such as Netware or Windows NT would have to communicate call set-up protocol information to the frame relay network before sending a data request or transaction update to a remote server.

Frame relay transmission rates are commonly as high as 1.544 Mbps and occasionally as high as 44.736 Mbps. Remembering that multiple PVCs can exist within the frame relay network cloud, another key advantage of frame relay over circuit-switched options such as leased lines is the ability to have multiple PVCs supported from only one access line. From a cost justification standpoint, this would allow a frame relay user to replace multiple leased line connections with a single access line to a frame relay network. Remember also, that frame relay network charges are based on usage, whereas circuit-switched leased lines charges are based on flat monthly fees whether or not they are used. Figure 8-35 illustrates the concept of multiple PVCs per single access line.

Dynamic Bandwidth Allocation Another important characteristic afforded by the many transmission options available with the mesh network of the frame relay cloud is the ability to allocate bandwidth dynamically. In other words, up to the transmission limit of the access line and the circuits between the frame relay switches, the frame relay network will handle bursts of data by simply assembling and forward more frames per second onto the frame relay network, over multiple PVCs if required.

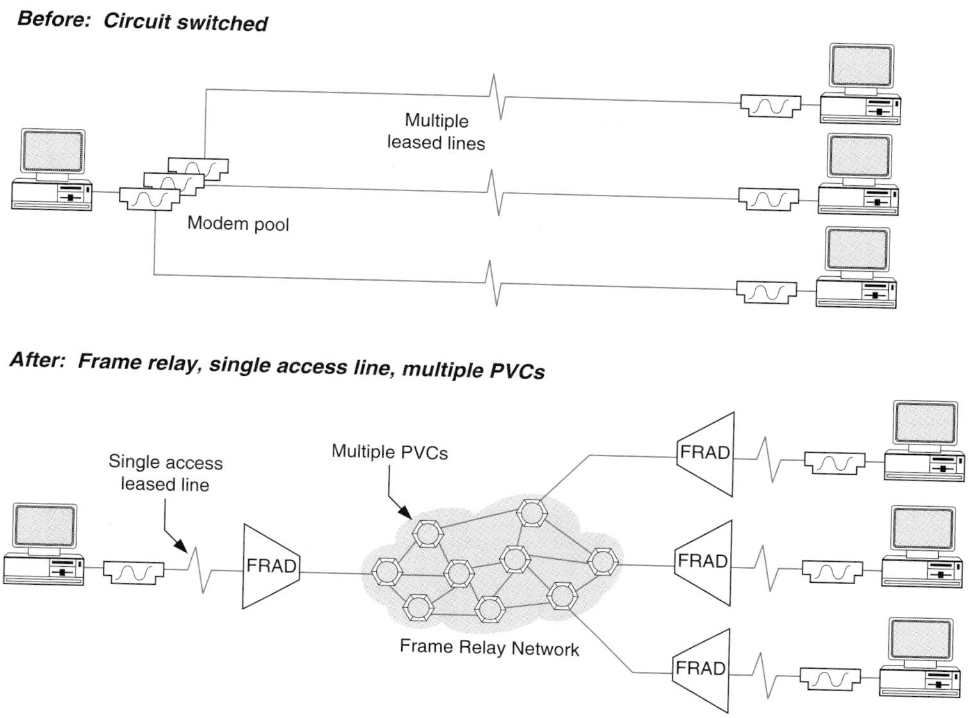

Figure 8-35 Multiple PVCs per Access Line

This ability to handle bursty traffic is especially appealing for LAN interconnection. Inter-LAN communication tends to be bursty, with intermittent requests for data and file transfers. Remembering that this Inter-LAN communication should be as transparent as possible, frame relay's ability to handle bursty traffic by dynamic bandwidth allocation is a real advantage. In the case of frame relay network access for LAN interconnection, the internetwork bridge or router is often integrated with a frame relay assembler/disassembler or frame relay protocol software.

A word of caution however. "Bursty" traffic is not easy to define. How large a burst, in terms of maximum bandwidth demand, and of what duration the frame relay network is expected to be able to handle are important questions. An attempt has been made to structure burstiness according to the following two characteristics:

- **CIR** or **committed information rate** refers to the minimum bandwidth guaranteed to users for "normal" transmission.
- **CBS** or **committed burst size** defines the extent to which a user can exceed the CIR over a period of time. If a user exceeds the CBS, the frame relay network reserves the right to discard frames to deliver guaranteed CIRs to other users.

Protocol Independence and Network to Network Interface Another frame relay feature that is appealing for LAN interconnection is that frame relay merely encapsulates user data into frames and forwards it to the destination. Frame relay is merely a delivery service. It does not process user data and is therefore protocol independent or protocol transparent. It can forward SNA/SDLC traffic just as easily as it can forward TCP/IP or Novell IPX traffic.

An issue hindering widespread global use of frame relay is the need for better coordination among the different frame relay network vendors in order to offer transparent access between them in a manner similar to the standard interfaces developed by phone companies for voice traffic. A conceptual standard known as **NNI** or **network to network interface** would be the functional equivalent of the X.75 internetwork standard for X.25 packet-switched networks.

Technology

As can be seen in Figure 8-33, the technology configuration for the X.25 packet-switched network and the frame relay network are amazingly similar. In the case of the frame relay network, the access device is known as a **FRAD** or **FAD** (frame relay or frame assembler/disassembler) rather than a PAD, and the switching device is known as a **frame relay switch,** rather than a packet or X.25 switch. FRADs are also known as **frame relay access devices.** FRADs and frame relay switches are available in numerous configurations and integrated with numerous other internetworking devices such as bridges, routers, multiplexers, and concentrators.

Conclusion: What Is Frame Relay?

First and foremost, frame relay is an interface specification. The LAP-D data link layer protocol defines a frame structure that contains destination address, error checking, control information, and user data all in a single protocol layer frame. It is this interface specification that allows faster processing to take place within the frame relay network.

Second, frame relay is also a network service, offered by several regional and long-distance phone companies primarily for the purpose of LAN interconnection. Frame relay's ability to dynamically allocate bandwidth over a single access line to the frame relay network make it particularly well suited for the bursty nature of inter-LAN traffic. Private frame relay networks can be established as well.

Finally, frame relay could also be considered a switching architecture. What goes on inside the frame relay network cloud is transparent to end-users, as long as the interface specification allows frame relay frames to enter the cloud and exit the cloud. However, there are true frame relay switches designed specifically to forward frame relay frames at an optimal rate. A mesh network composed of these "native" frame relay switches could legitimately be considered a switching architecture.

SMDS

SMDS, switched multimegabit data service, is a connectionless network service delivering switched LAN internetworking and data dial tone in a metropolitan area network deployment while adhering to the **IEEE 802.6** and **DQDB (distributed queue dual bus)** protocols by delivering fixed length cells of data to their destinations via a SONET transmission system at speeds up to T-3 (45 Mbps). Architecturally, it differs from frame relay primarily because it is a connectionless service and does not support virtual circuits.

Cell Relay—ATM

Architecture

As seen in Figure 8-32 (switched network services hierarchy), **cell relay** is another "fast packet" switching methodology and a key part of future network architectures. **ATM** or **asynchronous transfer mode** is the widely accepted standardized cell relay transmission service. The key physical difference between cell relay and frame relay is that, unlike the variable length frame relay frames, all cells in ATM networks are of a fixed length, 53 octets long (an octet is 8 bits). Forty-eight of the octets per cell are reserved for user data or information from higher layer protocols plus a 5-octet header.

ATM Protocol Model Because of the constant-length cells, cell relay switches can perform much faster than frame relay switches by depending on constant cell length, because more instructions for processing can be included in firmware and hardware. The constant-sized cells also lead to a predictable and dependable processing rate and forwarding or delivery rate. The lack of a predictable maximum delivery delay was a key weakness in frame relay.

This predictable delivery time of each and every cell makes cell relay a better choice for transmission of voice or video applications as well as data. Cell relay switching can provide switching capability on a similar scale to the highest capacity transmission alternatives such as T-3s (45 Mbps) and fiber optic transmission circuits with capacity of up to 2.4 gigabytes/psec.

ATM is presently defined by two different cell formats. One is called the **UNI (user-network interface)** and carries information between the user and the ATM network. The second cell standard is known as **NNI (network-network interface)** and carries information between ATM switches. Figure 8-36 depicts the ATM UNI protocol model that conceptually illustrates how inputs of data, voice, or video can all be processed and transmitted as homogeneous ATM cells, whereas Figure 8-37 relates the layers of the ATM model to the layers of the OSI model.

ATM Cell Structures User inputs of data, video, or voice must be processed into fixed-length ATM cells before they can be forwarded and delivered by ATM switches. This processing is done on the **AAL** or **ATM adaptation layer.** Depending on the type of input (voice, video, or data) a different type of adaptation process may be used, and different types of delivery requirements or priorities can be assigned within the ATM network. After emerging from the ATM adaptation layer, all cells are in an identical format as illustrated and explained in Figure 8-38.

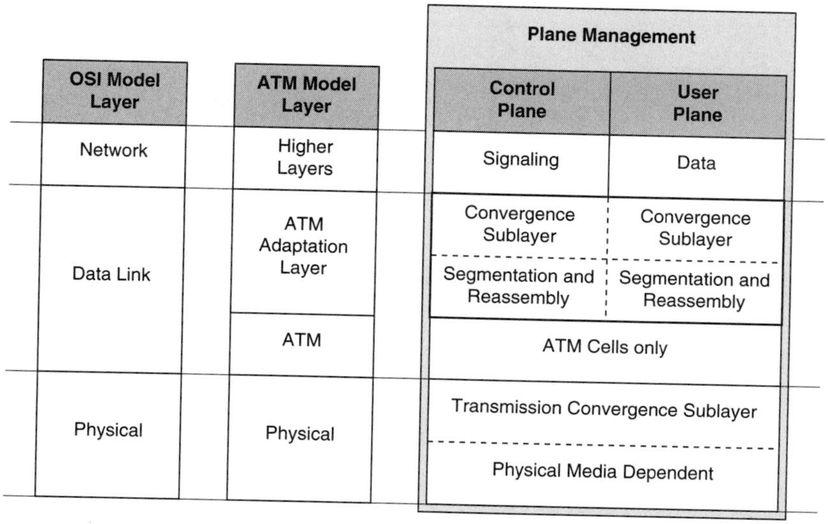

Figure 8-36 ATM UNI Protocol Model

OSI Layer	ATM Layer	Explanation
Network	Signaling	Fault management, performance management, connection management
	Data	User data, voice, video input that must be adapted into ATM cells
Data Link	AAL — ATM adaptation Layer	Divided further into CS, convergence sublayer, and SAR, Segmentation and reassembly sublayer. Converts input data, video, and voice into ATM cells
	ATM — asynchronous transfer mode	ATM cell processing layer, flow control, Address assignment and translation
Physical	TCS — transmission convergence sublayer	Cell delineation, header error check, path overhead signals, multiplexing
	PMD — physical medium dependent	Physical transport and connectivity, framing, bit timing, line coding, loopback testing

Figure 8-37 ATM Model vs. OSI Model

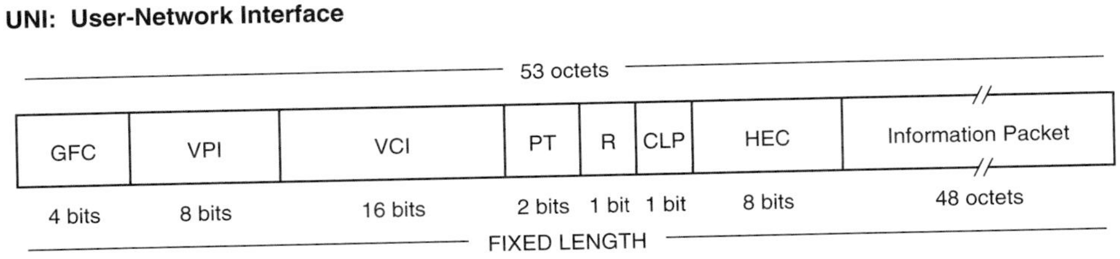

ATM Cell Field Name	Explanation
GFC: Generic Flow Control	Multiple devices of various types (voice, video, data) can gain access to an ATM network through a single access circuit. These different devices may require different flow control signaling.
VPI: Virtual Path Identifier	The virtual path identifier uniquely identifies the connection between two end-nodes and is equivalent to the virtual circuits of X.25 or frame relay networks. A VPI consists of several VCIs (see next entry).
VCI: Virtual Channel Identifier	Because ATM can carry multiple types of information (voice, video, data), several channels of information could be traveling along the same end-to-end connection simultaneously. The VCI uniquely identifies a particular channel of information within the virtual path.
PT: Payload Type	Payload type indicates whether cell contains user information or network control information.
CLP: Cell Loss Priority	If an ATM transmission exceeds its allotted bandwidth, including concessions for burstiness, a cell can be marked by the ATM network in a process known as policing. If congestion occurs on the network, these marked cells are the first to be discarded.
HEC: Header Error Control	Header error control ensures that header information contains no errors. The biggest concern is that the VPI and VCI are correct.

Figure 8-38 ATM Cell Structure

ATM AAL Protocols ATM adaptation layer protocols are designed to optimize the delivery of a wide variety of possible types of user inputs or traffic. However, all of these different types of traffic vary in a relatively small number of ways:

- Delay sensitivity—Can the traffic tolerate variable delay, or must end-to-end timing be preserved?
- Cell loss sensitivity—Can the traffic tolerate the occasional cell loss associated with connectionless transmission services, or must connection-oriented transmission services be employed to avoid cell loss?
- Guaranteed bandwidth—Must the traffic receive a constant amount of guaranteed bandwidth, or can it tolerate variable amounts of bandwidth?
- Additional overhead required—In addition to the 5 octets of overhead in the ATM cell header, some AAL protocols require additional overhead to properly manage payloads. This additional overhead is taken from the 48-octet payload. This can raise overhead percentages to as high as 13%.

To date, four different types of ATM adaptation protocols have been defined and are summarized in Figure 8-39.

ATM Bandwidth Management As illustrated in Figure 8-39, the type of bandwidth required for a given type of traffic varies according to which AAL protocol was employed. Currently three different categories of bit rates or bandwidth management schemes are supported by ATM standards:

- **CBR** or **constant bit rate** provides a guaranteed amount of bandwidth to a given virtual path, thereby producing the equivalent of leased T-1 or T-3 line. The disadvantage side of CBR is that if this guaranteed amount of bandwidth is not required 100% of the time, no other applications can use the unused bandwidth.

ATM AAL Protocol	Timing	Cell Loss	Bandwidth	Payload	Application/Notes
AAL-1	Preserved end-to-end	Connection oriented	Constant bit rate	47 octets	Used for mapping TDM services such as T-1, T-3
AAL-2	Preserved end-to-end	Connection oriented	Variable bit rate	45–47 octets	Variable rate compressed video
AAL-3/4	Variable delay acceptable	Connectionless	Variable bit rate	44 octets	Compatible with connectionless WAN data services such as SMDS
AAL-5	Variable delay acceptable	Connection oriented	Variable bit rate	48 octets	Currently most popular AAL protocol; also known as SEAL (simple and efficient adaptation layer)

Figure 8-39 ATM AAL Protocols

- **VBR** or **variable bit rate** provides a guaranteed minimum threshold amount of constant bandwidth below which the available bandwidth will not drop. However, as bursty traffic requires more bandwidth than this constant minimum, that required bandwidth will be provided.
- **ABR** or **available bit rate** provides leftover bandwidth whenever it is not required by the variable bit rate traffic.

Figure 8-40 illustrates the relationship between CBR, VBR, and ABR.

Technology The key benefits that ATM architecture affords actual implementations of ATM technology are as follows:

- Constant cell length affords faster, predictable delivery times.
- Constant cell length and predictable delivery times allow voice, video, and data to be transported effectively via ATM.
- ATM protocols are supported from the LAN to the WAN, from network interface cards to ATM WAN switches, thereby removing the necessity for multiple protocol conversions from the desktop across enterprise networks.

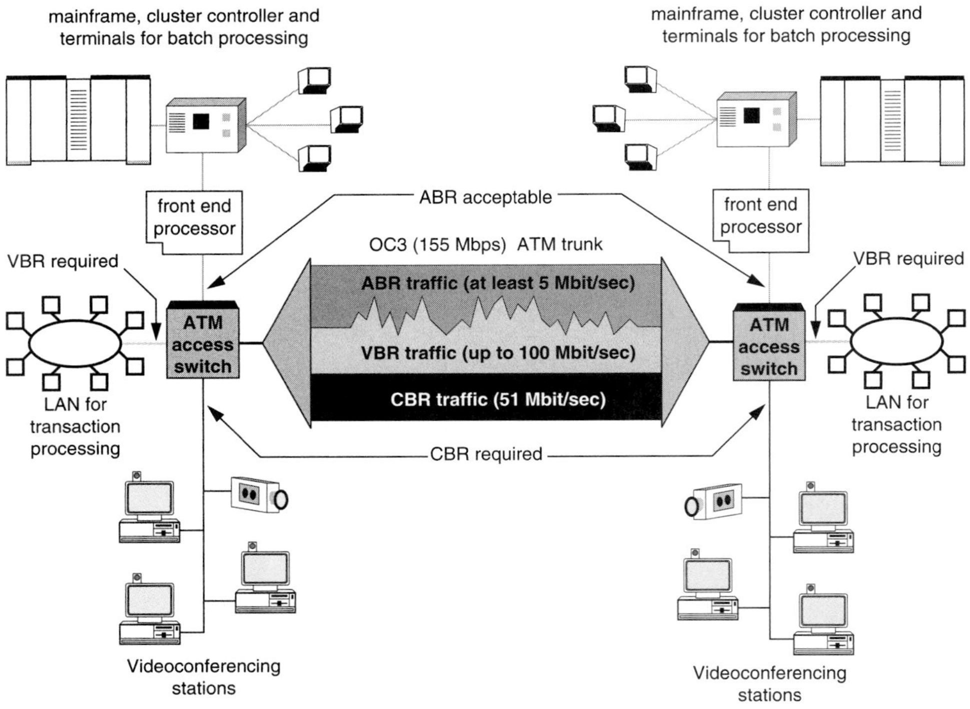

Figure 8-40 CBR, VBR, and ABR Bandwidth Management for ATM

ATM on the LAN ATM network interface cards are currently available at speeds from 25 to 155 Mbps. Workstations equipped with ATM NICs would be linked to each other via an ATM hub that would usually have a higher speed ATM up-link to a higher speed ATM enterprise switch. Workstations with Ethernet or token ring NICs do not have to have those NICs replaced to access ATM enterprise networks. **ATM gateway switches,** otherwise known as **ATM access switches,** can provide switched access for an entire legacy shared media LAN to an ATM enterprise network. Ethernet switches with ATM uplinks are a common example of an ATM gateway switch.

A virtual LAN refers to a group of workstations that appear to be all locally connected to each other but that, in fact, are geographically dispersed. Virtual LANs can be created across an enterprise-wide ATM network among geographically distributed workstations via an ATM capability known as **ATM LAN emulation.** In ATM LAN emulation, LAN MAC layer addresses are converted to ATM network addresses and forwarded via switched ATM connections across the enterprise network to their destination workstation. This capability allows workstations and legacy LANs to take advantage of ATM's speed without having to make any hardware or software modifications to the LAN workstations themselves.

ATM Across the WAN An implementation of an ATM-based enterprise network would consist of ATM access devices as well as a "cloud" of ATM switches. The ATM access devices would take user information in the form of variable-length data frames from a LAN or workstation, digitized voice from a PBX, or digitized video from a video codec and format all of these various types of information into fixed-length ATM cells. The local ATM switch could route information to other locally connected ATM devices as well as to the wide area ATM network.

In a sense, the general makeup of the ATM network is not unlike the X.25 or frame relay networks. Access devices ensure that data are properly formatted before entering "the cloud" where the data are forwarded by switches specially designed to handle that particular type of properly formatted data. However, the functionality that an ATM network can offer far exceeds that of either the X.25 or frame relay networks. Figure 8-41 illustrates a possible implementation of a variety of ATM technology.

Broadband ISDN

SONET is the optical transmission interface and mechanism that will deliver **broadband ISDN** services. ATM is the switching architecture which will ensure that video, voice, data, and image packets delivered by **B-ISDN** services are delivered to the proper destination. Together, ATM and SONET form the underlying network architecture of the B-ISDN of the future. ATM provides the cell relay switching fabric providing bandwidth on demand for bursty data from any source (voice, video, etc.), and SONET's synchronous payload envelope provides empty boxcars for ATM's cargo. Simply stated, SONET possesses the flexibility to carry multiple types of data cargo (voice, video, etc.) simultaneously, and ATM has the ability to switch multiple types of data simultaneously. That the complementary nature of the two architectures produces a network service known as B-ISDN should come as no surprise.

Much of the excitement concerning B-ISDN is due to its ability to support existing services (T-1, T-3), emerging services (SMDS, frame relay), as well as future services (HDTV, medical imaging) and services as yet undiscovered. B-ISDN should be the service that finally delivers true bandwidth on demand in an uncomplicated, transparent, and affordable manner.

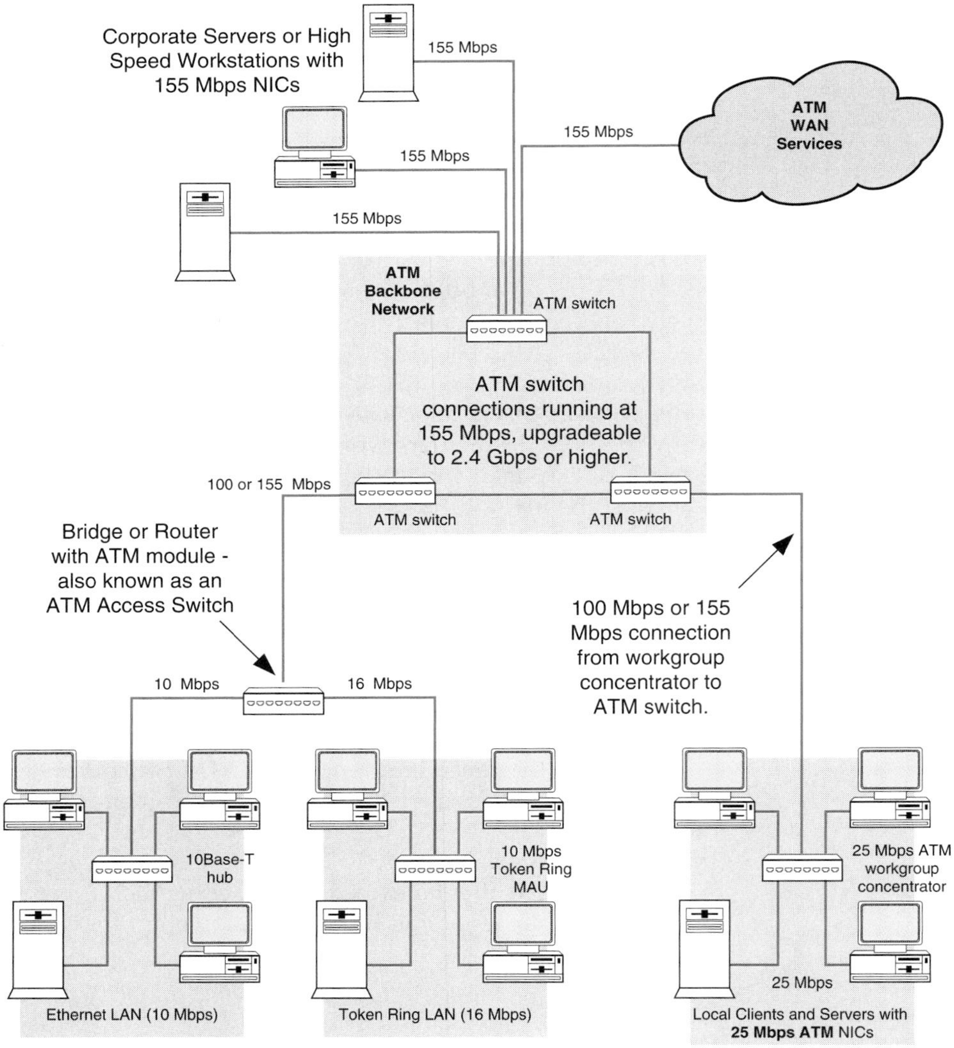

Figure 8-41 Implementation of ATM Technology

SUMMARY

In order to understand the basic technical principles of Wide Area Networking, one must really start by looking at the basic business principles of wide area networking. In wide area networking as in most areas of business, the desire to maximize the impact of any investment in technology is a central focus.

The two most basic principles involved in sharing a single data link among multiple sessions are packetizing and multiplexing. Packetizing is the segmenting of data transmissions between devices into structured blocks or packets of data which contain enough "overhead" or management information in addition to the transmitted data itself, to assure delivery of the packet of data to its intended destination. Multiplexing then takes this packetized data and sends the information over a shared wide area connection along with other packetized data from other sources.

An overall wide area network architecture is a simple model defining how packetizing, multiplexing and other wide area networking principles combine to create all of the current and emerging wide area networking technologies and services. Switching architectures and transmission architectures combine to enable network services.

Packet switching and circuit switching are the two major categories of switching architectures. Transmission architectures include local loop transmission alternatives such as POTS, ISDN, ADSL, and Cable, while broadband transmission alternatives include T-1, T-3, and SONET. Among the network services enabled by these switching and transmission architectures are X.25, Frame Relay, SMDS, ATM, and broadband ISDN.

It is important to note that there is no single best network service for all applications. Network analysts must carefully match business applications to appropriate network services through careful and thorough analysis of data traffic as well as business objectives.

KEY TERMS

23B+D
2B+D
30B+D
AAL
ABR
access line
ADSL
Asymmetric digital subscriber line
asynchronous transfer mode
AT&T 5ESS Switch
ATM
ATM access switches
ATM adaptation layer
ATM gateway switches
ATM LAN emulation
automatic number identification
available bit rate
B-ISDN
backward explicit congestion notification
bandwidth on demand interoperability group
basic rate interface
bearer channels
BECN
BER
bit error rate
BONDING
BRI
Broadband ISDN
broadband transmission
call set-up packets
CAP
carrierless amplitude & phase
CBR
CBS
cell relay
central clock
CIR
circuit switched network
circuit switching
clear request packet
committed burst size
committed information rate
composite message frame
connection-oriented
connectionless
constant bit rate
CPE
CRC
customer premises equipment
cyclical redundancy check
d channel
D-4
data over voice
datagrams
DE
digital service hierarchy
discard eligibility
discrete multitone
distributed queue dual bus
DMT
DQDB
DS
DS-1
DSE
E-1
error correction
error detection
ESF
extended superframe
EZ-ISDN
FAD
FCS
FDM
FECN
flow control
forward explicit congestion notification
fractional T-1
Fractional T-1 multiplexers
FRAD
frame check sequence
frame relay
frame relay access device
frame relay switch
frames
framing
framing bit
frequency division multiplexing
FT-1
global address
guardbands
HDLC
HDSL
HDSL2
high level data link control
IEEE 802.14
IEEE 802.6
in-band signalling
interface specification
inverse multiplexing
IOC
ISDN
ISDN ordering codes
ISDN switch
ISDN terminal adapters
LAP-B
LAP-D
link access procedure-balanced

link access procedure- D channel
local loop transmission
logical channel
logical channel number
multiplexing
multirate ISDN
Narrowband ISDN
National ISDN-1
network architecture
network convergence
network service
network termination unit-1
network-to-network interface
NISDN-1
NNI
Northern Telecom DMS100 Switch
NT-1
NTU-1
OC
OC-1
octet
optical carrier
optical switching
out of band signalling
packet assembler/disassembler
packet layer protocol
packet switched network
packet switches
packet switching
packetizing
PAD
payload
PDN
periodic framing
permanent virtual circuit
PLP
polling
POTS
PSE
public data network
PVC
RADSL
rate adaptive DSL
reliable
RJ48c
SDSL
Service Profile Identifier Numbers
sinks
SMDS
SONET
SONET superframe
SPE
SPID
statistical time division multiplexing
STDM
store-and-forward
STS-1
superframe
SVC
switched multimegabit data service
switched virtual circuit
switching
switching architecture
symmetric DSL
synchronous optical network
synchronous payload envelope
synchronous TDM
T-1
T-1 channel bank
T-1 CSU/DSU
T-1 IMUX
T-1 inverse multiplexer
T-1 multiplexers
T-1 switches
TDM
time division multiplexing
time slot
transmission architecture
UNI
unreliable
user demands
user network interface
variable bit rate
VBR
VDSL
very high speed DSL
virtual circuit table
virtual circuits
virtual tributary
VT
VT1.5
Wavelength division multiplexing
WDM
X.25

REVIEW QUESTIONS

1. Differentiate between the following multiplexing techniques in terms of mechanics, technology, and application:
   a. frequency division multiplexing
   b. time division multiplexing
   c. statistical time division multiplexing
2. Are multiplexers from different manufacturers interoperable? If not, why not?
3. What limitations in network design or operation would a lack of interoperability cause?
4. What are some of the technological differences between an X.25 network and a frame relay network?
5. What are some of the performance or architectural differences between an X.25 network and a frame relay network?
6. What are frame relay's underlying assumptions regarding transmission media and bit error rates?
7. What types of information are included in packets other than the actual data message itself?
8. How is it possible with a DOV unit that the voice and data don't necessarily have to share the same destination?
9. What are the key shortcomings of TDM and how does STDM seek to overcome these?

10. What is polling and what does it have to do with multiplexer efficiency?
11. What is the difference between switching and transmission and how do the two architectures compliment each other?
12. What is the difference between circuit switching and packet switching?
13. What is the difference between a packet assembler/disassembler and a packet switch?
14. What are the positive and negative aspects of a datagram delivery service?
15. What is the difference between connectionless and connection-oriented packet services in terms of overhead, physical transmission path, and reliability?
16. What do connection oriented services use in place of global addressing?
17. What overhead is involved with the establishment and maintenance of logical channel numbers?
18. What are the differences between PVCs and SVCs in terms of establishment, maintenance, and termination?
19. Which part of the packet switched network does X.25 actually define?
20. What is meant by the term bursty data and what unique transmission challenge does it pose?
21. What is the most common source of bursty data?
22. Name the major components of the wide area network architecture and the significance of each.
23. Give examples of switching and transmission architecture in today's network architectures.
24. Differentiate between X.25 and frame relay in terms of error control.
25. How is flow control handled in a frame relay network?
26. What is the significance of frame relay's variable length frames in terms of types of payloads that can be effectively delivered?
27. Why is dynamic allocation of bandwidth an important feature of frame relay?
28. Why is multiple PVCs per access line an important feature of frame relay?
29. What are the primary differences between frame relay and cell relay in terms of architecture and network performance?
30. What is the relationship between cell relay and ATM?
31. Differentiate between CBR, VBR, and ABR in terms of architecture and applications.
32. What is the purpose of the AAL protocols?
33. What are the differences between ISDN and B-ISDN?
34. What are the differences between POTS and ISDN?
35. What have been the traditional stumbling blocks to widespread ISDN deployment and what progress has been made in overcoming these?
36. What is SONET and where does it fit in the wide area network architecture?
37. What unique performance characteristics does SONET offer and what type of application might require such characteristics?
38. What is the difference between a T-1 and an E-1?
39. Differentiate between the following: time slot, frame, superframe, ESF.
40. What is the significance of NISDN-1?
41. What is the difference between DS-1 and T-1?
42. What is fractional T-1 and what is the business motivation behind such a service?
43. What is ADSL and what performance characteristics does it offer subscribers?
44. Why might carriers be especially interested in deploying ADSL services?
45. What are some other potential DSL services and how do they differ from ADSL?
46. What are some of the limitations facing the widespread use of cable modems?
47. What are the roles of the virtual tributaries in SONET?
48. What is B-ISDN and what switching and transmission architectures does it require?
49. What are some of the services which may be supported by B-ISDN?
50. What is the purpose of the D-channel in ISDN?
51. What is the difference between BRI and PRI ISDN?
52. What is inverse multiplexing and what applications are well suited to it?
53. What is SMDS and why has it not been adopted as widely as frame relay?

ACTIVITIES

1. Contact your local phone carrier. Is ISDN available in your area? What are the nonrecurring and monthly charges for service? What are the performance guarantees? What special equipment is required? What is the cost of such equipment and must it be purchased from the carrier? Are both PRI and BRI services available? What intelligent services are available via ISDN? Can all 128 Kbps be used?
2. Contact your local phone carrier. Is ADSL available in your area? What are the nonrecurring and monthly charges for service? What are the performance guarantees? What special equipment is required? What is the cost of such equipment and must it be purchased from the carrier? Is Internet access available? at an additional cost?
3. Contact your local Cable TV provider. Is cable modem service available in your area? ? What are the nonrecurring and monthly charges for service? What are the performance guarantees? What special equipment in required? What is the cost of such equipment and must it be purchased from the carrier? Is Internet access available? at an additional cost?
4. Gather articles on ATM from trade journals. Create a bulletin board or prepare a research topic summarizing the current issues facing ATM, focusing particularly on obstacles to widespread deployment, such as the pace of the standards development process.
5. Contact the ATM Forum and request literature concerning current standards development activities.
6. Investigate the installation and on-going costs of an X.25 packet switched service. What are the performance limitations?
7. Investigate the installation and on-going costs of an frame relay packet switched service. What are the performance limitations?
8. How are frame relay services tariffed in your local area? How are committed information rates and committed burst size negotiated? Is zero CIR available? What happens if you exceed your CIR? How do frame relay CIRs compare with X.25 transmission speeds?
9. Choose two cities within your LATA. Contact your local carrier for a quote on the cost of a leased line between these two cities. Compare pricing for both analog and digital lines of various sizes. Are switched digital services available? What are the installation and recurring costs?
10. Now choose another city just outside your local LATA. Contact multiple long distance carriers for quotes similar to the previous question. How do the quotes from the various long distance companies compare? How do the long distance carrier quotes compare to the local carrier quotes? What was the impact on cost of leaving your LATA? Did recurring or nonrecurring costs increase more? Explain your results.
11. Can your local carrier now offer inter-LATA data services thanks to the Telecommunications Act of 1996?
12. Research the wavelength division multiplexing technology market. How large is the market currently? What are the expected growth rates over the next 5 years? Who are the major vendors and who are the major customers? How exactly does WDM work? Report on the results of your research.

CASE STUDY

Rockers Megadeth Eye Broadband Access for Fans

Heavy-metal band Megadeth is moving toward megabits.

Through an alliance with digital subscriber line provider Covad Communications, the band is now able to merge its megadeth.net virtual domain with DSL broadband access. DSL can let fans log on at broadband speeds, opening up new possibilities, such as streaming video.

"High-speed connectivity has one of its biggest benefits in the entertainment industry. If we want to make a video or a song available on the Internet, fans can go in and actually make some use of that instead of using a RealAudio player that's buffering for 15 minutes trying to download," says Doug Brooks, megadeth.net's administrative director.

Megadeth didn't develop these broad-band ideas on its own. The fast-access dreams came up when LaserLink, which handled the band's megadeth.net domain business, was bought by DSL provider Covad earlier this year. The band had been selling fans megadeth.net e-mail addresses and Web space. Covad's strategy was to combine its expertise setting up and wholesaling DSL services with LaserLink's personalized domain services.

Until the Covad/LaserLink deal, Megadeth was satisfied with just offering dial-up Internet access as part of its megadeth.net offering, which includes e-mail and a personal Web site.

Megadeth is still mulling how exactly to incorporate DSL in its strategy. Initially, the Internet service was just a novelty. "We wanted to give fans the cool factor of having the band's name in their e-mail address," says Dave Mustaine, Megadeth's lead singer, who works directly on the band's Internet efforts.

But already the band sees ways to integrate its music and the Internet. Megadeth.net registration software comes included on the band's latest CD, Risk. And those who sign up separately for the service receive the registration software on a CD that includes videos of two songs—"Train of Consequences" and "Almost Honest"—that are available nowhere else.

The band isn't really interested in turning a big profit on the service it buys from Covad/LaserLink, Brooks says. "Even if it's a minimal profit, it's much more beneficial as a marketing tool," he says.

DING-DONG, DSL CALLING

While the personal domain service is auxiliary to Megadeth, the cosmetics company Avon is pinning its future on the Internet and its personalized Web site, Avon.com, that is being handled by Covad/LaserLink.

The company is working to get as many of its 500,000 representatives as possible to use the Internet to sell products and do paperwork electronically: Just processing the biweekly, 53-page purchase orders cuts the cost from $3 to 50 cents apiece. "This is an absolute necessity," says Len Edwards. Avon president and general manager.

To make the online scheme work. Avon has pieced together a deal under which representatives can lease a PC, get Internet access and a customized portal for reps to enter Avon's site to do business. That costs $19.95 per month, and at the end of three years, the reps own the PC.

DSL is potentially attractive because many of the sales reps have one home telephone and don't want to tie up the line. This would give them a separate DSL line that would leave the telephone free, Edwards says.

With the new online effort, reps will get their own Web pages where their customers can check in for the personalized treatment that is part of the Avon package, Edwards says.

Source: Tim Greene, "Rockers Megadeth eye broadband access for fans," *Network World*, vol. 17, no. 19 (May 8, 2000), p. 70. Copyright Network World. Reprinted with permission.

BUSINESS CASE STUDY QUESTIONS

Activities

1. Complete a top-down model for this case by gleaning facts from the case and placing them in the proper layer of the top-down model. After completing the top-down model, analyze and detail those instances where requirements were clearly passed down from upper layers to lower layers of the model and where solutions to those requirements were passed up from lower layers to upper layers of the model.
2. Detail any questions about the case that may occur to you for which answers are not clearly stated in the article.

Business

1. What was the business motivation or problem that initiated the search for the implemented solution?
2. What was the productivity impact of the implemented solution?
3. Were business performance metrics and associated infrastructure performance metrics identified? If so,

were they achieved? If not, what might be some suitable business and infrastructure performance metrics for this case?
4. How did an unrelated business merger enable the new business opportunity?
5. Is this business opportunity primarily marketing or profit driven?

Application

1. What new possibilities for applications are now possible with broadband access?
2. What had been the customary practice before broadband access to hear audio or view video via the Internet?
3. How does e-mail service fit with the business opportunity described?

Data

1. What are the amounts of data that typically must be transferred in this application?

Network

1. What underlying network technologies were key to the achievement of stated business objectives?

Technology

1. What specific technologies were employed to deliver the described solution?

CHAPTER 9

INTERNETWORKING

Concepts Reinforced

OSI Model
Protocols and Standards
Network Operating Systems Architecture
Network Addressing
Internet Suite of Protocols Model
Interoperability
Network Operating Systems Functionality
TCP/IP Protocols

Concepts Introduced

Internetwork Design
Bridging
Switching vs. Routing
Bridges
Repeaters
SNA/SDLC
Layer 2,3,4 Switches
Virtual LANs
Storage Area Networks
Internetworking Technology
Routing
Routing Protocols
Routers
Bridging Protocols
SNA/LAN Integration
ATM LAN Emulation
Quality of Service Protocols

OBJECTIVES

Upon successful completion of this chapter, you should:

1. Understand why an organization would want to implement LAN-to-LAN internetworking.
2. Understand the basics of internetwork design including decisions as to bridging, routing, or switching.
3. Understand the importance of protocols to successful internetworking design and implementation.
4. Understand the functionality and proper application of the following types of internetworking technology: repeaters, bridges, branch office routers, edge routers, boundary routers, route servers, distributed routers, dial-up routers, ISDN bridges and routers, wireless bridges, source routing bridges, layers 2, 3, and 4 switches, and software-only routers.
5. Understand the options available for integrating LAN traffic with SNA/SDLC mainframe traffic.

INTRODUCTION

The two basic goals of this chapter are:

- To introduce the reader to the complexities and basic principles of internetwork design such as bridging, routing, and switching.
- To introduce the reader to the available technology with which to implement designed internetworking solutions.

Internetwork design and technology issues are explored in this chapter for both LAN-to-LAN internetworking and LAN-to-mainframe internetworking. To understand the importance of internetworking in general, it is first necessary to understand the business motivation for seeking internetworking solutions in the first place.

INTERNETWORKING DESIGN

Managerial Perspective

BUSINESS MOTIVATION AND INTERNETWORKING CHALLENGES

Local area networks tend to grow by a natural process until the shared media network architecture (Ethernet, token ring, FDDI, etc.) becomes too congested and network performance begins to suffer. This scenario is one of the two primary reasons for investigating **internetworking** solutions. The other situation that often leads to internetworking design occurs when independently established and operated LANs wish to begin to share information. Each of these scenarios really boils down to business issues. The poor performance of the overloaded shared media LAN leads to a decrease in worker productivity with potential ripple effects that lead to decreases in customer satisfaction, sales, market share, etc.

The ability to provide decision makers with instantaneous access to the right information at the right place and time, regardless of the location of that information, is really the key motivation for internetworking. The key challenge or stumbling block to achieving transparent information access is the numerous incompatibilities caused by the multiple vendor hardware and software technologies that make up individual LANs to be linked. The operational characteristics of LANs are defined by protocols, which, when organized into a layered model such as the OSI model, are referred to as a protocol stack. A LAN's protocol stack is really a definition of that LAN's personality. In other words, if transparent LAN-to-LAN interoperability is to be achieved, each protocol in a given LAN's protocol stack must be either matched or converted to transparently interoperate with the corresponding protocol in the neighboring LAN to which the given LAN is to be linked. Overall LAN-to-LAN transparent interoperability is achieved only when corresponding protocols are able to achieve transparent interoperability.

Overall Internetworking Design Strategies

To improve performance on overburdened shared media LANs, several proven design strategies can be followed:

- **Segmentation** is usually the first approach to reducing shared media congestion. By having fewer workstations per segment, there is less contention for the shared bandwidth. Segmentation improves performance for both CSMA/CD (Ethernet) and token passing (token ring) access methodologies. Some type of internetworking device, such as a bridge or router, is required to link the LAN segments.
- When segmentation is taken to the extreme of limiting each LAN segment to only a single workstation, the design strategy is known as **microsegmentation.** A microsegmented internetwork requires a LAN switch that is compatible with the NICs installed in the attached workstations. Both Ethernet and token ring switches are readily available.
- Instead of assigning all workstations to their own LAN segment as in microsegmentation, only selected high-performance devices such as servers can be assigned to their own segment in a design strategy known as **server isolation.** By isolating servers on their own segments, guaranteed access to network bandwidth is ensured.
- **Hierarchical networking** isolates local LAN traffic on a local network architecture such as Ethernet or token ring while transmitting internetwork traffic over a higher speed network architecture such as FDDI, fast Ethernet, or ATM. Servers are often connected directly to the **backbone network** and individual workstations access the backbone network only as needed through routers.

Figure 9-1 illustrates these overall internetworking design strategies.

Bridging, routing, and switching are the three primary internetworking processes that offer LAN segmentation and isolation of network resources. All three internetworking processes are basically address processors, making decisions as to how to forward internetwork traffic based on data-link layer and network layer addresses. The three processes differ in their use of network addresses, in their overall sophistication, and in their advantages and limitations. The bridging, routing, and switching internetworking processes are reviewed here; differences between their associated internetworking technologies are reviewed later in the chapter.

MANs—Metropolitan Area Networks Occasionally, multiple LANs belonging to a single corporate entity all located within a single metropolitan area must be internetworked. In such cases, a **metropolitan area network** or **MAN** may be used to link these LANs together. Most often, these MAN services are provided by the local carrier, although in some circumstances a single corporation may maintain its own MAN. These MANs usually employ fiber optic cable and SONET as a basic transport mechanism. A key decision facing network architects these days in the MAN arena is

- What transport protocols should be carried on the MAN?

Among the choices for MAN transport protocols are gigabit Ethernet, ATM, packet over SONET, and Cisco's dynamic packet transport. Wavelength division multiplexing could allow multiple transport protocols to be carried simultaneously over multiple wavelengths over a single fiber.

SANs—Storage Area Networks A logical extension of the previously mentioned server isolation internetworking design technique is the **storage area network** or **SAN.**

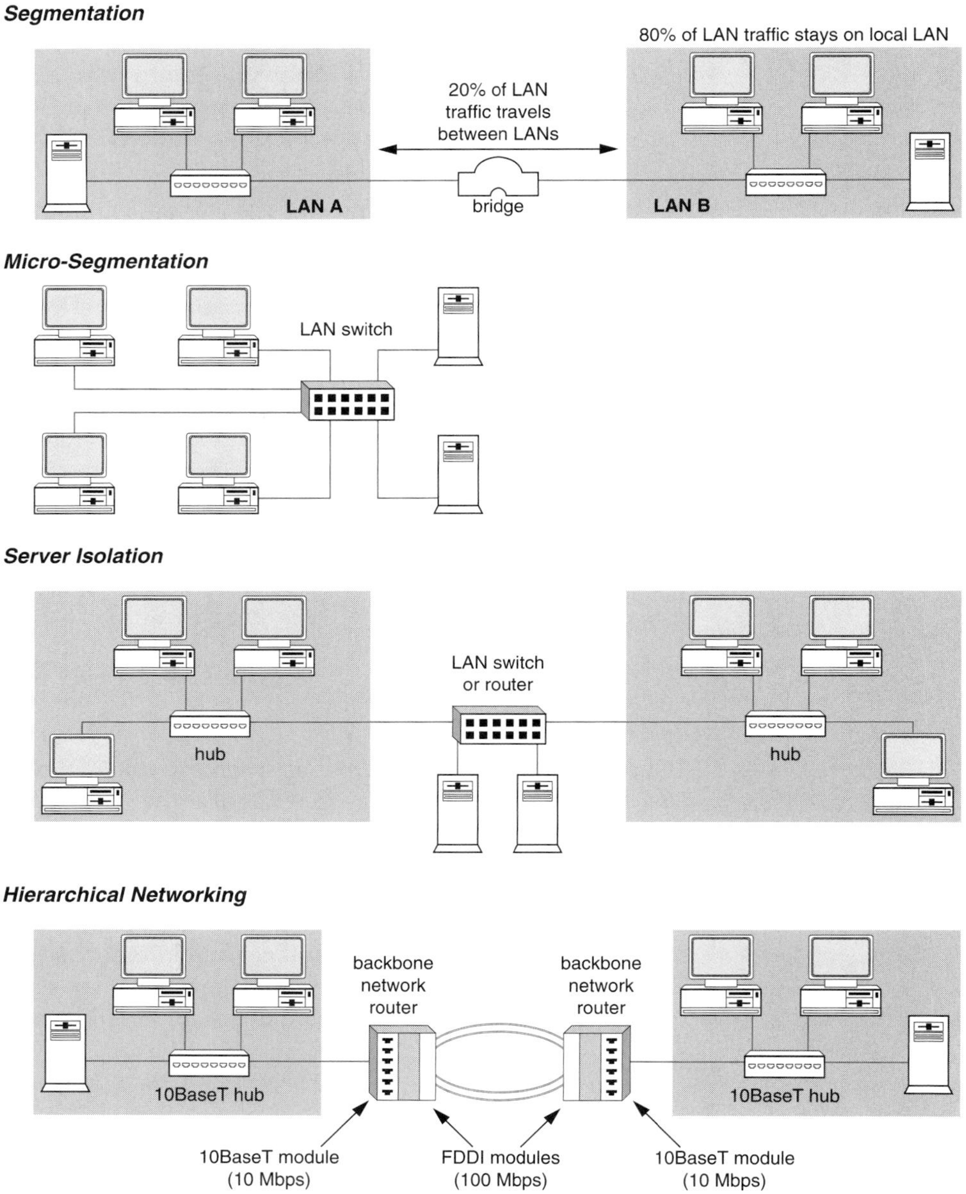

Figure 9-1 Overall Internetworking Design Strategies

Storage area networks seek to separate data storage from particular application-oriented servers sometimes referred to as storage islands by consolidating storage systems such as disk arrays or tape libraries and attaching them to the enterprise network via redundant, high-capacity network connections. Although numerous protocol alternatives exist in the construction of a SAN, fibre channel (up to 1 Gbps over 10 km) is becoming the protocol of choice for interconnection of the storage devices themselves. Although storage area networks hold great potential for providing an enterprise-based storage solution, integration and interoperability issues exist. Fibre channel devices from various vendors may not be fully compatible either with each other or with the SCSI interfaces often found on storage devices such as disk arrays. Also, not all client or server operating systems are able to access SAN-based storage directly. Figure 9-2 provides a representative view of a SAN and its associated topology and protocols.

Bridging

Bridging is often the first internetworking or LAN segmentation strategy employed because of its ease of installation and effective results. Dividing a single overburdened LAN into two LAN segments linked by a bridge must be done with some forethought to minimize the amount of internetwork traffic and thereby avoiding having the bridge become an internetwork bottleneck. The 80/20 rule is often used in deciding which workstations and servers should be assigned to each side of the bridge. The goal should be that 80% of all LAN traffic should stay on the local LAN, with no more than 20% of overall traffic requiring processing and forwarding by the bridge.

Addressing Bridging is a data-link layer process, making forwarding decisions based on the contents of the MAC layer or data-link layer addresses. Bridges are passive or transparent devices, receiving every frame broadcast on a given LAN. Bridges are known as **transparent** due to their ability to process only data-link layer addresses while transparently forwarding any variety of upper layer protocols safely embedded within the data field of the data-link layer frame. Rather than merely transferring all data between LANs or LAN segments, a bridge reads the **destination address** (MAC layer address of destination NIC) of each data frame on a LAN, decides whether the destination is local or remote (on the other side of the bridge),

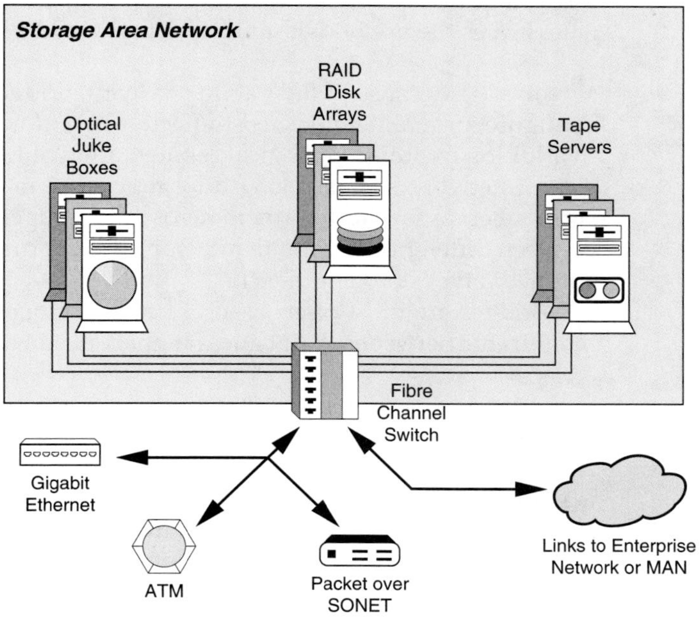

Figure 9-2 Storage Area Network

Data Link Layer Frame

Data Link Header		Data Link Data Field	Data Link Trailer
Source Address	**Destination Address**	**Upper layer protocols including network layer address information**	
Contains MAC address of original source workstation	Contains MAC address of ultimate destination workstation		
These addresses are used by bridges to determine whether or not packets should be forwarded across the bridge.			
Data Link layer addresses are ***NOT*** changed by bridges.			

Figure 9-3 Use of Data-link Addressing by Bridges

and allows only those data frames with nonlocal destination addresses to cross the bridge to the remote LAN.

Data-link protocols such as Ethernet contain **source addresses** as well as the destination addresses within the predefined Ethernet frame layout. A bridge checks the source address of each frame it receives and adds that source address to a table of **known local nodes.** In doing so, the bridge is learning without having to be manually reconfigured about new workstations that might have been added to the local LAN. Some bridges broadcast requests to all locally attached workstations, thereby forcing responses that can then be stored in the known local nodes table.

After each destination address is read, it is compared with the contents of the "known local nodes" table to determine whether the frame should be allowed to cross the bridge (i.e., whether or not the destination is local). Since only frames with destination addresses not found in the known local nodes table are forwarded across the bridge, bridges are sometimes known as a **forward-if-not-local** devices. Figure 9-3 illustrates the use of data-link layer frame addresses by bridges.

Advantages Because of their ability to learn, bridges are relatively easy to install and configure, providing quick, cost-effective relief for overburdened network segments. In addition to providing logical segmentation of LAN traffic, bridges also are able to extend network segment length by repeating, retiming, and regenerating received signals before forwarding them across the bridge. Bridges are also able to translate between different network architectures (token ring to Ethernet) and between different media types (UTP to fiber).

Bridges are most often used either to segment traffic between LANs or to segment traffic between a LAN and a higher speed backbone network.

Limitations The primary limitation of bridges is also one of their strengths. Because bridges learn and do not require ongoing configuration, they only know to forward all packets that are addressed to nonlocal nodes. In the case of a destination node that is many LANs and connecting bridges away from its source workstation, all workstations on all LANs between the source and destination workstation will be broadcast with the frame bound for the distant destination. Forwarding messages to all workstations on all intermittent LANs is known as **propagation.** In the case of improperly addressed frames or frames destined for nonexistent addresses, frames can be infinitely perpetuated or flooded onto all bridged LANs in a condition known as a **broadcast storm.** Bridges are generally not able to support networks containing redundant paths because the multiple active loops between LANs can lead to the propagation of broadcast storms.

Routing

Although both processes examine and forward data packets discriminately, routing and bridging differ significantly in several key functional areas:

- Although a bridge reads the destination address of every data packet on the LAN to which it is attached, a router examines only those data packets that are specifically addressed to it.
- Rather than just merely allowing the data packet access to the internetwork in a manner similar to a bridge, a router is both more cautious and more helpful.

Before indiscriminately forwarding a data packet, a router first confirms the existence of the destination address as well as the latest information on available network "paths" to reach that destination. Next, based on the latest network traffic conditions, the router chooses the best path for the data packet to reach its destination and sends the data packet on its way.

Addressing Whereas bridges make their forwarding decisions based on the contents of the MAC layer addresses contained in the header of the data-link layer frame, routers make their forwarding decisions based on the contents of the network layer addresses embedded within the data field of the data-link layer frame.

The router itself is a data-link layer destination address, available to receive, examine, and forward data packets from anywhere on any network to which it is either directly or indirectly internetworked.

How do data packets arrive at a router? The destination address on an Ethernet or token ring packet must be the MAC address of the router that will handle further internetwork forwarding. Thus, a router is addressed in the data-link layer destination address field. The router then discards this MAC sublayer "envelope" that contained its address and proceeds to read the contents of the data field of the Ethernet or token ring frame. Data-link layer addressing is functionally referred to as point-to-point addressing.

Just as in the case of the data-link layer protocols, network layer protocols dictate a bit-by-bit data frame structure that the router understands. What looked like just "data" and was ignored by the data-link layer internetworking device, the bridge, is "unwrapped" by the router and examined thoroughly to determine further processing.

After reading the network layer destination address, which is actually the network address of the ultimate destination workstation, the router consults its **routing tables** to determine the best path on which to forward this data packet. Routing tables contain at least some of the following fields on which to base their "best path" decisions:

- Network number of the destination network. This field serves as the key field or lookup field used to find the proper record with further information concerning the best path to this network.

- MAC address of the next router along the path to this target network.
- Port on this router out of which the readdressed data-link layer frame should be sent.
- Number of hops, or intermediate routers, to the destination network.
- The age of this entry in order to avoid making routing decisions based on outdated information.

Having found the best path, the router has the ability to repackage the data packet as required for the delivery route (best path) it has chosen. Although the network layer addresses remain unchanged, a fresh data-link layer frame is created. The destination address on the new data-link layer frame is filled in with the MAC address of the next router along the best path to the ultimate destination, and the source address on the new data-link layer frame is filled in with the MAC address of the router that just completed examination of the network layer addresses. Network layer addressing is functionally referred to as end-to-end addressing.

Unlike the bridge, which merely allows access to the internetwork (forward-if-not-local logic), the router specifically addresses the data packet to a distant router. However, before a router actually releases a data packet onto the internetwork, it confirms the existence of the destination address to which this data packet is bound. Only once the router is satisfied with both the viability of the destination address and the quality of the intended path will it release the carefully packaged data packet. This meticulous processing activity on the part of the router is known as **forward-if-proven-remote** logic. Figure 9-4 illustrates router's user of data-link and network layer addresses.

Advantages Compared with bridging, routing is able to make more efficient use of bandwidth on large networks containing redundant paths. The effective use of a network's redundant paths allows routers to perform **load balancing** of total network traffic across two or more links between two given locations. Choice of "best path"

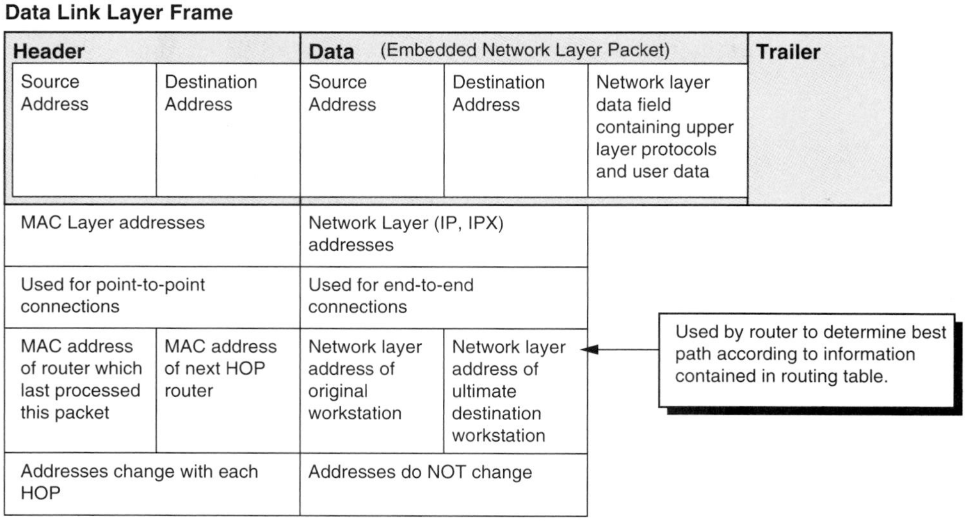

Data Link Layer Frame
Header
Data (Embedded Network Layer Packet)
Trailer
Source Address
Destination Address
Source Address
Destination Address
Network layer data field containing upper layer protocols and user data
MAC Layer addresses
Network Layer (IP, IPX) addresses
Used for point-to-point connections
Used for end-to-end connections
MAC address of router which last processed this packet
MAC address of next HOP router
Network layer address of original workstation
Network layer address of ultimate destination workstation
Used by router to determine best path according to information contained in routing table.
Addresses change with each HOP
Addresses do NOT change

Figure 9-4 Router's Use of Data-Link and Network Layer Addresses

by routers can be determined by a variety of factors including number of hops, transmission cost, and current line congestion. Routers are able to dynamically maintain routing tables, thereby adjusting performance to changing network conditions. Thanks to the forward-if-proven-remote logic, routers are more able to keep misbehaving or misaddressed traffic off the network through filtering of network layer addresses. In this role, routers can be considered as firewalls between connected networks. Router-based networks are much more scaleable than bridge-based networks. Routers are able to forward more sophisticated and informative management information to enterprise network management systems via SNMP.

When LANs are connected over a long distance via WAN links, it is more likely that routers, rather than bridges, should be employed to interface to the WAN link. Thanks to the router's ability to more accurately identify upper layer protocols, unnecessary or unwanted traffic can be kept off the relatively low-speed, high-cost WAN links.

Perhaps the most significant advantage of routers is their ability to process multiple network layer protocols simultaneously. A properly configured router could process IP, IPX, and AppleTalk packets simultaneously while forwarding each protocol type to the proper destination network. In addition, some routers are also able to handle nonroutable protocols such as NetBIOS, LAT, or SNA/SDLC that don't possess any network layer addressing scheme. In these cases, the data-link layer frames are either bridged or upper layer protocols are encapsulated in a network layer envelope such as IP.

To summarize, routers provide the following services to the internetwork:

- Create firewalls to protect connected LANs.
- Filter unwanted broadcast packets from the internetwork.
- Discriminate and prioritize processing of packets according to network layer protocol.
- Provide security by filtering packets by either data-link or network layer addresses.
- Provide transparent interconnection between LANs.

Limitations Owing to the sophisticated processing offered, routers are considerably more complicated to configure and manage than bridges. As the number of routers increases in a router-based network, the complexity level of network management increases proportionately. If routers are expected to be able to process multiple network layer protocols, they must have all supported protocol stacks installed and properly configured.

The router's sophisticated processing also has an impact in terms of the sophistication and cost of the router technology compared to the bridging technology.

Switching

Switching, otherwise known as LAN switching, is very similar in function to bridging. The key difference between switching and bridging is that switching is done in hardware, or ASIC (application-specific integrated circuit) chips and is extremely fast compared to bridging. The primary purpose for employing a switch is to increase available bandwidth within a shared media LAN by implementing microsegmentation on the local LAN. Because the switch creates point-to-point connections for each packet received, shared media LANs that employ switches become switched media LANs.

Addressing Switching uses addresses in a manner similar to bridging. LAN switches read the destination MAC addresses on incoming data-link layer frames and quickly build a switched connection to the switched LAN segment that contains the destination workstation. The switch ports for LAN segments that contain multiple workstations are able to discriminate between traffic between locally attached workstations and traffic that must be switched to another LAN switch port.

Switches work best when traffic does not have to leave the LAN segments linked to a particular LAN switch. In other words, to minimize the use of expensive WAN links or filter the traffic allowed onto high-speed backbone networks, layer 3 protocols will need to be examined by a router. In some cases, this routing functionality is being incorporated into the LAN switch. Basic LAN switches are layer 2 devices that must be complemented by either external layer 3 routers or by internal layer 3 routing functionality.

Much like a bridge would handle "nonlocal" traffic, when a LAN switch receives a data-link frame bound for a destination off the local network, it merely builds a switched connection to the switch port to which a router is connected or to a virtual router within the switch where the switch's routing functionality can be accessed.

Practical Advice and Information

In discriminating between the proper roles of switching and routing, the best advice may be: Switch for bandwidth; route for filtering and internetwork segmentation.

Advantages LAN switches are able to produce dramatic increases in bandwidth compared with shared media LANs if sufficient thought has gone into organizing workstations and servers on LAN switch segments in a logical manner.

Virtual LANs, which are thoroughly explored later in the chapter, are enabled by the LAN switch's ability to quickly make any two workstations or servers appear to be physically attached to the same LAN segment. Virtual LANs take advantage of this switching capability by logically defining those workstations and computers that belong to the same virtual LAN regardless of the physical location of those workstations and servers. A given workstation or server can belong to more than one virtual LAN.

Limitations A LAN switch's limitations are largely a result of its bridging heritage. Switching cannot perform sophisticated filtering or security based on network layer protocols because LAN switches are unable to read network layer protocols. Switches are not able to discriminate among multiple paths and make best path decisions. Management information offered to enterprise network management systems by LAN switches is minimal compared to that available from routers.

Perhaps more important, because switched LAN connections may exist only for a matter of microseconds, monitoring and management of traffic within the LAN switch are considerably more challenging than performing similar tasks on routers. Traditional LAN analyzers constructed for use on shared-media LANs are of no use on switched-media LANs. Potential solutions to this and other switching limitations, such as buffering between high- and low-speed network architectures within a single switch, are covered in the LAN switch technology analysis section in Chapter 6.

INTERNETWORKING TECHNOLOGY

Internetworking Technology and the OSI Model

Internetworking technology can be categorized according to the OSI model layer corresponding to the protocols that a given internetworking device is able to process. In this way, the following internetworking devices can be categorized with the following OSI layers:

• Repeaters:	OSI layer 1	physical layer
• Bridges:	OSI layer 2	data-link layer
• Routers:	OSI layer 3	network layer
• Layer 2 switches:	OSI layer 2	data-link layer
• Layer 3 switches:	OSI layers 2 and 3	data-link, network layers
• Layer 4 switches:	OSI layers 2, 3, and 4	data-link, network, transport layers

Each of these categories of internetworking devices is explored in more detail in the following sections. Although switching was dealt with in this chapter as an internetworking design issue based on future directions such as virtual LANs and integrated routing, LAN switch technology was previously explored in the chapter on LAN hardware because of its current deployment largely in local area networks, rather than in internetworks.

A few characteristics are true of all internetworking devices in relation to the protocols of the OSI layer with which they are associated.

- Any given network device can translate or convert protocols associated with OSI layers lower than or equal to the OSI layer of the internetworking device.
- Any given network device is unable to process protocols associated with OSI layers higher than the OSI layer of the internetworking device.

The relationship between the OSI model and internetworking devices is illustrated in Figure 9-5.

Repeaters

Functionality All data traffic on a LAN is in a digital format of discrete voltages of discrete duration traveling over one type of physical media or another. The only exception to this statement would be in the case of wireless-based LANs in which case the transmission would be through the air in an analog format. Given this, a **repeater**'s job is fairly simple to understand:

- Repeat the digital signal by regenerating and retiming the incoming signal.
- Pass all signals between all attached segments.
- Do not read destination addresses of data packets.
- Allow for the connection of and translation between different types of media.

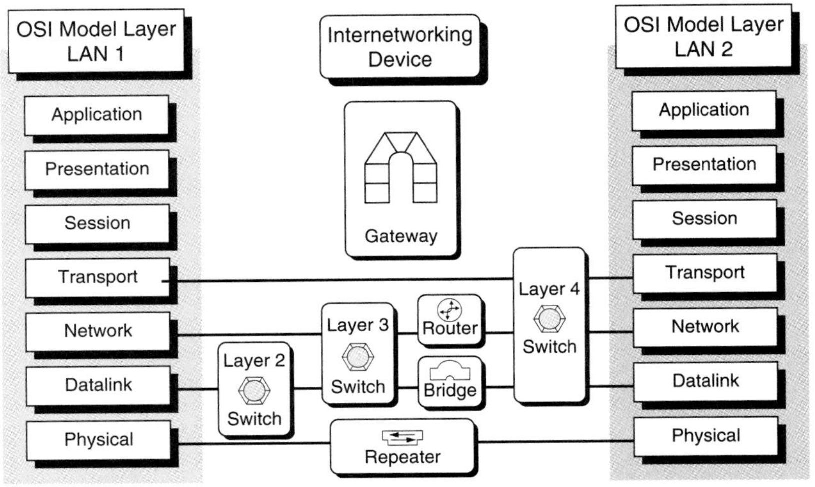

Figure 9-5 Relationship Between the OSI Model and Internetworking Devices

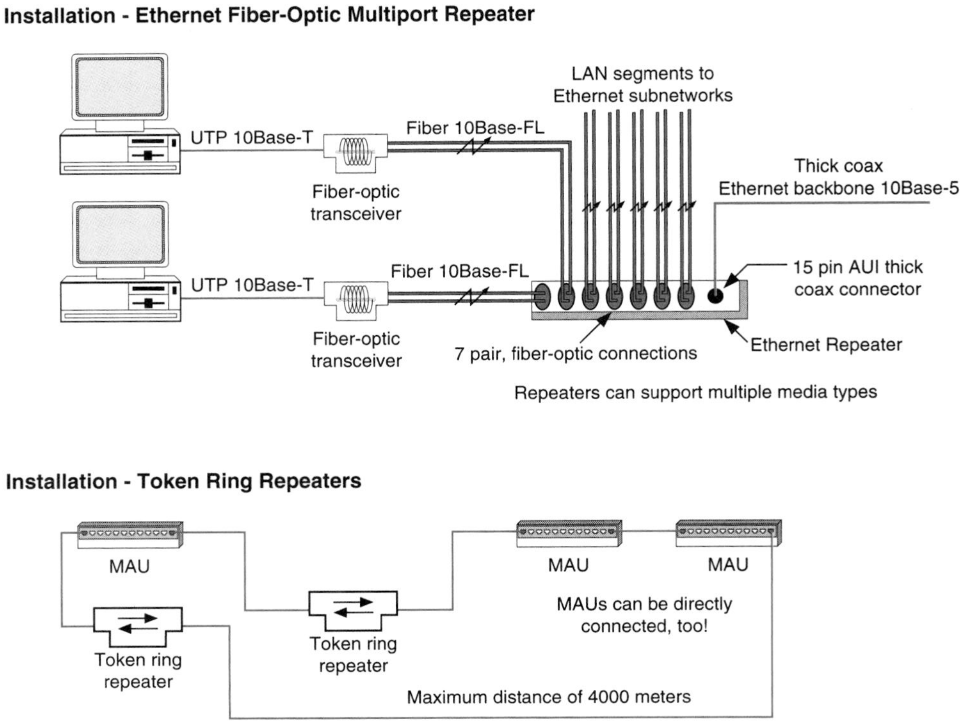

Figure 9-6 Repeater Installations

- Effectively extend overall LAN distance by repeating signals between LAN segments.

A repeater is a nondiscriminatory internetworking device. It does not discriminate between data packets. Every signal that comes into one side of a repeater gets regenerated and sent out the other side of the repeater. Repeaters are available for both Ethernet and token ring network architectures for a wide variety of media types. A repeater is a physical layer device concerned with physical layer signaling protocols relating to signal voltage levels and timing. The primary reasons for employing a repeater are as follows:

- Increase the overall length of the network media by repeating signals across multiple LAN segments. In a token ring LAN, several MAUs can be linked together by repeaters to increase the size of the LAN.
- Isolate key network resources onto different LAN segments to ensure greater survivability.
- Translate between different media types supported for a given network architecture.

Figure 9-6 illustrates typical installations of repeaters.

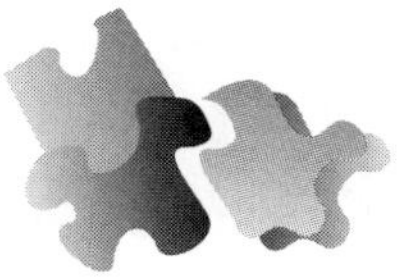

Applied Problem Solving

TECHNOLOGY ANALYSIS

Figure 9-7 outlines some of the technology analysis issues that should be considered before purchasing Ethernet or token ring repeaters.

Network Architecture	Technology Analysis Issue	Importance/Implications
Ethernet	Media type/interface support	• 10BaseT: UTP, RJ-45 • 10Base2: Thin coax, BNC • 10Base5: Thick Coax, AUI • 10BaseFL: fiber optic cable, ST or SMA connectors
	Long extended distance repeaters	• Work over single-pair telephone wire • Extend Ethernet LANs up to 1250 ft • Must be used in pairs • Fiber optic links yield distances of up to 1.2 miles
	Local repeaters	• Used to extend and segment local LANs
	Modular repeaters	• Hot-swappable modules allow flexible use for a variety of different media types and interfaces
	Workgroup repeaters	• Used for media conversion • All possible media combinations are available

Figure 9-7 Repeater Technology Analysis *(figure continues)*

	Auto-partitioning	• An important feature that prevents failure of one connected segment from affecting other segments • Auto-restoral upon segment reestablishment is often also included
	Number of segments per repeater	• Repeaters vary in segment capacity • Typical segment capacities range from 2 to 8
	Cascadability	• Some repeaters can be daisy-chained or cascaded to increase overall LAN length
	Price range	• \$250—\$2500
Token Ring	Transmission speed	• Token ring is available in 4 Mbps and 16 Mbps • Some repeaters are able to convert between speeds • Repeaters must support proper speed
	MAU ring length vs. lobe length	• Token ring repeaters can extend either the overall ring length, as measured by the distance between MAUs, or the Lobe length, which is the distance from the workstation to the MAU • Some token ring repeaters can be used to extend either ring length or lobe length
	Fiber optic repeaters	• Token ring fiber optic repeaters can extend ring length to 8200 ft
	Media type/interface support	• Type 1 cabling: STP, type 1 connectors • Type 3 cabling: UTP, RJ-45 connectors
	Price range	• \$815–\$2,300

Figure 9-7 Continued

Bridges

Functionality When users on one LAN need occasional access to data or resources from another LAN, an internetworking device that is more sophisticated and discriminating than a repeater is required. From a comparative outlook on the functionality of **bridges** vs. repeaters, one could say that bridges are more discriminating.

This reading, processing, and discriminating indicates a higher level of sophistication of the bridge, afforded by installed software, and also implies a higher price-tag than repeaters (repeaters: \$250—\$2500; bridges: \$2,000—\$6000). Bridges come in many varieties as determined by the characteristics of the two LANs joined by a particular bridge. Physically, bridges may be network interface cards that can be plugged into an expansion slot of a PC along with additional bridging software, or they may be standalone devices.

Bridge performance is generally measured by two criteria:

- **Filtering rate:** Measured in packets/sec or frames/sec. When a bridge reads the destination address on an Ethernet frame or token ring packet and decides whether or not that packet should be allowed access to the internetwork through the bridge, that process is known as **filtering.** Filtering rates for bridges range from 7000 to 60,000 frames per second.
- **Forwarding rate:** Also measured in packets/sec or frames/sec. Having decided whether or not to grant a packet access to the internetwork in the filtering process, the bridge now must perform a separate operation of **forwarding** the packet onto the internetwork media whether local or remote. Forwarding rates range from as little as 700 packets/sec for some remote bridges to as much as 30,000 packets/sec for RISC-based high-speed local bridges.

Although bridging functionality has already been reviewed in the section on internetwork design, two issues specific to bridging deserve further explanation:

- Dealing with redundant paths and broadcast storms.
- Source route bridging.

Spanning Tree Algorithm The **spanning tree algorithm (STA)** has been standardized as **IEEE 802.1** for the purposes of controlling redundant paths in bridged networks and thereby reducing the possibility of broadcast storms. When installing multiple bridges in a complex internetworking arrangement, a looping topology containing multiple active loops could be accidentally introduced into the internetwork architecture. The spanning tree algorithm (IEEE 802.1), which is implemented as software installed on STA-compliant bridges, can sense multiple paths and can disable all but one. In addition, if the primary path between two LANs becomes disabled, the spanning tree algorithm can reenable the previously disabled redundant link, thereby preserving the inter-LAN link. STA bridges accomplish this path management by communicating with each other via **configuration bridge protocol data units** (configuration BPDU). The overall effect of STA-compliant bridges is that they enable the positive aspects of redundant paths in bridged networks while eliminating the negative aspects.

Fast Spanning Tree The time that it takes the spanning tree algorithm to reenable links and reconfigure an Ethernet network is known as **recovery time. Fast spanning tree,** officially known as **IEEE 802.1w,** is an update to the spanning tree algorithm that seeks to reduce recovery time from 30 to 60 seconds to less than 10 seconds. Reducing the recovery time is required to avoid data loss and session timeouts on large switched Ethernet LANs. Until fast spanning tree, otherwise known as rapid reconfiguration, is finalized, vendor-specific solutions are available to overcome the slow recovery time from vendors such as 3Com, Cisco, and Foundry. However, these vendor-specific solutions are not interoperable.

Source Route Bridging **Source routing bridges** are not to be confused with routers since the capture of the routing information that delineates the chosen path to the destination address is done by the source device, usually a LAN-attached PC, and not by the bridge. The PC sends out a special **explorer packet** that determines the best path to the intended destination of its data message. The explorer packets are continually propagated through all source routing bridges until the destination workstation is finally reached by the explorer packet. Along the journey to the destination workstation, each source routing bridge enters its address in the **routing information field (RIF)** of the explorer packet. The destination workstation sends the completed RIF field back directly to the source workstation. All subsequent data messages include the suggested path to the destination embedded within the header of the token ring frame. Having determined the best path to the intended destination, the source PC sends the data message along with the path instructions to the local bridge that forwards the data message according to the received path instructions.

Data messages arrive at a source routing bridge with a detailed map of how they plan to reach their destination. One very important limitation of source routing bridges as applied to large internetworks is known as the **7 hop limit.** Because of the limited space in the RIF (router information field) of the explorer packet, only 7 hop locations can be included in the path to any remote destination. As a result, routers with larger routing table capacity are often employed for larger internetworks.

To avoid constantly flooding the network with explorer packets seeking destinations, source routing bridges may employ some type of **address caching** or RIF caching, so that previously determined routes to known destinations are saved and reused.

Applied Problem Solving

TECHNOLOGY ANALYSIS

Bridges can be categorized in a number of different ways. Perhaps the major criterion for categorizing bridges is the network architecture of the LANs to be joined by the bridge.

First and foremost are the two LANs that are to be bridged Ethernet or token ring? Bridges that connect LANs of similar data-link format are known as **transparent bridges.** Transparent bridges exhibit the following characteristics:

- **Promiscuous listen,** meaning that transparent bridges receive all data packets transmitted on the LANs to which they are connected.
- Store-and-forward bridging between LANs means that messages that are not destined for local workstations are forwarded through the bridge as soon as the target LAN is available.
- Learning is achieved by examining all MAC source addresses on data-link frames received to understand which workstations are locally attached to which LANs through which ports on the bridge.
- The IEEE 802.1 spanning tree algorithm is implemented to manage path connectivity between LANs.

A special type of bridge that includes a **format converter** can bridge between Ethernet and token ring. These special bridges may also be called **multiprotocol bridges** or **translating bridges.**

A third type of bridge, somewhat like a translating bridge, is used to bridge between Ethernet and FDDI networks. Unlike the translating bridge that must actually manipulate and rewrite the data-link layer frame, the **encapsulating bridge** merely takes the entire Ethernet data-link layer frame and stuffs it in an "envelope" (data frame) that conforms to the FDDI data-link layer protocol.

Source routing bridges are specifically designed for connecting token ring LANs that have source routing enabled. Not all token ring LANs are source-routing LANs, but only token ring LANs can be source-routing LANs. Bridges that can support links between source-routing token ring LANs or transparent LANs are known as **source routing transparent (SRT) bridges.** These bridges are able to identify whether frames are to be bridged transparently or source routed by reading the flags setting in the data-link frame header.

Figure 9-8 illustrates typical bridge installations and Figure 9-9 identifies some of the technology analysis issues that should be considered before purchasing bridge technology.

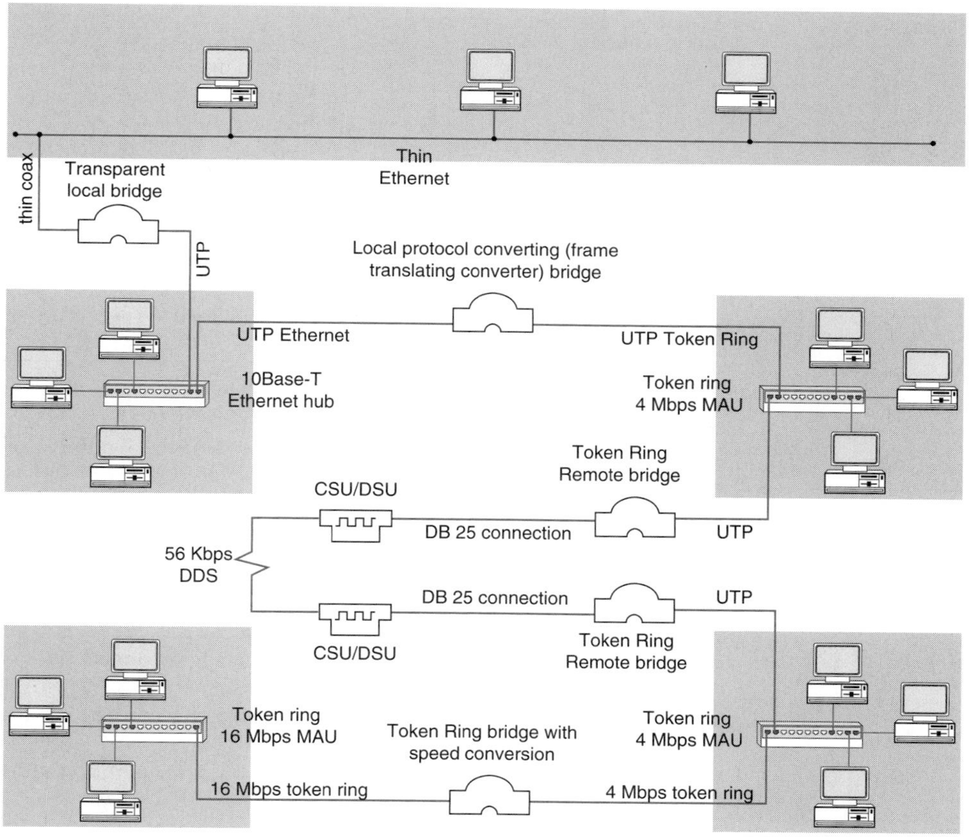

Figure 9-8 Bridge Installations

Bridge Technology Analysis Issue	Importance/Implication
Network Architectures to Be Connected	• Bridges for Ethernet and token ring are common • Bridges for FDDI, 100BaseT, and 100VGAnyLAN are less common • Network architecture determines LAN speed • Network architecture determines supported network media
Transparent Bridges	• Used for connecting Ethernet to Ethernet or non-source-routing token ring to non-source-routing token ring • Must be able to support promiscuous listen, store-and-forward bridging, learning, and spanning tree algorithm
Translating Bridges	• Ethernet/token ring is the most common translating bridge • Can become a serious network bottleneck due to incompatibilities between Ethernet and token ring frame layouts, transmission speeds, and frame lengths
Source Routing Bridges	• Used to connect two or more source-routing enabled token ring LANs • Source routes are determined by explorer packet broadcasts • Explorer packet broadcasts can negatively affect network performance • Routes are limited to 7 hops (intermediate bridges)
Source Routing Transparent Bridges	• An intelligent bridge that is able to distinguish between transparent bridge traffic and source routing bridge traffic and is able to bridge each appropriately

Bridge Performance Testing	• Bridge performance can be measured in any of the following ways:
	  • Throughput: Maximum sustained transmission rate with zero errors or lost packets
	  • Packet loss rate: % of packets lost at maximum theoretical transmission speed of the bridge
	  • Latency: The time it takes for a bridge to process a single packet. In other words, the delay per packet introduced by the bridge

Local Bridges	• Local bridges connect two or more LANs directly via network media • Local bridges contain two or more network interface cards • Local bridges are used to translate between media types
Multiport Bridges	• Multiport bridges contain more than two network interface cards

Figure 9-9 Bridge Technology Analysis *(figure continues)*

Bridge Technology Analysis Issue	Importance/Implication
	• If the bridge has learned which ports a destination workstation is attached to (by building known local nodes table for each port), it will forward the data-link layer frame to that port • If the bridge does not know which port a destination workstation is attached to, it will broadcast the data-link layer frame to all ports except the one from which it came
Remote Bridges	• Remote bridges contain network interface cards as well as serial ports for connection to WAN links via modems or CSU/DSUs • Most remote bridges contain one network interface card, specific to a particular network architecture, and one serial interface. (RS-232 or V.35) • A compatible remote bridge must be used on the far end of the WAN link to complete the LAN-to-LAN connection • Data compression is particularly important to remote bridges as the WAN links possess significantly less bandwidth than the LANs. Although compression rates depend on the file being compressed, 3:1 compression ratios are possible • SNMP management information from remote bridges is important to allow these bridges to be monitored and managed by an SNMP-compliant enterprise network management system • To be able to configure remote bridges from a centralized support location, the remote bridges must support Telnet login
WAN Services for Remote Bridges	• Among the WAN services available for remote bridges are 56K DDS, ISDN, T-1 (1.544 Mbps)
Hot-Swappable Modules	• Some bridges may support hot-swappable modules allowing users to flexibly configure the network interfaces in a bridge without disabling the network
RISC Processors	• Bridge performance is directly related to the speed of the processor within the bridge • RISC processors produce superior performance results
Price Range	• $2,000–$6,000

Figure 9-9 Continued

Wireless Bridges When corporate LAN locations are located up to 3 miles apart, remote bridges linked by WAN services such as 56 Kbps or faster lines are a common internetworking solution. This design implies monthly recurring expenses of approximately $500 for the WAN services in addition to fixed costs for the acquisition of the remote bridges and associated transmission equipment. An increasingly popular alternative for bridging remote LANs within 3 miles of each other are **wire-**

less bridges. Wireless bridges use spread spectrum radio transmission between LAN sites and are primarily limited to Ethernet networks at this time.

Like most Ethernet bridges, most wireless bridges support the spanning tree algorithm, filtering by MAC addresses, protection against broadcast storms, SNMP management, encryption, and a variety of different Ethernet network media. Like other remote bridges, wireless bridges must be used in pairs. List prices can range from $2700 to $13,500, with the majority of wireless bridges in the $4000 to $5000 range. These prices make wireless bridges comparable to remote WAN bridges in initial cost but have the added advantage of not requiring ongoing monthly expense for WAN services.

Routers

Functionality Among the advanced functionality offered by routers, perhaps the most important is their ability to discriminate between multiple network layer protocols. For instance, remembering that multiple protocols can be "sealed" within Ethernet data-link layer "envelopes," a router may be programmed to open the Ethernet envelopes and forward all NetWare (IPX) traffic to one network and all TCP/IP (IP) or AppleTalk (AFP) to another. In some cases, a certain protocol may require "priority" handling due to session time-out restrictions or the time sensitivity of the embedded data.

Routers are made to read specific network layer protocols to maximize filtering and forwarding rates. If a router has to route only one type of network protocol, then it knows exactly where to look for destination addresses every time and can process packets much faster. However, realizing that different network layer protocols will have different packet structures with the destination addresses of various lengths and positions, some more sophisticated routers known as **multiprotocol routers** have the capability to interpret, process, and forward data packets of multiple protocols.

In the case of an Ethernet data-link frame, the multiprotocol router knows which network layer protocol is embedded within the data-link frame's information field by the contents of the TYPE field in the Ethernet frame.

Some common network layer protocols and their associated network operating systems or upper layer protocols are as follows:

- IPX NetWare
- IP TCP/IP
- VIP Vines
- AFP AppleTalk
- XNS 3Com
- OSI Open Systems

Other protocols processed by some routers are actually data-link layer protocols without network-layer addressing schemes. These protocols are considered nonroutable. **Nonroutable protocols** can be processed by routers either by having the routers act as bridges or by encapsulating the nonroutable data-link layer frame's upper layer protocols in a routable network layer protocol such as IP. At one time, specialized devices which could either bridge or route were referred to as **brouters;**

however, today most advanced routers include bridging functionality. The following are some of the more common nonroutable protocols and their associated networking environments:

- LAT — Digital DECNet
- SNA/SDLC — IBM SNA
- NetBIOS — DOS-based LANs
- NetBEUI — LAN Manager

In Sharper Focus

ROUTING PROTOCOLS

Routers manufactured by different vendors need a way to talk to each other to exchange routing table information concerning current network conditions. Routing protocols used among routers within a given enterprise network are generally referred to as **interior gateway protocols.** Every network operating system contains an associated routing protocol as part of its protocol stack. Figure 9-10 lists common routing protocols (interior gateway protocols) and their associated protocol suites or network environments.

RIP, routing information protocol, at one time the most popular router protocol standard, is largely being replaced by **OSPF, open shortest path first.** OSPF offers several advantages over RIP including its ability to handle larger internetworks and a smaller impact on network traffic for routing table updates.

A major distinction between routing protocols is the method or algorithm by which up-to-date routing information is gathered by the router. For instance, RIP uses a **distance vector** algorithm, which measures only the number of hops to a distant router, to a maximum of 16, whereas the OSPF protocol uses a more comprehensive **link state** algorithm, which can decide between multiple paths to a given router based on variables other than number of hops such as delay, capacity, throughput, and reliability of the circuits connecting the routers. Perhaps more important, OSPF uses much less bandwidth in its efforts to keep routing tables up to date.

Distance vector routing requires each router to maintain a table listing the distances in hops, sometimes referred to as link cost, between itself and every other

Routing Protocol		Network Environment
RIP/RIP2	(routing information protocol)	XNS, NetWare, TCP/IP
OSPF	(open shortest path first)	TCP/IP
NLSP	(NetWare link state protocol)	NetWare 4.1
IS-IS	(Intermediate system to intermediate system)	DECnet, OSI
IGRP	(interior gateway protocol)	Cisco
EIGRP	(enhanced interior gateway protocol)	Cisco
RTMP	(routing table maintenance protocol)	AppleTalk
RTP	(router table protocol)	Vines

Figure 9-10 Router-to-Router Protocols

reachable network. These distances are computed by using the contents of neighboring routers' routing tables and adding the distance between itself and the neighboring router that supplied the routing table information. Routing tables must be kept up-to-date to reflect any changes in the network. The key problem with distance vector routing protocols is that changes in the network are not always known by all routers immediately due to the delays in having routers recalculate their own routing tables before retransmitting updated information to neighboring routers. This phenomenon is referred to as **slow convergence.**

Link state protocols such as OSPF (TCP/IP) and NLSP (NetWare) are able to overcome slow convergence and offer a number of other performance enhancements as well. One important distinction between distance vector and link state routing protocols is that distance vector routing protocols only use information supplied by directly attached neighboring routers, whereas link state routing protocols employ network information received from all routers on a given internetwork.

Link state routing protocols are able to maintain a complete and more current view of the total internetwork than distance vector routing protocols by adhering to the following basic processes:

- Link state routers use specialized datagrams known as **link state packets (LSP)** to determine the names of and the cost or distance to any neighboring routers and associated networks.
- All information learned about the network is sent to all known routers, not just neighboring routers, using LSPs.
- All routers have all other routers' full knowledge of the entire internetwork via the receipt of LSPs. The collection of LSPs is stored in an LSP database. This full internetwork view is in contrast to a view of only one's immediate neighbors using a distance vector protocol.
- Each router is responsible for compiling the information contained in all of the most recently received LSPs to form an up-to-the-minute view of the entire internetwork. From this full view of the internetwork, the link state routing protocol is able to calculate the best path to each destination network as well as a variety of alternate paths with varying costs.
- Newly received LSPs can be forwarded immediately, whereas distance vector routing protocols had to recalculate their own routing tables before forwarding updated information to neighboring routers. The immediate forwarding of LSPs allows quicker convergence in the case of lost links or newly added nodes.

Figure 9-11 summarizes the key differences between distance vector and link state interior gateway protocols.

Exterior Gateway Protocols Whereas interior gateway protocols are used by routers within a given enterprise network, **exterior gateway protocols (EGP)** are required by routers belonging to different enterprise networks or **autonomous systems.** An autonomous system is rather arbitrarily defined as a network under the authority of a single entity whose interior routing policies or interior gateway protocols (IGP) are independent of those of any other autonomous system.

The most common exterior gateway protocol currently is **BGP4 (border gateway protocol version 4).** BGP (border gateway protocol) is an exterior gateway protocol

	Distance Vector	Link State
Examples	RIPv1, RIPv2, IGRP, EIGRP	OSPF, NLSP, ISIS
Updates	Entire routing table exchanged with neighbor every 30–90 seconds, depending on protocol	Updates to routing table are sent out only as needed
Processing	After receiving neighboring router's routing table, each router recomputes all routing table entries based on its distance from the sending router	Link state packets are processed immediately; information contained therein is added to update the overall view of the network
Extent of View	Can see only its neighboring routers whom it depends on for broader view of network	Each router has a view of the entire network since all link state packets are received and incorporated by all routers
Bandwidth Usage	More	Less
Processor and Memory Usage	Less	More
Metric	RIP:Hop Count IGRP: bandwidth, delay, load, reliability, maximum transmission unit	Cost, shortest path algorithm
Advantages	• Low processing and memory usage • Simpler to implement	• No routing table exchange • No hop count limit • Link bandwidth and delay are considered in routing decisions • Fast convergence • Support for VLSM and CIDR • Hierarchical view of network scales better for large internet-work
Disadvantages	• Doesn't consider bandwidth of links when making routing decisions • Slow convergence • Hop count limit of 15, 16 = unreachable • Exchanging entire routing tables is inefficient • Don't support variable length subnet masks and classless inter domain routing (RIPv1) • No hierarchy to network view, can't scale to large internetworks	• More processor and memory intensive • More complicated to implement

Figure 9-11 Distance Vector vs. Link State Protocols

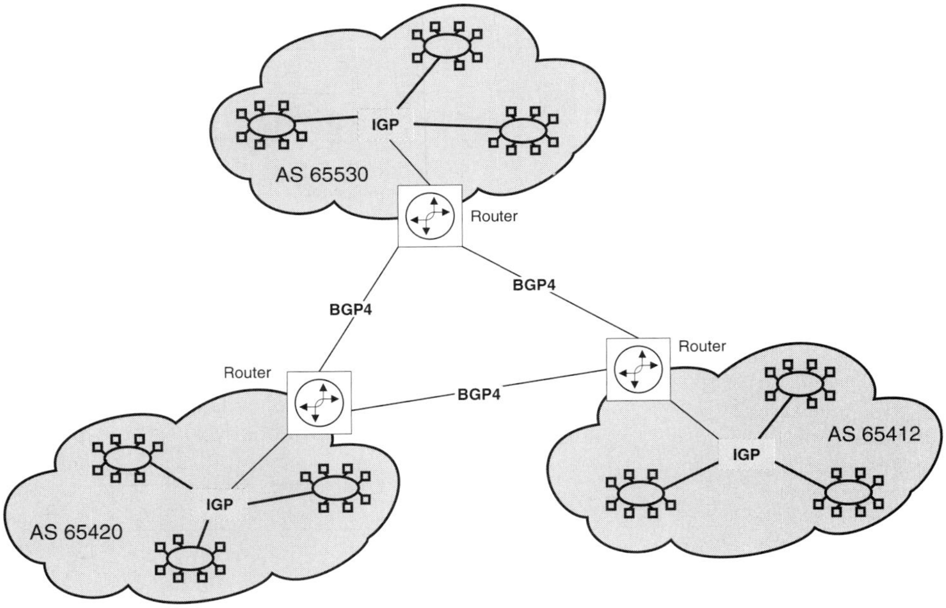

Figure 9-12 Autonomous Systems and Exterior Gateway Protocols

that performs routing between multiple autonomous systems or domains and exchanges routing and reachability information with other BGP systems. To the outside world, the AS is seen as a single entity. Each AS runs its own IGP (interior gateway protocol) independent of any other AS. Simply stated, any network can talk to any other network via the Internet because, regardless of what routing protocols those networks may speak internally, they all speak the same language (BGP) externally. Strictly speaking, BGP is a **path vector protocol.** This means that BGP routers exchange path information, which is a series of AS numbers, to indicate paths between autonomous systems. Routing policy in BGP can be very finely defined by manipulating BGP attributes and by setting route filtering. Figure 9-12 is a simple diagram illustrating these concepts.

BGP depends on TCP for path vector information delivery and is therefore considered a reliable protocol. BGP works on the concept of neighboring autonomous systems. Once a neighbor to a given autonomous system is discovered, keep-alive messages are continuously exchanged between neighboring autonomous systems to ensure the viability of advertised paths. In this manner, BGP routers know when neighboring routers fail and when path information becomes invalid. Each BGP router on an autonomous system is configured to advertise the summarized networks within that autonomous system and to define which routers on neighboring autonomous systems it will exchange path vector information with. Administrative weights can be assigned to different paths to make one path more attractive than another.

In the case of autonomous systems, static routing may be preferable to dynamic routing. Because routing information is not shared over the link connecting the various autonomous systems, the danger of having a misbehaving router from another autonomous system negatively affect the routers within a given autonomous system is minimized.

OSPF Areas If the interior gateway protocol in a given network is OSPF, then an additional layer of network hierarchy known as the **OSPF area** is introduced. All OSPF networks have at least one area, known as area 0 or the backbone area, configured. Depending on the size of the network, to keep the topological databases of manageable size and to reduce the amount of OSPF information that needs to be transmitted between routers, additional areas can be defined. All areas would communicate with each other through area 0, the backbone area.

Private Addressing and Network Address Translation As previously mentioned, routers make routing decisions based on information stored in routing tables. That information is organized according to subnet IDS that represent collections of IP addresses organized into logical groups. As more and more enterprises and individuals have wished to be linked to enterprise networks and the Internet, the demand for IP addresses has grown exponentially. IP address depletion has resulted from the explosion of the Internet as well as the inefficient use of existing IP addresses forced by classfull addressing. One way to cope with the rapid depletion of IP addresses is the use of **private addressing.**

When organizations connect to the Internet, the IP addresses that they send out must be globally unique. In most cases, these globally unique addresses are specified by an organization's Internet service provider.

However, traffic that remains only on an organization's private network does not need to be globally unique but only unique across that organization's private network. In support of this need, the Internet assigned numbers authority (IANA) has set aside the following three ranges of private IP addresses:

- 10.0.0.0–10.255.255.255 (equal to a single Class A Network ID)
- 172.16.0.0–172.31.255.255 (equal to 16 contiguous Class B Network IDs)
- 192.168.0.0–192.168.255.255 (equal to 256 contiguous Class C Network IDs)

Traffic using any of these address ranges must remain on the organization's private network. Because anyone is welcome to use these address ranges, they are not globally unique and therefore cannot be used on the Internet.

Computers on a network using the private IP address space can still send and receive traffic to and from the Internet by using **network address translation (NAT).** Network address translation can be provided by a router or by a stand-alone network translation software package running on a multihomed server. A multihomed server is the term used to describe a server that has one network interface card that is a member of the internal private IP address space network and one network interface card that is assigned a globally unique IP address. A version of such a program that is included as a networking feature of Linux is known as IP Masquerade, and a version that runs on Windows NT is known as WinRoute (www.winroute.com). A Linux IP Masquerade resource page can be found at bookmark http://ipmasq.cjb.net/. An added benefit of NAT is that the organization's private network is not visible from the Internet. Figure 9-13 illustrates how network translation allows an organization to use private addressing while still benefiting from global Internet connectivity.

As can be seen in Figure 9-13, all of the workstations on the private network can share a single IP address (195.75.16.65) to the global Internet because the NAT software maintains a table of connections and maps each private workstation to a unique TCP port number. In the case of WinRoute, these port numbers are in the range of 61000–61600 so as not to be confused with more commonly used port numbers.

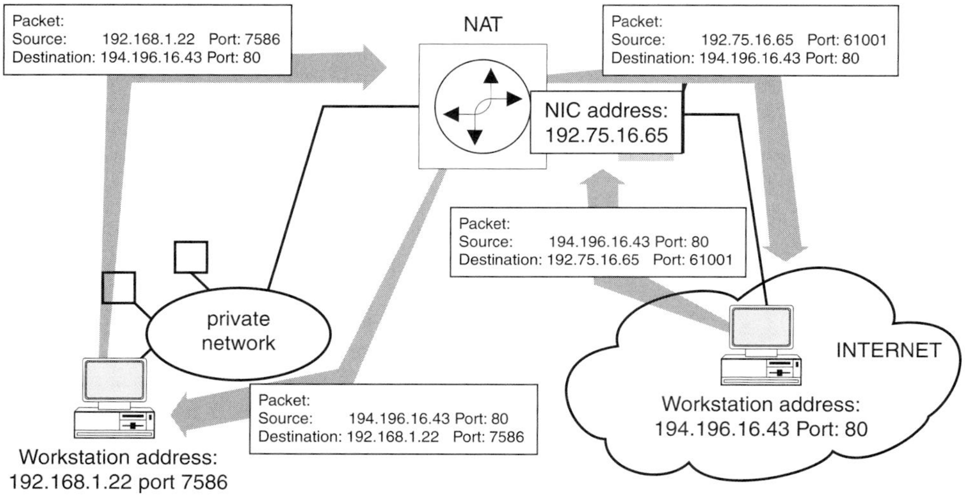

NAT Source/Destination Table

Private Source IP Address	Private Source Assigned Port ID
192.168.1.22	61001
192.168.1.23	61002
192.168.1.24	61003
192.168.1.25	61004
..and so on..	..and so on..

Figure 9-13 Network Address Translation

Applied Problem Solving

TECHNOLOGY ANALYSIS

The most significant distinguishing factor among routers is directly related to the location and associated routing requirements into which the router is to be deployed. As a result, **central site routers,** otherwise known as enterprise or backbone routers are employed at large corporate sites, while **boundary** or branch office **routers** are employed at remote corporate locations with less routing requirements and fewer technical support personnel. For branch offices whose amount of internetwork traffic does not warrant the constant bandwidth and higher cost of leased lines, **dial-up routers,** often using ISDN, are employed. Figure 9-14 illustrates the installation of various types of routers.

Boundary Routers In the case of boundary routers, all routing information is kept at the central site router. This allows the boundary router to require less technical configuration and to be available for a lower cost than central site routers. Boundary routers generally have just two interfaces, one WAN link and one LAN link. A boundary router's logic is fairly simple. All locally generated packets are either destined for the local LAN, in which case they are ignored, or they are nonlocal, in which case they are forwarded over the single WAN link to the central site router for further processing.

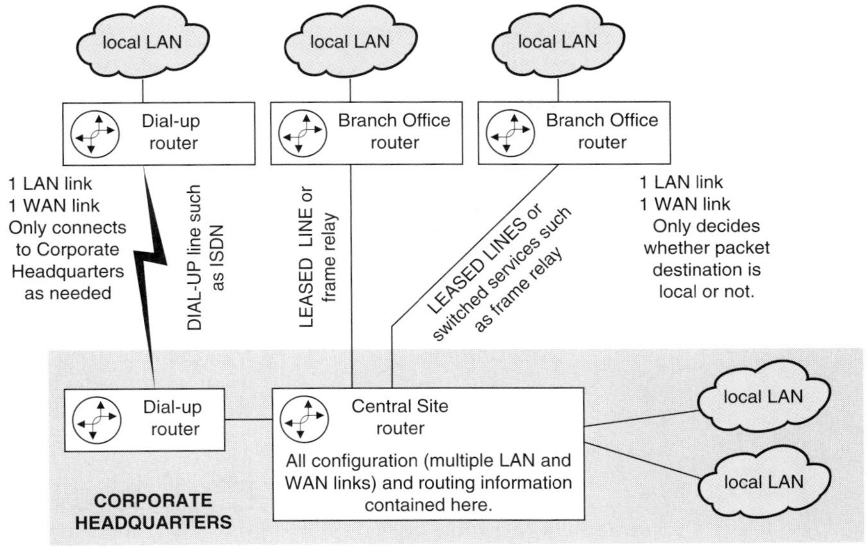

Figure 9-14 Router Installations

The obvious limitation of such a topology is that there is no direct communication between boundary routers and that the central routers must include redundancy because all internetwork communication depends on them. Also, a particular vendor's boundary routers must be matched with that vendor's central office routers, as there are no interoperability standards for this configuration. Figure 9-15 outlines some of the technical analysis issues to be considered with boundary routers.

Dial-Up Routers If the amount of inter-LAN traffic from a remote site does not justify the cost of a leased line, dial-up routers may be the appropriate choice of internetworking equipment. This is especially true if the dial-up digital WAN service known as ISDN (integrated services digital network) is available at the two ends of the LANs to be linked. ISDN BRI (basic rate interface) provides up to 128 Kbps of bandwidth on demand, and ISDN PRI (primary rate interface) provides up to 1.536 Mbps of usable digital bandwidth on demand. There are currently no interoperability standards for dial-up routers. As a result, dial-up routers should always be bought in pairs from the same manufacturer.

In addition to all of the technical features that are important to boundary routers, perhaps the most important feature of dial-up routers is **spoofing.** Spoofing is a method of filtering chatty or unwanted protocols from the WAN link while assuring that remote programs that require on-going communication from these filtered protocols are still reassured via emulation of these protocols by the local dial-up router. Among the chatty protocols that are most in need of filtering are:

- RIP (routing information protocol): NetWare and TCP/IP.
- SAP (service advertising protocol): NetWare.
- Watchdog, otherwise known as keep-alive messages: NetWare.
- Serialization, looking for duplicate license numbers: NetWare.

Technical Analysis Issue	Importance/Implication
Ability to Deal with Non - Routable Traffic	• Must be able to deal with nonroutable protocols such as SNA/SDLC and NetBIOS • Must be able to deal with timing requirements such as SDLC's session time-out limitation
Remote Configuration Support	• Must be able to be configured remotely • Software upgrades must be able to be performed remotely from central site • What happens if the transmission line or power fails during a remote update?
SNMP Compatibility	• Must be able to output SNMP-compatible management information for interaction with enterprise network management systems
WAN Services Supported	• May be any of the following: 56K DDS, T-1, frame relay
Frame Relay Support	• If frame relay is to be used as the WAN service, can the device interact properly with frame relay's congestion control mechanism to avoid packet loss?
Backup WAN Services	• Are switched WAN services available for backup if the leased line fails? • Examples: ISDN, dial-up Async, switched 56K
WAN Protocols Supported	• Examples: HDLC, X.25 frame relay, PPP
LAN Network Architectures Supported	• Examples: Ethernet, token ring. Others?
LAN Protocols Routed	• Example; IP, IPX, DECnet, AppleTalk, Vines, XNS, OSI
LAN Protocols Filtered	• Some LAN protocols are very chatty and can waste precious WAN bandwidth • Boundary routers should be able to filter these protocols to keep them off the WAN link: SAP, RIP, NetBIOS broadcasts, source routing explorer packets

Figure 9-15 Boundary Routers Technology Analysis

The reason filtering is so important to dial-up routers is that these unwanted protocols can easily establish or keep a dial-up line open, thereby unnecessarily leading to excessive line charges. Spoofing as a combination of filtering and emulation is illustrated in Figure 9-16.

Occasionally, updated information such as session status or services availability must be exchanged between dial-up routers so that packets are not routed in error and sessions are not terminated incorrectly. The manner in which these required updates of overhead information are performed can make a significant difference in the efficiency of the dial-up routers and the size of the associated charge for the use of dial-up bandwidth. It is important to remember that these routers only communicate via dial-up connections and that it would be economically unwise to create or maintain immediate dial-up connections for every update of overhead information.

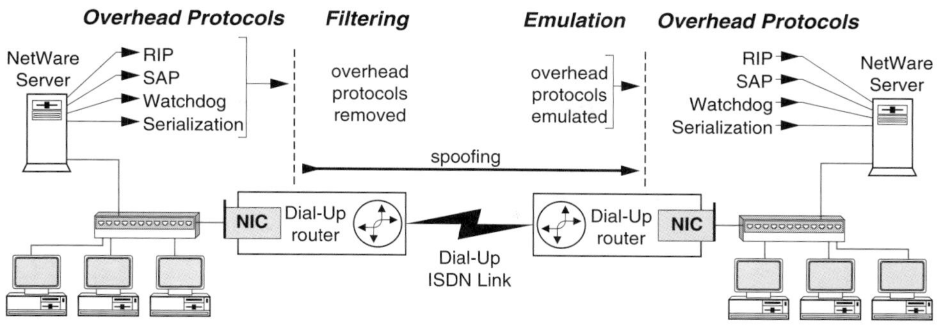

Figure 9-16 Dial-Up Router Spoofing

Different dial-up routers use different update mechanisms. Three primary methods for efficient updating are as follows:

- **Timed updates** are performed at regular predetermined intervals.
- **Triggered updates** are performed whenever a certain programmable event, such as a change in available services, occurs.
- **Piggyback updates** are performed only when the dial-up link has already been established for the purposes of exchanging user data.

ISDN router technology analysis issues other than spoofing are summarized in Figure 9-17.

Routing Evolution Although no one knows for sure what the future of internetworking design and technology holds, most people seem to agree that some combination of switching and routing will be the likely scenario in the foreseeable future. Although switching is excellent for providing large amounts of switched LAN bandwidth, it is a layer 2 technology and is unable to offer advanced filtering, security, and internetwork segmentation associated with layer 3 routing technology.

Three different possible internetwork design evolutionary scenarios are as follows:

- **Distinct layer 2 switching and layer 3 routing** in which separate layer 2 switches and layer 3 routers cooperatively contribute what each does best to deliver internetwork traffic as efficiently as possible.
- **Distributed routing** in which layer 2 switching and layer 3 routing functionality are combined into a single device sometimes referred to as a **multilayer or layer 3 switch.**
- **Route servers** will provide a centralized repository of routing information and **edge switches** deployed within the LANs will be programmed with minimal routing information. Edge switches will consult distributed route servers for "directory assistance" when they encounter routing situations they are not equipped to handle. In this scenario, routing information and

Technical Analysis Issue	Importance/Implication
Categorization	• LAN modems: less than 24 users, local LAN, dial-up BRI ISDN, shared IP address • Branch office routers: voice support, more than 24 users; supports routing tables, firewalls, virtual private networks
Automatic SPID Detection	• Service profile identifier number (see Chapter 8) must be configured into the ISDN router; Auto-detection can be a real time saver
Voice Disguise	• Some carriers charge more for voice transmission over ISDN; these charges can be avoided if the ISDN router can disguise the voice as data on a B channel
Network Address Translation	• Allows a single assigned IP address to be shared by multiple workstations on the interior or private network (see explanation in previous section)
Bandwidth on Demand	• Among the protocols that should be supported are MLPPP (multilink point-to-point protocol) and BACP (bandwidth allocation control protocol)
Transport Protocols	• All routers support IP, but some also support IPX and/or AppleTalk
Routing Protocols	• Most ISDN routers support only RIP, hopefully RIP2
Security	• Some ISDN routers include built-in firewall capability
Compression	• Given the relatively limited bandwidth of ISDN, it is important to make the most of it by compressing data; ISDN routers may differ in the number of compression algorithms supported
Port Density	• ISDN routers differ in the number of integrated 10Base-T ports and analog voice ports supported

Figure 9-17 ISDN Router Technology Analysis

processing overhead are kept to a minimum at the switches, which are primarily responsible for providing local bandwidth.

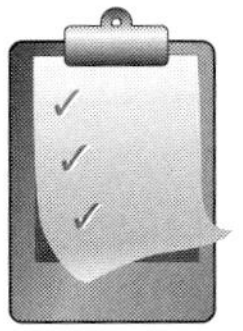

Practical Advice and Information

In differing manners, each of these scenarios implements the future of internetwork design as described by the currently popular phrase, "Switch when you can, route when you must." These three internetworking design scenarios combining switching and routing are illustrated in Figure 9-18.

Terabit Routers Another aspect of router evolution is the substantial increase in router processing power. Such routers are referred to by a variety of names including terabit routers, wire-speed routers, or wire-rate routers. Such routers can perform more than 40 million route lookups per second and possess aggregate throughput rates ranging from 10 Gbps to 160 Gbps. Theoretical maximum capacity of such devices are as high as 184 terabits per second. However, to compute the actual maximum usable capacity, one should multiply the maximum number of ports on a single chassis by the maximum port speed. They are able to support a variety of interfaces including gigabit Ethernet, ATM, and SONET (OC-48). Vendors of terabit routers

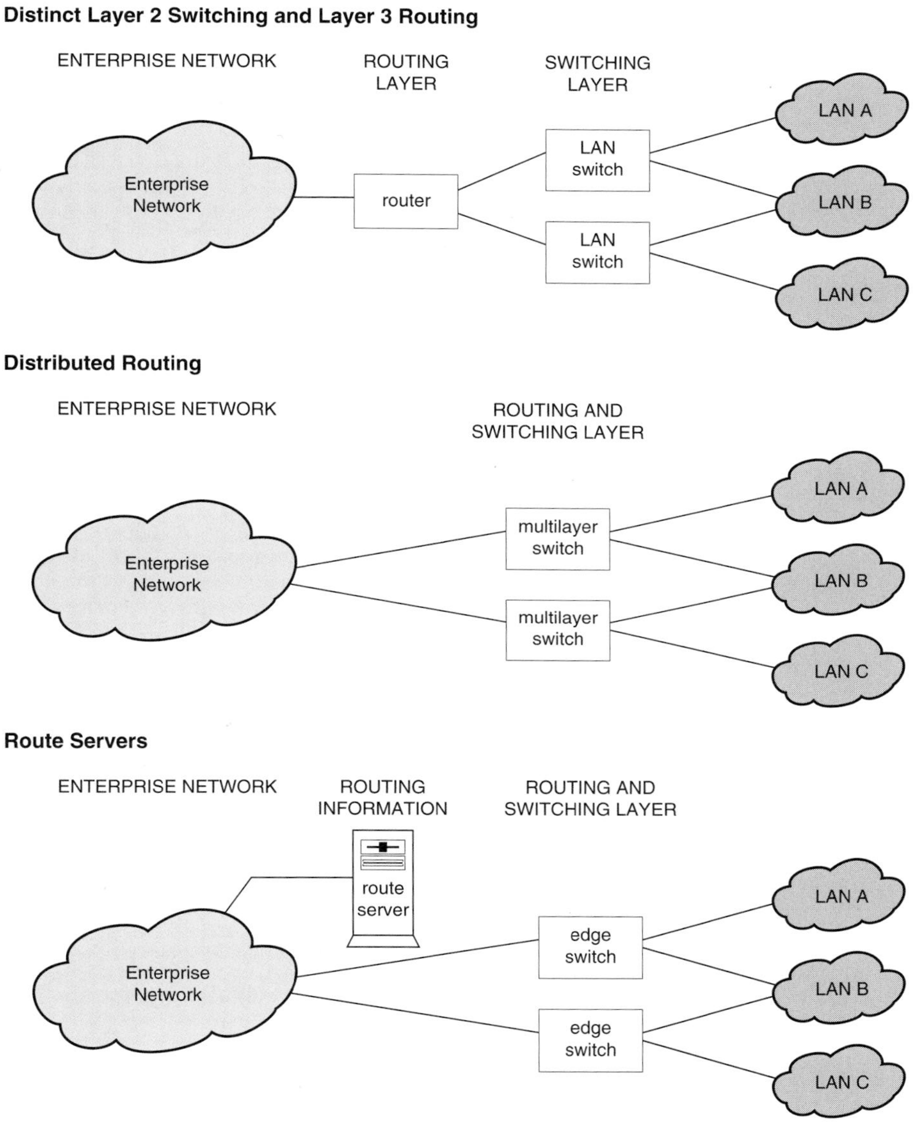

Figure 9-18 Routing Evolution Scenarios

include Argon, Avici, Charlotte's Web, Cisco, Juniper, Lucent, NetCore, Nexabit, Nortel, Packet, and Pluris.

IP Switching and Quality of Service Another possible evolutionary scenario combining switching and routing is known as **IP switching.** By implementing IP routing software directly on ATM switching hardware, IP switching combines switching and routing capabilities into a single device and discriminates between which traffic should be switched and which should be routed. For streaming data such as file transfers or multimedia sessions, ATM-switched virtual circuits are established, and the traffic is allowed to flow through the virtual circuit without the typical packet-by-packet processing associated with routers. For connectionless datagrams and shorter transmissions, IP routing software is implemented. Protocols to distinguish which traffic should be switched and which should be routed have been proposed by at least three different companies and will eventually be considered by the IETF. The early entries for IP switching management protocols are flow management protocol from IPsilon Networks, tag distribution protocol from Cisco, and aggregate route-based IP switching from IBM. IPsilon was an early promoter of IP switching that was later acquired by Nokia. Cisco's tag switching protocol became known as **MPLS (multiprotocol label switching)** when it began deliberation by the IETF.

Although MPLS was originally intended for use within a switched internetwork environment, the scope of its application has broadened to include the Internet. MPLS provides the following functionality:

- Uses labels to provide shortcuts to specific circuits for fast routing of IP packets without the typical packet-by-packet routing table lookups.
- Labels can also be used to represent **QoS (quality of service)** requirements or a virtual private network through the Internet.
- Defined for use over frame relay, ATM, and PPP (point-to-point protocol) WAN connections, and IEEE 802.3 LANs
- Supports explicit routing that allows certain types of traffic, video for instance, to be explicitly assigned to specific circuits.

However, it is this last functionality, explicit routing, which may delay the adoption of MPLS. Cisco and Juniper Networks are in favor of using RSVP (resource reservation protocol) to implement explicit routing, whereas other vendors such as Nortel and Ericsson are in favor of using LDP (label distribution protocol).

As a total alternative to MPLS, **Diff-Serv (differentiated services)** is being prepared by another IETF working group. Diff-Serv provides the following functionality:

- Uses the type of service (ToS) bits already in the IP header to differentiate among different levels of service required by different applications.
- Allows support of service level agreements between users and service providers.

Using the OSI model to differentiate between MPLS and Diff-Serv, it should be noted that MPLS is a layer 2 solution, whereas Diff-Serv is a layer 3 solution. For this reason, the two standards are not really competing, although many people perceive that to be the situation. MPLS, a layer 2 service, will work with or without Diff-Serv on layer 3. In fact, the best solution may be for the two protocols to work together, with MPLS enabling switching labels for circuit assignment after reading the ToS bits in the layer 3 IP header.

Switches and Virtual LANs

Basic Functionality The logical network design known as a virtual LAN is dependent on a physical device, the LAN switch, for its functionality. Although the original LAN switches delivered abundant bandwidth to locally attached workstations and segments, they lacked the ability to partition the switch into multiple segregated broadcast zones and to segment users into corresponding separate workgroups.

Virtual LANs are software definable through configuration software contained within the LAN switch. The use of virtual LANs allows workgroup members to be assigned, quickly and easily, to more than one workgroup if necessary. Subsequently, each virtual workgroup is assigned some portion of the LAN switch's backplane capacity. LAN switches that support virtual LANs use OSI layer 2 bridging functionality to logically segment the traffic within the switch into distinct virtual LANs.

Any message received by a LAN switch destined for a single workstation is delivered to that destination workstation via an individual switched network connection. The key difference between a LAN switch that does not support virtual LANs and one that does is the treatment of broadcast and multicast messages. In a virtual LAN, broadcasts and multicasts are limited to the members of that virtual LAN only, rather than to all connected devices. This prevents propagation of data across the entire network and reduces network traffic. To simplify, virtual LANs are nothing more than logically defined broadcast/multicast groups within layer 2 LAN switches because point-to-point traffic is handled by switched dedicated connections.

Limitations A key limitation of virtual LANs is that when members of the same virtual LAN are physically connected to separate LAN switches, the virtual LAN configuration information must be shared among multiple LAN switches. Currently, no interoperability standards exist for transmitting or sharing virtual LAN information between layer 2 LAN switches. As a result, only proprietary switch-to-switch protocols between a single vendor's equipment is possible for multiswitch virtual LANs.

Management of and monitoring virtual LANs are more difficult than for traditional LANs owing to the virtual LAN's dependence on LAN switches for physical connectivity. Because the switched LAN connections are established, used, and terminated in a matter of microseconds for most transmissions, it is difficult if not impossible to monitor these transmissions in real time by traditional means. One solution to this dilemma is known as traffic duplication in which traffic between two switch ports is duplicated onto a third port to which traditional LAN analyzers can be attached.

Figure 9-19 illustrates the differences between a LAN switch, a virtual LAN, and a multiswitch virtual LAN.

In Sharper Focus

TRANSMISSION BETWEEN LAYER 2 LAN SWITCHES

Among the alternative methods used by switch vendors to share virtual LAN information across layer 2 LAN switches are the following:

- Signaling message: Switches inform each other whenever new workstations come on line as to the MAC address and virtual LAN number of that workstation. To keep all switches' information synchronized, each switch's virtual LAN tables are broadcast periodically to all other switches. In larger switched networks, this virtual LAN table transfer can introduce significant amounts of broadcast traffic.

- Frame Tagging: A tag indicating the virtual LAN number of the source workstation is appended to every data-link layer frame that must travel between LAN switches. In this way, the recipient switch knows immediately to which virtual LAN workstations the received frame must be forwarded. One difficulty with frame tagging is that the added bits may exceed the maximum frame length of the data-link layer protocol, thereby requiring additional proprietary methods to cope with this limitation.

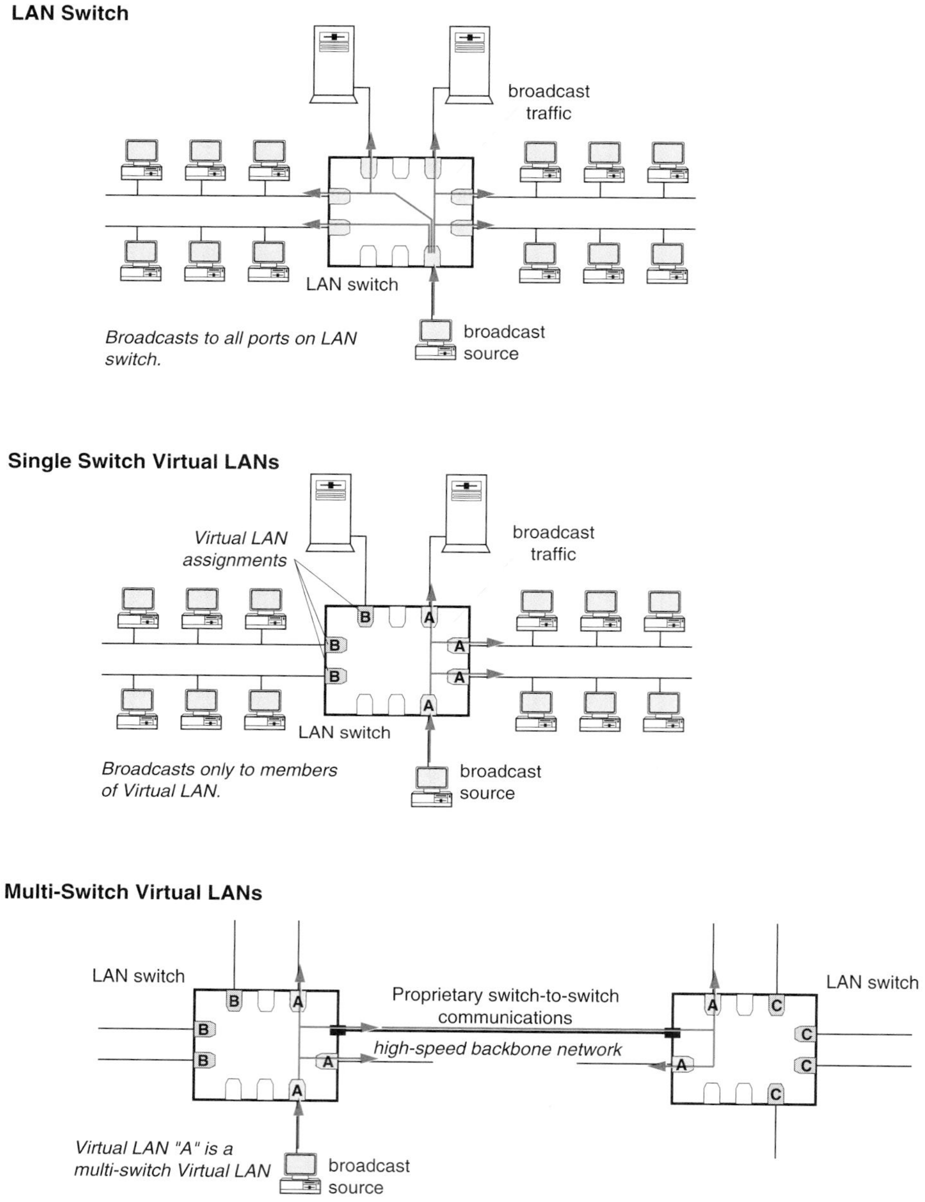

Figure 9-19 LAN Switches and Virtual LANs

- Time division multiplexing: Each virtual LAN is assigned a specific portion of the bandwidth available on the LAN switches' backplanes. Only the assigned virtual LAN is allowed to use designated bandwidth. In this way, each virtual LAN has a virtual private backplane and traffic from various virtual LANs does not interfere with each other. However, assigned but unused bandwidth cannot be shared among other virtual LANs.

One possibility for standardization of switch-to-switch communication in support of virtual LANs that span multiple switches is **IEEE 802.10.** Originally conceived as a standard for secure data exchange on LANs that would allow workstations to set encryption and authentication settings, this standard is of interest to virtual LAN switch vendors because of the addition of a 32-bit header to existing MAC sublayer frames. Instead of just holding security information, this additional 32-bit header could hold virtual LAN identifiers. To overcome the limitation on maximum data-link layer frame length, IEEE 802.10 also includes specifications for segmentation and reassembly of any frames that should exceed maximum length due to the addition of the 32-bit header.

Transmission Between Virtual LANs Virtual LANs are built using LAN switches that are OSI layer 2 devices that are only able to distinguish between MAC layer addresses. As a result, LAN switches are only able to offer the forward-if-not-local internetworking logic of bridges. To selectively transmit traffic between virtual LANs requires routing functionality. This routing functionality may be supplied by an external router or by specialized router software included in the LAN switch. LAN switches with built-in routing capabilities are sometimes referred to as layer 3 switches. Because traffic cannot move between virtual LANs without the benefit of routing, the virtual LAN logical design has been credited with offering firewall functionality owing to the filtering capabilities of intermediary routers.

Classification of Virtual LANs Virtual LANs are often classified in terms of the OSI layer that represents their highest level of functionality.

Layer 2 virtual LANs are built using LAN switches that act as microsegmenting bridges. In fact, some say that a **layer 2 switch** is nothing more than a multiport bridge. A LAN switch that supports a layer 2 virtual LAN distinguishes only between the MAC addresses of connected workstations. No differentiation is possible based on layer 3, network layer, protocols. One or more workstations can be connected to each switch port.

Layer 3 virtual LANs are built using LAN switches that are able to process layer 3 network addresses. Such devices may be called **routing switches** or **layer 3 switches.** Because these devices are able to perform filtering based on network layer protocols and addresses, they are able to support multiple virtual LANs using different network layer protocols.

In other words, one virtual LAN might support only TCP/IP, while another might only support IPX/SPX. Because layer 3 switches understand layer 3 addressing schemes, they are able to use the subnetwork numbers embedded within layer 3 addresses to organize virtual LANs. Because these subnetwork numbers are previously assigned to workstations, some layer 3 switches are able to query all connected workstations and auto-configure or automatically assign workstations to virtual LANs based on these subnetwork numbers. Workstations using nonroutable protocols such as LAT, NetBEUI, or NetBIOS are likewise segregated into their own virtual LANs.

Figure 9-20 illustrates the architectural differences between layer 2 and layer 3 virtual LANs, whereas Figure 9-21 details the functional differences between the two virtual LAN designs.

Managerial Perspective

VIRTUAL LAN REALITIES—THE BOTTOM LINE

Virtual LANs were initially touted as the ultimate solution for increasing LAN manageability and broadcast control. By implementing the "route once, switch many" concept, VLAN technologies promised to increase LAN performance while reducing management effort.

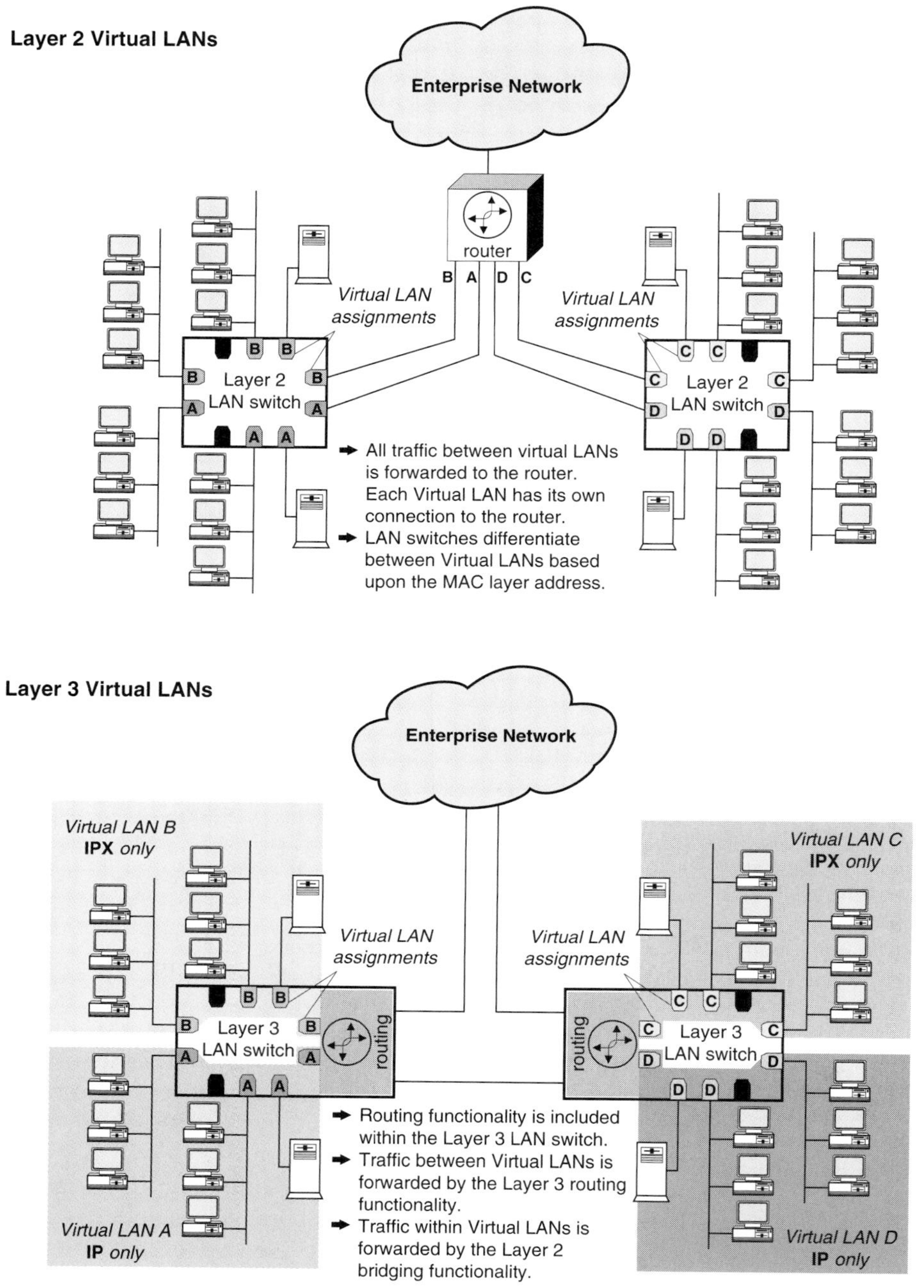

Figure 9-20 Layer 2 vs. Layer 3 Virtual LANs: An Architectural Comparison

Based on OSI network reference model layer 2 switching technologies, VLANs initially required a separate layer 3 routing device to allow traffic to flow between VLANs. To resolve this dependency on routing technologies, routing capabilities were added to layer 2 switches.

Virtual LAN Characteristic	Layer 2 Virtual LAN Functionality	Layer 3 Virtual LAN Functionality
Configuration	Simpler	More difficult
Expense	Less expensive, but may require external routers	More expensive, but include internal routing capability
Performance	Faster since they only process layer 2 addresses	Up to 30% slower since they must process layer 3 protocols.
Nonroutable Protocols	No problem since this is a layer 2 only device	May be able to segregate into a separate VLAN or may not be able to handle
Routable Protocols	No ability to differentiate between layer 3 protocols	Can differentiate between layer 3 protocols and can build separate virtual LANs based on the layer 3 protocol; layer 3 switches vary in the number of routable protocols supported
Multi-Switch Virtual LANs	Must use proprietary switch-to-switch communication, which adds to network traffic congestion in most cases	Able to use subnetwork numbers in network layer addresses to keep track of virtual LANs that span multiple switches without the need for proprietary switch-to-switch protocols
Broadcasts	Broadcasts to all segments that belong to a particular virtual LAN	Can broadcast only to appropriate subnetwork within a virtual LAN
Filtering	No filtering on network layer addresses or protocols possible	Filtering on network layer addresses and protocols for security and virtual LAN segmentation by protocol
Routing Capabilities	Must be supplied by external router	Included with built-in routing software that provides traffic management and protocol isolation. Some layer 3 switches are able to communicate with routers via RIP or OSPF while others are not able to.

Figure 9-21 Layer 2 vs. Layer 3 Virtual LANs: A Functional Comparison

LAN switches that include routing capabilities, known as layer 3 switches or routing switches, perform the traditional routing process for the first packet in a series, add the layer 2 addresses (MAC addresses) to an address table, and switch the remaining packets in the data flow at layer 2. In addition to allowing a series of switches to handle all traffic within and between VLANs, layer 3 switching can provide routing between LAN segments much faster than traditional routers.

As layer 3 switching technologies matured, the ability to analyze traffic flows based on the type of flow (as defined by the port number) was added. The resulting layer 4 switches provide a means to prioritize traffic flows based on traffic type, increase security by filtering, and collect application level traffic statistics on a per port basis.

Although the promise of VLANs to provide broadcast control has been fully realized, increasing manageability has been less successful. When a packet needs to be delivered to a VLAN node on a different physical switch, a means of identifying the VLAN to which the packet is to be delivered must be implemented.

One of the biggest issues with VLAN implementation has been the late arrival of standards for managing such multiswitch VLAN packet identification. In the absence of clear standards, VLAN technology manufacturers implemented various proprietary solutions. With these technologies currently in place, manufacturers are reluctant to replace their proprietary solutions with newer standard solutions such as IEEE 802.10 packet tagging. As a result, VLAN solutions are mostly limited to single-vendor solutions. Manageability varies widely among vendors, making it impossible to draw a definitive conclusion about overall VLAN manageability.

In addition to the growing pains experienced by VLANs, several significant technological changes have been introduced since the advent of VLAN technologies. Changes to both the normal broadcast environment and routing technologies have affected the viability of VLANs.

One of the primary reasons for implementing VLANs has traditionally been to control LAN broadcast traffic. Broadcast traffic has traditionally represented a high level of traffic overhead from ARP, RIP, and SAP broadcasts. Occasionally network nodes would error and propagate these broadcast packets repeatedly, wasting significant bandwidth. The control of broadcast activity was important because network bandwidth was very limited. In addition to the network capacity issue, each broadcast packet sent causes the network stack of each node on the network segment to analyze the packet, generating interrupts and using CPU cycles.

Research indicates, however, that broadcast control is no longer the important issue it once was. Newer network software has optimized ARP functionality, RIP is rapidly being replaced in favor of more efficient routing protocols, and IPX with its associated SAP broadcasts, is rapidly being replaced by IP. In conjunction with this reduction in broadcast frequency, bandwidth on LAN segments has been so increased that the percentage of broadcast activity is now relatively inconsequential for most LANs. The need for broadcast management has been further reduced because the increased processing power and standardization of bus mastering NIC cards have reduced the amount of node processor power wasted to processing broadcast packets to irrelevant levels for most LANs.

Based on this information, a case can be made that a network based entirely on layer 2 switching technologies is a viable option. No longer constrained by broadcast traffic concerns, such a network is significantly easier to troubleshoot and manage than a series of VLANs. As long as the backbone capacity of the layer 2 switches is adequate to meet the overall traffic needs, this type of solution would allow a node to simply be attached to any available switched port.

Routing technologies have also significantly changed. Newer routers that implement the routing function in hardware-based, application-specific integrated circuits (ASICS) have greatly reduced the latency traditionally associated with routers. These new "wire speed" routers offer IP routing performance similar to layer 3 switches while maintaining the familiar, easy to troubleshoot and manage routing paradigm. These new products also include many layer 4 switching features for packet prioritization, security, and application level packet flow data collection purposes.

Whereas wire speed routing technologies are new to the marketplace, companies such as Rapid-City Communications, Foundry Networks, and Cisco Systems (with technology acquired from Granite Systems) have developed or are developing products using this approach. These products offer gigabit speed LAN routing at costs relatively similar to layer 3 enabled VLAN switches. The use of such "wire speed" routers offers new life to the traditional routed network paradigm.

Although VLANs continue to offer excellent broadcast control and reasonable (though not standard) manageability, changes in other LAN technologies have significantly clouded the VLAN issue. It is no longer necessary to implement a VLAN solution to get many of the results associated with VLAN technologies.

Traditional switched networks can now offer similar performance to VLANs with significantly less management overhead and no standards issues. One potential concern with such large switched network designs is network address allocation. For IPX-based networks, this is not of concern, as the node section of the network layer address is not fixed. For IP-based networks, considerable network address redesign may be necessary to implement such a solution.

The advent of "wire speed" LAN routers also infringes on the market segment initially held by VLAN solutions. For an organization currently built on traditional shared media or switched LANs interconnected by routers, this solution has the added advantage of retaining the existing network design and time-tested analysis and troubleshooting techniques while increasing network performance. However, these solutions are new to the marketplace and have little to no real-world record on which to make definitive performance conclusions.

The final decision as to the best technologies to use to gain manageability and broadcast control ultimately depends on the existing network design and exact features required. For IPX-based networks, VLANs or large-switched solutions are the only viable choices, as the market for wire-speed IPX routers will probably never be strong enough to merit their development. For those solutions that require the collection of detailed information on data flows, layer 3/4 enabled VLAN solutions have the most mature data collection capabilities of the technologies reviewed.

Layer 3 and Layer 4 Switches Whereas layer 3 switches process network layer (layer 3) IP addresses and build point-to-point connections very quickly based on routing table information, layer 4 switches process TCP port numbers and can distribute multiple requests for a given service to multiple different physical servers, thus providing load balancing.

A layer 3 switch is nothing more than routing functionality delivered on ASIC (application specific integrated circuits) chips. By forcing the routing functionality onto silicon, significant price/performance gains can be realized when migrating from traditional software based routers to layer 3 switches. Layer 3 switches also simplify moves, adds, and changes for network administrators through their support of layer 3 virtual LANs, which don't require the network administrators to know which physical ports users are attached to.

A **layer 4 switch** uses a virtual IP address to balance traffic across multiple servers based on session information and status. This process is sometimes referred to as service-based load balancing. Layer 4 switches are best used when multiple servers are offering the same applications and require load balancing across those multiple servers. The layer 4 switch is capable of determining which session is being requested and submitting that request to the most available server by substituting the IP address of the virtual server with the IP address of the actual server to which the request is being forwarded. However, because of the virtual IP address running NAT (network address translation), the multiple load balanced servers in the background are transparent to users and their applications. Layer 4 switching is sometimes referred to application redirection. In some cases, switches can examine content above layer 4 and make switching decisions accordingly. For example, HTTP (web traffic) could be identified on layer 4 (port 80). However, layer 4 switches can also load balance or redirect based on actual session content, thereby allowing different types of web content to be stored on different physical servers, even though they are all accessed via a single server address.

Layer 4 switches can also be used to provide filtering of unwanted layer 4 protocols such as IPX SAP (service advertising protocol) or can also be used to provide prioritization. Depending on whether the packet is destined for a LAN or WAN, the layer 4 switch will assign prioritization with an 802.1p priority tag (layer 2) or set the priority in the IP ToS (type of service) field in the IP header (layer 3).

Still other layer 4 switches that use TCP and UDP port numbers to make decisions are more concerned with bandwidth management and traffic shaping. The PacketShaper from Packeteer classifies data traffic according to port number and then assigns guaranteed and excess bandwidth amounts along with a prioritization number to each of these traffic classes. The objective of such devices is a smooth and controlled traffic flow.

ATM Switching on the LAN

Although different vendors of enterprise networking equipment may each be promoting their own view of the enterprise network of the future, one view is that ATM will serve as the high-speed switched backbone network service used to connect geographically dispersed corporate networks. As was previously discussed in the section on virtual LANs, layer 2 switching, no matter how fast, is not by itself a sufficient enterprise network platform. As a result, routing capabilities must be added to the underlying switching capabilities offered by ATM. How the routing capabilities are added to the ATM switching fabric and the subsequent enterprise network performance characteristics exhibited as a result of those routing capabilities are the basic differences between alternative enterprise network physical topologies.

ATM LAN Emulation Because ATM acts as a layer 2 switching service, and because layer 2 LAN switches support virtual LANs, it would stand to reason that ATM switches ought to be able to support virtual LANs as well. In fact, through a process known as ATM LAN emulation, virtual LANs are able to be constructed over an ATM-switched network regardless of the geographic scope of that network. ATM LAN emulation is considered a bridging solution, like LAN switch-based virtual LANs, because traffic is switched based on MAC layer addresses. Unlike LAN switch-based virtual LANs, however, MAC layer addresses must be translated into, or resolved into, ATM addresses in a process known as ATM address resolution. In ATM LAN emulation, the ATM switching fabric adds an entire layer of its own addressing schemes, which it uses to forward virtual LAN traffic to its proper destination.

In Sharper Focus

ATM LAN EMULATION ARCHITECTURE

How MAC layer addresses are resolved into ATM addresses is defined by an ATM forum specification known as LAN emulation or more formally as L-UNI (LAN emulation user to network interface) or LANE (LAN emulation). The ATM LAN emulation specification actually defines an entire architecture of interacting software components to accomplish the ATM-to-MAC layer address resolution. Among the interacting components that cooperate to accomplish ATM LAN emulation as illustrated in Figure 9-22 are the following:

- LAN emulation client (LEC) software may physically reside within ATM-to-LAN conversion devices or may be included within a router that supports ATM interfaces. The job of the LEC is to appear to be an ATM end-station on behalf of the LAN clients it represents. As a result, the LEC is sometimes referred to as a proxy ATM end-station. The LEC is also responsible for converting the LAN's data-link layer protocols (Ethernet, token ring, FDDI) into fixed length ATM cells. Once the local LEC knows the ATM address of the remote LEC that is acting as an ATM proxy for the remote LAN destination, it sets up a switched virtual circuit, or switched network connection, to the remote LEC, which subsequently delivers the information payload to the remote LAN workstation in a unicast (point-to-point) transmission.
- LAN emulation server (LES) software resides on a server or workstation that is directly attached to the ATM network and has a unique ATM address. The LES software performs three major tasks or services, which can actually be accomplished by separate software programs executed on separate servers:
    - LES configuration services are responsible for keeping track of the types of virtual LANs that are being supported over the ATM switching fabric and the LECs that belong to which type of LAN. MAC addresses and corresponding ATM addresses of attached workstations are stored by the configuration server. LAN type (Ethernet, token ring, FDDI) is important

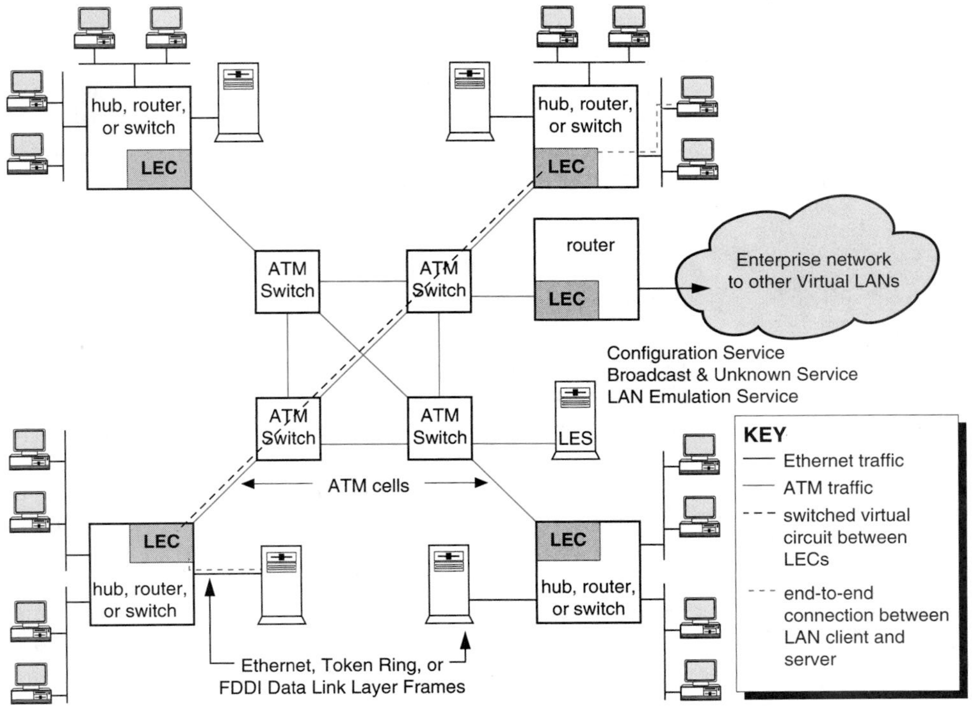

Figure 9-22 ATM LAN Emulation Architecture

to keep track of owing to the variability of the maximum frame length accepted by workstations attached to each type of LAN.

- LES broadcast and unknown services (BUS) are responsible for handling requests for broadcasts and multicasts within the virtual LANs that exist across the ATM switching fabric. In addition, if a LEC does not know the destination ATM address of a destination LAN workstation, it will forward that frame to the broadcast and unknown server that will broadcast that frame throughout the virtual LAN on behalf of the LEC.
- LES LAN emulation services receive address resolution protocol (ARP) requests from LECs seeking the ATM addresses of destination LAN workstations for which the MAC address is known. Once the LES responds to the LEC with the requested ATM address, the LEC is able to set up the point-to-point connection to the destination LEC. If the LES does not respond right away, the LEC continues to use the BUS to broadcast the destination frame throughout the virtual LAN.

Managerial Perspective

It is important to understand that ATM LAN emulation, like other virtual LAN architectures built on layer 2 switching, is basically a bridged topology that suffers from the same limitations as other layer 2 switched networks:

- Flat network topology.
- Broadcast storms (although limited to a particular virtual LAN).
- No layer 3 filtering for security or segmentation.

On the other hand, because it does not discriminate among network layer (layer 3) protocols, ATM LAN emulation is able to support, or transport, multiple network layer protocols between virtual LANs.

Perhaps more important, however, ATM LAN emulation offers no routing capability. As a result, each virtual LAN that is emulated using ATM emulation must still have a dedicated connection to a router that is able to process layer 3 addresses and make appropriate route determination and forwarding decisions between virtual LANs.

Layer 3 Protocols Over ATM Networks A variety of initiatives are underway by both the IETF (Internet engineering task force) and the ATM forum to somehow integrate layer 3 functionality with ATM networks. IETF RFC (request for comment) 1577 is known as classical IP over ATM. The goal of classical IP over ATM is to allow IP networks, as well as all upper layer TCP/IP protocols, utilities, and APIs encapsulated by IP, to be delivered over an ATM network without requiring modification to the TCP/IP protocols. Using classical IP over ATM, the ATM network is treated by IP like just another subnet or data-link protocol such as Ethernet or token ring. IP routers see the entire ATM network as only a single hop, regardless of the actual size of the ATM network. IP subnets established over ATM networks using this protocol are known as logical IP subnets or LIS.

A significant limitation of classical IP over ATM is that it only works within a given subnet. As a result, to use IP addresses to properly route data between classical IP subnets, an IP router must still be employed. Just as with ATM LAN emulation, classical IP over ATM also requires address resolution. In this case a new protocol known as ATMARP (ATM address resolution protocol) runs on a server in the logical

IP subnet and provides address resolution between IP addresses and ATM addresses. ATM addresses may actually be the virtual circuit ID numbers of the virtual circuits or connections that are established between two ATM end-points on the ATM network.

Understandably, classical IP over ATM only supports IP as a network layer protocol over ATM networks. Other initiatives are underway to support multiple network layer protocols over ATM. The ATM forum is currently working on MPOA (multiprotocols over ATM), which will not only support IP, IPX, AppleTalk and other network protocols over ATM, but will also be able to route data directly between virtual LANs, thereby precluding the need for additional external routers. Routing implemented on switches using protocols such as MPOA is sometimes referred to as **cut-through routing** and uses ATM LAN emulation as its layer 2 switching specification. Like ATM LAN emulation, MPOA operates transparently to end-devices and does not require any hardware or software changes to those end-devices or their applications. Multiprotocol over ATM is actually an entire architecture, as illustrated in Figure 9-23, comprised of the following key components:

- **Edge devices,** which might be a kind of hybrid hub, switch, and router, would act as interfaces or gateways between LANs and the ATM network. Once the ATM address is known, edge devices would be capable of establishing new virtual circuits over the ATM network.
- A **route server** would supply edge devices with their routing information including ATM addresses and virtual circuit IDs. The route server may actu-

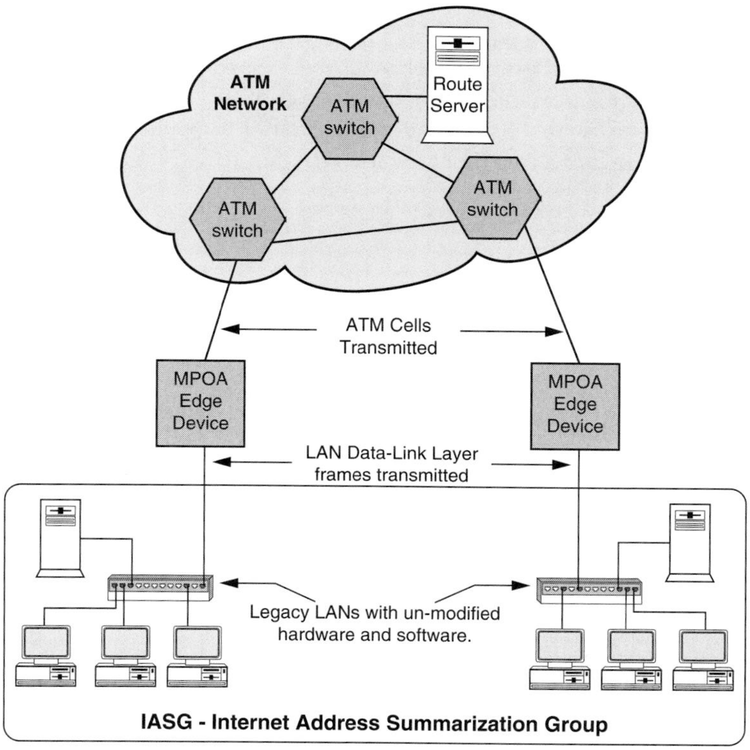

Figure 9-23 Multiprotocol Over ATM Architecture

ally be located within one of the ATM switches in the ATM backbone. Routing tables within the route server are organized according to layer 3 protocol specific subnets, which are referred to as **Internet address summarization groups (IASG).**

Whereas MPOA defines multiprotocol communications between ATM end-stations and a given route server, another ATM forum specification known as **integrated private network-to-network interface (IPNNI)** defines how route servers are able to communicate path and address information to each other and to/from ATM switches over an ATM network. If multiple route servers are required on a given enterprise network, then a protocol such as IPNNI must be implemented to share the layer 3 information between ATM switches and route servers to allow the best path through the network to be selected dynamically.

The IETF is currently working on RFC 1483, **multiprotocol encapsulation over ATM adaptation layer 5.** One of the significant contributions of this proposal is that it defines two different ways in which multiple network layer protocols can be transmitted simultaneously over an ATM network. The first method, LLC/SNAP encapsulation, places indicators in the ATM data-link layer frame to identify which network layer protocols are embedded within that data-link layer frame. The second method, virtual channel-based multiplexing, establishes a separate virtual circuit, or connection, through the ATM network, for each network layer protocol transported from one workstation to another.

Another alternative to add routing capabilities to ATM switching fabrics is known as **IP switching.** IP switching technology distinguishes between the length of data streams and switches or routes accordingly on a case-by-case basis. In the case of long data streams associated with file transfers or voice or video transmissions, the IP switch sets up a virtual circuit through the ATM switching fabric and then forwards packets immediately via layer 2 switching to that virtual circuit. In the case of datagram-oriented, short messages, each message is forwarded through the layer 3 routing software located in the IP switch. Protocols that distinguish between the types of transmissions and that decide whether to switch or route were covered previously.

LAN-TO-MAINFRAME INTERNETWORKING

Introduction

Micro–Mainframe Connectivity vs. Peer-to-Peer Internetworking Strictly speaking, micro–mainframe connectivity and internetworking are two different concepts. In **micro–mainframe connectivity,** the micro (stand-alone or LAN-attached PC) pretends to be or "emulates" a mainframe terminal such as an **IBM 3270** attached and logged into the mainframe. Although file transfer utilities may allow more capability than mere remote login, this is not the peer-to-peer networking implied by the term internetworking.

With full **peer-to-peer internetworking,** the PC can exchange data with any mainframe or any other PC on a host-to-host level rather than acting like a "dumb" terminal, as in the case of micro–mainframe connectivity. Although these two mainframe connectivity alternatives have their differences, they still have much in common. The truth is that most "IBM Shops" have a mixture of 3270 terminal connections, mainframes, and LANs that must communicate with each other on a number of different levels.

Hierarchical Networks and Peer-to-Peer Communications Networks A hierarchical network structure such as the "classic" **SNA** (systems network architecture) centers around the mainframe. If two devices other than the mainframe on an SNA network wanted to communicate, they would have to establish, maintain, and terminate that communication through the mainframe. This model is in direct contrast to a peer-to-peer network communications structure, typical of most LANs, in which any device may communicate directly with any other LAN-attached device.

Classic SNA Architecture

Figure 9-24 illustrates a simple SNA architecture and introduces some key SNA network elements.

Figure 9-24 illustrates two devices in a classic SNA environment:

1. **Front end processor (FEP)** (IBM 3745, 3746): A front-end processor is a computer that offloads the communications processing from the mainframe, allowing the mainframe to be dedicated to processing activities. A high-speed data channel connects the FEP to the mainframe locally, although FEPs can be deployed remotely as well. The FEP, also known as a communications controller, can have devices such as terminals or printers connected directly to it, or these end-user devices may be concentrated by another device known as a **cluster controller.** There are two options for high-speed data channels between FEPs and IBM mainframes:
   - **Bus and tag** has a transmission rate of 4.5 Mbps and has been available since 1967.

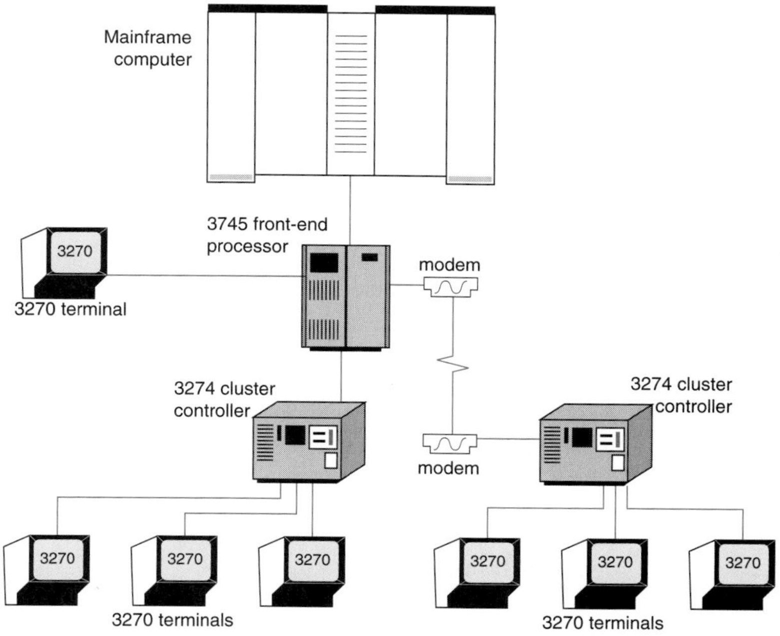

Figure 9-24 Classic SNA Architecture

- **ESCON II** (enterprise system connection) has a maximum transmission rate of 70 Mbps, has been available since 1990, and is able to transmit up to 30 miles over fiber optic cable.
- **FICON** (fiber connectivity) provides 100 megabyte/sec bi-directional link rates at unrepeated distances of up to 20 km over fiber optic cables.

2. **Cluster controller** (IBM 3174, 3274): A cluster controller allows connection of both 3270 terminals and LANs with possible wide area links to packet-switched networks (X.25) or high-speed leased lines. A cluster controller concentrates the transmissions of its numerous input devices and directs this concentrated data stream to the FEP either locally or remotely.

The hierarchical nature can be seen in Figure 9-24, as data received from the lowly terminals are concentrated by multiple cluster controllers for a front-end processor, which further manages the data for the almighty mainframe. As additional processors and minicomputers such as an IBM AS/400 are added, the hierarchical nature of classic SNA can be seen even more clearly.

The network illustrated in Figure 9-24 will be modified one step at a time until the goal of an architecture that seamlessly transports SNA and LAN traffic is reached.

Micro–Mainframe Connectivity

PCs as 3270 Terminals The first step of PC or LAN integration with classic SNA is to allow a stand-alone PC to emulate a 3270 terminal and conduct a communication session with the mainframe. To accomplish this step, **protocol conversion** must take place to allow the PC to appear to be a 3270 terminal in the eyes of the mainframe.

A 3270 protocol conversion card is inserted into an open expansion slot of a PC. Additional protocol conversion software, which may or may not be included with the protocol conversion card, must be loaded onto the PC to make the PC keyboard behave like a 3270 terminal keyboard (keyboard remapping). The media interface on the card is usually RG-62 Thin Coax for local connection to cluster controllers. Synchronous modems could also be employed for remote connection. Figure 9-25 illustrates possible configurations for stand-alone PC-3270 terminal emulation.

LAN-based SNA Gateways The next scenario is how to deliver mainframe connectivity to LAN-attached PCs. One way would be to mimic the method for attaching stand-alone PCs. That is, for every LAN-attached PC, buy and install the 3270 protocol conversion hardware and software and provide a dedicated link to a cluster controller. Whereas most of these LAN-attached PCs need mainframe connectivity only on an occasional basis, this would not be a very cost-effective solution. It would be wasteful not only in terms of the number of PC boards purchased, but also in the number of cluster controller ports monopolized but under-utilized.

Instead, it would be wiser to take advantage of the shared resource capabilities of the LAN to share a protocol conversion attachment to the mainframe. Such a LAN server-based, shared protocol converted access to a mainframe is known as a **gateway.** Popular SNA gateway software packages associated with LAN network operating are as follows:

- Microsoft SNA Server 4.0 for linking to Windows NT LANs
- NetWare for SAA 4.0 for linking to NetWare LANs

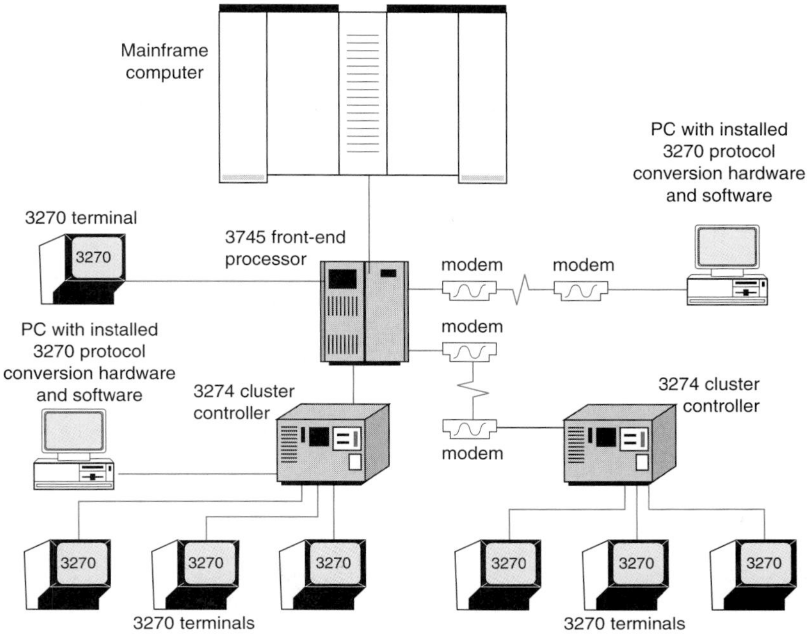

Figure 9-25 Stand-alone PC 3270 Terminal Emulation

- IBM's SecureWay Communication Server For NT
- Attachmate's E-Vantage Gateway 2.0
- Wall Data's Rumba

Such software may offer any or all of the following functionality:

- Client and print connectivity
- APPC, Tn3270, Tn3270e, Tn5250, OS/2, Macintosh, Unix, DOS client support
- Remote management
- Load balancing
- Host data and transaction processing integration
- Web-to-host integration
- Programming APIs
- Network drive support
- Integrated data access to VSAM and DB2 via OLE and ODBC
- Up to 30,000 simultaneous sessions
- Synchronization of password databases for single sign on support

Figure 9-26 illustrates both a LAN-based local gateway and remote gateway.

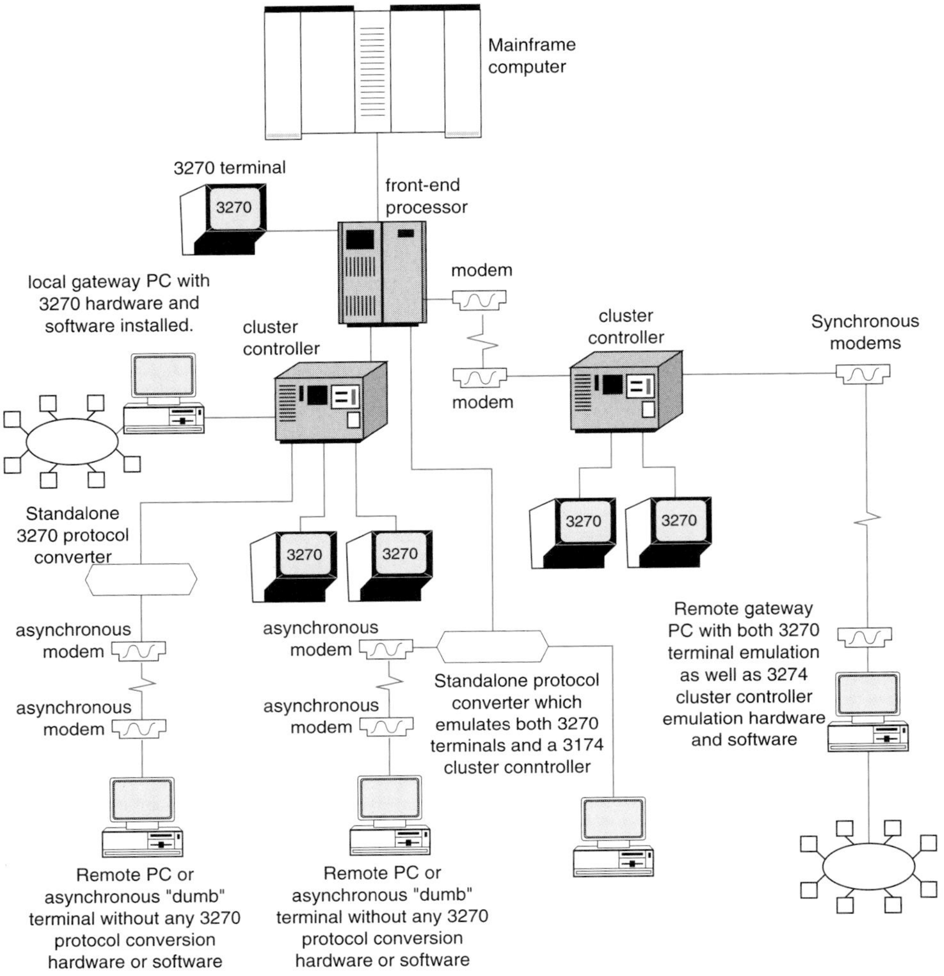

Figure 9-26 LAN-based SNA Gateways

As can be seen in Figure 9-26, a gateway configuration allows multiple simultaneous 3270 mainframe sessions to be accomplished via a single gateway PC and a single port on the cluster controller. A remote PC-based LAN gateway needs additional hardware and software to emulate not only the 3270 terminal but also the 3274 cluster controller. Such remote 3274 cluster controller boards and software are as available as 3270 terminal emulation hardware and software. As a slight variant on the PC-based emulation hardware and software previously mentioned, stand-alone protocol conversion devices for both 3270 terminal and 3274 cluster controller emulation are available as illustrated in Figure 9-26.

Mainframe Channel-Attached Gateways As an alternative to LAN-based gateways, **channel-attached gateways** are able to interface directly to the mainframe's high-speed data channel, thereby bypassing the FEP entirely. Physically, the channel-attached gateways, otherwise known as channel interface processors or CIPS, are often modules that are added to enterprise routers. Depending on the amount of actual 3270 terminal traffic required in a given network, the use of channel-attached

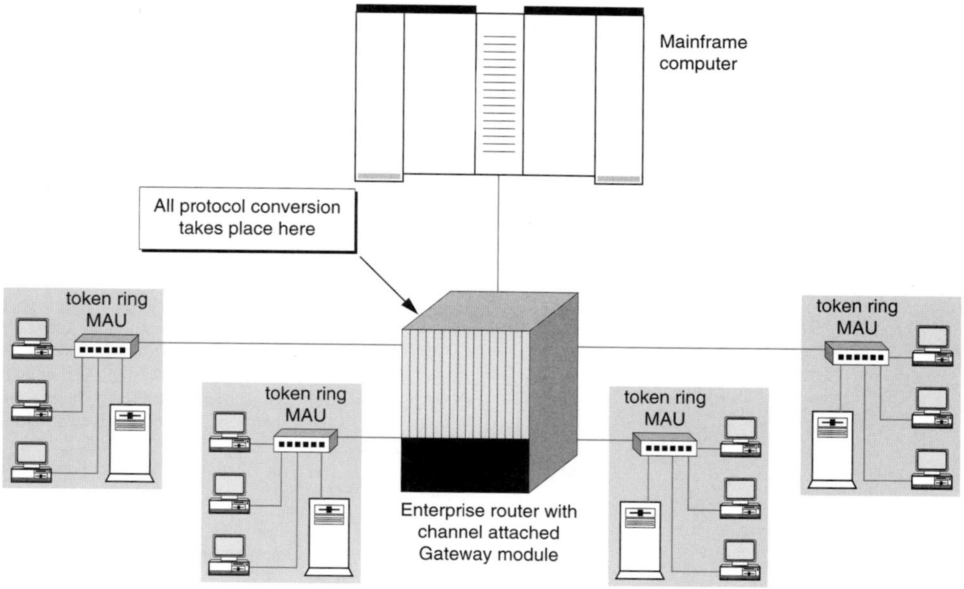

Figure 9-27 Channel-attached LAN/SNA Gateways

gateways may either preclude the need for additional FEP purchases or allow FEPs to be replaced altogether.

The price difference between channel-attached gateways and FEPs is significant. An ESCON-attached IBM 3745 FEP costs approximately $225,000, and an equivalent router-based Cisco channel interface processor costs approximately $69,000. Figure 9-27 illustrates the installation of channel-attached gateways for linking LAN-based PCs as 3270 terminals to mainframes.

IBM's Answer to Channel-Attached Gateways In response to the challenge presented by channel-attached, router-based gateways, IBM has introduced a series of stand-alone devices that are able to interface SNA mainframes to IP networks. Whereas enterprise router-based, channel-attached gateways from companies such as Cisco are priced at $69,000, the network utility devices from IBM cost $29,500 and are capable of handling 16,000 SNA sessions simultaneously. These devices have the ability to interface to a variety of LAN architectures including token ring, Ethernet, FDDI, and ATM, as well as to either ESCON or bus-and-tag channel interfaces.

In August 1999, IBM sold its network hardware division to Cisco, thereby eliminating the previous competition in router-based access to SNA networks.

The SNA Architecture

Figure 9-28 illustrates a 7-layer model of the SNA hierarchy. Like the OSI model, the SNA model starts with media issues in layer 1—the physical control layer—and ends up at layer 7—the transaction services layer, which interfaces to the end-user. The layers in between, however, do not match up perfectly with the corresponding numbered layer in the OSI model, although general functionality at each layer is similar. "Similar general functionality" will not suffice when it comes to internetworking. As

Layer number	Sublayer number	Layer/Sublayer Name	Function
7		Transaction Services	Provide network management services. Control document exchange and distributed database access.
6		Presentation Services	Formats data, data compression, and data transformation.
5		Data Flow Control	Synchronous exchange of data supports communications session for end-user applications, assures reliability of session.
4		Transmission Control	Matches the data exchange rate, establishes, maintains, and terminates sessions. Guarantees reliable delivery of data between end points. Error control, flow control.
3		Path Control	Overall layer: Creates the link between two end-points for the transmission control protocols to manage. Divided into 3 sublayers.
	3 (Path Control)	Virtual Route Control	Create virtual route (virtual circuit), manage end-to-end flow control.
	2 (Path Control)	Explicit Route Control	Determines actual end-to-end route for link between end nodes via intermediate nodes.
	1 (Path Control)	Transmission Group Control	If multiple possible physical paths exist between the end-points, this protocol manages to use these multiple lines to assure reliability and load balancing.
2		Data Link Control	Establishes, maintains, and terminates data transmission between two adjacent nodes. Protocol is SDLC.
1		Physical Control	Provides physical connections specifications from nodes to shared media.

Figure 9-28 The SNA Architecture Model

a result, options will be seen for merging SNA (SDLC) and OSI (LAN-based) data transmissions on a single internetwork involving various methods to overcome the discrepancies between the two architectures.

The SDLC Protocol Figure 9-29 illustrates the structure of the **SDLC (synchronous data link control)** protocol. Although the protocol structure itself does not look that unusual, it is the fact that the information block of the SLDC frame does not contain anything equivalent to the OSI network layer addressing information for use by routers which makes SDLC a **nonroutable protocol.** SDLC is nonroutable because there is simply no network layer address information available for the routers to process. This shortcoming can be overcome in a number of different ways. However, it is important to understand that this nonroutability is one of the key challenges facing SNA/LAN integration.

Given that SDLC cannot be routed, network managers had no choice but to implement multiple networks between corporate enterprises. One network would

Flag 1 byte	Address 1 byte	Control 1 byte	Information	Frame Check Sequence 2 bytes	Flag 1 byte

Figure 9-29 SDLC Data-Link Control Frame Layout

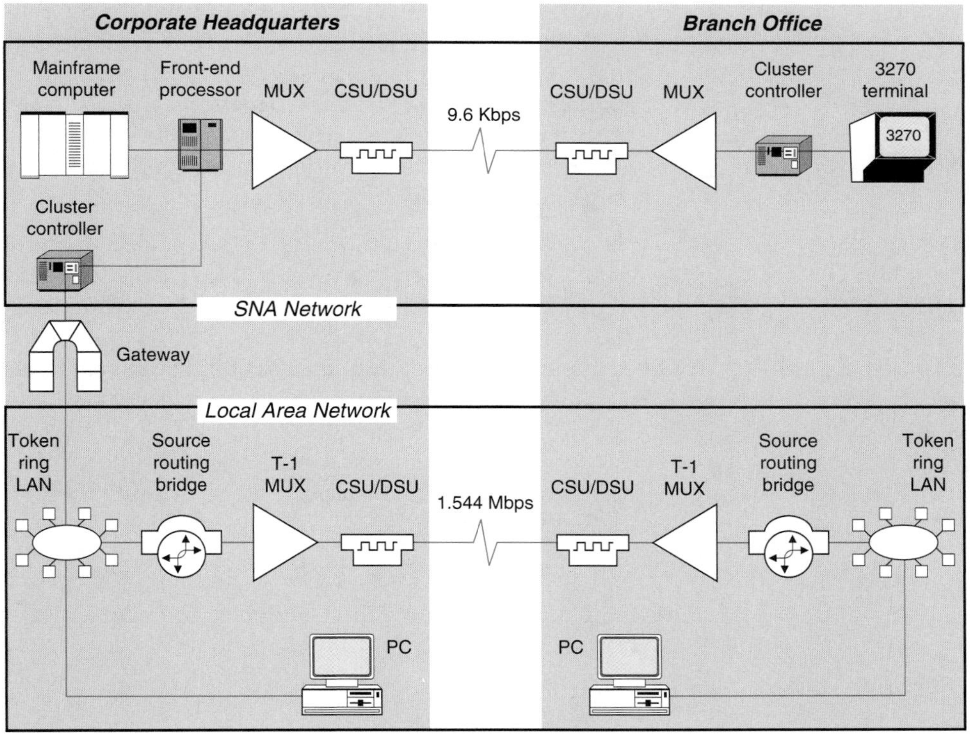

Figure 9-30 SNA/LAN Incompatibilities Yield Multiple Networks

carry SDLC traffic between remote cluster controllers and FEPs to local cluster controllers, FEPs, and mainframes, and a second network would support remote bridged/routed LANs linking with local LANs between the same corporate locations. Such an implementation is sometimes referred to as a **parallel networks model.** Obviously, it would be advantageous from both business and network management perspectives to somehow combine the two traffic streams into a single network. Figure 9-30 illustrates this multiple network scenario.

Challenges to SNA/LAN Integration

To understand how SNA and LAN traffic can be integrated, the incompatibilities between SNA networks and local area networks must first be delineated.

- The first characteristic of SNA that can cause trouble on a LAN is the great amount of **acknowledgment and polling traffic** between SNA processors and SNA end-user devices. This constant chatter could quickly monopolize the better part of the LAN bandwidth.
- The second SNA characteristic that can cause problems when run over a shared LAN backbone is that SNA has **timing limitations** for transmission duration between SNA hosts and end-user devices. Thus on wide area, internetworked LANs over shared network media, SNA sessions can "time-out," effectively terminating the session.

- Another traffic contributor that can easily monopolize internetwork bandwidth comes from the LAN side of the house. As described earlier in this chapter, token ring LANs use an internetworking device known as a source routing bridge. To define their source routed internetworking paths, source PCs send out numerous explorer packets as a means of gaining a sense of the best route from source to destination. All of these discovery packets mean only one thing—significantly more network traffic.
- As previously stated, SDLC is a nonroutable protocol. To maximize the efficiency of the integrated SNA/LAN network, some way must be found to route SDLC or otherwise transparently incorporate it with LAN traffic.

Given the aforementioned incompatibilities, it would seem clear that there are three major challenges to allowing SNA and LAN traffic to share an internetwork backbone:

- Reduce unnecessary traffic (source routing explorer packets and SDLC polling messages).
- Find some way to prioritize SNA traffic to avoid time-outs.
- Find a way to allow internetwork protocols to transport or route SDLC frames.

SNA/LAN Integration Solutions

Several major categories of SNA/LAN integration solutions are currently possible. Each varies in both approach and extent to which SNA/LAN incompatibilities are overcome:

- Add a token ring adapter to a compatible cluster controller.
- TCP/IP encapsulation.
- SDLC conversion.
- APPN (advanced peer-to-peer networking).

Token Ring Adapter into Cluster Controller The first method, as illustrated in Figure 9-31, is the least expensive and, predictably, also the least effective in terms of meeting the SNA/LAN integration challenges. A token ring network adapter is attached to an available cluster controller port and attached to a token ring network. The SNA traffic is transported using the standard source route bridging (SRB) to its destination.

However, that is only one of the three challenges to be met. Failure to deal with unnecessary traffic and prioritization of SNA traffic make this a less than ideal solution. This is a bridged approach, dealing only with OSI layer 2 protocols. Notice, however, the significant potential reduction to hardware and networking costs offered by this simple approach.

TCP/IP Encapsulation The second method is known alternatively as **TCP/IP encapsulation,** passthrough, or tunneling. Simply stated, each upper layer SNA packet is

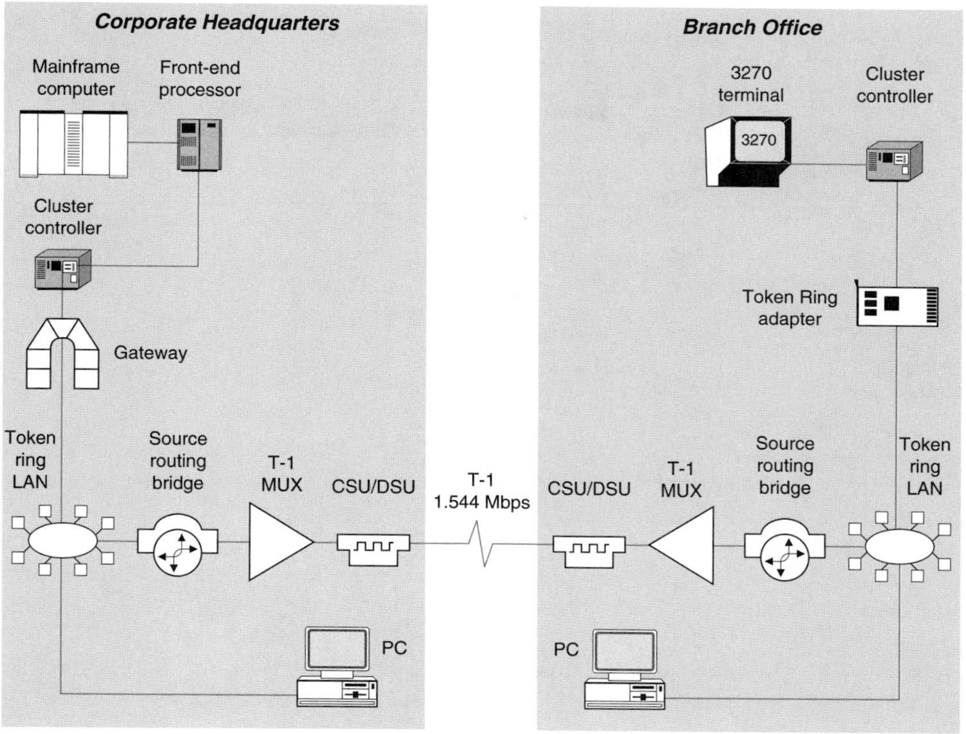

Figure 9-31 Token Ring Adapter into Cluster Controller

"stuffed" into an IP "envelope" for transport across the network and processing by routers supporting TCP/IP internetworking protocol. This IP passthrough methodology for SDLC transport is a common feature or option on internetworking routers. In this methodology IP is supplying the network layer addressing that was lacking from the native SDLC protocol, thereby enabling routing. Figure 9-32 illustrates a passthrough architecture. On close examination of Figure 9-32, it may become obvious that, in fact, there is no SNA/LAN integration. What the SNA and LAN traffic share is the T-1 wide area network between routers. The SNA traffic never travels over shared LAN media. Cost savings compared to the parallel networks model (Figure 9-30) includes eliminating one wide area link and associated internetworking hardware. The actual TCP/IP encapsulation may take place in either a gateway or a router.

IBM's version of TCP/IP encapsulation is known as **data link switching** or **DLSw** and has been proposed as a standard to the IETF (Internet Engineering Task Force) as RFC (Request for Comment) 934. DLSw does not propose anything radically new but incorporates many vendor-specific TCP/IP encapsulation features into a single standard that will, it is hoped, be widely supported. DLSw is implemented as a software feature on supported routers.

In addition to encapsulating SNA packets in IP-addressed envelopes, DLSw also deals with the polling traffic and session time-out issues of SDLC traffic. **Poll spoofing** is the ability of an internetworking device, such as an SDLC converter or router, to respond directly to, or acknowledge, the FEP's constant polling messages to the remote cluster controller. By answering these status check messages locally, the

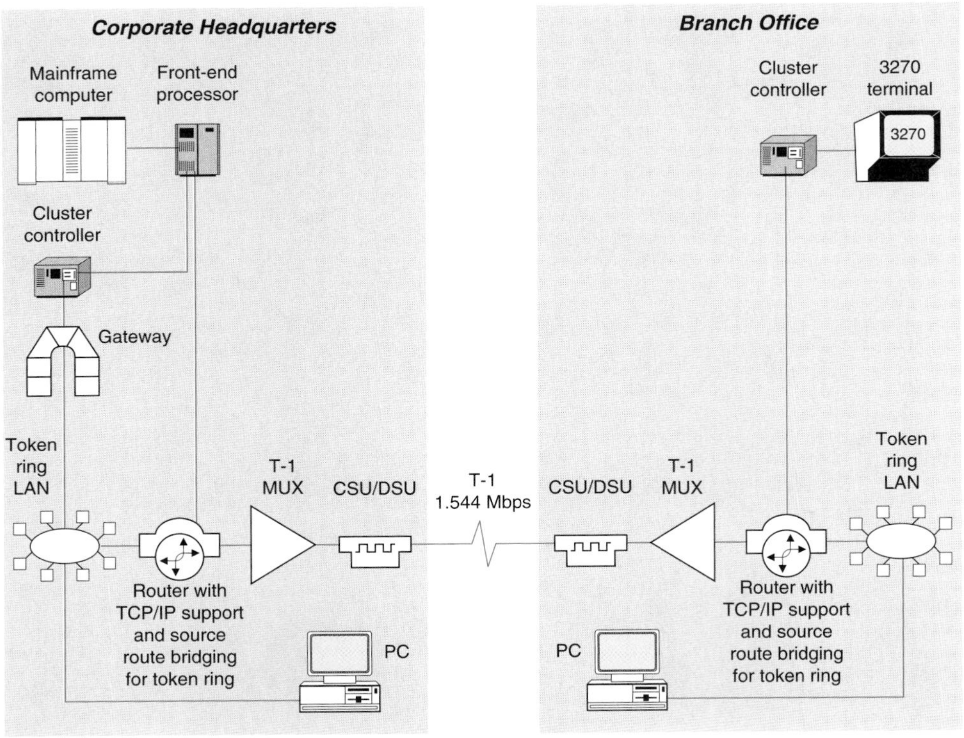

Figure 9-32 TCP/IP Encapsulation

inquiry and its answer never enter the wide area link portion of the internetwork. **Proxy polling,** on the other hand, emulates the FEP's polling messages on the remote side of the network, thereby ensuring the remote cluster controller that it is still in touch with an FEP.

Broadcast filtering addresses a bad habit of the LAN side of SNA/LAN integration. In token ring source route bridging, individual PCs send out multiple broadcast packets or explorer packets, causing potential congestion on the internetwork links. Instead of allowing these packets onto the internetwork, routers can filter these broadcast packets out of the traffic, read the destination address to which the PC is seeking a route, and supply the PC directly with that information after consulting its own routing tables.

Cisco is planning to add a new protocol to its IOS software called **SNA switching services (SNASw),** which will allow SNA traffic to ride directly on IP networks rather than having to be first encapsulated in an IP packet as with DLSw. SNASw integrates with IBM's HPR (high performance routing) architecture and uses UDP (user datagram protocol) rather than TCP (transmission control protocol) as its layer 4 protocol. The SNA data itself are given a hybrid SNA/IP header that can be processed by both the IP routing portion and the SNASw portion of a Cisco router supporting SNASw.

SDLC Conversion The third possible solution to SNA/LAN traffic integration is known as **SDLC conversion** and is characterized by SDLC frames actually being

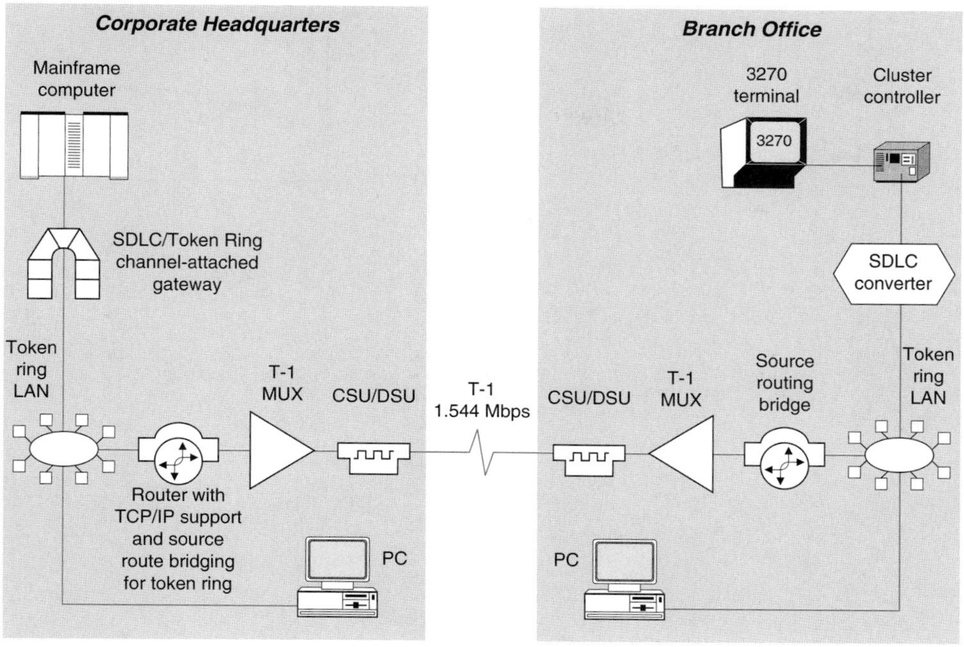

Figure 9-33 SDLC Conversion

converted to token ring frames by a specialized internetworking device known as a **SDLC converter.** The SDLC converter may be a stand-alone device or may be integrated into a bridge/router. As can be seen in Figure 9-33, in the SDLC conversion configuration, the cluster controller is attached to the token ring LAN via a stand-alone or integrated SDLC converter.

SDLC frames are converted to token ring frames, transported across the token ring internetwork, and routed to a gateway that transforms the token ring frames back into SDLC frames and forwards them to the mainframe. Also, notice the absence of the FEP from the illustration, a potential savings of several thousand dollars. Eliminating the FEP assumes that all 3270 traffic could be routed through attached LANs and gateways.

APPN: IBM's Alternative to LAN-Based SNA/LAN Integration **APPN (advanced peer-to-peer network)** is IBM's answer to multiprotocol networking on a peer-to-peer basis using the SNA architecture, rather than a LAN-based network architecture. Simply put, attached computers, whether PC's, AS/400s, or mainframes, are welcome to talk directly with each other without having the communications session established, maintained, and terminated by the almighty mainframe as was required in the classic SNA architecture. Recent enhancements to APPN known as **HPR (high performance routing)/AnyNET** now allow multiple transport protocols such as IP and IPX to travel over the APPN network simultaneously with SNA traffic. In such an implementation, APPN, rather than TCP/IP, serves as the single backbone protocol able to transport multiple LAN protocols as well as SNA traffic simultaneously. The specific APPN protocol that deals with SNA/LAN integration is known as DLUR/S (dependent logical unit requester/server).

APPN is a software-based solution that consists of only three basic components:

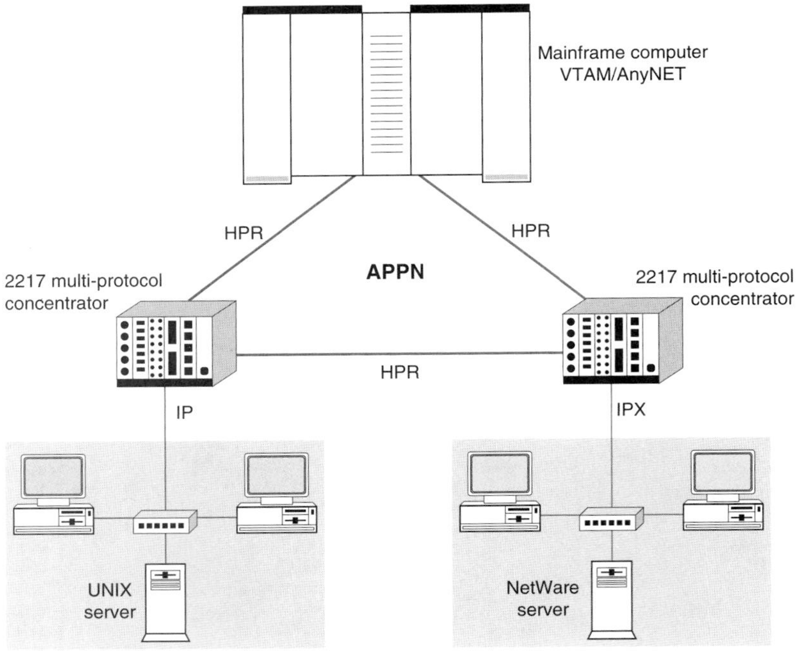

Figure 9-34 APPN with HPR/AnyNET for SNA/LAN Integration

- **End nodes** are end-user processing nodes, either clients or servers without any information on the overall network, available internetwork links, or routing tables.
- **Network nodes** are processing nodes with routing capabilities. They have the ability to locate network resources, maintain tables of information regarding internetwork links, and establish a session between the requesting end-node and the internetwork service requested.
- The **central directory server** can save time as well as network traffic for the network nodes. Instead of each network node on an internetwork doing its own information gathering and internetwork exploration and inquiry, it can simply consult the central directory server.

A simple example of an APPN network with HPR/AnyNET is illustrated in Figure 9-34.

If the functionality of APPN sounds a lot like what was just reviewed in the other SNA/LAN integration solutions, that should come as no surprise. IBM is not proposing any radical new methodologies. Rather, it is offering an IBM-backed migration from the hierarchical SNA network to a more effective peer-to-peer environment. Alternatively stated, rather than running SNA over a TCP/IP-based LAN internetwork, APPN runs TCP/IP and other protocols over an SNA mainframe-based internetwork.

Managerial Perspective

Although it now supports multiple protocols, APPN should not be misconstrued as an open architecture. APPN is a single-vendor solution, with only limited support from third-party internetworking hardware vendors.

SNA/LAN Integration and Frame Relay Although all of the SNA/LAN integration solutions illustrated thus far have used a leased T-1 (1.544 Mbps) as their WAN service, this is by no means the only option. A WAN packet-switched network service known as **frame relay** has become a popular alternative SNA/LAN integration WAN service. The key positive attribute of frame relay is that charges are based on actual amounts of traffic transmitted rather than fixed monthly rates. The key negative aspect of using frame relay as a WAN service for SNA/LAN integration is that the frame relay network is being shared with numerous other subscribers and is subject to congestion. At such times, the access device to the frame relay network, known as a **frame relay access device** or **FRAD,** must be able to respond to requests from the frame relay network to "throttle back" or slow down the input to the network or risk losing transmitted packets as a result of network overload.

Specifications for the transmission of integrated SNA/LAN traffic over frame relay networks, including proper reaction to congestion notification, is contained in the IETF RFC 990. Rather than converting SNA to IP and then using a FRAD before transmitting data over a frame relay network, RFC 1490 allows SNA traffic to be natively encapsulated from an IBM device directly onto a frame relay network. This method allows for less overhead than using DLSw as previously discussed. SNA/SDLC's need for prioritization to avoid session time-outs must still be addressed within the frame relay network. This is most often accomplished by circuit or bandwidth assignment capabilities offered by frame relay service vendors.

SUMMARY

Internetworking represents an evolutionary stage of LAN development brought on by either poor network performance or a need to share information between two different LANs. Internetworking design includes techniques such as segmentation and hierarchical networking, as well as processing methodologies such as bridging, routing, and switching.

Bridging is an OSI layer 2 process that makes forwarding decisions based on the contents of data-link layer addresses. Routing is an OSI layer 3 process that makes forwarding decisions based on the contents of network layer addresses. Switching is actually an implementation of microsegmented bridging designed to supply ample bandwidth to a local area network.

Switching and routing functionality must be combined to deliver optimal performance on the internetwork. Switching is used for supplying bandwidth, whereas routing is used for security, filtering by network layer protocols, and internetwork segmentation.

Repeaters are a physical layer internetworking device used to extend LAN segment length and to convert between media types. Bridges are a data-link layer internetworking device used to logically segment LANs, thereby supporting fewer workstations and more bandwidth on each LAN. Division of workstations onto bridged LANs should be done with some forethought to avoid having the bridge become an internetwork bottleneck.

Routers are network layer devices that are able to deal with larger internetworks than bridges and are able to determine best paths to destination workstations. Routers must keep routing tables up to date with the latest internetwork status through the use of routing protocols. Routing protocols can add significantly to bandwidth usage.

LAN–mainframe connectivity can be as simple as 3270 terminal emulation or as sophisticated as SNA/LAN integration via a single backbone protocol. In either case, alternatives are available that vary in their ability to meet the challenges of SNA/LAN integration, as well as in their cost and complexity.

KEY TERMS

3270 protocol conversion card
7 hop limit
acknowledgment and polling traffic
address caching
advanced peer-to-peer networking
APPN
autonomous systems
backbone network
BGP4
border gateway protocol version 4
boundary router
bridges
broadcast filtering
broadcast storm
brouters
bus and tag
central directory server
central site router
channel-attached gateways
cluster controller
configuration bridge protocol data units
data-link switching
destination address
dial-up routers
distance vector
distinct layer 2 switching and layer 3 routing
Diff-Serv
differentiated services
distributed routing
DLSw
edge switches
EGP
encapsulating bridge
end nodes
ESCON
explorer packet
exterior gateway protocols
fast spanning tree
FEP
filtering
filtering rate
format converter
forward if not local
forward if proven remote
forwarding
forwarding rate
FRAD
frame relay
frame relay access device
front-end processor
gateway
hierarchical networking
HPR/AnyNET
IBM3270
IEEE 802.1w
IEEE 802.1
IEEE 802.10
IGRP
interior gateway protocols
internetworking
IP switching
known local nodes
layer 2 switch
layer 3 switch
layer 4 switch
link state
link state packets
load balancing
LSP
MAN
metropolitan area network
micromainframe connectivity
microsegmentation
MPLS
multi-layer switch
multiprotocol bridges
multiprotocol label switching
multiprotocol routers
network address translation
network nodes
nonroutable
nonroutable protocol
open shortest path first
OSPF
OSPF area
parallel networks model
path vector protocol
peer-to-peer internetworking
piggyback updates
poll spoofing
private addressing
promiscuous listen
propagation
protocol conversion
proxy polling
QoS
quality of service
recovery time
repeater
RIF
RIP
router servers
routing information field
routing information protocol
routing switches
routing tables
SAN
SDLC
SDLC conversion
SDLC converter
segmentation
server isolation
slow convergence
SNA
SNA switching services
SNASw
source addresses
source routing bridges
source routing transparent bridges
spanning tree algorithm (STA)
spoofing
Storage Area Network
Synchronous data-link control
TCP/IP encapsulation
timed updates
timing limitations
translating bridges
transparent
transparent bridges
triggered updates
wireless bridges

REVIEW QUESTIONS

1. What is internetworking?
2. What are some of the factors that can lead an organization to seek internetworking solutions?
3. Differentiate among the four basic internetwork design strategies in terms of proper application.
4. Describe the use of data-link layer addresses by bridges.
5. What is meant by the phrase forward-if-not-local?
6. What are some of the key limitations of bridges?
7. How do routers overcome some of the key limitations of bridges?
8. Describe the use of data-link layer addresses by routers.
9. Describe the use of network layer addresses by routers.
10. What is meant by the phrase forward-if-proven-remote?
11. What are some of the key services that routers are able to provide to the internetwork?
12. Is switching more like bridging or routing? Explain.
13. What types of functionality are switches not able to deliver?
14. What can be said of all internetworking devices in relation to the OSI model layers and protocols?
15. What types of functionality is a repeater able to deliver?
16. What is auto-partitioning and why is it important to repeaters?
17. What is the difference between ring length and lobe length in token ring networks?
18. What is the difference between filtering and forwarding in bridge functionality?
19. What is the importance of the spanning tree algorithm?
20. What are the advantages and disadvantages of source route bridging?
21. Name and describe the functional characteristics of transparent bridges.
22. Differentiate between translating bridges and encapsulating bridges.
23. Differentiate between source routing bridges and source routing transparent bridges.
24. What implementation scenario is particularly well suited for wireless bridges?
25. What makes a protocol nonroutable?
26. What is slow convergence and why is it a problem?
27. Differentiate between distance vector and link state routing protocols in terms of delivered functionality.
28. From a business standpoint, when should boundary routers and dial-up routers be employed?
29. What functionality is of particular importance to boundary or branch office routers? Why?
30. What functionality is of particular importance to dial-up routers? Why?
31. What is spoofing and why is it important?
32. Differentiate among the three major methods for updating spoofed protocols on dial-up routers.
33. Differentiate among the three major alternatives for combining routing and switching functionality.
34. Differentiate between micro—mainframe connectivity and peer-to-peer internetworking in terms of where presentation, data management, and application processing take place in each alternative.
35. Why is a classic SNA architecture considered hierarchical?
36. What is the difference in terms of functionality between a front-end processor and a cluster controller?
37. Differentiate between LAN-based SNA gateways and channel-attached SNA gateways in terms of cost and functionality.
38. What is SDLC?
39. Why is SDLC considered nonroutable?
40. What is the parallel networks model and what is its cause?
41. Describe each of the challenges to SNA/LAN integration introduced by either SDLC or LAN protocols.
42. Differentiate among the four major SNA/LAN integration solutions in terms of their ability to meet the previously identified SNA/LAN integration challenges.
43. What is DLSw? Describe its functionality.
44. What is the importance of poll spoofing and proxy polling to DLSw?
45. Differentiate between TCP/IP encapsulation and SDLC conversion in terms of functionality, advantages, and disadvantages.
46. What are some of the major differences between APPN and TCP/IP encapsulation?
47. What is IP switching and how does it differ from conventional switching and routing?

ACTIVITIES

1. Find an organization that has implemented internetworking solutions. Interview the individuals who initiated the internetwork design. What were the motivating factors? Were they primarily business-oriented or technology-oriented?
2. Survey a number of organizations with internetworks to determine how many use primarily bridges vs. routers. Explain your results.
3. Research the expected market forecast for bridges, routers, and other internetwork technology. Many professional periodicals publish such surveys in January. Report on the results of your study.
4. Research broadcast storms and the spanning tree algorithm. Draw diagrams depicting how broadcast storms are created and how the spanning tree algorithm controls multiple active loops.
5. Print out the contents of a routing table from two different routers on the same internetwork. Trace the logical path that a packet would take from a local workstation on a LAN connected to either router.
6. Conduct a survey among organizations with internetworks. Research how many organizations are currently employing or plan to implement LAN switches. What do all of the situations have in common? How do they differ?
7. Research the topic of source route bridging. What percentage of token ring LANs employ source route bridging? Is this percentage increasing or decreasing? How is source route bridging being dealt with in multiprotocol internetworks by either bridges or routers?
8. Conduct a survey of organizations with router-based internetworks as to the router-to-router protocol currently employed and planned within the next year. What percentage use RIP vs. OSPF? What percentage are planning a change? Analyze and present your results.
9. Review trade magazines, professional periodicals, and product literature to determine the alternative methods for combining switching and routing technology. Is one method dominant? Report on and explain your results.
10. Conduct a survey of organizations with both SNA/SDLC traffic and LAN internetwork traffic. What percentage run parallel networks? What percentage have achieved SNA/LAN integration? How was SNA/LAN integration achieved? What are the plans for the 1-year horizon? Report on and explain your results.
11. Research IP switching technology and protocol development efforts. Have protocols been standardized? Who are the technology market leaders? How widespread is the deployment of IP switching technology? What are the projected growth rates for the IP switching market? Report on and explain your results.

CASE STUDY

Secure Extranet Is Just What the Doctor Ordered

The National Board of Medical Examiners (NBME), whose job is to accredit physicians in the U.S., has set up an extranet to provide online access to doctors' test scores and other data.

Medical schools, state medical licensing authorities, hospitals and other organizations need to know how medical students have scored on the tough exams given by the NBME, which also keeps track of whether or not physicians are in good standing.

The NBME decided it could disseminate such information much more quickly over the Web than it could via paper. The NBME's main challenge was finding a way to really be sure of the online user's identity and restrict access to the appropriate information, all housed in an Oracle database.

"Once we decided to use the Web, we needed to have a good way to qualify users online to make sure they are who they say they are," says Steve Lopez, the

NBME's director of IT. Simple passwords and IDs, used over and over again, were seen as inadequate because they can easily be compromised through sharing with others, he says.

The better answer for the extranet, Lopez says, was what security experts call "two-factor authentication"—which means generating a one-time password through a software or hardware token given to the user along with a unique PIN number.

Because the NBME was satisfied with the Raptor firewall from Axent Technologies it has been using for a long time, Lopez last year looked at adding two other Axent products—the SecureLink Bridge Server and WebDefender. These two products work inside the intranet to provide the remote user with single signon to Web pages.

The Unix-based SecureLink Bridge Server acts as a proxy to the firewall for the remote user—in this case, an individual at a medical school or other organization who wants to obtain physicians' records. The outsider has to prove his identity over the Web by entering a one-time password created by the WebDefender software token issued by the NBME.

The bridge server passes this identity authentication request to the WebDefender server, and if the remote user's identity checks out, WebDefender issues a software ticket. The ticket grants restricted access to a Web application server.

"We have about 130 outside people from medical schools using this to get test score information from the NBME," says Lopez, who notes the system has been in place since the fall.

The NBME's IT staff made sure to keep the organization's business divisions fully informed about the extranet project to encourage future use of the technology.

The next extranet application under way at the NBME will give college professors a way to discuss testing online rather than in person.

Source: Ellen Messmer, "Secure Extranet is just what the doctor ordered," *Network World,* vol. 17, no. 2 (January 10, 2000), p. 31.
Copyright © Network World. Reprinted with permission.

BUSINESS CASE STUDY QUESTIONS

Activities

1. Complete a top-down model for this case by gleaning facts from the case and placing them in the proper layer of the top-down model. After completing the top-down model, analyze and detail those instances where requirements were clearly passed down from upper layers to lower layers of the model and where solutions to those requirements were passed up from lower layers to upper layers of the model.
2. Detail any questions about the case that may occur to you for which answers are not clearly stated in the article.

Business

1. What was the business motivation or problem that initiated the search for the implemented solution?
2. What was the productivity impact of the implemented solution?
3. Were business performance metrics and associated infrastructure performance metrics identified? If so, were they achieved? If not, what might be some suitable business and infrastructure performance metrics for this case?

Application

1. What was the key challenge to deploying this application successfully?
2. What is two-factor authentication?
3. What are the advantages of single sign on?

Data

1. How were the data ultimately secured?

Network

1. What underlying network technologies were key to the achievement of stated business objectives?
2. What are the differences between the intranet and extranet in this case?

Technology

1. What specific technologies were employed to deliver the described solution?

2. How does the security technology implemented go beyond token generated one-time passwords?
3. Describe the interaction between the various security technologies? Would this work as well in a multivendor environment?
4. What is the difference between a proxy and a firewall?

CHAPTER 10

REMOTE ACCESS AND WIRELESS NETWORKING

Concepts Reinforced

OSI Model
Top-Down Model
Internetwork Design
Network Operating Systems
Internet Suite of Protocols Model
Protocols and Compatibility
Internetworking Technology

Concepts Introduced

Remote Access
Remote Node
Remote Access Security
Wireless WAN Services
Remote Access Network Design
Wireless PDAs
Remote Control
Mobile Computing
Wireless LANs
Remote Access Technology
IEEE 802.11
Wireless Middleware

OBJECTIVES

Upon successful completion of this chapter, you should:

1. Understand the difference between and proper application of remote node and remote control computing.
2. Understand the business motivation behind the need for remote access network design.
3. Understand the importance and networking implication of mobile computing.
4. Understand how to successfully design logical and physical topologies for remote access networks, including wireless LAN and WAN services.
5. Understand how to evaluate remote access technology including hardware, software, and WAN services.
6. Understand the unique security issues introduced by remote access and mobile computing.

INTRODUCTION

To understand the importance of remote access and wireless technology, it is first important to appreciate the business forces that have created the increased demand for such technology.

One of the most important things to understand about LAN remote access is the relatively limited bandwidth of the wide area network links that individuals will use to connect to corporate information resources. Although the goal of LAN remote access may be to offer transparent remote LAN connectivity, decreases in bandwidth by a factor of 100 on WAN links compared to LAN links cannot be ignored.

The goal of this chapter is to outline a methodology for the proper design of remote access solutions based on a thorough understanding of user needs, network architecture alternatives, available technology, and available WAN services.

Managerial Perspective

BUSINESS ISSUES OF REMOTE ACCESS

As information has come to be seen as a corporate asset to be leveraged to competitive advantage, the delivery of that information to users working at remote locations has become a key internetworking challenge. Corporate downsizing has not only increased remaining employees' responsibilities, but pushed those responsibilities ever closer to the corporation's customers. As a result, the voice mail message, "I'll be virtual all day today," is becoming more and more common. The business-oriented motivations for remote access to local LAN resources fall into about three general categories:

The first category of remote LAN access is often referred to as **telecommuting,** or more simply, working from home with all the information resources of the office LAN at one's fingertips. This category of connectivity and computing is often referred to as **SOHO,** or **small office home office.**

Studies have indicated that some of the ways in which telecommuting can increase overall worker productivity are the following:

- Better, quicker, more effective customer service.
- Increased on-time project completion and quicker product development.
- Increased job satisfaction among highly mobile employees, leading to both greater productivity and employee retention.
- Decreased worker turnover, leading to decreased training and recruiting budgets.
- Increased sales.

A variation of telecommuting, **mobile computing,** addresses the need for field representatives to be able to access corporate information resources to offer superior customer service while working on the road. These field representatives may or may not have a corporate office PC into which to dial.

Although some of the positive results of enabling remote access to corporate data for mobile workers are similar to those of telecommuters, the increased customer focus of the mobile worker is evident in the following benefits:

- Faster responses to customer inquiries.

- Improved communications with co-workers and support staff at corporate offices.
- Better, more effective customer support.
- Increased personal productivity by the mobile workers such as being able to complete more sales calls.
- Increased ability to be "on the road" in front of customers.
- More efficient service from service personnel.

The third major usage of remote computing is for **technical support** organizations that must be able to dial-in to client systems with the ability to appear as a local workstation, or take control of those workstations, to diagnose and correct problems remotely. Being able to diagnose and solve problems remotely can have significant impacts such as

- Quicker response to customer problems.
- Increased ability to avoid having to send service personnel for on-site visits.
- More efficient use of subject matter experts and service personnel.
- Increased ability to avoid revisits to customer sites due to a lack of proper parts.
- Greater customer satisfaction.

Managerial Perspective

THE HIDDEN COSTS OF TELECOMMUTING

To fully understand the total costs involved in supporting telecommuters, it is first essential to understand which employees are doing the telecommuting. Telecommuting employees generally fall into either one of the following categories:

- Full-time, day shift, at-home workers.
- After-hours workers who have a corporate office but choose to extend the workday by working remotely from home during evenings and weekends.

Most studies indicate that more than 75% of telecommuters are of the occasional, after-hours variety. However, corporate costs to set up and support these occasional users are nearly equal to the costs for setting up and supporting full-time at-home users, over $4000 per year. Among the hidden costs to be considered when evaluating the cost/benefit of telecommuting are the following:

- Workers may not be within local calling area of corporate resources, thereby incurring long-distance charges.
- It may be necessary to add wiring from street to home or within home to support additional phone lines.
- If existing phone lines are used, personnel time is used to sort personal calls from business calls.
- To provide sufficient bandwidth, more expensive ISDN or ADSL lines are often installed, if available.

- Some applications, especially those not optimized for remote access, run very slowly over dial-up lines, leading to decreased productivity.

ARCHITECTURAL ISSUES OF REMOTE ACCESS

There are basically only four steps to designing a dial-in/dial-out capability for a network:

- Needs analysis
- Logical topology choice
- Physical topology choice
- Current technology review and implementation

Logical Design Issues

Needs Analysis As dictated by the top-down model, before designing network topologies and choosing technology, it is essential to first determine what is to be accomplished in terms of LAN-based applications and use of other LAN-attached resources. Among the most likely possibilities for the information sharing needs of remote users are the following:

- Exchange e mail.
- Upload and download files.
- Run interactive application programs remotely.
- Utilize LAN-attached resources.

The purpose of examining information sharing needs in this manner is to validate the need for the remote PC user to establish a connection to the local LAN that offers all of the capabilities of locally attached PCs.

In other words, if the ability to upload and download files is the extent of the remote PC user's information sharing needs, then file transfer software, often included in asynchronous communications software packages, would suffice at a very reasonable cost. A network-based bulletin-board service (BBS) package is another way in which information can be shared by remote users easily. Likewise, if e-mail exchange is the total information-sharing requirement, then e-mail gateway software loaded on the LAN would meet that requirement.

However, to run LAN-based interactive application programs or utilize LAN attached resources such as high speed printers, CD-ROMs, mainframe connections, or fax servers, a full-powered remote connection to the local LAN must be established. From the remote user's standpoint, this connection must offer transparency. In other words, the remote PC should behave as if it were connected locally to the LAN. From the LAN's perspective, the remote user's PC should virtually behave as if it were locally attached.

Logical Topology Choice: Remote Node vs. Remote Control In terms of logical topology choices, two different logical methods for connection of remote PCs to LANs are possible. Each method has advantages, disadvantages, and proper usage situations. The two major remote PC operation mode possibilities are:

- Remote node
- Remote control

The term **remote access** is most often used to generally describe the process of linking remote PCs to local LANs without implying the particular functionality of that link (remote node vs. remote control). Unfortunately, the term remote access is also sometimes more specifically used as a synonym for remote node.

Figure 10-1 outlines some of the details, features, and requirements of these two remote PC modes of operation, and Figure 10-2 highlights the differences between remote node and remote control installations.

Remote node or remote client computing implies that, in theory, the remote client PC should be able to operate as if it were locally attached to network resources. In other words, the geographic separation between the remote client and the local LAN resources should be transparent. That's a good theory, but in practice, the comparative bandwidth of a typical dial-up link (theoretically 56 Kbps for a V. 90 modem, more likely 34–42 Kbps average) compared with the Mbps bandwidth of the LAN is anything but transparent. Whereas a NIC would normally plug directly into an expansion slot in a computer, a remote node connection merely extends that link via a relatively low speed dial-up link. Client applications run on the remote client rather than a local LAN-attached client.

Functional Characteristic	Remote Node	Remote Control
Also Called	Remote Client Remote LAN Node	Modem Remote Control
Redirector Hardware/ Software Required?	Yes	No
Traffic Characteristics	All client/server traffic	Keystrokes and screen images
Application Processing	On the remote PC	On the LAN-attached local PC
Relative Speed	Slower	Faster
Logical Role of WAN Link	Extends connection to NIC	Extends keyboard and monitor cables
Best Use	With specially written remote client applications which have been optimized for execution over limited band width WAN links	DOS applications. Graphics on Windows apps. can make response time unacceptable.

Figure 10-1 Remote Node vs. Remote Control Functional Characteristics

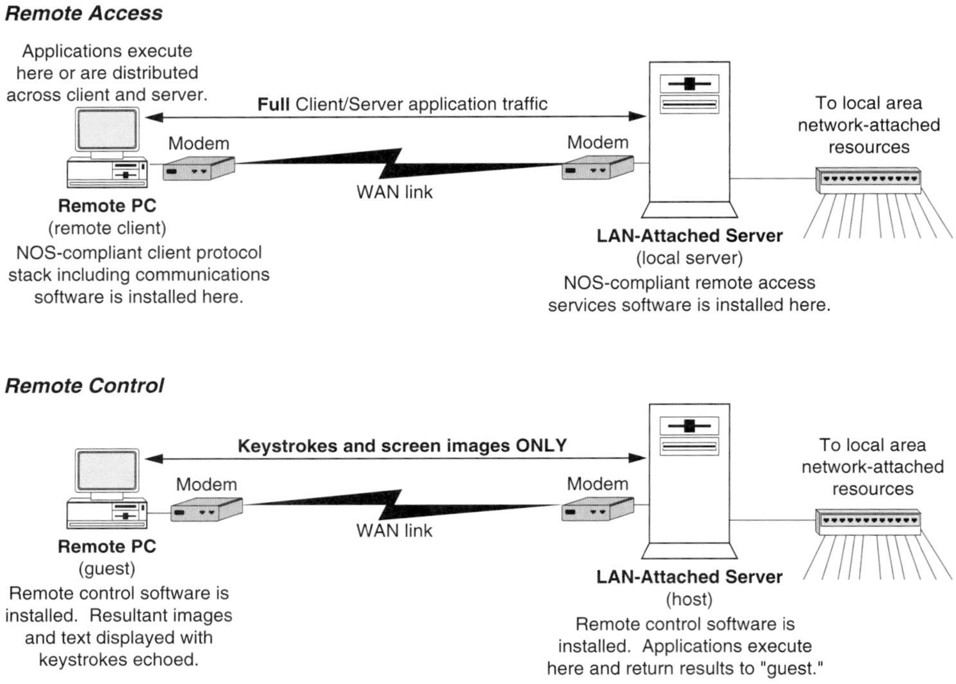
Remote Access
Applications execute here or are distributed across client and server.
Full Client/Server application traffic
Modem
Modem
To local area network-attached resources
WAN link
Remote PC
(remote client)
NOS-compliant client protocol stack including communications software is installed here.
LAN-Attached Server
(local server)
NOS-compliant remote access services software is installed here.
Remote Control
Keystrokes and screen images ONLY
Modem
Modem
To local area network-attached resources
WAN link
Remote PC
(guest)
Remote control software is installed. Resultant images and text displayed with keystrokes echoed.
LAN-Attached Server
(host)
Remote control software is installed. Applications execute here and return results to "guest."

Figure 10-2 Remote Node vs. Remote Control Installations

Client/server applications that require large transfers of data between client and server will not run well in remote node mode. Most successful remote node applications are rewritten to minimize large data transfers. For example, modified remote node e-mail client software allows just the headers of received messages that include sender, subject, and date/time to be transferred from the local e-mail server to the remote client. The remote client selects which e-mail messages should have the actual e-mail message body and attachments transferred. Local e-mail client software, which assumes plenty of LAN bandwidth, does not bother with such bandwidth-conserving modifications. Other client/server applications must be similarly modified if they are to execute acceptably in remote node mode.

Although transparent interoperability was discussed as one of the goals of remote access, that does not necessarily mean that a worker's mobile computer programs must be identical to those running on one's desktop at the price of terrible performance. One of the most commonly overlooked aspects in deploying remote access solutions is the need to customize applications for optimal performance in a remote access environment.

Remote node mode requires a full client network operating system protocol stack to be installed on the remote client. In addition, wide area network communication software must be incorporated with the remote client NOS protocol stack. Remote node software often also includes optional support of remote control functionality.

Remote control differs from remote node mode both in the technology involved and the degree to which existing LAN applications must be modified. In remote control mode, the remote PC is merely supplying input and output devices for the local client, which interacts as normal with the local server and other locally attached LAN resources. Client applications still run on the local client, which is able to communicate with the local server at native LAN speeds, thereby precluding the need to rewrite client applications for remote client optimization.

Remote control mode requires only remote control software to be installed at the remote PC rather than a full NOS client protocol stack, which is compatible with the NOS installed at the local LAN. The purpose of the remote control software is only to extend the input/output capabilities of the local client out to the keyboard and monitor attached to the remote PC. The host version of the same remote control package must be installed at the host or local PC. There are no interoperability standards for remote control software.

One of the most significant difficulties with remote control software is confusion by end-users as to logical disk assignments. Recalling that the remote PC supplies only the keyboard and monitor functionality, remote users fail to realize that a C: prompt refers to the C: drive on the local LAN-attached PC and not the C: drive of the remote PC that they are sitting in front of. This can be particularly confusing with file transfer applications.

Protocols and Compatibility At least some of the shortcomings of both remote node and remote control modes are caused by the underlying transport protocols responsible for delivering data across the WAN link.

In the case of remote control, the fact that proprietary protocols are used between the guest and host remote control software is the reason that remote control software from various vendors is not interoperable.

In the case of remote node, redirector software in the protocol stack must take LAN-based messages from the NDIS or ODI protocols and convert them into proper format for transmission over asynchronous serial WAN links.

Some remote node software uses TCP/IP as its protocol stack, and PPP as its data-link layer WAN protocol. In this manner, remote node sessions can be easily established via TCP/IP, even using the Internet as the connecting WAN service if that connection satisfies the security needs of the company in question. Once the TCP/IP link is established, the remote control mode of this software can be executed over TCP/IP as well, overcoming the proprietary protocols typically associated with remote control programs. In addition, due to PPP's ability to transport upper layer protocols other than TCP/IP, these remote node clients can support communications with a variety of different servers.

Figure 10-3 illustrates the protocol-related issues of typical remote control and remote node links, as well as TCP/IP based links.

Security Although security from an enterprise-wide perspective is dealt with in Chapter 13 security issues specifically related to remote access of corporate information resources are briefly summarized here. Security related procedures can be logically grouped into the following categories:

- Password assignment and management: Change passwords frequently, even considering single-use passwords. Passwords should not be actual words found in a dictionary, but ideally should be a random or meaningless combination of letters and numbers.
- Intrusion response: User accounts should be locked after a preset number of unsuccessful logins. These accounts should only be able to be unlocked by a system administrator.

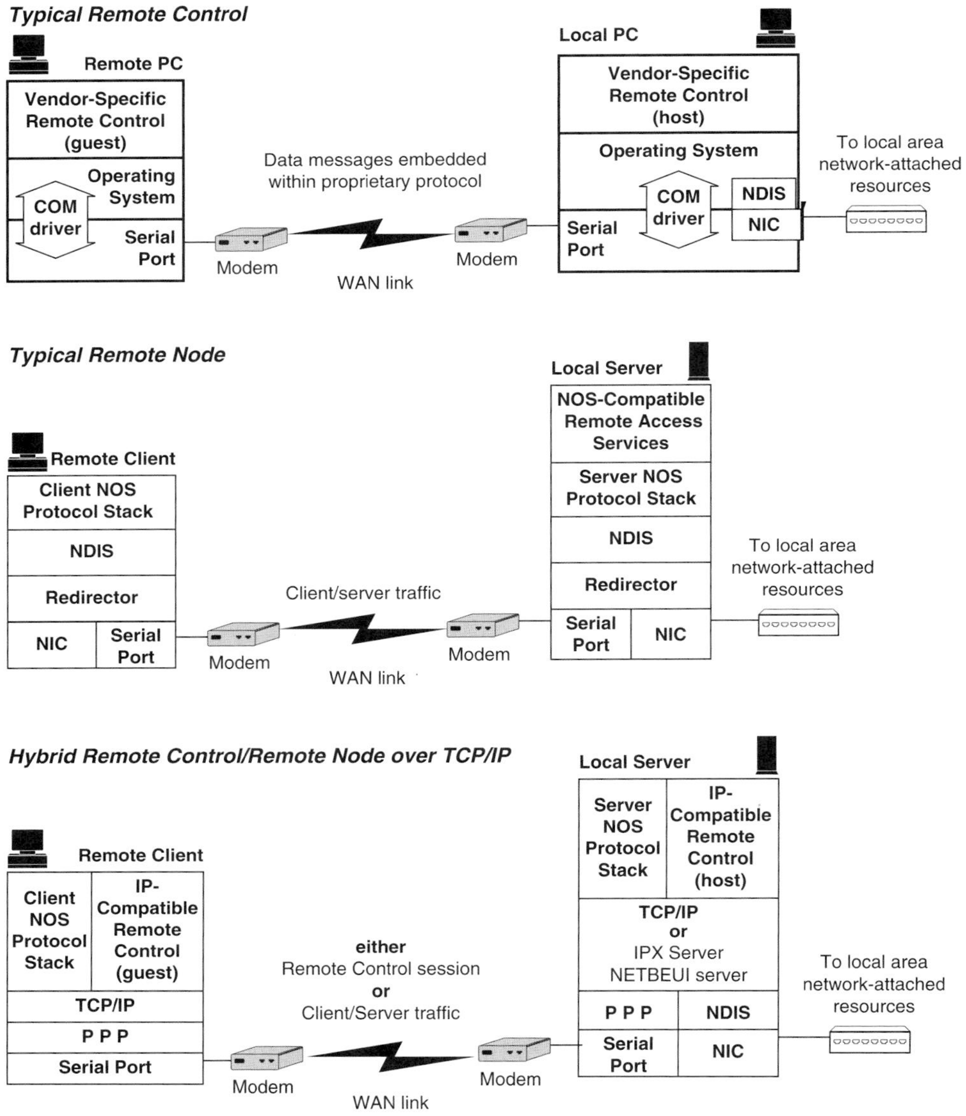

Figure 10-3 Protocol Issues of Remote Control and Remote Node Links

- Logical/physical partitioning of data: Separate public, private, and confidential data onto separate physical servers to avoid users with minimum security clearances gaining unauthorized access to sensitive or confidential data.
- Encryption: Although it is important for any sensitive or proprietary corporate data to be encrypted, it is especially important that passwords be encrypted to avoid interception and unauthorized reuse.
- Dial-back systems: After remote users enter proper UserID and passwords, these systems terminate the call and dial the authorized user back at preprogrammed phone numbers.

- Remote client software authentication protocols: Remote client protocol stacks often include software-based authentication protocols such as PAP (password authentication protocol) or CHAP (challenge handshake authentication protocol).
- Remote client authentication devices: Although exact implementation details may vary from one vendor to the next, all token authentication systems include server components linked to the communications server, and client components that are used with the remote access clients. Physically, the token authentication device employed at the remote client location may be a hand-held device resembling a calculator or just a small LCD screen capable of displaying 6 digits, a floppy disk, or it may be an in-line device linked to either the remote client's serial or parallel port. Token authentication devices are explained further in Chapter 13.

Physical Design Issues

Physical Topology: Alternative Access Points As Figure 10-4 illustrates, there are three basic ways in which a remote PC user can gain access to the local LAN resources.

- Serial port of a LAN attached PC: Perhaps the simplest physical topology or remote access arrangement is to establish a communications link to a user PC located in the corporate office. However, many field representative or mobile computing users no longer have permanent offices and workstations at a corporate building and must depend on remote access to shared computing resources.
- Communications server: As an alternative to having a dedicated PC at the corporate office for each remote user to dial into, remote users could attach to a dedicated multiuser server, known as a **remote access server** or **communications server** through one or more modems. Depending on the software loaded on the communications server, it may deliver remote node functionality, remote control functionality, or both. As telecommuting and demand for Internet access have increased, remote access servers have become the dominant means for accessing networks remotely. The 1999 revenue for remote access servers in the United States was $2.1 billion, growing at a 21% growth rate.
- LAN modem: Another alternative is to install a specialized device known as a **LAN modem,** also known as a **dial-in server,** to offer shared remote access to LAN resources. LAN modems come with all necessary software preinstalled and, therefore, do not require additional remote control or remote node software. LAN modems are often limited to a single network architecture such as Ethernet or token ring, and/or to a single network operating system protocol such as IP, IPX (NetWare), NetBIOS, NetBEUI, or AppleTalk.

The physical topology using the communications server (Figure 10-4, Illustration 2) actually depicts two different possible remote LAN connections. Most communications servers answer the modem, validate the user ID and password, and log the remote user onto the network. Some communications servers go beyond this to

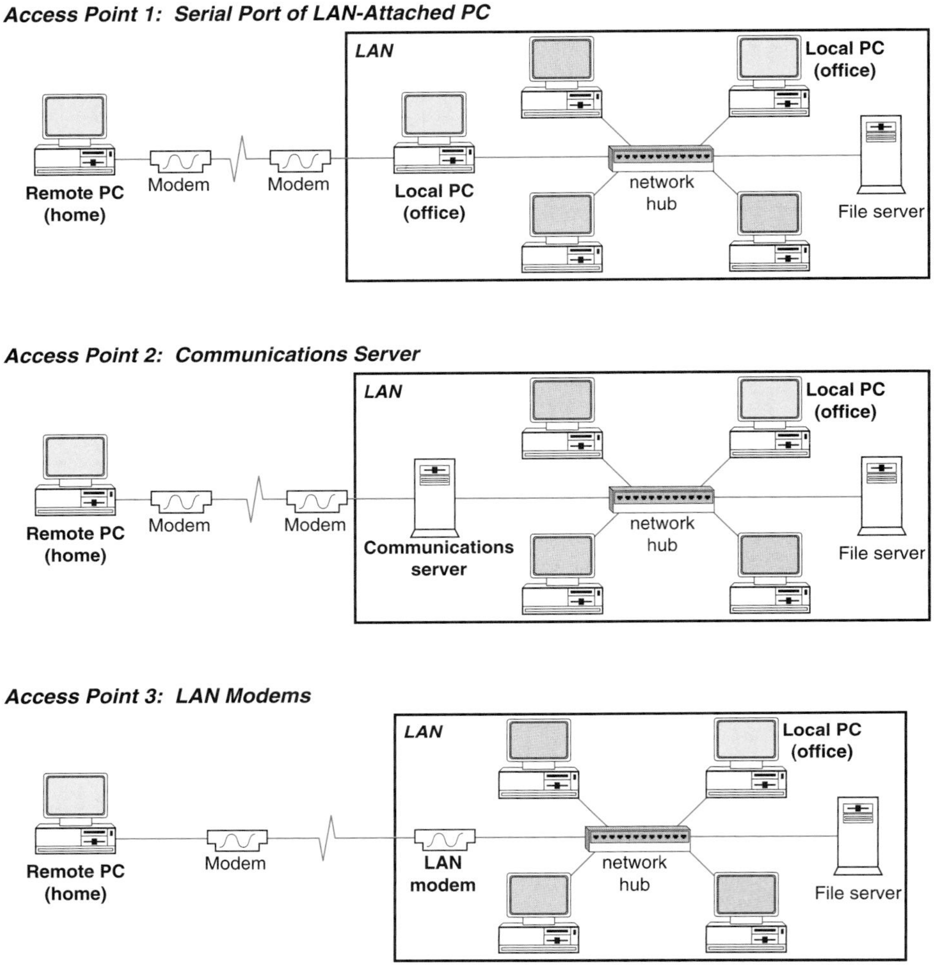

Figure 10-4 Physical Topology: Alternative Access Points

allow a remote user to access and/or remotely control a particular networked workstation. This scenario offers the same access capabilities as if the networked workstation had its own modem and software, but also offers the centralized management, security, and possible financial advantage of a network-attached communications server.

The three access arrangements illustrated are examples of possible physical topologies and do not imply a given logical topology such as remote node, remote control, or both. It is important to understand that the actual implementation of each of these LAN access arrangements may require additional hardware and/or software. They may also be limited in their ability to utilize all LAN-attached resources, or to dial out of the LAN through the same access point.

Network Topology: Alternative Network Access Services Whereas Figure 10-4 illustrated alternative access points within an enterprise network, numerous network access service alternatives exist that a remote access client can employ to reach an enterprise

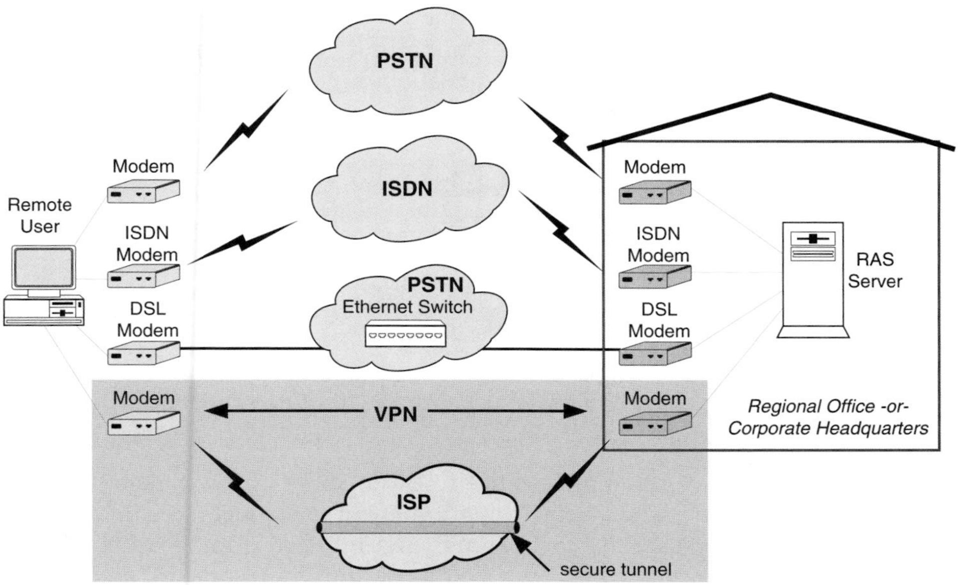

Figure 10-5 Alternative Network Access Services

network's access point. Among these alternatives are the following, many of which were introduced in Chapter 8.

- PSTN (public switched telephone network): Switched analog service; requires a modem; highest current modem standard is V.90; theoretically 56 Kbps, in reality closer to 33 Kbps.
- ISDN (integrated services digital network): A switched digital service; requires an ISDN "modem"; 64 Kbps per B channel; may be able to combine 2 B channels for 128 Kbps.
- XDSL (digital subscriber line) Fixed point-to-point digital service rides over PSTN circuit; requires DSL "modem"; bandwidth ranges from 64 Kbps to 1.5 Mbps; may be symmetrical or asymmetrical.
- VPN (virtual private network): Builds secure communication channels through the Internet to connect remote corporate sites with the regional or headquarters sites; requires VPN hardware and software and access to an Internet service provider. VPNs are explored in detail in Chapter 13.

Figure 10-5 illustrates alternative network access services that might be used to construct a remote access network topology.

■ REMOTE ACCESS TECHNOLOGY

Hardware

Communications Servers and Remote Access Servers As is often the case in the wonderful but confusing world of data communications, communications servers are also known by many other names. In some cases these names may imply, but don't guarantee, variations in configuration, operation, or application. Among these varied labels for the communications server are:

- Access servers
- Remote access servers
- Remote node servers
- Telecommuting servers
- Network resource servers
- Modem servers (usually reserved for dial-out only)
- Asynchronous communications servers

A communications server offers both management advantages and financial payback when large numbers of users wish to gain remote access to/from a LAN. Besides the cost savings of a reduced number of modems, phone lines, and software licenses, perhaps more important are the gains in control over the remote access to the LAN and its attached resources. By monitoring the use of the phone lines connected to the communications server, it is easier to determine exactly how many phone lines are required to service those users requiring remote LAN access.

Multiple remote users can dial into a communications server simultaneously. Exactly how many users can gain simultaneous access varies with the sophistication and cost of the communications server and the installed software. Most communications servers service at least four simultaneous users and possibly more than 1000.

Figure 10-6 provides an I-P-O (input-processing-output) diagram illustrating options for the key functional components of a communications server.

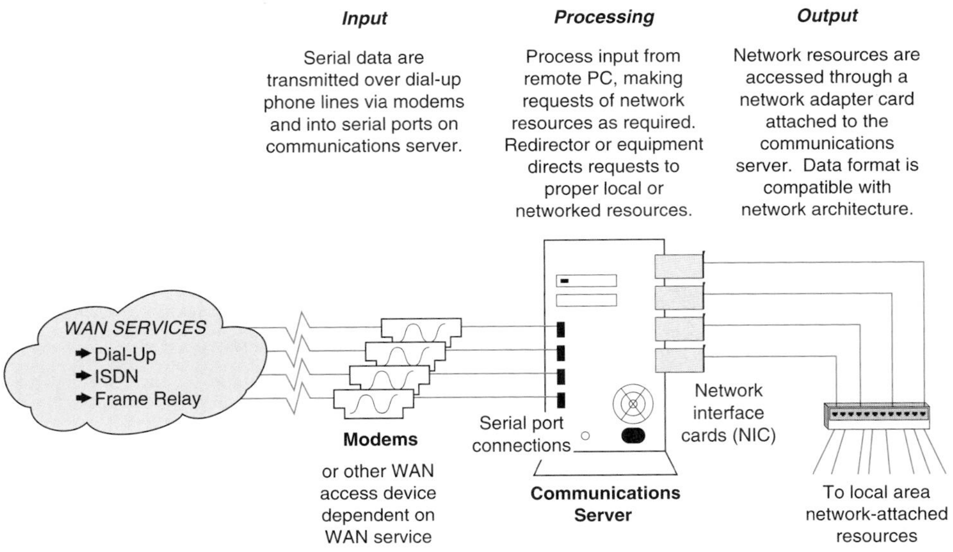

Figure 10-6 Communications Server Components

As can be seen from Figure 10-6, the key hardware components of the communications server are:

- Serial ports
- CPU(s)
- Network interface card(s)

Sometimes modems are also included in the remote access server usually in the form of multiport modem cards. The relative number of each of these three components included in a particular communications server is a key differentiating factor in communications server architectures or configurations. Although not guaranteed, the differentiation between communications servers and remote node servers is generally considered the following:

- **Communications servers** include several CPU boards inside a single enclosure. These servers combine both applications server functionality and remote node server functionality. Applications are physically loaded and executed on the communications server. Communications servers are often used for remote control functionality as an alternative to having several separate desktop PCs available for remote control. Consolidating the CPUs into a single enclosure provides additional fault tolerance and management capabilities over the separate PCs model.
- **Remote node servers** are strictly concerned with controlling remote access to LAN-attached resources and acting as a gateway to those resources. Applications services are supplied by the same LAN-attached applications servers that are accessed by locally attached clients.

The functional differences between communications servers and remote node servers are illustrated in Figure 10-7.

Currently, remote node server solutions fall into four major categories:

- Software-only solutions in which the user supplies a sufficiently powerful server and adds a remote node server software package such as Windows NT RAS or NetWare Connect or other third-party remote node software package. In some cases, a multiport serial board may be included with the software to add sufficient serial ports to the user's server. More information about software-only solutions is offered in the section on remote node software.
- Turnkey or hardware/software solutions in which fully configured remote node servers are compatible with existing network architectures and operating systems. Integrated modems may or may not be included. The remote node server software included on these turnkey systems must be compatible with the installed network operating system.
- LAN modems, also occasionally known as dial-up servers, could be thought of as a remote node server with one or more integrated modems. Included security and management software are also installed on the LAN modem. Given the rapid increase in modem transmission speeds due to evolving modem transmission standards, integrating a modem that cannot be

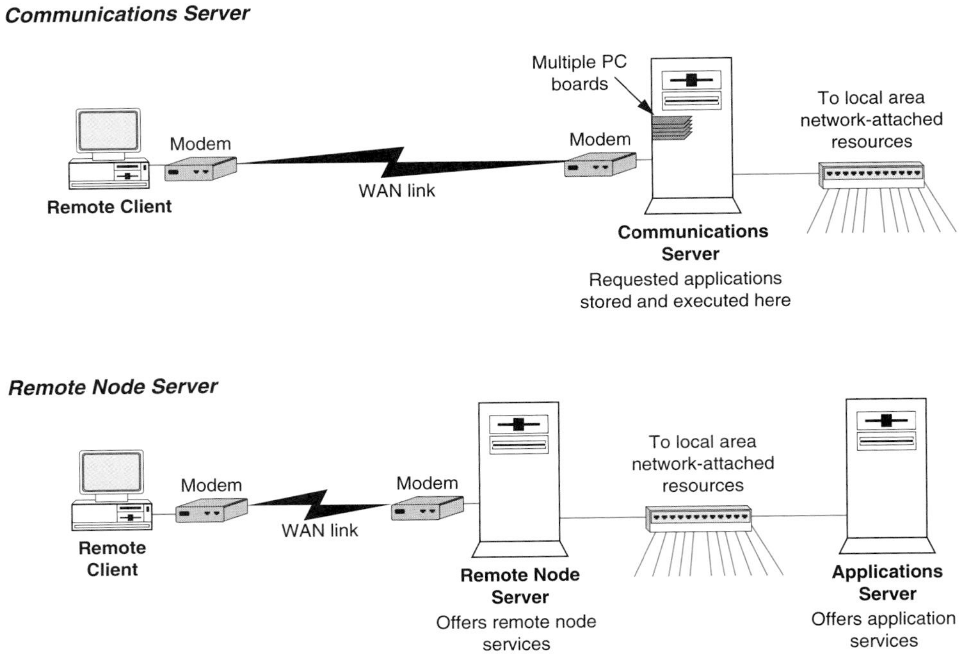

Figure 10-7 Communications Servers vs. Remote Node Servers

upgraded within a remote node server may be less beneficial than using external modems that can be more easily upgraded. Perhaps in a response to this need for convenient modem upgrades, some remote node servers now come with four or eight PC card (PCMCIA) slots into which the latest modem technology can be easily inserted. LAN modems are generally included in reviews of remote node servers rather than being looked on as a distinct product category.

- **Large scale remote access servers (RAS)** also known as **monster RAS** are differentiated from previously mentioned RAS hardware by their scalability (number of modem ports), manageability, and security. These are enterprise class machines boasting modem port counts up to 1344 per chassis, fast Ethernet LAN interfaces, and ATM DS3 (45 Mbps) or OC3 (155 Mbps) WAN connections. This functionality doesn't come cheap, as fully configured prices range from $114,000 to $255,000. Among monster RASs are AS5800 from Cisco, MAX TNT from Ascend, Portmaster 4 from Lucent, CVX 1800 from Nortel, and Total Control Multiservice Access Platform from 3Com.

When employing a self-contained remote node server including both hardware and software, compatibility with existing network resources on a number of different levels must be taken into account. These compatibility issues as well as key functional issues of remote node servers are outlined in Figure 10-8.

Remote Node Server Compatibility/Functional Issue	Importance/Implication
Network Architecture Compatibility	• Since the remote node server includes network interface cards, these must be compatible with the network architecture (Ethernet, fast Ethernet, token ring) of the network in which it is to be installed. • Most remote node servers have Ethernet models, but fewer offer token ring models. • Media compatibility must also be ensured. For example, Ethernet may use AUI, BNC, or RJ-45 interfaces.
Network Operating System Compatibility	• The remote node server software installed in the server must be compatible with the network operating system installed in the network-attached applications servers. • Since these are third-party hardware/software turnkey systems, the remote node server software is not the same as the native software-only solutions such as Windows NT RAS or NetWare Connect, which imply guaranteed compatibility with their respective network operating systems. • The remote node server must also be compatible with the underlying transport protocols used by the installed network operating system. • Can the remote node server access the network operating system's user authorization files to avoid having to build and maintain a second repository of user IDs and passwords? • In the case of NetWare LANs, integration with NetWare Bindery (3.12) or NDS (4.1) should be provided.
Remote Client Software Compatibility	• The remote node server software must be compatible with the remote node software executed on the remote clients. • This remote client software must be compatible with the native operating system on the remote client. • If compatible remote client software is not supplied with the remote node server, is compatibility with third-party PPP client or remote client software guaranteed? • Cost of remote client software may be included in remote node server purchase cost or may be an additional $50/client.
Physical Configuration	• Number of serial ports: Most models start at 8, some are expandable to over 1000 multiport modem ports. • Serial port speed: Most support serial port speeds of 110.2 Kbps, and some support speeds of 230.4 Kbps.
Transmission Optimization	• Use of the limited bandwidth WAN link can be optimized in a variety of ways: • Compression—Are both headers and data compressed? • Spoofing—Are chatty protocols restricted from the WAN link? • Are users warned before launching remote applications that may bog down the WAN link and offer poor performance?
Routing Functionality	• Routing functionality would allow LAN-to-LAN or remote server-to-local server connectivity rather than from a single remote client to the local server. • Routing functionality allows the remote node server to also act as a dial-up router. Dial-up routers must be used in pairs.

Figure 10-8 Compatibility and Functional Issues of Remote Node Servers *(figure continues)*

Remote Node Server Compatibility/Functional Issue	Importance/Implication
WAN Services Supported	• Is connectivity to ISDN, X.25, frame relay, ATM, ADSL, SONET and dial-up lines supported? • Some remote node servers have high-speed serial ports for connection to higher speed WAN services such as T-1 (1.544 Mbps) and T-3 (45 Mbps).
Call Management	• Are dropped calls automatically redialed? • Can connect-time limits be enforced? • Can status of all remote access calls be viewed and controlled form a single location? • Are event logs and reports generated? • Are status and alarm messages output via SNMP agents? • Is fixed and variable callback supported? • Is encryption supported?

Figure 10-8 Continued

In Sharper Focus

DIALING-OUT FROM THE LAN

Normally, when a modem is connected directly to a PC, the communications software expects to direct information to the local serial port to which the modem is attached. However, in the case of a pool of modems attached to a remote node server, the communications software on the local clients must redirect all information for modems through the locally attached network interface card, across the local LAN, to the remote node server, and ultimately to an attached modem. This ability to redirect information for **dial-out** modem applications from LAN-attached PCs is a cooperative task accomplished by the software of the remote node server and its corresponding remote client software. Not all remote node servers support dial-out functionality.

The required redirection is accomplished through the use of industry standard software redirection interrupts. The interrupts supported or enabled on particular remote node servers can vary.:

- **Int14,** or Interrupt 14, is one of the supported dial-out software redirectors and is most often employed by Microsoft network operating systems. Int14 is actually an IBM BIOS serial port interrupt used for the purpose of redirecting output from the local serial port. A TSR (terminate-and-stay-resident) program running on the client intercepts all of the calls and information passed to Int14 and redirects that information across the network to the modem pool.
- **NASI,** or NetWare asynchronous services interface, is a software interrupt that links to the NetWare shell on NetWare clients. As with the Int14 implementation, a TSR intercepts all of the information passed to the NASI interrupt and forwards it across the network to the dial-out modem pool.

Figure 10-9 illustrates some of the issues involved in dialing out from the LAN.

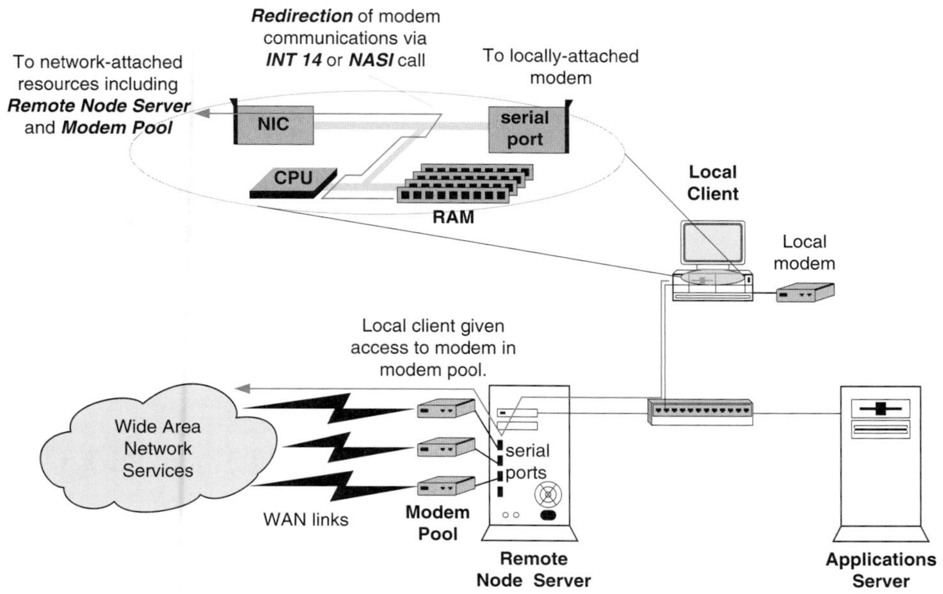

Figure 10-9 Dialing Out from the LAN

Wireless LANs Although not limited to use strictly in a remote access setting, wireless LANs do play a role in the overall objective of untethering workers to increase productivity and customer satisfaction. Although wireless LANs may have been initially marketed as a means of replacing wire-bound LANs, that marketing strategy has not been reflected in their applied uses to date

Mobile computing can be performed within the confines of a corporate or campus environment as well as over longer distances with the assistance of wireless bridges or WAN services. Portable or notebook PCs equipped with their own wireless LAN adapters can create an instant LAN connection merely by getting within range of a server-based wireless LAN adapter or wireless hub. In this way, a student or employee can sit down anywhere and log into a LAN as long as he/she is within range of the wireless hub and has the proper wireless adapter installed in their portable PC. These implementations are especially helpful in large warehouse or inventory settings.

Meeting rooms could be equipped with wireless hubs to allow spontaneous workgroups to log into network resources without running cables all over the meeting room. Similarly, by quickly installing wireless hubs and portable PCs with wireless adapters, temporary expansion needs or emergency/disaster recovery situations can be handled quickly and with relative ease—no rerunning of wires or finding the proper cross-connects in the wiring closet.

Finally, wireless LAN technology allows entire LANs to be preconfigured at a central site and shipped "ready to run" to remote sites. The nontechnical users at the remote site literally just have to plug the power cords into the electrical outlets and they have an instant LAN. For companies with a great number of remote sites and limited technical staff, such a technology is ideal. No preinstallation site visits are necessary. Also avoided are costs and supervision of building wiring jobs and troubleshooting building wiring problems during and after installation.

Although they have been called a technology looking for a market or, perhaps more aptly, a solution looking for a problem, wireless LANs do offer significant flexibility and spontaneity not possible with traditional wire-bound LANs. It is important to note that, in general, wireless LANs cannot match the speed of their wired equivalent network architectures. For example, most Ethernet wireless LANs are limited to around 2 Mbps compared to Ethernet's 10 Mbps wire-based capacity, although IEEE 802.11b wireless LANs are able to transmit at greater than 10 Mbps.

There are currently two popular wireless transmission technologies in the local area network technology area:

- **Spread spectrum transmission**
- **Infrared transmission**

In Sharper Focus

FREQUENCY-HOPPING VS. DIRECT-SEQUENCE SPREAD SPECTRUM

Spread spectrum transmission, as its name implies, spreads a data message across a wide range or spectrum of frequencies. This technique was originally employed as a security measure since a receiver would need to know exactly how the message was spread across the frequency spectrum to intercept the message in meaningful form. Spread spectrum transmission for wireless LANs is most often limited to two frequency ranges:

- 902–928 MHz
- 2.4–2.4835 GHz

However, vendors are also evaluating wireless products using the 5 GHz frequency bandwidth, and the IEEE 802.11 committee has completed development of an 11 Mbps standard.

In addition, only two spread spectrum techniques are allowed by the FCC for wireless LANs:

- **Frequency-hopping spread spectrum**
- **Direct-sequence spread spectrum**

As can be seen in Figure 10-10, direct-sequence spread spectrum is more commonly employed in wireless LAN technology, and in general, is capable of delivering higher data throughput rates than frequency-hopping spread spectrum. Direct-sequence spread spectrum (DSSS) transmits at a particular frequency within the allowable range. To distinguish between transmissions from multiple wireless workstations, DSSS adds at least 10 bits to the data message to uniquely identify a particular transmission. DSSS receivers must be able to differentiate between these bits, known as chips, to properly distinguish transmissions. The addition, removal, and interpretation of chips in DSS adds complexity, cost, and processing overhead. Nonetheless, DSSS generally delivers superior throughput to FHSS.

Frequency-hopping spread spectrum (FHSS) hops from one frequency to another throughout the allowable frequency range. The pattern of frequency hopping must be known by the wireless receiver so that the message can be recon-

Wireless LAN	Manufacturer	Network Architecture	Wireless Transmission Technology	Data Throughput	Maximum Distance
AirLAN	Solectek Corp.	Ethernet	Direct sequence Spread spectrum 902–928 MHz	2 Mbps	800 ft
Aironet	Aironet Wireless Communi-cations Inc (purchased by Cisco)	Ethernet or Token ring	Direct sequence Spread spectrum 902–928 MHz Direct sequence spread spectrum 2.4–2.4835 GHz	860 Kbps 2 Mbps 11 Mbps	1000 ft 500 ft 30 ft
BayStack 660	Nortel	Ethernet	Direct sequence 2.4 GHz	1.11 Mbps	32 ft
Collaborative	Photonics Corp	Ethernet	Diffuse infrared	1 Mbps	30-ft radius
FreePort	Windata	Ethernet	Direct sequence spread spectrum 902–928 MHz	5.7 Mbps	260 ft
Infranet	JVC	Ethernet	360–degree infrared	10 Mbps	16.5-ft radius
InfraLAN	InfraLAN Wireless	Ethernet	Line-of-sight Infrared	10 Mbps	90 ft
NetWave	Xircom Inc	Ethernet	Frequency hopping Spread spectrum 2.4–2.4835 GHz	1.6 Mbps	750 ft
RangeLAN2	Proxim Inc	Ethernet	Frequency hopping spread spectrum 2.4–2.4835 GHz	1.6 Mbps	1000 ft
Roamabout 2400	Cabletron	Ethernet	Direct sequence spread spectrum 2.4–2.4835 GHz	1.35 Mbps 2 Mbps	32 ft 800 ft
WaveLAN	Lucent	Ethernet	Direct sequence spread spectrum 902–928 MHz	1.15 Mbps 2 Mbps	32 ft 800 ft

Figure 10-10 Wireless LAN Functional and Technical Analysis

structed correctly. A given wireless transceiver's signal is on a given frequency for less than 1 second. Another desirable effect of all of the hopping from one frequency to another is that the transmission tends to be less affected by interference, an especially desirable characteristic for mobile computing applications.

Practical Advice and Information

Interference with wireless LANs using the 2.4–2.4835 GHz frequency range can be generated by microwave ovens. Other electronic devices such as cordless phones and wireless scanners are also licensed to use the 902–928 MHz frequency range.

Some of the technical and functional differences between these wireless LAN technologies are summarized in Figure 10-10. Internetworking devices that are able to link wireless LANs with wire-based LANs are known as wireless bridges or wireless access points and were reviewed in Chapter 9.

Some functional issues of wireless LANs not addressed in Figure 10-10 are as follows:

- Network Interface Cards: Since wireless LAN technology seems to be shifting toward an emphasis on mobile computing via laptops and portables, it should come as no surprise that most wireless LAN network interface cards are available as PC cards (PCMCIA). In such a case, card and socket services compatibility should be verified. Parallel port adapters that can also be attached to portable computers are also available on some wireless LANs, as are ISA adapters.
- Encryption: Since data being sent through the air, it is especially important to consider security with wireless LANs. Some wireless LANs support DES (data encryption standard) encryption directly on the network interface card, usually through the installation of an optional encryption chip.

In Sharper Focus

WIRELESS LAN STANDARDS: IEEE 802.11 AND MOBILE IP

One of the key shortcomings to date of wireless LANs has been a lack of interoperability among the wireless LAN offerings of different vendors. In an effort to address this shortcoming, a proposal for a new wireless LAN standard known as **IEEE 802.11** was approved in 1997 after 7 years of debate. Key points included in the standard are as follows:

- Physical layer: The standard defined physical layer protocols for each of the following transmission methods:
  - Frequency-hopping spread spectrum.
  - Direct-sequence spread spectrum.
  - Pulse position modulation infrared (diffuse infrared rather than line of sight).
- Media access control layer: The standard defined **CSMA/CA (carrier sense multiple access with collision avoidance)** as the MAC layer protocol. The standard is similar to CSMA/CD except that collisions cannot be detected in wireless environments as they can in wire-based environments. CSMA/CA avoids collisions by listening to the network before transmission and not transmitting if other workstations on the same network are transmitting. Before transmitting, workstations wait a predetermined amount of time to avoid collisions and set up a point-to-point wireless circuit to the destination workstation. Data-link layer header and information fields such as Ethernet or token ring are sent to the destination workstation. It is the responsibility of the wireless LAN access device to convert IEEE 802.3 or 802.5 frames into IEEE 802.11 frames. The wireless point-to-point circuit remains in place until

the sending workstation receives an acknowledgment that the message was received error-free.

- Data rate: Either 1 or 2 Mbps selectable either by the user or the by system, depending on transmissions conditions, 11 Mbps supported by IEEE 802.11b systems.

One important issue not included in the IEEE 802.11 standard is **roaming** capability, which allows a user to transparently move between the transmission ranges of wireless LANs without interruption. Proprietary roaming capabilities are currently offered by many wireless LAN vendors. **Mobile IP,** under consideration by the IETF as RFCs 2002, 2003–2006, 2334, and 2290, may be the roaming standard that wireless LANs require. Mobile IP, limited to TCP/IP networks, employs two pieces of software to support roaming:

- A mobile IP client is installed on the roaming wireless client workstation.
- A mobile IP home agent is installed on a server or router on the roaming user's home network.

The mobile IP client keeps the mobile IP home agent informed of its changing location as it travels from network to network. The mobile IP home agent forwards any transmissions it receives for the roaming client to its last reported location.

Work continues in wireless LAN standards development. The IEEE 802.11 committee has completed work on an 11 Mbps standard (802.11b) as well as a standard for a 54 Mbps wireless LAN known as 802.11a. Another standards-making body known as ETSI (European Telecommunications Standards Institute) is also working on a 54 Mbps wireless LAN standard using the 5 GHz range known as HiperLAN/2 or H2.

Practical Advice and Information

In January 1997, the FCC set aside an additional 300 MHz of bandwidth for a new class of wireless LANs and other wireless devices. The frequencies, from 5150 to 5350 MHz and from 5725 to 5825 MHz are collectively known as the Unlicensed National Information Infrastructure (U-NII). Compliant devices could include PCs and laptops with built-in or external radio receivers.

Software

Remote Control Software **Remote control software,** especially designed to allow remote PCs to "take-over" control of local PCs, should not be confused with the asynchronous communications software used for dial-up connections to asynchronous hosts via modems. Modem operation, file transfer, scripting languages, and terminal emulation are the primary features of asynchronous communications software.

Taking over remote control of the local PC is generally available only via remote control software. Remote control software allows the keyboard of the remote PC to control the actions of the local PC with screen output being reflected on the remote PC's screen. The terms remote and local are often replaced by **guest** (remote) and **host** (local) when referring to remote control software.

Operating remote control software requires installation of software programs on both the guest and host PCs. Various remote control software packages do not interoperate. The same brand of remote control software must be installed on both guest and host PCs. Both the guest and host pieces of the remote control software may or may not be included in the software package price. Remote control software must have modem operation, file transfer, scripting language, and terminal emulation capabilities similar to those of asynchronous communications software. However, in addition, remote control software should possess features to address the following situations unique to its role:

- Avoid lockups of host PCs
- Allow the guest PC to disable the keyboard and monitor the host PC
- Provide additional security precautions to prevent unauthorized access
- Provide virus detection software

Additionally, Windows-based applications pose a substantial challenge for remote control software. The busy screens of this graphical user interface can really bog down even with V.34or V.90 modems. Some remote control software vendors have implemented proprietary Windows screen transfer utilities that allow Windows-based applications to run on the guest PC as if they were sitting in front of the host PC, but other do not support Windows applications remotely at all.

Figure 10-11 summarizes the important features of Remote Control Software as well as their potential implications. Among the more popular Remote Control Software Enterprise or LAN-enabled packages are the following:

Software	*Vendor*
COSessions Remote 32	Artisoft
ReachOut Enterprise	Stac
PCAnywhere32 9.0	Symantec
Timbuktu Pro	Netopia
Carbon Copy 5.0	Compaq
Proxy 3.0	Funk Software
LapLink 7.5	Traveling Software

Prices range from $119 to $199, with most in the $149 range.

The remote control software loaded onto a communications server for use by multiple simultaneous users is not the same as the remote control software loaded onto single remote (guest) and local (host) PCs. Communications servers' remote control software has the ability to handle multiple users and, in some cases, multiple protocols.

Remote Node Software Traditionally remote node client and server software were supplied by the vendor of the network operating system on the server to be remotely accessed. **Windows NT RAS** (remote access service) and **NetWare Connect** are two examples of such NOS-specific **remote node server** software. It is important to note that these are software-only solutions, installed on industry standard, Intel applica-

Feature Category	Feature	Importance/Implication
Protocol Compatibility	Windows support	• How are Windows applications supported? Are full bit-mapped screens transmitted or only the changes? • Is there proprietary coded transmission of Windows screens?
	Windows '95/98 support	• Are Windows '95/98 applications supported?
	Network operating system protocols	• Which network operating system protocols are supported? (IP, IPX, NetBIOS)
LAN Compatibility	LAN versions	• Are specific multiuser LAN server versions available or required?
	Host/guest	• Are both host and guest (local and remote) versions included?
	Operating system	• Some remote control packages require the same operating system as host and guest PCs, but others do not
Operational Capabilities	Printing	• Can remote PC print on local or network-attached printers?
	File transfer	• Which file transfer protocols are supported? (Kermit, XModem, YModem, ZModem, proprietary) • **Delta file transfer** allows only changes to files to be transferred • Automated file and directory synchronization is important to mobile workers who also have desktop computers at home or at the office.
	Drive mapping	• Can guest (remote PC) drives be mapped for host access? • Can local (host PC) drives be mapped for guest access?
	Scripting language	• Allows repetitive call setups and connections to be automated
	On-line help system	• Context sensitive, which gives help based on where the user is in the program is preferable
	Color/resolution limitations	• Different packages vary from 16 to 16 million colors and 800 × 600 to 2048 × 1280 pixels resolution
	Terminal emulation	• How many different terminals are emulated? Most common are VT100, VT102, VT320, TTY
	Simultaneous connections	• Some packages allow more than one connection or more than one session per connection, for example, simultaneous file transfer and remote control
Security	Password access	• This should be the minimum required security for remote login
	Password encryption	• Since passwords must be transmitted over WAN links, it would be more secure if they were encrypted
	Keyboard disabling	• Since the local PC is active but controlled remotely, it is important that the local keyboard be disabled to prevent unauthorized access
	Monitor blanking	• Similar to rationale for keyboard disabling, since output is being transmitted to the remote PC, it is important to blank the local monitor so that processing cannot be viewed without authorization

Figure 10-11 Remote Control Software Technology Analysis *(figure continues)*

Feature Category	Feature	Importance/Implication
Security *(cont'd)*	Callback system	• Added security, although not hacker-proof, hangs up on dial in, and calls back at preprogrammed or entered phone number
	Access restriction	• Are remote users able to be restricted to certain servers, directories, files, or drives? Can the same user be given different restrictions when logging in locally or remotely?
	Remote access notification	• Can system managers or enterprise network management systems be notified when remote access or password failures have occurred?
	Call logging	• Can information about all calls be logged, sorted, and reported?
	Remote host reboot	• Can the remote PC (guest) reboot the local host if it becomes locked up?
	Limited logon attempts	• Are users locked out after a given number of failed login attempts?
	Virus protection	• This feature is especially important given file transfer capabilities from remote users • Can remote users be restricted to read-only access?
	Logoff after inactivity time-out	• To save on long-distance charges, can users be logged off (and calls dropped) after a set length of time?

Figure 10-11 Continued

tion servers as opposed to the proprietary hardware of specialized remote access or communications servers. A representative list of remote node server software, required operating system or network operating system, and vendors are listed Figure 10-12.

Some of the important functional characteristics of remote node server software other than operating system/network operating system compatibility are listed in Figure 10-13.

Most of the remote node server software packages also included compatible **remote node client software.** A problem arises, however, when a single remote node client needs to login to a variety of different servers running a variety of different network operating systems or remote node server packages. What is required is some sort of universal remote access client. In fact, such remote node clients are available. These standardized remote clients with the ability to link to servers running a variety of different network operating systems are sometimes referred to as

Remote Node Server Software	Required Operating System or Network Operating System	Vendor
Windows NT RAS	Windows NT	Microsoft
NetWare Connect	NetWare	Novell

Figure 10-12 Remote Node Server Software Operating System Compatibility

Remote Node Server Software Functional Characteristic	Importance/Implication
NOS Protocols Supported	• While most remote node server software supports IP and IPX, support of NetBIOS, NetBEUI, Appletalk, Vines, LANtastic, and SNA was more limited • If IP is supported, is the full IP protocol stack including applications and utilities supplied?
WAN Data-Link Layer Protocol	• Most remote node server software now supports PPP, while others support proprietary protocols. Proprietary protocols are fine in single-vendor environments
Modem Support	• How many serial ports can be supported simultaneously? Numbers vary from 32 to over 1000 • How many modem setup strings are included? If the setup string for a particular type of modem is not included, configuration could be considerably more difficult. Numbers vary from 75 to over 400 • Does the remote node server software support modem pools, or does there have to be a modem dedicated to every user? • Does the remote node server software support dial-out functionality over the attached modems?
Management	• How is the remote node server managed? via a specialized console or any attached workstation with proper software? • Does the remote node server software output management information in SNMP format? • Can remote users be limited as to connect time or by inactivity time-out?
Security	• Is forced password renewal (password aging) supported? • Are passwords encrypted? • Is the remote node server software compatible with third-party security servers such as token authentication servers? • Does the remote node server support callback (dial-back) capabilities?
Client Support	• Which types of client platforms are supported? (DOS, Mac, Windows, Windows for Workgroups, Windows 95/98, Windows NT, OS/2, Windows 2000) • Are both NDIS and ODI driver specifications supported?

Figure 10-13 Remote Node Server Software Functional Characteristics

PPP clients. In general, they can link to network operating systems that support IP, IPX, NetBEUI, or XNS as transport protocols. Those that support IPX are generally installable as either NetWare VLMs (virtual loadable modules) or NLMs (NetWare loadable modules). In addition, these PPP client packages include sophisticated authentication procedures to ensure secure communications, compression to ensure optimal use of the WAN link, as well as most of the important features of remote control software. PPP client software is most often included with remote control software. The inclusion of remote control software allows users to choose between remote node and remote control for optimal performance.

Among the specialized compression and authentication algorithms included with a majority of these PPP clients are:

- **CIPX** for compression of IPX headers
- **VJ** for compression of IP headers
- **CHAP MD5** for PPP-encrypted authentication
- **CHAP MD80** authentication for Windows NT RAS
- **SPAP**—Shiva's proprietary authentication protocol that includes password encryption and callback capability

Mobile-Aware Operating Systems The mobile computer user requires flexible computing functionality to easily support at least three possible distinct computing scenarios:

- Stand-alone computing on the laptop or notebook computer
- Remote node or remote control computing to corporate headquarters
- Synchronization of files and directories with desktop workstations at home or in the corporate office

Operating systems that are able to easily adapt to these different computing modes with a variety of included supporting accessory programs and utilities are sometimes referred to as **mobile-aware operating systems.** Windows95/98 is perhaps the best current example of such an operating system. Among the key functions offered by such mobile-aware operating systems are the following:

- Auto-detection of multiple configurations: If external monitors or full-size keyboards are used when at home or in the corporate office, the operating system should automatically detect these and load the proper device drivers.
- Built-in multiprotocol remote node client: Remote node software should be included that can automatically and transparently dial into a variety of different network operating system servers including Windows NT RAS or NetWare Connect. The remote node client should support a variety of network protocols including IP, IPX, and NetBEUI, as well as open data-link WAN protocols such as SLIP and PPP.
- Direct cable connection: When returning from the road, portables should be able to be easily linked to desktop workstations via direct connection through existing serial or parallel ports or perhaps an infrared port adhering to the IrDA spec. Software utilities to initiate and manage such connections should be included.
- File transfer and file/directory synchronizations: Once physical connections are in place, software utilities should be able to synchronize files and directories between either the laptop and the desktop or the laptop and the corporate LAN server.

- Deferred printing: This feature allows printed files to be spooled to the laptop disk drive and saved until the mobile user is next connected to corporate printing resources. At that point, instead of having to remember all of the individual files requiring printing, the deferred printing utility is able to automatically print all of the spooled files.
- Power management: Since most mobile computing users depend on battery-powered computers, anything that the operating system can do to extend battery life would be very beneficial. The demand for higher resolution screens has meant increased power consumption in many cases. Power management features offered by operating systems have been standardized as the **advanced power management (APM)** specification.
- Infrared connection: To avoid the potential hassle of physical cable connections, mobile-aware operating systems are including support for infrared wireless connections between laptops and desktops. To ensure multivendor interoperability, the infrared transmission should conform to the **IrDA (Infrared Data Association)** standards. The IrDA standard defines line-of-sight infrared transmission parameters rather than diffuse infrared transmission as defined by IEEE 802.11 IR. IrDA is currently limited to point-to-point distances of only 3 ft.

Mobile-Aware Applications Beyond the shortcomings of remote node applications already delineated, mobile applications that are dependent on inherently unreliable wireless transmission services must be uniquely developed or modified to optimize performance under these circumstances.

Oracle Mobile Agents, formerly known as Oracle-in-Motion is perhaps the best example of the overall architecture and components required to produce **mobile-aware applications.** As illustrated in Figure 10-14, the Oracle Mobile Agents architecture adheres to an overall **client-agent-server** architecture, compared to the more common LAN-based client/server architecture. The overall objective of such an architecture is to reduce the amount of client to server network traffic by building as much intelligence as possible into the server-based agent so that it can act on behalf of the client application. Oracle's testing of applications developed and deployed in this wireless architecture have produced performance improvements of up to 50:1.

The agent portion of the client/agent/server architecture consists of three cooperating components:

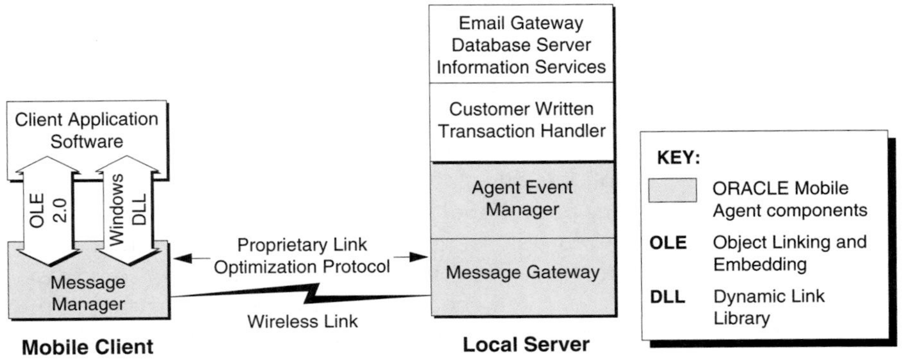

Figure 10-14 Client/Agent/Server Architecture Support Mobile-Aware Applications

- The **message manager** executes on the mobile client and acts as an interface between client applications requesting services and the wireless link over which the requests must be forwarded. It keeps track of requests pending on various servers that are being handled by intelligent agents. Oracle Mobile Agents also operate over LAN links or PPP based dial-up links.
- The **message gateway** can execute on the local server or on a dedicated Unix or Windows workstation and acts as an interface between the client's message manager and the intelligent agent on the local server. The gateway also acts as a holding station for messages to and from mobile clients that are temporarily unreachable. The client-based message manager and the message gateway communicate with each other via a communications protocol developed by Oracle that provides reliable message delivery over wireless transmission services while minimizing acknowledgment overhead.
- The **agent event manager** is combined with a customer written transaction handler to form an entity known as the **intelligent agent,** which resides on the local server. Once the agent event manager receives a request from a mobile client, it acts on behalf of that client in all communications with the local server until the original client request is totally fulfilled. During this processing time in which the intelligent agent is representing the mobile client, the wireless connection can be dropped. Once the original client request has been fulfilled, the entire response is sent from the intelligent agent to the client-based message manager in a single packet, thereby conserving bandwidth and transmission time. Having received the response to a pending request, the client-based message manager deletes the original request from its pending request queue.

Mobile Middleware An emerging category of software that seeks to offer maximum flexibility to mobile computing users while optimizing performance is known as **mobile middleware** sometimes also referred to as wireless middleware. Although specific products within this software category can vary significantly, the ultimate goal of mobile middleware is to offer mobile users transparent client/server access independent of the following variables:

- Client or server platform (operating system, network operating system)
- Applications (client/server or client/agent/server)
- Wireless transmission services

Figure 10-15 illustrates the basic components and interactions of mobile middleware.

As can be seen in Figure 10-15, the primary purpose of mobile middleware is to consolidate client/server traffic from multiple applications for transmission over a variety of potential wireless (or wire-based) transmission services. By consolidating client requests from multiple applications into a single transmission, overall transmission time and expense can be reduced. In some cases, the mobile middleware has sufficient intelligence to inform clients or servers if the intended destination is currently reachable or not, thereby saving wasted time and transmission expense. Some mobile middleware also has the ability to evaluate among available wireless services

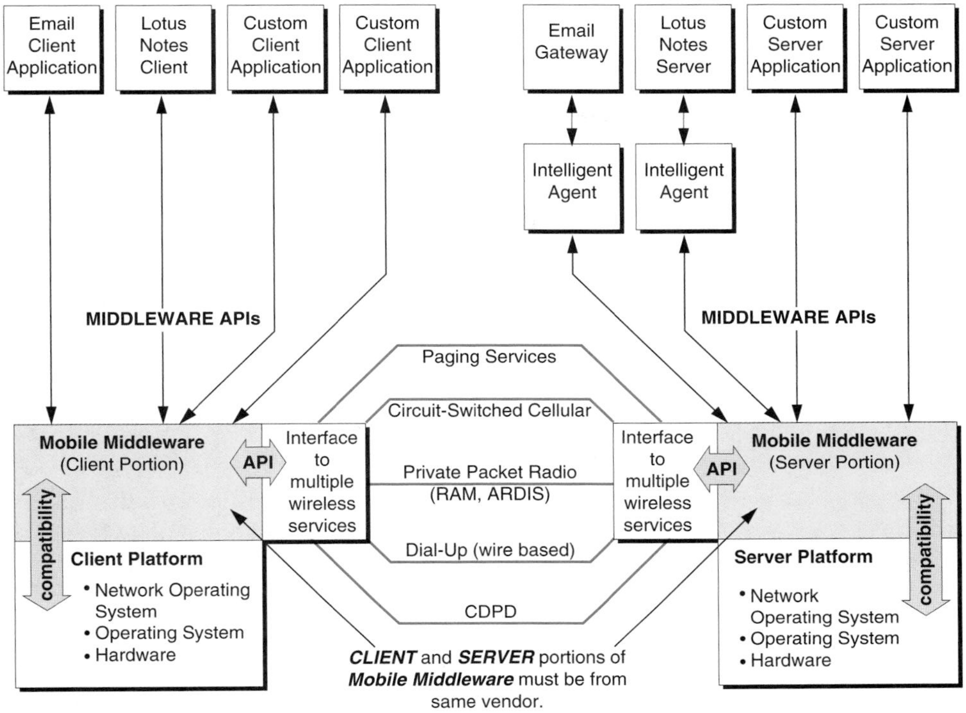

Figure 10-15 Mobile Middleware

between the mobile client and the local server and to choose an optimal wireless transmission service based on performance and/or expense.

Mobile middleware is an emerging category of software characterized by proprietary APIs and a resultant lack of interoperability. As a result, applications written to interact with one vendor's mobile middleware probably won't interact with another vendor's mobile middleware. As can be seen in Figure 10-15, mobile middleware interacts with two sets of APIs: one between the mobile middleware and the applications, and one between the middleware and the wireless transmission services. In an effort to standardize wireless APIs for mobile middleware, two standardization efforts are currently underway:

- The Winsock 2 Forum is developing standardized Winsock 2 APIs for linking mobile middleware with Windows-based applications. This API would be able to deliver transmission related information such as signal strength and transmission characteristics to the applications themselves. Such information could make the applications more intelligent and responsive to changing transmission quality.
- The PCCA (Portable Computer and Communications Association) is developing the standardized API for linking mobile middleware to a variety of wireless transmission services. This API will provide extensions to existing multiprotocol data-link layer device specifications such as NDIS and ODI.

Management and Configuration of Remote Access Technology

Practical Advice and Information

OPTIMIZING REMOTE NODE AND REMOTE CONTROL SOFTWARE PERFORMANCE

As previously described in the section on the remote node logical topology, suitable performance of remote client applications is severely hampered by the limited transmission speed of the WAN links combined with the high bandwidth demands of client/server applications. Besides rewriting the client/server application to minimize the amount of remote client to local server traffic, several other opportunities to improve over remote access performance are available. These optimization techniques will also improve performance of remote control applications as well:

- Use V.90 modems: This new modem specification can support transmission speeds of up to 56 Kbps over dialup lines (in theory).
- Use ISDN (integrated services digital network) services, if available, as an alternative to asynchronous dial-up with the V.90 modem. ISDN BRI (basic rate interface) delivers up to 144 Kbps of switched digital bandwidth. Using ISDN requires ISDN terminal adapters, the equivalent of an ISDN modem, and compatible communications software.
- Use 16550 UARTs and matching serial port drivers The UART (universal asynchronous receiver transmitter) transmits and receives data to and from a PC's serial port that interfaces to the modem. The 16550 UART includes increased buffering capacity to match the performance of faster modems such as the V.90. Transmission via serial ports and UARTS is controlled by operating system software known as serial or COM drivers. Some of these COM drivers have limitations of 19.2 Kbps. More recent operating systems, such as Windows 95/98 and many asynchronous communications packages support serial transmission rates of at least 110.2 Kbps.
- Use data compression software/hardware and set communications software transmission speed to/from the modem to the PC (DTE rate) high enough to take full advantage of the compression software's capabilities. V.90 modems include V.42bis built-in data compression capabilities that can yield compression ratios of up to 4:1 dependent on file content. Since V.90 modems have a maximum transmission speed of 56 Kbps and V.42bis supplies 4:1 data compression, maximum serial transmission rates of 224 Kbps (56 ×4) should be supported by PC hardware and software.
- Make sure that the remote control or remote node software being used supports **screen caching,** which allows only changes to screens, rather than entire screens to be transmitted over the limited bandwidth WAN links. Screen caching reduces the amount of actual traffic transmitted over the WAN link.
- Not to be confused with screen caching software, **network caching** or **LAN caching** software is able to improve overall remote node performance up to five times by caching repetitive applications commands and systems calls. These add-on packages are composed of both client and server pieces that work cooperatively to cache application commands and reduce network traffic over relatively low-speed WAN links. Network caching software is network operating system and protocol dependent, requiring that compatibility be ensured before purchase.

Mobile MIB To integrate the management of mobile computing users into an overall enterprise network management system such as HP Openview or IBM Systemview, a specialized MIB was required to store configuration and location information specific to remote users. The Mobile Management Task Force (MMTF) has proposed a **mobile MIB** capable of feeding configuration and location information to enterprise network management systems via SNMP. A key to the design of the mobile MIB was to balance the amount of information required to effectively manage remote clients while taking into account the limited bandwidth and expense of the remote links over which the management data must be transmitted. From the enterprise network management system's side, controls will need to be installed as to how often remote clients are to be polled via dial-up or wireless transmission for the purpose of gathering up-to-date management information. Among the fields of information included in the proposed mobile MIB are the following:

- Current user location
- Type and speed of connection device
- Type of remote client or remote control software installed on remote device
- Battery power
- Memory

NETWORK SERVICES

Wireless WAN Services

Whereas wireless LANs offer mobility to users across a local scope of coverage, a variety of wireless services are available for use across wider geographic spans. These **wireless WAN services** vary in many ways including availability, applications, transmission speed, and cost. Among the available wireless WAN services that will be explained further are the following:

- Circuit-switched analog cellular
- CDPD (cellular digital packet data)
- Private packet radio
- Enhanced paging and two-way messaging
- ESMR (enhanced specialized mobile radio)
- Microcellular spread spectrum
- PCS (personal communications services)

Applied Problem Solving

A TOP-DOWN APPROACH TO WIRELESS WAN SERVICES ANALYSIS

Because of the many variable factors concerning these wireless WAN services, it is important to take a top-down approach when considering their incorporation into an organization's information systems solution. Questions and issues to be considered on each layer of the top-down model for wireless WAN services are summarized in Figure 10-16.

Top Down Layer	Issues/Implications
Business	• What is the business activity that requires wireless transmission? • How will payback be calculated? Has the value of this business activity been substantiated? • What are the anticipated expenses for the 6-month, 1-year, and 2-year horizons? • What is the geographic scope of this business activity? Localized? National? International?
Application	• Have applications been developed especially for wireless transmission? • Have existing applications been modified to account for wireless transmission characteristics? • Have training and help-desk support systems been developed?
Data	• What is the nature of the data to be delivered via the wireless WAN service? Short bursty transactions, large two-way messages, faxes, file transfers? • Is the data time-sensitive or could transmissions be batched during off-peak hours for discounted rates? • What is the geographic scope of coverage required for wireless data delivery?
Network	• Must the WAN service provide error correction? • Do you wish the WAN service to also provide and maintain the access devices?
Technology	• Which wireless WAN service should be employed? • What type of access device must be employed with the chosen WAN service? • Are access devices proprietary or standards-based?

Figure 10-16 Top-Down Analysis for Wireless WAN Services

As a practical example of how to use the top-down model for wireless WAN services analysis, start with the business situation that requires wireless support and examine the applications and data characteristics that support the business activity in question. For example, which of the following best describes the data to be transmitted by wireless means?

- Fax
- File transfer
- E-mail
- Paging
- Transaction processing
- Database queries

The nature of the content, geographic scope, and amount and urgency of the data to be transmitted has a direct bearing on the particular wireless WAN service employed. Unfortunately, no single wireless WAN service fits all application and data needs. Once a wireless WAN service is chosen, compatibility with existing local area network architectures and technology must be assured. Typical uses of the currently most widely available wireless WAN services are as follows:

- Transaction processing and database queries: CDPD
  - Advantages: Fast call setup, inexpensive for short messages
  - Disadvantages: Limited availability but growing, expensive for large file transfers
- Large file transfers and faxes: Circuit-switched cellular
  - Advantages: Widely available, call duration pricing is more reasonable for longer transmissions than per kilopacket pricing
  - Disadvantages: Longer call setup time than CDPD (up to 30 seconds vs. less than 5 seconds), expensive for short messages
- Short bursty messages and e-mail: Private packet radio
  - Advantages: Wide coverage area and links to commercial e-mail systems
  - Disadvantage: Proprietary networks, expensive for larger file transfers

The key characteristics of these and other wireless WAN services are summarized in Figure 10-17.

Broadband Wireless Broadband wireless technology supports transmission rates of 128 Kbps to 155 Mbps and supports multiple simultaneous transmissions. Wireless T-1 (1.544 Mbps) is very popular at the present time. The frequency ranges most often used in the United States for broadband wireless transmission are 2.4, 2.5, 5, 24, 28, 38, and 42 GHz. Some of these frequency ranges are licensed but others are not, as illustrated in Figure 10-18.

The IEEE 802.16 working group is working on developing standards for broadband wireless access. Wireless T-1 technology operating in the unlicensed 2.4 and 5.8 GHz range has become very popular, ranging in price from $4500 to $9000 per wireless transmission unit (two required per link). Among wireless T-1 vendors and products are the following: Wave Wireless Speedcom, BreezeCom BreezeLink, GWM Lynx.sc, and Adtran Tracer.

Two-Way Messaging

Two-way messaging, sometimes referred to as enhanced paging, allows short text messages to be transmitted between relatively inexpensive transmission devices such as PDAs (personal digital assistants) and alpha-numeric pagers. Two distinct architectures and associated protocols have the potential to deliver these services.

One such architecture is based on **CDPD (cellular digital packet data)** and is being proposed and supported by AT&T Wireless Services, formerly known as McCaw Cellular. CDPD is a service that uses idle capacity in the circuit-switched cellular network to transmit IP-based data packets. The fact that CDPD is IP-based allows it to easily interface to IP-based private networks, as well as to the Internet and other e-mail services.

By adding a protocol known as **LSM (limited size messaging),** CDPD will be able to transport two-way messaging that will offer the following key services beyond simple paging:

Wireless WAN Service	Geographic Scope	Directionality	Data Characteristics	Billing	Access Device	Standards and Compatibility
Circuit-Switched Analog Cellular	National	Full-duplex circuit switched	14 Kbps max	Call duration	Modems with specialized error correction for cellular circuits	MNP-10 (adverse channel enhancements) and ETC (enhanced throughput cellular)
Private Packet Radio	Nearly national, more cities than CDPD but less than circuit-switched cellular	Full-duplex packet-switched digital data	4.8 Kbps	Per character	Proprietary modem compatible with particular private packet radio service	Proprietary; two major services: RAM mobile data and Ardis
CDPD	Limited to large metropolitan areas	Full-duplex Packet-switched digital data	19.2 Kbps max	Flat monthly charge plus usage charge per kilopacket	CDPD modem	Compatible with TCP/IP for easier internetwork integration
Enhanced Paging	National	One or two way; relatively short messages	100 characters or less	Flat monthly charges increasing with coverage area	Pagers	
ESMR	Currently limited	One or two way, voice, paging or messaging	4.8 Kbps	Unknown; service is under development	Proprietary Integrated voice/data devices	
Microcell Spread Spectrum	Limited those areas serviced by microcells; good for college and corporate campuses	Full duplex	10–45 Mbps	Monthly flat fee	Proprietary modem	Most provide access to Internet, e-mail services
PCS	Evolution of digital cellular network	Full duplex, all digital voice and data services	up to 25 Mbps		Two-way pagers; personal digital assistants, PCS devices	Standards-based, should ensure device/service interoperability

Figure 10-17 Wireless WAN Services Technology Analysis

Frequency Range	Distance Limitation	Application/Comments
2.4–2.483 GHz and 5.725–5.875 GHz	25 miles	ISM (industrial, scientific, medical) band—no license required; 83.5 MHz of bandwidth in 2.4 GHz band and 125 MHz of bandwidth in 5.8 GHz band
27.5–28.35 GHz and 29.1–29.25 GHz	2 miles	LMDS (local multipoint distribution service) licensed; more than 1 GHz of bandwidth
2.5–2.690 GHz	35 miles	MMDS (multichannel multipoint distribution service) licensed; 200 MHz of bandwidth
38–39.5 GHz	2 miles	Licensed

Figure 10-18 Broadband Wireless Frequency Ranges

- Guaranteed delivery to destination mobile users even if those devices are unreachable at the time the message was originally sent.
- Return receipt acknowledgments to the party that originated the message.

An alternative two-way messaging architecture is proposed by the PCIA (personal communicator industry association). Rather than building on existing IP-based networks as the CDPD/LSM architecture did, the **TDP (telocator data protocol)** architecture is actually a suite of protocols defining an end-to-end system for two-way messaging to and from paging devices. Figure 10-19 illustrates the differences between the LSM and TDP two-way messaging protocols.

Wireless Personal Digital Assistants (PDAs)

As personal digital assistants have become more versatile and powerful and as digital cellular transmission has become more widespread, it seems inevitable that these two trends will merge, creating a new market for wireless PDAs. These devices are most often web-enabled and are capable of accessing the Internet. It is estimated that there will be 750 million mobile wireless Internet users by the year 2004. To deliver transparent wireless web-based services to users, a combination of hardware devices, specialized protocols, and wireless middleware and services must be properly combined. Each of these components is described in more detail in the following paragraphs.

Devices Among the numerous different hardware devices capable of supporting web-based wireless transmission, some of which support voice transmission, are the following:

- Palm Pilot VII (Palm Computing [3Com])
- Omnibrowse (Microsoft)
- Blackberry (Dell)

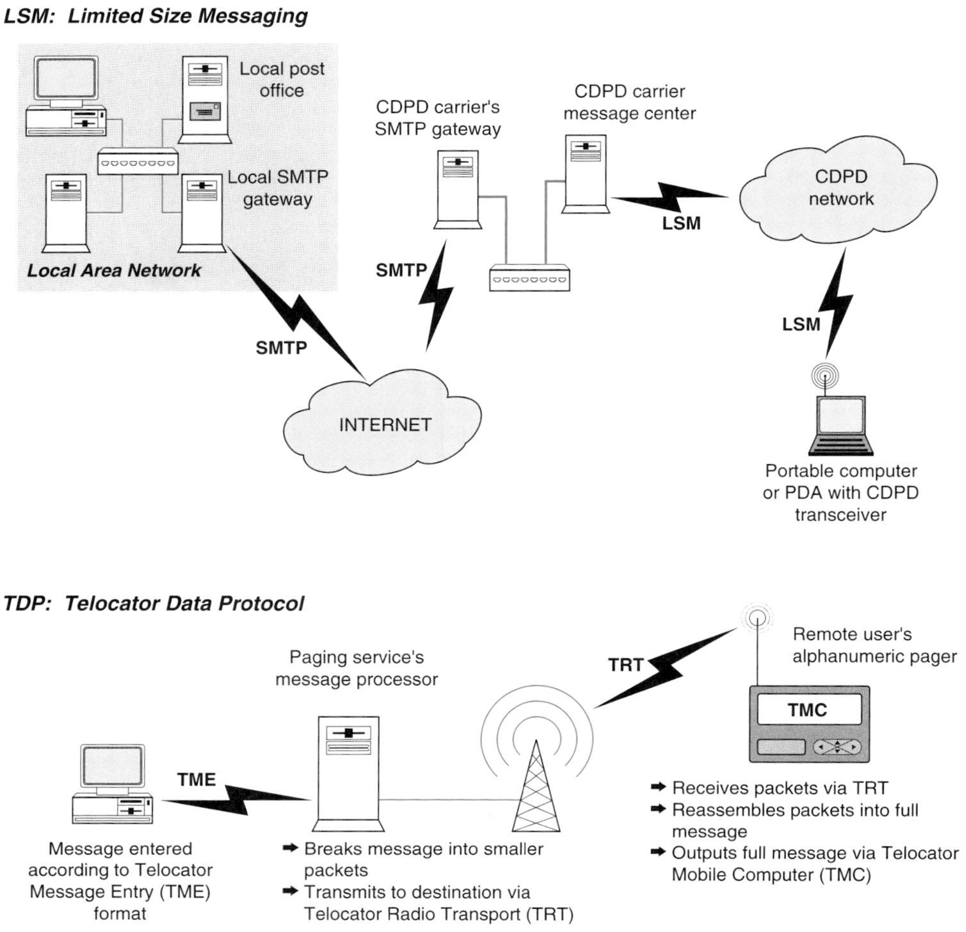

Figure 10-19 Two-Way Messaging Protocols: LSM and TDP

- 9000il (Nokia)
- 5mx (Psion)
- Netvision Data Phone (Symbol Technologies)
- PocketNet (AT&T)

Otherwise known as wireless smartphones or portable microbrowsers, the portability and power of these devices are key to the success and expansion of this market. The two primary operating systems for PDA are the Palm OS (Palm Pilot) and Windows CE from Microsoft. Although Palm OS has gained significant market share, it still lacks transparent interoperability with Windows desktop applications offered by Windows CE.

Protocols and Middleware Following are a few of the key wireless application-oriented protocols and middleware:

WAP (wireless access protocol) brings web browsing to mobile phones, allowing users of WAP 1.1-compliant PDAs to browse the Internet and download bitmap images. In addition, WAP supports secure wireless business transactions.

Bluetooth is a wireless transmission standard for linking mobile phones, computers, and other devices using unlicensed 2.45 GHz frequency for transmission rates of up to 1 Mbps over 10 meters. If is supported by over 700 vendors. Although often thought of as competing standards, WAP and Bluetooth are actually designed for two distinct purposes.

Applications for handhelds are often written in a software development environment known as satellite forms, which is part of a software development kit known as Vulcan from Puma Technologies. Satellite forms allows applications to be created, deployed, and integrated for the Palm OS.

Applications written for the Palm Pilot VII can be transmitted in a wireless manner by accessing wireless value-added networks such as Palm.net. Depending on geographic location, wireless access to Palm.net may be available both indoors and outdoors.

Figure 10-20 illustrates a wireless PDA protocol stack including WAP; Figure 10-21 illustrates the role of a WAP gateway including the Palm.net wireless service.

Next Generation Wireless Services These wireless PDAs require specialized high-bandwidth wireless services. The standards for this next generation of wireless transmission services are most often grouped under the name of **3G (third generation) mobile telephony,** otherwise known as UWC (universal wireless communications)–136. Specific 3G transmission technologies are summarized in Figure 10-22. The ITU's overall initiative for 3G wireless telephony is known as IMT 2000 (Interna-

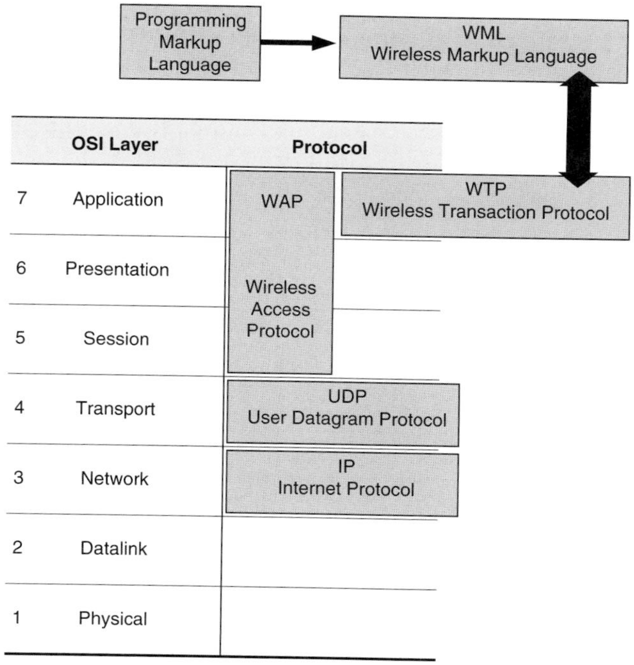

Figure 10-20 Wireless PDA Protocol Stack

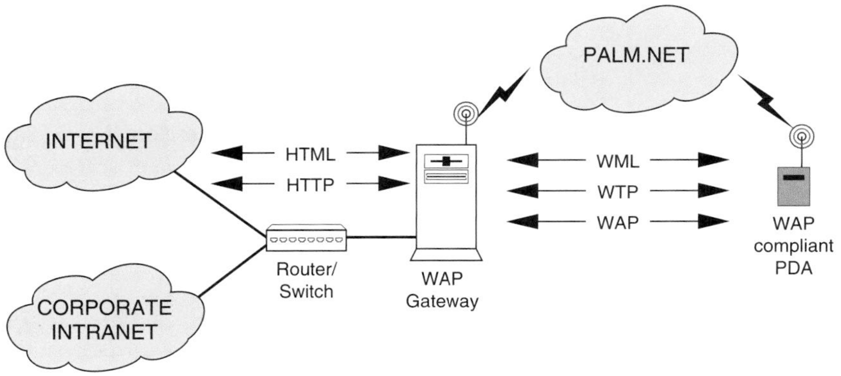

Figure 10-21 Role of a WAP Gateway

tional Mobile Telecommunications) and consists of three separate initiatives: UMTS (ETSI), UWC-136 (TIA), and CDMA2000 (TIA).

Analog Cellular

The current circuit-switched analog cellular network is more properly known by the transmission standard to which it adheres known as **advanced mobile phone service (AMPS)** and operates in the 800 MHz frequency range. Transmitting data over analog cellular networks requires modems that support specialized cellular transmission protocols on both ends of the cellular transmission to maximize throughput. Examples of such protocols are **MNP-10 adverse channel enhancements** and **enhanced throughput cellular (ETC).** In some cases, cellular service providers are deploying modem pools of cellular enhanced modems at the **mobile telephone switching office (MTSO)** where all cellular traffic is converted for transmission over the wireline public switched telephone network (PSTN). Figure 10-23 illustrates data transmission over the circuit-switched analog cellular network.

3G Transmission Technology	Maximum Transmission Rate	Upstream	Downstream
GPRS (general packet radio service)	115 Kbps	22 Kbps	44 Kbps
EDGE (enhanced data rates for global evolution)	384 Kbps	40 Kbps	100 Kbps
W-CDMA (wideband code division multiple access)	2 Mbps	100 Kbps	384 Kbps
UMTS (universal mobile telecommunications system)	2 Mbps	100 Kbps	384 Kbps
HSCSD (high-speed circuit-switched data)	57.6 Kbps	28.8 Kbps	28.8 Kbps

Figure 10-22 3G Mobile Telephony Standards

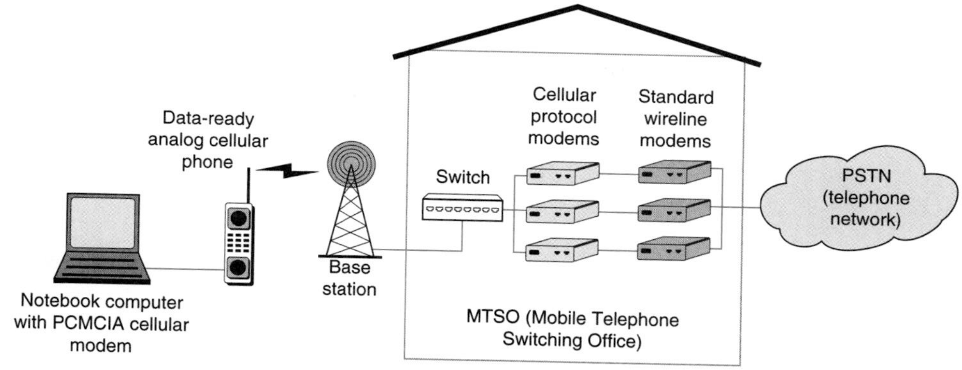

Figure 10-23 Data Transmission over the Circuit-Switched Analog Cellular Network

Digital Cellular/Personal Communications Services

PCS or **personal communications services** is a visionary concept of an evolving all-digital network architecture that could deliver a variety of telecommunications services transparently to users at any time regardless of their geographic location. PCS is not a totally new "from the bottom up" telecommunications architecture. In fact, it is the integration of a number of existing telecommunications environments. PCS seeks to combine the capabilities of the PSTN, otherwise known as the **landline telephone network,** with a new all digital cellular network, along with paging networks and satellite communications networks.

The need for seamless delivery of a combination of all of the preceding services is easily illustrated by the plight of today's mobile professional. A single person has a phone number for the home phone, a voice and fax number for the office, a cellular phone number for the automobile, a pager phone number for the pager, and perhaps even another phone number for the satellite service phone for use outside of cellular phone areas. The premise of PCS is rather straightforward: one person, one phone number.

This **personal phone number** or **PPN** would become the user's interface to PCS and the vast array of transparently available telecommunications services. This personal phone number is a key concept to PCS. It changes the entire focus of the interface to the telecommunications environment from the current orientation of a number being associated with a particular location, regardless of the individual using the facility, to a number being associated with particular individual, regardless of the location, even globally, of the accessed facility. Figure 10-24 illustrates the basic elements of PCS.

Digital Cellular Standards Given the limited bandwidth (only about 140 MHz from 1.85 GHz to 1.99 GHz, referred to as the 2 GHz band) allocated to PCS and the potentially large number of subscribers needing to share that limited bandwidth, a key challenge for PCS is the ability to maximize the number of simultaneous conversations over a finite amount of bandwidth. Just as multiplexing was originally introduced in the study of wide area networks as a means of maximizing the use of wire-based circuits, two variations of multiplexing are being field tested as a means of maximizing the use of the allocated bandwidth of these air-based circuits.

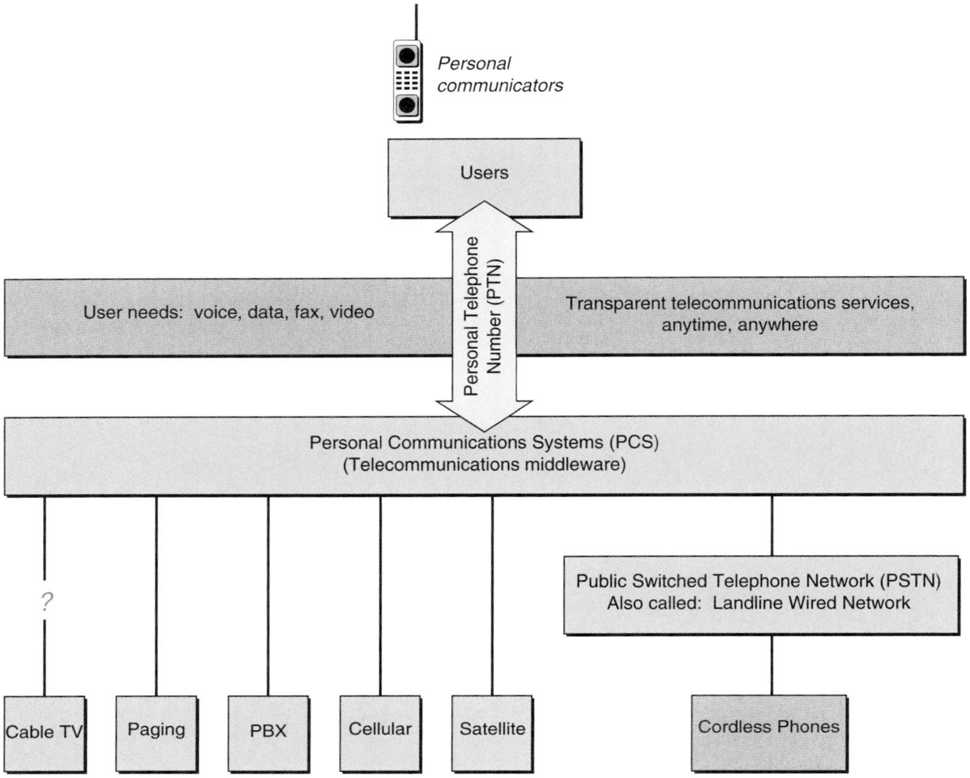

Figure 10-24 Basic Elements of PCS

TDMA (time division multiple access) and **CDMA (code division multiple access)** are the two methodologies currently being researched in PCS field trials. TDMA-based digital cellular may be able to support three times (some tests indicate six or seven times) the transmission capacity of analog cellular, and CDMA could offer as much as a tenfold increase. Note that the names of each of these techniques end in the words "multiple access" rather than "multiplexing." The "multiple access" refers to multiple phone conversations having access to the same bandwidth and yet not interfering with each other.

TDMA achieves more than one conversation per frequency by assigning timeslots to individual conversations. Ten timeslots per frequency are often assigned, with a given cellular device transmitting its digitized voice only during its assigned timeslot. Receiving devices must be in sync with the time slots of the sending device to receive the digitized voice packets and reassemble them into a natural sounding analog signal. TDMA should be able to transmit data at 9.6 Kbps. TDMA digital standards to handle call setup, maintenance, and termination have been defined by the Telecommunications Industry Association (TIA) as follows:

- IS-130: TDMA radio interface and radio link protocol 1
- IS-135: TDMA services, Async data and fax

CDMA is the newest and most advanced technique for maximizing the number of calls transmitted within a limited bandwidth by using a spread spectrum transmission technique. Rather than allocate specific frequency channels within the allocated bandwidth to specific conversations, as is the case with TDMA, CDMA transmits digitized voice packets from numerous calls at different frequencies spread all over the entire allocated bandwidth spectrum.

The *code* in CDMA reflects that to keep track of these various digitized voice packets from various conversations spread over the entire spectrum of allocated bandwidth, a code is appended to each packet indicating which voice conversation it belongs to. This technique is not unlike the datagram connectionless service used by packet-switched networks to send packetized data over numerous switched virtual circuits within the packet-switched network. By identifying the source and sequence of each packet, the original message integrity is maintained while maximizing the overall performance of the network. CDMA should be able to transmit data at up to 16 Kbps. The CDMA standards defined by the TIA are IS-95a and IS-99: Data services option for wideband spread spectrum digital cellular systems, commonly known as CDMAone. Upgrades to the CDMA standard include:

- IS-95b, which gives each user up to four 16 Kbps circuits.
- IS-95c, which employs packet switching and gives each user up to ten 14.4 Kbps channels.

Figure 10-25 illustrates both TDMA and CDMA.

TDMA and CDMA are being pursued and implemented primarily by cellular carriers in North America. In Europe and much of the rest of the world, **global system for mobile communication (GSM)** is either currently deployed or planned for implementation, and **personal handyphone system (PHS)** is the digital cellular standard being implemented in Japan. At the present time, these various digital cellular transmission standards are not interoperable, thereby precluding the possibility of transparent global access to digital cellular services.

Digital cellular systems will be deployed on an as-needed basis in the most congested metropolitan areas. As a result, existing analog cellular networks will be required to coexist and interoperate with newer digital cellular networks. Transmission protocols such as TDMA and CDMA must be compatible with analog transmission protocols, and next-generation cellular phones must be able to support both analog and digital transmission.

Transmitting digital data from a notebook computer over digital cellular networks will not require modulation as was required with analog cellular networks. As a result, notebook computers should be able to interface directly to TDMA- or CDMA-based digital cellular phones via serial ports. Figure 10-26 illustrates data transmission over a digital cellular network.

Managerial Perspective

THE FUTURE OF PCS

PCS faces significant challenges on its way to worldwide deployment. Required changes in thinking and behavior on the part of PCS users should not be overlooked. For instance, if a person can be called regardless of location thanks to the PPN, who should pay for that call, the called party or the calling party? Caller ID services will now display the calling party's name or personal number rather than the number of the phone from which that person is calling. Remember, with PCS, numbers are associated with people, not with equipment and phone lines.

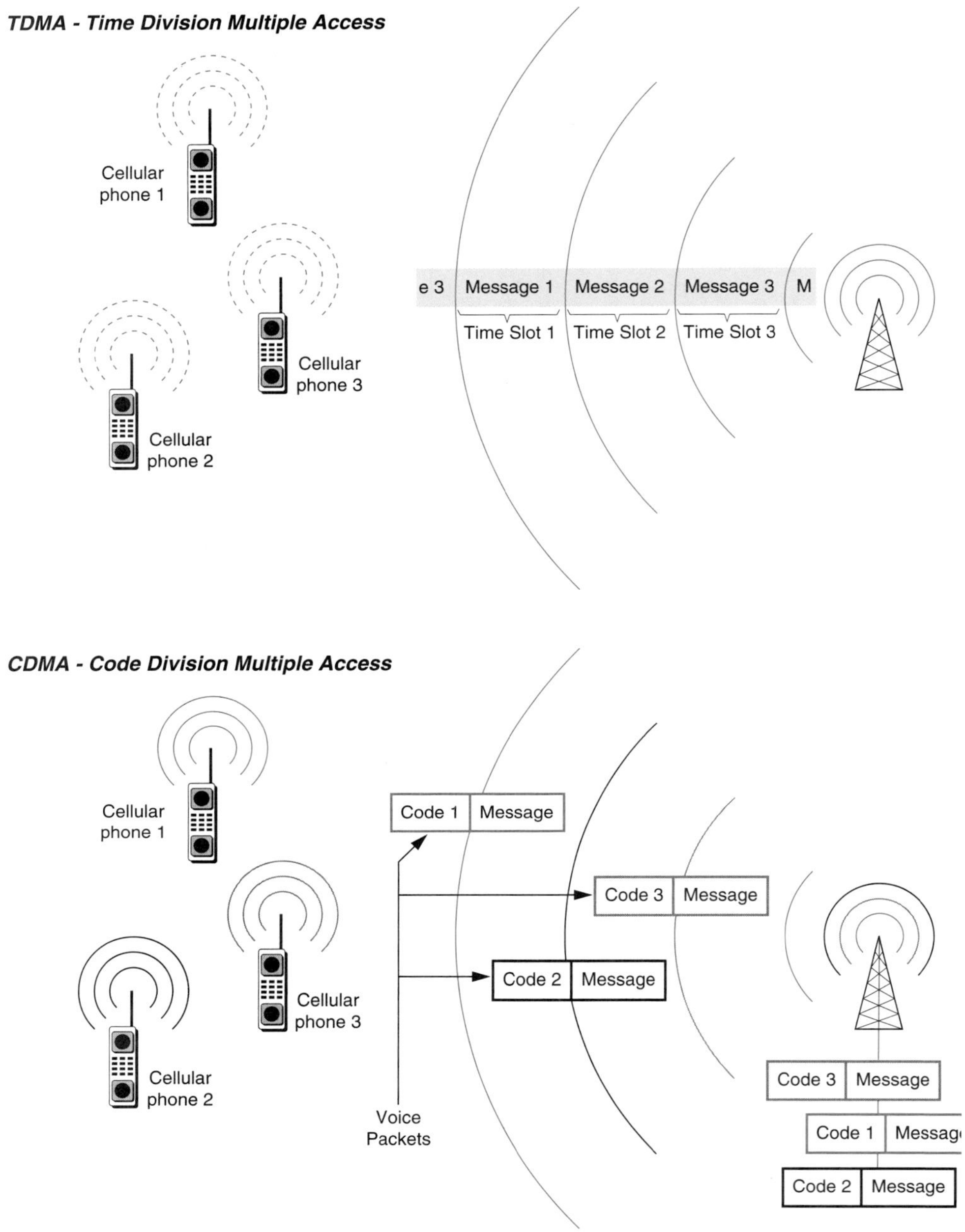

Figure 10-25 Maximizing Minimum Bandwidth: TDMA and CDMA

If the calling party is to be responsible for payment, the person would probably like to know where he/she is calling before placing the call. However, as a potentially called party, would you want just anybody knowing your location? Vandals or your supervisor could pinpoint your location without even placing a call. Advanced call screening services could allow only certain PPN calls to be received on a person's personal communicator, while forwarding others to voice mail. As with any dramat-

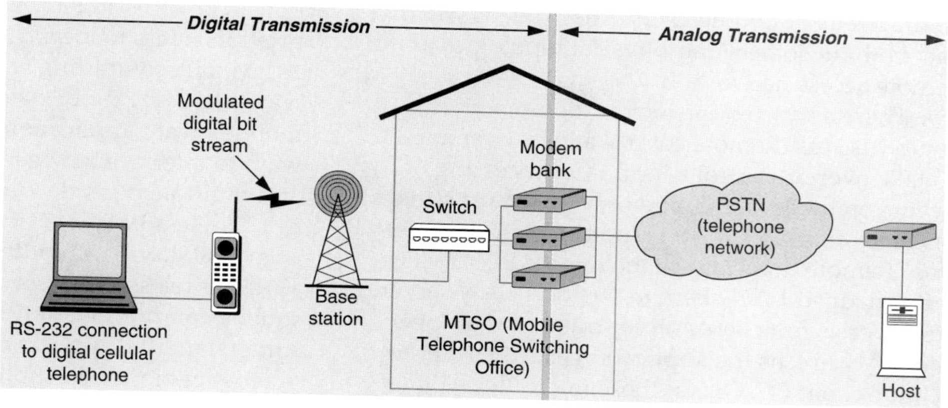

Figure 10-26 Data Transmission over a Digital Cellular Network

ically new technology, societal impact and changes will result. PCS should be no exception.

Perhaps the most significant hurdles are the individual and, at times, conflicting business missions of the various industries that must somehow achieve a metamorphosis that will produce a comprehensive, seamless, global, transparent personal communications service for subscribers. Another industry with its own distinct mission and on a possible collision course with the telecommunications industry is the cable television industry. PCS spread-spectrum communicators have been successfully demonstrated on CATV networks.

PCS vendors bid $7.7 billion for auctioned spectrum in 1995/1996. It is estimated that somewhere between an additional $10 billion and $50 billion must be spent on PCS infrastructure before services can be deployed. The dilemma is that PCS vendors must price their services attractively enough to gain market share while maintaining enough cash flow to surrender a tremendous amount of debt.

Finally, future PCS deployment levels may be determined by simple market demand. There is always the possibility that a seamless, comprehensive, location-independent communications system such as PCS is of more interest to the companies that stand to profit from it than to the buying public who are supposedly demanding it.

SUMMARY

Remote access to LANs has taken on increased importance in response to major changes in business conditions. As indicated by the top-down model, network functionality must respond to changing business conditions. Expectations of LAN remote access are significant. Remote users expect the same level of data accessibility, application services, and performances on the road as they receive at the office. Delivering this equivalent functionality is the challenge faced by networking professionals today. The major obstacle to this lofty objective is the bandwidth, availability, and quality of the wide area network services that are expected to deliver remote connectivity to mobile users. Increasingly, wireless WAN services are at the forefront of remote access solutions.

In designing remote access solutions, it is essential to start with a thorough understanding of the needs of remote users. These needs will dictate both the logical and physical topologies of the remote access network.

There are two basic logical topologies for remote access. Remote control allows a remote PC to take over or control a local PC. Processing occurs on the local PC, and only keyboard strokes and screen images are transported over the WAN link. Remote node allows the remote PC to act as a full-fledged LAN client to the local LAN server. In this case, full client/server traffic travels over the WAN link as the application executes on the remote client PC. One of these logical topologies is not preferable in all cases. Each situation must be analyzed on an individual basis.

Physical topologies include accessing a local LAN-attached PC directly via modem, accessing a shared communications server that might include PC boards for embedded shared computing power, or accessing a LAN modem that would provide access to local LAN computing resources.

Mobile computing requires specialized software including mobile-aware operating systems, mobile-aware applications, and mobile middleware to interface between multiple applications and multiple possible wireless WAN services.

Wireless WAN services vary widely in terms of availability, bandwidth, reliability, and cost. No single wireless WAN service is appropriate for all mobile computing applications. It is important to understand the application needs and data characteristics of mobile applications before choosing a wireless WAN service. Digital cellular and personal communications services may hold the promise of higher bandwidth, reliable wireless transmission. However, substantial infrastructure development remains before such services will be universally available.

KEY TERMS

3G Mobile Telephony
advanced mobile phone service
advanced power management
adverse channel enhancements
agent event manager
AMPS
APM
Blue tooth
Carrier sense multiple access with collision avoidance
CDMA
CDPD
cellular digital packet data
CHAP MD5
CHAP MD80
CIPX
circuit-switched analog cellular
client-agent-server
code division multiple access
communications server
CSMA/CA
delta file transfer
dial-in server
dial-out
direct-sequence spread spectrum
enhanced paging
enhanced throughput cellular
ESMR
ETC
frequency-hopping spread spectrum
global system for mobile communication
GSM
guest host
IEEE 802.11
Infrared Data Association
infrared transmission
Int14
intelligent agent
IrDA
LAN caching
LAN modem
landline telephone network
large scale RAS
limited size messaging
LSM
message gateway
message manager
microcell spread spectrum
MNP-10
mobile computing
mobile IP
mobile MIB
mobile middleware
mobile telephone switching office
mobile-aware applications
mobile-aware operating systems
monster RAS
MTSO
NASI
NetWare Connect
network caching
Oracle mobile agents
PCS
personal communications services
personal handyphone system
personal phone number
PHS
PPN
PPP clients
private packet radio
remote access
remote access server
remote control
remote control software
remote node
remote node client software
remote node server software
remote node servers
remote node software
roaming
screen caching
small office home office

SOHO
SPAP
spread spectrum transmission
TDMA
TDP
technical support
telecommuting
telocator data protocol
time division multiple access
two-way messaging
VJ
WAP
Windows NT RAS
wireless access protocol
wireless WAN services

REVIEW QUESTIONS

1. What are some of the key business trends that have led to an increased interest in LAN remote access?
2. What is the importance of needs analysis to LAN remote access design?
3. Differentiate between remote node and remote control in terms of functionality and network impact.
4. What is the major limitation in terms of delivering transparent access to remote LAN users?
5. Describe how it is possible to run remote control software via a remote node connection. What are the advantages of such a setup?
6. What are some of the security issues unique to remote access situations?
7. What added security capability can token authentication systems offer?
8. What advantages does a communications server offer over separate remote access links to multiple PCs? Disadvantages?
9. What is the common differentiation between communications servers and remote node servers?
10. Differentiate among the three major categories of remote node servers.
11. Why are dial-out solutions for remote node servers different from dial-in solutions?
12. How can dial-out solutions be implemented on LANs equipped with remote node servers?
13. Differentiate between the two spread spectrum transmission techniques approved by the FCC in terms of functionality and application.
14. Why are wireless LAN NICs most often PCMCIA?
15. Differentiate between CSMA/CD and CSMA/CA.
16. What is roaming and why is it important to remote access users?
17. How does mobile IP work?
18. What is the relationship between the guest and host remote control software?
19. Why is remote control software not interoperable?
20. Differentiate between remote control and remote node software in terms of transport protocols and client protocol stacks.
21. Differentiate between LAN (multiuser) remote control software and point-to-point remote control software.
22. What are some of the unique functional requirements of remote control software beyond being able to control local (host) PCs?
23. What are some of the unique functional requirements of remote node server software?
24. What advantage do PPP clients offer?
25. What are some of the unique functional requirements of mobile-aware operating systems?
26. Differentiate between the client-agent-server architecture and the client/server architecture.
27. How do mobile-aware applications need to adjust to or compensate for wireless transmission services?
28. Describe the interaction between the components of Oracle Mobile Agents.
29. What two distinct interfaces do mobile middleware products transcend?
30. What are the functional objectives of mobile middleware?
31. How can the proprietary nature of mobile middleware products be overcome?
32. Describe standards development efforts that may affect mobile middleware.
33. What are some of the ways that remote node or remote control applications can be optimized?
34. What is the difference between screen caching and network caching?
35. What unique information is required in a mobile MIB and why?
36. What are the conflicting objectives or limitations of mobile management software and the Mobile MIB?
37. Why is CDPD of such interest to circuit-switched cellular vendors?
38. What standards are important to a person wishing to purchase a "cellular-ready" modem?
39. Match each of the following to the most appropriate wireless WAN service and justify your answer: transaction processing, short messages, large file transfers.

40. What are the advantages of two-way messaging systems for data transfer?
41. Differentiate between analog and digital cellular transmission systems in terms of data transfer capabilities and equipment requirements.
42. How is the notion of a personal phone number central to PCS, and what changes in thinking about phone systems does it require?
43. Differentiate between TDMA and CDMA.
44. What are some of the obstacles to the vision of universal PCS?

ACTIVITIES

1. Gather articles regarding business trends that have contributed to the rise in LAN remote access. Relate these business trends to market trends for remote access technology and wireless WAN services. Use graphical presentation wherever possible.
2. Find an organization currently supporting LAN remote access. Analyze the situation from a business perspective. Which business activities are being supported? Was cost/benefit or payback period analysis performed or considered?
3. In the organization being studied, what is the physical topology employed? Links to multiple PCs? Communications server? LAN modems? Prepare a diagram of the physical topology including all software components such as network operating systems and transport protocols.
4. In the organization being studied, is remote node functionality supported? If so, which remote client software is installed? Are remote users able to access servers with multiple different network operating systems? Are PPP clients installed?
5. In the organization being studied, are dialout capabilities supplied? If so, how?
6. In the organization being studied, have any efforts been made to optimize the performance of remote node or remote control applications? If so, what were those adjustments, and what impact did they have?
7. What types of additional security precautions, if any, are instituted for remote users?
8. Investigate infrared wireless LANs. What is the difference between line-of-sight and diffuse infrared? Where are infrared wireless LANs being deployed? What is the percentage market share of infrared wireless LANs vs. spread spectrum wireless LANs?
9. Why did the FCC choose the frequency bands that they did for spread spectrum transmission?
10. What devices other than wireless LANs use the 902–928 MHz frequency range? Could this be a problem?
11. What is the difference between the CSMA/CA employed in IEEE 802.11 and that employed in AppleTalk networks?
12. What is the current status of IEEE 802.11? What are the perceived shortcomings of the standard?
13. Research current PCS or digital cellular pilot tests. Compare how many use TDMA and how many use CDMA. What have been the results of these pilot tests?

Case Study

Hospital Marries Wireless Net with Thin Clients

Thin client computing coupled with wireless LANs seem to be just what the doctor ordered.

At University Medical Center, Stony Brook, N.Y., a low-speed wireless LAN links tablet-sized portable terminals with server-based Windows applications. Respiratory therapists now capture more accurate information faster than ever before, says Michael McPeck, director of respiratory care and biomedical engineering and the center's wireless guru. This data becomes the basis of faster, more accurate decisions on patient care.

"We wanted to go wireless because the therapists don't work out of an office. They visit one patient after another," he says.

Previously, therapists visited patients, took notes and then recorded the information later on paper charts at nursing stations.

"You can't help seeing that time is saved because they're not endlessly visiting a nursing station and making pen notations on the patient's chart," McPeck says.

Two years ago—before ratification of the IEEE 802.11 wireless Ethernet standard—McPeck selected wireless LAN equipment as well as the handheld tablets from Symbol Technologies, located in nearby Holtsville. The 802.11b standard, with a bandwidth of 11M bit/sec, was approved last fall. The center's IT staff is planning an upgrade in the future.

For the 504-bed hospital, part of the State University of New York at Stony Brook, McPeck did most of the installation and deployment himself.

"It's not as simple as just plugging in a few wires. But it's certainly not as complex as people might believe," he says. Today, as a growing number of users and departments start to use the technology, the center's IT department has embraced it enthusiastically.

"Others see you using wireless, and very suddenly, they see the benefits and advantages that could take place in their line of work," McPeck says.

The 1M-bit/sec speed of the current wireless link serves the hospital well. "That's the data transfer rate between the mobile client and the Access Point [the interface between the wireless and wired nets]," he says. "The radio speed is only for the clients, not for the backbone."

Interference with the hospital's radio-based heart monitors and other equipment has not been a problem. "Sometimes, when I have visitors in to see the wireless LAN, I take them to our telemetry unit, where we monitor hearts with radio telemetry," McPeck says. "I show them the monitors with their antennae peacefully coexisting next to our Access Point antennae."

The Symbol wireless LAN was to be the connection medium. McPeck decided to use a portable Window-based terminal—a thin client—to access applications on an NT server, via the Citrix Systems software.

"The handheld computers didn't have the horsepower to run Windows applications locally," he says. "Worst of all, they would have had a spinning PCMIA hard drive, which would have been expensive, delicate, hot-running and power-draining."

The Symbol tablet terminal that McPeck selected has an Intel 486-MHz processor with MS DOS. McPeck added a card with 4M bytes of RAM and loaded into it TCP/IP software and the Citrix ICA client to access the server-based applications.

The Citrix software makes administration a snap. McPeck loads new or upgraded software on the one server, and all the users have immediate access. The respiratory therapy department has 10 tablets deployed.

The software also lets an administrator troubleshoot problems by "shadowing" a user's session—the administrator can see from his desktop PC exactly what appears on the user's screen.

Besides upgrading to a faster wireless LAN topology, McPeck is looking to client devices that are lighter and less cumbersome than the tablets.

"The terminal still weighs about three pounds. So, for a mobile worker on their feet for eight hours, it gets pretty heavy," he says.

McPeck is looking at handhelds running the PalmOS operating system. They're much lighter and smaller than the tablets, but one drawback is the lack of software that lets the Palm act as a thin client to server-based applications.

"I think there's a screaming need for thinner applications that can work with PalmOS-based devices and the Palm database structures," McPeck says.

Source: John Cox, "Hospital marries wireless net with thin clients," *Network World,* vol. 17, no. 20 (May 15, 2000), p. 27. Copyright Network World. Reprinted with permission.

BUSINESS CASE STUDY QUESTIONS

Activities

1. Complete a top-down model for this case by gleaning facts from the case and placing them in the proper layer of the top-down model. After completing the top-down model, analyze and detail those instances where requirements were clearly passed down from upper layers to lower layers of the model and where solutions to those requirements were passed up from lower layers to upper layers of the model.
2. Detail any questions about the case that may occur to you for which answers are not clearly stated in the article.

Business

1. What was the business motivation or problem that initiated the search for the implemented solution?
2. What was the productivity impact of the implemented solution?
3. What was the old business process before the implemented solution?
4. Were business performance metrics and associated infrastructure performance metrics identified? If so, were they achieved? If not, what might be some suitable business and infrastructure performance metrics for this case?

Application

1. What is a thin client?
2. What applications are actually being run via thin client software?
3. How are software updates loaded on the thin clients?
4. What operating system is used on the thin client currently?
5. What operating system for the thin client is being considered for the future?

Data

1. How does the thin client software employed impact the amount of data that must be transmitted via the network?

Network

1. What underlying network technologies were key to the achievement of stated business objectives?
2. What standards issues had an impact on this case?
3. What is the current transmission rate?
4. What upgrades are being planned?

Technology

1. What specific technologies were employed to deliver the described solution?
2. Has interference been a problem? Why or why not?
3. Draw a diagram showing all interoperating technologies highlighting protocols used for interfacing between the various technologies.

CHAPTER 11

THE NETWORK DEVELOPMENT LIFE CYCLE

Concepts Reinforced

Top-Down Model
Business Process Reengineering
Cost/Benefit Analysis

Concepts Introduced

Network Development Life Cycle
Comprehensive Systems and Networking Budget Model
Integrated Computer Assisted Network Engineering
Network Analysis and Design Methodology
Physical Network Design
Logical Network Design
Total Cost of Ownership
Return on Investment
IT Project Portfolio Management

OBJECTIVES

Upon successful completion of this chapter, you should:

1. Understand how the network development life cycle (NDLC) relates to other systems development architectures and life cycles and, consequently, how the network analyst/designer must interact with analyst/designers involved in these related processes.
2. Understand the network development life cycle including: overall issues, process structure, detailed activities for each step of the process, coping with the reality of today's multiprotocol, multivendor environments.
3. Understand how one remains focused with a business perspective throughout the network development life cycle.
4. Understand what automated tools are available to assist in the NDLC process as well as the cost justification necessary for the acquisition of such tools.
5. Understand the current shortcomings of these automated tools as well as possible proposals for solutions to these shortcomings.
6. Understand the role of vendors at various stages of the NDLC and how to maximize the effectiveness of these vendors.

INTRODUCTION

This chapter is perhaps the most important chapter in this entire book. Although a process-orientation and top-down approach have been taken throughout the entire text as data communications concepts and technology have been introduced, the focus of this chapter is solely on the data communications process known as the network development life cycle. All of the concepts and technology mastered in previous chapters will serve as available resources for the actual network development process outlined in this chapter. Simply stated, this chapter should tie together much of the material covered to this point in the text, which talked *about* data communications by explaining how to *do* data communications.

In addition, this chapter provides a business context for the technically oriented network development life cycle. Important concepts such as alignment of IT projects with strategic business initiatives and the calculation of total cost of ownership and return on investment are stressed.

This chapter does not include instruction in network traffic engineering. Although this is an introductory text, an appropriate level of complexity will be presented for the more technical aspects of network design. Reemphasizing the practical aspect of this chapter, techniques for effective interaction with consultants and vendors who possess the technical expertise to perform network traffic engineering are stressed.

WHERE DOES NETWORK DESIGN FIT IN OVERALL INFORMATION SYSTEMS DEVELOPMENT?

To be able to fully understand the importance of a properly designed network to a smoothly operating information system, one must first understand how the network design process relates to other information system development processes. The top-down model, which has been a constant strategic framework throughout the text, is an appropriate way to portray the relationship between the network development process and other information systems-related development processes. This relationship is illustrated in Figure 11-1.

As can be seen in Figure 11-1, the network development life cycle depends on previously completed development processes such as strategic business planning, applications development life cycle, and data distribution analysis. If an implemented network is to effectively deliver the information systems that will, in turn, fulfill strategic business goals, then a top-down approach must be taken to the overall information systems development process, as well as to the network development life cycle.

Cooperative Application and Network Development

As applications have been increasingly deployed on a globally distributed basis over network links of limited bandwidth or uncertain reliability, it has become essential for application developers and networking specialists to work more closely together during the early stages of the application development process. Automated application monitoring and simulation tools discussed later in the chapter are now available to show application developers how distributed applications will actually perform

Top-Down Model	Information Systems Development Process
Business	• Strategic business planning • Business process reengineering
Application	• Systems development life cycle • Systems analysis and design • Application development life cycle
Data	• Database analysis and design • Database distribution analysis
Network	• Network development life cycle • Network analysis and design • Logical network design
Technology	• Physical network design • Network implementation • Technology analysis

Figure 11-1 The Top-Down Model and the Network Development Life Cycle

over a variety of different network conditions. In this manner, application developers and networking specialists can cooperatively ensure that applications are developed in a proactive manner with assurance that the deployed application will operate successfully and meet stated business objectives.

Understanding Systems Development: Process and Product

Two key components to any systems development effort are the **process** and the **product** of each stage of that development life cycle. Simply stated, the process describes activities that should be taking place at any point during the development cycle, and the product is the outcome or deliverable from a particular stage of the overall cycle.

A focus on the process allows one to visualize what they will be or should be doing at any point in the development life cycle. The product, meanwhile, could be interpreted as a milestone or deliverable, indicating completion of one stage of the development cycle and a readiness to proceed with subsequent stages.

A focus on product and process facilitates understanding of any systems development life cycle, not only the network development life cycle. Alternatively stated, by staying focused on the questions: "What are we supposed to be doing?" and "How will we know when we are done?" we are more likely to be productive. Identification of process and product can be beneficial on high-level or summarized development cycles as well as on more detailed methodologies. Figure 11-2 takes the high-level processes identified in Figure 11-1 and lists possible products, or outcomes, from each of the corresponding processes.

Figure 11-2 clearly points out the need for significant analysis and design, and associated products or deliverables, before the commencement of any network analysis and design activities. As has been stated many times in this text, network analysis and design cannot be successfully performed in a vacuum. Rather, network analysis and design is but one step in an overall comprehensive information systems development cycle, commencing with business layer analysis and concluding with

Information Systems Development Process	Product or Milestone
Strategic business planning Business process reengineering	• Strategic business plan • Long-range business goals • Business process models, methods, or rules
Systems development life cycle Systems analysis and design Application development life cycle	• Information systems design • Applications program design
Database analysis and design Database distribution analysis	• Database design • Database distribution design
Network development life cycle Network analysis and design Logical network design	• Network requirements document • Network design proposal
Physical network design Network implementation Technology analysis	• Detailed network diagram • Network product specifications • Network circuit diagrams

Figure 11-2 Understanding Systems Development: Process and Product

an analysis of the technology currently available to implement the system as designed.

THE NETWORK DEVELOPMENT LIFE CYCLE

The key model behind the network design process is known as the **network development life cycle (NDLC)** as illustrated in Figure 11-3.

The word "cycle" is a key descriptive term of the network development life cycle as it clearly illustrates the continuous nature of network development. A network designed "from scratch" clearly has to start somewhere, namely with an analysis phase.

Existing networks, however, are constantly progressing from one phase to another within the network development life cycle. For instance, the monitoring of

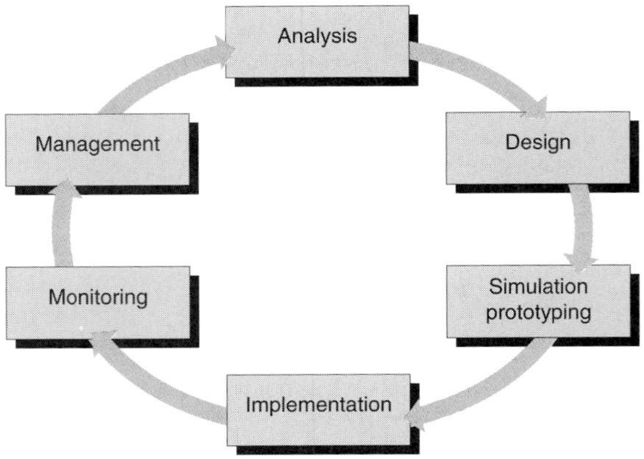

Figure 11-3 Network Development Life Cycle

existing networks would produce management and performance statistics perhaps using a network management protocol such as SNMP. Qualified network analysts would then analyze these performance statistics of this existing network. Design changes may or may not be implemented based on the analysis of these performance statistics. As will be described later in the chapter, network designs may be physical or logical in nature. **Physical network designs** involve the arrangement and interconnection of the physical network circuits and devices, whereas **logical network designs** involve configuration and definition of services that will run over that physical network such as addressing schemes, routing schemes, traffic prioritization, security, and management. Many times, proposed network design changes are first simulated using sophisticated network simulation software packages or prototyped in a test environment, safely removed from a company's production network, before being deployed or implemented.

This cycle of monitoring, management, analysis, design, simulation, and implementation is ongoing. Just as demands on a network are in a constant state of change due to changes in business, application, or data requirements, so must the network design itself be of a dynamic nature to successfully support these changing requirements. The network development life cycle serves as a logical framework in which this dynamic network design is able to thrive.

STRATEGIC ALIGNMENT OF THE NETWORK DEVELOPMENT LIFE CYCLE

It is important to understand the business-oriented nature of the environment in which the network development life cycle must operate. Network design projects are not undertaken at random or on the whim of any network manager. Rather, network design projects must be aligned with strategic business initiatives and/or the strategic development of the overall corporate IT infrastructure. Figure 11-4 illustrates the overall alignment of the network development life cycle with strategic business and IT infrastructure initiatives.

IT Project Portfolio Management

All networking projects or IT projects are not of equal strategic importance to the enterprise. Some projects may depend on other projects. Some projects may be focused on basic infrastructure improvements, whereas others may be tied to specific business units or projects. Funding for network projects is limited and must be budgeted with a view toward those projects that can have the greatest positive impact on the enterprise and that are most closely aligned with corporate business strategy and the overall strategy of the IT infrastructure. Given the multitude of projects seeking, funding, today's chief information officer (CIO) often views individual projects as potential investments and the sum total of all potential projects as a project portfolio, much like a stock portfolio. Some percentage of investment must be with "blue chip" conservative projects with more likely but more modest returns, whereas another percentage of investment must be with more risky projects with potentially greater payback to the enterprise. Determining how much to invest in which types of projects is a difficult job with serious consequences.

From a strategic process standpoint, as illustrated in Figure 11-4, a given network design project must be aligned with the overall strategic plan of the IT infrastructure as a whole, as well as with the strategic business initiatives of the corporation. A

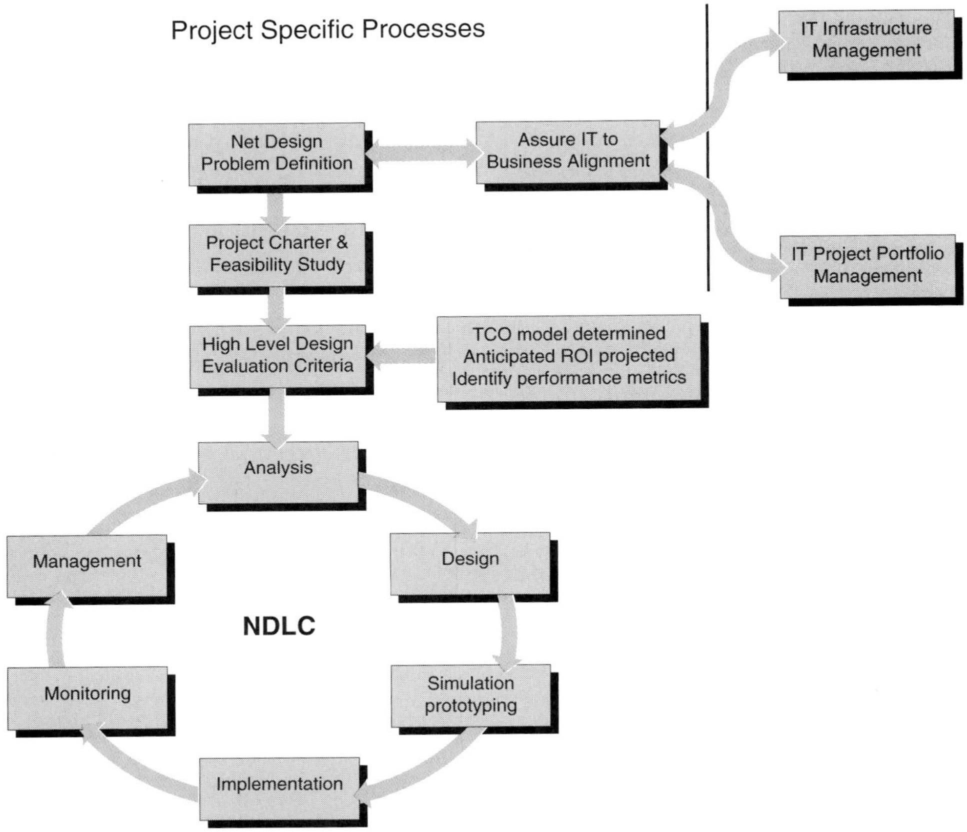

Figure 11-4 Alignment of Network Design Projects with Strategic Business and IT Infrastructure Initiatives

process known as **IT project portfolio management** often manages the overall strategic development direction of the IT infrastructure. In such a process, all potential IT-related projects from component architectures such as network, application development, computing platforms, or data management are evaluated for potential support and funding. In today's business climate, it is simply unrealistic for all IT-related projects to be funded. Tough choices must be made according to a defined process using justifiable criteria. The exact process used for IT portfolio management varies from one organization to another. Some processes are more quantitative and others are more subjective. Figure 11-5 illustrates one potential strategy for IT portfolio management.

As illustrated in Figure 11-5, the two criteria chosen in this case to evaluate potential IT projects are "alignment with business initiatives" and "projected return on investment." The actual criteria chosen vary from one situation to another depending on corporate circumstances and priority. Other possible choices include

- Maturity level of technology
- Alignment with current IT infrastructure
- Required support and management

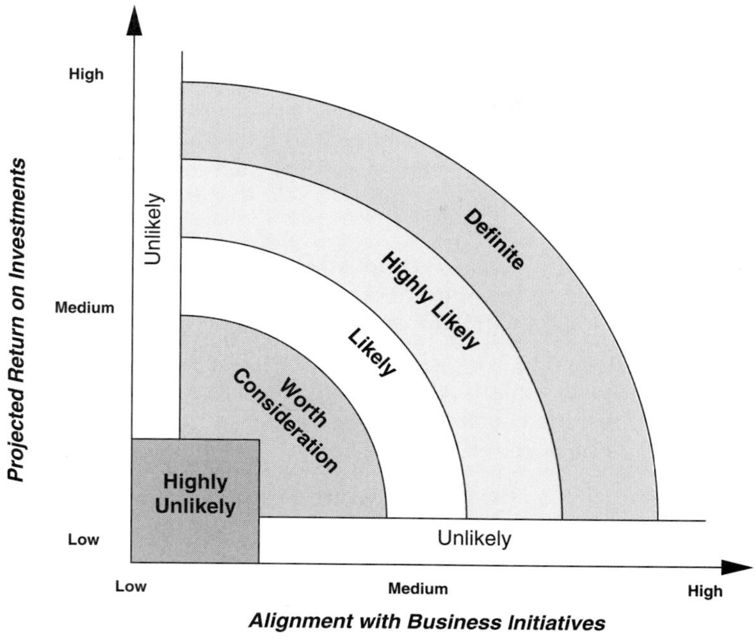

Figure 11-5 IT Project Portfolio Management

- Initial investment cost
- Long-term expense

Each potential project is evaluated according to each of the chosen criteria in a qualitative manner by assigning a value of low, medium, or high. Quantitative methods can be used as a justification for the assignment of these values. Once each project is evaluated in terms of both criteria, the intersection of those assigned values will place each project in one of the portfolio management ranges of the grid. Again, the exact number, arrangement, and assigned names of each section of the grid will vary by organization. In the example shown in Figure 11-5, this organization has decided that if projects score low in either alignment *or* return on investment, then it is unlikely that these projects will be pursued. Furthermore, any project that scores low in alignment *and* return on investment is highly unlikely to be pursued. Other categories of recommended actions are arranged according to relative strengths of alignment with business initiatives and return on investment.

Project Specific Processes

As illustrated in Figure 11-4, once a project has been deemed as properly aligned with both the overall IT infrastructure and with the strategic business initiatives of the corporation, it goes through a number of project management steps before the initiation of actual network design activity. Each of these project-specific processes and the overall critical success factors are explained next.

Critical Success Factors of the Network Development Life Cycle

Also associated with the overall network development process, rather than with any specific step of the process, are several key behaviors or things to remember that can be of critical importance to the overall successful outcome of the network development life cycle. These **critical success factors** are summarized in Figure 11-6 and explained next.

Identification of All Potential Customers The best source of information for system performance requirements is the people who must use the system most frequently. However, all user groups and levels of management must be consulted during the analysis and design phase to ensure that no individuals or groups feel left out of the development process. Although one would like to think it isn't true, the best designed systems can be doomed to failure owing to the effective internal sabotage of disenchanted users.

Political Awareness At the very least, it is imperative to be aware of the so-called corporate culture of an organization. Corporate culture is sometimes described in terms related to network design. For instance, corporate cultures can be described as "hierarchical" or "distributed" or "open." If the corporate culture of the organization in which a network analyst is working is hierarchical, then it would be a mistake to make an appointment to interview an end-user without first interviewing and seeking approval of the required levels of management. On the other hand, "open-door"

Critical Success Factor	Explanation
Identification of All Potential Customers and Constituencies	No one likes to feel left out or that his/her input does not matter. It is better to include too many as representative user groups than to inadvertently exclude anyone.
Political Awareness	Awareness of the corporate political environment as well as the overall corporate culture can have a large impact on a project's success.
Buy-In	As each stage is concluded, buy-in or agreement as to conclusions from all effected customer groups is of critical importance.
Communication	Do not assume others know what is going on with the project. Write memos or newsletters, send e-mail, or communicate with key people in person.
Detailed Project Documentation	Document every phone call and every meeting. Keep the project well organized from day one with copies of all correspondence.
Process/Product Awareness	As a simple means of staying focused and on track, keep in mind the process and product for each step in the network analysis and design methodology
Be Honest with Yourself	Be your own harshest critic. Identify weak points in your proposal and address them accordingly. Play "devil's advocate" with your proposal and prepare for the possible objections.

Figure 11-6 Critical Success Factors of the Network Development Life Cycle

corporate cultures are less concerned with hierarchies of authority, thereby allowing quicker and simpler access to end-users.

Unfortunately, so-called "back room" politics can play an important role in systems design as well. The best researched and planned network design may go unimplemented if the company president's brother-in-law or golf partner is in the computer business and has a different idea. Sad, but true. The best way to defend against such situations is to first be aware of any such possible political situations. Specific strategies for ensuring the objectivity of the analysis and design process will be highlighted as the overall network analysis and design methodology is described further.

Buy-In All of the critical success factors listed in Figure 11-6 are important. However, one of the most important yet easiest to accomplish is **buy-in.** After having chartered the project and identified all potential customers and constituencies, it is imperative to gain buy-in from each of these groups for the deliverable or product of each stage of the overall network analysis and design methodology.

By reaching consensus on the acceptability of the results or deliverables of each and every stage, one avoids having initial assumptions or work on earlier stages brought into question during the presentation of the final proposal. In other words, the approved results of one stage become the foundation or starting point for the next stage. If buy-in from all affected parties is ensured at each stage, the presentation of the final proposal should be much smoother with a minimum of back-tracking or rework required.

Communication Many of the other critical success factors listed in Figure 11-6 depend on effective communication, both verbal and written. Often in network or systems development projects, it is assumed that because network analysts and designers are aware of the project status, everyone must be fully informed as well. Unfortunately, this is not the case. As previously pointed out, no one likes to feel left out. More important, networks often cross the "territory" or authority of numerous individuals and departments. To keep these people supportive of the project, it is imperative to keep them informed and to make them feel that they are an important part of the process.

Communication can take many forms. Newsletters, project status reports, web sites, and e-mail are all suitable means of keeping people informed and up-to-date. More ambitious communications schemes such as videoconferencing or the production of a VCR tape or CD-ROM might be appropriate for critical tasks, public relations, or training opportunities.

Detailed Project Documentation A project manager must not only manage the overall network analysis and design project effectively with task schedules, project lists, and to-do lists, but also document every aspect of the project. During every conversation, by phone or in person, notes should be entered into a log book indicating such things as date, time, persons involved, topics of conversation, and required follow-up. E-mail messages should be printed and filed. Meetings should be documented in a similar fashion, with agendas and action item assignments included in a project binder as well as being sent to responsible parties and key managers.

Organization of this project documentation is of equal importance. A large binder with several sections for different portions of the project can be a very effective way to be able to quickly access any piece of project documentation required.

This documentation is of particular importance in the latter stages of the project when consultants and vendors become a part of the project. Document everything in writing and take no action on any agreement until it has been presented in writing.

Process/Product Awareness As a facilitator in meetings of end-users trying to define system requirements, it is the network analyst's job to keep the participants focused and the meeting on track. To accomplish this goal, it is important to have a clear understanding of the process involved at that particular stage of the network analysis and design methodology as well as the nature of the product or deliverable that is to be the outcome of this process.

Meetings can easily get off on tangents and aggressive users can easily sway meetings toward personal agendas. By remaining focused on the proper topics of discussion and a clear visualization of the product of that discussion, a facilitator can maximize the effectiveness of the analysis and design process. As the leader of the meeting, it is important not to go overboard on controlling the discussion of the meeting however. With practice and patience, experienced facilitators can direct meetings that foster imaginative solutions and proposals without either stifling creativity or allowing discussion to wander ineffectively.

Be Honest With Yourself One of the greatest advantages of being totally honest with oneself is that no one else knows the potential weaknesses or areas for improvement in a proposal better than the person who wrote it. The difficulty comes when forcing oneself to be totally honest and acknowledging the potential weaknesses in a proposal to either correct them or be prepared to defend them.

Peer review and egoless programming are other systems development techniques employed to identify potential weaknesses in programs or proposals before implementation. Not all weaknesses can necessarily be corrected. Financial or time constraints may have restricted potential solutions. If that is the case, an honest self-review of the proposal will allow one to prepare an objective explanation of such weaknesses in advance.

Critical Success Factors Are Learned Behaviors Although many of the critical success factors listed in Figure 11-6 may seem to be nothing more than common sense, it has been the author's experience that more network analysis and design projects suffer from difficulties caused by a failure to address one or more of these critical success factors than from any other cause of failure. These critical success factors must be applied throughout the entire life of the network development project and are therefore best seen as habits or behaviors, rather than discrete events to be scheduled or planned.

NETWORK ANALYSIS AND DESIGN METHODOLOGY

Although the Network Development Life Cycle is useful as a logical model of the overall processes involved in network development, it is not at all specific as to how the various stages within the life cycle are to be accomplished. What is required is a more detailed step-by-step methodology which compliments the overall logical framework as outlined by the Network Development Life Cycle.

The **Network Analysis and Design Methodology** is a practical, high-level, step-by-step approach to network analysis and design and is illustrated in a summarized fashion in Figure 11-7.

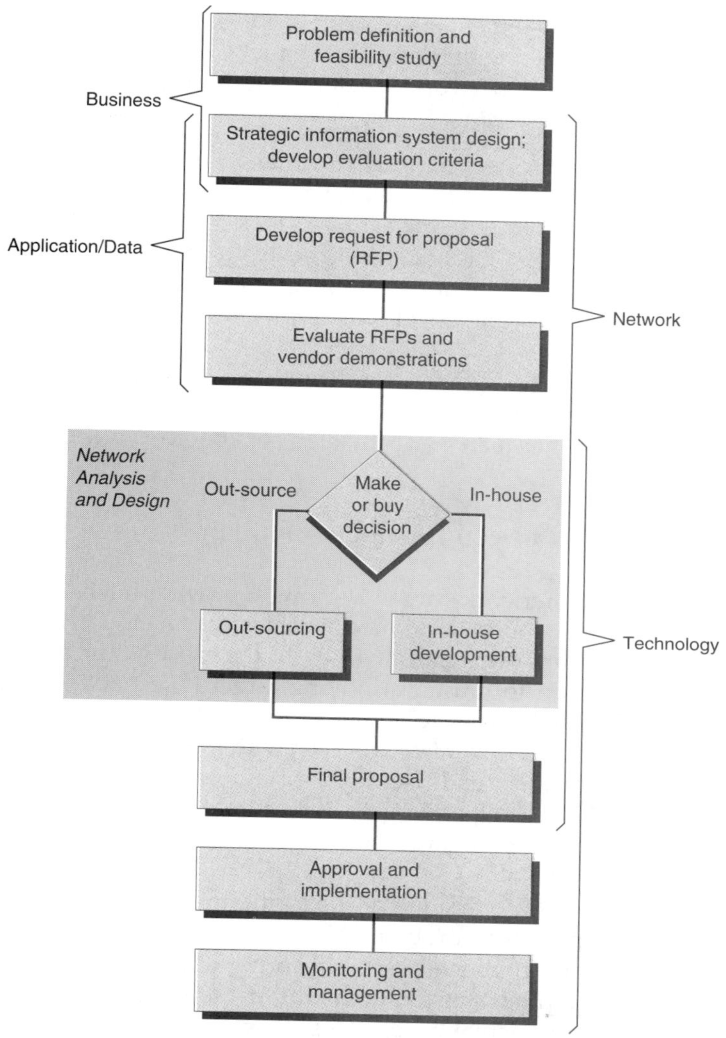

Figure 11-7 Network Analysis and Design Methodology

Overall Characteristics

Before describing each of the major categories of the methodology as illustrated in Figure 11-7 in detail, a few important characteristics of the overall methodology are worth noting.

- First, the Network Analysis and Design Methodology is consistent with previous information systems development models in that business, application, and data requirements definition are prerequisites to network design activities.
- Second, this methodology treats both in-house personnel as well as outside consultants as potential service providers by clearly documenting require-

ments in a formalized RFP (Request for Proposal) and expecting compliance with those requirements by whomever may be eventually chosen to perform network development duties.

- Finally, although any diagram of a systems development methodology would indicate that activities are of a serial nature, occurring one after another, with discrete starting and ending points, such is very often not the case. In fact, activities from various stages of the methodology often take place simultaneously. In addition, network analysts often must backtrack to previous activities when new or contradictory information is uncovered as the development process progresses.

Thus, the network analysis and design methodology as illustrated in Figure 11-7 should be looked upon as an overall guideline to the network development process rather than a step-by-step cookbook-style set of instructions.

Net Design Problem Definition

A network cannot very well provide effective solutions to problems that have not been clearly defined in objective terms. To attempt to implement networks before everyone agrees to (buy-in) the exact nature of the problem to be solved is somewhat akin to hitting a moving target. The network will never satisfy all constituencies' needs because no one agreed what those needs were in the first place. All network development efforts start with a problem as perceived by someone, be they management or end-users. At some point, management agrees that a problem exists that is worth expending resources to at least investigate. The responsibility for conducting the investigation may be given to in-house personnel or to an outside consultant or facilitator.

The first job of the facilitator is to identify all parties potentially affected by the perceived problem. Next, representatives of each of these constituencies are selected and convened for brainstorming sessions to determine the nature of the problem and perhaps, the requirements of a solution. To make these problem definition sessions as productive as possible, it is important that representatives do their "homework" before the meetings.

Project Charter and Feasibility Study

To effectively control multiple projects simultaneously in large organizations, it is essential that all projects requiring allocation of manpower, technical, or financial resources be carefully planned. A **project charter** is the mechanism by which a project is organized and initial expectations are documented and agreed on. Network-related projects are likely to interact with numerous business units and other areas of IT such as application development. It is important to get involvement and buy-in from all affected organizations in the form of project sponsorship. When all parties can agree before the project is launched what the expected outcomes of the project are and what it will take to reach those objectives in a given amount of time, then that project stands a much greater chance of success.

Among the sections that could be included in a project charter are the following:

- Description: 2 or 3 sentences briefly describing what, why, how, and when this project will be accomplished.
- Objectives: often divided into separate categories of business and technical objectives. Objectives should be measurable and serve as the evaluation criteria for the completed project.
- Scope: often divided into "within scope" and "out of scope" sections to assure that the project remains on target and is not subjected to "scope creep" where side issues and amendments to the project charter cause the project to lose focus.
- Phases: What are the major logical sections of the project? Give some thought as to what must be accomplished in each phase in order to move on to the next phase. This is where initial thought to overall process design for the project is considered.
- Deliverables: can be either presented as overall project deliverables or phase by phase deliverables. What tangible work or documents will the project team actually be producing?
- Stakeholders and Key Reporting Relationships: Which departments or business units within an organization or corporation will be impacted by this project? Which departments will have to supply personnel to complete this project? Which individuals have budget responsibility for these departments and will have to approve the participation of team members? Who will provide technical leadership, project management, and technical team participation?
- Project Schedule: when will milestones, phases, and overall project be completed?
- Project Budget: what is the anticipated budget for the project?
- Assumptions, Concerns, and Constraints: any other issues (technical, business, political) that could have an impact on the project that should be shared with all concerned before project kick-off.
- Sponsor Approval Signatures: Executive level approval to proceed with the project as described in the previous charter.

Understand Strategic Business Objectives Once the group has been assembled, it is time to remember the top-down model. To keep the problem definition session and the subsequent solution proposal session on track, it is vital to start with the strategic business goals of the organization as articulated by senior management. Whenever the author consulted as a user group facilitator, he always strived to have either the chief executive officer or chief financial officer (or both) present at the initial meeting to say a few words about the importance of the user group's work and the strategic direction of the corporate business goals. In addition, if strategic corporate goals had been prepared in writing, these were shared with the group, as allowed by company policy. In this way, the whole group starts off with the same focus and strategic business direction with the proper attitude about the overall process.

Importance of Baseline Data To measure the eventual impact, hopefully positive, of the installed network, one has to have baseline data, or the current status of the system and network, from which to measure that eventual network impact. This baseline data can often be collected from the various customer groups or constituencies of the information system and network who are chosen to attend the problem definition sessions. Depending on the extent, in terms of both geography and sophistication, to which current systems have been implemented, a structured framework may be required to record this systems information in a standardized manner. Fortunately, the top-down model is an excellent example of such a framework. Chapter 12, Network Management, provides more detailed information on the technology and processes involved with network performance baselining.

Top-Down Model Organizes Baseline Data Using the top-down model as a framework for organizing the baseline data to reflect the current system and network status does not necessarily imply that a separate top-down model must be completed for every corporate location attached to the network or that every layer of the top-down model must be filled in for every location. Just enough data should be collected at this point in the network analysis and design methodology to clearly define the problem in measurable terms.

Information that is gathered in the top-down models at this stage should relate directly to the problems as perceived by the user groups. It is hoped that the problems have some business layer impact; otherwise this whole process may be a waste of time. In other words, although the source of the problem may be in the application, data, network, or technology layers, if it has no impact on the business layer, why should time be spent studying it?

Questions should deal with business problems or situations. Once these business problems are identified, the sources of these business problems within the lower layers of top-down model would be subsequently investigated as part of the problem definition process. Conversely, these same lower layers of the top-down model will be redesigned to become the source of business solutions as delivered by the new network.

Feasibility Studies and Buy-In Once sufficient information has been gathered to document the current status of the systems and networks in objective, measurable terms, the required product for this process, the problem definition, has been completed and it is time to ensure buy-in. The problem definition and its associated alternative recommendations for further study are sometimes referred to as a **feasibility study.**

The need for buy-in on a problem definition or feasibility study will vary from one case to another. Much of the need for management buy-in and the associated approval to proceed depend on the nature of the original charge from management.

In other words, if management's initial charge were, "Look into this problem and get back to me," then a feasibility study followed by management buy-in and approval before further study is clearly appropriate. Conversely, if management's charge were, "Figure out what's wrong and fix-it," then a formalized feasibility report with formal presentation may not be called for. However, remember one of the key critical success factors—communications. Even if a formal feasibility report is not required, timely management reports should be completed and submitted on a regular basis to keep management abreast of progress and in tune with overall project strategic direction. Figure 11-8 summarizes the key points (process and product) of the problem definition phase.

Process	1. Problem is perceived 2. Management perceives problem as worth investigating 3. Management delegates responsibility for problem definition 4. User/constituency groups are identified and representatives chosen 5. Representative groups are convened 6. Senior management commitment and priorities are conveyed to representative group 7. Representative groups produce baseline data of current system status 8. Depending on the extent of the current system and network implementation, the top-down model may be used to organize this baseline data into a standardized format. 9. Buy-in
Product	1. Baseline data describing current system status in objective, measurable terms. Can be organized into multiple top-down models. 2. A formalized feasibility study may be required depending on the initial charge/direction from management.

Figure 11-8 Key Points of Problem Definition and Feasibility Study

High-Level Design Evaluation Criteria

The problem definition phase provided a starting point of baseline data for the new system, and the strategic information systems design provides the operational goals for the new system to attain. Just as the baseline data have to be objective and measurable, so must the evaluation criteria associated with these operational goals.

These goals may have a direct impact on network design when defined in terms such as maximum response time, transactions/second, or mean time between failures. By producing objective, measurable goals or performance evaluation criteria and getting subsequent management buy-in on those goals, one helps to ensure the objectivity of the entire network analysis and design process. For example, if a substandard system is suggested solely because of "back-room" politics, it is simply

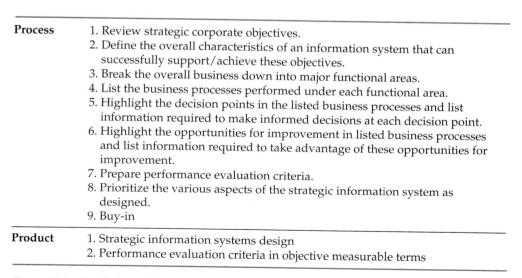

Process	1. Review strategic corporate objectives. 2. Define the overall characteristics of an information system that can successfully support/achieve these objectives. 3. Break the overall business down into major functional areas. 4. List the business processes performed under each functional area. 5. Highlight the decision points in the listed business processes and list information required to make informed decisions at each decision point. 6. Highlight the opportunities for improvement in listed business processes and list information required to take advantage of these opportunities for improvement. 7. Prepare performance evaluation criteria. 8. Prioritize the various aspects of the strategic information system as designed. 9. Buy-in
Product	1. Strategic information systems design 2. Performance evaluation criteria in objective measurable terms

Figure 11-9 Key Points of Strategic Information System Design

evaluated against the evaluation criteria as previously agreed on by all appropriate levels of management. Figure 11-9 summarizes the key points of the strategic information system design phase in terms of both process and product.

Total Cost of Ownership

Evaluation criteria based on performance are an important starting point for an overall assessment of a project's relative success or failure. However, performance criteria consider only whether the project was successful from a technical perspective. It is equally important to consider a project's relative success from a financial perspective. Cost-oriented evaluation criteria must also be established. Today, IT projects are often evaluated from a financial standpoint in terms of **total cost of ownership.** Total cost of ownership implies that all cost aspects of a project are properly identified including ongoing costs such as support, management, and maintenance. Hidden costs such as those included in budgets other than the IT department are also an important component of an accurate total cost of ownership. Projected total cost of ownership figures should be completed for every proposed project and used as a financially oriented set of evaluation criteria during project development and after project implementation.

A **comprehensive systems and networking budget model,** presented in Figure 11-22, would be a suitable instrument for developing a total cost of ownership model for a network development project. Costing models for ongoing network services provided to business units or end-user organizations require a different type of costing model. Such an activity-based costing model is introduced in Chapter 12, as part of the discussion of service management and costing.

Return on Investment

Increasingly, networking and information systems professionals are being called on to quantify the positive impact of their projects and implemented systems in financial terms. A variety of options exist for this quantification. **return on investment (ROI)** is perhaps the most traditional approach to measuring cost/benefit and is well suited to incremental upgrades of existing systems. However, for entirely new or innovative projects, although costs may be accurately projected, projected benefits are more intangible and are far more difficult to quantify in real terms. **Return on opportunity (ROO)** attempts to quantify benefits that may be unanticipated or indirectly related to the immediate investment. This methodology recognizes the fact that improvements in IT infrastructure aimed at one project may enable unanticipated benefits and uses not related to that initiating project.

In a similar manner, **total benefit of ownership (TBO)** tries to quantify the usability and associated benefits of technological options. TBO attempts to quantify productivity increases as well as cost reduction. However, to properly quantify increased productivity, one must first measure current levels of productivity by developing evaluation criteria so that baseline data can be gathered.

Performance Metrics

Performance metrics refer to quantifiable, measurable performance criteria by which the success of an implemented system can be judged. Performance metrics must be defined in both business terms and IT infrastructure terms. Given that the alignment of a given IT project with a strategic business initiative has already been assured, the performance metrics required to validate that alignment should be able to be defined. Business-oriented performance metrics that reflect the achievement of the intended business outcomes must first be defined. The ability to report on the status of these business performance metrics should be embedded within the components of the IT infrastructure supporting this new initiative.

On a technical level, the performance levels required from each element of the IT infrastructure, in order for the overall system to achieve its business objectives, must be individually identified. Technology-specific performance metrics must be identified for each technical component of the overall system. The definition, monitoring, and management of these performance metrics are part of an area of IT known as service management. Definitions of required levels of service from the IT infrastructure to achieve intended business goals are delineated in service level agreements. Service management and service level agreements are explained further in Chapter 12.

DESIGN AND ANALYSIS PROCESSES

Identify Overall System Characteristics

The word *strategic* is used in the context of information systems design to portray the top-down, strategic business goal orientation of the entire information design process. As can be seen in Figure 11-9, the strategic information systems design process starts with a review of the strategic business goals as articulated by senior management.

With these strategic business goals in mind, the next step in the process is to describe the overall characteristics of an information system that could fulfill these strategic business goals. Examples might be the following. To fulfill our corporation's strategic business goals, this information system must:

1. Enable delivery of improved customer service
2. Enable improved inventory control
3. Allow for more flexible pricing
4. Enable shorter shelf restocking cycles
5. Allow for more efficient use of manpower

Many other examples could have been included. The point of these overall characteristics, in terms of the top-down model, is to ensure and specify that the application layer solutions will deliver on the business layer requirements. As can be seen from Figure 11-9, one of the key products of this strategic information system design phase is the performance evaluation criteria. The overall required system characteristics as listed previously serve as one set of evaluation criteria for proposed information systems designs. Other more objective evaluation criteria will be developed further along in the overall design process. However, the importance of the strategic system performance evaluation criteria lies in their ability to measure the extent to which proposed information systems designs deliver on strategic business goals.

Identify Major Business Functional Areas

Once overall system performance characteristics have been established, the overall business can be broken down into large functional areas. These functional areas may correspond to corporate departments or divisions. Examples might include manufacturing, inventory control, project management, customer service, accounting and payroll, and human resources.

In practice, each of these identified major **business functional areas** can be written on a separate large sheet of flip-chart paper and taped over the walls of the room in which the user groups were meeting. It is not important to argue about which functional areas deserve their own sheet of paper at this point. Consolidation and editing take place later in the process.

Identify Business Processes Associated with Each Business Functional Area

Once the major functional areas of the business have been established, the business processes that take place in each major functional area are listed. This presents a wonderful opportunity for **business process reengineering.** Oftentimes, user groups are made up of individuals from various business units who have not had the time to really understand each other's jobs and responsibilities. As business processes are described, brainstorming quickly takes over and problems that seemed deeply imbedded in current systems are solved as new or modified business processes are defined for the new strategic information system design. This process is repeated for every major business functional area identified in the previous step.

It is important for the facilitator of this process to keep the discussions on a fairly strategic level, thereby avoiding lower level implementation issues such as screen design and report layouts. Continuing with the flip chart scenario, each major business functional area should now have its own flip chart(s) with detailed business processes described for each large business functional area.

Managerial Perspective

THE NETWORK ANALYST AND BUSINESS PROCESS REENGINEERING

As current business processes are discussed during the network development life cycle, opportunities abound for improvement of those business processes. It is important, however, to take an organized approach to business process improvement, more popularly known as business process reengineering. Part of that required organized approach hinges on maintaining one's common sense. For example:

- If it isn't broken, don't fix it: In searching for opportunities for improvement, concentrate on the processes that are in the greatest need of improvement.
- How will you know if the new process is better if you never measured how bad the old process was? Baseline data must be gathered to document the performance of current processes before redesign takes place. These same evaluation criteria and methods must be used to evaluate the new processes to objectively evaluate improvement levels.
- Learn from others' mistakes: Pay attention to other business process reengineering efforts, especially those in closely related industries that have failed. What lessons can be learned and what mistakes can avoid being repeated?

- Don't be afraid to admit mistakes: If the reengineered business process does not produce anticipated results based on objective evaluation criteria, don't be afraid to admit the mistake early and make corrections as soon as possible to minimize negative impact.

As information systems and networking professionals are increasingly called on to justify their budgets and corporate contributions in the face of outsourcing alternatives, it is imperative that network analysts understand the importance of a realistic approach to business process reengineering.

Identify Decision Points and Opportunities for Improvement

Recalling that one of the primary goals of a well-designed strategic information system is to deliver the right information to the right decision-maker, the next logical step in the design process is to identify the key **decision points** in all of the documented business processes where decision-makers must make decisions.

Once identified, each decision point is then analyzed as to what information (the "right" information) is required for the decision-maker to make an informed decision at each respective decision point. This analysis process often brings out the fact that decision-makers are getting much more information than they need to make informed decisions. Entire reports hundreds of pages long may contain only one or two pieces of information that are of critical importance to a decision-maker at any given decision point.

One of the key areas in which user group members can contribute is in the identification of **opportunities for improvement** that can be enabled by this strategic information system design. Opportunities for improvement may imply improvement in any one of a number of areas: financial, productivity, inventory control, accounts receivable collections, customer service, customer satisfaction, repeat customers, employee retention, etc.

The important thing to remember is that if these opportunities for improvement support the strategic business goals of the corporation then they should be identified along with the information required to turn these opportunities into reality. Figure 11-10 illustrates the relationship of the various processes described thus far in the strategic information system design.

Prioritization

Once the strategic information system has been designed as described previously, priorities can be assigned to each of the major functional areas, business processes, decision points, and opportunities. These priorities may assist in the evaluation process by identifying those systems that exhibit the most important elements of the strategic information systems design. A simple yet effective approach to systems design prioritization is known as the **three-pile approach.** In this prioritization scheme, there are only three priorities, defined as follows:

- Priority 1 items are so important that the system is simply not worth implementing without them.

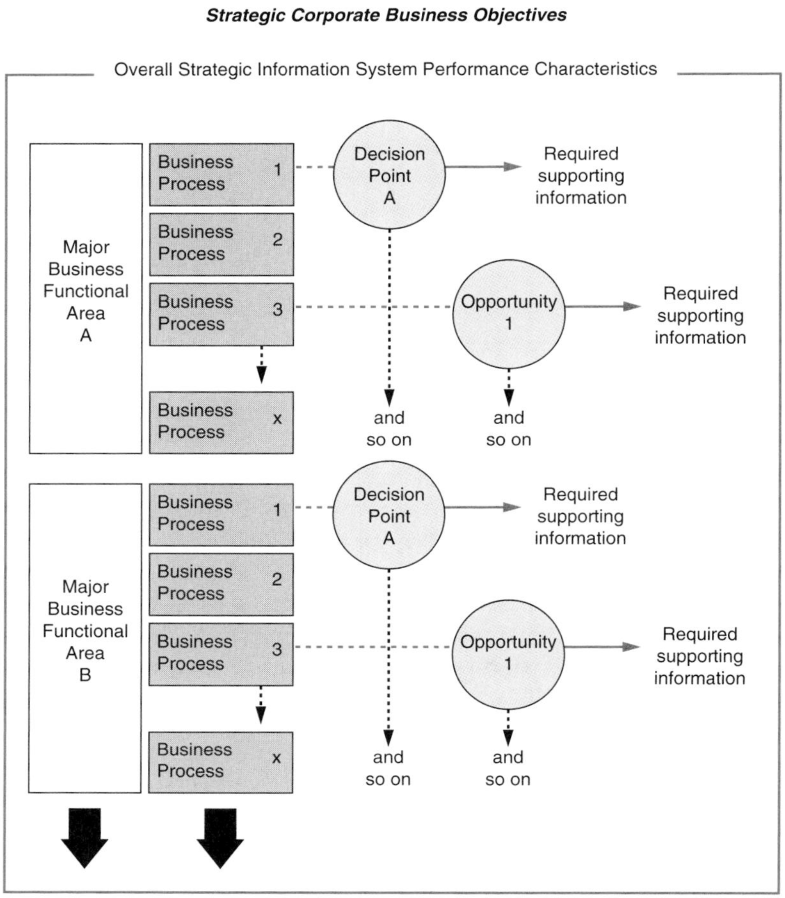

Figure 11-10 Process Relationship of Strategic Information System Design

- Priority 2 items can be lived without or "worked around" but really need to be implemented as soon as possible.
- Priority 3 items would be nice to have but can be lived without.

One important point to remember is that these priorities should be considered in terms of business impact. At this point, a strategic, or high-level, information system design has been completed. Many details need to be added to this requirements document before proposals can accurately reflect their ability to meet not only the business and application layer system requirements, but the data and networking requirements that must support this strategic information system as well.

Finding and Managing Required Technical Talent

Once a clear understanding of system requirements and evaluation criteria have been established, the next major task is to find the technical talent required to pro-

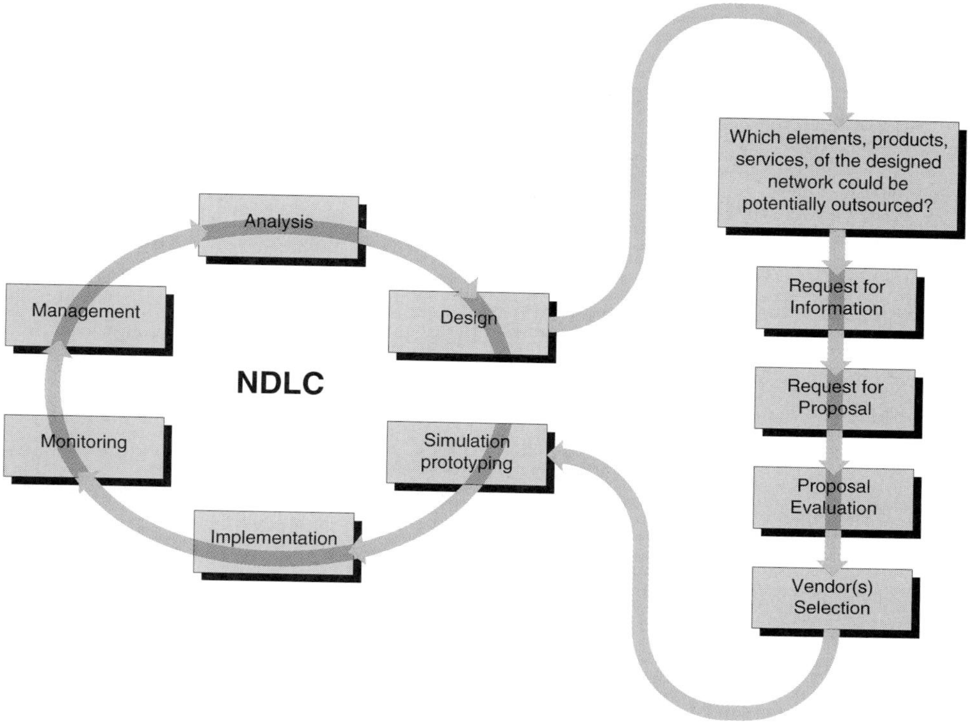

Figure 11-11 NDLC and the Proposal Process

duce the designed system. This talent may be either in-house or may be hired from the outside, often referred to as outsourcing. The overall process for finding system development talent is illustrated in Figure 11-11 and explained in the following sections.

Request for Information (RFI)

Before sending out a detailed request for proposal to numerous potential vendors, it is often prudent to narrow the field of potential respondents by issuing a **request for information (RFI).** The purpose of an RFI is to gather enough information about potential vendors that they can be quickly and easily evaluated as to their suitability for further consideration. The RFI should be easy to comply with for the potential vendors and easy to evaluate the responses from for the corporation issuing the RFI.

Among the sections that could be included in a request for information are the following:

- Technical requirements: a high-level description of technical performance requirements that must be met by the proposed technology or system. These requirements should be of high importance to the overall system. In other words, vendors that cannot meet these technical requirements will not be considered further.

- Business requirements: ask for price structure of technology or services in order to gauge whether or not potential vendors are even in the ballpark of your budget. Do not share your budget with potential vendors at this point.
- References: the purpose of this section is to gauge the experience of this vendor in supplying this technology or service. How many have been sold or installed? Will you be their first customer for this new technology or service?

Remember, the overall purpose of the RFI is to narrow the field of vendors that will be sent the RFP so that you are not wasting time with nonqualified vendors. Keep the RFI short, to the point, and ask questions regarding those system or business requirements that you regard as absolute necessities or "show-stoppers".

Request for Proposal (RFP)

By organizing the strategic information system design information into an understandable format and by adding detailed information concerning performance evaluation criteria for the data and network layers, a document known as a **RFP (request for proposal)** is produced. It is important to understand the benefits of an RFP to be able to justify the work that goes into it.

By taking the time to prepare a detailed RFP, a company ensures that its priorities and unique business processes and requirements are fulfilled by the information system and network that is eventually installed. All vendor proposals are measured against the users' predefined requirements regardless of whom the vendor may be related to. If a vendor's proposal does not meet minimum standards for meeting the requirements of the RFP, it is dropped from further consideration regardless of how nice the screens look or how colorful the brochures are. The RFP ensures that the delivered system, whether developed in-house or purchased from an outside vendor, will be flexible enough to change as business needs and requirements change. Unfortunately, the alternative is all too often the case, in which businesses are forced to mold their business practices according to the constraints of the purchased information system and network. Figure 11-12 summarizes both the processes and products involved in the RFP preparation phase of the network design.

Examine Each Corporate Location Now that the strategic information system design has been completed, the next step is to carefully examine each corporate location at which the information system will eventually be deployed. The purpose of gathering all of this data about each of the corporate locations is to compile an accurate representation of the scope and requirements of the network over which this strategic information system will be implemented.

As each location is examined, the information gathered will help determine the unique data and processing requirements for those locations. This detailed location-specific information is distinct from the high-level information gathered in top-down model format as part of the problem definition phase.

Some corporate locations may be regional offices, concentrating data or transactions from several branch offices. These, along with many other facts must be recorded to accurately define data and network layer requirements for the overall information system. Although each company may differ in what location-specific statistics are important in terms of strategic network design, many of the points in Figure 11-13 may warrant consideration:

Process	1. Examine each corporate location 2. Produce evaluation criteria for application and data layer considerations as required 3. Survey all existing system resources: people, hardware-software-media, data, network, physical plant 4. Prepare preliminary overall project schedule 5. Determine information required from vendor 6. Determine potential vendors 7. Determine percent-of-fit goal 8. Compile and distribute RFP to selected vendors
Product	1. Formalized request for proposal 2. Percent-of-fit goal

Figure 11-12 Preparing the Request for Proposal

Category	**Questions/Issues**
People	• Number of total employees • Number of employees performing each business function as listed in strategic information system design • Feeling about the "new" system • Key political situations • Number of network-oriented/technically-oriented employees • Training needs

Hardware-Software-Media	• Current level of computerization
	• Current applications software
	• Current networking status
	• Local phone company
	• Availability of data services from local phone company
	• Software performance requirements
	  • Maximum time for customer look-up
	  • Maximum time for part number or pricing look-up
	  • Maximum time for order entry
	• How "mission-critical" is each application?
	• Must backup systems be ready at a moment's notice?

Data	• Number of customers • Number of inventory items • Number of open orders • Need for sharing data with other locations, regional offices, corporate headquarters • Special security needs for data or transmission
Network	• Current network configuration • Network traffic volumes • Network protocols • Network monitoring and management technology • Current problems with network to be corrected • Expected growth of network, traffic volume, user community
Physical Plant	• What is the condition of each remote site? • Will additional electrical, heating, data wiring, space, or security systems be required at any sights to accommodate the new systems?

Figure 11-13 Possible Location-Specific Statistics

The information gathered in such location-by-location surveys adds to the evaluation criteria of any potential system proposal. Any need identified must be met by a proposed system solution in accordance with the determined priority of each of these requirements. It is of critical importance that this survey is done as accurately as possible because this is the data upon which the initial network design will largely be based. Buy-in by all affected groups at this stage is especially important, as outside vendors and in-house staffs will be using this data to prepare detailed application, database, and network designs.

Final RFP Preparation The two major components of the RFP that should have been completed at this point are

1. Strategic information systems design.
2. Corporate location survey results.

To put the finishing touches on the RFP, a few more pieces of information must be either supplied to or requested from potential system and network suppliers. This additional information is often included in a section of the RFP known as the **management abstract** or executive summary. Figure 11-14 illustrates a sample table of contents from an RFP including the items that might be included in a management abstract.

Information Supplied to Vendors Among the information included in the management abstract that should be supplied to potential vendors to give them as accurate a description as possible of the opportunity are the following items:

- Company profile: A brief description of the company issuing the request for proposal. Number of corporate locations, approximate yearly sales, anticipated growth rate, and a brief statement concerning the current state of computerization or networking could all be elements of this section.

Management Abstract	• Company profile • Statement of the problem • Overall system characteristics—anticipated outcomes • Project phase prioritization • Proposed project schedule summary • Constraints • Contact information • Evaluation criteria for proposals • Legal-terms and nondisclosure agreements • Information requested from vendor; system development experience; hardware, software, networking experience; references; pricing; support; training and documentation; vendor background
System Design	• Summary review • Details of geographic locations • System requirements of each software module

Figure 11-14 Sample RFP Table of Contents

- Statement of the problem: From a business perspective, what was the source of the initiation of the problem definition process and what did the problem definition team conclude?
- Overall system characteristics: It is important to include overall system characteristics at the beginning of the RFP as some of these requirements may be beyond the capabilities of possible vendors and their systems. In this way, these vendors won't waste their time or yours in submitting a proposal that can't meet these basic overall requirements. Figure 11-15 lists some possible overall system characteristics that might be included in an RFP. Although some of the requirements listed in Figure 11-15 may seem obvious or unnecessary, it is important not to assume anything when shopping for information systems.
- Project phase prioritization: If some modules (business area computerization plans) of the overall strategic information systems design are more critical than others, this prioritization should be conveyed to potential vendors. Often, a vendor may be able to supply some, but not all, of the information systems modules. If the vendors have a sense of which modules are most important, they will be better able to know whether or not to submit a proposal.
- Proposed project schedule summary: Figure 11-16 illustrates a sample proposed project schedule with key events that may be of concern to potential vendors listed. Before taking the time to prepare detailed proposals, many vendors appreciate knowing the implementation timetable of the proposed project. If the vendor already has projects underway or anticipated, he/she may lack sufficient staff to meet this RFP's proposed implementation schedule.

1. Source code must be owned by the client company.
2. The system must be easy to use and maintain and must contain on-line help as well as extensive input editing and verification to help prevent errors.
3. The system must require a minimum of training.
4. The system must be easy to install (hardware and software) to expedite installation throughout all corporate locations.
5. The system must allow multiple users simultaneous access to information. The system must have the capability to ensure information integrity through record locking and must have adequate security to ensure against unauthorized access to information.
6. The system must have windowing capabilities allowing drop-down menus and screens to allow simultaneous access to multiple files and/or modules.
7. The system must be easily transportable to numerous hardware and operating system platforms on both minicomputers and microcomputers.
8. The system must have the ability to output and input ASCII data files to ensure necessary informational ties to regional centers.
9. The system must have database/file rollback capabilities to ensure data integrity in the event of a system failure or power outage.

Figure 11-15 Possible Required Overall System Characteristics

Event	Proposed Completion Date
Requests for Proposals Sent to Selected Vendors	07/29/01
Proposals Due to Consultant from Vendors	08/29/01
Selection and Notification of Vendor Finalists	09/14/01
Presentation/Demonstration by Vendor Finalists	09/21/01-10/07/01
Make-or-Buy Decision	10/14/01
Pilot Test	12/14/01
Projected System Implementation Date	04/01/02

Figure 11-16 Proposed Project Schedule Summary

Information Requested from Vendors At least as important as the information supplied to potential vendors is the information required from potential vendors. To avoid being sent standard proposals with preprinted product literature and brochures, it is advantageous to list specific information required from vendors and to evaluate only those proposals that supply the requested information.

Figure 11-17 lists some of the information that may be requested of vendors, although the list is by no means authoritative or exhaustive. Information requested should satisfy corporate policies as well as business layer concerns from initial problem definition analysis. The overall purpose of this section is to ensure that

1. The vendor has significant experience in developing and implementing systems of a similar nature to the one described in the RFP.
2. The vendor has a sufficiently large organization to support the smooth and successful implementation of such a system.
3. The vendor is financially solvent so as not to be likely to declare bankruptcy in the middle of the project implementation

Percent-of-Fit Goal The RFP should now be fairly complete and ready to send to prospective system vendors. In addition to the RFP itself, one other important product of this phase of the overall network analysis and design methodology is known as the **percent-of-fit goal.** This is an especially important element if in-house development of the system and network is a possibility. The percent-of-fit goal is a rather arbitrary percentage that is determined by the user representative group preparing the RFP and is subject to the same overall buy-in as the RFP itself.

The purpose of the percent-of-fit goal is to set a minimum threshold of compliance for vendor proposals to warrant further consideration and invitations for demonstrations. As an example, perhaps the users group feels that any proposal that meets at least 50% of the priority 1 features deserves further consideration.

This percent-of-fit goal offers an element of objectivity to the proposal evaluation process. The percent-of-fit goal, combined with the specific descriptions of required features in the RFP, constitutes an objective, comprehensive evaluation mechanism for evaluating proposals according to what is important to the corporation. By having this evaluation mechanism clearly defined before receipt of the first proposal,

System Development	• Vendor's experience in client's industry • Number of installed systems • Date of first installation • Integration with related manufacturing and financial modules • Scope of installed systems
Hardware/Operating Systems/Software	• Which hardware platforms does system run on? • Multiuser? • Operating systems • Programming languages • 4GL/DBMS experience • Ease of/availability of customization • Source code availability
References	• Names, addresses, and phone numbers of three customers with similar systems implemented
Pricing	• Hardware: If vendor will supply hardware, list cost by component including manufacturer and model number • Software: List cost per module, additional per user license costs, source code costs, cost for software customization, cost for maintenance and support agreements, cost for operating or runtime systems
Training	• Include information regarding: facilities, courses, materials, instructor availability, schedule, media used, cost
Support	• Hours—hotline available? • Cost—800 number? • Experience of support personnel • Software guarantees • Bug fixes—turnaround time • Software updates—maintenance
Vendor Background	• Number of employees • Yearly sales (approximate) • Growth pattern • Strategic direction • Research and development

Figure 11-17 Information Requested From Vendor

evaluators are less likely to be swayed by fancy brochures or systems' "bells and whistles."

If an in-house systems development group feels that they should rightfully be developing and/or implementing this system, they must submit a proposal in compliance with the requirements outlined in the RFP. Their proposal will be evaluated along with all of the outside vendors' proposals.

The percent of fit of a particular proposal can be easily calculated. Recalling that all features or requirements of the RFP were given a priority of 1, 2, or 3, by merely counting how many features of each priority are present in a given proposal, an overall objective "score" can be determined for each proposal. The process is fair, objective, and, to a large extent, eliminates politics from the proposal evaluation process.

Proposal Evaluation and Vendor Selection

Having determined a percent-of-fit score for each proposal as well as a percent-of-fit goal for proposals to warrant further consideration, invitations to selected vendors might be the next logical step. However, before selected vendors are invited for demonstrations, it is important once again to gain buy-in from all effected parties, especially management, on not only the selected vendors, but perhaps more important, the vendor selection process. Only when all groups agree that the vendor screening and proposal process has been fair and objective should the overall process move forward to the vendor demonstration stage.

At vendor demonstrations, it is important once again for the users, rather than the vendors, to be in charge. Have a copy of the vendor's proposal at the demonstration and ask to see each and every feature demonstrated that was described as included or supported in the vendor's initial proposal. Score should be kept on those features successfully demonstrated, and this score should be compared to the score received based on the proposal evaluation.

After all of the vendor demonstrations, it is time for the **make-or-buy decision.** Were any of the vendors' systems worth further consideration, or should the system be developed in-house? Once again, before proceeding, buy-in of the vendor demonstration evaluation and the make-or-buy decision should be assured.

Managerial Perspective

OUTSOURCING

Outsourcing allows information systems and networking administrators to hire outside contractors to operate and maintain corporate information systems and networks. This option has become increasingly popular with companies whose primary business is not related to information systems or networking. Early ventures into outsourcing were not always ideal, as corporations and outsourcing vendors wrestled with where one entity's control terminated and the other's began.

As corporations have gained more experience with outsourcing, the delineation of control has become clearer. Corporations should maintain control over which services can be subcontracted by the outsourcing vendor and should maintain the right to exclude certain subcontractors. The relationship between the corporation and the outsourcing company should be viewed as a strategic partnership rather than as a typical supplier–customer relationship. Partnership agreements can be written to include mutual benefits for mutually achieved goals or shared successes. In this manner, both the client and outsourcing company stand to gain by working together to reach mutually beneficial goals—a truly win–win situation.

NETWORK ANALYSIS AND DESIGN

Although it may seem as if a great deal of analysis and design have been done already, it is important to note that the network layer requirements are now ready to be addressed, having designed satisfactory solutions for business, application, and data requirements. As stated several times before, a network cannot be designed in a vacuum, but rather must be designed to deliver solutions and performance in response to specific and well-defined data, application, and business layer requirements.

The term *network analysis and design* really refers more specifically to wide area network analysis and design. LAN design considerations and internetworking (LAN to LAN) connectivity issues were covered in their respective chapters. In this chapter, a more corporate-wide view of networking is taken by designing a network that will effectively support the strategic information system design across geographically dispersed corporate locations. Figure 11-18 illustrates the key points, both process and product, of the network analysis and design phase. Each of these steps is explained in detail.

The overall network analysis and design process can be broken down into three major steps:

1. **Data traffic analysis** examines all aspects and characteristics of the traffic that will be passed between corporate locations over the proposed network. Since this data traffic is what the network must carry effectively, it is important to start with a thorough analysis of the data traffic to design an effective network. As an analogy, it would be equally wise to understand the driving patterns and transportation needs of an urban area before designing a new highway system.

2. Once the nature of the data traffic is thoroughly understood, **circuit analysis and configuration alternatives** explores the possibilities for delivering that data traffic in a reliable and effective manner. Although there are often alternative ways to transport data from point A to point B, it is important to document alternative network configurations along with an understanding of the advantages and disadvantages of each alternative.

3. Finally, given the nature of the data traffic, especially its protocol-related characteristics, and the possible circuit configurations over which that data may be transported, **network hardware analysis and configuration alternatives** explores the possible data communications hardware devices that may be required to tie the various circuit configurations together into a reliable, manageable network.

Process	1. Data traffic analysis • Flow Analysis • Payload type analysis • Transaction analysis • Protocol stack analysis • Time studies • Mission critical analysis • Traffic volume analysis 2. Circuit analysis and configuration alternatives 3. Network hardware analysis and configuration alternatives
Product	1. Data traffic analysis report for each geographic location 2. Alternative network configuration diagrams including circuit and network hardware details

Figure 11-18 In-House Network Analysis and Design

Baseline Existing Network Infrastructure

In most cases, network design projects are actually upgrades or additions to existing networks. As a result, it is essential to be aware of the existing network infrastructure to which the new network or upgrade must interface. Hopefully, detailed records and network diagrams have been kept up to date documenting current network configuration and layout. If this is not the case, then the existing network infrastructure must be thoroughly analyzed and documented to ensure accurate baseline information.

Data Traffic Analysis

The exact types of analysis performed in the major step known as data traffic analysis may vary from one networking design to another. Figure 11-19 details some of the

Data Traffic Analysis Category	Description
Flow Analysis	Flow analysis is concerned with which workstations and servers are talking to each other. In other words, who is talking to whom? Who are the "top-talkers"? It is important to identify not only the amount of traffic to be transmitted but the end-points of these transmissions. Only in this manner can proper traffic consolidation be achieved.
Payload Type Analysis	Most locations will require at least voice and data service. Videoconferencing and multimedia also may need to be supported. All payload types should be considered and documented before selecting circuit and networking hardware.
Transaction Analysis	Use process flow analysis and document flow analysis to identify each type of transaction. Analyze detailed data requirements for each transaction type. Some types of transactions, database replication for example, may be especially bursty.
Time Studies	Once all transaction types have been identified, analyze when and how often each transaction type occurs.
Traffic Volume Analysis	By combining all known types of transactions with the results of the time study, a time-sensitive traffic volume requirements profile can be produced. This is a starting point for mapping bandwidth requirements to circuit capacity.
Mission-Critical Analysis	Results of this analysis phase may dictate the need for special data security procedures such as encryption or special reliability/fault tolerance features such as redundant circuits and networking components.
Protocol Stack Analysis	Each corporate location's data traffic is analyzed as to protocols that must be transported across the corporate wide area network. Many alternatives for the transport of numerous protocols exist, but first these protocols must be identified.

Figure 11-19 Data Traffic Analysis

possible types of data traffic analysis. The required outcome from this step is a data traffic analysis report that will form the basis for circuit and networking hardware selection. It is the obligation of the network analyst to perform whatever types of data traffic analysis are necessary to ensure that the data traffic analysis report is as complete as possible while forming the foundation on which to build a network design.

Flow Analysis The first step toward a thorough understanding of data traffic analysis is to analyze the flow of that data. Understanding the source and destination of each data "conversation" and the nature of the data in that conversation is fundamental to a proper network design. Flow analysis may involve the identification and classification of different types or groups of users of information and the sources of the information that they must access. Traffic flow can vary greatly depending on the types of applications or equipment at either end of a traffic flow. Among some of these types are:

- SNA traffic from mainframes to dumb terminals
- Client/server traffic from client applications to back-end servers
- Server-to-server traffic between transaction and/or database servers
- Browser-to-Internet traffic between client browsers and Internet-based servers

Only after documenting all flows to be handled by a given network can the various types of flows be summarized or conglomerated in an optimal manner.

Payload Type Analysis For the most cost-effective network design, voice as well as data requirements should be considered during the network analysis and design phase. Videoconferencing, imaging, and multimedia requirements should also be considered due to their bandwidth-intensive transport demands. Digitized video and voice represent streaming data and often require isochronous transmission, whereas inter-LAN data tends to be of a more busty nature. These data characteristics may have a major impact on network design decisions.

Transaction Analysis To determine the actual data traffic requirements from a given corporate location, the network analyst has to examine the source of that data: transactions of one type or another. Examples might include customer entry or inquiry, order entry, inventory receipt, order fulfillment, part number or pricing lookup, etc.

Each of these different transaction types should be identified from the business process definitions of the strategic information systems design. **Process flow analysis** and **document flow analysis** are also employed to identify and analyze transaction types. Once each transaction type has been identified, the amount of data required to complete that transaction is calculated and documented. Some transactions such as credit card verifications or ATM machine transactions are composed of short bursts of data that must be handled quickly and accurately. Some nightly backup or file transfer applications may not require the same type of high-speed, high-priority transmission. The difference in the characteristics of these transactions may warrant a difference in the network design in each case. Perhaps one type of transaction is better suited to a packet-switched approach, whereas the other may require a leased line.

Time Studies Once all transaction types have been identified, the next step is to analyze when and how often these transactions are executed. One method of determining both the frequency and time distribution of these transactions is through a time study. Simply stated, a time study merely counts how often and at what time of day, week, or month a given transaction or process is executed. For instance, a retail store's daily close-out procedure is executed once per day. However, is it the same time each day and are all stores executing the same process as the same time each day? What are the network implications of month-end closing procedures? The answers to these types of questions can have a major bearing on bandwidth requirements and the resultant network design.

Traffic Volume Analysis Traffic volume analysis could be looked on as the product of transaction analysis and time studies. By knowing the data and network requirements of every transaction type and by further knowing the frequency and time distribution of the execution of a given transaction type, a time-sensitive traffic volume requirements profile can be constructed. Such a profile shows average network bandwidth requirements as well as peak or maximum requirements. Seasonality of transaction volume should not be overlooked. The transaction frequency of retail businesses can easily double or even triple during the Christmas shopping season. An undersized network must not be the cause of poor customer service during important periods of increased customer activity. As another example, power companies must design voice and data networks that can easily accommodate higher than normal demand to provide adequate customer service during power outages or other emergencies.

Traffic volume analysis should also be viewed from a location-oriented perspective. To have an accurate representation of overall traffic volumes, one must consider the average and peak traffic volume levels between all identified corporate locations or network nodes. Such point-to-point traffic volume analysis data can then be fed into network design and simulation software packages for further analysis and what-if scenario development.

Mission-Critical Analysis Although all data could be considered important, some transactions are so important to a business that they are known as mission critical. Electronics funds transfer is a good example of a mission-critical transaction. The mission-critical nature of some transactions can spawn further analysis and design in two other areas. Data security may require investigation. Encryption of data transmitted over wide area networks may be a requirement. If so, this fact should be stated as part of the overall data traffic analysis report.

Second, it is a fact of life that data circuits fail from time to time. If certain mission-critical transactions cannot tolerate an occasional faulty data circuit, then redundant links may need to be designed into the initial network design configuration.

Protocol Stack Analysis As has been seen in both the LAN and internetworking design processes, protocol stack analysis is of critical importance. Some protocols, such as SNA, are extremely time sensitive. Some protocols are routable, but others are not. Others, such as SNA and some LAN protocols are very "chatty," sending constant status-checking and keep-alive messages onto the network and occupying precious bandwidth. As each corporate location's data traffic is analyzed, special attention must be paid to the various protocol stacks of that data.

Will the wide area network be required to support more than one protocol? What are the bandwidth and network hardware implications of a multiprotocol WAN? Is

TCP/IP encapsulation an option, or is SDLC conversion a more appealing alternative? Before reaching any conclusions as to how various protocols are to be transported over the corporate network, those protocols must be accurately identified and documented. This is the role of the protocol stack analysis.

The type of network design concerned with the proper accommodation of all necessary protocols is referred to as logical network design.

Physical Design Concepts

As opposed to logical network design, physical network design is most concerned with the specification of the transmission and switching elements that must be combined to deliver analyzed levels of traffic to its proper destination. Some of the key activities involved with physical network design are described next.

Circuit Analysis and Configuration Alternatives

A thorough data traffic analysis should produce sufficient information to configure various network design alternatives that will effectively support the strategic information system design to all corporate locations. Evaluating alternative network configurations and computing circuit capacity are beyond the reasonable expectations of a person who may be using this textbook in support of a first course in data communications. Upper level courses in traffic engineering, wide area networking, or network analysis and design would better prepare a person to perform such a task.

Wide area network design software has greatly simplified the design process but is relatively expensive. In most cases, even using the software requires a great deal of network design expertise. As a result, in most cases, only companies that can afford to have full-time network analysts and designers on staff are likely to own copies of network design software. The various categories of network design software are explored in greater detail later in this chapter.

A second alternative for circuit analysis and network configuration would be to hire a data communications/networking consultant. This too may be a very expensive alternative. Furthermore, there is little or no regulation as to the level of expertise required to call oneself a telecommunications consultant.

Third, telecommunications companies, both local carriers and interexchange carriers, have the ability to design networks according to customer data requirements. The network design process is part of preparing a quote and is done at no charge. Therefore, it may be advisable for the small company or novice data communications person to let the experts design the network. Talk to several carriers and get a network design proposal with associated costs from each. If the carriers design the network and quote a price, they can be held accountable for delivering service at a quoted price in accordance with the data traffic analysis and performance evaluation criteria.

Consideration of Network Alternatives

It is important to consider more than just the data traffic analysis when considering network configuration alternatives. The detailed survey of existing system resources should also be considered. For instance, local carriers servicing some remote corporate locations may be limited in their ability to offer certain data transmission services. This should be documented in the survey of existing system resources.

Regardless of who actually designs the network configuration alternatives, it is important to ensure that sufficient bandwidth has been allocated to handle sudden increases in demand. More gradual increases in bandwidth demand due to expanding business opportunities can usually be accommodated with upgrades to higher capacity lines and their associated data communications equipment.

A second performance evaluation criterion for network configurations involves reliability. Based on the data traffic analysis study, sufficient redundancy should be implemented in the network to properly support mission critical applications. Third, is the data transmission provided by these circuits sufficiently secure? The overall goal of this portion of the network design is to find a network configuration that has sufficient bandwidth to reliably deliver the data as described in the data traffic analysis report in a secure manner at a reasonable cost.

Alternative configurations must be understood in terms of both performance and costs. Comprehensive methodologies for project budgeting are presented later. However, the point remains that the choice of a given network configuration may come down to a business decision. That decision may be that a given network configuration is all a company can afford, and, as a result, that company will have to live with the associated performance and reliability. Conversely, the business decision may be that the business requires optimum network performance, regardless of cost.

In any case, it is not the role of the network analyst to dismiss network design alternatives on the basis of cost. The network analyst's job is to deliver network design alternatives capable of delivering required network functionality. Only senior management should determine the feasibility of any particular network design in terms of its affordability. The person presenting the various network configurations to senior management for buy-in must know the pros and cons of each configuration. The ability of each configuration to handle expansion or business growth should be anticipated.

Network Hardware Analysis and Configuration Alternatives Before describing the process of network hardware analysis, it is important to first reiterate the information gathered thus far that will assist in the decision-making process. Two key products of earlier analysis efforts form the basis of the supporting material for selection of the particular networking devices that will be placed throughout the corporate wide area network. These two key products are

1. Data traffic analysis reports for each corporate location.
2. Circuit configuration alternatives diagrams.

Recall briefly the process involved in producing each of these products. The data traffic analysis report was based on a detailed study of numerous aspects of the data traveling to or from each corporate location. The circuit configuration alternatives were designed, in turn, based on a careful study of the required bandwidth and delay sensitivity of the transactions performed at each corporate location as identified in the data traffic analysis study. If the results of these two analysis efforts are valid, then the networking devices chosen to tie the network together that are based on these results should also be valid.

Use of the I-P-O Model The actual decision-making process for network device selection utilizes a model of data communications that was first introduced very early in the text. By compiling the results of the data traffic analysis report and the circuit configuration diagram in an I-P-O diagram, the required processing ability of the sought-after device can be documented. Once the performance characteristics of the required network device have been identified, product specifications can be reviewed and vendor presentations can be scheduled to find the proper networking device for each location.

As with the data traffic analysis and circuit analysis, the network device analysis were done on a location-by-location basis. Figure 11-20 shows a sample use of an I-P-O diagram as a tool for network device analysis.

Figure 11-20 is not meant to be all-inclusive. Rather, it attempts to portray that by knowing the data characteristics of the local data, with particular attention paid to the protocol stack, and by knowing the circuit alternatives available for carrying that data over the wide area network, the choices among network devices that can join the two are relatively limited.

Careful analysis of the available alternatives that can join the input and output characteristics can then be further analyzed from a business or strategic planning objective. Additional information to assist in this evaluation may come from the detailed reports of each corporate location that were part of the preparation of the RFP.

Input	**Processing**	**Output**
Local Data Characteristics	**Required Network Device Characteristics**	**Wide Area Network Circuit Characteristics**

Host-terminal data
  IBM 3270 (synchronous)
  VT-100 (asynchronous)
Transport protocols
  SNA
  DecNet
  TCP/IP
  IPX/SPX
  AppleTalk
Payload types
  LAN data
  Terminal data
  Voice
  Video
  Fax
  Imaging/multimedia
Internet access
	Host-terminal data
	  Cluster controllers
	  STDMs
	  T-1 MUXs and switches
	  X.25 MUXs and switches
	  Frame relay MUXs and switches
	  ATM access devices and switches
	LAN data
	  Bridges
	  Routers
	  Switches
	Voice
	  T-1 channel banks
	Video
	  Inverse MUXs
	Internet access
	  Modems
	  ADSL devices
	  Cable Modems
		Circuit-switched WAN services
		  POTS
		  ISDN
		  Switched 56K
		Leased WAN services
		  DDS
		  T-1
		  T-3
		  SONET
		Packet/Cell Switched Services
		  X.25
		  Frame relay
		  ATM

Figure 11-20 I-P-O Diagram as Tool for Network Device Analysis

Review of Overall Network Analysis and Design Process

Once the network hardware analysis, circuit analysis, and data analysis have been completed, the finishing touches can now be put on the final proposal. Before doing so, a brief review of the network analysis and design process is in order.

Notice that the network design process did not start with a discussion of network hardware device alternatives. To do so would have been to ignore the importance of the top-down model, a central theme of this book. Many so-called data communications experts still start with their favorite hardware alternative and adjust data and circuit characteristics to match the chosen network hardware.

In this case, just the opposite approach was taken:

- Determine data characteristics based on a thorough examination of the transactions that generate the data.
- Determine circuits based on required bandwidth and delay-sensitivity as determined by the data analysis study.
- Determine the networking hardware devices capable of transporting this data over these circuits while remaining responsive to business and location-specific influences.

Preparing the Final Proposal

Figure 11-21 summarizes the key points of wrapping up the network analysis and design methodology. After preparing and presenting the final proposal, buy-in is

Final Proposal	Process	1. Prepare a detailed comprehensive budget 2. Prepare detailed implementation timetable 3. Prepare project task detail 4. Prepare formal presentation 5. SELL!
	Product	1. Comprehensive systems and networking budget model 2. Project management details 3. Presentation graphics
Approval	Process	1. Final buy-in by all affected parties 2. Contract negotiation—outsourcing only 3. Executive approval
Implementation	Process	1. Pilot test 2. In-house trial—outsourcing only 3. Performance evaluation 4. Prepare deployment schedule 5. Roll-out
	Product	1. Detailed list of tasks and responsible parties with due dates 2. Identify and satisfy needs for management, support, and training on new system/network

Figure 11-21 Final Proposal, Approval, and Implementation

sought from all affected constituencies, followed, it is hoped, by final approval and funding by senior management. One element of the final proposal process deserves further explanation.

Preparing a Comprehensive Budget

It has been the author's experience that senior management can accept well-organized, comprehensive budgets representing large sums of money. What has been found to be unacceptable are the so-called hidden or forgotten costs of network and systems implementation often left out of budgets.

As a result, a comprehensive budget format needed to be developed that would help to identify as many elements of potential implementation and operation costs as possible. Figure 11-22 illustrates a sample budget page from the **comprehensive systems and networking budget model.** Along the vertical axis, major budget categories are listed including

- Hardware/equipment
- Software
- Personnel
- Communications (carrier services)
- Facilities

Proposal Number		**Description:**		
	Acquisition	Operation	Incremental Change/ Anticipated Growth	**TOTALS**
Hardware	Data center: Network operations: Application development:	Data center: Network operations: Application development:	Data center: Network operations: Application development:	Data center: Network operations: Application development:
Software	Data center: Network operations: Application development:	Data center: Network operations: Application development:	Data center: Network operations: Application development:	Data center: Network operations: Application development:
Personnel	Data center: Network operations: Application development:	Data center: Network operations: Application development:	Data center: Network operations: Application development:	Data center: Network operations: Application development:
Communications	Data center: Network operations: Application development:	Data center: Network operations: Application development:	Data center: Network operations: Application development:	Data center: Network operations: Application development:
Facilities	Data center: Network operations: Application development:	Data center: Network operations: Application development:	Data center: Network operations: Application development:	Data center: Network operations: Application development:
TOTALS	Data center: Network operations: Application development:	Data center: Network operations: Application development:	Data center: Network operations: Application development:	Data center: Network operations: Application development:

Figure 11-22 Comprehensive Systems and Networking Budget Model

There is nothing sacred about these categories. Change them to whatever best reflects your situation. The important point is to organize the budget grid in such a way that all possible costs are identified in advance.

The horizontal access has three columns representing the major categories of costs with respect to time. Networking and systems budgets typically focused only on the **acquisition costs** of the new system. Even within the acquisition category, costs associated with personnel additions, changes, and training were often omitted. Likewise, costs involved with facilities upgrades or changes such as electrical wiring, cabinets, wiring closets, or security systems were also likely to be overlooked or unanticipated. Preventing surprises such as these requires a two-step approach:

1. Required or anticipated facilities upgrades and personnel needs are identified during the location-by-location survey as part of the final preparation of the RFP.
2. Any legitimate need that was identified in the location-by-location survey should be budgeted for in the comprehensive systems and networking budget model.

Even a budget that identifies all acquisition costs is still neither complete nor accurate. Two other major categories of costs must be accounted for:

1. Operations
2. Incremental change/anticipated growth

Operations Costs **Operations costs** include estimated monthly costs for leased-line or dial-up line usage, as well as the estimated cost for the additional electricity required to run new equipment. If additional cooling, heating, or environmental control is required as a result of system implementation, these costs should be included as well. Service contracts, maintenance agreements, or budgeted time and materials for repairs should be also be considered as operation costs. Also, don't forget budgeting for taxes, contingency or "rainy day" funds, and other hidden costs.

Practical Advice and Information

ANTICIPATING AND BUDGETING FOR NETWORK GROWTH

Another aspect of project budgeting often overlooked at proposal time is the cost associated with the anticipated growth of the system during the first 3 to 5 years after implementation. These **incremental change costs** may be significant if certain elements of the system or network design are not expandable or only moderately so. As an example, perhaps a remote site starts with a four-port STDM as its networking device. To add four more users, an upgrade kit could be installed for $1300. However, to add a ninth user would require replacing the entire STDM with a higher capacity unit at a cost of $5000. Although the costs in this example may not be precise, the point of the example remains. Anticipated growth should be budgeted. In some cases, this budgeting process of the anticipated growth may cause changes in the equipment choices at acquisition time.

To accurately budget for anticipated systems and network growth, the network analyst must have access to strategic business plans that outline the anticipated growth of the business. After all, the implemented system and network are a direct result of the business requirements, including the required ability to respond to changing business conditions in accordance with the overall business vision as articulated in a strategic business plan. Depending on the corporate culture, network analysts may not be allowed access to such strategic business planning information.

As shown in Figure 11-22, each budget category that is formed by an intersection of a column and row can be further subdivided if such department budgeting is required within the overall project budget. In Figure 11-22, the three abbreviated categories stand for three typical departments within an overall M.I.S. operation: DC (data center), NO (network operations), and AD (application development). Make this budget grid fit your business. If departmental or cost center budgeting is not required for your business, ignore these subcategories. If other departmental designations are more appropriate, substitute them.

THE NETWORK IMPLEMENTATION PROCESS

Although specific details of an implementation process will vary from one project to the next, there are a few general points worth making. Perhaps most important, regardless of how well designed an information system or network may be, it is still essential to test that design in as safe a manner as possible. "Safe" in this case could be defined as the least likely to have a tragic effect on production systems or networks.

Pilot tests are a popular way to safely roll out new systems or networks. For example, bring one retail store on-line and monitor performance, fix unanticipated problems, and gain management experience before deploying the system on a wider scale. Honest feedback and performance evaluations are essential to smooth system implementations. User groups can be a helpful feedback mechanism if managed skillfully to prevent degeneration into nothing more than gripe sessions.

Project Management

Another important skill to a smooth implementation process is effective project management. Detailed task lists including task description, scheduled start and finish dates, actual start and finish dates, and responsible parties are at the heart of good project management. Some systems and network professionals use project management software. The author has used project management software on occasion but found, in general, that loading and maintaining all of the project detail in the project management software was more work than managing the project manually. Although perhaps overly simplistic, the general rule of thumb as to when to use project management software goes something like this:

- When a project is too complicated to manage manually, then you may benefit from the use of project management software.

People Are Important

Despite this book's focus on networking hardware and software, people are the most important element of any systems implementation. Buy-in at every stage by all affected parties was stressed throughout the network analysis and design process to ensure that everyone gets behind the new system and network and that everyone feels that they had an opportunity to make their thoughts known. The best designed network will fail miserably without the support of people.

Therefore, a key element of system and network implementation is to ensure that people-related needs such as management, support, and training have been thoroughly researched and appropriately addressed.

AUTOMATING THE NETWORK DEVELOPMENT LIFE CYCLE

Sophisticated software packages now exist to assist network analysts in the analysis and design of large and complicated networks. These software tools can vary greatly in sophistication, functionality, scope, and price.

Managerial Perspective

THE BUSINESS CASE FOR COMPUTER-ASSISTED NETWORK ENGINEERING

The entire network development life cycle is sometimes referred to as **network engineering.** The use of software tools of one type or another to assist in this process is known as **computer-assisted network engineering (CANE).** Companies must be able to make a strong business case for the payback of this computer-assisted network engineering software when the prices for the software generally range from $10,000 to $30,000 per copy. Besides the obvious use of the software for designing new networks "from scratch," several other uses of computer-assisted network engineering software can offer significant paybacks.

By using analysis and design software to model their current network, companies are able to run **optimization routines** to reconfigure circuits and/or network hardware to deliver data more efficiently. In the case of optimization software, "efficiently" can mean maximized performance, minimized price, or a combination of both.

When current networks have grown over time in a somewhat helter-skelter manner without any major redesigns, network optimization software can redesign networks that can save from thousands of dollars per month to millions of dollars per year depending on the size of the network.

Another important use of analysis and design software on a corporation's current network is for **billing verification.** Most analysis and design packages have up-to-date tariff information from multiple regional and long-distance carriers. By inputting a company's current network design in the analysis and design software and by using the tariff tables to price individual circuits within that network, prices generated from the tariff tables can be compared to recent phone bills. Such verification often uncovers discrepancies in billing amounts, some of which can be significant.

Either of the two previous uses of computer-assisted network engineering software could pay back the cost of that software within 6 months to 1 year. Another very common use of this type of software with a less tangible short-term financial payback but significant future benefits is **proactive performance assurance**

Figure 11-23 illustrates the various categories of computer-assisted network engineering software along with a few examples of each type. Many other software packages are available in each category that offer a range of features at a range of prices. Differentiation between network design tools, network simulation tools, and network management tools is not as definitive as Figure 11-23 might imply. In fact,

Top Category	Examples

Application Monitoring	• Optimal Networks
	  • Optimal Application Preview
	  • Optimal Application Expert
	  • Optimal Application Vantage

Network Monitoring	• Concord Net Health • NextPoints S3 • NetMetrix • VitalNet
Network Management	• Tivoli/IBM TME • CA—Unicenter • HP—Openview

Network Simulation	• CACI COMNET III
	  • COMNET Predictor
	  • COMNET Baseliner

Network Design	• NetMaker Mainstation • Smart Metrics • NetCracker Professional • WANWise

Figure 11-23 Computer-Assisted Network Engineering Software

most network design tools now include at least some network simulation and management capabilities, as well as network design intelligence to actively assist in the network design.

In addition, recognizing the interdependence between application performance and network performance, many network-based analysis and monitoring tools are able to monitor and/or simulate application performance on a given network. This capability is essential if applications and networks are to be designed in an optimal fashion. Otherwise, network designers fall prey to the rule of thumb of network design: "when in doubt, over-provision the bandwidth until the application performs acceptably." Unfortunately, for latency-constrained applications, no amount of bandwidth will produce acceptable performance results. However, financial consequences of such a network design philosophy could be disastrous.

Analysis and Design Tools

Figure 11-24 lists some of the more common elements of network design tools in an input-processing-output model format.

Following is a listing of some of the important features to look for when considering network analysis and design tools:

- Tariff databases: How current are they? How many carriers and types of circuits are included? How often are the tariff databases updated? Is there an additional charge for tariff database updates? Tariff structures have become very complicated and are calculated in a variety of different ways. Confirm that the tariff database in the analysis and design software includes all necessary tariffs.

Phase	Network Design Tool Features
Input	• Input requirements definitions • Drop network objects • Auto-discovery on existing networks from enterprise network management packages such as HP's Openview, IBM's NetView, or CA-Unicenter • Assign traffic characteristics and distribution • Link objects with circuits • Assign attributes and protocols to network devices and circuits • Build a computer-assisted network model • Accept input (traffic data) from network analysis tools or sniffers
Processing	• Validate the design (which objects can be connected to which other objects) • Roll up and simulate a fully loaded network • Ensure protocol compatibility • Assess reliability and security • Test alternative configurations for cost and performance optimization • Conduct what-if testing
Output	• Detailed network equipment requirements by vendor • Detailed transmission circuit requirements • Detailed protocol design • Bill of materials listing all items to be purchased

Figure 11-24 Input-Processing-Output Model for Network Design Tools

- Response time calculation: Does the software consider the processing time of the particular host computer that may be a part of the network? Can user-defined elements be taken into account in the response time calculation, for example, applications programs of various types, different types of networking equipment?
- Multiple transport protocols: Can the software consider the effect of various transport protocols on response time? How many protocols are included? SNA, DECNET, ISDN, TCP/IP, X.25, frame relay, ATM, satellite, microwave, cellular?
- Multiple topologies: How many different topologies can the software model? Examples: hierarchical, hub and spoke, mesh, point-to-point multipoint, concentrated, packet-switched, multiple host.
- Circuit design: Can the software configure circuits for a combination of simultaneous voice and data traffic, or must voice and data circuits be designed separately? Can multiplexers be cascaded? Are tail circuits allowed?
- Financial: Can the software roll up costs for network equipment as well as for circuits? Can costs and performance be optimized simultaneously? Can costs be compared across multiple carriers?
- Input/output: Can protocol analyzers or network monitoring or management systems be interfaced directly to the analysis and design software for

automatic input of current system performance data? Can analysis and design results be output directly to spreadsheet, database, and word processing packages?

- Operating platforms: What platform does the design software run over? NT, Unix, SunOS, Win'95,98,2000?
- Design platforms: What types of networks can the software design? LAN only, WAN only, LAN/WAN and internetworking?
- Product library: Different network design packages can contain varying numbers of network device objects that contain manufacturer-specific information and specifications.
- Design validation: The software should validate that all devices are accounted for, that all segment lengths conform to standards, and that all hardware is properly matched according to protocols.

Simulation Tools

Simulation software tools are also sometimes known as **performance engineering** software tools. All simulation systems share a similar trait in that the overall network performance that they are able to model is a result of the net effect of a series of mathematical formulas. These mathematical formulas represent and are derived from the actual performance of the circuits and networking equipment that make up the final network design.

The value of a simulation system is in its ability to predict the performance of various networking scenarios otherwise known as **what-if analysis.** Simulation software uses the current network configuration as a starting point and applies what-if scenarios. The benefits of a good network simulation package include

- Ability to spot network bottlenecks such as overworked servers, network failures, or disk capacity problems.
- Ability to test new applications and network configurations before actual deployment. New applications may run well in a controlled test environment, but may perform quite differently on the shared enterprise network.
- Ability to recreate circumstances to reproduce intermittent or occasional network problems.
- Ability to replicate traffic volume as well as traffic transaction type and protocol mix.

The key characteristics that distinguish simulation software are as follows:

- Network types: Which different types of networks can be simulated? Circuit-switched, packet-switched, store-and-forward, packet-radio, VSAT, microwave?
- Network scope: How many of the following can the simulation software model either individually or in combination with one another: modems and multiplexers, LANs, Internetworks, WANs, MANs?

- Network services: How many of the following advanced services can be modeled: frame relay, ISDN (BRI and PRI), SMDS, X.25, ATM, SONET.
- Network devices: Some simulation systems have developed performance profiles of individual networking devices to the point where they can model particular networking devices (bridges, routers, switches, MUXs) made by particular manufacturers.
- Network protocols: In addition to the network transport protocols listed in the analysis and design section, different router-to-router protocols can have a dramatic impact on network performance. Examples: RIP, OSPF, PPP, BGP.
- Different data traffic attributes: As studied in previous chapters, all data traffic does not have identical transmission needs or characteristics. Can the software simulate data with different traits? For example: bursty LAN data, streaming digitized voice or video, real-time transaction-oriented data, batch-oriented file transfer data.
- Traffic data entry: Any simulation needs traffic statistics to run. How these traffic statistics may be entered can make a major difference in the ease of use of the simulation system. Possibilities include manual entry by users of traffic data collected elsewhere, traffic data entered "live" through a direct interface to a protocol analyzer, a traffic generator that generates simulated traffic according to the user's parameters or auto-discovery from enterprise network management systems.
- User interface: Many simulation software tools now offer easy-to-use graphical user interfaces with point-and-click network design capability for flexible "what-if" analysis. Some, but not all, produce graphical maps that can be output to printers or plotters. Others require users to learn a procedure-oriented programming language.
- Simulation presentation: Some simulation tools have the ability to animate the performance of the simulated network in real time, and others perform all mathematical calculations and then play back the simulation when those calculations are complete.

Object-Oriented Technology Meets Network Engineering As network simulation software has shifted its intended audience from network engineers well versed in the intricacies of network performance optimization to network analysts most familiar with networking requirements, the designers of that software have had to make some fairly radical changes in the ease of use as well as the sophistication of the software.

The mathematical formulas representing the performance characteristics of individual networking elements become the methods of the network objects, and the attributes describe the details such as manufacturer, model, price, and capacity. By merely clicking on one of these network objects representing a particular network device or circuit, the user automatically adds all of the associated methods and attributes of that network object to the network simulation. Particular applications programs or transport protocols can also be represented as network objects and be clicked on to be added to the overall network simulation. In this way, all seven layers of the OSI model can be included in the final simulation run.

Management: Proactive LAN Management

Sophisticated proactive network management software has the ability to monitor network performance on an ongoing basis and to report unusual network conditions or activities to a network management workstation. The term *unusual network conditions* is really user definable. **Thresholds,** or desired limits of certain performance characteristics, are set by the user. In some cases the user may have no idea where to set these thresholds. To aid in such a situation, some management systems can record "normal" performance characteristics over an extended time to gather valid **baseline data.**

Some management software systems even have the ability to feed this "alarm data" back to certain simulation systems that can simulate the "threshold crossing" and allow what-if analysis to be performed in order to diagnose the cause of the problem and propose a solution.

THE FUTURE OF THE AUTOMATED NETWORK DEVELOPMENT LIFE CYCLE

Some of the trends mentioned in previous sections will continue as computer-assisted network engineering software tools continue to evolve and mature. The key word in terms of the future of these various tools that make up the automated network development life cycle is integration. The real potential of network engineering software integration has just barely scratched the surface and only in a few vendor-specific cases.

For instance, certain protocol analyzers such as Network General's Distributed Sniffer have the ability to interface directly into certain network simulation systems. In such a scenario, actual traffic statistics from the current network configuration are fed directly into the mathematical engines underlying the simulation software. Such vendor-specific, product-specific integration is significant. However, to have true transparent integration of all computer-assisted network engineering tools, a more open and standardized approach must be undertaken.

Horizontal Integration

Figure 11-25 illustrates, on a conceptual level, how such a standardized open architecture offering seamless **horizontal integration** might be constructed. Rather than having to know the intricacies and, in some cases, the trade secrets of how each other's products work, vendors of computer-assisted network engineering software merely pass the output from their particular software product to a "neutral" data platform known as **CNIP** or **common network information platform.** Any other CANE tool that could use that output to provide transparent integration with other CANE tools would import the standardized, formatted data from the common network information platform. The end result of the use of such a standardized platform for CANE tool data output and retrieval is the seamless integration of a variety of CANE tools spanning all phases of the network development life cycle.

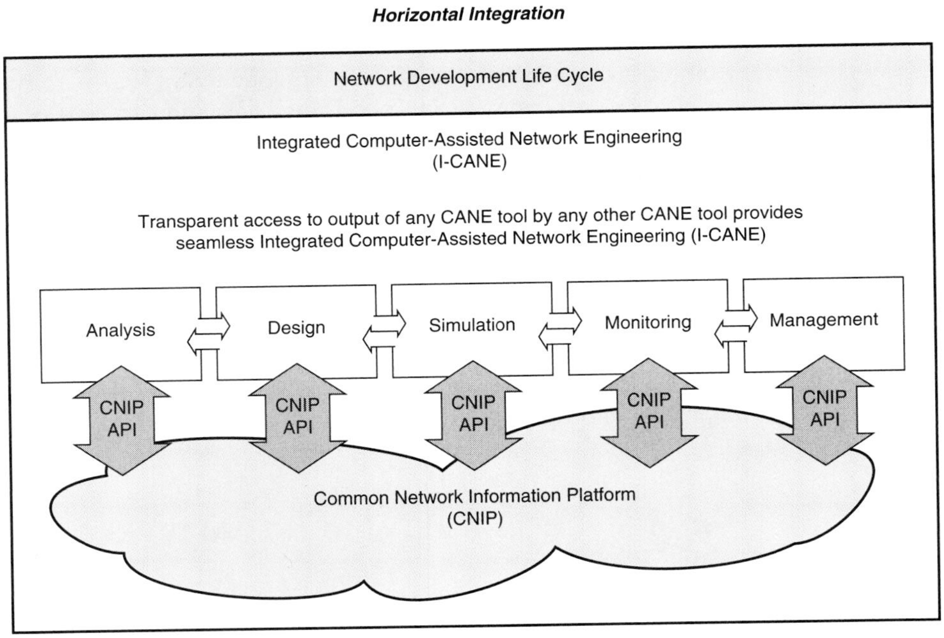

Figure 11-25 The Future of the Automated Network Development Life Cycle—Horizontal Integration

The Final Frontier: Vertical Integration

Integration implies not only horizontal integration with software from other categories of the CANE family but also **vertical integration** with applications development platforms such as CASE (computer assisted software engineering) tools. Integrated CASE (I-CASE) tools could generate code for a new corporate-wide application and could download key information concerning that new application to the CANE suite of software products to predict network impact of the new proposed application.

Proactive network management is the result when the network implications of the deployment of new network-intensive applications are known before the actual release of the software.

As can be seen in Figure 11-26, the actual gateway between the I-CASE and **I-CANE** tools may not be a simple API. Because of the sophistication of the interface between these two platforms, expert systems may be required to dynamically model the relationships between the objects underlying the CASE tools and those underlying the CANE tools.

Extending the vertical integration above the CASE tools and the strategic information systems that they produce, expert systems could again maintain the relationships between major software platforms. Applications layer objects used by the CASE tools could be dynamically linked via expert systems to the objects representing the business rules and processes that, in turn, support strategic business goals and objectives.

Thus, although current technology may not possess the capability, the business information system of the future may interface to the strategic business planning

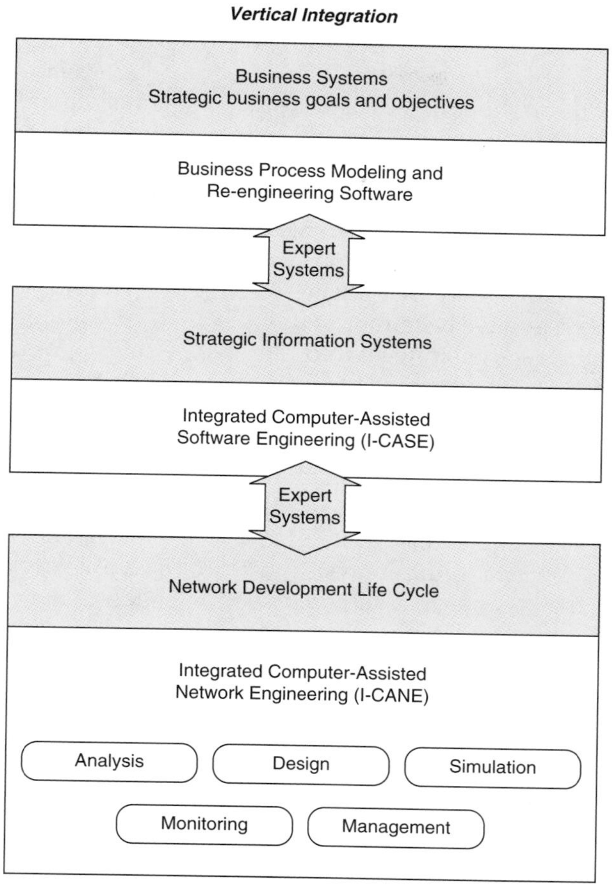

Figure 11-26 The Future of the Automated Network Development Life Cycle—Vertical Integration

person who amends strategic business goals and objects via a graphical user interface and point-and-click manipulation of business process objects. The changes caused by this business process reengineering are immediately forwarded via an expert system interface to the strategic information systems design that supports these business processes. Changes to application programs would be automatically generated by integrated CASE tools.

Resultant changes in the applications programs produced by the CASE tools are immediately forwarded via expert systems to the integrated computer-assisted network engineering platform. Finally, network objects, circuits, and networking devices are amended as necessary due to the impact of the new applications programs. Network simulation programs are automatically run to assess network impact while network design optimization programs automatically reconfigure the network design to adjust most appropriately to the new network impacts. The amazing part of this whole process is that it was initiated originally by a change in strategic business objectives. The future of computer-assisted network engineering software represents one of the most exciting opportunities in data communications and networking while adhering to the overall top-down model philosophy of network design.

SUMMARY

As has been stated throughout the text, network design cannot be done in a vacuum. Effective network designs will only result from strict adherence to the top-down model by beginning with an analysis of business objectives rather than networking technology. Strategic information systems design must be conducted after business objectives and processes have been thoroughly examined. The importance of strategic information systems design lies not only in its delivery of business objectives but also in its role as a template for network design.

Information systems may be developed in-house or may be outsourced. In either case, it is essential to have a thorough and accurate RFP (request for proposal). Data traffic analysis is a multi-step process that assures that all potential sources of network traffic are identified and accurately quantified. Circuit analysis and configuration alternatives match the proper WAN service to each location's data delivery needs, while network hardware analysis and configuration alternatives match the proper networking hardware with the location's input data and the installed WAN service.

Comprehensive budgets go beyond the typical proposal focus of acquisition costs to include categories for operations and anticipated network growth for a variety of cost centers and categories. Finally, although network design has been a manual process for many years, automated network design and simulation tools are beginning to become more popular as network scope and complexity make "back of the napkin" network design both impractical and unwise.

KEY TERMS

acquisition costs
baseline data
billing verification
business functional areas
business process reengineering
buy-in
CANE optimization routines
circuit analysis and configuration alternatives
CNIP
common network information platform
comprehensive systems & networking budget model
computer assisted network engineering
critical success factors
data traffic analysis
decision points
document flow analysis
evaluation criteria
feasibility study
flow analysis
horizontal integration
I-CANE
incremental change costs
IT project portfolio management
logical network design
make-or-buy decision
management abstract
mission-critical analysis
NDLC
network analysis & design methodology
network development life cycle
network engineering
network hardware analysis and configuration alternatives
operations costs
opportunities for improvement
payload type analysis
percent of fit goal
performance engineering
performance metrics
physical network design
pilot tests
proactive performance assurance process
process flow analysis
project charter product
protocol stack analysis
request for information
request for proposal
return on investment
return on opportunity
RFI
RFP
ROI
ROO
strategic information system design
TBO
TCO
three-pile approach
thresholds
time studies
total benefit of ownership
total cost of ownership
traffic volume analysis
transaction analysis
vertical integration
what-if analysis

REVIEW QUESTIONS

1. Explain how one can assure that IT projects are aligned with strategic business initiatives.
2. Explain how IT project portfolio management works and how it is able to adapt to different corporate business situations.
3. What is the difference between total cost of ownership and total benefit of ownership?
4. What is the difference between return on investment and return on opportunity?
5. Why does total cost of ownership calculation not lend itself easily to IT projects?
6. What is flow analysis and why is it important?
7. Explain how the NDLC interacts with strategic level business and IT infrastructure alignment.
8. Explain how the NDLC interacts with project specific activities such as RFP generation.
9. What are performance metrics and how can they help to assure IT/business alignment?
10. Where does the network development life cycle fit in the overall systems development life cycle?
11. How can one insure that a network design will meet strategic business requirements?
12. How can a company cost justify the expense of network analysis and design software?
13. What does optimization accomplish in network design software?
14. What are the two major characteristics on which networks are optimized?
15. Can these two optimization characteristics conflict with each other?
16. How is horizontal integration of CANE tools likely to be enabled?
17. How is vertical integration of CANE tools likely to be enabled?
18. What is so significant about the comprehensive systems and networking budget model?
19. What is meant by the term critical success factor? Discuss three.
20. What is the significance of process and product in the network analysis and design methodology?
21. What are the important elements of data traffic analysis?
22. Explain the relationship of data traffic analysis, circuit analysis, and network hardware analysis.
23. Explain the importance of evaluation criteria and percent of fit goals to the overall network design process.
24. What is the purpose of an RFP?
25. What are the major components of an RFP?
26. How can the RFP process be kept as objective and non-political as possible?
27. What types of information must be gathered about each corporate location?
28. How can a network analyst assure widespread support of new systems or network implementations?
29. What is cyclic about the network development life cycle?
30. How can computer-assisted network engineering software products exhibit the same cyclic nature?
31. Why are seasonal or occasional differences in transaction volumes or processes so important to network design?
32. What are some of the potential advantages and disadvantages of outsourcing network analysis and design functions?
33. How can so-called backroom politics affect network development and how can a network analyst minimize such effects?
34. What does corporate culture have to do with the method in which a network development project is carried out?
35. What does buy-in imply beyond simple agreement and why is it important to the network development life cycle?
36. How can responses to RFPs be objectively evaluated to determine those vendors worthy of further consideration?
37. What is the role of protocol analyzers in the network development life cycle and in the functionality of network optimization tools?
38. How do network analysts assure that they have a clear understanding of a business problem before proceeding to a network solution?
39. What is the importance of baseline data to the ability to articulate the eventual success or failure of a network development effort?
40. How can too much information be as detrimental as too little information for decision makers? What effect on network design might this have?
41. What is the danger in not starting the network development life cycle with an examination of business layer issues but merely networking business operations as they currently exist?
42. How can the amount of work invested in the development of an RFP be justified?
43. Why is the customer's proposed project schedule important to potential vendors?
44. What is the importance of the corporate location by location survey?
45. Although specific questions asked of vendors in an RFP may vary, what are the overall objectives in asking for this information?

46. How can a network analysis project leader assure that vendor demonstrations are objective and useful and don't revert to "dog and pony" shows?
47. What are some of the difficulties in transporting voice and data simultaneously?
48. What are some of the promising network technologies for transmission of video and data on both the LAN and WAN?
49. How can an I-P-O diagram be used to assist in the proper selection of network hardware devices?
50. Describe those items beyond acquisition costs which should be included in a network budget as well as the importance of those items.
51. What impact has object-oriented programming had on network design and simulation tools?
52. What is so proactive about proactive LAN management? What is the likely business impact of proactive LAN management?
53. Differentiate between ROI, TCO, and TBO is terms of methodology as well as appropriateness for network development projects.

ACTIVITIES

1. You have been asked to design a network for a state lottery commission connecting between 1500 and 2000 outlets to lottery headquarters. Without knowing any further details, what might some of the strategic requirements for such a network be? In other words, from a business perspective, if the state lottery is to prosper as a business, what characteristics must the network supporting this business venture exhibit?
2. Concerning the state lottery example, how important are seasonality or peak transaction periods to network design and performance? What network characteristics might reflect this level of required performance?
3. You have been asked to be project leader of a network design team. Rumor has it that the company president's golf partner already has been hired to install the network and that this network design project is intended to give the appearance of an objective process. Prepare a detailed outline of your approach including long-range project plan, detailed task list, meetings to schedule, and alternative courses of action based on the results of those scheduled meetings.
4. You are in charge of a nationwide voice and data network that has grown in a piecemeal fashion and may benefit from design optimization using automated network design software. It is essential to demonstrate a relatively short payback period for the software investment. The software must contain current tariff information from a number of different carriers so that actual installation and operating costs are generated along with various network design scenarios. Use buyer's guides found in professional periodicals or the Internet to find product information and pricing information. Determine which packages might best meet your needs and write a memo to your company president outlining your recommendation.
5. Modify the requirements in the previous question to include a need to model all seven layers of the OSI model rather than the more typical ability of network design/simulation packages to model only layers 1-3. By modeling all seven layers, you should be able to model the impact of a given application or transport protocol. This package must allow you to define your own objects for any layer of the OSI model.
6. Modify the requirements in question 4 to include a need to model the performance of network devices from a particular manufacturer. For example, it may be a requirement to differentiate between network performance using switches and routers manufactured by Cisco and Bay Networks.
7. Prepare a technology analysis grid for network design and simulation software that shows the difference in features to justify the differences in software costs.
8. Investigate an opportunity to perform a network analysis and design project within your department or business. By dividing the entire project into sections to be performed by various teams, more can be accomplished in a shorter time. Perhaps your instructor, supervisor, or department chairperson has such an opportunity in mind. If not, consider one of the following scenarios:
   a. develop a network to deliver local and remote e-mail interoperability
   b. develop a network to deliver transparent database distribution
   c. develop a network to support remote access and transparent telecommuting
   d. develop a network to support Internet access and a corporate web site

e. develop a network to support desktop videoconferencing
f. develop a network to deliver CAD/CAM engineering drawings to a manufacturing environment or shop floor
g. develop a network that can handle electronic funds transfer between banks on an international basis
h. develop a network with a bandwidth hierarchy scheme including frame relay, T-1 and ATM

The outcome of such studies may not be a physical network design. A great deal of meaningful learning can take place on the way to a physical design. Take a top-down approach by starting with strategic business layer concerns. Try to get through the development of the RFP and the data traffic analysis stages.

9. Choose a networked application for your department or business.
   a. Gather baseline data on this process.
   b. What is the nature of the transactions involved?
   c. How much data is transmitted per transaction?
   d. Perform a time study to produce a traffic volume requirements profile.
   e. What networking resources are currently involved?
10. Describe how a network analyst might cope with a "Because that's the way we've always done it" attitude during the business process analysis phase of the network development life cycle.
11. Develop a corporate location survey covering people, hardware, software, media, data, networking, and physical plant. Use this survey on at least five corporate locations or academic departments. Reevaluate the survey and modify and/or improve it as necessary.
12. Prepare a data traffic analysis report on the data transmitted between these 5 locations by performing as many types of data traffic analysis as possible from the types listed in the chapter. Protocol stack analysis must be completed for each location.
13. Contact your local or long distance carrier to determine how one gets a quote for various types of data services. Are there different contacts for:
   a. analog leased lines
   b. DDS services
   c. ISDN
   d. Switched 56K
   e. X.25
   f. frame relay
   g. ATM
   h. ADSL
14. One of the vendors that responded favorably to the RFP has been in business less than three years. What are your concerns and should these concerns be addressed?
15. Invite a local vendor of data communications equipment to present a guest lecture or demonstration. Notice how the vendor responds to questions.
16. Prepare a comprehensive budget proposal for one of the networks proposed in question 8 above.

CASE STUDY

Lands' End Builds Custom Web Sites

Known primarily for consumer sales of apparel through its print catalog and the Web, billion-dollar retailer Lands' End is pursuing an aggressive strategy to boost sales to businesses by letting them order merchandise online from customized Web pages.

To sell on the Web to businesses, Lands' End realized it would have to provide a customer-specific Web view displaying only the merchandise the corporate employee was allowed to buy, along with the prearranged volume pricing.

This requirement makes business-to-business sales far more complex on the Web than landsend.com's business-to-consumer sales, in which prices and merchandise are the same for everyone. Business sales aren't wholly new for Lands' End. Several dozen companies spend about $140 million each year at Lands' End for clothing with corporate logos.

But after some success making specialized Web sites for General Motors' Saturn division and Carolina Power & Light, the clothing retailer says it is ready to provide custom catalogs to all its corporate customers. The Web site set up for Saturn, for instance, serves 8,000 employees. Lands' End is also setting up a store for use by electronics retailer RadioShack.

"It's done as a free service, and we create each site separately," says Mike Grasee, director of Internet business development, adding that the technical work is being done in-house with help from IBM. Lands' End consults with each business customer to define the content and establish which employees are allowed to buy directly online.

As a security measure, "some companies may want to restrict access to the site only to employees coming through the company intranet," Grasee notes. This is done by checking and verifying the IP address of each Web visitor. Lands' End expects to have more than two dozen Web stores ready by year-end.

Later this spring, the retailer expects to offer Web-based real-time interactive customer support. This will be done using Cisco's Web-Line collaboration software, which lets customer-support representatives guide shoppers through Web pages while simultaneously carrying on a phone discussion. The service is already available to Lands' End's consumer customers.

In addition to the custom Web development for business, Lands' End is looking to make sure its Web business catalogs will work with procurement management software from Ariba and Commerce One.

Ariba and Commerce One offer software to let corporations set up order approval processes and restrict the nature and price of products employees can buy online. Ariba's product is called PunchOut, and Commerce One's is called Round Trip, Grasee says.

Lands' End is adding the Ariba and Commerce One API sets to the company's business Web sites. The APIs "allow us to trade the shopping data back and forth from the Web site to the Ariba or Commerce One network," Grasee says.

The effort is intended to inspire loyalty from business customers so that they keep buying Lands' End apparel and other goods.

"Our customers want this case in online purchasing, so we're going to do this level of personalization," Grasee says.

Source: Ellen Messmer, "Lands' End builds custom web sites," *Network World,* vol. 17, no. 13 (March 27, 2000), p. 37. Copyright Network World. Reprinted with permission.

BUSINESS CASE STUDY QUESTIONS

Activities

1. Complete a top-down model for this case by gleaning facts from the case and placing them in the proper layer of the top-down model. After completing the top-down model, analyze and detail those instances where requirements were clearly passed down from upper layers to lower layers of the model and where solutions to those requirements were passed up from lower layers to upper layers of the model.
2. Detail any questions about the case that may occur to you for which answers are not clearly stated in the article.

Business

1. What was the business motivation or problem that initiated the search for the implemented solution?
2. What was the productivity impact of the implemented solution?
3. Were business performance metrics and associated infrastructure performance metrics identified? If so, were they achieved? If not, what might be some suitable business and infrastructure performance metrics for this case?

Application

1. How does the application in the case differ from the "normal" Lands' End Web site applications?
2. What are some of the key differences between business-to-business and business-to-consumer Web applications?
3. What new customer service applications are being planned?
4. What software must the Web pages be compatible with?
5. What functionality will software from Ariba and Commerce One add?

Data

1. How is security assured?

Network

1. What underlying network technologies were key to the achievement of stated business objectives?
2. How can simultaneous voice and Internet transmissions be achieved?

Technology

1. What specific technologies were employed to deliver the described solution?
2. Describe the interaction between the various technologies employed or planned for this solution.

CHAPTER 12

NETWORK MANAGEMENT

Concepts Reinforced

OSI Model
Enterprise Network Architectures
Distributed Information Systems
Top-Down Model
Network Development Life Cycle
Protocols and Interoperability

Concepts Introduced

Enterprise Network Management
Server Management
Desktop Management
Distributed Applications Management
Internetwork Device Management
Distributed Network Management
Service Management
Traffic Shaping
Systems Administration
Help Desk Management
Consolidated Services Desk
LAN Management
Internet/WWW Management
Network Management Technology
Quality of Service
Bandwidth Management

OBJECTIVES

Upon successful completion of this chapter, you should:

1. Understand the business motivations and forces at work in the current systems administration and network management arena.
2. Understand the relationship between network management processes, personnel, and technology to produce a successful network management system.
3. Understand the differences between systems administration processes and network management processes.
4. Understand the protocols and technology associated with each area of systems administration and network management.
5. Understand how systems administration and network management technology can be most effectively implemented.

INTRODUCTION

At this point in the text, it should be clear to all readers that a network is a complex combination of hardware and software technologies linked by networking technologies. Once these various categories of technologies are successfully integrated, they must be properly managed. The purpose of this chapter is to expose the reader to how each of the elements of a network can be managed to achieve stated business objectives. Although entire texts are written on network and information systems management, this chapter provides an overview of the key issues surrounding the management of several aspects of networks including business alignment, standards and protocols, interoperability issues, currently available technology, key vendors, and market trends.

SERVICE MANAGEMENT PROVIDES BUSINESS ALIGNMENT WITH NETWORK MANAGEMENT

To ensure that networks and their associated information systems are delivering expected levels of service to achieve strategic business initiatives, a verifiable methodology to measure service performance levels must be developed. **Service management** is concerned with the management of IT services and the business processes that depend on them. Service management is achieved through the controlled operation of ongoing service by formalized and disciplined processes. Because of the predictable service environment enabled by strictly defined service processes, the following benefits or characteristics of IT services can be realized:

- Higher quality
- Lower cost
- Greater flexibility and responsiveness
- More consistent service
- Faster responses to customer needs
- Proactive rather than reactive service definition

A service management architecture is developed to map required IT services to specific business unit or customer needs.

Service Management Architecture

Service management architectures provide metrics for service evaluation on both a business and IT infrastructure level. Business expectations as stated by business unit management, the customer, are translated into business performance metrics. These business performance metrics are then mapped to the IT infrastructure expected levels of service that will be required to meet the previously mentioned business expectations. These IT infrastructure expected levels of service are then mapped to IT performance metrics that will objectively measure the IT infrastructure's ability to meet expected levels of service. Figure 12-1 provides a high level view of the components and interaction of a service management architecture.

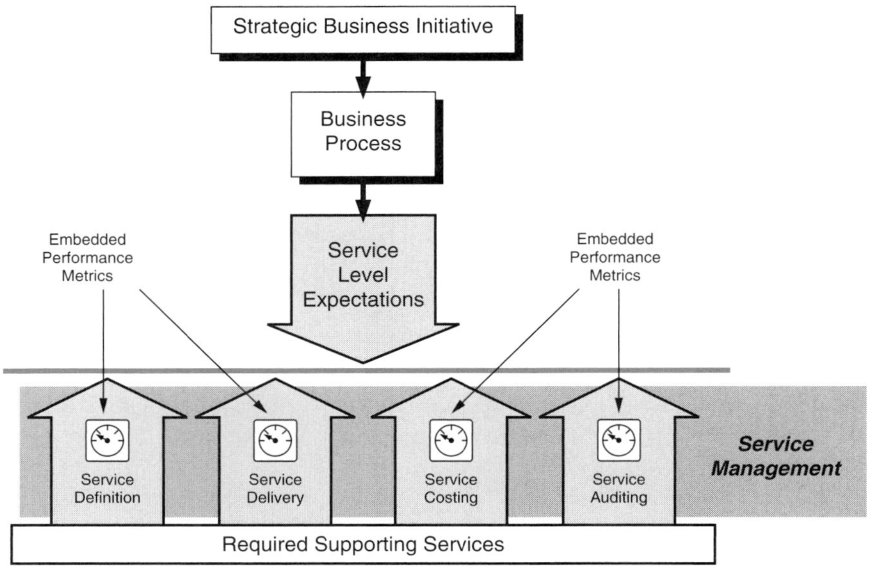

Figure 12-1 Service Management Architecture

Service Definition and Frameworks

Services are defined in terms of the processes, technical expertise (people), and technology that are required to deliver those services. A given service can vary in terms of several characteristics contributing to measurable differences in cost and price:

- Complexity
- Risk (or lack thereof)
- Required service or support level
- Level of deviation from "basic" service

Service definition implies that a baseline level of service and the costs associated with that level of service are first determined. Modifications or upgraded levels of that service are available at customer specification for a predetermined cost above the baseline service.

Defined services and their associated processes are often organized into categories. Workflow and document flow analysis defines the interaction among these various categories of service management processes. Although network management is only one element of overall IT infrastructure and service management, the OSI Network Management Framework can serve as the basis for a larger list of management services incorporating the broader service management category.

The Network Management Forum associated with the OSI Reference Model has divided the field of network management into five major categories in a document known as the **ISO Management Framework** (ISO 7498-4). This categorization is somewhat arbitrary as standards and network management technology apply to multiple categories, and even the categories themselves are interdependent. However, it is important for the network analyst to be aware of this categorization, as it

OSI Category of Network Management	Explanation/Importance
Fault Management	• Monitoring of the network or system state • Receipt and processing of alarms • Diagnosis of the causes of faults • Determination of the propagation of errors • Initiation and checking of error recovery measures • Introduction of trouble ticket system • Provision of a user help desk
Configuration Management	• Compile accurate description of all network components • Control updating of configuration • Control of remote configuration • Support for network version control • Initiation of jobs and tracing of their execution
Performance Management	• Determination of quality of service parameters • Monitor network for performance bottlenecks • Measure system and network performance • Process measurement data and produce reports • Capacity planning and proactive performance planning
Security Management	• Monitor the system for intrusions • Provide authentication of users • Provide encryption in order to assure message privacy • Implement associated security policy
Accounting Management	• Record system and network usage statistics • Maintain usage accounting system for chargeback purposes • Allocation and monitoring of system or network usage quotas • Maintain and report usage statistics

Figure 12-2 OSI Categories of Network Management

is often referred to when discussing network management architectures and technology. Figure 12-2 lists and explains the five OSI categories of network management.

Other service management frameworks may include other categories of management that further expand the list presented in Figure 12-2. Many of these categories are concerned with the definition, costing, reporting, support, management, and auditing of the services that must be collectively delivered by the combined elements of the IT infrastructure. Some of the potential additional categories of service management include:

- Service level management: Concerned with the definition and management of offered service levels.
- Incident management: Reactive process to resolve issues as quickly as possible.
- Problem management: Proactive process that attempts to prevent incidents from recurring.

- Change management: Concerned with the management and documentation of changes to the IT infrastructure.
- Capacity management: Proactive management practice concerned with ensuring that the IT infrastructure has sufficient capacity to support current service level agreements as well as unforeseen sudden increases in demand.
- Asset management: Concerned with the monitoring and management of the hardware and software technology that comprises the IT infrastructure.
- Availability management, risk management, and contingency planning: All are related to the desire to be able to meet or exceed system availability commitments as contained in service level agreements.

Many of these categories of management are described in more detail in the remainder of the chapter. Another network management model or framework that is more specifically focused on public telecommunications networks owned by carriers, as opposed to privately owned enterprise networks, is the **Telecommunication Management Network (TMN).** Standards for TMN are issued by the ITU-T (International Telecommunications Union – Telecommunications Standardization Sector). TMN standards are organized according to the particular focus areas such as: architecture, functional requirements, information models, protocols, conformance, profiles, and methodology. Overall TMN management functionality can be organized into a four-layer TMN Model consisting of the following four functional layers, following an overall top-down model approach:

- Business management: focus on high-level business aspects of telecomm management including strategic business and financial planning.
- Service management: focus on the implementation, support, and management of telecommunications services that will meet business and financial strategic goals described in the business management layer. This layer includes all customer service interaction with end users of services. Quality assurance and billing processes are included on this layer.
- Network management: focus on the end-to-end management of the network infrastructure that will be delivering the services described in the service management layer. Functionality on this layer is considered vendor independent.
- Element management: In TMN, all networks are comprised of a combination of network elements (NE). The element management layer is concerned with the management of the distributed individual network elements that comprise the networks that deliver the services. Functionality on this layer is considered vendor dependent, based on the vendor of a particular network element.

Service Level Agreements

Once services are defined and a given level of service is agreed upon between the customer and the IT services department, a formally documented **service level agreement** is negotiated. The service level agreement clearly describes expected levels of service, how that service will be measured, what that service will cost, and what the consequences will be if the agreed upon service levels are not met. Measurements defined in service level agreements must be able to clearly show how effective services are in meeting business objectives, not how much of an IT commodity was used. For example, it is no longer appropriate to report bandwidth consumed, CPU cycles consumed, or amount of disk space consumed. What really matters is whether or not the total IT infrastructure was able to support the success of the business initiative. Among the network management tools capable of monitoring service level agreements, especially with carriers for wide area network services, are the following:

Service Level Monitoring Tool	Vendor
Visual Uptime	Visual Networks
Vital Suite	Lucent
WiseWAN	Net Reality
OpenLANE	Paradyne

Service Costing

Once services have been defined, they must be assigned a cost. Costing IT services is not a simple matter. Initially costs can be differentiated as follows:

- Direct costs: Those that can be directly attributed to the provision of a given service.
- Indirect costs: Those that go to support the overall IT infrastructure on which all services depend.
- Variable costs: Those that vary directly with the amount or level of service required or purchased.
- Fixed costs: Those that do not vary as additional amounts or levels of service are required or delivered.

Figure 12-3 provides a simple model of how variable levels of services can be effectively costed.

As illustrated in Figure 12-3, different types of customers from different business units or business initiatives would interact with IT account managers to assist them in defining their IT service needs. This represents a customercentric approach to IT services. Conversely, a systemcentric approach requires the customer to interact individually with all of the managers of the various components of the IT infrastructure (e.g., network, application development, data management, systems management). The systemcentric approach requires the customer to act as a general contractor, whereas the customercentric approach offers the customer one-stop shopping for business-oriented IT services.

Customers are free to choose distinct levels of different services to meet their IT needs. The variable levels of service imply variable, direct costs associated with the chosen level of service. A given level of service requires a combination of technical expertise, defined processes, and requisite technology. The IT infrastructure repre-

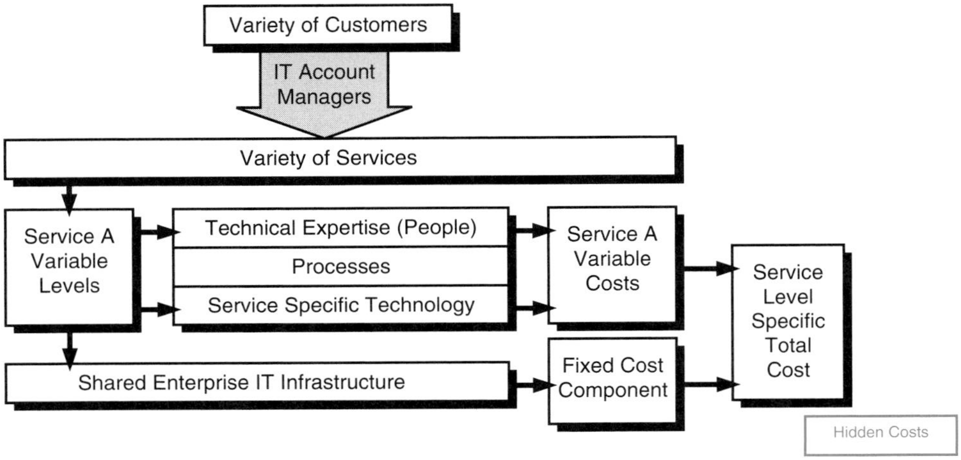

Figure 12-3 Service Costing Model

sents a fixed or indirect cost to the services purchased by the customer. An allocation formula, sometimes called a cost generator, must be calculated to determine how much of the fixed IT infrastructure costs should be passed to the service level cost. Hidden costs are those costs that must still be covered by organizations other than IT. Informal support of systems and applications by end-user departments or business units is a commonly cited source of hidden costs.

IT INFRASTRUCTURE MANAGEMENT

Whereas service management provides the methodology to measure business performance expectations, the achievement of these expectations depends on properly managed components of the IT infrastructure. An IT infrastructure is made of a combination of separately managed and monitored elements. This presents a challenge as these different management tools often do not interoperate or share data. As a result, multiple different categories of management and monitoring tools are required to ensure end-to-end performance of the overall IT infrastructure. Figure 12-4 illustrates some of the different categories of IT infrastructure management that are explained further in the remainder of the chapter.

APPLICATION AND DATABASE MANAGEMENT

Distributed Application Management

Although distributed applications can be developed for local area networks that possess the power equivalent to those deployed on mainframes, distributed applications have not yet matched mainframe applications in terms of reliability and manageability. This is primarily due to a lack of effective application management tools and underlying application management protocols that can expose an application's dependencies and measure numerous aspects of performance. This lack of applica-

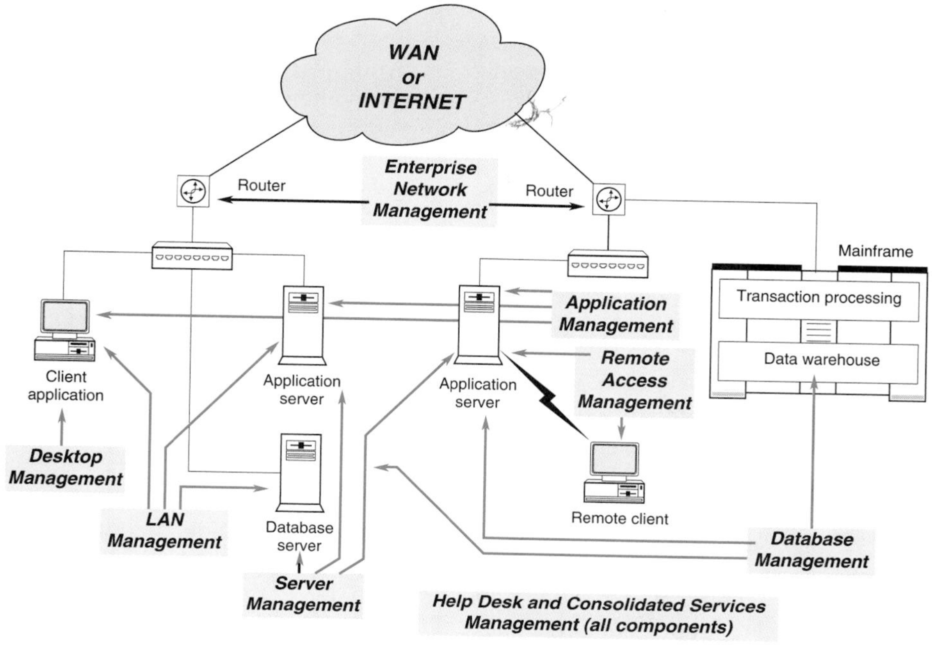

Figure 12-4 Elements of IT Infrastructure That Must Be Managed

tion management tools can make it impossible to diagnose and correct application problems ranging from poor performance to system crashes.

Fortunately, an effort is underway to build self-diagnosing intelligence into applications during the development stage. By having these predefined events and **performance metrics** included within the application, management consoles will be able to detect problems with application performance and take corrective action. These embedded performance metrics are sometimes referred to as **instrumentation.** Two such development environments are Unify VISION and Forte Application Environment. In between the intelligent application, reporting on event conditions and performance metrics, and the management console is an autonomous piece of software known as an **agent** that collects these performance statistics and properly formats them for transmission to the application management console. In turn, these agents are able to communicate with a variety of application management consoles or any SNMP-based administrative program. Examples of agents include AgentWorks from Computer Associates and AppMan from Unify. Eventually, it is hoped that such application management information can be consolidated into enterprise management frameworks such as CA-Unicenter and Tivoli Management Environment.

Application monitoring tools such as Application Expert from Optimal Networks provide real-time statistics on application behavior and network impact as well as the ability to perform "what-if" simulation analysis on captured applications. The two primary network-related variables that can affect distributed application performance are bandwidth and **latency.** It should be obvious at this point in the text how network bandwidth can have a significant impact on application performance. The effect of latency on applications performance, however, is not as widely understood. Latency is simply the delay introduced by any computer or processing node that takes part in the execution of a distributed application. Downloading the client portion of an application from a server, processing SQL queries, or server-to-server queries all introduce latency to an application. The part of application optimization that is surprising to some people is that more bandwidth is not always the answer. If an application is constrained by latency, introducing more bandwidth will have little or no impact on application performance. Application monitoring and simulation tools are extremely valuable in their ability to pinpoint bandwidth and latency constraints before distributed applications are deployed throughout a global enterprise.

An alternative to developing your own applications with embedded management intelligence is to purchase a prewritten **event management tool** that has been written to monitor specific commercially available applications such as Lotus Notes, SAP R2/R3, Oracle Financials, or a variety of databases including IBM DB2, Oracle, Informix, and Sybase. An event can be thought of as a transaction or database update. PATROL from BMC Software, Inc. is an example of such an event management tool. Although effective, PATROL supports only proprietary protocols for application management data.

One of the key stumbling blocks to widespread deployment and support of distributed application management is the lack of a standard of what application performance information should be gathered and how that information should be reported. One proposal for standardizing how instrumentation should be developed within applications is known as the **applications management specification (AMS).** AMS defines a set of management objects that define distribution, dependencies, relationships, monitoring and management criteria, and performance metrics that can subsequently be processed by agents and forwarded to management consoles. These AMS agents are placed into applications through the use of the ARM software developers kit. An API that can be used by applications developers is known as **application response measurement (ARM)** and can measure several key application statistics. Agents are able to forward application performance statistics to ARM-compatible application management consoles. ARM 2.0 added the capability to track applications to multiple servers, to track business-specific transaction information, and to more effectively explain application performance problems. Vendors such as Hewlett Packard, Tivoli, Oracle, and Compuware have committed to supporting the ARM specification. Figure 12-5 illustrates some of the key concepts involved in a distributed application management architecture.

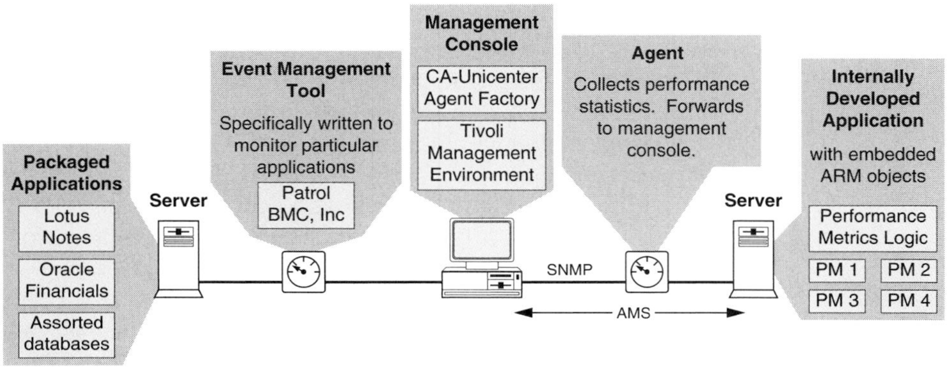

Figure 12-5 Distributed Application Management Architecture

Another possible standard for distributed application management is a proposed IETF standard known as **web-based enterprise management (WBEM),** which integrates SNMP, HTTP, and DMI (desktop management interface) into an application management architecture that can use common web browser software as its user interface. Another IETF initiative is developing a two-part applications MIB, the first part of which is known as the SysAppl MIB dealing with collection of applications performance data without the use of instrumentation, and the second part of which deals with the collection of performance data that requires instrumentation (performance metrics). The RMON Application MIB is explained in more detail later in this chapter. As can be seen from the previous paragraph, when it comes to application management, the standards arena is anything but decided.

Among the application management/monitoring technology available are the following:

Application Management/Monitoring Tools	Vendors
Opitmal Application Suite	Optimal Networks
Visualizer & Analyzer	Apptitute
EcoScope	Compuware
IWatch	Exact Solutions
FirstSense Enterprise	FirstSense Software
Pegasus	Ganymede Software
VitalSuite	Lucent
SMA	Jyra Research
Nextpoint	Nextpoint Networks
Progress IPQoS	Progress Software
ResponseWeb	Response Networks

Enterprise Database Management

Distributed database management is also important to overall enterprise information system management. Although most distributed data management platforms provide their own management system for reporting performance statistics, there is currently no way to consolidate these separate management systems into a single enterprise-wide view. As a result of corporate mergers and the need to consolidate once isolated departmental databases, it is a very common phenomenon for a corporation to have data stored in a wide variety of incompatible database systems. The IETF has been working on a **database MIB** specification that would allow any enterprise data management system to report performance statistics back to any SNMP-compliant enterprise network management system.

Enterprise database management tools that are able to manage a variety of different databases should include the following important major functional areas:

- Global user administration: User and group authorization and security management across a variety of different databases are important characteristics for an enterprise-wide database management system.

- Heterogeneous data schema and content manipulation: In other words, from one console, an administrator can change the database record layout or the contents of those records, regardless of the particular database management system. In some cases, these changes can be automated across an entire enterprise's databases, scheduled to be run at a later time, or saved for future reuse. Such systems should be able to add columns to or otherwise modify database tables automatically across a variety of different databases. In some cases, databases may need to be replicated from one platform to another or one databases schema, or a portion thereof, may need to be copied to a different database platform.
- Effective troubleshooting: Enterprise database management systems must be able to monitor a variety of different databases for such critical events as: inadequate free space, runaway processes, high CPU utilization, or low swap space. Events and alarms should be able to trigger e-mail, pagers, or on-screen events. In some cases, the enterprise database management system can take corrective action as defined by user-supplied script files.
- Among the databases such an enterprise database management system should support are Oracle, Informix, SQL Server, adaptive server, and DB2. In addition, it could run on the following computing platforms: Windows NT, OS/2, Windows 95/98, Windows 2000, and any of the following flavors of Unix on such platforms as SPARC, AIX, Irix, Digital Alpha, and HP-UX.

CLIENT AND DESKTOP MANAGEMENT

Desktop Management

Desktop management is primarily concerned with the configuration and support of desktop workstations or client computers. In most cases, this management is more concerned with the assorted hardware and operating systems software of the desktop machines than with the applications or database software discussed in the previous section.

Desktop Management Architecture and Protocols Desktop management systems rely on an architecture and associated protocols proposed by the **desktop management task force (DMTF),** which is composed of over 50 companies including Intel, Microsoft, IBM, Digital, Hewlett-Packard, Apple, Compaq, Dell, and Sun. The overall desktop management architecture is known as the **DMI** or **desktop management interface** and is illustrated in Figure 12-6.

Although they differ in both strategic intent and governing standards-making organizations, desktop management and enterprise management systems must still be able to transparently interoperate. Since DMI-compliant desktop management systems store performance and configuration statistics in a **MIF (management information format),** and enterprise management systems employ a MIB, a MIF-to-MIB mapper is required to link desktop and enterprise management systems. The DMI architecture is composed of four primary components:

- **DMI services layer** is the DMI application that resides on each desktop device to be managed. The DMI services layer does the actual processing of

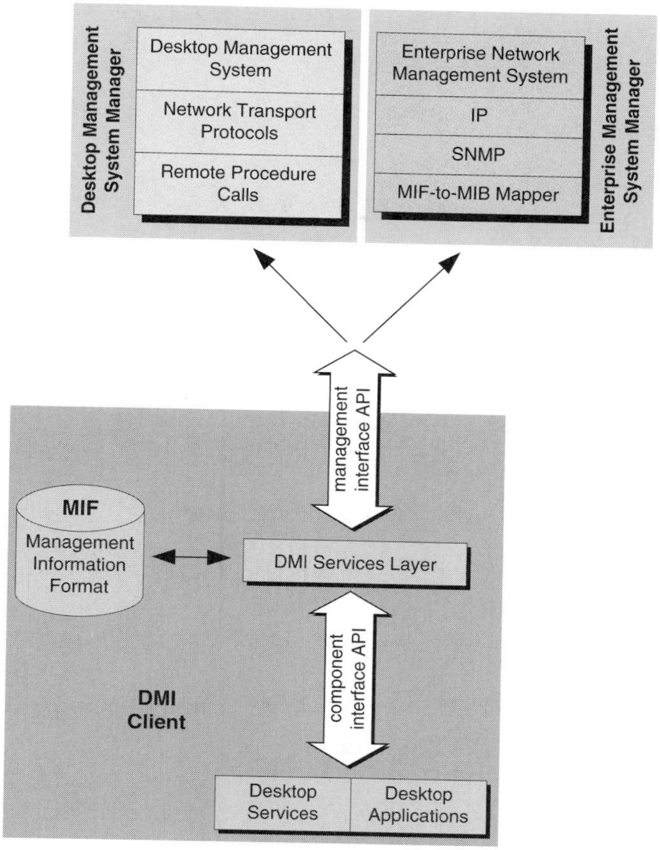

Figure 12-6 Desktop Management Interface Architecture

desktop management information on the client platform and serves as an interface to two APIs.

- The **management interface API** is designed to interface to the desktop system management program that will consolidate the information from this client with all other desktop information.
- The **component interface API** is designed to interface to the individual application programs or desktop components that are to be managed and monitored on the local client.
- Information about the local desktop components is stored locally in a MIF or **management information format.**

Desktop Management Technology Desktop management technology offerings from different vendors are best characterized as suites of associated desktop management applications. Current offerings differ in the variety of management modules within a given suite as well as the extent of integration between suite modules. Among the modules that some, but not necessarily all, desktop management suites include are the following:

- Hardware and software inventory.
- Asset management.
- Software distribution.
- License metering.
- Server monitoring.
- Virus protection.
- Help desk support.

Among the desktop management technology available are the following:

Desktop Management Technology	Vendors
LANDesk Management Suite	Intel
Desktop Management suite	VERITAS Software
NetWizard Plus	Attachmate Corp.
ZENWorks	Novell Inc.
IT Director	Tivoli
System Management Server	Microsoft
LANUtil Suite	Vector Networks

Key functional characteristics of desktop management systems are listed in Figure 12-7. Many of the functional areas described briefly in Figure 12-7 are explained in further detail later in the chapter.

Mobile Desktop Management Extending desktop management functionality such as software distribution, change analysis, job scheduling, asset monitoring, and backup to mobile laptop computers linked only occasionally to corporate headquarters over relatively low bandwidth network links presents some unique challenges. The need for such management software is indeed important when one considers that laptop usage in supposed to at least double between 1998 and 2002 from 50 to 108 million users. Mobile users have a need to receive not only updates to their application software but also corporate data such as product and pricing information. It is equally important for support personnel at corporate headquarters to know exactly what is installed on each laptop computer in terms of hardware and software technology.

XcelleNet, Inc produces a series of remote management modules known collectively as RemoteWare that are able to manage software distribution, antivirus protection, backup, and inventory management for laptop computers. RemoteWare differs from traditional desktop management software packages in that all files transmitted between the management software and the remote laptop computers are in a compressed format. If the transmission is interrupted midstream, the transmission is able to restart where it left off, rather than having to start over from the beginning. Once received at the remote laptop computer after disconnection from the transmission line, the installation application is executed locally on the laptop. Backup management software saves time and bandwidth by only transmitting changes to files rather than the entire file in a process known as delta file synchronization.

Functional Category	Importance/Implication
Integration	• Are all desktop management applications tied together through a single interface to a single console? • Do all desktop management applications share information with each other via a single database? • Can software modules be added individually as needed? Suites may be either modular or tightly integrated in design. • Does the system support the DMI architecture? Output data in MIF format?
Network Operating System Compatibility	• Which network operating system must the desktop management console or server run over? • Which network operating systems is the desktop management system able to monitor? Some desktop management systems can monitor only a single NOS. For example, Novell ManageWise is able to monitor only NetWare networks and Microsoft's System Management Server is able to manage only Microsoft networks, although this may not always be the case. • Examples of supported network operating systems include NetWare, Windows NT, IBM LAN Server, Banyan Vines, Artisoft LANtastic, DEC Pathworks, and AppleTalk
Desktop Compatibility	• Since the primary objective of this software category is to manage desktops, it is essential that as many desktop platforms as possible are supported • Examples of supported client platforms include DOS, Macintosh, OS/2, Windows 95/98, Windows NT Workstation, Windows for Workgroups, or Windows 2000
Hardware and Software Inventory (Asset Management)	• Can the inventory software auto-detect client hardware and software? • Can changes in files or configuration be tracked? • Can versions of software be detected and tracked? • How many applications can be identified? Libraries of 6000 are not uncommon • Can CPU types and speeds be correctly identified? • Is a query utility included to identify workstations with given characteristics?
Server Monitoring	• Does the software support the setting of threshold limits for CPU activity, remaining disk space, etc.? • What server attributes can be tracked? CPU activity, memory usage, free disk space, number of concurrent logins or sessions
Network Monitoring	• Can data-link layer traffic be monitored and reported on? • Can network layer protocol traffic activity be monitored and reported on? • Can MAC layer addresses be sensed and monitored? • Can activity thresholds be established for particular data-link or network layer protocols?

Figure 12-7 Functional Categories of Desktop Management Systems *(figure continues)*

Functional Category	Importance/Implication
Software Distribution	• Can software be distributed to local client drives as well as network servers? • Can updates be automatically installed? • Can the system track which software needs to be updated through ties with the software inventory system? • Can updates be uninstalled automatically? • Can progress and error reports be produced during and after software distribution?

License Metering	• Where can software licenses be tracked?
	  • Clients
	  • Server
	  • Across multiple servers
	• Can license limit thresholds be set?
	• Will the manager be notified before the license limit is reached?
	• Will users be notified if license limit has been reached?
	• Will users be put into a queue for next available license after license limit has been reached?

Virus Protection	• Can virus protection be provided for both clients and servers? • Can both diskette drives and hard drives be protected? • Can viruses embedded within application programs be detected?
Help Desk Support	• Are trouble ticketing and call tracking utilities included? • Are query capabilities included to search for similar problems and solutions? • Are reports available to spot trends and track help desk effectiveness and productivity?
Alarms	• Can managers be notified of changes to files or configuration? • Can violations or preset thresholds be reported? • Can alarms be sent by e-mail, pager, fax, cellular phone?
Remote Control Management	• Can managers take over remote client workstations for monitoring or troubleshooting purposes? • Can this be done via modem as well as over the local LAN? • Can files be transferred to/from the remote client? • Can files on remote client be viewed without taking over complete control of the remote client? • Can remote reboots be initiated?
Reporting Capabilities	• How many predefined reports are available? • Can users define their own reports? • Can information be exported to documents, spreadsheets, or databases? • Which export file formats are supported?

Figure 12-7 Continued

Callisto markets similar remote laptop management software known as Orbiter. A key difference between Orbiter and RemoteWare is that the Orbiter software uses a mobile agent architecture that works in conjunction with the management server at headquarters. In such a scenario, the client-based agent software executes applications and updates on a timed basis in an off-line manner as programmed by the management software. The next time that the laptop and management server are connected, the client agent updates the management server with the status of all of the jobs that it was scheduled to execute in the interim.

In terms of standardized protocols for mobile desktop management, the desktop management task force has created a **mobile MIF** as an extension to the desktop management interface (DMI) 2.0. Among the types of information that management software supporting the Mobile MIF will be able to gather from compliant laptops are the following:

- Battery levels.
- AC lines.
- Docking status.
- Infrared ports.
- Video display types.
- Pointing devices.
- Device bays.

Configuration Management

Single Sign-On Providing single sign-on services for distributed applications deployed across multiple servers is a benefit to users as well as systems administrators. By establishing a distributed security directory housed on a central security server, single sign-on software is able to provide a single login location for multiple, different types of computing platforms. This precludes users from having to remember multiple passwords and allows systems administrators to maintain user accounts and privileges for an entire enterprise from a single location. Single sign-on software is ideally deployed as part of the consolidated service desk.

Among the single-sign-on technology available are the following:

Single Sign On Technology	Vendors
V-GO-PRO	Passlogix
VPN – 1	Checkpoint Software
SafeWord Plus	Secure Computing

Configuration or Policy-based Management Tools Once hardware and software desktop configuration standards have been established and enforced, ongoing maintenance and monitoring of those standards can be ensured by configuration management tools such as electronic software distribution tools, license metering tools, and automated inventory tools. To more easily integrate configuration management tools with corporate policy and standards regarding desktop configurations, a new breed of **policy-based management tools** has emerged. These desktop-oriented, policy-based management tools should not be confused with policy-based network management tools, discussed later in the chapter, which are designed to ensure end-to-end quality of service via bandwidth management.

Policy-based management tools in their simplest form are able to automate certain tasks by using job scheduling utilities to schedule background and after-hours jobs. Another key point about these tools is that they are able to administer multiple different types of client platforms such as DOS, Windows 2000, Windows 95/98, Windows NT, OS/2, HP-UX, AIX, SunOS, and Solaris, to name but a few. More advanced tools not only automate administrative tasks, but also provide an interface for managing the corporate desktop configuration policies themselves. Administrators are able to set policies for an entire global enterprise, for specified domains, or for individual workstations. For example, some policy-based management software can store policies in a knowledge base that arranges the policies in a hierarchical fashion to identify policy conflicts. However, once again, mere throwing technology at a problem will not provide an adequate solution. First, internal policies must be developed within the corporate environment before they can be entered into the policy-based management system. This policy development may involve a tremendous amount of work before the software can ever be implemented. Examples of the types of policies that might be enforced by policy-based management tools are the following:

- User access rights to files, directories, servers, and executables.
- Desktop start-up applications and background colors, or corporate-approved screen savers.
- Deny user access to network if desktop virus checking or metering has been disabled.
- Facilitate changes when applications move or devices are added to the network.
- Prevent users from trying to install and run programs their desktops can't support.

Among the Policy Based Network Management technology available are the following:

Policy Based Network Management	Vendors
NetPolicy	Allot Communications
QPM 1.1 & URT 1.2	Cisco
ExtremeWare Enterprise Manager	Extreme Networks
Open View Policy Expert	Hewlett Packard
Open Policy System	IP Highway
Realnet Rules	Lucent
Optivity Policy Services	Nortel
Spectrum Policy Based Management Suite	Cabletron

Help Desks

As processing power has moved from the centralized mainframe room to the user's desktop, the support organization required to facilitate that processing power has undergone significant changes. When mission-critical business applications are shifted to distributed architectures, effective help desk operations must be in place and ready to go.

Although some help desk management technology is aimed at setting up small help desks on a single PC or workstation to provide simple trouble ticketing and tracking, the higher end of help desk technology supports such additional processes as

- Asset management
- Change management
- Integration with event management systems
- Support of business-specific processes and procedures

The basic objective of this higher end technology is to proactively manage system and network resources to prevent problems rather than merely reacting to system or network problems.

Because the help desk is held accountable for its level of service to end-users, it is essential that help desk management technology be able to gather the statistics necessary to measure the impact of its efforts. Since a significant amount of the interaction with a help desk is via the phone, it is important for help desk management software to be able to interact with call center management technology such as **automatic call distributors (ACD)** and **interactive voice response units (IVRU).** The overall integration of computer-based software and telephony equipment in known as **computer telephony integration (CTI).**

The heart of any help desk management software package is the **knowledge base** that contains not just the resolutions or answers to problems, but the logic structure or decision tree that takes a given problem and leads the help desk staff person through a series of questions to the appropriate solution. Interestingly, the knowledge bases supplied with help desk management software may be supplied by third parties under license to the help desk management software vendor. Obviously, the knowledge base is added to by help desk personnel with corporate-specific problems and solutions, but the amount of information supplied initially by a given knowledge base can vary. The portion of the software that sifts through the knowledge base to the proper answer is sometimes referred to as the **search engine.**

Figure 12-8 summarizes some of the other key functional areas for help desk management software.

Asset Management

Asset management is a broad category of management software that has traditionally been divided into three subcategories:

- Electronic software distribution
- License metering software
- LAN inventory management software

Help Desk Management Software Functionality	Explanation/Importance
Administration, Security and Utilities	• What types of adds, deletes, and changes can be made with the system up and running and what types require a system shutdown? • Must all help desk personnel be logged out of the system to perform administrative functions? • Can major changes be done on a separate version off-line, followed by a brief system restart with the new version? • Can changes be tested in an off-line environment before committing to live installation? • Is security primarily group level or individual? Can agents belong to more than one group? • Can priorities and response times be flexibly assigned? • Can information be imported and exported in a variety of formats?
Call Logging	• How easy is it to log calls? • Can call logging link to existing databases to minimize amount of data that must be entered? • Can number of steps and keystrokes required to add a user or log a call be controlled? • Can multiple calls be logged at once? • Can one call be suspended (put on hold) while another one is logged? • Can special customers or users be flagged as such?
Call Tracking and Escalation	• How flexible are the call escalation options? • Are escalation options able to support internally defined problem resolution and escalation policies and processes? • Can the system support both manual and automatic escalation? • Can automatic escalation paths, priorities, and criteria be flexibly defined? • Can calls be timed as part of service level reporting? • How flexibly can calls be assigned to individual or groups of agents? • Is escalation system tied to work schedule system? • Can subject area or problem experts be identified and used as part of the escalation process?
Customizability	• Customizability is an issue at both the database level and the screen design level • How easy is it to add knowledge and new problems/solutions to the knowledge base? • Does the software offer customizability for multinational companies? • Can entire new screens or views be designed? • Do existing screens contain undefined fields?

Figure 12-8 Help Desk Management Software *(figure continues)*

Help Desk Management Software Functionality	Explanation/Importance
Integration with Other Products	• Computer telephony integration with automatic call distributors and interactive voice response units • Which other integrated modules are included: asset management, change management, scheduling, training, workstation auditing? • Does the software link to enterprise network management software such as HP Open View or IBM System View?
Performance	• Variables to consider when evaluating performance: number of simultaneous users on-line, number of calls per hour, required platform for database/knowledge base and search engine, required platform for agents. • Which SQL-compliant databases are supported? • Can searches be limited to improve performance?
Problem Resolution	• Products can differ significantly in how they search knowledge bases. This can have a major impact on performance. Decision trees, case-based retrieval, troubleshooting tools and embedded expert systems or artificial intelligence are the most intelligent, most complicated, and most expensive options for problem resolution methodologies. • Many products provide more than one search engine or problem resolution method. • Some problem resolution products learn about your environment as more problems are entered. • Some problem resolution methods can use numerous different knowledge sources or problem databases.
Reporting	• How many standard reports are included? • How easily can customized reports be created? • How easily can data (especially agent performance data) be exported to spreadsheet or database programs for further analysis?

Figure 12-8 Help Desk Management Software

Electronic Software Distribution As the distributed architecture has taken hold as the dominant information systems paradigm, the increased processing power possessed by client workstations had been matched by increasing amounts of sophisticated software installed on these client workstations. The distribution of client software to multiple locally and remotely attached client workstations could be a very personnel-intensive and expensive task were it not for a new category of LAN-enabled software known as **ESD** or **electronic software distribution.** ESD software can vary widely in the types of services and features offered as well as the costs for the convenience offered. For example, in addition to simply delivering software to LAN-attached clients, ESD software may also:

- Update configuration files
- Edit other files

- Capture commands entered during a manual software installation and convert the captured text into an automated script to control subsequent electronic software distribution

Figure 12-9 summarizes some of the key functional characteristics of ESD software.

License Metering Software Although **license metering software** was originally intended to monitor the number of executing copies of a particular software package vs. the number of licenses purchased for that package, an interesting and beneficial side effect of license metering software has occurred. In recognition of this beneficial side effect, this category of software is now sometimes referred to as **license management software.** The previously mentioned beneficial side effect stems from the realization that at any one point in time, less than 100% of the workstations possess-

ESD Software Functional Category	Description/Implication
NOS Support	• Since ESD software distributes software via the LAN, it is important to know which network operating systems are supported. Options: NetWare, LANManager, Vines, LANServer, Windows NT, Windows for Workgroups, PathWorks, LANtastic, Windows 2000
Update Control	• Can updates be scheduled? • Can updates be selectively done based on hardware configuration? • Can updates be done only on selected machines? • Can only certain files be searched for and replaced? • Can files be edited or updated? Examples: CONFIG.SYS, AUTOEXEC.BAT, WIN.INI, SYSTEM.INI • Can files in use be replaced? • Can files be moved and renamed? • Can the update be done in the background on client workstations? • How secure is the update control? • Can updates be scripted? • Can update keystrokes be captured and converted to an automated update control file? • Can users perform their own selected updates from a distribution server? • Are unattended updates possible? • Are in-progress status screens available? • Can outside distribution lists be imported? • Can remote workstations be shut down and rebooted? • How extensive are the update reporting and logging capabilities?
Interoperability	• Is the ESD software integrated with license metering or LAN hardware/software inventory software? • Are other software packages required in order to execute the ESD software?
Licensing	• Are licensing fees based on numbers of clients or numbers of distribution servers?

Figure 12-9 Electronic Software Distribution Functionality

ing legitimate licenses for a given software product are actually executing that software product.

As a result, with the aid of license management software, fewer licenses can service an equal or greater number of users, thereby reducing the numbers of software licenses purchased and the associated cost of software ownership. License management software is able to dynamically allocate licenses to those users wishing to execute a particular software package in a process known as **license optimization.** Three of the more popular license optimization techniques are as follows:

1. **Dynamic allocation** gives out either single user or suite licenses based on the number of suite applications used. As an example, a user who starts a word processing package within an application suite would be issued a single user license for the word processing package. However, if the user were to subsequently also execute a spreadsheet package within the same suite, he/she would be issued a suite license rather than a second single user license.
2. **Load balancing** shifts licenses between servers to meet demands for licenses put on those servers by locally attached users. Licenses are loaned between servers on an as-needed basis. In this way, every server does not need to have a full complement of licenses to meet all anticipated user demands. This technique is also known as **license pooling.**
3. **Global license sharing** recognizes the opportunity for license sharing presented by the widely distributed nature of today's global enterprise networks. While users on one side of the globe are sleeping, users on the other side of the globe are sharing the same pool of licenses.

License metering and management software has traditionally been supplied as add-on products written by third-party software developers. However, this trend may change abruptly. Novell and Microsoft have cooperated (an unusual circumstance in itself) on a **licensing server API (LSAPI).** This API would build license metering capability into Microsoft and Novell's network operating systems and would eliminate the need for third-party license metering software.

LSAPI-compliant applications would communicate with a specialized **license server** that would issue **access tokens,** more formally known as **digital license certificates,** based on the license information stored in the license server database. Applications wishing to take advantage of the NOS-based license metering service would need only to include the proper commands as specified in the LSAPI.

LAN Inventory Management Software **LAN Inventory Management Software** is often included or integrated with electronic software distribution or license metering software. However, it has a unique and important mission of its own in a widely distributed architecture in which hardware and software assets are located throughout an enterprise network. A quality LAN inventory management software system is especially important when it comes to the planning efforts for network hardware and software upgrades. An enormous amount of human energy, and associated expense, can be wasted going from workstation to workstation figuring out what the hardware and software characteristics of each workstation are when LAN inventory management software can do the job automatically and can report gathered data in useful and flexible formats. Figure 12-10 highlights some of the key functional capabilities of LAN Inventory Management software.

LAN Inventory Management Functional Category	Description/Functionality
Platforms	• Client platforms supported: DOS, Macintosh, Windows, OS/2 • Server platforms supported: NetWare, LANManager, LANServer, PathWorks, Vines, NetBIOS (DOS-Based), Windows NT, Windows 2000
Data Collection	• Scheduling: How flexibly can inventory scans be scheduled? • Can inventory scans of client workstations be completed incrementally during successive logins? • Does the inventory software flag unknown software which it finds on client workstations? • How large a catalog of known software titles does the inventory software have? 6000 titles is among the best. • Can software titles be added to the known software list? • Are fields for data collection user-definable? • Can the inventory management software audit servers as well as client workstations? • Are hardware and software inventory information stored in the same database? • What is the database format? • Can the inventory management software differentiate between and track the assets of multiple laptop computers that share a single docking bay?
Reporting	• How many predefined reports are available? • Are customized reports available? • How easy is it to produce a customized report? • Can reports be exported in numerous formats such as popular word processing, spreadsheet, and presentation graphics formats?
Query	• How user-friendly and powerful are the query tools? • Can queries be generated on unique hardware and software combinations? • Can inventory information be gathered and displayed on demand?

Figure 12-10 LAN Inventory Management Software Functionality

DISTRIBUTED IT INFRASTRUCTURE ARCHITECTURE

Having covered the issues involved in the management of client workstations whether mobile or desktop oriented, it is now time to look at what is involved with the management of the remainder of the distributed IT infrastructure. To delineate the processes and technology involved with the management of the infrastructure that underlies an enterprise-wide local area network, one must first define those components that make up the infrastructure to be managed. Traditionally, a distributed IT infrastructure is composed of a wide variety of servers and the various networks that connect those servers to each other and to the clients that they serve. There is no single right or wrong way to divide the processes or responsibility for the management of these various components. For the purposes of this chapter, the topic of distributed IT infrastructure management is segmented into the following components:

- **Systems administration** focuses on the management of client and server computers and the operating systems and network operating systems that allow the client and server computers to communicate. This could also be considered as local area network administration.

- **Enterprise network management** focuses on the hardware, software, media, and network services required to seamlessly link and effectively manage distributed client and server computers across an enterprise. This could also be considered internetwork (between LANs) administration.

Both systems administration and enterprise network management are comprised of several subprocesses as illustrated in Figure 12-11

As local area networks, internetworks, and wide area networks have combined to form enterprise networks, the management of all of these elements of the enterprise has been a key concern. LANs, internetworks, and WANs have traditionally each had their own set of management tools and protocols. Once integrated into a single enterprise, these disparate tools and protocols do not necessarily meld together into an integrated cohesive system.

Figure 12-12 summarizes the key functional differences between enterprise network management and systems administration and lists some representative technologies of each category as well.

Consolidated Service Desk

Although the division of distributed IT infrastructure management processes into systems administration and enterprise network management is helpful in terms of distin-

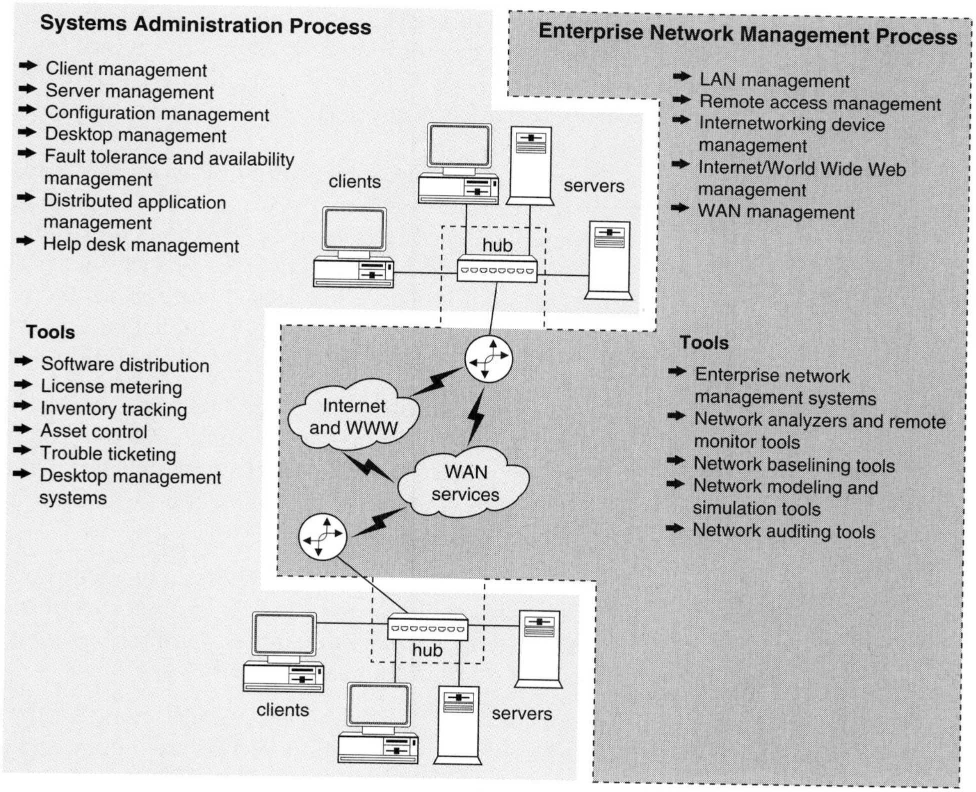

Figure 12-11 Distributed IT Infrastructure Architecture: Systems Administration and Enterprise Network Management

	Functionality	Technology
Enterprise Network Management	• Monitor and manage internetwork technology: switches, routers, hubs • Monitor and manage WAN links	• HP Openview • Tivoli TME/IBM • Sun Solstice Enterprise Manager • CA Unicenter
Systems Administration Also Known As Desktop Management	• Track hardware and and software inventory • Perform license metering • Monitor LAN and server activity • Software distribution • Asset management • Server monitoring	• SaberLAN Workstation - McAfee • Brightworks -McAfee • LANDesk Suite – Intel • Norton Administrator for Networks – Symantec • Frye Utilities for Desktops – Seagate • System Management Server-Microsoft • Manage Wise – Novell

Figure 12-12 Systems Administration vs. Enterprise Network Management

guishing between associated function, protocols, and technology, how are these various processes actually supported or implemented in an enterprise? Reflective of the evoluation of information systems in general, distributed IT infrastructure management has undergone an evolution of its own. The current trend in distributed IT infrastructure management is to offer a **consolidated service desk** (CSD) approach to end-user and infrastructure support. Such an approach offers a number of benefits:

- As a single point of contact for all network and application problem resolution, appropriate personnel processes can be matched with associated network management technologies. This match of standardized processes with technology yields more predictable service levels and accountability. CSD software should include features to support problem escalation, trouble ticketing and tracking, and productivity management reporting. Users should be able to easily check on the status of the resolution of reported problems.
- The consolidation of all problem data at a single location allows correlation between problem reports to be made, thereby enabling a more proactive rather than reactive management style. Incorporated remote control software will allow CSD personnel to take over end-user computers and fix problems remotely in a swift manner.
- Resolutions to known user inquiries can be incorporated into intelligent help desk support systems to expedite problem resolution and make the most effective use of support personnel. On-line knowledge bases allow users to solve their own problems in many cases.
- The consolidated services desk can also handle other processes not directly related to problem resolution such as inventory and asset tracking and asset optimization through the use of such technology as license metering software. It can also coordinate hardware and/or software upgrades. Software upgrades could be centrally handled by electronic software distribution tech-

nology. The management of these systems changes is referred to as change management.

- Network security policies, procedures, and technology can also be consolidated at the CSD.
- The consolidated services desk eliminates or reduces "console clutter" in which every monitored system has its own console. In large multinational corporations, this can lead to well over 100 consoles. Recalling that all of these consoles must be monitored by people, console consolidation can obviously lead to cost containment.

Figure 12-13 illustrates how policy, procedures, personnel, and technology all merge at the consolidated service desk. It is important to note the inclusion of policy and procedures in the illustration. The formation of a CSD provides a marvelous opportunity to define or redesign processes to meet specific business and management objectives. Any technology incorporated in the CSD should be chosen based on

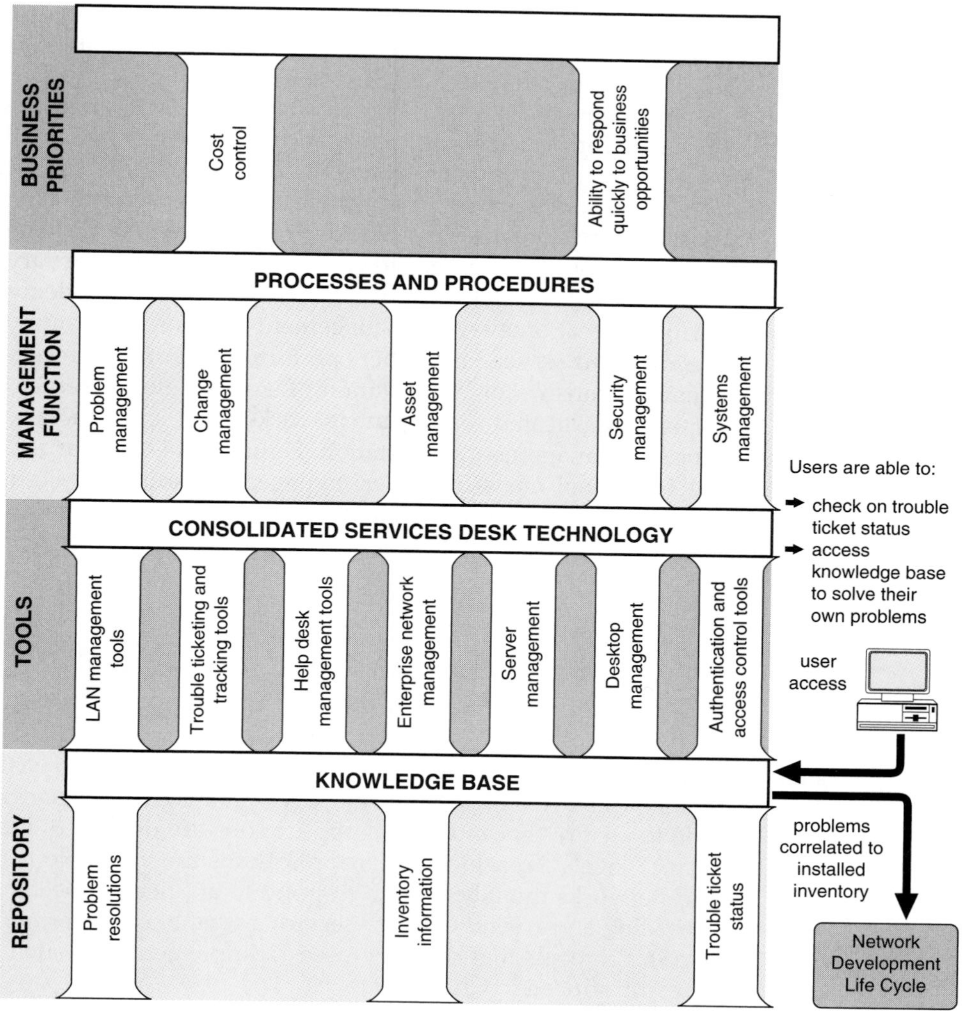

Figure 12-13 Consolidated Service Desk

its ability to support the previously defined corporate policies and procedures in its area of influence. It is important not to first choose a CSD tool and let that tool dictate the corporate processes and procedures in that particular area of management.

SERVER MANAGEMENT AND SYSTEMS ADMINISTRATION

Server Management

At the heart of systems administration is the administration of the servers that are the workhorses and providers of basic system functionality. As servers are continuing to take on increasingly important roles for the entire enterprise such as electronic messaging servers and enterprise directory servers, it is becoming more important to be able to effectively manage, troubleshoot, and remotely configure these critical elements of the enterprise infrastructure. Server management software seeks to ease systems administrators' chores by effectively monitoring, reporting, troubleshooting, and diagnosing server performance. Some server management software is particular to a certain brand of server, whereas other server management software is able to manage multiple different brands of servers. Ultimately, to be especially useful in meeting overall goals of systems reliability and end-user satisfaction, server management software must provide **server capacity planning** capabilities by monitoring server performance trends and making recommendations for server component upgrades in a proactive manner.

An important point to remember about server management software is that it most often requires a software and/or hardware module to be installed on all servers to be monitored and managed. This module will require varying amounts of system resources (CPU cycles, memory) and will have varying degrees of impact on system performance. Some server management systems perform most of the processing on the managed servers, but others perform most of the processing on the server management console or workstation. Likewise, some server management systems require a dedicated management workstation, but others will operate on a multifunction management workstation. Figure 12-14 summarizes some of the key potential functional areas of server management software; Figure 12-15 illustrates the implemented architecture of a server management system.

ENTERPRISE NETWORK MANAGEMENT

Quality of Service, Traffic Shaping, and Bandwidth Management

Enterprise network management is no longer limited to ensuring that a network is available and reliable. To provide service management guarantees, networks must be able to ensure that individual applications are delivered according to agreed upon service levels. To achieve this, applications must be able to be uniquely identified, and networks must be able to respond to application needs on an individual basis. Providing end-to-end delivery service guarantees is referred to as **quality of service (QoS).** Protocols that could be used to implement QoS such as MPLS and Diff-Serv were introduced in Chapter 9.

Bandwidth management, often used interchangeably with the term **traffic shaping,** can be defined as the appropriate allocation of bandwidth to support application

Server Management System Function	Importance/Explanation
Diagnose Server Hardware Problems	• Can alarm thresholds and status be flexibly defined? • How many alarm levels are possible? • Can RAID drive arrays be monitored and diagnosed? • Is predictive hardware failure analysis offered? • Is a diagnostic hardware module required? • Can server temperature and voltage be monitored? • Can bus configuration and utilization be reported?
Diagnose Server Software Problems	• Does the server management software track version control and correlate with currently available versions? • Can version control indicate potential impacts of version upgrades? • What diagnostics or routines are supplied to diagnose server software problems?
Server Capacity Planning and Performance Enhancement	• Are performance enhancement and capacity planning capabilities included? • Trend identification routines included? • Are inventory, asset management, and optimization modules included?
Share Data with Other Management Platforms	• Can data be passed to frameworks and integrated suites such as HP Open View or Tivoli TME? • Can alerts and alarms trigger pagers, e-mail, dial-up? • Can data be exported to ODBC-compliant database?
Remote Configuration Capability	• Can servers be remotely configured from a single console? • Is out-of-band (dial-up) management supported? • Is remote power cycling supported? • Is screen redirection/remote console control supported?
Report Generation	• Are alert logs automatically generated? • Can reports be flexibly and easily defined by users?
Protocol Issues	• Is TCP/IP required for the transport protocol? • Is IPX supported? • Is SNMP the management protocol? • Are any proprietary protocols required?
Server Platforms Managed	• Possibilities include Windows NT, NetWare, SCO Unix and other Unix varieties, OS2, Vines, Windows 2000
Console Requirements	• Is a Web browser interface supported? • Is a dedicated workstation required for the console? • What are the operating system requirements for a console? • Hardware requirements for console?
Statistics Tracked and Reported	• Logged in users • Applications running • CPU utilization • I/O bus utilization • Memory utilization • Network interface card(s) utilization • Disk(s) performance and utilization • Security management • System usage by application, user
Mapping Capabilities	• Can the administrator map or group servers flexibly? • Can statistics be viewed across multiple server groups defined by a variety of characteristics? • How effective is the server topology map? • Can screen displays be easily printed?

Figure 12-14 Server Management Software Functionality

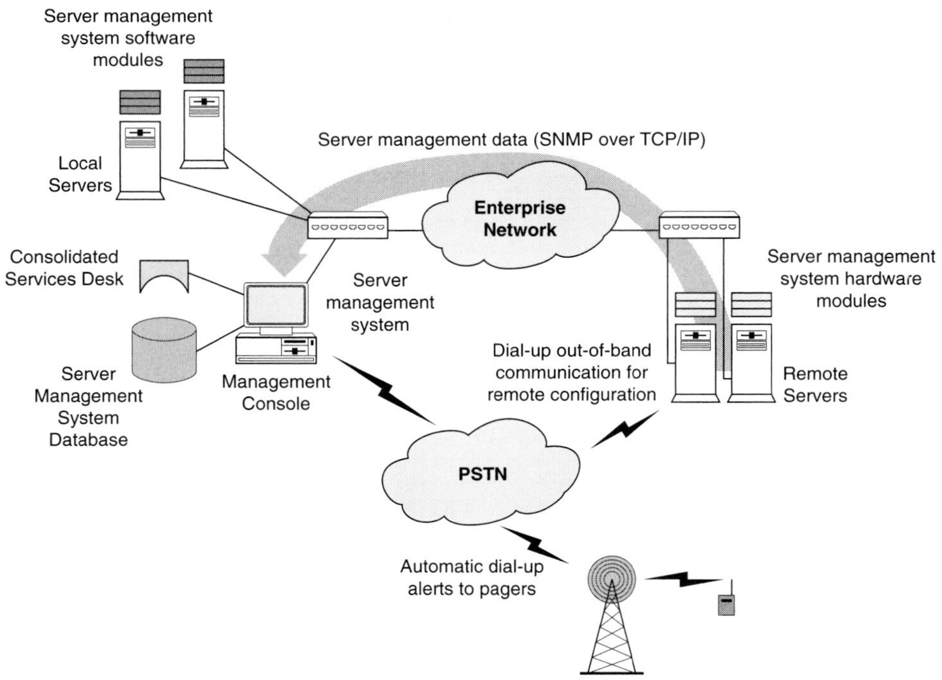

Figure 12-15 Server Management Architecture

requirements. Although a wide variety of terms may be used to describe different bandwidth management techniques, nearly all of these techniques and their associated technologies use either **rate control** or **queueing** or a combination of the two. Traffic shaping can provide bandwidth-constrained or time sensitive applications the bandwidth necessary to potentially improve application performance. Traffic shaping devices will NOT improve the performance of latency-constrained applications. Figure 12-16 compares and contrasts the key characteristics of rate control and queueing while Figure 12-17 introduces several other bandwidth management protocols in addition to those introduced in Chapter 9.

Standards activity would indicate that bandwidth management will be incorporated as a part of an overall **policy-based network management** system. Such policy-based network management systems exist now, although they are largely limited to single-vendor solutions such as CiscoAssure. The vision of policy based networking is the delivery of an integrated, rules-based implementation of traffic prioritization providing end-to-end quality of service and security. Among the required standards being developed are COPS, Dynamic DNS/DHCP, Directory Services Integration, LDAP, and DEN.

Enterprise Network Management Architecture and Protocols

As illustrated in Figure 12-18, today's enterprise network management architectures are composed of a relatively few elements.

Agents are software programs that run on networking devices such as servers, bridges, and routers to monitor and report the status of those devices. Agent soft-

	Rate Control	Queueing
Otherwise known as	• Traffic Shaping	• Flow Control
Functionality	• Smooths bursty TCP traffic • Bidirectional including return path • Improves on default behavior of TCP connections by adjusting TCP window size (standard field in TCP header) • Controls flow by TCP window size adjustment • Some traffic shapers can also limit bandwidth based on allocation to a Port ID, or UDP stream	• Not normally bidirectional, but can be if implemented on both routers at the choke point • Algorithms assign traffic with different priorities to different queues
Limitations	• Due to its dependency on TCP window size adjustment, traffic shaping is ineffective on connectionless networks unless a company has strict service level agreements with its network services provider • Relatively slow reaction to congestion can result in a series of overcorrections that may take several seconds to stabilize	• Traffic classification and queue management may have an impact on router performance • Difficulty of setting admission policies to limit new flows on full links
Requirements	• Since different applications require different TCP window sizes, round-trip latency and end-to-end bandwidth must be considered • This requires precise measurement of variables in real time and an associated ability to adjust TCP window sizes quickly	• Requires queueing and prioritization functionality in router and switch operating systems • Queueing and prioritization must be processed at each hop (router or switch)
Dependencies	• Future developments in protocols (policy servers, directory enabled networking) will likely interfere with rate control schemes	• If done in routers, depends on level of queueing functionality supported by routers

Figure 12-16 Rate Control vs. Queueing Bandwidth Management Techniques *(figure continues)*

	Rate Control	Queueing
Otherwise known as	• **Traffic Shaping**	• **Flow Control**
Deployment Scenarios	• Use traffic shaping to ensure that traffic flows do not exceed CIR (committed information rate) with network providers to avoid discarded frames and associated retransmissions	• Weighted fair Queueing—all queues get an established amount of bandwidth, divides bandwidth across queues of traffic based on weights; prevents low priority traffic from being stranded • Class based Queueing—provides support for user defined classes by criteria such as protocol, IP address, access control list, input interfaces; one queue for each class. Queue can be limited by minimum bandwidth, weight, or maximum packet limit
Technology	• Packet shaper by packeteer—uses TCP for rate control, uses queues for UDP and SNA traffic. Provides a hierarchical policy specification architecture in which policies are set, flows are measured for end-to-end latency, and associated with policies; necessary flow rates are predicted and TCP windows sizes are modified to release packets into smooth (shaped) traffic flows	• Xedia access point—dedicated hardware devices work at different maximum throughput levels. Include integrated CSU/DSU, interface directly to T1, T3, ATM, Ethernet. Popular with ISPs. Implements class based queueing algorithm; defines hierarchy of traffic classes, assigns bandwidth commitments and priorities to classes

Figure 12-16 Continued

ware must be compatible with the device that it is reporting management statistics for as well as with the protocols supported by the enterprise network management system to which those statistics are fed. Agents from the numerous individual networking devices forward this network management information to **enterprise network management systems** that compile and report network operation statistics to the end user, most often in some type of graphical format. Enterprise network management systems are really management application programs running on a management server.

The network management information gathered must be stored in some type of database with an index and standardized field definitions so that network management workstations can easily access these data. A **MIB,** or **management information base** as these databases are known, can differ in the fields defined for different vendor's networking devices. These fields within the MIBs are known as **objects.** One fairly standard MIB is known as the **RMON MIB,** which stands for remote network monitoring MIB. Finally, a protocol is required to encapsulate the management data for delivery by network and transport layer protocols. Partly due to the dominance

Standard	Description/Functionality
Diff-Serv	• Uses type of service field in IP header, can define up to 8 priority classes and queues • Must be supported in hardware (multiple queue network interface cards) • Implemented in routers and switches • Based on policy • No per flow state and processing, scales well over large networks
RSVP+	• Extensions to RSVP (resource reservation protocol) • Intended for use with Diff-Serv • Enables application to identify itself to network devices for prioritization vs. other applications
COPS	• Common open policy service • Query and response protocol between policy server and clients • Switches and routers are policy clients • Query policy as to proper prioritization of user/applications • Goal is more efficient resource allocation based on business-oriented priorities and rules
Diameter	• Enables communication between network clients for authorization, authentication, and accounting • Viewed as a replacement for RADIUS • Driven by desire to charge for mobile computing usage
MPLS	• Multiprotocol label switching—derived from Cisco's tag switching • Tags added to routing tables and sent to other network devices • Allows flows to be switched rather than having to route every packet with a routing table lookup • Tag identifies next hop in path • This explicit routing avoids potentially overburdening paths by using only shortest path algorithms
RAP	• Resource allocation protocol—under development by IETF • Policy-based networking including QOS • Scalable policy control model for RSVP • Defines policy decision points (PDP), policy enforcement points (PEP), policy information base (PIB) for schema and architecture, and policy framework definition language (PFDL); device and vendor independent policy encoding language
DEN	• Directory enabled networking—DMTF standard; part of the CIM (common information model) specification

Figure 12-17 Bandwidth Management Protocols

of TCP/IP as the internetworking protocol of choice, **SNMP (simple network management protocol)** is the de facto standard for delivering enterprise management data.

As originally conceived, the enterprise management console would collect the performance data from all of the devices, or elements, comprising an enterprise network in a single, centralized location. However, as networks grew in both complexity and size, and the numbers of devices to be managed exploded, the amount of

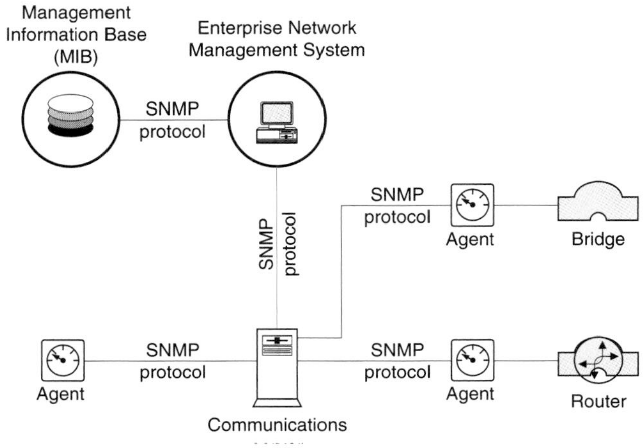

Figure 12-18 Enterprise Network Management Architecture

management traffic flowing over the enterprise network has begun to reach unacceptable levels. In some cases, management traffic alone can account for 30% of network bandwidth usage, thereby reporting on the problems that it is itself creating.

An alternative to the centralized enterprise management console approach known as the **distributed device manager (DDM)** has begun to emerge. DDM takes more of an end-to-end full network view of the enterprise network as opposed to the centralized enterprise management console architecture that takes more of an individual device or element focus. A DDM architecture relies on **distributed network probes** that are able to gather information from a variety of network devices manufactured by multiple vendors and relay that information to numerous distributed device manager consoles. Probes are strategically placed throughout the enterprise network, especially at junctions of LAN and WAN segments to isolate the source of network traffic problems. Management traffic is minimized and remains localized rather than monopolizing enterprise network bandwidth supplying the centralized enterprise management console. Figure 12-19 provides a conceptual view of a distributed device manager architecture.

Web-Based Management Another possible evolutionary stage in enterprise network management architectures is web-based enterprise management, first mentioned in the section on distributed application management. The WBEM logical architecture is illustrated in Figure 12-20. The overall intention of the architecture is that the network manager could manage any networked device or application from any location on the network, via any **HMMP (hypermedia management protocol)**-compliant browser. Existing network and desktop management protocols such as SNMP and DMI may either interoperate or be replaced by HMMP. Current plans call for HMMP to communicate either via Microsoft's DCOM (distributed component object model) or by CORBA (common object request broker architecture). Management data from a variety of software agents would be incorporated into the web-based enterprise management architecture via the **HMMS (hypermedia management schema).** All web-based management information is stored and retrieved by the request broker formerly known as **HMOM (hypermedia object manager),** now known simply as Object Manager.

A proposed protocol currently under development by the DMTF (desktop management task force) that would support HMMS is known as **CIM** or **common infor-**

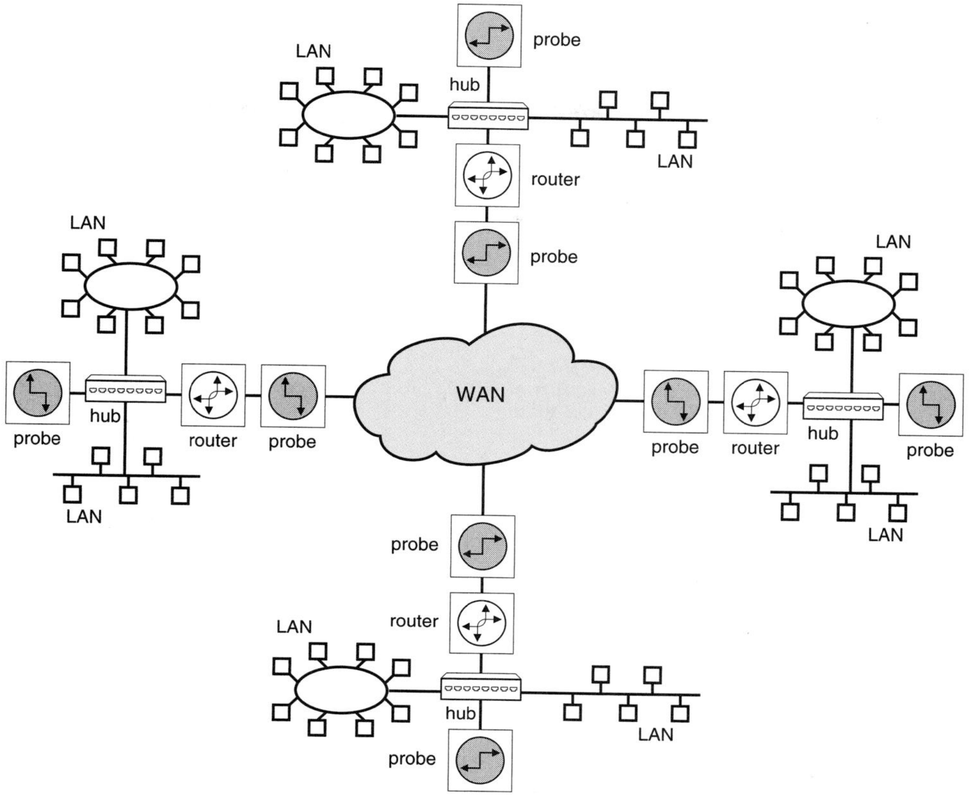

Figure 12-19 Distributed Device Manager Architecture

mation model. CIM would permit management data gathered from a variety of enterprise and desktop voice and data technology to all be transported, processed, displayed, and stored by a single CIM-compliant web browser. Management data to be used by CIM would be stored in **MOF (modified object format)** as opposed to DMI's MIF format or SNMP's MIB format. Figure 12-21 illustrates the interaction of the various types of management data.

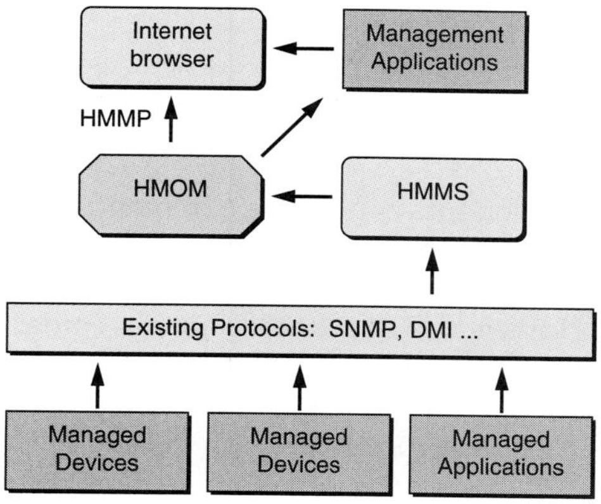

Figure 12-20 Web-Based Enterprise Management Logical Architecture

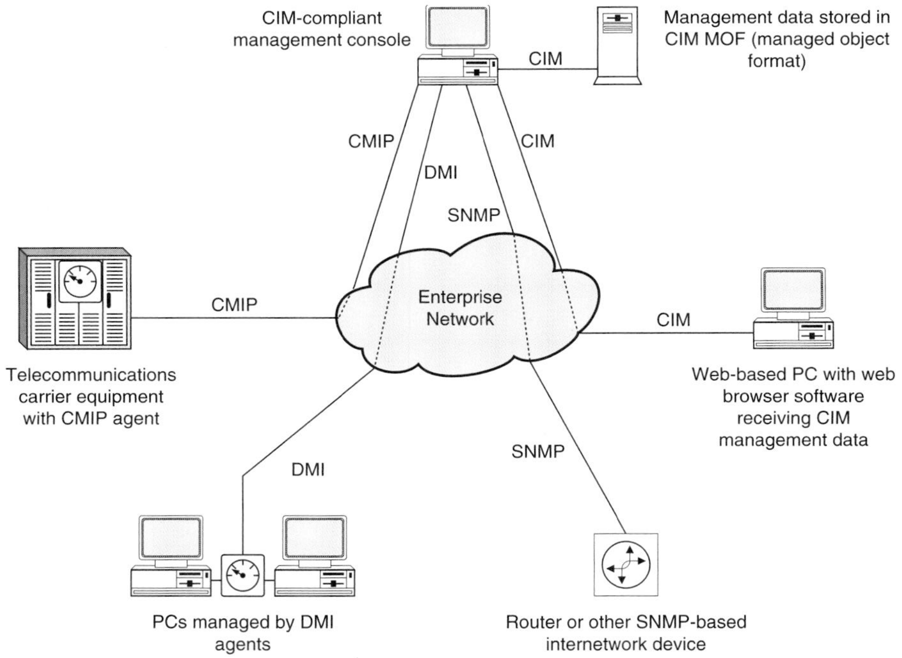

Figure 12-21 Management Data: CIM, CMIP, DMI, and SNMP

Managerial Perspective

Some would argue that CIM is the answer to finally being able to achieve transparency of enterprise management technology. Others would argue that CIM is nothing more than an added layer of complexity on top of an enterprise management system that is already overly complex. An alternative would be to make existing management protocols such as SNMP, DMI, and CMIP more interoperable without the need for additional layers of protocols. However, because of political issues and turf wars, achieving such interoperability is easier said than done, thereby creating opportunities for new all-encompassing protocols such as CIM.

From a practical standpoint, web-based management could benefit both vendors and users:

- Users would have to deal with only one common interface regardless of the enterprise network device that was to be managed.
- Vendors could save a tremendous amount of development costs by only having to develop management applications for a single platform.

However, the fact that a management tool is web-based is not enough. It must deliver all of the functionality of the proprietary management software packages written for specific devices. Some of the most important functions for such software are listed in Figure 12-22.

Web-based network management technology is relatively new, and the market is still being defined. Current technology in this category provides a web browser interface to the user in one of two ways:

Functional Category	Importance/Explanation
Configuration	• Ability to remotely configure network attached devices • Ability to detect changes to remote device configurations
Polling	• Ability to poll network attached devices for performance and traffic statistics
Analysis	• Ability to consolidate and analyze statistics from multiple devices across the network • Ability to discern initial errors from cascading errors • Ability to detect trends • Ability to proactively predict potential trouble spots
Response	• Ability to respond in an appropriate manner to alarms and preset thresholds • Ability to detect false alarms • Ability to escalate problems as appropriate • Ability to notify proper personnel by a variety of means

Figure 12-22 Web-Based Management Tool Functionality

- A web server application is embedded with the enterprise network management platform and the user accesses that embedded web server via a web browser. Communications between the actual network devices being managed and the enterprise network management platform is still via SNMP as illustrated in Figure 12-18.
- A web server application is embedded within a given network device, thereby giving a user direct access to the management data of that device via any client-based web browser. Communication between the user and the network device is via HTTP.

Which SNMP Is the Real SNMP? The original SNMP protocol required internetworking device specific agents to be polled for SNMP encapsulated management data. Alarm conditions or exceptions to preset thresholds could not be directly reported on an as-needed basis from the agents to the enterprise network management software. The lack of ability of agents to initiate communications with enterprise network management systems causes constant polling of agents to transpire. As a result of the constant polling, considerable network bandwidth is consumed.

Also, the original SNMP protocol did not provide for any means of manager-to-manager communication. As a result, only one enterprise network manager could be installed on a given network, forcing all internetworked devices to report directly to the single enterprise network manager. Hierarchical arrangements in which regional managers are able to filter raw management data and pass only exceptional information to enterprise managers is not possible with the original SNMP.

Another major shortcoming of the original SNMP is that it was limited to using TCP/IP as its transport protocol. It was therefore unusable on NetWare (IPX/SPX), Macintosh (AppleTalk), or other networks. Finally, SNMP does not offer any security features that would authenticate valid polling managers or encrypt traffic between agents and managers.

The need to reduce network traffic caused by the SNMP protocol and to deal with other aforementioned SNMP shortcomings led to a proposal for a new version of SNMP known as **SNMP2,** or **SMP (simple management protocol).**

SNMP2's major objectives can be summarized as follows:

- Reduce network traffic
- Segment large networks
- Support multiple transport protocols
- Increase security
- Allow multiple agents per device

Through a new SNMP2 procedure known as **bulk retrieval mechanism,** managers can retrieve several pieces of network information at a time from a given agent. This precludes the need for a constant request and reply mechanism for each and every piece of network management information desired. Agents have also been given increased intelligence that enables them to send error or exception conditions to managers when request for information cannot be met. With SNMP, agents simply sent empty datagrams back to managers when requests could not be fulfilled. The receipt of the empty packet merely caused the manager to repeat the request for information, thus increasing network traffic.

SNMP2 allows the establishment of multiple manager entities within a single network. As a result, large networks that were managed by a single manager under SNMP can now be managed by multiple managers in a hierarchical arrangement in SNMP2. Overall network traffic is reduced as network management information is confined to the management domains of the individual network segment managers. Information is passed from the segment managers to the centralized network management system via manager-to-manager communication only on request of the central manager or if certain predefined error conditions occur on a subnet. Figure 12-23 illustrates the impact of SNMP2 manager-to-manager communications.

SNMP was initially part of the internet suite of protocols and therefore was deployed only on those networks equipped with the TCP/IP protocols. SNMP2 works transparently with AppleTalk, IPX, and OSI transport protocols.

Increased security in SNMP2 allows not just monitoring and management of remote network devices, but actual **remote configuration** of those devices as well. Furthermore, SNMP2, or a variation of SNMP known as **secure SNMP,** allows users to access carriers' network management information and incorporate it into the wide area component of an enterprise network management system. This ability to actually access data from within the carrier's central office has powerful implications for users and enables many advanced user services such as SDN, or software defined network.

Perhaps the most significant SNMP2 development in terms of implication for distributed IT infrastructure management is the ability to deploy multiple agents per device. As a practical example, on a distributed server, one agent could monitor the processing activity, a second agent could monitor the database activity, and a third could monitor the networking activity, with each reporting back to its own manager. In this way, rather than having merely distributed enterprise network management, the entire distributed information system could be managed, with each major element of the client-server architecture managed by its own management infrastructure.

Unfortunately, considerable debate over portions of the SNMP2 protocol has delayed its deployment for years. Some people believe that features of SNMP2, especially the security aspects, are too difficult to implement and use, whereas others

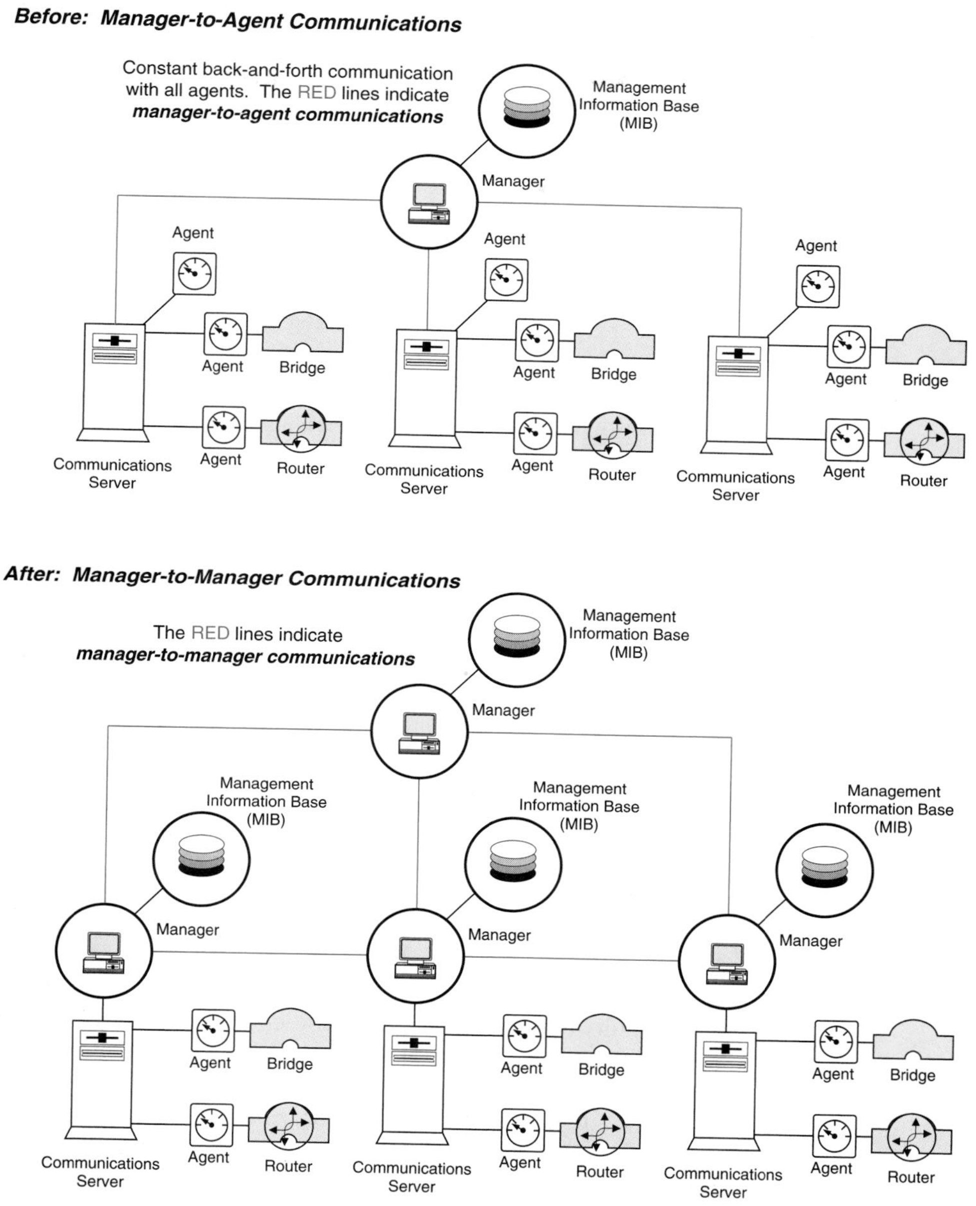

Figure 12-23 SNMP2 Supports Manager-to-Manager Communications

blame the delay on concerns over marketing position and competitive advantage from technology vendors. In the interim, alternative upgrades to SNMP have been proposed by both officially sanctioned organizations such as the IETF and ad hoc forums. Figure 12-24 summarizes key points of the various SNMP2 alternatives.

MIBs Management information bases serve as repositories for enterprise network performance information to be displayed in meaningful format by enterprise net-

SNMP Standard	Also Known As	Advantages	Disadvantages
SNMP		• Part of TCP/IP suite • Open standard • Works with defined MIBs	• Excessive polling • No manager-to-manager communication • Only supports TCP/IP • No security
SNMP2	SMP Secure SNMP	• Supports bulk retrieval • Supports manager-to-manager communication • Supports multiple protocols • Provides security • Remote configuration	• Never implemented due to squabbling among standards bodies
Updated SNMP2	SNMP2t SNMP2C SNMP1.5	• Supposedly easier to implement due to removal of security features	• No security features • No manager-to-manager communications • No remote configuration
Interim SNMPV2	SNMP2u SNMP2*	• Added back some of features taken out of updated SNMP2	• SNMP2u and SNMP2* are incompatible
SNMP3	SNMP2	• Adds security features back in to SNMP2 • Merges concepts and technical elements of SNMP2u and SNMP*	• Lack of support from official standards-making organization • Vendor-specific solutions are being offered as alternatives

Figure 12-24 Alternative SNMP2 Proposals

work management systems. The original RMON MIB standard that was developed in 1991 has been updated as **RMON2.** Whereas the original RMON MIB only required compatible technology to be able to collect and analyze statistics on the physical and data-link layers, RMON2 requires collection and analysis of network layer protocols as well. In addition, RMON2 requires compatible technology to be able to identify from which applications a given packet was generated. RMON2-compatible agent software that resides within internetworking devices and reports performance statistics to enterprise network management systems is referred to as an **RMON probe.** Overall, RMON2 should enable network analysts to more effectively pinpoint the exact sources and percentages of the traffic that flows through their enterprise networks. Figure 12-25 summarizes some of the key functional areas of the RMON 2 specification.

To implement RMON2-based monitoring, a network manager would purchase RMON2 probes and associated RMON2 management software.

Besides differing in the number of RMON2 options and groups implemented, probes and RMON2 management software also differ significantly in their ability to integrate transparently with enterprise network management systems such as HP Openview, IBM/Tivoli TME 10, and CA Unicenter.

One shortcoming of RMON2 is its inability to collect and provide data regarding wide area network (WAN) performance. **RMON3** is expected to provide much needed standards for the WAN monitoring and management technology category. RMON3 would provide a way for many of the current proprietary WAN management tools to interoperate and share data. In addition, RMON3 is supposed to offer management and statistics gathering support for switched networks and virtual

RMON2 Function	Explanation/Importance
Protocol Distribution	• Tracks and reports data-link layer protocols by percentage • Tracks and reports network layer protocols by percentage • Tracks and reports application source by percentage
Address Mapping	• Maps network layer addresses to MAC layer addresses • Maps MAC layer addresses to hub or switch port
Network Layer Host Table	• Tracks and stores in table format network layer protocols and associated traffic statistics according to source host
Network Layer Matrix Table	• Tracks and stores in a matrix table format network layer protocols and associated traffic statistics according to sessions established between two given hosts
Application Host Table	• Tracks and stores in table format application-specific traffic statistics according to source host
Application Matrix Table	• Tracks and stores in a matrix table format application-specific traffic statistics according to sessions established between two given hosts
Probe Configuration	• Defines standards for remotely configuring probes that are responsible for gathering and reporting network activity statistics
History	• Tracks and stores historical traffic information according to parameters determined by the user

Figure 12-25 RMON2 Specifications

LANs, as well as the ability to measure application program response times to monitor distributed applications for degraded performance. Another effort to monitor distributed applications is known as the **application MIB.** Proposals for such an application MIB identify three key groups of variables for proper application tracking and management:

- **Definition variables** would store background information concerning applications such as application name, manufacturer, version, release, installation date, license number, and number of consecutive users.
- **State variables** would report on the current status of a given application. Three possible states are up, down, and degraded.
- **Relationship variables** would define all other network attached resources on which a given distributed application depends. This would include databases, associated client applications, and other network resources.

One of the major difficulties with developing and implementing an application MIB is the vast difference that exists among distributed applications.

Enterprise Network Management Technology

Technology Architectures All of the systems administration and network management processes reviewed in this chapter can be enabled by associated technology. In most cases, network management products offer functionality across more than one category of network or systems management. One way to distinguish between network management technology is to focus on the architecture of that technology. In general, network management technology can be categorized into one of three possible architectures:

- **Point products,** also known as **element managers,** are specifically written to address a particular systems administration or network management issue. The advantage of point products is that they are narrow in scope, provide the sought after solution, and are usually relatively easy to install and understand. The disadvantage to point solutions is that they do not necessarily integrate with other systems administration and network management tools. Any necessary correlation between point products must be done by network management personnel. Backup and restoral tools, license optimization tools, and management tools specifically written for a particular vendor's equipment are examples of point solutions.
- **Frameworks** offer an overall systems administration or network management platform with integration between modules and a shared database into which all alerts, messages, alarms, and warnings can be stored and correlated. Perhaps more important, most frameworks also offer open APIs or an entire application development environment so that third-party application developers can create additional systems administration or network management modules that will be able to plug-in to the existing framework and share management information with other modules. The advantage of a well-integrated framework is that it can offer the network administrator a single, correlated view of all systems and network resources. The disadvantage of frameworks is the development or integration of modules within the framework can be difficult and time consuming. In addition, not all management modules may be compatible with a given framework.
- **Integrated suites** could perhaps be looked upon as a subset of frameworks, although the two terms are often used interchangeably. The difference between integrated suites and frameworks is that integrated suites are filled with their own network management and systems administration applications rather than offering the user an open framework into which to place a variety of chosen applications. The advantage of integrated suites is that the applications are more tightly integrated and linked by a set of common services that tend to offer the user a more consolidated view of network resources. The disadvantage of integrated suites is that they usually do not offer the open pick-and-choose architecture of the framework. Some products in this category offer an integrated suite of applications but also support open APIs to accommodate third-party systems administration and network management applications.

Managerial Perspective

FRAMEWORKS VS. POINT PRODUCTS

The original intention of frameworks was to provide a standards-based shell into which both the framework vendor and independent third-party software vendors could offer framework compatible applications for sale. The idea behind the framework was that all of these various applications would be able to talk to each other and share data. From a functional standpoint, frameworks have often fallen short of this goal. From a financial standpoint, although the frameworks themselves were expensive enough, they provide little functionality without the proper combination of added-cost applications. The other major problem faced by framework adopters is the complexity of framework configuration. Delivered with a pricetag of as much as $500,000, frameworks can add little value without a significant amount of complex setup and configuration. This configuration requires highly specialized skills, often brought in on a consulting basis. These consulting and training costs should be considered when purchasing a framework.

As an alternative to frameworks, point products can offer specific solutions at a more reasonable price, with far less configuration complexity. However, point products do not provide the integration capability afforded by the frameworks. The bottom line to the frameworks vs. point products debate is that each is appropriate in certain circumstances. However, network managers would be wise to clearly understand their needs and the characteristics of the various product categories before making a purchasing decision.

Desired Functionality Beyond the choices of architecture, systems administration and network management technology also differ in the level of functionality offered. For example, although most network management software can report on network activity and detect abnormal activities and report alarms, fewer packages can diagnose or fix problems. Among the commonly listed functions that network administrators would like to see delivered by systems administration and network management technology are the following:

- The ability to track the operational status of distributed applications.
- The ability to automate reporting of system status information.
- The ability to automate repetitive system management tasks.
- The ability to integrate application management and systems administration information with network management information.
- The ability to improve application performance by properly responding to system status messages.

Currently Available Technology Enterprise network management systems must be able to gather information from a variety of sources throughout the enterprise network and display that information in a clear and meaningful format. Furthermore, enterprise network management systems are being called on to monitor and manage additional distributed resources such as:

- Workstations and servers
- Distributed applications
- Distributed data management systems

One of the current difficulties with actually implementing enterprise network management systems is a lack of interoperability between different enterprise network management systems and third-party or vendor-specific network management systems. Popular enterprise network management systems that could be considered frameworks or integrated suites include

- HP Openview
- Sun Soft Solstice Enterprise Manager
- Computer Associates' CA-Unicenter TNG (The Next Generation)
- TME 10—IBM/Tivoli Systems (includes IBM System View)
- PatrolView—BMC Software Inc.
- Spectrum enterprise manager—Cabletron

Examples of third-party or vendor-specific network management systems, sometimes known as element managers or point products include:

- 3Com Transcend Enterprise Manager
- Cisco Cisco Works
- Bay Networks Optivity Enterprise. (Nortel)
- Legato Networker
- Cabletron Spectrum Element Manager
- American Power Conversion PowerNet

Among the manifestations of the lack of interoperability between third-party applications and enterprise network management systems are:

- Separate databases maintained by each third-party application and enterprise network management system.
- Redundant polling of agent software to gather performance statistics.
- Multiple agents installed and executed on networked devices to report to multiple management platforms.

The lack of interoperability between different enterprise network management systems makes it difficult if not impossible to:

- Exchange network topology information and maps.
- Exchange threshold performance parameter and alarm information.

The major cause of all of this lack of interoperability is the lack of common APIs, both between different enterprise network management systems, and between a given enterprise network management system and a variety of third-party network management systems. Figure 12-26 illustrates an architectural view of how enterprise network management systems interface to other enterprise network components. Interoperability APIs included in Figure 12-26 are either proposed or under development.

In addition to interoperability issues previously discussed, key functional areas of enterprise network management software are listed in Figure 12-27.

Analysis—Network Analyzers

The only really effective way to diagnose problems with network performance is to be able to unobtrusively peer into the network transmission media and actually see

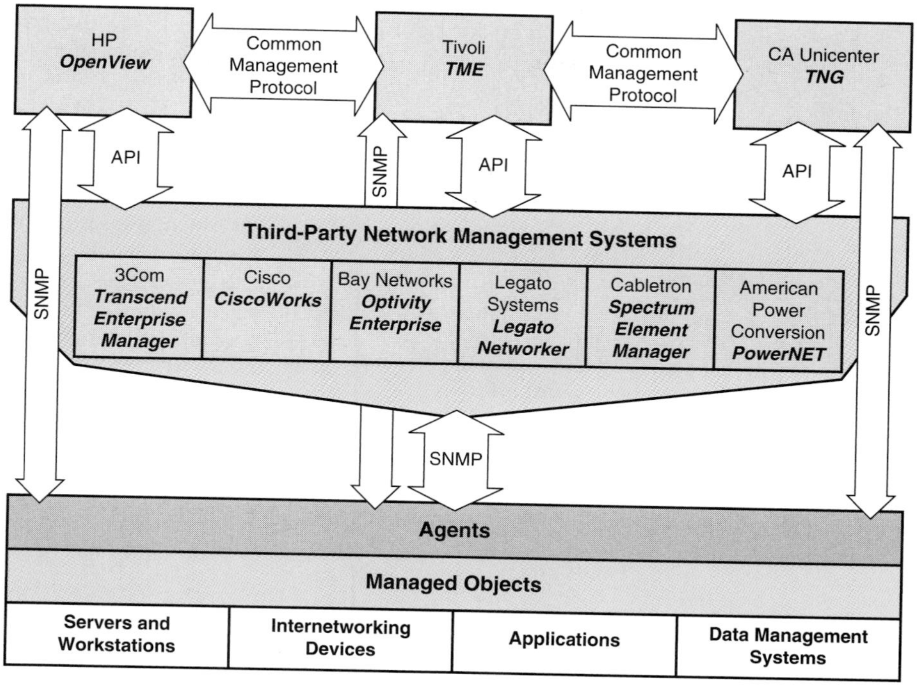

Figure 12-26 Enterprise Network Management System Architecture

the characteristics of the packets of data that are causing performance problems. LAN and WAN **network analyzers** are able to capture network traffic in real time without interrupting normal network transmission. In addition to capturing packets of data from the network, most network analyzers are able to decode those packets, monitor packet traffic statistics, and simulate network traffic through traffic generators. Filtering provided by network analyzers can isolate certain types of protocols or traffic from only particular workstations or servers. Given the multitude of protocols and the tidal wave of packets on a given network, effective filtering capabilities are enormously important to network analyzer usefulness.

Some network analyzers are software based (you supply the PC), hardware-based (come fully installed in their own dedicated PC), or hybrid in which an add-on hardware device with installed software is linked to the notebook PC via the parallel port. Still other analyzers, such as the Network General Sniffer are shipped with a PCMCIA (PC card) Ethernet adapter and software for installation on a limited number of supported notebook computers. Preconfigured sniffers are also available. Network analyzers can also differ in the number of LAN and WAN protocols that can be analyzed, the number of nodes from which traffic can be captured, and the ease of use, understanding, and flexibility of the user interface. Some network analyzers include expert systems that are able to predict oncoming problems based on observed traffic trends.

Network analyzer capabilities are most easily compared and categorized according to the seven-layer OSI model as outlined in Figure 12-28. In some cases, devices are specific to particular layers. For example, layer 1 testers are more commonly known as **cable scanners** or cable testers, whereas devices that test layers 2 through 7 are often called **protocol analyzers.**

Functional Category	Importance/Implication
Operating System Compatibility	• Which operating systems does the enterprise network management system run over? • HP UX • Sun OS • Solaris SPARC • IBM AIX • Windows NT/2000 • How many simultaneous operators of the enterprise network management system are supported? • Can multiple operators be distributed across the enterprise network?
Database Compatibility	• With which databases can the enterprise network management system interoperate? • Oracle • Ingres • SyBase • Informix • Proprietary • DB2 • Flat file
Network Size and Architecture	• Is there a limit to the number of nodes supported? • Can the software map all network architectures? Ethernet, token-ring, FDDI, switched LANs, WANs, ATM • Can mainframes be integrated into the enterprise network management system? • Can IPX and IP devices be managed?
Third-Party Application Support	• How many third-party applications are guaranteed to interoperate with this enterprise network management system?
MIB and Management Protocol Support	• How many different MIBs are supported? MIBs can be both IETF sanctioned or vendor specific. Enterprise network management systems can easily support over 200 different MIBs. • Are management protocols other than SNMP supported? CMIP (common management information protocol), proprietary, SNMP2
Self-Configuration	• To what extent is the enterprise network management software able to self-configure or auto-discover the enterprise network topology? • Can the self-configuration process be customized or controlled?
Cascading or Effect Alarms	• Is the system able to identify and report alarms triggered by other alarms to more easily pinpoint the cause of problems? This capability may be known as event correlation.

Figure 12-27 Functional Categories of Enterprise Network Management Systems

OSI Model Layer	Network Analyzer Functionality
Layer 7—Application	• Some analyzers are able to display actual text and numbers being transmitted across a medium. Since passwords and credit card numbers can be displayed by such a device, it is understandable why network analyzers are sometimes considered a security threat. Displaying protocols from layers 4 through 7 is referred to as embedded protocol decodes.
Layer 6—Presentation	• Embedded protocol decodes
Layer 5—Session	• Embedded protocol decodes
Layer 4—Transport	• Embedded protocol decodes
Layer 3—Network	• Network layer protocols: X.25, ISDN Q.931, IP, IPX, AppleTalk
Layer 2—DataLink	• Hardware Interface Modules (LAN): Ethernet, token ring, switched Ethernet, fast Ethernet, FDDI • Hardware interface modules (WAN): ISDN BRI, DDS, ATM • DataLink WAN Protocols: BiSync, HDLC, SDLC, PPP, LAPB, LAPD, SLIP, frame relay, SNA
Layer 1—Physical **(Also Known As Cable Scanners or Cable)**	• Cable scanners are able to pinpoint cable problems including locations of breaks, short-circuits, mis-wiring, and polarity problems • Although a variety of different media types might be tested, the two most popular are Category 5 unshielded twisted pair and fiber optic cable • Layer 1 protocols: V.35, RS-232, RS-449, 423, 422, 530, T-1 (variety of interfaces)
Testers	Among the key features and measurements of cable testers are the following: • Ambient noise: level of external noise (from fluorescent lights, motors) where a cable is installed • Attenuation: loss of signal strength over the distance traveled through media • Attenuation-to-crosstalk: extent to which a medium resists crosstalk • BERT (bit error rate tester): able to determine percent of received bits received in error • Capacitance: capacity of the medium to store an electrical charge • Continuity: an uninterrupted electrical path along the medium • Impedance: opposition to flow of a signal within a medium, measured in ohms; the lower the impedance, the better the conductor • Loopback device: cable tester function that sends transmitted signal out through medium and back into device for test and measurement • Loop resistance: resistance encountered in completing a full electrical circuit • Injector device: part of cable tester that creates signal, verifies transmission, and manages testing

Figure 12-28 Network Analyzer Functional Capabilities by OSI Model Layer *(figure continues)*

OSI Model Layer	Network Analyzer Functionality
Testers (cont'd)	• NeXT (near-end crosstalk): signals being transmitted on one end overcoming and interfering with the weaker signals being received on the same end • NVP (nominal velocity of propagation): the speed of the data transmission through the tested media compared to speed of light transmission through a vacuum • OTDR (optical time division reflectometer): device that measures the time it takes for light to be reflected through a medium to detect breaks, crimps, etc. • SNR (signal to noise ratio): comparison of signal strength to background noise measured in dB (decibels) • Split pair: when a wire of one pair gets spliced to the wire of an adjacent pair • TDR (time domain reflectometer: able to measure cable lengths, distance to breaks, etc. by reflected electrical signals through a medium • Two way NeXT: measures near-end crosstalk as well as far-end crosstalk, which is crosstalk in same direction as signal • Wire map: verifies pin-to-pin continuity and checks for polarity reversal, short-circuits, and open circuits; displayed graphically

Figure 12-28 Continued

Among the Network Performance Monitoring technology available are the following:

Network/Protocol Analyzer Technology	Vendors
Prism	RADCOM
Surveyor	Shomiti
LANSleuth	Systems & Synchronous
InterWATCH	GN Nettest
HP Internet Advisor	Hewlett Packard
SmartBits Network	NetCom Systems
NetScout Probe	NetScout
Sniffer	Network Associates
Meterware	Technically Elite
Domino	Wandel & Goltermann

Monitoring—Network Baselining Tools

By combining the ability to monitor and capture SNMP, RMON, and RMON2 data from multivendor networking technology with the abilities to analyze the captured data and report on trends and exceptions, **network baselining tools** are able to track network performance over extended periods of time and report on anomalies or deviations from the accumulated baseline data. Also known as **proactive network management tools** or **network trending products,** such tools usually need several weeks of SNMP data to establish realistic baseline network performance averages. Network baselining tools may possess auto-discovery or auto-DNS capabilities that allow them to build graphical representations of networks by monitoring network management traffic. Such tools also exhibit characteristics such as flexible polling and event correlation that allow them to proactively seek information from network-attached devices and assimilate that information with previously collected data to form conclusions and make recommendations. Most network baselining tools share the results of their efforts through a wide variety of predefined and user-defined reports.

Typical reports would offer such statistics such as:

- Current network volume by day, week, and month compared to historical averages
- Network traffic volume leaders by node, actual vs. expected in terms of utilization, errors, or collisions
- Nodes that are in violation of a variety of user-defined thresholds
- Predicted number of days before a node will cross a user threshold
- Nodes whose performance is degrading

Among the Network Performance Monitoring technology available are the following:

Network Performance Monitoring Technology	Vendors
NetMetrix	Agilent
Network Health	Concord
VitalSuite	Lucent
Nextpoint S3	Nextpoint
Trend	DeskTalk Systems
Traffix	3COM

Simulation—Network Modeling and Simulation Tools

Simulation software tools are also sometimes known as **performance engineering** software tools. All simulation systems share a similar trait in that the overall network performance they are able to model is a result of the net effect of a series of mathematical formulas. These mathematical formulas represent and are derived from the actual performance of the circuits and networking equipment that compose the final network design.

The value of a simulation system is in its ability to predict the performance of various networking scenarios otherwise known as **what-if analysis.** Simulation software uses the current network configuration as a starting point and applies what-if scenarios. The benefits of a good network simulation package include:

- Ability to spot network bottlenecks such as overworked servers, network failures, or disk capacity problems.

- Ability to test new applications and network configurations before actual deployment. New applications may run well in a controlled test environment, but may perform quite differently on the shared enterprise network.
- Ability to recreate circumstances to reproduce intermittent or occasional network problems.
- Ability to replicate traffic volume as well as traffic transaction type and protocol mix.

The key characteristics that distinguish simulation software are listed in Figure 12-29.

Among the Network Simulation technology available are the following:

Network Simulation Technology	Vendors
NetRule	Analytical Engines
IT Decision Guru	Opnet Technologies
EcoPredictor	CompuWare
NetCracker Professional	NetCracker Technology

BUSINESS ISSUES

The successful implementation of a network management strategy requires a combination of policy, process, people, and technology. Merely throwing management technology in a vacuum at a management opportunity will not produce the desired results. What these desired results are may be a matter of perspective.

From the top-down, or business-first perspective, senior management may look to the proper management of information resources to enable a competitive advantage and to be able to deploy new network services quickly and as needed at a reasonable cost. Meanwhile, the desired result of business unit management might be that end users can successfully execute those applications that have been implemented to enable business processes and achieve business objectives. Successful execution of applications can be quantified in terms such as transactions per second, mean time between failures, and average response time to database queries. Such guarantees of proper execution and delivery of end-user applications are sometimes quantified in terms of a quality of service (QoS) guarantees. Network management personnel tend to take a more infrastructurecentric approach by concentrating on those elements of the network infrastructure that support the enterprise applications. Examples of such infrastructure components could be server performance, network traffic analysis, internetwork device performance, and WAN analysis.

How can network managers simultaneously deploy new services, control costs, provide competitive advantage, and provide guaranteed quality of service in an increasingly complicated, multivendor, multiplatform, multiprotocol environment? To a great extent, the answer is to combine the processes embedded in the top-down model and the network development life cycle. The top-down model forces the network manager to constantly evaluate business objectives, the nature of the applications that will meet those business objectives, the nature of the data that will support those applications, the functional requirements of the network that will deliver that data, and finally, the configuration of the technology that will provide the required

Network Simulation Software Characteristic	Importance/Explanation
Network Types	• Which different types of networks can be simulated: Circuit-Switched, Packet-Switched, Store-and-Forward, Packet-Radio, VSAT, Microwave?
Network Scope	• How many of the following can the simulation software model either individually or in combination with one another? modems and multiplexers, LANs, Netware only, Internetworks, WANs, MANs?
Network Services	• How many of the following advanced services can be modeled: frame relay, ISDN (BRI and PRI), SMDS, X.25, SONET, ATM?
Network Devices	• Some simulation systems have developed performance profiles of individual networking devices to the point where they can model particular networking devices (bridges, routers, MUXs) made by particular manufacturers
Network Protocols	• In addition to the network transport protocols listed in the analysis and design section, different router-to-router or WAN protocols can have a dramatic impact on network performance. Examples: RIP, OSPF, PPP, BGP
Different Data Traffic Attributes	• As studied in previous chapters, all data traffic does not have identical transmission needs or transmission needs or characteristics. Can the software simulate data with different traits? For example: bursty LAN data, streaming digitized voice or video, real-time transaction-oriented data, batch-oriented file transfer data.
Traffic Data Entry	• Any simulation needs traffic statistics to run. How these traffic statistics may be entered can make a major difference in the ease of use of the simulation system. Possibilities include: manual entry by users of traffic data collected elsewhere, traffic data entered "live" through a direct interface to a protocol analyzer, a traffic generator that generates simulated traffic according to the user's parameters, or auto discovery from SNMP, and RMON data generated by enterprise network management systems
User Interface	• Many simulation software tools now offer easy to use graphical user interfaces with point-and-click network design capability for flexible "what-if" analysis. Some, but not all, produce graphical maps that can be output to printers or plotters. Others require users to learn a procedure-oriented programming language.
Simulation Presentation	• Some simulation tools have the ability to animate the performance of the simulated network in real time, whereas others perform all mathematical calculations and then play back the simulation when those calculations are complete.

Figure 12-29 Network Simulation Software Functionality

network functionality. The network development life cycle forces the network manager to engage in an ongoing process of network monitoring, planning, analysis, design, modeling, and implementation based on network performance.

Network infrastructures must be both flexible and reliable. The ability to have networks change in response to changing business conditions and opportunities is of critical importance to the successful network manager.

Cost Containment

Before a network manager can contain or reduce costs, it is first necessary to have an accurate representation of the source of those costs. Although this may sound like simple common sense, it is easier said than done, and sometimes not done at all. Figure 12-30 lists some practical suggestions for systems administration and network management cost containment.

Outsourcing

In terms of cost control, one of the key weapons in the arsenal of network managers is **outsourcing,** or the selective hiring of outside contractors to perform specific network management duties. Outsourcing is also becoming increasingly necessary for global corporations to cost effectively secure required systems and network support personnel throughout the world. There are several keys to outsourcing success:

- The successful identification of those processes that can be most appropriately outsourced is the first key issue. Which processes do the company really need to manage themselves and which could be more cost effectively managed by a third party? Which skills are worth investing in for the strategic needs of the corporation itself, and which skills are better hired on an as-needed basis? Which tasks can an outsourcer do more cheaply than internal personnel? Which tasks can outsourcers supply new or on-demand expertise for? Which tasks can be outsourced to free corporate personnel for more strategically important issues? Are there tasks that could be more effectively managed by outside experts?
- The successful management of the outsourcing process is required once network management activities have been outsourced as appropriate. It is a good idea to establish communication and evaluation mechanisms as part of the contract negotiation. Issues to be discussed include reporting requirements from the outsourcer to the customer. Among these issues are performance reports on systems the outsourcers are responsible for problem resolution mechanisms, change negotiation mechanisms, performance criteria to be used for outsourcer evaluations, and penalties or bonuses based on outsourcer performance.
- Choosing the right outsourcing provider for the right job. For example, any or all of the following areas may be outsourced, although it is unlikely that any one outsourcer could be considered as expert in all areas: application development, application maintenance, client/server systems migration, data center operation, server management, help desk operations, LAN management, end-user support, PC and workstation management, network

Cost Containment Issue	Importance/Explanation
Take Inventory	• Gather accurate statistics and information as to every device, including hardware and software configuration information, that is currently requiring support • This initial inventory will produce an overall accounting of how many different platforms and standards must be supported
Determine Support Costs	• Perform task analysis on network support personnel to determine how costly personnel are spending their time • Are there too many fires? • Are networking personnel being managed effectively? • What is the cost of supporting multiple platforms and standards? • Are networking personnel required at all corporate sites? • Are more networking personnel required as networks become more complex?
Consolidate and Centralize	• Consolidate support personnel and deliver one-stop-support for end-users • Centralize purchasing authority • Pool network support personnel to optimize use of costly personnel • Implement centralized license metering and software distribution to help standardize software platforms deployed throughout the enterprise • How can network management functions and technology be centralized to cap or reduce the number of network personnel required to support enterprise networks? • Centralize standardized applications on a server rather than allowing desktops to install a wide variety of applications
Support Process Redesign	• Once task analysis has been performed on network support personnel, redesign network support processes to optimize end-user support while minimizing support costs • Use consolidated help desk and trouble ticketing systems to organize user support efforts while minimizing fire-fighting mentality
Standardize	• Standardize on hardware and software platforms, network architectures, network protocols, and network management platforms to simplify management tasks and reduce costs • Standardized desktop platforms will lead to reduced support and maintenance costs • Implement a software version control program so that network support people don't have to deal with multiple versions of multiple software packages

Figure 12-30 Systems Administration and Network Management Cost Containment

monitoring, off-site backup and recovery, remote network access, user training and support, and WAN management. The two most common outsourcing areas are application development and data center operation. Among the key evaluation criteria that could be used to narrow the choices of outsourcing vendors are the following: financial stability, networking skill set, geographic coverage, customer references, and pricing structure.

Flexibility

Delivering network flexibility at a reasonable cost to respond quickly to pending business opportunities has become a priority for many network managers. Most network managers that have achieved success in this area cite a few key underlying philosophies:

- Remove dependencies on customized or proprietary hardware and software.
- Move toward adoption of open protocols and off-the-shelf hardware and software technologies. Examples of open protocols include TCP/IP for network transport and SNMP for management information.
- Adopt network management and systems administration packages that support open APIs and can easily accommodate add-in modules.

How can such an acquisition process be managed? Again the top-down model provides the framework to build the technology analysis grid in which technologies to be considered are measured against requirements as dictated by the upper layers of the top-down model.

SUMMARY

Network management, like other network-related, technology-based solutions, can only be effectively implemented when combined with the proper processes, people, and procedures. As information technology departments have had to become more business-oriented, network management has become more focused on cost containment. Outsourcing is one way in which costs may be contained. However, outsourcing opportunities must be properly analyzed and managed to ensure the delivery of quality network management.

The overall field of network management can be logically segmented into systems administration, which is most concerned with the management of clients, servers, and their installed network operating systems, and enterprise network management, which is more concerned with the elements of the enterprise network that connect these distributed systems. One solution to providing comprehensive systems administration and enterprise management services is known as the consolidated service desk.

Server management, help desk management, configuration management, desktop management, LAN management, and distributed application management are all segments of systems administration. Although each of these segments may contain unique functionality and require unique technology, there is a great deal of integration of functionality and overlap of technology.

Enterprise network management architectures and protocols can vary from one installation to the next. New architectures and protocols are under development to bring some order to the multiplatform, multivendor, multiprotocol mix of today's enterprise networks.

A variety of enterprise network management technology is available to allow network managers to be proactive rather than reactive. Besides a wide variety of enterprise network management integrated suites and element managers, other enterprise network management tools include network analyzers, network baselining tools, network modeling and simulation tools, and network auditing tools.

KEY TERMS

access to kens
ACD
agents
AMS
application MIB
application response measurement
applications management specification
ARM
automatic call distributors
bandwidth management
bulk retrieval mechanism
cable scanners
CIM
common information model
component interface API
computer telephony integration
consolidated service desk
CTI
database MIB
DDM
definition variables
desktop management interface
desktop management task force
digital license certificates
distributed device manager
distributed network probes
DMI
DMI services layer
DMTF
dynamic allocation
electronic software distribution
element managers
enterprise network management
enterprise network management systems
ESD
event management tool
frameworks
global license sharing
HMMP
HMMS
HMOM
hypermedia management protocol
hypermedia management schema
hypermedia object manager
instrumentation
integrated suites
interactive voice response unit
ISO Management Framework
IVRU
knowledge base
LAN Inventory Management Software
latency
license management software
license metering software
license optimization
license pooling
license server
licensing server API (LSAPI)
load balancing
management information base
management information format
management interface API
MIB
MIF
mobile MIF
modified object format
MOF
network analyzers
network auditing tools
network baselining tools
network modeling and simulation tools
network trending products
objects
outsourcing
performance engineering
performance metrics
point products
policy-based management tools
policy-based network management
proactive network management tools
protocol analyzers
queueing
QoS
quality of service
rate control
relationship variables
remote configuration
RMON MIB
RMON probe
RMON2
RMON3
search engine
secure SNMP
server capacity planning
service level agreement
service management
service management architectures
simple management protocol
simple network management protocol
SMP
SNMP
SNMP2
state variables
systems administration
telecommunication management network
traffic shaping
TMN
WBEM
web-based enterprise management
what-if analysis

REVIEW QUESTIONS

1. Differentiate between rate control and queueing as traffic-shaping techniques.
2. Describe circumstances in which bandwidth management could help application performance and those in which it could not.
3. What is service management and how does it differ from IT infrastructure management?
4. What are some of the various categories of service management and what are the roles of each category?
5. How can IT services be effectively costed?
6. What is a service level agreement and why is it important?
7. What is quality of service and how does it relate to IT infrastructure management?

8. Describe some of the business-oriented pressures faced by network managers as well as some of the responses to those pressures.
9. What are some of the advantages and disadvantages to outsourcing?
10. Differentiate between systems administration and enterprise network management.
11. Differentiate between the various layers of management defined by the OSI management framework.
12. What is a consolidated service desk and what unique functionality or advantages does it offer? How does it differ from previous network management technologies?
13. What are some of the important advantages and disadvantages of server management software?
14. Why is it important for help desk software to be able to integrate with call center technology?
15. What is the difference between a knowledge base and a search engine and why is each important?
16. What are the unique features of policy-based management tools and what is the significance of such features?
17. What is the purpose and structure of the DMI?
18. How does desktop management software functionality differ from enterprise network management software functionality?
19. What are the key limitations of distributed application management and how are these limitations overcome?
20. What is the difference between distributed device management and centralized enterprise network management?
21. What disadvantage of centralized network management does distributed network management attempt to overcome?
22. Differentiate among the following terms: agent, MIB, RMON, object, SNMP.
23. What is a distributed network probe and how does it differ from an SNMP agent or an RMON probe?
24. What is CIM and what interoperability issues does it hope to overcome?
25. Describe the relationship between the various components of WBEM.
26. What are some of the shortcomings of SNMP and how are they overcome in SNMP2?
27. Why has SNMP2 not been widely accepted and implemented?
28. Differentiate between RMON and RMON2.
29. Differentiate between point products, frameworks, and integrated suites as alternate enterprise network management technology architectures.
30. What are some of the most important functional characteristics of enterprise network management systems?
31. What are some of the important functional characteristics of network analyzers?
32. What is the difference between a cable scanner and a protocol analyzer?
33. What is the overall purpose or value of a network baselining tool?
34. What is the overall purpose or value of a network modeling and simulation tool?
35. What are some of the ways in which current network configuration information can be loaded into a network modeling and simulation package?
36. What is the overall purpose of network auditing tools?
37. Why are network auditing tools becoming more popular than they once were?

ACTIVITIES

1. Investigate the current status of SNMP2. Is the IETF still working on the standard? What are businesses doing in the meantime? What key issues are the cause of debate?
2. Survey businesses or organizations that have implemented enterprise network management systems. Which enterprise network management system was chosen? Why? Which third-party network management systems (if any) does the enterprise system interface with? What functionality of the enterprise network management system has actually been implemented? What do the organizations think has been the benefit of these systems? What has been the investment in terms of effort to implement and support these systems?
3. Investigate the current state of the desktop management systems market. What percentage of products support the DMI architecture? What percentage of products interface directly to enterprise network management systems? Does one product have a dominant market share? Analyze and report on your results.
4. Research the outsourcing phenomenon. Is outsourcing still increasing in popularity? What has been learned about the advantages and disadvantages of outsourcing? Which types of activities are most often outsourced? Find an organization that has hired an outsourcer and interview them. Find a company that provides outsourcing services and interview them. Do you think outsourcing is a passing phenomenon?

5. Review currently available help desk technology and report on your findings. Find a corporation using help desk software and determine how well the software fits the corporation's business processes and policies. Investigate the technology selection process to determine whether evaluation criteria were established before the purchase.
6. Review currently available policy-based management technology and report on your findings. Find a corporation using policy-based management software and determine how well the software fits the corporation's business processes and policies. Investigate the technology selection process to determine whether evaluation criteria were established before the purchase.
7. Investigate the field of distributed application management. Has the percentage of applications managed via embedded instrumentation increased? Are application developers including more embedded instrumentation within their applications? Survey corporations in your area to determine how many are using or planning to use distributed application management.
8. Investigate the current status and availability of products supporting the WBEM architecture.
9. Investigate the extent to which network simulation, network baselining, and network auditing tools are being used by corporations in your area. What common characteristics do the corporations using these tools share?

CASE STUDY

Software Maker "Rents" System Management Expertise

Corporate IT groups can now rent the systems management expertise they need from a new breed of third-party service company that uses networks as delivery routes.

Software vendor Rogue Wave, for example, pays a monthly fee for start-up StrataSource to monitor and manage the company's Boulder, Colo., data center from afar. Rogue Wave gets round-the-clock coverage without having to find, hire and train three shifts of data center staff. The company has been using this arrangement for about nine months.

Remote management is made possible through a set of small StrataSource programs, called agents, that are loaded onto each of Rogue Wave's three multiprocessor Windows NT servers. The servers host business applications and a Microsoft SQL Server database. The agents schedule various management tasks, monitor an array of operating system and database event logs, and report trend information and problems to StrataSource administrators 1,500 miles away via Internet-based e-mail.

Before turning to StrataSource, Rogue Wave's technical staff was plagued with late night and early morning alarms concerning its NT servers and SQL Server database, says Keith Spitz, director of IT.

"They watch our systems for us 24-7 and try to correct problems any time of the day or night," he says.

StrataSource experts did a thorough, highly detailed assessment of Rogue Wave's servers, database and applications. Then the staff recommended a passel of changes to the systems for improved performance and reliability.

When the software agents alert StrataSource managers of a potential problem, the managers can log on to Rogue Wave's servers. In most cases, the managers can fix the problem or at least start fixing it. "There's a lot they can do as long as NT itself hasn't failed," Spitz says.

The StrataSource staff doesn't simply sit around waiting to be alerted.

"They do proactive monitoring, nightly systems logs, database consistency checks, disk free-space management and so on," Spitz says. "They call us with this information or alert us that we have to increase the size of the database."

The decision to rely on an outsider to watch over critical systems was fairly easy for Rogue Wave. For one thing, managers were impressed by the skills and expertise of the StrataSource staff, which currently includes 22 full-time technicians. StrataSource, based in Menlo Park, Calif., spun off last year from Relational Data Systems, a systems management consultancy in Irvine, Calif.

The economics of using a third party also appealed to Rogue Wave. Although hard numbers are lacking, Spitz's team was able to identify some of the costs associated with every hour of down-time, such as loss of sales momentum and decreased customer service.

"It was mainly a preventative argument—they could prevent problems from ever happening in the first place," Spitz says.

StrataSource charges $45,000 to $65,000 yearly for its service, depending on the number of servers. According to StrataSource President and CEO Thomas Jones, customers get a return on their investment in about two months. That's because hiring round-the-clock staff for even a small data center will cost a customer about $500,000 per year, he says.

Jones claims StrataSource is unique, but other vendors offer similar services. Resonate of Sunnyvale, Calif., offers an Internet management service that is designed to monitor a customer's entire infrastructure: network, servers and applications.

Currently, StrataSource doesn't focus on applications but on their associated databases.

Source: John Cox, "Software maker `rents' system management expertise," *Network World*, vol. 17, no. 4 (January 24, 2000), p. 44.
Copyright © Network World. Reprinted with permission.

BUSINESS CASE STUDY QUESTIONS

Activities

1. Complete a top-down model for this case by gleaning facts from the case and placing them in the proper layer of the top-down model. After completing the top-down model, analyze and detail those instances where requirements were clearly passed down from upper layers to lower layers of the model and where solutions to those requirements were passed up from lower layers to upper layers of the model.
2. Detail any questions about the case that may occur to you for which answers are not clearly stated in the article.

Business

1. What was the business motivation or problem that initiated the search for the implemented solution?
2. What was the productivity impact of the implemented solution?
3. How long has the described solution been implemented?
4. What processes were employed before remote system management was initiated?
5. Were business performance metrics and associated infrastructure performance metrics identified? If so, were they achieved? If not, what might be some suitable business and infrastructure performance metrics for this case?
6. What are some of the economic factors or costs that could be used to evaluate the effectiveness of this solution?
7. What have been typical returns on investment according to the article?

Application

1. What is the role of software agents in this solution?
2. What types of services does the remote system management service offer the software company?

Data

1. How are systems management information and problems reported and transmitted?

Network

1. What underlying network technologies were key to the achievement of stated business objectives?

Technology

1. What specific technologies were employed to deliver the described solution?
2. Describe the interaction between the various technologies employed or planned for this solution.

CHAPTER 13

NETWORK SECURITY

Concepts Reinforced

OSI Model
Top-Down Model
Internet Suite of Protocols Model
Standards and Protocols

Concepts Introduced

Security Policy Development
Security Architecture
Firewalls
Encryption
Active content monitoring
Virus Protection
Security Principles
Authentication
Applied Security Technology
Intrusion Detection

OBJECTIVES

Upon successful completion of this chapter, you should:

1. Understand the many processes involved with the development of a comprehensive security policy and security architecture.
2. Understand the importance of a well-developed and implemented security policy and associated people processes to effective security technology implementation.
3. Understand the concepts, protocols, standards, and technology related to virus protection.
4. Understand the concepts, protocols, standards, and technology related to firewalls.
5. Understand the concepts, protocols, standards, and technology related to authentication.
6. Understand the concepts, protocols, standards, and technology related to encryption.

INTRODUCTION

As interest and activity concerning the Internet has mushroomed, and as telecommuters and remote users are increasingly in need of access to corporate data, network security has become a dominant topic in data communications. As the various processes, concepts, protocols, standards, and technology associated with network security are reviewed in this chapter, it is important to remember the importance of people and their basic honesty and integrity as the underlying foundation for any successful network security implementation. Merely throwing network security technology at a problem without the benefit of a comprehensive, vigorously enforced network security policy including sound business processes will surely not produce desired results. As the saying goes, such action "Is like putting a steel door on a grass hut."

BUSINESS IMPACT

What is the impact on business when network security is violated by on-line thieves? Consider these facts:

- According to federal law enforcement estimates, more than $10 billion worth of data is stolen annually in the United States.
- In a single incident, 60,000 credit and calling card numbers were stolen.
- Fifty % of computer crimes are committed by a company's current or ex-employees.

One of the problems with gauging the true business impact of security breaches is that many companies are understandably reluctant to publicly admit that they have suffered significant losses due to failed network security. Network security is a business problem. It is not merely a network problem or an information technology problem. The development and implementation of a sound network security policy must start with strategic business assessment followed by strong management support throughout the policy development and implementation stages.

However, this management support for network security policy development and implementation cannot be assumed. For example, 71% of executives surveyed stated that they lacked confidence in the ability of their company's network security to fend off attacks from within or without. This stated lack of confidence has not translated into an infusion of support for network security efforts. From the same survey previously referenced, 73% of responding companies had three or fewer employees dedicated to network security, and 55% of respondents said that less than 5% of their information technology budgets went to network security. Enterprise network security goals must be set by corporate presidents and/or board of directors. The real leadership of the corporation must define the vision and allocate sufficient resources to send a clear message that corporate information and network resources are valuable corporate assets that must be properly protected.

SECURITY POLICY DEVELOPMENT

The Security Policy Development Life Cycle

One methodology for the development of a comprehensive network security policy is known as the **security policy development life cycle (SPDLC).** As illustrated in

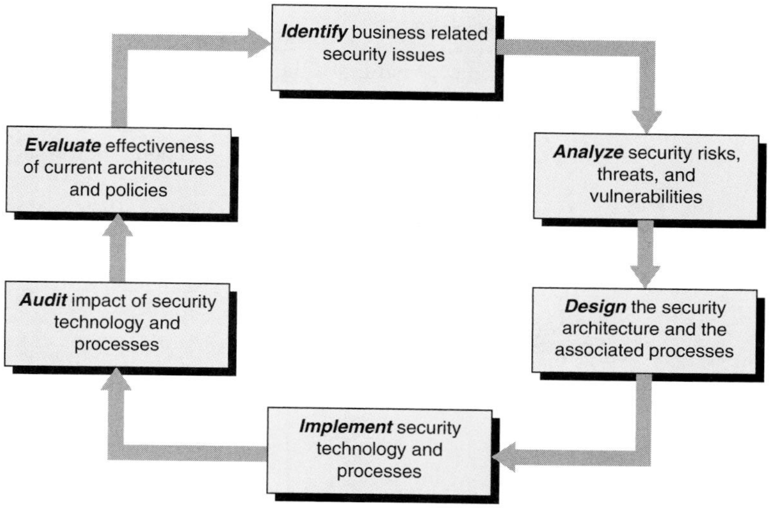

Figure 13-1 The Security Policy Development Life Cycle

Figure 13-1, the SPDLC is aptly depicted as a cycle since evaluation processes validate the effectiveness of original analysis stages. Feedback from evaluation stages causes renewed analysis with possible ripple effects of changes in architecture or implemented technology. The feedback provided by such a cycle is ongoing, but will work only with proper training and commitment from the people responsible for the various processes depicted in the SPDLC.

Each of the processes identified in the SPDLC is explained further in Figure 13-2.

A successful network security implementation requires a marriage of technology and process. Roles and responsibilities and corporate standards for business processes and acceptable network-related behavior must be clearly defined, effectively shared, universally understood, and vigorously enforced for implemented network security technology to be effective. Process definition and setting of corporate security standards must precede technology evaluation and implementation.

Security Requirements Assessment

Proper security requirements assessment implies that appropriate security processes and technology have been applied for any given user group's access to/from any potential corporate information resource. The proper development and application of these security processes and technology require a structured approach to ensure that all potential user group/information resource combinations have been considered.

To begin to define security requirements and the potential solutions to those requirements, a network analyst can create a matrix grid mapping all potential user groups against all potential corporate information resources. An example of such a security requirements assessment grid is illustrated in Figure 13-3. Whereas the user groups and corporate information resources form the row and column headings of the grid, the intersections of these rows and columns are the suggested security processes and policies required for each unique user group/information resource

SPDLC Process	Explanation/Importance
Identification of Business-Related Security Issues	• Security requirements assessment • What do we have to lose? • What do we have worth stealing? • Where are the security holes in our business processes? • How much can we afford to lose? • How much can we afford to spend on network security?
Analysis of Security Risks, Threats, Vulnerabilities	• Information asset evaluation—what do you have that's worth protecting? • Network architecture documentation—What is the current state of your network? • How many unauthorized modems are dialing in? • Identify all assets, threats, and vulnerabilities • Determine risks and create protective measures
Architecture and Process Design	• Logical design of security architecture and associated processes • What must be the required functionality of the implemented technology? • What business processes implemented and monitored by people must complement this security architecture?
Security Technology and Process Implementation	• Choose security technology based on logical design requirements • Implement all security technology with complementary people processes • Increase the overall awareness of network security and implement training • Design ongoing education process for all employees including senior management
Audit Impact of Security Technology and Processes	• Ensure that implemented policy and technology are meeting initial goals • Institute a method to identify exceptions to security policy standards and deal with these exceptions swiftly
Evaluate Effectiveness of Current Architecture and Processes	• Based on results of ongoing audits, evaluate effectiveness of current policy and architecture of meeting high-level goals • Adjust policy and architecture as required and renew the cycle

Figure 13-2 Processes of the Security Policy Development Life Cycle

combination. These security processes refer to not just restrictions to information access imposed on each user group, but also the responsibilities of each user group for security policy implementation and enforcement. Another category of information for each intersection is the security technology to be applied to each unique user group/information resource combination to implement the documented security processes.

User Group	Legacy Data Access	Intranet Access	Internet Inbound Access	Internet Outbound Access	Global E-Mail Access
Corporate HQ employees					
Executives					
I.S. development staff					
Network management					
Network technicians					
Dept. management					
End-users					
Remote branch employees					
Telecommuters					
Trading partners					
Customers					
Vendors					
Browsers					
Casual browsers					
Prospective customers					
Consultants and outsourcers					

Figure 13-3 Security Requirements Assessment Grid

The security requirements assessment grid is meant to provide only an example of potential user groups and information resource categories. The grid should be modified to provide an accurate reflection of each different corporate security environment. Furthermore, the grid should be used as a dynamic strategic planning tool. It should be reviewed on a periodic basis and should be modified to reflect changes in either user groups or information resources. Only through on-going auditing, monitoring, evaluation, and analysis, can a security requirements assessment plan remain accurate and reflective of a changing corporate network environment.

Scope Definition and Feasibility Studies

Before proceeding blindly with a security policy development project, it is important to properly define the scope or limitations of the project. In some cases, this scope may be defined in advance due to a management edict to develop a corporate-wide security policy, perhaps in response to an incident of breached security. In other cases, feasibility studies may be performed in advance of the decision that determines the scope of the full security policy development effort.

The pilot project or feasibility study provides an opportunity to gain vital information on the difficulty of the security policy development process as well as the assets (human and financial) required to maintain such a process. In addition, vital information concerning corporate culture, especially management attitudes, and its readiness to assist in the development and implementation of corporate network security can be gathered. Only after the feasibility study has been completed can one truly assess the magnitude of the effort and assets required to complete a wider scope policy development effort.

One of the key issues addressed during scope definition or feasibility studies is deciding on the balance between security and productivity. Security measures that

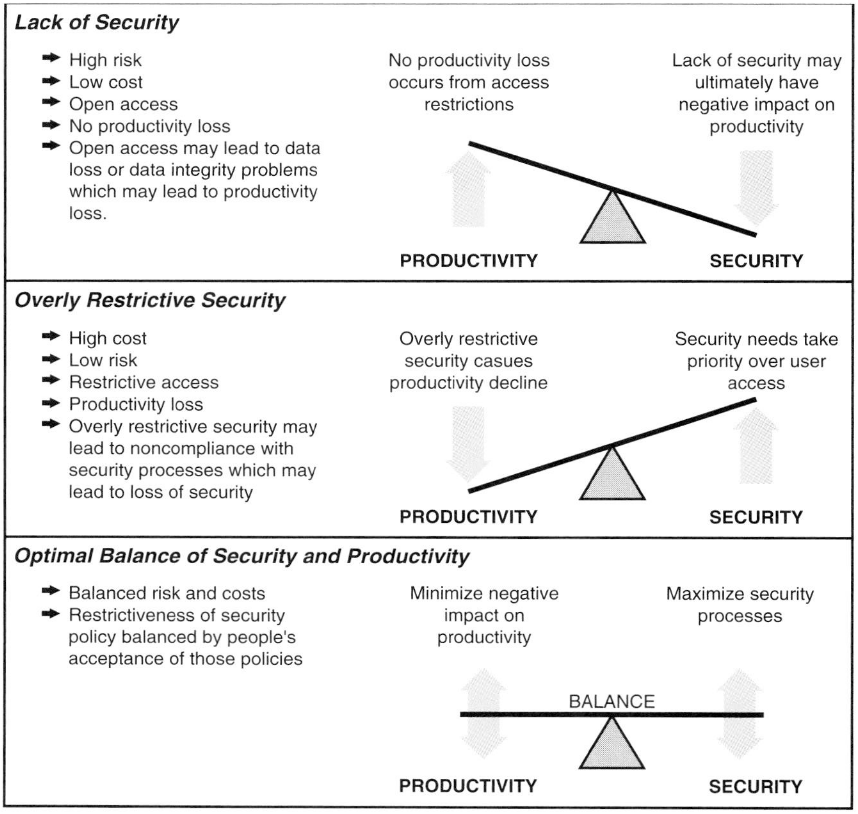

Figure 13-4 Security vs. Productivity Balance

are too stringent can be just as damaging to user productivity as can a total lack of enforced security measures. The optimal balance point that is sought is the proper amount of implemented security process and technology that will adequately protect corporate information resources while optimizing user productivity. Figure 13-4 attempts to graphically depict this balance.

Another issue that is commonly dealt with during the scope definition stage is the identification of those key values that a corporation expects an implemented security policy and associated technology to be able to deliver. By defining these key values during scope definition, policy and associated architecture can be developed to assure that each of these values are maintained. These key values represent the objectives or intended outcomes of the security policy development effort. Figure 13-5 lists and briefly explains the five most typical fundamental values of network security policy development.

Yet another way to organize an approach to security policy and architecture development is to use a model or framework such as **ISO 7498/2,** the **OSI Security Architecture.** This framework maps 14 different security services to specific layers of the OSI 7 Layer Reference Model. The OSI Model Security Architecture can be used as an open framework in which to categorize security technology and protocols, just as the OSI 7 Layer Model can be used to categorize internetworking technology and protocols. Although more specific and varying slightly in terminology from the five fundamental values listed in Figure 13-5, the OSI Security Architecture is consistent

Value of Network Security Policy Development	Explanation/Implication
Identification/Authentication	Want to be assured that users can be accurately identified and that only authenticated users are allowed access to corporate resources
Access Control/Authentication	Want to be assured that even authenticated users are only allowed access to those information and network resources that they are supposed to access
Privacy/Confidentiality	Want to be assured that network based communication is private and not subject to eavesdropping
Data Integrity	Want to be assured that data is genuine and cannot be changed without proper controls
Nonrepudiation	Want to be assured that users cannot deny the occurrence of given events or transactions

Figure 13-5 Fundamental Values of Network Security Policy Development

with and includes all of these fundamental values. As illustrated in Figure 13-6, the ISO 7498-2 Security Architecture could be used as a grid or checklist to assess whether or not the listed security service has been provided for each associated OSI Model layer protocols and by what technologies each service is to be provided. Not all services will necessarily be provided to all suggested layers in all corporate settings. This does not diminish the values of the OSI Security Architecture as a planning framework however.

Assets, Threats, Vulnerabilities, and Risks

Although Figure 13-4 graphically illustrates the theoretical goal of the security policy development process, balance between productivity, and security, how can such a balance actually be delineated within the context of a structured methodology such as the security requirements assessment grid? Most security policy development methodologies boil down to the following six major steps:

1. Identify assets
2. Identify threats
3. Identify vulnerabilities
4. Consider the risks
5. Identify risk domains
6. Take protective measures

The terms used within these six major steps are related in a process-oriented manner.

Assets are corporate property of some value that require varying degrees of protection. In the case of network security, assets most often include corporate data and the network hardware, software, and media used to transport and store that data.

ISO 7498-2 Security Architecture	Associated OSI Model Layer(s)
Peer entity authentication: Verifies that a peer entity in an association is the one claimed. Verification is provided to the next layer	Application, transport network
Data origin authentication: Verifies that the source of the data is as claimed. Verificationis provided to the next layer	Application, transport network
Access control service: This service protects against unauthorized access of network resources, including by authenticated users	Application, transport network
Connection confidentiality: Provides for the confidentiality of all data at a given layer for its connection to a peer layer elsewhere, provided primarily by encryption technology	Application, transport network, data-link
Connectionless confidentiality: Same security as above applied to a connectionless communication environment	Application, transport network, data-link
Selective field confidentiality: Provides for the confidentiality of selected fields of application level information on a connection. For example, a customer's PIN (personal ID number) on an ATM transaction	Application, transport network, data-link
Traffic flow confidentiality: Protects against unauthorized traffic analysis such as capture of source and destination addresses	Application, network physical
Connection integrity with recovery: Provides for data integrity for data on a connection at a given time and detects any modifications with recovery attempted	Application, transport
Connection integrity without recovery: Same as above except no recovery attempted	Application, transport network
Selective field connection integrity: Provides for the integrity of selected fields transferred over a connection and determines whether the fields have been modified in any manner	Application
Connectionless integrity: Provides integrity assurances to the layer above it, and may also determine if any modifications have been performed	Application, transport network
Selective field connectionless integrity: Provides for the integrity of selected fields and may also determine if any modifications have been performed	Application
Nonrepudiation, origin: The recipient of the data is provided with proof of the origin of the data; provides protection against the sender denying the transmission of the data	Application
Nonrepudiation, delivery: The sender is provided with proof that the data was delivered. Protects against attempts by the recipient to falsify the data or deny receipt of the data	Application

Figure 13-6 OSI 7498-2 Security Architecture

Data or Information Classification Because the most common asset to be protected in an information systems environment is the information or data itself, it is important for an organization to adopt an information classification scheme that is easily understood and globally implemented. As will be seen in the discussion of security architectures, properly classified data are an input assumption for a security architecture. If information is not properly classified, the security architecture will be unable to protect it appropriately. Most information classification schemes are based on some variation of the classification scheme used by the Department of Defense:

- Unclassified or public: Information that is readily available to the public. No restrictions as to storage, transmission, or distribution.
- Sensitive: Information whose release could not cause damage to the corporation but could cause potential embarrassment or measurable harm to individuals. Salary and benefits data would be examples of sensitive data.
- Confidential: Information whose release could cause measurable damage to the corporation. Corporate strategic plans and contracts would be considered confidential.
- Secret: Information whose release could cause serious damage to a corporation. Trade secrets or engineering diagrams would be examples of secret information.
- Top Secret: Information whose release could cause grave or permanent damage. Release of such information could literally put a company out of business. Secret formulas for key products would be considered top secret.

Threats are processes or people that pose a potential danger to identified assets. A given asset can be potentially threatened by numerous threats. Threats can be intentional or unintentional, natural or man-made. Network-related threats include hackers, line outages, fires, floods, power failures, equipment failures, dishonest employees, or incompetent employees.

Vulnerabilities are the manner or path by which threats are able to attack assets. Vulnerabilities can be thought of as weak links in the overall security architecture and should be identified for every potential threat/asset combination. Vulnerabilities that have been identified can be blocked.

Once vulnerabilities have been identified, how should a network analyst proceed in developing defenses to these vulnerabilities? Which vulnerabilities should be dealt with first? How can a network analyst determine an objective means to prioritize vulnerabilities? By considering the **risk,** or probability of a particular threat successfully attacking a particular asset in a given amount of time via a particular vulnerability, network analysts are able to quantify the relative importance of threats and vulnerabilities. A word of caution, however. Risk analysis is a specialized field of study, and quantification of risks should not be viewed as an exact science. In identifying the proper prioritization of threats and vulnerabilities to be dealt with, network analysts should combine subjective instincts and judgment with objective risk analysis data.

A **risk domain** consists of a unique group of networked systems sharing both common business function and common elements of exposure. These common business functions and risks are identified during initial risk analysis or assessment. Risk domains are differentiated or isolated from each other based on the differences in risks associated with each risk domain. Because each risk domain has unique business functions and risks, it would stand to reason that each should have a uniquely designed set of technology control processes and technology to offer the required level of security for that particular risk domain. The column headings in Figure 13-3 could potentially be considered as risk domains. Risk domains are important to security analysts because of their use as a means to organize security strategies and technology.

Once the order in which threats and vulnerabilities will be attacked has been determined, **protective measures** are designed and taken that effectively block the vulnerability to prevent threats from attacking assets. Recalling that multiple vulnerabilities (paths) may exist between a given asset and a given threat, it should be obvious that multiple protective measures may need to be established between given threat/asset combinations. Among the major categories of potential protective measures are

- Virus protection
- Firewalls
- Authentication
- Encryption
- Intrusion detection

An explanation of each of these categories of protective measures and examples and applications of each category are supplied in the remainder of this chapter. Figure 13-7 illustrates the relationships between assets, threats, vulnerabilities, risks, and protective measures.

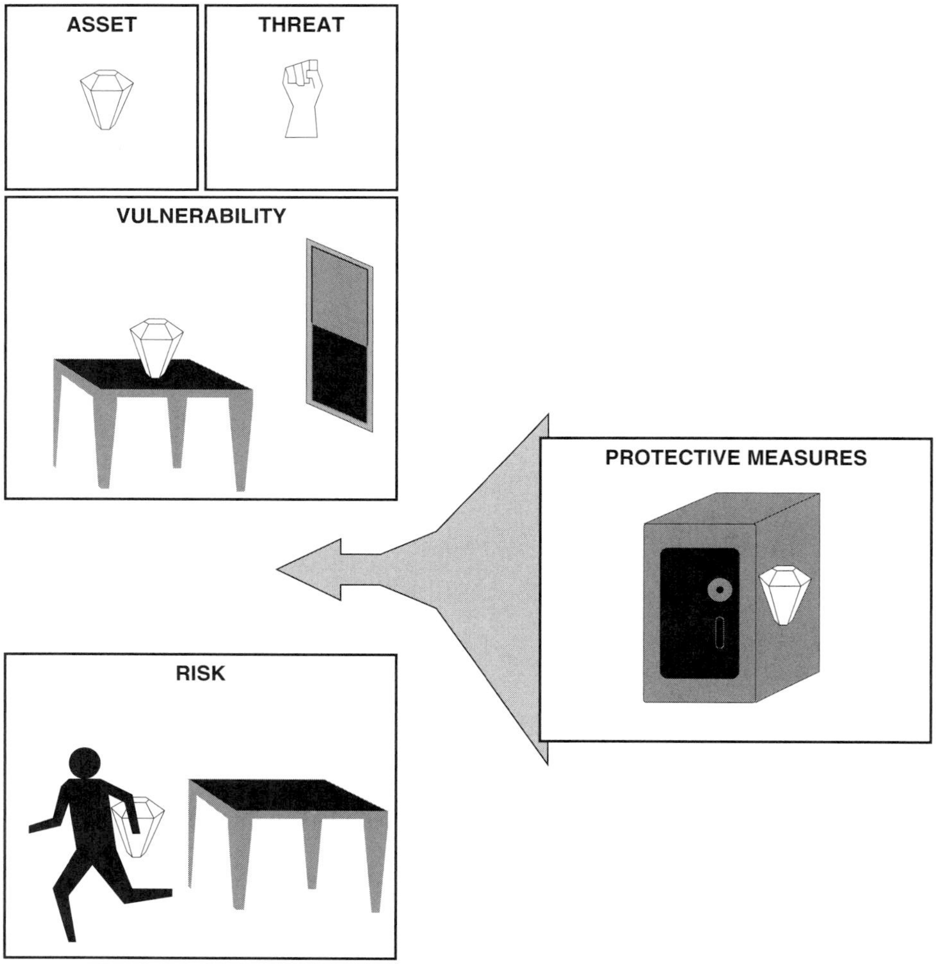

Figure 13-7 Assets, Threats, Vulnerabilities, Risks, and Protective Measures

Attack Strategies

Attack strategies often concentrate on vulnerabilities of specific network operating systems. For example, attack strategies for NetWare servers differ from those intended for Windows NT or Unix servers. Often, such attack strategies are openly shared on the Internet. To understand how to properly protect servers, it is important to use all possible means to discover the server's vulnerabilities. Paying attention to hackers' forums on the Internet is one way to stay on top of these issues.

Figure 13-8 lists some of the more common attack strategies and potential protective measures.

Rather than attacking a specific network operating system, some hackers choose to attack the underlying transport protocols that are used to communicate between servers. The most common transport protocol is **TCP** or **transmission control protocol.** When two servers that are communicating via TCP wish to set up a connection to each other, they engage in a three-step exchange of addresses and confirmations known as a **three-way handshake.** The following two attack strategies take advantage of this three-way handshake in slightly different ways:

- **Denial of service attack:** In the denial of service attack, the hacker flooded the server with requests to connect to other servers that did not exist. The server would try to establish connections with the nonexistent servers and wait for a response while being flooded with thousands of other bogus connection requests. This caused the server to deny service to legitimate users because it was overwhelmed trying to handle the bogus requests
- **Land attack:** The land attack is a variation on the denial of service attack in which the hacker substitutes the targeted server's own address as the address of the server requesting a connection. This causes the attacked server to constantly try to establish connections to itself, thereby often crashing the server.

Network/Information System Attack Strategies	Protective Measure
Masquerading	Authentication
Eavesdropping	Encryption
Man-in-the-Middle-Attack	Digital certificates, digital signatures
Address Spoofing	Firewalls
Data Diddling	Encrypted message digest
Dictionary Attack	Strong passwords, intruder detection
Replay Attack	Time stamping or sequence numbering
Virus Attack	Virus management policy
Trojan Horse Attack	Firewalls
Denial of Service Attack	Authentication, service filtering

Figure 13-8 Network/Information System Vulnerabilities and Protective Measures

Web-Specific Attack Strategies All web servers employ some type of operating or network operating system and are subject to any of the previously mentioned attack strategies. In addition, there are other web specific vulnerabilities and associated attack strategies. To minimize the possibility of attack the following techniques should be considered:

- Eliminate all unused user accounts, especially default accounts such as GUEST.
- Remove or disable all unused services such as FTP, Telnet, and Gopher. If such services must be enabled, consider installing a proxy server or application layer firewall.
- Remove unused Unix command shells and interpreters so that hackers can't access the web server's operating system directly.
- Be sure that permission levels on files and directories are properly set. Default permissions often grant access to too many user groups or individual user accounts.
- Consult WWW security frequently asked questions (FAQ) sites on an ongoing basis to stay up-to-date with current attack strategies and defenses.
- Common gateway interface (CGI) programs are capable of extracting a Unix-based web server's password file.
- Server side includes (SSIs) can be embedded in web pages such as guest books and can instruct a web server to remove an entire directory's contents.

Management Roles and Responsibilities

Once the scope of the security policy development effort has been determined and assets, threats, vulnerabilities, risks, and protective measures have been identified, it is time to secure management buy-in for the security policy development process before proceeding. Results of the feasibility study form the basis of the presentation for management.

Be certain that this presentation for management is objective and that any estimates of financial losses caused by security threats can be substantiated. You will be asking for financial and moral support from management. Your success at securing this success will be a simple matter of management's perception of the cost/benefit analysis of your threat/asset/protective measure scenarios. In other words, have you clearly proven that the costs involved to provide protective measures for corporate assets are outweighed by the benefits of ensuring proper protection of those assets?

Once you have substantiated the existence of security threats and vulnerabilities, propose your plan of action to develop and implement a solution. It is important not to underestimate the manpower and time requirements necessary to scale up your security analysis from a limited scope feasibility study to a full-fledged, enterprise-wide security policy development and implementation process.

What are the responsibilities of executives and managers beyond merely approving budgets and providing policy enforcement? Figure 13-9 provides a brief listing of key executive responsibilities, and Figure 13-10 provides a brief list of management

Executive's Responsibilities for Protection of Information Resources (excerpted from NIST Special Pub. SP 500:169 Executive Guide to the Protection of Information Resources)
1. Set the security policy (acceptable use policy) of the entire organization
2. Allocate sufficient staff, funding, and positive incentives to successfully implement policy
3. State the value of information as a corporate resource to your organization
4. Demonstrate your organization's commitment to the protection of its information resources
5. Make it clear that the protection of the corporate information resources is everyone's responsibility
6. Assign ultimate responsibility for information and network security to specific individuals
7. Require computer and network security and awareness training
8. Hold employees personally responsible for the resources in their care including network access and corporate information
9. Monitor and assess security through external and internal audits (overt and covert)
10. State and follow through on penalties for nonadherence to network security policies
11. Lead by example

Figure 13-9 Executive's Responsibilities for Protection of Information Resources

Management's Responsibilities for Protection of Information Resources (excerpted from NIST Special Pub. SP 500-170, Management Guide to the Protection of Information Resources)
1. Assess the consequences of a security breach in the area for which you are responsible. Risks include inability or impairment to perform necessary duties; waste, misuse, or theft of funds or resources; and internal or external loss of credibility
2. Find the optimal balance between security needs and productivity needs
3. Assess vulnerabilities. How long can each information resource be unavailable before business processes become threatened?
4. Assure data integrity within the systems for which you are responsible
5. Maintain required confidentiality and data privacy
6. Ensure that nonrepudiation and auditing are present in the systems for which you are responsible
7. Adhere by and enforce corporate acceptable use policies

Figure 13-10 Management's Responsibilities for the Protection of Information Resources

responsibilities. Each of these lists was summarized from publications available from the National Institute of Standards and Technology. The NIST publishes a series of Federal Information Processing Standards (FIPS) as well as a series of special publications on a variety of computer and network security-related topics.

Policy Development Process

It is important to reiterate that although technology may well be implemented as part of the protective measures to eliminate vulnerabilities and protect assets from their associated threats, it is the processes and policies associated with each of those protective measures that really determine the success or failure of a network security policy implementation.

Be sure that all effected user groups are represented on the policy development task force. Start from a business perspective with a positive philosophy and a universally supportable goal: "The purpose of this policy is to protect our vital corporate resources to ensure that we can all keep our jobs. This is in our collective best interests...." The emphasis should be on corporate-wide awareness and shared values as to the importance of protecting corporate resources such as information and network access. The policy should not be portrayed as administrative edicts to be obeyed under consequence of termination.

Areas that may be considered for development of acceptable use policies are listed in Figure 13-11.

Potential Areas for Development of Acceptable Use Policies
1. Password protection and management (i.e., it is against corporate policy to write your password on a Post-it note and paste it to your monitor; it is against corporate policy to allow anyone else to use your user ID or password)
2. Software license policy (policies on using illegal or pirated software on corporate machines, policy on use of shareware on corporate machines, policy regarding who is allowed to install any type of software on corporate machines)
3. Virus protection policy (policies re: use of diskettes on network attached PCs, use of corporate computing resources by consultants and outsource personnel, related to Internet access policies)
4. Internet access policy (policies re: acceptable use of Internet for corporate business
5. Remote access policy (policies re: use of single use passwords, Smart Cards, secure transfer of corporate data)
6. E-mail policy (policies re: enrollment in e-mail news groups, personal use of e-mail systems)
7. Policies regarding penalties, warnings, and enforcements for violation of corporate acceptable use policies
8. Physical access policies (policies re: access to locked areas, offices, computer and telecom rooms, combinations for limited access areas, visitor policies, logging out or locking keyboard when leaving office)

Figure 13-11 Potential Areas for Development of Acceptable Use Policies

The list of suggested areas for policy development in Figure 13-11 is not meant to be exhaustive or all-inclusive. Each corporation should amend such a list to include those areas of policy development most appropriate to their corporation. Once policies have been developed for those agreed-on areas, those policies should be measured against the user group/information resource matrix produced in the security requirements assessment grid (Figure 13-3) to be sure that all potential needs for acceptable use policies have been met.

Policy Implementation Process

Once policies have been developed, it is up to everyone to support those policies in their own way. The required support of executives and managers was listed in Figures 13-9 and 13-10, respectively. Having been included in the policy development process, users should also be expected to actively support the implemented acceptable use policies. Users' responsibilities for the protection of information resources are included in Figure 13-12.

Users' Responsibilities for Protection of Information Resources (excerpted from NIST Special Pub. SP 500-171, Computer Users' Guide to the Protection of Information Resources)
1. You are ultimately responsible for protecting the data to which you have access
2. Know which information is especially sensitive or confidential. When in doubt, ask.
3. Information is a valuable, shared corporate asset—as valuable as buildings, stock price, sales, or financial reserves
4. The computing resources that the company provides for you are the property of the company and should only be used for purposes that benefit the company directly
5. Familiarize yourself with the acceptable use policies of your company and abide by them
6. Understand that you will be held accountable for whatever actions you take with corporate computing or networking resources
7. If you ever observe anything or anyone unusual or suspicious, inform your supervisor immediately
8. Never share your password or user ID with anyone
9. If you are allowed to choose a password, choose one that could not be easily guessed
10. Always log off before leaving your computer or terminal
11. Keep sensitive information, whether on diskettes or on paper, under lock and key
12. Don't allow others to look over your shoulder if you are working on something confidential
13. Don't smoke, eat, or drink near computer equipment
14. Know the location of the nearest fire extinguisher
15. Backup your data onto diskettes early and often

Figure 13-12 Users' Responsibilities for the Protection of Information Resources

Organizing Policy Implementation: The Security Architecture Once security policy has been determined, appropriate technology and associated processes must be implemented to execute that policy. It is difficult to organize all security technologies and processes and map them to security policies without overlooking something. What is required is an overall security model or architecture that starts with business drivers and ends with a combination of available security tools, mapping policy to processes and technology controls.

A security architecture implies an open framework into which business-driven security processes and requirements can be quickly and easily organized, now or in the future. Security architectures map clearly justified security functional requirements to currently available security technical solutions. Security architectures imply that standardized security solutions have been predefined for a given corporation's variety of computing and network platforms. In this manner, security solutions are implemented consistently across an enterprise without the need for security personnel to become personally involved in every implementation. The use of a well-designed security architecture should provide both a more secure and a more cost-effective information systems environment.

Information systems architectures in general and information security architectures in particular separate business needs from the logical requirements that meet those business needs and the physically implemented technology that meets those logical requirements. In doing so, the architecture enables security analysts to separately analyze these major elements of the security architecture while understanding the relationship among the various layers of the architecture. This allows the architecture to stand the test of time by allowing changing business drivers to be mapped to changing logical requirements to be mapped to changing security technology without having to change the overall architecture into which all of these changing elements are organized. As new threats or vulnerabilities are discovered, a well-designed security architecture should provide some structure to the manner in which protective measures are designed to counteract these new threats and vulnerabilities.

Information security architectures could, and perhaps should, vary from one organization to the next. Figure 13-13 is a representative example of a security architecture that clearly maps business and technical drivers through security policy and processes to implemented security technology. One or more of the layers of the security architecture could be subsequently expanded into more detailed multilayer models. Figure 13-14 explains each layer of the representative architecture in terms of the significance of each layer, as well as the relationships or impacts between layers.

At this point, an effective security policy, including associated technology and processes, should have been developed and be ready for implementation. If user involvement was substantial during the policy development stage and if buy-in was assured at each stage of the policy development, then implementation stands a better chance of succeeding. However, policy implementation will inevitably force changes in people's behaviors, which can cause resistance. Resistance to change is both natural and to be expected. Handled properly, resistance to change can be just a temporary implementation hurdle. Handled improperly, it can spell disaster for an otherwise effective network security policy. Figure 13-15 summarizes some of the key behaviors and attitudes that can help ensure a successful network security policy implementation.

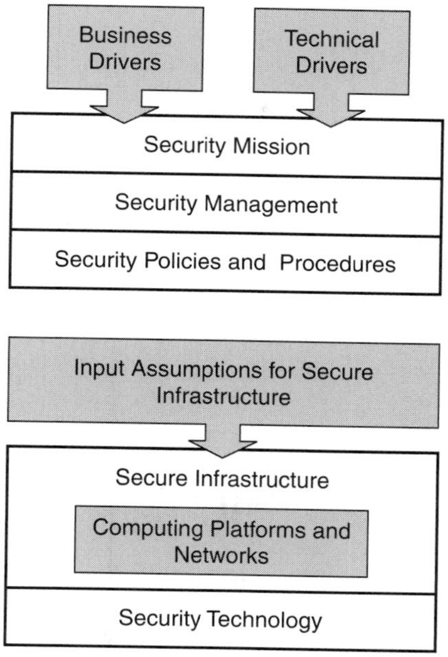

Figure 13-13 Representative Security Architecture

Auditing

Manual Audits To judge whether or not a corporate security policy is successful, it must be audited and monitored on a continual basis. Auditing as it relates to network security policy may be either automated or manual. Manual audits can be done by either internal or external personnel. Manual audits serve to verify the effectiveness of policy development and implementation, especially the extent to which people understand and effectively execute their assigned processes in the overall corporate security policy. Manual audits are also referred to as **policy audits** or **off-line** audits. Consulting firms that specialize in network security have generated some rather startling results during security audits when they were able to gain entry to a corporate president's office, access her e-mail account, and send e-mail to the chief information officer informing him he was fired for his lack of effective security policy. As it turns out, the CIO was not really fired. In fact, it was poorly designed and poorly executed people processes that allowed this incident to occur. A receptionist was solely responsible for physical access security to the executive offices and the president left her PC logged in.

Automated Audits Automated audits, otherwise known as **event detection** or **real-time audits** depend on software that is able to assess the weaknesses of your network security and security standards. Most audit software depends on capturing large amounts of event data and then filtering that data for exceptional or unusual events. Captured events can be telephone calls, login attempts, network server direc-

Security Architecture Layer	Importance/Implication/Examples
Business and Technical Drivers	Business drivers are inherited from the corporation's overall strategic business plan. The security architecture must play its part in the achievement of the corporation's overall business mission. Technical drivers are enablers or limiting factors that determine the extent to which technology can contribute to the security architecture's achievement of the overall corporate business mission.
Security Mission	The security mission is the definition of the role of the security architecture as driven by the business and technical drivers. An example would be: "To enable secure information sharing and protect information resources throughout the corporate enterprise."
Security Management	Security management bridges the gap between the high-level security mission statement and the policies and procedures that actually implement and achieve the security mission. These are the parts of the security architecture that do not change, even though security policies and procedures may change. Examples include communications mechanisms, educational programs, and other efforts that ensure that security policies and procedures are well understood, widely observed, and strictly enforced.
Security Policies and Procedures	Security policies and procedures are meant to protect identified assets from identified threats by neutralizing identified vulnerabilities through the implementation of appropriate protective measures.
Input Assumptions for Secure Infrastructure	Examples of input assumptions might be the following: • All information will be properly classified before entering the secure infrastructure so that the secure infrastructure is able to handle each type of information classification accordingly. • All users will be properly categorized in terms of what resources they have a right to access so that if the secure infrastructure properly authenticates an individual, it will know what resources that individual can access.
Secure Infrastructure	The secure infrastructure is a combination of technology and associated procedures applied to a corporation's computing platforms and networks.
Computing Platforms and Networks	Since vulnerabilities are specific to different computing platforms and networks, proper technology controls must be applied to specific computing platforms and networks. Likewise, security analysts must be constantly vigilant, looking for new vulnerabilities on any installed computing platform or network.
Security Technology	Security technology, sometimes known as the security toolkit, is the constantly changing combination of potential solutions that can be implemented to achieve a secure infrastructure. As vulnerabilities change, security technology constantly changes to keep pace. It is essential for security analysts to be students of security technology, constantly seeking the best and most effective security solutions for their corporations.

Figure 13-14 Layers of the Security Architecture

Critical Success Factors for Network Security Policy Implementation
1. The policy must have been developed in a team effort with all affected parties feeling that they had input to the process. Policy development must be a bottom-up, grassroots effort rather than a top-down, administration imposed effort.
2. The security policy must be coordinated with and in compliance with other corporate policies re: disaster recovery, employee rights, and personnel policies.
3. It is important to ensure that no part of the security policy is illegal. This is particularly important for corporations that do business in multiple states or countries. For example, in some localities, it is illegal to monitor phone conversations of employees.
4. Technology must not be promoted as a security solution. Dedicated people, implementing well-designed processes on a consistent basis, combined with the effective use of technology, are the only means to a true security solution.
5. The network security policy must not be put on a shelf and forgotten. Security awareness must be a priority, and ongoing auditing and monitoring should ensure that security remains at the forefront of people's thoughts.
6. An attitude must be fostered that security threats are indeed real and that they can and will happen in the company if people do not follow corporate security procedures.
7. Management must be ready to impose prescribed penalties on employees who fail to follow corporate security policy. To do otherwise will quickly send the message that the security policy is a farce.
8. Corporate culture may indeed need to change. This is especially true for growing companies that started out as very open, entrepreneurial cultures. Such companies often have difficulty adjusting to structure and controlled access to corporate resources imposed by corporate security policies.

Figure 13-15 Critical Success Factors for Network Security Policy Implementation

tory access attempts, access to Internet news groups or web sites, or remote access attempts via dial-up lines. To generate meaningful exception reports, audit software allows users to create filters that will allow only those events deemed exceptional by the users to appear on reports.

Some automated audit tools are able to analyze the network for potential vulnerabilities and make recommendations for corrective action, whereas others merely capture events so that you can figure out who did what and when after a security breach has occurred. Other automated tools are able to benchmark or compare events and security-related parameters to a set of government-issued security standards known as C2 or Orange Book standards (officially known as the Trusted Computer System Evaluation Criteria or TCSEC) and issue a report card or "Top 10 Risks" list as to how well a given network measures up. The C2 standards and other security standards are explained later in the chapter. Some audit tools are able to save previous audit data as baseline information so that network analysts and security specialists can measure improvement in network security including the impact of any security improvements that may have been implemented.

Security Probes and Intrusion Detection Systems Rather than passively gathering network statistics like auditing tools, **security probes** (otherwise known as vulnerability scanners) actively test various aspects of enterprise network security and report results and suggest improvements. **Intrusion detection systems** (sometimes referred to as host-based intrusion detection systems) monitor systems, ports, files and applications. When an unauthorized access or intrusion is detected, the software can respond with alarms. In addition to merely detecting intrusions, such as unsuccessful login attempts over a preset limit, some tools are also able to provide automated responses, or countermeasures to these intrusion attempts. Also, some of the more sophisticated intrusion detection systems are dynamic or self-learning and are able to become better at detecting intrusions or to adjust exception parameters as they gain experience in a given enterprise network environment. Examples of host-based intrusion detection systems include CyberCop from Network Associates, Kane Security Monitor from Security Dynamics, and Intruder Alert from Axent Technologies.

Network-based intrusion detection systems often use network traffic probes distributed throughout a network to identify traffic patterns that may indicate some type of attack may be underway. Rather than wait until such attacks reach a particular host, network-based intrusion detection systems keep a big picture view of overall suspicious network activity. Examples of network-based intrusion detection systems include Cisco Secure from Cisco Systems, NetProwler from Axent Technologies, and Real Secure from Internet Security Systems.

Real Secure also acts as a security probe that looks for as many as 600 known security weaknesses on firewalls, routers, Unix machines, Windows machines, or Windows NT machines or any other device that uses TCP/IP as its transport protocol stack. RealSecure combines network-analyzer, attack signature recognition, and attack response in a single unit. If an attack is detected, Real Secure is able to terminate the connection by spoofing both hosts involved in the communication.

A security probe known as **Security Analyzer Tool for Analyzing Networks (SATAN)** is able to probe networks for security weak spots. The SATAN probe is especially written to analyze Unix- and TCP/IP-based systems, and once it has found a way to get inside an enterprise network, it continues to probe all TCP/IP machines within that enterprise network. Once all vulnerabilities have been found, SATAN generates a report that not only details the vulnerabilities found, but also suggests methods for eliminating the vulnerabilities. SATAN tries to start TCP/IP sessions with target computers by launching applications such as Telnet, FTP, DNS, NFS, and TFTP. It is able to target specific computers because all TCP/IP-based machines use the same 16-bit address or port number for each of these previously mentioned applications. This application-specific port address plus the 32-bit IP address is known as a socket. Although SATAN was developed as a tool for network managers to detect weaknesses in their own networks, it is widely available on the Internet and can easily be employed by hackers seeking to attack weaknesses in target networks of their choice. Because of the potential for unscrupulous use of SATAN, tools such as Courtney, from the Department of Energy's Computer Incident Advisory Capability, and Gabriel, from Los Altos Technologies, are able to detect the use of SATAN against a network and are able to trigger alarms.

Like intrusion detection systems, vulnerability scanners may be host-based or network-based. Examples of host-based vulnerability scanners include Kane Security Analyst from Security Dynamics, ESM from Axent Technologies, and System Scanner from Internet Security Systems. Some host-based vulnerability scanners are customized to particular network operating systems or databases such as NOSAdmin for NetWare and NOSAdmin for NT from Bindview Development, and SFProtect for Enterprise SQL Server from Agilent Technologies. Examples of network-based vulnerability scanners include CyberCop Scanner from Network Associates, Internet Scanner from Internet Security Systems, and NetRecon from Axent Technologies.

VIRUS PROTECTION

Virus protection is often the first area of network security addressed by individuals or corporations. A comprehensive virus protection plan must combine policy, people, processes, and technology to be effective. Too often, virus protection is thought to be a technology-based quick fix. Nothing could be further from the truth. A survey conducted by the National Computer Security Association revealed the following:

- Computer viruses are the most common microcomputer security breach.
- Ninety percent of the organizations surveyed with 500 or more PCs experience at least one virus incident per month.
- Complete recovery from a virus infection costs an average of $8300 and 44 hours over a period of 22 working days.
- In January 1998 there were over 16,000 known viruses, with as many as 200 new viruses appearing per month. There were over 2000 macro viruses, with this category experiencing exponential growth.

Virus Categories

Although definitions and parameters may vary, the term *computer virus* is generally used to describe any computer program or group of programs that gains access to a computer system or network with the potential to disrupt the normal activity of that system or network. Virus symptoms, methods of infection, and outbreak mechanisms can vary widely, but all viruses do share a few common characteristics or behaviors:

- Most viruses work by infecting other legitimate programs and causing them to become destructive or disrupt the system in some other manner.
- Most viruses use some type of replication method to get the virus to spread and infect other programs, systems, or networks.
- Most viruses need some sort of trigger or activation mechanism to set them off. Viruses may remain dormant and undetected for long periods.

Viruses that are triggered by the passing of a certain date or time are referred to as **time bombs,** and viruses that require a certain event to transpire are known as **logic bombs.** Logic bombs in event-driven or visual programs may appear as a button supposedly providing search or some other function. However, when the button is pushed, the virus is executed, causing a wide range of possibilities from capturing passwords to wiping out the disk drive. One of the ways in which viruses are able to infect systems in the first place is by a mechanism known as a **trojan horse.** In such a scenario, the actual virus is hidden inside an otherwise benign program and delivered to the target system or network to be infected. The Microsoft Word Macro (or Concept) Virus is an example of a trojan horse virus because the virus itself is innocently embedded within otherwise legitimate Word documents and templates. **Macro viruses** can infect Macintosh as well as Windows-based computers and are not limited to Word, but can also infect files through such programs as Corel WordPerfect, Lotus WordPro, and Microsoft Excel.

A particular disruptive variation of the macro virus affecting Word 97 and Word 2000 documents was known as the Melissa virus. Launched in March of 1999, the Melissa virus arrived via e-mail with the message, "Here is the document you asked for ... don't show anyone else.;-)." Once opened, the virus would replicate itself and e-mail itself via mail servers to the first 50 users in the Microsoft Outlook local address book with the subject line "Important message from [username]." Because the username was probably known to the intended recipient, it was more likely to be opened, thereby perpetuating the virus infection. Before long, an estimated 100,000 computer systems were infected, and entire corporate e-mail systems were forced to shut down. Virus protection experts quickly posted fixed to the virus, and the FBI launched the largest Internet suspect hunt ever. David Smith of Aberdeen, NJ, was arrested for and has admitted to creating the Melissa virus but contends that he never intended to do anything wrong.

Although new types of viruses will continue to appear, Figure 13-16 lists the major virus categories and gives a brief explanation of each.

Antivirus Strategies

An effective antivirus strategy must include policy, procedures, and technology. Policy and procedures must be tied to those vulnerabilities that are specific to virus infection. Viruses can attack systems at the client PC, the server PC, or the network's connection to the Internet. By far, the most common physical transport mechanism for the spread of viruses is the diskette. Effective antivirus policies and procedures must first focus on the use and checking of all diskettes before pursuing technology-based solutions. In fact, 61% of all viral infections are caused by infected diskettes. However, the macro viruses that infect Word documents and Excel spreadsheets are becoming a predominant virus transport mechanism because of the frequency at which such documents are shared between co-workers and across networks as e-mail attachments. Figure 13-17 lists some examples of antivirus strategies, although this list should be tailored for each situation and reviewed and updated on a regular basis.

As collaborative applications such as groupware have become more commonplace in corporations, a new method of virus infection and virus reinfection has emerged. Because groupware messages and data are stored in a shared database, and because documents can be distributed throughout the network for document conferencing or workflow automation, the virus is spread throughout the network. Moreover, because groupware servers usually replicate their databases to ensure that all servers on the network are providing consistent information, the virus will continue to spread. Even if the virus is eliminated from the originating server, responses from still-infected replicated servers will reinfect the original server as the infection/reinfection cycle continues. Virus scanning software specially designed for groupware databases has been designed to combat this problem. Norton AntiVirus for Lotus Notes is an example of such a specialized antivirus tool. Figure 13-18 illustrates the collaboration software infection/reinfection cycle.

Virus Category	Explanation/Implication

File Infectors	• Attach themselves to a variety of types of executable files.
	• Subcategories of file infectors include the following:
	  • Direct action file infectors infect a program each time it is executed
	  • Resident infectors use the infected program to become resident in memory from where they attack other programs as they are loaded into memory
	  • Slow infectors infect files as they are changed or created thus assuring that the infection is saved
	  • Sparse infectors seek to avoid detection by striking only certain programs on an occasional basis.
	  • Companion viruses create new infected programs that are identical to the original uninfected programs
	  • Armored viruses are equipped with defense mechanisms to avoid detection and antivirus technology. **Polymorphic viruses** change their appearance each time an infected program is run to avoid detection.

System/Boot Infectors	• Attack the files of the operating system or boot sector rather than application programs • System/boot sector viruses are memory resident
Multipartite Viruses	• Also known as boot-and-file viruses, attack both application files and system and boot sectors
Hostile Applets	• Although specific to web technology and Java-embedded programs, hostile applets could still be considered viruses. **Attack applets** are intent on serious security breaches, whereas **malicious applets** tend to be annoying rather than destructive. Hostile applets are unknowingly downloaded while web surfing. Hostile ActiveX components present a similar threat. Some people would argue that such malicious code is not technically a virus. However, there is little doubt as to the potential destructiveness of the code.
E-mail Viruses	• Some sites report that 98% of viruses are introduced through e-mail attachments. • Antivirus software must be version specific to the e-mail messaging system (i.e., Exchange Server 5.5) • Such software scans files after decryption before releasing the files to the users, and questionable files are quarantined.
Cluster/File System Viruses	• Attack the file systems, directories, or file allocation tables so that viruses can be loaded in to memory before requested files

Figure 13-16 Virus Categories

Managerial Perspective

Antivirus awareness and a mechanism for quickly sharing information regarding new virus outbreaks must accompany the deployment of any antivirus technology. These antivirus awareness and communications mechanisms must be enterprise wide in scope rather than being confined to a relatively few virus-aware departments. Procedures and policies on how and when antivirus technology is to be employed must be universally understood and implemented.

Antivirus Strategies
1. Identify virus infection vulnerabilities and design protective measures.
2. Install virus scanning software at all points of attack. Assure that network-attached client PCs with detected viruses can be quarantined to prevent the spread of the virus over the network.
3. All diskettes must be scanned at a stand-alone scanning PC before being loaded onto network-attached clients or servers.
4. All consultants and third-party contractors are prohibited from attaching notebook computers to the corporate network until the computer has been scanned in accordance with security policy.
5. All vendors must run demonstrations on their own equipment.
6. Shareware or downloaded software should be prohibited or controlled and scanned.
7. All diagnostic and reference diskettes must be scanned before use.
8. Write protect all diskettes with .exe, .com files.
9. Create a master boot record that disables writes to the hard drive when booting from a floppy or disable booting from a floppy, depending on operating system.

Figure 13-17 Antivirus Strategies

Antivirus Technology

Since viruses can attack locally or remotely attached client platforms, server platforms, and/or the entrance to the corporate network via the Internet, all four points of attack must be protected. Viruses must be detected and removed at each point of attack. **Virus scanning** is the primary method for successful detection and removal. However, virus scanning software most often works off a library of known viruses, or more specifically the unique digital signatures of these viruses, but new viruses are appearing at the rate of nearly 200 per month. Because of this, it is important to buy virus scanning software whose vendor supplies updates of virus signatures at least once per month. As virus introduction accelerates, it is likely that virus signature updates to virus scanning software will become more frequent as well. Vendors are currently updating virus signatures files every 4 hours, with hourly updates expected in the near future. Also, some virus scanners can remove a virus from an infected file, while others merely destroy the infected file as a remedy. Because virus scanners are really scanning for known digital signatures or viruses, they are sometimes referred to as **signature scanners.**

In an effort to be more proactive than reactive, **emulation technology** attempts to detect as yet unknown viruses by running programs with a software emulation program known as a **virtual PC.** In so doing, the executing program can be examined in a safe environment for any unusual behavior or other tell-tale symptoms of resident viruses. The advantage of such programs is that they identify potentially unknown viruses based on their behavior rather than by relying on identifiable signatures of known viruses. Because of their ability to monitor behavior of programs, this category of antivirus technology is also sometimes known as **activity monitors** or **heuristic analysis.** Such programs are also capable of trapping encrypted or polymorphic viruses that are capable of constantly changing their identities or signatures.

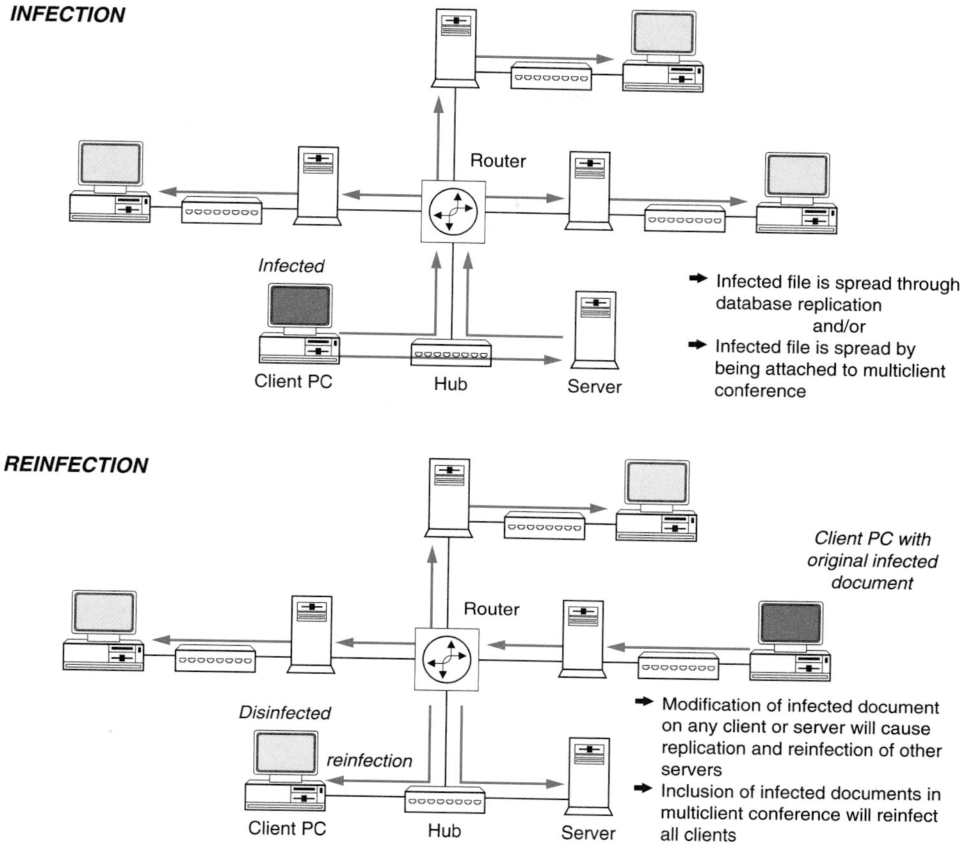

Figure 13-18 Collaborative Software Infection/Reinfection Cycle

In addition, some of these programs are self-learning, thereby increasing their knowledge of virus-like activity with experience. Obviously, the key operational advantage is that potentially infected programs are run in the safe, emulated test environment before they are run on actual PCs and corporate networks.

A third category of antivirus technology, known as **CRC checkers** or **hashing checkers,** creates and saves a unique cyclical redundancy check character or hashing number for each file to be monitored. Each time that file is subsequently saved, the new CRC is checked against the reference CRC. If the CRCs do not match, then the file has been changed. These changes are then evaluated by the program to determine the likelihood that the change was caused by a viral infection. The shortcoming of such technology is that it is only able to detect viruses after infection, which may already be too late. Perhaps as a solution to this problem, **decoys** are files that are allowed to become infected to detect and report on virus activity.

To identify viruses and malicious content such as Java applets or Active X controls that may be introduced via Internet connectivity, a new defensive tool category known as **active content monitors** is able examine transmissions from the Internet in real time and identify known malicious content based on contents of reference or definition libraries.

Antivirus software is now available for clients, servers, e-mail gateways, web browsers, firewalls, and groupware. It is even being installed in the firmware on net-

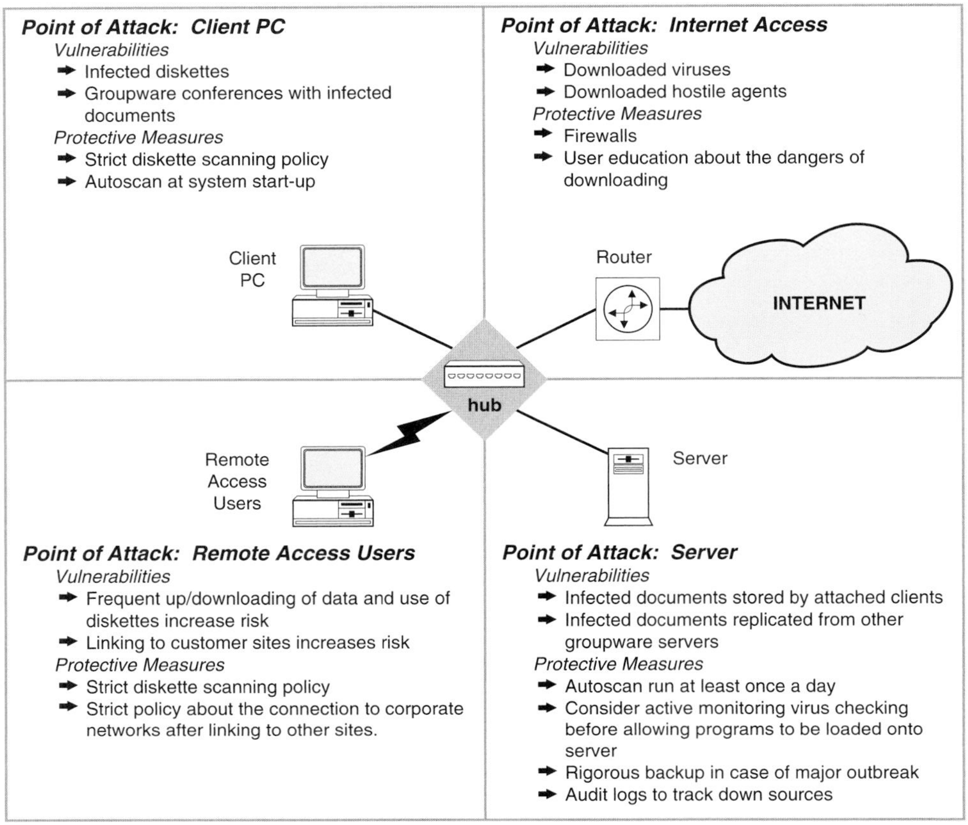

Figure 13-19 Virus Infection Points of Attack and Protective Measures

work interface cards. Overall, the trend is to catch Internet-borne viruses before they reach servers and clients computers by installing virus protection technology at the Internet gateways capable of scanning FTP, HTTP, and SMTP traffic. Antivirus products are now certified by the **National Computer Security Association (NCSA),** which also maintains a list of known or sighted viruses. Figure 13-19 illustrates the typical points of attack for virus infection as well as potential protective measures to the combat those attacks.

FIREWALLS

When a company links to the Internet, a two-way access point out of as well as *into* that company's confidential information systems is created. To prevent unauthorized access from the Internet into a company's confidential data, specialized software known as a **firewall** is often deployed. Firewall software usually runs on a dedicated server that is connected to, but outside of, the corporate network. All network packets entering the firewall are filtered or examined to determine whether those users have authority to access requested files or services and whether the information contained within the message meets corporate criteria for forwarding over the internal network. Firewalls provide a layer of isolation between the inside network and the outside network. The underlying assumption in such a design scenario is that all of the threats come from the outside network. As evidenced by the statistic cited earlier, this is often not the case. In addition, outside threats may be able to circumvent the firewall entirely if dial-up modem access remains uncontrolled or unmonitored. In addition, incorrectly implemented firewalls can actually exacerbate the situation by creating new, and sometimes undetected, security holes.

Firewall Architectures

Another difficulty with firewalls is that there are no standards for firewall functionality, architectures, or interoperability. As a result, users must be especially aware of how firewalls work to evaluate potential firewall technology purchases. Firewall functionality and architectures are explained in the next few sections.

Packet Filtering Every packet of data on the Internet is uniquely identified by the source address of the computer that issued the message and the destination address of the Internet server to which the message is bound. These addresses are included in a portion of the packet called the header.

A **filter** is a program that examines the source address and destination address of every incoming packet to the firewall server. Network access devices known as routers are also capable of filtering data packets. **Filter tables** are lists of addresses whose data packets and embedded messages are either allowed or prohibited from proceeding through the firewall server and into the corporate network. Filter tables can also limit the access of certain IP addresses to certain directories. This is how anonymous FTP users are restricted to only certain information resources. It obviously takes time for a firewall server to examine the addresses of each packet and compare those addresses to filter table entries. This filtering time introduces **latency** to the overall transmission time. A filtering program that only examines source and destination addresses and determines access based on the entries in a filter table is known as **a port level filter, network level filter,** or **packet filter.**

Packet filter gateways can be implemented on routers. This means that an existing piece of technology can be used for dual purposes. However, maintaining filter tables and access rules on multiple routers is not a simple task, and packet filtering does have its limitations in terms of the level of security it is able to provide. Dedicated packet-filtering firewalls are usually easier to configure and require less in-depth knowledge of protocols to be filtered or examined. Packet filters can be breached by hackers in a technique known as **IP spoofing.** Since packet filters make all filtering decisions based on IP source and destination addresses, if a hacker can make a packet appear to come from an authorized or trusted IP address, then it can pass through the firewall.

Application Gateways **Application level filters,** otherwise known as **assured pipelines, application gateways,** or **proxies,** go beyond port level filters in their attempts to prevent unauthorized access to corporate data. Whereas port level filters determine the legitimacy of the party asking for information, application level filters ensure the validity of what they are asking for. Application level filters examine the entire request for data rather than just the source and destination addresses. Secure files can be marked as such, and application level filters will not allow those files to be transferred, even to users authorized by port level filters.

Certain application level protocols commands that are typically used for probing or hacking into systems can be identified, trapped, and removed. For example, SMTP (simple mail transfer protocol) is an e-mail interoperability protocol that is a member of the TCP/IP family and used widely over the Internet. It is often used to mask attacks or intrusions. MIME (multipurpose Internet mail extension) is also often used to hide or encapsulate malicious code such as Java applets or ActiveX components. Other application protocols that may require monitoring include World Wide Web protocols such as HTTP, as well as Telnet, FTP, Gopher, and Real Audio. Each of these application protocols requires its own proxy and each application-specific proxy must be intimately familiar with the commands within each application that will need to be trapped and examined. For example an SMTP proxy should be able to filter SMTP packets according to e-mail content, message length, and type of attachments. A given application gateway may not include proxies for all potential application layer protocols.

Circuit-level proxies provide proxy services for transport layer protocols such as TCP. **Socks** creates a proxy data channel to the application server on behalf of the application client. Since all data goes through Socks, it can audit, screen, and filter all traffic in between the application client and server. Socks can control traffic by disabling or enabling communication according to TCP port numbers. Socks4 allowed outgoing firewall applications, whereas Socks5 supports both incoming and outgoing firewall applications. Socks5 also supports authentication. The key negative characteristic is that applications must be "socksified" to communicate with the Socks protocol and server. In the case of Socks4, this meant that local applications had to literally be recompiled. However, with Sock5, a launcher is employed that avoids "socksification" and recompilation of client programs that don't natively support Socks in most cases. Socks5 uses a private routing table and hides internal network addresses from outside networks.

Application gateways are concerned with what services or applications a message is requesting in addition to who is making that request. Connections between requesting clients and service providing servers are created only after the application gateway is satisfied as to the legitimacy of the request. Even once the legitimacy of the request has been established, only proxy clients and servers actually communicate with each other. A gateway firewall does not allow actual internal IP addresses or names to be transported to the external nonsecure network. To the external network, the proxy application on the firewall appears to be the actual source or destination as the case may be.

An architectural variation of an application gateway that offers increased security is known as a **dual-homed gateway.** In this scenario, the application gateway is physically connected to the private secure network, and the packet filtering router is connected to the nonsecure network or the Internet. Between the application gateway and the packet filter router is an area known as the screened subnet, or DMZ. Also attached to this screened subnet are information servers, WWW servers, or other servers that the company may wish to make available to outside users. However, all outside traffic still goes through the application gateway first, and then to the information servers. TCP/IP forwarding is disabled, and access to the private network is available only through one of the installed proxies. Remote logins are only allowed to the gateway host.

An alternative to the dual-homed gateway that seeks to relieve all the reliance on the application gateway for all communication, both inbound and outbound, is known as a **trusted gateway** or trusted application gateway. In a trusted gateway, certain applications are identified as trusted and are able to bypass the application gateway entirely and establish connections directly rather than be executed by proxy. In this way, outside users can access information servers and WWW servers without

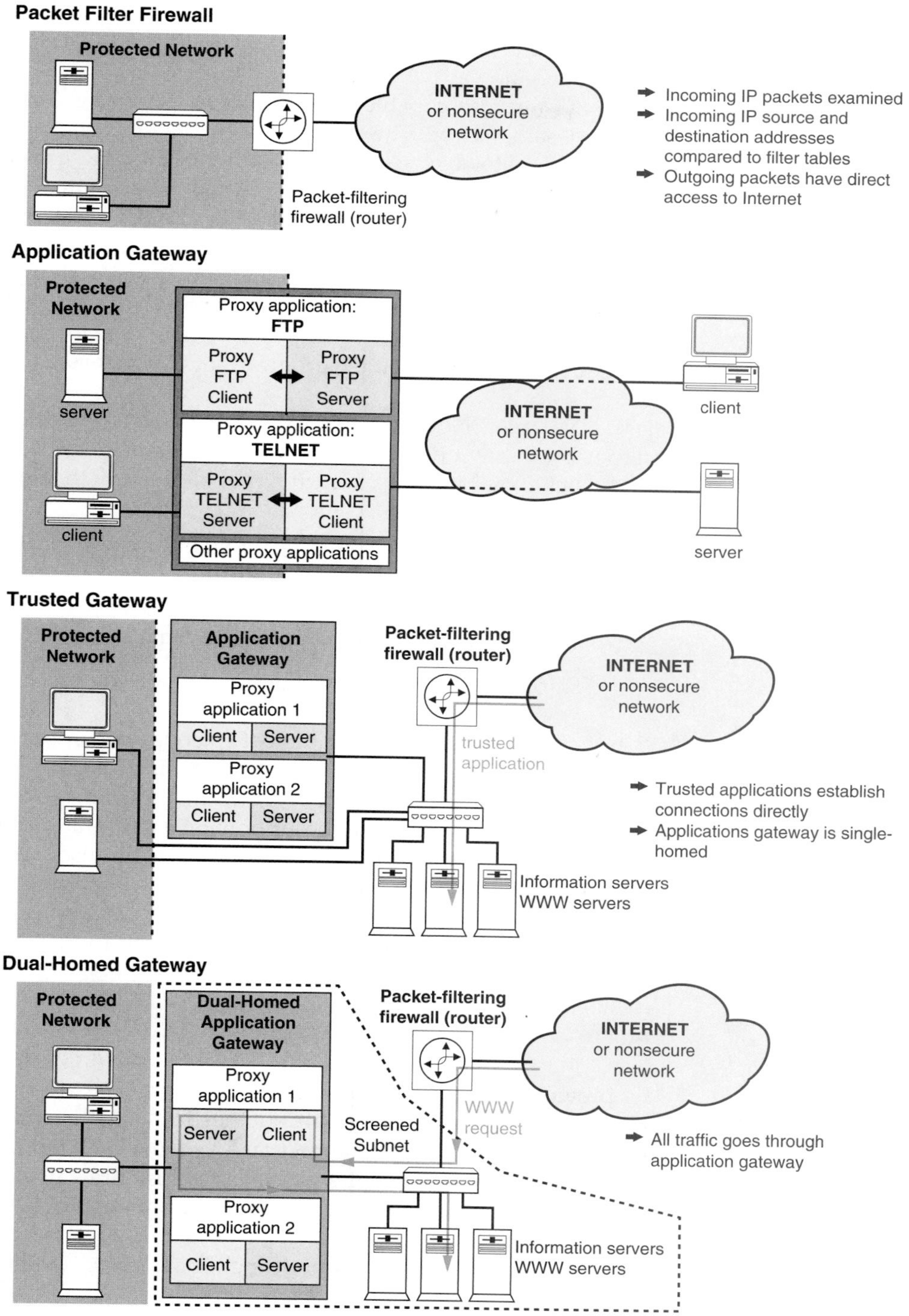

Figure 13-20 Packet Filters, Application Gateways, Proxies, Trusted Gateways, and Dual-Homed Gateways

tying up the proxy applications on the application gateway. Figure 13-20 differentiates between packet filters, application gateways, proxies, trusted gateways, and dual-homed gateways.

Proxies are also capable of approving or denying connections based on directionality. Users may be allowed to upload files but not download them. Some application level gateways have the ability to encrypt communications over these established connections. The level of difficulty associated with configuring application level gateways vs. router-based packet filters is debatable. Router-based gateways tend to require a more intimate knowledge of protocol behavior, whereas application level gateways deal with more upper level, application layer protocols. Proxies introduce increased latency compared with port level filtering. The key weakness of an application level gateway is its inability to detect embedded malicious code such as trojan horse programs or macro viruses.

Internal Firewalls Not all threats to a corporation's network are perpetrated from the Internet by anonymous hackers, and firewalls are not a stand-alone, technology-based quick fix for network security as evidenced by the following facts:

- Sixty percent of network attacks are made by internal users, people inside the firewall.
- Disgruntled employees, former employees, or friends of employees are responsible for 568 of 600 incidents of network hacking.
- Thirty percent of Internet sites that reported breaches had firewalls in place.

In response to the reality that most episodes of computer crime are inside jobs, a new category of software known as **internal firewalls** has begun to emerge. Internal firewalls include filters that work on the datalink, network, and application layers to examine communications that occur only on a corporation's internal network, inside the reach of traditional firewalls. Internal firewalls also act as access control mechanisms, denying access to any application for which a user does not have specific access approval. To ensure the security of confidential or private files, encryption may also be used, even during internal communication of such files.

Enterprise Firewall Architectures

The previous section described different approaches to firewall architecture on an individual basis; key decisions are still needed as to the number and location of these firewalls in relation to the Internet and a corporation's public and private information resources. Each of the alternative enterprise firewall architectures explored next is attempting to segregate the following three distinct networks or risk domains:

- The Internet contains both legitimate customers and business partners as well as hackers.
- The demilitarized zone, DMZ, otherwise known as the external private network, contains web servers and mail servers.
- The internal private network, otherwise known as the secure network or intranet, contains valuable corporate information.

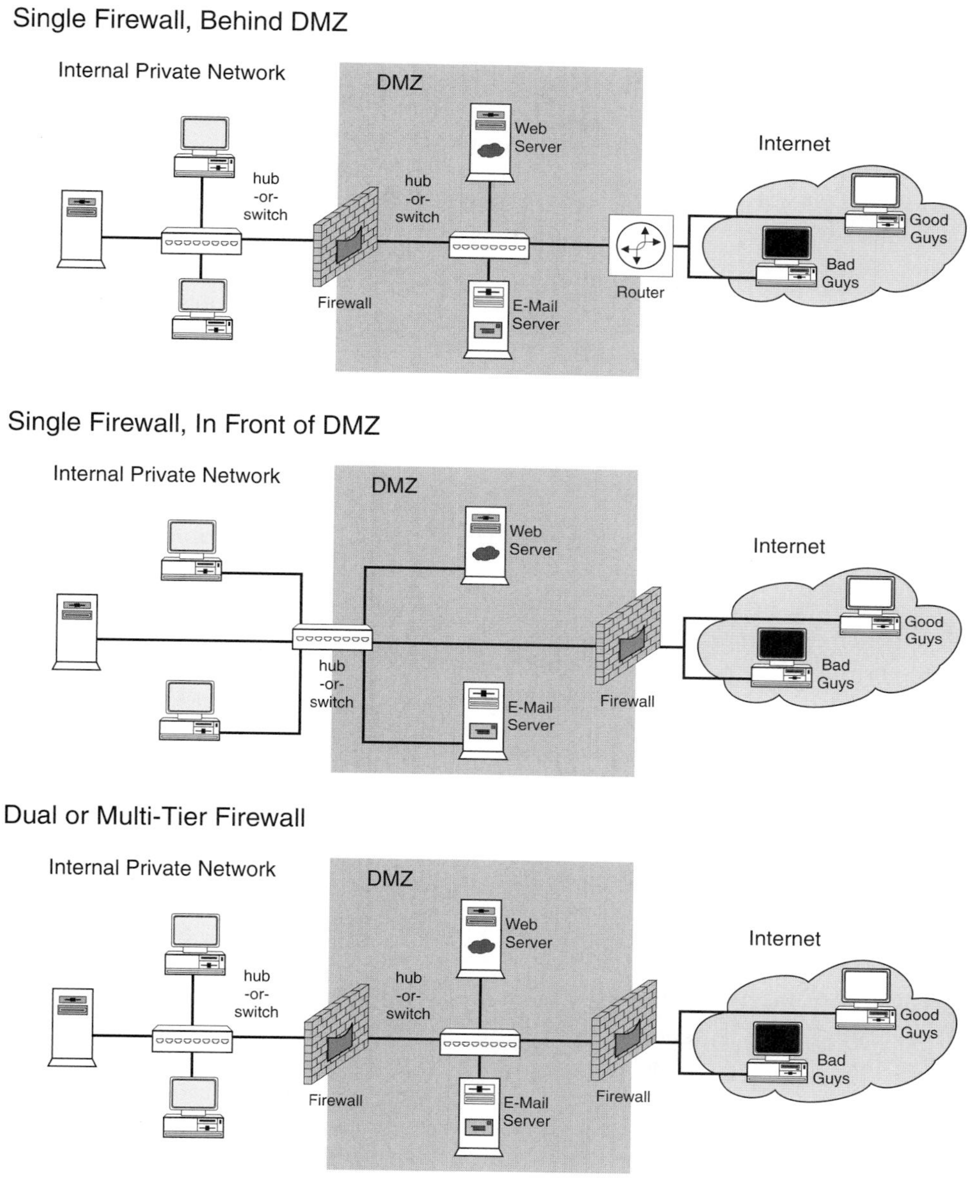

Figure 13-21 Enterprise Firewall Architectures

Figure 13-21 illustrates the various ways in which one or two firewalls can be arranged in an enterprise firewall architecture; Figure 13-22 describes the functionality of each alternative.

Firewall Functionality and Technology Analysis

Commercially available firewalls usually employ either packet filtering or proxies as a firewall architecture and add an easy-to-use graphical user interface to ease the

Enterprise Firewall Architecture	Key Functional Characteristics
Single Firewall, Behind DMZ	• Exposes web servers and mail servers to Internet without protection
Single Firewall, in Front of DMZ	• Must open paths through single firewall to allow public access to web server and mail server • No firewall protection to internal private network since it is on the same physical network as the DMZ
Dual or Multitier Firewall	• Allows controlled access to DMZ while blocking unauthorized access to secure network • Same functionality may be offered in a single product known as a trihomed firewall.

Figure 13-22 Comparative Functionality of Enterprise Firewall Architectures

configuration and implementation tasks. Some firewalls even use industry standard web browsers as their GUIs. Firewall technology is now certified by the **National Computer Security Association.** The NCSA certifies the following:

- That firewalls meet the minimum requirements for reliable protection.
- That firewalls perform as advertised.
- That Internet applications perform as expected through the firewall.

Figure 13-23 summarizes some of the key functional characteristics of firewall technology.

Examples of some of the more popular firewall technology include Firewall-1 from Checkpoint, Gauntlet from Network Associates, Raptor Firewall from Axent Technologies, and AltaVista Firewall from Compaq.

Small Office Home Office (SOHO) Firewalls As telecommuting has boomed and independent consultants have set up shop in home offices, the need for firewalls for the SOHO market has grown as well. These devices are most often integrated with ISDN-based multiprotocol routers that supply bandwidth on demand capabilities for Internet access. Some of these SOHO firewalls offer sophisticated features such as support for virtual private networks and NCSA certification at a reasonable price, less than $3000. Some of these devices combine additional functionality such as network address translation, built-in hub/switch ports, and load balancing in a combined hardware/software device known as a **security appliance.** Examples of such appliances include VPN-1 Appliance from CheckPoint Software, Interceptor from Technologic, and OpenGate from FreeGate.

AUTHENTICATION AND ACCESS CONTROL

The overall purpose of **authentication** is to ensure that users attempting to gain access to networks are really who they claim to be. Password protection was the traditional means to ensure authentication. However, password protection by itself is no longer sufficient to ensure authentication. As a result, a wide variety of technol-

Firewall Functional Characteristic	Explanation/Importance
Encryption	• Allows secure communication through firewall • Encryption schemes supported: DES, • Encryption key length supported: 40, 56, 128 bits
Virtual Private Network Support	• Allows secure communication over the Internet in a virtual private network topology • VPN Security protocols supported: IPsec
Application Proxies Supported	• How many different application proxies are supported? Internet application protocols? (HTTP, SMTP, FTP, Telnet, NNTP, WAIS, SNMP, rlogin, ping traceroute) Real Audio? • How many controls or commands are supported for each application?
Proxy Isolation	• In some cases, proxies are executed in their own protected domains to prevent penetration of other proxies or the firewall operating system if a given proxy is breached
Operating Systems Supported	• Unix and varieties, Windows NT, UnixWare, Windows 2000
Virus Scanning Included	• Since many viruses enter through Internet connections, it would stand to reason that the firewall would be a logical place to scan for viruses
Web Tracking	• To assure compliance with corporate policy regarding use of the World Wide Web, some firewalls provide web tracking software. The placement of the web tracking software in the firewall makes sense because all Web access must pass through the firewall. Access to certain URLs can be filtered
Violation Notification	• How does the firewall react when access violations are detected? Options include SNMP traps, e-mail, pop-up windows, pagers, reports
Authentication Supported	• As a major network access point, the firewall must support popular authentication protocols and technology. Options include SecureID, Cryptocard, Enigma Logic, DES Gold, DES Silver, Safeword, Radius, ASSUREnet, FW-1, Digital Pathways, S/Key, OS Login
Network Interfaces Supported	• Which network interfaces and associated data-link layer protocols are supported? Options include Ethernet, fast Ethernet, FDDI, token ring, high speed serial for CSU/DSUs, ATM, ISDN, T-1, T-3, HDLC, PPP
System Monitoring	• Are graphical systems monitoring utilities available to display such statistics as disk usage or network activity by interface?
Auditing and Logging	• Is auditing and logging supporting? • How many different types of events can be logged? • Are user-defined events supported? • Can logged events be sent to SNMP managers?

Figure 13-23 Functional Characteristics of Firewall Technology *(figure continues)*

Firewall Functional Characteristic	Explanation/Importance
Attack Protection	• Following is a sample of the types of attacks that a firewall should be able to guard against: TCP denial-of-service attack, TCP sequence number prediction, Source routing and routing information protocol (RIP) attacks, exterior gateway protocol infiltration and Internet control message protocol (ICMP) attacks, authentication server attacks, finger access, PCMAIL access, domain name server (DNS) access, FTP authentication attacks, anonymous FTP access, SNMP access remote access remote booting from outside networks; IP, media access control (MAC) and address resolution protocol (ARP) spoofing and broadcast storms: trivial FTP and filter to/from the firewall, reserved port attacks, TCP wrappers, Gopher spoofing, and MIME spoofing
Administration Interface	• Is the administration interface graphical in nature? Forms-based? • Is a mastery of Unix required to administer the firewall?

Figure 13-23 Functional Characteristics of Firewall Technology

ogy has been developed to ensure that users really are who they say they are. Authentication products break down into three overall categories:

- *What you know:* Authentication technology that delivers **single sign-on (SSO)** access to multiple network-attached servers and resources via passwords. Examples of single sign-on technology includes TrustBroker from CyberSafe, PassGo SSO from Axent Technologies, and Global Sign On from IBM.
- *What you have:* Authentication technology that uses one-time or session passwords or other techniques to authenticate users and validate the authenticity of messages or files. This category of technology requires the user to possess some type of smart card or other token authentication device to generate these single use passwords. Examples of one-time password programs include OPIE and S/Key
- *What you are:* Authentication technology that validates users based on some physical characteristic such as fingerprints, hand geometry, or retinal scans.

Token Authentication—Smart Cards

Token authentication technology provides one-time-use session passwords that are authenticated by associated server software. This token authentication technology may take multiple forms:

- Hardware-based **smart cards** or Smart IDs that are about the size of a credit card with a numeric keypad, or key fob.

- In-line token authentication devices that connect to the serial port of a computer for dial-in authentication through a modem.
- Software tokens that are installed on the client PC and authenticate with the server portion of the token authentication product transparently to the end user. The user must only enter a personal ID number (PIN) to activate the authentication process.

Token authentication technology is really a system of interacting components that could include any or all of the following:

- A smart card to generate the session password.
- Client software to enter session passwords and communicate with the token authentication server software.
- Server software to validate entries for session passwords and keep track of which smart cards are issued to which users.
- Application development software to integrate the token authentication technology with existing information systems.

There are two overall approaches to the token authentication process:

- **Challenge-response token authentication.**
- **Time synchronous token authentication.**

Challenge-response token authentication involves the following steps:

1. The user enters an assigned user ID and password at the client workstation.
2. The token authentication server software returns a numeric string known as a challenge.
3. The challenge number and a personal ID number are entered on the handheld smart card.
4. The smart card displays a response number on the LCD screen.
5. This response number is entered on the client workstation and transmitted back to the token authentication server.
6. The token authentication server validates the response against the expected response from this particular user and this particular smart card. If the two match, the user is deemed authentic and the login session is enabled.

Time-synchronous token authentication uses slightly more sophisticated technology to simplify the challenge-response procedure. The result is that in time-synchronous token authentication, there is no server-to-client challenge step. SecureID tokens from Security Dynamics are examples of time-synchronous token authentication using a protocol known as SecureID ACE (access control encryption).

1. Every 60 seconds, the time-synchronous smart card and the server-based software generate a new access code.

2. The user enters a userID, a personal ID number, and the access code currently displayed on the smart card.

3. The server receives the access code and authenticates the user by comparing the received access code to the expected access code unique to that smart card that was generated at the server in time-synchronous fashion.

Figure 13-24 differentiates between challenge-response token authentication and time-synchronous token authentication.

Besides SecureID from Security Dynamics, other examples of authentication tokens include Praesidium SpeedCard from Hewlett-Packard, PrivateCard from Cylink, CryptCard from Global Technologies Group, TrustBroker from CyberSafe, and Defender from Axent Technologies.

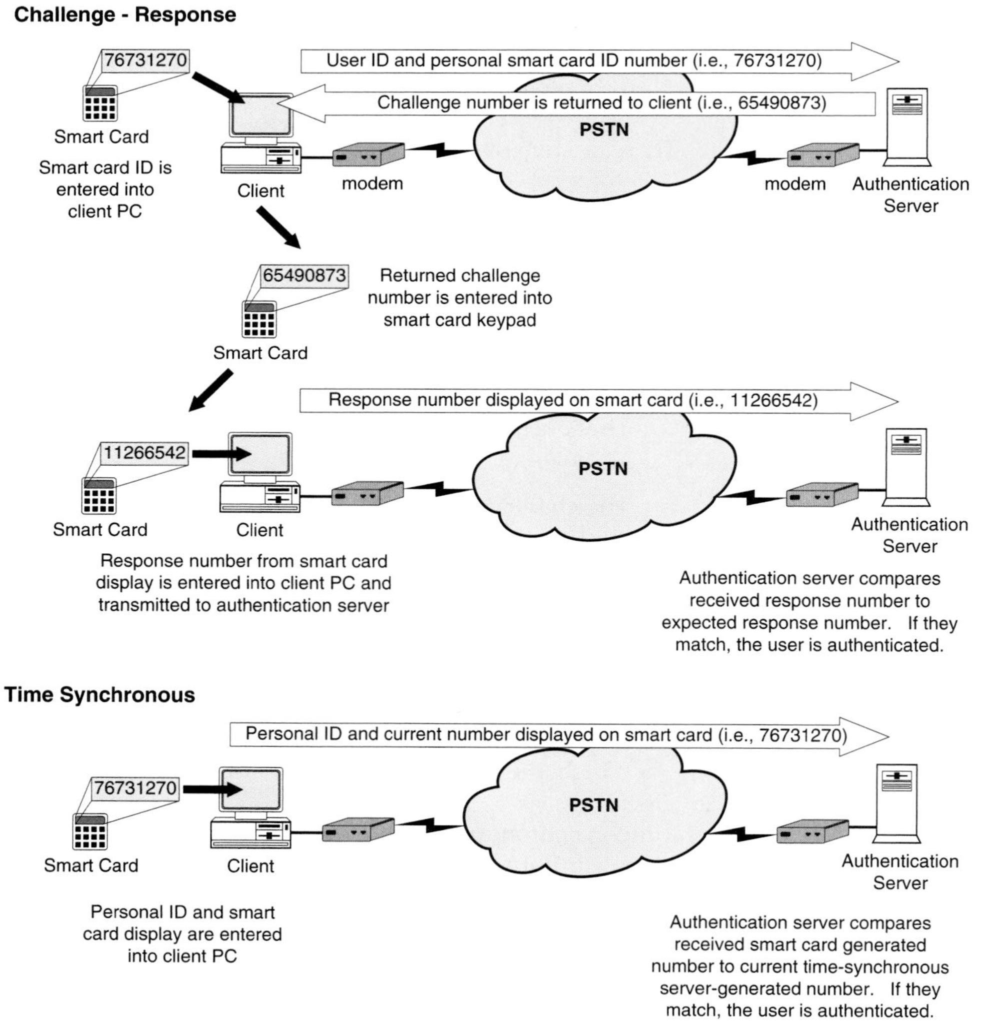

Figure 13-24 Challenge-Response vs. Time-Synchronous Token Authentication

Biometric Authentication

If the security offered by token authentication is insufficient, **biometric authentication** can authenticate users based on fingerprints, palm prints, retinal patterns, hand geometry, facial geometry, voice recognition, or other physical characteristics. Passwords and smart cards can be stolen, but fingerprints and retinal patterns cannot. All biometric authentication devices require that valid users first register by storing copies of their fingerprints, voice, or retinal patterns in a validation database. This gives the biometric device something to reference each time an intended user logs in.

Biometric authentication devices are not yet perfect or foolproof. Most biometric authentication devices must be calibrated for sensitivity. If the biometric device comparison algorithm is set too sensitively, then **false rejects** will occur when valid users are denied access because of slight variations detected between the reference biometric characteristic and the current one. If the biometric device comparison algorithm is not set sensitively enough, then **false accepts** will occur when impostors are allowed access because the comparison was not detailed enough. Users of biometric authentication equipment must calibrate the sensitivity of the equipment to produce acceptable levels of false rejects and false accepts.

Authorization

Sometimes perceived as a subset of authentication, authorization is concerned with ensuring that only properly authorized users are able to access particular network resources or corporate information resources. In other words, while authentication ensures that only legitimate users are able to log into the network, authorization ensures that these properly authenticated users only access the network resources for which they are properly authorized. This assurance that users are able to log into a network, rather than each individual server and application, and be only able to access only resources for which they are properly authorized is known as **secure single login.**

The authorization security software can be either server-based, also known as **brokered authorization,** or workstation-based, also referred to as **trusted node.** TrustBroker from Cybersafe and AccessMaster from BullSoft are two examples of this category of software.

Kerberos

Perhaps the most well-known combination authentication/authorization software is **Kerberos,** developed originally at Massachusetts Institute of Technology and marketed commercially by a variety of firms. The Kerberos architecture is illustrated in Figure 13-25.

A Kerberos architecture consists of three key components:

- Kerberos client software
- Kerberos authentication server software
- Kerberos application server software

To be able to ensure that only authorized users are able to access a particular application, Kerberos must be able to communicate directly with that application. As

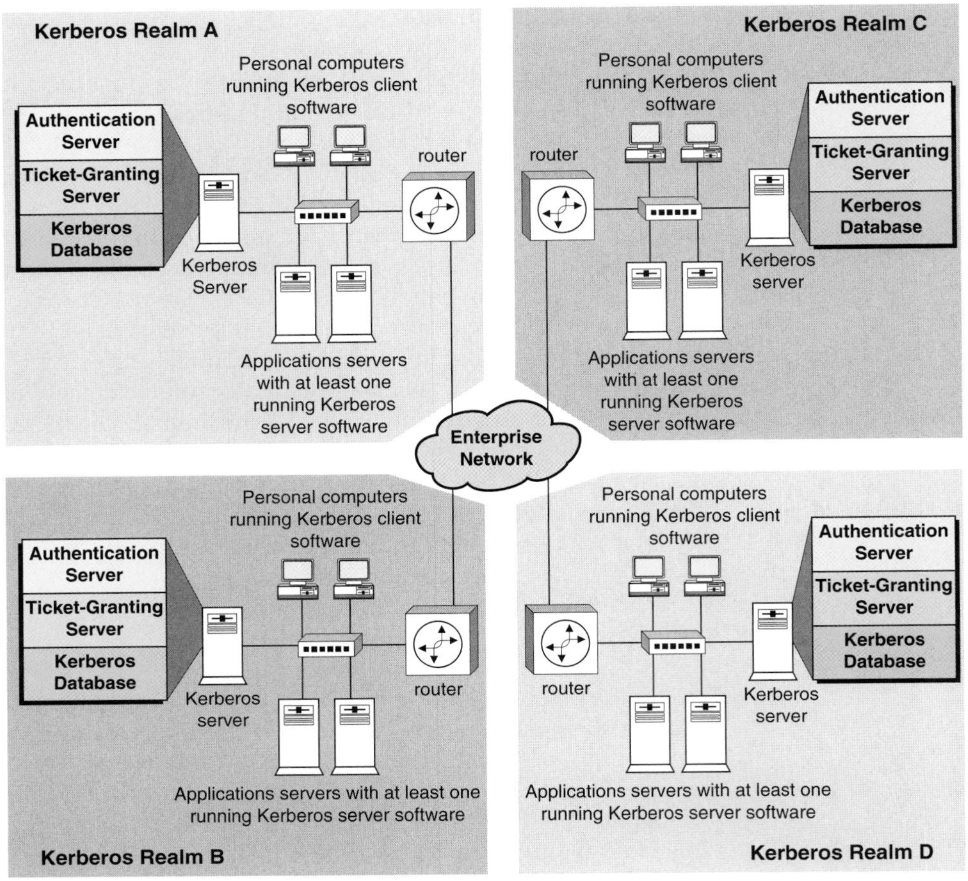

Figure 13-25 Kerberos Architecture

a result, the source code of the application must be "Kerberized" or modified to be compatible with Kerberos. If the source code is not available, perhaps the software vendor sells Kerberized versions of their software. Kerberos is not able to offer authorization protection to applications with which it cannot communicate. Kerberos enforces authentication and authorization through the use of a ticket-based system. An encrypted **ticket** is issued for each server-to-client session and is valid only for a preset amount of time. The ticket is valid only for connections between a designated client and server, thus precluding users from accessing servers or applications for which they are not properly authorized.

Logically, Kerberos works as follows:

1. Users are first authenticated by the Kerberos authentication server, which consults its database and grants a ticket for the valid user to communicate with the ticket granting server (TGS). This ticket is known as a **ticket-granting ticket.**
2. Using this ticket, the user sends an encrypted request to the TGS requesting a ticket for access to a particular applications server.

3. If the TGS determines that the request is valid, a ticket is issued that will allow the user to access the requested server. This ticket is known as a **service-granting ticket.**

4. The user presents the validated ticket to the application server, which evaluates the ticket's validity. If the application determines that the ticket is valid, a client/server session is established. This session can optionally be encrypted.

Enterprise networks implementing Kerberos are divided into Kerberos **realms,** each served by its own Kerberos server. If a client wishes to access a server in another realm, it requests an **inter-realm** ticket granting ticket from its local ticket granting server to authorize access to the remote ticket granting server that can authorize access to the remote applications server.

Managerial Perspective

From a network analyst's perspective, concern should be centered on the amount of overhead or network bandwidth consumed by the addition of Kerberos security. Research has indicated that, in fact, the network impact is minimal. However, the additional administrative responsibility of maintaining the Kerberos databases that indicate which users are authorized to access which network resources should not be ignored.

ENCRYPTION

Encryption involves the changing of data into an indecipherable form before transmission. In this way, even if the transmitted data are somehow intercepted, they cannot be interpreted. The changed, unmeaningful data is known as **ciphertext.** Encryption must be accompanied by decryption, or changing the unreadable text back into its original form.

DES—Private Key Encryption

The decrypting device must use the same algorithm or method and key to decode or decrypt the data as the encrypting device used to encrypt the data. For this reason **private key encryption** is sometimes also known as symmetric encryption. Although proprietary standards do exist, a standard known as **DES (data encryption standard),** originally approved by the National Institute of Standards and Technology (NIST) in 1977, is often used, allowing encryption devices manufactured by different manufacturers to interoperate successfully. The DES encryption standard actually has two parts, which offer greater overall security. In addition to the standard algorithm or method of encrypting data 64 bits at a time, the DES standard also uses a 64-bit key.

The encryption key customizes the commonly known algorithm to prevent anyone without this private key from possibly decrypting the document. This private key must be known by the both the sending and receiving encryption devices and allows so many unique combinations (nearly 2 to the 64th power), that unauthorized decryption is nearly impossible. The safe and reliable distribution of these private keys among numerous encryption devices can be difficult. If this private key is somehow intercepted, the integrity of the encryption system is compromised.

RSA—Public Key Encryption

As an alternative to the DES private key standard, **public key encryption** can be utilized. The current standard for public key encryption is known as **RSA,** named after the three founders of the protocol (Rivest-Shamir-Adelman). Public key encryption could perhaps more accurately be named public/private key encryption, as the process actually combines usage of both public and private keys. In public key encryption, the sending encryption device encrypts a document using the intended recipient's public key and the originating party's private key. This public key is readily available in a public directory or is sent by the intended recipient to the message sender. However, to decrypt the document, the receiving encryption/decryption device must be programmed with its own private key and the sending party's public key. In this method, the need for transmission of private keys between sending and receiving parties is eliminated.

Digital Signature Encryption

As an added security measure, **digital signature encryption** uses this public key encryption methodology in reverse as an electronic means of guaranteeing authenticity of the sending party and assurance that encrypted documents have not been altered during transmission.

With digital signature encryption, a document's digital signature is created by the sender using a private key and the original document. The original document is processed by a hashing program such as Secure Hash Algorithm, Message Digest 2, or Message Digest 5, to produce a mathematical string that is unique to the exact content of the original document. This unique mathematical string is then encrypted using the originator's private key. The encrypted digital signature is then appended to and transmitted with the encrypted original document.

To validate the authenticity of the received document, the recipient uses a public key associated with the apparent sender to regenerate a digital signature from the received encrypted document. The transmitted digital signature is then compared by the recipient to the regenerated digital signature produced by using the public key and the received document. If the two digital signatures match, the document is authentic (really produced by alleged originator) and has not been altered. Figure 13-26 illustrates the differences between private key encryption, public key encryption, and digital signature encryption; Figure 13-27 summarizes some key facts about currently popular encryption standards.

Examples of encryption technology capable of encrypting files either while being stored or transmitted include Secure PC from Security Dynamics, F-Secure Workstation Suite from Data Fellows, and PrivaCD from Global Technologies Group.

Key Management Alternatives

Before two computers can communicate in a secure manner, they must be able to agree on encryption and authentication algorithms and establish keys in a process known as key management. Two standards for key management are:

- **ISAKMP (Internet security association and key management protocol)** from the IETF: now largely replaced by IKE (internet key exchange) described later in the section on IPSec.

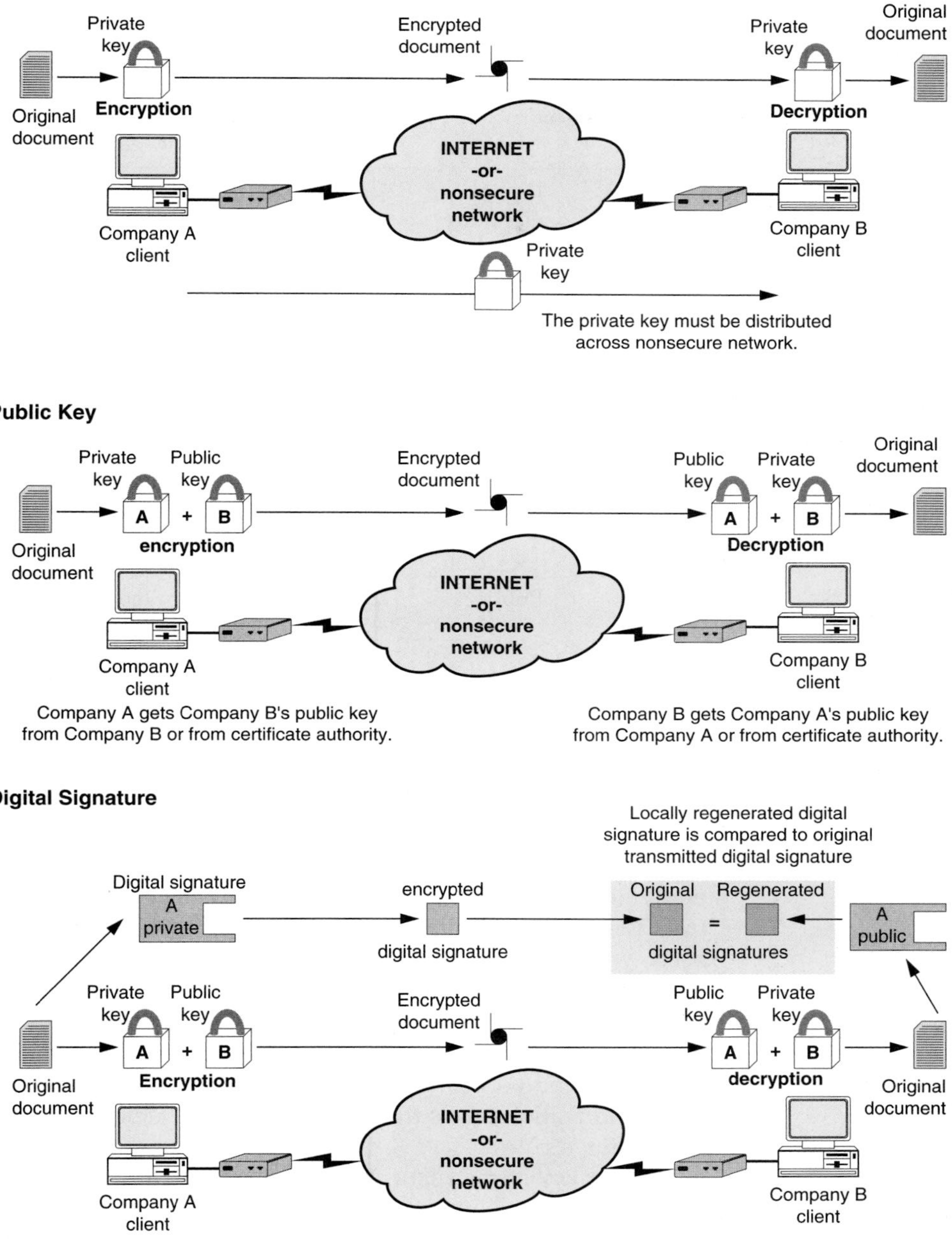

Figure 13-26 Private Key Encryption, Public Key Encryption, and Digital Signature Encryption

- **SKIP (simple key management for IP)** from Sun.

Public key dissemination must be managed in such a way that users can be assured that public keys received are actually the public keys of the companies or organizations that they are alleged to be. This added level of assurance is provided by **public key certificates.** The organization required to manage digital keys is gen-

Standard	Type	Key Size	Explanation
3DES	Private	40, 56 bits	Triple DES, uses 2 or 3 keys and multiple passes
DES	Private	40, 56 bits	Digital encryption standard, widely used for private key encryption
DSA	Digital Signature	1024	Digital signature algorithm generates appended digital signatures based on original document to ensure document has not been altered
ECC	Public	160	Elliptical curve cryptography, claims to produce equivalent security of 1024 bit RSA key in only 160 bits
IDEA	Private	128 bit	International data encryption algorithm, generates one-time use session keys, used in PGP (pretty good privacy)
MD5	Digest		Produces 128-bit hash number based on original document, can then be incorporated into digital signature, replaced MD4 and MD2
RSA	Public	512 to 2048 bits	Rivest-Shamir-Adelman, popular public key encryption standard, minimum key length of 1024 recommended
Skipjack	Private	80	Used for Clipper and Capstone encryption chips and Defense Messaging System (DMS)

Figure 13-27 Encryption Standards

erally described as the public key infrastructure (PKI). **PKIX (public key infrastructure X.509)** is an international ISO standard for public key certificates. The IETF has been working on an alternative public key infrastructure standard that is oriented toward varying authorization levels rather than personal identities by using what are known as privilege-based certificates. This draft standard, known as **SPKI/SDSI (simple public key infrastructure/simple distributed security infrastructure),** specifies a distributed client/server model in which humanly readable certificates and the authorization levels they represent can be delegated and processed according to user-defined rules.

Public key infrastructures that link a particular user to a particular public key are implemented through the use of server-based software known as **certificate servers.** Certificate server software also supports encryption and digital signatures while flexibly supporting directory integration, multiple certificate types, and a variety of request fulfillment options. Third-party key certification services, or **certificate authorities (CA),** issue the public keys along with a certificate ensuring the authenticity of the key. Such certification authorities issue public keys of other organizations, along with certificates of authenticity, ensured by their own digital signature. VeriSign is one example of a trusted third-party issuer of X.509 public-key certificates. Other certificate authorities include CyberTrust from GTE and CommercePoint from IBM. Interoperability among digital certificates issued by different certificate authorities is now beginning to emerge, but should not be assumed. The U.S. Postal

Service has also announced plans to begin issuing public key certificates. Organizations can install their own certificate servers as well. Examples of certificate server software include NetScape Certificate Server from NetScape, Microsoft Certificate Server from Microsoft, and Entrust from Entrust.

Digital certificates or **Digital IDs** issued from CAs such as VeriSign contain an organization's encrypted public key along with a minimal amount of information about the organization such as e-mail address, department, company, state or province, and country. Once a certificate has been issued by a CA, an organization can post its Digital ID on a web page and be assured that the CA will stand behind the Digital ID's authenticity.

Digital IDs may one day replace passwords for Internet-based communications. Recognizing the potential for electronic commerce vendors to quickly gather demographic data about their customers, VeriSign has enhanced its Class 1 Digital ID format to include additional fields in which to store demographic data such as gender, age, address, zip code, or other personal data. Information stored in the encrypted Class 2 Digital ID could allow customized web pages to be built based on the information contained therein. The Digital ID service from VeriSign costs $6.00 per year for a Class 1 Digital ID and $12.00 per year for a Class 2 Digital ID.

APPLIED SECURITY SCENARIOS

Overall Design Strategies

Although it is impossible to prescribe a network security design that would be appropriate for any given situation, some general guidelines that would apply to most situations are as follows:

- Install only software and hardware that you really need on the network. Every time that hardware or software is installed on a network, potential security vulnerabilities resulting from misconfiguration or design flaws are introduced.
- Allow only essential traffic into and out of the corporate network and eliminate all other types by blocking with routers or firewalls. E-mail and domain name service (DNS) queries are a good place to start.
- Investigate the business case for outsourcing web-hosting services so that the corporate web server is not physically on the same network as the rest of the corporate information assets.
- Use routers to filter traffic by IP address. Allow only known authorized users to have access through the router and into the corporate information network.
- Make sure that router operating system software has been patched to prevent denial of service and land attacks by exploiting TCP vulnerabilities, or better still, block all incoming TCP traffic.
- Identify those information assets that are most critical to the corporation, and protect those servers first. It is better to have the most important assets well protected than to have all of the information assets somewhat protected.

- Implement physical security constraints to hinder physical access to critical resources such as servers.
- Monitor system activity logs carefully, paying close attention to failed login attempts and file transfers.
- Develop a simple, effective, and enforceable security policy and monitor its implementation and effectiveness.
- Consider installing a proxy server or applications layer firewall.
- Block incoming DNS queries and requests for zone transfers. This is how hackers are able to map a corporation's internal network resources.
- Don't publish the corporation's complete DNS map on DNS servers that are outside the corporate firewall. Publish only those few servers that the Internet needs to know: e-mail gateway, DNS server, web site.
- Disable all TCP ports and services that are not essential so that hackers are not able to exploit and use these services.

Integration with Information Systems and Application Development

Authentication products must be integrated with existing information systems and applications development efforts. APIs (application program interfaces) are the means by which authentication products are able to integrate with client/server applications. Beyond APIs are application development environments or software development kits that combine an application development language with the supported APIs. APIs or application development environments must be compatible with the programming language in which applications are to be developed.

AT&T provides a software development kit that includes a library of C language security APIs and software modules for integrating digital signature and other security functionality into Windows NT and Windows 95 applications.

Security Dynamics, who markets SecurID time-synchronous token authentication products, also provides software development kits known as BSAFE 3.0 and Toolkit for Interoperable Privacy Enhanced Messaging.

Microsoft's CryptoAPI (CAPI) allows security services such as authentication, encryption, certificate management services, and digital signatures to be integrated with applications. Obviously, these applications must then be executed over Microsoft platforms.

Intel, IBM, and Netscape have collaborated on a multi-API security framework for encryption and authentication known as common data security architecture (CDSA) that can be integrated with Java bases objects. Other security APIs may be forthcoming from Sun and Novell also.

An open API which would allow applications to communicate with a variety of security authorization programs is known as **GSS-API (generic security service-applications program interface)** and is documented in RFCs 1508 and 1509. Security products companies such as Nortel, producers of the Entrust file signing and encryption package, and Cybersafe Corporation support the GSS-API. GSS-API is described as open because it interfaces between user applications and a variety of security services such as Kerberos, secure FTP, or encryption services. The applications developer does not need to understand the intricacies of these security services and is able to flexibly choose those security services that best meet the needs of the application under development. The GSS-API can also be integrated with Intel's CDSA.

Remote Access Security

The biggest challenge facing remote access security is how to manage the activity of all of the remote access users that have logged in via a variety of multivendor equipment and authentication technology. A protocol and associated architecture known as **remote authentication dial-in user service (RADIUS)** (RFC 2058) is supported by a wide variety of remote access technology and offers the potential to enable centralized management of remote access users and technology. The RADIUS architecture is illustrated in Figure 13-28. This architecture is referred to as three-tiered because it enables communication between the following three tiers of technology:

- Remote access devices such as remote access servers and token authentication technology from a variety of vendors, otherwise known as network access servers (NAS).
- Enterprise database that contains authentication and access control information.
- RADIUS authentication server.

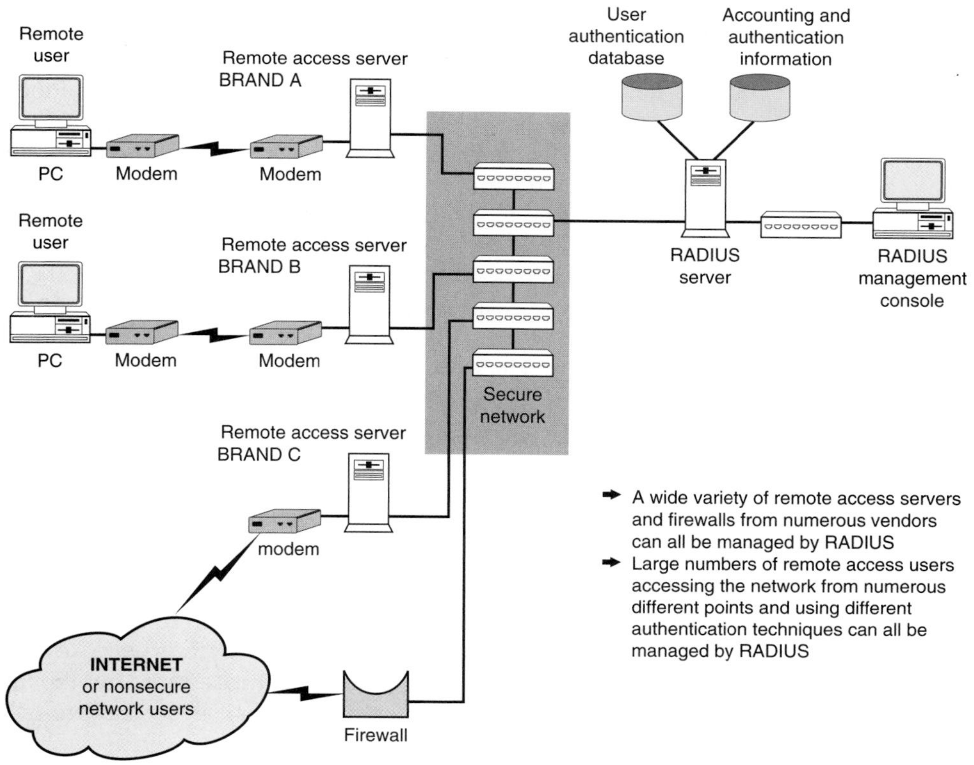

Figure 13-28 Remote Authentication Dial-In User Services (RADIUS) Architecture

In this architecture, users request connections and provide user IDs and passwords to the network access servers, which, in turn, pass the information along to the RADIUS authentication server for authentication approval or denial.

RADIUS allows network managers to centrally manage remote access users, access methods, and logon restrictions. It allows centralized auditing capabilities such as keeping track of volume of traffic sent and amount of time on-line. RADIUS also enforces remote access limitations such as server access restrictions or on-line time limitations. For authentication, it supports **password authentication protocol (PAP), challenge handshake authentication protocol (CHAP),** and SecurID token authentication. RADIUS transmits passwords in encrypted format only. Some RADIUS-based centralized management products may require that a new centralized database of remote access user information be built, whereas others, such as Funk Software's Steel Belted RADIUS, are able to use an existing network operating system's directory services, such as NetWare's NDS, as the management database.

RADIUS is not the only open protocol for communication between centralized remote access management technology and multivendor remote access technology. **Extended terminal access controller access-control system (XTACACS),** also known simply as TACACS or the updated version known as TACACS+ (RFC 1492), is another example of remote access management protocol that supports three-tiered remote access management architectures. The most widely known implementation of TACACS is Cisco System's server-based security protocol. TACACS transmits authentication information in cleartext format, whereas TACACS+ employs MD hashing and encrypts the entire packet. TACACS+ can also handle multiprotocol logins (IP and IPX) and incorporate PAP/CHAP as well.

PAP/CHAP PAP and CHAP, incorporated within RADIUS as previously described, are two other protocols that can be used on a stand-alone basis for remote access authentication. **Password authentication protocol** (RFC 1334) is the simpler of the two authentication protocols designed for dial-in communication. PAP repeatedly sends the user ID and password to the authenticating system in clear text pairs until it is either acknowledged or the connection is dropped. Otherwise known as a two-way handshaking protocol, PAP does not perform encryption.

Challenge handshake authentication protocol (RFC 1994) provides a more secure means for establishing dial-in communication. It uses a three-way challenge or handshake that includes the user ID, password and also a key that encrypts the ID and password. The process of sending the pair to the authentication system is the same as with PAP, but the encryption reduces the chance that someone will be able to pick up the ID and password and use it to access a system. CHAP is initiated by the server by issuing a challenge to the client that wishes to log in. The client must calculate a value using a one-time key and the challenge that it just received from the server. The server would then verify the calculated value based on the challenge it had initially sent the client. The problem with this system, and any single key system for that matter, is that some mechanism must be in place for both the receiver and sender to know and have access to the key. To address this problem, a public key technique may be used to encrypt the single private key for transmission. In addition, CHAP repeats the authentication procedure after the link is initially established to ensure that the session or link has not been compromised or taken over by an unauthorized party.

E-Mail, Web, and Internet/Intranet Security

The two primary standards for encrypting traffic on the World Wide Web are

- **S-HTTP: secure hypertext transport protocol.**
- **SSL: secure sockets layer.**

S-HTTP Secure HTTP is a secure version of HTTP that requires both client and server S-HTTP versions to be installed for secure end-to-end encrypted transmission. S-HTTP, based on public key encryption, is described as providing security at the document or application level since it works with the actual HTTP applications to secure documents and messages. S-HTTP uses digital signature encryption to ensure that the document possesses both authenticity and message integrity. The use of S-HTTP has diminished with the growing popularity of Netscape's Secure browser and server as well as other alternatives for secure web-based transmissions.

SSL SSL is described as wrapping an encrypted envelope around HTTP transmissions. Whereas S-HTTP can only be used to encrypt Web documents, SSL can be wrapped around other Internet service transmissions such as FTP, Telnet, and Gopher, as well as HTTP. SSL is a connection level encryption method providing security to the network link itself. SSL Version 3 (SSL3) added support for more key exchange and encryption algorithms as well as separate keys for authentication and encryption.

SSL and S-HTTP are not competing or conflicting standards, although they are sometimes viewed that way. In an analogy to a postal service scenario, SSL provides the locked postal delivery vehicle, and S-HTTP provides the sealed, tamper-evident envelope that allows only the intended recipient to view the confidential document contained within.

Another Internet security protocol directed specifically toward securing and authenticating commercial financial transactions is known as **secure courier** and is offered by Netscape. Secure Courier is based on SSL and allows users to create a secure digital envelope for transmission of financial transactions over the Internet. Secure Courier also provides consumer authentication for the cybermerchants inhabiting the commercial Internet.

PCT Microsoft's version of SSL is known as **PCT** or **private communications technology.** The key difference between SSL and PCT is that PCT supports secure transmissions across unreliable (UDP rather TCP based) connections by allowing decryption of transmitted records independently from each other, as transmitted in the individual datagrams. PCT is targeted primarily toward on-line commerce and financial transactions, whereas SSL is more flexibly targeted toward web and Internet applications in general.

PEM **Privacy enhanced mail** was the application standard encryption technique for e-mail use on the Internet, and used with SMTP (simple mail transport protocol). It was designed to use both DES and RSA encryption techniques, but it would work with other encryption algorithms as well. PEM did not receive much support, however, and has been placed in "historical status" by the IETF, meaning that it is no longer being implemented. The reason for this is that PEM did not gain support from either the vendor or user populations. The vendors supported their own products and users preferred using other e-mail programs and protocols such as PGP and S/MIME.

PGP An Internet e-mail-specific encryption standard that also uses digital signature encryption to guarantee the authenticity, security, and message integrity of received e-mail is known as **PGP,** which stands for **pretty good privacy** (RFC 1991). PGP overcomes inherent security loopholes with public/private key security schemes by implementing a web of trust in which e-mail users electronically sign each other's public keys to create an interconnected group of public key users. Digital signature encryption is provided using a combination of RSA and **MD5** (message direct version 5) encryption techniques. Combined documents and digital signatures are then encrypted using **IDEA (international data encryption algorithm),** which makes use of one-time 128-bit keys known as **session keys.** PGP is also able to compress data transmissions as well. PGP/MIME overcomes PGP's inability to encrypt multimedia (MIME) objects.

SET **Secure electronic transactions (SET)** are a series of standards to ensure the confidentiality of electronic commerce transactions. These standards are being largely promoted by credit card giants VISA and MasterCard. SET standards are specifically aimed at defining how bank-card transactions can be conducted in a secure manner over the Internet. However, the assurance of e-commerce confidentiality is not without costs in terms of processing overhead. A single SET-compliant electronic transaction could require as many as six cryptographic functions, taking from one-third to one-half second on a high-powered Unix workstation. The impact of thousands or millions of transactions per second could be enormous.

A large part of ensuring the authenticity of e-commerce depends on trusting that the e-customers and e-vendors are really who they say they are. An important aspect of the SET standards is the incorporation of digital certificates or digital IDs, more specifically known as SET Digital IDs that are issued by such companies as VeriSign.

S/MIME **Secure multipurpose Internet mail extension** secures e-mail traffic in e-mail applications that have been **S/MIME** enabled. S/MIME encrypts and authenticates e-mail messages for transmission over SMTP-based e-mail networks. S/MIME enables different e-mail systems to exchange encrypted messages and is able to encrypt multimedia as well as text-based e-mail.

Virtual Private Network Security

To provide virtual private networking capabilities using the Internet as an enterprise network backbone, specialized **tunneling protocols** needed to be developed that could establish private, secure channels between connected systems. Two rival standards are examples of such tunneling protocols:

- Microsoft's **point-to-point tunneling protocol (PPTP).**
- Cisco's **layer two forwarding (L2F).**

An effort is underway to have the Internet Engineering Task Force (IETF) propose a unification of the two rival standards known as **layer 2 tunneling protocol**

(L2TP). One shortcoming of the proposed specification is that it does not deal with security issues such as encryption and authentication. Figure 13-29 illustrates the use of tunneling protocols to build virtual private networks using the Internet as an enterprise network backbone.

Two rival specifications currently exist for establishing security over VPN tunnels:

- **IPsec** is largely supported by the firewall vendor community and is intended to provide interoperability between VPN firewalls from different vendors.
- PPTP is Microsoft's tunneling protocol that is specific to Windows NT servers and remote access servers. It has the backing of several remote access server vendors.

Examples of VPN technology include Cisco Secure Integrated VPN Software from Cisco Systems, VPN-1 from Checkpoint, Raptor Power VPN Server from Axent Technologies, Cyberwall PLUS-VPN from Network 1 Security Solutions, and PPTP-RAS from Microsoft.

IPSec—Secure IP IPsec is a protocol that ensures encrypted (56-bit key DES) communications across the Internet via virtual private networks through the use of manual key exchange. IPsec supports only IP-based communications. IPsec is a standard that, in theory at least, should enable interoperability between firewalls supporting the protocol. Although firewalls of the same brand seem to interoperate sufficiently via IPsec, that does not seem to be the case between different brands of firewall technology.

IPsec is also proposed to be able to support both authentication and encryption. These capabilities are optional for IPv4 and mandatory for **IPv6** and are outlined in IETF RFCs 1825 through 1829. In addition to encryption and authentication, IPsec also includes the ISAKMP (Internet security association key management protocol),

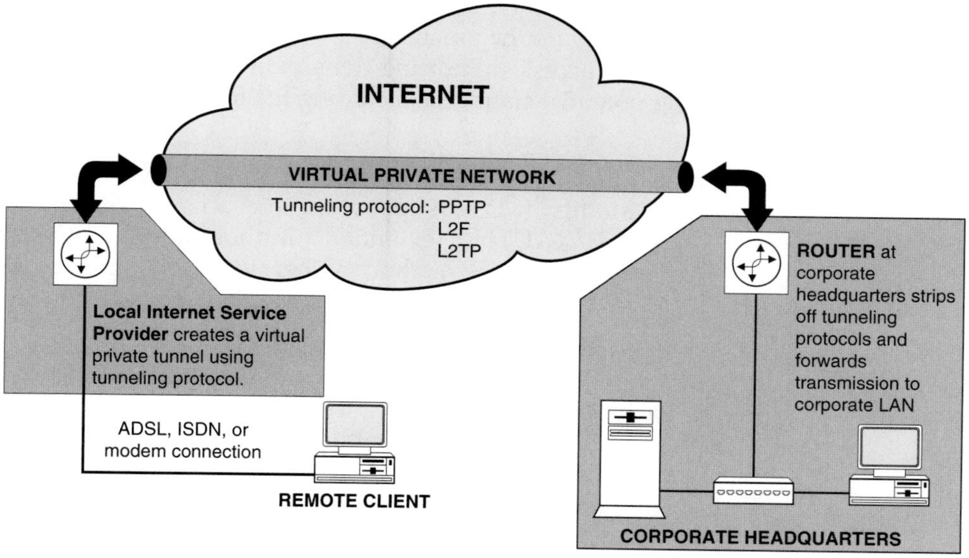

Figure 13-29 Tunneling Protocols Enable Virtual Private Networks

now largely replaced by IKE. To deliver these functions, two new headers are added to the existing IP header:

- The **authentication header** (RFC 1826) provides data integrity and allows for the authentication of IP packets. It can specify the security association to provide authentication between the source and destination parties, and it can also supply data to be used by the agreed on particular authentication algorithm to be used.
- The **encapsulating security payload header (ESP)** (RFC 1827) ensures the privacy of the transmission. The ESP header can be used in two different modes depending on the user's privacy needs:
    - **Transport Mode ESP** is used to encrypt the data carried by the IP packet. The contents of the data field of an IP (network layer) packet are the upper layer or transport layer protocols TCP (connection-oriented) or UDP (connectionless). These transport layer envelopes encapsulate upper layer data.
    - **Tunnel Mode ESP** encrypts the entire IP packet including its own header. This mode is effective at countering network analyzers or sniffers from capturing IP address information. Tunnel mode is most often used in a network topology that includes a firewall that separates a protected network from an external nonsecure network.

It is important to note that the mere inclusion of fields in a protocol does not ensure implementation. Applications, authentication products, and trusted security associations would all have to modify hardware and/or software technology to avail themselves of the protocol's new functionality. Figure 13-30 illustrates an IPsec packet with authentication and encryption headers added.

IKE (internet key exchange) is the handshaking portion of the IPSec protocol used to establish sessions across a VPN. It is referred to as a replacement for ISAKMP. However, IKE requires preshared keys and static IP addresses, neither of which may be practical with dial-up users and/or trading partners with whom sharing keys may not be practical. How to get IPSec to work in an interoperable fashion for remote access supporting dynamic IP addresses has generated numerous competing potential standards including the following:

- Use L2TP with IPSec.
- Modify IKE to support remote access over the Internet—referred to as IKE/XAUTH (extended authorization) otherwise known as the IKE/RADIUS method. Other variations include IKE Mode Config and Hybrid Authentication Mode for IKE.
- Modify IKE to support DHCP.

Each of these alternatives has technical advantages and disadvantages. Some efforts are being developed within the IETF and others are vendor driven. There are no clear choices and users must educate themselves as to the intricacies of each protocol and force vendors to be truthful as to functionality and interoperability of their products.

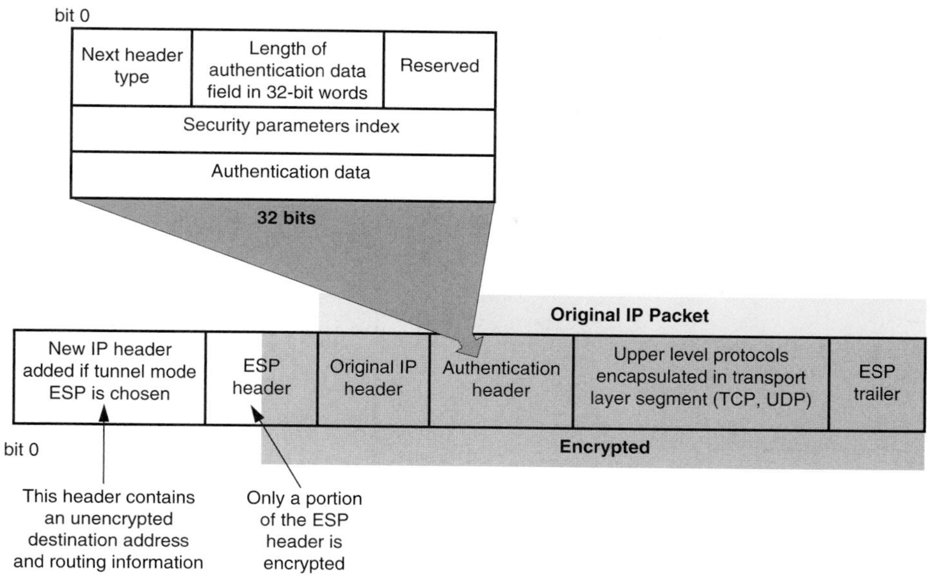

Figure 13-30 IP Packet Plus Authentication and Encryption Headers

PPTP—Point-to-Point Tunneling Protocol

PPTP is essentially just a tunneling protocol that allows managers to choose whatever encryption or authentication technology they wish to hang off either end of the established tunnel. PPTP supports multiple network protocols including IPX, NetBEUI, and IP. PPTP is primarily concerned with secure remote access in that PPP-enabled clients would be able to dial in to a corporate network via the Internet.

Enterprise Network Security

To maintain proper security over a widely distributed enterprise network, it is essential to be able to conduct certain security-related processes from a single, centralized, security management location. Among these processes or functions are the following:

- **Single point of registration (SPR)** allows a network security manager to enter a new user (or delete a terminated user) from a single centralized location and assign all associated rights, privileges, and access control to enterprise resources from this single point rather than having to enter this new user's information on multiple resources distributed throughout the enterprise.
- **Single sign-on (SSO),** also sometimes known as secure single sign-on (SSSO), allows the user to login to the enterprise network and to be authenticated from the client PC location. It is not necessary for the user to remember a variety of different user IDS and passwords to the numerous different enterprise servers from which they may request services. Since this is the sin-

gle entry point onto the enterprise network for this user, auditing software can be used to keep nonrepuditable records of all activities and transactions. Any of the variety of authentication technologies discussed earlier can be used in support of single sign-on.

- **Single access control view** allows the user's access from the client workstation to display only those resources that the user actually has access to. Any differences between server platforms should be shielded from the user. The user should not need to memorize different commands or control interfaces for the variety of enterprise servers that a user may need to access.
- **Security auditing and intrusion detection** is able to track and identify suspicious behaviors from both internal employees and potential intruders. In addition to detecting and reporting these instances, it is essential to be able to respond in an appropriate and automated fashion to these events. Although the intrusions may take place anywhere on the widely distributed network, the detection and response to such events must be controlled from a centralized security management location.

Tying It All Together—Security Frameworks

An enterprise-wide security solution currently involves the deployment of a wide variety of different security technologies, sometimes referred to as point products, from a multitude of vendors. The centralized management of such a wide array of technology is very challenging. In response to this challenge, **security frameworks** have begun to emerge that attempt to consolidate security management into a single architecture or console, allowing centralized policy management and automated incident response. Obviously, interoperability standards are required to get security tools from various vendors to all interact with a single overall framework. The **OPSEC (open platform for security) alliance** is one example of a multivendor interoperable security architecture. More than 200 vendors of security technology have joined the OPSEC alliance, which offers certification for OPSEC-compliant security products.

GOVERNMENT IMPACT

Government agencies play a major role in the area of network security. The two primary functions of these various government agencies are

- Standards-making organizations that set standards for the design, implementation, and certification of security technology and systems.
- Regulatory agencies that control the export of security technology to a company's international locations.

Standards-Making Organizations

Although many standards-making organizations are involved to varying degrees in the field of network security, following are some of the most significant ones.

ANSI The American National Standards Institute, or ANSI, is the United States representative to the International Standards Organization, or ISO. Any submissions to the ISO from other U.S. standards organizations must first be submitted to ANSI.

NIST The National Institute of Standards and Technology, or the NIST, was formed in 1987, but it was formerly known as the National Bureau of Standards. This organization issues publications called the Federal Information Processing Standards, or FIPS publications. Category 5 FIPS publications deal with computer security standards and guidelines and include subcategories of access control, cryptography, general computer security, risk analysis and contingency planning, and security labels. The NIST also publishes a series of special publications related to computer security included in the SP500 and SP800 series. The NIST also operates a very useful Computer Security Resource Clearinghouse on the World Wide Web at http://csrc.ncsl.nist.gov/

IAB The Internet Architecture Board is the policy setting and decision review board for the Internet. The IETF or Internet Engineering Task Force is a subgroup of the IAB that is responsible for setting the technical standards that run the Internet. This group is responsible for issuing and gathering the responses to RFC (requests for comments).

ISO The International Standards Organization is a voluntary organization sanctioned by the United Nations. It is responsible for international standards in a variety of fields, not just data communications. Besides the OSI seven-layer reference model, the ISO is also responsible for the security-related addendum to the OSI model known as **ISO 7498/2,** the OSI Security Architecture.

NSA The National Security Agency is a secretive governmental organization that works closely with the NIST and is responsible for the design and use of nonmilitary encryption technology. The NSA also runs the NCSC, or the National Computer Security Center (www.nsa.gov).

NCSC The purpose of this organization is to work with members of the computer industry to provide guidelines that are designed to help them develop trusted systems and computer products. This organization is also known for a security certification program called the Trusted Computer System Evaluation Criteria (TCSEC). It is commonly known as the Orange Book because of the color of the jacket. There is also a Red Book from the NCSC, which was developed in 1987 as a supplement to the Orange Book. These "colored book" security guidelines have been criticized for their focus primarily on computer security rather than network security.

Orange Book Certification The primary focus of the Orange Book is to provide confidential protection of sensitive information based on six fundamental requirements:

1. Security policy: An explicit and well-defined security policy must be enforced by the system.
2. Marking: Access control labels must be associated with all objects.
3. Identification: Individual users must be identified.

Division	Protection	Class	Protection	Description
D	Minimal	D	Minimal	Evaluated but does not meet any higher class requirements
C	Discretionary	C1	Discretionary security	Confidence in hardware and software controls
				Isolates and authenticates users and data
		C2	Controlled access	Encapsulates resources; login and explicit auditing
B	Mandatory	B1	Labeled security	Explicit protection model; execution domains, file labels, system security officer and documentation required
		B2	Structured	Formal security model, kernelized, covert channel ID, mandatory controls including communication lines required
		B3	Security domains	Central encapsulation, reference monitor, tamper proof, recovery procedures, protected against authentication attacks
A	Verified	A1	Verified design	Extensive security considerations during all developmental phases. Math tools, formal models with explicit math theorems, formal top level specifications, trusted software distribution required
		Beyond A1		Developmental; source verification

Figure 13-31 Orange Book Certification Criteria

4. Accountability: Audit information must be kept and protected so that actions affecting security can be traced to the responsible party.
5. Assurance: The system must contain hardware and/or software components that can be evaluated independently to provide sufficient assurance that the security policy and accountability criteria can be enforced.
6. Continuous protection: The components above that enforce these basic requirements must be continuously protected against tampering and/or unauthorized changes

The Orange Book is broken into two primary parts. The first part is illustrated in Figure 13-31. It specifies the criteria that must be met to achieve a specific rating. The criteria are defined in hierarchical fashion, with four different ratings possible. The "A" rating is the most secure possible and the "D" rating corresponds to the least secure rating possible. The second portion contains information about the basic objectives, rationale, and government policy behind the development of each of the criteria. It is also intended to provide guidelines for product developers to aid them in achieving a specific criteria.

The Orange Book certification process is both costly and lengthy. Typically, the certification process is projected to take 2 years to complete at a cost of 17 million dollars. To date, both NetWare and NT Server have achieved the C-2 certification. An important point to be aware of is that many products may advertise a certification compliance with an Orange Book level; however, compliance and certification are two very different terms. Any vendor can claim compliance, but only vendors that have spent the time and money to pursue the certification process can claim that their products are C-2 certified.

Encryption Export Policy and Key Recovery

Many corporations and organizations depend on the need for private and confidential communication on an international basis. However, in the United States, export of encryption software is tightly controlled. The traditional limit on exportable encryption technology was a 40-bit key. However, 40-bit keys can be cracked in a matter of minutes and do not offer much protection. Businesses conducting operations internationally obviously want to be able to use stronger encryption technology. The government, on the other hand, wishes to gain greater control over international encrypted communication as evidenced by its **Clipper chip** initiative.

The Clipper Chip initiative proposed that every phone and data communications device in the United States would be equipped with a Clipper Chip to support encryption. The part of the proposal that had businesses and individuals concerned was that the government would hold a spare set of keys that could decrypt any messaged encrypted by a Clipper Chip device. The notion of trusting the government with a spare set of keys caused quite an uproar and the proposal was subsequently not pursued. However, the initiative clearly showed the government's intention to seek greater control of international encrypted communications.

A proposal announced in September 1999 and clarified in January 2000 allows U.S. companies to export retail encryption technology to commercial firms, individuals, and nongovernment agencies without a license after a technical review. U.S. companies can export encryption technology to their own foreign subsidiaries without review or restriction. The new regulations also relax restrictions on publicly available encryption technology posted to the Internet. Exports to Cuba, Iran, Iraq, Libya, North Korea, Sudan, and Syria are still prohibited. Export of encryption technology is now administered by the Commerce Department's Bureau of Export Administration.

Key recovery schemes basically ensure that a spare set of encryption keys is always available. With key recovery, the actual information used to reconstruct a key travels with the message header. However, someone with the key decryption codes (the spare set of keys) must combine the decryption codes with the key information in the message header to decrypt the message. The big question seems to be, "Who will hold the keys?" **Key escrow agencies,** otherwise known as trusted third parties, are the most commonly proposed solution. Other proposals say that large multinational corporations should be able to act as their own key escrow agents. At the moment there are about 13 different **key recovery mechanisms,** and no single standard has been proposed, although an IBM-led key-recovery alliance with 40 corporate members has been formed. If key recovery were to be extended to a domestic basis, the implications could be phenomenal. Everyone who uses the Internet for communication would need a key and a key escrow agent. This could mean tens of millions of keys unless some type of key sharing was initiated.

SUMMARY

Without question, the overriding theme in this chapter has been that the implementation of security technology in the absence of a comprehensive security policy including senior management support is a waste of time and money. Security policy must be developed as part of an overall increase in security awareness on the part of all users. It must be accompanied by a clear understanding of business processes and personal responsibilities as they relate to security policy implementation. Only in the context of a dynamic, constantly audited security policy can security technology implementation be successful.

The first security process that is generally addressed is virus protection, most often in response to a virus incident. Virus scanning technology is of little use without comprehensive, enforced policies regarding use and handling of diskettes and downloaded files. Activity monitors and signature scanners are two major types of virus scanning software.

The next security process that is generally addressed is authentication, ensuring that users attempting to log into network resources are really whom they claim to be. Authentication technology includes challenge response and time synchronous token authentication systems.

Authorization and access control ensure that authenticated users are only able to access those files, directories, and applications to which they are entitled. Kerberos is the best example of a comprehensive authentication/authorization system.

Firewalls are an effective means of shielding private, secure, internal networks from nonsecure external networks. Like other security technology, they must be implemented correctly and in accordance with the overall security policy. Two major categories of firewalls are packet filters, which discriminate between traffic based on source and destination addresses, and application gateways of proxies, which examine individual commands within applications.

Privacy of network communications is ensured by encryption. Private key encryption, public key encryption, and digital signature encryption are the major categories of encryption technology. Encryption sessions are customized through the use of keys. The longer the key, in bits, the more secure the transmission.

KEY TERMS

active content monitors
activity monitors
application gateways
application level filters
assets
assured pipelines
attack applets
authentication
authentication header
biometric authentication
brokered authorization
C-2 certification
CA
certificate authorities
certificate servers
challenge handshake authentication protocol
challenge-response token authentication
CHAP
ciphertext
circuit-level proxies
clipper chip
CRC checkers
data encryption standard
decoys
denial of service attack
DES
Digital IDs
digital signature encryption
DMZ
dual firewalls
dual-homed gateway
emulation technology
encapsulating security payload header
ESP
event detection
Extended terminal access control access system
false accepts
false rejects
filter
filter tables
firewall
generic security service-applications program interface
GSS-API
hashing checkers
heuristic analysis
IDEA

IKE
inter-realm
internal firewalls
international data encryption algorithm
Internet key exchange
Internet security association and key management protocol
intrusion detection systems
IP spoofing
IPsec
IPv6
ISAKMP
ISO 7498/2
Kerberos
key escrow agencies
key recovery mechanisms
L2F
L2TP
land attack
latency
layer 2 tunneling protocol
layer two forwarding
logic bombs
macro viruses
malicious applets
MD5
Multi-tiered firewall
National Computer Security Association
NCSA
network-based intrusion detection systems
network level filter
off-line audits
OPSEC Alliance open platform for security
OSI security architecture
packet filter
PAP
password authentication protocol
PCT
PEM
PGP
PKIX
point-to-point tunneling protocol
policy audits
polymorphic viruses
port level filter
PPTP
pretty good privacy
privacy enhanced mail
private communications technology
private key encryption
protective measures
proxies
public key certificates
public key encryption
public key infrastructure X 509
RADIUS
real-time audits
realms
remote authentication dial-in user service
risk
risk domain
RSA
S-HTTP
S/MIME
SATAN
Secure Courier
Secure Electronic Transactions
secure hypertext transport protocol
secure multipurpose Internet mail extension
secure single login
secure sockets layer
Security Analyzer Tools for Analyzing Networks
security appliance
security auditing and intrusion detection
security frameworks
security policy development life cycle
security probes
service-granting ticket
session keys
SET
signature scanners
simple distributed security infrastructure
simple key management for IP
simple public key infrastructure
single access control view
single point of registration
single sign-on
SKIP
smart cards
Socks
SPDLC
SPKI/SDSI
SPR
SSL
SSO
TCP
threats
three-way handshake
ticket
ticket-granting ticket
time bombs
time-synchronous token authentication
token authentication
transmission control protocol
transport mode ESP
trojan horse
trusted gateway
trusted node
tunnel mode ESP
tunneling protocols
virtual PC
virus scanning
vulnerabilities
XTACACS

REVIEW QUESTIONS

1. What are some recent changes in the business and networking worlds that have brought network security to the forefront?
2. What is the importance of the cyclical nature of the security policy development life cycle?
3. What is the purpose of the security requirements assessment grid?
4. What is the dilemma involved with the security/productivity balance?
5. How do the critical success factors introduced with the network development life cycle apply to security policy development?
6. What is the purpose of the OSI Security Architecture and how does it relate to the OSI seven-layer reference model?
7. Differentiate between and give an example, in a network security context, of each of the following: asset, threat, vulnerability, risk, protective measures.
8. Are all of the entities listed in the previous question related by one-to-one relationships? Give an example to defend your answer.
9. Briefly summarize the roles of executives, management, and users in the successful development and implementation of security policy.
10. What is the difference between off-line audits and real-time audits?
11. What is the difference between event detection technology and intrusion detection technology?
12. What is the difference between security audit tools and security probes?
13. What is a virus?
14. What is the difference between a logic bomb and a time bomb?
15. What is a trojan horse?
16. What is a polymorphic virus?
17. What are hostile applets and which environment are they particular to?
18. Why are collaborative applications such as groupware an especially friendly environment for viruses?
19. Differentiate between virus scanning and activity monitors as antivirus technology.
20. What is the shortcoming of CRC and hashing checkers as antivirus solutions?
21. What is a firewall?
22. Differentiate between packet filtering firewalls and application gateway firewalls.
23. Describe the advantages and disadvantages of proxies.
24. What is a dual-homed gateway?
25. What is a trusted gateway?
26. How does a trusted gateway differ from a dual-homed gateway?
27. What is an internal firewall and what is the motivation for such a device?
28. What is authentication?
29. Differentiate between challenge-response authentication and time-synchronous authentication.
30. What is biometric authentication? Give some examples of biometric authentication technology.
31. What is Kerberos?
32. How does Kerberos ensure both authentication and authorization?
33. Differentiate between private key encryption, public key encryption, and digital signature encryption.
34. Why are public key certificates and certificate authorities necessary?
35. Why are APIs and application development environments required to integrate security services with information systems? What would be the alternative?
36. What is RADIUS and what added functionality does it offer over an environment without a three-tiered approach?
37. Differentiate between S-HTTP and SSL.
38. Differentiate between PAP and CHAP.
39. What is PGP? What are its advantages and disadvantages?
40. What is SET and what industry is it targeted toward?
41. What is a tunneling protocol and why is it necessary?
42. What is Secure IP (IPv6) and what services can it offer?
43. What is the difference between transport mode ESP and tunnel mode ESP?
44. What is the difference between single sign-on, single point of registration, and single access control view? What do they all have in common?
45. What is Orange Book or C-2 certification?
46. What is the Clipper Chip?
47. What is the purpose of a key recovery mechanism and how does it work?
48. What is the role of key escrow agencies in enabling a key recovery mechanism?
49. What are the potential implications if all Internet users were required to use key recovery mechanisms?
50. Discuss the advantages and disadvantages of the alternative enterprise firewall architectures discussed in the text. Are there other viable alternatives that were not mentioned?

ACTIVITIES

1. Research topics such as network security losses or computer crime and report on your results. What is the trend of the statistics over the last 5 years? How valid are the statistics in terms of being an accurate reflection of the entire extent of the problem?
2. Find an organization or business that will let you prepare a security policy document. Run the entire process as a well-organized project using project management software if possible. Start with a small feasibility and report your results before defining the full project scope. Use the planning tools supplied in the chapter and adapt them to your own situation as needed.
3. Choose any network security-related topic of interest and research it using only Internet resources. Two good sites to start with are http://www.ncsa.com and http://csrc.ncsl.nist.gov/
4. Consider the statement: The implementation of security technology in the absence of a comprehensive security policy is like putting a steel door on a grass hut. Find actual examples of network security implementations to either support or refute the statement.
5. Download a copy of Security Analyzer Tool for Analyzing Networks from ftp://ftp.win.tue.nl/pub/security/index.html After obtaining proper permissions, run the analysis tool and report on your results.
6. Log into Internet Security Systems web site at www.iss.net and review information regarding their RealSecure network-based attack analyzer. Compare its features with those of SATAN. What would be the most appropriate use for each technology?
7. Create a virus clearinghouse and information center for your school, business, or organization if one does not already exist. Does your organization have a published antivirus strategy? If not, create one. Report on your results.
8. Research the problem of hostile applets and components. What are the potential solutions to the problem? Is this a problem with the development languages?
9. What is Word Macro Concept virus? Find out exactly how it works and figure out how it can be eradicated and kept from spreading. How much of the solution is technology vs. procedures?
10. Design and prepare a budget for a safe remote access network including remote access server, firewall, authentication technology, and modems. Prepare alternative budget proposals for challenge-response vs. time-synchronous token authentication technology. Was the price difference significant? If so, how could the price difference be justified?
11. Research the field of biometric authentication technology. What are the most stable and dependable products? What are the latest products? Can you find data on false-accept and false-reject rates of biometric authentication technology?
12. What is the current rate of acceptance and implementation of Kerberos in industry? What are the strengths and limitations of the architecture?
13. Research the issue of privacy in the age of electronic commerce. What impact might digital IDs and key recovery schemes have on an individual's right to privacy? Consider debating the issue in class. What are the conflicting motivations or goals behind the issue?
14. Research virtual private networks. What is the extent of actual implementation of virtual private networks as opposed to the amount of press coverage and technology development? Explain your results.
15. Research and prepare a presentation, time-line, bulletin board on the government's role in encryption technology control, especially in terms of export control. Begin with the Clipper Chip initiative and follow it through the present day.

CASE STUDY

Swedish Lottery Takes A Chance on Public-Key Certificates

The Swedish government last spring decided to allow the Swedish National Lottery to expand its 8-year-old gaming operations to provide gambling over the Internet—as long as the security was as tight as a bank vault.

The country's lottery system has a tradition of relying on Swedish banks to move money on a real-time basis to and from gamblers' bank accounts—with their permission, of course—whenever they play casino-style games in venues such as restaurants. Out of a population of 8.9 million, Sweden has a whopping 750,000 registered gamblers who do this.

Svenska Spel, as the gaming operation is known, wanted online gamblers to have something better than just passwords to safeguard transactions, given that real-time money transfers would be involved in every online bet. So the lottery organization opted to give online gamblers in Sweden free public-key digital certificates to prove their identity and to digitally sign and encrypt bets.

The system works like this: Each approved online gambler gets a mailed letter with a PIN number that he can enter via his browser at the lottery Web site to download the digital certificate required to place bets.

The www.svenskaspel.se site so far has distributed about 7,000 public-key certificates to Sweden's registered online gamblers, says Ralph Gelfgren, vice president for IT development at the Swedish National Lottery, which is a quasi-governmental organization. The lottery is using software from Celo Communications of Dublin, Ireland at its Web site to help distribute the certificates.

Going with software from a U.S. firm was not an option, in light of laws preventing U.S. firms from exporting products with strong 128-bit encryption, Gelfgren says.

He adds that a handful of other European nations, including Finland and Norway, have online gambling, but that Sweden is the first nation to offer certificates to gamblers.

"The challenge for us in Sweden is the high security standard that the banks have set," Gelfgren says. The banks, such as Nordbanken, typically require that gamblers sign a paper to put a limit on fund transfers before they are allowed to play offline. The same applies in online gambling.

Gelfgren says Svenska Spel has gained momentum by making the registration process as easy as possible. The first online betting game is wagering on sports events.

Though he doesn't know exactly why, online gamblers seem to be higher rollers than those who gamble offline, Gelfgren says.

Source: Ellen Messmer, "Swedish lottery takes a chance on public-key certificates," *Network World*, vol. 16, no. 49 (December 6, 2000), p. 44. Copyright © Network World. Reprinted with permission.

BUSINESS CASE STUDY QUESTIONS

Activities

1. Complete a top-down model for this case by gleaning facts from the case and placing them in the proper layer of the top-down model. After completing the top-down model, analyze and detail those instances where requirements were clearly passed down from upper layers to lower layers of the model and where solutions to those requirements were passed up from lower layers to upper layers of the model.
2. Detail any questions about the case that may occur to you for which answers are not clearly stated in the article.

Business

1. What was the business motivation or problem that initiated the search for the implemented solution?
2. What was the productivity impact of the implemented solution?

3. What was the current business process that moved money on a real-time basis from gamblers' bank accounts?
4. What was the proposed new business process?

Application

1. What applications are executed to implement the described solution?
2. How many public key certificates have been distributed to date?

Data

1. What were the security requirements for transferring data?

Network

1. What underlying network technologies were key to the achievement of stated business objectives?

Technology

1. What specific technologies were employed to deliver the described solution?
2. Describe the interaction between the various technologies employed or planned for this solution.
3. What technology restrictions limited the choices of available technology options?

Glossary

10/100 NICs Most 100BaseT NICs are called 10/100 NICs, which means that they are able to support either 10BaseT or 100BaseT, but not simultaneously.

1000BaseCX Uses copper twinaxial cable and transceivers for distances of only 25 meters; used primarily to link servers within a data center or high speed network devices within a wiring closet.

1000BaseLX Uses long wavelength (1300 nanometers) laser fiber optic media, used primarily for high speed campus backbone applications.

1000BaseSX Uses short wavelength (850 nanometers) laser fiber optic media; used primarily for horizontal building cabling on a given floor.

1000BaseTX This standard allows gigabit Ethernet to travel over 4 pair of Category 5 unshielded twisted pair at a distance of 100 meters.

100BaseFX Physical layer standard for 100Mbps transmission over fiber optic cable.

100BaseT4 Physical layer standard for 100Mbps transmission over 4 pair of Category 3, 4, or 5 UTP.

100BaseTX The most common of the three 100BaseX standards and the one for which the most technology is available. It specifies 100Mbps performance over 2 pair of Category 5 UTP (Unshielded Twisted Pair) or 2 pair of Type 1 STP (Shielded Twisted Pair).

100VG-AnyLAN A 100Mbps alternative to 100BaseT which replaces the CSMA/CD access methodology with Demand Priority Access or DPA, otherwise known as Demand Priority Protocol or DPP.

10Base2 A 10Mbps Ethernet standard for thin coaxial cable media.

10Base5 A 10Mbps Ethernet standard for thick coaxial cable media.

10BaseF A 10Mbps Ethernet standard for fiber optic cable media.

10BaseT A 10Mbps Ethernet standard for unshielded twisted pair media.

16-bit subsystem A shared memory address space, sometimes referred to as a 16-bit subsystem, allows 16 bit applications to execute in a 32 bit operating environment.

16QAM A 16 point quadrature amplitude modulation; a modulation scheme with 16 different potential detectable events would allow 4 bits/baud or quadbits to be produced or detected per signaling event. In this case the transmission rate in bps would be 4 times the baud rate.

1Base5 A 1Mbps Ethernet standard for unshielded twisted pair.

23B+D 23 bearer channels (64Kbps ea.) plus one 64K D channel. Configuration of PRI ISDN.

2B+D 2 64Kbps B channels plus one 16K D channel. Configuration of BRI ISDN.

30B+D 30 64Kbps bearer channels plus one 64K D channel. European PRI which maps to an E-1.

3270 protocol conversion card Card inserted into an open expansion slot of a PC. Additional protocol conversion software, which may or may not be included with the protocol conversion card, must be loaded onto the PC in order to make the PC keyboard behave like a 3270 terminal keyboard.

3G Mobile Telephony Service This next generation of wireless transmission services is most often grouped under the name of 3G (Third Generation) Mobile Telephony, otherwise known as UWC (Universal Wireless Communications)—136.

4 conductor station wire RYGB; the type of phone wire installed in most homes consists of a tan plastic jacket containing four untwisted wires: red, yellow, green, and black.

7 Hop limit One very important limitation of source routing bridges as applied to large internetworks. Because of the limited space in the RIF (Router Information Field) of the explorer packet, only 7 hop locations can be included in the path to any remote destination.

AAL ATM adaptation layer protocols convert user input payloads into ATM cells.

ABR Available bit rate; ATM bandwidth management scheme that takes a fixed minimum amount of bandwidth plus whatever VBR (variable bit rate) is not using.

access charges RBOCs were allowed to charge access charges for co-location of the alternate carrier's equipment in their COs.

Access Control List *See* ACL.

access line Local loop from customer premises to network service entry point.

access methodologies Because the LAN media is to be shared by numerous PC users, there must be some way to control access by multiple users to that media. These media sharing methods are properly known as access methodologies.

access server *See* Communications server.

ACD Incoming calls are routed directly to certain extensions without going through a central switchboard. Calls can be routed according to the incoming trunk or phone number. Often used in customer service organizations in which calls may be distributed to the first available agent.

ACE Adverse Channel Enhancements; a collection of 4 MNP 10 protocols designed to work with circuits subject to impairment such as cellular.

ACE/NAK Acknowledgment/negative acknowledgment, used with ARQ error correction to indicate whether or not retransmission is required.

acknowledgment Postive acknowledgment indicating data block was received without error.

acknowledgment & polling traffic The first characteristic of SNA that can cause trouble on a LAN is the great amount of acknowledgment and polling traffic between SNA processors and SNA end-user devices. This constant chatter could quickly monopolize the better part of the LAN bandwidth.

ACL A list of users authorized to access a given resource. An ACL is located on the server containing the resource and includes the effective rights or permissions that the user has to the resource.

acquisition costs Networking and systems budgets typically focused only on the acquisition costs of the new system. Even within the acquisition category, costs associated with personnel additions, changes, and training were often omitted.

ACR Attenuation to Crosstalk Ratio—measured in dB or decibels. A decibel is a logarithmic rather than linear measurement of the ratio between two powers, often a data signal and some type of noise or interference.

active management MAUs Able to send alerts to management consoles regarding malfunctioning token ring adapters and can also forcibly remove these misbehaving adapters from the ring.

active monitor In a token passing access methodology, the token is generated in the first place by a designated PC known as the active monitor and passed among PCs until one PC would like to access the network.

activity monitors A category of antivirus technology with the ability to monitor behavior of programs.

Adaptive Differential Pulse Code Modulation *See* ADPCM.

adaptive protocols Protocols that are able to change transmission characteristics as circuit quality varies.

Adaptive Size Packet Assembly A MNP 4 protocol that changes the amount of data transmitted in each block dependent on circuit quality.

Adaptive switching *See* Error-free cut-through switches.

address bit order reversal In the case of IEEE 802.3, the least significant bit is the right-most bit of the byte and, in the case of IEEE 802.5, the least significant bit is the left-most bit of the byte. This bit order reversal is especially troublesome for translating bridges which must translate between token ring and Ethernet frames.

address caching In order to avoid constantly flooding the network with explorer packets seeking destinations, source routing bridges may employ some type of address caching or RIF caching, so that previously determined routes to known destinations are saved and reused.

address classes IP addresses are categorized into address classes A, B, C, D, or E.

address resolution The process of resolving a hardware (MAC) address from a layer three network layer address.

address resolution protocol *See* ARP.

address resolution server LAN emulation is most often implemented by the ATM vendor by the installation of an address resolution server, which provides translation between the ATM addressing scheme and the addressing scheme that is native to a particular emulated LAN.

ADPCM By transmitting only the approximate difference or change in amplitude of consecutive amplitude samples, rather than the absolute amplitude, only 32Kbps of bandwidth is required for each conversation digitized via ADPCM as opposed to PCM.

ADSL Asymmetric digital subscriber line. Local loop data service able to offer 6Mbps download and 640Kbps upload over existing copper pairs without interfering with existing POTS service.

ADSP A connectionless session layer protocol used in the AppleTalk protocol suite.

advanced intelligent network *See* AIN.

Advanced mobile phone service *See* AMPS.

Advanced Parallel Technology *See* APT.

Advanced Peer to Peer Networking *See* APPN.

Advanced Power Management *See* APM.

Adverse Channel enchancements Transmitting data over analog cellular networks requires modems that support specialized cellular transmission protocols on both ends of the cellular transmission in order to maximize throughput. Examples of such protocols are MNP-10 Adverse Channel Enhancements and Enhanced Throughput Cellular (ETC).

Adverse Channel Enhancements *See* ACE.

AEP A protocol used to test network connectivity on AppleTalk networks through echo-reply packets.

AFP The file sharing application layer protocol used in the AppleTalk protocol suite.

agent In between the intelligent application, reporting on event conditions and performance metrics, and the management console is an autonomous piece of software known as an **agent,** which collects these performance statistics and properly formats them for transmission to the application management console.

agent event manager One of three cooperating components of the agent portion of the client/agent/server architecture. The agent event manager is combined with a customer-written transaction handler to form an entity known as the intelligent agent which resides on the local server. Once the agent event manager receives a request from a mobile client, it acts on behalf of that client in all communications with the local server until the original client request is totally fulfilled.

agents Network statistics and information are gathered in the first place and packetized in SNMP format by specialized software known as agents which reside within the monitored network device and are supplied by the network device's manufacturer.

AIN Signaling System 7 and the intelligent services that it enables are often described as part of an all-encompassing interface between users and the PSTN (Public Switched Telephone Network) known as AIN or Advanced Intelligent Network.

American Standard Code for Information Interchange *See* ASCII.

Amplifier amplitude Device used on analog circuits to strengthen and retransmit signals carrier wave characteristic which is manipulated to represent 1s and 0s (wave height).

amplitude modulation A modulation scheme in which amplitude is manipulated in order to represent discrete detectable events which are then interpreted into 1s and 0s.

AMPS The current circuit switched analog cellular network is more properly known by the transmission standard to which it adheres known as Advanced Mobile Phone Service (AMPS) and operates in the 800MHz frequency range.

AMS **Applications management specification;** one proposal for standardizing how instrumentation should be developed within applications.

analog Transmission method characterized by continuously varying tones within a given bandwidth or range of frequencies.

analog simultaneous voice/data *See* ASVD.

ANI Automatic number identification; also known as caller ID.

API Application program interface; a set of standard commands supported by both application programs and the operating systems with which they interact.

APM Power management features offered by operating systems have been standardized as the Advanced Power Management (APM) specification.

AppleTalk Included as a communications protocol in order to support NT's Services for Macintosh (SFM).

AppleTalk Data Stream Protocol *See* ADSP.

AppleTalk Echo Protocol *See* AEP.

AppleTalk Filing Protocol *See* AFP.

AppleTalk Session Protocol *See* ASP.

AppleTalk Transaction Protocol *See* ATP.

application gateways Concerned with what services or applications a message is requesting in addition to who is making that request. Connections between requesting clients and service providing servers are created only after the application gateway is satisfied as to the legitimacy of the request. Even when the legitimacy of the request has been established, only proxy clients and servers actually communicate with each other.

Application level filters Examine the entire request for data rather than just the source and destination addresses. Secure files can be marked as such and application level filters will not allow those files to be transferred, even to users authorized by port level filters.

Application MIB Identifies three key groups of variables for proper application tracking and management.

Application program interface *See* API.

application response measurement *See* ARM.

application services It is the server network operating system that is responsible for application services, which includes not only executing the back-end engine portion of the application, but also supplying the messaging and communications services to enable interoperability between distributed clients and servers.

applications layer The application layer, layer 7 of the OSI Model is also open to misinterpretation. Application layer protocols do not include end-user application programs. Rather, they include utilities that support end-user application programs. Some people include network operating systems in this category. Strictly speaking, the best examples of application layer protocols are the OSI protocols X.400 and X.500.

applications management specification *See* AMS.

APPN Advanced Peer to Peer Network, IBM's answer to multiprotocol networking on a peer to peer basis using the SNA architecture, rather than a LAN-based network architecture.

APT Microcom protocol that allows modems to connect to PCs via parallel port in order to avoid serial port bottlenecks.

ARM Application response measurement; an API that can be used by applications developers, and can measure several key application statistics.

ARP Address Resolution Protocol (RFC 826); used if an IP address of workstation is known but a data-link layer address for the same workstation is required.

ARQ Automatic retransmission request; error correction protocol that requires retransmission of data blocks received in error.
ASCII Standardized method for encoding humanly readable characters; uses a series of 7 bits to represent 128 ($2^7 = 128$) different characters.
ASP The session layer protocol used in the AppleTalk protocol suite.
assets Corporate property of some value that require varying degrees of protection.
assured pipelines *See* Application gateways.
ASVD Analog simultaneous voice/data; does not transmit voice and data in a truly simultaneous manner. Instead, it switches quickly between voice and data transmission. Voice transmission always takes priority, so data transfers are paused during data transmissions. ASVD has been formalized as ITU standard V.61.
asymmetric digital subscriber line *See* ADSL.
asymmetrical transmission A data transmission where the two directions operate at different speeds.
asynchronous frames In FDDI, while synchronous frames are being transmitted, any unused network capacity can still be used by other workstations transmitting asynchronous frames.
asynchronous transfer mode *See* ATM.
asynchronous transmission Synchronization is reestablished with the transmission of each character in asynchronous transmission via the use of start and stop bits.
AT&T 5ESS Switch One of the switches that supports ISDN.
ATM Asynchronous Transfer Mode; a switch-based WAN service using fixed length frames, more properly referred to as cells. Fixed length cells assure fixed length processing time by ATM switches, thereby enabling predictable, rather than variable, delay and delivery time.
ATM access switches Interface between ATM switches and legacy LANs.
ATM adaptation layer *See* AAL.
ATM gateway switches *See* ATM access switches.
ATM LAN emulation ATM service that allows Ethernet or token ring traffic to travel across higher speed ATM networks without requring changes to LAN workstations.
ATP The transport layer protocol used in the AppleTalk protocol suite.
Attachment Units *See* AU.
Attack applets Attack applets are Java applets, downloaded from the Web, intent on serious security breaches.
attenuation The decrease in the power of signal over a distance in a particular type of wire or media.
Attenuation to crosstalk ratio *See* ACR.
AU Iso-Ethernet hubs are known as Attachment Units (AU) and cost between $400–$500 per port.
Audiotex These systems deliver audio information to callers based on responses on the touch-tone keypad to prerecorded questions. Primarily used for information hotlines.
authentication The process of proving that a user is who they claim to be. Authentication is a two-step process: identification and proof of identification.
authentication credentials The means used to authenticate a user. Most commonly a user ID and a password.
Authentication Header In Secure IP, provides data integrity and allows for the authentication of IP packets.
authorization The process of determining the access rights a user should have for a resource. Authorization is usually accomplished through the use of Access Control Lists.
auto restoral Ability of dial backup units to restore communications to leased lines from dial-up backup lines once the leased lines have been repaired.
auto-detection & configuration Auto-detection & configuration of installed controllers, interface cards, and peripherals by network operating systems are dependent on the network operating system possessing a compatible driver for that device.
automated attendant Allows callers to direct calls to a desired individual at a given business without necessarily knowing that person's extension number.
automatic call distribution *See* ACD.
automatic number identification Service available via either ISDN or in-band signaling.
Automatic retransmission request *See* ARQ.
available bit rate *See* ABR.
AWG American Wire Gauge; wire thickness is measured by gauge and represented with the unit AWG.

B channel In Isochronous Ethernet, the 6.144 Mbps C channel is in fact further subdivided into 96 64Kbps ISDN B channels, which carry the actual multimedia traffic. Applications are able to aggregate these B channels as needed up to the 6.144Mbps limit.
backbone network In a hierarchial enterprise network design, the high speed inter-LAN portion of the network is often referred to as the backbone network.
backbone/data center switch Offer high capacity, fault tolerant, switching capacity with traffic management capabilities. These high-end switches are actually a self-contained backbone network that is sometimes referred to as a collapsed backbone network.

backbone-attached LAN switch Offer all of the local switching capabilities of the stand-alone workgroup/departmental LAN switch plus switched access to higher speed backbone networks.

backplane capacity The number of simultaneous point to point connections that a given switch can support.

backpressure In the case of Ethernet switches, backpressure prevents lost frames during overload conditions by sending out false collision detection signals in order to get transmitting clients and servers to time-out long enough to give the switch a chance to forward buffered data.

backward compatibility An important aspect of any migration plan to a new client network operating system is the extent of support for backward compatibility is terms of application support, also known as legacy application support. In other words, will current applications run without modification on the new network operating system?

backward explicit congestion notification *See* BECN.

bandwdith management Often used interchangeably with the term traffic shaping, can be defined as the appropriate allocation of bandwidth to support application requirements.

bandwidth Range of frequencies.

bandwidth on demand interoperability group *See* BONDING.

Base I/O address This address defines a memory location through which the data will flow between the network interface card and the CPU.

Base memory address Not to be confused with Base I/O address, some NICs require a base memory address to indicate the starting location in the computer's memory that can be used by the NIC as a buffer memory.

baseband transmission Means that the entire bandwidth of the media is devoted to one data channel.

baseline data In order to properly quantify increased productivity, one must first measure current levels of productivity by developing evaluation criteria so that baseline data can be gathered.

Basic input output system *See* BIOS.

basic rate interface *See* BRI.

baud Timed opportunities to identify ones and zeros by sampling the carrier wave are known as signaling events. The proper name for one signaling event is a baud.

baud rate The number of baud, or signaling events, per second.

bearer channels ISDN channels that actually bear, or carry, data and voice.

BECN Backward explicit congestion notification; a frame relay flow control mechanism.

Bell 103 Bell system modem standard for 300bps modem using FSK modulation.

Bell 212A Bell system modem standard for 1200bps modem using 4PSK.

benchmarking A process of demonstrating the impact of implemented technology by tying networking costs to business value.

BER Bit error rate; measurement of errors on a given transmission line.

BGP Border Gateway Protocol; an exterior gateway protocol used to exchange routing information between autonomous systems.

billing verification By inputting a company's current network design in the analysis and design software and by using the tariff tables to price individual circuits within that network, prices generated from the tariff tables can be compared to recent phone bills.

bindery Network operating systems have always depended on some sort of naming service or directory in which to store information about users as well as systems resources such as disks, servers, and printers. NetWare 3.x servers stored this type of information in a bindery.

binding NDIS specifies a binding operation that is managed by a separate program known as the Protocol Manager, which combines separate NDIS compliant driver software supplied by NIC and NOS vendors.

biometric authentication Can authenticate users based on fingerprints, palm prints, retinal patterns, voice recognition, or other physical characteristics.

BIOS Basic input system; interface between operating system and PC hardware components.

B-ISDN Broadband ISDN; ATM switching plus SONET transmission.

bit A binary digit, a 1 or 0.

bit error rate *See* BER.

Block Sequence Number Used in ARQ error control to identify which data blocks were received in error.

bluetooth A wireless transmission standard for linking mobile phones, computers, and other devices using unlicensed 2.45GHz frequency for transmission rates of up to 1Mbps over 10 meters. Supported by more than 700 vendors.

BONDING Bandwidth on demand interoperability group Inverse multiplexing standard.

BootP Originally designed to configure local diskless workstations that were unable to store IP configuration information locally. In the case of BootP, the MAC address of the BootP client had to be known beforehand, entered into a database in the BootP server, and permanently associated with an IP address.

boundary router In the case of boundary or branch office routers, all routing information is kept at the central site router. This allows the boundary router to require less technical configuration and to be available for a lower cost than central site routers.

bps Bits per second.

breakout boxes A device used to monitor and manipulate transmission signals.

BRI Basic rate interface; 2B+D ISDN.

bridge Uses MAC layer addressing to logically segment traffic between attached LANs.

Broadband ISDN *See* B-ISDN.

broadband transmission In general, any transmission service at the T-1 level or greater is considered broadband.

broadcast In a broadcast logical topology, a data message is sent simultaneously to all nodes on the network. Each node decides individually if the data message was directed toward it. If not, the message is simply ignored.

broadcast address A special network address that identifies all nodes on a network segment rather than a single node.

broadcast filtering Instead of allowing explorer packets onto the internetwork, routers can filter these broadcast packets out of the traffic, read the destination address to which the PC is seeking a route, and supply the PC directly with that information after consulting its own routing tables.

broadcast storm In the case of improperly addressed frames or frames destined for nonexistent addresses, frames can be infinitely perpetuated or flooded onto all bridged LANs in a condition known as a broadcast storm.

brokered authorization Authorization security software can be either server-based, also known as brokered authorization, or workstation-based, also referred to as trusted node.

brouters At one time, specialized devices that could either bridge or route were referred to as brouters; today, however, most advanced routers include bridging functionality.

Buffer Memory Memory included in modems to hold transmitted blocks of data in order to implement sliding window or continuous ARQ.

bulk retrieval mechanism A new SNMP2 procedure whereby managers can retrieve several pieces of network information at a time from a given agent.

bus A linear arrangement with terminators on either end and devices connected to the "bus" via connectors and/or transceivers.

bus and tag A standard for high speed data channels between FEPs and IBM mainframes, Bus and Tag has a transmission rate of 4.5Mbps and has been available since 1967.

bus mastering DMA The CPU on the network adapter card manages the movement of data directly into the PC's RAM memory without interruption of the system CPU by taking control of the PC's expansion bus.

business functional areas Once overall system performance characteristics have been established, the overall business can be broken down into large functional areas. These functional areas may correspond to corporate departments or divisions.

business process reengineering As business processes are described, brainstorming quickly takes over and problems that seemed deeply imbedded in current systems are solved as new or modified business processes are defined for the new strategic information system design.

buy-in As each stage is concluded, buy-in or agreement as to conclusions from all affected customer groups is of critical importance.

byte A collection of 8 bits which represents a character.

C channel In Isochronous Ethernet, A 6.144Mbps ISDN C channel is reserved for streaming time-sensitive traffic such as multimedia applications.

C-2 certification The Orange Book certification process is both costly and lengthy. Typically, the certification process is projected to take 2 years to complete at a cost of $17 million. To date, both NetWare and NT Server have achieved the C-2 certification.

C2 level security A standard security level required by the U.S. government for stand-alone systems.

CA Third-party key certification services, or certificate authorities (CA), issue the public keys along with a certificate assuring the authenticity of the key.

cable modem A high speed data communications device that encodes digital data onto a cable television distribution system.

cable scanners Layer 1 testers are more commonly known as **cable scanners** or cable testers.

CAI PBX-integrated wireless phones support the CT2 (Cordless Telephony Generation 2) Common Air Interface (CAI) global standard for low-power wireless transmission.

call accounting system Systems that can pay for themselves in a short amount of time by spotting and curtailing abuse as well as by allocating phone usage charges on a departmental basis.

call control Using computer-based applications users can more easily use all of the features of their phone system or PBX, especially the more complicated but seldom used features. Includes use of features like on-line phone books, auto-dialing, click-and-point conference calls, on-line display, and processing of voice mail messages.

call pickup Allows a user to pick up or answer another user's phone without having to actually forward calls.

call set-up packets Used to establish virtual circuits in frame relay networks.

callback security Modem security feature that verifies users and dials them back at predetermined numbers.

CANE Computer Assisted Engineering; the use of software tools of one type or another to assist in network engineering.

CAP A de facto standard, deployed in many trial ADSL units; developed by AT&T Paradyne.

card and socket services *See* CSS.

card services The card services sub-layer of PCMCIA Card & Socket Services is hardware independent and interfaces to the client operating system or network operating system driver software.

CardBus Version 3.0 of the PCMCIA standard; supports bus widths to 32 bits and clock speeds as high as 33MHz.

Carrier Sense Multiple Access with Collision Avoidance *See* CSMA/CA.

Carrier Sense Multiple Access with Collision Detection *See* CSMA/CD.

carrier wave A reference wave that is manipulated by modems to represent 1s and 0s.

carrierless amplitude & phase *See* CAP.

carriers A carrier, or phone company, that offers phone services to the general public in a given geographic area.

cascading ports Hubs may also be cascadable or stackable via cascading ports which may be specialized ports on the hub or may be switch configurable "normal" ports allowing repeated data to flow out of a cascading port to the next hub rather than the normal inbound-only port traffic flow.

CAT 5 Category 5 UTP -22 or 24 AWG; tested for attenuation and near-end crosstalk to 100MHz. Capable of transmitting up to 100Mbps when strictly installed to EIA/TIA 568 specifications. Currently the most commonly installed category of UTP.

CBR Constant Bit Rate; voice is currently transmitted across ATM networks using a bandwidth reservation scheme known as CBR, which is analogous to a Frame Relay virtual circuit.

CBS Commited Burst Size; defines the extent to which a user can exceed their CIR over a period of time in a frame relay network.

CCIS Common Channel Interoffice Signaling; a more official name for out-of-band signaling.

CDDI Copper Distributed Data Interface; employs FDDI over twisted pair media. The official ANSI standard for CDDI is known as TP-PMD (Twisted Pair-Physical Media Dependent).

CDMA Code division multiple access; transmits digitized voice packets from numerous calls at different frequencies spread throughout the entire allocated bandwidth spectrum.

CDPD Cellular Digital Packet Data; a service that uses idle capacity in the circuit-switched cellular network to transmit IP-based data packets. The fact that CDPD is IP-based allows it to easily interface to IP-based private networks as well as to the Internet and other e-mail services.

cell relay Fast packet switching technology employing fixed length cells.

cells ATM (Asynchronous Transfer Mode) is a switch-based WAN service using fixed length frames, more properly referred to as cells.

Cellular Digital Packet Data *See* CDPD.

central clock A timing device in the TDM that gives each input device its allotted time to empty its buffer into an area of the TDM where the combined data from all of the polled input devices are conglomerated into a single message frame for transmission over the composite circuit.

Central Directory Server In APPN, the Central Directory Server can save time as well as network traffic for the Network Nodes. Instead of each Network Node on an internetwork doing its own information gathering and internetwork exploration and inquiry, they can simply consult the Central Directory Server.

central office *See* CO.

central site router Otherwise known as enterprise or backbone routers; employed at large corporate sites, whereas boundary or branch office routers are employed at remote corporate locations with less routing requirements and fewer technical support personnel.

certificate authorities *See* CA.

Certificate servers Public key infrastructures that link a particular user to a particular public key are implemented through the use of server-based software known as certificate servers. Certificate server software also supports encryption and digital signatures while flexibly supporting directory integration, multiple certificate types, and a variety of request fulfillment options.

Challenge Handshake Authentication Protocol *See* CHAP.

Challenge Response Token Authentication A token authentication protocol in which a user uses a Smart Card to generate a one-time session key response to a server initiated challenge.

channel bank When a bank of codes are arranged in a modular chassis to not only digitize analog voice conversations but also load them onto a shared high capacity (T-1:1.544Mbps) circuit, the hybrid device is referred to as a channel bank.

Channel Service Unit/Data Service Unit *See* CSU/DSU.

channel-attached gateways As an alternative to LAN-based gateways, they have the ability to interface directly to the mainframe's high speed data channel, thereby bypassing the FEP entirely. Physically, the channel attached gateways are often modules that are added to enterprise routers.

CHAP Challenge Handshake Authentication Protocol; provides a more secure means for establishing dial-in communication. Uses a three-way challenge that includes the user ID, password and also a key that encrypts the ID and password.

CHAP MD5 A protocol for PPP encrypted authentication included with most PPP clients.

CHAP MD80 A protocol for authentication for Windows NT RAS included with most PPP clients.

character encoding Process required to render humanly readable characters into machine language through representation of characters as a series of 1s and 0s.

checksums Error check character calculated using decimal face values of characters in transmitted data blocks.

CIM **Common Information Model;** proposed protocol currently under development by the DMTF (Desktop Management Task Force) would support HMMS. CIM would permit management data gathered from a variety of enterprise and desktop voice and data technology to all be transported, processed, displayed, and stored by a single CIM-compliant Web browser.

ciphertext In encryption, the changed, meaningless data.

CIPX A protocol for compression of IPX headers included with most PPP clients.

CIR Committed Information Rate; refers to the minimum bandwidth guaranteed to users for "normal" transmission in a frame relay network.

circuit analysis and configuration alternatives Explores the possibilities for delivering data traffic in a reliable and effective manner, once the nature of the data traffic is thoroughly understood.

circuit-level proxy Provide proxy services for transport layer protocols such as TCP.

circuit switched network A network based on circuit switched services in which users are able to use the entire bandwidth of physical circuits created solely for their transmissions.

circuit switching A switching process in which physical circuits are created, maintained, and terminated for individual point-to-point or multi-point connections.

circuit-switched cellular Analog cellular service capable of supporting 14.4Kbps max.

Class 1 regional center Highest capacity switching office in PSTN network hierarchy.

Class 2 sectional center 2nd highest capacity switching office in PSTN network hierarchy.

Class 3 primary center 3rd highest capacity switching office in PSTN network hierarchy.

Class 4 toll center 4th highest capacity switching office in PSTN network hierarchy.

Class 5 office Local switching office.

class of service A method of prioritizing traffic to ensure that important packets are not delayed at routers or switches.

classfull address An IP address that is broken into network segment and node portions at octet boundaries.

classical IP *See* IP over ATM.

classless address An IP address that is broken into network segment and node portions at locations other than octet boundaries.

clear request packet In frame relay networks, the special packet that terminates virtual circuits.

CLEC Competitive Local Exchange Carriers; companies that seek to offer local access service in competition with RBOCs.

Client network operating systems Integrate traditional operating system functionality with advanced network operating system features to enable communication with a variety of different types of network operating system servers.

Client/server CTI In this CTI architecture, a CTI server computer interfaces to the PBX or ACD to provide overall system management while individual client-based CTI applications execute on multiple client PCs.

client/server network operating systems Offer the ability to support hundreds of users, and the ability to interact with other network operating systems via gateways. These client/server network operating systems are considerably more expensive and considerably more complicated to install and administer than peer-to-peer network operating systems.

client-agent-server The overall objective of a client-agent-server architecture, as opposed to the more common LAN-based client/server architecture, is to reduce the amount of mobile client-to-server network traffic by building as much intelligence as possible into the server-based agent so that it can act on behalf of the mobile client application.

Clipper Chip An initiative proposed that every phone and data communications device in the United States would be equipped with a Clipper Chip to support encryption.

cluster controller A device that allows connection of both 3270 terminals as well as LANs with possible wide area links to packet switched networks (X.25) or high speed leased lines. Concentrates the transmissions of its numerous input devices and directs this concentrated data stream to the FEP either locally or remotely.

CNIP Common Network Information Platform. Rather than having to know the intricacies, and, in some cases, the trade secrets, of how each other's products work, vendors of computer assisted network engineering software merely pass the output from their particular software product to a "neutral" data platform known as CNIP.

CO Central office; a facility belonging to the local phone company in which calls are switched to their proper destination.

Code division multiple access *See* CDMA.

codec Coder/decoder used to digitize analog voice signals.

collapsed backbone network A switched network architecture that employs backbone/data center switches to offer high capacity, fault tolerant, switching capacity with traffic management capabilities.

co-location A mandated process through which RBOCs had to allow alternate local loop carriers to install their equipment in the RBOC's central office.

committed burst size *See* CBS.

committed information rate *See* CIR.

Common Air Interface *See* CAI.

common channel interoffice signalling *See* CCIS.

Common Control Area Software programs that reside in and are executed on specialized computers within the PBX in an area sometimes referred to as the PBX CPU, Stored Program Control or Common Control Area.

common information model *See* CIM.

common network information platform *See* CNIP.

communications server Remote users could attach to a dedicated multi-user server, known as an access server or communications server through one or more modems. Depending on the software loaded on the communications server, it may deliver remote node functionality, remote control functionality, or both.

competitive local exchange carrier *See* CLEC.

component interface API Designed to interface to the individual application programs or desktop components that are to be managed and monitored on the local client.

composite message frame The frame that is built by combining the contents of individual channel buffers in a multiplexer.

comprehensive systems and networking budget model A comprehensive budget format needed to be developed that would help to identify as many elements of potential implementation and operation costs as possible associated with systems and networking implementations.

computer assisted network engineering *See* CANE.

Computer telephony integration *See* CTI.

configuration bridge protocol data unit Spanning Tree Algorithm bridges accomplish path management by communicating with each other via configuration bridge protocol data units (Configuration BPDU).

connectionless IP allows each packet to be processed individually within the network and provides no guarantees as to whether packets will arrive at their intended destination in sequence, if at all. As such, IP is described as a connectionless, unreliable protocol.

connection-oriented Implying that specific paths known as virtual circuits are explored and determined prior to the first packet being sent. Once the virtual circuit is established directly from the source host or node to destination node, then all packets bound for that address follow each other in sequence down the same physical path.

consolidated service desk A single point of contact for all network and application problem resolution, appropriate personnel processes can be matched with associated network management technologies.

constant bit rate *See* CBR.

constellation points A plotted point on a quadrant that represents a particular phase shift and amplitude of a modulation scheme.

Continuous ARQ Also known as sliding window ARQ, continues to transmit data while waiting for ACK/NAK. Slides back to NAK'd block and begins retransmission from there.

convolutional encoding Encoding methodology used with trellis coded modulation, a forward error correction protocol.

Copper Distributed Data Interface *See* CDDI.

Cordless Telephony Generation 2 *See* CT2.

CPE Customer premises equipment; generic name for customer owned PBX.

CRC A 32 bit cyclical redundancy check (CRC) is generated over the address, type, and data fields as a frame check sequence in Ethernet networks.

CRC Checkers Category of antivirus technology also known as Hashing Checkers; creates and saves a unique cyclical redundancy check character or hashing number for each file to be monitored.

CRC-16 16 bit cyclic redundancy check; traps multiple bit errors up to 15 bits 100% of the time.

CRC-32 32 bit cyclic redundancy check; traps multiple bit errors up to 31 bits 100% of the time.

critical success factors Several key behaviors or things to remember that can be of critical importance to the overall successful outcome of the network development life cycle.

CSMA/CA Carrier Sense Multiple Access with Collision Avoidance; part of the IEEE 802.11 standard. Similar to CSMA/CD except that collisions cannot be detected in wireless environments as they can in wire-based environments. Before transmitting, workstations wait a predetermined amount of time in order to avoid collisions, and set up a point-to-point wireless circuit to the destination workstation.

CSMA/CD Carrier Sense Multiple Access with Collision Detection; the access methodology used by Ethernet media sharing LANs.

CSS Card and Socket Services; the driver specification for PCMCIA devices that enables the following capabilities and is supposed to be relatively self-configuring: hot swappable devices allowing PCMCIA cards to be removed and inserted while the notebook computer is powered up, automatic PCMCIA card configuration, multiple PCMCIA card management, standby mode, I/O conflict management.

CSU/DSU Channel service unit/data service unit; used to interface to carriers' digital transmission services.

CT2 PBX-integrated wireless phones support the CT2. (Cordless Telephony Generation 2) Common Air Interface (CAI) global standard for low-power wireless transmission.

CTI It is important for help desk management software to be able to interact with call center management technology such as **automatic call distributors (ACD)** and **interactive voice response units (IVRU).** The overall integration of computer-based software and telephony equipment in known as **computer telephony integration (CTI).**

CTI application development tool Generates application code in a language such as Visual Basic and incorporates TAPI or TSAPI system commands into the program.

CTI voice card Key functions are as follows: Record and playback digitized video, Create and recognize DTMF tones (Dual Tone Multiple Frequency), Answer and place phone calls, Recognize and process incoming Caller ID (Automatic Number Identification) information.

customer premises equipment *See* CPE.

cut-through switches Read only the address information in the MAC layer header before beginning processing. Cut-through switching is very fast. However, because the Frame Check Sequence on the forwarded frame was not checked, bad frames are forwarded.

cyclical redundancy check *See* CRC.

D channel In Isochronous Ethernet, one 64Kbps ISDN D channel is used for management tasks such as call control and signaling.

D-4 A type of T-1 framing in which 24 8 bit time slots are combined with a framing bit to form 193 bit frames.

DARPA TCP/IP was developed during the 1970s and widely deployed during the 1980s under the auspices of DARPA or Defense Advanced Research Projects Agency.

DAS Dual Attachment Station devices attach to both of FDDI's rings.

data circuit terminating equipment *See* DCE.

data communications The encoded transmission of data via electrical or optical means.

Data Compression Procedure in which redundant data are removed from the data stream and represented by shorter codes thereby increasing overall throughput for a given transmisssion rate.

data display channel *See* DDC.

Data Encryption Standard *See* DES.

Data Link Control *See* DLC.

Data Link Switching *See* DLSw.

data migration Utilities that manage the migration of data among different types of storage devices as part of a comprehensive hierarchical storage management (HSM) program.

data over voice A type of frequency division multiplexer.

data terminal equipment *See* DTE.

data traffic analysis Examines all aspects and characteristics of the traffic that will be passed between corporate locations over the proposed network.

database MIB The IETF has been working on a Database MIB specification that would allow any enterprise data management system to report performance statistics back to any SNMP-compliant enterprise network management system.

Datagram Delivery *See* DDP.

Protocol datagrams Globally addressed message packets found in connectionless frame relay networks.

data-link layer Layer 2 of the OSI model; responsible for providing protocols that deliver reliability to upper layers for the point-to-point connections established by the physical layer protocols. The data-link layer is of particular interest to the study of local area networks because this is the layer in which network architecture standards are defined.

DB-25 A 25 pin physical connector associated with both serial and parallel transmission protocols.

DB-9 A 9 pin physical connector associated with a variety of serial protocols.

DCE Data circuit terminating equipment; a generic designation to indicate directionality in a serial transmission. Modems are DCE.

DDM Distributed device manager. A DDM architecture relies on distributed network probes that are able to gather information from a variety of network devices manufactured by multiple vendors and relay that information to numerous distributed device manager consoles.

DDP The network layer protocol associated with the AppleTalk protocol suite.

DDS Digital data service; a digital carrier transmission service offering speeds up to 56Kbps.

DE Discard eligibility. Flag in frame relay frame indicating those frames that can be discarded in the event of network congestion.

decision points Points in all of the documented business processes where decision makers must make decisions.

de-encapsulation Each successive layer of the OSI model removes headers and/or trailers and processes the data that were passed to it from the corresponding layer protocol on the source client.

definition variables In Application MIB, variables that would store background information concerning applications such as application name, manufacturer, version, release, installation data, license number, number of consecutive users, etc.

delta file synchronization Perhaps the most significant file synchronization option in terms of its potential impact on reducing required bandwidth and file transfer time to accomplish the synchronization. Rather than sending entire files across the dial-up or LAN link, delta file synchronization only transfers the changes to those files.

delta file transfer Allows only changes to files to be transferred.

Demand Priority Access *See* DPP.

Demand Priority Protocol *See* DPP.

demodulation Conversion of an analog signal to equivalent digital data.

Denial of service attack The hacker floods the server with requests to connect to other nonexistent servers. The server tries to establish connections with the nonexistent servers and waits for a response while being flooded with thousands of other bogus connection requests. This causes the server to deny service to legitimate users because it is overwhelmed trying to handle the bogus requests.

deregulation As a result of deregulation, both AT&T and the RBOCs were allowed to enter into other nonregulated industries by forming additional subsidiaries.

DES Data Encryption Standard; a private key encryption standard originally approved by the National Institute of Standards and Technology (NIST) in 1977.

desktop CTI In this CTI architecture, individual PCs are equipped with telephony boards and associated call control software. Each Desktop CTI-equipped PC controls only the phone to which it is directly attached.

desktop management interface *See* DMI.

desktop management task force *See* DMTF.

destination address Rather than merely transferring all data between LANs or LAN segments, a bridge reads the destination address (MAC layer address of destination NIC) of each data frame on a LAN, decides whether the destination is local or remote (on the other side of the bridge), and only allows those data frames with nonlocal destination addresses to cross the bridge to the remote LAN.

DHCP Dynamic Host Control Protocol; dynamically assigns IP upon requests from clients. With DHCP, IP addresses are leased for a fixed length of time rather than being permanently assigned.

dial backup Ability of leased line modems to restore transmission via dial-up circuits in the event of a leased line failure,

dial-in server *See* LAN modem.

dial-up line Circuit switched connection or local loop used to access PSTN.

dial-up router In those cases where the amount of inter-LAN traffic from a remote site does not justify the cost of a leased line, dial-up routers may be the appropriate choice of internetworking equipment.

dial-up server *See* Remote node server.

dibit Two bits.

DID Direct inward dialing allows calls to bypass the central switchboard and go directly to a particular user's phone.

Diff-Serv Provides the following functionality: Uses the type of service (ToS) bits already in the IP header to differentiate between different levels of service required by different applications; allows service level agreements between users and service providers to be supported.

digital A transmission method characterized by discrete voltage levels used to represent logical is and 0s.

digital data services *See* DDS.

Digital IDs Digital certificates or Digital IDs issued from CAs such as VeriSign contain an organization's encrypted public key along with a minimal amount of information about the organization such as e-mail address, department, company, state or province, and country.

digital service hierarchy Series of standards defining high speed digital services (DS-1 = 1.544Mbps).

digital signal processors Take the digitized PCM code and further manipulate and compress it.

digital signal processors *See* DSP.

Digital Signature Encryption Provides an electronic means of guaranteeing authenticity of the sending party and assurance that encrypted documents have not been altered during transmission.

digital simultaneous voice/data *See* DSVD.

Digital subscriber line *See* DSL.

direct enablers If compatible CSS drivers are not available for a particular PC Card/Controller combination, or if the amount of memory CSS drivers require is unacceptable, then lower-level drivers known as direct enablers must be configured and installed.

direct inward dial *See* DID.

direct sequence spread spectrum DSSS; transmits at a particular frequency within the allowable range. In order to distinguish between transmissions from multiple wireless workstations, DSSS adds at least 10 bits to the data message in order to uniquely identify a particular transmission. DSSS receivers must be able to differentiate between these bits, known as chips, in order to properly distinguish transmissions.

directory services Network operating systems have always depended on some sort of directory or naming service in which to store information about users as well as systems resources such as disks, servers, and printers.

directory synchronization software *See* File synchronization.

discard eligibility *See* DE.

Discrete ARQ Also known as stop and wait ARQ. Transmitting modem waits for an ACK or NAK for each transmitted block before transmitting the next block.

discrete multitone *See* DMT.

distance vector RIP uses a distance vector algorithm that only measures the number of hops to a distant router, to a maximum of 16.

distance vector protocols Router to router protocols, such as RIP, which only consider the distance between networks in hops as a determination of the best internetwork path.

distinct layer 2 switching & layer 3 routing An internetwork evolutionary design scenario in which separate Layer 2 switches and Layer 3 routers cooperatively contribute what each does best in order to deliver internetwork traffic as efficiently as possible.

distributed database A database application that consists of a central data repository with separate clients connecting to it.

distributed device manager *See* DDM.

distributed network probes A DDM architecture relies on **distributed network probes** that are able to gather information from a variety of network devices manufactured by multiple vendors and relay that information to numerous distributed device manager consoles.

distributed queue dual bus *See* DQDB.

distributed routing An internetwork evolutionary design scenario in which layer 2 switching and layer 3 routing functionality are combined into a single device sometimes referred to as a multi-layer switch.

divestiture Broke up the network services of AT&T into separate long-distance and local service companies.

DLC Data Link Control; a Windows NT communication protocol that has been traditionally reserved for communication with IBM mainframe computers. Recently, this same communication protocol has been used to communicate between Windows NT servers and printers that are attached directly to the network by network interface cards such as the Hewlett-Packard LaserJet 4Si equipped with a JetDirect card.

DLSw Data Link Switching; IBM's version of TCP/IP encapsulation has been proposed as a standard to the IETF (Internet Engineering Task Force) as RFC (Request for Comment) 1434. DLSw does not propose anything radically new but incorporates many vendor-specific TCP/IP encapsulation features into a single standard which, it is hoped, will be widely supported.

DMI Desktop management systems rely on an architecture and associated protocols proposed by the Desktop Management Task Force (DMTF), which is comprised of more than 50 companies including Intel, Microsoft, IBM, Digital, Hewlett-Packard, Apple, Compaq, Dell, and Sun. The overall desktop management architecture is known as the DMI or Desktop Management Interface.

DMI services layer The DMI application that resides on each desktop device to be managed.

DMT Discrete multitone; has been approved as an ADSL standard (ANSI Standard T1.413) by the ANSI T1E1.4 working group.

DMTF Desktop management systems rely on an architecture and associated protocols proposed by the Desktop Management Task Force (DMTF), which is comprised of more than 50 companies including Intel, Microsoft, IBM, Digital, Hewlett-Packard, Apple, Compaq, Dell, and Sun. The overall desktop management architecture is known as the DMI or Desktop Management Interface.

DMZ The De-militarized zone, otherwise known as the external private network; contains Web servers and mail servers.

DNS The Domain Name System; has been created to provide the following key services: Uniquely identify all hosts connected to the Internet by name, Resolve, or translate, host names into IP addresses (and vice versa), identify which services are offered by each host such as gateway or mail transfer, and to which networks these services are offered.

DNS server DNS is physically implemented in a client/server architecture in which client-based DNS software known as the DNS or name resolver, sends requests for DNS name resolution to a DNS (or name) Server.

domain directory services Network operating systems have always depended on some sort of naming service or directory in which to store information about users as well as systems resources such as disks, servers, and printers. Windows NT uses a domain directory service.

domain name system *See* DNS.

domains Domain directory services see the network as a series of linked subdivisions known as domains.

DPA *See* DPP.

DPP Demand Priority Protocol (Demand Priority Access); the access methodology of 100VG-AnyLAN. Ports can be designated as high priority, thereby giving priority delivery status to time-sensitive types of traffic such as video or voice which require guaranteed delivery times for smooth presentation. This makes 100VG-AnyLAN especially suitable for multimedia traffic.

DQDB Distributed queue dual bus; SMDS network architecture.

DS Digital service; *see* Digital service hierarchy.

DS-0 A 64Kbps digital carrier transmission service.

DS-1 1.544Mbps.

DSE Data Switching Exchanges; otherwise known as packet switched networks.

DSL Digital Subscriber Line services use frequency division multiplexing to analog encode a high speed data channel over a traditional POTS local loop connection.

DSP Digital signal processor; specialized computer chip able to process digital signals quickly; used in echo cancellation.

DSVD Digitizes all voice transmissions and combines the digitized voice and data over the single analog transmission line (ITU V.70).

DTE Data terminal equipment; a generic designation to indicate directionality in a serial transmission. PCs are DTE in a point to point, PC to modem transmission.

DTMF Touch-tone dialing is technically known as DTMF, or Dual Tone Multi-Frequency, because the tone associated with each number dialed is actually a combination of two tones selected from a matrix of multiple possible frequencies.

Dual Attachment Station *See* DAS.

Dual firewalls An enterprise firewall architecture that allows controlled access to DMZ while blocking unauthorized access to secure network, Same functionality may be offered in a single product known as a tri-homed firewall.

dual homing In FDDI, a given server may be connected to more than one FDDI concentrator to provide redundant connections and increased fault tolerance. Dual connecting servers in this manner are known as dual homing.

dual ring of trees Multiple concentrators attaching multiple devices to the FDDI rings as illustrated in Figure 7-13.

dual tone multi frequency *See* DTMF.

dual-homed gateway The application gateway is physically connected to the private secure network and the packet filtering router is connected to the nonsecure network or the Internet. Between the application gateway and the packet filter router is an area known as the screened subnet.

Dynamic Host Configuration Protocol *See* DHCP.

dynamic reconfiguration PnP standards also include support for dynamic reconfiguration which will enable such things as: PCMCIA cards being inserted into and removed from computers without a need to reboot, Hot docking (powered up) of laptop computers into docking bays or stations, Dynamic reconfiguration-aware applications software that could automatically respond to changes in system configuration.

Dynamic Speed Shifts MNP 10 protocol that allows modems to automatically raise or lower transmission speeds in response to variable circuit conditions.

E-1 European standard for high speed digital transmission 2.048Mbps.

early token release mechanism A modified form of token passing access methodology, used by 16 Mbps Token Ring network architectures, in which the token is set free and released as soon as the transmission of the data frame is completed rather than waiting for the transmitted data frame to return to the source workstation.

EBCDIC Extended binary coded decimal interchange code; 8 bit encoding scheme, 256 characters.

echo cancellation Sophisticated technique that allows some moderms to offer full duplex transmission over two wire circuits.

edge switches Edge switches deployed within the LANs will be programmed with minimal routing information. Edge switches will consult distributed route servers for "directory assistance" when they encounter routing situations which they are not equipped to handle.

EGP Exterior gateway protocol.

EIA/TIA 568 Electronics Industry Association/Telecommunications Industry Association; in addition to specifying UTP specifications, EIA/TIA 568 also specifies: the topology, cable types, and connector types to be used in EIA/TIA 568 compliant wiring schemes; the minimum performance specifications for cabling, connectors, and components such as wall plates, punch down blocks, and patch panels to be used in an EIA/TIA 568 compliant installation.

element managers **Point products** (also known as **element managers**) are specifically written to address a particular systems administration or network management issue.

EMI Electro Magnetic Interference.

emulation technology Attempts to detect as yet unknown viruses by running programs with a software emulation program known as a virtual PC.

encapsulating bridges The encapsulating bridge merely takes the entire Ethernet data-link layer frame and stuffs it in an "envelope" (data frame) that conforms to the FDDI data-link layer protocol.

Encapsulating Security Payload Header *See* ESP.

encapsulation A process in which a data message emerges from a client front end program and proceeds down the protocol stack of the network operating system installed in the client PC. Each successive layer of the OSI model adds a header according to the syntax of the protocol that occupies that layer.

encryption The process of "scrambling" a message for transmission to ensure that it is not intercepted along the way.

end nodes In APPN, end nodes are end user processing nodes, either clients or servers without any information on the overall network, available internetwork links, or routing tables.

end-to-end network links The network layer protocols are responsible for the establishment, maintenance, and termination of end-to-end network links. Network layer protocols are required when computers that are not physically connected to the same LAN must communicate.

Enhanced CAT 5 **Enhanced Category 5 UTP (EC5),** otherwise known as **Category 5+** or **CAT5e,** offers enhanced performance over CAT5 UTP due to the following improvements in electrical specifications: Attenuation to Crosstalk ratio of 10dB at 155 MHz, a minimum 400% improvement in capacitance, or ability of a wire to store an electrical charge, a 250% improvement in frequency, a 35% improvement in resistance, an average of 5% improvement in attenuation, an average of a 6dB improvement in NEXT.

enhanced paging A pager based wireless service capable of delivering one- or two-way messages of 100 characters or less.

Enhanced throughput cellular *See* ETC.

enterprise hubs Modular by design, offering a chassis-based architecture to which a variety of different modules can be inserted. In some cases, these modules can be inserted and/or removed while the hub remains powered-up, a capability known as hot-swappable.

enterprise network management Focuses on the hardware, software, media, and network services required to seamlessly link and effectively manage distributed client and server computers across an enterprise.

enterprise network management systems Systems such as HP OpenView, IBM NetView, and Sun Net Manager are able to manage a variety of multi-vendor network attached devices distributed throughout an enterprise network.

equal access Any other long-distance carrier must be treated equally by the local BOCs in terms of access to the local carrier switching equipment, and ultimately to their customers.

error correction Process of re-transmitting data blocks received in error.

error detection Comparison of CRCs in order to detect transmission errors.

error prevention Process of trying to prevent data errors by either reducing interference on circuits or by employing adaptive protocols that are able to adjust to impairments of varying circuit quality.

error-free cut-through switches Switches that read both the addresses and Frame Check Sequences for every frame. Frames are forwarded immediately to destinations nodes in an identical fashion to cut-through switches. Should bad frames be forwarded, however, the error-free cut-through switch is able to reconfigure those individual ports producing the bad frames to use store-and-forward switching.

ESCON Enterprise System CONnection; a standard for high speed data channels between FEPs and IBM mainframes, ESCON II has a maximum transmission rate of 70Mbps, has been available since 1990, and is able to transmit up to 30 miles over fiber optic cable.

ESF 24 D-4 frames.

ESMR Enhanced specialized mobile radio; currently under development, this wireless WAN service offers one- or two-way voice, paging, or messaging at speeds up to 4.8Kbps over proprietary integrated voice/data devices.

ESP Encapsulating Security Payload Header; in Secure IP, ESP assures the privacy of the transmission.

ETC Enhanced Throughput Cellular; transmitting data over analog cellular networks requires modems that support specialized cellular transmission protocols on both ends of the cellular transmission in order to maximize throughput. Examples of such protocols are MNP-10 Adverse Channel Enhancements and ETC.

Ethernet Although strictly speaking, Ethernet and IEEE 802.3 are conflicting standards, the term *Ethernet* is commonly used to refer to any IEEE 802.3 compliant network.

Ethernet II The first Ethernet standard was developed by Digital, Intel, and Xerox Corporation in 1981 and was known as DIX 1.0, sometimes referred to as Ethernet I. This standard was superseded in 1982 by DIX 2.0, the current Ethernet standard, also known as Ethernet II.

evaluation criteria These goals may have a direct impact on network design when defined in terms such as maximum response time, transactions per second, or mean time between failures.

event detection Most audit software depends on capturing large amounts of event data and then filtering that data for exceptional or unusual events.

event management tool An alternative to developing your own applications with embedded management intelligence is to purchase a prewritten **event management tool** that has been written to monitor specific commercially available applications.

explorer packet In an internetwork connected via source routing bridges, the PC sends out a special explorer packet that determines the best path to the intended destination of its data message. The explorer packets are continually propagated through all source routing bridges until the destination workstation is finally reached.

extended binary coded decimal interchange code *See* EBCDIC.

extended superframe *See* ESF.

Extended Terminal Access Control Access System *See* XTACACS.

EZ-ISDN In order to try to further simplify the ISDN ordering process, an alternative ordering code scheme known as EZ-ISDN has been proposed by the National ISDN Users Forum.

fallback When an analog circuit, dial-up or leased, degrades or has some kind of transmission impairment, many modems automatically use fallback or lower speeds and continue with data transmissions.

false accepts In biometric authentication, false accepts will occur when impostors are allowed access because the comparison was not detailed enough.

false rejects In biometric authentication, false rejects will occur when valid users are denied access because of slight variations detected between the reference biometric characteristic and the current one.

fast packet forwarding *See* Packet overlapping.

Fax-on-demand By combining computer-based faxing with interactive voice response, users can dial in and request that specific information be transmitted to their fax machine.

FCS Frame check sequence, error detection technique.

FDDI Fiber Distributed Data Interface; a 100Mbps network architecture that was first specified in 1984 by the ANSI (American National Standards Institute) subcommittee entitled X3T9.5.

FDM Frequency division multiplexing; each channel gets a portion of the bandwidth for 100% of the time.

feasibility study The problem definition and its associated alternative recommendations for further study are sometimes referred to as a feasibility study.

FECN Forward explicit congestion notification; a flow control mechanism in frame relay networks.

FEP Front end processor; a computer that offloads the communications processing from the mainframe, allowing the mainframe to be dedicated to processing activities. A high speed data channel connects the FEP to the mainframe locally although FEPs can be deployed remotely as well.

Fiber Distributed Data *See* FDDI.

Interface file synchronization software Software that is able to synchronize versions of files on laptops and desktop workstations and is now often included as a standard or optional feature in client network operating systems. Also known as version control software or directory synchronization software.

filter A program that examines the source address and destination address of every incoming packet to the firewall server.

Filter tables Lists of addresses whose data packets and embedded messages are either allowed or prohibited from proceeding through the firewall server and into the corporate network.

filtering A bridge reads the destination address on an Ethernet frame or Token Ring packet and decides whether or not that packet should be allowed access to the internetwork through the bridge.

filtering rate Measured in Packets/sec or Frames/sec, a measure of the filtering performance of a given bridge.

firewall Specialized software often deployed to prevent unauthorized access from the Internet into a company's confidential data. All network packets entering the firewall are filtered, or examined, to determine whether those users have authority to access requested files or services and whether the information contained within the message meets corporate criteria for forwarding over the internal network.

firewire *See* IEEE-1394.

first-party call control Also known as desktop CTI.

fixed callback Callback mechanism that is only able to call remote uses back at predetermined phone numbers entered in a directory.

flat gray modular Wiring, also known as gray satin or silver satin, that contains either 4, 6, or 8 wires which get crimped into either RJ-11 (4 wire), RJ-12 (6 wire), or RJ-45 plugs (8 wire) using a specialized crimping tool.

Flow analysis The first step toward a thorough understanding of data traffic analysis is to analyze the flow of that data. Understanding the source and destination of each data "conversation" and the nature of the data in that conversation is fundamental to a proper network design.

Flow Control Mechanism that stops and starts data transmission in order to avoid overflow of buffer memory.

format converter A special type of bridge that includes a format converter can bridge between Ethernet and Token Ring. These special bridges may also be called multi-protocol bridges or translating bridges.

Forward Error Correction Error correction protocols that seek to avoid the need for retransmission by sending redundant data along with actual data in order to assist the receiving modem in correctly interpreting received signals.

forward explicit congestion notification *See* FECN.

forward if not local Since only frames with destination addresses not found in the known local nodes table are forwarded across the bridge, bridges are sometimes known as a "Forward-if-not-local" devices.

forward if proven remote Once the router is satisfied with both the viability of the destination address as well as with the quality of the intended path, it will release the carefully packaged data packet via processing known as forward-if-proven-remote logic.

forwarding Forwarding is the bridge process necessary to load the packet onto the internetwork media whether local or remote.

forwarding rate Measured in Packets/sec or Frames/sec, a measure of the forwarding performance of a given bridge.

four-wire circuit Comprised of two wires capable of simultaneously carrying a data signal each with its own dedicated ground wire. Typically, four-wire circuits are reserved for leased lines.

fractional T-1 *See* FT-1.

Fractional T-1 multiplexers A T-1 multiplexer that is able to use less than a full T-1 as its composite output channel.

FRAD Frame relay access device; the access device to the frame relay network must be able to respond to requests from the frame relay network to "throttle back" or slow down the input to the network or risk losing transmitted packets due to network overload.

fragmentation As contiguous blocks of memory of varying sizes are continuously cut out of a finite amount of primary memory, that primary memory suffers from fragmentation where numerous, small leftover pieces of contiguous memory remain unused.

frame check sequence FCS; is an error detection mechanism generated by the transmitting Ethernet network interface card.

frame check sequence *See* FCS.

Frame relay A switch based service that packages voice and data into variable length frames.

frame relay access device *See* FRAD.

frame relay switch Network switch capable of switching frame relay frames.

frame status flags In a token passing access methodology, successful delivery of the data frame is confirmed by the destination workstation setting frame status flags to indicate successful receipt of the frame and continuing to forward the original frame around the ring to the sending PC.

frames The data-link layer provides the required reliability to the physical layer transmission by organizing the bit stream into structured frames that add addressing and error checking information.

frameworks Offer an overall systems administration or network management platform with integration between modules and a shared database into which all alerts, messages, alarms, and warnings can be stored and correlated.

framing In T-1 framing, differentiating between channels is accomplished through a technique known as framing, which is an adaptation of the TDM.

framing bit The 193rd bit added to the 24 8 bit time slots to indicate the end of one D-4 frame.

frequency A wave characteristic that can be manipulated in order represent 1s and 0s.

frequency division multiplexing *See* FDM.

frequency hopping spread spectrum FHSS hops from one frequency to another throughout the allowable frequency range. The pattern of frequency hopping must be known by the wireless receiver so that the message can be reconstructed correctly.

frequency modulation Process of manipulating carrier wave frequency in order to represent 1s and 0s.

frequency shift keying *See* FSK.

front end processor *See* FEP.

FSK Frequency shift keying; shifting carrier wave frequency on analog circuits in order to represent digital 1s and 0s.

FT-1 Fractional T-1, broadband service that allows customer to access less than the full 24 DS-0s in a T-1.

Full duplex Ethernet Requires specialized full duplex Ethernet NICs, NIC drivers, and full duplex Ethernet switches. Should allow twice the normal Ethernet performance speed by offering a dedicated 10Mpbs communication channel in each direction for a total available bandwidth 20Mbps.

full-duplex Simultaneous transmission in both directions on a given circuit.

gateway A LAN server-based, shared protocol converted access to a mainframe is known as a gateway.

Generic Security Service-Applications Program Interface *See* GSS-API.

Gigabit Ethernet Also known as 1000Base-X; an upgrade to Fast Ethernet that was standardized as the **IEEE 802.3z** standard by the IEEE on June 25, 1998.

global address Address attached to a datagram in a frame relay network that allows it to be properly delivered.

global directory services *See* NDS.

Global system for mobile communication *See* GSM.

granularity How finely access can be controlled (by disk, directory, or file level) is sometimes referred to as the granularity of the access control scheme.

GSM **Global System for Mobile Communication;** in Europe and much of the rest of the world, is either currently deployed or planned for implementation as the digital cellular standard.

GSS-API An open API that would allow applications to communicate with a variety of security authorization programs.

guardbands Portions of the 4000Hz voice bandwidth, reserved to protect against interference.

guest The terms *remote* and *local* are often replaced by guest (remote) and host (local), when referring to Remote Control Software.

half-duplex Transmission in both directions, only one direction at a time on a given circuit.

Handshaking Modem initialization that takes place in order to allow modems to agree on carrier wave frequency, modulation scheme, error correction protocols, etc.

Hashing Checkers Flow control mechanism that uses RS-232 pins CTS/RTS, clear-to-send/request to send, category of antivirus technology known as CRC Checkers or Hashing Checkers. Creates and saves a unique cyclical redundancy check character or hashing number for each file to be monitored.

Hayes AT Command Set Series of commands understood by both communications software and modems that allows the communications software to control and respond to modem activity.

Hayes compatible Term that indicates a modem is able to understand and respond to commands in the Hayes AT command set.

HDLC High level data-link control; data-link layer protocol for X.25.

header Additional information added to the front of data.

Heuristic analysis Because of their ability to monitor behavior of programs, this category of antivirus technology is also sometimes known as **activity monitors** or **heuristic analysis.** Such programs are also capable of trapping encrypted or polymorphic viruses that are capable of constantly changing their identities or signatures.

hierarchical networking An internetworking design strategy that isolates local LAN traffic on a local network architecture such as Ethernet or Token Ring while transmitting internetwork traffic over a higher speed network architecture such as FDDI or Fast Ethernet. Servers are often directly connected to the backbone network while individual workstations access the backbone network only as needed through routers.

high level data link control *See* HDLC.

High speed token ring *See* HSTR.

HMMP Hypermedia Management Protocol; The overall intention of the WBEM architecture is that the network manager could manage any networked device or application from any location on the network, via any **HMMP** compliant browser.

HMMS Hypermedia Management Schema; management data from a variety of software agents would be incorporated into the Web-based enterprise management architecture via the **HMMS.**

HMOM Hypermedia Object Manager; all Web-based management information is stored and retrieved by the request broker known as **HMOM.**

horizontal integration A standardized open architecture offering seamless horizontal integration between a variety of CANE products might be constructed. Rather than having to know the intricacies, and, in some cases, the trade secrets, of how each other's products work, vendors of computer assisted network engineering software merely pass the output from their particular software product to a "neutral" data platform.

host The terms *remote* and *local* are often replaced by guest (remote) and host (local), when referring to Remote Control Software.

hot swappable A capability in which enterprise hub modules can be inserted and/or removed while the hub remains powered-up.

HPR/AnyNET Recent enhancements to APPN known as HPR (High Performance Routing)/AnyNET now allow multiple transport protocols such as IP and IPX to travel over the APPN network simultaneously with SNA traffic. In such an implementation, APPN rather than TCP/IP serves as the single backbone protocol able to transport multiple LAN protocols as well as SNA traffic simultaneously.

HSTR High Speed Token Ring; a 100Mbps token ring network architecture, otherwise known as HSTR has been approved by an organization known as the High Speed Token Ring Alliance, which is also supposedly working on a gigabit token ring standard.

hubs Wiring centers for network architectures other than token ring.

Huffman encoding Encoding mechanism that replaces ASCII code with variable length codes, shorter codes (4 bits) for most frequently used characters, longer (11 bit) codes for least frequently used characters.

hunting Hunt groups are established to allow incoming calls to get through on alternate trunks when a primary trunk is busy.

hypermedia management protocol *See* HMMP.

hypermedia management schema *See* HMMS.

Hypermedia object manager *See* HMOM.

IBM3270 In micro-mainframe connectivity, the micro (Standalone or LAN-attached PC) pretends to be or "emulates" a mainframe terminal such as an IBM 3270 attached and logged into the mainframe.

I-CANE Integration of CANE software with CASE software and business process expert systems via vertical integration.

ICMP Internet Control Message Protocol; although IP is by definition an unreliable transport mechanism, ICMP does deliver a variety of error status and control messages related to the ability of IP to deliver its encapsulated payloads.

ICP Intelligent Call Processing service; customers are able to reroute incoming 800 calls among multiple customer service centers in a matter of seconds.

IDEA International Data Encryption Algorithm; makes use of one-time 128-bit keys known as session keys.

IEEE 1394 A high speed multipoint serial bus based solution used in digital video and high speed data applications. Also known as firewire and I-link.

IEEE 802 Local area network architecture standards are defined, debated, and established by the IEEE (Institute of Electrical and Electronic Engineers) 802 committee.

IEEE 802.1 *See* Spanning Tree Algorithm.

IEEE 802.11 A lack of interoperability among the wireless LAN offerings of different vendors is a shortcoming being addressed by a proposal for a new wireless LAN standard known as IEEE 802.11.

IEEE 802.12 Details of the 100VG-AnyLAN network architecture are contained in the proposed IEEE 802.12 standard.

IEEE 802.14 The access methodologies for sharing cable bandwidth via cable modems are being standardized as IEEE 802.14 cable network specifications.

IEEE 802.2 The upper sub-layer of the data-link layer that interfaces to the network layer is known as the logical link control or LLC sub-layer and is represented by a single IEEE 802 protocol (IEEE 802.2).

IEEE 802.3 Although strictly speaking, Ethernet and IEEE 802.3 are conflicting standards, the term *Ethernet* is commonly used to refer to any IEEE 802.3 compliant network.

IEEE 802.3u The details of the operation of 100BaseT are in the IEEE 802.3u proposed standard.

IEEE 802.3x Full duplex Ethernet has gathered sufficient interest from the networking technology vendor and user communities so as to warrant the formation of the IEEE 802.3x committee to propose standards for full duplex Ethernet.

IEEE 802.3z *See* Gigabit Ethernet.

IEEE 802.5 IBM has been the driving force behind the standardization and adoption of Token Ring with a prototype in IBM's lab in Zurich, Switzerland, serving as a model for the eventual IEEE 802.5 standard.

IEEE 802.6 IEEE specification for DQDB, the SMDS network architecture.

IEEE 802.9a Details of the Iso-Ethernet network architecture are contained in the IEEE 802.9a standard, which is officially known as Isochronous Ethernet Integrated Services.

IGRP Interior Gateway Routing Protocol; Cisco's proprietary distance vector protocol.

i-link hardware flow control *See* IEEE-1394.

in-band signaling Occurs when signal bandwidth is robbed to transport managerial or control information.

incremental change costs An important element of the comprehensive systems and networking budget model that highlights costs for anticipated growth over the next five years.

Infrared Data Association In order to assure multivendor interoperability between laptops and mobile aware operating systems, the infra-red transmission should conform to the IrDA standards.

Infrared transmission A wireless LAN transmission methodology limited by its line-of-sight requirement.

Institute of Electrical and Electronic Engineers 802 Committee *See* IEEE 802.

instrumentation Embedded performance metrics are sometimes referred to as instrumentation.

Int14 Interrupt 14; one of the supported dial-out software re-directors and most often employed by Microsoft network operating systems. Int14 is actually an IBM BIOS serial port interrupt used for the purpose of redirecting output from the local serial port.

integrated service digital network *See* ISDN.

Integrated Services Terminal Equipment *See* ISTE.

integrated suites The difference between integrated suites and frameworks is that integrated suites are filled with their own network management and systems administration applications rather then offering the user an open framework into which to place a variety of chosen applications.

integration Refers to that transitionary period of time in the migration process when both network operating systems must be running simultaneously and interacting to some degree.

integration/migration services Integration refers to that transitionary period of time in the migration process when both network operating systems must be running simultaneously and interacting to some degree. Migration features are aimed at easing the transition from NetWare 3.12 to either NetWare 4.1 or Windows NT.

intelligent agent *See* Agent event manager.

intelligent call processing *See* ICP.

interactive voice response *See* IVR.

Interdomain Trust In the case of a domain directory service such as Windows NT 3.51, the remote or foreign server receives the user authentication from the user's primary domain controller (local server) in a process known as Interdomain Trust (IT).

inter-exchange carriers *See* IXC.

interface The logical gap between two communicating hardware or software components.

interface specification Bit by bit layout of frames that user data must be transformed into before entering network switches.

internal firewalls Include filters that work on the data-link, network, and application layers to examine communications that occur only on a corporation's internal network, inside the reach of traditional firewalls.

International Data Encryption Algorithm *See* IDEA.

internet control message protocol *See* ICMP.

Internet Packet Exchange *See* IPX.

Internet protocol *See* IP.

Internet Security Association and Key Management Protocol *See* ISAKMP.

Internet Suite of Protocols TCP/IP (Transmission Control Protocol/Internet Protocol); the term generally used to refer to an entire suite of protocols used to provide communication on a variety of layers between widely distributed different types of computers. Strictly speaking, TCP and IP are just two of the protocols contained within the family of protocols more properly known as the Internet Suite of Protocols.

internet suite of protocols model A four-layered communications architecture in which upper layers use the functionality offered by the protocols of the lower layers.

internetworking Linking multiple LANs together in such as way as to deliver information more efficiently from cost, business, and performance perspectives.

inter-realm In Kerberos, if a client wishes to access a server in another realm, it requests an inter-realm ticket granting ticket from its local ticket granting server to authorize access to the remote ticket granting server which can authorize access to the remote applications server.

inter-ring gate calls NLMs executing in Ring 3 access operating systems services in Ring 0 by issuing structured inter-ring gate calls, thereby protecting the operating system from misbehaving NLMs overwriting its memory space.

Interrupt 14 *See* Int14.

Interrupt request *See* IRQ.

intersymbol interference Interference between constellation points in a given modulation scheme which can cause misinterpretation is known as intersymbol interference.

intranets Internet type services available for use by in-house, authorized employees.

Intrusion detection systems Test the perimeter of the enterprise network through dial modems, remote access servers, Web servers, or Internet access.

inverse multiplexing A process in which MLPPP compliant devices are able to deliver "bandwidth on demand."

IOC Depending on what combinations of voice, video, or data traffic a user wishes to transmit over ISDN, up to 20 or more ISDN Ordering Codes are possible.

IP Internet Protocol; the network layer protocol of the TCP/IP suite of protocols. As such, it is primarily responsible for providing the addressing functionality necessary to assure that all reachable network destinations can be uniquely and correctly identified.

IP over ATM Otherwise known as Classical IP, adapts the TCP/IP protocol stack to employ ATM services as a native transport protocol directly. This is an IP specific proposal and is not an option for LANs using other protocol stacks such as NetWare's IPX/SPX.

IP spoofing A technique in which packet filters can be breached by hackers. Since packet filters make all filtering decisions based on IP source and destination addresses, if a hacker can make a packet appear to come from an authorized or trusted IP address, then it can pass through the firewall.

IP Switching Technology that distinguishes between the length of data streams and switches or routes accordingly on a case-by-case basis.

IPng IP next generation, otherwise known as IPv6 (IP version 6), offers significant increases in functionality as well as increased address space in comparison to IPv4 (current version, IP version 4).

I-P-O model Provides a framework in which to focus on the difference between the data that came into a particular networked device (1) and the data that came out of that same device(O). By defining this difference, the processing (P) performed by the device is documented.

IPsec For establishing security over VPN tunnels. IPsec is largely supported by the firewall vendor community and is intended to provide interoperability between VPN firewalls from different vendors.

IPv4 Current version, IP version 4.

IPv6 *See* IPng.

Ipv6 IPsec is also proposed to be able to support both authentication and encryption. These capabilities are optional for IPv4 and mandatory for **IPv6** and are outlined in IETF RFCs 1825 through 1829.

IPX Internet Packet Exchange like most OSI network layer protocols, serves as a basic delivery mechanism for upper layer protocols such as SPX, RIP, SAP, and NCP. It is connectionless and unreliable.

IrDA *See* Infrared Data Association.

IRQ Interrupt request—The network interface card, like every other hardware device in the computer, must interrupt and request resources such as CPU cycles and memory from the CPU itself. It must be assigned an IRQ or interrupt request number so that the CPU knows that it is the NIC requesting these services.

ISAKMP Internet Security Association and Key Management Protocol; a key management protocol from the IETF.

ISDN Integrated Services Digital Network; a circuit-switched digital WAN service that is the support network transport service for Isochronous Ethernet.

ISDN data/voice modem Not truly a modem, but a ISDN terminal adapter that supports analog phones as well as data transmission.

ISDN ordering codes *See* IOC.

ISDN switch Switch that supports circuit switching for ISDN services.

ISDN terminal adapters Allows analog devices (phones, fax machines) to hook to ISDN services.

ISO 10646 More commonly known as Unicode, this encoding scheme used 16 bit characters to represent most known languages and symbols (more than 65,000 possible characters).

ISO 7498/2 This framework maps 14 different security services to specific layers of the OSI 7 Layer Reference Model.

ISO Management Framework The Network Management Forum associated with the OSI Reference Model has divided the field of network management into five major categories in a document known as the ISO Management Framework (ISO 7498-4).

isochronous Refers to any signaling system in which all connections or circuits are synchronized using a single common clocking reference. This common clocking mechanism allows such systems to offer guaranteed delivery times that are very important to streaming or time-sensitive traffic such as voice and video.

Isochronous Ethernet *See* Iso-Ethernet.

Iso-Ethernet Isochronous Ethernet; offers a combination of services by dividing the overall 16.144Mbps bandwidth delivered to each workstation into several service-specific channels.

ISTE Integrated Services Terminal Equipment; a workstation with an Iso-Ethernet NIC installed.

IT *See* Interdomain Trust.

IT project portfolio management A process that often manages the overall strategic development direction of the IT infrastructure.

ITU H.323 The standard for interoperability among client software for low bandwidth audio (voice) and video conferencing.

IVR Interactive voice response; systems that support on-line transaction processing rather than just information hot-line applications.

IVRU It is important for help desk management software to be able to interact with call center management technology such as automatic call distributors (ACD) and interactive voice response units (IVRU). The overall integration of computer-based software and telephony equipment in known as **computer telephony integration (CTI).**

IXC Inter-Exchange Carrier; any phone traffic destined for locations outside of the local LATA must be handed off to the long distance or IXC of the customer's choice.

Kerberos Perhaps the most well-known combination authentication/authorization software; originally developed at Massachusetts Institute of Technology and marketed commercially by a variety of firms.

Kermit Kermit is a popular file transfer protocol best known for being available on nearly any computing platform of any type.

Key Escrow agencies Otherwise known as Trusted Third Parties, these agencies will hold the keys necessary to decrypt key recovery documents.

key recovery mechanism U.S. companies with international subsidiaries may now export 56 bit key-based encryption technology provided that they establish within two years a key recovery mechanism that will offer a back door into encrypted data for the government.

knowledge base Contains not just the resolutions or answers to problems, but the logic structure or decision tree that takes a given problem and leads the help desk staff person through a series of questions to the appropriate solution.

known local nodes Data-link protocols such as Ethernet contain source addresses as well as the destination addresses within the predefined Ethernet Frame layout. A bridge checks the source address of each frame it receives and adds that source address to a table of known local nodes.

L2F Cisco's Layer Two Forwarding tunneling protocol for virtual private networks.

L2TP Layer 2 Tunneling Protocol; an effort is underway to have the Internet Engineering Task Force (IETF) propose a unification of the two rival virtual private network tunneling standards known as L2TP.

LAN caching *See* Network caching.

LAN emulation Provides a translation layer that allows ATM to emulate existing Ethernet and token ring LANs and allows all current upper-layer LAN protocols to be transported by the ATM services in an unmodified fashion.

LAN modem Also known as a Dial-In Server; offers shared remote access to LAN resources. LAN modems come with all necessary software preinstalled and therefore require no additional remote control or remote node software. LAN modems are often limited to a single network architecture such as Ethernet or Token Ring, and/or to a single network operating system protocol such as IP, IPX (NetWare), NetBIOS, NetBEUI, or Appletalk.

LAN switch *See* Switching hub.

Land attack A variation on the denial of service attack in which the hacker substituted the targeted server's own address as the address of the server requesting a connection. This caused the attacked server to constantly try to establish connections to itself, thereby often crashing the server.

Landline telephone network PSTN, otherwise known as the Landline Telephone Network.

LAP-B Link access procedure-balanced, data-link layer protocol for X.25.

LAP-D The frame definition for frame relay networks. This frame definition is said to be a subset of the LAP-D protocol. LAP-D stands for Link Access Procedure - D Channel, where the D channel refers to the 16Kbps Delta Channel in BRI (Basic Rate Interface) ISDN (Integrated Services Digital Network).

LAP-M Link Access Protocol for Modems; V.42 error control protocol that implements selective ARQ.

Large Internet Packets *See* LIP.

Large Packet IPX *See* LIP.

Large scale RAS **Large Scale Remote Access Servers (RAS)** also known as **Monster RAS** are differentiated from previously mentioned RAS hardware by their scalability (number of modem ports), manageability, and security. These are enterprise class machines boasting modem port counts up to 1,344 per chassis, fast Ethernet LAN interfaces, and ATM DS3 (45 Mbps) or OC3 (155Mbps) WAN connections.

LATA All local phone traffic within a local access transport area is handled by the local phone company, more formally known as a local exchange carrier or LEC, most often one of the RBOCs.

latency Filtering time introduces latency to the overall transmission time.

Layer 2 switch A LAN switch that supports a layer 2 virtual LAN distinguishes only between the MAC addresses of connected workstations.

Layer 2 Tunneling Protocol *See* L2TP.

Layer 3 switch Devices able to perform filtering based on network layer protocols and addresses; able to support multiple virtual LANs using different network layer protocols.

Layer 4 switch Process TCP port numbers and can distribute multiple requests for a given service to multiple different physical servers, thus providing load balancing.

Layer Two Forwarding *See* L2F.

LCR Using routing and pricing information supplied by the user, the PBX chooses the most economical path for any given call.

LDAP A subset of the X.500 directory service standardized by the IETF for use on TCP/IP networks.

leased line A dedicated phone circuit that bypasses central office switching equipment; no dial tone.

Least cost routing *See* LCR.

least significant bit Both Ethernet and token ring believe that bit 0 on byte 0, referred to as the least significant bit, should be transmitted first.

LEC Local exchange carriers, or local phone company that handles all local phone traffic within a LATA.

legacy applications *See* Backward compatibility.

Lightweight Directory Access Protocol *See* LDAP.

limited size messaging *See* LSM.

line cards PBX cards that attach to users' phones.

Line conditioning Value added service available from carriers in order to reduce interference on analog leased lines.

link access procedure-D channel *See* LAP-D.

link access procedure-balanced *See* LAP-B.

link access protocol for modems *See* LAP-M.

link state OSPF protocol uses a more comprehensive link state algorithm that can decide between multiple paths to a given router based upon variables other than number of hops such as delay, and capacity, throughput, and reliability of the circuits connecting the routers.

link state packets *See* LSP.

link state protocols Routing protocols known as link state protocols take into account other factors regarding internetwork paths such as link capacity, delay, throughput, reliability, or cost.

link support layer A layer of the ODI Architecture; LSL.COM is the program that orchestrates the operation of ODI drivers.

LIP Large Internet Packets; applies only to NetWare 4.1 LANs that are linked to each other via a wide area network through routers. LIP, also known as Large

Packet IPX, allows NetWare clients to negotiate with the routers as to the size of the IPX frame. From the NetWare client's perspective, the larger the IPX frame, the larger the IPX frame's data field, and the greater the amount of data that the client can cram into a single IPX frame.

LLC In order for an IEEE 802.3 compliant network interface card to be able to determine the type of protocols embedded within the data field of an IEEE 802.3 frame, it refers to the header of the IEEE 802.2 Logical Link Control (LLC) data unit.

LLC sub-layer The upper sub-layer of the data-link layer that interfaces to the network layer is known as the logical link control or LLC sub-layer and is represented by a single IEEE 802 protocol (IEEE 802.2).

load balancing The effective use of a network's redundant paths allows routers to perform load balancing of total network traffic across two or more links between two given locations.

local access transport area *See* LATA.

local exchange carrier *See* LEC.

local hub management software Usually supplied by the hub vendor and runs over either DOS or Windows. This software allows monitoring and management of the hub from a locally attached management console.

local loop transmission Narrowband transmission services from customer premises to CO.

local loops The circuits between a residence or business and the local Central Office or CO.

local session number A NetBIOS variable that typically limits NetBIOS and NetBEUI clients and servers to a 254 session limit.

logic bombs Viruses that require a certain event to transpire are known as logic bombs.

logical channel Virtual circuit in frame relay network.

logical channel number Identifier assigned to virtual circuit in frame relay network.

logical link control *See* LLC.

logical network design Network performance criteria could be referred to as *what* the implemented network must do in order to meet the business objectives outlined at the outset of this top-down analysis. These requirements are also sometimes referred to as the logical network design.

Logical Ring Physical Star IBM's Token Ring network architecture, adhering to the IEEE 802.5 standard, utilizes a star configuration, sequential message delivery, and a token passing access methodology scheme. Since the sequential logical topology is equivalent to passing messages from neighbor to neighbor around a ring, the token ring network architecture is sometimes referred to as Logical Ring, Physical Star.

logical topology The particular message passing methodology, or how a message will be passed from workstation to workstation until the message ultimately reaches its intended destination workstation, is more properly known as a network architecture's logical topology.

longitudinal redundancy checks *See* LRC.

LRC Longitudinal redundancy checks; two-dimensional parity that overcomes simple parity's inability to detect multiple bit errors.

LSL *See* Link support layer.

LSM By adding a protocol known as LSM (Limited Size Messaging), CDPD will be able to transport two-way messaging that will offer the following key services beyond simple paging: guaranteed delivery to destination mobile users even if those devices are unreachable at the time the message was originally sent, return receipt acknowledgments to the party that originated the message.

LSP Link state packets; specialized datagrams used by link state routers to determine the names of and the cost or distance to any neighboring routers and associated networks.

M block connector Physical connector most often associated with V. 35 serial transmission standard.

MAC sub-layer The media access control or MAC sub-layer is a sub-layer of the data-link layer that interfaces with the physical layer and is represented by protocols that define how the shared local area network media is to be accessed by the many connected computers.

make or buy decision Follows all of the vendor demonstrations; will systems and networks be developed in-house or outsourced?

malicious applets Java applets downloaded from the Web; tend to be annoying rather than destructive.

MAN *See* Metropolitan Area networks.

management abstract A section of the RFP that includes important information regarding the project other than project specifications.

management information base *See* MIB.

management information format *See* MIF.

management interface API Designed to interface to the desktop system management program which will consolidate the information from this client with all other desktop information.

MAU Multistation Access Unit; Token Ring wiring centers.

Maximum Transmission Unit *See* MTU.

MD5 Produces 128 bit hash number based on original document. Can then be incorporated into digital signature. Replaced MD4 and MD2.

media access control *See* MAC.

media sharing LANs Local area networks that use access methodologies to control the access of multiple users to a shared media.

message Transport layer protocols also provide mechanisms for sequentially organizing multiple network layer packets into a coherent message.

message gateway One of three cooperating components of the agent portion of the client/agent/server architecture. The message gateway can execute on the local server or on a dedicated Unix or Windows workstation, and acts as an interface between the client's message manager and the intelligent agent on the local server. The gateway also acts as a holding station for messages to and from mobile clients that are temporarily unreachable.

message manager One of three cooperating components of the agent portion of the client/agent/server architecture. Executes on the mobile client and acts as an interface between client applications requesting services and the wireless link over which the requests must be forwarded.

Metropolitan area networks Occasionally, multiple LANs belonging to a single corporate entity that are all located within a single metropolitan area must be internetworked. In such cases, a metropolitan area network or MAN may be used to link these LANs together.

MIB Management Information Base; the network management information gathered must be stored in some type of database with an index and standardized field definitions so that network management workstations can easily access this data. An MIB can differ in the fields defined for different vendor's networking devices.

microcell spread spectrum Limited to areas such as college and corporate campuses that are served by microcells, this wireless WAN service offers full-duplex transmission at rates up to 104.5Mbps via proprietary modems.

Microcom Networking Protocols *See* MNP.

micro-mainframe connectivity In micro-mainframe connectivity, the micro (Standalone or LAN-attached PC) pretends to be or "emulates" a mainframe terminal such as an IBM 3270 attached and logged into the mainframe.

micro-segmentation When segmentation is taken to the extreme of limiting each LAN segment to only a single workstation, the internetworking design strategy is known as micro-segmentation. A micro-segmented internetwork requires a LAN switch that is compatible with the NICs installed in the attached workstations.

MIF Management Information Format; DMI-compliant desktop management systems store performance and configuration statistics in an **MIF.**

migration Migration features are aimed at easing the transition from NetWare 3.12 to either NetWare 4.1 or Windows NT.

mini-PBX Offer multiple workers the ability to share a small number of phone lines with integrated advanced features.

mission-critical analysis A data traffic analysis process that examines which data must be specially handled due to its mission critical nature.

MLID Multi-Link Drivers; Network interface card drivers in an ODI-compliant environment.

MLPPP Multilink Point-to-Point Protocol or MLPPP (RFC 1717); able to support multiple simultaneous physical WAN links and also able to combine multiple channels from a variety of WAN services into a single logical link.

MNP A series of 10 classes of error control and data compression protocols that have become de facto standards for modem transmission.

MNP-10 Transmitting data over analog cellular networks requires modems that support specialized cellular transmission protocols on both ends of the cellular transmission in order to maximize throughput. Examples of such protocols are MNP-10 Adverse Channel Enhancements and Enhanced Throughput Cellular (ETC).

MNP Class 5 MNP protocol that offers data compression at up to a 2:1 ratio.

mobile computing Enables field representatives to access corporate information resources in order to offer superior customer service while working on the road. These field reps may or may not have a corporate office PC into which to dial.

Mobile IP Under consideration by the IETF, may be the roaming standard that wireless LANs require. Mobile IP, limited to TCP/IP networks, employs two pieces of software in order to support roaming: a mobile IP client is installed on the roaming wireless client workstation; a mobile IP home agent is installed on a server or router on the roaming user's home network.

mobile MIB The Mobile Management Task Force (MMTF) has proposed a mobile MIB capable of feeding configuration and location information to enterprise network management systems via SNMP. A key to the design of the mobile MIB was to balance the amount of information required in order to effectively manage remote clients while taking into account the limited bandwidth and expense of the remote links over which the management data must be transmitted.

mobile middleware The ultimate goal of mobile middleware is to offer mobile users transparent client/server access independent of the following variables: Client or server platform (operating system, network operating system). Applications (client/server or client/agent/server), Wireless transmission services.

Mobile telephone switching office *See* MTSO.

mobile-aware applications The overall objective of mobile-aware applications is to reduce the amount of mobile client to server network traffic by building as much intelligence as possible into the server-based agent so that it can act on behalf of the mobile client application.

mobile-aware operating systems Operating systems that are able to easily adapt to these different computing modes with a variety of included supporting accessory programs and utilities.

modem Data communications device that modulates/demodulates analog/digital conversion.

modem cable Attaches a modem to a PC. Pinned straight through.

modem setup string Initialization string of Hayes AT commands that establishes communication between a modem and the local PC's communication software.

modified object format *See* MOF.

modular concentrators *See* Enterprise hubs.

modulation Process of converting discrete digital signals in continuously varying analog signals.

MOF Modified Object Format; management data to be used by CIM would be stored in MOF as opposed to DMI's MIF format or SNMP's MIB format.

monolithic drivers Network interface card drivers written for specific adapter card/network operating system combinations.

Monster RAS *See* Large scale RAS.

MPLS Multi-protocol label switching; Cisco's Tag Switching protocol became known as MPLS when it began deliberation by the IETF. Although originally intended for use within a switched internetwork environment, the scope of its application has broadened to include the Internet. MPLS uses labels to provide shortcuts to specific circuits for fast routing of IP packets without the typical packet-by-packet routing table lookups.

MPOA Provides support for multiple local area network protocols running on top of the ATM cell switched network.

MTSO Mobile Telephone Switching Office; cellular service providers are deploying modem pools of cellular enhanced modems at the MTSO where all cellular traffic is converted for transmission over the wireline public switched telephone network (PSTN).

MTU The maximum capacity of a layer two data frame.

multi-casting The process of sending a single packet to multiple nodes on one or more network segments.

multi-function telephony boards *See* Mini-PBX.

multi-homed A node that has NICs on more than one network segment.

multi-layer switch A single device in which layer 2 switching and layer 3 routing functionality are combined.

multi-link interface drivers *See* MLID.

Multilink Point-to-Point Protocol *See* MLPPP.

multimode In a Multimode or Multimode Step Index fiber optic cable, the rays of light will bounce off the cladding at different angles and continue down the core while others will be absorbed in the cladding. These multiple rays at varying angles cause distortion and limit the overall transmission capabilities of the fiber.

multimode graded index By gradually decreasing a characteristic of the core known as the refractive index from the center to the outer edge, reflected rays are focused along the core more efficiently, yielding higher bandwidth (3 GBps) over several kilometers in a type of fiber optic cable known as Multimode Graded Index Fiber.

multimode step index *See* Multimode.

multiplexing Process that combines outputs of several channels into a single composite output.

multiprotocol bridges *See* Translating bridge.

Multi-Protocol Over ATM *See* MPOA.

multiprotocol routers Have the capability to interpret, process, and forward data packets of multiple routable and nonroutable protocols.

Multiprotocol routing Provides the functionality necessary to actually process and understand multiple network protocols as well as translate between them. Without multiprotocol routing software, clients speaking multiple different network protocols cannot be supported.

Multiprotocol Transport Networking Layer *See* MPTN.

multirate ISDN Uses a technique known as inverse multiplexing in which a collection of 64Kbps B channels are dialed up and combined into a single logical channel of sufficient bandwidth to meet application needs such as videoconferencing.

multistation access unit *See* MAU.

Multi-tier firewall Allows controlled access to DMZ while blocking unauthorized access to secure network. Same functionality may be offered in a single product known as a tri-homed firewall.

narrowband digital services Digital carrier services offering bandwidth of less than 1.544Mbps.

Narrowband ISDN A switched digital network service offering both voice and non-voice connectivity to other ISDN end users.

NASI NetWare Asynchronous Services Interface; a software interrupt that links to the NetWare shell on NetWare clients. As with the Int14 implementation, a TSR intercepts all of the information passed to the

NASI interrupt and forwards it across the network to the dial-out modem pool.

National Computer Security Association Now certifies firewall technology.

National ISDN-1 *See* NISDN-1.

NBF NetBEUI Frame; the Windows NT version of the NetBEUI protocol stack included for backward compatibility purposes with such NetBEUI-based network operating systems as Microsoft LAN Manager and OS/2 LAN Server.

NCP NetWare Core Protocols; provide a standardized set of commands or messages that can be used to communicate requests and responses for services between clients and servers.

NDIS Network Driver Interface Specification; a driver specification that offers standard commands for communications between NDIS-compliant network operating system protocol stacks (NDIS Protocol Driver) and NDIS-compliant network adapter card drivers (NDIS MAC Drivers). In addition NDIS specifies a binding operation that is managed by a separate program known as the Protocol Manager.

NDLC Network development life cycle.

NDS Network operating systems have always depended on some sort of naming service or directory in which to store information about users as well as systems resources such as disks, servers, and printers. NetWare 4.1 employs a global directory service known as NDS or NetWare Directory Services.

near-end crosstalk *See* NExT.

negative acknowledgment NAK; control character sent to the transmitting modem from the receiving modem when a data block is received in error.

NetBEUI Frame *See* NBF.

NetWare Connect Novell's remote node server software.

NetWare Directory Services *See* NDS.

NetWare Link Services Protocol *See* NLSP.

network analysis and design methodology The key model behind the network design process is known as the Network Development Life Cycle. Its major phases include analysis, design, simulation, prototyping, monitoring, and management.

network analyzers LAN and WAN **network analyzers** are able to capture network traffic in real time without interrupting normal network transmission. In addition to capturing packets of data from the network, most network analyzers are able to decode those packets, monitor packet traffic statistics, and simulate network traffic through traffic generators.

network architecture Switching architecture + transmission architecture = network architecture.

network auditing tools All network auditing tools seem to have in common the ability to provide records of which network files have been accessed by which users.

network baselining tools By combining the ability to monitor and capture SNMP and RMON data with the abilities to analyze the captured data and report on trends and exceptions, network baselining tools are able to track network performance over extended periods of time and report on anomalies or deviations from the accumulated baseline data.

network byte order The IP header can be either 20 or 24 bytes long, with the bits actually being transmitted in network byte order or from left to right.

network caching Network caching or LAN caching software is able to improve overall remote node performance up to five times by caching repetitive applications commands and systems calls. These add-on packages are comprised of both client and server pieces that work cooperatively with cache application commands and reduce network traffic over relatively low-speed WAN links. Network caching software is network operating system and protocol dependent, requiring that compatibility be assured prior to purchase.

Network convergence The merging (or converging) of data, voice, and video traffic onto a single physical network. The achievement of network convergence is dependent on a combination of business drivers, technology drivers, and technology industry drivers.

network development life cycle *See* NDLC.

network device interface specification *See* NDIS.

network engineering Field of study concentrated largely on processes represented in the NDLC.

network hardware analysis and configuration alternatives Analysis of networking hardware requirements to link data sources with chosen WAN services.

network hierarchy A hierarchy of switching offices from class 5 to class 1. Higher levels on the network hierarchy imply greater switching and transmission capacity as well as greater expense.

network interface card Data-link layer frames are built within the network interface card installed in a computer according to the predetermined frame layout particular to the network architecture of the installed network interface card. Network interface cards are given a unique address in a format determined by their network architecture.

network interface card drivers Small software programs responsible for delivering full interoperability and compatibility between the NIC and the network operating system installed in a given computer.

network interface cards *See* NICs.

network layer Network layer protocols are responsible for the establishment, maintenance, and termination of end-to-end network links. Network layer protocols are required when computers that are not physically connected to the same LAN must communicate.

network level filter A filtering program that only examines source and destination addresses and determines access based on the entries in a filter table is known as a port level filter or network level filter or packet filter.

network modeling and simulation tools Simulation software uses the current network configuration as a starting point and applies what-if scenarios.

network nodes Processing nodes with routing capabilities in APPN. They have the ability to locate network resources, maintain tables of information regarding internetwork links, and establish a session between the requesting end-node and the internetwork service requested.

network objects In some cases, directory services may view all users and network resources as network objects with information concerning them stored in a single database, arranged by object type. Object attributes can be modified and new network objects can be defined.

network segment address The portion of a network layer address that determines the network segment upon which the node resides.

network service Services offered to customers by carriers dependent upon the capabilities of their network architecture.

network termination unit-1 *See* NTU-1.

Network trending tools Tools that are able to track network performance over extended periods of time and report on anomalies or deviations from the accumulated baseline data. Also known as proactive network management tools or network trending products, such tools usually need several weeks of SNMP data in order to establish realistic baseline network performance averages.

network-network interface *See* NNI.

network-to-network interface *See* NNI.

NExT Near-End Crosstalk; signal interference caused by a strong signal on one-pair (transmitting) overpowering a weaker signal on an adjacent pair (receiving).

NICs Network Interface Cards; installed either internally or externally to client and server computers in order to provide a connection to the local area network of choice.

night mode Many companies close their switchboard at night but still have employees on duty who must be able to receive and make phone calls.

NISDN-1 NISDN-1 (National ISDN-1); defines a national standard for ISDN switches as well as interswitch communication.

NLSP NetWare Link Services Protocol; introduced in NetWare 4.1 in an effort to overcome the inefficiencies introduced by RIP. NLSP only broadcasts as changes occur, or every 2 hours at a minimum. Real world implementations of NLSP have reported 15 to 20 times (not %) reduction in WAN traffic with Novell claiming a possibility of up to 40-fold decreases in router-to-router traffic.

NNI Network-Network Interface; defines interoperability standards between various vendors' ATM equipment and network services. These standards are not as well defined as UNI.

node address The portion of a network layer address that determines to which NIC the network layer address correlates.

non-routable Protocols processed by some routers are actually data link layer protocols without network layer addressing schemes. These protocols are considered non-routable.

non-routable protocol Non-routable protocols can be processed by routers by either having the routers act as bridges or by encapsulating the non-routable data link layer frame's upper layer protocols in a routable network layer protocol such as IP.

Northern Telecom DMS100 Switch One of the switches able to support ISDN services.

NT-1 *See* NTU-1.

NTU-1 Network Termination Unit-1 (NTU-1) or (NT-1); required to physically connect the ISDN line to a user's ISDN CPE. Most integrated ISDN equipment includes built-in NT-1s, although stand-alone models are available.

object oriented user interfaces Present the user with a graphical desktop on which objects such as files, directories, folders, disk drives, programs, or devices can be arranged according to the user's whim.

objects The fields within the MIBs are known as objects.

OC Optical carrier; standards for optical transmission.

OC-1 Optical transmission standard, 51.84Mbps.

octet A unit of data 8 bits long. The term *byte* is often used to refer to an 8 bit character or number. Since today's networks are likely to carry digitized voice, video, and images as well as data, the term *octet* is more often used to refer to these 8 bit packets of digital network traffic.

ODI Open DataLink Interface operates in a manner similar to the basic functionality of NDIS and is orchestrated by a program known as LSL.COM where LSL stands for Link Support Layer.

open data-link interface *See* ODI.

open shortest path first *See* OSPF.

operations costs A cost category from the comprehensive systems and network budget model that focuses on the incremental costs to operate new equipment.

opportunities for improvement During stratgic information systems design, opportunities for improvement of business processes and the associated required information are identified.

OPSEC **Open Platform for Security Alliance;** one example of a multivendor interoperable security architecture. More than 200 vendors of security technology have joined the OPSEC alliance that offers certification for OPSEC compliant security products.

optical carrier *See* OC.

Optical switching A switching process that can be accomplished directly on optical signals without the need to first convert to electronic or digital signals.

optimization routines By using analysis and design software to model their current network, companies are able to run optimization routines to reconfigure circuits and/or network hardware to deliver data more efficiently. In the case of optimization software, "efficiently" can mean maximized performance, minimized price, or a combination of both.

Oracle Mobile Agents Formerly known as Oracle-in-Motion; perhaps the best example of the overall architecture and components required to produce mobile-aware applications. The Oracle Mobile Agents architecture adheres to an overall client-agent-server architecture, as opposed to the more common LAN-based client/server architecture.

OSI Model Consists of a hierarchy of 7 layers that loosely group the functional requirements for communication between two computing devices. The power of the OSI Model lies in its openness and flexibility. It can be used to organize and define protocols involved in communicating between two computing devices in the same room as effectively as two devices across the world from each other.

OSI Security Architecture A framework that maps 14 different security services to specific layers of the OSI 7 Layer Reference Model.

OSI Seven Layer Model Divides the communication between any two networked computing devices into seven layers or categories and allows data communications technology developers as well as standards developers to talk about the interconnection of two networks or computers in common terms without dealing in proprietary vendor jargon.

OSPF Open Shortest Path First (RFC 1247); an example of a link state protocol that was developed to overcome some of RIP's shortcomings such as the 15 hop limit and full routing table broadcasts every 30 seconds. OSPF uses IP for connectionless transport.

out-of-band signaling A process in which interswitch signaling should travel out of the voice conversation's band or channel.

outsourcing The purchase of services from outside vendors rather than supporting internal staffs.

outsourcing The selective hiring of outside contractors to perform specific network management duties.

P channel In Isochronous Ethernet, a 10Mbps ISDN P channel is reserved for Ethernet traffic and is completely compatible with 10BaseT Ethernet.

packet assembler/disassembler *See* PAD.

packet filter A filtering program that examines only source and destination addresses and determines access based on the entries in a filter table. Known as a port level filter or network level filter or packet filter.

packet layer protocol *See* PLP.

packet overlapping A technology in which the next packet of information is immediately forwarded as soon as its start of frame is detected rather than waiting for the previous frame to be totally onto the network media before beginning transmission of the next packet.

packet switched network As opposed to circuit switched networks, physical circuits are shared by numerous users transmitting their own packets of data between switches.

packet switches Used to route user's data from source to destination.

packet switching As opposed to circuit switching, user's data shares physical circuits with data from numerous other users.

packetizing Process of adding overhead or management data to raw user data in order to assure proper delivery.

packets Network layer protocols are responsible for providing network layer (end-to-end) addressing schemes and for enabling inter-network routing of network layer data packets. The term *packets* is usually associated with network layer protocols while the term *frames* is usually associated with data-link layer protocols.

PAD Device that transforms raw data into properly formatted packets.

paging Ability to use paging speakers in a building. May be limited to specific paging zone.

PAM Pulse amplitude modulation; a voice digitization technique.

PAP The remote network printing protocol used in the AppleTalk protocol suite.

PAP Password Authentication Protocol; repeatedly sends the user ID and password to the authenticating system in clear text pairs until it is either acknowledged or the connection is dropped. There is no encryption performed with PAP.

parallel networks model A network design in which separate networks for SNA and LAN traffic had to be established between the same corporate locations.

parallel transmission Transmission method in which all bits in a given character travel simultaneously through a computer bus or parallel transmission cable.

parity Simple error checking mechanism that adds a single bit per character.

Password Authentication *See* PAP.

Protocol password protection Modem security mechanism that requires passwords for access to dial-up network resources.

payload Generic term referring to data, voice, or video that may be transmitted over WANs.

payload type analysis A type of data traffic analysis concerned with whether traffic is data, voice, video, image, or multimedia.

PBX Private branch exchange; a customer owned telephone switch.

PBX CPU Software program execution area in a PBX.

pbx-to-host interfaces Interface between PBXs and host computers for sharing information in order to enable CTI.

PC Card Expansion cards that support the PCMCIA standards.

PCM Pulse code modulation; voice digitization technique that digitizes voice into 64Kbps by assigning voice levels to one of 256 eight bit codes.

PCMCIA A nonprofit trade association and standards body that promotes PC Card technology along with Miniature Card and SmartMedia cards by defining technical standards and educating the market.

PCS Personal Communications Services; will provide national full duplex digital voice and data at up to 25Mbps via 2-way pagers, PDAs, and PCS devices.

PCT Private Communications Technology; Microsoft's version of SSL. The key difference between SSL and PCT is that PCT supports secure transmissions across unreliable (UDP rather TCP based) connections by allowing decryption of transmitted records independently from each other, as transmitted in the individual datagrams.

PDC Primary Domain Controller; domain directory services associate network users and resources with a primary server.

PDM Pulse duration modulation; a voice digitization technique.

PDN Public data network; another name for packet switched network.

peer-to-peer internetworking With full peer-to-peer internetworking, the PC can exchange data with any mainframe or any other PC on a host-to-host level rather than acting like a "dumb" terminal as in the case of micro-mainframe connectivity.

peer-to-peer network operating systems Also known as DOS-based LANs or low-cost LANs, offer easy to install and use file and print services for workgroup and departmental networking needs.

PEM Privacy Enhanced Mail; the application standard encryption technique for e-mail use on the Internet, and used with SMTP, Simple Mail Transport Protocol. It was designed to use both DES and RSA encryption techniques, but it would work with other encryption algorithms as well.

percent of fit goal Sets a minimum threshold of compliance for vendor proposals in order to warrant further consideration and invitations for demonstrations.

performance engineering Simulation software tools are also sometimes known as Performance Engineering software tools.

Performance metrics Refer to quantifiable, measurable performance criteria by which the success of an implemented system can be judged. Must be defined in both business terms and IT infrastructure terms.

performance monitoring Software that should offer the ability to set thresholds for multiple system performance parameters. If these thresholds are exceeded, alerts or alarms should notify network management personnel of the problem, and offer advice as to possible diagnoses or solutions. Event logging and audit trails are often included as part of the performance monitoring package.

periodic framing Framing used in T-1 services to combine 24 DS-0s into a D-4 frame.

permanent virtual circuit *See* PVC.

Personal Communications Services *See* PCS.

Personal Computer Memory Card International Association *See* PCMCIA.

Personal Handyphone System *See* PHS.

PGP Pretty Good Privacy; an Internet e-mail specific encryption standard that also uses digital signature encryption to guarantee the authenticity, security, and message integrity of received e-mail.

phase One characteristic (analogous to the wave's pattern) of a wave that can be manipulated in phase modulation schemes in order to represent logical 1s and 0s.

phase modulation Manipulation of a carrier wave's phase via phase shifting in order to represent logical 1s and 0s on an analog transmission circuit.

phase shift keying *See* PSK.

PHS **Personal Handyphone System;** the digital cellular standard, being implemented in Japan.

physical layer Also known as layer 1 of the OSI model; responsible for the establishment, maintenance, and termination of physical connections between communicating devices. These connections are sometimes referred to as point-to-point data links.

physical network design The delineation of required technology determining *how* various hardware and software components will be combined to build a functional network that will meet predetermined business objectives is often referred to as the physical network design.

physical topology Clients and servers must be physically connected to each other according to some configuration and be linked by the shared media of choice. The physical layout of this configuration can have a significant impact on LAN performance and reliability and is known as a network architecture's physical topology.

piggyback updates A dial-up router update mechanism in which updates are performed only when the dial-up link has already been established for the purposes of exchanging user data.

pilot tests A popular way to safely roll out new systems or networks. For example, bring one retail store on-line and monitor performance, solve unanticipated problems, and gain management experience, before deploying the system on a wider scale.

PKIX **Public Key Infrastructure X.509** is an international ISO standard for public key certificates.

Plain Old Telephone Service *See* POTS.

PLP Network layer protocol for X.25.

Plug-n-play *See* PnP.

PnP The goal of plug-n-play is to free users from having to understand and worry about such things as IRQs (Interrupt Requests), DMA (Direct Memory Access) channels, memory addresses, COM ports, and editing CONFIG.SYS whenever they want to add a device to their computer.

PnP BIOS Basic Input Output System required to interface directly to both PnP and non-PnP compliant hardware.

point of presence *See* POP.

point products Also known as **element managers;** specifically written to address a particular systems administration or network management issue.

point-to-point data links The physical layer, also known as layer 1 of the OSI model, is responsible for the establishment, maintenance, and termination of physical connections between communicating devices. These connections are sometimes referred to as point-to-point data links.

Point-to-Point Protocol *See* PPP.

Point-to-Point Tunneling Protocol *See* PPTP.

policy audits Manual audits serve to verify the effectiveness of policy development and implementation, especially the extent to which people understand and effectively execute their assigned processes in the overall corporate security policy.

policy-based management tools In order to more easily integrate configuration management tools with corporate policy and standards regarding desktop configurations, a new breed of policy-based management tools has emerged.

poll spoofing The ability of an internetworking device, such as an SDLC converter or router, to respond directly to, or acknowledge, the FEP's constant polling messages to the remote cluster controller. By answering these status check messages locally, the inquiry and its answer never enter the wide area link portion of the internetwork.

polling In TDM multiplexing, the process of emptying each channel's buffer in order to build the composite frame.

Polymorphic viruses Change their appearance each time an infected program is run in order to avoid detection.

POP Point of Presence; competing long-distance carriers wishing to do business in a given LATA maintain a switching office in that LATA known as a POP.

port cards Also known as line cards or station cards. PBX cards through which user phones are attached.

port level filter A filtering program that only examines source and destination addresses and determines access based on the entries in a filter table is known as a port level filter or network level filter or packet filter.

port mirroring Copies information from a particular switch port to an attached LAN analyzer. The difficulty with this approach is that it only allows one port to be monitored at a time.

ports Ports are specific addresses uniquely related to particular applications.

POTS Plain old telephone service. Analog voice service.

Powersum crosstalk Taking into account the crosstalk influence from all pairs in the cable, whether four-pair or 25-pair rather than just crosstalk between adjacent pairs, or pair-to-pair.

PPM Pulse position modulation; a voice digitization technique.

PPN **Personal Phone Number;** would become the user's interface to PCS, a number associated with a particular individual regardless of the location, even globally, of the accessed facility.

PPP A WAN data-link layer protocol that is able to support multiple network layer protocols simultaneously over a single WAN connection. In addition, PPP is able to establish connections over a variety of WAN services including: ISDN, Frame Relay, SONET, X.25, as well as synchronous and asynchronous serial links.

PPP clients Standardized remote clients with the ability to link to servers running a variety of different network operating systems are sometimes referred to as

PPP clients. In general, they can link to network operating systems that support IP, IPX, NetBEUI, or XNS as transport protocols.

PPTP Microsoft's tunneling protocol that is specific to Windows NT Servers and remote access servers. It has the backing of several remote access server vendors.

predictive dialing Also known as outbound dialing; uses a database of phone numbers, automatically dials those numbers, recognizes when calls are answered by people, and quickly passes those calls to available agents.

presentation layer Protocols that provide an interface between user applications and various presentation-related services required by those applications. For example, data encryption/decryption protocols are considered presentation layer protocols as are protocols that translate between encoding schemes such as ASCII to EBCDIC.

Pretty Good Privacy *See* PGP.

primary domain controller *See* PDC.

Principle of Shifting Bottlenecks Principle that states that as one network bottleneck is overcome, the network bottleneck merely shifts to a different network location (from the modem to the serial port).

Printer Access Protocol *See* PAP.

prioritization Gives priority access to available trunks to certain users.

Privacy Enhanced Mail *See* PEM.

private branch exchange *See* PBX.

Private Communications Technology *See* PCT.

private key encryption The decrypting device must use the same algorithm or method to decode or decrypt the data as the encrypting device used to encrypt the data. For this reason private key encryption is sometimes also known as symmetric encryption.

private packet radio Proprietary wireless WAN service offered by RAM and Ardis in most major U.S. cities. Offers full duplex packet switched data at speeds of up to 4.8Kbps via proprietary modems.

Proactive network management tool Network baselining tools are able to track network performance over extended periods of time and report on anomalies or deviations from the accumulated baseline data. Also known as proactive network management tools or network trending products, such tools usually need several weeks of SNMP data in order to establish realistic baseline network performance averages.

proactive performance assurance For the rapidly growing network, the ability of simulation software to simulate different possible future combinations of traffic usage, circuits, and networking equipment can avoid costly future network congestion problems or failures.

process Network analysts focus on what processes should be taking place at each stage of the NDLC in order to stay on track.

product Network analysts focus on what the deliverables should be at each stage of the NDLC in order to stay on track.

productivity paradox The fact that little if any documented increase in productivity results from massive investments in technology.

Project charter The mechanism by which a project is organized and initial expectations are documented and agreed upon.

promiscuous listen Transparent bridges receive all data packets transmitted on the LANs to which they are connected.

propagation Forwarding messages by bridges to all workstations on all intermittent LANs.

propagation delay The time it takes a signal from a source PC to reach a destination PC. Because of this propagation delay, it is possible for a workstation to sense that there is no signal on the shared media, when in fact another distant workstation has transmitted a signal that has not yet reached the carrier sensing PC.

protected memory mode Client network operating systems may execute 32 bit applications in their own address space, otherwise known as protected memory mode.

protective measures Measures designed and taken that effectively block the vulnerability in order to prevent threats from attacking assets.

protocol A set of rules that govern communication between hardware and/or software components.

protocol analyzers Devices that test layers 2 through 7.

protocol conversion Must take place to allow the PC to appear to be a 3270 terminal in the eyes of the mainframe.

protocol discriminator In order to differentiate which particular noncompliant protocol is embedded, any packet with AA in the DSAP and SSAP fields also has a 5 octet SNAP header known as a protocol discriminator following the Control field.

protocol manager The NDIS program which controls the binding operation that combines separate NDIS compliant software from NOS and NIC vendors into a single compatible driver.

protocol stack The sum of all of the protocols employed in a particular computer.

protocol stack analysis A data traffic analysis process that focuses on the protocols used at each network node.

protocols Rules for how communicating hardware and software components bridge interfaces or talk to one another.

proxies *See* Application gateways.

proxy polling Emulates the FEP's polling messages on the remote side of the network, thereby assuring the remote cluster controller that it is still in touch with an FEP.

PSE Packet switched exchange; another name for packet switched network.

PSK A type of phase modulation in which different phase shifts represent different combinations of 1s and 0s.

PSTN The Public Switched Network or dial-up phone system through which local access to phone services is gained.

public data network *See* PDN.

public key certificates A certificate assuring the authenticity of the public encryption key.

Public Key Encryption Could perhaps more accurately be named Public/Private Key Encryption since the process actually combines usage of both public and private keys.

public switched telephone network *See* PSTN.

pulse Older style of dialing with rotary phone that produces pulses of electricity to represent numbers.

Pulse Amplitude Modulation *See* PAM.

Pulse Code Modulation *See* PCM.

Pulse Duration Modulation *See* PDM.

Pulse Position Modulation *See* PPM.

Pulse Width Modulation *See* PWM.

PVC Packet switched equivalent of a leased line.

PWM Pulse width modulation; a voice digitization technique.

Q.931 An ISDN Standard that allows PBX features to interoperate with Public Switched Network Features.

Q.sig Q.Sig standardizes features among different PBX manufacturers and delivers those standardized features within the limitations of the feature set offered by ISDN.

QAM Quadrature amplitude modulation; modulation scheme in which both phase and amplitude are manipulated.

QoS Quality of Service; general term for being able to differentiate between the level of network performance and reliability required by different applications.

QPSK Quadrature phase shift keying; phase shift modulation with four different phases.

quadrature amplitude modulation *See* QAM.

quadrature phase shift keying *See* QPSK.

quality of service *See* QOS.

quantization error When an analog signal is converted to a digital signal and back to an analog signal, some data are lost. The difference between the original signal and the final signal is known as quantization error.

queueing Bandwidth management technique, otherwise known as flow control that uses algorithms to assign traffic with different priorities to different queues.

RADIUS Remote Authentication Dial-In User Service; A protocol and associated architecture supported by a wide variety of remote access technology and offers the potential to enable centralized management of remote access users and technology.

RADSL Rate adaptive digital subscriber line; able to adapt its data rate to the level of noise and interference on a given line. Currently, it is unable to support this adaptive rate on a dynamic basis.

RARP Reverse Address Resolution Protocol; used if the data-link layer address of the workstation is known but the IP address of the same workstation is required.

RAS Windows NT's remote access server software.

rate adaptive DSL *See* RADSL.

Rate control Bandwidth management technique, otherwise known as traffic shaping, that controls flow by TCP window size adjustment.

RBOC Regional Bell Operating Company Divestiture; caused the former Local Bell Operating Companies to be grouped into new Regional Bell Operating Companies (RBOCs) to offer local telecommunications service.

real-mode device drivers Programs or sub-routines that write directly to computer hardware are sometimes referred to as employing real-mode device drivers.

realms Enterprise networks implementing Kerberos are divided into Kerberos realms, each served by its own Kerberos server.

real-time audits Most audit software depends on capturing large amounts of event data and then filtering that data for exceptional or unusual events.

receiver Earpiece on a phone handset.

recursion A process whereby if the local DNS cannot resolve an address itself, it may contact the higher authority DNS server, thereby increasing its own knowledge while meeting the client request.

regulatory agencies State, local, and federal authorities charged with overseeing the operation of companies in the telecommunications industry.

relationship variables In Application MIB, **relationship variables** would define all other network attached resources on which a given distributed application depends. This would include databases, associated client applications, or other network resources.

reliable Reliable transmission for upper layer application programs or utilities is assured through the additional fields contained within the TCP header which offer the following functionality: flow control, acknowledgments of successful receipt of packets after error checking, retransmission of packets as required, proper sequencing of packets.

remote access A term most often used to describe the process of linking remote PCs to local LANs without implying the particular functionality of that link (remote node vs. remote control). Unfortunately, the term *remote access* is also sometimes more specifically used as a synonym for remote node.

remote access server Dedicated LAN-based server that controls remote access via modems to LAN based resources.

Remote Authentication Dial-In User Service *See* RADIUS.

remote configuration Increased security in SNMP2 allows not just monitoring and management of remote network devices, but actual remote configuration of those devices as well.

remote control A mode in which the remote PC is merely supplying input and output devices for the local client which interacts as normal with the local server and other locally attached LAN resources.

remote control software Especially designed to allow remote PC's to "take-over" control of local PCs; should not be confused with the Asynchronous Communications Software used for dial-up connections to asynchronous hosts via modems.

remote monitoring *See* RMON.

remote node Remote node or remote client computing implies that, in theory, the remote client PC should be able to operate as if it were locally attached to network resources. In other words, the geographic separation between the remote client and the local LAN resources should be transparent.

remote node client software Most of the remote node server software packages also include compatible remote node client software. A problem arises, however, when a single remote node client needs to login to a variety of different servers running a variety of different network operating systems or remote node server packages.

remote node server An alternative to server-based remote access software is a standalone device also known as a dial-up server or remote node server. Such a self-contained unit includes modems, communications software, and NOS-specific remote access server software in a turnkey system.

remote node server software Traditionally remote node client and server software were supplied by the vendor of the network operating system on the server to be remotely accessed. Windows NT RAS (Remote Access Service) and NetWare Connect are two examples of such NOS-specific remote node server software.

remote node servers Servers strictly concerned with controlling remote access to LAN attached resources and acting as a gateway to those resources. Applications services are supplied by the same LAN-attached applications servers that are accessed by locally attached clients.

remote node software Requires both remote node server and compatible remote node client software in order to successfully initiate remote node sessions.

Repeater Device used by carriers on digital transmission lines to regenerate digital signals over long distances.

repeater A repeater's job is to: Repeat the digital signal by regenerating and retiming the incoming signal, pass all signals between all attached segments, do not read destination addresses of data packets, allow for the connection of and translation between different types of media, effectively extend overall LAN distance by repeating signals between.

replicate The process of automatically copying a database from one server to another.

request for proposal *See* RFP.

resolver DNS is physically implemented in a client/server architecture in which client-based DNS software known as the DNS or name resolver, sends requests for DNS name resolution to a DNS (or name) Server.

return on investment *See* ROI.

Return on opportunity *See* ROO.

reverse address resolution protocol *See* RARP.

reverse poison *See* Split horizon.

RFI Radio Frequency Interference.

RFP Request for proposal; by organizing the Strategic Information System Design information into an understandable format and by adding detailed information concerning performance evaluation criteria for the data and network layers, a document known as a RFP (Request for Proposal) is produced.

RIF Router Information Field; one very important limitation of source routing bridges as applied to large internetworks is known as the 7 Hop Limit. Because of the limited space in the RIF of the explorer packet, only 7 hop locations can be included in the path to any remote destination.

ring logical topology *See* Sequential.

ring physical topology Each PC is actually an active part of the ring, passing data packets in a sequential pattern around the ring. If one of the PCs dies, or a network adapter card malfunctions, the "sequence" is broken, the token is lost, and the network is down.

RIP A router-to-router protocol used to keep routers synchronized and up-to-date via broadcasts every 30 seconds.

risk Probability of a particular threat successfully attacking a particular asset in a given amount of time via a particular vulnerability.

Risk domains Consists of a unique group of networked systems sharing both common business function and common elements of exposure.

RJ48c Jack in which T-1 services are typically terminated.

RMON Remote Monitoring; the most commonly used MIB for network monitoring and management.

RMON MIB Remote Network Monitoring MIB.

RMON probe RMON2 compatible agent software that resides within internetworking devices and reports performance statistics to enterprise network management systems.

RMON2 While the original RMON MIB only required compatible technology to be able to collect and analyze statistics on the physical and data-link layers, RMON2 requires collection and analysis of network layer protocols as well.

RMON3 roaming One important issue not included in the IEEE 802.11 standard is roaming capability that allows a user to transparently move between the transmission ranges of wireless LANs without interruption. Proprietary roaming capabilities are currently offered by many wireless LAN vendors.

ROI Return on investment; a form of cost/benefit analysis commonly used in networking and systems projects.

ROO **Return on Opportunity;** attempts to quantify benefits that may be unanticipated or indirectly related to the immediate investment. This methodology recognizes that improvements in IT infrastructure aimed at one project may enable unanticipated benefits and uses not related to that initiating project.

round robin polling scheme In 100VG-AnyLAN, the Demand Priority Protocol access methodology uses a round robin polling scheme in which the hubs scan each port in sequence to see if the attached workstations have any traffic to transmit. The round robin polling scheme is distributed through a hierarchical arrangement of cascaded hubs.

router A device that forwards packets between layer three segments based on the layer three network address.

router servers An internetwork evolutionary design scenario in which route servers will provide a centralized repository of routing information while edge switches deployed within the LANs will be programmed with minimal routing information.

Routing Information Field *See* RIF.

Routing Information Protocol *See* RIP.

Routing Table Maintenance Protocol *See* RTMP.

routing tables Routers consult routing tables in order to determine the best path on which to forward a particular data packet.

roving port mirroring Creates a roving RMON (Remote Monitoring) probe that gathers statistics at regular intervals on multiple switch ports. The shortcoming with this approach remains that at any single point in time, only one port is being monitored.

RS-232-C An EIA serial transmission standard officially limited to 20Kbps over 50 ft distance.

RSA The current standard for public key encryption.

RSVP Resource Reservation Protocol; enables routing software to reserve a portion of network bandwidth known as a virtual circuit.

RT24 A voice compression algorithm.

RTMP A routing protocol used in the AppleTalk protocol suite.

run length encoding Encoding mechanism that looks for repeating characters and replaces multiple repeating characters with a repetition count code.

RYGB The type of phone wire installed in most homes consists of a tan plastic jacket containing four untwisted wires: red, yellow, green, and black and is also known as 4 conductor station wire or RYGB.

S/MIME Secure Multipurpose Internet Mail Extension; secures e-mail traffic in e-mail applications that have been S/MIME enabled. S/MIME encrypts and authenticates e-mail messages for transmission over SMTP-based e-mail networks.

S/N Signal to noise ratio; expressed in decibels, measures power of data signal as compared to power of circuit interference or noise.

SAN *See* Storage area network.

SAP Service Advertising Protocol; used by all network servers to advertise the services they provide to all other reachable networked servers. SAP uses IPX packets as its means of delivering its service advertising requests or responses throughout the network.

SAP filtering In order to eliminate the every 60 second broadcast of SAP packets, an associated feature of advanced IPX known as SAP filtering, assures that SAP broadcasts are synchronized to take place only with NLSP updates.

SAS Single Attachment Stations; attach to only one of FDDI's two rings.

SATAN A probe written especially to analyze Unix and TCP/IP based systems, and once it has found a way to get inside an enterprise network, it continues to probe all TCP/IP machines within that enterprise network.

SBA Synchronous bandwidth allocation; in FDDI, frames transmitted in a continuous stream are known as synchronous frames and are prioritized according to a methodology known as SBA, which assigns fixed amounts of bandwidth to given stations.

screen caching Allows only changes to screens, rather than entire screens to be transmitted over the limited bandwidth WAN links. Screen caching will reduce the amount of actual traffic transmitted over the WAN link.

SDLC IBM SNA's data-link layer protocol. SLDC frames do not contain anything equivalent to the OSI network layer addressing information for use by routers, which makes SDLC a nonroutable protocol.

SDLC conversion SDLC frames are converted to Token Ring Frames by a specialized internetworking device known as a SDLC Converter.

SDLC converter *See* SDLC conversion.

SDSL Symmetric digital subscriber line; differs from ADSL in that it offers upstream and downstream channels of equal bandwidth.

search engine The portion of the software that sifts through the knowledge base to the proper answer.

Secure Courier Based on SSL; allows users to create a secure digital envelope for transmission of financial transactions over the Internet.

Secure Electronic Transactions *See* SET.

Secure Hypertext Transport Protocol *See* S-HTTP.

Secure Multipurpose Internet Mail Extension *See* S/MIME.

secure single login Assurance that users are able to log into a network, rather than each individual server and application, and be able to access only resources for which they are properly authorized.

secure SNMP SNMP2 or a variation of SNMP known as **Secure SNMP,** will allow users to access carriers' network management information and incorporate it into the wide area component of an enterprise network management system.

Secure Sockets Layer *See* SSL.

Security Analyzer Tool for Analyzing Networks *See* SATAN.

Security architecture Implies an open framework into which business-driven security processes and requirements can be quickly and easily organized, now or in the future.

Security Auditing and Intrusion Detection Able to track and identify suspicious behaviors from both internal employees as well as potential intruders.

Security framework Frameworks that have begun to emerge which attempt to consolidate security management into a single architecture or console allowing centralized policy management and automated incident response.

security policy development life cycle *See* SPDLC.

security probes Actively test various aspects of enterprise network security and report results and suggest improvements.

segmentation Usually the first internetworking approach employed to reduce shared media congestion. By having fewer workstations per segment, there is less contention for the shared bandwidth.

selective ARQ ARQ error control mechanism that is able to retransmit only those particular data blocks received in error.

send window With an adaptive sliding window protocol, the number of packets allowed to be sent before the receipt of an acknowledgment determines the size of the send window.

Sequenced Packet *See* SPX.

Exchange sequential In a sequential logical topology, also known as a ring logical topology, data are passed from one PC (or node) to another. Each node examines the destination address of the data packet to determine if this particular packet is meant for it. If the data were not meant to be delivered at this node, the data are passed along to the next node in the logical ring.

Serial Line Internet Protocol *See* SLIP.

serial transmission Method of transmission in which all bits of a given character are transmitted in linear fashion, one after the other.

server capacity planning Server management software must provide server capacity planning capabilities by monitoring server performance trends and making recommendations for server component upgrades in a proactive manner.

server front-end LAN switch A switched network architecture in which dedicated LAN switch ports are only necessary for servers, while client workstations share a switch port via a cascaded media-sharing hub.

server isolation Instead of assigning all workstations to their own LAN segment as in micro-segmentation, only selected high-performance devices such as servers can be assigned to their own segment in an internetworking design strategy known as server isolation. By isolating servers on their own segments, guaranteed access to network bandwidth is assured.

Server MONitoring *See* SMON.

server network operating systems Able to be chosen and installed based on their performance characteristics for a given required functionality. For example, NetWare servers are often employed as file and print servers, whereas Windows NT, OS/2, or UNIX servers are more likely to be employed as application servers.

Service Advertising Protocol *See* SAP.

Service level agreement Clearly describes expected levels of service, how that service will be measured, what that service will cost, and what the consequences will be if the agreed upon service levels are not met.

Service management Concerned with the management of IT services and the business processes that depend on them.

Service management architectures Provide metrics for service evaluation on both a business and IT infrastructure level.

Service Profile Identifier Numbers *See* SPID.

service-granting ticket In kerberos, if the Ticket Granting Server determines that the request is valid, a ticket is issued that will allow the user to access the requested server.

session keys Unique, one-time use keys used for encryption.

session layer Protocols responsible for establishing, maintaining, and terminating sessions between user application programs. Sessions are interactive dialogues between networked computers and are of particular importance to distributed computing applications in a client/server environment.

session limits The second major improvement of NBF over NetBEUI involves session limits. Since NetBEUI is NetBIOS-based, it was forced to support the 254 session limit of NetBIOS. With NBF, each client to server connection can support 254 sessions, rather than a grand total for all connections of 254 sessions.

SET Secure Electronic Transactions; a series of standards to assure the confidentiality of electronic commerce transactions. These standards are being largely promoted by credit card giants VISA and MasterCard.

Shared media network architecture Architectures that employ media-sharing network wiring centers such as hubs, which offer all attached workstations shared access to a single LAN segment.

shielding Shielding may be a metallic foil or copper braid. The function of the shield is rather simple. It "shields" the individual twisted pairs as well as the entire cable from either EMI (Electromagnetic Interference) or RFI (Radio Frequency Interference).

S-HTTP Secure HTTP is a secure version of HTTP, which requires both client and server S-HTTP versions to be installed for secure end-to-end encrypted transmission.

signal to noise ratio *See* S/N.

signaling system 7 *See* SS7.

signature scanners Because virus scanners are actually scanning for known digital signatures or viruses they are sometimes referred to as signature scanners.

Simple key management for IP *See* SKIP.

simple management protocol *See* SMP.

simple network management protocol *See* SNMP.

simultaneous RMON view Allows all network traffic to be monitored simultaneously. Such a monitoring scheme is only possible on those switches that incorporate a shared memory multi-gigabit bus as opposed to a switching matrix internal architecture. Furthermore, unless this monitoring software is executed on a separate CPU, switch performance is likely to degrade.

Single Access Control View Allows the users access from their client workstation to display only those resources to which the user actually has access.

Single Attachment Station *See* SAS.

single mode Fiber optic cable that is able to focus the rays of light so that only a single wavelength can pass through at a time. Without numerous reflections of rays at multiple angles, distortion is eliminated and bandwidth is maximized.

single point of failure Any network attached device or piece of technology whose failure would cause the failure of the entire network.

Single Point of Registration *See* SPR.

single sign-on *See* SSO.

sinks Packet destinations.

SKIP Simple Key Management for IP; a proposed key management protocol from Sun.

Sliding Window Protocols Continuous ARQ, for example, continues to transmit and slides back to NAK'd data blocks when a NAK is received.

SLIP Serial Line Interface Protocol; able to establish asynchronous serial links between two computers that support both SLIP and TCP/IP over any of the following connections: via modems and a dial-up line, via modems and a point-to-point private or leased line, via hard-wired or direct connections.

slot time In Ethernet networks, the time required for a given workstation to detect a collision is known slot time and is measured in bits.

slow convergence The delay that occurs while all of the routers are propagating their routing tables using RIP, known as slow convergence, could allow certain routers to assume that failed links to certain networks are still viable.

Small Office Home Office *See* SOHO.

Smart Cards Used in token authentication systems, Hardware-based Smart Cards or Smart IDs that are about the size of a credit card with or without a numeric keypad.

SMDR Station message detail recording. An individual detail record is generated for each call for call accounting systems.

SMDS Switched multimegabit data service; a connectionless high speed data service.

SMON The newest addition to the SNMP family of monitoring standards. SMON expands RMON's monitoring ability by offering a mechanism to collect data from all network segments connected to a LAN switch.

SMP Simple Management Protocol; the need to reduce network traffic caused by the SNMP protocol as well as to deal with other aforementioned SNMP shortcomings, led to a proposal for a new version of SNMP known as **SNMP2,** or **SMP.**

SNA Systems Network Architecture; IBM's proprietary network architecture, originally designed to link mainframes.

SNAP In order to ease the transition to IEEE 802 compliance, an alternative method of identifying the embedded upper layer protocols was developed, known as SNAP or Sub-Network Access Protocol. Any protocol can use SNAP with IEEE 802.2 and appear to be an IEEE 802 compliant protocol.

SNMP Simple Network Management Protocol; partly due to the dominance of TCP/IP as the internetworking protocol of choice, **SNMP** is the de facto standard for delivering enterprise management data.

SNMP2 The need to reduce network traffic caused by the SNMP protocol as well as to deal with other aforementioned SNMP shortcomings, led to a proposal for a new version of SNMP known as **SNMP2,** or **SMP** (Simple Management Protocol).

socket The unique port address of an application combined with the unique 32 bit IP address of the computer on which the application is executing.

socket services The socket services sub-layer of the PCMCIA Card & Socket Services driver specification is written specifically for the type of PCMCIA controller included in a notebook computer.

SOCKS Used by Circuit level proxy programs, **Socks** creates a proxy data channel to the application server on behalf of the application client. Since all data go through Socks, it can audit, screen, and filter all traffic in between the application client and server.

software flow control Uses control characters XON, XOFF to control data transmission into and out of buffer memory.

SOHO New market for mini-PBXs and desktop CTI.

SONET Synchronous optical network, dual ring, high speed fiber-based transmission architecture.

SONET superframe Rather than fitting 24 channels per frame delineated by a single framing bit, a single SONET frame or row is delineated by 3 octets of overhead for control information followed by 87 octets of payload. Nine of these 90 octet rows are grouped together to form a SONET superframe.

source address Data-link protocols such as Ethernet contain source addresses as well as the destination addresses within the predefined Ethernet Frame layout. A bridge checks the source address of each frame it receives and adds that source address to a table of known local nodes.

source routing bridge Used to connect two source-routing enabled Token Ring LANs. Data messages arrive at a source routing bridge with a detailed map of how they plan to reach their destination.

source routing transparent bridge Bridges that can support links between source routing Token Ring LANs or transparent LANs.

Spanning Tree Algorithm STA; has been standardized as IEEE 802.1 for the purposes of controlling redundant paths in bridged networks, thereby reducing the possibility of broadcast storms.

SPAP Shiva's proprietary authentication protocol that includes password encryption and callback capability.

SPDLC Security Policy Development Life Cycle; one methodology for the development of a comprehensive network security policy.

SPE Synchronous Payload Envelope; the 87 octets of payload per row in each of the time rows or the Superframe.

SPID Service Profile Identifier Numbers; in order to properly interface an end-user's ISDN equipment to a carrier's ISDN services, desired ISDN features must be specified. In some cases, end-user equipment such as remote access servers must be programmed with SPIDs so as to properly identify the carrier's equipment with which the user equipment must interface.

split horizon In order to reduce slow convergence in RIP based router networks, split horizon and reverse poison prevent routers from wasting time broadcasting routing table changes back to the routers that just supplied them with the same changes in the first place.

spoofing A method of filtering chatty or unwanted protocols from the WAN link while assuring that remote programs that require ongoing communication from these filtered protocols are still reassured via emulation of these protocols by the local dial-up router.

SPR Single Point of Registration; allows a network security manager to enter a new user (or delete a terminated user) from a single centralized location and assign all associated rights, privileges, and access control to enterprise resources from this single point rather than having to enter this new user's information on multiple resources distributed throughout the enterprise.

Spread spectrum transmission Spreads a data message across a wide range or spectrum of frequencies. This technique was originally employed as a security measure since a receiver would need to know exactly how the message was spread across the frequency spectrum in order to intercept the message in meaningful form.

SPX NetWare's connection-oriented, reliable transport layer protocol.

SS7 Signaling system 7; a common inter-switch signaling protocol for call management and control.

SSL A connection level encryption method providing security to the network link itself. SSL Version 3

(SSL3) added support for more key exchange and encryption algorithms as well as separate keys for authentication and encryption.

SSO Authentication technology that delivers single sign-on (SSO) access to multiple network attached servers and resources via passwords.

stackable hubs Add expandability and manageability to the basic capabilities of the stand-alone hub. Can be linked together, or cascaded, to form one larger virtual hub of a single type of network architecture and media.

stand-alone hubs Fully configured hubs offering a limited number (12 or fewer) ports of a particular type of network architecture (Ethernet, Token Ring) and media.

stand-alone LAN switches Stand-alone Workgroup/Departmental LAN switches; offer dedicated connections to all attached client and server computers via individual switch ports.

standards An agreed-upon protocol as determined by officially sanctioned standards-making organizations, market share, or user group concensus.

star The star physical topology employs some type of central management device. Depending on the network architecture and sophistication of the device, it may be called a hub, a wiring center, a concentrator, a MAU (Multiple Access Unit), a repeater, or a switching hub.

state variables In Application MIB, **state variables** would report on the current status of a given application. Three possible states are: up, down, or degraded.

station cards PBX cards that attach to users' phones.

station message detail recording *See* SMDR.

statistical time division multiplexing *See* STDM.

STDM Advanced form of TDM multiplexing that seeks to overcome TDM inefficiencies by dynamically adapting polling of channels.

Storage area network Seek to separate data storage from particular application-oriented servers (sometimes referred to as storage islands) by consolidating storage systems such as disk arrays or tape libraries and attaching them to the enterprise network via redundant, high capacity network connections.

store-and-forward switches Switches that read the entire frame into a shared memory area in the switch. The contents of the transmitted Frame Check Sequence field is read and compared with the locally recalculated Frame Check Sequence. Store-and-forward switching is slower than cut-through switching but does not forward bad frames.

Stored Program Control Location in PBX where software is executed.

strategic information system design A high level information systems design that will meet agreed upon business objectives and serve as a starting point for network design.

streaming protocol File transfer protocol that continues to transmit until it encounters an end of file indicator. Relies on modems to provide error control.

STS-1 Synchronous Transport Signal: the electrical equivalent of the OC-1, the optical SONET Superframe standard is known as the STS-1.

subnet mask By applying a 32 bit subnet mask to a Class B IP address, a portion of the bits that comprises the host ID can be reserved for denoting subnetworks, with the remaining bits being reserved for host IDs per subnetwork.

subnetwork access protocol *See* SNAP.

subnetworking Subnetworking allows organizations that were issued an IP address with a single network ID to use a portion of their host ID address field to provide multiple subnetwork IDs in order to implement internetworking.

superframe 12 D-4 frames.

SVC Switched virtual circuit; packet switched equivalent of a circuit switched dial-up line.

switched LAN network architecture Architectures that depend on wiring centers called LAN switches or switching hubs which offer all attached workstations access to a switching matrix that provides point-to-point, rather than shared, connections between any two ports.

switched line Unlike a leased line, a switched line is connected to a CO switch, provides dial tone, and reaches different destinations by dialing different phone numbers.

switched multimegabit data service *See* SMDS.

switched virtual circuit *See* SVC.

switching Process by which messages are routed from switch to switch en route to their final destination.

switching architecture Major component of network architecture along with transmission architecture.

switching hub Able to create connections, or switch, between any two attached Ethernet devices on a packet-by-packet basis in as little as 40 milliseconds. The "one-at-time" broadcast limitation previously associated with shared media Ethernet is overcome with an Ethernet switch.

switching matrix Location in CPU where circuits are switched to complete calls.

symmetric DSL *See* SDSL.

synchronous bandwidth allocation *See* SBA.

Synchronous Data Link Control *See* SDLC.

synchronous frames Frames transmitted in a continuous stream in FDDI; prioritized according to a methodology known as synchronous bandwidth allocation or SBA, which assigns fixed amounts of bandwidth to given stations.

synchronous optical network *See* SONET.

synchronous payload envelope *See* SPE.

synchronous TDM In a technique used in T-1 transmission service known as periodic framing or synchronous TDM, 24 channels of eight bits each (192 bits total) are arranged in a frame.

synchronous transmission Transmission method in which timing is provided by a clocking signal supplied by either modems or the carrier.

systems administration Focuses on the management of client and server computers and the operating systems and network operating systems that allow the client and server computers to communicate.

Systems Network Architecture *See* SNA.

T.120 Standard for multipoint audioconferences.

T-1 1.544Mbps digital WAN service adhering to the DS-1 standard.

T-1 channel bank Device that can take a variety of voice and data inputs, digitize them, and multiplex them onto a T-1 circuit.

T-1 CSU/DSU Device that interfaces between a T-1 circuit and another device such as a mux, bridge, or router.

T-1 IMUX Inverse multiplexer that can combine four or more T-1s for bandwidth on demand applications.

T-1 inverse multiplexer *See* T-1 IMUX.

T-1 multiplexers Multiplexers that combine several digitized voice or data inputs into a T-1 output.

T-1 switches Switches able to redirect T-1s or the DS-0s contained therein.

T-3 A leased line digital broadband service of 44.736Mbps.

tandem office Establishes the intra-LATA circuit and also handles billing procedures for the long-distance call.

TAPI CTI API promoted by Microsoft and Intel.

TBO Total benefit of ownership; a cost benefit measurement methodology used in networking that concentrates on comparing projects based on perceived benefits.

TCM Trellis coded modulation; a forward error correction technique that transmits redundant data in hopes of avoiding retransmission.

TCO Total cost of ownership; a cost benefit measurement methodology used in networking that concentrates on comparing projects based on perceived costs.

TCP Transmission control protocol, connection oriented transport layer protocol whose 3-way handshake for connection setup is vulnerable to attack.

TCP/IP Transmission Control Protocol/Internet Protocol; the term generally used to refer to an entire suite of protocols used to provide communication on a variety of layers between widely distributed different types of computers. Strictly speaking, TCP and IP are just two of the protocols contained within the family of protocols more properly known as the Internet Suite of Protocols.

TCP/IP encapsulation Each nonroutable SNA SDLC frame is "stuffed" into an IP "envelope" for transport across the network and processing by routers supporting TCP/IP internetworking protocol.

TDM Time division multiplexing; With TDM, from a connected terminal's point of view, 100% of the bandwidth is available for a portion of the time.

TDMA Time Division Multiple Access; achieves more than one conversation per frequency by assigning time slots to individual conversations. Ten time slots per frequency are often assigned, with a given cellular device transmitting its digitized voice only during its assigned time slot.

TDP Telocator Data Protocol; an alternative two-way messaging architecture is proposed by the PCIA (Personal Communicator Industry Association). Rather than building on existing IP-based networks as the CDPD/LSM architecture did, the TDP architecture is actually a suite of protocols defining an end-to-end system for two-way messaging to and from paging devices.

technical support The third major usage of remote computing is for technical support organizations that must be able to dial-in to client systems with the ability to appear as a local workstation, or take control of those workstations, in order to diagnose and correct problems remotely.

Technology Push/Demand Pull In a technology push scenario, new technologies may be introduced to the market in order to spawn innovative uses for this technology and thereby generate demand. Conversely, business needs may create a demand for services or technological innovation that are currently unavailable. However, the demand pull causes research and development efforts to accelerate, thereby introducing the new technology sooner than it would have otherwise been brought to market.

Telecommunications Usually used to indicate a broader market than data communications, including voice, video, and image services.

Telecommunications Act of 1996 Seeks to encourage competition in all aspects and markets of telecommunications services, including switched and dedicated local and inter-LATA traffic as well as cable TV companies and wireless services such as paging, cellular, and satellite services.

telecommuting Working from home with all the information resources of the office LAN at one's fingertips, is often referred to as SOHO, or Small Office Home Office.

telephony API *See* TAPI.

telocator data protocol *See* TDP.

threats Processes or people that pose a potential danger to identified assets.

three pile approach Prioritization method for elements of strategic information systems design.

Three-way handshake TCP vulnerability that can be exploited for denial of service or land attacks.

thresholds Desired limits of certain performance characteristics that are set by the user and monitored by network management software.

throughput PC to PC data rate, transmission rate × data compression ratio.

ticket In Kerberos, an encrypted ticket is issued for each server to client session and is valid only for a preset amount of time.

ticket-granting ticket Users are first authenticated by the Kerberos Authentication server which consults its database and grants a ticket for the valid user to communicate with the Ticket Granting Server (TGS). This ticket is known as a ticket-granting ticket.

time bombs Viruses triggered by the passing of a certain date or time.

Time division multiple access *See* TDMA.

time division multiplexing *See* TDM.

time slot 8 bits of digitized information collected in one sample and assigned to one of 24 channels in a T-1 D-4 frame.

time studies A data traffic analysis process that measures how often different types of transactions occur.

time synchronous authentication Owing to the time synchronization, the server authentication unit should have the same current random authentication number which is compared to the one transmitted from the remote client.

Time Synchronous Token Authentication A token authentication process in which no challenge is sent because both the SecureID card and the server are time synchronized, so only the displayed one-time session key is transmitted.

timed updates A dial-up router update mechanism in which updates are performed at regular predetermined intervals.

timing limitation The second SNA characteristic that can cause problems when run over a shared LAN backbone is that SNA has timing limitations for transmission duration between SNA hosts and end-user devices. Thus on wide area, internetworked LANs over shared network media, SNA sessions can "time-out," effectively terminating the session.

token In a token passing access methodology, a specific packet (24 bits) of data is known as a token.

token authentication All token authentication systems include server components linked to the communications server, and client components that are used with the remote access clients. Physically, the token authentication device employed at the remote client location may be a hand-held device resembling a calculator, a floppy disk, or it may be an in-line device linked to either the remote client's serial or parallel port.

token passing An access methodology that assures that each PC user has 100% of the network channel available for their data requests and transfers by insisting that no PC accesses the network without first possessing a specific packet (24 bits) of data known as a token.

token response authentication Schemes that begin when the transmitted challenge response is received by the authentication server and compared with the expected challenge response number that was generated at the server. If they match, the user is authenticated and allowed access to network attached resources.

toll quality The ITU standard for 32Kbps ADPCM is known as G.721 and is generally used as a reference point for the quality of voice transmission.

tone Common name for DTMF dialing.

top-down model Insisting that a top-down approach to network analysis and design is undertaken, through the use of the top-down model, should assure that the network design implemented will meet the business needs and objectives that motivated the design in the first place.

total benefit of ownership *See* TBO.

total cost of ownership *See* TCO.

TP-PMD Twisted Pair-Physical Media Dependent; the official ANSI standard for CDDI.

Traffic shaping Can provide bandwidth-constrained or time sensitive applications with the bandwidth necessary to potentially improve application performance. Traffic shaping devices will *not* improve the performance of latency-constrained applications.

traffic volume analysis A data traffic analysis process that combines transaction analysis and time studies to yield a traffic volume profile.

trailer Information added to the back of data.

transaction analysis A data traffic analysis process that examines the amount of data transmitted for every different type of identified transaction.

translating bridges A special type of bridge that includes a format converter which can bridge between Ethernet and Token Ring. These special bridges may also be called multi-protocol bridges or translating bridges.

transmission architecture Key component of network architecture along with switching architecture.

Transmission control protocol *See* TCP.

transmission control protocol/internet protocol *See* TCP/IP.

transmission rate Rate of actual bits transmitted end-to-end measured in bps, equal to bits/baud × baud rate.

transmitter Mouthpiece on telephone handset.

transparent Bridges are passive or transparent devices, receiving every frame broadcast on a given LAN. Bridges are known as transparent due to their ability to only process data-link layer addresses while transparently forwarding any variety of upper layer protocols safely embedded within the data field of the data-link layer frame.

transparent bridge Bridges that connect LANs of similar data-link format.

transport layer Protocols responsible for providing reliability for the end-to-end network layer connections. Provide end-to-end error recovery and flow control and also provide mechanisms for sequentially organizing multiple network layer packets into a coherent message.

Transport Mode ESP In Secure IP, used to encrypt the data carried by the IP packet.

Trellis Coded Modulation *See* TCM.

triggered updates In order to reduce slow convergence in RIP based router networks, allow routers to immediately broadcast routing table updates regarding failed links rather than having to wait for the next 30 sec. periodic update.

trojan horse The actual virus is hidden inside an otherwise benign program and delivered to the target system or network to be infected.

trunk cards Cards in PBX that attach to local loops.

trusted gateway Certain applications are identified as trusted and are able to bypass the application gateway entirely and also are able to establish connections directly rather than be executed by proxy.

trusted node Authorization security software can be either server-based, also known as brokered authorization, or workstation-based, also referred to as trusted node.

Tunnel Mode ESP In Secure IP, encrypts the entire IP packet including its own header. This mode is effective in countering network analyzers or sniffers from capturing IP address information.

tunneling protocols In order to provide virtual private networking capabilities using the Internet as an enterprise network backbone, specialized tunneling protocols needed to be developed that could establish private, secure channels between connected systems.

turnaround time Time it takes two half-duplex modems to change from transmit to receive mode by manipulating RTS and CTS signals.

two-way messaging Sometimes referred to as enhanced paging, allows short text messages to be transmitted between relatively inexpensive transmission devices such as PDAs (Personal Digital Assistants) and alphanumeric pagers.

two-wire circuits Common local loop circuit in which one of these two wires serves as a ground wire for the circuit, thereby leaving only one wire between the two ends of the circuit for data signaling.

UART Universal Asynchronous Receiver Transmitter; acts as the interface between the parallel transmission of the computer bus and the serial transmission of the serial port.

UDP User datagram protocol; transport protocol that is part of the Internet suite of protocols, used in IP voice transmission.

UNI User network interface; in ATM, cell format that carries information between the user and the ATM network.

Unicode 16 bit character encoding scheme identical to ISO 10646.

unified messaging Also known as the Universal In-Box; will allow voice mail, e-mail, faxes, and pager messages to be displayed on a single graphical screen. Messages can then be forwarded, deleted, or replied to easily in point and click fashion.

universal asynchronous receiver transmitter *See* UART.

universal client capability A client workstation's ability to interoperate transparently with a number of different network operating system servers without the need for additional products or configurations.

universal in-box *See* Unified messaging.

Universal Serial Bus *See* USB.

unreliable An unreliable protocol does not require error checking and acknowledgment of error-free receipt by the destination host.

unshielded twisted pair *See* UTP.

USB A fast multi-point serial interface commonly installed in current generation PCs. USB can be used to support a wide variety of peripherals from network adapters to scanners and digital cameras.

User Datagram Protocol *See* UDP.

user demands The top layer of the wide area network architecture.

user-network interface *See* UNI.

UTP Twisted pair wiring consists of one or more pairs of insulated copper wire that are twisted at varying lengths, from 2 to 12 twists per foot, to reduce interference both between pairs and from outside sources such as electric motors and fluorescent lights. No additional shielding is added before the pairs are wrapped in the plastic covering.

V.32 ITU standard for modem transmitting at 9600bps, 4 QAM & TCM modulation.

V.32bis ITU standard for modem transmitting at 14.4Kbps, 6QAM & TCM modulation.

V.32ter Proprietary standard for modem transmitting at 19.2Kbps, 8 QAM & TCM modulation.

V.34 ITU standard for modem transmitting at 28.8Kbps, 9QAM & TCM.

V.42 ITU standard for error control, supports MNP 4 and LAP-M.

V.42bis ITU standard for data compression, compression ratios up to 4:1.

V.90 ITU standard for modems that operate at speeds up to 56Kbps by using directly connected digital servers.

variable bit rate *See* VBR.

variable callback Callback security mechanism for modems that supports callback to phone numbers entered at dial-in time after password verification.

VBR Variable Bit Rate; provides a guaranteed minimum threshold amount of constant bandwidth below which the available bandwidth will not drop. However, as bursty traffic requires more bandwidth than this constant minimum, that required bandwidth will be provided.

VDSL Very High Speed DSL; provides 52Mbps downstream and between 1.6–2.3Mbps upstream over distances of up to only 1,000 ft. It is being explored primarily as a means to bring video on demand services to the home.

vector Once a NDIS driver is bound and operating, packets of a particular protocol are forwarded from the adapter card to the proper protocol stack by a layer of software known as the vector.

version control software *See* File synchronization.

vertical integration Integration of CANE software with I-CASE software and business process reengineering software through the use of expert systems.

vertical redundancy check *See* VRC.

very high speed DSL *See* VDSL.

virtual circuit Dedicated path for voiceover frame relay that minimizes or eliminates delay usually associated with frame relay.

virtual circuit table Details that relate the LCN to a physical circuit consisting of an actual series of specific packet switches within the packet switched network are stored in a virtual circuit table.

virtual circuits Paths set up in connection-oriented packet switched networks.

virtual device drivers *See* VxDs.

virtual machines Some client network operating systems, such as Windows NT, have the ability to support multiple APIs and multiple different operating system subsystems, sometimes known as virtual machines.

virtual PC Emulation technology attempts to detect as yet unknown viruses by running programs with a software emulation program known as a virtual PC.

virtual tributary *See* VT.

Virus scanning The primary method for successful detection and removal.

VJ A protocol for compression of IP headers included with most PPP clients.

voice digitization Technique by which analog voice is converted into digital signals.

voiceover IP Also known as IP-based voice.

voice/data multiplexers Device that interfaces to T-1 leased lines to carry voice and data.

voice-grade leased line Analog leased line with 3100Hz of bandwidth.

VRC Simple parity checking; adds one parity bit per character.

VT Virtual tributaries; flexibly defined channels within the SONET payload area.

VT1.5 SONET virtual tributary equivalent to a mapped T-1.

vulnerabilities The manner or path by which threats are able to attack assets.

VxDs More secure 32 bit operating systems control access to hardware and certain system services via virtual device drivers. otherwise known as VxDs.

WAP *See* Wireless access protocol.

wavelength The distance between the same spots on two subsequent waves. The longer the wavelength, the lower the frequency and the shorter the wavelength, the greater the frequency.

Wavelength Division Multiplexing *See* WDM.

WBEM Web-Based Enterprise Management; another possible standard for distributed application management is a proposed IETF standard (WBEM) that integrates SNMP, HTTP, and DMI (desktop management interface) into an application management architecture that can use common Web browser software as its user interface.

WDM Wavelength Division Multiplexing; technique in fiber optic transmission in which multiple bits of data can be transmitted simultaneously over a single fiber by being represented by different light wavelengths.

web-based enterprise management *See* WBEM.

what-if analysis A feature of network simulation software that allows users to modify their current network in a variety of hypothetical scenarios.

Windows NT RAS Microsoft's remote node server software for Windows NT.

Wireless access protocol A protocol that brings Web browsing to mobile phones allowing users of WAP 1.1 compliant PDAs to browse the Internet and download bitmap images. In addition, WAP supports secure wireless business transactions.

wireless bridge Uses spread spectrum radio transmission between LAN sites (up to 3 miles); at present, primarily limited to Ethernet networks.

wireless WAN services A variety of wireless services are available for use across wider geographic spans. These wireless WAN services vary in many ways including availability, applications, transmission speed, and cost.

X.25 Packet switching standard that defines interface specification for packet switched networks.

X.500 As enterprise networks become more heterogeneous comprised of network operating systems from a variety of different vendors, the need will arise for different network operating systems to share each other's directory services information. A directory services specification known as X.500 offers the potential for this directory services interoperability.

X.509 An international standard for public key certificates.

XMODEM Public domain file transfer protocol, widely used, 128 bytes/block, checksum error control.

XON/XOFF Control characters used in software flow control. XOFF stops data transmission; XON restarts it.

XTACACS Extended Terminal Access Control Access System; another example of a remote access management protocol that supports three-tiered remote access management architectures.

YMODEM File transfer protocol, 1KB data blocks, CRC-16 error control, batch execution.

zero slot LANs The name "zero slot" refers to the fact that by using existing serial or parallel ports for network communications, zero expansion slots are occupied by network interface cards.

ZMODEM File transfer protocol, dynamically adjusts data packet size, automatic recovery from aborted file transfers.

zone The scope of coverage, or collection of domains, for which a given DNS server can resolve names.

INDEX

F

G

H